1004901375

Corporate Governance and Corporate Finance

This impressive collection defines the current status of corporate governance and corporate finance from a European perspective. The book brings together a comprehensive range of contemporary and classic articles, with a major emphasis on recent research, accompanied by a new and authoritative editorial commentary.

Topics discussed include:

- Alternative perspectives on corporate governance systems
- Equity ownership structure and control
- Corporate governance, underperformance and management turnover
- Directors' remuneration
- Governance, performance and financial strategy
- The market for corporate control

Addressing both the theory and practice of corporate governance and corporate finance, this book is an invaluable resource for scholars and students engaged with managerial finance, financial economics and business law, as well as the role of the corporation in the modern economy. It is also fascinating reading for practitioners interested in managerial finance.

Ruud A. I. van Frederikslust is Associate Professor of Finance at Erasmus University, the Netherlands.

James S. Ang is Professor of Finance at Florida State University, USA.

P. Sudi Sudarsanam is Professor of Finance and Corporate Control at Cranfield School of Management, UK.

Corporate Governance and Corporate Finance

A European perspective

Edited by
Ruud A. I. van Frederikslust,
James S. Ang and
P. Sudi Sudarsanam

Routledge
Taylor & Francis Group

LONDON AND NEW YORK

First published 2008
by Routledge
2 Park Square, Milton Park, Abingdon, Oxon OX14 4RN

Simultaneously published in the USA and Canada
by Routledge
270 Madison Ave, New York, NY 10016

*Routledge is an imprint of the Taylor & Francis Group,
an informa business*

Typeset in Bell Gothic by
Newgen Imaging Systems (P) Ltd, Chennai, India
Printed and bound in Great Britain by
Cromwell Press Ltd, Trowbridge, Wiltshire

British Library Cataloguing in Publication Data
A catalogue record for this book is available from the British Library

Library of Congress Cataloging in Publication Data
Corporate governance and corporate finance : a European
perspective / edited by Ruud A. I. van Frederikslust, James S. Ang
and P. Sudi Sudarsanam.
     p. cm.
   Includes bibliographical references and index.
   1. Corporate governance – Europe. 2. Corporations – Europe –
Finance. I. Van Frederikslust, R. A. I. II. Ang, James S.
III. Sudarsanam, P. S.

   HD2741.C77485 2007
   658.15094 – dc22   2007007573

ISBN10: 0–415–40531–9 (hbk)
ISBN10: 0–415–40532–7 (hbk)
ISBN10: 0–203–94013–X (hbk)

ISBN13: 978–0–415–40531–7 (hbk)
ISBN13: 978–0–415–40532–4 (pbk)
ISBN13: 978–0–203–94013–6 (ebk)

Contents

Tables

Figures

About the editors

Ruud A. I. van Frederikslust, until 1 January 2007 has held various positions at RSM Erasmus University since the graduate management programme was first established in 1970. His most recent position was Associate of Professor of Corporate Finance. He is author of the work *Predictability of Corporate Failure* (Kluwer Academic Publishers), and editor-in-chief of the volumes: *Science, Management and Entrepreneurship* (Kluwer Academic Publishers), *Mergers & Acquisitions* and *Corporate Restructuring and Recovery* (Elsevier Business Intelligence). He has participated in the organisation of leading conferences in Europe and the USA and also presented numerous research papers at the conferences. He has published in leading journals such as the *Multinational Finance Journal* and the *Journal of Financial Transformation*. He is a former member of the Board of the European Finance Association.

James S. Ang, Bank of America Eminent Scholar, Professor of Finance, College of Business, Florida State University. He joined the College of Business of Florida State University as the William O. Cullom Chair Professor of Finance in 1980 from Purdue University. His main areas of research interest are amongst others, corporate restructuring, corporate governance and control. He has published extensively in leading academic journals such as *Journal of Finance, Journal of Financial Economics, Journal of Financial and Quantitative Analysis, Journal of Business, Journal of Corporate Finance, The Bell Journal of Economics, Journal of Money, Credit and Banking* and *The Review of Economics and Statistics*. He was a two term Editor of the journal *Financial Management*, and a past president of the Financial Management Association International. He is a member (current and past) of the Editorial Board of several Journals. He was a member of the Board of Directors of the European Financial Management Association, and a Visiting Professor at the London Business School.

P. Sudi Sudarsanam, Professor of Finance and Corporate Control, School of Management, Cranfield University. Formerly Professor of Finance and Accounting at the Cass Business School in London, he has also been a Visiting Professor at universities in Vienna, Innsbruck, Athens, Szczecin and Chapel Hill, North Carolina. His main areas of research interest are corporate restructuring, mergers and acquisitions, executive compensation, corporate behavioral finance and corporate governance. He is one of the leading authorities on mergers and acquisitions in Europe and author of *The Essence of Mergers and Acquisitions* (Prentice Hall, 1995), which has been translated into five European and Asian languages. His more recently published second book, *Creating Value from Mergers and Acquisitions: The Challenges, an International and Integrated Perspective* (FT Prentice Hall, 2003) has been acclaimed by both practitioners and academics. He has published extensively in leading academic journals such as *Financial Management, Journal of Banking & Finance, European Finance Review, European Financial Management* and *Journal of Industrial Economics*. He has presented numerous research papers at leading conferences in Europe and the USA. He has also contributed to *Acquisitions Monthly*. He is on the editorial board of the *Journal of Business Finance & Accounting*. He is a member of the UK Competition Commission and of its Expert Committee on Cost of Capital.

Preface[*]

The last few years have probably seen more articles and books on both Corporate Governance and Corporate Finance than ever before. Whilst much has happened in the field of Corporate Governance following a number of serious accidents such as Enron and Ahold, there are still some very fundamental issues, which will have to be addressed. Moreover this is a field where globalisation of rules and attitudes has not, or not yet, been achieved.

First of all there is the fundamental difference between the US approach of strict and often detailed legislation on the one side and the European attitude that a Company Board can deviate from the required – or, more appropriately, recommended – course of action by giving an explanation which then has to be accepted by the shareholders. Or to put it in the vernacular, the well known 'comply or explain' possibility most European codes offer has a counterpart in 'comply or go to jail' on the other side of the Atlantic. Sarbanes Oxley is a case in point and European companies with a New York listing frequently are confronted with this.

A second issue is the question of whether more supervision by independents (however defined) also means more effective supervision. The problem remains that in the end the supervision of a group of relative outsiders can never be complete but will depend on the work of other outsiders, notably the external auditors. As an aside I would like to mention that the almost endemic inclination to change accounting conventions and definitions with disturbing regularity has been a further impediment to clarity in reporting. Even the most active and experienced Audit Committee will have to accept that there are limits to what they can control. In other words, in the end the supervisors will have, above all, to judge the integrity of the company management and in case of doubt be prepared to take action.

The third fundamental question is whether more and better supervision leads to better company results. Here some more research seems to be in order but the few articles I have seen are inconclusive. That is a serious matter because the new approach to corporate government, notably Sarbanes Oxley, allegedly generates very high costs and amounts of a $100 million and more are mentioned as the cost of introducing the system in major multinational companies.

Many publications address other important issues, such as the legitimacy of Boards, whom they represent, how they should be nominated/elected or how their independence can be assured. Over the past decade the Anglo-American tradition of giving primacy of place to the shareholder has by now in fact been accepted in most European countries, with the probable exception of Germany, where codetermination still has in important place in corporate governance. Another topic for discussion is the question of the requirements for a good Board member. Integrity, transparency and activity – meaning the willingness to take action when necessary – are probably the most important for independent Board members. For the sake of completeness I mention the European debate on the one-tier/two-tiers Board, an issue that, in my view, will gradually disappear with the de facto convergence between the two systems, which one can see in practice. This would especially be the case for UK Boards where the recommended split of the CEO and the Board Chairmanship (duality) in practice means that the board functioning is in many respects comparable to the Rhineland model.

Corporate Finance and notably the merger and acquisition aspect of it, has also recently drawn more attention from the public, the experts and the lawmakers. This is not the place to discuss the dangers and merits of the growth of private equity groups and hedge funds, two phenomena that are rather different, though sometimes confused in popular perception. Suffice it here to mention that one of the reasons for the rapid growth of private equity, which is mentioned with increasing frequency, is the increasing burden of corporate governance requirements as imposed by the authorities.

There is obviously another more direct relationship between Corporate Governance and Corporate Finance, certainly in the case of a takeover by a financial – as opposed to an industrial – party. The financial party will also be inclined, at least initially, to be hostile, although in the course of the process this may gradually change by applying techniques such as the 'bear hug'. A threat of a takeover or acquisition by a financial consortium will often – though not always – be a reflection of the market judgement of the performance of the management. The bidders feel, rightly or wrongly, that they can use the company's assets more productively than the present management. In effect the hostile bidders criticise by implication the attitude and judgement of the independent directors. They are seen as responsible for maintaining and tolerating a performance that outsiders apparently consider below the required standards. A new owner, allegedly, would be able to improve profitability by changing the existing situation, probably by first replacing (part of) the management and then proceeding by hiving off non-core assets, however defined. A further step is splitting the company in parts and selling these to interested parties, the 'buy and break' scenario. Burdening the acquired company with considerable loans at relatively heavy costs would then usually finance the investment.

The risk of an undesired offer from a hostile financial partner increases therefore if the Board has not been able or willing to exercise a proper level of quality control on the performance of the senior executives. To avoid this, the non-executive Board members have to be absolutely independent and sufficiently courageous to take action if and when necessary. Related to this is the problem of formulating and implementing a fair remuneration policy, which encourages and rewards good performance but does not accept compromises if the target results are not achieved. The recent reports on the development of some practices with the pricing of options in the US demonstrate that not every Board is sufficiently aware of its responsibility to hold the management to established targets.

The subjects of Corporate Governance and Corporate Finance are therefore related in a number of interesting and often complex ways and this book makes a timely contribution to the discussion.

FLORIS MALJERS

NOTE

*   Floris Maljers is former Chairman of the Advisory Board for RSM Erasmus University and former CEO of Unilever. With his outstanding business experience and contacts he still helps companies like Philips, KLM, Guinness and BP in a series of non-executive roles. He is emeritus professor of strategic management at RSM Erasmus University.

Acknowledgements

The editors and publishers wish to thank the authors and the following publishers who have kindly given permission for the use of copyright material.

Academic Press Inc. for article: Julian Franks, Colin Mayer and Luc Renneboog (2001), 'Who disciplines management in poorly performing companies?', *Journal of Financial Intermediation*, 10(3–4), 209–248.

Blackwell Publishing Ltd for articles: Michael C. Jensen (1993),'The modern industrial revolution, exit and the failure of internal control systems', *Journal of Finance*, 48(3), 831–880; Andrei Shleifer and Robert W. Vishny (1997), 'A survey of corporate governance', *Journal of Finance*, 52(2), 737–784; James S. Ang, Rebel Cole, and James Wuh Lin (2000), 'Agency costs and ownership structure', *Journal of Finance*, 55(1), 81–106; Martin J. Conyon and Kevin J. Murphy (2000), 'The prince and the pauper? CEO pay in the United States and United Kingdom', *The Economic Journal*, 110(Nov), 640–671; Jay Dahya, John J. McConnell and Nickolaos Travlos (2002), 'The Cadbury Committee, corporate performance and management turnover', *Journal of Finance*, 57(1), 461–483; Jorge Farinha (2003), 'Dividend policy, corporate governance and the managerial entrenchment hypothesis: an empirical analysis', *Journal of Business Finance & Accounting*, 30(9–10), 1173–1210.

Elsevier Ltd for articles: Julian Franks and Colin Mayer (1996), 'Hostile takeovers and the correction of managerial failure', *Journal of Financial Economics*, 40(1), 163–181; Wayne R. Guay (1999), 'The sensitivity of CEO wealth to equity risk: an analysis of the magnitude and determinants', *Journal of Financial Economics*, 53(1), 43–71; Marco Becht and Ailisa Röell (1999), 'Blockholdings in Europe: an international comparison', *European Economic Review*, 43(4–6), 1049–1056; Rafael La Porta, Florencio Lopez-de-Silanes, Andrei Shleifer and Robert Vishny (2000), 'Investor protection and corporate governance', *Journal of Financial Economics*, 58(1–2), 3–27; Mara Faccio and M. Ameziane Lasfer (2000), 'Do occupational pension funds monitor companies in which they hold large stakes?', *Journal of Corporate Finance*, 6(1), 71–110; Luc Renneboog (2000), 'Ownership, managerial control and the governance of companies listed on the Brussels stock exchange', *Journal of Banking & Finance*, 24(12), 1959–1995; John E. Core and David F. Larcker (2001), 'Performance consequences of mandatory increases in executive stock ownership', *Journal of Financial Economics*, 64(3), 317–340; Tim Jenkinson and Alexander Ljungqvist (2001), 'The role of hostile stakes in German corporate governance', *Journal of Corporate Finance*, 7(4), 397–446; Paolo F. Volpin (2002), 'Governance with poor investor protection: evidence from top executive turnover in Italy', *Journal of Financial Economics*, 64(1), 61–90; Mara Faccio and Larry H. P. Lang (2002),

'The ultimate ownership of Western European corporations', *Journal of Financial Economics*, 65(3), 365–395; N. K. Chidambaran and Nagpurnanand R. Prabhala, (2003),'Executive stock option repricing, internal governance mechanisms, and management turnover', *Journal of Financial Economics*, 69(1), 153–189; Julie Ann Elston and Lawrence G. Goldberg (2003), 'Executive compensation and agency costs in Germany', *Journal of Banking & Finance*, 27(7), 1391–1410; Christian Leuz, Dhananjay Nanda and Peter D. Wysocki (2003), 'Earnings management and investor protection: an international comparison', *Journal of Financial Economics*, 69(3), 505–527; Jens Köke (2004), 'The market for corporate control in a bank-based economy: a governance device?' *Journal of Corporate Finance*, 10(1), 53–80.

John Wiley & Sons Ltd for article: Rezaul Kabir, Dolph Cantrijn and Andreas Jeunink (1997), 'Takeover defences, ownership structure and stock returns: an empirical analysis with Dutch data', *Strategic Management Journal*, 18(2), 97–109.

MIT Press Journals for article: Paul Gompers, Joy Ishii and Andrew Metrick (2003), 'Corporate governance and equity prices', *The Quarterly Journal of Economics*, 118(1), 107–155.

Multinational Finance Society for article: Gertjan Schut and Ruud van Frederikslust (2004), 'Shareholder wealth effects of joint venture strategies', *Multinational Finance Journal*, 8(3–4), 211–225.

Oxford University Press for article: Marc Goergen and Luc Renneboog (2003), 'Why are the levels of controls so different in German and UK companies? Evidence from initial public offerings', *Journal of Law, Economics and Organization*, 19(1), 141–175.

Springer Science B.V. for articles: Jim Lai and Sudi Sudarsanam (1997), 'Corporate restructuring in response to performance decline: impact of ownership, governance and lenders', *European Finance Review*, 1(2), 197–233; Hiroshi Osano (1999), 'Security design, insider monitoring, and financial market equilibrium', *European Finance Review*, 2(3), 273–302; Erik Lehmann and Jürgen Weigand (2000), 'Does the governed corporation perform better? Governance structures and corporate performance in Germany', *European Finance Review*, 4(2), 157–195.

In addition the editors and publishers wish to thank the Library of RSM Erasmus University for their assistance in obtaining these articles.

General introduction[1]

ALTHOUGH MUCH HAS BEEN PUBLISHED ON corporate governance in recent years, the predominant paradigm is a US one. Yet the European context is highly significant in both its differences and similarities to the US experience. Continental Europe is characterised by a governance system in which large block shareholders play a key role, whereas the US system is driven by the needs of dispersed shareholders articulated through the stock market. The UK, however, shares much similarities with the US system although it has its own idiosyncratic features and institutional characteristics. There has been much debate over the relative merits of the block holder-dominated and stock market-dominated systems in promoting economic efficiency and growth, but this remain an inconclusive debate. There is also a trend towards greater convergence of some, or all, aspects of corporate governance driven in part by the forces of globalisation of product and capital markets but also inspired by political visions of greater harmonisation within Europe and between Europe and the rest of the world. Thus corporate governance, far from being monochromatic, presents a rich variety of laws, practices and institutional structures. An understanding of this variety is a necessary precondition to understanding how corporate governance is likely to evolve in the future and affect the functioning of companies and capital markets, as well as influence the practice of corporate finance.

The architecture of corporate governance differs across countries but consists broadly of the internal managerial control and monitoring mechanisms and the external monitoring and control mechanisms. The former include the board of structures, the presence of block shareholders, managerial incentive contracts and other devices to ensure alignment of shareholder and manager interests. The external mechanisms include the stock market and the market for corporate control (i.e. hostile takeovers). The relative balance among these mechanisms and their relative efficiencies differ among countries. The present collection of papers focuses on corporate governance and its impact in several European countries.

This volume brings together many of the most important classic and contemporary published articles on the main elements of corporate governance and their impact on various aspects of corporate finance within a European perspective. This collection illustrates and explains the differing perspectives on corporate governance frameworks and the interrelated set of mechanisms that constitute the corporate governance architecture. Some papers discuss the structural design features such as the ownership structure (e.g. institutional shareholders and block shareholders), financial structure, and structure of the board of directors. Other papers deal with the governance processes (e.g. executive compensation arrangements and pay-for-performance sensitivities). The role of takeovers as a managerial control device is also discussed. The impact of corporate governance structure as well as the related processes on certain corporate strategic and financing policies is the subject of a few other papers.

The articles in this volume are organised under six subject headings:

1. Alternative perspectives on corporate governance systems
2. Equity ownership structure and control
3. Corporate governance, underperformance and management turnover
4. Directors' remuneration
5. Governance, performance and financial strategy
6. On takeover as disciplinary mechanism

BROAD OVERVIEW OF THE COLLECTED PAPERS

Part 1   Alternative perspectives on corporate governance systems

This part deals with corporate governance systems and presents alternative typologies of such systems based on the institutional character (i.e. bank-centred or stock market-centred), the legal traditions of countries and the extent of legal protection of investor rights against firms. The legal traditions are also shown as the outcome of long political and economic processes in different countries. The papers provide the historical backdrop to the observed differences in corporate governance systems. The relationship between corporate governance systems on the one hand and cost of capital and sources of corporate finance on the other is explored. One element of the cost of capital in the form of agency costs is shown to depend on the ownership structure of firms and the extent of owner–manager alignment (Ang et al., 2000).

Part 2   Equity ownership structure and control

The efficacy of a corporate governance system requires effective monitoring of managers by the shareholders. Shleifer and Vishny (1997) have argued that large shareholders can perform this monitoring function. They also acknowledge that this role imposes costs such as free riding by non-block shareholders who may avoid the monitoring effort but reap the benefits of the block shareholder's monitoring. Large shareholders in this event may only be willing to undertake monitoring if they can expect to receive compensation for their efforts including an appropriate share of the added value that monitoring generates. They may also look to design the securities they hold in the firms with features that guarantee such reward. In the first paper of this part, Hiroshi Osano (1999) addresses the problem of security design that will satisfy a large investor and motivate her to undertake monitoring. The author shows that the optimal security is a debt-like security such as standard debt with a positive probability of default, or debt with call options. Such a design also leads to the financial market equilibrium being Pareto optimal. The remaining three papers by Becht and Röell (1999), Faccio and Lang (2002) and Goergen and Renneboog (2003) present empirical evidence on the ownership structure of European corporations with particular focus on block shareholdings and control exercised through pyramidal structures. Pyramidal structures allow block holders to control vast groups of companies with relatively small investment capital.

Part 3   Corporate governance, underperformance and management turnover

Part 3 comprises papers that deal with the effectiveness of corporate governance mechanisms in disciplining top managers. A measure of such discipline is the removal or turnover of such managers in response to poor corporate performance. Where such managers are entrenched owing to their ownership of the company's voting shares, connections to controlling shareholders or both, this form of disciplining is unlikely and the corporate governance mechanism is rendered ineffective. The controlling large block shareholder may in theory have an incentive to improve corporate performance, if necessary by disciplining top mangers of underperformers but this concern may be overridden by their enjoyment of private benefits of control. Minority shareholders, however, do not enjoy such countervailing private benefits. Large shareholding may thus align the interest of managers and large shareholders but create another agency problem (i.e. between large, controlling shareholders and minority shareholders). The phenomenon whereby controlling shareholders manage to receive private benefits at the expense of minority shareholders is called 'tunnelling'.

Part 4 Directors' remuneration

One of the important tools in the armoury of the board of directors to align the interests of shareholders and mangers is the executive compensation contract for the CEO and other executive managers. In theory, a properly written contract should achieve such alignment by making level of compensation conditional upon performance. However, in practice, there are problems in both contract writing and enforcement and in specifying the appropriate performance measures and the time horizon for the award of compensation. Many scholars (e.g. Bebchuk and Fried, 2004) have argued that entrenched top managers capture the pay setting process and manipulate the boards into awarding them excessive pay. They argue that such managers often get rewarded for failure rather than success in delivering performance and shareholder value. Thus, far from being a solution to the agency problem, executive compensation may itself be a manifestation of an agency problem and reflect failure of the governance arrangements in firms. The sensitivity of pay to performance is therefore an important test of governance effectiveness. Executive compensation arrangements may vary from country to country depending on governmental and public attitudes to 'high' managerial remuneration. The papers in this part deal with many of these issues and provide empirical evidence.

Part 5 Governance, performance and financial strategy

The papers in this part deal with the impact of governance structure on corporate performance and its financial strategy.

Corporate governance and performance

Although there has been an intensive debate on the relative merits of different systems of corporate governance, empirical evidence on the link between corporate governance and firm performance almost exclusively refers to the market-oriented Anglo-American system. The paper of Lehmann and Weigand (2000) therefore investigates the more network- or bank-oriented German system. In panel regressions for 361 German corporations over the time period 1991 to 1996, significantly, the authors find ownership concentration to negatively affect profitability. However, this effect depends intricately on stock market exposure, the location of control rights, and the time horizon (short-run vs long-run). They conclude that (1) the presence of large shareholders does not necessarily enhance profitability, (2) ownership concentration seems to be sub-optimal for many German corporations, and, finally, (3) having financial institutions as largest shareholders of traded corporations improves corporate performance.

Corporate governance and corporate financial strategy

The governance structure of strategic investments and its impact on both the investment itself and the investing firms is a matter of interest to firms. Often strategic investments may fail due to poor governance structures as evidenced by numerous studies on post-merger integration (Sudarsanam, 2003, chapter 22). Such governance problems also plague joint ventures and strategic alliances (Sudarsanam, 2003, chapter 10). Schut and Van Frederikslust (2004) show that strategic intention, the context in which the strategy is unfolded and the extent to which the company has ownership and managerial control over the implementation of the joint venture, strongly explains the extent to which it can create value.

Financial distress is another context in which the influence of corporate governance on the strategic and other decisions a firm makes can be studied. Firms in performance decline may choose a variety of restructuring strategies for recovery with conflicting welfare implications for different stakeholders such as shareholders, lenders and managers. Choice of recovery strategies is therefore determined by the complex interplay of ownership structure, corporate governance and lender monitoring of such firms. The paper of Lai and Sudarsanam (1997) points to the rich and complex ways in which different corporate governance mechanisms interact, sometimes conflicting with and, at others, complementing one another.

Part 6   On takeover as disciplinary mechanism

In Part 3 we collected papers that examine the relationship between different corporate control devices and top management turnover as a manifestation of their disciplinary effect. The control devices are generally internal to the control or ownership structure of the underperforming firms. In his part, we present papers that deal with an external control device. This is the market for control in which management teams compete for control of corporate assets. Manne (1995) was the first to conceptualise the market for corporate control as a managerial disciplinary device with underperforming firms becoming targets of bidders with presumably greater ability to correct underperformance and create greater value for target shareholders.

Hostile takeover is the means by which corporate control is wrested from the underperforming target managers. In theory such an external disciplinary device may be considered redundant if the internal control mechanisms are effective. The incidence of a hostile takeover may thus be an indictment of the failure of the internal controls. This argument pre-supposes that internal controls and hostile takeover are substitutes. A contrary perspective is that efficient internal controls facilitate hostile takeovers by preventing the entrenched incumbent management of the target firm from raising the barricades against managerial change. In his view hostile takeover and robust internal controls are complementary tools serving the same purpose. The papers in this part deal with the role of hostile takeovers as a disciplinary device and how governance regimes in certain countries substitute for them or facilitate them.

This volume brings together key articles, which represent the current state of theories and practices of corporate governance and corporate finance, ensuring that this collection will be an invaluable resource for scholars, students and practitioners in business law, managerial finance, and financial economics.

NOTE

1   We acknowledge comments and suggestions on prior drafts by W. Koppelman and S. Witteman.

REFERENCES

Ang, J.S., Cole, R. and Wuh Lin, J. (2000), 'Agency costs and ownership structure', *Journal of Finance*, 55(1): 81–106.

Bebchuk, L. and Fried, J. (2004), *Pay without performance*, Cambridge, Mass: Harvard University Press.

Becht, M. and Röell, A. (1999), 'Block holdings in Europe: an international comparison', *European Economic Review*, 43(4–6): 1049–1056.

Faccio M. and Lang, Larry H.P. (2002), 'The ultimate ownership of Western European corporations', *Journal of Financial Economics*, 65(3): 365–395.

Goergen, M. and Renneboog, L. (2003), 'Why are the levels of controls (so) different in German and UK companies? Evidence from initial public offerings', *Journal of Law, Economics and Organization*, 19(1): 141–175.

Lai, J. and Sudarsanam, S. (1997), 'Corporate restructuring in response to performance decline: impact of ownership, governance and lenders', *European Finance Review*, 1(2): 197–233.

Lehmann, E. and Weigand, J. (2000), 'Does the governed corporation perform better? Governance structures and corporate performance in Germany', *European Finance Review*, 4(2): 157–195.

Manne, H.G. (1965), 'Merger and the market for corporate control', *Journal of Political Economy*, 73: 110–120.

Osano, H. (1999), 'Security design, insider monitoring, and financial market equilibrium', *European Finance Review*, 2(3): 273–302.

Schut G.J. and van Frederikslust R. (2004), 'Shareholder wealth effects of joint venture strategies', *Multinational Finance Journal*, 8(3–4): 211–225.

Shleifer A. and Vishny R.W. (1997), 'A survey of corporate governance', *Journal of Finance*, 52(2): 737–783.

Sundarsanam, P.S. (2003), *Creating value from mergers and acquisitions. The challenges, an international and integrated perspective*, New York: FT Prentice Hall.

Part 1

Alternative perspectives on corporate governance systems

INTRODUCTION

PART 1 DEALS WITH CORPORATE GOVERNANCE SYSTEMS, and presents alternative typologies of such systems based on the institutional character (i.e. bank-centred or stock market-centred), the legal traditions of countries and the extent of legal protection of investor rights against firms. The legal traditions are also shown as the outcome of long political and economic processes in different countries. The papers provide the historical backdrop to the observed differences in corporate governance systems. The relationship between corporate governance systems on the one hand and cost of capital and sources of corporate finance on the other is explored. One element of the cost of capital in the form of agency costs is shown to depend on the ownership structure of firms and the extent of owner-manager alignment.

In the first paper Jensen (Ch.1) identifies alternative corporate control mechanisms and how failures in the internal control mechanism (i.e. the internal corporate governance failed to prevent excessive and unprofitable investments, for example, in R&D). He compares the 1980s restructuring of US industry with a similar restructuring of the 1890s. He traces the failure of the internal governance mechanism to the processes and characteristics of the board of directors and argues that the market for corporate control played a key role in the 1980s in unravelling the excess capacity built up in earlier decades. In his view corporate boards in the US have been 'captured' by management. Jensen argues for the organisational and governance innovations introduced by the venture capital and leveraged buyout firms as more effective corporate control mechanisms. The paper provides a long historical perspective on the evolution of alternative corporate control mechanisms and how they complement, or substitute for, one another. The role of corporate governance in corporate restructuring and in turn in promoting efficient allocation of resources is an important focus of this seminal paper.

Shleifer and Vishny (Ch.2) focus on legal protection of shareholder rights as a way of preventing managers from stealing the funds entrusted to them by shareholders and ensuring that managers deliver adequate returns on their investments. While legal protection may solve extreme cases of expropriation and stealing, it may be inadequate in ensuring that managers make investment decisions in the shareholders' interests and not in their own. Concentrated ownership may provide a solution to this agency problem by allowing large shareholders to monitor and control managers but this solution creates problems of its own (i.e. excessive risk exposure, potential expropriation of dispersed owners by the large shareholder in collusion with managers, and enhancing their own private benefits rather than the firm value). Moreover, incompetence of entrenched managers may be costlier to shareholders than managerial malfeasance or self-interest pursuit.

Shleifer and Vishny survey corporate governance systems around the world covering shareholders' legal rights and their enforcement regime, the monitoring role of banks as creditors, and concentrated ownership structures that result from leveraged buyouts (LBOs). They identify three principal governance systems – US and the UK with strong shareholder rights, Germany with permanent large shareholders and weak shareholder rights and Japan that falls between the other two. Comparing corporate governance systems around the world, Shleifer and Vishny conclude that legal protection of shareholder rights in combination with large shareholders provides the elements of effective corporate governance and cite the US, UK, Germany and Japan as examples of such optimal combination. They note, in contrast, how weak shareholder rights and concentrated ownership by family interests have reduced Italian firms' access to stock and loan markets.

In Chapter 3, La Porta, Lopez-de-Silanes, Shleifer and Vishny follow the same legalistic line of exposition by elevating shareholder rights protection as a central framework for examining corporate governance systems in different countries. They define corporate governance as a set of mechanisms by which outside investors – shareholders and creditors – protect themselves against expropriation by insiders (i.e. large controlling shareholders and managers). By rendering expropriation technology expensive or ineffective, the legal mechanism increases the access corporations have to external finance. La Porta et al. compare the efficiency of private contracts subject to enforcement by the court (the Coase theorem, 1937) to that of laws and regulations that explicitly limit the scope for expropriation and argue that even in countries with a judiciary that can arbitrate private contracts, such laws and regulations can be efficient and add value. They classify countries into four groups based on their legal origin – common law in the UK, the US and the British Commonwealth, French civil law, German civil law and Scandinavian civil law. They find that common law countries afford better investor protection than civil law countries while, within civil law countries, Germany is more efficient than France in enforcement of investor rights. La Porta et al. explore the impact of investor protection on ownership structure of firms, financial development and resource allocation and conclude that the impact is positive. They also find the classification of governance systems as bank-centred or stock market-centred is unhelpful in evaluating their relative efficiencies or in explaining the prevalent patterns of corporate financing. They advocate strong legal protection of investor rights, a reliable enforcement mechanism and, in the absence of these, a robust market regulator such as the SEC in the US to enhance corporate governance that promotes financial development. The paper thus clearly establishes the linkage between shareholder rights as an element of corporate governance and corporate finance.

While agency cost resulting from the divorce of managerial control of a firm from its ownership has emerged, since Jensen and Meckling's seminal paper in 1976, as a central problem of corporate governance and its reduction a measure of the efficiency of a corporate governance structure, plausible proxies for agency cost have eluded empirical researchers. As Ang et al. (Ch.4) argue, the base case of a firm free of any agency cost is one owned and managed by the same person/s. However empirical data on such firms have been difficult to obtain since such firms are not publicly listed and are small. Using unique data from the National Survey of Small Business Finances in the US, the authors' test many of the implications of the Jensen and Meckling model. They are able to use proxies for agency costs between owner-managed firms and firms with nonmanaging shareholders. They find that the former are significantly more efficient in using their assets (i.e. they display less shirking and incur significantly lower levels of operating costs, that is, they display less perquisite consumption). Ang et al. also report that agency costs decrease as ownership becomes more concentrated and creditors provide additional, but much weaker, monitoring of managers. These results are consistent with the benign role of large shareholders advocated by Shleifer and Vishny, and of leverage recommended by Jensen, in the first three papers in this part.

REFERENCES

Coase, Ronald (1937) 'The nature of the firm', *Economica,* 4: 386–405.
Jensen, Michael and William Meekling (1976) 'Theory of the firm: managerial behavior, agency costs, and ownership structure', *Journal of Financial Economics,* 3: 305–360.

Chapter 1

Michael C. Jensen

THE MODERN INDUSTRIAL REVOLUTION, EXIT, AND THE FAILURE OF INTERNAL CONTROL SYSTEMS

Source: *Journal of Finance*, 48(3) (1993): 831–880.

ABSTRACT

Since 1973 technological, political, regulatory, and economic forces have been changing the worldwide economy in a fashion comparable to the changes experienced during the nineteenth century Industrial Revolution. As in the nineteenth century, we are experiencing declining costs, increasing average (but decreasing marginal) productivity of labor, reduced growth rates of labor income, excess capacity, and the requirement for downsizing and exit. The last two decades indicate corporate internal control systems have failed to deal effectively with these changes, especially slow growth and the requirement for exit. The next several decades pose a major challenge for Western firms and political systems as these forces continue to work their way through the worldwide economy.

I. INTRODUCTION

Parallels between the modern and historical industrial revolutions

FUNDAMENTAL TECHNOLOGICAL, POLITICAL, regulatory, and economic forces are radically changing the worldwide competitive environment. We have not seen such a metamorphosis of the economic landscape since the Industrial Revolution of the nineteenth century. The scope and pace of the changes over the past two decades quality this period as a modern industrial revolution, and I predict it will take decades for these forces to be fully worked out in the worldwide economy.

Although the current and historical economic transformations occurred a century apart, the parallels between the two are strikingly similar: most notably, the widespread technological and organizational change leading to declining costs, increasing average but decreasing marginal productivity of labor, reduced growth rates in labor income, excess capacity, and—ultimately—downsizing and exit.

The capital markets played a major role in eliminating excess capacity both in the nineteenth century and in the 1980s. The merger boom of the 1890s brought about a massive consolidation of independent firms and the closure of marginal facilities. In the 1980s the capital markets helped eliminate excess capacity through leveraged acquisitions, stock buybacks, hostile takeovers, leveraged buyouts, and divisional sales. Just as the takeover specialists of the 1980s were disparaged by managers, policymakers, and the press, the so-called Robber Barons were criticized in the nineteenth century. In both cases the criticism was followed by public policy changes that restricted the capital markets: in the nineteenth century the passage of antitrust laws restricting combinations, and in the late 1980s the reregulation of the credit markets, anti-takeover legislation, and court decisions that restricted the market for corporate control.

Although the vast increases in productivity associated with the nineteenth century industrial revolution increased aggregate welfare, the large costs associated with the obsolescence of human and physical capital generated substantial hardship, mis-understanding, and bitterness. As noted in 1873 by Henry Ward Beecher, a well-known commentator and influential clergyman of the time,

> The present period will always be memo-rable in the dark days of commerce in America. We have had commercial dark-ness at other times. There have been these depressions, but none so obstinate and none so universal . . . Great Britain has felt it; France has felt it; all Austria and her neighborhood has experienced it. It is cosmopolitan. It is distinguished by its obstinacy from former like periods of commercial depression. Remedies have no effect. Party confidence, all stimulat-ing persuasion, have not lifted the pall, and practical men have waited, feeling that if they could tide over a year they could get along; but they could not tide over the year. If only one or two years could elapse they could save themselves. The years have lapsed, and they were worse off than they were before. What is the matter? What has happened? Why, from the very height of prosperity with-out any visible warning, without even a cloud the size of a man's hand visible on the horizon, has the cloud gathered, as it were, from the center first, spreading all over the sky? (Price (1933), p. 6).

On July 4, 1892, the Populist Party plat-form adopted at the party's first conven-tion in Omaha reflected similar discontent and conflict:

> We meet in the midst of a nation brought to the verge of moral, political, and

> material ruin. . . . The fruits of the toil of millions are boldly stolen to build up colos-sal fortunes for the few, unprecedented in the history of mankind; and the posses-sors of these in turn despise the republic and endanger liberty. From the same prolific womb of government injustice are bred two great classes of tramps and millionaires. (McMurray (1929), p. 7).

Technological and other developments that began in the mid-twentieth century have culminated in the past two decades in a similar situation: rapidly improving pro-ductivity, the creation of overcapacity and, consequently, the requirement for exit. Although efficient exit—because of the ramifications it has on productivity and human welfare—remains an issue of great importance, research on the topic has been relatively sparse since the 1942 publication of Schumpeter's insights on creative destruction.[1] These insights will almost cer-tainly receive renewed attention in the coming decade:

> Every piece of business strategy acquires its true significance only against the background of that process and within the situation created by it. It must be seen in its role in the perennial gale of creative destruction; it cannot be under-stood irrespective of it or, in fact, on the hypothesis that there is a perennial lull . . . The usual theorist's paper and the usual government commission's report practically never try to see that behavior, on the one hand, as a result of a piece of past history and, on the other hand, as an attempt to deal with a situa-tion that is sure to change presently—as an attempt by those firms to keep on their feet, on ground that is slipping away from under them. In other words, the problem that is usually being visual-ized is how capitalism administers existing structures, whereas the relevant problem is how it creates and destroys them. (Schumpeter (1976), p. 83).

Current technological and political changes are bringing this issue to the forefront. It is important for managers, policymakers, and researchers to understand the magnitude and generality of the implications of these forces.

Outline of the paper

In this paper, I review the industrial revolutions of the nineteenth century and draw on these experiences to enlighten our understanding of current economic trends. Drawing parallels to the 1800s, I discuss in some detail the changes that mandate exit in today's economy. I address those factors that hinder efficient exit, and outline the control forces acting on the corporation to eventually overcome these barriers. Specifically, I describe the role of the market for corporate control in affecting efficient exit, and how the shutdown of the capital markets has, to a great extent, transferred this challenge to corporate internal control mechanisms. I summarize evidence, however, indicating that internal control systems have largely failed in bringing about timely exit and downsizing, leaving only the product market or legal/political/regulatory system to resolve excess capacity. Although overcapacity will in the end be eliminated by product market forces, this solution generates large, unnecessary costs. I discuss the forces that render internal control mechanisms ineffective and offer suggestions for their reform. Lastly, I address the challenge this modern industrial revolution poses for finance professionals; that is, the changes that we too must undergo to aid in the learning and adjustments that must occur over the next several decades.

II. THE SECOND INDUSTRIAL REVOLUTION

The Industrial Revolution was distinguished by a shift to capital-intensive production, rapid growth in productivity and living standards, the formation of large corporate hierarchies, overcapacity, and, eventually, closure of facilities. (See the excellent discussions of the period by Chandler (1977, 1990, 1992), McCraw (1981, 1992), and Lamoreaux (1985).) Originating in Britain in the late eighteenth century, the First Industrial Revolution—as Chandler (1990, p. 250) labels it—witnessed the application of new energy sources to methods of production. The mid-nineteenth century witnessed another wave of massive change with the birth of modern transportation and communication facilities, including the railroad, telegraph, steamship, and cable systems. Coupled with the invention of high-speed consumer packaging technology, these innovations gave rise to the mass production and distribution systems of the late nineteenth and early twentieth centuries—the Second Industrial Revolution (Chandler (1990), p. 62).

The dramatic changes that occurred from the middle to the end of the century clearly warranted the term "revolution." The invention of the McCormick reaper (1830s), the sewing machine (1844), and high-volume canning and packaging devices (mid-1880s) exemplified a worldwide surge in productivity that "substituted machine tools for human craftsmen, interchangeable parts for hand-tooled components, and the energy of coal for that of wood, water, and animals" (McCraw (1981), p. 3). New technology in the paper industry allowed wood pulp to replace rags as the primary input material (Lamoreaux (1985), p. 41). Continuous rod rolling transformed the wire industry: within a decade, wire nails replaced cut nails as the main source of supply (Lamoreaux (1985), p. 64). Worsted textiles resulting from advances in combining technology changed the woolen textile industry (Lamoreaux (1985), p. 98). Between 1869 and 1899, the capital invested per American manufacturer grew from about $700 to $2,000; In the period 1889 to 1919, the annual growth of total factor productivity was almost six times higher than that which had occurred for most of the nineteenth century (McCraw (1981), p. 3).

As productivity climbed steadily, production costs and prices fell dramatically. The 1882 formation of the Standard Oil Trust, which concentrated nearly 25 percent of the world's kerosene production into three refineries, reduced the average cost of a gallon of kerosene by 70 percent between 1882 and 1885. In tobacco, the invention of the Bonsack machine in the early 1880s reduced the labor costs of cigarette production 98.5 percent (Chandler (1992), p. 5). The Bessemer process reduced the cost of steel rails by 88 percent from the early 1870s to the late 1890s, and the electrolytic refining process invented in the 1880s reduced the price of a kilo of aluminum by 96 percent between 1888 and 1895 (Chandler (1992), pp. 4–6). In chemicals, the mass production of synthetic dyes, alkalis, nitrates, fibers, plastics, and film occurred rapidly after 1880. Production costs of synthetic blue dye, for example, fell by 95 percent from the 1870s to 1886 (Chandler (1992), p. 5). New lost-cost sources of superphosphate rock and the manufacture of superphosphates changed the fertilizer industry. In sugar refining, technological changes dramatically lowered the costs of sugar production and changed the industry (Lamoreaux (1985), p. 99).

Lamoreaux (1985) discusses other cases where various stimuli led to major increases in demand and, in turn, expansion that led to excess capacity (the page numbers in parentheses reference her discussions). This growth occurred in cereals (when "Schumacher broke down the American prejudice against eating oats" (p. 98)), whisky (when crop failures in Europe created a sudden large demand for U.S. producers (p. 99)), and tin plate (when the McKinley tariff raised domestic demand and prices (p. 97)).

The surplus capacity developed during the period was exacerbated by the fall in demand brought about by the recession and panic of 1893. Although attempts were made to eliminate overcapacity through pools, associations, and cartels (p. 100), not until the capital markets motivated exit in the 1890s' mergers and acquisitions (M&A) boom was the problem substantially resolved. Capacity was reduced through the consolidation and closure of marginal facilities in the merged entities. Between 1895 and 1904, over 1,800 firms were bought or combined by merger into 157 firms (Lamoreaux (1985), p. i.).

III. THE MODERN INDUSTRIAL REVOLUTION

The major restructuring of the American business community that began in the 1970s and is continuing in the 1990s is being brought about by a variety of factors, including changes in physical and management technology, global competition, regulation, taxes, and the conversion of formerly closed, centrally planned socialist and communist economies to capitalism, along with open participation in international trade. These changes are significant in scope and effect; indeed, they are bringing about the Third Industrial Revolution. To understand fully the challenges that current control systems face in light of this change, we must understand more about these general forces sweeping the world economy, and why they are generating excess capacity and thus the requirement for exit.

What has generally been referred to as the "decade of the 80s" in the United States actually began in the early 1970s with the ten-fold increase in energy prices from 1973 to 1979, and the emergence of the modern market for corporate control, and high-yield nonrated bonds in the mid-1970s. These events, among others, were associated with the beginnings of the Third Industrial Revolution which—if I were to pick a particular date—would be the time of the oil price increases beginning in 1973.

The decade of the 80s: capital markets provided an early response to the modern industrial revolution

The macroeconomic data available for the 1980s shows major productivity gains (Jensen (1991)). 1981 was in fact a watershed year: Total factor productivity growth in the manufacturing sector more than doubled after 1981 from 1.4 percent per year in the period 1950 to 1981 to 3.3 percent in the period 1981 to 1990.[2] Nominal unit labor costs stopped their 17-year rise, and real unit labor costs declined by 25 percent. These lower labor costs came not from reduced wages or employment, but from increased productivity: Nominal and real hourly compensation increased by a total of 4.2 and 0.3 percent per year respectively over the 1981 to 1989 period.[3] Manufacturing employment reached a low in 1983, but by 1989 had experienced a small cumulative increase of 5.5 percent.[4] Meanwhile, the annual growth in labor productivity increased from 2.3 percent between 1950 and 1981 to 3.8 percent between 1981 and 1990, while a 30-year decline in capital productivity was reversed when the annual change in the productivity of capital increased from −1.03 percent between 1950 and 1981 to 2.03 percent between 1981 and 1990.[5]

During the 1980s, the real value of public firms' equity more than doubled from $1.4 to $3 trillion.[6] In addition, real median income increased at the rate of 1.8 percent per year between 1982 and 1989, reversing the 1.0 percent per year decrease that occurred from 1973 to 1982.[7] Contrary to generally held beliefs, real research and development (R&D) expenditures set record levels every year from 1975 to 1990, growing at an average annual rate of 5.8 percent.[8] *The Economist* (1990), in one of the media's few accurate portrayals of this period, noted that from 1980 to 1985 "American industry went on an R&D spending spree, with few big successes to show for it."

Regardless of the gains in productivity, efficiency, and welfare, the 1980s are generally portrayed by politicians, the media, and others as a "decade of greed and excess." In particular, criticism was centered on M&A transactions, 35,000 of which occurred from 1976 to 1990, with a total value of $2.6 trillion (1992 dollars). Contrary to common beliefs, only 364 of these offers were contested, and of those only 172 resulted in successful hostile takeovers (*Mergerstat Review* (1991)).

Indeed, Marty Lipton, prominent defender of American CEOs, expresses a common view of the 1980s when he states that "the takeover activity in the United States has imposed short-term profit maximization strategies on American Business at the expense of research, development and capital investment. This is minimizing our ability to compete in world markets and still maintain a growing standard of living at home" (Lipton (1989), p. 2).

On average, selling-firm shareholders in all M&A transactions in the period 1976 to 1990 were paid premiums over market value of 41 percent,[9] and total M&A transactions generated $750 billion in gains to target firms' shareholders (measured in 1992 dollars).[10] This value change represents the minimum forecast value change by the buyer (the amount the buyer is willing to pay the seller), and does not include further gains (or losses) reaped by the buyer after execution of the transaction.[11] It includes synergy gains from combining the assets of two or more organizations and the gains from replacing inefficient governance systems, as well as possible wealth transfers from employees, communities, and bondholders.[12] As Shleifer and Summers (1988) point out, if the value gains are merely transfers of wealth from creditors, employees, suppliers, or communities, they do not represent efficiency improvements. Thus far, however, little evidence has been found to support substantial wealth transfers from any group,[13] and it appears that most of these gains represent increases in efficiency.

Part of the attack on M&A transactions was centered on the high-yield (or so-called "junk") bond market, which eliminated mere size as an effective deterrent against takeover. This opened the management of America's largest corporations to monitoring and discipline from the capital markets. It also helped provide capital for newcomers to compete with existing firms in the product markets.

High-yield bonds opened the public capital markets to small, risky, and unrated firms across the country, and made it possible for some of the country's largest firms to be taken over. The sentiment of J. Richard Munro (1989, p. 472), Chairman and CEO of Time Inc., exemplifies the critical appraisal of their role:

> Notwithstanding television ads to the contrary, junk bonds are designed as the currency of "casino economics" . . . they've been used not to create new plants or jobs or products but to do the opposite: to dismantle existing companies so the players can make their profit. . . . This isn't the Seventh Cavalry coming to the rescue. It's a scalping party.

The high leverage incurred in the eighties contributed to an increase in the bankruptcy rate of large firms in the early 1990s. That increase was also encouraged by the recession (which in turn was at least partly caused by the restriction in the credit markets implemented in late 1989 and 1990 to offset the trend toward higher leverage), and the revisions in bankruptcy procedures and the tax code (which made it much more difficult to restructure financially distressed firms outside the courts, see Wruck (1990)). The unwise public policy and court decisions that contributed significantly to hampering private adjustment to this financial distress seemed to be at least partially motivated by the general antagonism towards the control market at the time. Even given the difficulties, the general effects of financial distress in the high-yield markets were greatly overemphasized, and the high-yield bond market has recently experienced near-record levels of new issues. While precise numbers are difficult to come by, I estimate the total bankruptcy losses to junk bond and bank HLT (highly levered transaction) loans from inception of the market in the mid-1970s through 1990 amounted to less than $50 billion (Jensen (1991), footnote 9). In comparison, IBM alone lost $51 billion (almost 65 percent of the total market value of its equity) from its 1991 high to its 1992 close.[14]

Mistakes were made in the takeover activity of the 1980s; indeed, given the far reaching nature of the restructuring, it would be surprising if none occurred. However, the negative assessment characteristic of general opinion is inconsistent with both the empirical evidence and the almost universal opinion of finance scholars who have studied the phenomenon. In fact, takeover activities were addressing an important set of problems in corporate America, and doing it before the companies faced serious trouble in the product markets. They were, in effect, providing an early warning system that motivated healthy adjustments to the excess capacity that began to proliferate in the worldwide economy.

Causes of excess capacity

Excess capacity can arise in at least four ways, the most obvious of which occurs when market demand falls below the level required to yield returns that will support the currently installed production capacity. This *demand-reduction* scenario is most familiarly associated with recession episodes in the business cycle.

Excess capacity can also arise from two types of technological change. The first type, *capacity-expanding* technological change, increases the output of a given capital stock and organization. An example of the capacity-expanding type of change is the Reduced Instruction Set CPU (RISC) processor innovation in the computer workstation market. RISC processors bring about a ten-fold increase in power, but can be produced by adapting the current production technology. With no increase in the quantity demanded, this change implies that production capacity must fall by 90 percent. Price declines increase the quantity demanded in these situations, and therefore reduce the capacity adjustment that would otherwise be required. If demand is elastic, output of the higher-powered units will grow as it did for much of the computing industry's history; now, however, the new workstation technology is reducing the demand for mainframe computers.

The second type is *obsolescence-creating* change—that is, one that obsoletes the current capital stock and organization. Wal-Mart and the wholesale clubs that are revolutionizing retailing are examples of such change. These new, focused, large scale, low-cost retailers are dominating old-line department stores which can no longer compete. Building these new low-cost stores means much current retail capacity becomes obsolete—when Wal-Mart enters a new market total retail capacity expands, and it is common for some of the existing high-cost retail capacity to go out of business.[15] More intensive use of information and other technologies, direct dealing with manufacturers, and the replacement of high-cost, restrictive work-rule union labor are several sources of the competitive advantage of these new organizations.

Finally, excess capacity also results when many competitors simultaneously rush to implement new, highly productive technologies without considering whether the aggregate effects of all such investment will be greater capacity than can be supported by demand in the final product market. Sahlman and Stevenson's (1985) analysis of the winchester disk drive industry provides an example of this phenomenon. Between 1977 and 1984, venture capitalists invested over $400 million in 43 different manufacturers of winchester disk drives; initial public offerings of common stock infused additional capital in excess of $800 million. In mid-1983, the capital markets assigned a value of $5.4 billion to 12 publicly traded, venture-capital-backed hard disk drive manufacturers—yet by the end of 1984, the value assigned to those companies had plummeted to $1.4 billion. In his study of the industry, Christensen (1993) finds that over 138 firms entered the industry in the period from its invention in 1956 to 1990, and of these 103 subsequently failed and six were acquired. Sahlman and Stevenson (p. 7) emphasize the lack of foresight in the industry: "The investment mania visited on the hard disk industry contained inherent assumptions about the long-run industry size and profitability and about future growth, profitability and access to capital for each individual company. These assumptions, had

they been stated explicitly, would not have been acceptable to the rational investor." There are clues in the history of the nineteenth century that similar overshooting occurred then as well. In Jensen (1991), I analyze the incentive, information, and contracting problems that cause this overshooting and argue that these problems of boom-bust cycles are general in venture markets—but that they can be corrected by reforming contracts that currently pay promoters for doing deals, rather than for doing successful deals.

Current forces leading to excess capacity and exit

The ten-fold increase in crude oil prices between 1973 and 1979 had ubiquitous effects, forcing contraction in oil, chemicals, steel, aluminum, and international shipping, among other industries. In addition, the sharp crude oil price increases that motivated major changes to economize on energy had other, perhaps even larger, implications. I believe the reevaluation of organizational processes and procedures stimulated by the oil shock also generated dramatic increases in efficiency beyond the original pure energy-saving projects. The original energy-motivated reexamination of corporate processes helped initiate a major reengineering of company practices and procedures that still continues to accelerate throughout the world.

Since the oil price increases of the 1970s, we again have seen systematic overcapacity problems in many industries similar to those of the nineteenth century. While the reasons for this overcapacity nominally differ among industries, I doubt they are independent phenomena. We do not yet fully understand all the causes propelling the rise in excess capacity in the 1980s, yet I believe there were a few basic forces in operation.

Macro policies

Major deregulation of the American economy (including trucking, rail, airlines, telecommunications, banking and financial services industries) under President Carter contributed to the requirements for exit in these industries,[16] as did important changes in the U.S. tax laws that reduced tax advantages to real estate development, construction, and other activities. The end of the cold war has had obvious ramifications for the defense industry, as well as less direct effects on the industry's suppliers. In addition, two generations of managerial focus on growth as a recipe for success caused many firms, I believe, to overshoot their optimal capacity, setting the stage for cutbacks, especially in white collar corporate bureaucracies. Specifically, in the decade from 1979 to 1989 the *Fortune* 100 firms lost 1.5 million employees, or 14 percent of their workforce.[17]

Technology

Massive changes in technology are clearly part of the cause of the current industrial revolution and its associated excess capacity. Both within and across industries, technological developments have had far-reaching impact. To give some examples, the widespread acceptance of radial tires (lasting three to five times longer than the older bias ply technology and providing better gas mileage) caused excess capacity in the tire industry; the personal computer revolution forced contraction of the market for mainframes; the advent of aluminum and plastic alternatives reduced demand for steel and glass containers; and fiberoptic, satellite, digital (ISDN), and new compression technologies dramatically increased capacity in telecommunication. Wireless personal communication such as cellular phones and their replacements promise to further extend this dramatic change.

The changes in computer technology, including miniaturization, have not only revamped the computer industry, but also redefined the capabilities of countless other industries. Some estimates indicate the price of computing capacity fell by a factor of 1,000 over the last decade.[18] This means that computer production lines now produce boxes with 1,000 times the capacity for a given price. Consequently, computers are becoming commonplace—in cars, toasters, cameras, stereos, ovens, and so on. Nevertheless, the increase in quantity demanded has not been sufficient to avoid overcapacity, and we are therefore witnessing a dramatic shutdown of production lines in the industry—a force that has wracked IBM as a high-cost producer. A change of similar magnitude in auto production technology would have reduced the price of a $20,000 auto in 1980 to under $20 today. Such increases in capacity and productivity in a basic technology have unavoidably massive implications for the organization of work and society.

Fiberoptic and other telecommunications technologies such as compression algorithms are bringing about similarly vast increases in worldwide capacity and functionality. A Bell Laboratories study of excess capacity indicates, for example, that given three years and an additional expenditure of $3.1 billion, three of AT&T's new competitors (MCI, Sprint, and National Telecommunications Network) would be able to absorb the entire long distance switched service that was supplied by AT&T in 1990 (Federal Communications Commission (1991), p. 1140).

Organizational innovation

Overcapacity can be caused not only by changes in the physical technology, but also by changes in organizational practices and management technology. The vast improvements in telecommunications, including computer networks, electronic mail, teleconferencing, and facsimile transmission are changing the workplace in major ways that affect the manner in which people work and interact. It is far less valuable for people to be in the same geographical location to work together effectively, and this is encouraging smaller, more efficient, entrepreneurial organizing units that cooperate through technology.[19] This encourages even more fundamental changes. Through competition "virtual organizations"—networked or transitory organizations where people come together temporarily to complete a task, then separate to pursue their individual specialties—are changing the structure of the standard large bureaucratic organization and contributing to its shrinkage. Virtual organizations tap talented specialists, avoid many of the regulatory costs imposed on permanent structures, and bypass the inefficient work rules and high wages imposed by unions. In doing so, they increase efficiency and thereby further contribute to excess capacity.

In addition, Japanese management techniques such as total quality management, just-in-time production, and flexible manufacturing have significantly increased the efficiency of organizations where they have been successfully implemented throughout the world. Some experts argue that, properly implemented, these new management techniques can reduce defects and spoilage by an order of magnitude. These changes in managing and organizing principles have contributed significantly to the productivity of the world's capital stock and economized on the use of labor and raw materials, thus also contributing to the excess capacity problems.[20]

Globalization of trade

With the globalization of markets, excess capacity tends to occur worldwide. Japan, for example, is currently in the midst of substantial excess capacity caused, at least partially, by the breakdown in its own corporate control system;[21] it is now in the process of a massive restructuring of its economy.[22] Yet even if the requirement for exit were isolated in the United States, the interdependency of today's world economy would ensure that such overcapacity would have reverberating, global implications. For example, the rise of efficient high-quality producers of steel and autos in Japan and Korea has contributed to excess capacity in those industries worldwide. Between 1973 and 1990 total capacity in the U.S. steel industry fell by 38 percent from 156.7 million tons to 97 million tons, and total employment fell over 50 percent from

509,000 to 252,000.[23] From 1985 to 1989 multifactor productivity in the industry increased at an annual rate of 5.3 percent compared to 1.3 percent for the period 1958 to 1989 (Burnham (1993), Table 1 and p. 15).

The entry of Japan and other Pacific Rim countries such as Hong Kong, Taiwan, Singapore, Thailand, Korea, Malaysia, and China into worldwide product markets has contributed to the required adjustments in Western economies over the last several decades. Moreover, competition from new entrants to the world product markets promises to get considerably more intense.

Revolution in political economy

The movement of formerly closed communist and socialist centrally planned economies to more market-oriented open capitalist economies is likely to generate huge changes in the world economy over the next several decades. These changes promise to cause much conflict, pain, and suffering as world markets adjust, but also large profit opportunities.

More specifically, the rapid pace of development of capitalism, the opening of closed economies, and the dismantlement of central control in communist and socialist states is occurring to various degrees in China, India, Indonesia, Pakistan, other Asian economies, and Africa. This evolution will place a potential labor force of almost a billion people—whose current average income is less than $2 per day—on world markets.[24,25] Table 1.1 summarizes some of the population and labor force estimates relevant to this issue. The opening of Mexico and other Latin American countries and the transition of communist and socialist central and eastern European economies to open capitalist systems (at least some of which will make the transition in some form) could add almost 200 million laborers with average incomes of less than $10 per day to the world market.

For perspective, Table 1.1 shows that the average daily U.S. income per worker is slightly over $90, and the total labor force numbers about 117 million, and the

Table 1.1 Labor Force and Manufacturing Wage Estimates of Various Countries and Areas Playing an Actual or Potential Role in International Trade in the Past and in the Future

Country/Area	Total Population[a] (Millions)	Potential Labor Force[b] (Millions)	Average Daily Earnings[c] (U.S.$)
Major potential entrants from Asia			
China	1,155.8	464.4	$1.53
India	849.6	341.4	$2.46
Indonesia	187.8	75.4	NA[d]
Pakistan	115.5	46.4	$3.12
Sri Lanka	17.2	6.9	$1.25
Thailand	56.9	23.0	$1.49
Vietnam	68.2	27.4	NA
Total/Average: Total pop./labor force & average earnings	2,451.0	984.9	$1.97[e]
Potential entrant under NAFTA			
Mexico	87.8	35.5	$10.29
Major potential entrants from central and eastern Europe			
Czechoslovakia	15.6	6.3	$6.45
Hungary	10.3	4.2	$9.25
Poland	38.2	15.4	$6.14
Romania	23.2	9.4	$8.98
Yugoslavia	23.8	9.6	NA
Former U.S.S.R.	286.7	115.8	$6.69
Total/Average: Mexico, central & eastern Europe	485.6	196.2	$7.49
Previous world market entrants from Asia			
Hong Kong	5.8	2.3	$25.79
Japan	123.9	50.1	$146.97
Korea	43.3	17.5	$45.37
Malaysia	17.9	7.4	NA
Singapore	2.8	1.1	$27.86
Taiwan	20.7	8.4	NA
Total/Average	214.4	86.8	$116.16
U.S. and E.E.C. for comparison			
United States	252.7	117.3	$92.24
European Economic Community	658.4	129.7	$78.34
Total/Average	911.1	246.7	$84.93

a Population statistics from *Monthly Bulletin of Statistics* (United Nations, 1993), 1991 data.
b Potential labor force estimated by applying the 40.4 percent labor force participation rate in the European Economic Community to the 1991 population estimates, using the most recent employment estimates (*Statistical Yearbook*, United Nations, 1992) for each member country.
c Unless otherwise noted, refers to 1991 earnings from the *Monthly Bulletin of Statistics* (United Nations, 1993) or earnings from *Statistical Yearbook* (United Nations, 1992) adjusted to 1991 levels using the Consumer Price Index. Earnings for Poland were calculated using 1986 earnings and 1986 year-end exchange rate, while earnings for Romania were calculated using 1985 earnings and 1985 exchange rate. An approximation for the former U.S.S.R. was made using 1987 data for daily earnings in the U.S.S.R. and the estimated 1991 exchange rate for the former U.S.S.R. from the *Monthly Bulletin of Statistics*.
d NA = Not available. In the case of Yugoslavia, inflation and currency changes made estimates unreliable. For Indonesia, Vietnam, Malaysia, and Taiwan data on earnings in manufacturing are unavailable.
e Average daily wage weighted according to projected labor force in each grouping.

European Economic Community average wage is about $80 per day with a total labor force of about 130 million. The labor forces that have affected world trade extensively in the last several decades total only about 90 million (Hong Kong, Japan, Korea, Malaysia, Singapore, and Taiwan).[26]

While the changes associated with bringing a potential 1.2 billion low-cost laborers onto world markets will significantly increase average living standards throughout the world, they will also bring massive obsolescence of capital (manifested in the form of excess capacity) in Western economies as the adjustments sweep through the system. Western managers cannot count on the backward nature of these economies to limit competition from these new human resources. Experience in China and elsewhere indicates the problems associated with bringing relatively current technology on line with labor forces in these areas is possible with fewer difficulties than one might anticipate.[27]

One can confidently forecast that the transition to open capitalist economies will generate great conflict over international trade as special interests in individual countries try to insulate themselves from competition and the required exit. The transition of these economies will require large redirection of Western labor and capital to activities where it has a comparative advantage. While the opposition to global competition will be strong, the forces are likely to be irresistible in this day of rapid and inexpensive communication, transportation, miniaturization, and migration.

The bottom line, of course, is that with even more excess capacity and the requirement for additional exit, the strains put on the internal control mechanisms of Western corporations are likely to worsen for decades to come.

In the 1980s managers and employees demanded protection from the capital markets. Many are now demanding protection from international competition in the product markets (often under the guise of protecting jobs). The current dispute over the NAFTA (North American Free Trade Act, which will remove trade barriers between Canada, the United States, and Mexico) is but one general example of conflicts that are also occurring in the steel, automobile, computer chip, computer screen, and textile industries. In addition it would not be surprising to see a return to demands for protection from even domestic competition. This is currently underway in the deregulated airline industry, an industry that is faced with significant excess capacity.

We should not underestimate the strains this continuing change will place on worldwide social and political systems. In both the First and Second Industrial Revolutions, the demands for protection from competition and for redistribution of income became intense. It is conceivable that Western nations could face the modern equivalent of the English Luddites who destroyed industrial machinery (primarily knitting frames) in the period 1811 to 1816, and were eventually subdued by the militia (Watson (1993)). In the United States during the early 1890s, large groups of unemployed men (along with some vagrants and criminals), banding together under different leaders in the West, Midwest, and East, wandered cross-country in a march on Congress. These "industrial armies" formed to demand relief from "the evils of murderous competition; the supplanting of manual labor by machinery; the excessive Mongolian and pauper immigration; the curse of alien landlordism . . ." (McMurray (1929), p. 128). Although the armies received widespread attention and enthusiasm at the onset, the groups were soon seen as implicit threats as they roamed from town to town, often stealing trains and provisions as they went. Of the 100,000 men anticipated by Coxey, only 1,000 actually arrived in Washington to protest on May 1, 1893. At the request of the local authorities, these protesters disbanded and dispersed after submitting a petition to Congress (McMurray (1929), pp. 253–262).

We need look no further than central and eastern Europe or Asia to see the effects of policies that protect organizations from foreign and domestic competition. Hundreds of millions of people have been condemned to poverty as a result of governmental policies that protect firms from competition in the product markets (both domestic and foreign) and attempt to ensure prosperity and jobs by protecting organizations against decline and exit. Such policies are self-defeating, as employees of state-owned factories in these areas are now finding. Indeed, Porter (1990) finds that the most successful economies are those blessed with intense internal competition that forces efficiency through survival of the fittest.

Our own experience in the 1980s demonstrated that the capital markets can also play an important role—that capital market pressures, while not perfect, can significantly increase efficiency by bringing about earlier adjustments. Earlier adjustments avoid much of the waste generated when failure in the product markets forces exit.

IV. THE DIFFICULTY OF EXIT

The asymmetry between growth and decline

Exit problems appear to be particularly severe in companies that for long periods enjoyed rapid growth, commanding market positions, and high cash flow and profits. In these situations, the culture of the organization and the mindset of managers seem to make it extremely difficult for adjustment to take place until long after the problems have become severe, and in some cases even unsolvable. In a fundamental sense, there is an asymmetry between the growth stage and the contraction stage over the life of a firm. We have spent little time thinking about how to manage the contracting stage efficiently, or more importantly how to manage the growth stage to avoid sowing the seeds of decline.

In industry after industry with excess capacity, managers fail to recognize that they themselves must downsize; instead they leave the exit to others while they continue to invest. When all managers behave

this way, exit is significantly delayed at substantial cost of real resources to society. The tire industry is an example. Widespread consumer acceptance of radial tires meant that worldwide tire capacity had to shrink by two-thirds (because radials last three to five times longer than bias ply tires). Nonetheless, the response by the managers of individual companies was often equivalent to: "This business is going through some rough times. We have to make major investments so that we will have a chair when the music stops." A. William Reynolds (1988), Chairman and CEO of GenCorp (maker of General Tires), illustrates this reaction in his testimony before the Subcommittee on Oversight and Investigations (February 18, 1988), U.S. House Committee on Energy and Commerce:

> The tire business was the largest piece of GenCorp, both in terms of annual revenues and its asset base. Yet General Tire was not GenCorp's strongest performer. Its relatively poor earnings performance was due in part to conditions affecting all of the tire industry. . . . In 1985 worldwide tire manufacturing capacity substantially exceeded demand. At the same time, due to a series of technological improvements in the design of tires and the materials used to make them, the product life of tires had lengthened significantly. General Tire, and its competitors, faced an increasing imbalance between supply and demand. The economic pressure on our tire business was substantial. Because our unit volume was far below others in the industry, we had less competitive flexibility. . . . We made several moves to improve our competitive position: We increased our investment in research and development. We increased our involvement in the high performance and light truck tire categories, two market segments which offered faster growth opportunities. We developed new tire products for those segments and invested heavily in an aggressive marketing program designed to enhance our presence in both markets.

We made the difficult decision to reduce our overall manufacturing capacity by closing one of our older, less modern plants in Waco, TX . . . I believe that the General Tire example illustrates that we were taking a rational, long-term approach to improving GenCorp's overall performance and shareholder value. . . . As a result of the takeover attempt, . . . [and] to meet the principal and interest payments on our vastly increased corporate debt, GenCorp had to quickly sell off valuable assets and abruptly lay-off approximately 550 important emloyees.

GenCorp sold its General Tire subsidiary to Continental AG of Hannover, West Germany for approximately $625 million. Despite Reynolds's good intentions and efforts, Gen Corp's increased investment seems not to be a socially optimal response for managers in a declining industry with excess capacity.

Information problems

Information problems hinder exit because the high-cost capacity in the industry must be eliminated if resources are to be used efficiently. Firms often do not have good information on their own costs, much less the costs of their competitors; it is therefore sometimes unclear to managers that they are the high-cost firm which should exit the industry.[28] Even when managers do acknowledge the requirement for exit, it is often difficult for them to accept and initiate the shutdown decision. For the managers who must implement these decisions, shutting plants or liquidating the firm causes personal pain, creates uncertainty, and interrupts or sidetracks careers. Rather than confronting this pain, managers generally resist such actions as long as they have the cash flow to subsidize the losing operations. Indeed, firms with large positive cash flow will often invest in even more money-losing capacity — situations that illustrate vividly what I call the agency costs of free cash flow (Jensen (1986)).

Contracting problems

Explicit and implicit contracts in the organization can become major obstacles to efficient exit. Unionization, restrictive work rules, and lucrative employee compensation and benefits are other ways in which the agency costs of free cash flow can manifest themselves in a growing, cash-rich organization. Formerly dominant firms became unionized in their heyday (or effectively unionized in organizations like IBM and Kodak) when managers spent some of the organization's free cash flow to buy labor peace. Faced with technical innovation and worldwide competition (often from new, more flexible, and nonunion organizations), these dominant firms cannot adjust fast enough to maintain their market dominance (see DeAngelo and DeAngelo (1991) and Burnham (1993)). Part of the problem is managerial and organizational defensiveness that inhibits learning and prevents managers from changing their model of the business (see Argyris (1990)).

Implicit contracts with unions, other employees, suppliers, and communities add to formal union barriers to change by reinforcing organizational defensiveness and inhibiting change long beyond the optimal time — even beyond the survival point for the organization. In an environment like this a shock must occur to bring about effective change. We must ask why we cannot design systems that can adjust more continuously, and therefore more efficiently.

The security of property rights and the enforceability of contracts are extremely important to the growth of real output, efficiency, and wealth. Much press coverage and official policy seems to be based on the notion that all implicit contracts should be unchangeable and rigidly enforced. Yet it is clear that, given the occurrence of unexpected events, not all contracts, whether explicit or implicit can (or even should) be fulfilled. Implicit contracts, in addition to avoiding the costs incurred in the writing process, provide opportunity to revise the obligation if circumstances change;

presumably, this is a major reason for their existence.

Indeed the gradual abrogation of the legal notion of "at will" employment is coming close to granting property rights in jobs to all employees.[29] While casual breach of implicit contracts will destroy trust in an organization and seriously reduce efficiency, all organizations must evolve a way to change contracts that are no longer optimal. For example, bankruptcy is essentially a state-supervised system for breaking (or more politely, rewriting) contracts that are mutually inconsistent and therefore, unenforceable. All developed economies evolve such a system. Yet, the problem is a very general one, given that the optimality of changing contracts must be one of the major reasons for leaving many of them implicit. Research into the optimal breach of contracts, and the bonding against opportunistic behavior that must accompany it, is an important topic that has received considerable attention in the law and economics literature (see Polinsky (1989)) but is deserving of more attention by organization theorists.

V. THE ROLE OF THE MARKET FOR CORPORATE CONTROL

The four control forces operating on the corporation

There are only four control forces operating on the corporation to resolve the problems caused by a divergence between managers' decisions and those that are optimal from society's standpoint. They are the

- capital markets,
- legal/political/regulatory system,
- product and factor markets, and
- internal control system headed by the board of directors.

As explained elsewhere (Jensen (1989a, 1989b, 1991), Roe (1990, 1991)), the capital markets were relatively constrained by law and regulatory practice from about 1940 until their resurrection through

hostile tender offers in the 1970s. Prior to the 1970s capital market discipline took place primarily through the proxy process. (Pound (1993) analyzes the history of the political model of corporate control.)

The legal/political/regulatory system is far too blunt an instrument to handle the problems of wasteful managerial behavior effectively. (The breakup and deregulation of AT&T, however, is one of the court system's outstanding successes. As we shall see below, it helped create over $125 billion of increased value between AT&T and the Baby Bells.)

While the product and factor markets are slow to act as a control force, their discipline is inevitable—firms that do not supply the product that customers desire at a competitive price cannot survive. Unfortunately, when product and factor market disciplines take effect it can often be too late to save much of the enterprise. To avoid this waste of resources, it is important for us to learn how to make the other three organizational control forces more expedient and efficient.

Substantial data support the proposition that the internal control systems of publicly held corporations have generally failed to cause managers to maximize efficiency and value.[30] More persuasive than the formal statistical evidence is the fact that few firms ever restructure themselves or engage in a major strategic redirection without a crisis either in the capital markets, the legal/political/regulatory system, or the product/factor markets. But there are firms that have proved to be flexible in their responses to changing market conditions in an evolutionary way. For example, investment banking firms and consulting firms seem to be better at responding to changing market conditions.

Capital markets and the market for corporate control

The capital markets provided one mechanism for accomplishing change before losses in the product markets generate a crisis. While the corporate control activity of the 1980s has been widely criticized as counterproductive to American industry, few have recognized that many of these transactions were necessary to accomplish exit over the objections of current managers and other constituencies of the firm such as employees and communities. For example, the solution to excess capacity in the tire industry came about through the market for corporate control. Every major U.S. tire firm was either taken over or restructured in the 1980s.[31] In total, 37 tire plants were shut down in the period 1977 to 1987 and total employment in the industry fell by over 40 percent. (U.S. Bureau of the Census (1987), Table 1a-1.) The pattern in the U.S. tire industry is repeated elsewhere among the crown jewels of American business.

Capital market and corporate control transactions such as the repurchase of stock (or the purchase of another company) for cash or debt creates exit of resources in a very direct way. When Chevron acquired Gulf for $13.2 billion in cash and debt in 1984, the net assets devoted to the oil industry fell by $13.2 billion as soon as the checks were mailed out. In the 1980s the oil industry had to shrink to accommodate the reduction in the quantity of oil demanded and the reduced rate of growth of demand. This meant paying out to shareholders its huge cash inflows, reducing exploration and development expenditures to bring reserves in line with reduced demands, and closing refining and distribution facilities. The leveraged acquisitions and equity repurchases helped accomplish this end for virtually all major U.S. oil firms (see Jensen (1986b, 1988)).

Exit also resulted when Kohlberg, Kravis, and Roberts (KKR) acquired RJR-Nabisco for $25 billion in cash and debt in its 1986 leveraged buyout (LBO). Given the change in smoking habits in response to consumer awareness of cancer threats, the tobacco industry must shrink, and the payout of RJR's cash accomplished this to some extent. Furthermore, the LBO debt prohibits RJR from continuing to squander its cash flows on the wasteful projects it had undertaken prior to the buyout. Thus, the buyout laid the groundwork for the

efficient reduction of capacity by one of the major firms in the industry. Also, by eliminating some of the cash resources from the oil and tobacco industries, these capital market transactions promote an environment that reduces the rate of growth of human resources in the industries or even promotes outright reduction when that is the optimal policy.

The era of the control market came to an end, however, in late 1989 and 1990. Intense controversy and opposition from corporate managers, assisted by charges of fraud, the increase in default and bankruptcy rates, and insider trading prosecutions, caused the shutdown of the control market through court decisions, state antitakeover amendments, and regulatory restrictions on the availability of financing (see Swartz (1992), and Comment and Schwert (1993)). In 1991, the total value of transactions fell to $96 billion from $340 billion in 1988.[32] LBOs and management buyouts fell to slightly over $1 billion in 1991 from $80 billion in 1988.[33] The demise of the control market as an effective influence on American corporations has not ended the restructuring, but it has meant that organizations have typically postponed addressing the problems they face until forced to by financial difficulties generated by the product markets. Unfortunately the delay means that some of these organizations will not survive—or will survive as mere shadows of their former selves.

VI. THE FAILURE OF CORPORATE INTERNAL CONTROL SYSTEMS

With the shutdown of the capital markets as an effective mechanism for motivating change, renewal, and exit, we are left to depend on the internal control system to act to preserve organizational assets, both human and nonhuman. Throughout corporate America, the problems that motivated much of the control activity of the 1980s are now reflected in lackluster performance, financial distress, and pressures for restructuring. Kodak, IBM, Xerox, ITT, and many others have faced or are now facing severe challenges in the product markets. We therefore must understand why these internal control systems have failed and learn how to make them work.

By nature, organizations abhor control systems, and ineffective governance is a major part of the problem with internal control mechanisms. They seldom respond in the absence of a crisis. The recent GM board revolt (as the press has called it) which resulted in the firing of CEO Robert Stempel exemplifies the failure, not the success, of GM's governance system. General Motors, one of the world's high-cost producers in a market with substantial excess capacity, avoided making major changes in its strategy for over a decade. The revolt came too late: the board acted to remove the CEO only in 1992, after the company had reported losses of $6.5 billion in 1990 and 1991 and (as we shall see in the next section) an opportunity loss of over $100 billion in its R&D and capital expenditure program over the eleven-year period 1980 to 1990. Moreover, the changes to date are still too small to resolve the company's problems.

Unfortunately, GM is not an isolated example. IBM is another testimony to the failure of internal control systems: it failed to adjust to the substitution away from its mainframe business following the revolution in the workstation and personal computer market—ironically enough a revolution that it helped launch with the invention of the RISC technology in 1974 (Loomis (1993)). Like GM, IBM is a high-cost producer in a market with substantial excess capacity. It too began to change its strategy significantly and removed its CEO only after reporting losses of $2.8 billion in 1991 and further losses in 1992 while losing almost 65 percent of its equity value.

Eastman Kodak, another major U.S. company formerly dominant in its market, also failed to adjust to competition and has performed poorly. Its $37 share price in 1992 was roughly unchanged from 1981. After several reorganizations, it only recently began to seriously change its incentives and strategy, and it appointed a chief financial officer well-known for turning around troubled companies.

(Unfortunately he resigned only several months later—after, according to press reports, running into resistance from the current management and board about the necessity for dramatic change.)

General Electric (GE) under Jack Welch, who has been CEO since 1981, is a counterexample to my proposition about the failure of corporate internal control systems. GE has accomplished a major strategic redirection, eliminating 104,000 of its 402,000 person workforce (through layoffs or sales of divisions) in the period 1980 to 1990 without the motivation of a threat from capital or product markets.[34] But there is little evidence to indicate this is due to anything more than the vision and persuasive powers of Jack Welch rather than the influence of GE's governance system.

General Dynamics (GD) provides another counterexample. The appointment of William Anders as CEO in September 1991 (coupled with large changes in its management compensation system which tied bonuses to increases in stock value) resulted in its rapid adjustment to excess capacity in the defense industry—again with no apparent threat from any outside force. GD generated $3.4 billion of increased value on a $1 billion company in just over two years (see Murphy and Dial (1992)). Sealed Air (Wruck (1992)) is another particularly interesting example of a company that restructured itself without the threat of an immediate crisis. CEO Dermot Dumphy recognized the necessity for redirection, and after several attempts to rejuvenate the company to avoid future competitive problems in the product markets, created a crisis by voluntarily using the capital markets in a leveraged restructuring. Its value more than tripled over a three-year period. I hold these companies up as examples of successes of the internal control systems, because each redirection was initiated without immediate crises in the product or factor markets, the capital markets, or in the legal/political/regulatory system. The problem is that they are far too rare.

Although the strategic redirection of General Mills provides another counterexample (Donaldson (1990)), the fact that it took more than ten years to accomplish the change leaves serious questions about the social costs of continuing the waste caused by ineffective control. It appears that internal control systems have two faults. They react too late, and they take too long to effect major change. Changes motivated by the capital market are generally accomplished quickly—within one and a half to three years. As yet no one has demonstrated the social benefit from relying on purely internally motivated change that offsets the costs of the decade-long delay exhibited by General Mills.

In summary, it appears that the infrequency with which large corporate organizations restructure or redirect themselves solely on the basis of the internal control mechanisms in the absence of crises in the product, factor, or capital markets or the regulatory sector is strong testimony to the inadequacy of these control mechanisms.

VII. DIRECT EVIDENCE OF THE FAILURE OF INTERNAL CONTROL SYSTEMS

The productivity of R&D and capital expenditures

The control market, corporate restructurings, and financial distress provide substantial evidence on the failings of corporate internal control systems. My purpose in this section is to provide another and more direct estimate of the effectiveness of internal control systems by measuring the productivity of corporate R&D and capital expenditures. The results reaffirm that many corporate control systems are not functioning well. While it is impossible to get an unambiguous measure of the productivity of R&D and capital expenditures, by using a period as long as a decade we can get some approximations. We cannot simply measure the performance of a corporation by the change in its market value over time (more precisely the returns to its shareholders) because this measure does not take account of the efficiency with which the management team manages internally

generated cash flows. For example, consider a firm that provides dividends plus capital gains to its shareholders over a ten-year period that equal the cost of capital on the beginning of period share value. Suppose, however, that management spent $30 billion of internally generated cash flow on R&D and capital expenditures that generated no returns. In this case the firm's shareholders suffered an opportunity loss equal to the value that could have been created if the firm had paid the funds out to them and they had invested it in equivalently risky projects.

The opportunity cost of R&D and capital expenditures thus can be thought of as the returns that would have been earned by an investment in equivalent-risk assets over the same time period. We don't know exactly what the risk is, nor what the expected returns would be, but we can make a range of assumptions. A simple measure of performance would be the difference between the total value of the R&D plus capital and acquisition expenditures invested in a benchmark strategy and the total value the firm actually created with its investment strategy. The benchmark strategy can be thought of as the ending value of a comparable-risk bank account (with an expected return of 10 percent) into which the R&D and capital expenditures in excess of depreciation (hereafter referred to as net capital expenditures) had been deposited instead of invested in real projects. For simplicity I call this the benchmark strategy. The technical details of the model are given in the Appendix. The calculation of the performance measure takes account of all stock splits, stock dividends, equity issues and repurchases, dividends, debt issues and payments, and interest.

Three measures of the productivity of R&D and net capital expenditures

Measure 1

Consider an alternative strategy which pays the same dividends and stock repurchases as the firm actually paid (and raises the same outside capital) and puts the R&D

and capital and acquisition expenditures (in excess of depreciation) in marketable securities of the same risk as the R&D and capital expenditures, yielding expected returns equal to their cost of capital, *i*. Under the assumption that the zero investment and R&D strategy yields a terminal value of the firm equal to the ending debt plus the beginning value of equity (that is, investment equal to depreciation is sufficient to maintain the original equity value of the firm), Measure 1 is the difference between the actual ending total value of the firm and the value of the benchmark. The exact equation is given in the Appendix for this measure as well as the next two measures of performance.

Unless capital and R&D expenditures are completely unproductive, this first crude measure of the productivity of R&D and capital expenditures will be biased downward. I define two additional measures that use different assumptions about the effect of the reduced R&D and capital expenditures on the ending value of the firm's equity and on the ability of the firm to make the intermediate cash dividend and stock repurchase payouts to shareholders. If R&D is required to maintain a competitive position in the industry, the ending value of the equity in the benchmark strategy is likely to be less than the initial value of equity even though nominal depreciation of the capital stock is being replaced. Moreover, with no R&D and maintenance only of the nominal value of the capital stock, the annual cash flows from operations are also likely to be lower than those actually realized (because organizational efficiency and product improvement will lag competitors, and new product introduction will be lower). Therefore I use two more conservative measures that will yield higher estimates of the productivity of these expenditures.

Measure 2

The second measure assumes that replacement of depreciation and zero expenditures on R&D are sufficient to maintain the intermediate cash flows but,

like a one-horse shay, the firm arrives at the end of the period still generating cash returns, but then collapses with no additional cash payments to equityholders, and equity value of zero as of the horizon date.

Measure 3

To allow for the effects of the reduced investment and R&D on intermediate cash flows my third measure assumes that all intermediate cash flows are reduced in the benchmark investment strategy by the amount paid out to shareholders in the form of dividends and net share repurchases and that the original value of the equity is maintained. This measure is likely to yield an upward biased estimate of the productivity of R&D and capital expenditures.

The data and results

The data for this analysis consist of all 432 firms on COMPUSTAT with 1989 sales of $250 million or more for which complete data on R&D, capital expenditures, depreciation, dividends, and market value were available for the period December 31, 1979 through December 31, 1990. The estimates of the productivity of R&D are likely to be upward biased because the selection criteria use only firms that managed to survive through the period and eliminate those that failed. I have calculated results for various rates of interest but report only those using a 10 percent rate of return. This rate is probably lower than the cost of capital for R&D expenditures at the beginning of the period when interest rates were in the high teens, and probably about right or on the high side at the end of the period when the cost of capital was probably on the order of 8 to 10 percent. A low approximation of the cost of capital appropriate to R&D and capital expenditures will bias the performance measures up, so I am reasonably comfortable with these conservative assumptions.

Because they are interesting in their own right, Table 1.2 presents the data on annual R&D and capital expenditures of nine selected *Fortune* 500 corporations and the

Table 1.2 Total R&D and Capital Expenditures for Selected Companies and the Venture Capital
Industry, 1980–1990 ($ Billions)

Year	GM	IBM	Xerox	Kodak	Intel	GE	Venture Capital Industry	Merck	AT&T
				Total R&D Expenditures					
1980	2.2	1.5	0.4	0.5	0.1	0.8	0.6	0.2	0.4
1981	2.2	1.6	0.5	0.6	0.1	0.8	1.2	0.3	0.5
1982	2.2	2.1	0.6	0.7	0.1	0.8	1.5	0.3	0.6
1983	2.6	2.5	0.6	0.7	0.1	0.9	2.6	0.4	0.9
1984	3.1	3.1	0.6	0.8	0.2	1.0	2.8	0.4	2.4
1985	4.0	3.5	0.6	1.0	0.2	1.1	2.7	0.4	2.2
1986	4.6	4.0	0.7	1.1	0.2	1.3	3.2	0.5	2.3
1987	4.8	4.0	0.7	1.0	0.3	1.2	4.0	0.6	2.5
1988	5.3	4.4	0.8	1.1	0.3	1.2	3.9	0.7	2.6
1989	5.8	5.2	0.8	1.3	0.4	1.3	3.4	0.8	2.7
1990	5.9	4.9	0.9	1.3	0.5	1.5	1.9	0.9	2.4
Total	42.7	36.8	7.1	10.1	2.5	11.9	27.8	5.4	19.3
				Total Capital Expenditures					
1980	7.8	6.6	1.3	0.9	0.2	2.0	NA	0.3	17.0
1981	9.7	6.8	1.4	1.2	0.2	2.0	NA	0.3	17.8
1982	6.2	6.7	1.2	1.5	0.1	1.6	NA	0.3	16.5
1983	4.0	4.9	1.1	0.9	0.1	1.7	NA	0.3	13.8
1984	6.0	5.5	1.3	1.0	0.4	2.5	NA	0.3	3.5
1985	9.2	6.4	1.0	1.5	0.2	2.0	NA	0.2	4.2
1986	11.7	4.7	1.0	1.4	0.2	2.0	NA	0.2	3.6
1987	7.1	4.3	0.3	1.7	0.3	1.8	NA	0.3	3.7
1988	6.6	5.4	0.5	1.9	0.5	3.7	NA	0.4	4.0
1989	9.1	6.4	0.4	2.1	0.4	5.5	NA	0.4	3.5
1990	10.1	6.5	0.4	2.0	0.7	2.1	NA	0.7	3.7
Total	87.5	64.2	9.9	16.1	3.3	27.0	NA	3.7	91.2
			Net Capital Expenditures (Capital Expenditures less Depreciation)						
1980	3.6	3.8	0.5	0.5	0.1	1.2	NA	0.2	9.9
1981	5.3	3.5	0.6	0.7	0.1	1.1	NA	0.2	9.9
1982	1.7	3.1	0.4	0.9	0.1	0.6	NA	0.2	7.7
1983	−1.1	1.3	0.3	0.2	0.1	0.6	NA	0.1	3.9
1984	1.1	2.3	0.5	0.2	0.3	1.3	NA	0.1	0.7
1985	3.5	3.4	1.2	0.6	0.1	0.8	NA	0.07	0.9
1986	5.6	1.3	0.2	0.5	0.0	0.6	NA	0.04	−3.2
1987	0.8	0.7	−0.3	0.6	0.1	0.2	NA	0.07	−0.6
1988	−0.7	1.5	−0.2	0.7	0.3	0.3	NA	0.2	−5.9
1989	2.0	2.2	−0.2	0.8	0.2	0.7	NA	0.2	1.1
1990	2.7	2.3	−0.3	0.7	0.4	0.6	NA	0.4	0.3
Total	24.5	25.4	2.7	6.4	1.0	8.0	NA	1.8	24.7
			Total Value of R&D plus Net Capital Expenditures						
	67.2	62.2	9.8	16.7	4.3	19.9	27.8	7.2	44.0
			Ending Equity Value of the Company, 12/90						
	26.2	64.6	3.2	13.5	13.5	50.0	>60	34.8	32.9

NA = Not available. Source: Annual reports, COMPUSTAT, *Business Week R&D Scoreboard*, William
Sahlman. *Venture Economics* for total disbursements by industry. Capital expenditures for the venture capital
industry are included in the R&D expenditures which are the total actual disbursements by the industry.

total venture capital industry from January 1, 1980 through December 31, 1990. Table 1.3 contains calculations that provide some benchmarks for evaluating the productivity of these expenditures.

Total R&D expenditures over the eleven-year period range from $42.7 billion for General Motors to $5.4 billion for Merck. The individual R&D expenditures of GM and IBM were significantly greater than the $27.8 billion spent by the entire U.S. venture capital industry over the eleven-year period. Because venture capital data include both the R&D component and capital expenditures, we must add in corporate capital expenditures to get a proper comparison to the venture industry figures. Total capital expenditures range from $91.2 billion for AT&T and $87.5 billion for GM to $3.7 billion for Merck. Capital expenditures net of depreciation range from $25.4 billion for IBM to $1.8 billion for Merck.

It is clear that GM's R&D and investment program produced massive losses. The company spent a total of $67.2 billion in excess of depreciation in the period and produced a firm with total ending value of equity (including the E and H shares) of $26.2 billion. Ironically, its expenditures were more than enough to pay for the entire equity value of Toyota and Honda, which in 1985 totaled $21.5 billion. If it

had done this (and not changed the companies in any way), GM would have owned two of the world's low-cost, high-quality automobile producers.

As Table 1.3 shows, the difference between the value of GM's actual strategy and the value of the equivalent-risk bank account strategy amounts to $ −100.7 billion by Measure 2 (which assumes the ending value of the company given no R&D or net capital expenditures is zero in the benchmark strategy), $ −115.2 billion for Measure 1 (which assumes the original value of the equity is maintained), and $ −90 billion by Measure 3 (which assumes cash flows fall by the amount of all intermediate cash outflows to shareholders and debtholders). I concentrate on Measure 2 which I believe is the best measure of the three. By this measure, IBM lost over $11 billion relative to the benchmark strategy (and this is prior to the $50 billion decline in its equity value in 1991 and 1992), while Xerox and Kodak were down $8.4 billion and $4.6 billion respectively. GE and Merck were major success stories, with value creation in excess of the benchmark strategy of $29.9 billion and $28 billion respectively. AT&T gained $2.1 billion over the benchmark strategy, after having gone through the court-ordered breakup and deregulation of the Bell system in 1984. The value gains of

Table 1.3 Benefit-Cost Analysis of Corporate R&D and Investment Programs: Actual Total Value of Company at 12/31/90 Less Total Value of the Benchmark Strategy $r = 10$ percent (billions of dollars)

GM	IBM	Xerox	Kodak	Intel	GE	Venture Capital Industry	Merck	AT&T
Measure 1: Gain (Loss) [Assumes beginning value of equity is maintained]								
($115.2)	($49.4)	($13.6)	($12.4)	$1.8	$18.4	>$17	$22.6	($34.5)
Measure 2: [Assumes ending equity value is zero]								
($100.7)	($11.8)	($8.4)	($4.6)	$3.2	$29.9	> $17	$28.0	$2.1
Measure 3: [Assumes ending equity value equals beginning value and intermediate cash flows are smaller by the amount paid to equity under company's strategy]								
($90.0)	($5.4)	($8.0)	($1.8)	$1.8	$36.4	> $17	$28.1	$21.3

the seven Baby Bells totaled $125 billion by Measure 2 (not shown in the table), making the breakup and deregulation a nontrivial success given that prices to consumers have generally fallen in the interim.

The value created by the venture capital industry is difficult to estimate. We would like to have estimates of the 1990 total end-of-year value of all companies funded during the eleven-year period. This value is not available so I have relied on the $60 billion estimate of the total value of all IPOs during the period. This overcounts those firms that were funded prior to 1980 and counts as zero all those firms that had not yet come public as of 1990. Because of the pattern of increasing investment over the period from the mid-1970s, the over-counting problem is not likely to be as severe as the undercounting problem. Thus, the value added by the industry over the bank account strategy is most probably greater than $17 billion as shown in Table 1.3. Since the venture capital industry is in Table 1.3 as another potential source of comparison, and since virtually its entire value creation is reflected in its ending equity value, I have recorded its value creation under each measure as the actual estimate of greater than $17 billion.

Because the extreme observations in the distribution are the most interesting, Table 1.4 gives the three performance measures for the 35 companies at the bottom of the list of 432 firms ranked in reverse order on Measure 2 (Panel A), and on the 35 companies at the top of the ranked list (Panel B), also in reverse order. As the tables show, GM ranked at the bottom of the performance list, preceded by Ford, British Petroleum, Chevron, Du Pont, IBM, Unisys, United Technologies, and Xerox. Obviously many of the United States' largest and best-known companies appear on this list (including GD prior to its recent turn-around), along with Japan's Honda Motor company. Panel B shows that Philip Morris created the most value in excess of the benchmark strategy, followed by Wal-Mart, Bristol Myers, GE, Loews, Merck, Bellsouth, Bell Atlantic, Procter & Gamble, Ameritech, and Southwestern Bell.[35]

Table 1.5 provides summary statistics (including the minimum, mean, five fractiles of the distribution, maximum, and standard deviation) on R&D expenditures, net capital expenditures, and the three performance measures. The mean ten-year R&D and net capital expenditures are $1.296 billion and $1.367 billion respectively; the medians are $146 million and $233 million. The average of Measure 2 over all 432 firms is slightly over $1 billion with a t-value of 3.0, indicating that on average this sample of firms created value above that of the benchmark strategy. The average for Measures 1 and 2 are $ −221 million and $1.086 billion respectively. All productivity measures are upward biased because failed firms are omitted from the sample, and because the decade of the eighties was an historical outlier in stock market performance. The median performance measures are $24 million, $200 million, and $206 million respectively. The maximum performance measures range from $37.7 billion to $47 billion.

Although the average performance measures are positive, well-functioning internal control systems would substantially truncate the lower tail of the distribution. And given that the sample is subject to survivorship bias,[36] and that the period was one in which stock prices performed historically above average, the results demonstrate major inefficiencies in the capital expenditure and R&D spending decisions of a substantial number of firms.[37] I believe we can improve these control systems substantially, but to do so we must attain a detailed understanding of how they work and the factors that lead to their success or failure.

VIII. REVIVING INTERNAL CORPORATE CONTROL SYSTEMS

Remaking the board as an effective control mechanism

The problems with corporate internal control systems start with the board of directors. The board, at the apex of the

Table 1.4 Difference between Value of Benchmark Strategy for Investing R&D and Net Capital Expenditure and Actual Strategy under Three Assumptions regarding Ending Value of Equity and Intermediate Cash Flows for Benchmark Strategy (Performance Measures 1–3)

Panel A: Performance measures for the 35 companies at the bottom of the ranked list of 432 companies in the period 1980–1990 on performance measure 2. r = 10 percent

		Performance Measure (Millions)		
Rank	Company	1	2	3
432	General Motors Corp.	(115,188)	(100,720)	(90,024)
431	Ford Motor Co.	(29,304)	(25,447)	(20,392)
430	British Petroleum P.L.C. (ADR)	(35,585)	(23,699)	(19,958)
429	Chevron Corp.	(25,497)	(15,859)	(10,586)
428	Du Pont (E.I.) de Nemours	(21,122)	(15,279)	(8,535)
427	Intl. Business Machines Corp.	(49,395)	(11,826)	(5,394)
426	Unisys Corp.	(14,655)	(11,427)	(11,899)
425	United Technologies Corp.	(10,843)	(9,032)	(7,048)
424	Xerox Corp.	(13,636)	(8,409)	(7,978)
423	Allied Signal Inc.	(8,869)	(7,454)	(5,002)
422	Hewlett-Packard Co.	(9,493)	(6,373)	(8,605)
421	ITT Corp.	(9,099)	(6,147)	(3,611)
420	Union Carbide Corp.	(8,673)	(5,893)	(3,341)
419	Honeywell Inc.	(7,212)	(5,361)	(5,677)
418	Lockheed Corp.	(5,744)	(5,339)	(5,149)
417	Digital Equipment	(7,346)	(5,082)	(7,346)
416	Penn Central Corp.	(5,381)	(4,846)	(4,938)
415	Eastman Kodak Co.	(12,397)	(4,630)	(1,762)
414	Chrysler Corp.	(5,054)	(4,604)	(3,041)
413	Atlantic Richfield Co.	(13,239)	(3,977)	(1,321)
412	Northrop Corp.	(4,489)	(3,904)	(3,743)
411	Goodyear Tire & Rubber Co.	(4,728)	(3,805)	(2,532)
410	Phillips Petroleum Co.	(11,027)	(3,614)	(5,427)
409	Honda Motor Ltd. (Amer. shares)	(4,880)	(3,435)	(3,898)
408	Texaco Inc.	(11,192)	(3,354)	3,830
407	Texas Instruments Inc.	(5,359)	(3,350)	(4,276)
406	NEC Corp. (ADR)	(4,803)	(3,326)	(3,736)
405	National Semiconductor Corp.	(3,705)	(3,246)	(3,632)
404	General Dynamics Corp.	(4,576)	(2,966)	(3,783)
403	Grace (W.R.) & Co.	(4,599)	(2,776)	(2,314)
402	Imperial Chem. Inds. P.L.C. (ADR)	(7,223)	(2,575)	(1,287)
401	Tektronix Inc.	(3,414)	(2,500)	(3,070)
400	Advanced Micro Devices	(2,647)	(2,419)	(2,603)
399	Wang Laboratories (CLB)	(2,815)	(2,368)	(2,564)
398	Motorola Inc.	(3,863)	(2,270)	(2,588)

Panel B: Performance measures for the 35 companies ranked at the top of the list of 432 companies in the period 1980–1990 on performance measure 2. r = 10 percent.

		Performance Measure (Millions)		
Rank	Company	1	2	3
35	Kellogg Co.	5,747	7,190	8,245
34	Pfizer Inc.	4,607	7,477	8,650
33	General Mills Inc.	6,205	7,605	8,256
32	Kyocera Corp. (ADR)	7,194	7,959	7,709
31	Minnesota Mining & Mfg. Co.	2,375	8,270	10,008
30	Canon Inc. (ADR)	7,717	8,326	8,285

Rank	Company	Performance Measure (Millions)		
		1	2	3
29	Matsushita Electric (ADR)	5,356	8,694	6,999
28	Tele-Communications (CLA)	8,692	8,998	8,698
27	Kubota Corp. (ADR)	7,383	9,246	8,280
26	Marion Merrell Dow Inc.	9,489	9,606	9,865
25	Unilever N.V. (N.Y. shares)	8,642	10,574	12,510
24	Fuji Photo Film (ADR)	10,102	10,858	10,518
23	Hitachi Ltd. (ADR)	8,412	10,863	10,800
22	Amoco Corp.	(331)	11,437	14,838
21	Sony Corp. (Amer. shares)	10,001	11,591	11,019
20	Lilly (Eli) & Co.	7,462	11,818	12,001
19	Ito Yokado Co. Ltd. (ADR)	12,415	13,178	12,982
18	Abbot Laboratories	11,076	13,555	14,043
17	Johnson & Johnson	8,945	13,796	13,199
16	Nynex Corp.	7,971	13,975	14,856
15	U.S. West Inc.	8,696	14,398	14,430
14	Exxon Corp.	(9,213)	14,976	40,096
13	Pacific Telesis Group	11,530	16,846	17,648
12	Glaxo Holdings P.L.C. (ADR)	16,215	17,007	18,348
11	Southwestern Bell Corp.	11,807	17,702	17,880
10	Ameritech Corp.	11,883	18,453	18,516
9	Procter & Gamble Co.	12,900	19,247	20,293
8	Bell Atlantic Corp.	13,146	19,921	20,235
7	Bellsouth Corp.	15,205	23,921	24,644
6	Merck & Co.	22,606	28,045	28,092
5	Loews Corp.	28,540	29,265	29,579
4	General Electric Co.	18,411	29,945	36,363
3	Bristol Myers Squibb	27,899	30,321	33,296
2	Wal-Mart Stores	37,701	38,239	38,486
1	Philip Morris Cos. Inc.	37,548	42,032	47,029

Table 1.5 Summary Statistics on R&D, Capital Expenditures, and Performance Measures for 432 Firms with Sales Greater than $250 Million in the Period 1980–1990 $r = 10$ percent (millions of dollars)

Statistic	R&D Expenditures	Net Capital Expenditures	Performance Measure 1	Performance Measure 2	Performance Measure 3
Mean	1,296	1,367	−221	1,086	1,480
Minimum	0	−377	−115,188	−100,720	−90,023
0.1 fractile	0	23	−3,015	−1,388	1,283
0.25 fractile	19	66	−693	−109	103
0.5 fractile	146	233	24	200	206
0.75 fractile	771	1012	577	1,220	1,386
0.9 fractile	3,295	3,267	3,817	5,610	6,385
Maximum	42,742	34,456	37,701	42,032	47,029
Standard Deviation	3,838	3,613	8,471	7,618	7,676

internal control system, has the final responsibility for the functioning of the firm. Most importantly, it sets the rules of the game for the CEO. The job of the board is to hire, fire, and compensate the CEO, and to provide high-level counsel. Few boards in the past decades have done this job well in the absence of external crises. This is particularly unfortunate given that the very purpose of the internal control mechanism is to provide an early warning system to put the organization back on track before difficulties reach a crisis stage. The reasons for the failure of the board are not completely understood, but we are making progress toward understanding these complex issues. The available evidence does suggest that CEOs are removed after poor performance,[38] but the effect, while statistically significant, seems too late and too small to meet the obligations of the board. I believe bad systems or rules, not bad people, underlie the general failings of boards of directors.

Some caution is advisable here because while resolving problems with boards can cure the difficulties associated with a nonfunctioning court of last resort, this alone cannot solve all the problems with defective internal control systems. I resist the temptation in an already lengthy paper to launch into a discussion of other organizational and strategic issues that must be attacked. A well-functioning board, however, is capable of providing the organizational culture and supporting environment for a continuing attack on these issues.

Board culture

Board culture is an important component of board failure. The great emphasis on politeness and courtesy at the expense of truth and frankness in boardrooms is both a symptom and cause of failure in the control system. CEOs have the same insecurities and defense mechanisms as other human beings; few will accept, much less seek, the monitoring and criticism of an active and attentive board. Magnet (1992, p. 86) gives an example of this environment. John Hanley, retired Monsanto CEO, accepted an invitation from a CEO

> to join his board—subject, Hanley wrote, to meeting with the company's general counsel and outside accountants as a kind of directorial due diligence. Says Hanley: "At the first board dinner the CEO got up and said, 'I think Jack was a little bit confused whether we wanted him to be a director or the chief executive

officer.' I should have known right there that he wasn't going to pay a goddamn bit of attention to anything I said." So it turned out, and after a year Hanley quit the board in disgust.

The result is a continuing cycle of ineffectiveness: by rewarding consent and discouraging conflicts, CEOs have the power to control the board, which in turn ultimately reduces the CEO's and the company's performance. This downward spiral makes the resulting difficulties likely to be a crisis rather than a series of small problems met by a continuous self-correcting mechanism. The culture of boards will not change simply in response to calls for change from policy makers, the press, or academics. It only will follow, or be associated with, general recognition that past practices have resulted in major failures and substantive changes in the rules and practices governing the system.

Information problems

Serious information problems limit the effectiveness of board members in the typical large corporation. For example, the CEO almost always determines the agenda and the information given to the board. This limitation on information severely hinders the ability of even highly talented board members to contribute effectively to the monitoring and evaluation of the CEO and the company's strategy.

Moreover, the board requires expertise to provide input into the financial aspects of planning—especially in forming the corporate objective and determining the factors which affect corporate value. Yet such financial expertise is generally lacking on today's boards. Consequently, boards (and management) often fail to understand why long-run market value maximization is generally the privately and socially optimal corporate objective, and they often fail to understand how to translate this objective into a feasible foundation for corporate strategy and operating policy.

Legal liability

The factors that motivate modern boards are generally inadequate. Boards are often motivated by substantial legal liabilities through class action suits initiated by shareholders, the plaintiff's bar, and others—lawsuits which are often triggered by unexpected declines in stock price. These legal incentives are more often consistent with minimizing downside risk rather than maximizing value. Boards are also motivated by threats of adverse publicity from the media or from the political/regulatory authorities. Again, while these incentives often provide motivation for board members to cover their own interests, they do not necessarily provide proper incentives to take actions that create efficiency and value for the company.

Lack of management and board member equity holdings

Many problems arise from the fact that neither managers nor nonmanager board members typically own substantial fractions of their firm's equity. While the average CEO of the 1,000 largest firms (measured by market value of equity) holds 2.7 percent of his or her firm's equity in 1991, the median holding is only 0.2 percent and 75 percent of CEOs own less than 1.2 percent (Murphy (1992)).[39] Encouraging outside board members to hold substantial equity interests would provide better incentives. Stewart (1990) outlines a useful approach using levered equity purchase plans or the sale of in-the-money options to executives to resolve this problem in large firms, where achieving significant ownership would require huge dollar outlays by managers or board members. By requiring significant outlays by managers for the purchase of these quasi equity interests, Stewart's approach reduces the incentive problems created by the asymmetry of payoffs in the typical option plan.

Boards should have an implicit understanding or explicit requirement that new members must invest in the stock of the company. While the initial investment could vary, it should seldom be less than $100,000 from the new board member's personal funds; this investment would force new board members to recognize from the outset that their decisions affect their own wealth as well as that of remote shareholders. Over the long term the investment can be made much larger by options or other stock-based compensation. The recent trend to pay some board member fees in stock or options is a move in the right direction. Discouraging board members from selling this equity is important so that holdings will accumulate to a significant size over time.

Oversized boards

Keeping boards small can help improve their performance. When boards get beyond seven or eight people they are less likely to function effectively and are easier for the CEO to control.[40] Since the possibility for animosity and retribution from the CEO is too great, it is almost impossible for those who report directly to the CEO to participate openly and critically in effective evaluation and monitoring of the CEO. Therefore, the only inside board member should be the CEO. Insiders other than the CEO can be regularly invited to attend board meetings in an ex officio capacity. Indeed, board members should be given regular opportunities to meet with and observe executives below the CEO—both to expand their knowledge of the company and CEO succession candidates, and to increase other top-level executives' understanding of the thinking of the board and the board process.

Attempts to model the process after political democracy

Suggestions to model the board process after a democratic political model in which various constituencies are represented are likely to make the process even weaker. To see this we need look no farther than the inefficiency of representative political democracies (whether at the local, state, or federal level), or at their management of quasi-business organizations such as the Post Office, schools, or power generation entities such as the TVA. This does not mean, however, that the current corporate system is satisfactory as it stands; indeed there is significant room for rethinking and revision.

For example, proxy regulations by the SEC make the current process far less efficient than it otherwise could be. Specifically, it has been illegal for any shareholder to discuss company matters with more than ten other shareholders without prior filing with, and approval of, the SEC. The November 1992 relaxation of this restriction allows an investor to communicate with an unlimited number of other stockholders provided the investor owns less than 5 percent of the shares, has no special interest in the issue being discussed, and is not seeking proxy authority. These restrictions still have obvious shortcomings that limit effective institutional action by those shareholders most likely to pursue an issue.

As equity holdings become concentrated in institutional hands, it is easier to resolve some of the free-rider problems that limit the ability of thousands of individual shareholders to engage in effective collective action. In principle such institutions can therefore begin to exercise corporate control rights more effectively. Legal and regulatory restrictions, however, have prevented financial institutions from playing a major corporate monitoring role. (Roe (1990, 1991), Black (1990), and Pound (1991) provide an excellent historical review of these restrictions.) Therefore, if institutions are to aid in effective governance, we must continue to dismantle the rules and regulations that have prevented them and other large investors from accomplishing this coordination.

The CEO as chairman of the board

It is common in U.S. corporations for the CEO to also hold the position of chairman of the board. The function of the chairman is to run board meetings and oversee the process of hiring, firing, evaluating, and compensating the CEO. Clearly, the CEO cannot perform this function apart from his or her personal interest. Without the direction of an independent leader, it is much more difficult for the board to perform its critical function. Therefore, for the board to be effective, it is important to separate the CEO and chairman positions.[41] The independent chairman should, at a minimum, be given the rights to initiate board appointments, board committee assignments, and (jointly with the CEO) the setting of the board's agenda. All these recommendations, of course, will be made conditional on the ratification of the board.

An effective board will often evidence tension among its members as well as with the CEO. But I hasten to add that I am not advocating continuous war in the boardroom. In fact, in well-functioning organizations the board will generally be relatively inactive and will exhibit little conflict. It becomes important primarily when the rest of the internal control system is failing, and this should be a relatively rare event. The challenge is to create a system that will not fall into complacency and inactivity during periods of prosperity and high-quality management, and therefore be unable to rise early to the challenge of correcting a failing management system. This is a difficult task because there are strong tendencies for boards to evolve a culture and social norms that reflect optimal behavior under prosperity, and these norms make it extremely difficult for the board to respond early to failure in its top management team.[42]

Resurrecting active investors

A major set of problems with internal control systems are associated with the curbing of what I call active investors (Jensen (1989a, 1989b)). Active investors are individuals or institutions that simultaneously hold large debt and/or equity positions in a company and actively participate in its strategic direction. Active investors are important to a well-functioning governance system because they have the financial interest and independence to view firm management and policies in an unbiased way. They have the incentives to buck the system to correct problems early rather than late when the problems are obvious but difficult to correct. Financial institutions such as banks, pensions funds, insurance companies, mutual funds, and money managers are natural active investors, but they have been shut out of board rooms and firm strategy by the legal structure, by custom, and by their own practices.[43]

Active investors are important to a well-functioning governance system, and there is much we can do to dismantle the web of legal, tax, and regulatory apparatus that severely limits the scope of active investors in this country.[44] But even absent these regulatory changes, CEOs and boards can take actions to encourage investors to hold large positions in their debt and equity and to play an active role in the strategic direction of the firm and in monitoring the CEO.

Wise CEOs can recruit large block investors to serve on the board, even selling new equity or debt to them to induce their commitment to the firm. Lazard Freres Corporate Partners Fund is an example of an institution set up specifically to perform this function, making new funds available to the firm and taking a board seat to advise and monitor management performance. Warren Buffet's activity through Berkshire Hathaway provides another example of a well-known active investor. He played an important role in helping Salomon Brothers through its recent legal and organizational difficulties following the government bond bidding scandal. Dobrzynski (1993) discusses many varieties of this phenomenon (which she calls relationship investing) that are currently arising both in the United States and abroad.

Using LBOs and venture capital firms as models of successful organization, governance, and control

Organizational experimentation in the 1980s

Founded on the assumption that firm cash flows are independent of financial policy,

the Modigliani-Miller (M&M) theorems on the independence of firm value, leverage, and payout policy have been extremely productive in helping the finance profession structure the logic of many valuation issues. The 1980s control activities, however, have demonstrated that the M & M theorems (while logically sound) are empirically incorrect. The evidence from LBOs, leveraged restructurings, takeovers, and venture capital firms has demonstrated dramatically that leverage, payout policy, and ownership structure (that is, who owns the firm's securities) do in fact affect organizational efficiency, cash flow, and, therefore, value.[45] Such organizational changes show these effects are especially important in low-growth or declining firms where the agency costs of free cash flow are large.[46]

Evidence from LBOs

LBOs provide a good source of estimates of value gain from changing leverage, payout policies, and the control and governance system because, to a first approximation, the company has the same managers and the same assets, but a different financial policy and control system after the transaction.[47] Leverage increases from about 18 percent of value to 90 percent, large payouts to prior shareholders occur, equity becomes concentrated in the hands of managers (over 20 percent on average) and the board (about 20 and 60 percent on average, respectively), boards shrink to about seven or eight people, the sensitivity of managerial pay to performance rises, and the companies' equity usually become nonpublicly traded (although debt is often publicly traded).

The evidence of DeAngelo, DeAngelo, and Rice (1984), Kaplan (1989), Smith (1990), and others indicates that premiums to selling-firm shareholders are roughly 40 to 50 percent of the prebuyout market value, cash flows increase by 96 percent from the year before the buyout to three years after the buyout, and value increases by 235 percent (96 percent market adjusted) from two months prior to the buyout offer to the time of going public, sale, or recapitalization about three years later on average.[48] Palepu and Wruck (1992) show that large value increases also occur in voluntary recapitalizations where the company stays public but buys back a significant fraction of its equity or pays out a significant dividend. Clinical studies of individual cases demonstrate that these changes in financial and governance policies generate value-creating changes in behavior of managers and employees.[49]

A proven model of governance structure

LBO associations and venture capital funds provide a blueprint for managers and boards who wish to revamp their top-level control systems to make them more efficient. LBOs and venture capital funds are, of course, the preeminent examples of active investors in recent U.S. history, and they serve as excellent models that can be emulated in part or in total by virtually any corporation. The two have similar governance structures, and have been successful in resolving the governance problems of both slow growth or declining firms (LBO associations) and high growth entrepreneurial firms (venture capital funds).[50]

Both LBO associations and venture capital funds, of which KKR and Kleiner Perkins are prominent examples, tend to be organized as limited partnerships. In effect, the institutions which contribute the funds to these organizations are delegating the task of being active investors to the general partners of the organizations. Both governance systems are characterized by:

a. limited partnership agreements at the top level that prohibit headquarters from cross-subsidizing one division with the cash from another,
b. high equity ownership on the part of managers and board members,
c. board members (who are mostly the LBO association partners or the venture capitalists) who in their funds directly represent a large fraction of the equity owners of each subsidiary company,
d. small boards of directors (of the operating companies) typically

consisting of no more than eight people,
e. CEOs who are typically the only insider on the board, and finally
f. CEOs who are seldom the chairman of the board.

LBO associations and venture funds also solve many of the information problems facing typical boards of directors. First, as a result of the due diligence process at the time the deal is done, both the managers and the LBO and venture partners have extensive and detailed knowledge of virtually all aspects of the business. In addition, these boards have frequent contact with management, often weekly or even daily during times of difficult challenges. This contact and information flow is facilitated by the fact that LBO associations and venture funds both have their own staff. They also often perform the corporate finance function for the operating companies, providing the major interface with the capital markets and investment banking communities.

Finally, the close relationship between the LBO partners or venture fund partners and the operating companies facilitates the infusion of expertise from the board during times of crisis. It is not unusual for a partner to join the management team, even as CEO, to help an organization through such emergencies. Very importantly, there are market forces that operate to limit the human tendency to micromanage and thereby overcentralize management in the headquarters staff. If headquarters develops a reputation for abusing the relationship with the CEO, the LBO or venture organization will find it more difficult to complete new deals (which frequently depend on the CEO being willing to sell the company to the LBO fund or on the new entrepreneur being willing to sell an equity interest in the new venture to the venture capital organization).

IX. IMPLICATIONS FOR THE FINANCE PROFESSION

One implication of the foregoing discussion is that finance has failed to provide firms with an effective mechanism to achieve efficient corporate investment. While modern capital-budgeting procedures are implemented by virtually all large corporations, it appears that the net present value (or more generally, value-maximizing) rule imbedded in these procedures is far from universally followed by operating managers. In particular, the acceptance of negative-value projects tends to be common in organizations with substantial amounts of free cash flow (cash flow in excess of that required to fund all value-increasing investment projects) and in particular in firms and industries where downsizing and exit are required. The finance profession has concentrated on how capital investment decisions should be made, with little systematic study of how they actually *are* made in practice.[51] This narrowly normative view of investment decisions has led the profession to ignore what has become a major worldwide efficiency problem that will be with us for several decades to come.

Agency theory (the study of the inevitable conflicts of interest that occur when individuals engage in cooperative behavior) has fundamentally changed corporate finance and organization theory, but it has yet to affect substantially research on capital-budgeting procedures. No longer can we assume managers automatically act (in opposition to their own best interests) to maximize firm value.

Conflicts between managers and the firm's financial claimants were brought to center stage by the market for corporate control in the last two decades. This market brought widespread experimentation, teaching us not only about corporate finance, but also about the effects of leverage, governance arrangements, and active investors on incentives and organizational efficiency. These events have taught us much about the interdependencies among the implicit and explicit contracts specifying the following three elements of organizations:

1. Finance—I use this term narrowly here to refer to the definition and structure of financial claims on the firm's cash flows (e.g., equity, bond, preferred stock, and warrant claims).[52]

2. Governance—the top-level control structure, consisting of the decision rights possessed by the board of directors and the CEO, the procedures for changing them, the size and membership of the board, and the compensation and equity holdings of managers and the board.[53]

3. Organization—the nexus of contracts defining the internal "rules of the game" (the performance measurement and evaluation system, the reward and punishment system, and the system for allocating decision rights to agents in the organization).[54]

The close interrelationships between these factors have dragged finance scholars into the analysis of governance and organization theory.[55] In addition, the perceived "excesses of the 1980s" have generated major reregulation of financial markets in the United States affecting the control market, credit markets (especially the banking, thrift, and insurance industries), and market microstructure.[56] These changes have highlighted the importance of the political and regulatory environment to financial, organizational, and governance policies, and generated a new interest in what I call the "politics of finance."[57]

The dramatic growth of these new research areas has fragmented the finance profession, which can no longer be divided simply into the study of capital markets and corporate finance. Finance is now much less an exercise in valuing a given stream of cash flows (although this is still important) and much more the study of how to increase those cash flows—an effort that goes far beyond the capital asset pricing model, Modigliani and Miller irrelevance propositions, and capital budgeting. This fragmentation is evidence of progress, not failure; but the inability to understand this maturation causes conflict in those quarters where research is judged and certified, including the academic journals and university departments. Specialists in different subfields have tended to react by labeling research in areas other than their own as "low-quality" and "illegitimate." Acknowledging this separation and nurturing communication among the subfields will help avoid this intellectual warfare with substantial benefit to the progress of the profession.

My review of macro and organizational trends in the previous pages has highlighted many areas for future research for finance scholars. They include understanding:

- the implications of the modern (or Third) Industrial Revolution, and how it will affect financial, product, and labor markets, as well as the level and distribution of worldwide income and wealth.

  - how industry-wide excess capacity arises, how markets and firms respond to such market pressures, and why exit is so difficult for organizations to deal with.
  - the implications of new technology for organizational downsizing.
  - the financial policies appropriate for the new virtual or network organizations that are arising.

- the weaknesses that cause internal corporate control systems to fail and how to correct them.

  - the reasons for the asymmetry between corporate growth and decline, and how to limit the organizational and strategic inefficiencies that seem to creep into highly successful rapidly growing organizations.
  - how capital budgeting decisions are actually made and how organizational practices can be implemented that will reduce the tendency to accept negative value projects.

  - the nature of implicit contracts, the optimal degree to which private contracts should be left open to abrogation or change, and how to bond or monitor to limit opportunistic behavior regarding those implicit contracts.

- how politics, the press, and public opinion affect the types of governance, financial, and organizational policies that firms adopt.

  - how capital market forces can be made a politically and economically efficient part of corporate control mechanisms.
  - how active investors can be resurrected and reconciled with a legal structure that currently favors liquid and anonymous markets over the intimate illiquid market relations that seem to be required for efficient governance.

X. CONCLUSION

For those with a normative bent, making the internal control systems of corporations work is the major challenge facing economists and management scholars in the 1990s. For those who choose to take a purely positive approach, the major challenge is understanding how these systems work, and how they interact with the other control forces (in particular the product and factor markets, legal, political, and regulatory systems, and the capital markets) impinging on the corporation. I believe the reason we have an interest in developing positive theories of the world is so that we can understand how to make things work more efficiently. Without accurate positive theories of cause and effect relationships, normative propositions and decisions based on them will be wrong. Therefore, the two objectives are completely consistent.

Financial economists have a unique advantage in working on these control and organizational problems because we understand what determines value, and we know how to think about uncertainty and objective functions. To do this we have to understand even better than we do now the factors leading to organizational past failures (and successes): we have to break open the black box called the firm, and this means understanding how organizations and the people in them work. In short, we're facing the problem of developing a viable theory of organizations. To be successful we must continue to broaden our thinking to new topics and to learn and develop new analytical tools.

This research effort is a very profitable venture. I commend it to you.

APPENDIX: DIRECT ESTIMATES OF THE PRODUCTIVITY OF R&D—THE MODEL

Consider a firm in period t with cash flow from operations, C_t, available for:

R_t = R&D expenditures,
K_t = capital investment,
d_t = payments to shareholders in the form of dividends and net share repurchases,
b_t = interest and net debt payments,
a_t = acquisitions net of asset sales.
$d < 0, b < 0, a < 0$ mean respectively that a new equity is raised in the form of capital contributions from equityholders, net bond issues exceed interest and debt repayments, and asset sales exceed acquisitions.

By definition $C_t = R_t + K_t + d_t + b_t + a_t$ The initial value of the firm equals the sum of the market values of equity and debt, $V_0 = S_0 + B_0$ and the final value at the end of period n, is V_n. Assume for simplicity that taxes are zero, and debt is riskless. If r is the riskless interest rate and ρ is the cost of equity capital, the total value, V_T, created by the firm's investment, R&D, and payout policy measured at the future horizon date n, is the final value of the firm plus the ending value of the dividend payments

plus stock repurchases plus the ending value of the interest payments plus debt payments

$$V_T = V_n + \Sigma d_t(1 + \rho)^{n-t} + b_t(1 + r)^{n-t},$$

where the investor is assumed to reinvest all intermediate payouts from the firm at the cost of equity and debt, ρ and r respectively.

Consider an alternative strategy which pays the same dividends and stock repurchases, d_t, (and raises the same outside capital) and puts the R&D and capital and acquisition expenditures (in excess of depreciation) in marketable securities of the same risk as the R&D and capital expenditures, yielding expected returns equal to their cost of capital, i. Under the assumption that the zero investment and R&D strategy yields a terminal value, V'_n, equal to the ending debt, B_n, plus the beginning value of equity, S_0, (that is, investment equal to depreciation is sufficient to maintain the original equity value of the firm), the value created by this strategy is

$$V'_T = S_0 + B_n + \Sigma(K_t + R_t + a_t)$$
$$(1 + i)^{n-t} + \Sigma d_t(1 + \rho)^{n-t}$$
$$+ b_t(1 + r)^{n-t}$$

The difference between the terminal values of the two strategies is

$$V_T - V'_T = V_n - V'_n - \Sigma(K_t + R_t + a_t)$$
$$(1 + i)^{n-t}$$
$$= S_n - S_0 - \Sigma(K_t + R_t + a_t)$$
$$(1 + i)^{n-t} \quad (1)$$

This is my first crude measure of the productivity of R&D and capital expenditures. Unless capital and R&D expenditures are completely unproductive, this measure will be biased downward. Therefore I define two more conservative measures that will yield higher estimates of the productivity of these expenditures. The second assumes that replacement of depreciation and zero expenditures on R&D are sufficient to maintain the intermediate cash flows but at the end of the period the firm has equity value of zero. This second measure is:

$$V_T - V'_T = V_n - B_n - \frac{\Sigma(K_t + R_t + a_t)}{(1 + i)^{n - t}} \qquad (2)$$

Alternatively, to allow for the effects of the reduced investment and R&D on intermediate cash flows my third measure assumes that all intermediate cash flows are reduced in the benchmark investment strategy by the amount paid out to shareholders in the form of dividends and net share repurchases and that the original value of the equity is maintained. This measure is likely to yield an upward biased estimate of the productivity of R&D and capital expenditures. The measure is:[58]

$$\begin{aligned} V_T - V'_T &= V_n + \Sigma d_t (1 + r)^{n - t} \\ &= S_0 - B_n - \frac{\Sigma(K_t + R_t + a_t)}{(1 + i)^{n - t}} \end{aligned} \qquad (3)$$

NOTES

* Harvard Business School. Presidential Address to the American Finance Association, January 1993, Anaheim, California. I appreciate the research assistance of Chris Allen, Brian Barry, Susan Brumfield, Karin Monsler, and particularly Donna Feinberg, the support of the Division of Research of the Harvard Business School, and the comments of and discussions with George Baker, Carliss Baldwin, Joe Bower, Alfred Chandler, Harry and Linda DeAngelo, Ben Esty, Takashi Hikino, Steve Kaplan, Nancy Koehn, Claudio Loderer, George Lodge, John Long, Kevin Murphy, Malcolm Salter, René Stulz, Richard Tedlow, and especially Richard Hackman, Richard Hall, and Karen Wruck on many of these ideas.
1   In a rare finance study of exit, DeAngelo and DeAngelo (1991) analyze the retrenchment of the U.S. steel industry in the 1980s. Ghemawat and Nalebuff (1985) have an interesting paper entitled "Exit," and Anderson (1986) provides a detailed comparison of U.S. and Japanese retrenchment in the 1970s and early 1980s and their respective political and regulatory policies toward the issues. Bower (1984, 1986) analyzes the private and political responses to decline in the petrochemical industry. Harrigan (1988,

1980) conducts detailed firm and industry studies. See also Hirschman's (1970) work on exit.
2   Measured by multifactor productivity, U.S. Department of Labor (USDL) (1990, Table 3). See Jensen (1991) for a summary. Multifactor productivity showed no growth between 1973 and 1980 and grew at the rate of 1.9 percent per year between 1950 and 1973. Manufacturing labor productivity grew at an annual rate of 2.3 percent in the period 1950 to 1981 and at 3.8 percent in 1981 to 1990 (USDL, 1990, Table 3). Using data recently revised by the Bureau of Economic Analysis from 1977 to 1990, the growth rate in the earlier period was 2.2 and 3.0 percent in the 1981 to 1990 period (USDL, 1991, Table 1). Productivity growth in the nonfarm business sector fell from 1.9 percent in the 1950 to 1981 period to 1.1 percent in the 1981 to 1990 period (USDL, 1990, Table 2). The reason for the fall apparently lies in the relatively large growth in the service sector relative to the manufacturing sector and the low measured productivity growth in services.
There is considerable controversy over the adequacy of the measurement of productivity in the service sector. The USDL has no productivity measures for services employing nearly 70 percent of service workers, including, among others, health care, real estate, and securities brokerage. In addition, many believe that service sector productivity growth measures are downward biased. Service sector price measurements, for example, take no account of the improved productivity and lower prices of discount outlet clubs such as Sam's Club. The Commerce Department measures output of financial services as the value of labor used to produce it. Since labor productivity is defined as the value of total output divided by total labor inputs it is impossible for measured productivity to grow. Between 1973 and 1987 total equity shares traded daily grew from 5.7 million to 63.8 million, while employment only doubled—implying considerably more productivity growth than that reflected in the statistics. Other factors, however, contribute to potential overestimates of productivity growth in the manufacturing sector. See Malabre and Clark (1992) and Richman (1993).
3   Nominal and real hourly compensation, *Economic Report of the President*, Table B42 (1993).
4   USDL (1991).
5   USDL (1990). Trends in U.S. producivity have been controversial issues in academic and policy circles in the last decade. One reason,

I believe, is that it takes time for these complicated changes to show up in the aggregate statistics. In their recent book Baumol, Blackman, and Wolff (1989, pp. ix-x) changed their formerly pessimistic position. In their words: "This book is perhaps most easily summed up as a compendium of evidence demonstrating the error of our previous ways. . . . The main change that was forced upon our views by careful examination of the long-run data was abandonment of our earlier gloomy assessment of American productivity performance. It has been replaced by the guarded optimism that pervades this book. This does *not* mean that we believe retention of American leadership will be automatic or easy. Yet the statistical evidence did drive us to conclude that the many writers who have suggested that the demise of America's traditional position has already occurred or was close at hand were, like the author of Mark Twain's obituary, a bit premature. . . . It should, incidentally, be acknowledged that a number of distinguished economists have also been driven to a similar evaluation . . . "

6   As measured by the Wilshire 5,000 index of all publicly held equities.

7   Bureau of the Census (1991).

8   *Business Week Annual R&D Scoreboard.*

9   Annual premiums reported by *Mergerstat Review* (1991, fig. 5) weighted by value of transaction in the year for this estimate.

10   I assume that all transactions without publicly disclosed prices have a value equal to 20 percent of the value of the average publicly disclosed transaction in the same year, and that they have average premiums equal to those for publicly disclosed transactions.

11   In some cases buyers overpay, perhaps because of mistakes or because of agency problems with their own shareholders. Such overpayment represents only a wealth transfer from the buying firm's claimants to those of the selling firm and not an efficiency gain.

12   Healy, Palepu, and Ruback (1992) estimate the total gains to buying- and selling-firm shareholders in the 50 largest mergers in the period 1979 to 1984 at 9.1 percent. They also find a strong positive cross-sectional relation between the value change and the cash flow changes resulting from the merger.

13   See Kaplan (1989), Jensen, Kaplan, and Stiglin (1989), Pontiff, Shleifer, and Weisbach (1990), Asquith and Wizman (1990), and Rosett (1990).

14   Its high of $139.50 occurred on 2/19/91 and it closed at $50.38 at the end of 1992.

15   Zellner (1992) discusses the difficulties traditional retailers have in meeting Wal-Mart's prices.

16   Vietor, Forthcoming.

17   Source: COMPUSTAT.

18   "In 1980 IBM's top-of-the-line computers provided 4.5 MIPS (millions of instructions per second) for $4.5 million. By 1990, the cost of a MIP on a personal computer had dropped to $1,000 . . ." (Keene (1991)), p. 110). By 1993 the price had dropped to under $100. The technological progress in personal computers has itself been stunning. Intel's Pentium (586) chip, introduced in 1993, has a capacity of 100 MIPS—100 times the capacity of its 286 chip introduced in 1982 (Brandt (1993)). In addition, the progress of storage, printing, and other related technology has also been rapid (Christensen (1993)).

19   The *Journal of Financial Economics* which I have been editing with several others since 1973 is an example. The *JFE* is now edited by seven faculty members with offices at three universities in different states and the main editorial administrative office is located in yet another state. North Holland, the publisher, is located in Amsterdam, the printing is done in India, and mailing and billing is executed in Switzerland. This "networked organization" would have been extremely inefficient two decades ago without fax machines, high-speed modems, electronic mail, and overnight delivery services.

20   Wruck and Jensen (1993) provide an analysis of the critical organizational innovations that total quality management is bringing to the technology of management.

21   A collapse I predicted in Jensen (1989a).

22   See Neff, Holyoke, Gross, and Miller (1993).

23   Steel industry employment is now down to 160,000 from its peak of 600,000 in 1953 (Fader (1993)).

24   I am indebted to Steven Cheung for discussions on these issues.

25   Although migration will play a role it will be relatively small compared to the export of the labor in products and services. Swissair's 1987 transfer of part of its reservation system to Bombay and its 1991 announcement of plans to transfer 150 accounting jobs to the same city are small examples (Economist Intelligence Unit (1991)).

26   Thailand and China have played a role in the world markets in the last decade, but since it has been such a small part of their potential I have left them in the potential entrant category.

27 In a recent article focusing on the prospects for textile manufacturer investment in Central European countries, van Delden (1993, p. 43) reports: "When major French group Rhone Poulenc's fibres division started a discussion for a formal joint venture in 1991, they discovered an example of astonishing competitiveness. Workers—whose qualifications matched those normal in the West—cost only 8% of their West European counterparts, and yet achieved productivity rates of between 60% and 75% compared to EC level. Moreover, energy costs of the integrated power station are 50% below West German costs, and all of this is complemented by extremely competitive raw material prices."

The textile industry illustrates the problems with chronic excess capacity brought on by a situation where the worldwide demand for textiles grows fairly constantly, but growth in the productivity of textile machinery through technological improvements is greater. Moreover, additional capacity is being created because new entrants to the global textile market must upgrade outdated (and less productive) weaving machinery with new technology to meet minimum global quality standards. This means excess capacity is likely to be a continuing problem in the industry and that adjustment will have to occur through exit of capacity in high-cost Western textile mills.

28 Total quality management programs strongly encourage managers to benchmark their firm's operations against the most successful worldwide competitors, and good cost systems and competitive benchmarking are becoming more common in well-managed firms.

29 Shleifer and Summers (1988) seem to take the position that all implicit contracts should be enforced rigidly and never be breached.

30 A partial list of references is: Dann and DeAngelo (1988), Mann and Sicherman (1991), Baker and Wruck (1989), Berger and Ofek (1993), Bhide (1993), Brickley, Jarrell, and Netter (1988), Denis (1992), Donaldson (1990), DeAngelo and DeAngelo (1991), DeAngelo, DeAngelo, and Rice (1984), Esty (1992, 1993), Grundfest (1990), Holderness and Sheehan (1991), Jensen (1986a, 1986b, 1988, 1989a, 1989b, 1991), Kaplan (1989a, 1989b, 1992), Lang, Poulsen, and Stulz (1992), Lang, Stulz, and Walkling (1991), Lewellen, Loderer, and Martin (1987), Lichtenberg (1992), Lichtenberg and Siegel (1990), Ofek (1993), Palepu (1990), Pound (1988, 1991, 1992), Roe (1990, 1991), Smith (1990), Tedlow (1991), Tiemann (1990), Wruck and Stephens (1992a, 1992b), Wruck (1990, 1991, 1992), Wruck and Palepu (1992).

31 In May 1985, Uniroyal approved an LBO proposal to block hostile advances by Carl Icahn. About the same time, BF Goodrich began diversifying out of the tire business. In January 1986, Goodrich and Uniroyal independently spun off their tire divisions and together, in a 50–50 joint venture, formed the Uniroyal-Goodrich Tire Company. By December 1987, Goodrich had sold its interest in the venture to Clayton and Dubilier; Uniroyal followed soon after. Similarly, General tire moved away from tires: the company, renamed GenCorp in 1984, sold its tire division to Continental in 1987. Other takeovers in the industry during this period include the sale of Firestone to Bridgestone and Pirelli's purchase of the Armstrong Tire Company. By 1991, Goodyear was the only remaining major American tire manufacturer. Yet it too faced challenges in the control market: in 1986, following three years of unprofitable diversifying investments, Goodyear initiated a major leveraged stock repurchase and restructuring to defend itself from a hostile takeover from Sir James Goldsmith. Uniroyal-Goodrich was purchased by Michelin in 1990. See Tedlow (1991).

32 In 1992 dollars, calculated from *Mergerstat Review*, 1991, p. 100f.

33 In 1992 dollars, *Mergerstat Review*, 1991, figs. 29 and 38.

34 Source: GE annual reports.

35 Because of the sharp decline in Japanese stock prices, the Japanese firms ranked in the top 35 firms would have performed less well if the period since 1990 had been included.

36 I am in the process of creating a database that avoids the survivorship bias. Hall (1993a, 1993b) in a large sample free of survivorship bias finds lower market valuation of R&D in the 1980s and hypothesizes that this is due to a higher depreciation rate for R&D capital. The Stern Stewart Performance 1000 (1992) ranks companies by a measure of the economic value added by management decisions that is an alternative to performance measures 1–3 summarized in Table 1.4 GM also ranks at the bottom of this list.

37 Changes in market expectations about the prospects for a firm (and therefore changes in its market value) obviously can affect the interpretation of the performance measures. Other than using a long period of time there is no simple way to handle this problem. The large

increase in stock prices in the 1980s would indicate that expectations were generally being revised upward.

38   CEO turnover approximately doubles from 3 to 6 percent after two years of poor performance (stock returns less than 50 percent below equivalent-risk market returns, Weisbach (1988)), or increases from 8.3 to 13.9 percent from the highest to the lowest performing decile of firms (Warner, Watts, and Wruck (1988)). See also DeAngelo (1888) and DeAngelo and DeAngelo (1989).

39   See also Jensen and Murphy (1990a, 1990b) for similar estimates based on earlier data.

40   In their excellent analysis of boards, Lipton and Lorsch (1992) also criticize the functioning of traditionally configured boards, recommend limiting membership to seven or eight people, and encourage equity ownership by board members. Research supports the proposition that as groups increase in size they become less effective because the coordination and process problems overwhelm the advantages gained from having more people to draw on (see Steiner (1972) and Hackman (1990)).

41   Lipton and Lorsch (1992) stop short of recommending appointment of an independent chairman, recommending instead the appointment of a "lead director" whose functions would be to coordinate board activities.

42   Gersick and Hackman (1990) and Hackman (1993) study a similar problem: the issues associated with habitual behavior routines in groups to understand how to create more productive environments. They apply the analysis to airline cockpit crews.

43   See Roe (1990, 1991), Black (1990), and Pound (1991).

44   See Porter (1992a, 1992b, 1992c). Hall and Hall provide excellent empirical tests of the myopic capital market hypothesis on which much of debate on the functioning of U.S. capital markets rests.

45   See Kaplan (1989a, 1989b, 1989c, 1992), Smith (1990), Wruck (1990), Lichtenberg (1992), Lichtenberg and Siegel (1990), Healy, Palepu, and Ruback (1992), and Ofck (1993).

There have now been a number of detailed clinical and case studies of these transactions that document the effects of the changes on incentives and organizational effectiveness as well as the risks of bankruptcy from overleveraging. See Baker and Wruck (1989), Wruck (1991, 1992a), Holderness and Sheehan (1988, 1991), Wruck and Keating (1992a,

1992b), Wruck and Stephens (1992a, 1992b), Jensen and Barry (1992), Jensen, Burkhardt, and Barry (1992), Jensen, Dial, and Barry (1992), Lang and Stultz (1992), Denis (1992).

46   See Jensen (1986), and the references in the previous footnote.

47   Assets do change somewhat after an LBO because such firms often engage in asset sales after the transaction to pay down debt and to get rid of assets that are peripheral to the organization's core focus.

48   See Palepu (1990) for a review of research on LBOs, their governance changes, and their productivity effects. Kaplan and Stein (1993) show similar results in more recent data.

49   See references in footnote 45 above. In a counterexample, Healy and Palepu argue in their study of CUC that the value increase following its recapitalization occurred not because of incentive effects of the deal, but because of the information the recapitalization provided to the capital markets about the nature of the company's business and profitability.

50   Jensen (1989a, 1989b) and Sahlman (1990) analyze the LBO association and venture capital funds respectively.

51   Counterexamples are Bower (1970), Baldwin and Clark (1992), Baldwin (1982, 1988, 1991), Baldwin and Trigeorgis (1992), and Shleifer and Vishny (1989).

52   See Harris and Raviv (1988, 1991), and Stulz (1990).

53   Jensen (1989a, 1989b), Kester (1991), Sahlman (1990), Pound (1988, 1991, 1992).

54   Jensen (1983), Jensen and Meckling (1992).

55   Examples of this work include Gilson, Lang, and John (1990), Wruck (1990, 1991), Lang and Stulz (1992), Lang, and Poulsen, and Stulz (1992) on bankruptcy and financial distress, Warner, Watts, and Wruck (1989), Weisbach (1988), Jensen and Murphy (1990a, 1990b) and Gibbons and Murphy (1990) on executive turnover, compensation, and organizational performance, Esty (1992, 1993) on the effects of organizational form on thrift losses, Gilson and Kraakman (1991) on governance, Brickley and Dark (1987) on franchising, Boycko, Shleifer, and Vishny (1993), Kaplan (1989a, 1989b, 1989c, 1992), Smith (1990), Kaplan and Stein (1993), Palepu (1990), and Sahlman (1990) on leverage buyouts and venture capital organizations.

56   The 1989 Financial Institutions Reform, Recovery, and Enforcement Act increased federal authority and sanctions by shifting

regulation of the S&L industry from the FDIC to the Treasury, and insurance of the industry from FSLIC to the Federal Home Loan Bank Board. The act banned thrift investment in high-yield bonds, raised capital ratios and insurance premiums. The 1990 Comprehensive Thrift and Bank Fraud Prosecution and Tax Payer Recovery Act increased criminal penalties for financial institution-related crimes. The 1991 FDIC Improvement Act tightened examination and auditing standards, recapitalized the Bank Insurance Fund and limited foreign bank powers. The Truth in Banking Act of 1992 required stricter disclosure of interest rates and fees on deposit accounts and tightened advertising guidelines. The National Association of Insurance Commissioners (NAIC) substantially restricted the ability of insurance companies to invest in high-yield debt in 1990 to 1991.

57   See Jensen (1989b, 1991), Roe (1990, 1991), Grundfest (1990), Bhide (1993), Black (1990), Pound (1988, 1991, 1992), and DeAngleo, DeAngelo, and Gilson (1993).

58   Most conservatively, we could assume that the cutback in R&D and capital expenditures under the alternative strategy results in a reduction in intermediate cash flows by the amount of the net cash paid to shareholders in the form of dividends and share repurchases and a final equity value of zero.

$$V_T - V'_T = V_n + \Sigma d_t (1 + r)^{n-t} - B_n \\ - \Sigma (K_t + R_t)(1 + i)^{n-t} \quad (4)$$

I expect this measure provides an unreasonably high estimate of the productivity of R&D and investment expenditures and therefore do not report it.

REFERENCES

Anderson, Douglas, 1986, Managing retreat: Disinvestment policy, in Thomas K. McCraw, ed.: *America versus Japan* (Harvard Business School Press, Boston), pp. 337–372.

Argyris, Chris, 1990, *Overcoming Organizational Defenses* (Allyn and Bacon, Needham, Mass.).

Asquith, Paul, and Thierry A. Wizman, 1990, Event risk, convenants, and bondholder returns in leveraged buyouts, *Journal of Financial Economics* 27, 195–213.

Baker, George, and Karen Wruck, 1989, Organizational changes and value creation in leveraged buyouts: The case of O. M. Scott and Sons Company, *Journal of Financial Economics* 25, 163–190.

Baldwin, Carliss Y., 1982, Optimal sequential investment when capital is not readily reversible, *Journal of Finance* 37, 763–782.

——, 1988, Time inconsistency in capital budgeting, Working paper, Harvard Business School.

——, 1991, How capital budgeting deters innovation—and what companies can do about it, *Research-Technology Management*, November-December, 39–45.

—— and Kim B. Clark, 1992. Capabilities and capital investment: New perspectives on capital budgeting, *Journal of Applied Corporate Finance* 5, 67–82.

—— and Lenos Trigeorgis, 1992, Toward remedying the underinvestment problem: Competitiveness, real options, capabilities, and TQM, Working paper, Harvard Business School.

Baumol, William, Sue Anne Beattey Blackman, and Edward Wolff, 1989, *Productivity and American Leadership* (MIT Press, Boston).

Berger, Philip, and Eli Ofek, 1993, Leverage and value: The role of agency costs and taxes, Unpublished manuscript, The Wharton School.

Bhide, Amar, 1993, The hidden costs of stock market liquidity, *Journal of Financial Economics* 34, 31–55.

Black, Bernard S., 1990, Shareholder passivity reexamined, *Michigan Law Review* 89, 520–608.

Bower, Joseph L., 1970, *Managing the Resource Allocation Process: A Study of Corporate Planning and Investment* (Division of Research, Graduate School of Business Administration, Harvard University, Boston).

——, 1984, Restructuring petrochemicals: A comparative study of business and government to deal with a declining sector of the economy, in Bruce R. Scott and George C. Lodge, eds.: *U.S. Competitiveness in the World Economy* (Harvard Business School Press, Boston).

——, 1986, *When Markets Quake* (Harvard Business School Press, Boston).

Boycko, Maxim, Andrei Shleifer, and Robert W. Vishny, 1993, Voucher privatization, Unpublished manuscript, Harvard University.

Brandt, Richard, 1993, Tiny transistors and gold pizza, *Business Week*, March 29.

Brickley, James A., and Frederick H. Dark, 1987, The choice of organizational form: The case of franchising, *Journal of Financial Economics* 18, 401–420.

——, Gregg A. Jarrell, and Jeffrey M. Netter, 1988, The market for corporate control: The empirical evidence since 1980, *Journal of Economic Perspectives* 2, 49–68.

——, Ronald C. Lease, and Clifford W. Smith, Jr., 1988, Ownership structure and voting on antitakeover amendments, *Journal of Financial Economics* 20, 267–291.

Burnham, James D., 1993, *Changes and Challenges: The Transformation of the U.S. Steel Industry*, Policy Study No. 115 (Center for the Study of American Business, Washington University, St. Louis, Mo.).

Chandler, Alfred D., Jr., 1977, *The Visible Hand: The Managerial Revolution in American Business* (Harvard University Press, Cambridge, Mass.).

——, 1990, *Scale and Scope, The Dynamics of Industrial Capitalism* (The Belknapp Press of Harvard University Press, Cambridge, Mass.).

——, 1992, The emergence of managerial capitalism, Harvard Business School Case No. 9-384-081, revised by Thomas J. McCraw.

Christensen, Clayton, 1993, The rigid disk drive industry, 1956–1990: A history of commercial and technological turbulence, Working paper, Harvard Business School.

Comment, Robert, and G. William Schwert, 1993, Poison or placebo? Evidence on the deterrent and wealth effects of modern antitakeover measures. Unpublished manuscript, Simon School of Business, University of Rochester.

Dann, Larry Y., and Harry DeAngelo, 1988, Corporate financial policy and corporate control: A study of defensive adjustments in asset and ownership structure, *Journal of Financial Economics* 20, 07–127.

DeAngelo, Harry, and Linda DeAngelo, 1989, Proxy contests and the governance of publicly held corporations, *Journal of Financial Economics* 23, 29–59.

——, 1991, Union negotiations and corporate policy: A study of labor concessions in the domestic steel industry during the 1980s, *Journal of Financial Economics* 30, 3–43.

—— and Edward Rice, 1984, Going private: Minority freezeouts and stockholder wealth, *Journal of Law and Economics* 27, 367–401.

—— and Stuart C. Gilson, 1993, The collapse of First Executive Corporation: Junk bonds, adverse publicity, and the "run on the bank" phenomenon, Unpublished manuscript, University of Southern California.

DeAngelo, Linda, 1988, Managerial competition, information costs, and corporate governance: The use of accounting performance measures in proxy contests, *Journal of Accounting and Economics* 10, January, 3–36.

Denis, David J., 1992, Organizational form and the consequences of highly leveraged transactions: Kroger's recapitalization and Safeway's LBO, Unpublished manuscript, Virginia Polytechnic Institute.

Dobrzynski, Judith, 1993, Relationship investing, *Business Week*, March 15.

Donaldson, Gordon, 1990, Voluntary restructuring: The case of General Mills, *Journal of Financial Economics* 27, 117–141.

Economic Report of the President, 1993 (U.S. Government Printing Office, Washington, D.C.).

Economist Intelligence Unit, 1991, *Switzerland Country Report*, No. 3.

Economist, 1990, Out of the ivory tower, February 3.

Esty, Benjamin C., 1992, Organizational form, leverage and incentives: A study of risk-taking in the S&L industry, Unpublished manuscript, Harvard Business School.

——, 1993, A tale of two thrifts, Unpublished manuscript, Harvard Business School.

Fader, Barnaby J., 1993, Struggle to survive in the town that steel forgot, *New York Times*, April 27.

Federal Communications Commission, 1991, *Competition in the Interstate Interexchange Marketplace*, FCC 91–251, Sept. 16.

Gersick, Connie J., and J. Richard Hackman, 1990, Habitual routines in task-performing teams, *Organizational Behavior and Human Decision Processes* 47, 65–97.

Ghemawat, Pankaj, and Barry Nalebuff, 1985, Exit, *Rand Journal of Economics* 16, 184–194.

Gibbons, Robert, and Kevin J. Murphy, 1990, Relative performance evaluation for chief executive officers, *Industrial and Labor Relations Review* 43, 30S–51S (Special issue, Cornell University).

Gilson, Ronald, and Reinier Kraakman, 1991, Reinventing the outside director: An agenda for institutional investors, *Stanford Law Review* 43, 863–900.

Gilson, Stuart C., Kose John, and Larry H. P. Lang, 1990, Trouble debt restructurings: An empirical study of private reorganization of firms in default, *Journal of Financial Economics* 27, 315–353.

Grossman, Sanford J., and Oliver D. Hart, 1988, One share/one vote and the market for corporate control, *Journal of Financial Economics* 20, 175–202.

Grundfest, Joseph, 1990, Subordination of American capital, *Journal of Financial Economics* 27, 89–117.

Hackman, J. Richard, ed., 1990, *Groups That Work* (Jossey-Bass, San Francisco).

——, 1993, Teams, leaders, and organizations: New directions for crew-oriented flight training, in E. L. Weiner, B. G. Kanki, and R. L. Helmreich, eds.: *Cockpit Resource Management* (Academic Press, Orlando, Fla.).

Hall, Bronwyn H., 1993a, The stock market's valuation of R&D investment during the 1980's, *American Economic Review*, 83, 259–264.

——, 1993b, New evidence on the impacts of research and development, Unpublished manuscript, Stanford University.

—— and Robert E. Hall, 1993, The value and performance of U.S. corporations, Unpublished manuscript, Stanford University.

Harrigan, Kathryn R., 1980, *Strategies for Declining Businesses* (Lexington Books, Lexington, Mass.).

——, 1988, *Managing Maturing Businesses: Restructuring Declining Industries and Revitalizing Troubled Operations* (Lexington Books, Lexington, Mass.).

Harris, Milton, and Artur Raviv, 1988, Corporate governance: Voting rights and majority rules, *Journal of Financial Economics* 20, 203–235.

——, 1991, The theory of capital structure, *Journal of Finance* 46, 297–355.

Healy, Paul M., Krishna G. Palepu, and Richard S. Ruback, 1992, Does corporate performance improve after mergers?, *Journal of Financial Economics* 31, 135–175.

Hirschman, Albert, 1970, *Exit, Voice and Loyalty: Responses to Decline in Firms,* *Organizations and States* (Harvard University Press, Cambridge, Mass.).

Holderness, Clifford G., and Dennis P. Sheehan, 1988, The role of majority shareholders in publicly held corporations: An exploratory analysis, *Journal of Financial Economics* 20, 317–346.

——, 1991, Monitoring an owner: The case of Turner Broadcasting, *Journal of Financial Economics* 30, 325–346.

Jensen, Michael C., 1983, Organization theory and methodology, *Accounting Review* 58, 319–339.

——, 1986a, The agency costs of free cash flow: Corporate finance and takeovers, *American Economic Review* 76, 323–329.

——, 1986b, The takeover controversy: Analysis and evidence, *Midland Corporate Finance Journal* 4(2), 6–32.

——, 1988, Takeovers: Their causes and consequences, *Journal of Economic Perspectives* 2, 21–48.

——, 1989a, Eclipse of the public corporation, *Harvard Business Review* 67(5), 61–74.

——, 1989b, Active investors, LBOs, and the privatization of bankruptcy, *Journal of Applied Corporate Finance* 2, 35–44.

——, 1991, Corporate control and the politics of finance, *Journal of Applied Corporate Finance* 4, 13–33.

—— and Brian Barry, 1992, Gordon Cain and the Sterling Group (A) and (B), Harvard Business School Case Nos. 9–942–021 and 9–942–022.

Jensen, Michael C., Willy Burkhardt, and Brian K. Barry, 1992, Wisconsin Central Ltd. Railroad and Berkshire Partners (A): Leverage buyouts and financial distress, Harvard Business School Case No. 9–190–062.

Jensen, Michael C., Jay Dial, and Brian K. Barry, 1992, Wisconsin Central Ltd. Railroad and Berkshire Partners (B): LBO associations and corporate governance, Harvard Business School Case No. 9–190–070.

Jensen, Michael C., Steven Kaplan, and Laura Stiglin, 1989, Effects of LBOs on tax revenues of the U.S. Treasury, *Tax Notes* 42, 727–733.

Jensen, Michael C., and William H. Meckling, 1992, Knowledge, control and organizational structure, in Lars Werin and Hans Wijkander, eds.: *Current Economics* (Blackwell, Oxford), pp. 251–274.

Jensen, Michael C., and Kevin J. Murphy, 1990a, Performance pay and top-management incentives, *Journal of Political Economy* 98, 225–264.

——, 1990b, CEO incentives—It's not how much you pay, but how, *Harvard Business Review*, 68(3), 138–153.

Jensen, Michael C., and Jerold B. Warner, 1988, The distribution of power among corporate managers, shareholders, and directors. *Journal of Financial Economics* 20, 3–24.

Kaplan, Steven N., 1989a, The effects of management buyouts on operating performance and value, *Journal of Financial Economics* 24, 581–618.

——, 1989b, Campeau's acquisition of Federated: Value added or destroyed, *Journal of Financial Economics* 25, 191–212.

——, 1989c, Management buyouts: Evidence on taxes as a source of value, *Journal of Finance* 44, 611–632.

——, 1992, Campeau's acquisition of Federated: A post-petition post-mortem, working paper, University of Chicago.

—— and Jeremy Stein, 1990, How risky is the debt in highly leveraged transactions?, *Journal of Financial Economics* 27, 215–245.

——, 1993, The evolution of buyout pricing and financial structure in the 1980s, *Quarterly Journal of Economics* 108, 313–358.

Keene, Peter G., 1991, *Every Manager's Guide to Information Technology* (Harvard University Press, Boston).

Kester, Carl, 1991, *Japanese Takeovers: The Global Contest for Corporate Control* (Harvard Business School Press, Cambridge, Mass.).

Lamoreaux, Naomi, R., 1985, *The Great Merger Movement in American Business, 1895–1904* (Cambridge University Press, Cambridge).

Lang, Larry H. P., Annette Poulsen, and Rene M. Stulz, 1992, Asset sales, leverage, and the agency costs of managerial discretion, Unpublished manuscript, Ohio State University.

Lang, Larry H. P., and Rene M. Stulz, 1992, Contagion and competitive intra-industry effects of bankruptcy announcements: An empirical analysis, *Journal of Financial Economics* 32, 45–60.

—— and Ralph A. Walkling, 1991, A test of the free cash flow hypothesis: The case of bidder returns, *Journal of Financial Economics* 29, 315–335.

Lewellen, Wilbur, Claudio Loderer, and Kenneth Martin, 1987, Executive compensation and executive incentive problems: An empirical analysis, *Journal of Accounting and Economics* 9, 287–310.

Lichtenberg, Frank R., 1992, *Corporate Takeovers and Productivity* (M.I.T. Press: Cambridge, Mass.).

—— and Donald Siegel, 1990, The effects of leveraged buyouts on productivity and related aspects of firm behavior, *Journal of Financial Economics* 27, 165–194.

Lipton, Martin, 1989, Corporate governance: Major issues for the 1990's, Address to the Third Annual Corporate Finance Forum at the J. Ira Harris Center for the Study of Corporate Finance, University of Michigan School of Business, April 6.

—— and Jay Lorsch, 1992, A modest proposal for improved corporate governance, *Business Lawyer* 48, 59–77.

Loomis, Carol J., 1993, Dinosaurs?, *Fortune*, June 15, 85–000.

McCraw, Thomas K., 1981, Rethinking the trust question, in T. McCraw, ed.: *Regulation in Perspective* (Division of Research, Harvard University, Graduate School of Business, distributed by Harvard University Press, Boston), pp. 1–55.

——, 1992, Antitrust: The perceptions and reality in coping with big business, Harvard Business School Case No. 9-391-292.

McMurray, Donald L., 1929, *Coxey's Army: A Study of the Industrial Army Movement of 1894* (Little, Brown, Boston).

Magnet, Myron, 1992, Directors, wake up! *Fortune*, June 15, 85–92.

Malabre, Alfred L., Jr., and Lindley H. Clark, Jr., 1992, Dubious figures: Productivity statistics for the service sector may understate gains, *Wall Street Journal*, August 12.

Mann, Steven V., and Neil W. Sicherman, 1991, The agency costs of free cash flow: Acquisition activity, and equity issues, *Journal of Business* 64, 213–227.

Mergerstat Review, 1991 (Merrill Lynch, Schaumburg, Illinois).

Munro, J. Richard, 1989, Takeovers: The myths behind the mystique, *Vital Speeches*, May 15.

Murphy, Kevin, 1992, *Executive Compensation in Corporate America, 1992* (United Shareholders Association, Washington, D.C.).

—— and Jay Dial, 1992, Compensation and strategy at General Dynamics (A) and (B), Harvard Business School Case Nos. N9–493–032 and N9–493–033.

Neff, Robert, Larry Holyoke, Neil Gross, and Karen Lowry Miller, 1993, Fixing Japan, *Business Week*, March 29.

Ofek, Eli, 1993, Capital structure and firm response to poor performance: An empirical analysis, *Journal of Financial Economics* 34, 3–30.

Palepu, Krishna G., 1990, Consequences of leveraged buyouts, *Journal of Financial Economics* 27, 247–262.

Polinsky, A. Mitchell, 1989, *An Introduction to Law and Economics* (Little, Brown & Co., Boston).

Pontiff, Jeffrey, Andrei Shleifer, and Michael S. Weisbach, 1990, Reversions of excess pension assets after takeovers, *Rand Journal of Economics* 21, 600–613.

Porter, Michael E., 1990, *Competitive Advantage of Nations* (Free Press, New York).

——, 1992a, Capital choices: Changing the way America invests in industry, *Journal of Applied Corporate Finance* 5, 4–16.

——, 1992b. Capital choices: Changing the way America invests in industry, A Research Report presented to The Council on Competitiveness and co-sponsored by Harvard Business School.

——, 1992c, Capital disadvantage: America's failing capital investment system, *Harvard Business Review* 70(5), 65–82.

Pound, John, 1988, Proxy contests and the efficiency of shareholder oversight, *Journal of Financial Economics* 20, 237–265.

——, 1991, Proxy voting and the SEC: Investor protection versus market efficiency, *Journal of Financial Economics* 29, 241–285.

——, 1992, Beyond takeovers: Politics comes to corporate control, *Harvard Business Review* 70(2), 83–93.

——, 1993, The rise of the political model of corporate governance and corporate control, Unpublished manuscript, Harvard University, Kennedy School of Government.

Price, Walter W., 1933, *We Have Recovered Before!* (Harper & Brothers, New York).

Reynolds, A. William, 1988, Chairman and Chief Executive Officer, GenCorp Inc., before the Subcommittee on Oversight and Investigations, U.S. House Committee on Energy and Commerce, February 8.

Richman, Louis S., 1993, Why the economic data mislead us, *Fortune*, March 8.

Roe, Mark J., 1990, Political and legal restraints on ownership and control of public companies, *Journal of Financial Economics* 27, 7–42.

——, 1991, a political theory of American corporate finance, *Columbia Law Review* 91, 10–67.

Rosett, Joshua G., 1990, Do union wealth concessions explain takeover premiums? The evidence on contract wages, *Journal of Financial Economics* 27, 263–282.

Sahlman, William A., 1990, The structure and governance of venture-capital organizations. *Journal of Financial Economics* 27, 473–521.

Sahlman, William A., and Howard H. Stevenson, 1985, Capital market myopia, *Journal of Business Venturing* 1, 7–30.

Schumpeter, Joseph A., 1976, *Capitalism Socialism, and Democracy* (Harper & Row, New York).

Shleifer, Andrei, and Larry Summers, 1988, Breach of trust in hostile takeovers, in A. Auerbach, ed.: *Corporate Takeovers: Causes and Consequences* (University of Chicago Press, Chicago), pp. 33–56.

Shleifer, Andrei, and Robert W. Vishny, 1989, Management entrenchment: The case of manager-specific investments, *Journal of Financial Economics* 25, 123–139.

Smith, Abbie J., 1990, Corporate ownership structure and performance: The case of management buyouts, *Journal of Financial Economics* 27, 143–164.

Steiner, I. D., 1972, *Group Process and Productivity* (Academic Press, New York).

Stern Stewart Performance 1000, 1992, *Corporate Finance*, October/November, 33–45.

Stewart, G. Bennett, III, 1990, Remaking the public corporation from within, *Harvard Business Review* 68(4), 126–137.

Stulz, Rene M., 1990, Managerial discretion and optimal financing policies, *Journal of Financial Economics* 26, 3–00.

Swartz, L. Mick, 1992, The impact of third generation antitakeover laws on security value, Unpublished manuscript, University of Manitoba.

Tedlow, Richard, 1991, Hitting the skids: Tires and time horizons, Unpublished manuscript, Harvard Business School.

Tiemann, Jonathan, 1990, The economics of exit and restructuring: The Pabst Brewing Company, Unpublished manuscript, Harvard Business School.

United Nations, 1993, *Monthly Bulletin of Statistics*, February (United Nations, New York).

United Nations, 1992, *1988/89 Statistical yearbook, thirty-seventh issue* (United Nations, New York).

U.S. Bureau of the Census, 1987, *Census of Manufacturing* (U.S. Government Printing Office, Washington, D.C.)

U.S. Bureau of the Census, Housing and Household Economic Statistics Division, 1991 (U.S. Government Printing Office, Washington, D.C.).

U.S. Department of Labor, Bureau of Labor Statistics, Office of Productivity and Technology, 1990, *Multifactor Productivity Measures*, Report No. USDL 91–412.

——, 1991, *International Comparisons of Manufacturing Productivity and Unit Labor Cost Trends*, Report No. USDL 92–752.

van Delden, Hendrik H., 1993, Czech and Slovak Republics: Lands of opportunity, *ITS Textile Leader*, Spring, 43–48.

Vietor, Richard, 1994, *Contrived Competition* (Harvard University Press, Cambridge, Mass.) Forthcoming.

Warner, Jerold B., Ross L. Watts, and Karen H. Wruck, 1989, Stock prices and top management changes, *Journal of Financial Economics* 20, 461–492.

Watson, Bruce, 1993, For a while the Luddites had a smashing success, *Smithsonian*, April, pp. 140–154.

Weisbach, Michael S., 1988, Outside directors and CEO turnovers, *Journal of Financial Economics* 20, 431–460.

Wruck, Karen H. 1990, Financial distress, reorganization, and organizational efficiency, *Journal of Financial Economics* 27, 420–444.

——, 1991, What really went wrong at Revco?, *Journal of Applied Corporate Finance* 4, 79–92.

——, 1992, Changing the rules of the game: Sealed Air Corporation's leveraged recapitalization, Working paper, Harvard Business School.

—— and Michael C. Jensen, 1993, Science, specific knowledge, and total quality management, Unpublished manuscript, Harvard Business School.

Wruck, Karen H., and A. Scott Keating, 1992a, Sterling Chemicals, Inc., quality and productivity improvement program, Harvard Business School Case No. 9–493–026.

——, 1992b, Sterling Chemicals, Inc., Harvard Business School Case No. 9–493–025.

Wruck, Karen H., and Krishna Palepu, 1992, Consequences of leveraged shareholder payouts: Defensive versus voluntary recapitalizations, Working paper, Harvard Business School.

Wruck, Karen H. and Steve-Anna Stephens, 1992a, Leveraged buyouts and restructuring: The case of Safeway, Inc., Harvard Business School Case No. 192–095.

——, 1992b, Leveraged buyouts and restructuring: The case of Safeway, Inc.: Media response, Harvard Business School Case No. 192–094.

Zellner, Wendy, 1992, Not everybody loves Wal-Mart's low prices, *Wall Street Journal*, October 12.

## Chapter 2

Andrei Shleifer and Robert W. Vishny*

A SURVEY OF CORPORATE GOVERNANCE

Source: *Journal of Finance,* 52(2) (1997): 737–784.

ABSTRACT

This article surveys research on corporate governance, with special attention to the importance of legal protection of investors and of ownership concentration in corporate governance systems around the world.

CORPORATE GOVERNANCE DEALS WITH the ways in which suppliers of finance to corporations assure themselves of getting a return on their investment. How do the suppliers of finance get managers to return some of the profits to them? How do they make sure that managers do not steal the capital they supply or invest it in bad projects? How do suppliers of finance control managers?

At first glance, it is not entirely obvious why the suppliers of capital get anything back. After all, they part with their money, and have little to contribute to the enterprise afterward. The professional managers or entrepreneurs who run the firms might as well abscond with the money. Although they sometimes do, usually they do not. Most advanced market economies have solved the problem of corporate governance at least reasonably well, in that they have assured the flows of enormous amounts of capital to firms, and actual repatriation of profits to the providers of finance. But this does not imply that they have solved the corporate governance problem perfectly, or that the corporate governance mechanisms cannot be improved.

In fact, the subject of corporate governance is of enormous practical importance. Even in advanced market economies, there is a great deal of disagreement on how good or bad the existing governance mechanisms are. For example, Easterbrook and Fischel (1991) and Romano (1993a) make a very optimistic assessment of the United States corporate governance system, whereas Jensen (1989a, 1993) believes that it is deeply flawed and that a major move from the current corporate form to much more highly leveraged organizations, similar to LBOs, is in order. There is also constant talk of replacing the Anglo-Saxon corporate governance systems with those patterned after Germany and Japan (see, for example, Roe (1993) and Charkham (1994)). But the United States, Germany, Japan, and the United Kingdom have some of the best corporate governance systems in the world, and the differences between them are probably small relative to their differences from other countries. According to Barca (1995) and Pagano, Panetta, and Zingales (1995), Italian corporate governance mechanisms are so undeveloped as to substantially retard the flow of external capital to firms. In less developed countries, including some of the transition economies, corporate governance mechanisms are practically nonexistent. In Russia the weakness of corporate governance mechanisms leads to substantial diversion of assets by managers of many privatized firms, and the virtual nonexistence of external capital supply to firms (Boycko, Shleifer, and Vishny (1995)). Understanding corporate governance not only enlightens the discussion of perhaps marginal improvements in rich economies, but can also stimulate major institutional changes in places where they need to be made.

Corporate governance mechanisms are economic and legal institutions that can be altered through the political process—sometimes for the better. One could take a view that we should not worry about governance reform, since, in the long run, product market competition would force firms to minimize costs, and as part of this cost minimization to adopt rules, including corporate governance mechanisms, enabling them to raise external capital at the lowest cost. On this evolutionary theory of economic change (Alchian (1950), Stigler (1958)), competition would take care of corporate governance.

While we agree that product market competition is probably the most powerful force toward economic efficiency in the world, we are skeptical that it alone can solve the problem of corporate governance. One could imagine a scenario in which entrepreneurs rent labor and capital on the spot market every minute at a competitive price, and hence have no resources left over to divert to their own use. But in actual practice, production capital is highly specific and sunk, and entrepreneurs cannot rent it every minute. As a result, the people who sink the capital need to be assured that they get back the return on this capital. The corporate governance mechanisms provide this assurance. Product market competition may reduce the returns on capital and hence cut the amount that managers can possibly expropriate, but it does not prevent the managers from expropriating the competitive return after the capital is sunk. Solving that problem requires something more than competition, as we show in this survey.

Our perspective on corporate governance is a straightforward agency perspective,

sometimes referred to as separation of ownership and control. We want to know how investors get the managers to give them back their money. To begin, Section I outlines the nature of the agency problem, and discusses some standard models of agency. It also focuses on incentive contracts as a possible solution to the agency problem. Finally, Section I summarizes some evidence pointing to the large magnitude of this problem even in advanced market economies.

Sections II through IV outline, in broad terms, the various ways in which firms can attract capital despite the agency problem. Section II briefly examines how firms can raise money without giving suppliers of capital any real power. Specifically, we consider reputation-building in the capital market and excessive investor optimism, and conclude that these are unlikely to be the only reasons why investors entrust capital to firms.

Sections III and IV then turn to the two most common approaches to corporate governance, both of which rely on giving investors some power. The first approach is to give investors power through legal protection from expropriation by managers. Protection of minority rights and legal prohibitions against managerial self-dealing are examples of such mechanisms. The second major approach is ownership by large investors (concentrated ownership): matching significant control rights with significant cash flow rights. Most corporate governance mechanisms used in the world—including large share holdings, relationship banking, and even takeovers—can be viewed as examples of large investors exercising their power. We discuss how large investors reduce agency costs. While large investors still rely on the legal system, they do not need as many rights as the small investors do to protect their interests. For this reason, corporate governance is typically exercised by large investors.

Despite its common use, concentrated ownership has its costs as well, which can be best described as potential expropriation by large investors of other investors and stakeholders in the firm. In Section V, we focus on these potential costs of ownership by large investors.

In Section VI, we turn to several specific examples of widely used corporate governance mechanisms, which illustrate the roles of legal protection and concentrated ownership in corporate governance. We begin by discussing debt governance and equity governance as alternative approaches to addressing the agency problem. We then turn to a brief discussion of a hybrid form — the leveraged buy out — which reveals both the benefits and the costs of concentrated ownership. Finally, we look at state enterprises as a manifestation of a radical failure of corporate governance.

In Section VII, we bring sections III through VI together by asking: which system is the best? We argue that a good corporate governance system should combine some type of large investors with legal protection of both their rights and those of small investors. Indeed, corporations in successful market economies, such as the United States, Germany, and Japan, are governed through somewhat different combinations of legal protection and concentrated ownership. Because all these economies have the essential elements of a good governance system, the available evidence does not tell us which one of *their* governance systems is the best. In contrast, corporate governance systems in most other countries, ranging from poor developing countries, to transition economies, to some rich European countries such as Italy, lack some essential elements of a good system. In most cases, in fact, they lack mechanisms for legal protection of investors. Our analysis suggests that the principal practical question in designing a corporate governance system is not whether to emulate the United States, Germany, or Japan, but rather how to introduce, significant legal protection of at least some investors so that mechanisms of extensive outside financing can develop.

Finally, in Section VIII, we summarize our argument and present what we take to be some of the major unresolved puzzles in the analysis of corporate governance.

Before proceeding, we should mention several important topics closely related to corporate governance that our article does not deal with, as well as some of the references on these topics. Our article does not deal with foundations of contract theory; for that, see Hart and Holmstrom (1987), Hart (1995, part I), and Tirole (1994). Second, we do not deal with some of the basic elements of the theory of the firm, such as the make or buy decision (vertical integration). On this topic, see Williamson (1985), Holmstrom and Tirole (1989), and Hart (1995, part I). Third, while we pay some attention to cooperatives, we do not focus on a broad variety of noncapitalist ownership patterns, such as worker ownership or nonprofit organizations. A major new treatise on this subject is Hansmann (1996). Finally, although we talk about the role of financial intermediaries in governance, we ignore their function as collectors of savings from the public. For recent overviews of intermediation, see Allen and Gale (1994), Dewatripont and Tirole (1995) and Hellwig (1994). In sum, this survey deals with the separation of financing and management of firms, and tries to discuss how this separation is dealt with in theory and in practice.

The last preliminary point is on the selection of countries we talk about. Most of the available empirical evidence in the English language comes from the United States, which therefore receives the most attention in this article. More recently, there has been a great surge of work on Japan, and to a lesser extent on Germany, Italy, and Sweden. In addition, we frequently refer to the recent experience of privatized firms in Russia, with which we are familiar from our advisory work, even though there is little systematic research on Russia's corporate governance. Unfortunately, except for the countries just mentioned, there has been extremely little research done on corporate governance around the world, and this dearth of research is reflected in our survey.

I. THE AGENCY PROBLEM

A. Contracts

The agency problem is an essential element of the so-called contractual view of the firm, developed by Coase (1937), Jensen and Meckling (1976), and Fama and Jensen (1983a,b). The essence of the agency problem is the separation of management and finance, or—in more standard terminology—of ownership and control. An entrepreneur, or a manager, raises funds from investors either to put them to productive use or to cash out his holdings in the firm. The financiers need the manager's specialized human capital to generate returns on their funds. The manager needs the financiers' funds, since he either does not have enough capital of his own to invest or else wants to cash out his holdings. But how can financiers be sure that, once they sink their funds, they get anything but a worthless piece of paper back from the manager? The agency problem in this context refers to the difficulties financiers have in assuring that their funds are not expropriated or wasted on unattractive projects.

In most general terms, the financiers and the manager sign a contract that specifies what the manager does with the funds, and how the returns are divided between him and the financiers. Ideally, they would sign a complete contract, that specifies exactly what the manager does in all states of the world, and how the profits are allocated. The trouble is, most future contingencies are hard to describe and foresee, and as a result, complete contracts are technologically infeasible. This problem would not be avoided even if the manager is motivated to raise as much funds as he can, and so tries hard to accommodate the financiers by developing a complete contract. Because of these problems in designing their contract, the manager and the financier have to allocate residual control rights—i.e., the rights to make decisions in circumstances not fully foreseen by the contract (Grossman and Hart (1986), Hart and Moore (1990)). The theory of ownership addresses the question of how these residual control rights are allocated efficiently.

In principle, one could imagine a contract in which the financiers give funds to the manager on the condition that they retain all the residual control rights. Any time something unexpected happens, they get to decide what to do. But this does not quite work, for the simple reason that the financiers are not qualified or informed enough to decide what to do—the very reason they hired the manager in the first place. As a consequence, the manager ends up with substantial residual control rights and therefore discretion to allocate funds as he chooses. There may be limits on this discretion specified in the contract—and much of corporate governance deals with these limits, but the fact is that managers do have most of the residual control rights.

In practice, the situation is more complicated. First, the contracts that the managers and investors sign cannot require too much interpretation if they are to be enforced by outside courts. In the United States, the role of courts is more extensive than anywhere else in the world, but even there the so-called business judgment rule keeps the courts out of the affairs of companies. In much of the rest of the world, courts only get involved in massive violations by managers of investors' rights (e.g., erasing shareholders' names from the register). Second, in the cases where financing requires collection of funds from many investors, these investors themselves are often small and too poorly informed to exercise even the control rights that they actually have. The free rider problem faced by individual investors makes it uninteresting for them to learn about the firms they have financed, or even to participate in the governance, just as it may not pay citizens to get informed about political candidates and vote (Downs (1957)). As a result, the effective control rights of the managers—and hence the room they have for discretionary allocation of funds—end up being much more extensive than they would have been if courts or providers of finance became actively involved in detailed contract enforcement.

B. Management discretion

The upshot of this is that managers end up with significant control rights (discretion) over how to allocate investors' funds. To begin, they can expropriate them. In many pyramid schemes, for example, the organizers end up absconding with the money. Managerial expropriation of funds can also take more elaborate forms than just taking the cash out, such as transfer pricing. For example, managers can set up independent companies that they own personally, and sell the output of the main company they run to the independent firms at below market prices. In the Russian oil industry, such sales of oil to manager-owned trading companies (which often do not even pay for the oil) are evidently common. An even more dramatic alternative is to sell the assets, and not just the output, of the company to other manager-owned businesses at below market prices. For example, the Economist (June 1995) reports that Korean chaebol sometimes sell their subsidiaries to the relatives of the chaebol founder at low prices. Zingales (1994) describes an episode in which one state-controlled Italian firm sold some assets to another at an excessively high price. The buying firm, unlike the selling firm, had a large number of minority shareholders, and these shareholders got significantly diluted by the transaction. In short, straight-out expropriation is a frequent manifestation of the agency problem that financiers need to address. Finally, before the reader dismisses the importance of such expropriation, we point out that much of the corporate law development in the 18th and 19th centuries in Britain, Continental Europe, and Russia focused precisely on addressing the problem of managerial theft rather than that of shirking or even empire-building (Hunt (1936), Owen (1991)).

In many countries today, the law protects investors better than it does in Russia, Korea, or Italy. In the United States, for example, courts try to control managerial diversion of company assets to themselves, although even in the United States there are cases of executive compensation or transfer pricing that have a bad smell. For example, Victor Posner, a Miami financier, received in 1985 over $8 million in salary from DWG; a public company he controlled, at the time the company was losing money (New York Times, June 23, 1986). Because such expropriation of investors by managers is generally kept down by the courts in the United States, more typically managers use their discretion to allocate investors' funds for less direct personal benefits. The least costly of this is probably consumption of perquisites, such as plush carpets and company airplanes (Burrough and Helyar 1990). Greater costs are incurred when managers have an interest in expanding the firm beyond what is rational, reinvesting the free cash, pursuing pet projects, and so on. A vast managerialist literature explains how managers use their effective control rights to pursue projects that benefit them rather than investors (Baumol (1959), Marris (1964), Williamson (1964), Jensen (1986), etc.). Grossman and Hart (1988) aptly describe these benefits as the private benefits of control.

Finally, and perhaps most important, managers can expropriate shareholders by entrenching themselves and staying on the job even if they are no longer competent or qualified to run the firm (Shleifer and Vishny (1989)). As argued in Jensen and Ruback (1983), poor managers who resist being replaced might be the costliest manifestation of the agency problem.

Managerial opportunism, whether in the form of expropriation of investors or of misallocation of company funds, reduces the amount of resources that investors are willing to put up ex ante to finance the firm (Williamson (1985), Grossman and Hart (1986)). Much of the subject of corporate governance deals with constraints that managers put on themselves, or that investors put on managers, to reduce the ex post misallocation and thus to induce investors to provide more funds ex ante. Even with these constraints, the outcome is in general less efficient than would occur if the manager financed the firm with his own funds.

An equally interesting problem concerns the efficiency of the ex post resource allocation, after investors have put up their funds. Suppose that the manager of a firm cannot expropriate resources outright, but has some freedom not to return the money to investors. The manager contemplates going ahead with an investment project that will give him $10 of personal benefits, but will cost his investors $20 in foregone wealth. Suppose for simplicity that the manager owns no equity in the firm. Then, as argued by Jensen and Meckling (1976), the manager will undertake the project, resulting in an ex post inefficiency (and of course an ex ante inefficiency as investors cut down finance to such a firm).

The Jensen-Meckling scenario raises the obvious point: why don't investors try to bribe the manager with cash, say $11, not to undertake the inefficient project? This would be what the Coase (1960) Theorem predicts should happen, and what Grossman and Hart (1986) presume actually happens ex post. In some cases, such as golden parachutes that convince managers to accept hostile takeover bids, we actually observe these bribes (Walkling and Long (1984), Lambert and Larcker (1985)). More commonly, investors do not pay managers for individual actions and therefore do not seem to arrive at efficient outcomes ex post. The Jensen-Meckling view is empirically accurate and the Coase Theorem does not seem to apply. Moreover, the traditional reason for the failure of the Coase Theorem, namely that numerous investors need to agree in order to bribe the manager, does not seem relevant, since the manager needs only to agree on his bribe with a small board of directors.

The reason we do not observe managers threatening shareholders and being bribed not to take inefficient actions is that such threats would violate the managers' legal "duty of loyalty" to shareholders. While it is difficult to describe exactly what this duty obligates the managers to do (Clark (1985)), threats to take value-reducing actions unless one is paid off would surely violate this duty. But this only raises the question of why this legal duty exists at all

if it prevents efficient ex post bargaining between managers and shareholders. The reason for introducing the duty of loyalty is probably to avoid the situation in which managers constantly threaten shareholders, in circumstances that have not been specified in the contract, to take ever less efficient actions unless they are bribed not to. It is better for shareholders to avoid bargaining altogether than to expose themselves to constant threats. This argument is similar to that of why corruption in general is not legal, even if ex post it improves the resource allocation: the public does not want to give the bureaucrats incentives to come up with ever increasing obstacles to private activity solely to create corruption opportunities (Shleifer and Vishny (1993)). But the consequence is that, with limited corruption, not all the efficient bargains are actually realized ex post. Similarly, if the duty of loyalty to shareholders prevents the managers from being paid off for not taking self-interested actions, then such actions will be taken even when they benefit managers less than they cost shareholders.

C. Incentive contracts

In the previous section, we discussed the agency problem when complete, contingent contracts are infeasible. When contracts are incomplete and managers possess more expertise than shareholders, managers typically end up with the residual rights of control, giving them enormous latitude for self-interested behavior. In some cases, this results in managers taking highly inefficient actions, which cost investors far more than the personal benefits to the managers. Moreover, the managers' fiduciary duty to shareholders makes it difficult to contract around this inefficiency ex post.

A better solution is to grant a manager a highly contingent, long term incentive contract ex ante to align his interests with those of investors. While in some future contingencies the marginal value of the personal benefits of control may exceed the marginal value of the manager's contingent compensation, such instances will be relatively rare if the incentive component of pay is substantial. In this way, incentive contracts can induce the manager to act in investors' interest without encouraging blackmail, although such contracts may be expensive if the personal benefits of control are high and there is a lower bound on the manager's compensation in the bad states of the world. Typically, to make such contracts feasible, some measure of performance that is highly correlated with the quality of the manager's decision must be verifiable in court. In some cases, the credibility of an implicit threat or promise from the investors to take action based on an observable, but not verifiable, signal may also suffice. Incentive contracts can take a variety of forms, including share ownership, stock options, or a threat of dismissal if income is low (Jensen and Meckling (1976), Fama (1980)). The optimal incentive contract is determined by the manager's risk aversion, the importance of his decisions, and his ability to pay for the cash flow ownership up front (Ross (1973), Stiglitz (1975), Mirrlees (1976), Holmstrom (1979, 1982)).

Incentive contracts are indeed common in practice. A vast empirical literature on incentive contracts in general and management ownership in particular dates back at least to Berle and Means (1932), who argue that management ownership in large firms is too small to make managers interested in profit maximization. Some of the early studies take issue with Berle and Means by documenting a positive relationship between pay and performance, and thus rejecting the extreme hypothesis of complete separation of ownership and control (Murphy (1985), Coughlan and Schmidt (1985), Benston (1985)). More recently, Jensen and Murphy (1990) look at the sensitivity of pay of American executives to performance. In addition to looking at salary and bonuses, Jensen and Murphy also examine stock options and the effects on pay of potential dismissal after poor performance. Jensen and Murphy arrive at a striking number that executive pay rises (and falls) by about $3 per every $1000 change in the wealth of a firm's shareholders.

Similarly to Berle and Means, Jensen and Murphy interpret their findings as evidence of inefficient compensation arrangements, although in their view these arrangements are driven by politically motivated restrictions on extremely high levels of pay.

Kaplan (1994a,b) shows that the sensitivity of pay (and dismissal) to performance is similar in the United States, Germany, and Japan, although average levels of pay are the highest in the United States. The question is whether there is a similar failure to pay for performance in all countries, or, alternatively, the results found by Jensen and Murphy are not so counterintuitive. In particular, even the sensitivity of pay to performance that Jensen and Murphy find would generate enormous swings in executive wealth, which require considerable risk tolerance. More sensitivity may not be efficient for risk-averse executives (Haubrich (1994)).

The more serious problem with high powered incentive contracts is that they create enormous opportunities for self-dealing for the managers, especially if these contracts are negotiated with poorly motivated boards of directors rather than with large investors. Managers may negotiate for themselves such contracts when they know that earnings or stock price are likely to rise, or even manipulate accounting numbers and investment policy to increase their pay. For example, Yermack (1997) finds that managers receive stock option grants shortly before good news announcements and delay such grants until after bad news announcements. His results suggest that options are often not so much an incentive device as a somewhat covert mechanism of self-dealing.

Given the self-dealing opportunities in high powered incentive contracts, it is not surprising that courts and regulators have looked at them with suspicion. After all, the business judgment rule that governs the attitude of American courts toward agency problems keeps the courts out of corporate decisions *except* in the matters of executive pay and self-dealing. These legal and political factors, which appear to be common in other countries as well as in the United

States, have probably played an important role in keeping down the sensitivity of executive pay to performance (Shleifer and Vishny (1988), Jensen and Murphy (1990)). While it is a mistake to jump from this evidence to the conclusion that managers do not care about performance at all, it is equally problematic to argue that incentive contracts completely solve the agency problem.

D. Evidence on agency costs

In the last ten years, a considerable amount of evidence has documented the prevalence of managerial behavior that does not serve the interests of investors, particularly shareholders. Most of this evidence comes from the capital market in the form of "event" studies. The idea is that if the stock price falls when managers announce a particular action, then this action must serve the interests of managers rather than those of the shareholders. While in some circumstances this inference is not justified because the managerial action, while serving the interests of shareholders, inadvertently conveys to the market some unrelated bad news about the firm (Shleifer and Vishny (1986a)), in general such event study analysis is fairly compelling. It has surely become the most common empirical methodology of corporate governance and finance (see Fama, Fisher, Jensen, and Roll (1969) for the first event study).

We have pointed out above that managerial investment decisions may reflect their personal interests rather than those of the investors. In his free cash flow theory, Jensen (1986) argues that managers choose to reinvest the free cash rather than return it to investors. Jensen uses the example of the oil industry, where in the mid-1980s integrated oil producers spent roughly $20 per barrel to explore for new oil reserves (and thus maintain their large oil exploration activities), rather than return their profits to shareholders or even buy proven oil reserves that sold in the marketplace for around $6 per barrel. McConnell and Muscarella (1986) look more generally at announcement effects of investment projects of oil and other firms, and find negative returns on such announcements in the oil industry, although not in others. The study of investment announcements is complicated by the fact that managers in general are not obligated to make such announcements, and hence those that they do make are likely to be better news than the average one. Still, the managers in the oil industry announce even the bad news.

The announcement selection problem does not arise in the case of a particular kind of investment, namely acquisitions, since almost all acquisitions of public companies are publicly announced. Some of the clearest evidence on agency problems therefore comes from acquisition announcements. Many studies show that bidder returns on the announcement of acquisitions are often negative (Roll (1986) surveys this evidence). Lewellen, Loderer, and Rosenfeld (1985) find that negative returns are most common for bidders in which their managers hold little equity, suggesting that agency problems can be ameliorated with incentives. Morck, Shleifer, and Vishny (1990) find that bidder returns tend to be the lowest when bidders diversify or when they buy rapidly growing firms. Bhagat, Shleifer, and Vishny (1990), Lang and Stulz (1994), and Comment and Jarrell (1995) find related evidence of adverse effects of diversification on company valuation. Diversification and growth are among the most commonly cited managerial, as opposed to shareholder, objectives. Kaplan and Weisbach (1992) document the poor history of diversification by the U.S. firms and the common incidence of subsequent divestitures. Finally, Lang, Stulz, and Walkling (1991) find that bidder returns are the lowest among firms with low Tobin's Qs and high cash flows. Their result supports Jensen's (1986) version of agency theory, in which the worst agency problems occur in firms with poor investment opportunities and excess cash. In sum, quite a bit of evidence points to the dominance of managerial rather than shareholder motives in firms' acquisition decisions.

Even clearer evidence of agency problems is revealed by the studies that focus on managers directly threatened with the loss of private benefits of control. These are the studies of management resistance to takeovers, which are now too numerous to survey completely. Walkling and Long (1984) find that managerial resistance to value-increasing takeovers is less likely when top managers have a direct financial interest in the deal going through via share ownership or golden parachutes, or when top managers are more likely to keep their jobs. Another set of studies finds that, when managers take anti-takeover actions, shareholders lose. For example, DeAngelo and Rice (1983) and Jarrell and Poulsen (1988a) find that public announcements of certain anti-takeover amendments to corporate charters, such as super-majority provisions requiring more than 50 percent of the votes to change corporate boards, reduce shareholder wealth. Ryngaert (1988) and Malatesta and Walkling (1988) find that, for firms who have experienced challenges to management control, the adoption of poison pills— which are devices to make takeovers extremely costly without target management's consent—also reduce shareholder wealth. Comment and Schwert (1995), however, question the event study evidence given the higher frequency of takeovers among firms with poison pills in place. Taken as a whole, the evidence suggests that managers resist takeovers to protect their private benefits of control rather than to serve shareholders.

Some of the evidence on the importance of agency costs is less direct, but perhaps as compelling. In one of the most macabre event studies ever performed, Johnson, Magee, Nagarajan, and Newman (1985) find that sudden executive deaths—in plane crashes or from heart attacks—are often accompanied by increases in share prices of the companies these executives managed. The price increases are the largest for some major conglomerates, whose founders built vast empires without returning much to investors. A plausible interpretation of this evidence is that the flow of benefits of control diminishes after the deaths of powerful managers.

There is also a great deal of evidence that control is valued, which would not be the case if controlling managers (or shareholders) received the same benefits as the other investors. Barclay and Holderness (1989, 1992) find that, in the United States, large blocks of equity trade at a substantial premium to the posttrade price of minority shares, indicating that the buyers of the blocks that may have a controlling influence receive special benefits. Several studies compare the prices of shares with identical dividend rights, but differential voting rights. Lease, McConnell, and Mikkelson (1983, 1984), DeAngelo and DeAngelo (1985), and Zingales (1995) all show that, in the United States, shares with superior voting rights trade at a premium. On average, this premium is very small, but Zingales (1995) shows that it rises sharply in situations where control over firms is contested, indicating yet again that controlling management teams earn benefits that are not available to minority investors.

Even more dramatic evidence comes from other countries. Levy (1982) finds the average voting premium of 45.5 percent in Israel, Rydqvist (1987) reports 6.5 percent for Sweden, Horner (1988) shows about 20 percent for Switzerland, and, most recently, Zingales (1994) reports the 82 percent voting premium on the Milan Stock Exchange. Zingales (1994) and Barca (1995) suggest that managers in Italy have significant opportunities to divert profits to themselves and not share them with nonvoting shareholders.

The evidence on the voting premium in Israel and Italy suggests that agency costs may be very large in some countries. But how large can they get? Some evidence from Russia offers a hint. Boycko, Shleifer, and Vishny (1993) calculate that, in privatization, manufacturing firms in Russia sold for about $100 per employee, compared to market valuations of about $100,000 per employee for Western firms. The one thousandfold difference cannot be explained by a difference in living standards, which in Russia are about one tenth of those in the West. Even controlling for this difference, the Russian assets sold at a 99 percent discount. Very similar evidence comes from the oil industry, where Russian companies were valued at under 5 cents per barrel of proven reserves, compared to typical $4 to $5 per barrel valuations for Western oil firms. An important element of this 99 percent discount is surely the reality of government expropriation, regulation, and taxation. Poor management is probably also a part of the story. But equally important seems to be the ability of managers of Russian firms to divert both profits and assets to themselves. The Russian evidence suggests that an upper bound on agency costs in the regime of minimal protection of investors is 99 percent of value.

II. FINANCING WITHOUT GOVERNANCE

The previous section raised the main question of corporate governance: why do investors part with their money, and give it to managers, when both the theory and the evidence suggests that managers have enormous discretion about what is done with that money, often to the point of being able to expropriate much of it? The question is particularly intriguing in the case of investors because, unlike highly trained employees and managers, the initial investors have no special ability to help the firm once they have parted with their money. Their investment is sunk and nobody—especially the managers—needs them. Yet despite all these problems, outside finance occurs in almost all market economies, and on an enormous scale in the developed ones. How does this happen?

In this section, we begin to discuss the various answers to the puzzle of outside finance by first focusing on two explanations that do not rely on governance proper: the idea that firms and managers have reputations and the idea that investors are gullible and get taken. Both of these approaches have the common element that investors do not get any control rights in

exchange for their funds, only the hope that they will make money in the future.

Reputation-building is a very common explanation for why people deliver on their agreements even if they cannot be forced to (see, for example, Kreps (1990)). In the financing context, the argument is that managers repay investors because they want to come to the capital market and raise funds in the future, and hence need to establish a reputation as good risks in order to convince future investors to give them money. This argument has been made initially in the context of sovereign borrowing, where legal enforcement of contracts is virtually nonexistent (Eaton and Gersovitz (1981), Bulow and Rogoff (1989)). However, several recent articles have presented reputation-building models of private financing. Diamond (1989, 1991) shows how firms establish reputations as good borrowers by repaying their short term loans, and Gomes (1996) shows how dividend payments create reputations that enable firms to raise equity.

There surely is much truth to the reputation models, although they do have problems. As pointed out by Bulow and Rogoff (1989), pure reputational stories run into a backward recursion problem. Suppose that at some point in the future (or in some future states of the world), the future benefits to the manager of being able to raise outside funds are lower than the costs of paying what he promised investors already. In this case, he rationally defaults on his repayments. Of course, if investors expect that such a time or state is reached in the future, they would not finance the firm in the first place. Under some plausible circumstances discussed by Bulow and Rogoff, the problem unravels and there is no possibility of external finance. While reputation is surely an important reason why firms are able to raise money, the available research suggests that it is probably not the whole explanation for external financing. For example, in Diamond's (1989) model of corporate borrowing, reputation plays a role alongside other protections of creditors that prevent managers from removing assets from the firm.

An alternative theory of how investors give their money to companies without receiving control rights in exchange appeals to excessive investor optimism. Investors get excited about companies, and hence finance them without thinking much about getting their money back, simply counting on short run share appreciation. An extreme version of this story is a Ponzi scheme, in which promoters raise external funds sequentially, and use the funds raised from later investors to pay off initial investors, thereby creating an illusion of high returns. Even without Ponzi schemes, if investors are sufficiently optimistic about short term capital gains and are prepared to part with their money without regard for how the firm will ultimately pay investors back, then external finance can be sustained without effective governance. Delong, Shleifer, Summers, and Waldmann (1989, 1990) provide early models of external finance based on excessive investor optimism.

Pyramid schemes have been an essential element of all major financial markets, going back at least to the Louisiana and the South Sea Bubbles (Kindleberger (1978)). Most railroad booms in the world were financed by investors who had virtually no protection, only hope. In the United States, such schemes were very common as recently as the 1920s (Galbraith (1955)), and still happen occasionally today. They also occur in many transition economies, as Russia's famous pyramid scheme, MMM, in which millions of people subscribed to shares of a company that used the proceeds to advertise on television while running a Ponzi scheme, vividly illustrates. Nor is it crazy to assume that enormous volumes of equity financing in the rapidly growing East Asian economies are based in part on investor optimism about near-term appreciation, and overlook the weakness of mechanisms that can force managers to repay investors.

In recent years, more systematic statistical evidence has pointed to the importance of investor optimism for financing in at least some markets. Kaplan and Stein (1993), for example, present evidence suggesting that the high yield bonds that were used to finance takeovers in the United States in the late 1980s were systematically overvalued by investors. Evidence from both the United States and other countries also indicates that the shares of companies issuing equity in initial or secondary offerings are systematically overvalued (Ritter (1991), Loughran, Ritter, and Rydqvist (1994), Pagano, Panetta, and Zingales (1995), Teoh, Welch, and Wong (1995)). This evidence points to concentration of new issues during times when stock prices are high, to poor long run performance of initial public offerings, to earnings manipulation prior to the issue, and to deterioration of profitability following the issue. In short, excessive investor optimism as an explanation of security issues appears to have at least some explanatory power.

Still, we do not believe that investors as a general rule are prepared to pay good money for securities that are actually worthless because managers can steal everything. As the evidence on agency theory indicates, managers can expropriate only limited wealth, and therefore the securities that investors buy do have some underlying value. To explain why these securities have value, we need theories that go beyond investor overoptimism.

III. LEGAL PROTECTION

The principal reason that investors provide external financing to firms is that they receive control rights in exchange. External financing is a contract between the firm as a legal entity and the financiers, which gives the financiers certain rights vis a vis the assets of the firm (Hart (1995), part II). If firm managers violate the terms of the contract, then the financiers have the right to appeal to the courts to enforce their rights. Much of the difference in corporate governance systems around the world stems from the differences in the nature of legal obligations that managers have to the financiers, as well as in the differences in how courts interpret and enforce these obligations.

The most important legal right shareholders have is the right to vote on important corporate matters, such as mergers and liquidations, as well as in elections of boards of directors, which in turn have certain rights vis a vis the management (Manne (1965), Easterbrook and Fischel (1983)). (We discuss voting rights as the essential characteristic of equity in Section VI.) Voting rights, however, turn out to be expensive to exercise and to enforce. In many countries, shareholders cannot vote by mail and actually have to show up at the shareholder meeting to vote—a requirement that virtually guarantees nonvoting by small investors. In developed countries, courts can be relied on to ensure that voting takes place, but even there managers often interfere in the voting process, and try to jawbone shareholders into supporting them, conceal information from their opponents, and so on (Pound (1988), Grundfest (1990)). In countries with weaker legal systems, shareholder voting rights are violated more flagrantly. Russian managers sometimes threaten employee-shareholders with layoffs unless these employees vote with the management, fail to notify shareholders about annual meetings, try to prevent hostile shareholders from voting based on technicalities, and so on. Besides, as Stalin noted, "it is important not how people vote, but who counts the votes," and managers count shareholders' votes. Still, even in Russia, courts have protected a large shareholder when a firm's management erased his name from the register of shareholders. In sum, both the legal extent and the court protection of shareholder voting rights differ greatly across countries.

Even if shareholders elect the board, directors need not necessarily represent their interests. The structure of corporate boards varies greatly even across developed economies, ranging from two-tier supervisory and management boards in Germany, to insider-dominated boards in Japan, to mixed boards in the United States (Charkham (1994)). The question of board effectiveness in any of these countries has proved to be controversial. The available systematic evidence is mixed. In the United States, boards, especially those dominated by outside directors, sometimes remove top managers after poor performance (Weisbach (1988)). However, a true performance disaster is required before boards actually act (Warner, Watts, and Wruck (1988)). The evidence on Japan and Germany (Kaplan (1994a,b)) similarly indicates that boards are quite passive except in extreme circumstances. Mace (1971) and Jensen (1993) argue very strongly that, as a general rule, corporate boards in the United States are captured by the management.

In many countries, shareholder voting rights are supplemented by an affirmative duty of loyalty of the managers to shareholders. Loosely speaking, managers have a duty to act in shareholders' interest. Although the appropriateness of this duty is often challenged by those who believe that managers also ought to have a duty of loyalty to employees, communities, creditors, the state, and so on (see the articles in Hopt and Teubner, Eds. (1985)), the courts in Organization for Economic Cooperation and Development (OECD) countries have generally accepted the idea of managers' duty of loyalty to shareholders. There is a good reason for this. The investments by shareholders are largely sunk, and further investment in the firm is generally not needed from them. This is much less the case with employees, community members, and even creditors. The employees, for example, get paid almost immediately for their efforts, and are generally in a much better position to hold up the firm by threatening to quit than the shareholders are. Because their investment is sunk, shareholders have fewer protections from expropriation than the other stakeholders do. To induce them to invest in the first place, they need stronger protections, such as the duty of loyalty.

Perhaps the most commonly accepted element of the duty of loyalty are the legal restrictions on managerial self-dealing, such as outright theft from the firm, excessive compensation, or issues of additional securities (such as equity) to the management and its relatives. In some cases, the law explicitly prohibits self-dealing; in other cases, courts enforce corporate charters that prohibit it (see Easterbrook and Fischel (1991)). Some legal restrictions on managers constrain their actions, by for example demanding that managers consult the board of directors before making major decisions, or giving shareholders appraisal remedies to stop asset sales at low prices. Other restrictions specify that minority shareholders be treated as well as the insiders (Holderness and Sheehan (1988a)).

Although the duty of loyalty is accepted in principle in most OECD countries, the strictness with which the courts enforce it varies greatly. In the United States, courts would interfere in cases of management theft and asset diversion, and they would surely interfere if managers diluted existing shareholders through an issue of equity to themselves. Courts are less likely to interfere in cases of excessive pay, especially if it takes the complex form of option contracts, and are very unlikely to second guess managers' business decisions, including the decisions that hurt shareholders. Perhaps most importantly, shareholders in the United States have the right to sue the corporation, often using class action suits that get around the free rider problem, if they believe that the managers have violated the duty of loyalty.

The United States is generally viewed as relatively tough on managers in interpreting the duty of loyalty, although some, including Bebchuk (1985) and Brudney and Chirelstein (1978), believe it is not tough enough. For example, in France the doctrine of corporate opportunities, which prohibits managers from personally profiting from business opportunities that are offered to the corporation, is not accepted by courts (Tunc (1991)). Outside the United States and Canada, class action suits are not generally permitted and contingent fees are prohibited (Romano (1993a)). Outside the OECD, the duty of loyalty is a much weaker concept, at least in part because courts have no capability or desire to interfere in business.

Like shareholders, creditors have a variety of legal protections, which also vary across countries. (Again, we say more about this in the discussion of debt and bankruptcy in Section VI.) These may include the right to grab assets that serve as collateral for the loans, the right to liquidate the company when it does not pay its debts, the right to vote in the decision to reorganize the company, and the right to remove managers in reorganization. Legal protection of creditors is often more effective than that of the shareholders, since default is a reasonably straightforward violation of a debt contract that a court can verify. On the other hand, when the bankruptcy procedure gives companies the right of automatic stay of the creditors, managers can keep creditors at bay even after having defaulted. Repossessing assets in bankruptcy is often very hard even for the secured creditors (White (1993)). With multiple, diverse creditors who have conflicting interests, the difficulties of collecting are even greater, and bankruptcy proceedings often take years to complete (Baird and Jackson (1985), Gertner and Scharfstein (1991), Weiss (1990)). This, of course, makes debt a less attractive financing instrument to begin with (Bolton and Scharfstein (1996)). Still, while costly to the creditors, bankruptcy is very tough on the debtor firms as well, since their managers typically get fired, assets liquidated, and debt kept largely in place (Baird (1995)). Creditors' legal rights are thus enforced in a costly and inefficient way, but they are enforced.

Because bankruptcy procedures are so complicated, creditors often renegotiate outside of formal bankruptcy proceedings both in the United States (Gilson, John, and Lang (1990), Asquith, Gertner, and Scharfstein (1994)) and in Europe (OECD (1995)). The situation is worse in developing countries, where courts are even less reliable and bankruptcy laws are even less complete. The inefficiency of existing bankruptcy procedures has prompted some economists (Bebchuk (1988), Aghion, Hart, and Moore (1992)) to propose new ones, which try to avoid complicated negotiations by first converting all the claims of a bankrupt company into equity, and then allowing the equity holders to decide what to do with the bankrupt firm. It is possible that in the long run, these proposals will reduce the cost of enforcing creditor rights.

In sum, the extent of legal protection of investors varies enormously around the world. In some countries, such as the United States, Japan, and Germany, the law protects the rights of at least some investors and the courts are relatively willing to enforce these laws. But even in these countries, the legal system leaves managers with considerable discretion. In most of the rest of the world, the laws are less protective of investors and courts function less well and stop only the clearest violations of investor rights. As a result, legal protection alone becomes insufficient to ensure that investors get their money back.

IV. LARGE INVESTORS

If legal protection does not give enough control rights to small investors to induce them to part with their money, then perhaps investors can get more effective control rights by being large. When control rights are concentrated in the hands of a small number of investors with a collectively large cash flow stake, concerted action by investors is much easier than when control rights, such as votes, are split among many of them. In particular, this concerted action is possible with only minimal help from the courts. In effect, concentration of ownership leverages up legal protection. There are several distinct forms that concentration can take, including large shareholders, takeovers, and large creditors. In this section, we discuss these forms of concentrating ownership, and how they address the agency problem. In the following section, we discuss some costs of having large investors.

A. Large shareholders

The most direct way to align cash flow and control rights of outside investors is to concentrate share holdings. This can mean that one or several investors in the firm have substantial minority ownership stakes, such as 10 or 20 percent. A substantial minority shareholder has the incentive to collect information and monitor the management, thereby avoiding the traditional free rider problem. He also has enough voting control to put pressure on the management in some cases, or perhaps even to oust the management through a proxy fight or a takeover (Shleifer and Vishny (1986b)). In the more extreme cases, large shareholders have outright control of the firms and their management with 51 or more percent ownership. Large shareholders thus address the agency problem in that they both have a general interest in profit maximization, and enough control over the assets of the firm to have their interests respected.

In the United States, large share holdings, and especially majority ownership, are relatively uncommon—probably because of legal restrictions on high ownership and exercise of control by banks, mutual funds, insurance companies, and other institutions (Roe (1994)). Even in the United States, however, ownership is not completely dispersed, and concentrated holdings by families and wealthy investors are more common than is often believed (Eisenberg (1976), Demsetz (1983), Shleifer and Vishny (1986b)). Holderness and Sheehan (1988a,b) in fact found several hundred cases of over 51 percent shareholders in public firms in the United States. One other country where the rule is broadly dispersed ownership by diversified shareholders is the United Kingdom (Black and Coffee (1994)).

In the rest of the world, large share holdings in some form are the norm. In Germany, large commercial banks through proxy voting arrangements often control over a quarter of the votes in major companies, and also have smaller but significant cash flow stakes as direct shareholders or creditors (Franks and Mayer (1994), OECD (1995)). In addition, one study estimates that about 80 percent of the large German companies have an over

25 percent nonbank large shareholder (Gorton and Schmid (1996)). In smaller German companies, the norm is family control through majority ownership or pyramids, in which the owner controls 51 percent of a company, which in turn controls 51 percent of its subsidiaries and so on (Franks and Mayer (1994)). Pyramids enable the ultimate owners to control the assets with the least amount of capital (Barca (1995)). In Japan, although ownership is not nearly as concentrated as in Germany, large cross-holdings as well as share holdings by major banks are the norm (Prowse (1992), Berglof and Perotti (1994), OECD (1995)). In France, cross-ownership and so-called core investors are common (OECD (1995)). In most of the rest of the world, including most of Europe (e.g., Italy, Finland, and Sweden), as well as Latin America, East Asia, and Africa, corporations typically have controlling owners, who are often founders or their offspring. In short, heavily concentrated share holdings and a predominance of controlling ownership seems to be the rule around the world.

The evidence on the role of large shareholders in exercising corporate governance is beginning to accumulate. For Germany, Franks and Mayer (1994) find that large shareholders are associated with higher turnover of directors. Gorton and Schmid (1996) show that bank block holders improve the performance of German companies in their 1974 sample, and that both bank and nonbank block holders improve performance in a 1985 sample. For Japan, Kaplan and Minton (1994) and Kang and Shivdasani (1995) show that firms with large shareholders are more likely to replace managers in response to poor performance than firms without them. Yafeh and Yosha (1996) find that large shareholders reduce discretionary spending, such as advertising, Research & Development (R&D), and entertainment expenses, by Japanese managers. For the United States, Shivdasani (1993) shows that large outside shareholders increase the likelihood that a firm is taken over, whereas Denis and Serrano (1996) show that, if a takeover is defeated, management turnover is higher in poorly performing firms that have block holders. All these findings support the view that large shareholders play an active role in corporate governance (Shleifer and Vishny (1986b)).

Because large shareholders govern by exercising their voting rights, their power depends on the degree of legal protection of their votes. Majority ownership only works if the voting mechanism works, and the majority owner can dictate the decisions of the company. This may require fairly little enforcement by courts, since 51 percent ownership is relatively easy to prove, and a vote count is not required once the majority shareholder expresses his preferences. With large minority shareholders, matters are more complicated, since they need to make alliances with other investors to exercise control. The power of the managers to interfere in these alliances is greatly enhanced, and the burden on courts to protect large shareholder rights is much greater. For this reason, large minority share holdings may be effective only in countries with relatively sophisticated legal systems, whereas countries where courts are really weak are more likely to have outright majority ownership.

Again, the most vivid example comes from Russia. As one Russian investment banker has pointed out, a Western investor can control a Russian company with 75 percent ownership, whereas a Russian investor can do so with only 25 percent ownership. This comment is easy to understand once it is recognized that the management can use a variety of techniques against foreign investors, including declaring some of their shares illegal, requiring super majorities to bring issues on the agenda of shareholder meetings, losing voting records, and so on. While managers can apply these techniques against domestic investors as well, the latter have more mechanisms of their own to protect their power, including better access to other shareholders, to courts, as well as in some cases to physical force. The effectiveness of large shareholders, then, is intimately tied to their ability to defend their rights.

B. Takeovers

In Britain and the United States, two of the countries where large shareholders are less common, a particular mechanism for consolidating ownership has emerged, namely the hostile takeover (Jensen and Ruback (1983), Franks and Mayer (1990)). In a typical hostile takeover, a bidder makes a tender offer to the dispersed shareholders of the target firm, and if they accept this offer, acquires control of the target firm and so can replace, or at least control, the management. Takeovers can thus be viewed as rapid-fire mechanisms for ownership concentration.

A great deal of theory and evidence supports the idea that takeovers address governance problems (Manne (1965), Jensen (1988), Scharfstein (1988)). The most important point is that takeovers typically increase the combined value of the target and acquiring firm, indicating that profits are expected to increase afterwards (Jensen and Ruback (1983)). Moreover, takeover targets are often poorly performing firms (Palepu (1985), Morck, Shleifer, and Vishny (1988a, 1989)), and their managers are removed once the takeover succeeds (Martin and McConnell (1991)). Jensen (1986, 1988) argues that takeovers can solve the free cash flow problem, since they usually lead to distribution of the firm's profits to investors over time. Takeovers are widely interpreted as the critical corporate governance mechanism in the United States, without which managerial discretion cannot be effectively controlled (Easterbrook and Fischel (1991), Jensen (1993)).

There remain some questions about the effectiveness of takeovers as a corporate governance mechanism. First, takeovers are sufficiently expensive that only major performance failures are likely to be addressed. It is not just the cost of mounting a takeover that makes them expensive. As Grossman and Hart (1980) point out, the bidder in takeovers may have to pay the expected increase in profits under his management to target firm's shareholders, for otherwise they will not tender and simply hold on to their shares, which automatically

become more valuable if the takeover succeeds. If minority rights are not fully protected, then the bidder can get a slightly better deal for himself than the target shareholders get, but still he may have to surrender much of the gains resulting from his acquisition of control.

Second, acquisitions can actually increase agency costs when bidding managements overpay for acquisitions that bring them private benefits of control (Shleifer and Vishny (1988)). A fluid takeover market might enable managers to expand their empires more easily, and not just stop excessive expansion of empires. Jensen (1993) shows that disciplinary hostile takeovers were only a small fraction of takeover activity in the 1980s in the United States.

Third, takeovers require a liquid capital market, which gives bidders access to vast amounts of capital on short notice. In the 1980s in the United States, the firm of Drexel, Burnham, Lambert created such a market through junk bond financing. The collapse of this firm may have contributed to the end of that takeover wave.

Last but not least, hostile takeovers are politically an extremely vulnerable mechanism, since they are opposed by the managerial lobbies. In the United States, this political pressure, which manifested itself through state anti-takeover legislation, contributed to ending the 1980s takeovers (Jensen (1993)). In other countries, the political opposition to hostile takeovers in part explains their general nonexistence in the first place. The takeover solution practiced in the United States and the United Kingdom, then, is a very imperfect and politically vulnerable method of concentrating ownership.

C. Large creditors

Significant creditors, such as banks, are also large and potentially active investors. Like the large shareholders, they have large investments in the firm, and want to see the returns on their investments materialize. Their power comes in part because of a variety of control rights they receive when firms default or violate debt covenants (Smith and Warner (1979)) and in part because they typically lend short term, so borrowers have to come back at regular, short intervals for more funds. As a result of having a whole range of controls, large creditors combine substantial cash flow rights with the ability to interfere in the major decisions of the firm. Moreover, in many countries, banks end up holding equity as well as debt of the firms they invest in, or alternatively vote the equity of other investors (OECD (1995)). As a result, banks and other large creditors are in many ways similar to the large share-holders. Diamond (1984) presents one of the first models of monitoring by the large creditors.

Although there has been a great deal of theoretical discussion of governance by large creditors, the empirical evidence of their role remains scarce. For Japan, Kaplan and Minton (1994) and Kang and Shivdasani (1995) document the higher incidence of management turnover in response to poor performance in companies that have a principal banking relationship relative to companies that do not. For Germany, Gorton and Schmid (1996) find evidence of banks improving company per-formance (to the extent they hold equity) more so than other block holders do in 1974, although this is not so in 1985. For the United States, DeLong (1991) points to a significant governance role played by J. P. Morgan partners in the companies J. P. Morgan invested in in the early 20th century. More recently, U.S. banks play a major governance role in bankruptcies, when they change managers and directors (Gilson 1990).

The effectiveness of large creditors, like the effectiveness of large shareholders, depends on the legal rights they have. In Germany and Japan, the powers of the banks vis a vis companies are very signifi-cant because banks vote significant blocks of shares, sit on boards of directors, play a dominant role in lending, and operate in a legal environment favorable to creditors. In other countries, especially where proce-dures for turning control over to the banks

are not well established, bank governance is likely to be less effective (see Barca (1995) on Italy).

The need for at least some legal protec-tion is shared by all large investors. Large shareholders need courts to enforce their voting rights, takeover artists need court-protected mechanisms for buying shares and changing boards of directors, and creditors need courts to enable them to repossess collateral. The principal advantage of large investors (except in takeovers) is that they rely on relatively simple legal interventions, which are suitable for even poorly informed and motivated courts. Large investors put a lighter burden on the legal system than the small investors might if they tried to enforce their rights. For this reason, perhaps, large investors are so prevalent in most countries in the world, where courts are less equipped to meddle in corporate affairs than they are in the United States.

V. THE COSTS OF LARGE INVESTORS

The benefits of large investors are at least theoretically clear: they have both the interest in getting their money back and the power to demand it. But there may be costs of large investors as well. The most obvious of these costs, which is also the usual argument for the benefits of dispersed ownership, is that large investors are not diversified, and hence bear excessive risk (see, e.g., Demsetz and Lehn (1985)). However, the fact that ownership in companies is so concentrated almost everywhere in the world suggests that lack of diversification is not as great a private cost for large investors to bear as relinquishing control.

A more fundamental problem is that the large investors represent their own interests, which need not coincide with the interests of other investors in the firm, or with the interests of employees and man-agers. In the process of using his control rights to maximize his own welfare, the large investor can therefore redistribute wealth—in both efficient and inefficient ways—from others. This cost of concen-trated ownership becomes particularly important when others—such as employees or minority investors—have their own firm-specific investments to make, which are distorted because of possible expropriation by the large investors. Using this general framework, we discuss several potential costs of having large investors: straightforward expropriation of other investors, managers, and employees; inefficient expropriation through pursuit of personal (nonprofit-maximizing) objectives; and finally the incentive effects of expropriation on the other stakeholders.

To begin, large investors might try to treat themselves preferentially at the expense of other investors and employees. Their ability to do so is especially great if their control rights are significantly in excess of their cash flow rights. This happens if they own equity with superior voting rights or if they control the firm through a pyramid structure, i.e., if there is a substantial departure from one-share-one-vote (Grossman and Hart (1988), Harris and Raviv (1988)). In this case, large investors have not only a strong preference, but also the ability not to pay out cash flows as pro-rata distributions to all investors, but rather to pay themselves only. They can do so by paying themselves special dividends or by exploiting other business relationships with the companies they control. Greenmail and targeted share repurchases are examples of special deals for large investors (Dann and DeAngelo 1983).

A small number of papers focus on measuring the degree of expropriation of minority shareholders. The very fact that shares with superior voting rights trade at a large premium is evidence of significant private benefits of control that may come at the expense of minority shareholders. Interestingly, the two countries where the voting premium is the lowest—Sweden and the United States—are the two countries for which the studies of expropriation of minorities have been made. Not surprisingly, Bergström and Rydqvist (1990) for Sweden and Barclay and Holderness (1989, 1992) for the United States do not find evidence of substantial expropriation. In contrast, the casual evidence provided by Zingales (1994) suggests that the expropriation problem is larger in Italy, consistent with a much larger voting premium he finds for that country.

Some related evidence on the benefits of control and potential expropriation of minority shareholders comes from the studies of ownership structure and performance. Although Demsetz (1983) and Demsetz and Lehn (1985) argue that there should be no relationship between ownership structure of a firm and its performance, the evidence has not borne out their view. Morck, Shleifer, and Vishny (1988b) present evidence on the relationship between cash flow ownership of the largest shareholders and profitability of firms, as measured by their Tobin's Qs. Morck et al. find that profitability rises in the range of ownership between 0 and 5 percent, and falls afterwards. One interpretation of this finding is that, consistent with the role of incentives in reducing agency costs, performance improves with higher manager and large shareholder ownership at first. However, as ownership gets beyond a certain point, the large owners gain nearly full control and are wealthy enough to prefer to use firms to generate private benefits of control that are not shared by minority shareholders. Thus there are costs associated with high ownership and entrenchment, as well as with exceptionally dispersed ownership. Stulz (1988) presents a formal model of the roof-shaped relationship between ownership and performance, which has also been corroborated by subsequent empirical work (McConnell and Servaes (1990), Wruck (1989)).

It has also been argued that German and Japanese banks earn rents from their control over industrial firms, and therefore effectively benefit themselves at the expense of other investors. Rajan (1992) presents a theoretical model explaining how banks can extract rents from investors by using their informational advantage. Weinstein and Yafeh (1994) find that, controlling for other factors, Japanese firms with main banks pay higher average interest rates on their liabilities than do unaffiliated firms. Their evidence is consistent with rent-extraction by the main banks. Even more telling is the finding of Hoshi, Kashyap, and Scharfstein (1993) that, when regulatory change enabled Japanese firms to borrow in public capital markets and not just from the banks, high net worth firms jumped at the opportunity. This evidence suggests that, for these firms, the costs of bank finance exceeded its benefits. Franks and Mayer (1994) present a few cases of German banks resisting takeovers of their customer companies, either because they were captured by the management or because they feared losing profits from the banking relationship. On the other hand, Gorton and Schmid (1996) find no evidence of rent extraction by the German banks.

The problem of expropriation by large investors becomes potentially more significant when other investors are of a different type, i.e., have a different pattern of cash flow claims in the company. For example, if the large investor is an equity holder, he may have an incentive to force the firm to take on too much risk, since he shares in the upside while the other investors, who might be creditors, bear all the costs of failure (Jensen and Meckling (1976)). Alternatively, if the large investor is a creditor, he might cause the company to forego good investment projects because he bears some of the cost, while the benefits accrue to the shareholders (Myers (1977)). Finally, large investors might have a greater incentive to redistribute rents from the employees to themselves than the managers do (Shleifer and Summers (1988)).

The available evidence of redistributions between different types of claim holders in the firm comes largely from corporate control transactions. Several studies, for example, ask whether shareholders expropriate bondholders in leveraged buy outs or leveraged recapitalizations. Typically, these redistributions are relatively small (Asquith and Wizman (1990)). Another group of studies ask whether takeovers lead to large redistributions of wealth from the employees in the form of wage reductions, layoffs, and pension cutbacks. Again, these redistributions typically do not appear to be large (Bhagat et al. (1990), Rosett (1990), Pontiff et al. (1990)). Of course, the significant protection of investors and employees in the United States may give an unrepresentative picture of expropriation in other countries.

Expropriation by large investors can be detrimental to efficiency through adverse effects on the incentives of managers and employees, who might reduce their firm-specific human capital investments when they are closely monitored by financiers or may be easily dismissed with the consequent loss of rents. Schmidt (1996) and Cremer (1995) make the general point of how a principal's high powered incentives can reduce an agent's effort. In the case of large shareholders, a similar point is made by Burkart, Grom, and Panunzi (1997), in the case of takeovers by Shleifer and Summers (1988), and in the case of banks by Rajan (1992). In all these examples, the idea is that a large investor cannot commit himself not to extract rents from the manager ex post, and this adversely affects ex ante managerial and employee incentives.

When the targets of expropriation by large investors are other investors, the adverse incentive effect of such expropriation is the decline of external finance. Many countries, for example, do not do much to protect minority investor rights, yet have large investors in the form of families or banks. While this governance structure may control managers, it leaves potential minority investors unprotected and hence unwilling to invest. Perhaps for this reason, countries in Continental Europe, such is Italy, Germany, and France, have relatively small public equity markets. In this regard, the existence of a large equity market in Japan despite the weak protection of minority investors is puzzling. The puzzle may be explained by the predominance of low powered incentives within large Japanese institutions or in the workings of reputations and implicit contracts in Japan.

The Japanese example brings up a very different view of large investors, namely that they are too soft rather than too tough. This can be so for several reasons.

First, large investors, whether shareholders or creditors, may be soft when they themselves are corporations with their own agency problems. Charkham (1994) shows, for example, that German banks virtually control themselves. "At general meetings in recent years, Deutsche Bank held voting rights for 47.2 percent of its shares, Dresdner for 59.25 percent, and Commerzbank for 30.29 percent" (p. 36). Moreover, banks have no incentive to discipline managers, and some incentive to cater to them to get more business, as long as the firm is far away from default (Harris and Raviv (1990)). Edwards and Fischer (1994) summarize evidence suggesting that German banks are not nearly as active in corporate governance as might be expected given their lending power and control over equity votes. Second, some recent articles show that, even if they don't suffer from their own agency problems, large investors such as banks may be too soft because they fail to terminate unprofitable projects they have invested in when continuation is preferred to liquidation (Dewatripont and Maskin (1995), Gertner, Scharfstein, and Stein (1994)). Finally, a large investor may be rich enough that he prefers to maximize private benefits of control rather than wealth. Unless he owns the entire firm, he will not internalize the cost of these control benefits to the other investors. While these arguments suggest a different set of problems with large investors, they too point to failures of large investors to force managers to maximize profits and pay them out.

VI. SPECIFIC GOVERNANCE ARRANGEMENTS

In the previous sections, we discussed the roles of legal protection and concentrated ownership in assuring that investors can collect their returns from firms. We have postponed the discussion of specific contractual mechanisms used to address the agency problem until this section. In particular, we now focus on debt and equity as instruments of finance. In addition, we discuss state ownership—a particular organizational form that, for reasons discussed in this article, is rarely conducive to efficiency.

A. The debt versus equity choice

Recent years saw a veritable flood of research on the debt contract as a mechanism for solving agency problems. In this new work, unlike in the Modigliani-Miller (1958) framework, where debt is associated only with a particular pattern of cash flows, the defining feature of debt is the ability of creditors to exercise control. Specifically, debt is a contract in which a borrower gets some funds from the lender, and promises to make a prespecified stream of future payments to the lender. In addition, the borrower typically promises not to violate a range of covenants (Smith and Warner (1979)), such as maintaining the value of assets inside the firm. If the borrower violates any covenant, and especially if he defaults on a payment, the lender gets certain rights, such as the ability to repossess some of the firm's assets (collateral) or the opportunity to throw the firm into bankruptcy. An essential feature of debt, then, is that a failure by the borrower to adhere to the contract triggers the transfer of some control rights from him to the lender.

The literature on debt can be usefully divided into that before Grossman-Hart (1986), and that after. Townsend (1978) and Gale and Hellwig (1985) consider models in which the borrower can abscond with the profits of the firm. However, if the lender is not repaid, he has the right to investigate the books of the firm, and grab its cash before the borrower can steal it. Thus failure to repay triggers the transfer of control over the assets from the borrower to the lender. Gale and Hellwig (1985) show that the optimal contract that minimizes the expected investigation costs is a debt contract. Grossman and Hart (1982) and Jensen (1986) model the role of debt in committing the payout of free cash flows to investors. In Grossman and Hart (1982), in particular, default enables creditors to deprive the manager of the benefits of control. A final important early article, which is not cast in the agency context, but contains a highly relevant idea, is Myers and Majluf (1984). They show that, because management has superior information, external finance is costly. Moreover, they argue that this adverse selection problem is minimized by the issuance of the "safest" security, i.e., the security whose pricing is least sensitive to the manager's private information. Thus highly rated debt with a fairly certain payoff stream is issued before equity, since equity is difficult to price without knowing the precise value of the firm's assets in place and future growth opportunities. Debt is particularly easy to value where there is abundant collateral, so that investors need only concern themselves with the value of the collateral and not with the valuation of the entire firm, as equity investors would need to.

The next generation of papers adopts the incomplete contracts framework more explicitly, and focuses on the transfer of control from managers to creditors. Aghion and Bolton (1992) use incomplete contract theory to characterize debt as an instrument whose holders take control of the firm in a bad state of the world. They show that if the managerial benefits of control are higher in good states of the world, then it may be efficient for managers to have control of assets in good states, and for creditors to have it in bad states. Their model does not incorporate the idea that control reverts to the creditors in the case of default as opposed to some general bad state. Bolton and Scharfstein (1990) present a model in which upon default, creditors have enough power to exclude the firm from the capital market, and hence stop future financing altogether. Hart and Moore (1989, 1994a) explicitly model the idea that debt is a contract that gives the creditor the right to repossess collateral in case of default. Fear of such liquidation keeps money flowing from the debtors to the creditors. Hart and Moore's models of debt show exactly how the schedule of debt repayments depends on what creditors can realize once they gain control.

Several other articles model the costs and benefits of the debt contract. The benefit is usually the reduction in the agency cost, such as preventing the manager from investing in negative net present value projects, or forcing him to sell assets that are worth more in alternative use. The main costs of debt are that firms may be prevented from undertaking good projects because debt covenants keep them from raising additional funds, or else they may be forced by creditors to liquidate when it is not efficient to do so. Stulz (1990), Diamond (1991), Harris and Raviv (1990), and Hart and Moore (1995) present some of the main models incorporating these ideas, whereas Lang, Ofek, and Stulz (1996) present evidence indicating that leverage indeed curtails investment by firms with poor prospects. Williamson (1988) and Shleifer and Vishny (1992) argue that liquidations might be particularly costly when alternative use of the asset is limited or when the potential buyers of the asset cannot raise funds themselves. Dewatripont and Tirole (1994) derive the optimal amount of debt in a model where the tough negotiating stance of debt holders after default deters managerial shirking ex ante. The model explains how the cash flow structure of debt as senior claimant with little upside potential makes debt holders tough on managers after a default. This makes it optimal to combine the specific form of cash flow rights of debt with contingent control of the firm in the bad state. Berglof and von Thadden (1994) similarly show why short term debt holders—who are the tough financiers in their model—should have control in the bad states. Many of these articles take advantage of Myers' (1977) insight that debt overhang might be an effective deterrent to new financing and investment.

Because the rights of creditors are clearer, and violations of those rights are easier to verify in courts, the existing literature has anointed debt as providing better protection to outside investors than equity. However, the focus on large investors sheds new light on the relative powers of debt and equity. Specifically, debt and equity ought be compared in terms of the combination of legal protections and ease of ownership concentration that each typically provides.

First, does debt promote concentrated ownership? By far the dominant form of lending around the world is bank lending. Banks are usually large investors, who gain numerous control rights in the firm at the time of or even before default. For example, the main bank can often take physical control of the firm's bank account—which resides at that very bank—if it misses a payment, thereby assuring fairly complete control of the firm by the bank without much involvement of the courts. This control is often bolstered by direct equity ownership in the firm, as well as a large degree of monopoly power over any future credit extended to the firm (OECD (1995)). In contrast, American, Canadian, and British firms make more extensive use of syndicated bank lending and even of public debt, in which creditors are fairly dispersed (Mayer (1990)).

But even where debt is not very concentrated, the effective legal protection afforded creditors is likely to be greater than that enjoyed by dispersed equity holders. The crucial feature of the creditors' legal rights is that concerted action by multiple creditors is not required to take action against a delinquent debtor. The legal obligation of the firm is an obligation to each and every creditor, and any of these creditors can typically sue the firm for payment of what is owed or for sale of assets. Of course, once action is taken by one creditor, the other creditors and the courts will take action to ensure that the first creditor does not grab a disproportionate share for himself. In fact, this ability to unilaterally initiate the grab for assets in a multiple creditor situation lends the theoretical justification for bankruptcy protection.

Unlike equity, debt in a peculiar way may be tougher when it is not concentrated. If a borrower defaults on debt held by a large number of creditors, renegotiating with these creditors may be extremely difficult, and the borrower might be forced into bankruptcy (Gertner and Scharfstein

(1991), Bolton and Scharfstein (1996)). In contrast, it may be easier to renegotiate with a bank. The difficulty of renegotiation, and the power of dispersed creditors, might explain why public debt is an extremely uncommon financing instrument, used only in a few developed countries, and even there much less than bank debt (Mayer (1990)).

Unlike creditors, *individual* shareholders are not promised any payments in return for their financial investment in the firm, although often they receive dividends at the discretion of the board of directors. Unlike creditors, individual shareholders have no claim to specific assets of the firm, and have no right to pull the collateral (one commonly studied exception is mutual funds, in which individual equity holders can force a liquidation of their pro rata share of the assets and a repayment of its value). Unlike creditors, shareholders do not even have a final date at which the firm is liquidated and the proceeds are distributed. In principle, they may never get anything back at all.

In addition to some relatively weak legal protections, the principal right that equity holders typically get is the right to vote for the board of directors. Even this right is not universal, since many countries have multiple classes of common stock, and hence equity holders with inferior voting rights get proportionately fewer votes than their financial investment in the company. Because concerted action by a large group of shareholders is required to take control via the voting mechanism, voting rights are of limited value unless they are concentrated. Most small shareholders do not even have an incentive to become informed on how to vote. Contacting and persuading a large group of small shareholders through the proxy mechanism is difficult and expensive, especially when the management stands in the way (Dodd and Warner (1983)). In contrast, when votes are concentrated—either in a large share holding block or through a takeover—they become extremely valuable, since the party that controls the concentrated votes can make virtually *all* corporate decisions.

Concentrated equity in this respect is more powerful than concentrated debt. The value of individual shares comes from the fact that the votes attached to them are valuable to those trying to control the firm, and the protection of minority shareholders assures that those who have control must share some of the benefits with the minority (Grossman and Hart (1988), Harris and Raviv (1988)).

Because the equity holders have voting power and legal protection of minority shareholders, they have the ability to extract some payments from the managers in the form of dividends. Easterbrook (1984) articulates the agency theory of dividend payments, in which dividends are for equity what interest is for debt: pay out by the managers supported by the control rights of the financiers, except in the case of equity these control rights are the voting rights. More recently, Fluck (1995) and Myers (1995) present agency-theoretic models of dividends, based on the idea that shareholders can threaten to vote to fire managers or liquidate the firm, and therefore managers pay dividends to hold off the shareholders. These models do not explicitly address the free rider problem between shareholders; namely, how do they manage to organize themselves to pose a threat to the management when they are small and dispersed? Concentration of equity ownership, or at least the threat of such concentration, must be important to get companies to pay dividends.

One of the fundamental questions that the equity contracts raise is how—given the weakness of control rights without concentration—do firms manage to issue equity in any substantial amounts at all? Equity is the most suitable financing tool when debt contracts are difficult to enforce, i.e., when no specific collateral can be used to back credit and when near-term cash flows are insufficient to service debt payments. Young firms, and firms with intangible assets, may need to be equity financed simply because their assets have little or no liquidation value. If they are financed by debt, their managers effectively give full control to the bank from the start.

This may be especially problematic when the firm's value consists primarily of future growth opportunities, but the bank's debt claim and unwillingness to take equity give it little interest in the upside and a distorted incentive to liquidate (Diamond (1991), Hart and Moore (1995), Dewatripont and Tirole (1994)). Rather than give away control to the bank, such firms often have highly concentrated equity ownership by the entrepreneur and a venture capitalist. This may pave the way for some dispersed outside equity ownership as long as minority rights are well enough protected.

In fact, we do observe equity financing primarily for young, growing firms, as well as for firms in rapidly growing economies, whereas mature economies and mature firms typically use bank finance when they rely on external funds at all (see Mayer (1990), Singh (1995)). In the same spirit, Titman and Wessels (1988) and Rajan and Zingales (1995) show for the United States and several OECD economies respectively that debt finance is most common for firms with tangible assets.

This analysis of equity financing still leaves an important question open: how can firms raise equity finance in countries with virtually no protection of minority investors, even if these countries are rapidly growing? Singh (1995) provides some evidence on the importance of equity financing in LDCs, although some of his data on equity financing might include privatizations and equity exchanges within industrial groups, both of which often take the form of sales of large blocks and hence need not reflect any minority purchases. One possible explanation is that, during a period of rapid economic growth, reputational effects and the prospects of coming back soon to the capital market sustain good behavior until the requisite institutions and legal protections are put in place (Gomes (1996)). Investors can thus count on reputation in the short run, and legal protection in the longer run when the firm's needs for access to capital markets are smaller. Also, in some rapidly growing countries, such as Korea, the rates of return on investment may exceed the rates of appropriation by the insiders. However, another possibility is that speculative bubbles and investor overoptimism are playing an important role in equity financing in rapidly growing economies. The available evidence does not satisfactorily account for the puzzle of external equity financing in countries with only minimal legal protection of investors.

B. LBOs

A remarkable recent phenomenon in the United States that illustrates both the benefits and the costs of having large investors is leveraged buy outs. In these transactions, shareholders of a publicly owned company are bought out by a new group of investors, that usually includes old managers, a specialized buyout firm, banks and public debt holders (Jensen (1989a, 1989b)). With fewer constraints on compensation arrangements than when the firm was public, managers typically sharply increase their percentage ownership of the new company, even though they take out some of their money invested in the firm (Kaplan and Stein (1993)). The buyout firm typically buys enough equity to control the firm. Most of the financing, however, comes from banks and from buyers of subordinated public debt, which in the 1980s became known as junk bonds. In some cases, the decisions of the dispersed holders of junk debt were coordinated by its underwriters. In short, LBOs had concentrated equity ownership by managers and LBO funds, as well as debt ownership by banks, and, in effect, the holders of public debt.

Consistent with the idea that large investors reduce agency problems, the available evidence indicates that LBOs are efficient organizations. First, like other takeovers, LBOs usually buy out the old shareholders at a substantial premium, meaning at least prima facie that they were going to increase profits (DeAngelo, DeAngelo, and Rice (1984)). Second, there is direct evidence from the sample of LBOs that subsequently went public that they do increase profits (Kaplan (1989)). Third,

there is some evidence that the way in which profits are increased has to do with lower agency costs. Many LBOs are targeted at highly diversified firms, which sell off many of their noncore divisions shortly after the LBO (Bhagat, Shleifer, and Vishny (1990)). If the agency problem expresses itself in the form of excessive size and diversification, then the effect of debt overhang and large shareholders is to reduce agency costs.

At the same time, LBOs illustrate the potential costs of heavily concentrated ownership. Jensen (1989a) conjectures that because LBOs are so efficient, they would become a predominant organizational form in the United States. Rappaport (1990) in contrast argues that the heavy oversight from investors might prevent future investment and growth, and hence be unattractive to the management. Bhagat, Shleifer, and Vishny (1990) argue that the principal purpose of LBOs in the 1980's was to serve as a temporary financing tool for implementation of drastic short-run improvements, such as divestitures. Kaplan (1991) looks empirically at the question of whether LBOs are permanent organizations, or whether, alternatively, they eventually return to the public equity market. His evidence suggests that, while LBOs are not very short lived organizations, the median firm sells equity to the public within five to six years. Although this suggests that LBOs are not permanent organizations, Kaplan also finds that even those firms issuing equity to the public retain a very heavy concentration of both debt and equity ownership. Large investors remain even when the original financing structure is too tough to be permanent.

C. Cooperatives and state ownership

We have suggested that, in some situations, concentrated ownership may not be optimal because nonshareholder constituencies such as managers, employees, and consumers are left with too few rents, and too little incentive to make relationship-specific investments. In these situations, cooperatives might be a more efficient ownership structure (Hansmann (1988), Hart and Moore (1994b)). For example, private firms with large investors might under-provide quality or otherwise shortchange the firm's stakeholders because of their single-minded focus on profits. This logic has been used to explain why health care, child care, and even retailing are sometimes best provided by cooperatives, including consumer cooperatives. By voting on prices and quality, stakeholders achieve a better outcome than would a profit-maximizing owner.

A similar argument has been used to justify state ownership of firms. Where monopoly power, externalities, or distributional issues raise concerns, private profit-maximizing firms may fail to address these concerns. A publicly spirited politician can then improve efficiency by controlling the decisions of firms. Such social welfare arguments underlie the traditional case for state ownership of railroads, electricity, prisons, schools, health care, and many other activities (Laffont and Tirole (1993), Sappington and Stiglitz (1987)). Versions of this argument are used to justify state ownership of industrial firms as well.

With a few exceptions of activities where the argument for state ownership carries the day, such as police and prisons (Hart, Shleifer, and Vishny (1997)), the reality of state ownership is broadly inconsistent with this efficiency argument. First, state firms do not appear to serve the public interest better than private firms do. For example, in many countries state enterprises are much worse polluters than private firms. Indeed, the pollution problems are most severe in the former communist countries that were dominated by state firms (Grossman and Krueger (1993)). Second, contrary to the theory, state firms are typically extremely inefficient, and their losses result in huge drains on their countries' treasuries (Kikeri, Nellis, and Shirley (1992) and Boycko, Shleifer, and Vishny (1995) survey the relevant evidence). In their frequent disregard of social objectives, as well as in their extreme inefficiency, the behavior of state firms is inconsistent with the efficiency justification for their existence.

The view of corporate governance taken in this article helps explain the principal elements of the behavior of state firms. While in theory these firms are controlled by the public, the de facto control rights belong to the bureaucrats. These bureaucrats can be thought of as having extremely concentrated control rights, but no significant cash flow rights because the cash flow ownership of state firms is effectively dispersed amongst the taxpayers of the country. Moreover, the bureaucrats typically have goals that are very different from social welfare, and are dictated by their political interests (Shapiro and Willig (1990), Boycko et al. (1996), Shleifer and Vishny (1994)). For example, they often cater to special interest groups that help them win elections, such as public employee trade unions, which not surprisingly typically strongly support state ownership (Lopez-de-Silanes, Shleifer, and Vishny (1997)). In sum, the bureaucrats controlling state firms have at best only an indirect concern about profits (because profits flow into the government budget), and have objectives that are very different from the social interest. Nonetheless, they have virtually complete power over these firms, and can direct them to pursue any political objective. State ownership is then an example of concentrated control with no cash flow rights *and* socially harmful objectives. Viewed from this perspective, the inefficiency of state firms is not at all surprising.

The recognition of enormous inefficiency of state firms, and the pressures on public budgets, have created a common response around the world in the last few years, namely privatization. In most cases, privatization replaces political control with private control by outside investors. At the same time, privatization in most countries creates concentrated private cash flow ownership to go along with control. The result of the switch to these relatively more efficient ownership structures is typically a significant improvement in performance of privatized firms (Megginson et al. (1994), Lopez-de-Silanes (1994)).

The cases where privatization does not work as well as intended can also be understood from the corporate governance perspective. For example, when firms are privatized without the creation of large investors, agency costs of managerial control may rise even when the costs of political control fall. In the United Kingdom, managers of privatized firms such as water utilities receive large wage increases (Wolfram (1995)). This outcome is not surprising, given that the controlling outside shareholders no longer exist in these firms, leaving managers with more discretion. At the same time, we doubt that the problems of managerial discretion in these companies are nearly as serious as the prior problems of political control.

Another example of postprivatization difficulties with corporate governance is Russia (Boycko et al. (1995)). For political reasons, the Russian privatization has led to controlling ownership by the management of many companies. The management has almost complete control and substantial cash flow rights, which can in principle lead to dramatically improved incentives. However, there are two problems—both of which could have been predicted from the theory. First, the virtual absence of protection of minority shareholders makes it attractive for managers to divert resources from the firms despite their large personal cash flow stakes, since in this way they do not need to share with outside investors at all. Second, managers in many cases are not competent to restructure the privatized firms, yet in virtue of their control rights remain on the job and "consume" the benefits of control. In fact, some of the most successful privatizations in Russia have been the ones where outside investors have accumulated enough shares to either replace or otherwise control the management. Such outside investors have typically been less capable of diverting the profits for themselves than the managers, as well as better capable of maximizing these profits. The example of the Russian privatization vividly illustrates both the benefits and the costs of concentrated ownership without legal protection of minority investors.

VII. WHICH SYSTEM IS THE BEST?

Corporate governance mechanisms vary a great deal around the world. Firms in the United States and the United Kingdom substantially rely on legal protection of investors. Large investors are less prevalent, except that ownership is concentrated sporadically in the takeover process. In much of Continental Europe as well as in Japan, there is less reliance on elaborate legal protections, and more reliance on large investors and banks. Finally, in the rest of the world, ownership is typically heavily concentrated in families, with a few large outside investors and banks. Legal protection of investors is considerably weaker than in Japan and Germany, let alone in Britain and the United States. This diversity of systems raises the obvious question: what arrangement is the best from the viewpoint of attracting external funds to firms? In this section, we attempt to deal with this question.

A. Legal protection and large investors

Our analysis leads us to conclude that both the legal protection of investors and some form of concentrated ownership are essential elements of a good corporate governance system. Large investors appear to be necessary to force managers to distribute profits. These investors require at least some basic legal rights, such as the voting rights or the power to pull collateral, to exercise their power over the management. If small investors are to be attracted to the business of financing companies, they as well require some legal protection against expropriation by both the managers and the large investors. Legal protection and large investors are complementary in an effective corporate governance system.

Indeed, the successful corporate governance systems, such as those of the United States, Germany, and Japan, rely on some combination of concentrated ownership and legal protection of investors. In the United States, both small and large shareholders are protected through an extensive system of rules that protects minority rights, allows for easy transfer of shares, keeps elections of directors relatively uninhibited by managers, and gives shareholders extensive powers to sue directors for violations of fiduciary duty, including through class-action suits. Because of extensive bankruptcy protection of companies, however, creditors in the United States have relatively fewer rights than do creditors in Germany and Japan. These legal rules support a system of active public participation in the stock market, concentration of ownership through takeovers, but little governance by banks.

In Germany, creditors have stronger rights than they do in the United States, but shareholder rights are weaker. Germany then has a system of governance by both permanent large shareholders, for whom the existing legal rules suffice to exercise their power, and by banks, but has virtually no participation by small investors in the market. Japan falls between the United States and Germany in the degree of protection of both shareholder and creditor rights, and as a result has powerful banks and powerful long term shareholders, although neither is evidently as powerful as they are in Germany. In addition, the Japanese governance system has succeeded in attracting small investors into the stock market. Because both Germany and Japan have a system of permanent large investors, hostile takeovers are rare in both countries. Although we compare the merits of the three systems below, it is essential to remember that all of them have effective legal protection of at least some types of investors.

In much of the rest of the world, legal protection of investors is less substantial, either because laws are bad or because courts do not enforce these laws. As a consequence, firms remain family-controlled and, even in some of the richest countries, have difficulty raising outside funds, and finance most of their investment internally (Mayer 1990). Pagano, Panetta, and Zingales (1995) report the extraordinary difficulties that firms face raising outside funds in Italy. Over an 11-year period between 1982 and 1992, only 123 firms

went public in Italy, compared to several thousand in the United States. Barca (1995) suggests that bank finance is also difficult to obtain. Although Mayer (1990) reports a significant amount of bank financing in Italy, most of it comes from state bank financing of state firms. In Italy, most large firms not supported by the government are family controlled and internally financed.

Although there is little systematic evidence available, most of the world appears to be more like Italy than like the United States, Germany, or Japan. A recent study of India, for example, shows that large firms tend to be family controlled, and to rely almost entirely on internal financing except when they get money from the government (Khanna and Palepu (1996)). Latin American firms also face little external corporate governance, and financing tends to be either internal or from government-controlled banks. The conclusion we draw is simple: corporate governance systems of the United States, Germany, and Japan have more in common than is typically thought, namely a combination of large investors and a legal system that protects investor rights. Corporate governance systems elsewhere are less effective because they lack the necessary legal protections.

B. Evolution of governance systems

The above discussion does not address the question that has interested many people, namely which of the developed corporate governance systems works the best? One could argue that, since all these systems survived and the economies prospered, the governance systems of the United States, Japan, and Germany must be about equally good. However, recent research has shown that, historically, political pressures are as important in the evolution of corporate governance systems as the economic ones.

In a much-discussed recent book, Roe (1994) argues that politics rather than economic efficiency shaped American corporate law, at least at the Federal level. Roe provides a detailed account on how the American political system systematically discouraged large investors. Banks, insurance companies, mutual funds, and pension funds were all prevented from becoming influential in corporate affairs. The hostile political response to the 1980s takeovers can be viewed as a continuation of the promanagement and antilarge-shareholder policies (Grundfest (1990), Jensen (1993)). Roe does not explain whether the extremely fine development of the legal protection of small shareholders in the United States is in part a response to the suppression of large investors, but this conclusion is actually suggested by some other work (e.g., Douglas (1940), Coffee (1991), Bhide (1993)). Roe's conclusion is nonetheless that the American system is far from efficient because of its discouragement of the large investors.

The trouble is, the argument that the political process accommodates the powerful interests in the economy rather than maximizing social welfare applies to Germany and Japan as well. Both countries have shaped their systems of powerful banks at the end of the 19th century, during the period of rapid economic growth, and with strong support from the state (Gerschenkron (1962)). In both countries, the United States attempted to destroy the powerful financial institutions during the occupation after World War II (Adler (1949)), and in both countries it failed. Moreover, once German banks became sufficiently powerful, they discouraged the introduction of disclosure rules, prohibitions on insider trading, and other protections of minority shareholders—thus making sure that these investors never became a significant economic or political force to protect their rights. Through this political channel, the legal system has developed to accommodate the prevailing economic power, which happened to be the banks. Evolutionary arguments evidently do not adjudicate the question of which system is more efficient.

C. What kind of large investors?

The question that many of the comparisons of the United States, Japan, and Germany

have focused on is: what type of large investors are best? How do U.S.-style takeovers compare to more permanent large shareholders and creditors in West Germany and Japan? We do not believe that the available research provides a firm answer to this question.

Not surprisingly, the most enthusiastic assessments of American corporate governance system come from those who put greater emphasis on the role of legal protection than on that of large investors (Easterbrook and Fischel (1991), Romano (1993a)). Romano (1993a) argues that competition between U.S. states has caused the State of Delaware, where many large companies are incorporated, to adopt corporate laws that effectively serve the interests of shareholders, and thus secure effective corporate governance. Romano (1993a) even argues that Delaware adopted the most benign antitakeover legislation of all the states, thereby not precluding a future role for hostile takeovers. Easterbrook and Fischel (1991) do not discuss the role of large shareholders at all. Romano (1993b) believes that the frequently mentioned hopes that institutional investors in the United States become active, value-maximizing shareholders (e.g., Black (1990)) are exaggerated. She is also skeptical about the potential governance role of banks. In short, the bet among these scholars is on the legal protection of investors. To the extent that takeovers complement this legal protection, they are viewed as sufficient.

In contrast, advocates of the German and Japanese corporate governance system point to the benefits of permanent long term investors relative to those of takeovers. Hoshi, Kashyap, and Scharfstein (1990, 1991) show that firms with a main banking relationship in Japan go through financial distress with less economic distress and better access to financing. In addition, a large theoretical and anecdotal literature argues that the American corporate governance system, particularly takeovers, imposes short horizons on the behavior of corporate managers, and hence reduces the efficiency of investment

(Stein (1988, 1989), Shleifer and Vishny (1990)). The theories and the arguments (Porter (1992)) in this area are remarkably short of any empirical support (see Poterba and Summers (1995)). Still, the superior performance of the Japanese and German economies, at least until the 1990s, has caused many to prefer their governance systems to the American one (see Aoki (1990), Roe (1993), and Charkham (1994)).

We do not think that these debates have been conclusive. True, American takeovers are a crude governance mechanism. But the U.S. economy has produced mechanisms of this kind repeatedly during the 20th century, including mergers, proxy fights, LBOs, and more recently vulture funds. Although many of these mechanisms run into political trouble, new ones keep being invented. The end of 1980s hostile takeovers probably does not spell the end of active large investors. Moreover, partly as a result of takeovers, the American economy in the 1980s went through a more radical, and possibly effective, restructuring than the economies of Japan and Western Europe. Finally, because of extensive legal protection of small investors, young American firms are able to raise capital in the stock market better than firms elsewhere in the world. It is difficult to dismiss the U.S. corporate governance system in light of these basic facts.

On the other hand, permanent large shareholders and banks, such as those dominating corporate governance in Japan and Germany, obviously have some advantages, such as the ability to influence corporate management by patient, informed investors. These investors may be better able to help distressed firms as well. Still, there are serious questions about the effectiveness of these investors, largely because their toughness is in doubt. As Charkham (1994) has shown, German banks are large public institutions that effectively control themselves. There is little evidence from either Japan or Germany that banks are very tough in corporate governance. Finally, at least in Germany, large-investor-oriented governance system discourages small investors from participating in financial markets. In sum, despite a great deal of controversy, we do not believe that either the theory or the evidence tells us which of the three principal corporate governance systems is the best. In this regard, we are not surprised to see political and economic pressures for the three systems to move toward each other, as exemplified by the growing popularity of large shareholders in the United States, the emergence of public debt markets in Japan, and the increasing bank-bashing in Germany.

At the same time, in thinking about the evolution of governance in transition economies, it is difficult to believe that either significant legal protection of investors or takeovers are likely to play a key role. In all likelihood, then, unless Eastern Europe is stuck with insider domination and no private external finance at all (a risk in Russia), it will move toward governance by banks and large shareholders. The early evidence from the Czech Republic (van Wijnbergen and Mancini (1995)) and Russia (Blasi and Shleifer (1996)) indeed suggests that large shareholders, which in the Czech Republic are often bank-controlled mutual funds, play a central role in corporate governance. It would be extremely fortunate if transition economies managed to approach the corporate governance systems of Germany and Japan, particularly in the dimension of the legal protection of investors. But this does not imply that the United States should move in the same direction as well.

VIII. CONCLUSION

In the course of surveying the research on corporate governance, we try to convey a particular structure of this field. Corporate governance deals with the agency problem: the separation of management and finance. The fundamental question of corporate governance is how to assure financiers that they get a return on their financial investment. We begin this survey by showing that the agency problem is serious: the opportunities for managers to abscond with financiers' funds, or to squander them on pet projects, are plentiful and well-documented.

We then describe several broad approaches to corporate governance. We begin by considering the possibility of financing based on reputations of managers, or on excessively optimistic expectations of investors about the likelihood of getting their money back. We argue that such financing without governance is unlikely to be the whole story. We then discuss legal protection of investors and concentration of ownership as complementary approaches to governance. We argue that legal protection of investor rights is one essential element of corporate governance. Concentrated ownership—through large share holdings, takeovers, and bank finance—is also a nearly universal method of control that helps investors to get their money back. Although large investors can be very effective in solving the agency problem, they may also inefficiently redistribute wealth from other investors to themselves.

Successful corporate governance systems, such as those of the United States, Germany, and Japan, combine significant legal protection of at least some investors with an important role for large investors. This combination separates them from governance systems in most other countries, which provide extremely limited legal protection of investors, and are stuck with family and insider-dominated firms receiving little external financing. At the same time, we do not believe that the available evidence tells us which one of the successful governance systems is the best.

In writing this survey, we face a variety of still open questions. In conclusion, we simply raise some of them. While the literature in some cases expresses opinions about these questions, we are skeptical that at the moment persuasive answers are available.

First, given the large impact of executives' actions on values of firms, why aren't very high powered incentive contracts used more often in the United States and elsewhere in the world? Is their use limited by optimal design of incentives, by fear of self-dealing, or by distributive politics?

Second, what is the nature of legal protection of investors that underlies corporate governance systems in various countries? How do corporate laws differ, and how does enforcement of these laws vary across countries? Although a lot has been written about law and corporate governance in the United States, much less is written (in English) about the rest of the world, including other wealthy economies. Yet legal rules appear to play a key role in corporate governance.

Third, are the costs and benefits of concentrated ownership significant? In particular, do large investors effectively expropriate other investors and stakeholders? Are they tough enough toward managers? Resistance to large investors has driven the evolution of corporate governance in the United States, yet they dominate corporate governance in other countries. We need to know a great deal more about these questions to objectively compare the successful corporate governance systems.

Fourth, do companies in developing countries actually raise substantial equity finance? Who are the buyers of this equity? If they are dispersed shareholders, why are they buying the equity despite the apparent absence of minority protections? What are the real protections of shareholders in most countries anyway? We were surprised to find very little information on equity finance outside the United States.

Finally, and perhaps most generally, what are the political dynamics of corporate governance? Do political and economic forces move corporate governance toward greater efficiency or, alternatively, do powerful interest groups, such as the managers in the United States or the banks in Germany, preserve inefficient governance systems? How effective is the political and economic marketplace in delivering efficient governance? While our survey has described some evidence in this area from the United States, our understanding of the politics of corporate governance around the world remains extremely limited.

NOTE

* Shleifer is from Harvard University. Vishny is from the University of Chicago. Prepared for the Nobel Symposium on Law and Finance, Stockholm, August 1995. We are grateful to Oliver D. Hart for many conversations, to Doug Diamond, Frank Easterbrook, Milton Harris, Martin Hellwig, James Hines, Tor Jonsson, Steve Kaplan, Rafael La Porta, Florencio Lopez-de-Silanes, Raghu Rajan, David Scharfstein, René Stulz, and Luigi Zingales for comments, and to the NSF for financial support.

REFERENCES

Adler, Hans, 1949, The post-war reorganization of the German banking system, Quarterly Journal of Economics 63, 322–341.

Aghion, Philippe, and Patrick Bolton, 1992, An "incomplete contracts" approach to financial contracting, Review of Economic Studies 59, 473–494.

Aghion, Philippe, Oliver Hart, and John Moore, 1992, The economics of bankruptcy reform, Journal of Law, Economics, and Organization 8, 523–546.

Alchian, Armen, 1950, Uncertainty, evolution, and economic theory, Journal of Political Economy 58, 211–221.

Allen, Franklin, and Douglas Gale, 1994, Financial Innovation and Risk Sharing (MIT Press, Cambridge, Mass.).

Aoki, Masahiko, 1990, Towards an economic model of the Japanese firm, Journal of Economic Literature 28, 1–27.

Asquith, Paul, Robert Gertner, and David Scharfstein, 1994, Anatomy of financial distress: An examination of junk bond issuers, Quarterly Journal of Economics 109, 625–658.

Asquith, Paul, and Thierry Wizman, 1990, Event risk, covenants, and bondholders' returns in leveraged buyouts, Journal of Financial Economics 27, 195–214.

Baird, Douglas, 1995, The hidden virtues of chapter 11: An overview of the law and economics of financially distressed firms, manuscript, University of Chicago Law School.

Baird, Douglas, and Thomas Jackson, 1985, Cases, Problems, and Materials on Bankruptcy (Little, Brown and Co., Boston).

Barca, Fabrizio, 1995, On corporate governance in Italy: Issues, facts, and agency, manuscript, Bank of Italy, Rome.

Barclay, Michael, and Clifford Holderness, 1989, Private benefits from control of public corporations, Journal of Financial Economics 25, 371–395.

Barclay, Michael, and Clifford Holderness, 1992, The law and large-block trades, The Journal of Law and Economics 35, 265–294.

Baumol, William, 1959, Business Behavior, Value and Growth (Macmillan, New York).

Bebchuk, Lucian, 1985, Toward undistorted choice and equal treatment in corporate takeovers, Harvard Law Review 98, 1693–1808.

Bebchuk, Lucian, 1988, A new method for corporate reorganization, Harvard Law Review 101, 775–804.

Benston, George, 1985, The self-serving management hypothesis: Some evidence, Journal of Accounting & Economics 7, 67–83.

Berglof, Erik, and Enrico Perotti, 1994, The governance structure of the Japanese financial keiretsu, Journal of Financial Economics 36, 259–284.

Berglof, Erik, and Ernst-Ludwig von Thadden, 1994, Short-term versus long-term interests: Capital structure with multiple investors, Quarterly Journal of Economics 109, 1055–1084.

Bergström, Clas, and Kristian Rydqvist, 1990, Ownership of equity in dual-class firms, Journal of Banking and Finance 14, 255–269.

Berle, Adolf, and Gardiner Means, 1932, The Modern Corporation and Private Property (Macmillan, New York).

Bhide, Amar, 1993, The hidden costs of stock market liquidity, Journal of Financial Economics 34, 31–51.

Bhagat, Sanjay, Andrei Shleifer, and Robert Vishny, 1990, Hostile takeovers in the 1980s: The return to corporate specialization, Brookings Papers on Economic Activity: Microeconomics, Special Issue, 1–72.

Black, Bernard, 1990, Shareholder passivity reexamined, Michigan Law Review 89, 520–591.

Black, Bernard, and John Coffee, 1994, Hail Britannia?: Institutional investor behavior under limited regulation, Michigan Law Review 92, 1997–2087.

Blasi, Joseph, and Andrei Shleifer, 1996, Corporate governance in Russia: An initial look, in Roman Frydman, Cheryl W. Gray, and Andrzej Rapaczynski, Eds.: *Corporate Governance in Central Europe and Russia: Vol. 2 Insiders and the State* (Central European University Press, Budapest).

Bolton, Patrick, and David Scharfstein, 1990, A theory of predation based on agency problems in financial contracting, *American Economic Review* 80, 94–106.

Bolton, Patrick, and David Scharfstein, 1996, Optimal debt structure and the number of creditors, *Journal of Political Economy* 104, 1–25.

Boycko, Maxim, Andrei Shleifer, and Robert W. Vishny, 1993, Privatizing Russia, *Brookings Papers on Economic Activity*, 139–192.

Boycko, Maxim, Andrei Shleifer, and Robert W. Vishny, 1995, *Privatizing Russia* (M.I.T. Press, Cambridge, Mass.).

Boycko, Maxim, Andrei Shleifer, and Robert W. Vishny, 1996, A theory of privatization, Paish lecture, *Economic Journal* 106, 309–319.

Brudney, Victor, and Marvin A. Chirelstein, 1978, A restatement of corporate freeze-outs, *Yale Law Journal* 87, 1354–1375.

Bulow, Jeremy, and Kenneth Rogoff, 1989, A constant recontracting model of sovereign debt, *Journal of Political Economy* 97, 155–178.

Burkart, M., Denis Gromb, and Fausto Panunzi, 1997, Large shareholders, monitoring, and fiduciary duty, *Quarterly Journal of Economics* 112.

Burrough, Bryan, and John Helyar, 1990, *Barbarians at the Gate: The Fall of RJR Nabisco*, (Harper & Row, New York).

Charkham, Jonathan, 1994, *Keeping Good Company: A Study of Corporate Governance in Five Countries* (Clarendon Press, Oxford).

Clark, Robert, 1985, Agency costs versus fiduciary duties, in John Pratt and Richard Zeckhauser, Eds.: *Principals and Agents: The Structure of Business* (Harvard Business School Press, Cambridge, Mass.).

Coase, Ronald, 1937, The nature of the firm, *Economica* 4, 386–405.

Coase, Ronald, 1960, The problem of social cost, *Journal of Law and Economics* 3, 1–44.

Coffee, John, 1991, Liquidity versus control: The institutional investor as corporate monitor, *Columbia Law Review* 91, 1277–1368.

Comment, Robert, and Gregg Jarrell, 1995, Corporate focus and stock returns, *Journal of Financial Economics* 37, 67–87.

Comment, Robert, and G. William Schwert, 1995, Poison or placebo? Evidence on the deterrent and wealth effects of modern antitakeover measures, *Journal of Financial Economics* 39, 3–44.

Coughlan, Anne, and Ronald Schmidt, 1985, Executive compensation, management turnover, and firm performance: An empirical investigation, *Journal of Accounting and Economics* 7, 43–66.

Cremer, Jacques, 1995, Arm's length relationships, *Quarterly Journal of Economics* 110, 275–296.

Dann, Larry, and Harry DeAngelo, 1983, Standstill agreements, privately negotiated stock repurchases, and the market for corporate control, *Journal of Financial Economics* 11, 275–300.

DeAngelo, Harry, and Linda DeAngelo, 1985, Managerial ownership of voting rights, *Journal of Financial Economics* 14, 33–69.

DeAngelo, Harry, Linda DeAngelo, and Edward Rice, 1984, Going private: Minority freezeouts and stockholder wealth, *Journal of Law and Economics* 27, 367–401.

DeAngelo, Harry, and Edward Rice, 1983, Antitakeover amendments and stockholder wealth, *Journal of Financial Economics* 11, 329–360.

De Long, J. Bradford, 1991, Did Morgan's Men Add Value? An Economist's Perspective on Financial Capitalism, in Peter Temin, Ed.: *Inside the Business Enterprise: Historical Perspectives on the Use of Information* (University Press, Chicago).

De Long, J. Bradford, Andrei Shleifer, Lawrence Summers, and Robert Waldmann, 1989, The size and incidence of the losses from noise trading, *Journal of Finance* 44, 681–696.

De Long, J. Bradford, Andrei Shleifer, Lawrence Summers, and Robert Waldmann, 1990, Noise trader risk in financial markets, *Journal of Political Economy* 98, 703–738.

Demsetz, Harold, 1983, The structure of ownership and the theory of the firm, *Journal of Law and Economics* 26, 375–390.

Demsetz, Harold, and Kenneth Lehn, 1985, The structure of corporate ownership: Causes and consequences, *Journal of Political Economy* 93, 1155–1177.

Denis, David, and Jan Serrano, 1996, Active investors and management turnover following unsuccessful control contests, *Journal of Financial Economics* 40, 239–266.

Dewatripont, Mathias, and Eric Maskin, 1995, Credit and efficiency in centralized and decentralized economies, *Review of Economic Studies* 62, 541–556.

Dewatripont, Mathias, and Jean Tirole, 1994, A theory of debt and equity: Diversity of securities and manager-shareholder congruence, *Quarterly Journal of Economics* 109, 1027–1054.

Dewatripont, Mathias, and Jean Tirole, 1995, *The Prudential Regulation of Banks* (MIT Press, Cambridge).

Diamond, Douglas, 1984, Financial intermediation and delegated monitoring, *Review of Economic Studies* 51, 393–414.

Diamond, Douglas, 1989, Reputation acquisition in debt markets, *Journal of Political Economy* 97, 828–862.

Diamond, Douglas, 1991, Debt maturity structure and liquidity risk, *Quarterly Journal of Economics* 106, 1027–1054.

Dodd, Peter, and Jerold Warner, 1983, On corporate governance: A study of proxy contests, *Journal of Financial Economics* 11, 401–439.

Douglas, William O., 1940, *Democracy and Finance* (Yale University Press, New Haven).

Downs, Anthony, 1957, *An Economic Theory of Democracy* (Harper, New York).

Easterbrook, Frank, 1984, Two agency-cost explanations of dividends, *American Economic Review* 74, 650–659.

Easterbrook, Frank, and Daniel Fischel, 1983, Voting in corporate law, *Journal of Law and Economics* 26, 395–427.

Easterbrook, Frank, and Daniel Fischel, 1991, *The Economic Structure of Corporate Law* (Harvard University Press, Cambridge, Mass.).

Eaton, Jonathan, and Mark Gersovitz, 1981, Debt with potential repudiation: Theoretical and empirical analysis, *Review of Economic Studies* 48, 289–309.

Edwards, Jeremy, and Klaus Fischer, 1994, *Banks, Finance and Investment in West Germany Since 1970* (Cambridge University Press, Cambridge).

Eisenberg, Melvin, 1976, *The Structure of the Corporation: A Legal Analysis* (Little, Brown and Co., Boston).

Fama, Eugene, 1980, Agency problems and the theory of the firm, *Journal of Political Economy* 88, 288–307.

Fama, Eugene, Lawrence Fisher, Michael Jensen, and Richard Roll, 1969, The adjustment of stock prices to new information, *International Economic Review* 10, 1–21.

Fama, Eugene, and Michael Jensen, 1983a, Separation of ownership and control, *Journal of Law and Economics* 26, 301–325.

Fama, Eugene, and Michael Jensen, 1983b, Agency problems and residuals claims, *Journal of Law and Economics* 26, 327–349.

Fluck, Zsussanna, 1995, The optimality of debt versus outside equity, manuscript, New York University.

Franks, Julian, and Colin Mayer, 1990, Takeovers: Capital markets and corporate control: A study of France, Germany, and the UK, *Economic Policy: A European Forum* 10, 189–231.

Franks, Julian, and Colin Mayer, 1994, The ownership and control of German corporations, manuscript, London Business School.

Galbraith, John Kenneth, 1955, *The Great Crash, 1929* (Houghton Mifflin, Boston).

Gale, Douglas, and Martin Hellwig, 1985, Incentive-compatible debt contracts: The one-period problem, *Review of Economic Studies* 52, 647–663.

Gerschenkron, Alexander, 1962, *Economic Backwardness in Historical Perspective* (Harvard University Press, Cambridge MA).

Gertner, Robert, and David Scharfstein, 1991, A theory of workouts and the effects of reorganization law, *Journal of Finance* 46, 1189–1222.

Gertner, Robert, David Scharfstein, and Jeremy Stein, 1994, Internal versus external capital markets, *Quarterly Journal of Economics* 109, 1211–1230.

Gilson, Stuart, 1990, Bankruptcy, boards, banks, and block holders, *Journal of Financial Economics* 27, 355–387.

Gilson, Stuart, Kose John, and Larry Lang, 1990, Troubled debt restructurings: an empirical study of private reorganization of firms in default, *Journal of Financial Economics* 27, 315–355.

Gomes, Armando, 1996, Dynamics of stock prices, manager ownership, and private benefits of control, manuscript, Harvard University.

Gorton, Gary, and Frank Schmid, 1996, Universal banking and the performance of German firms, Working Paper 5453, National Bureau of Economic Research, Cambridge, MA.

Grossman, Sanford, and Oliver Hart, 1980, Takeover bids, the free-rider problem, and the theory of the corporation, *Bell Journal of Economics* 11, 42–64.

Grossman, Sanford, and Oliver Hart, 1982, Corporate financial structure and managerial incentives, in J. J. McCall Ed.: *The Economics of Information and Uncertainty* (University of Chicago Press, Chicago), 123–155.

Grossman, Sanford, and Oliver Hart, 1986, The costs and benefits of ownership: A theory of vertical and lateral integration, *Journal of Political Economy* 94, 691–719.

Grossman, Sanford, and Oliver Hart, 1988, One share-one vote and the market for corporate control, *Journal of Financial Economics* 20, 175–202.

Grossman, Gene, and Alan Krueger, 1993, Environmental impact of a North-American free trade agreement, in *The U.S.-Mexico Free Trade Agreement*, P. Garber, Ed.: (MIT Press, Cambridge, Mass.).

Grundfest, Joseph, 1990, Subordination of American capital, *Journal of Financial Economics* 27, 89–114.

Hansmann, Henry, 1988, Ownership of the firm, *Journal of Law, Economics, and Organization* 4, 267–304.

Hansmann, Henry, 1996, *The Ownership of Enterprise* (Harvard University Press, Cambridge, MA).

Harris, Milton, and Artur Raviv, 1988, Corporate governance: Voting rights and majority rules, *Journal of Financial Economics* 20, 203–235.

Harris, Milton, and Artur Raviv, 1990, Capital structure and the informational role of debt, *Journal of Finance* 45, 321–350.

Hart, Oliver, 1995, *Firms, Contracts, and Financial Structure* (Oxford University Press, London).

Hart, Oliver, and Bengt Holmstrom, 1987, The Theory of Contracts, in T. Bewley, Ed.: *Advances in Economic Theory* (University Press, Cambridge, U.K.), 294–351.

Hart, Oliver, and John Moore, 1989, Default and renegotiation: A dynamic model of debt, manuscript, Harvard University.

Hart, Oliver, and John Moore, 1990, Property rights and the nature of the firm, *Journal of Political Economy* 98, 1119–1158.

Hart, Oliver, and John Moore, 1994a, A theory of debt based on the inalienability of human capital, *Quarterly Journal of Economics* 109, 841–879.

Hart, Oliver, and John Moore, 1994b, The governance of exchanges: Members' cooperatives versus outside ownership, manuscript, Harvard University.

Hart, Oliver, and John Moore, 1995, Debt and seniority: An analysis of the role of hard claims in constraining management, *American Economic Review* 85, 567–585.

Hart, Oliver, Andrei Shleifer, and Robert Vishny, 1997, The proper scope of government: Theory and an application to prisons, *Quarterly Journal of Economics* 112.

Haubrich, Joseph, 1994, Risk aversion, performance pay, and the principal-agent problem, *Journal of Political Economy* 102, 258–276.

Hellwig, Martin, 1994, Banking and finance at the end of the twentieth century, Wirtschaftswissenschaftliches Zentrum Discussion Paper No. 9426, University of Basel.

Holderness, Clifford, and Dennis Sheehan, 1988a, What constrains managers who own large blocks of stock? Managerial Economics Research Center Working Paper 88–07, University of Rochester.

Holderness, Clifford, and Dennis Sheehan, 1988b, The role of majority shareholders in publicly held corporations: An exploratory analysis, *Journal of Financial Economics* 20, 317–346.

Holmstrom, Bengt, 1979, Moral hazard and observability, *Bell Journal of Economics* 10, 4–29.

Holmstrom, Bengt, 1982, Managerial incentive problems: A dynamic perspective, in *Essays in Economics and Management in Honor of Lars Wahlbeck* (Swedish School of Economics, Helsinki), 210–235.

Holmstrom, Bengt, and Jean Tirole, 1989, The theory of the firm, in R. Schmalensee and R. D. Willig, Eds.: *Handbook of Industrial Organization*, Vol. 1, (North-Holland, Amsterdam), 61–133.

Hopt, Klaus, and Gunther Teubner, Eds., 1985, *Corporate Governance and Directors' Liabilities*, (de Gruyter, Berlin).

Horner, M., 1988, The value of the corporate voting right, *Journal of Banking and Finance* 12, 69–83.

Hoshi, Takeo, Anil Kashyap, and David Scharfstein, 1990, The role of banks in reducing the costs of financial distress in Japan, *Journal of Financial Economics* 27, 67–88.

Hoshi, Takeo, Anil Kashyap, and David Scharfstein, 1991, Corporate structure, liquidity, and investment: Evidence from Japanese industrial groups, *Quarterly Journal of Economics* 106, 33–60.

Hoshi, Takeo, Anil Kashyap, and David Scharfstein, 1993, The choice between public and private debt: An analysis of post-deregulation corporate finance in Japan, National Bureau of Economic Research Working Paper 4421, Cambridge, Mass.

Hunt, Bishop Carleton, 1936, *The Development of the Business Corporation in England, 1800–1867*, (Harvard University Press, Cambridge, Mass.).

Jarrell, Gregg, and Annette Poulsen, 1988a, Shark repellents and stock prices: The effects of antitakeover amendments since 1980, *Journal of Financial Economics* 19, 127–168.

Jarrell, Gregg, and Annette Poulsen, 1988b, Dual-class recapitalizations as antitakeover mechanisms: The recent evidence, *Journal of Financial Economics* 20, 129–152.

Jensen, Michael, 1986, Agency costs of free cash flow, corporate finance, and takeovers, *American Economic Review* 76, 323–329.

Jensen, Michael, 1988, Takeovers: Their causes and consequences, *Journal of Economic Perspectives* 2, 21–48.

Jensen, Michael, 1989a, Eclipse of the public corporation, *Harvard Business Review* 67, 60–70.

Jensen, Michael, 1989b, Active investors, LBOs and the privatization of bankruptcy, *Journal of Applied Corporate Finance* 2, 35–44.

Jensen, Michael, 1993, The modern industrial revolution, exit, and the failure of internal control systems, *Journal of Finance* 48, 831–880.

Jensen, Michael, and William Meckling, 1976, Theory of the firm: Managerial behavior, agency costs, and ownership structure, *Journal of Financial Economics* 3, 305–360.

Jensen, Michael, and Kevin Murphy, 1990, Performance pay and top management incentives, *Journal of Political Economy* 98, 225–263.

Jensen, Michael, and Richard Ruback, 1983, The market for corporate control: The scientific evidence, *Journal of Financial Economics* 11, 5–50.

Johnson, W. Bruce, Robert Magee, Nandu Nagarajan, and Harry Newman, 1985, An analysis of the stock price reaction to sudden executive deaths: Implications for the management labor market, *Journal of Accounting & Economics* 7, 151–174.

Kang, Jun-Koo, and Anil Shivdasani, 1995, Firm performance, corporate governance, and top executive turnover in Japan, *Journal of Financial Economics* 38, 29–58.

Kaplan, Steven, 1989, The effects of management buyouts on operating performance and value, *Journal of Financial Economics* 24, 217–254.

Kaplan, Steven, 1991, The staying power of leveraged buyouts, *Journal of Financial Economics* 29, 287–313.

Kaplan, Steven, 1994a, Top executives, turnover, and firm performance in Germany, *Journal of Law, Economics, and Organization* 10, 142–159.

Kaplan, Steven, 1994b, Top executive rewards and firm performance: A comparison of Japan and the United States, *Journal of Political Economy* 102, 510–546.

Kaplan, Steven, and Bernadette Minton, 1994, Appointments of outsiders to Japanese boards: Determinants and implications for managers, *Journal of Financial Economics* 36, 225–257.

Kaplan, Steven, and Jeremy Stein, 1993, The Evolution of Buy out Pricing and Financial Structure in the 1980s, *Quarterly Journal of Economics* 108, 313–357.

Kaplan, Steven, and Michael Weisbach, 1992, The success of acquisitions: Evidence from divestitures, *Journal of Finance* 47, 107–138.

Khanna, Tarun, and Krishna Palepu, 1996, Corporate scope and severe market imperfections: An empirical analysis of diversified business groups in India, manuscript, Harvard University.

Kikeri, Sunita, John Nellis, and Mary Shirley, 1992, *Privatization: The Lessons of Experience*, (The World Bank, Washington, D.C.).

Kindelberger, Charles P., 1978, *Manias, Panics, and Crashes*, (Basic Books, New York).

Kreps, David, 1990, Corporate Culture and Economic Theory, in J. Alt and K. Shepsle, Eds.: *Perspectives on Positive Political Economy* (University Press, Cambridge).

Laffont, Jean-Jacques, and Jean Tirole, 1993, *A Theory of Incentives in Regulation and Procurement* (MIT Press, Cambridge, Mass.).

Lambert, Richard, and David Larcker, 1985, Golden parachutes, executive decision-making, and shareholder wealth, *Journal of Accounting & Economics* 7, 179–203.

Lang, Larry, and René Stulz, 1994, Tobin's Q, corporate diversification, and firm performance, *Journal of Political Economy* 102, 1248–1280.

Lang, Larry, Eli Ofek, and René Stulz, 1996, Leverage, investment, and firm growth, *Journal of Financial Economics* 40, 3–30.

Lang, Larry, René Stulz, and Ralph Walkling, 1991, A test of the free cash flow hypothesis: The case of bidder returns, *Journal of Financial Economics* 29, 315–336.

Loughran, Timothy, Jay Ritter, and Kristian Rydqvist, 1994, Initial public offerings: International insights, *Pacific-Basin Finance Journal* 2, 165–199.

Lease, Ronald, John McConnell, and Wayne Mikkelson, 1983, The market value of control in publicly traded corporations, *Journal of Financial Economics* 11, 439–471.

Lease, Ronald, John McConnell, and Wayne Mikkelson, 1984, The market value of differential voting rights in closely held corporations, *Journal of Business* 57, 443–467.

Levy, Haim, 1982, Economic valuation of voting power of common stock, *Journal of Finance* 38, 79–93.

Lewellen, Wilbur, Claudio Loderer, and Ahron Rosenfeld, 1985, Merger decisions and executive stock ownership in acquiring firms, *Journal of Accounting & Economics* 7, 209–231.

Lopez-de-Silanes, Florencio, 1994, Determinants of privatization prices, manuscript, Harvard University.

Lopez-de-Silanes, Florencio, Andrei Shleifer, and Robert W. Vishny, 1997, Privatization in the United States, *Rand Journal of Economics* 28.

Mace, Myles, 1971, *Directors, Myth, and Reality* (Harvard Business School Press, Boston).

Malatesta, Paul, and Ralph Walkling, 1988, Poison Pill Securities: Stockholder Wealth, Profitability, and Ownership Structure, *Journal of Financial Economics* 20, 347–376.

Manne, Henry, 1965, Mergers and the market for corporate control, *Journal of Political Economy* 75, 110–126.

Marris, Robin, 1964, *The Economic Theory of Managerial Capitalism* (Free Press of Glencoe, Illinois).

Martin, Kenneth, and John McConnell, 1991, Corporate performance, corporate takeovers, and management turnover, *Journal of Finance* 46, 671–688.

Mayer, Colin, 1990, Financial systems, corporate finance, and economic development, in R. G. Hubbard, Ed.: *Asymmetric Information, Corporate Finance, and Investment* (University of Chicago Press, Chicago).

McConnell, John, and Chris Muscarella, 1986, Corporate capital expenditure decisions and the market value of the firm, *Journal of Financial Economics* 14, 399–422.

McConnell, John, and Henri Servaes, 1990, Additional evidence on equity ownership and corporate value, *Journal of Financial Economics* 27, 595–612.

Megginson, William, Robert Nash, and Matthias van Randenborgh, 1994, The financial and operating performance of newly privatized firms, *Journal of Finance* 49, 403–452.

Mirrlees, James, 1976, The optimal structure of incentives and authority within an organization, *Bell Journal of Economics* 7, 105–131.

Modigliani, Franco, and Merton Miller, 1958, The cost of capital, corporation finance, and the theory of investment, *American Economic Review* 48, 261–297.

Morck, Randall, Andrei Shleifer, and Robert Vishny, 1988a, Characteristics of targets of hostile and friendly takeovers, in A. Auerbach, Ed.: *Corporate Takeovers: Causes and Consequences* (University of Chicago Press, Chicago).

Morck, Randall, Andrei Shleifer, and Robert Vishny, 1988b, Management ownership and market valuation: An empirical analysis, *Journal of Financial Economics* 20, 293–315.

Morck, Randall, Andrei Shleifer, and Robert Vishny, 1989, Alternative Mechanisms of Corporate Control, *American Economic Review* 79, 842–852.

Morck, Randall, Andrei Shleifer, and Robert Vishny, 1990, Do managerial objectives drive bad acquisitions? *Journal of Finance* 45, 31–48.

Murphy, Kevin J., 1985, Corporate performance and managerial remuneration: An empirical analysis, *Journal of Accounting & Economics* 7, 11–41.

Myers, Stuart, 1977, Determinants of corporate borrowing, *Journal of Financial Economics* 5, 147–175.

Myers, Stuart, 1995, Inside and outside equity financing, manuscript, Massachusetts Institute of Technology.

Myers, Stuart, and Nicholas Majluf, 1984, Corporate financing and investment decisions when firms have information that investors do not have, *Journal of Financial Economics* 13, 187–221.

New York Times, 1986, Tax trial only one of Posner problems, June 23, Section D, 3.

Organization for Economic Cooperation and Development, 1995, Corporate governance environments in OECD countries, February 1.

Owen, Thomas, 1991, *The Corporation under Russian Law, 1800–1917: A Study in Tsarist Economic Policy* (Cambridge University Press, New York).

Pagano, Marco, F. Panetta, and Luigi Zingales, 1995, Why do companies go public? An empirical analysis, manuscript, Graduate School of Business, University of Chicago.

Palepu, Krishna, 1986, Predicting takeover targets: A methodological and empirical analysis, *Journal of Accounting and Economics* 8, 3–35.

Pontiff, Jeffrey, Andrei Shleifer, and Michael Weisbach, 1990, Reversions of excess pension assets after takeovers, *Rand Journal of Economics* 21, 600–613.

Porter, Michael, 1992, Capital disadvantage: America's failing capital investment system, *Harvard Business Review*, Sept.–Oct., 65–83.

Poterba, James M., and Lawrence H. Summers, 1995, A survey of U.S. companies, time horizons, and hurdle rates, *Sloan Management Review* 37, 43–53.

Pound, John, 1988, Proxy contests and the efficiency of shareholder oversight, *Journal of Financial Economics* 20, 237–265.

Prowse, Stephen, 1990, Institutional investment patterns and corporate financial behavior in the United States and Japan, *Journal of Financial Economics* 27, 43–66.

Rajan, Raghuram, 1992, Insiders and Outsiders: The choice between relationship and arms-length debt, *Journal of Finance* 47, 1367–1400.

Rajan, Raghuram, and Luigi Zingales, 1995, What do we know about capital structure? Some evidence from international data, *Journal of Finance* 50, 1421–1460.

Rappaport, Alfred, 1990, The staying power of the public corporation, *Harvard Business Review* 1, 96–104.

Ritter, Jay, 1991, The long run performance of IPOs, *Journal of Finance* 46, 3–27.

Roe, Mark, 1993, Some differences in corporate structure in Germany, Japan, and the United States, *The Yale Law Review* 102, 1927–2003.

Roe, Mark, 1994, *Strong Managers Weak Owners: The Political Roots of American Corporate Finance* (University Press, Princeton, N.J.).

Roll, Richard, 1986, The hubris hypothesis of corporate takeovers, *Journal of Business* 59, 197–216.

Ross, Stephen, 1973, The economic theory of agency: The principal's problem, *American Economic Review* 63, 134–139.

Rossett, Joshua, G., 1990, Do union wealth concessions explain takeover premiums? The evidence on contract wages, *Journal of Financial Economics* 27, 263–282.

Romano, Roberta, 1993a, *The Genius of American Corporate Law* (American Enterprise Institute Press, Washington, D.C.).

Romano, Roberta, 1993c, Public pension fund activism in corporate governance reconsidered, *Columbia Law Review* 93, 795–853.

Rydqvist, Kristian, 1987, Empirical investigation of the voting premium, Working Paper 35, Northwestern University.

Ryngaert, Michael, 1988, The effect of poison pill securities on shareholder wealth, *Journal of Financial Economics* 20, 377–417.

Sappington, David, and Joseph Stiglitz, 1987, Privatization, information, and incentives,

Journal of Policy Analysis and Management 6, 567–582.

Scharfstein, David, 1988, The disciplinary role of takeovers, *Review of Economic Studies* 55, 185–199.

Schmidt, Klaus, 1996, The costs and benefits of privatization, *The Journal of Law, Economics & Organization* 12, 1–24.

Shapiro, Carl, and Robert D. Willig, 1990, Economic rationales for the scope of privatization, in E. N. Suleiman and J. Waterbury, Eds.: *The Political Economy of Public Sector Reform and Privatization* (Westview Press, London), 55–87.

Shivdasani, Anil, 1993, Board composition, ownership structure, and hostile takeovers, *Journal of Accounting and Economics* 16, 167–198.

Shleifer, Andrei, and Lawrence Summers, 1988, Breach of trust in hostile takeovers, in A. J. Auerbach, Ed.: *Corporate Takeovers: Causes and Consequence* (University of Chicago Press, Chicago), 65–88.

Shleifer, Andrei, and Robert Vishny, 1986a, Greenmail, white knights, and shareholder's interest, *Rand Journal of Economics* 17, 293–309.

Shleifer, Andrei, and Robert Vishny, 1986b, Large shareholders and corporate control, *Journal of Political Economy* 94, 461–488.

Shleifer, Andrei, and Robert Vishny, 1988, Value maximization and the acquisition process, *Journal of Economic Perspectives* 2, 7–20.

Shleifer, Andrei, and Robert Vishny, 1989, Management entrenchment: The case of manager-specific investments, *Journal of Financial Economics* 25, 123–140.

Shleifer, Andrei, and Robert Vishny, 1990, Equilibrium short horizons of investors and firms, *American Economic Review Papers and Proceedings* 80, 148–153.

Shleifer, Andrei, and Robert Vishny, 1992, Liquidation values and debt capacity: A market equilibrium approach, *Journal of Finance* 47, 1343–1366.

Shleifer, Andrei, and Robert Vishny, 1993, Corruption, *Quarterly Journal of Economics* 108, 599–618.

Shleifer, Andrei, and Robert Vishny, 1994, Politicians and firms, *Quarterly Journal of Economics* 109, 995–1025.

Singh, Ajit, 1995, Corporate financial patterns in industrializing economies: A comparative international study, Technical Paper 2, April, Washington, DC: World Bank and International Finance Corporation.

Smith, Clifford, and Jerold Warner, 1979, On financial contracting: An analysis of bond covenants, *Journal of Financial Economics* 7, 117–161.

Stein, Jeremy, 1988, Takeover threats and managerial myopia, *Journal of Political Economy* 96, 61–80.

Stein, Jeremy, 1989, Efficient capital markets, inefficient firms: A model of myopic corporate behavior, *Quarterly Journal of Economics* 104, 655–669.

Stigler, George, 1958, The economies of scale, *Journal of Law and Economics* 1, 54–71.

Stiglitz, Joseph, 1975, Incentives, risk, and information: Notes toward a theory of hierarchy, *Bell Journal of Economics* 6, 552–579.

Stulz, René, 1988, Managerial control of voting rights, *Journal of Financial Economics* 20, 25–59.

Stulz, René, 1990, Managerial discretion and optimal financing policies, *Journal of Financial Economics* 26, 3–27.

The Economist, June 1995, A Survey of Korea.

Teoh, S. H., Ivo Welch, and T. J. Wong, 1995, Earnings management and post-issue under performance of seasoned equity offerings, manuscript, University of California.

Tirole, Jean, 1994, Incomplete contracts: Where do we stand? manuscript, IDEI, Toulouse, France.

Titman, Sheridan, and Roberto Wessels, 1988, The determinants of capital structure choice, *Journal of Finance* 43, 1–19.

Townsend, Robert, 1978, Optimal contracts and competitive markets with costly state verification, *Journal of Economic Theory* 21, 265–293.

Tunc, Andre, 1991, Corporate Law, in R. Buxbaum, G. Hertig, A. Hirsch, and K. Hopt, Eds.: *European Business Law: Legal and Economic Analysis of Integration and Harmonization* (de Gruyter, Berlin).

Walkling, Ralph, and Michael Long, 1984, Agency theory, managerial welfare, and takeover bid resistance, *Rand Journal of Economics* 15, 54–68.

Warner, Jerold, Ron Watts, and Karen Wruck, 1988, Stock prices and top management changes, *Journal of Financial Economics* 20, 461–492.

Weinstein, David E., and Yishay Yafeh, 1994, On the costs of a bank-centered financial system: Evidence from the changing main bank relations in Japan, manuscript, Harvard University.

Weisbach, Michael, 1988, Outside directors and CEO turnover, *Journal of Financial Economics* 20, 431–460.

Weiss, Lawrence, 1990, Bankruptcy resolution: Direct costs and violation of priority of claims, *Journal of Financial Economics* 27, 285–314.

White, Michelle, 1993, The costs of corporate bankruptcy: a U.S.-European comparison, manuscript, University of Michigan.

van Wijnbergen, Sweder, and Anton Mancini, 1995, Voucher privatization, corporate control, and the cost of capital: An analysis of the Czech privatization program, manuscript, LSE.

Williamson, Oliver, 1964, *The Economics of Discretionary Behavior: Managerial Objectives in a Theory of the Firm* (Prentice Hall, Englewood Cliffs, N.J.).

Williamson, Oliver, 1985, *The Economic Institutions of Capitalism* (Free Press, New York).

Williamson, Oliver, 1988, Corporate finance and corporate governance, *Journal of Finance* 43, 567–592.

Wolfram, Catherine, 1995, Increases in executive pay following privatization, manuscript, MIT.

Wruck, Karen, 1989, Equity ownership concentration and firm value, *Journal of Financial Economics* 23, 3–28.

Yafeh, Yishay, and Oved Yosha, 1996, Large shareholders and banks: Who monitors and how? manuscript, Hebrew University, Jerusalem, Israel.

Yermack, David, 1997, Good timing: CEO stock option awards and company news announcements, *Journal of Finance* 52, 449–476.

Zingales, Luigi, 1994, The value of the voting right: A study of the Milan stock exchange experience, *The Review of Financial Studies* 7, 125–148.

Zingales, Luigi, 1995, What determines the value of corporate votes? *Quarterly Journal of Economics* 110, 1075–1110.

## Chapter 3

Rafael La Porta, Florencio Lopez-de-Silanes, Andrei Shleifer[†] and Robert Vishny

INVESTOR PROTECTION AND CORPORATE GOVERNANCE*

Source: *Journal of Financial Economics*, 58(1–2)(2000): 3–27.

ABSTRACT

Recent research has documented large differences among countries in ownership concentration in publicly traded firms, in the breadth and depth of capital markets, in dividend policies, and in the access of firms to external finance. A common element to the explanations of these differences is how well investors, both shareholders and creditors, are protected by law from expropriation by the managers and controlling shareholders of firms. We describe the differences in laws and the effectiveness of their enforcement across countries, discuss the possible origins of these differences, summarize their consequences, and assess potential strategies of corporate governance reform. We argue that the legal approach is a more fruitful way to understand corporate governance and its reform than the conventional distinction between bank-centered and market-centered financial systems.

1. INTRODUCTION

RECENT RESEARCH ON CORPORATE GOVERNANCE around the world has established a number of empirical regularities. Such diverse elements of countries' financial systems as the breadth and depth of their capital markets, the pace of new security issues, corporate ownership structures, dividend policies, and the efficiency of investment allocation appear to be explained both conceptually and empirically by how well the laws in these countries protect outside investors. According to this research, the protection of shareholders and creditors by the legal system is central to understanding the patterns of corporate finance in different countries.

Investor protection turns out to be crucial because, in many countries, expropriation of minority shareholders and creditors by the controlling shareholders is extensive. When outside investors finance firms, they face a risk, and sometimes near certainty, that the returns on their investments will never materialize because the controlling shareholders or managers expropriate them. (We refer to both managers and controlling shareholders as "the insiders".) Corporate governance is, to a large extent, a set of mechanisms through which outside investors protect themselves against expropriation by the insiders.

Expropriation can take a variety of forms. In some instances, the insiders simply steal the profits. In other instances, the insiders sell the output, the assets, or the additional securities in the firm they control to another firm they own at below market prices. Such transfer pricing, asset stripping, and investor dilution, though often legal, have largely the same effect as theft. In still other instances, expropriation takes the form of diversion of corporate opportunities from the firm, installing possibly unqualified family members in managerial positions, or overpaying executives. In general, expropriation is related to the agency problem described by Jensen and Meckling (1976), who focus on the consumption of "perquisites" by managers and other types of empire building. It means that the insiders use the profits of the firm to benefit themselves rather than return the money to the outside investors.

If extensive expropriation undermines the functioning of a financial system, how can it be limited? The legal approach to corporate governance holds that the key mechanism is the protection of outside investors – whether shareholders or creditors – through the legal system, meaning both laws and their enforcement. Although reputations and bubbles can help raise funds, variations in law and its enforcement are central to understanding why firms raise more funds in some countries than in others. To a large extent, potential shareholders and creditors finance firms because their rights are protected by the law. These outside investors are more vulnerable to expropriation, and more dependent on the law, than either the employees or the suppliers, who remain continually useful to the firm and are thus at a lesser risk of being mistreated.

The legal approach to corporate governance is a natural continuation of the field as it has developed over the last 40 years. Modigliani and Miller (1958) think of firms as collections of investment projects and the cash flows these projects create, and hence naturally interpret securities such as debt and equity as claims to these cash flows. They do not explain why the managers would return the cash flows to investors. Jensen and Meckling (1976) point out that the return of the cash flows from projects to investors cannot be taken for granted, and that the insiders of firms

may use these resources for their own benefit. Jensen and Meckling view financial claims as contracts that give outside investors, such as shareholders and creditors, claims to the cash flows. In their model, the limitation on expropriation is the residual equity ownership by entrepreneurs that enhances their interest in dividends relative to perquisites.

Research by Grossman, Hart, and Moore, summarized in Hart (1995), makes a further key advance by focusing squarely on investor power vis a vis the insiders, and distinguishing between the contractual and residual control rights that investors have. Economists have used this idea to model financial instruments not in terms of their cash flows, but in terms of the rights they allocate to their holders. In this framework, investors get cash only because they have power. This can be the power to change directors, to force dividend payments, to stop a project or a scheme that benefits the insiders at the expense of outside investors, to sue directors and get compensation, or to liquidate the firm and receive the proceeds. Unlike in the Modigliani-Miller world, changing the capital structure of the firm changes the allocation of power between the insiders and the outside investors, and thus almost surely changes the firm's investment policy.

In both the contractual framework of Jensen and Meckling and the residual control rights framework of Grossman, Hart, and Moore, the rights of the investors are protected and sometimes even specified by the legal system. For example, contract law deals with privately negotiated arrangements, whereas company, bankruptcy, and securities laws specifically describe some of the rights of corporate insiders and outside investors. These laws, and the quality of their enforcement by the regulators and courts, are essential elements of corporate governance and finance (La Porta et al., 1997, 1998). When investor rights such as the voting rights of the shareholders and the reorganization and liquidation rights of the creditors are extensive and well enforced by regulators or courts, investors are willing to finance firms. In contrast, when the legal system does not protect outside investors, corporate governance and external finance do not work well.

Jensen and Meckling (1976) recognize the role of the legal system when they write:

This view of the firm points up the important role which the legal system and the law play in social organizations, especially, the organization of economic activity. Statutory law sets bounds on the kinds of contracts into which individuals and organizations may enter without risking criminal prosecution. The police powers of the state are available and used to enforce performance of contracts or to enforce the collection of damages for non-performance. The courts adjudicate contracts between contracting parties and establish precedents which form the body of common law. All of these government activities affect both the kinds of contracts executed and the extent to which contracting is relied upon (p. 311).

One way to think about legal protection of outside investors is that it makes the expropriation technology less efficient. At the extreme of no investor protection, the insiders can steal a firm's profits perfectly efficiently. Without a strong reputation, no rational outsider would finance such a firm. As investor protection improves, the insiders must engage in more distorted and wasteful diversion practices such as setting up intermediary companies into which they channel profits. Yet these mechanisms are still efficient enough for the insiders to choose to divert extensively. When investor protection is very good, the most the insiders can do is overpay themselves, put relatives in management, and undertake some wasteful projects. After a point, it may be better just to pay dividends. As the diversion technology becomes less efficient, the insiders expropriate less, and their private benefits of control diminish. Firms then obtain outside finance on better terms. By shaping the expropriation technology, the

law also shapes the opportunities for external finance.

The legal approach to corporate governance has emerged as a fruitful way to think about a number of questions in finance. In Section 2, we discuss the differences in legal investor protection among countries and the possible judicial, political, and historical origins of these differences. In Section 3, we summarize the research on the economic consequences of investor protection. In Section 4, we compare the legal approach to corporate governance to the more standard focus on the relative importance of banks and stock markets as ways to explain country differences. In Section 5, we discuss both the difficulties and the opportunities for corporate governance reform. Section 6 concludes.

2. INVESTOR PROTECTION

When investors finance firms, they typically obtain certain rights or powers that are generally protected through the enforcement of regulations and laws. Some of these rights include disclosure and accounting rules, which provide investors with the information they need to exercise other rights. Protected shareholder rights include those to receive dividends on pro-rata terms, to vote for directors, to participate in shareholders' meetings, to subscribe to new issues of securities on the same terms as the insiders, to sue directors or the majority for suspected expropriation, to call extraordinary shareholders' meetings, etc. Laws protecting creditors largely deal with bankruptcy and reorganization procedures, and include measures that enable creditors to repossess collateral, to protect their seniority, and to make it harder for firms to seek court protection in reorganization.

In different jurisdictions, rules protecting investors come from different sources, including company, security, bankruptcy, takeover, and competition laws, but also from stock exchange regulations and accounting standards. Enforcement of laws is as crucial as their contents. In most countries, laws and regulations are enforced in part by market regulators, in part by courts, and in part by market participants themselves. All outside investors, be they large or small, shareholders or creditors, need to have their rights protected. Absent effectively enforced rights, the insiders would not have much of a reason to repay the creditors or to distribute profits to shareholders, and external financing mechanisms would tend to break down.

The emphasis on legal rules and regulations protecting outside investors stands in sharp contrast to the traditional "law and economics" perspective on financial contracting. According to that perspective, most regulations of financial markets are unnecessary because financial contracts take place between sophisticated issuers and sophisticated investors. On average, investors recognize a risk of expropriation, penalizing firms that fail to contractually disclose information about themselves and to contractually bind themselves to treat investors well. Because entrepreneurs bear these costs when they issue securities, they have an incentive to bind themselves through contracts with investors to limit expropriation (Jensen and Meckling, 1976). As long as these contracts are enforced, financial markets do not require regulation (Stigler, 1964; Easterbrook and Fischel, 1991).

This point of view, originating in the Coase (1961) theorem, crucially relies on courts enforcing elaborate contracts. In many countries, such enforcement cannot be taken for granted. Indeed, courts are often unable or unwilling to invest the resources necessary to ascertain the facts pertaining to complicated contracts. They are also slow, subject to political pressures, and at times corrupt. When the enforcement of private contracts through the court system is costly enough, other forms of protecting property rights, such as judicially-enforced laws or even government-enforced regulations, may be more efficient. It may be better to have contracts restricted by laws and regulations that are enforced than unrestricted contracts that are not.

Whether contracts, court-enforced legal rules, or government-enforced regulations are the most efficient form of protecting financial arrangements is largely an empirical question. As the next section shows, the evidence rejects the hypothesis that private contracting is sufficient. Even among countries with well functioning judiciaries, those with laws and regulations more protective of investors have better developed capital markets.

La Porta et al. (1998) discuss a set of key legal rules protecting shareholders and creditors and document the prevalence of these rules in 49 countries around the world. They also aggregate these rules into shareholder (antidirector) and creditor rights indices for each country, and consider several measures of enforcement quality, such as the efficiency of the judicial system and a measure of the quality of accounting standards. La Porta, Lopez-de-Silanes, Shleifer, and Vishny use these variables as proxies for the stance of the law toward investor protection to examine the variation of legal rules and enforcement quality across countries and across legal families.

Legal scholars such as David and Brierley (1985) show that commercial legal systems of most countries derive from relatively few legal "families," including the English (common law), the French, and the German, the latter two derived from the Roman Law. In the 19th century, these systems spread throughout the world through conquest, colonization, and voluntary adoption. England and its former colonies, including the U.S., Canada, Australia, New Zealand, and many countries in Africa and South East Asia, have ended up with the common law system. France and many countries Napoleon conquered are part of the French civil law tradition. This legal family also extends to the former French, Dutch, Belgian, and Spanish colonies, including Latin America. Germany, Germanic countries in Europe, and a number of countries in East Asia are part of the German civil law tradition. The Scandinavian countries form their own tradition.[1]

Table 3.1 presents the percentage of countries in each legal family that give investors the rights discussed by La Porta, Lopez-de-Silanes, Shleifer, and Vishny, as well as the mean for that family antidirector and creditor rights scores. How well legal rules protect outside investors varies systematically across legal origins. Common law countries have the strongest protection of outside investors − both shareholders and creditors − whereas French civil law countries have the weakest protection. German civil law and Scandinavian countries fall in between, although comparatively speaking they have stronger protection of creditors, especially secured creditors. In general, differences among legal origins are best described by the proposition that some countries protect all outside investors better than others, and not by the proposition that some countries protect shareholders while other countries protect creditors.

Table 3.1 also points to significant differences among countries in the quality of law enforcement as measured by the efficiency of the judiciary, (lack of) corruption, and the quality of accounting standards. Unlike legal rules, which do not appear to depend on the level of economic development, the quality of enforcement is higher in richer countries. In particular, the generally richer Scandinavian and German legal origin countries receive the best scores on the efficiency of the judicial system. The French legal origin countries have the worst quality of law enforcement of the four legal traditions, even controlling for per capita income.

Because legal origins are highly correlated with the content of the law, and because legal families originated before financial markets had developed, it is unlikely that laws were written primarily in response to market pressures. Rather, the legal families appear to shape the legal rules, which in turn influence financial markets. But what is special about legal families? Why, in particular, is common law more protective of investors than civil law? These questions do not have accepted answers. However, it may be useful here to

distinguish between two broad kinds of answers: the "judicial" explanations that account for the differences in the legal philosophies using the organization of the legal system, and the "political" explanations that account for these differences using political history.

The "judicial" explanation of why common law protects investors better than civil law has been most recently articulated by Coffee (2000) and Johnson et al. (2000b). Legal rules in the common law system are usually made by judges, based on precedents and inspired by general principles such as fiduciary duty or fairness. Judges are expected to rule on new situations by applying these general principles even when specific conduct has not yet been described or prohibited in the statutes. In the area of investor expropriation, also known as self-dealing, the judges apply what Coffee calls a "smell test," and try to sniff out whether even unprecedented conduct by the insiders is unfair to outside investors. The expansion of legal precedents to additional violations of fiduciary duty, and the fear of such expansion, limit the expropriation by the insiders in common law countries. In contrast, laws in civil law systems are made by legislatures, and judges are not supposed to go beyond the statutes and apply "smell tests" or fairness opinions. As a consequence, a corporate insider who finds a way not explicitly forbidden by the statutes to expropriate outside investors can proceed without fear of an adverse judicial ruling. Moreover, in civil law countries, courts do not intervene in self-dealing transactions as long as these have a plausible business purpose. The vague fiduciary duty principles of the common law are more protective of investors than the bright line rules of the civil law, which can often be circumvented by sufficiently imaginative insiders.

The judicial perspective on the differences is fascinating and possibly correct, but it is incomplete. It requires a further assumption that the judges have an inclination to protect the outside investors rather than the insiders. In principle, it is easy to imagine that the judges would use their discretion in common law countries to narrow

Table 3.1 Legal origin and investors rights

This table presents data on measures of investor protection for 49 countries classified by their legal origin. The source of the data is La Porta et al. (1998). Panel A shows the measures of shareholder protection across legal origins. The "antidirector rights index" is a summary measure of shareholder protection. This index ranges from zero to six and is formed by adding one when: the country allows shareholders to mail their proxy vote to the firm; shareholders are not required to deposit their shares prior to the General Shareholders'. Meeting; cumulative voting or proportional representation of minorities in the board of directors is allowed; an oppressed minorities mechanism is in place; the minimum percentage of share capital that entitles a shareholder to call for an Extraordinary Shareholders'. Meeting is less than or equal to 10 percent (the sample median); shareholders have preemptive rights that can only be waved by a shareholders', vote. The rest of the rows in Panel A show the percentage of countries within each legal origin for which each component of the "antidirector rights index" is provided by the law. Panel B shows the measures of creditor protection across legal origins. The "creditor rights index" is a summary measure of creditor protection. This index ranges from zero to four and is formed by adding one when: the country imposes restrictions, such as creditors' consent or minimum dividends to file for reorganization; secured creditors are able to gain possession of their security once the reorganization petition has been approved (no automatic stay); the debtor does not retain the administration of its property pending the resolution of the reorganization. The rest of the rows in Panel B show the percentage of countries within each legal origin for which each component of the "creditor rights index" is provided by the law. Panel C shows measures of legal enforcement. "Efficiency of the judicial system" is an index ranging from zero to ten representing the average of investors' assessments of conditions of the judicial system in each country between 1980–1983 (lower scores represent lower efficiency levels). "Corruption" is an index ranging from zero to ten representing the average of investors' assessments of corruption in government in each country between 1982 and 1995 (lower scores represent higher corruption). "Accounting standards" is an index created by examining and rating companies' 1990 annual reports on their inclusion or omission of 90 items falling in the categories of general information, income statements, balance sheets, funds flow statement, accounting standards, stock data, and special items.

	Legal origin				
Variables	Common law (18 countries)	French civil law (21 countries)	German civil law (6 countries)	Scandinavian civil law (4 countries)	World average (49 countries)
Panel A: Measures of shareholder protection					
Antidirector rights index	4.00	2.33	2.33	3.00	3.00
Proxy by mail	39%	5%	0%	25%	18%

Shares not blocked before meeting	100%	57%	17%	100%	71%
Cumulative voting/proportional represent'n	28%	29%	33%	0%	27%
Oppressed minority	94%	29%	50%	0%	53%
Preemptive right to new issues	44%	62%	33%	75%	53%
% Share of capital to call and ESM ≤ 10%	94%	52%	0%	0%	78%

Panel B: Measures of creditor protection

Creditor rights index	3.11	1.58	2.33	2.00	2.30
No automatic stay on secured assets	72%	26%	67%	25%	49%
Secured creditors first	89%	65%	100%	100%	81%
Paid restrictions for going into reorganization	72%	42%	33%	75%	55%
Management does not stay in reorganization	78%	26%	33%	0%	45%

Panel C: Measures of enforcement

Efficiency of of the judicial system	8.15	6.56	8.54	10.00	7.67
Corruption	7.06	5.84	8.03	10.00	6.90
Accounting standards	69.92	51.17	62.67	74.00	60.93

the interpretation of fiduciary duty and to sanction expropriation rather than prohibit it. Common law judges could also in principle use their discretion to serve political interests, especially when the outside investors obstruct the government's goals. To explain investor protection, it is not enough to focus on judicial power; a political and historical analysis of judicial objectives is required. From this perspective, important political and historical differences between mother countries shape their laws. This is not to say that laws never change (in Section 5 we focus specifically on legal reform) but rather to suggest that history has persistent effects.

La Porta et al. (1999a) argue that an important historical factor shaping laws is that the state has a relatively greater role in regulating business in civil law countries than in common law ones. One element of this view, suggested by Finer (1997) and other historians, points to the differences in the relative power of the king and the property owners across European states. In England from the seventeenth century on, the crown partially lost control of the courts, which came under the influence of the parliament and the property owners who dominated it. As a consequence, common law evolved to protect private property against the crown. Over time, courts extended this protection of property owners to investors. In France and Germany, by contrast, parliamentary power was weaker. Commercial Codes were adopted only in the nineteenth century by the two great state builders, Napoleon and Bismarck, to enable the state to better regulate economic activity. Over time, the state maintained political control over firms and resisted the surrender of that power to financiers.[2] Perhaps as importantly, the state in civil law countries did not surrender its power over economic decisions to courts, and hence maintained the statutory approach to commercial laws. As we noted above, however, fairness assessments of self-dealing transactions, for which judicial power and discretion are essential, may be central to limiting expropriation.

Recent research supports the proposition that civil law is associated with greater government intervention in economic activity and weaker protection of private property than common law. La Porta et al. (1999a) examine the determinants of government performance in a large number of countries. To measure government interventionism, they consider proxies for the amount and quality of regulation, the prevalence of corruption and of red tape, and bureaucratic delays. As a general rule, they find that civil law countries, particularly French civil law countries, are more interventionist than common law countries. The inferior protection of the rights of outside investors in civil law countries may be one manifestation of this general phenomenon. This evidence provides some support for interpreting the differences in legal families based on political history.[3]

3. CONSEQUENCES OF INVESTOR PROTECTION

Three broad areas in which investor protection has been shown to matter are the ownership of firms, the development of financial markets, and the allocation of real resources.

3.1. Patterns of ownership and control

The focus on expropriation of investors and its prevention has a number of implications for the ownership structures of firms. Consider first the concentration of control rights in firms (as opposed to the dividend or cash flow rights). At the most basic level, when investor rights are poorly protected and expropriation is feasible on a substantial scale, control acquires enormous value because it gives the insiders the opportunity to expropriate efficiently. When the insiders actually do expropriate, the so called private benefits of control become a substantial share of the firm's value. This observation raises a question: will control in such an environment be concentrated in the hands of an entrepreneur or dispersed among many investors?

The research in this area originates in the work of Grossman and Hart (1988) and Harris and Raviv (1988), who examine the optimal allocation of voting and cash flow rights in a firm. The specific question of how control is likely to be allocated has not received a clear answer. For several reasons, entrepreneurs may wish to keep control of their firms when investor protection is poor. La Porta et al. (1999) note that if expropriation of investors requires secrecy, sharing control may restrain the entrepreneur beyond his wishes. Zingales (1995), La Porta et al. (1999), and Bebchuk (1999) argue that if entrepreneurs disperse control between many investors, they give up the "private benefits" premium in a takeover. In Bebchuk's (1999) model, diffuse control structures are unstable when investors can concentrate control without fully paying for it. Finally, an entrepreneur or his family may need to retain control of the firm because the family's reputation is needed to raise external funds when the legal protection of outside investors is poor. For all these reasons, firms in countries with poor investor protection may need concentrated control.

Bennedsen and Wolfenzon (2000) make a countervailing argument. When investor protection is poor, dissipating control among several large investors – none of whom can control the decisions of the firm without agreeing with the others – may serve as a commitment to limit expropriation. When there is no single controlling shareholder, and the agreement of several large investors (the board) is needed for major corporate actions, these investors might together hold enough cash flow rights to choose to limit expropriation of the remaining shareholders and pay the profits out as efficient dividends. When the dissipation of control reduces inefficient expropriation, it may emerge as an optimal policy for a wealth-maximizing entrepreneur.

An entrepreneur has a number of ways to retain control of a firm. He can sell shares with limited voting rights to the outsiders and still retain control by holding on to the shares with superior voting rights. He can also use a pyramidal structure, in which a holding company he controls sells shares in a subsidiary that it itself controls. Wolfenzon (1999) shows that an entrepreneur can then control the subsidiary without owning a substantial fraction of its cash flow rights, and that such schemes are more attractive when the protection of outside investors is weaker. An entrepreneur can also keep control through cross-shareholdings among firms, which make it harder for outsiders to gain control of one group firm without buying all of them.

What about the distribution of cash flow rights between investors as opposed to control? If an entrepreneur retains control of a firm, how can he raise any external funds from outside investors – for financing or for diversification – who expect to be expropriated? Jensen and Meckling (1976) would suggest that cash flow ownership by an entrepreneur reduces incentives for expropriation and raises incentives to pay out dividends. La Porta et al. (1999b) show that this need for higher cash flow ownership as a commitment to limit expropriation is higher in countries with inferior shareholder protection.

The available evidence on corporate ownership patterns around the world supports the importance of investor protection. This evidence was obtained for a number of individual countries, including Germany (Edwards and Fischer, 1994; Gorton and Schmid, 2000), Italy (Barca, 1995), and seven Organization for Economic Cooperation and Development countries (European Corporate Governance Network, 1997). La Porta et al. (1998) describe ownership concentration in their sample of 49 countries, while La Porta et al. (1999) examine patterns of control in the largest firms from each of 27 wealthy economies. The data show that countries with poor investor protection typically exhibit more concentrated control of firms than do countries with good investor protection. In the former, even the largest firms are usually controlled either by the state or by the families that founded or acquired these firms. In the latter countries, the Berle and Means corporation – with dispersed shareholders and professional managers in control – is more common.[4]

Claessens et al. (2000) examine a sample of nearly 3,000 firms from 9 East Asian economies. Except in Japan, which has fairly good shareholder protection, they find a predominance of family control and family management of the corporations in their sample, with some state control as well. They also present remarkable evidence of "crony capitalism" in Asia: outside Japan, the top 10 families in each of the remaining 8 countries studied control between 18 and 58 percent of the aggregate value of listed equities.

In sum, the evidence has proved to be broadly consistent with the proposition that the legal environment shapes the value of the private benefits of control and thereby determines the equilibrium ownership structures. Perhaps the main implications of this evidence for the study of corporate governance are the relative irrelevance of the Berle and Means corporation in most countries in the world and the centrality of family control. Indeed, La Porta et al. (1999) and Claessens et al. (2000) find that family-controlled firms are typically managed by family members so that the managers appear to be kept on a tighter leash than what Berle and Means describe. As Shleifer and Vishny (1997) have argued, in large corporations of most countries, the fundamental agency problem is not the Berle and Means conflict between outside investors and managers, but rather that between outside investors and controlling shareholders who have nearly full control over the managers.

3.2. Financial markets

The most basic prediction of the legal approach is that investor protection encourages the development of financial markets. When investors are protected from expropriation, they pay more for securities, making it more attractive for entrepreneurs to issue these securities. This applies to both creditors and shareholders.

Creditor rights encourage the development of lending, and the exact structure of these rights may alternatively favor bank lending or market lending. Shareholder rights encourage the development of equity markets, as measured by the valuation of firms, the number of listed firms (market breadth), and the rate at which firms go public. For both shareholders and creditors, protection includes not only the rights written into the laws and regulations but also the effectiveness of their enforcement. Consistent with these predictions, La Porta et al. (1997) show that countries that protect shareholders have more valuable stock markets, larger numbers of listed securities per capita, and a higher rate of IPO (initial public offering) activity than do the unprotective countries. Countries that protect creditors better have larger credit markets.

Several recent studies have also established a link between investor protection, insider ownership of cash flows, and corporate valuation.[5] Gorton and Schmid (2000) show that higher ownership by the large shareholders is associated with higher valuation of corporate assets in Germany. Claessens et al. (1999) use a sample of East Asian firms to show that greater insider cash flow ownership is associated with higher valuation of corporate assets, whereas greater insider control of voting rights is associated with lower valuation of corporate assets. Using a sample of firms from 27 wealthy economies, La Porta et al. (1999b) find that firms in countries with better shareholder protection have higher Tobin's Q than do firms in countries with inferior protection. They also find that higher insider cash flow ownership is (weakly) associated with higher corporate valuation, and that this effect is greater in countries with inferior shareholder protection. These results support the roles of investor protection and cash flow ownership by the insiders in limiting expropriation.

Johnson et al. (2000a) draw an ingenious connection between investor protection and financial crises. In countries with poor protection, the insiders might treat outside investors well as long as future prospects are bright and they are interested in continued external financing. When future prospects deteriorate, however, the insiders step up expropriation, and the outside investors, whether shareholders or creditors, are unable to do anything about it. This escalation of expropriation renders security price declines especially deep in countries with poor investor protection. To test this hypothesis, Johnson et al. (2000a) examine the depreciation of currencies and the decline of the stock markets in 25 countries during the Asian crisis of 1997–1998. They find that governance variables, such as investor protection indices and the quality of law enforcement, are powerful predictors of the extent of market declines during the crisis. These variables explain the cross-section of declines better than do the macroeconomic variables that have been the focus of the initial policy debate.

3.3. Real consequences

Through its effect on financial markets, investor protection influences the real economy. According to Beck et al. (2000), financial development can accelerate economic growth in three ways. First, it can enhance savings. Second, it can channel these savings into real investment and thereby foster capital accumulation. Third, to the extent that the financiers exercise some control over the investment decisions of the entrepreneurs, financial development allows capital to flow toward the more productive uses, and thus improves the efficiency of resource allocation. All three channels can in principle have large effects on economic growth.

A large body of research links financial development to economic growth. King and Levine (1993) initiate the modern incarnation of this literature by showing that countries with larger initial capital markets grow faster in the future. Demirguc-Kunt and Maksimovic (1998), Levine and Zervos (1998), Rajan and Zingales (1998), and Carlin and Mayer (1999) extend these findings. Several of these papers show that an exogenous component of financial market development, obtained by using legal origin as an instrument, predicts economic growth.

More recent research distinguishes the three channels through which finance can contribute to growth: saving, factor accumulation, and efficiency improvements. Beck et al. (2000) find that banking sector development exerts a large impact on total factor productivity growth and a less obvious impact on private savings and capital accumulation. Moreover, this influence continues to hold when an exogenous component of banking sector development, obtained by using legal origin as an instrument, is taken as a predictor. Wurgler (2000) finds that financially developed countries allocate investment across industries more in line with the variation in growth opportunities than do financially underdeveloped countries. Morck et al. (2000) find that stock markets in more developed countries incorporate firm-specific information better, helping to allocate investment more effectively. This research suggests that financial development improves resource allocation. Through this channel, investor protection may benefit the growth of productivity and output.

4. BANK AND MARKET CENTERED GOVERNANCE

Traditional comparisons of corporate governance systems focus on the institutions financing firms rather than on the legal protection of investors. Bank-centered corporate governance systems, such as those of Germany and Japan, are compared to market-centered systems, such as those of the United States and the United Kingdom (see, e.g., Allen and Gale, 2000). Relatedly, relationship-based corporate governance, in which a main bank provides a significant share of finance and governance to each firm, is contrasted with market-based governance, in which finance is provided by large numbers of investors and in which takeovers play a key governance role.

These institutional distinctions have been central to the evaluation of alternative corporate governance regimes and to policy proposals for improvement. In the 1980s, when the Japanese economy could do no wrong, bank-centered governance was widely regarded as superior because, as Aoki and Patrick (1993) and Porter (1992) argue, far-sighted banks enable firms to focus on long term investment decisions. According to Hoshi et al. (1991), banks also deliver capital to firms facing liquidity shortfalls, thereby avoiding costly financial distress. Finally, banks replace the expensive and disruptive takeovers with more surgical bank intervention when the management of the borrowing firm under-performed.

In the 1990s, as the Japanese economy collapsed, the pendulum swung the other way.[6] Kang and Stulz (1998) show that, far from being the promoters of rational investment, Japanese banks perpetrate soft budget constraints, over-lending to declining firms that require radical reorganization. And according to Weinstein and Yafeh (1998) and Morck and Nakamura (1999), Japanese banks, instead of facilitating governance, collude with enterprise managers to deter external threats to their control and to collect rents on bank loans. In the recent assessments by Edwards and Fischer (1994) and Hellwig (1999), German banks are likewise downgraded to ineffective providers of governance. Market-based systems, in contrast, rode the American stock market bubble of the 1990s into the stratosphere of wide support and adulation.

Unfortunately, the classification of financial systems into bank and market centered is neither straightforward nor particularly fruitful. One way to do this is by looking at the actual outcomes. It is easy to classify Germany as bank-centered because its banks influence firms through both debt and equity holdings and its stock market is underdeveloped.[7] But what about Japan, which boasts both powerful banks with influence over firms and a highly developed and widely-held equity market (second or third in the world by size) with thousands of listed securities? Or what about the French civil law based financial systems, in which neither credit markets nor stock markets are especially well developed? Sapienza (1999), for example, finds that in Italy the stock market is extremely underdeveloped, but so is the banking system, with a typical firm raising a small amount of money from each of a dozen banks. More generally, La Porta et al. (1997) show that, on average, countries with bigger stock markets also have higher ratios of private debt to gross domestic product (GDP), contrary to the view that debt and equity finance are substitutes for each other. The prevalent financing modes generally do not help with the classification.

Another way to classify financial systems is based on the existence of Glass-Steagall regulations restricting bank ownership of corporate equity. This approach is again useful for distinguishing the United States from Germany, which does not have such regulations. On the other hand, most countries in the world do not have these regulations. Some of them, like the United Kingdom, have a highly developed stock market and few equity holdings by banks, even though banks are not prevented by law from holding equity. Other countries have neither a developed banking system nor a developed stock market. Glass-Steagall regulations in themselves do not assure a development of a market system by interfering with corporate governance by banks. Consistent with our skepticism about the usefulness of such regulations for classifying financial systems, La Porta et al. (1999) show that Glass-Steagall regulations have no predictive power for ownership concentration across countries.

Perhaps most important, the reliance on either the outcomes or the Glass-Steagall regulations to classify corporate governance regimes misses the crucial importance of investor rights. All financiers depend on legal protection to function. A method of financing develops when it is protected by the law that gives financiers the power to get their money back. Germany and some other German civil law countries have developed banking systems because they have strong legal protection of creditors, particularly of secured creditors. Without such rights German banks would have much less power. The United Kingdom also has a large banking and public debt sector, again because creditors have extensive rights, as well as a large equity market. Italy and Belgium, by contrast, have developed neither debt nor equity markets because no outside investors are protected there.[8] The point here is simple: all outside investors, be they large or small, creditors or shareholders, need rights to get their money back. Investor rights are a more primitive determinant of financial development than is the size of particular institutions.

Despite the difficulty of classifying financial systems into bank- and market centered, economists at least since Gerschenkron (1962) have engaged in a lively debate as to which one is superior, focusing on the hypothesis that bank-centered systems are particularly suitable for developing economies. This is not a place to review this debate. Rather, our concern is that the interest in monopoly bank lending distracts attention from the important role that stock markets play in external finance. Equity financing is essential for the expansion of new firms whose main asset are the growth opportunities. In principle, firms could utilize private equity financing, but it has many of the same problems of excessive investor power suppressing entrepreneurial initiative as does monopoly banking (see, e.g., Myers, 1977; Burkart et al., 1997). Public equity financing, for which a developed stock market is needed, has other advantages over private equity financing. It allows the buyers of equity to diversify. It offers the initial equity holders, such as venture capitalists, an attractive exit option through the public equity markets. Last but not least, it allows firms to time their equity issues to take advantage of favorable investor sentiment toward their industry, or toward the market as a whole. Such sentiment may play a beneficial role when shareholders are skeptical about the likelihood of getting back a return on their money. Indeed, Keynes

(1931) and others have argued that bubbles play an important and positive role in stimulating investment.

To summarize, bank-versus market centeredness is not an especially useful way to distinguish financial systems. Investor rights work better to explain differences among countries, and in fact are often necessary for financial intermediaries to develop. Moreover, even if some countries go through monopoly banking in their development process, this stage has little to recommend it other than as a stepping stone toward more developed markets. And to get to more developed markets, it is essential to improve the rights of outside investors.

5. POSSIBILITIES FOR REFORM

In the last decade, the reform of corporate governance has attracted interest in Western and Eastern Europe, Latin America, and Asia. The discussions have intensified since the Asian financial crisis, and took on the flavor of reforming "the global financial architecture". To discuss any reform, it is important to start with its goals. Our analysis suggests that one objective of corporate governance reform is to protect the rights of outside investors, including both shareholders and creditors. As the evidence described in Section 3 shows, the benefits of such reform would be to expand financial markets, to facilitate external financing of new firms, to move away from concentrated ownership, to improve the efficiency of investment allocation, and to facilitate private restructuring of financial claims in a crisis.

So what, if anything, can be done to achieve these goals, and what are the obstacles? To organize this discussion, we follow Coffee (1999) and Gilson (2000) in drawing a distinction between legal and functional convergence. Legal convergence refers to the changes in rules and enforcement mechanisms toward some successful standard. To converge to effective investor protection in this way, most countries require extensive legal, regulatory, and judicial reform. Alternatively, functional convergence refers to more decentralized, market-based changes, which do not require legal reform per se, but still bring more firms and assets under the umbrella of effective legal protection of investors. We discuss these paths of reform in turn.

For most countries, the improvement of investor protection requires radical changes in the legal system. Securities, company, and bankruptcy laws generally need to be amended. The particular list of legal protections of investors studied by La Porta et al. (1998) is neither necessary nor sufficient for such reforms. There may be significant complementarities between various laws in protecting minority shareholders: securities laws, for example, can mandate disclosure of material information while company laws enable minority shareholders to act on it. Moreover, the regulatory and judicial mechanisms of enforcing shareholders and creditor rights would need to be radically improved. In fact, the evidence on the importance of the historically determined legal origin in shaping investor rights – which could be thought of as a proxy for the law's general stance toward outside investors – suggests at least tentatively that many rules need to be changed simultaneously to bring a country with poor investor protection up to best practice.

The political opposition to such change has proved intense. Governments are often reluctant to introduce laws that surrender to the financiers the regulatory control they currently have over large corporations. Important objections to reform also come from the families that control large corporations. From the point of view of these families, an improvement in the rights of outside investors is first and foremost a reduction in the value of control due to the deterioration of expropriation opportunities. The total value of these firms may increase as a result of legal reform, as expropriation declines and investors finance new projects on more attractive terms; still, the first order effect is a tax on the insiders for the benefit of minority shareholders and creditors. What the

reformers see as protection of investors, the founding families call "expropriation of entrepreneurs". No wonder, then, that in all countries – from Latin America to Asia to Europe – the families have opposed legal reform.

There is a further reason why the insiders in major firms oppose corporate governance reform and the expansion of capital markets. As Mayer (1988) shows, existing large firms typically finance their own investment projects internally or through captive or closely connected banks. In fact, La Porta et al. (1997) show that the lion's share of credit in countries with poor creditor protection goes to the few largest firms. These firms obtain the finance they need, the political influence that comes with the access to such finance, and the protection from competition that would come if smaller firms could also raise external capital. When new entrepreneurs have good projects, they often have to come to the existing firms for capital. Poor corporate governance delivers the insiders secure finance, secure politics and secure markets. They have an interest in keeping the system as is.

Consistent with the dominance of interest group politics, successful reforms have occurred only when the special interests could be destroyed or appeased. In this respect, corporate governance reform is no different from most other reforms in developing or industrialized countries (see, e.g., Hirschman, 1963; Shleifer and Treisman, 2000). But examples of significant legal reform of corporate governance do exist. Ramseyer and Nakazato (1999) describe legal reform in Japan after World War II, when General McArthur, assisted by attorneys from Chicago and an occupying army, introduced an Illinois-based company law. Another example is securities markets regulation in the United States in 1933–1934, introduced in the middle of the Great Depression, which substantially increased corporate disclosure. A third example is some streamlining of bankruptcy procedures in East Asia following the crisis of 1997.

Although such opportunities for corporate governance reform do arise, they often have been wasted, in part because of a lack of appreciation of the need to protect investors. Recent research points to some crucial principles of investor protection that reforms need to focus on.

The first such principle is that legal rules do matter. It is not just the stance of the law or the political sentiment of the day that shapes financial markets. One illustration of this principle, described by Johnson (1999), is the Neuer Markt in Germany, a segment of the Frankfurt Stock Exchange created especially for listing new firms. Because the Neuer Markt operates in Germany, the corporate law, the securities law, and other basic laws and regulations that are applied to the companies listing there are the general German rules. The politics are German as well. As part of a private contract with firms wishing to list on the Neuer Markt, the Deutsche Bourse – which operates the Frankfurt Stock Exchange – has mandated that these firms must comply with international accounting standards and agree to greater disclosure than that required of already listed firms. The new listing venue, with its greater restrictions on the entrepreneurs, has sharply accelerated the pace of initial public offerings in Germany. At the same time, the captains of German industry have accepted it because their firms were not directly affected. This points to one possible strategy of overcoming political opposition to reform.

A second principle is that good legal rules are the ones that a country can enforce. The strategy for reform is not to create an ideal set of rules and then see how well they can be enforced, but rather to enact the rules that can be enforced within the existing structure. One example of the success of such a policy is the U.S. securities legislation of 1933–1934, described by Landis (1938) and McCraw (1984). This legislation placed much of the responsibility for accurate corporate accounting and disclosure on intermediaries, and focused the regulatory oversight by the Securities and Exchange Commission (SEC) on these relatively few intermediaries. The SEC also emphasized self-regulation by the intermediaries. Thus the accounting profession, once it recognized the increased demand for its services, became an independent private force in assuring the compliance with disclosure regulations. As a consequence, a small Commission was able to regulate a huge market with relatively few resources. The principle of recruiting private intermediaries into the enforcement of securities regulations has since been followed by a number of countries, including Germany and Poland.

A third and related principle of successful reform, stressed by Glaeser et al. (2001), is that government regulation of financial markets may be useful when court enforcement of private contracts or laws cannot be relied upon. An example of how regulation can work when judicial enforcement is limited comes from the securities law reform in Poland and the Czech Republic, two transition economies whose judiciaries in the early 1990s were generally viewed as ineffective. At that time the Polish government introduced a tough securities law focused on shareholder protection. Like the U.S. securities law, the Polish regulations focused on significant disclosure by new issuers and already listed firms, as well as on licensing and close administrative oversight of intermediaries. The law also provided for a creation of a powerful SEC with significant enforcement powers that did not require reliance on courts. This reform was followed by a remarkable development of the Polish stock market, with both new and already listed companies raising equity in the market.

By contrast, the Czech government chose neither to introduce tough securities laws nor to create a powerful market regulator at the time of privatization. Perhaps as a consequence, the Czech markets have been plagued by massive expropriation of minority shareholders – the so-called "tunneling" of assets from both firms and mutual funds. In contrast to the Polish market, the Czech market stagnated, with hundreds of companies getting delisted and virtually no public equity financing by firms (see Coffee, 1999; Pistor, 1999; Glaeser et al., 2001).

The comparison of Poland to the Czech Republic is especially instructive because the two countries share roughly similar incomes, economic policies, and quality of judiciaries. Under these circumstances, regulation of the stock market and listed firms in Poland, with its focus on investor protection, appeared to play a beneficial role.

The successful regulations of the U.S. securities markets, the Polish financial markets, and the Neuer Markt in Germany share a common element: the extensive and mandatory disclosure of financial information by the issuers, the accuracy of which is enforced by tightly regulated financial intermediaries. Although such disclosure is not sufficient by itself without the right of the shareholders to act on it, it does appear to be a key element of shareholder protection.

With the legal reform slow and halting in most countries, "functional convergence" may play a role in improving investor protection. The liberalization of capital markets in many countries has increased not only the flow of foreign investment into them, as Henry (2000) and Stulz (1999) document, but also the economic and political pressure to create financial instruments acceptable to foreign investors. These pressures give rise to several forms of functional convergence. When contracts are enforced well, companies in unprotective legal regimes can offer their investors customized contracts such as corporate charters with greater rights than the law generally provides. This strategy relies on perhaps a greater enforcement capacity of courts than is warranted, and also ignores the public good benefit of standard rules. A more promising approach is for companies to opt into the more investor friendly legal regimes. One way of doing this is to list a company's securities on an exchange that protects minority shareholders through disclosure or other means. In fact, this is done by many companies that list their shares as American Depositary Receipts (ADRs) in the U.S. But such listing imposes only limited constraints on the insiders: although it improves disclosure, it typically does not give minority shareholders many effective rights.

A related and increasingly important mechanism of opting into a more protective legal regime is being acquired by a firm already operating in such a regime. When a British firm fully acquires a Swedish firm, the possibilities for legal expropriation of investors diminish. Because the controlling shareholders of the Swedish company are compensated in such a friendly deal for the lost private benefits of control, they are more likely to go along. By replacing the wasteful expropriation with publicly shared profits and dividends, such acquisitions enhance efficiency.

It is important to recognize the limitations of functional convergence, particularly in the area of creditor rights. Assets located in particular countries generally remain under the jurisdiction of these countries' laws. Without bankruptcy reform, opt-in mechanisms are unlikely to address the legal problems faced by creditors. Thus, despite the benefits of opting into the more protective legal regime for external finance, this mechanism is unlikely to fully replace bona fide legal reform.

6. CONCLUSION

This paper describes the legal protection of investors as a potentially useful way of thinking about corporate governance. Strong investor protection may be a particularly important manifestation of the greater security of property rights against political interference in some countries. Empirically, strong investor protection is associated with effective corporate governance, as reflected in valuable and broad financial markets, dispersed ownership of shares, and efficient allocation of capital across firms. Using investor protection as the starting point appears to be a more fruitful way to describe differences in corporate governance regimes across countries than some of the more customary classifications such as bank- or market-centeredness.

An important implication of this approach is that leaving financial markets alone is not a good way to encourage them.

Financial markets need some protection of outside investors, whether by courts, government agencies, or market participants themselves. Improving such protection is a difficult task. In part, the nature of investor protection, and more generally of regulation of financial markets, is deeply rooted in the legal structure of each country and in the origin of its laws. Marginal reform may not successfully achieve the reformer's goals. In part, the existing corporate governance arrangements benefit both the politicians and the entrenched economic interests, including the families that manage the largest firms in most countries in the world. Corporate governance reform must circumvent the opposition by these interests. Despite these difficulties, reform of investor protection is politically feasible in some circumstances, and can bring significant benefits. It can take the form of opting into more protective legal regimes or introducing more radical changes in the legal structure. The integration of world capital markets makes such reforms more likely today than they have been in decades.

NOTES

* We are grateful to Nicholas Barberis, Simeon Djankov, Oliver Hart, Michael Jensen, Simon Johnson, Ross Levine, and Daniel Wolfenzon for helpful comments, and also to the NSF for financial support of this research.
† Corresponding author. Tel.: 617–495–5046; fax: 617–496–1708. E-mail address: ashleifer@harvard.edu (A. Shleifer).

1   Socialist countries had a legal tradition based on Soviet law, but because the laws of these countries are changing rapidly during the transition out of socialism, La Porta et al. (1998) do not consider them.
2   According to Cameron (1961), France had a lively stock market in the nineteenth century. Nearly all firms listed on it, however, benefitted from government concessions, investment, ownership, subsidies, protection, and often outright guarantees to investors.
3   Berglof and von Thadden (1999) and Rajan and Zingales (1999) argue that political factors affect corporate governance through channels other than the law itself. This may be true, but

the law remains a crucial channel through which politics affects corporate governance.
4   The evidence also reveals that control is valued, and specifically that voting premiums increase as shareholder protection deteriorates (see, for example, Modigliani and Perotti, 1998; Nenova, 1999; Zingales, 1994).
5   In addition, La Porta et al. (2000) show that better minority shareholder protection is associated with higher dividend pay-outs in a cross-section of firms from around the world.
6   Jensen (1989) expresses some early skepticism about the Japanese financial system.
7   Hellwig (1999) doubts that banks are so powerful, even in the case of Germany.
8   Levine et al. (2000) find that the La Porta et al. (1998) measure of creditor rights is correlated with measures of financial intermediaries development across countries, while their measure of shareholder rights is correlated with stock market development.

REFERENCES

Allen, F., Gale, D., 2000. Comparing Financial Systems. MIT Press, Cambridge, MA.

Aoki, M., Patrick, H., 1993. The Japanese Main Bank System: Its Relevance for Developing and Transforming Economies. Oxford University Press, New York.

Barca, F., 1995. On corporate governance in Italy: issues, facts, and agency. Unpublished working paper. Bank of Italy, Rome.

Bebchuk, L., 1999. The rent protection theory of corporate ownership and control. Unpublished working paper. Harvard Law School, Cambridge, MA.

Beck, T., Levine, R., Loayza, N., 2000. Finance and the sources of growth. Journal of Financial Economics 58, 261–300.

Bennedsen, M., Wolfenzon, D., 2000. The balance of power in closely held corporations. Journal of Financial Economics 58, 113–139.

Berglof, E., von Thadden, L., 1999. The changing corporate governance paradigm: implications for transition and developing countries. Unpublished working paper. Stockholm Institute of Transition Economics, Stockholm, Sweden.

Burkart, M., Gromb, D., Panunzi, F., 1997. Large Shareholders, monitoring, and fiduciary duty. Quarterly Journal of Economics 112, 693–728.

Cameron, R., 1961. France and the Economic Development of Europe. Princeton University Press, Princeton, NJ.

Carlin, W., Mayer, C., 1999. Finance, investment and growth. Unpublished working paper. University College, London.

Claessens, S., Djankov, S., Lang, L., 2000. The separation of ownership and control in East Asian corporations. Journal of Financial Economics 58, 81–112.

Claessens, S., Djankov, S., Fan, J., Lang, L., 1999. Expropriation of minority shareholders in East Asia. Unpublished working paper. The World Bank, Washington, DC.

Coase, R., 1961. The problem of social cost. Journal of Law and Economics 3, 1–44.

Coffee, J., 1999. The future as history: the prospects for global convergence in corporate governance and its implications. Northwestern Law Review 93, 631–707.

Coffee, J., 2000. Privatization and corporate governance: the lessons from securities market failure. Working paper no. 158. Columbia Law School, New York.

David, R., Brierley, J., 1985. Major Legal Systems in the World Today. Stevens and Sons, London.

Demirguc-Kunt, A., Maksimovic, V., 1998. Law, finance, and firm growth. Journal of Finance 53, 2107–2139.

Easterbrook, F., Fischel, D., 1991. The Economic Structure of Corporate Law. Harvard University Press, Cambridge, MA.

Edwards, J., Fischer, K., 1994. Banks, Finance and Investment in West Germany Since 1970. Cambridge University Press, Cambridge, UK.

European Corporate Governance Network (ECGN). 1997. The Separation of Ownership and Control: A Survey of 7 European Countries Preliminary Report to the European Commission. Volumes 1–4. Brussels, European Corporate Governance Network.

Finer, S., 1997. The History of Government, Vol. III. Cambridge University Press, Cambridge, UK.

Gerschenkron, A., 1962. Economic Backwardness in Historical Perspective. Belknap Press of Harvard University Press, Cambridge, MA.

Gilson, R., 2000. Globalizing corporate governance: convergence of form or function.

Unpublished working paper. Stanford University, Stanford, CA.

Glaeser, E., Johnson, S., Shleifer, A., 2001. Coase versus the Coasians. Quarterly Journal of Economics, forthcoming.

Gorton, G., Schmid, F., 2000. Universal banking and the performance of German firms. Journal of Financial Economics 58, 29–80.

Grossman, S., Hart, O., 1988. One-share-one-vote and the market for corporate control. Journal of Financial Economics 20, 175–202.

Harris, M., Raviv, A., 1988. Corporate governance: voting rights and majority rules. Journal of Financial Economics 20, 203–236.

Hart, O., 1995. Firms, Contracts, and Financial Structure. Oxford University Press, London.

Hellwig, M., 1999. On the economics and politics of corporate finance and corporate control. Unpublished working paper. University of Mannheim, Mannheim.

Henry, P., 2000. Do stock market liberalizations cause investment booms? Journal of Financial Economics 58, 301–334.

Hirschman, A., 1963. Journeys Toward Progress. The Twentieth Century Fund, New York.

Hoshi, T., Kashyap, A., Scharfstein, D., 1991. Corporate structure, liquidity, and investment: evidence from Japanese industrial groups. Quarterly Journal of Economics 106, 33–60.

Jensen, M., 1989. Eclipse of the modern corporation. Harvard Business Review 67, 61–74.

Jensen, M., Meckling, W., 1976. Theory of the firm: managerial behavior, agency costs, and ownership structure. Journal of Financial Economics 3, 305–360.

Johnson, S., 1999. Does investor protection matter? Evidence from Germany's Neuer Markt. Unpublished working paper. MIT Press, Cambridge, MA.

Johnson, S., Boone, P., Breach, A., Friedman, E., 2000a. Corporate governance in the Asian financial crisis, Journal of Financial Economics 58, 141–186.

Johnson, S., La Porta, R., Lopez-de-Silanes, F., Shleifer, A., 2000b. Tunneling. American Economic Review Papers and Proceedings 90, 22–27.

Kang, J., Stulz, R., 1998. Do banking shocks affect borrowing firm performance? An analysis of the Japanese experience. Unpublished working paper. Ohio State University, Columbus, OH.

Keynes, J., 1931. An economic analysis of unemployment. In Collected Writings, Vol. XII. Macmillan, London.

King, R., Levine, R., 1993. Finance and growth: Schumpeter might be right. Quarterly Journal of Economics 108, 717–738.

Landis, J., 1938. The Administrative Process. Yale University Press, New Haven, CT.

La Porta, R., Lopez-de-Silanes, F., Shleifer, A., 1999. Corporate ownership around the world. Journal of Finance 54, 471–517.

La Porta, R., Lopez-de-Silanes, F., Shleifer, A., Vishny, R., 1997. Legal determinants of external finance. Journal of Finance 52, 1131–1150.

La Porta, R., Lopez-de-Silanes, F., Shleifer, A., Vishny, R., 1998. Law and finance. Journal of Political Economy 106, 1113–1155.

La Porta, R., Lopez-de-Silanes, F., Shleifer, A., Vishny, R., 1999a. The quality of government. Journal of Law, Economics and Organization 15, 222–279.

La Porta, R., Lopez-de-Silanes, F., Shleifer, A., Vishny, R., 1999b. Investor protection and corporate valuation. NBER Working Paper 7403. National Bureau of Economic Research, Cambridge, MA.

La Porta, R., Lopez-de-Silanes, F., Shleifer, A., Vishny, R., 2000. Agency problems and dividend policies around the world. Journal of Finance 55, 1–33.

Levine, R., Zervos, S., 1998. Stock markets, banks and economic growth. American Economic Review 88, 537–558.

Levine, R., Loayza, N., Beck, T., 2000. Financial intermediary development and economic growth: causality and causes. Journal of Monetary Economics, 46, 31–77.

Mayer, C., 1988. New issues in corporate finance. European Economic Review 32, 1167–1188.

McCraw, T.K., 1984. Prophets of Regulation. The Belknap Press of Harvard University Press, Cambridge, MA.

Modigliani, F., Miller, M., 1958. The cost of capital, corporation finance, and the theory of investment. American Economic Review 48, 261–297.

Modigliani, F., Perotti, E., 1998. Security versus bank finance: the importance of a proper enforcement of legal rules. Unpublished working paper. MIT Press, Cambridge, MA.

Morck, R., Nakamura, M., 1999. Banks and corporate control in Japan. Journal of Finance 54, 319–340.

Morck, R., Yeung, B., Yu, W., 2000. The information content of stock markets: why do emerging markets have synchronous price movements? Journal of Financial Economics 58, 215–260.

Myers, S., 1977. Determinants of corporate borrowing. Journal of Financial Economics 5, 147–175.

Nenova, T., 1999. The value of a corporate vote and private benefits: a cross-country analysis. Unpublished working paper. Harvard University, Cambridge, MA.

Pistor, K., 1999. Law as a determinant of equity market development. Unpublished working paper. Harvard University, Cambridge, MA.

Porter, M., 1992. Capital disadvantage: America's falling capital investment system. Harvard Business Review 46, 65–72.

Rajan, R., Zingales, L., 1998. Financial dependence and growth. American Economic Review 88, 559–586.

Rajan, R., Zingales, L., 1999. The politics of financial development. Unpublished working paper. University of Chicago, Chicago, IL.

Ramseyer, M., Nakazato, M., 1999. Japanese Law: an Economic Approach. University of Chicago Press, Chicago, IL.

Sapienza, P., 1999. The effects of bank mergers on loan contracts. Unpublished working paper. Northwestern University, Chicago, IL.

Shleifer, A., Treisman, D., 2000. Without a Map: Political Tactics and Economic Reform in Russia. MIT Press, Cambridge, MA.

Shleifer, A., Vishny, R., 1997. A survey of corporate governance. Journal of Finance 52, 737–783.

Stigler, G., 1964. Public regulation of the securities market. Journal of Business 37, 117–142.

Stulz, R., 1999. International Portfolio Flows and Securities Markets. Working Paper 99–3, Fisher College of Business. The Ohio State University, Columbus, OH.

Weinstein, D., Yafeh, Y., 1998. On the costs of a bank-centered financial system: evidence from the main bank relations in Japan. Journal of Finance 53, 635–672.

Wolfenzon, D., 1999. A theory of pyramidal structures. Unpublished working paper. Harvard University, Cambridge, MA.

Wurgler, J., 2000. Financial markets and the allocation of capital. Journal of Financial Economics 58, this issue.

Zingales, L., 1994. The value of the voting right: a study of the Milan stock exchange. The Review of Financial Studies 7, 125–148.

Zingales, L., 1995. Inside ownership and the decision to go public. Review of Economic Studies 62, 425–448.

Chapter 4

James S. Ang, Rebel Cole, and James Wuh Lin*

AGENCY COSTS AND OWNERSHIP STRUCTURE

Source: *Journal of Finance*, 55(1) (2000): 81–106.

ABSTRACT

We provide measures of absolute and relative equity agency costs for corporations under different ownership and management structures. Our base case is Jensen and Meckling's (1976) zero agency-cost firm, where the manager is the firm's sole shareholder. We utilize a sample of 1,708 small corporations from the FRB/NSSBF database and find that agency costs (i) are significantly higher when an outsider rather than an insider manages the firm; (ii) are inversely related to the manager's ownership share; (iii) increase with the number of nonmanager shareholders, and (iv) to a lesser extent, are lower with greater monitoring by banks.

THE SOCIAL AND PRIVATE COSTS OF AN AGENT'S ACTIONS due to incomplete alignment of the agent's and owner's interests were brought to attention by the seminal contributions of Jensen and Meckling (1976) on agency costs. Agency theory has also brought the roles of managerial decision rights and various external and internal monitoring and bonding mechanisms to the forefront of theoretical discussions and empirical research. Great strides have been made in demonstrating empirically the role of agency costs in financial decisions, such as in explaining the choices of capital structure, maturity structure, dividend policy, and executive compensation. However, the actual measurement of the principal variable of interest, agency costs, in both absolute and relative terms, has lagged behind.

To measure absolute agency costs, a zero agency-cost base case must be observed to serve as the reference point of comparison for all other cases of ownership and management structures. In the original Jensen and Meckling agency theory, the zero agency-cost base case is, by definition, the firm owned solely by a single owner-manager. When management owns less than 100 percent of the firm's equity, shareholders incur agency costs resulting from management's shirking and perquisite consumption. Because of limitations imposed by personal wealth constraints, exchange regulations on the minimum numbers of shareholders, and other considerations, no publicly traded firm is entirely owned by management. Thus, Jensen and Meckling's zero agency cost base case cannot be found among the usual sample of publicly traded firms for which information is readily available. The absence of information about solo owner manager firms explains why agency costs are often inferred but not directly measured in the empirical finance literature.

No-agency-cost base case firms, however, can be found among non–publicly traded firms. Until recently, data on non–publicly traded firms, which tend to be much smaller than their publicly traded counterparts, have been sparse. In 1997, the Federal Reserve Board released its National Survey of Small Business Finances (NSSBF), which collected data from a nationally representative sample of small businesses. Data from the NSSBF enable us to analyze the relationship between agency costs and ownership structure because the survey provides financial data on a group of firms whose management owns 100 percent of equity. These firms enable us to estimate the expected expense for the no-outside-equity agency-cost base case. Furthermore, the database includes firms with a wide range of ownership and manager/owner structures, including firms owned by two individuals as well as firms managed by outsiders with no equity stake. As a consequence, small firms appear well suited for a study of equity-related agency costs.

We use two alternative measures of agency costs. The first is direct agency costs, calculated as the difference in dollar expenses between a firm with a certain ownership and management structure and the no-agency-cost base case firm. This measure captures excessive expenses including perk consumption. To facilitate cross-sectional comparisons, we standardize expenses by annual sales. Our second measure of agency costs is a proxy for the loss in revenues attributable to inefficient asset utilization, which can result from poor investment decisions (e.g., investing in negative net-present-value assets) or from management's shirking (e.g., exerting too little effort to help generate revenue). This second measure of agency costs is calculated as the ratio of annual sales to total assets, an efficiency ratio. We can then measure agency costs as the difference in the efficiency ratio, or, equivalently, the dollar revenues lost, between a firm whose manager is the sole equity owner and a firm whose manager owns less than 100 percent of equity.

Monitoring of managers' expenditures on perquisites and other personal consumption relies on the vigilance of the nonmanaging shareholders and/or related third parties, such as the company's bankers. The lack of specific operational knowledge on the part of nonmanaging shareholders, and the lack of an external market for shares, however, may offset the presence of dominant shareholders. Additionally, heavy reliance of the non–publicly traded firms on bank financing could give banks a special role in delegated monitoring on behalf of other shareholders. Thus, it would seem that determination of the size of agency costs for these firms is an empirical issue.

Our results provide direct confirmation of the predictions made by Jensen and Meckling (1976). Agency costs are indeed higher among firms that are not 100 percent owned by their managers, and these costs increase as the equity share of the owner-manager declines. Hence, agency costs increase with a reduction in managerial ownership, as predicted by Jensen and Meckling. These results hold true after controlling for differences across industries, the effects of economies of scale, and differences in capital structure. We also find some evidence that delegated monitoring of small firms by banks reduces agency costs.

The paper is organized as follows. In Section I, we discuss the nature of equity agency costs in various ownership structures and explain the broad outline of our empirical model. In Section II, we provide a description of the data. We present results and analysis in Section III, followed by a summary and conclusions in Section IV.

I. AGENCY COSTS AMONG SMALL BUSINESSES

When compared to publicly traded firms, small businesses come closest to the type of firms depicted in the stylized theoretical model of agency costs developed by Jensen and Meckling (1976). At one extreme of ownership and management structures are firms whose managers own 100 percent of the firm. These firms, by their definition, have no agency costs. At the other extreme are firms whose managers are paid employees with no equity in the firm. In between are firms where the managers own some, but not all, of their firm's equity.

Agency costs arise when the interests of the firm's managers are not aligned with those of the firm's owner(s), and take the form of preference for on-the-job perks, shirking, and making self-interested and entrenched decisions that reduce shareholder wealth. The magnitude of these costs is limited by how well the owners and delegated third parties, such as banks, monitor the actions of the outside managers.

To illustrate, consider those firms where a single owner controls 100 percent of the stock but hires an outsider to manage the business. On the one hand, agency costs may be small because the sole owner can internalize all monitoring costs and has the right to hire and fire the manager. More specifically, such an owner incurs 100 percent of the monitoring costs and receives 100 percent of the resulting benefits. On the other hand, the sole owner may not be able to monitor perfectly for the same reasons that he or she hired an outside manager, such as lack of time or ability. Owners of small firms typically lack financial sophistication, and may not be capable of performing random audits or fully understanding the operating or financial results. Consequently, these firms incur residual agency costs. If these costs are significant, they must reflect a failure of the owner's monitoring activities. Potential explanations for this failure are lax monitoring by the owners and the lack of an adequate monitoring technology available for the owners. In this case, the separation of the management function (initiation and implementation) versus the control function by nonmanaging owners/shareholders (ratification and monitoring), as suggested by Fama and Jensen (1983a, 1983b), may not be complete or effective. Thus, residual agency costs are still expected in a sole owner firm when the manager is an outsider.

Agency costs attributable to the divergence of interests vary inversely with the manager's ownership stake. As the number of shareholders increases from one, the ownership of the owner/manager falls to α, where $0 \leq \alpha < 1$. Because the manager gains 100 percent of each dollar spent on perks, but only α percent of each dollar in firm profit, the manager who owns less than 100 percent of the firm has the incentive to consume perks rather than to maximize the value of the firm to all shareholders. At the extreme is the manager with zero ownership ($\alpha = 0$), who gains 100 percent of perquisite consumption, but zero percent of firm profits (in the case when salary is independent of firm performance).

Aggregate expenditure on monitoring by the nonmanaging shareholders decreases as their individual ownership shares decline. This is due to the well-known free-rider problem in spending for quasi-public goods, such as monitoring effort. Each monitoring shareholder, with ownership λ_i must incur 100 percent of the monitoring costs, but realizes only λ_i percent of the monitoring benefits (in the form of reduced agency costs). A nonmonitoring shareholder, however, enjoys the full benefits of a monitoring shareholder's activity without incurring any monitoring cost. Thus, as the number of non-manager shareholders increases, aggregate expenditure on monitoring declines, and the magnitude of owner-manager agency-cost problems increases. Offsetting this relationship are concerns among shareholders about an increase in the probability that the firm will be unable to pay off bank debt or secure future financing from the same or new investors, which may produce some restraint in agency behavior. However, as noted by Williams (1987), these countervailing forces to agency behavior are expected to decline in effectiveness when the firm is not in imminent danger of insolvency.

To summarize, against the null hypothesis that agency costs are independent of the ownership and control structure,[1] we postulate the following hypotheses derived from agency theory when compared to the base case: (i) agency costs are higher at firms whose managers own none of the firm's equity, (ii) agency costs are an inverse function of the managers' ownership stake, and (iii) agency costs are an increasing function of the number of nonmanager shareholders.

II. DATA

Our empirical approach utilizes two fundamental assumptions about agency costs: (1) A firm managed by a 100 percent owner incurs zero agency costs and, (2) agency costs can be measured as the difference in the efficiency of an imperfectly aligned firm and the efficiency of a perfectly aligned firm. To operationalize this approach for measuring agency costs, we need certain data inputs: (i) data on firm efficiency measures; (ii) data on firm ownership structure, including a set of firms that are 100 percent owned by managers; and (iii) data on control variables, including firm size, characteristics, and monitoring technology.

Of these data requirements, the most demanding in terms of availability is item (ii) because sole-ownership firms typically are not publicly listed, and because financial information on U.S. private firms usually is not available to the public. The Federal Reserve Board's National Survey of Small Business Finances (NSSBF), fortunately, does provide financial information about privately held firms, including their ownership structure, and does include a set of firms entirely owned by managers. Consequently, we use data from the NSSBF to measure agency costs.[2]

The NSSBF is a survey conducted by the Federal Reserve Board to gather information about small businesses, which have largely been ignored in the academic literature because of the limited availability of data. The survey collected detailed information from a sample of 4,637 firms that is broadly representative of approximately 5 million small nonfarm, nonfinancial businesses operating in the United States as of year-end 1992. Cole and Wolken (1995) provide detailed information about the data available from NSSBF.

For this study, we limit our analysis to small C-corporations, collecting information on the governance structure, management alignment, extent of shareholder and external monitoring, size, and financial information. We focus on corporations to minimize problems associated with the financial statements of proprietorships, which typically commingle personal and business funds. We eliminate partnerships and S-corporations because, unlike C-corporations, they are not subject to corporate taxation, and this may lead owner-managers to take compensation in the form of partner distributions or dividends rather than salary expense because there is no double taxation of such earnings at the firm level. By focusing solely on C-corporations, we avoid the complications of comparing operating expenses across organizational forms. This restriction on the NSSBF database yields an analysis sample of 1,708 firms.[3]

A. Agency costs

To measure agency costs of the firm, we use two alternative efficiency ratios that frequently appear in the accounting and financial economics literature: the expense ratio, which is operating expense scaled by annual sales,[4] and the asset utilization ratio, which is annual sales divided by total assets. The first ratio is a measure of how effectively the firm's management controls operating costs, including excessive perquisite consumption, and other direct agency costs. More precisely, the difference in the ratios of a firm with a certain ownership and management structure and the no-agency-cost base case firm, multiplied by the assets of the former, gives the excess agency cost related expense in dollars.

The second ratio is a measure of how effectively the firm's management deploys its assets. In contrast to the expense ratio, agency costs are inversely related to the sales-to-asset ratio. A firm whose sales-to-asset ratio is lower than the base case firm experiences positive agency cost. These costs arise because the manager acts in some or all of the following ways: makes poor investment decisions, exerts insufficient effort, resulting in lower revenues; consumes executive perquisites, so that the firm purchases unproductive assets, such as excessively fancy office space, office furnishing, automobiles, and resort properties.

These efficiency ratios are not measured without error. Sources of measurement error include differences in the accounting methods chosen with respect to the recognition and timing of revenues and costs, poor record-keeping typical of small businesses, and the tendency of small-business owners to exercise flexibility with respect to certain cost items. For example, owners may raise/lower expenses, including their own pay, when profits are high/low. Fortunately, these items are sources of random measurement errors that may be reduced with a larger sample across firms in different industries and age.

B. Ownership structure

The corporate form of organization, with the limited-liability provision that makes it more efficient for risk-sharing than proprietorships or partnerships, allows the firm to expand and raise funds from a large number of investors.[5] Thus, it has a richer set of ownership and management structures. The NSSBF provides four variables that we use to capture various aspects of the ownership structure of small-business corporations: (i) the ownership share of the primary owner, (ii) an indicator for firms where a single family controls more than 50 percent of the firm's shares, (iii) the number of nonmanager shareholders,[6] and, (iv) an indicator for firms managed by a shareholder rather than an outsider.

According to theory, agency costs should be inversely related to the ownership share of the primary owner. For a primary owner who is also the firm's manager, the incentive to consume perquisites declines as his ownership share rises, because his share of the firm's profits rises with ownership while his benefits from perquisite consumption are constant. For a primary owner who employs an outside manager, the gains from monitoring in the form of reduced agency costs increase with his ownership stake. Here, the primary owner fulfills the monitoring role that large blockholders perform at publicly traded corporations.

Agency costs should be lower at firms where a single family controls more than 50 percent of the firm's equity. At a small, closely held corporation where a single family controls the firm, the controlling family also fulfills the monitoring role that large blockholders perform at publicly traded corporations. Due to more diffused ownership among older businesses with larger families, however, monitoring by family members whose interests may not always be aligned should be less effective than monitoring by a sole owner.

Agency costs should increase with the number of nonmanager shareholders. As the number of shareholders increases, the free-rider problem reduces the incentives for limited-liability shareholders to monitor. With less monitoring, agency costs increase. Hence, we hypothesize that the expense and asset-utilization ratios should be positively and negatively related to the natural logarithm of one plus the number of nonmanaging shareholders, respectively.[7]

Finally, agency costs should be higher at firms managed by an outsider. This relationship follows directly from the agency theory of Jensen and Meckling (1976). As noted above, this is the extreme case where the manager gains 100 percent of perquisite consumption, but little of the firm's profits.

C. External monitoring by banks

Banks play a pivotal role in small business financing because they are the major source of external funds for such firms. Cole, Wolken, and Woodburn (1996) report that more than 60 percent of the dollar amount of small business credit outstanding takes the form of bank loans. Petersen and Rajan (1994), Berger and Udell (1995), and Cole (1998) argue and present evidence that firm-creditor relationships generate valuable information about borrower quality.

Because banks generally require a firm's managers to report results honestly and to run the business efficiently with profit, bank monitoring complements shareholder monitoring of managers, indirectly reducing owner-manager agency costs. That is, by incurring monitoring costs to safeguard their loans, banks lead firms to operate

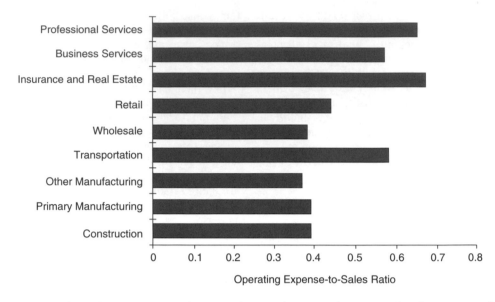

Figure 4.1 Operating expense-to-sales ratio by one-digit SIC for a sample of 1,708 small corporations.

more efficiently by better utilizing assets and moderating perquisite consumption in order to improve the firm's reported financial performance to the bank. Thus, lower priority claimants, such as outside shareholders, should realize a positive externality from bank monitoring, in the form of lower agency costs. Additionally, local bankers' ability to acquire knowledge concerning the firms from various local sources, such as churches, social gatherings, and interactions with the firm's customers and suppliers, makes them especially good monitors. We use two variables to represent bankers' incentive, cost, and ability to monitor: the number of banks used by the firm and the length of the firm's longest banking relationship.[8]

The bank's cost of monitoring is proxied by the number of banks from which the firm obtains financial services. The incentive for each bank to monitor may decrease as the number of banks with which the firm deals increases (Diamond (1984)). Part of the reduced incentive to monitor is due to a form of lenders' free-rider problems, and part is due to the shorter expected length of banking relationships when there is a greater perceived likelihood of the firm switching its banking business between banks.

The bank's ability to monitor is proxied by the length of a firm's relationship with its primary bank. A longer relationship enables the bank to generate information about the firm that is useful in deciding its creditworthiness (Diamond (1984)). Both Petersen and Rajan (1994) and Cole (1998) find that longer relationships improve the availability of credit to small firms while Berger and Udell (1995) find that longer relationships improve the terms of credit available to small firms.

The bank's incentive to monitor is proxied by the firm's debt-to-asset ratio. Because our sample consists entirely of small businesses, virtually all of the firm's debt is private rather than public, and the majority of this debt is in the form of bank loans. As leverage increases, so does the risk of default by the firm, hence the incentive for the lender to monitor the firm. While the primary purpose of this monitoring is to prevent risk-shifting by shareholders to debtholders, increased monitoring should also inhibit excessive perquisite consumption

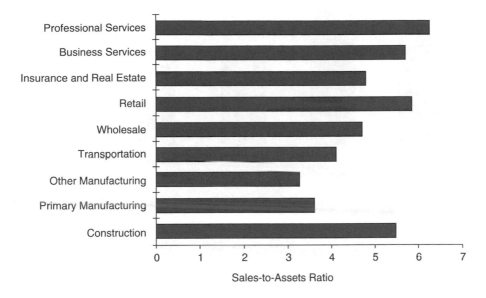

Figure 4.2 Sales-to-asset ratio by one-digit SIC for a sample of 1,708 small corporations.

by managers. (Most of the sample firms' nonbank debt is in the form of loans from finance companies and other nonbank private lenders, who also have greater incentive to monitor the firm as leverage increases.)

D. Control variables

We realize that the length of banking relationship variable may be correlated with firm age, which in turn could be related to a firm's efficiency. Due to the effects of learning curve and survival bias, older firms are likely to be more efficient than younger ones and, especially, than start-up firms. Hence, we include firm age as a control variable in all our tests involving the variable measuring the length of the firm's relationship with its primary bank.

Both of our efficiency ratios vary widely across industries because of the varying importance of inventory and fixed assets. Figure 4.1 shows the ratio of operating expenses to sales by one-digit SIC. These ratios vary from a low of 0.39 for construction and manufacturing to a high

of 0.65 for finance and real estate and professional services. Figure 4.2 shows the ratio of annual sales to total assets by one-digit SIC. This efficiency ratio ranges from 3.6 for manufacturing to 6.2 for professional services. Hence, these figures underscore the importance of controlling for differences across industries in our analysis of agency costs. We do this by including a set of 35 dummy variables, one for each two-digit SIC that accounts for more than one percent of our sample of firms.

Small firms such as those surveyed by the NSSBF seem likely to realize scale economies in operating expenses (e.g., overhead items). Thus, there is a need to control for firm size. This adjustment is especially important for comparisons of operating expenses across firms where the difference in average size is of several orders of magnitude, as it is with the small businesses in our sample. Figure 4.3 confirms this, showing that the operating-expense-to-sales ratio declines monotonically by sales quartile, decreasing from 0.56 for the smallest quartile to 0.38 for the largest quartile. If we regress the expense-to-sales ratio against annual sales, we find a

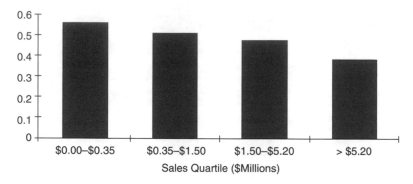

Figure 4.3 Operating expense-to-sales ratio by sales quartile for a sample of 1,708 small corporations.

negative relationship that is statistically significant at better than the 1 percent level ($t = -6.9$).

It is not clear, however, that efficiency in scale economies is realized as measured by the ratio of sales to assets, where both the numerator and denominator are popular alternative measures of size. Indeed, Figure 4.4 shows that the ratio of sales to assets is higher for the two middle sales quartiles than for either the largest or smallest quartile, suggesting, if any, a quadratic relationship. When we regress the sales-to-asset ratio against sales we find a positive but statistically insignificant relationship ($t = 0.18$). Similar results are obtained when the sales-to-asset ratio is regressed against the natural logarithm of sales.

III. RESULTS AND ANALYSIS

A. Some preliminary results regarding the separation of ownership and control

We first examine how agency costs vary with the separation of ownership and control—that is, whether the firm's manager is a shareholder or an outsider with no ownership stake. This analysis may offer some insights into the effects of managerial alignment with owners on equity agency costs.[9] Table 4.1 compares the agency costs of firms under two

types of managers: owners versus outsiders. Panel A shows results when agency costs are measured by the ratio of operating expenses to annual sales; Panel B shows results when agency costs are measured by the ratio of annual sales to total assets. It is important to note here and in all subsequent analyses that the expected signs for the expense ratio and the asset utilization ratio are opposite to each other. Higher sales-to-assets ratios are associated with greater efficiency and lower agency costs, whereas higher expense-to-sales ratios are associated with less efficiency and higher agency costs.

A.1. Agency costs as measured by the ratio of operating expenses to annual sales

In Panel A of Table 4.1, columns 2 and 3 show the number of observations and the mean (median) ratios of operating expenses (which does not include salary to managers), to sales for firms whose manager is an owner. Columns 4 and 5 show the same information for firms whose manager is an outsider. Consistent with our prior expectations, most small businesses are managed by shareholders rather than by outsiders (1,249, or 73 percent of the 1,708 sample firms). However, there is not an insignificant number of firms that hire outside managers (459, or 27 percent of the sample). Thus, there appear to be a sufficient number of

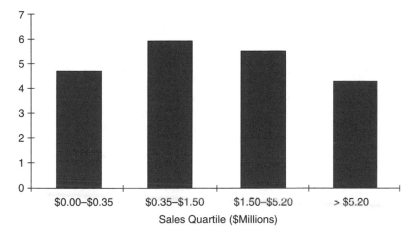

Figure 4.4 Sales-to-asset ratio by sales quartile for a sample of 1,708 small corporations.

firms in these two groups for making meaningful statistical comparisons of their operating expense ratios.

We find that both the median and average ratios of operating expenses to annual sales are considerably higher for firms managed by outsiders (column 5) than for firms owned by shareholders (column 3). For the full sample (line 1 of Panel A), the average ratios of operating expenses to assets at insider-managed firms and outsider-managed firms are 46.9 percent and 51.9 percent, respectively; the 5.0 percentage-point difference in these means is statistically significant at the 1 percent level.

Our data enable us to provide a rough estimate of the agency costs per year attributable to the nonalignment of outside managers and shareholders. A back-of-the-envelope calculation shows that, in absolute dollars, a five-percentage-point difference implies that the operating expenses at a firm with median annual sales of $1.3 million are $65,000 per year higher when an outsider rather than a shareholder manages the firm. The present values of these residual equity agency costs are of course several times higher.[10]

Included in the full sample are 515 firms in which the primary owner controls all of the firm's equity. At 368 of these 515 firms, the owner also serves as manager; at 147 firms, the owner employs an outsider as manager. The former group fits the definition of our no-agency-cost base case, where the manager owns 100 percent of the firm and the interests of manager and owner are completely aligned. For the latter group, the interests of owner and manager are completely unaligned. Thus, these groups are of interest because they represent the two ends of the Jensen and Meckling's spectrum of ownership and managerial structures. Line 2 of Panel A in Table 4.1 shows that the ratio of operating expenses to sales for the no-agency-cost base case firm, where the manager owns 100 percent of the firm's equity, is 46.4 percent, as compared with 49.8 percent for firms whose owners hold all of the firms' equity but hire an outside manager. For these two groups of firms, the difference in operating expense ratios is 3.4 percentage points. Although this univariate difference in means is not statistically significant, a multiple regression model that corrects for size and industry effect, shown in Table 4.3 later, indicates that firms hiring outside managers have operating expenses that are 5.4 percent greater than those at firms managed by a shareholder.

Also included in the full sample are 1,001 firms in which the primary owner holds a controlling interest of more than half of the firm's equity. As shown in Table 4.1, Panel A, line 3, the ratio of operating expenses to sales for these firms is 2.8 percentage points lower when the owner manages the firm than when the owner hires an outside manager. However, this difference is not statistically significant.

There are also 1,249 firms in which a single family holds a controlling interest of more than half of the firm's equity. As shown in line 4 of Panel A, the average ratio of operating expenses to sales for these firms is 3.9 percentage points higher when the firm is managed by an outsider than when the firm is managed by a shareholder. This difference is statistically significant at the 5 percent level.

One final group of interest is composed of 336 firms in which no person or family holds a controlling interest of more than 50 percent of the firm's equity. As predicted, because of the more diffuse ownership of these firms, the average ratio of operating expenses to sales is indeed much higher: 7.2 percentage points more at firms managed by outsiders than at firms managed by shareholders. This difference is statistically significant at the 5 percent level. To confirm that our finding is robust with respect to sample distributions, we also perform non-parametric tests on the difference between the medians, and find similar results.

A.2. Agency costs as measured by the ratio of annual sales to total assets

In Panel B of Table 4.1 we present results from a similar analysis of agency costs, but here we measure agency costs by the ratio of annual sales to total assets rather than the ratio of operating expenses to annual sales.[11] As predicted, the results show that the sales-to-asset ratios are higher in all categories of shareholder-managed firms versus outsider-managed firms. This is true for the full sample of 1,249 firms (line 1) and for the subsamples where the primary owner holds all of the firm's equity (line 2), where the primary owner holds a controlling

interest in the firm (line 3), where a single family holds a controlling interest in the firm (line 4), and where no individual or family owns more than half of the firm (line 5).

For the full sample, displayed in line 1, the average sales-to-asset ratio at insider-managed firms is almost 10 percent higher than at outsider-managed firms at 4.76 and 4.35, respectively. The 0.41 difference in these means is statistically significant at the 10 percent level. This difference implies that the revenues of a median-size firm, which has $438,000 in total assets, are $180,000 per year higher when a shareholder rather than an outsider manages the firm. In each of the remaining four comparisons (lines 2–5 of Panel B), the average ratio of annual sales to total assets also is greater when the firm is managed by a shareholder than when the firm is managed by an outsider. However, this difference is statistically significant at least at the 10 percent level only when the primary owner holds a controlling interest in the firm (line 3).

Overall, the results displayed in Table 4.1 suggest that both the ratio of operating expenses to annual sales and the ratio of annual sales to total assets are adequate proxies for small corporations' agency costs. Each provides results consistent with the predictions of agency theory for a wide range of potentially high to low agency cost organizational and management structures.

A.3. Determinants of high- and low-agency cost firms

Table 4.2 presents descriptive statistics for the variables hypothesized to explain agency costs. Statistics are presented both for the entire sample and for two groups of firms constructed by dividing the entire sample in half, based on the sample's median ratios of agency costs. For the entire sample (Panel A), ownership and control is highly concentrated. On average, a shareholder manages the firm 73 percent of the time, the primary owner controls 65 percent of the firm's equity, and a single family owns a controlling interest in the firm 73 percent of the time. The average

Table 4.1 Agency Costs, Ownership Structure, and Managerial Alignment with Shareholders

Agency costs are presented for a sample of 1,708 small corporations divided into two groups of firms: those managed by owners (aligned with shareholders) and those managed by an outsider (not aligned with shareholders). Agency costs are proxied alternatively by the ratio of operating expenses to annual sales and the ratio of annual sales to total assets. Separate analyses are presented for each agency cost proxy and for subgroups where the primary owner owns 100 percent of the firm, where the primary owner owns more than half of the firm, where a single family owns more than half of the firm, and where no owner or family owns more than half of the firm. The last column shows the difference between the mean (median) ratios of the outsider-managed firms and the insider-managed firms. Statistical significance of the differences in the mean ratios is based on the *t*-statistic from a parametric test (based on the assumption of unequal variances) of whether the difference in the mean ratios of the two groups of firms is significantly different from zero. Statistical significance of the differences in the median ratios is based on a chi-square statistic from a nonparametric test of whether the two groups are from populations with the same median (Mood (1950)). Data are taken from the Federal Reserve Board's National Survey of Small Business Finances.

| | Type of Manager | | | | |
| | Owner-Manager | | Outsider-Manager | | Difference |
	Number of Firms	Ratio Mean (Median)	Number of Firms	Ratio Mean (Median)	in Means (in Median)
Panel A: Operating Expense-to-Annual Sales Ratio					
All firms	1,249	46.9 (42.0)	459	51.9 (52.2)	5.0*** (10.2)***
Primary owner owns 100 percent of the firm	368	46.4 (41.7)	147	49.8 (47.6)	3.4 (5.9)**
Primary owner owns >50 percent of the firm	743	46.8 (41.5)	258	49.6 (47.7)	2.8 (6.2)**
A single family owns >50 percent of the firm	943	46.2 (41.7)	306	50.1 (49.0)	3.9** (7.3)***
No owner or family owns >50 percent of the firm	220	48.1 (42.7)	116	55.3 (55.6)	7.2** (12.9)***
Panel B: Annual Sales-to-Total Assets Ratio					
All firms	1,249	4.76 (3.18)	459	4.35 (2.88)	−0.41* (−0.30)*
Primary owner owns 100 percent of the firm	368	5.35 (3.54)	147	4.78 (3.33)	−0.57 (−0.21)
Primary owner owns >50 percent of the firm	743	5.08 (3.33)	258	4.49 (3.13)	−0.59* (−0.20)
A single family owns >50 percent of the firm	943	4.74 (3.19)	306	4.41 (3.07)	−0.33 (−0.12)
No owner or family owns >50 percent of the firm	220	4.63 (3.14)	116	3.89 (2.49)	−0.74 (−0.65)**

*, **,*** indicate statistical significance at the 10, 5, and 1 percent levels, respectively.

Table 4.2 Descriptive Statistics for Variables Used to Analyze Agency Costs

Selected variables used to study agency costs at a sample of 1,708 small corporations are identified in column 1, the sample means and medians appear in columns 2 and 3. In columns 4 and 5 (columns 7 and 8) are the means for two groups of firms constructed by splitting the sample into two equal-size groups of 854 firms based on the entire sample's median operating expense-to-annual sales ratio (annual sales-to-total asset ratio). Column 6 (column 9) shows the difference in the two groups' means, and the results from a t-test for significant differences in the means of the low- and high-ratio groups of firms. Data are from the Federal Reserve Board's National Survey of Small Business Finances.

(1)	Panel A		Panel B Operating Expense-to-Assets Ratio Groups			Panel C Sales-to-Assets Ratio Groups		
	Mean (2)	Median (3)	Below Median (4)	Above Median (5)	Difference (6)	Below Median (7)	Above Median (8)	Difference (9)
Ownership variables								
Firm manager is a shareholder	0.73	1	0.78	0.69	0.09***	0.71	0.75	−0.04*
One family owns >50 percent of the firm	0.73	1	0.75	0.71	0.04*	0.72	0.74	−0.02
Ownership share of primary owner	0.65	0.54	0.66	0.64	0.02	0.62	0.68	−0.06***
Number of nonmanager shareholders	3.51	1	3.89	3.14	0.75**	2.35	4.68	−2.33***
External monitoring variables								
Length of the longest banking relationship (years)	10.6	8	11.3	10.0	1.3***	11.5	9.7	1.8***
Number of banking relationships	1.65	1	1.75	1.56	0.19***	1.73	1.58	0.15***
Debt-to-asset ratio	0.60	0.52	0.61	0.58	0.03	0.55	0.64	−0.09***
Control variables								
Annual sales ($millions)	5.9	1.3	8.2	3.6	4.6***	6.1	5.7	0.4
Firm age (years)	17.6	14	18.4	16.8	1.6**	19.0	16.2	2.8***

*, **, *** indicate statistical significance at the 10, 5, and 1 percent levels, respectively.

number of nonmanager shareholders is 3.51, but this statistic is strongly influenced by extreme values, as the median number of nonmanager shareholders is one. The average firm's longest banking relationship is 10.6 years. The average firm maintains relationships with 1.65 banks, reports $5.9 million in annual sales, is 17.6 years old, and has a debt-to-asset ratio of 0.60.

When we split the sample into low-expense and high-expense ratio groups (Panel B), we observe strong differences in the two groups. Based on *t*-tests for significant differences in the means of the two groups, the high-expense firms are less likely to be managed by a shareholder, are less likely to be controlled by one family, have fewer nonmanaging shareholders, have shorter and fewer banking relationships, report lower sales, and are younger than the low-expense firms. Similar results are obtained when the top third and bottom third of the sample are compared.

When we split the sample into low and high asset-utilization groups (Panel C), we also find strong differences in the two groups. Low-efficiency firms are less likely to be managed by a shareholder, have lower percentage ownership by the primary owner, have fewer nonmanaging shareholders, have longer and more numerous banking relationships, have lower debt-to-asset ratios, and are older than high-efficiency firms.

B. Multivariate regression results explaining agency costs

Tables 4.3 and 4.4 present the results obtained from estimating multivariate regressions to explain the determinants of our two proxies for agency costs, the ratio of operating expenses to annual sales and of annual sales to total assets. Each proxy is regressed against the ownership, external monitoring, and control variables introduced and discussed in Section II These regressions compare the relative, as well as the absolute, agency costs of various ownership structures vis-à-vis the no-agency-cost base case—the 100 percent manager-owned firm.

B.1. Agency costs as measured by the ratio of operating expenses to annual sales

Table 4.3 presents the results from multivariate regressions analyzing agency costs as measured by the ratio of operating expenses to annual sales. Column 1 identifies the explanatory variable and columns 2 through 9 display parameter estimates for eight different model specifications. In columns 2 through 8 we analyze each of the seven ownership structures, external monitoring, and capital structure variables independently. In column 9 we test whether the independent results stand up when all seven variables are included in a single regression. Because of the importance of industry structure and economies of scale, as established in Section II, we include in each regression variables to control for firm size and industry effects. Our measure of size is the logarithm of annual sales, and our controls for industry are 35 two-digit SIC indicator variables, one for each two-digit standard industrial classification that accounts for more than one percent of our sample of firms.

In column 2 of Table 4.3 we find that a firm managed by a shareholder has agency costs that are 5.4 percentage points lower than those at firms managed by an outsider. This is very close to the 5.0 percentage point difference reported for all firms in Panel A of Table 4.1. For a firm with the $1.3 million median annual sales, the coefficient in column 2 of Table 4.3 implies agency costs of approximately $70,000.

In column 3 of Table 4.3 we find that a firm in which one family owns a controlling interest has agency costs that are 3.0 percentage points lower than other firms. For the median-size firm, this implies agency costs of approximately $39,000. In column 4, we find that agency costs decline by 0.082 percentage points for each percentage point increase in the ownership share of the firm's primary owner. This implies that a median-size firm where the primary owner has a 100 percent share has agency costs that are approximately $105,000, or

Table 4.3 Determinants of Agency Costs at Small Corporations

The dependent variable proxying for agency costs is the ratio of operating expense to annual sales. There are four groups of independent variables: common ownership/managerial alignment variables, external monitoring variables, capital structure variables, and control variables. Sample size is 1,708. Each specification includes a set of 35 dummy variables indicating each two-digit SIC that accounts for more than one percent of the sample of firms. Data are from the Federal Reserve Board's National Survey of Small Business Finances.

(1)	(2)	(3)	(4)	(5)	(6)	(7)	(8)	(9)
Intercept	94.7***	91.7***	74.9***	91.3***	88.3***	87.4***	88.7***	104.5***
	(17.4)	(16.9)	(17.1)	(17.2)	(16.9)	(16.6)	(16.9)	(17.3)
Ownership variables								
Manager is a shareholder	−5.4***							−5.7***
	(−4.1)							(−4.3)
One family owns >50 percent of the firm		−3.0**						−0.4
		(−2.2)						(−0.3)
Ownership share of primary owner			−8.2***					−8.6***
			(−3.9)					(−2.8)
Log of the number of nonmanager stockholders				1.9***				0.01
				(2.8)				(0.1)
External monitoring variables								
Length of the longest banking relationship					−0.22***			−0.3***
					(−3.2)			(−3.4)
Number of banking relationships						−1.1*		−1.0*
						(−1.9)		(−1.7)
Debt-to-asset ratio							−0.6	−0.7
							(−0.6)	(−0.7)
Control variables								
Two-digit SIC dummies	Yes	Yes	Yes	Yes	Yes	Yes	Yes	Yes
Log of annual sales	−2.9***	−3.1***	−3.1***	−3.1***	−2.6***	−2.6***	−2.8***	−2.9***
	(−8.8)	(−8.6)	(−9.0)	(−8.8)	(−7.8)	(−7.4)	(−8.3)	(−7.9)
Firm age					0.03			0.02
					(0.6)			(0.4)
Regression summary statistics								
Adjusted R^2	0.246	0.241	0.245	0.242	0.244	0.240	0.239	0.259
F-statistic	16.04***	15.63***	16.00***	15.73***	15.50***	15.57***	15.46***	14.57***

*, **, *** indicate statistical significance at the 10, 5, and 1 percent levels, respectively.

8.1 percentage points, lower than those at a firm where the primary owner has only a one percent share. Each of the variables analyzed in columns 2 through 4 is statistically significant at least at the 5 percent level.

In column 5 of Table 4.3 we analyze (the natural logarithm of one plus) the number of nonmanager shareholders. We expect a positive relationship between agency costs and this variable, as the returns to monitoring decrease and free-rider problems increase with the number of nonmanager shareholders. We use the natural logarithm rather than the level of this variable because we expect that the relationship is stronger at smaller values of the variable. The estimated coefficient is positive and significant at better than the one percent level, confirming our expectations. For a firm with 30 non-manager shareholders, the maximum value imposed by our cap at the 95th percentile, the estimated coefficient of 1.9 implies that agency costs are 6.5 percentage points higher, or $85,000 greater, than at a firm with zero nonmanager shareholders.

In columns 6 and 7 of Table 4.3 we analyze the two bank monitoring variables: the length of the firm's longest banking relationship and the firm's number of banking relationships. As discussed in Section II, we expect agency costs to vary inversely with the length of the longest banking relationship and directly with the number of banking relationships. To distinguish between the private information generated by bank monitoring and the public information generated by a firm's durability, we also include firm age in the specification analyzing the length of the firm's longest banking relationship.

As shown in column 6 of Table 4.3, agency costs are reduced by a statistically significant 0.22 percent for each additional year in the length of the firm's longest banking relationship. The coefficient on firm age is not significantly different from zero. In column 7, however, a related variable, the number of banking relationships, is negative and statistically significant at better than the 10 percent level. This

finding conflicts with our hypothesis in which multiple banking relationships reduce each bank's incentive to monitor, and, therefore, increase agency costs. One possible explanation reconciling the two seemingly contradictory results is that the number of banking relationships may proxy for factors other than the banks' incentive to monitor the firm. The most prominent explanations are the increasing financial sophistication and maturity of the firms and their managers, and regulatory limitations on loans to a single borrower, which may constrain a small bank's ability to supply funds to a larger firm.

In column 8 of Table 4.3 we analyze the complex relation between capital structure and ownership on agency costs. As discussed in Section II, we expect an inverse relationship between agency costs and the debt-to-asset ratio. We do, indeed, find a negative relationship, but the coefficient is not significantly different from zero.

In each of the seven specifications displayed in columns 2 through 8 of Table 4.3, observe that our size variable, the natural logarithm of annual sales, is negative and statistically significant at better than the 1 percent level, which is strong evidence of economies of scale. Not shown in Table 4.3 are statistics indicating that at least 20 of the 35 two-digit SIC indicator variables included in each specification are statistically significant at least at the 5 percent level. These findings underscore the critical importance of controlling for differences across industries when examining the operating expense-to-sales ratio. The adjusted R^2 for each of the seven specifications in columns 2 through 8 indicates that the models explain approximately one-quarter of the variability in the ratio of operating expenses to annual sales.

Our final specification appears in column 9 of Table 4.3, where we include each of four of the ownership variables, the two bank-monitoring variables, and the capital structure variable, along with the control variables for firm size, age, and industrial classification. We find that each of the four ownership variables has the predicted sign. However, only two of the four—the indicator variable for shareholder-managed firm and the variable for the ownership share of the primary owner—are statistically significant, but each is significant at better than the 1 percent level. The statistical insignificance of the other two ownership variables may be attributable to the high correlation among the ownership variables. The significant coefficients indicate that agency costs at a firm managed by a shareholder are 5.7 percentage points lower than those at a firm managed by an outsider, and that agency costs are reduced by 0.086 percentage points for each percentage point increase in the primary owner's ownership share. This latter result supports the hypothesis that large shareholders make more effective monitors (Shleifer and Vishny (1986) and Zeckhauser and Pound (1990)).[12]

Both of the external monitoring variables are negative and significant, just as they are in columns 6 and 7. The debt-to-asset ratio is negative but not significantly different from zero, just as it is in column 8. Overall, the results displayed in column 9 generally confirm the findings when the analysis variables are examined independently in columns 2 through 8.

B.2. Agency costs as measured by the ratio of annual sales to total assets

Table 4.4 displays the results from multivariate regressions analyzing agency costs as measured by the ratio of annual sales to total assets. In interpreting these results, it is important to remember that the sales-to-asset ratio varies inversely with agency costs. As in Table 4.3, column 1 identifies the explanatory variables and columns 2 through 9 display parameter estimates for different specifications of the regression model. In columns 2 through 8, we analyze each of seven ownership structure, external monitoring, and capital structure variables independently. In column 9, we test whether the independent results stand up when all seven are included in a single regression.

Because of the importance of industry structure, established in Section II, we include in each regression a series of 35 two-digit SIC indicator variables, one for each two-digit standard industrial classification that accounts for more than one percent of our sample of firms. We include the natural logarithm of annual sales as a measure of size, because Figure 4.4 suggests a possible quadratic relationship between sales and the ratio of sales-to-asset ratio.

Column 2 of Table 4.4 shows that a firm managed by a shareholder has a sales-to-asset ratio that is 0.51 greater than that of a firm managed by an outsider, and this coefficient is statistically significant at better than the 5 percent level. This evidence supports the hypothesis that agency costs are higher when an outsider manages the firm. In column 3, we see that the variable indicating those firms in which one family owns a controlling interest has a coefficient that is positive but not significantly different from zero. Column 4 shows that the coefficient on the ownership share of the primary owner is positive and significant at better than the 1 percent level. The coefficient indicates that the sales-to-asset ratio increases by 0.012 for each percentage point increase in the ownership share of the firm's primary owner. This finding supports the hypothesis that agency costs decrease as the ownership becomes more concentrated. Column 5 shows that the coefficient on (the natural logarithm of) the number of nonmanager stockholders is negative and statistically significant at better than the 1 percent level, supporting the hypothesis that agency costs increase as the free-rider problem worsens.

In columns 6 and 7 of Table 4.4 we analyze the two bank monitoring variables: the length of the firm's longest banking relationship and the number of the firm's banking relationships. Once again, to distinguish between the private information generated by bank monitoring and the public information generated by a firm's durability, we also include firm age in the specification analyzing the length of the firm's longest banking relationship. As shown in column 6, the length of the firm's longest banking relationship variable is

Table 4.4 Determinants of Agency Costs at Small Corporations

The dependent variable proxying for agency costs is the ratio of annual sales to total assets. There are four groups of independent variables: common ownership/managerial alignment variables, external monitoring variables, capital structure variables, and control variables. Sample size is 1,708. Each specification includes a set of 35 dummy variables indicating each two-digit SIC that accounts for more than one percent of the sample of firms. In column 10, the four ownership variables have been orthogonalized. Data are from the Federal Reserve Board's National Survey of Small Business Finances.

(1)	(2)	(3)	(4)	(5)	(6)	(7)	(8)	(9)	(10)
Intercept	2.01*	2.51**	1.27	1.27	2.49**	1.95*	3.26***	1.34	1.17
	(1.9)	(2.4)	(1.2)	(1.2)	(2.5)	(1.9)	(3.2)	(1.2)	(-1.0)
Ownership variables									
Manager is a shareholder	0.51**							0.30	0.46*
	(2.0)							(1.2)	(1.8)
One family owns >50% of the firm		0.087						-0.34	-0.22
		(0.3)						(-1.2)	(-0.8)
Ownership share of primary owner			0.012***					-0.011*	0.012***
			(3.0)					(-1.8)	(3.1)
Log of the number of nonmanager stockholders				-0.82***				-1.05***	-1.05***
				(-6.2)				(-5.4)	(-5.4)
External monitoring variables									
Length of the longest banking relationship					-0.025*			-0.01	-0.01
					(-1.7)			(-0.4)	(-0.4)
Number of banking relationships						-1.09***		-0.50***	-0.50***
						(-4.7)		(-4.3)	(-4.3)
Debt-to-asset ratio							1.05***	1.11***	1.11***
							(5.3)	(5.5)	(5.5)
Control variables									
Two-digit SIC dummies	Yes	Yes	Yes	Yes	Yes	Yes	Yes	Yes	Yes
Log of annual sales	0.05	0.03	0.07	0.18***	0.07	0.11*	0.02	0.28***	0.28***
	(0.7)	(0.5)	(1.1)	(2.7)	(1.1)	(1.7)	(0.3)	(3.9)	(3.9)
Firm age					-0.012			-0.01	-0.01
					(-1.2)			(-0.8)	(-0.8)
Regression summary statistics									
Adjusted R^2	0.032	0.030	0.035	0.051	0.035	0.042	0.045	0.080	0.080
F-statistic	2.51***	2.40***	2.65***	3.49***	2.63***	3.02***	3.23***	4.37***	4.37***

*, **, *** indicate statistical significance at the 10, 5, and 1 percent levels, respectively.

inversely related to the sales-to-asset ratio, and is statistically significant at better than the 10 percent level. This runs counter to our hypothesis that agency costs are lower when a firm's bank has had more time to develop valuable private information about the firm. However, this variable is not significantly different from zero in the full specification shown in column 9. In column 7 we see that a related variable, number of banking relationships, is negative and statistically significant at better than the 1 percent level. This latter finding supports the hypothesis that the values of a bank's monitoring effort and private information about a firm are dissipated when the firm obtains financial services from multiple sources, but, on the whole, the results regarding the bank monitoring variables are ambiguous.

In column 8 we analyze the effect of capital structure on the sales-to-asset ratio. The results indicate that firms with higher debt ratios have higher sales-to-asset ratios, and that this relationship is statistically significant at better than the 1 percent level. This finding is supportive of a version of the theory put forth by Williams (1987) that additional debt decreases agency costs.

Not shown in Table 4.4 are the results concerning the industry indicator variables. In each specification, at least 20 of the 35 two-digit SIC indicator variables are significant at the 5 percent level. Once again, this finding underscores the critical importance of controlling for differences across industries when comparing agency costs.

Our final specification appears in column 9 of Table 4.4, where we include each of the four ownership variables, the two monitoring variables, and the capital structure variable, along with the control variables for firm size, age, and industrial classification. We find that only two of the four correlated ownership variables are statistically significant at better than the 10 percent level. The natural logarithm of the number of nonmanager shareholders varies inversely with the sales-to-asset ratio and is significant at better than the 1 percent level. The primary owner's ownership share switches

from positive and significant at better than the 1 percent level in column 4 to negative and significant at better than the 10 percent level in column 9. This counterintuitive finding may be attributable to the high correlation of the ownership share variable with the log of number of nonmanager shareholders ($\rho = -0.75$).

Both of the external monitoring variables are inversely related to the sales-to-asset ratio, as they are in columns 6 and 7, when these variables are analyzed independently. However, the length of the longest banking relationship variable no longer even approaches statistical significance ($t = -0.3$), but the number of banking relationships is significant at better than the 1 percent level. The debt-to-asset ratio remains positive and significant at better than the 1 percent level, as it is in column 8. Overall, the results displayed in column 9 tend to confirm the findings previously discussed when the analysis variables are examined one-by-one in columns 2 through 8.

To test whether the correlations among the ownership variables are responsible for this finding, we orthogonalize the four ownership variables and then reestimate the model specification appearing in column 9. The results of this reestimation, which appear in column 10, confirm our suspicions. Three of the four ownership variables are statistically significant at least at the 10 percent level.[13] The log of the number of shareholders remains negative and significant at better than the 1 percent level, but the primary owner's ownership share switches back from negative to positive and also is significant at better than the 1 percent level. The dummy indicating that the firm is managed by a shareholder also is positive, but is significant at only the 10 percent level. The dummy indicating that a family controls the firm is not significantly different from zero. In sum, the results for the four ownership variables are not qualitatively different from those reported in columns 2 through 5, when each of these variables is examined independently, and provide strong support for the agency-cost theory of Jensen and Meckling (1976).[14]

IV. SUMMARY AND CONCLUSIONS

In this article, we use data on small businesses to examine how agency costs vary with a firm's ownership structure. Because the managerial ownership of small firms is highly variable, with a range from zero to 100 percent, we are able to estimate a firm's agency costs across a wide variety of management and ownership structures.[15] By comparing the efficiency of firms that are managed by shareholders with the efficiency of firms managed by outsiders, we can calculate the agency costs attributable to the separation of ownership and control.

We also examine the determinants of agency costs in a multivariate regression framework and find that our results support predictions put forth by the theories of Jensen and Meckling (1976) and Fama and Jensen (1983a) about ownership structure, organizational form, and the alignment of managers' and shareholders' interests. First, we find that agency costs are higher when an outsider manages the firm. Second, we find that agency costs vary inversely with the manager's ownership share. Third, we find that agency costs increase with the number of nonmanager shareholders. Fourth, we also find that, to a lesser extent, external monitoring by banks produces a positive externality in the form of lower agency costs.

NOTES

*   Ang is from Florida State University; Cole is from The University of Auckland, New Zealand; and Lin is from Montana State University. We appreciate the comments of David Mauer, Michael Long, René Stulz (the editor), and an anonymous referee.

1   Theoretical support for the null hypothesis is due to Demsetz (1983), who suggests that the sum of amenities for on-the-job consumption and take-home pay for similar quality managers is the same for both high-cost and low-cost monitoring organizations. The proportion paid to the managers, however, differs according to the cost of monitoring. Here, it would seem that total operating expense, which include direct pay to the managers as well as perks and firm level monitoring cost, is the appropriate measure to test the hypothesis.

2   Data from the NSSBF yield significant and interesting results that appear in several recent published papers. See the studies on banking relationships and credit markets by Petersen and Rajan (1994, 1995, 1997), Berger and Udell (1995), and Cole (1998).

3   The staff at the Federal Reserve Board partially edited the financial statement items for violations of accounting rules, such as when gross profit is not equal to sales less cost of goods sold, and some improbable events such as when accounts receivable are greater than sales, or cost of goods sold equals inventory.

4   Operating expenses are defined as total expenses less cost of goods sold, interest expense, and managerial compensation. Excessive expense on perks and other nonessentials should be reflected in the operating expenses. Strictly speaking, agency costs that are measured by this ratio are those incurred at the firm level (i.e., shirking and perquisite consumption by the managers). This may underestimate total agency costs since this ratio does not fully measure firm-level indirect agency costs, such as the distortion of operating decisions due to agency problems. (See Mello and Parsons (1992) for an attempt to measure such costs in the presence of debt.) Nor does it measure off-income-statement agency costs, such as the private monitoring costs by the nonmanagement shareholders or the private costs of bonding incurred by the manager.

5   Manne (1967) and Alchian and Demsetz (1972) agree that limited liability is an attractive feature of the corporate form of organization. Jensen and Meckling (1976) point out that although unlimited liability gives more incentive for each shareholder to monitor, in the aggregate it leads to excessive monitoring. Thus, it may be more economical to offer a single high premium to creditors to bear risk of nonpayment and, thus, monitoring in exchange for limited liability.

6   Technically, the survey does not provide a variable for the number of nonmanager shareholders. Rather, we define this variable as the number of shareholders for firms that have an outside manager and as the number of shareholders less one for firms that have an insider manager.

7   This formulation recognizes the unequal and diminishing role of additional shareholders, and the problem of undefined zero when there is no other shareholder.

8   These are also the same governance variables used by Berger and Udell (1995) and Cole (1998) in their studies of banking relationship. However, none of their variables, except for the corporate form dummy, are found to significantly affect either the loan term or the use of collateral.

9   In Fama and Jensen (1983a), the delegation of decision control management and residual owner (i.e., hiring of outsiders as managers) is related to the decision skill and the accompanying specialized knowledge that are needed to run the firm. Shareholders, however, still have to bear the costs of monitoring.

10   As a way of comparison, Dong and Dow (1993) estimate that 10 to 20 percent of total labor hours are attributed to supervision or monitoring in the Chinese collective farms. Dobson (1992) finds that X-inefficiency measures 0.2 percent of sales among large U.S. manufacturing firms.

11   The distribution of the sales-to-asset ratio is highly skewed by the presence of large outliers. Consequently, the ratio is capped at the value found at the 95th percentile, a ratio of 19.0.

12   Fama and Jensen (1983) realize that for shareholders to monitor the firm's management they must hold sufficient ownership; however, the cost of large ownership shares is suboptimal risk-taking, and, possibly, underinvestment. Also, Demsetz (1983) suggests that firms with concentrated ownership have lower monitoring costs.

13   The sales-to-asset ratio is likely subject to additional biases that render it much noisier than the operating expense-to-sales ratio. Note that the adjusted-R^2 statistics appearing at the bottoms of Tables 4.3 and 4.4 indicate that we are able to explain about 26 percent of the variability in the latter ratio but only about eight percent of the variability in the former ratio. This led us to investigate additional control variables in the sales-to-asset regression, including the ratio of operating expenses to sales. Results from specifications including the operating expense-to-sales ratio as an additional regressor are not qualitatively different from those in Table 4.4. In no case was the operating expense-to-sales ratio statistically significant at even the 20 percent level. Because we view the operating expense-to-sales ratio as an endogenous variable, we also tested a specification that included a predicted value of this ratio rather than the actual value. The predicted value was obtained using the model appearing in column 9 of Table 4.3. Again, the results from this robustness check are not qualitatively different from those appearing in Table 4.4

14   For the sake of completeness, we also perform the same procedure on the regression equation in column 9 of Table 4.3. We find that orthogonalizing the ownership variables does not qualitatively affect the results. Only the same two ownership variables are statistically significant. Overall, although both measures of agency costs provide qualitatively similar results, the expense ratio regression yields greater explained variations.

15   There are few empirical studies in related areas of corporate finance that analyze ownership, organizational, and management structures in detail. For example, see a study of executive compensation in Israel by Ang, Hauser, and Lauterbach (1997).

REFERENCES

Alchian, Armen A., and Harold Demsetz, 1992, Production, information costs, and economic organization, *American Economic Review* 62, 777–795.

Ang, James S., Samuel Hauser, and Beni Lauterbach, 1997, Top executive compensation under alternate ownership and governance structure, in Mark Hirschey and M. Wayne Marr, eds.: *Advances in Financial Economics* (JAI Press Inc., Greenwich, Conn.).

Arnold, R. J., 1985, Agency costs in banking firms: An analysis of expense preference behavior, *Journal of Economics and Business*, 103–112.

Barclay, Michael J., and Clifford W. Smith Jr., 1995, The maturity structure of corporate debt, *Journal of Finance* 50, 609–632.

Berger, Allen N., and Gregory F. Udell, 1995, Relationship lending and lines of credit in small firm finance, *Journal of Business* 68, 351–382.

Cole, Rebel A., 1998, The importance of relationships to the availability of credit, *Journal of Banking and Finance*, forthcoming.

Cole, Rebel A., and Hamid Mehran, 1998, CEO compensation, ownership structure, and taxation: Evidence from small businesses, mimeo, Northwestern University.

Cole, Rebel A., and John D. Wolken, 1995, Sources and uses of financial services by small businesses: Evidence from the 1993 National Survey of Small Business Finances, *Federal Reserve Bulletin* 81, 629–667.

Cole, Rebel A., John D. Wolken, and Louise Woodburn, 1996, Bank and nonbank competition for small business credit: Evidence from the 1987 and 1993 National Surveys of Small Business Finances, *Federal Reserve Bulletin* 82, 983–995.

Demsetz, Harold, 1983, The structure of ownership and theory of the firm, *Journal of Law and Economics* 26, 375–393.

Demsetz, Harold, and Kenneth Lehn, 1985, The structure of corporate ownership: Causes and consequences, *Journal of Political Economy* 93, 1155–1177.

Denning, Karen C., and Kuldeep Shastri, 1993, Changes in organizational structure and shareholder wealth, *Journal of Financial and Quantitative Analysis* 28, 553–564.

Diamond, Douglas W., 1984, Financial intermediation and delegated monitoring, *Review of Economic Studies* 51, 393–414.

Dobson, John, 1992, Agency costs in U.S. manufacturing: An empirical measure using X-efficiency, *Journal of Economics and Finance* 16, 1–10.

Dong, Xiao Y., and Gregory K. Dow, 1993, Monitoring costs in Chinese agricultural teams, *Journal of Political Economy* 101, 539–553.

Fama, Eugene F., and Michael C. Jensen, 1983a, Separation of ownership and control, *Journal of Law and Economics* 26, 301–325.

Fama, Eugene F., and Michael C. Jensen, 1983b, Agency problems and residual claims, *Journal of Law and Economics* 26, 327–349.

Fama, Eugene F., and Michael C. Jensen, 1985, Organizational forms and investment decisions, *Journal of Financial Economics* 14, 101–119.

Jensen, Michael C., 1986, Agency costs of free cash flow, corporate finance and takeovers, *American Economic Review* 76, 323–329.

Jensen, Michael C., and William H. Meckling, 1976, Theory of the firm: Managerial behavior,

agency costs and capital structure, *Journal of Financial Economics* 3, 305–360.

Kim, Wi S., and Eric H. Sorensen, 1986, Evidence on the impact of the agency costs of debt in corporate debt policy, *Journal of Financial and Quantitative Analysis* 21, 131–144.

Knight, Frank H., 1921, *Risk, Uncertainty and Profit* (University of Chicago Press, Chicago).

Manne, Henry G., 1967, Our two corporate systems: Law and economics, *Virginia Law Review* 53, 259–284.

Mello, Antonio S., and John E. Parsons, 1992, Measuring the agency cost of debt, *Journal of Finance* 47, 1887–1904.

Milgrom, Paul, and John Roberts, 1995, *Economics, Organization, and Management* (Prentice Hall, Englewood Cliffs, N.J.).

Petersen, Mitchell A., and Raghuram G. Rajan, 1994, The benefits of lending relationships: Evidence from small business data, *Journal of Finance* 49, 3–38.

Petersen, Mitchell A., and Raghuram G. Rajan, 1995, The effect of credit market competition on lending relationships, *Quarterly Journal of Economics* 110, 407–442.

Petersen, Mitchell A., and Raghuram G. Rajan, 1997, Trade credit: Theories and evidence, *Review of Financial Studies* 10, 661–691.

Shleifer, Andrei, and Robert Vishny, 1986, Large shareholders and corporate control, *Journal of Political Economy* 94, 461–488.

Williams, Joseph, 1987, Perquisites, risk, and capital structure, *Journal of Finance* 42, 29–48.

Zeckhauser, Richard, and John Pound, 1990, Are large shareholders effective monitors? An investigation of share ownership and corporate performance, in R. G. Hubbard, ed.: *Asymmetric Information, Corporate Finance, and Investment* (University of Chicago Press, Chicago).

Part 2

Equity ownership structure and control

INTRODUCTION

AS SEEN IN PART 1, EFFICACY OF A CORPORATE governance system requires effective monitoring of managers by the shareholders. Shleifer and Vishny (Ch.2) have argued that large shareholders can perform this monitoring function. They also acknowledge that this role imposes costs such as free riding by non-block shareholders who may avoid the monitoring effort but reap the benefits of the block shareholder's monitoring. Large shareholders in this event may only be willing to undertake monitoring if they can expect to receive compensation for their efforts including an appropriate share of the added value that monitoring generates. They may also look to design the securities they hold in the firms with features that guarantee such reward. In the first paper of this part, Hiroshi Osano (Ch.5) addresses the problem of security design that will satisfy a large investor and motivate her to undertake monitoring. The author shows that the optimal security is a debt-like security such as standard debt with a positive probability of default, or debt with call options. Such a design also leads to the financial market equilibrium being Pareto optimal. The remaining three papers by Becht and Röell (Ch.6), Faccio and Lang (Ch.7) and Goergen and Renneboog (Ch.8) present empirical evidence on the ownership structure of European corporations with particular focus on block shareholdings and control exercised through pyramidal structures. Pyramidal structures allow block holders to control vast groups of companies with relatively small investment capital.

Becht and Röell (Ch.6) find the most salient finding is the extraordinarily high degree of concentration of shareholder voting power in Continental Europe relative to the USA and the UK. Thus the relationship between large controlling shareholders and weak minority shareholders is at least as important to understand as the more commonly studied interface between management and dispersed shareholders. Faccio and Lang (Ch.7) report similar findings of high concentration in Western Europe excluding the UK but they also provide a rich analysis of the ownership structure of Western European corporations including pyramids, cross-shareholdings, multiple control chains, etc. They employ a mechanism to differentiate control (i.e. voting rights from cash flow rights and report the relative importance of each). Faccio and Lang find that both dispersed shareholdings and family controlled shareholdings are prevalent with the former more common in the UK and Ireland and the latter in Continental Europe. This pattern also differs between financial and non-financial firms. This paper is important in order to understand the ownership pattern in Europe and how it may influence corporate financial behaviour.

Goergen and Renneboog (Ch.8) make an interesting comparison between the UK and Germany in terms of their ownership structure and how such a structure leads to different outcomes after initial public offerings in terms of takeover incidence, the ownership structure of bidders, and the differential characteristics of acquired firms that attract concentrated and dispersed acquirers. Goergen and Renneboog relate these differences to the differences in shareholder rights and laws protecting minority shareholders in Germany and the UK.

Although in the UK concentrated ownership of the kind observed in Germany is uncommon, as noted in the previous paper, large block shareholdings in the form of institutional shareholding are quite widespread in the UK. Institutional shareholders – insurance companies, pension funds, mutual funds, investment trusts – collectively hold a substantial majority of shares in UK listed companies. Given their dominance, do institutional large block shareholders monitor their investee companies effectively? This question is addressed by Faccio and Lasfer (Ch.9) with particular reference to occupational pension funds. By comparing companies in which these funds hold large stakes with a control group of companies listed on the London Stock Exchange, they show that occupational pension funds hold large stakes over a long time period mainly in small companies. However, the value added by these funds is negligible and their holdings do not lead companies to comply with the Code of Best Practice or outperform their industry counterparts. Overall, their results suggest that occupational pension funds are not effective monitors.

Chapter 5

Hiroshi Osano*

SECURITY DESIGN, INSIDER MONITORING, AND FINANCIAL MARKET EQUILIBRIUM

Source: *European Finance Review*, 2(3) (1999): 273–302.

ABSTRACT

This paper considers a problem of security design in the presence of monitoring done by a large investor to discipline the management of a firm. Since the large investor enjoys only part of the benefits generated by her monitoring activities but incurs all the associated costs, the design and amount of security need to be structured so as to motivate her to maintain an efficient level of monitoring, if no other mechanism exists to make her commit to specific levels of monitoring in advance. By assuming that the large investor takes account of the effect of the issued amount of security on the revenues received, we show that the optimal security is a debt-like security such as standard debt with a positive probability of default, or debt with call options. We also verify that the financial market equilibrium is constrained Pareto optimal.

1. INTRODUCTION

LARGE INVESTORS – INSTITUTIONAL INVESTORS such as pension funds, mutual funds, commercial banks, insurance companies, and finance companies, as well as private investors such as initial owners – monitor and control the management of companies on behalf of the other investors.[1] However, in recent years, the securitizing of financial assets and a shift away from bank borrowing toward bond and equity financing have grown significantly.[2] If this tendency increases the number of shares owned by small and passive investors, it may reduce the incentive for large investors to monitor the performance of the management of a given company. This possibility arises from a free-rider problem: small and passive investors realize part of the benefits of monitoring performed by large investors but they incur none of the costs of the monitoring. This paper investigates how the design and issued amount of security can

be organized so as to best enhance the role of the large investor as a delegated monitor who disciplines the performance of a company's management.

To attain our goal, we consider the problem of security design under asymmetric information when investors can freely trade in the market. In particular, we develop a model in which a large investor affects the return structure of a risky project by having access to costly monitoring technology but cannot be made to commit to monitoring the management of the firm at any particular level of intensity because her monitoring level is hidden from outside investors. In this framework, one natural question is whether standard debt or some other simple security design would be suitable under reasonable assumptions. Another question is how the interaction between the design of a security, amount of the security implemented, and the intensity of the large investor's monitoring is structured.

The main thesis of this paper depends on a mechanism in which the design and issued amount of security influences the intensity of the large investor's monitoring, not only through a direct effect on her ex ante payoff but also through an indirect effect via the market security price on her ex ante payoff. To clarify the basic idea, consider first an entrepreneur (a large investor) who holds a project that generates risky returns in future periods. She may keep some of the future returns for herself and securitize the other portion of the future returns to raise capital and maintain liquidity. Once the large investor issues a security, she turns effective control of the firm over to a manager. However, the large investor is assumed to have access to costly technology for monitoring the management of the firm and thus can affect the return structure of the project.[3] However, if the large investor carries out such monitoring, small and passive investors can free-ride on part of the benefits of the control function of the large investor, although these investors incur none of the costs of monitoring. This externality reduces the likelihood of the large investor's carrying out high intensity monitoring unless she can be made to commit to prior monitoring levels before she designs and issues the security.

In this model, the design and issued amount of security affects the large investor's monitoring because of both the direct effect on her ex ante payoff and the indirect effect on her ex ante payoff through a change in the security price. The logic of the indirect effect is explained as follows. If small and passive investors are aware that a change in the design and issued amount of security affects the large investor's monitoring, the security price at which the trade takes place will reflect this awareness.

More specifically, small and passive investors rationally anticipate a low intensity of monitoring if the large investor designs and sells to small and passive investors a security that is more sensitive to the variations of future returns or if she sells a security more aggressively. This expectation implies that in this situation a lower security price will prevail. Such an indirect effect of the design and issued amount of security causes a liquidity cost that is borne by the large investor, who issues the security. Thus, the large investor needs to consider not only the direct effect of the design and issued amount of security, including a *retention cost* associated with a high unsecuritized or unsold portion of the cash flows, but also the indirect effect of the design and issued amount of security through a change in the security price, including a *liquidity cost* associated with a low rate of monitoring.

The above arguments show that there is a potential conflict between the need for liquidity preference and the efficiency of monitoring. Furthermore, these arguments indicate that the design of the security and the amount issued are incentive devices independent of one another for reconciling the friction between these two aims. Nevertheless, the interaction between the design of the security, the amount issued, and the large investor's monitoring remains imperfectly understood in the literature of corporate governance or finance. Indeed, the literature reveals several difficulties. The first problem is that only a limited menu of debt and equity has been studied. The second problem is that most of the arguments in this field depend on the bilateral contract framework but not on the market equilibrium framework.[4]

To avoid these difficulties and formalize the trade-off between the retention cost and the liquidity cost, we incorporate four key issues into our model. First, to motivate the entrepreneur (large investor) to issue a security backed by future risky returns, we assume that she must sell her issued security for liquidity reasons, as studied in Allen and Gale (1988, 1991), Gale (1992), and DeMarzo and Duffie (1999). Thus, the retention cost arises from retaining a large amount of unsecuritized returns or unsold securities. Second, we assume that the large investor can choose a level of monitoring to discipline the management of the firm and affect the structure of risky returns in future periods, while she cannot be committed to any specific levels of monitoring until she designs and issues a security. As a result, the free-rider problem associated with monitoring in the presence of small and passive investors naturally occurs. This causes a liquidity cost to the large investor because her weaker incentive to monitor makes the security price lower. Third, we do not take the forms of financial claims as given, such as debt and equity, but rather try to derive these instruments as an optimal security design. By designing securities, the large investor can balance the retention cost against the liquidity cost. Finally, instead of a bilateral contract model, we set up a simple market (general) equilibrium model in which the large investor sells her issued security to small and passive investors, taking account of the effect of the amount sold on the revenues received. This framework enables us to investigate the price effect of the design and issued amount of security. This framework also allows us to consider how the recent trend in the financing patterns of nonfinancial firms away from (indirect) bank borrowing and toward (direct) bond financing in Germany and Japan affects their corporate governance systems.

By considering these four issues, we show that the optimal security is a debt-like security such as standard debt with a positive probability of default, or debt with call options in the presence of the monitoring problem. This result suggests that it cannot be necessarily optimal to issue risk free debt with zero default probability. The intuitive reason for this result is that in the present model, the large investor wants to sell some portion of the security and receive the revenues from the sale of the security in the initial period to maintain liquidity; as a result, to promote sales revenues, the large investor is motivated to set security claims at each possible contingency to increase by the maximum amount that the firm can pay by taking account of the adverse effect on monitoring. If the security claims were not constrained by monitoring considerations, then the optimal security would become equity. In fact, since the security claims must be constrained to

some extent by monitoring considerations, the optimal security becomes a debt-like security such as standard debt with a positive probability of default or debt with call options.

We also compare the allocation of the financial market equilibrium with three benchmark allocations. The first benchmark case is concerned with the competitive equilibrium allocation, in which the large investor does not take account of the effect of the amount of security issued on her sales revenues. The second benchmark case is the "passive" equilibrium allocation, in which the large investor becomes a passive investor, that is, she chooses the minimum monitoring level. The final benchmark case deals with the constrained social surplus maximizing allocation, in which the social planner maximizes the social surplus subject to the constraints: (i) that the large investor initially owns the risky project,[5] (ii) that her monitoring level is unobservable to outside investors, and (iii) that she cannot be committed to any specific levels of monitoring before she designs and issues the security. In the first two benchmark cases, we show that the competitive equilibrium allocation is identical with the passive one. More specifically, under these two equilibrium allocations, either the optimal security is equity or the financial market breaks down, and the monitoring level of the large investor is minimized. Compared to the final benchmark allocation, the allocation of the financial market equilibrium, in which the large investor considers the effect of the amount sold on the revenues received, is proved to be constrained Pareto optimal: it attains the constrained social surplus maximizing allocation.

Our research is related to two strands of the literature. One is concerned with security design under the bilateral contract or the general equilibrium model, while the other is involved with insider or speculator monitoring under the general equilibrium model. In the analysis of security design under the bilateral contract model, Hart and Moore (1989) and Bolton and Scharfstein (1990) show that standard debt is an optimal contract when managers can appropriate to themselves income not paid out. Berglöf and von Thadden (1994), incorporating partial liquidation and multiple investors into the Hart and Moore model, discuss whether short-term debt, long-term debt, or equity are the best securities the firm can issue. However, these papers do not investigate the monitoring activity of investors. Townsend (1979), Diamond (1984), Gale and Hellwig (1985), and von Thadden (1995) do consider the monitoring activity of investors under the bilateral contract model, and prove that standard debt is an optimal contract. Although these papers make important contributions, they shed little light on the effect of security design on the market security price because their framework is restricted to bilateral contracts.

The problem of optimal security design in the general equilibrium model is analyzed with symmetric information by Allen and Gale (1988, 1991), and with adverse selection by Boot and Thakor (1993), Nachman and Noe (1994), Demange and Laroque (1995), Ohashi (1995), Rahi (1995, 1996), and DeMarzo and Duffie (1999). This line of research, however, does not examine the implications of monitoring done by investors under asymmetric information.

In work most closely related to ours, Holmström and Tirole (1993) and Admati, Pfleiderer, and Zechner (1994) explore the implications of monitoring done by investors under the general equilibrium model with asymmetric information.[6] Holmström and Tirole develop a model in which the equity ownership structure of firms affects the value of market monitoring through its effect on market liquidity. Admati, Pfleiderer, and Zechner study the effect of monitoring done by large shareholders on security market equilibrium. Our analysis goes beyond these two interesting papers by considering the problem of security design endogenously instead of focusing on particular financial claims such as equity.

The paper is organized as follows. Section 2 describes the basic model. Section 3 characterizes the allocation at financial market equilibrium. Section 4 compares the allocation at financial market equilibrium with the three benchmark allocations. Section 5 summarizes our results and discusses some directions for future study.

2. THE MODEL

We consider a model in which there exist one large investor (the issuer) and a set of outside investors. The large investor owns a risky project that generates future cash flows, and also has access to some monitoring activities by which she can affect the structure of the returns of the risky project. We assume that all investors are risk neutral and normalize the market interest rate to zero.

The model has three periods, indexed $t = 0, 1, 2$. In the initial period, the large investor designs a security whose return represents a claim backed by some part of the risky project returns of the firm, with the total supply normalized to one. The large investor also offers the security for sale on the security market. The large investor then decides to sell a fraction $q_L \in [0, 1]$ of the security to the market at a price p. The large investor herself keeps the fraction $(1 - q_L)$ of the security.[7] On the other side of the market, outside investors establish their share of security allocations, $q_O \in [0, 1]$. Once the large investor issues the security, she turns effective control of the risky project (firm) over to the management. In period 1, the large investor has access to costly technology of monitoring the management, and can affect the return structure of the risky project. Given the costs and benefits of monitoring, the large investor chooses the level of monitoring. Note that the large investor makes the monitoring decision by taking into account the share of security allocations established in period 0. There is no further trading from period 1 to period 2. In period 2, the returns of the risky project are realized and the claims of the security are paid off to security holders. The large investor also receives the residual claims that remain after the security claims are paid to security holders including the large investor herself.

To formalize the model, we require specific assumptions about the liquidity motive of the large investor, the preference of outside investors, and the monitoring technology of the large investor.

To provide the motivation for liquidation, we assume that the large investor evaluates the period 2 cash flows at a rate $\delta \in (0, 1)$. This assumption implies that the large investor is indifferent as to whether she keeps future project returns or sells them for δ cents in the dollar in cash by securitizing them. This also means that, if the large investor retains a portion of the security, the private value of one dollar's worth of security returns to the large investor is δ. Similar assumptions are made in Allen and Gale (1988, 1991), Gale (1992), and DeMarzo and Duffie (1999).[8] Since we assume that high transaction costs deter the large investor and outside investors from building a bilateral contract relation, the large investor has an incentive to securitize some portion of the future risky project returns and sell the security to outside investors.

In contrast, outside investors are assumed to have no liquidity motives. Since outside investors do not care when asset returns are generated, they have no concern about the timing of payments.

The large investor has access to costly technology of monitoring the management. The technology affects the structure of the returns of the risky project as follows:[9,10]

$$\tilde{X} = \begin{cases} X_g, & \text{with probability } \sigma_g(m), \\ X_b, & \text{with probability } \sigma_b(m), \end{cases}$$

where $X_g > X_b > 0$, $(\sigma_g(m), \sigma_b(m)) \in \{(\sigma_g(m), \sigma_b(m)) \mid \sigma_g(m) + \sigma_b(m) = 1, \sigma_g(m) > 0, \sigma_b(m) > 0\}$, and m is the intensity of monitoring.[11] One part of the efficiency of monitoring is captured by the function $\sigma_g(m)$, where $\sigma_g'(m) > 0$ and $\sigma_g''(m) < 0$. The other part of the efficiency of monitoring is characterized by the cost of monitoring at level m, expressed by

cm, where c is the unit monitoring cost. Let $\underline{m}$ be the minimum monitoring level required to sustain the monitoring process.[12]

All the project returns at each state, (X_g, X_b), and the fraction of the security sold by the large investor to the market, q_L, can be verified with no cost. On the other hand, the monitoring level chosen by the large investor, m, cannot be observed by any outside agents. Thus, the large investor cannot be committed to any specific levels of monitoring until period 1. The functions $(\sigma_g(m), \sigma_b(m))$ and the parameters (X_g, X_b, c, δ) are assumed to be common knowledge.

The security is represented by a claim, that is, any promise to make a future payment, contingent on the state of nature (that is, the project returns). Let $\tilde{F}$ be a real-valued random variable that generates a security claim F_g at the good state, and a security claim F_b at the bad state, respectively. We focus our attention on the set of admissible securities. These are defined by a set of functions satisfying the following limited liability and monotonicity conditions:

$$0 \leq F_s \leq X_s, \quad s = g, b, \tag{1}$$

$$F_b \leq F_g. \tag{2}$$

In the subsequent discussion, we denote the set of admissible securities as Δ. In the limited liability condition (1), the restriction of $0 \leq F_s$ for $s = g, b$ expresses limited liability for security holders. The restriction of $F_s \leq X_s$ for $s = g, b$ implies limited liability for the large investor as a residual claimant. The monotonicity condition (2) shows that the security claim is nondecreasing in the available firm cash flows.[13] These assumptions are quite common in the finance literature, and are justified in Innes (1990), Nachman and Noe (1994), Hart and Moore (1994), and DeMarzo and Duffie (1999).

Now, the security represented by the claim (F_g, F_b) pays an amount min (F_s, X_s) for $s = g, b$ when the returns of the project are realized in period 2.[14] The large investor then receives the cash revenues from the sale of the fraction q_L of the security in period 1, and the residual cash flows of max $(X_s - F_s, 0)$ for $s = g, b$ and the claims for the unsold fraction $(1 - q_L)$ of the security in period 2.

The trading process is described as a Walrasian process in which the large investor is strategic. The large investor chooses the fraction of the security sold to the market, q_L, by taking into account the effect of the issued amount on the security price, p. We assume that the large investor perceives an inverse demand correspondence $p \in P(q_L; \tilde{F})$ for the issued security $\tilde{F}$, where $P : [0, 1] \to \mathfrak{R}_+$. In the next section, we specify how $P(q_L; \tilde{F})$ is determined. On the other hand, outside investors behave as representative, risk - neutral, price-taking investors. Thus, outside investors do not receive expected net gains from buying any security at market equilibrium.

The expected payoff of the large investor in period 0 is then given by

$$R_L(m, \tilde{F}, q_L) = \delta E \max(\tilde{X} - \tilde{F}, 0)$$
$$+ \delta(1 - q_L)E \min(\tilde{F}, \tilde{X})$$
$$+ q_L P(q_L; \tilde{F}) - cm, \quad (3)$$

where E is the expectation operator. The right-hand side of (3) consists of the expected residual claims retained by the large shareholder, $E \max (\tilde{X} - \tilde{F}, 0)$ the expected claims for the unsold fraction $(1 - q_L)$ of the security, $(1 - q_L)E \min (\tilde{F}, \tilde{X})$, the cash revenues raised from the sale of the security, $q_L P(q_L; \tilde{F})$, and the monitoring cost, $-cm$. The first two terms are discounted by the rate δ because the returns of these two claims accrue only in period 2. The monitoring cost is not discounted, since it must be paid in period 1. Note that the first two terms clearly depend on the monitoring level m because the realized probability of the state is affected by the choice of m.

The expected payoff of outsiders in period 0 is similarly represented by

$$R_o(q_o, p) = q_o [E \min (\tilde{F}, \tilde{X}) - p]. \quad (4)$$

Since outside investors do not behave strategically, they take the security price p as given.

A financial market equilibrium is now characterized by $(m^\circ, \tilde{F}^\circ, q_L^\circ, q_0^\circ, p^\circ)$ that satisfies the following conditions (see Figure 5.1):

FINANCIAL MARKET EQUILIBRIUM:
(i) *Sequential Optimality of the Large Investor.* In period 1, the large investor chooses a monitoring level m° such that

$$\prod_{L1}(\tilde{F}, q_L) = \max_{m \geq \underline{m}} R_L(m, \tilde{F}, q_L). \quad (5)$$

In period 0, given the knowledge of the price correspondence $P(q_L; \tilde{F})$, the large investor chooses a design $\tilde{F}^\circ$ and a fraction q_L° of the security sold to the market such that

$$\prod_{L0} = \max_{\tilde{F} \in \Delta, q_L \in [0,1]} \prod_{L1}(\tilde{F}, q_L), \quad (6)$$

where Δ is the set of admissible securities defined by (1) and (2).
(ii) *Optimality of Outsider Investors.* In period 1, outside investors purchase a fraction q_0° of the security supplied in the market, relative to an observed price p°, such that

$$\prod_0 (p^\circ) = \max_{q_0 \in [0,1]} R_o(q_o, p^\circ). \quad (7)$$

(iii) *Market Equilibrium.* The security price p° and the sold and purchased fractions (q_L°, q_0°) must satisfy

$$p^\circ \in P(q_L^\circ; \tilde{F}^\circ), \quad (8)$$
and
$$q_L^\circ = q_0^\circ. \quad (9)$$

Note that the large investor selects a security design $\tilde{F}$ from the set of admissible securities Δ, a sold fraction q_L from $[0, 1]$, and a monitoring level m from $(\underline{m}, \infty)$. Outside investors select a purchased fraction q_0 from $[0, 1]$. Since the large investor cannot be committed in advance to any specific levels of monitoring, she must solve the sequential problem made up of (5) and (6).

period 0

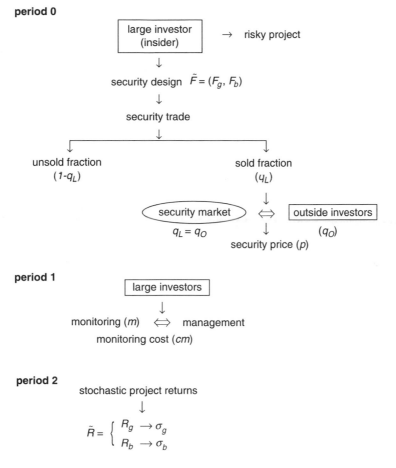

Figure 5.1 Sequence of the events.

3. FINANCIAL MARKET EQUILIBRIUM

In this section, we first derive the inverse demand correspondence $P(q_L; \tilde{F})$ from the condition of the optimality of outside investors and the condition of market equilibrium by taking as given a security design chosen by the large investor, $\tilde{F}$. We next solve the sequential optimization problem of the large investor in two steps, and determine the remaining variables endogenously.

3.1. Inverse demand correspondence

Solving the optimization problem of out-side investors, (7), with (4), we see

$$q_O = \begin{cases} = 0 & \text{if } E \min (\tilde{F}, \tilde{X}) < p, \\ \in [0,1] & \text{if } E \min (\tilde{F}, \tilde{X}) = p, \\ = 0 & \text{if } E \min (\tilde{F}, \tilde{X}) < p. \end{cases}$$

(10)

Combining (9) and (10), we have

$$q_L = \begin{cases} = 0 & \text{if } E \min (\tilde{F}, \tilde{X}) < p, \\ \in [0,1] & \text{if } E \min (\tilde{F}, \tilde{X}) = p, \\ = 0 & \text{if } E \min (\tilde{F}, \tilde{X}) > p. \end{cases}$$

(11)

The relation between q_L and p determined by (11) gives the inverse demand correspondence $p \in P(q_L; \tilde{F})$.

3.2. The monitoring problem faced by the large investor

We now proceed to the sequential optimization problem of the large investor. We discuss the optimality conditions for this problem by moving backward from period 1 to period 0.

We begin with solving the monitoring problem (5) faced in period 1 by the large investor, who designs a security $\tilde{F}$ and holds a fraction $1 - q_L$ of the security after trading. Since the large investor takes the price correspondence $p \in P(q_L; \tilde{F})$ as given because q_L and $\tilde{F}$ are determined in period 0, it follows from (11) that the following three cases are distinguished: $E \min (\tilde{F}, \tilde{X}) < p$, $E \min (\tilde{F}, \tilde{X}) = p$, or $E \min (\tilde{F}, \tilde{X}) > p$.

We first discuss the case of $E \min (\tilde{F}, \tilde{X}) < p$, where $q_L = 0$ from (11). Given (1), (3) and $q_L = 0$, the objective function of (5) is reduced to

$$R_L(m, \tilde{F}, 0) = \delta E\tilde{X} - cm. \tag{12}$$

Rewriting (12) with the definition of $\tilde{X}$, we specify the interim maximization problem of the large investor as follows:

$$\max_{m \geq \underline{m}} R_L(m, \tilde{F}, 0)$$

$$= \max_{m \geq \underline{m}} \left[\delta \sum_{i=g,b} X_i \sigma_i(m) - cm \right] \tag{13}$$

Let us assume that the maximization problem (13) has an interior solution. Since the objective function (13) is globally concave with respect to m under $X_g > X_b$, the first-order condition for this problem becomes a global optimality condition. Solving (13) with $\sigma_g(m) + \sigma_b(m) = 1$, we see the following first-order condition:

$$\delta(X_g - X_b)\sigma_g'(m) - c = 0. \tag{14}$$

In this case, the monitoring level is ex post efficient because the large investor holds all the issued security. However, she cannot satisfy her liquidity needs.

We next examine the case of $E \min (\tilde{F}, \tilde{X}) = p$, where $q_L \in [0, 1]$ from (11). Rearranging (3) with the definitions of $\tilde{X}$ and $\tilde{F}$, we explicitly describe the interim maximization problem (5) by

$$\max_{m \geq \underline{m}} R_L(m, \tilde{F}, q_L)$$

$$= \max_{m \geq \underline{m}} \left[\delta \sum_{i=g,b} \max(X_i - F_i, 0)\sigma_i(m) \right.$$

$$+ \delta(1 - q_L) \sum_{i=g,b} \min(F_i - X_i)$$

$$\left. \sigma_i(m) + pq_L - cm \right]. \tag{15}$$

We should again keep in mind that the security price p is determined in period 0. Thus, the large investor in this stage takes the security price p as given.

In the subsequent analysis, we assume that the maximization problem (15) has an interior solution that satisfies the second-order sufficient condition for m to be a local maximum of $R_L (m, \tilde{F}, q_L)$.[15] Then, the first-order condition for the problem (15) implies a local optimality condition, and is expressed by

$$\delta \sum_{i=g,b} \max(X_i - F_i, 0)\sigma_i'(m)$$

$$+ \delta(1 - q_L) \sum_{i=g,b} \min(F_i - X_i)$$

$$\sigma_i'(m) - c = 0. \tag{16}$$

Note that although the large investor pays the full cost of monitoring, she enjoys only a part of the benefits of the monitoring because the monitoring also affects the claims on the outsiders' holdings of the security. Thus, the monitoring level is always less than ex post efficient, which is achieved if the large investor is the sole owner of the security.

In fact, (16) is not easily tractable. To obtain a more manageable form, let us distinguish the following four cases by exploiting the monotonicity condition (2): (A) $F_b \leq F_g \leq X_b < X_g$ or $F_b \leq X_b \leq F_g \leq X_g$,

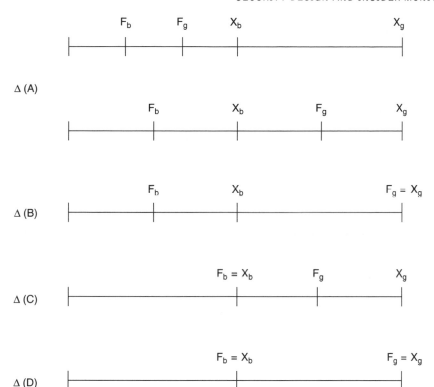

Figure 5.2 Four possible cases of $\tilde{F}$.

(B) $F_b \leq X_b < X_g \leq F_g$, (C) $X_b \leq F_b \leq F_g \leq X_g$, and (D) $X_b \leq F_b \leq X_g \leq F_g$ or $X_b < X_g \leq F_b \leq F_g$. Furthermore, given the limited liability condition (1), the four possible cases of $\tilde{F}$ introduced above are reduced to the following four possible sets $\tilde{F}$ (see Figure 5.2): $\Delta(A) \equiv \{(F_g, F_b) \mid F_b \leq F_g \leq X_g$ and $0 \leq F_b \leq X_b\}$, $\Delta(B) \equiv \{(F_g, F_b) \mid 0 \leq F_b \leq X_b < X_g = F_g\}$, $\Delta(C) \equiv \{(F_g, F_b) \mid X_b = F_b \leq F_g \leq X_g\}$, and $\Delta(D) \equiv \{(F_g, F_b) \mid X_b = F_b < X_g = F_g\}$. Note that $\Delta(A)$ is identical to the set $\tilde{F}$, $\{(F_g, F_b) \mid F_b \leq F_g \leq X_b < X_g$ or $F_b \leq X_b \leq F_g \leq X_g\}$, under conditions (1) and (2). Similarly, $\Delta(D)$ is identical with the set $\tilde{F}$, $\{(F_g, F_h) \mid X_h \leq F_h \leq X_g \leq F_g$ or $X_b < X_g \leq F_b \leq F_g\}$, under conditions (1) and (2). From now on, we divide the space $\tilde{F}$ into $\Delta(A)$, $\Delta(B)$, $\Delta(C)$, and $\Delta(D)$. For each division of the space of $\tilde{F}$, the first-order condition for an interior solution to the monitoring problem is specified in the Appendix. In Subsection 3.3

and Section 4, the optimality condition will be fully exploited.

Finally, we investigate the case of E min $(\tilde{F}, \tilde{X}) \geq p$, where q_L must be equal to 1 from (11). Then, it is immediately seen from (3) and $q_L = 1$ that the objective function of (5) is described by

$$R_L(m, \tilde{F}, 1) = \delta E \max (\tilde{X} - \tilde{F}, 0) \\ + P(1; \tilde{F}) - cm.$$

Because of E min $(\tilde{F}, \tilde{X}) \geq p$ for $p \in P(1; \tilde{F})$ from (11), we have E min $(\tilde{F}, \tilde{X}) \geq \sup P(1; \tilde{F})$. Thus, using the definitions of $\tilde{F}$ and $\tilde{F}$, we find

$$\max_{m \geq \underline{m}} R_L(m, \tilde{F}, 1)$$

$$= \max_{m \geq \underline{m}} \left[\delta \sum_{i=g,b} \max(X_i - F_i, 0)\sigma_i(m) \right. \\ \left. + P(1; \tilde{F}) - cm \right]$$

$$\leq \max_{m \geq \underline{m}} \left[\delta \sum_{i=g,b} \max(X_i - F_i, 0)\sigma_i(m) \right.$$

$$\left. + \sum_{i=g,b} \min(F_i - X_i)\sigma_i(m) - cm \right]$$

$$= \lim_{q_L \to 1} \max_{m \geq \underline{m}} R_L(m, \tilde{F}, q_L). \quad (17)$$

Here, the inequality in (17) is derived from $E \min (\tilde{F}, \tilde{X}) \geq \sup P(1; \tilde{F})$, and the final equality in (17) is obtained from the limit of the right-hand side of (15) with $E \min (\tilde{F}, \tilde{X}) = p$, as q_L converges to unity.

The arguments of the three cases examined above suggest the following. First, we can rule out the case of $E \min (\tilde{F}, \tilde{X}) < p$. In this case, we cannot examine the problem of the security issue because the large investor holds all the issued security ($q_L = 0$). Second, we can substitute the case of $E \min (\tilde{F}, \tilde{X}) = p$ for the case of $E \min (\tilde{F}, \tilde{X}) > p$ because the latter is included in the former as q_L converges to unity. We will, therefore, focus on the case of both $E \min (\tilde{F}, \tilde{X}) = p$ and $q_L > 0$ in the subsequent analysis.

3.3. The problem faced by the large investor of issuing the security.

We are now in a position to discuss the optimization problem of issuing the security, (6), faced by the large investor in period 0. To do so, we first solve the problem (6) with the restriction in which $\tilde{F} = (F_g, F_b)$ belongs to one of the four sets defined in the preceding subsection: (A) $\tilde{F} \in \Delta(A)$, (B) $\tilde{F} \in \Delta(B)$, (C) $\tilde{F} \in \Delta(C)$, and (D) $\tilde{F} \in \Delta(D)$. Then, we compute the optimal value for the problem (6) under each of the four possible restrictions, and choose the maximal value among the optimal values of the four possible cases. The corresponding solution gives an optimal security design $\tilde{F}^\circ = (F_g^\circ, F_b^\circ)$ and an optimal level of the sold fraction q_L° to the problem (6). In contrast to the analysis of the monitoring problem, the large investor must consider the effect of a change in her strategy on the security price. A detailed analysis of the optimizing conditions to the

problem (6) is provided by (A5)–(A8) in the Appendix.

The most notable feature of these optimality conditions is that changes in the design of the security, (F_g, F_b), or in the issued amount of security, q_L, has both a direct effect on the monitoring level and an indirect effect through a change in the security price. If the large investor did not take into account the effect of a change in (F_g, F_b) or q_L on sales revenues, the optimal strategy would be given by $F_g = X_g$, $F_b = X_b$, and $q_L = 1$ in all possible cases, unless the security market breaks down. However, this implies that the large investor would securitize all the project returns and sell all of the security. Thus, the monitoring level would be minimized, which might cause a collapse of the security market: outside investors would rationally anticipate the strategy of the large investor and participate in the security market only if the security price is low enough.

On the basis of the optimality conditions (A5)–(A8) given in the Appendix, we now have the following proposition on the optimal strategy of the large investor for each possible set of $\tilde{F}$. The detailed proof is presented in the Appendix.

PROPOSITION 1. (i) If $\tilde{F}$ is restricted to $\Delta(A)$ or $\Delta(C)$, the optimal solution to the constrained maximization problem, $(m^*, F_g^*, F_b^*, q_L^*)$, is characterized by

$$\delta[X_g - X_b - q_L^*(F_g^* - X_b)]\sigma_g'(m^*) = c, \quad (18a)$$

$$F_g^* = \min \left(X_b - (1 - \delta)\sigma_g(m^*) \right.$$
$$\left. \left[\sigma_g'(m^*)\frac{\partial m^*}{\partial F_g^*} \right]^{-1}, X_g \right), \quad (18b)$$

$$F_g^* = X_b, \quad (18c)$$

$$(1 - \delta)[F_g^*\sigma_g(m^*) + X_b\sigma_b(m^*)]$$
$$+ q_L^*(F_g^* - X_b)\sigma_g'(m^*)\frac{\partial m^*}{\partial q_L^*} = 0. \quad (18d)$$

The large investor's payoff is then

$$\prod_{Lo}^{A} = \prod_{Lo}^{C} = \delta \left[X_g \sigma_g(m^*) + X_b \sigma_b(m^*) \right]$$

$$+ q_L^*(1 - \delta)[F_g^* \sigma_g(m^*)$$

$$+ X_b \sigma_b(m^*)] - cm^*. \qquad (18e)$$

(ii) If $\tilde{F}$ is restricted to $\Delta(B)$ or $\Delta(D)$, the optimal solution to the constrained maximization problem, $(m^{**}, F_g^{**}, F_b^{**}, q_L^{**})$, is represented by

$$\delta(1 - q_L^{**})(X_g - X_b)\sigma_g'(m^{**}) = c, \qquad (19a)$$

$$F_g^{**} = X_{g\prime} \qquad (19b)$$

$$F_b^{**} = X_{b\prime} \qquad (19c)$$

$$(1 - \delta)[X_g \sigma_g(m^{**}) + X_b \sigma_b(m^{**})]$$

$$+ q_L^{**}(X_g - X_b)\sigma_g'(m^{**})\frac{\partial m^{**}}{\partial q_L^{**}} = 0. \qquad (19d)$$

The large investor's payoff is then

$$\prod_{Lo}^{B} = \prod_{Lo}^{D} = [\delta + q_L^{**}(1 - \delta)]$$

$$[X_g \sigma_g(m^{**}) + X_b \sigma_b(m^{**})] - cm^{**}. \qquad (19e)$$

Proposition 1 shows that, if $\tilde{F}$ is restricted to $\Delta(A)$ or $\Delta(C)$, the optimal security can be a debt-like security with $F_g^* < X_g$ and $F_b^* = X_b$. One interpretation of this kind of security is standard debt with default such as that analyzed in DeMarzo and Duffle (1999) and von Thadden (1995): F_g^* can be viewed as the face value, and F_b^* as the default payment of debt. Another interpretation is debt with call options (convertible bond or debt with warrant): $X_g - F_g^*$ can then be interpreted as the option premium. Proposition 1 also indicates that if $\tilde{F}$ is restricted to $\Delta(B)$ or $\Delta(D)$, the optimal security is equity whose claim fully reflects the project returns.

It is instructive to explore the implications of equations (18) and (19). Let us begin with (18a). Given the security price determined in period 0, an increase in the monitoring effort in period 1 affects the ex ante payoff of the large investor through two routes. One effect increases the expected project returns, thereby further increasing not only the discounted residual returns to be received by the large investor, that is, $\delta(X_g - F_g^* - X_b + F_b^*)\sigma_g'(m^*)$, but also the discounted security returns for the unsold portion to be received by the large investor, that is, $\delta(1 - q_L^*)(F_q^* - F_b^*)\sigma_g'(m^*)$. The combined effects *increase* the ex ante payoff of the large investor, expressed by the left-hand side of (18a). The other effect increases the total monitoring cost, c, thus *decreasing* the ex ante payoff of the large investor. This cost effect is represented by the right-hand side of (18a). The monitoring level is then chosen to balance the former benefit against the latter cost.

Before proceeding to (18b) and (18c), we discuss the implications of (18d) because it is then more straightforward to understand (18b) and (18c). An increase in the sold fraction has two potentially conflicting effects on the ex ante payoff of the large investor. One effect causes the large investor to receive higher revenues from the sale of the security. This effect enables the large investor to satisfy any desire to obtain as much revenue as possible at date 0 rather than at date 1 thus directly *increasing* her ex ante payoff, expressed by $(1 - \delta)p^* = (1 - \delta)[F_g^* \sigma_g(m^*) + X_b \sigma_b(m^*)]$. The other effect of an increase in q_L reduces the correlation between the ex post project returns and the ex post payoff of the large investor because she obtains the more deterministic sales revenues at period 0. Since this effect leads to a lower monitoring level, outside investors rationally anticipate a lower intensity of monitoring. This expectation reduces the security price, thus indirectly *decreasing* the large investor's revenues from the sale of the security, represented by $q_L^*(F_g^* - X_b)\sigma_g'(m^*)[\partial m^*/\partial q_L^*]$. The former direct benefit cancels out the latter indirect cost at the optimal level of the sold fraction.

We can now examine the implications of (18b) and (18c), and show how the design of the security affects the ex ante payoff of the large investor. If $F_g^* < X_g$, we multiply both sides of (18b) by q_L^* and rewrite it:

$$- q_L^* \delta \sigma_g(m^*) + q_L^* \sigma_g(m^*)$$
$$+ q_L^* (F_g^* - X_b) \sigma_g'(m^*) \frac{\partial m^*}{\partial F_g^*} = 0. \quad (20)$$

Given (20), an increase in F_g brings two direct effects to the ex ante payoff of the large investor. The first increases the discounted good state security returns to be received by the large investor, expressed by $\delta(1 - q_L^*)\sigma_g(m^*)$. The second direct effect in turn decreases the discounted good state residual returns to be obtained by the large investor, represented by $-\delta\sigma_g(m^*)$. The combined two direct effects are then summarized by $-q_L^* \delta\sigma_g(m^*)$, which is *negative* and is shown by the first term in the left-hand side of (20). An increase in F_g also leads to two indirect effects on the ex ante payoff of the large investor due to a change in the security price. Due to an increase in the security returns at the good state, one indirect effect raises the security price. This effect results in an increase in the large investor's revenues from the sale of the security, represented by $q_L^* \sigma_g(m^*)$, which is *positive* and is indicated by the middle term in the left-hand side of (20). The other indirect effect of an increase in F_g reduces the incentive for the large investor to attain the good state because the combined two direct effects represented by the first term in the left-hand side of (20) decrease her discounted good state returns. This indirect effect causes the large investor to choose a lower monitoring level. Since outside investors anticipate this, the security price and the large investor's revenues from the sale of the security *decrease*. This effect is captured by the final term in the left-hand side of (20). The claim at the good state, F_g, is thus determined by considering all of these effects.

In contrast, the claim at the bad state, F_b, is found to be on the boundary of $F_b \leq X_b$, since the total effect of an increase in F_b on the ex ante payoff of the large investor,

$q_L^*(1 - \delta)\sigma_b(m^*) + q_L^*(F_g^* - X_b) \sigma_g'(m^*)\partial m^*/\partial F_b^*$ becomes positive. The reason for $F_b^* = X_b$ mainly depends on these facts: (i) that an increase in F_b further motivates the large investor to attain the good state because its direct effects decrease her discounted bad state returns mainly through a decline in the discounted bad state residual returns to be received by the large investor, and (ii) that its positive indirect effects dominate its negative direct effects.

In a similar manner, we can investigate the implications of (19) by substituting X_g for F_g.

Using Proposition 1, an optimal solution to the sequential optimization problem faced by the large investor, $(m^\circ, F_g^\circ, F_b^\circ, q_L^\circ)$, is represented by

$(m^\circ, F_g^\circ, F_b^\circ, q_L^\circ)$

$$\begin{cases} = (m^*, F_g^*, F_b^*, q_L^*) & \text{if } \Pi_{LO}^A > \Pi_{LO}^B, \\ = (m^{**}, F_g^{**}, F_b^{**}, q_L^{**}) & \text{if } \Pi_{LO}^A \leq \Pi_{LO}^B. \end{cases}$$
$$(21)$$

Here, Π_{LO}^A and Π_{LO}^B are determined by (18e) and (19e), respectively.

Comparing Π_{LO}^A with Π_{LO}^B, we now obtain the following proposition that characterizes the optimal security design. The detailed proof is provided in the Appendix.

PROPOSITION 2. (i) In the presence of the monitoring problem, the optimal security is standard debt with default or debt with call options ($F_g^* < X_g$ and $F_b^* = X_b$). (ii) In the absence of the monitoring problem, the optimal security is equity.

One crucial implication of this proposition is that it is not optimal to issue risk-free debt such as $F_g^* = F_b^*$ because risk-free debt prevents the large investor from satisfying the desire to obtain the revenues as much as possible at date 0 rather than at date 1. Another important implication of this proposition is that in the presence of the monitoring problem, it is not optimal to issue equity.

A natural intuition is that risk-free debt would be an optimal security if we neglected the large investor's desire to receive the revenues as much as possible at date 0 rather than at date 1. This is because the large investor would receive the full margin benefit from monitoring as well as bearing the full marginal cost of monitoring. However, in the present case, the large investor can sell some portion of the security and receive the revenues from the sale of the security. Since the discount factor δ is less than one, the sales revenues received in period 0 are higher than the residual claims received in period 2. Hence, unless the monitoring level decreases through a change in security payments, the large investor is motivated to increase the sales revenues received in period 0. This implies that, in the absence of monitoring considerations, the large investor is motivated to set security claims at each state to increase by the maximum amount that the firm can pay. If the security claims need not be constrained by monitoring considerations, then the optimal security becomes equity because $F_g^* = X_g$ and $F_b^* = X_b$. On the other hand, if the security claims are constrained by monitoring considerations to some extent, the large investor needs to enhance her monitoring activity by increasing the residual revenues received at the good state in period 2. The large investor would therefore face the possibility that the optimal security becomes standard debt with default because she must set F_g^* less than X_g while keeping $F_b^* = X_b$.

More specifically, in the presence of monitoring considerations, the large investor needs to consider the trade-off between a decline in F_g from X_g and a rise in q_L. In other words, she needs to balance the costs of securitizing a smaller portion of the project returns against the costs of selling a smaller portion of the issued security.[16] Since the total effects of a decrease in F_g from X_g and an increase in q_L on the ex ante payoff of the large investor per issued amount are positive, the optimal security involves debt-like types such as standard debt with default or debt with call options.

Several remarks about this proposition are in order. First, we should notice that the result of this proposition depends on the simplifying assumptions such as two

possible outcomes and so on. Second, Admati, Pfleiderer, and Zechner (1994) discuss the monitoring activity of the large investor when only equity can be issued. However, Proposition 2 implies that the optimal security becomes debt-like in the presence of the monitoring problem, although our framework is restricted. This suggests that the security design problem needs to be analyzed endogenously in the study of the monitoring of the large investor.

4. NORMATIVE ANALYSIS OF THE FINANCIAL MARKET EQUILIBRIUM

In this section, we compare the financial market equilibrium in the preceding section with several benchmark cases: the competitive equilibrium allocation, the passive equilibrium allocation, and the constrained social surplus maximizing allocation.

The competitive equilibrium allocation deals with the situation in which the large investor does not take account of the effect of the issued amount of security on her sales revenues. The passive equilibrium allocation arises from the situation in which the large investor chooses the minimum monitoring level. The constrained social surplus maximizing allocation corresponds to the constrained Pareto optimal allocation such that the social planner maximizes the social surplus subject to several information constraints. In the analysis that follows, we show that the financial market equilibrium in the preceding section is constrained Pareto optimal, whereas the competitive and passive equilibrium allocations are not. With regard to the competitive and passive equilibrium allocations, we suggest that they are identical.

PROPOSITION 3. If the large investor does not take account of the effect of the issued amount of security on her sales revenues, the optimal allocation, $(\hat{m}, \hat{F}_g, \hat{F}_b, \hat{q}_L)$, would be given such that the monitoring level of the large investor, $\hat{m}$, is minimized: more specifically, $\hat{m} = \underline{m}$, $\hat{F}_g = X_g$, $\hat{F}_b = X_b$, and $\hat{q}_L = 1$.

Proof. If the large investor does not take into account the effect of the issued amount of security on her sales revenues, the optimality conditions for the problem (6) provided by (A5)–(A8) in the Appendix show that her optimal strategy is given by $\hat{m} = \underline{m}$, $\hat{F}_g = X_g$, $\hat{F}_b = X_b$, and $\hat{q}_L = 1$ in all possible cases, provided the security market does not collapse.

The intuitive explanation for Proposition 3 is clarified as follows. If the large investor does not consider the effect of the issued amount of security on her sales revenues, it is optimal for the large investor to securitize all the project returns and sell all of the security, because she evaluates the sales revenues received in period 0 more than the residual claims received in period 2. Since the large investor need not take account of the monitoring problem, she can minimize the monitoring level. However, this might cause the collapse of the security market because outside investors would rationally anticipate the large investor's strategy and participate in the security market only if the security price is low enough.

Proposition 2 indicates that in the presence of the monitoring problem, the optimal security is a debt-like security if the large investor takes account of the effect of the amount sold on the revenues received. On the other hand, Proposition 3 suggests that even in the presence of the monitoring problem, the optimal security is equity if the large investor does not take account of the effect of the amount of security issued on her sales revenues, that is, if she chooses the minimum monitoring level. The result of Proposition 3 depends on the assumption that the large investor cannot be committed to any prior levels of monitoring until she designs and issues the security.

We next examine the relation between the financial market equilibrium and constrained social surplus maximizing allocations, defined such that the social planner maximizes the social surplus subject to the constraints: (i) that the large investor initially owns the risky project,[17] (ii) that her monitoring level is unobservable to outside investors, and (iii) that she cannot be committed to any specific levels of monitoring before she designs and issues the security.

Let $S(m, \tilde{F}, q)$ be the social surplus defined by
$$S(m, \tilde{F}, q) = \delta E \tilde{X} + q(1 - \delta) E \min(\tilde{F}, \tilde{X}) - cm, \quad (23)$$

where the first term represents the project returns, the second term expresses the liquidity benefits of the large investor, and the third term indicates the monitoring cost.

Then, the constrained social surplus maximizing allocation is formally characterized by the following sequential maximization problem:

Constrained social surplus maximizing allocation. In period 1, the social planner chooses a monitoring level m such that

$$S^1(\tilde{F}, q) = \max_{m \geq \underline{m}} S(m, \tilde{F}, q). \quad (24)$$

In period 0, the social planner chooses a design $\tilde{F}$ and a fraction q of security sold to outside investors such that

$$S^0 = \max_{\tilde{F} \in \Delta, q \in [0,1]} S^1(\tilde{F}, q). \quad (25)$$

Given (A1) and (A3) with $E \min(\tilde{F}, \tilde{X}) = p$ in the Appendix, it can be seen immediately from (23) that the constrained social surplus maximization problem is equivalent to the sequential optimization problem of the large investor at financial market equilibrium. Thus, we obtain the following proposition:

PROPOSITION 4. If the large investor takes account of the effect of the amount sold on the revenues received, the financial market equilibrium characterized in the preceding section is constrained Pareto optimal in the sense that it attains the constrained social surplus maximizing allocation.

In view of Propositions 2–4, we see that the competitive equilibrium allocation is not constrained Pareto optimal. Thus, the large investor must take into account the effect of the issued amount of security on her sales revenues to attain the constrained social surplus maximizing allocation. This finding is reminiscent of the results of Allen and Gale (1991) in a different context.

The intuition behind this proposition is that the social surplus can be transformed into the surplus of the large investor as a result of the price adjustment at financial market equilibrium. This finding mainly depends on both the price-making behavior of the large investor and the risk neutrality of the large investor and outside investors.

5. CONCLUSION

This paper has developed a framework for analyzing a problem of security design in the presence of monitoring done by a large investor to discipline the management of a firm. Since the large investor enjoys only a part of the benefits brought about by her monitoring activities but incurs all the associated costs, she needs to structure the problem of security design to motivate herself to make an efficient level of monitoring if she cannot be committed to any prior levels of monitoring before she designs and issues the security. In fact, it is costly to design and issue the security to attain an efficient level of monitoring because of both the direct effect on the ex ante payoff of the large investor and the indirect effect on her ex ante payoff through a change in the security price.

By assuming that the large investor takes account of the effect on her sales revenues of the amount of security issued, we have shown that the optimal security is a debt-like security such as standard debt with a positive probability of default, or debt with call options in the presence of the monitoring problem. This result suggests that it is not necessarily optimal to issue a security with zero default probability such as risk-free debt, and that the monitoring model of Admati, Pfleiderer, and Zechner (1994) is restricted in the sense that only equity is permitted to be issued. We have also proved that the financial market equilibrium is constrained Pareto optimal. In contrast, if the large investor does not take into account the effect of the amount of security issued on her sales revenues, the competitive equilibrium allocation is not

constrained Pareto optimal or the market collapses. Furthermore, unless the market breaks down, the optimal security in this case is always equity; and the monitoring level of the large investor is minimized.

As suggested in DeMarzo and Duffie (1999), the model rather closely fits into the context of the design of corporated securities that are sold by an informed underwriter who retains some fraction of the security of issuing firms. In Germany and Japan, the recent trend in the financing patterns of nonfinancial firms away from (indirect) bank borrowing and toward (direct) bond financing has been affecting their corporate governance systems. However, since German house banks and Japanese main banks usually retain the security of their borrowing firms, our result indicates that these intermediaries may still discipline the management of firms by designing a debt-like security for their borrowing firms and retaining some portion of the security.

Within our framework, many issues remain to be investigated. Among other things, the problem of multi-security design is an important question that we hope to pursue in future research. Furthermore, the spanning issue caused by the risk averting actions of investors should also be examined. Finally, as has been recently studied under the incomplete contract model, the bankruptcy and liquidation problem is an important topic of corporate governance (see Hart and Moore (1989), Bolton and Scharfstein (1990), Aghion and Bolton (1992), Berglöf and von Thadden (1994), and Dewatripont and Tirole (1994)). It will be very interesting to explore how the design of securities can resolve the bankruptcy and liquidation problem at financial market equilibrium.

APPENDIX

5.1. First-order condition (16) for each division of the space $\tilde{F}$:

For each possible set of $\tilde{F}$, we obtain the corresponding value of the objective function of (5) and the corresponding expression for the first-order condition (16): *Objective function of (5) in the case of E* min $(\tilde{F}, \tilde{X}) = p$:

(A) $\tilde{F} \in \Delta(A)$:

$$
\begin{aligned}
R_L(m, \tilde{F}, q_L) = &\; \delta[(X_g - F_g)\sigma_g(m) \\
&+ (X_b - F_b)\sigma_b(m)] \\
&+ \delta(1 - q_L)[F_g\sigma_g(m) \\
&+ F_b\sigma_b(m) + pq_L - cm,
\end{aligned}
$$
(A1A)

(B) $\tilde{F} \in \Delta(B)$:

$$
\begin{aligned}
R_L(m, \tilde{F}, q_L) = &\; \delta(X_b - F_b)\sigma_b(m) \\
&+ \delta(1 - q_L)[X_g\sigma_g(m) \\
&+ F_b\sigma_b(m)] + pq_L - cm,
\end{aligned}
$$
(A1B)

(C) $\tilde{F} \in \Delta(C)$:

$$
\begin{aligned}
R_L(m, \tilde{F}, q_L) = &\; \delta(X_g - F_g)\sigma_g(m) \\
&+ \delta(1 - q_L)[F_g\sigma_g(m) \\
&+ X_b\sigma_b(m)] + pq_L - cm,
\end{aligned}
$$
(A1C)

(D) $\tilde{F} \in \Delta(D)$:

$$
\begin{aligned}
R_L(m, \tilde{F}, q_L) = &\; \delta(1 - q_L)[X_g\sigma_g(m) \\
&+ X_b\sigma_b(m)] + pq_L - cm.
\end{aligned}
$$
(A1D)

First-order condition (16):

(A) $\tilde{F} \in \Delta(A)$:

$$
\delta[X_g - X_b - q_L](F_g - F_b)]\sigma_g'(m) = c,
$$
(A2A)

(B) $\tilde{F} \in \Delta(B)$:

$$
\delta[X_g - X_b - q_L](X_g - F_b)]\sigma_g'(m) = c,
$$
(A2B)

(C) $\tilde{F} \in \Delta(C)$:

$$
\delta[X_g - X_b - q_L](F_g - X_b)]\sigma_g'(m) = c,
$$
(A2C)

(D) $\tilde{F} \in \Delta(D)$:

$$
\delta(1 - q_L)(X_g - X_b)\sigma_g'(m) = c.
$$
(A2D)

We should again notice that the large investor takes the security price as given when solving the monitoring problem in period 1.

In Subsection 3.3, we will use (A1) and (A2) to solve the problem (6) faced by the large investor in period 0.

5.2. Optimizing conditions for the problem (6):

For this analysis, we need to respecify the objective function $\Pi_{L1}(\tilde{F}, q_L)$ of the problem (6) for each possible case generated from the restriction of $\tilde{F}$. Substituting E min $(\tilde{F}, \tilde{X})$ for p in (A1A)–(A1D) yields:

(A) $\tilde{F} \in \Delta(A)$:

$$
\begin{aligned}
\Pi_{L1}^A(\tilde{F}, q_L) = &\; \delta[X_g\sigma_g(m_A) + X_b\sigma_b(m_A)] \\
&+ q_L(1 - \delta)[F_g\sigma_g(m_A) \\
&+ F_b\sigma_b(m_A)] - cm_A,
\end{aligned}
$$
(A3A)

(B) $\tilde{F} \in \Delta(B)$:

$$
\begin{aligned}
\Pi_{L1}^B(\tilde{F}, q_L) = &\; \delta[X_g\sigma_g(m_B) + X_b\sigma_b(m_B)] \\
&+ q_L(1 - \delta)[X_g\sigma_g(m_B) \\
&+ F_b\sigma_b(m_B)] - cm_B,
\end{aligned}
$$
(A3B)

(C) $\tilde{F} \in \Delta(C)$:

$$
\begin{aligned}
\Pi_{L1}^C(\tilde{F}, q_L) = &\; \delta[X_g\sigma_g(m_C) + X_b\sigma_b(m_C)] \\
&+ q_L(1 - \delta)[F_g\sigma_g(m_C) \\
&+ X_b\sigma_b(m_C)] - cm_C,
\end{aligned}
$$
(A3C)

(D) $\tilde{F} \in \Delta(D)$:

$$
\begin{aligned}
\Pi_{L1}^D(\tilde{F}, q_L) = &\; [\delta + q_L(1 - \delta)] \\
&[X_g\sigma_g(m_D) + X_b\sigma_b(m_D)] \\
&- cm_D,
\end{aligned}
$$
(A3D)

where m_A, m_B, m_C, and m_D denote the monitoring levels that satisfy the optimality conditions (A2A), (A2B), (A2C), and (A2D), respectively.

Now, for each possible set of $\tilde{F}$, we solve the following constrained maximization problem:

$$
\Pi_{L0}^i = \max_{\tilde{F} \in \Delta(i), q_L \in [0,1]} \Pi_{L1}^i(\tilde{F}, q_L),
$$

$$
i = A, B, C, D.
$$
(A4)

Using the envelope theorem and (A2A)–(A2D), the first-order conditions for each constrained maximization problem are described as follows:

(A) $\tilde{F} \in \Delta(A)$:

$$q_L\left[(1-\delta)\sigma_g(m_A) + (F_g - F_b)\right.$$

$$\left.\sigma_g'(m_A)\frac{\partial m_A}{\partial F_g}\right] + \eta_{g0} - \eta_{g1} = 0, \quad \text{(A5a)}$$

$$qL\left[(1-\delta)\sigma_b(m_A) + (F_g - F_b)\right.$$

$$\left.\sigma_g'(m_A)\frac{\partial m_A}{\partial F_b}\right] + \eta_{g0} + \eta_{b0} - \eta_{b1} = 0, \quad \text{(A5b)}$$

$$(1-\delta)[F_g\sigma_g(m_A) + F_b\sigma_b(m_A)]$$

$$+ q_L(F_g - F_b)\,\sigma_g'(m_A)\frac{\partial m_A}{\partial q_L} - s = 0, \quad \text{(A5c)}$$

where $\eta_{g0}, \eta_{g1}, \eta_{b0}, \eta_{b1},$ and ς are the nonnegative multipliers associated with $F_g \geq F_b$, $X_g \geq F_g$, $F_b \geq 0$, $X_b \geq F_b$, and $1 \geq q_L$, respectively. The partial derivatives $\partial m_A/\partial F_g$, $\partial m_A/\partial F_b$, and $\partial m_A/\partial q_L$ are derived by totally differentiating (A2A) with respect to m_A, F_g, F_b, and q_L.

(B) $\tilde{F} \in \Delta(B)$:

$$q_L\left[(1-\delta)\sigma_b(m_B) + (X_g - F_b)\sigma_g'\right.$$

$$\left.(m_B)\frac{\partial m_B}{\partial F_b}\right] + \eta_{b0} - \eta_{b1} = 0, \quad \text{(A6a)}$$

$$(1-\delta)[X_g\sigma_g(m_B) + F_b\sigma_b(m_B)]$$

$$+ q_L(X_g - F_b)\,\sigma_g'(m_B)\frac{\partial m_B}{\partial q_L} - s = 0, \quad \text{(A6b)}$$

where $\eta_{b0}, \eta_{b1},$ and ς are the nonnegative multipliers associated with $F_b \geq 0$, $X_b \geq F_b$, and $1 \geq q_L$, respectively. The partial derivatives $\partial m_B/\partial F_b$ and $\partial m_B/\partial q_L$ are obtained by totally differentiating (A2B) with respect to m_B, F_b, and q_L. Note that F_g is equal to X_g in this parameter constellation.

(C) $\tilde{F} \in \Delta(C)$:

$$q_L\left[(1-\delta)\sigma_g(m_C) + (F_g - X_b)\sigma_g'\right.$$

$$\left.(m_C)\frac{\partial m_C}{\partial F_g}\right] + \eta_{g0} - \eta_{g1} = 0, \quad \text{(A7a)}$$

$$(1-\delta)[F_g\sigma_g(m_C) + X_b\sigma_b(m_C)]$$

$$+ q_L(F_g - X_b)\,\sigma_g'(m_C)\frac{\partial m_C}{\partial q_L} - s = 0, \quad \text{(A7b)}$$

where $\eta_{g0}, \eta_{g1},$ and ς are the nonnegative multipliers associated with $F_g \geq X_b$, $X_g \geq F_g$ and $1 \geq q_L$, respectively. The partial derivatives $\partial m_C/\partial F_g$ and $\partial m_C/\partial q_L$ are constructed by totally differentiating (A2C) with respect to m_C, F_g, and q_L. Note that F_b is equal to X_b in this case.

(D) $\tilde{F} \in \Delta(D)$:

$$(1-\delta)[X_g\sigma_g(m_D) + X_b\sigma_b(m_D)]$$

$$+ q_L(X_g - X_b)\,\sigma_g'(m_D)\frac{\partial m_D}{\partial q_L} - s = 0, \quad \text{(A8)}$$

where ς is the nonnegative multiplier associated with $1 \geq q_L$. The partial derivative $\partial m_D/\partial q_L$ is derived by totally differentiating (A2D) with respect to m_D and q_L. Note that $F_g = X_g$ and $F_b = X_b$ in this case.

Proof of Proposition 1. We begin by evaluating the first-order conditions for $\tilde{F}$ and q_L, assuming $\tilde{F} \in \Delta(A)$, that is, (A5a)–(A5c). To do so, we first need to specify $\partial m_A/\partial F_g$, $\partial m_A/\partial F_b$, and $\partial m_A/\partial q_L$, which are obtained from (A2A). Totally differentiating (A2A) with respect to m_A, F_g, F_b, and q_L yields

$$\frac{\partial m_A}{\partial F_g} = \frac{\delta q_L \sigma_g'(m_A)}{\Lambda_A} < 0, \quad \text{(A9)}$$

$$\frac{\partial m_A}{\partial F_b} = -\frac{\delta q_L \sigma_g'(m_A)}{\Lambda_A} > 0, \quad \text{(A10)}$$

$$\frac{\partial m_A}{\partial q_L} = \frac{\delta(F_g - F_b)\sigma_g'(m_A)}{\Lambda_A} \leq 0, \quad \text{(A11)}$$

where $\Lambda_A = \delta[X_g - X_b - q_L(F_g - F_b)]\sigma_g''(m_A) < 0$. Note that Λ_A is negative because the second-order condition must be satisfied. The signs of (A9)–(A11) then follow from (2), $0 < q_L \leq 1$, and $\sigma'_g(m) > 0$. Since η_{g0}, η_{b0}, and η_{b1} are the nonnegative multipliers associated with $F_g \geq F_b \geq F_b \geq 0$, and $X_b \geq F_b$, (A5b) and (A10) show that $\eta_{g0} > 0$ or $\eta_{b1} > 0$ or both, that is, $F_g = F_b$ or $X_b = F_b$ or $F_g = F_b = X_b$. If $\eta_{g0} > 0$ so that $F_g = F_b$, it is seen from (A5a) that $\eta_{g1} > 0$, which means $X_g = F_g = F_b$. This contradicts $F_b \leq X_b < X_g$ for $\tilde{F} \in \Delta(A)$. Thus, we must have $\eta_{b1} > 0$ and $F_b = X_b$. Furthermore, if $F_g = F_b = X_b$, it again follows from (A5a) that $\eta_{g1} > 0$, which implies $X_g = F_g$. However, this contradicts $F_g = F_b = X_b < X_g$. Therefore, we must have $X_b = F_b < F_g$ and $\eta_{g1} = 0$. Given $\partial m_A / \partial F_g < 0$ from (A9) and $\partial m_A / \partial q_L < 0$ from (A11) with $X_b = F_b < F_g$, we can assume that F_g and q_L are determined as an interior solution by (A5a) and (A5c). Thus, rearranging (A2A), (A5a), and (A5c) with $X_b = F_b$ and $\eta_{g0} = \eta_{g1} = \varsigma = 0$, we obtain (18a)–(18e) if $\tilde{F} \in \Delta(A)$.

We next discuss the first-order conditions for $\tilde{F}$ and q_L, assuming $\tilde{F} \in \Delta(B)$, that is, (A6a) and (A6b). To specify $\partial m_B / \partial F_b$ and $\partial m_B / \partial q_L$, we totally differentiate (A2B) with respect to m_B, F_b, and q_L:

$$\frac{\partial m_B}{\partial F_b} = -\frac{\delta q_L \sigma'_g(m_B)}{\Lambda_B} > 0, \qquad \text{(A12)}$$

$$\frac{\partial m_B}{\partial q_L} = \frac{\delta(X_g - F_b)\sigma'_g(m_B)}{\Lambda_B} \leq 0, \qquad \text{(A13)}$$

where $\Lambda_B = \delta[X_g - X_b - q_L(X_g - F_b)]\sigma''_g(m_B) < 0$, which is negative from the second-order condition. It then follows from (A6a) and (A12) that $\eta_{b1} > 0$, that is, $X_b = F_b$. Given $\partial m_B / \partial q_L < 0$ from (A13) and $F_b = X_b < X_g$, we can assume that q_L is determined as an interior solution by (A6b). Thus, rearranging (A2B) and (A6b) with $\varsigma = 0$ and $(F_b, F_g) = (X_b, X_g)$ from $F_b = X_b$ and $\tilde{F} \in \Delta(B)$, we have (19a)–(19e) if $\tilde{F} \in \Delta(B)$.

To examine the first-order conditions for $\tilde{F}$ and q_L when $\tilde{F} \in \Delta(C)$, that is, (A7a) and

(A7b), we totally differentiate (A2C) with respect to m_C, F_g, and q_L:

$$\frac{\partial m_C}{\partial F_g} = -\frac{\delta q_L \sigma'_g(m_C)}{\Lambda_C} < 0, \qquad \text{(A14)}$$

$$\frac{\partial m_C}{\partial q_L} = \frac{\delta(F_g - X_b)\sigma'_g(m_C)}{\Lambda_C} \leq 0, \qquad \text{(A15)}$$

where $\Lambda_C = \delta[X_g - X_b - q_L(F_g - X_b)]$ $\sigma''_g(m_C) < 0$, which is negative from the second-order condition. Suppose that $X_b = F_b = F_g$. Then, it is found from (A7a) that $\eta_{g1} > 0$, that is, $X_g = F_g$. Since this contradicts $F_g = X_b$, we must have $X_b = F_b < F_g$ for $\tilde{F} \in \Delta(C)$. Given $\partial m_C / \partial F_g < 0$ from (A14) and $\partial m_C / \partial q_L < 0$ from (A15) with $F_g > X_b$, we can assume that F_g and q_L are determined as an interior solution by (A7a) and (A7b). Thus, rearranging (A2C), (A7a), and (A7b) with $X_b = F_b$ and $\eta_{g0} = \eta_{g1} = \varsigma = 0$, we have (18a)–(18e) if $\tilde{F} \in \Delta(C)$.

Finally, we investigate the first-order condition for q_L when $\tilde{F} \in \Delta(D)$, that is, (A8). We totally differentiate (A2D) with respect to m_D and qL, and see

$$\frac{\partial m_D}{\partial q_L} = \frac{\delta(X_g - X_b)\sigma'_g(m_D)}{\Lambda_D} < 0. \qquad \text{(A16)}$$

Here, $\Lambda_D = \delta(1 - q_L)(X_g - X_b)\sigma''_g(m_D) < 0$, which is negative due to the second-order condition. Given $\partial m_D / \partial q_L < 0$ from (A16), we can assume that q_L is determined as an interior solution by (A8). Thus, rearranging (A2D) and (A8) with $X_b = F_b$, $X_g = F_g$, and $\varsigma = 0$, we obtain (19a)–(19e) if $\tilde{F} \in \Delta(D)$.

Proof of Proposition 2. Since $(\tilde{F}^{**}, q_L^{**})$ is feasible in the problem (6) even if $\tilde{F}$ is restricted to the set $\Delta(A) \cup \Delta(C)$, we should notice that $\Pi_{L1}(\tilde{F}^*, q_L^*) \geq \Pi_{L1}(\tilde{F}^{**}, q_L^{**})$. Thus, the remaining problem is to check whether or not a solution with $F_g^* < X_g$ is really optimal.

In the absence of the monitoring problem, $\sigma_g(m)$ is independent of m so that $\sigma'_g(m) = 0$. Thus, the problem (6) has no interior solution with respect to F_g if $\tilde{F}$ is restricted to the set $\Delta(A) \cup \Delta(C)$. More specifically, it follows from (A5a) and

(A7a) that $\eta_{g1} > 0$ in this case. Thus, we see $F_g^* = X_g$ even if $\tilde{F}$ is restricted by the set $\Delta(A) \cup \Delta(C)$. This finding implies that the optimal security is equity.

We now return to the situation in which $\sigma_g'(m) > 0$. Let us take the solution $(F_g, F_b, q_L = (F_g^{**}, F_b^{**}, q_L^{**}) = (X_g, X_b, q_L^{**})$ as a starting point. Then, consider a permutation $(F_g^\lozenge, F_b^\lozenge, q_L^\lozenge)$ from the solution $(F_g^{**}, F_b^{**}, q_L^{**})$; that is, $(F_g^\lozenge, F_b^\lozenge, q_L^\lozenge) = (X_g - \epsilon, X_b, q_L^{**}(1 + \phi))$, where $X_g - X_b > \epsilon > 0$ and $\phi > 0$. Choose $m^\lozenge$ that satisfies

$$\delta[X_g - X_b - q_L^\lozenge(F_g^\lozenge - X_b)]\sigma_g'(m^\lozenge) = c,$$

which means

$$\delta[X_g - X_b - q_L^{**}(1 + \phi)(X_g - \epsilon - X_b)]\sigma_g'(m^\lozenge) = c. \tag{A17}$$

Since $(F_g^\lozenge, F_b^\lozenge) \in \Delta(A) \cap \Delta(C)$, the large investor's payoff is represented by

$$\prod_{L1}^A(\tilde{F}^\lozenge, q_L^\lozenge) = \delta[X_g\sigma_g(m^\lozenge) + X_b\sigma_g(m^\lozenge)]$$

$$+ q_L^{**}(1 + \phi)(1 - \delta)[(X_g - \epsilon)$$

$$\sigma_g(m^\lozenge) + X_b\sigma_b(m^\lozenge)] - cm^\lozenge.$$

Now, for $\prod_{L0}^B$ defined in Proposition 1, construct

$$\Gamma^{\epsilon,\phi} \equiv \prod_{L1}^A(\tilde{F}^\lozenge, q_L^\lozenge) - \prod_{L0}^B$$

$$= \delta(X_g - X_b)[\sigma_g(m^\lozenge) - \sigma_g(m^{**})]$$

$$+ q_L^{**}(1 + \phi)(1 - \delta)[(X_g - \epsilon - X_b)$$

$$[\sigma_g(m^\lozenge) - \sigma_g(m^{**})] - c(m^\lozenge - m^{**})$$

$$+ q_L^{**}\phi(1 - \delta)[(X_g - \epsilon)\sigma_g(m^{**})$$

$$+ X_b\sigma_b(m^{**})] - q_L^{**}(1 - \delta)\epsilon\sigma_g(m^{**}). \tag{A18}$$

Because of $\sigma_g'' < 0$, we find

$$\delta(X_g - X_b)[\sigma_g(m^\lozenge) - \sigma_g(m^{**})]$$

$$- \delta q_L^{**}(1 + \phi)(X_g - \epsilon - X_b)[\sigma_g(m^\lozenge)$$

$$- \sigma_g(m^{**})] > - \delta[X_g$$

$$- X_b - q_L^{**}(1 - \phi)$$

$$(X_g - \epsilon - X_b)]\sigma_g'(m^\lozenge)(m^{**} - m^\lozenge),$$

for $m^{**} \neq m^\lozenge$. \tag{A19}

Combining (A18) and (A19) yields

$$\Gamma^{\epsilon,\phi} > - \{\delta[X_g - X_b - q_L^{**}(1 + \phi)$$

$$(X_g - \epsilon - X_b)]\sigma_g'(m^\lozenge) - c\}(m^{**} - m^\lozenge)$$

$$+ q_L^{**}(1 + \phi)(X_g - \epsilon - X_b)$$

$$[\sigma_g(m^\lozenge) - \sigma_g(m^{**})]$$

$$+ q_L^{**}\phi(1 - \delta)[(X_g - \epsilon)$$

$$\sigma_g(m^{**}) + X_b\sigma_b(m^{**})]$$

$$- q_L^{**}(1 - \delta)\epsilon\,\sigma_g(m^{**}), \quad \text{for } m^{**} \neq m^\lozenge.$$

Since $m^\lozenge$ satisfies (A17), this inequality reduces to

$$\Gamma^{\epsilon,\phi} > q_L^{**}\{(1 + \phi)(X_g - \epsilon$$

$$- X_b)[\sigma_g(m^\lozenge) - \sigma_g(m^{**})]$$

$$+ \phi(1 - \delta)[(X_g - \epsilon)\sigma_g(m^{**})$$

$$+ X_b\sigma_b(m^{**})] - (1 - \delta)\epsilon\sigma_g(m^{**})\},$$

for $m^{**} \neq m^\lozenge$. \tag{A20}

Now, suppose that we can take a pair $(\epsilon, \phi) \in \{(\epsilon, \phi) \mid X_g - X_b > \epsilon > 0$ and $\phi > 0\}$ which satisfies

$$X_g - X_b - q_L^{**}(1 + \phi)$$

$$(X_g - \epsilon - X_b) \geq X_g - X_b$$

$$- q_L^{**}(X_g - X_b), \tag{A21}$$

$$\phi[(X_g - \epsilon)\sigma_g(m^{**}) + X_b\sigma_b$$

$$(m^{**})] \geq \epsilon\sigma_g(m^{**}). \tag{A22}$$

Condition (A21) with (19a), (A17), and $\sigma_g'' < 0$ leads to $m^\lozenge \geq m^{**}$, thereby ensuring that the first term in the large bracket of the right-hand side of (A20) is nonnegative. Condition (A22) also means that the sum of the remaining two terms in the large bracket of the right-hand side of (A20) are nonnegative. Thus, if (A21) and (A22) hold, the right-hand side of (A20) is nonnegative. Combining (A21) and (A22) under $(\epsilon, \phi) \in \{(\epsilon, \phi) \mid X_g - X_b > \epsilon > 0$ and $\phi > 0\}$, we now have the following sufficient condition for $\Gamma^{\epsilon,\phi} > 0$:

$$\Xi_1 \equiv \frac{\epsilon\sigma_g(m^{**})}{(X_g - \epsilon)\sigma_g(m^{**}) + X_b\sigma_b(m^{**})}$$

$$\leq \phi \leq \frac{\epsilon}{X_g - \epsilon - X_b} \equiv \Xi_2, \tag{A23}$$

where m^{**} is determined with q_L^{**} from (19a) and (19d). Note that $X_g - X_b > \epsilon$ is also fulfilled for any pair of $(\epsilon, \phi) > 0$ that satisfies (A23). Thus, if these exists a pair $(\epsilon, \phi) > 0$ that satisfies (A23), then $\Gamma^{\epsilon, \phi} > 0$ for $(\epsilon, \phi) \in \{(\epsilon, \phi) \mid X_g - X_b > \epsilon > 0$ and $\phi > 0\}$. This finding shows

$$\prod_{LO}^{A} \geq \prod_{L1}^{A}(\tilde{F}^{\diamond}, q_L^{\diamond}) > \prod_{LO}^{B}.$$

The remaining problem is to prove that a pair $(\epsilon, \phi) > 0$ that satisfies (A23) always exists. Given $\sigma_b(m^{**}) = 1 - \sigma_g(m^{**})$, we see

$$\frac{\epsilon \sigma_g(m^{**})}{(X_g - \epsilon)\sigma_g(m^{**}) + X_b\sigma_b(m^{**})}$$
$$\leq \frac{\epsilon}{X_g - \epsilon - X_b + \dfrac{X_b}{\sigma_g(m^{**})}}$$
$$< \frac{\epsilon}{X_g - \epsilon - X_b},$$

for any ϵ such that $X_g - X_b > \epsilon > 0$. This completes the proof of Proposition 2.

NOTE

* I am most grateful for helpful comments by Noriyuki Yanagawa and seminar participants at the ISER Seminar (Osaka University), the Finance Forum Seminar (Kansai Economic Research Center), and the Tezukayama University Workshop. I would also like to thank an anonymous referee for detailed and valuable comments.
1 In the United States, large shareholders are more common than is often believed (see Demsetz (1983), Shleifer and Vishny (1988), and Holderness and Sheehan (1988)). Furthermore, large investors such as pension funds and mutual funds have increasingly played active roles as delegated monitors in recent years (see Admati, Pfleiderer, and Zechner (1994)). In other countries, large investors are more prevalent. In Germany and Japan, commercial banks have significant powers because they vote significant blocks of shares, sit on boards of directors, play a dominant role in lending, and operate in a legal environment favorable to creditors (see Aoki (1990), Franks and Mayer (1994), OECD (1995), and Gorton and Schmid (1996)). Furthermore, in Japan, large crossholdings also strengthen the role of large investors (Prowse (1992), Berglöf and Perotti (1994), and OECD (1995)). In France, cross-ownership and core industries are the norm (OECD (1995)). Finally, in most of the rest of the world except the United Kingdom, firms are controlled by large owners such as the families of founders or the State. For the literature and empirical evidence on this issue, see Shleifer and Vishny (1997) and La Porta, Lopez-de-Silanes, and Shleifer (1999).

2 For the decline in the importance of bank financing in Japan, see Hoshi, Kashyap, and Scharfstein (1990) and Campbell and Hamao (1994). For the German evidence, see Baums (1994).

3 The monitoring level of the large investor may also be interpreted as her managerial effort or her investment level in the production or investment processes. If we follow this interpretation, our research enables us to investigate the underinvestment problem such as Williamson (1985), Klein, Crawford, and Alchian (1978), and Grout (1984) within the financial market equilibrium where the design and issued amount of security are endogenously determined.

4 Holmström and Tirole (1993) and Admati, Pfleiderer, and Zechner (1994) are the exceptional ones.

5 Unless we assume that the large investor initially owns the risky project, we cannot incorporate her liquidity benefits into the social surplus.

6 The recent work of Bolton and von Thadden (1998) and Maug (1998) compares the liquidity benefits obtained through dispersed corporate ownership with the benefits from efficient management control achieved by some degree of ownership concentration. Kahn and Winton (1998) also demonstrate that market liquidity can undermine effective control by a large shareholder because it gives the large shareholder excessive incentives to speculate rather than monitor.

7 The fraction q_L sold to the market does not necessarily equal to 1 because the large investor cannot sell all the holding fraction of the security even though she adjusts the design of the security. In other words, a change in the fraction of the security sold affects the revenues of the large investor in a different way from a change in the design of the security (see equation (3)). Thus, the fraction of the security sold is not a perfect substitute for the design of the security in our model.

8   More specifically, $\delta = 0$ in Allen and Gale (1988, 1991) and Gale (1992), while $\delta \in (0, 1)$ in De-Marzo and Duffie (1999). Another line of literature assumes the presence of noise or liquidity traders, instead of assuming the liquidity motive for the issuer. See Boot and Thakor (1993), Holmström and Tirole (1993), and Demange and Laroque (1995). As pointed out in DeMarzo and Duffie (1999), this kind of assumption ($\delta < 1$) is justified if the issuer faces strict credit constraints or binding minimal capital requirements. It is also plausible to impose this assumption if firms need to raise capital to fund other valuable investment opportunities under various forms of market imperfections.

9   To simplify the analysis, we do not specify the action of managers nor the structure of managerial contracts. Holmström and Tirole (1993) throw light on this problem in their model of market monitoring.

10   In the subsequent discussion, "tildes" is used to denote random variables.

11   As mentioned in note 3, the monitoring level of the large investor, m, may also be interpreted as her managerial effort or her investment level.

12   The minimum level of monitoring $\underline{m}$ may be set equal to zero.

13   As indicated in Innes (1990) and Nachman and Noe (1994), the monotonicity assumption is important in establishing the optimality of the debt-like security because this assumption can exclude the type of "do or die" contract under which the firm pays everything to investors in the bad state and nothing in the good state. Nachman and Noe (1994) additionally assume another monotonicity condition that the residual claims $X_s - F_s$ are nondecreasing in the available project returns, X_s. Even when this assumption is additionally imposed, all of our results in this paper still remain valid.

14   If the security belongs to the set of admissible securities, Δ, then we always have min $(X_s, F_s) = F_s$.

15   The second-order sufficient condition for m to be a local maximum of $R_L(m, \tilde{F}, q_L)$ is automatically satisfied if we also assume another monotonicity condition, that the residual claims $X_s - F_s$ are nondecreasing in X_s.

16   We should keep in mind that securitizing a larger portion of the project returns is not a perfect substitute for selling a larger portion of the issued security. This mainly depends on the assumption that a change in F_g can affect the payoff of the large investor in a different way from a change in q_L. See note 7.

17   See note 5.

REFERENCES

Admati, A. R., Pfleiderer, P., and Zechner, J. (1994) Large shareholder activism, risk sharing, and financial market equilibrium, *Journal of Political Economy* **102**, 1097–1130.

Aghion, P. and Bolton, P. (1992) An 'Incomplete contracts' approach to bankruptcy and the financial structure of the firm, *Review of Economic Studies* **59**, 473–494.

Allen, F. and Gale, D. (1988) Optimal security design, *Review of Financial Studies* **1**, 229–263.

Allen, F. and Gale, D. (1991) Arbitrage, short sales, and financial innovation, *Econometrica* **59**, 1041–1068.

Aoki, M. (1990) Towards an economic model of the Japanese firm, *Journal of Economic Literature* **28**, 1–27.

Baums, T. (1994) The German banking system and its impact on corporate finance and governance, in M. Aoki and H. Patrick (eds.), *The Japanese Main Bank System: Its Relevance for Developing and Transforming Economies*, Oxford University Press, Oxford, pp. 409–449.

Berglöf, E. and Perotti, E. (1994) The governance structure of the Japanese financial keiretsu, *Journal of Financial Economics* **36**, 259–284.

Berglöf, E. and von Thadden, E.-L. (1994) Short-term versus long-term investors: Capital structure with multiple investors, *Quarterly Journal of Economics* **109**, 1055–1084.

Bolton, P. and Scharfstein, D. S. (1990) A theory of predation based on agency problems in financial contracting, *American Economic Review* **80**, 93–106.

Bolton, P. and von Thadden, E.-L. (1998) Blocks, liquidity, and corporate control, *Journal of Finance* **53**, 1–25.

Boot, A. W. A. and Thakor, A. V. (1993) Security design, *Journal of Finance* **48**, 1349–1378.

Campbell, J. Y. and Hamao, Y. (1994) Changing patterns of corporate financing and the main bank system in Japan, in M. Aoki and H. Patrick (eds.), *The Japanese Main Bank System: Its Relevance for Developing and Transforming Economies*, Oxford University Press, Oxford, pp. 325–349.

Demange, G. and Laroque, G. (1995) Private information and the design of securities, *Journal of Economic Theory* **65**, 233–257.

DeMarzo, P. and Duffie, D. (1999) A liquidity-based model of security design, *Econometrica* **67**, 65–99.

Demsetz, H. (1983) The structure of ownership and the theory of the firm, *Journal of Law and Economics* **26**, pp. 375–390.

Dewatripont, M. and Tirole, J. (1994) A theory of debt and equity: Diversity of securities and manager-shareholder congruence, *Quarterly Journal of Economics* **109**, 1027–1054.

Diamond, D. W. (1984) Financial intermediation and delegated monitoring, *Review of Economic Studies* **51**, 393–414.

Franks, J. and Mayer, C. (1994) The ownership and control of German corporations, mimeo.

Gale, D. (1992) Standard securities, *Review of Economic Studies* **59**, 731–755.

Gale, D. and Hellwig, M. (1985) Incentive-compatible debt contracts: The one-period problem, *Review of Economic Studies* **52**, 647–664.

Gorton, G. and Schmid, F. (1996) Universal banking and the performance of German firms, *NBER Working Paper* No. 5453, National Bureau of Economic Research, Cambridge, Mass.

Grout, P. (1984) Investment and wages in the absence of binding contracts: A Nash bargaining approach, *Econometrica* **52**, 449–460.

Hart, O. and Moore, J. (1989) Default and renegotiation: A dynamic model of debt, mimeo.

Hart, O. and Moore, J. (1994) A theory of debt based on the inalienability of human capital, *Quarterly Journal of Economics* **109**, 841–879.

Holderness, C. and Sheehan, D. (1988) The role of majority shareholders in publicly held corporations: An exploratory analysis, *Journal of Financial Economics* **20**, 317–346.

Holmström, B. and Tirole, J. (1993) Market liquidity and performance monitoring, *Journal of Political Economy* **101**, 678–709.

Hoshi, T., Kashyap, A., and Scharfstein, D. (1990) Bank monitoring and investment: Evidence from the changing structure of Japanese corporate banking relationships, in G. Hubbard (ed.), *Asymmetric Information, Corporate Finance, and Investment*, University of Chicago Press, Chicago, pp. 105–126.

Innes, R. (1990) Limited liability and incentive contracting with ex-ante action choices, *Journal of Economic Theory* **52**, 45–67.

Kahn, C. and Winton, A. (1998) Ownership structure, speculation, and shareholder intervention, *Journal of Finance* **53**, 99–129.

Klein, B., Crawford, R., and Alchian, A. (1978) Vertical integration, appropriable rents, and the competitive contracting process, *Journal of Law and Economics* **21**, 297–326.

La Porta, R., Lopez-de-Silanes, F., and Shleifer, A. (1999) Corporate ownership around the world, *Journal of Finance* **54**, 471–517.

Maug, E. (1998) Large shareholders as monitors: Is there a trade-off between liquidity and control?, *Journal of Finance* **53**, 65–98.

Nachman, D. C. and Noe, T. H. (1994) Optimal design of securities under asymmetric information, *Review of Financial Studies* **7**, 1–44.

Organization for Economic Cooperation and Development, *Corporate Governance Environments in OECD countries* (1995).

Ohashi, K. (1995) Endogenous determination of the degree of market-incompleteness in future innovation, *Journal of Economic Theory* **65**, 198–217.

Prowse, S. (1992) The structure of corporate ownership in Japan, *Journal of Finance* **47**, 1121–1140.

Rahi, R. (1995) Optimal incomplete markets with asymmetric information, *Journal of Economic Theory* **65**, 171–197.

Rahi, R. (1996) Adverse selection and security design, *Review of Economic Studies* **63**, 287–300.

Shleifer, A. and Vishny, R. (1986) Large shareholders and corporate control, *Journal of Political Economy* **94**, 461–488.

Shleifer, A. and Vishny, R. (1997) A survey of corporate governance, *Journal of Finance* **52**, 737–783.

von Thadden, E.-L. (1995) Short-term versus long-term investors: Capital structure with multiple investors, *Review of Economic Studies* **62**, 557–575.

Townsend, R. (1979) Optimal contracts and competitive markets with costly state verification, *Journal of Economic Theory* **21**, 265–293.

Williamson, O. (1985) *The Economic Institutions of Capitalism*, Free Press.

## Chapter 6

Marco Becht[*] and Ailisa Röell

BLOCKHOLDINGS IN EUROPE: AN INTERNATIONAL COMPARISON[1]

Source: *European Economic Review*, 43(4–6) (1999): 1049–1056.

ABSTRACT

We preview empirical work by the European Corporate Governance Network on the size of block shareholdings in Europe. The most salient finding is the extraordinarily high degree of concentration of shareholder voting power in Continental Europe relative to the U.S.A. and the U.K. Thus the relationship between large controlling shareholders and weak minority shareholders is at least as important to understand as the more commonly studied interface between management and dispersed shareholders.

1. INTRODUCTION

THE PURPOSE OF THIS PRESENTATION IS TO DRAW attention to and briefly preview the work on large shareholding in Europe carried out in the context of an ongoing international research initiative, the European Corporate Governance Network (ECGN). The data and tables on which this article are based were collected for each country by participating 'country teams' (listed at the end of this paper), and are currently being prepared for publication in book form.

The structure of the paper is as follows. Section 2 discusses the quality and availability of the data, and describes the recent developments in Europe that have made the collection of reasonably comparable data on large blockholdings possible. Section 3 presents some comparative cross-country data and briefly discusses the findings and their relationship to differences among countries' legal and other institutions.

2. THE DATA

Data on large shareholders' stakes in listed companies has only recently become widely and publicly available throughout the European Union. The impetus for this development was given by the European Commission's 1988 Transparency Directive (more formally, Large Holdings Directive, 88/627/EEC). It requires member states to enact laws directing shareholders of companies listed on a member state exchange to notify the relevant authorities and the company itself within seven days whenever their voting rights cross the thresholds of 10%, 20%, 1/3 (or 25%), 50% and 2/3 (or 75%). The directive is quite strict as to the attribution of voting rights. Any voting rights controlled by a person or entity must be included, such as voting rights held indirectly through controlled companies, those obtained through written voting agreements, or those on shares lodged for safekeeping and exercised at discretion in the absence of instructions from the holders. As a result of member state legislation carrying out this directive, data on large shareholders' voting stakes has become available, starting in the early to mid-1990s, throughout the European Union.

There are several reasons why the data on large share stakes thus made available are imperfect in terms of quality and international comparability. The directive left countries with considerable leeway regarding how it was carried out; as a result, the information available varies greatly in quality and detail. For example, most countries do not require the notification of large ownership stakes (we will use the term 'ownership' to refer to cash-flow rather than voting rights) alongside voting stakes; a notable exception is the Netherlands. There is also some variation in the reporting thresholds used and in the accuracy of the snapshot of a company's control structure that can be obtained at any moment in time (as a result of reporting errors, deliberate omissions, changes in the total number of shares outstanding, etc.). More fundamentally, different countries have different legal devices available as a means of separating ownership from voting rights. Common examples are the use of dual class stock, the issue of essentially non-voting share certificates via trust offices, restrictions on voting rights of large share positions (voting caps), the issue of stock with contingent voting rights triggered by control disputes, and the use of pyramidal groups. Such intricacies are not always easy to reconstruct from the raw numbers reported in the context of the transparency legislation. The individual country teams of ECGN have thus to some degree found themselves working within the idiosyncrasies of their own country's situation; this has led to considerable differences in the focus, coverge and degree of detail in the different country reports.

Figure 6.1 describes the concept of 'ultimate' voting power that must be notified pursuant to the transparency legislation. Company 4 is a listed company whose control is at issue. While the largest *direct* stake in the company is 50%, in fact bank 2 controls 72% of the votes in company 4: 50% directly through its majority-held holding 3, plus the 20% owned by 1 via a voting pact, plus the 2% owned by individual 5 who has deposited the shares with 2, who controls the associated votes. Thus the *ultimate* voting block notified by 2 is 72%. The data presented in this paper concerns such ultimate voting blocks.

3. EVIDENCE ON BLOCKHOLDINGS

The most striking fact about blockholdings in Europe is that they are so much higher than in the U.S.A. Table 6.1 presents the median size of the largest ultimate voting block in listed industrial companies for various countries. In several countries, the median largest voting stake in listed companies is over 50%, suggesting that voting control by a large blockholder is the rule rather than the exception; and in no European country studied is the median largest shareholder small enough to fall below the 5% disclosure threshold. Table 6.2 provides a more detailed breakdown into ranges for the largest ultimate voting block. Note that, whereas in the U.S.A. over 50% of companies have a largest shareholder who holds less than 5% of the shares, in Austria and Germany there are virtually no such companies. These findings were summarised at the first ECGN conference in March 1997 under the heading 'Strong Blockholders–Weak Minority Owners' (see Becht, 1997a, b): the separation of ownership and control manifests itself in a fundamentally different way in Europe than in the U.S.A. While in the U.S.A. the main agency problems seem to stem from conflicts of interest between managers and dispersed, insufficiently interventionist shareholders, in much of continental Europe there are generally large blockholders present who can and do exercise control over management. Instead, the main potential conflict of interest lies between controlling shareholders and powerless minority shareholders. Recently LaPorta et al. (1998) have come to a similar conclusion focusing on a sample of 691 firms in a broader set of 27 countries.[2]

Within Europe, the level of concentration of voting power is by no means uniform; and these differences are rooted in differences in customs and the legal environment in different countries. To illustrate the striking differences in concentration of voting power among countries, consider the size of the largest voting block. In the U.K., the sample of 250 listed companies reports a very modest median value of 9.9%; while

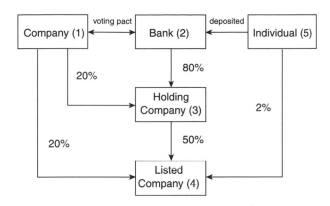

Figure 6.1 Direct stakes and voting blocks.

Table 6.1 Median size (%) of largest ultimate outside voting block for listed industrial companies

Country	Number of companies	Median largest voting block
Austria	50	52.0
Belgium	121	50.6
– BEL20	20	45.1
Germany	374	52.1
– DAX30	30	11.0
Spain	193	34.2
France – CAC40	40	20.0
Italy	216	54.53
The Netherlands	137	43.5
United Kingdom[a]	250	9.9
United States – NYSE	1309	0[b]
– NASDAQ	2831	0[b]

Sources: Austria: Gugler et al. (1999); Belgium: Becht et al. (1999); France: Bloch and Kremp (1999); Germany: Becht and Böhmer (1999); Italy: Bianchi et al. (1999); Spain: Crespí-Cladera and Garcia-Cestona (1999); The Netherlands: De Jong et al. (1999); UK: Goergen and Renneboog (1999); USA: Becht (1999a).

a Random sample of 250 companies.
b More precisely, below the 5% disclosure threshold.

at the other extreme, Germany, Austria and Italy all exceed 50%. The figures for the German DAX30 are somewhat atypical because there is a minimum turnover requirement for membership of the DAX30, leading these companies to widen their shareholder base in order to ensure their continued inclusion in the index. Similarly, the French CAC40 is an unrepresentative group of the largest and most liquid companies on the exchange. In general, voting power concentration is inversely related to company size: blocks held in smaller companies tend to be much larger on average, see some of the country reports forthcoming in Barca and Becht (1999).

The numbers mask strong differences in the way the large voting stakes are built up, which are discussed more fully in the various country reports. For example, in Italy, France and Belgium, pyramidal holding company groups are a preferred method of

Table 6.2 Voting power concentration, percentage of companies for which largest voting power stake lies in (in and below) various ranges

Range	Austria		Germany		Netherlands		USA (NYSE)		USA (NASDAQ)	
[x, y]	(%)	Cum (%)	(%)	Cum (%)	(%)	Cum (%)	(%)	Cum (%)	(%)	Cum (%)
0–5%	0	0	1.1	1.1	10.2	10.2	52.8	52.8	54.4	54.4
5–10%	0	0	1.9	3.0	11.7	21.9	21.1	73.9	17.4	71.9
10–25%	14	14	14.5	17.5	13.9	35.8	20.9	94.8	20.6	92.4
25–50%	18	32	18.3	35.8	24.8	60.6	3.5	98.3	5.5	98.0
50–75%	54	86	25.5	61.3	19.7	80.3	1.5	99.8	1.5	99.4
75–90%	8	94	17.5	78.8	6.6	86.9	0.2	100	0.5	99.9
90–95%	6	100	5.7	84.4	5.1`	92.0	0	100	0.0	99.9
95–100%	0	100	15.6	100	8.0	100	0	100	0.1	100

Sources: See Table 6.1.

amassing voting power without concentrating (cash flow) ownership. In the Netherlands, many companies use a device called an *Administratiekantoor,* a foundation controlled by company insiders that owns all or most of the voting stock and distributes non-voting share certificates to ordinary shareholders; as well as a defensive arsenal of preference or priority shares, with large blocks of potential voting power triggered by important control-relevant events. In Germany, voting pacts are a commonly used device for concentrating voting power, together with voting caps and the default voting power of banks where shares are placed in custody (a source of voting power excluded from the figures in Tables 6.1 and 6.2).

Figures 6.2 and 6.3, taken from the ECGN U.K. and Germany Country Reports, respectively, illustrate how countries' legal environment affects the pattern of voting power concentration. Thus is the U.K. the Takeover Panel's mandatory bid rule that prescribes a general cash offer to all shareholders whenever a blockholder crosses the 30% threshold, has effectively ensured that the growth of large blocks stops short of 30%. For the 250 companies examined, all blocks over 30% were held by founders and their families. In Germany, important thresholds induce clusters of holdings: the 10% anti-director threshold at which shareholders can take to court board members, the 25% blocking minority and 75% super majority for changes to company statutes,

and of course the 50% majority threshold. Such thresholds differ from country to country and are reflected in differences in clustering of voting blocks.

4. CONCLUSION

An immediate very clear conclusion from the EGCN's work on blockholdings in Europe is that voting power is highly concentrated in Continental Europe. Our survey, which was purely descriptive, raises more questions than it answers. Why is there this strong preference for voting power, and to what extent is it matched by concentration in cash flow ownership stakes (which, unfortunately, need not be disclosed under the EU transparency directive)? Becht (1999b) provides an analysis of the trade-offs involved. Is the current level of disclosure of voting and ownership stakes sufficient or excessive? Can EU policy on these matters do better in ensuring the smooth functioning of capital markets: in the words of U.S. Supreme Court justice Louis Brandeis, is transparency the best disinfectant? And Bianco and Casavola (1999) make progress towards tackling the most fundamental question: what are the effects of corporate governance variables such as (pyramidal) ownership concentration on company performance?[3] There is enormous scope for further empirical work on these issues.

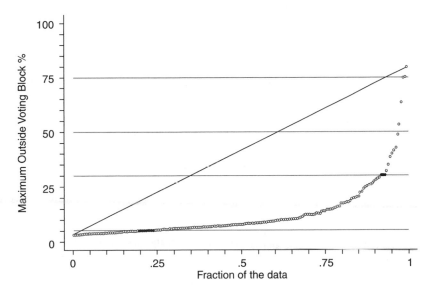

Figure 6.2 U.K.: Percentile plot of largest ultimate voting block.
Source: Goergen and Renneboog (1999).

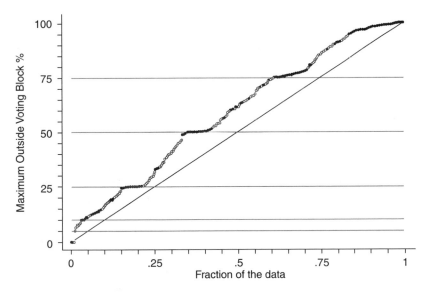

Figure 6.3 Germany: Percentile plot of largest ultimate voting block.
Source: Becht and Böhmer (1999).

NOTES

* Corresponding author.
1 The authors wish to stress that this paper reports on a collective research effort by the members of the European Corporate Governance Network. The ECGN was founded in 1996 as a vehicle for encouraging comparative empirical research on corporate governance in Europe. Lack of hard data has been a major impediment to such research, and the ECGN brings together local 'country teams' (listed in reference

section) familiar with the language and corporate culture of their own country to investigate issues of common interest. The data collection efforts focus on varibales for which there are common (and high) disclosure standards, such as those mandated by the European Union in various directives relating to company law and securities market; the current results regarding blockholdings are an example. The readers should consult the ECGN website, http://www.ecgn.org, for more detailed analysis and continuing updates of country reports and other work. During 1996–1998 the Network received financial support from the Directorate General for Industry of European Commission, Fondazione Eni Enrico Mattei and the Politecnico di Milano.

2 They also document that most companies in their sample are family or state controlled; see the ECGN country reports (Barca and Becht, 1999) for detailed information on this point for European listed companies.

3 See Gugler (1999) for a survey of work on this issue, including appendices by the various ECGN country teams on local research.

REFERENCES

Barca, F., Becht, M. (Eds.), 1999. Ownership and Control: A European Perspective, forthcoming.

Becht, M., 1997a. Strong blockholders, weak owners and the need for European mandatory disclosure. In: European Corporate Governance Network, The Separation of Ownership and Control: A Survey of 7 European Countries. Preliminary Report to the European Commission, Brussels.

Becht, M., 1997b. Strong blockholders – Weak minority owners. Fondazione Eni Enrico Mattei Newsletter, May.

Becht, M., 1999a. Beneficial ownership in the United States. In: Barca, F., Becht, M. (Eds.), Ownership and Control: A European Perspective, forthcoming.

Becht, M., 1999b. European corporate governance: Trading off liquidity against control. European Economic Reviews 43, this issue.

Becht, M., Böhmer, E., 1999. Ownership and voting power in Germany. In: Barca, F., Becht, M. (Eds.), Ownership and Control: A European Perspective, forthcoming.

Becht, M., Chapelle, A., Renneboog, L., 1999. Shareholding cascades: The separation of ownership and control in Belgium. In: Barca, F., Becht, M. (Eds.), Ownership and Control: A European Perspective, forthcoming.

Becht, M., Mayer, C. 1999. Ownership and voting power in Europe. In: Barca, F., Becht, M. (Eds.), Ownership and Control: A European Perspective, forthcoming.

Bianchi, M., Bianco, M., Enriques, L., 1999. Pyramidal groupe and the separation between ownership and control in Italy. In: Barca, F., Becht, M. (Eds.), Ownership and Control: A European Perspective, forthcoming.

Bianco, M., Casavola, P., 1999. Italian corporate governance: Effects of financial structure and firm performance. European Economic Reviews 43, this issue.

Bloch, L., Kremp, E., 1999. Ownership and voting power in France. In: Barca, F., Becht, M. (Eds.), Ownership and Control: A European Perspective, forthcoming.

Crespí-Cladera, R., Garcia-Cestona, M.A., 1999. Ownership and control: A Spanish survey. In: Barca, F., Becht, M. (Eds.), Ownership and Control: A European Perspective, forthcoming.

De Jong, A., Kabir, R., Marra, T., Röell, A., 1999. Ownership and control in The Netherlands. In: Barca, F., Becht, M. (Eds.), Ownership and Control: A European Perspective, forthcoming.

Goergen, M., Renneboog, L., 1999. Strong managers and passive institutional investors in the U.K. In: Barca, F., Becht, M. (Eds.), Ownership and Control: A European Perspective, forthcoming.

Gugler, K., 1999. Corporate governance and economic performance. Preliminary Report to the OECD, Paris.

Gugler, K., Kalss, S., Stomper, A., Zechner, J., 1999. The separation of ownership and control: An Austrian perspective. In: Barca, F., Becht, M. (Eds.), Ownership and Control: A European Perspective, forthcoming.

LaPorta, R., Lopez de Silanes, F., Shleifer, A., 1998. Corporate ownership around the world. Journal of Finance, forthcoming.

## Chapter 7

Mara Faccio* and Larry H. P. Lang

THE ULTIMATE OWNERSHIP OF WESTERN EUROPEAN CORPORATIONS[†]

Source: *Journal of Financial Economics,* 65(3) (2002): 365–395.

ABSTRACT

We analyze the ultimate ownership and control of 5,232 corporations in 13 Western European countries. Typically firms are widely held (36.93%) or family controlled (44.29%). Widely held firms are more important in the UK and Ireland, family controlled firms in continental Europe. Financial and large firms are more likely widely held, while non-financial and small firms are more likely family controlled. State control is important for larger firms in certain countries. Dual class shares and pyramids enhance the control of the largest shareholders, but overall there are significant discrepancies between ownership and control in only a few countries.

1. INTRODUCTION

RECENT STUDIES SUCH AS SHLEIFER AND VISHNY (1997), Claessens et al. (2000), and Holderness et al. (1999) suggest that Berle and Means' (1932) model of widely dispersed corporate ownership is not common, even in developed countries. In fact, large shareholders control a significant number of firms in many countries, including developed ones. To examine ownership and control by large shareholders, La Porta et al. (1999) traced the control chains of a sample of 30 firms in each of 27 countries. They documented the ultimate controlling owners and how they achieved control rights in excess of their ownership rights through deviations from the one-share-one-vote rule, pyramiding, and cross-holdings. Claessens et al. (2000) carried out a similar task for 2,980 listed firms in nine East Asian countries including Hong Kong, Indonesia, Japan, South Korea, Malaysia, the Philippines, Singapore, Taiwan, and Thailand. They found significant discrepancies

between ultimate ownership and control, allowing a small number of families to control firms representing a large percentage of stock market capitalization.

This paper answers two questions. What is the structure of the ultimate ownership of Western European firms? What are the means by which owners gain control rights in excess of ownership rights? To answer these questions, we collect ultimate ownership data for a sample of 5,232 listed firms in Austria, Belgium, Finland, France, Germany, Ireland, Italy, Norway, Portugal, Spain, Sweden, Switzerland, and the UK. We include a large number of medium- and small-sized corporations, and we include both non financial and financial companies. We measure ownership and control in terms of cash-flow and voting rights. For example, if a family owns 25% of Firm X that owns 20% of Firm Y, then this family owns 5% of the cash-flow rights of Firm Y (the product of the ownership stakes along the chain) and controls 20% of Firm Y (the weakest link along the control chain).

Western European firms are most likely to be widely held (36.93%) or family controlled (44.29%). Widely held firms are especially important in the UK and Ireland, while family control is more important in continental Europe. Widely held firms are more important for financial and large firms, while families are more important for non financial and small firms. In certain countries, widely held financial institutions also control a significant proportion of firms, especially financial firms. In some countries of continental Europe, the State also controls a significant proportion of firms, especially the largest. Widely held corporations control few firms.

We report the use of multiple classes of shares, pyramidal structures, holdings through multiple control chains, and cross-holdings, which are devices that give the controlling shareholders control rights in excess of their cash-flow rights. Pyramiding occurs when the controlling shareholder owns one corporation through another which he does not totally own. Firm Y is held through "multiple control chains" if it has an ultimate owner who controls it via *a multitude* of control chains, each of which includes at least 5% of the voting rights at each link. "Cross-holdings" means company Y directly or indirectly controls its own stocks. Dual class shares are used by few firms in Belgium, Portugal, and Spain, but by 66.07%, 51.17%, and 41.35% of firms in Sweden, Switzerland, and Italy. Pyramids and holdings through multiple control chains are used to control only 19.13% and 5.52% of listed firms respectively, being less important for family controlled firms and more important for firms controlled by the State and by widely held financial institutions. 53.99% of European firms have only one controlling owner. More than two-thirds of the family controlled firms have top managers from the controlling family. Overall, we find a substantial discrepancy between ownership and control in Belgium, Italy, Norway, Sweden, and Switzerland, but much less elsewhere.

Our results for the 20 largest firms differ slightly from those of La Porta et al. (1999), in that we find fewer State-controlled firms and more widely held firms, fewer pyramids, and more dual class shares. Compared to the findings of Claessens et al. (2000) for East Asia, we find that families control a higher proportion of firms; each family controls fewer firms on average; top families control a lower proportion of total stock market capitalization;[1] a higher proportion of family controlled companies have family members in top management; and the largest shareholder is less often alone, but averages much higher cash-flow rights, control rights, and ratio of cash-flow to voting rights. These differences may be due to weaker law enforcement in Asia that allows controlling owners to achieve effective control of a large number of firms by controlling and owning a smaller part of each firm.

Section 2 describes the data. Section 3 discusses ultimate ownership patterns. Section 4 discusses the means whereby owners gain control rights in excess of ownership rights and Section 5 measures the extent to which this has been achieved. Section 6 presents conclusions.

2. DATA

Some of the previous studies of corporate ownership and control, such as Lins and Servaes (1999a, b), rely primarily on Worldscope. However, we find its coverage inadequate. For example, Worldscope includes only 176 of 632 Spanish listed firms at the end of 1997. In this case, we instead rely upon the Spanish Stock Exchange regulatory authority's files (Comision Nacional del Mercado de Valores, 1998) which provides quarterly information on all shareholders with at least 5% of control rights, as well as directors' ownership for all listed firms. Moreover, ownership data is sometimes missing: in this case, Worldscope reports zero ownership stakes. To ensure accuracy, we include only countries for which we can obtain alternative sources (especially primary or official) to permit cross-checking. We do not rely on Worldscope if we have an official data source (i.e., the Stock Exchange ownership files). When official data sources are not available, we collect data from alternative sources. We use Worldscope for ownership data only when information for a specific firm can not otherwise be identified. Cross-checking excludes Luxembourg, Greece,[2] Denmark[3] and Holland[4] leaving comprehensive, reliable ownership data for 13 Western European countries: Austria, Belgium, Finland, France, Germany, Ireland, Italy, Norway, Portugal, Spain, Sweden, Switzerland, and the UK. For these countries, Table 7.1 lists the data sources for ownership and multiple classes of shares. Data limitations confined our sample to the period from 1996 to the end of 1999.[5] This is not a significant restriction since ownership structures tend to be rather stable, as noted in La Porta et al. (1999).

The European Corporate Governance Network (ECGN), too, has sponsored several studies on ownership structures within the European Union.[6] However, compliance with the European Union directive on large shareholdings (88/627/EEC) restricts meaningful cross-country analysis with non-European Union countries. In particular, the ownership measures documented in those studies represent neither ultimate ownership nor ultimate control stakes. Specifically, they do not consider the use of multiple voting shares, and simply add up direct and indirect control stakes without tracing them to the ultimate owners. The controlling owner is defined as the one who controls an absolute majority (i.e., over 50%) of voting rights, or holds enough voting rights to have de facto control. For example, French regulation defines de facto control as occurring when a person or a legal entity owns, directly or indirectly, more than 40% of voting rights and no other partners or shareholders own a higher percentage directly or indirectly (Bloch and Kremp, 1998). This corresponds to a control threshold of 40%. To illustrate the bias that this definition introduces, consider the ultimate control structure of Montedison (Italy). Montedison has two shareholders with a

stake above 2%: Compart with a stake of 33.45% and Mediobanca with a stake of 3.77%. Compart is indicated in the Italian supervisory authority's files as the "ultimate" owner of Montedison. However, we found that Compart has three shareholders with stakes above 10%: Credit (11.01%), Cassa di Risparmio di Roma (10.14%), and Mediobanca (15.26%). According to our definition, Compart is the ultimate controlling shareholder of Montedison at the 20% threshold. However, at the 10% threshold, Mediobanca would be the largest ultimate owner of Montedison, with a 15.26% + 3.77% = 19.03% control stake. Furthermore, mechanisms used to secure control rights in excess of ownership rights are not systematically analyzed.

Over the sample period, a total of 5,547 firms were listed in these 13 countries. Of these, we excluded 167 firms whose ownership was not recorded, 61 that use nominee accounts (mostly in the UK and Ireland, where firms are not required to disclose the identity of their "true" owners) and 87 affiliates of foreign firms (i.e., a foreign firm controls at least 50% of their voting rights) where we could not follow their ownership chain. We retain the affiliates of foreign firms in our database whenever the holding firm is included in our sample. This screening left 5,232 firms comprising 94.32% of the listed firms in the 13 countries.[7] For these firms, our database records all owners who control at least 5% of voting rights. In France, Germany, and Spain, such owners must disclose their identity. The disclosure threshold is 2% in Italy and 3% in the UK.

The difficulty of organizing dispersed shareholders means that if the largest shareholder holds a substantial block of shares, then that shareholder has effective control. In line with earlier studies, we shall assume that 20% of the voting shares suffices to ensure control. We shall also discuss some cases that assume a control threshold of 10%. If no shareholder exceeds a given control threshold, then the firm is said to be widely held at that threshold. Table 7.2 sets out the screening process and lists the samples of firms analyzed in later tables.

Table 7.1 List of country specific data sources used to collect data on direct ownership (i.e., names of large shareholders, and stakes held in the company), and dual class share structures

Countries	Direct ownership data	Dual class shares
Austria	Wiener Börse (2000), "Yearbook 1999" Worldscope (1998)	Wiener Börse (2000), "Yearbook 1999"
Belgium	Brussels Stock Exchange (www.bxs.be) Worldscope (1998)	Datastream Brussels Stock Exchange
Finland	Helsinki Media Blue Book, "Major Finnish Firms Internet Database" (http://www.bluebook.fi/en/tuotteet/haku/majorfinnishfirms.html) Hugin, Annual Report CD (1998) (http://www.huginonline.com)	Datastream Helsinki Media Blue Book, "Major Finnish Firms Internet Database"
France	The Herald Tribune (1997), "French Firm Handbook 1997," SFB-Paris Bourse Financial Times (1997), "Extel Financial" Worldscope (1998) http://www.bourse-de-paris.fr/fr/market8/fsg830.htm	Datastream Financial Times (1997), "Extel Financial" Les Echos (1996) Muus (1998)
Germany	Commerzbank (1997), "Wer gehört zu wem" (http://www.commerzbank.com/navigate/date_frm.htm) Financial Times (1997), "Extel Financial" Worldscope (1998)	Datastream Die Welt (1996), available at: http://www.welt.de/ Financial Times (1997), "Extel Financial" Becht and Boehmer (1998)
Ireland	http://www.hemscott.com/equities/firm/ Worldscope (1998)	Datastream Worldscope (1998)

Country		
Italy	CONSOB (1997), "Bollettino – edizione speciale n. 4/97 – Compagine azionaria delle società quotate in borsa o ammesse alle negoziazioni nel mercato ristretto al 31 dicembre 1996" (http://www.consob.it/trasparenza_soc_quot/trasp_soc_quot.htm) Il Sole 24 ore (1997), "Il taccuino dell'azionista"	Datastream Il Sole 24 ore (1997), "Il taccuino dell'azionista"
Norway	Hugin, Annual Report CD (1998) Worldscope (1998)	Datastream Hugin, Annual Report CD (1998)
Portugal	Bolsa de Valores de Lisboa, "Sociedades Cotadas 1997" (1998)	Bolsa de Valores de Lisboa, "Sociedades Cotadas 1997" ABC (1996)
Spain	Comision Nacional del Mercado de Valores (1998), "Participaciones significativas en sociedades cotizadas" (http://www.cnmv.es/english/cnmve.htm)	Financial Times (1997), "Extel Financial" Crespi-Cladera and Garcia-Cestona (1998)
Sweden	Hugin, Annual Report CD (1998) Worldscope (1998)	Datastream Hugin, Annual Report CD (1998)
Switzerland	Union Bank of Switzerland (1998), "Swiss Stock Guide 96/97," Zurich	Union Bank of Switzerland (1998), "Swiss Stock Guide 96/97," Zurich
United Kingdom	Financial Times (1997), "Extel Financial" London Stock Exchange (1997), "The London Stock Exchange Yearbook" Financial Times Worldscope (1998) http://www.hemscott.com/equities/firm/	Datastream Financial Times (1997), "Extel Financial" Financial Times (1996)

Table 7.2   Screenings used to identify and remove corporations without reliable ownership data, and sub-samples of firms used in the different sections of the paper. Panel A describes the procedure used to eliminate companies with insufficient or unreliable data on ownership, due to unavailable data, or related to the impossibility to trace ownership back to the ultimate owner (i.e., when the direct controlling shareholder is from a country for which we do not have ownership data, or when the direct owner is a nominee). Panel B reports the total number of firms remaining after this screening, as well as the number of firms with an ultimate owner at the 5% and 20% cutoffs. It also lists the different subsets of firms used in the various sections of the paper

Panel A: Selection criteria	*Number*	*Percentage*	
All listed firms	5,547	100.00	
Firms with no ownership data	(167)	(3.01)	
Firms majority-controlled by foreign investors	(87)	(1.57)	
Firms controlled by "nominees"	(61)	(1.10)	
Firms in our sample	5,232	94.32	
Panel B: Sample of firms analyzed in the various tables			*Tables*
All listed firms	5,232	100.00	7.3, 7.4, 7.5, 7.6
Firms where at least one shareholder holds at least 5% of voting rights	4,806	91.86	7.9
Firms where at least one shareholder holds at least 20% of voting rights	3,300	63.07	7.7, 7.8
Selected samples of firms			7.10; Figures 7.1 and 7.2

The exclusion of firms that use nominee accounts may overstate the proportion of widely held firms in our sample. However, nominee accounts are the largest shareholders in only a small proportion of firms (less than 5%), so any bias is likely to be marginal. Ireland and the UK have the highest proportion of nominee accounts so this bias would be strongest there. These countries also have the highest proportions of widely held firms, so the exclusion of firms using nominee accounts is unlikely to distort our cross-country comparisons.

A shareholder of a corporation is said to be an ultimate owner at a given threshold if he controls it via a control chain whose links all exceed that threshold. If a firm has two owners with 12% of control rights each, then we say that the firm is half controlled by each owner at the 10% threshold, but that the firm is widely held at the 20% threshold. In the case of a firm with two owners (a family with 20% of control rights and a widely held corporation with 19% of control rights) we would say that this firm is half controlled

by each owner at the 10% threshold, but family controlled at the 20% threshold.

2.1. Calculation of cash-flow rights and control rights

Corporate ownership is measured by cash-flow rights, and control is measured by voting rights. Ownership and control rights can differ because corporations can issue different classes of shares that provide different voting rights for given cash-flow rights. Ownership and control rights can also differ because of pyramiding and holdings through multiple control chains.

Firm Y is said to be controlled through pyramiding if it has an ultimate owner, who controls Y indirectly through another corporation that it does not wholly control. For example, if a family owns 15% of Firm X, that owns 20% of Firm Y, then Y is controlled through a pyramid at the 10% threshold. However, at the 20% threshold, we would say that Firm Y is directly controlled by Firm X (which is widely held at the

20% threshold) and no pyramiding would be recorded. If Firm X holds 100% of Firm Y, then again there is no pyramid. Pyramiding implies a discrepancy between the ultimate owner's ownership and control rights. In the above example, the family owns 3% of the cash-flow rights of Firm Y (the product of its ownership stakes along the control chain) but its control rights are measured by the weakest link in its control chain, i.e., 15%.

Firm Y is said to be controlled through a multiple control chain if it has an ultimate owner who controls it via *a multitude* of control chains, each of which includes at least 5% of the voting rights at each link. In the previous example, suppose that the family also owns 7% of Firm Y directly. Then the family owns 10% of the cash-flow rights of Firm Y (0.15 * 0.20 + 0.07) and controls 22% of its voting rights (min (0.15, 0.20) + 0.07). Claessens et al. (2000) defined "holdings through multiple control chain" as "cross-holdings."

A firm can be controlled by holdings through multiple control chains, even though it is not controlled by pyramiding. For example, suppose that Firm A controls 10% of B and 100% of C, which controls 15% of B. Since C is fully controlled by A in the control chain A-C-B, there is no pyramiding. However, Firm A controls Firm B directly and indirectly through Firm C, with control rights of 25%. We conclude that Firm A controls Firm B through multiple control chains because: (1) Firm B has a controlling owner at the 20% level; (2) B is controlled via multiple control chains; and (3) all links in each chain involve at least 5% of the control rights.

Firm Y is controlled by a cross-holding at the 20% threshold if Firm X holds a stake in Firm Y of at least 20%, and Y holds a stake in Firm X of at least 20%, or if firm Y holds directly at least 20% of its own stocks.

2.2. Types of ownership

This section discusses our classification of ultimate owners into the following six types:

Family: A family (including an individual) or a firm that is unlisted on any stock exchange.

Widely held financial institution: A financial firm (SIC 6000-6999) that is widely held at the control threshold.

State: A national government (domestic or foreign), local authority (county, municipality, etc.), or government agency.

Widely held corporation: A non financial firm, widely held at the control threshold.

Cross-holdings: The firm Y is controlled by another firm, that is controlled by Y, or directly controls at least 20% of its own stocks.

Miscellaneous: Charities, voting trusts, employees, cooperatives, or minority foreign investors.

Where the ultimate owner of a corporation is an unlisted firm, we tried to trace its owners using all available data sources. We had incomplete success because most of our sample countries do not require unlisted firms to disclose their owners. One exception is the UK, where the 3% disclosure rule also applies to unlisted firms. However, we were still not able to find ownership data for all unlisted firms. If we failed to identify the owners of an unlisted firm, then we classified them as a family. This approach is close to that of Claessens et al. (2000), who regard as a family any controlling shareholder that was an unlisted firm in a business group. Below, we offer both a general justification for this convention and statistical support for it in the largest European economies.

In the case of the Fiat group, for example, we traced the ownership of La Rinascente back to the Agnelli family from *Il Taccuino dell' Azionista*, although we find two unlisted firms in its chain of control (namely, Carfin and Eufin). In fact, La Rinascente is controlled by Eufin (with a 32.8% ownership and a 40.51% control stake), which is wholly controlled by Ifil. *Wer gehört zu wem* is particularly useful in a number of cases in Germany. However, it helps us identify the owners for only 20% of unlisted German firms. For example, we find that TCHIBO Holding AG is the largest owner of Beiersdorf AG (a listed firm) with a 25.87% O&C stake. TCHIBO Holding, however, is an unlisted firm. We identified its ultimate owner: the Herz family, which has a 100% O&C stake. Another case is Heidelberger Zement AG, whose largest owner (with a 19.07% O stake and a 21.8% C stake) is Schwenk Gmbh, again an unlisted firm. We find that Schwenk is 90% owned and controlled by the Schwenk family, and 10% owned by the Babette family. In some cases, the ownership structure of unlisted firms is more complex. For example, the direct owner of Thyssen AG is Thyssen Beteiligunsverw Gmbh, which is unlisted. We find that this firm is 49.999% owned and controlled by Commerzbank (a listed, widely held financial firm), and 49.981% owned and controlled by Allianz. A number of complex cases of ownership of unlisted firms were also reported by La Porta et al. (1999).

Our database records the unlisted subsidiaries of widely held corporation or financial institution, so any listed firm controlled by an unlisted firm that is controlled by a widely held corporation or financial institution is recorded as controlled by the latter in our database. Thus, an unlisted firm that we identify as the ultimate controller of a listed firm is unlikely to be, in fact, controlled by a widely held corporation or financial institution. The unlisted firm isn't likely controlled by the State because State-controlled firms tend to be listed. In any case, State ownership has decreased dramatically in Europe after the privatization wave of the 1990s. The low likelihood that an unlisted firm is, in fact, controlled by a widely held corporation, widely held financial institution, or the State leaves families as the most likely controller of an unlisted firm.

For Germany, we collected a sample of 500 unlisted firms with ultimate owners from *Wer gehört zu wem*. We considered firms in alphabetical order, including a firm in our sample if we could trace its ultimate owners. We stopped when our sample numbered 500. We found that the average control stake is 89.44%. In 68% of the cases, the largest owner is the sole owner; in the remainder, the largest owner holds an average stake of 67%. Families, both domestic and foreign, are the largest ultimate owners of 90.6% of these firms.

At the 20% level, financial firms control 4.9% of unlisted firms, the State 2.67%, and cross-holdings 1.83%. Thus, both State and widely held financial firms are insignificant as ultimate owners of unlisted firms. Furthermore, since the State and the largest financial institutions are included in the *Wer gehört zu wem* database, we were able to identify them and trace their ownership chain. This further reduces the possibility of bias in our sample.

For Italy, Bianchi et al. (1998) considered a sample of 1,000 manufacturing firms surveyed by the Bank of Italy. They reported that the largest immediate shareholder of these firms held, on average, a direct stake of 67.69%. Among all types of immediate shareholders, individuals held 48% of equity, non financial firms 36.9%, financial firms 0.17%, the State 4.6%, and foreign investors 8%. We secured a wider sample of 3,800 unlisted Italian firms with ultimate owners from the AIDA database.[8] We found that the State is the largest owner for 0.4% of firms, financial institutions for 0.2%, and families (domestic and foreign) for 99.4%. The average ultimate control stake of the largest controlling shareholder was 70.71%.

For France, Bloch and Kremp (1998) summarize the ownership structure of a sample of 282,322 (mostly unlisted) firms.[9] For firms with more than 500 employees, the largest owner held, on average, 88% of the capital. For 56% of the unlisted firms, the largest owner was a family; for the remaining 44% it was another corporation, usually an unlisted firm. For the UK, Goergen and Renneboog (1998) reported that 78% of unlisted firms are fully controlled by one shareholder, while the remaining 22% have a shareholder who (directly) holds a majority stake.[10]

2.3. Examples

Figure 7.1 illustrates dual class shares and pyramiding in the Nordström family group of Sweden. All holdings of more than 5% of a firm's shares are listed. All firms shown in Figure 7.1 have dual class shares: A-shares carry one voting right while B-shares

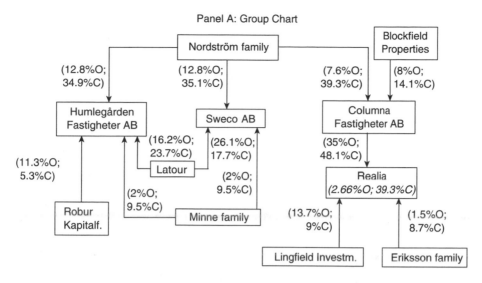

Panel A: Group Chart

Panel B: Calculating ownership and voting rights in Realia's capital structure

Type	Number of shares	Voting rights	Number of votes	Percent of share capital	Percent of votes
A-shares	2.641 million	1	2.641 million	5.8%	38.09%
B-shares	42.922 million	1/10	4.292 million	94.2%	61.91%
All	*45.563 million*		*6.933 million*	*100%*	*100%*

Shareholders	A-shares	B-shares	Ownership	Control
Columna Fastigheter	1.933 million	14.007 million	35.0%	48.1%
Lingfield Investments	—	6.259 million	13.7%	9.0%
The Eriksson family	0.591 million	0.101 million	1.5%	8.7%

Figure 7.1 The Nordström family group (Sweden). This figure describes the major listed firms controlled by the Nordström family. All control stakes of at least 5% are reported. All the firms have dual class shares with A-shares each carrying one voting right and B-shares each carrying a tenth of a vote. The procedure used to compute direct ownership and control rights is illustrated in Panel B. Ownership stakes are denoted by "O" and voting stakes by "C." Direct ownership and control stakes are shown alongside each of the arrows, while the resulting ultimate ownership and control stakes for Realia (the only case of pyramiding) by the Nordström family are reported in the firm's box.

carrying one-tenth of a voting right. Realia has two classes of shares: 2.641 million A-shares and 42.922 million B-shares. A- and B-shares have the same face value, so the total stock capital is 45.563 million shares. A-shares constitute 5.8% of stock capital (= 2.641 million/45.563 million) while B-shares constitute 94.2%. A-shares carry 2.641 million votes, while B-shares

carry 4.292 million votes (= one-tenth of 42.922 million). Thus, A-shares carry 38.09% of the votes (= 2.641 million/ (2.641 million + 4.292 million)), while B-shares carry 61.91% of votes.

Realia has three direct shareholders: Columna Fastigheter, Lingfield Investment, and the Eriksson family. Columna owns 1.933 million A-shares and 14.007 million

B-shares. Thus, Columna owns 35% (= (1.933 million + 14.007 million)/ 45.563 million) of cash-flow rights, and controls 48.1% (= (1.933 million + 1.401 million)/ (2.641 million + 4.292 million)) of votes in Realia. Realia's second largest direct shareholder, Lingfield Investments, owns no A-shares and only 6.259 million B-shares, which comprise 13.7% (6.259 million/ 45.563 million) of the cash-flow rights, and 9% (0.6259/(2.641 million + 4.292 million)) of the control rights. Finally, the Eriksson family owns 0.591 million A-shares and 0.101 million B-shares, comprising 1.5% (= (0.591 million + 0.101 million)/ 45.563 million) of the ownership rights and 8.7% (= (0.591 million + 0.0101 million)/ (2.641 million + 4.292 million)) of the control rights. Through Columna Fastigheter, the Nordström family has sole control of Realia at the 20% threshold. However, at the 10% threshold, Realia has a second large shareholder, Blockfield Properties. In Relia's control structure there are two pyramiding chains: Nordström family/Columna/Realia and Blockfield/Columna/Realia.

Figure 7.2 illustrates the control of Unicem by pyramiding, holdings through multiple control chains, and dual class shares within the Agnelli family group, the largest Italian group. The methodology presented in Figure 7.1 is used to compute cash-flow rights (O) and control rights (C), taking account of dual class shares. Unicem is directly controlled by two major shareholders: Ifi and Ifil. Ifil is controlled by Ifi with a direct stake (O = 7.97%; C = 14.6%) and an indirect stake (O = 20.55%; C = 37.64%) through Carfin, a wholly owned, non financial unlisted firm. Since Carfin is wholly controlled by Ifi, we consider Ifi's stake in Ifil as a direct holding rather than a pyramid, although we say there is holdings through multiple control chain (see section 2.1). Ifi is controlled by a single major shareholder, Giovanni Agnelli & C. S.p.A. (the Agnelli family). The Agnelli family's control of Unicem is thus exercised through pyramiding (Ifi-Carfin-Ifil-Unicem), non voting shares (within Ifi, Ifil, and Unicem), and two holdings through multiple control

chains (Ifi-Ifil and Ifi-Unicem, denoted by dotted lines in Figure 7.2).

To compute the Agnelli family's ultimate ownership of Unicem, we form the product of its ownership stakes along the pyramidal chain of Agnelli-Ifi-Carfin-Ifil-Unicem, namely 100% * 41.23% * 100% * 20.55% * 8.76% = 0.7422%. We then add the stake from the two further (i.e., multiple) control chains (the dotted lines). The first chain is from Ifi into Ifil (the left side of Figure 7.2) which gives the Agnelli family a stake of 100% * 41.23% * 7.97% * 8.76% = 0.2878%. The second chain is from Ifi to Unicem (the right side of Figure 7.2) which gives the Agnelli family a stake of 100% * 41.23% * 19.42% = 8.0069%. The family's overall ownership stake in Unicem is the sum of these three stakes: 0.7422% + 0.2878% + 8.0069% = 9.0369%.

The Agnelli family's ultimate control stake is the sum of the weakest links along each control chain. The weakest link in the pyramidal chain is min(100%; 82.45%; 100%; 37.64%; 14.81%) = 14.81%. In the control chain from Ifi to Ifil, the weakest link is min(100%; 82.45%; 14.16%; 0%) = 0%. Note that Ifil controls 14.81% of Unicem; this 14.81% stake has already been considered in the pyramidal chain, so we use 0%. In the control chain from Ifi to Unicem, the weakest link is min(100%; 82.45%; 32.83%) = 32.83%. The Agnelli family's control stake in Unicem is the sum of these three weakest links, namely 14.81% + 0% + 32.83% = 47.64%. The ratio of cash-flow to voting rights is 0.1897 (9.04%/47.64%).

We conclude that Unicem is controlled by the Agnelli family at both the 10% and the 20% thresholds. The company has only one controlling shareholder, and its control structure includes pyramiding, multiple control chains, and multiple class shares.

3. ULTIMATE OWNERSHIP PATTERNS

Table 7.3 analyzes the ultimate controlling owners of Western European corporations at the 20% threshold. In all countries,

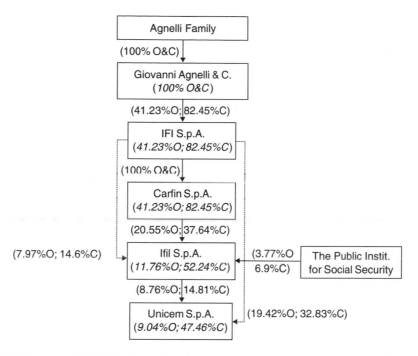

Figure 7.2 Unicem (Italy). This figure describes the principal shareholders of Unicem, a complex case of pyramiding, holdings through multiple control chains, and the use of dual class shares within the Agnelli family group, the largest Italian group. All control stakes of at least 5% are reported. The company has only one ultimate owner, the Agnelli family, which controls 47.64% of the voting rights and owns 9.04% of the cash-flow rights in Unicem. Hard lines indicate pyramiding while dotted lines indicate holdings through further (i.e., multiple) control chains. Ownership stakes are denoted by "O" and voting stakes by "C." Direct ownership and control stakes are shown alongside each arrow, while the Agnelli family's ultimate ownership and control stakes (when different from the direct stakes) are shown in each firm's box.

widely held and family controlled firms are the most important category. 36.93% of the firms in our sample are widely held and 44.29% are family controlled. However, there is a sharp cleavage between ownership patterns in continental Europe and in the UK and Ireland. Widely held firms comprise 63.08% of UK firms and 62.32% of Irish firms; in continental Europe the highest percentages of widely held firms are all in Scandinavia but are substantially lower (Sweden 39.18%, Norway 36.77%, Finland 28.68%). The lowest percentages of widely held firms are in Germany (10.37%), Austria (11.11%), and Italy (12.98%). The picture for family control is reversed. Here, the lowest

percentages are in the UK (23.68%) and Ireland (24.63%); in continental Europe, the lowest percentages are in Norway (38.55%), Sweden (46.94%), Switzerland (48.13) and Finland (48.84%). In every other Western European country, family controlled firms are in the majority.

The UK and Ireland also stand apart in the low percentages of corporations that are State controlled (0.08% and 1.45%). In continental Europe, the State controls more than 10% of the listed firms in Austria, Finland, Italy, and Norway.

9.03% of Western European firms are controlled by widely held financial institutions, this being especially significant in

Table 7.3 Ultimate control of publicly traded firms. Data relating to 5,232 publicly traded corporations are used to construct this table. The table presents the percentage of firms controlled by different controlling owners at the 20% threshold. Controlling shareholders are classified into six types. Family: A family (including an individual) or a firm that is unlisted on any stock exchange. Widely held financial institution: A financial firm (SIC 6000–6999) that is widely held at the control threshold. State: A national government (domestic or foreign), local authority (county, municipality, etc.), or government agency. Widely held corporation: A non financial firm, widely held at the control threshold. Cross-holdings: The firm Y is controlled by another firm, that is controlled by Y, or directly controls at least 20% of its own stocks. Miscellaneous: Charities, voting trusts, employees, cooperatives, or minority foreign investors. Companies that do not have a shareholder controlling at least 20% of votes are classified as widely held

Country	Number of Firm	Widely held	Family	Family of which:		State	Widely held Corporation	Widely held Financial	Miscellaneous	Cross-holdings
				Identified families	Unlisted firms					
Austria	99	11.11	52.86	12.12	40.74	15.32	0.00	8.59	11.11	1.01
Belgium	130	20.00	51.54	7.31	44.23	2.31	0.77	12.69	12.69	0.00
Finland	129	28.68	48.84	16.28	32.56	15.76	1.55	0.65	4.52	0.00
France	607	14.00	64.82	26.11	38.71	5.11	3.79	11.37	0.91	0.00
Germany	704	10.37	64.62	27.03	37.59	6.30	3.65	9.07	3.37	2.62
Ireland	69	62.32	24.63	13.04	11.59	1.45	2.17	4.35	5.07	0.00
Italy	208	12.98	59.61	39.50	20.11	10.34	2.88	12.26	1.20	0.72
Norway	155	36.77	38.55	10.59	27.96	13.09	0.32	4.46	4.54	2.27
Portugal	87	21.84	60.34	5.17	55.17	5.75	0.57	4.60	6.90	0.00
Spain	632	26.42	55.79	6.25	49.54	4.11	1.64	11.51	0.47	0.05
Sweden	245	39.18	46.94	22.65	24.29	4.90	0.00	2.86	5.71	0.41
Switzerland	214	27.57	48.13	22.66	25.47	7.32	1.09	9.35	6.31	0.23
UK	1,953	63.08	23.68	12.22	11.46	0.08	0.76	8.94	3.46	0.00
Total	5,232	36.93	44.29	16.93	27.36	4.14	1.68	9.03	3.43	0.51

Belgium (12.69%) and Italy (12.26%) but insignificant in Finland (0.65%). Control by widely held corporations is trivial (1.68%) in all sample countries. Cross-holdings are only marginally significant in Norway, Germany, and Austria (accounting for 2.27%, 2.62%, and 1.01% of cases respectively) but are insignificant elsewhere.

If we lower the threshold to 10%, then the proportion of widely held firms falls to 13.72%; family control increases from 44.29% to 55.87%; control by financial institutions also increases from 8.73% to 18.34%. This increase is especially significant in the UK and Ireland. By contrast, lowering the control threshold to 10% has little effect on the percentages of State-controlled firms, firms controlled by widely held firms, and firms with cross-holdings.

3.1. Financial versus non financial firms

Table 7.4 compares the ownership structure of financial firms and non-financial firms. Financial firms are slightly more likely to be widely held than non-financial firms (39.92% versus 36.39%), are much more likely to be controlled by a widely held financial institution (21.48% versus 5.96%), and are much less likely to be family controlled (26.54% versus 48.15%). For other types of controlling owners, the differences between financial and non financial firms are insignificant.

In both the UK and Ireland, the proportion of widely held financial firms is about the same as that of non financial firms. Financial firms are more likely than non-financial firms to be widely held for continental countries except Austria, Finland, and Portugal. Non-financial firms are more likely to be family controlled in all countries except Finland and Portugal.

Differences in patterns of ownership and control across countries can be explained by differences in the regulations on financial firms (Barth et al., 2000). Since the ownership structure of financial firms differs from that of non financial firms, a country's ratio of financial to non financial

firms will affect its results. Financial firms constitute only 10.1% of sample firms in Finland and 14.5% in Germany, but 30.3% in Austria and 39.2% in Belgium.

3.2. Size effects

To explore the relationship between ownership patterns and firm size, we identify in each country the 20 largest, the middle 50, and the 50 smallest firms by market capitalization. For Austria, Ireland, and Portugal which had less than 120 listed firms, we defined the 20 largest firms as "Large", then divided the rest equally into those that were "Medium" and "Small." Table 7.5 shows that family ownership is less likely for larger firms, being particularly weak among the largest firms in the UK and Sweden. In Austria, Finland, Italy, Norway, and Portugal, State control is quite important for the largest firms. Large firms are also more likely to be widely held than small firms in all our sample countries except Austria, Norway, and Portugal. In the UK, 90% of large firms are widely held at the 20% threshold, but only 14% of small firms are widely held at the 10% threshold. Cross-country differences become less significant among small firms.

4. MEANS OF ENHANCING CONTROL

This section reports the major mechanisms used to enhance control. We neglect less significant mechanisms such as firm-specific voting caps,[11] golden shares,[12] informal alliances (i.e., voting blocks), or transfer restrictions on shares.

4.1. Dual class share structures

Consistent with the hypothesis that control provides large private benefits (see, for example, Barclay and Holderness, 1989; Claessens et al., 2002; Jensen and Meckling, 1976; Johnson et al., 2000; La Porta et al., 1997, 2002) in Western Europe, several studies report that voting shares trade at a premium over non voting

Table 7.4 Concentration of control: financial versus non financial firms. Data relating to 5,232 publicly traded corporations are used to construct this table, which groups corporations into financial firms (SIC: 6000-6999) and non financial corporations. The table presents the percentage of firms controlled by different controlling owners at the 20% threshold. Controlling shareholders are classified into six types. Family: A family (including an individual) or a firm that is unlisted on any stock exchange. Widely held financial institution: A financial firm (SIC 6000-6999) that is widely held at the control threshold. State: A national government (domestic or foreign), local authority (county, municipality, etc.), or government agency. Widely held corporation: A non financial firm, widely held at the control threshold. Cross-holdings: The firm Y is controlled by another firm, that is controlled by Y, or directly controls at least 20% of its own stocks. Miscellaneous: Charities, voting trusts, employees, cooperatives, or minority foreign investors. Companies that do not have a shareholder controlling at least 20% of votes are classified as widely held

Country	Type of firm	% of firms	Widely held	Family	State	Widely held corporation	Widely held financial	Miscellaneous	Cross-holdings
Austria	Financial	30.3	10.00	38.33	13.33	0.00	18.33	16.67	3.33
	Non-financial	69.7	11.59	59.18	16.18	0.00	4.35	8.70	0.00
Belgium	Financial	39.2	37.25	32.35	1.96	1.96	13.73	12.75	0.00
	Non-financial	60.8	8.86	63.92	2.53	0.00	12.03	12.66	0.00
Finland	Financial	10.1	23.08	64.10	10.26	0.00	2.56	0.00	0.00
	Non-financial	89.9	31.71	44.11	17.07	1.22	0.61	5.28	0.00
France	Financial	16.1	22.45	33.16	6.63	0.00	36.22	1.53	0.00
	Non-financial	83.9	12.38	70.92	4.81	4.52	6.58	0.79	0.00
Germany	Financial	14.5	12.75	37.58	5.88	0.00	28.27	1.96	13.56
	Non-financial	85.5	9.97	69.20	6.37	4.26	5.82	3.61	0.76
Ireland	Financial	15.9	63.64	13.64	9.09	4.55	0.00	9.09	0.00
	Non-financial	84.1	62.07	26.72	0.00	1.72	5.17	4.31	0.00
Italy	Financial	23.6	24.49	18.37	8.16	7.14	38.78	0.00	3.06
	Non-financial	76.4	9.43	72.33	11.01	1.57	4.09	1.57	0.00
Norway	Financial	16.1	56.00	12.00	24.00	0.00	4.00	4.00	0.00
	Non-financial	83.9	33.08	43.65	10.99	0.38	4.55	4.64	2.71
Portugal	Financial	24.1	19.05	71.43	0.00	0.00	4.76	4.76	0.00
	Non-financial	75.9	23.44	55.47	7.81	0.78	4.69	7.81	0.00
Spain	Financial	16.1	29.41	23.37	7.35	0.00	38.40	1.47	0.00
	Non-financial	83.9	25.85	62.03	3.49	1.95	6.34	0.28	0.06
Sweden	Financial	17.1	50.00	40.48	4.76	0.00	2.38	2.38	0.00
	Non-financial	82.9	37.43	47.49	5.03	0.00	3.35	6.70	0.00
Switzerland	Financial	24.3	32.69	24.04	17.31	0.00	16.35	9.62	0.00
	Non-financial	75.7	25.93	55.86	4.12	1.44	7.10	5.25	0.31
UK	Financial	0.185	60.11	18.01	0.00	0.42	17.94	3.53	0.00
	Non-financial	0.815	63.76	24.97	0.09	0.84	6.90	3.44	0.00
All	Financial	0.183	39.92	26.54	5.05	1.31	21.48	4.00	1.71
	Non-financial	0.817	36.39	48.15	3.85	2.13	5.96	3.30	0.21

shares. For example, Zingales (1994) reports that in Italy this premium is 81.5%, Megginson (1990) reports a 13.3% premium in the UK, Muus and Tyrell (1999) find a 29% premium in Germany, and Muus (1998) documents a 51.35% premium in France. In addition, Horner (1988) documents a 27% premium in Switzerland and Rydqvist (1992) finds a 6.5% premium in Sweden. In the US, Lease et al. (1983) find a voting premium of 5.4%. Nenova (2000) analyzes a sample of 661 dual class share firms in 18 countries and reports that control benefits constitute 50% of firm value in Mexico, around 0% of firm value in Denmark, and between one-quarter and one-half of firm value for Brazil, Chile, France, Italy, and South Korea. Nenova adds that a large fraction (i.e., more than 70%) of the differences in benefits can be explained by the legal systems, in particular the quality of general investor protection, minority rights in the case of control transfer, and standards of law enforcement.

Panel A of Table 7.6 displays the legal restrictions in each country on dual class shares, the proportion of firms issuing dual class shares for each country, and the average minimum percentage of the stock capital required to control 20% of the voting rights (denoted by *Own = 20% Con*). For example, Realia (Figure 1) has 2.641 million A-shares with one vote per share and 42.922 million B-shares with one-tenth of a vote per share. A-shares represent 5.8% of stock capital (2.641 million/45.563 million) and 38.09% (i.e., 2.641 million/(2.641 million + 4.292 million)) of votes, while B-shares represent 61.91% of votes. Hence, it takes 3.05% (= 0.2 * (5.8%/38.09%)) of A-share capital to acquire 20% of the votes (*Own = 20% Con* is 0.0305).

Minimum percentages are calculated for each firm from its capital structure, then averaged over all sample firms to construct the table. These figures need not account for the use of multiple voting shares (except in Scandinavian countries). The issue of multiple voting shares was outlawed in Italy, Spain, the UK, and Germany,

as of May 1998. Prior to this, German firms could be authorized to issue shares with multiple voting rights by State authorities. For example, at the end of 1996, Rwe AG had multiple voting stocks with a $\times 20$ voting right, and Siemens AG had multiple voting stocks with a $\times 6$ voting right. Multiple voting shares were issued in Germany by Bewag, Frankisches Uberlandwerk, Hamburger Hochbahn, Hamburgische Electricitats Werke, Lech Elektrizitatswerke, and Uberlandwerk Unterfranken. Multiple voting shares are legal in France and most firms grant two votes for each ordinary share, as long as they have been held for at least two consecutive years; for publicly traded firms this minimum holding period can be extended up to four years. These multiple voting stocks do not represent a special category of stocks in France, so we treat them as ordinary shares.

Table 7.6 ranks countries by this last statistic. Some ironies emerge when we compare this ranking with the ranking of countries by the severity of legal restrictions on dual class shares, which are of four types: (1) the one-share-one-vote rule; (2) a cap on the proportion of non voting stocks; (3) a rule placing a minimum on the votes accruing to any type of share; (4) no restrictions on the type of stock issued.

The European countries with the lowest average minimum percentages of shares required to ensure 20% control are Sweden (9.83%), Switzerland (15.26%), and Finland (15.42%). Thus, Sweden and Finland, the only countries that impose a lower limit on the voting rights of shares, exhibit a greater discrepancy between ownership and control than countries that place no limits on voting rights, such as Austria and Ireland. Therefore, the explicit floor on the voting rights of a share provides a clear indication of the unfairness in voting rights that regulators will tolerate, as well as a defense against public criticism. Sweden also has the highest percentage of firms issuing dual class shares (66.07%), followed by Switzerland (51.17%), Italy (41.35%), and Finland (37.60%).

Table 7.5 Concentration of control and firm size. Data relating to 5,232 publicly traded corporations are used to construct this table, which groups corporations according to their size (market capitalization), and, for each variable, presents means for the largest 20 firms, 50 medium-size firms, and the smallest 50 firms. For countries with less than 120 firms, we group the largest 20 firms in the "Largest 20" group, and then divide the rest into two equal groups. The table presents the percentage of firms controlled by different controlling owners at the 20% threshold. Controlling shareholders are classified into six types. Family: A family (including an individual) or a firm that is unlisted on any stock exchange. Widely held financial institution: A financial firm (SIC 6000-6999) that is widely held at the control threshold. State: A national government (domestic or foreign), local authority (county, municipality, etc.), or government agency. Widely held corporation: A non financial firm, widely held at the control threshold. Cross-holdings: The firm Y is controlled by another firm, that is controlled by Y, or directly controls at least 20% of its own stocks. Miscellaneous: Charities, voting trusts, employees, cooperatives, or minority foreign investors. Companies that do not have a shareholder controlling at least 20% of votes are classified as widely held.

Country	Category	Average market cap (m US$)	Widely held	Family	State	Widely held corporation	Widely held financial	Misc.	Cross-holding
Austria	Largest 20	1,593.0	10.00	32.50	42.50	0.00	5.00	10.00	0.00
	Middle 40	227.8	14.29	47.14	11.43	0.00	15.71	8.57	2.86
	Smallest 39	33.5	11.76	71.57	4.90	0.00	2.94	8.82	0.00
Belgium	Largest 20	5,386.4	20.00	37.50	0.00	0.00	27.50	15.00	0.00
	Middle 50	722.2	18.00	47.00	4.00	0.00	20.00	11.00	0.00
	Smallest 50	58.0	16.00	65.00	0.00	2.00	2.00	15.00	0.00
Finland	Largest 20	2,310.2	38.10	33.33	28.57	0.00	0.00	0.00	0.00
	Middle 50	274.3	41.18	38.23	11.76	2.94	1.47	4.41	0.00
	Smallest 50	30.1	17.65	65.20	9.80	0.00	0.00	7.35	0.00
France	Largest 20	16,467.1	60.00	30.00	0.00	0.00	10.00	0.00	0.00
	Middle 50	149.9	14.00	68.00	6.00	2.00	10.00	0.00	0.00
	Smallest 50	6.8	8.00	77.00	2.00	4.00	9.00	0.00	0.00
Germany	Largest 20	27,510.2	45.00	15.00	10.00	0.00	12.50	5.00	12.50
	Middle 50	158.3	10.00	75.00	2.00	7.00	4.00	1.00	1.00
	Smallest 50	12.0	14.00	81.00	3.00	0.00	2.00	0.00	0.00

Ireland	Largest 20	2,260.2	70.00	20.00	0.00	2.50	0.00	7.50	0.00
	Middle 25	198.9	50.00	29.16	0.00	4.17	8.33	8.33	0.00
	Smallest 24	37.0	68.00	24.00	4.00	0.00	4.00	0.00	0.00
Italy	Largest 20	10,398.8	35.00	20.00	25.00	0.00	15.00	0.00	5.00
	Middle 50	320.4	8.00	63.00	6.00	6.00	14.00	2.00	1.00
	Smallest 50	70.4	14.00	67.00	6.00	2.00	10.00	1.00	0.00
Norway	Largest 20	2,302.7	30.00	45.00	20.00	0.00	0.00	5.00	0.00
	Middle 50	310.8	38.00	34.83	16.50	0.00	3.83	5.67	1.17
	Smallest 50	62.4	40.00	35.67	7.40	0.00	7.33	4.40	5.20
Portugal	Largest 20	2,338.9	15.00	60.00	17.50	2.50	0.00	5.00	0.00
	Middle 34	170.4	28.57	60.00	2.86	0.00	5.71	2.86	0.00
	Smallest 33	42.8	18.75	60.94	1.56	0.00	6.25	12.50	0.00
Spain	Largest 20	4,919.2	45.00	20.83	10.00	9.17	15.00	0.00	0.00
	Middle 50	302.4	34.00	46.00	8.00	2.00	10.00	0.00	0.00
	Smallest 50	65.3	36.00	56.00	2.00	0.00	6.00	0.00	0.00
Sweden	Largest 20	9,575.2	80.00	5.00	5.00	0.00	0.00	10.00	0.00
	Middle 50	397.9	49.02	42.16	2.94	0.00	0.98	4.90	0.00
	Smallest 50	44.0	32.00	63.00	0.00	0.00	3.00	2.00	0.00
Switzerland	Largest 20	24,589.9	50.00	35.00	0.00	0.00	15.00	0.00	0.00
	Middle 50	352.2	18.00	58.00	10.00	2.00	5.00	7.00	0.00
	Smallest 50	58.0	28.00	55.00	7.33	2.67	6.00	1.00	0.00
UK	Largest 20	40,563.4	90.00	0.00	0.00	0.00	10.00	0.00	0.00
	Middle 50	151.7	64.71	19.60	0.00	0.00	13.73	1.96	0.00
	Smallest 50	4.2	42.00	38.67	0.00	0.00	8.00	11.33	0.00
All	Largest	12,027.2	45.24	27.24	12.20	1.09	8.46	4.42	1.35
	Middle	295.0	29.28	48.82	6.53	2.01	8.65	4.25	0.46
	Smallest	38.9	25.32	59.66	3.72	0.90	5.17	4.80	0.44

Table 7.6 Legal restrictions on issuing dual class shares. Data relating to 5,232 publicly traded corporations are used to construct this table. *Own = 20% Con* is the average minimum percent of the book value of equity required to control 20% of votes (as computed for each firm in our sample); *Dual class shares (%)* is the percentage of firms with outstanding dual class shares.

Panel A: Country-level results

Country	Restrictions	Restriction details	Number of firms	Own = 20% Con	Dual class shares (%)
Belgium	One-share-one-vote		130	20.00	0.00
Portugal	Proportion of non-voting stocks capped	Non voting (and limited voting) capital may not exceed 50% of stock capital	87	20.00	0.00
Spain	Proportion of non voting stocks capped	Non voting (and limited voting) capital may not exceed 50% of stock capital	632	20.00	0.16
France	Proportion of non voting stocks capped	Non voting (and limited voting) capital may not exceed 25% of stock capital	607	19.93	2.64
UK	Non voting shares outlawed since 1968. Firms may issue "preference shares" provided these are given "adequate voting rights"	Minimum voting rights required for preference stocks include voting (1) when their dividend is in arrears, (2) on resolutions for reducing share capital and winding-up the firm, and (3) on resolutions which are likely to affect their class rights	1,953	19.14	23.91

Country	Restriction		N		Dual class shares (%)
Norway	One-share-one-vote rule	Governmental approval needed for exceptions	155	19.05	13.16
Austria	Unrestricted		99	18.96	23.23
Ireland	Unrestricted		69	18.91	28.07
Germany	Proportion of non-voting stocks capped	Non voting (and limited voting) capital may not exceed 50% of stock capital	704	18.83	17.61
Italy	Proportion of non-voting stocks capped	Non voting (and limited voting) capital may not exceed 50% of stock capital	208	18.38	41.35
Finland	Minimum vote ratio	Minimum vote ratio: one-tenth	129	15.42	37.60
Switzerland	Unrestricted		214	15.26	51.17
Sweden	Minimum vote ratio	Minimum vote ratio: one-tenth	245	9.83	66.07
All			5,232	18.74	19.91

Panel B: Results by type of restrictions

Restrictions	Own = 20% Con	Dual class shares (%)
Minimum voting ratio required	12.26 U, C, P	53.92 U, C, P
Unrestricted	16.86 M, C, P	40.11 M, C, P
Cap on the proportion of non voting stocks	19.47 U, M	10.14 U, M, P
Prohibited	19.56 U, M	6.15 U, M, C

U, M, C, P indicates that the ratio is significantly different (at the 5% level) from the sample of firms in countries where regulation is unrestricted (U), requires a minimum voting ratio (M), imposes a cap (C) to the proportion of non-voting stocks (with reference to the total stock capital), or prohibits (P) the issuance of non voting/limited-voting stocks. The UK is not included in any of these groups since its regulations prohibit the issue of stocks that carry no voting rights, but permit the issue of limited voting stocks (i.e., preference shares). Information about restrictions on voting rights is obtained from the national stock exchanges (or their supervisory authorities), as well as from the papers discussed in Section 4.

By contrast, Rydqvist's survey (1992) reported that 75% of Swedish firms issue non voting stocks. Bergström and Rydqvist (1990) reported that stocks issued by Swedish firms can be restricted or unrestricted to foreigners, but unrestricted shares cannot exceed 40% of equity and 20% of the votes. Swedish firms seem to have taken this as a license to issue shares with inferior voting rights to foreigners. Shares with superior voting rights are often not traded in Sweden. In Switzerland, firms can issue different classes of shares: Bearer (B-shares), registered (R-shares), and non-voting shares. R- and B-shares have identical cash-flow rights; however, R-shares have more voting power than B-shares since they are issued with a lower face value (Gardiol et al., 1997; Horner, 1988). Italian firms can issue limited voting (i.e., preference) shares and non voting shares. Only eight firms have limited voting shares outstanding. Both limited voting and non voting shares have legally prior claims on dividends, and on reimbursement in case of liquidation, see Zingales (1994). Finnish regulations require a control contestant to treat all classes of shares in a "fair and equitable" manner, so bidders need to offer all classes of shares the same tender price. The protection of minority shareholders during takeover contests may explain why small investors are willing to hold limited voting and non voting shares.

At the opposite extreme, dual class shares are rare in Portugal (0%), Belgium (0%), Spain (0.16%), and France (2.64%).[13] These countries have either a one-share-one-vote rule or a cap on the proportion of non voting stocks. In Norway, departures from the one-share-one-vote principle require governmental approval. This seems readily given since 13% of firms have multiple classes of shares. In the UK, non-voting shares have been outlawed since 1968, but firms can issue preference shares that have a prior claim on dividends and cumulative dividends, but limited voting rights. Preference shares may have no voting rights at general meetings. However, listing rules on the London Stock Exchange require firms to give these shares "adequate voting rights" on resolutions on (1) dividends in arrears, (2) reducing share capital and winding-up the firm, and (3) actions affecting their class rights. The voting rights attached to preference shares are defined by the articles of the firm and vary across firms. We combine limited voting (i.e., preference) shares with non-voting shares to calculate the ratio of votes to share capital. The consequence is that 19.91% of firms issue dual class shares and the *Own = 20% Con* ratio is 18.74%.

4.2. Pyramiding, holdings through multiple control chains, and cross-holdings

Table 7.7 displays the control enhancements employed by firms that have a controlling shareholder at the 20% threshold. Pyramids are used by 19.13% of such firms in our sample, being most prevalent in Norway (33.90%) and least prevalent in Finland (7.46%). Holdings through multiple control chains are used by 5.52% of controlling shareholders, being most prevalent in Norway (20.34%), Italy (8.78%), and Germany (7.22%) but insignificant elsewhere. Cross-holdings are used by 0.73% of the controlling shareholders, being most prevalent in Germany (2.69%) and Norway (2.04%)[14] but marginal in other countries, whose regulations typically set a 10% cap on these stakes.

4.3. Other control-enhancing mechanisms

A controlling shareholder is said to be "alone" if no other owner controls at least 10% of the voting rights. Table 7.7 shows that this is true of 53.99% of the firms that are not widely held. Austria exhibits the highest percentage of such firms (81.82%) and Norway the lowest (38.78%). Bennedsen and Wolfenzon (2000) and Gomes and Novaes (1999) discuss the role of the second largest shareholders.

Table 7.7 Percentage of firms adopting control-enhancing devices. We only include the 3,300 firms with controlling shareholders at the 20% level. *Pyramids* reports the percentage of firms whose largest controlling shareholder adopts pyramids as control devices. *Holdings through multiple control chains* reports the percentage of firms whose largest controlling shareholder adopts at least 5% of holdings through multiple control chains as control devices. *Cross-holdings* reports the percentage of firms whose largest controlling shareholder adopts cross-holdings as control devices. *Controlling owner alone* reports the percentage of firms that have single controlling owners. *Management* reports the percentage of firms whose top managers come from the largest shareholder's family. The table presents the percentage of firms controlled by different controlling owners at the 20% threshold.

Country	Number of firms	Pyramids	Holdings through multiple control chains	Cross-holdings	Controlling owner alone	Management
Austria	88	20.78	6.49	1.14	81.82	80.00
Belgium	104	25.00	2.38	0.00	71.15	80.00
Finland	92	7.46	1.49	0.00	41.30	69.23
France	522	15.67	2.87	0.00	64.75	62.20
Germany	631	22.89	7.22	2.69	59.90	61.46
Ireland	26	9.09	0.00	0.00	42.31	77.78
Italy	181	20.27	8.78	1.13	58.76	70.00
Norway	98	33.90	20.34	2.04	38.78	66.67
Portugal	68	10.91	0.00	0.00	60.29	50.00
Spain	465	16.00	5.43	0.22	44.30	62.50
Sweden	149	15.91	0.00	0.67	48.32	73.47
Switzerland	155	10.91	0.91	0.00	68.39	70.00
UK	721	21.13	4.93	0.00	43.00	75.85
Total	3,300	19.13	5.52	0.73	53.99	68.45

A member of the controlling family is said to be in "management" if he/she is the CEO, Honorary Chairman, Chairman, or Vice-Chairman. We assumed that individuals are in the same family if they have the same last names, a convention that understates family affiliation. Nevertheless, in more than two-thirds of the family controlled firms, the controlling owner is in management. The proportion is highest (above 70%) in Austria, Belgium, Ireland, Italy, Sweden, Switzerland, and the UK, and lowest in Portugal (50%).

4.4. Types of control-enhancing instruments by different types of shareholders

Table 7.8 details the means of enhancing control by families, the State, and widely held financial institutions. Pyramids and holdings through multiple control chains are used to enhance control in 13.81% and

3.22% of family controlled firms respectively, in 35.32% and 11.01% of State-controlled firms, and in 27.96% and 16.78% of firms controlled by widely held financial institutions. The State is most likely to be the controlling owner alone (58.72%), followed by families (54.74%), then by widely held financial institutions (44.74%); however, there are significant variations across countries.

5. DISCREPANCY BETWEEN OWNERSHIP AND CONTROL

Pyramids, holdings through multiple control chains, cross-holdings, and deviations from the one-share-one-vote rule all create discrepancies between ownership and control rights. Table 7.9 shows that, on average, the largest ultimate controlling shareholder owns 34.64% of cash-flow rights and 38.48% of voting rights.

Table 7.8 Means of enhancing control in Europe by types of controlling owners. We only include 3,012 firms with controlling shareholders at the 20% (2,332 firms controlled by families, 218 firms controlled by the State, and 462 firms controlled by widely held financial institutions) level. *Own = 20% Con* reports the average minimum percent of the book value of equity required to control 20% of votes. *Dual class shares (%)* reports the proportion of firms with dual class shares outstanding. *Pyramids* reports the percentage of firms whose largest controlling shareholder adopts pyramids as control devices. *Holdings through multiple control chains* reports the percentage of firms whose largest controlling shareholder adopts at least 5% of holdings through multiple control chains as control devices. *Controlling owner alone* reports the percentage of firms that have single controlling owners. Panel A presents percentages for family controlled firms, Panel B presents percentages for State-controlled firms, and Panel C presents percentages for firms controlled by widely held financial firms.

Country	Number of firms	Own = 20% Con	Dual class shares (%)	Pyramids	Holdings through multiple control chains	Controlling owner alone
Panel A: Family-controlled firms						
Austria	51	18.91	21.57	11.76	1.96	86.27
Belgium	67	20.00	0.00	8.96	4.48	61.19
Finland	65	14.82	43.55	6.15	1.54	36.92
France	395	19.96	1.01	13.16	3.04	63.80
Germany	460	18.75	18.26	14.57	3.04	66.96
Ireland	17	19.53	16.67	5.88	0.00	35.29
Italy	122	18.34	42.62	20.34	5.93	54.55
Norway	60	18.33	21.28	23.33	5.00	38.33
Portugal	54	20.00	0.00	16.67	3.70	61.11
Spain	351	20.00	0.00	11.97	5.41	39.32
Sweden	117	9.34	67.12	18.80	0.85	47.01
Switzerland	106	13.52	68.57	7.55	1.89	65.09
UK	467	19.16	18.84	13.70	2.14	46.47
Total	2,332	18.64	17.61	13.81	3.22	54.74
Panel B: State-controlled firms						
Austria	16	19.67	12.50	37.50	18.75	68.75
Belgium	3	20.00	0.00	33.33	0.00	100.00
Finland	19	16.81	21.05	5.26	0.00	47.37
France	30	19.93	3.33	36.67	3.33	73.33
Germany	41	19.90	4.88	43.90	4.88	17.07
Ireland	1	20.00	0.00	0.00	0.00	100.00
Italy	22	18.50	40.91	27.27	9.09	77.27
Norway	24	20.00	0.00	70.83	58.33	37.50
Portugal	5	20.00	0.00	0.00	0.00	80.00
Spain	26	20.00	0.00	57.69	3.85	88.46
Sweden	12	10.92	62.50	0.00	0.00	75.00
Switzerland	16	18.09	25.00	6.25	0.00	81.25
UK	3	20.00	0.00	33.33	33.33	0.00
Total	218	18.98	13.17	35.32	11.01	58.72
Panel C: Firms controlled by a widely held financial firm						
Austria	9	18.29	55.56	22.22	22.22	88.89
Belgium	16	20.00	0.00	0.00	0.00	93.75
Finland	0	n.a.	n.a.	n.a.	n.a.	n.a.
France	69	19.94	2.90	15.94	1.45	60.87

Table 7.8 (Continued)

Country	Number of firms	Own = 20% Con	Dual class shares (%)	Pyramids	Holdings through multiple control chains	Controlling owner alone
Germany	65	18.85	21.54	53.85	40.00	33.85
Ireland	3	20.00	0.00	33.33	33.33	100.00
Italy	27	18.39	33.33	29.63	14.81	40.74
Norway	5	20.00	0.00	40.00	20.00	40.00
Portugal	3	20.00	0.00	0.00	0.00	0.00
Spain	74	20.00	0.00	20.27	9.46	51.35
Sweden	6	13.72	60.00	33.33	33.33	16.67
Switzerland	19	15.51	31.58	15.79	0.00	68.42
UK	166	18.77	31.93	27.71	18.67	35.54
Total	462	18.98	20.67	27.96	16.78	44.74

n.a.: Not available.

These averages are computed over firms where at least one owner owns at least 5% of the control rights. The largest ultimate owners average the highest cash-flow rights in Germany (48.54%), Austria (47.16%) and France (46.68%), but the lowest cash-flow rights in Ireland (18.82%) and the UK (22.94%), followed by the Scandinavian countries of Norway (24.39%), Sweden (25.15%), and Finland (32.98%).

The largest ultimate owners average the highest voting rights in Germany (54.50%) and Austria (53.52%), but the lowest in Ireland (21.55%) and the UK (25.13%), again followed by the Scandinavian countries of Sweden (30.96%), Norway (31.47%), and Finland (37.43%).

Table 7.9, Panel C shows that the largest ultimate shareholder's average ratio of cash-flow to voting rights is 0.868, being lowest in Switzerland (0.740), Italy (0.743), and Norway (0.776), and highest in Spain (0.941), Portugal (0.924), and France (0.930).

To measure the concentration of corporate control in families, Table 7.10 displays the average number of firms controlled by each family via control chains that include at least 10% of the control rights at each link. For example, if a family controls 20% of Firm A, Firm A controls 15% of Firm B, and Firm B controls 9% of Firm C, then we include only A and B amongst the firms controlled by that family. Italy has the largest average number of firms controlled by a single family (1.46), while Finland (1.05) and Switzerland (1.10) have the smallest.

Another perspective on the concentration of family control is provided by the percentage of total market capitalization controlled by the top families in each country. For each family, we sum the market capitalization of all firms in which the family is the largest controlling shareholder, then divide by the market capitalization of all firms in our sample from that country. We then rank families by the share of market capitalization that they control and calculate the share of market capitalization controlled by the top 1, 5, 10, and 15 families.

The top family controls 17.89% of total market capitalization in Switzerland and 10.40% in Italy,[15] but only 1.40% in the UK, 1.66% in Spain and 3.40% in Ireland. The top 15 families control 36.77% of total market capitalization in Portugal and 36.63% in Belgium, but only 6.55% in the UK, 13.48% in Spain, and 15.38% in Ireland.

6. CONCLUSION

In this paper, we document the ultimate ownership of 5,232 listed firms in 13 Western European countries. Widely held and family controlled firms predominate.

Table 7.9 Cash-flow and control rights. This table includes data relating to 4,806 publicly traded
corporations (including both financial institutions and non financial institutions) where
the largest controlling owner has at least 5% of voting rights. *Cash-flow rights* represents the ultimate ownership stake held by the largest controlling shareholder. *Control
rights* the percentage of voting rights controlled by the largest controlling shareholder.

Country	Number of firms	Mean	Standard deviation	Median	1st quartile	3rd quartile
Panel A: Cash-flow rights						
Austria	95	47.16	23.52	50.00	25.50	65.00
Belgium	120	35.14	24.96	36.10	14.98	51.81
Finland	119	32.98	23.94	27.60	14.60	49.91
France	604	46.68	26.69	48.98	24.69	66.00
Germany	690	48.54	31.46	48.89	21.05	75.00
Ireland	68	18.82	17.32	14.24	6.76	26.03
Italy	204	38.33	25.13	39.68	16.61	56.83
Norway	149	24.39	21.26	19.42	8.91	36.12
Portugal	86	38.42	20.45	39.31	19.83	52.00
Spain	610	42.72	30.46	32.55	18.50	64.91
Sweden	244	25.15	23.06	17.30	9.45	33.55
Switzerland	189	34.66	24.69	29.00	12.85	51.00
UK	1,628	22.94	17.87	16.21	10.96	29.66
Total	4,806	34.64	26.76	25.90	13.02	51.00
Panel B: Control rights						
Austria	95	53.52	22.77	54.70	34.00	75.00
Belgium	120	40.09	23.20	39.56	19.49	55.86
Finland	119	37.43	22.44	33.70	20.80	52.36
France	604	48.32	25.55	50.00	28.70	66.00
Germany	690	54.50	28.70	50.76	27.00	76.91
Ireland	68	21.55	16.39	16.64	10.39	26.56
Italy	204	48.26	21.00	50.11	31.39	63.15
Norway	149	31.47	20.18	27.78	15.10	43.59
Portugal	86	41.00	19.18	44.95	22.28	52.30
Spain	610	44.24	29.59	35.73	20.00	65.03
Sweden	244	30.96	22.37	24.90	14.50	40.55
Switzerland	189	46.68	25.97	50.00	22.50	63.00
UK	1,628	25.13	17.87	18.02	13.28	30.19
Total	4,806	38.48	26.10	30.01	15.96	53.98
Panel C: Ratio of cash flow to control rights						
Austria	95	0.851	0.224	1.000	0.704	1.000
Belgium	120	0.779	0.360	1.000	0.596	1.000
Finland	119	0.842	0.246	1.000	0.800	1.000
France	604	0.930	0.189	1.000	1.000	1.000
Germany	690	0.842	0.267	1.000	0.709	1.000
Ireland	68	0.811	0.321	1.000	0.683	1.000
Italy	204	0.743	0.337	0.971	0.548	1.000
Norway	149	0.776	0.341	1.000	0.532	1.000
Portugal	86	0.924	0.218	1.000	1.000	1.000
Spain	610	0.941	0.178	1.000	1.000	1.000
Sweden	244	0.790	0.339	1.000	0.526	1.000
Switzerland	189	0.740	0.290	0.830	0.468	1.000
UK	1,628	0.888	0.228	1.000	0.907	1.000
Total	4,806	0.868	0.255	1.000	0.852	1.000

Table 7.10 How concentrated is control by families/unlisted firms? This table provides summary statistics on the concentration of control by families and unlisted firms. *Average number of firms per family* refers only to firms in the sample. *Percent of total market value of listed corporate assets that families control* is the aggregate market value of common equity of firms controlled by the largest, the top 5, the top 10, and the top 15 families divided by the total market value of common equity for all firms included in the sample for a given country.

Country	Average number of firms per family	Percent of total market value of listed corporate assets that families control			
		Top family	Top 5 families	Top 10 families	Top 15 families
Austria	1.16	5.64	15.59	19.47	22.15
Belgium	1.22	5.63	20.38	30.45	36.63
Finland	1.05	3.94	13.98	21.82	25.90
France	1.18	5.94	22.04	29.18	33.80
Germany	1.24	5.43	15.66	21.29	25.01
Ireland	1.16	3.40	11.88	14.46	15.38
Italy	1.46	10.40	16.83	20.18	21.92
Norway	1.29	3.73	16.01	23.13	27.18
Portugal	1.23	6.11	24.59	34.23	36.77
Spain	1.19	1.66	6.97	10.92	13.48
Sweden	1.27	3.37	9.29	13.26	15.66
Switzerland	1.10	17.89	24.35	28.94	30.93
UK	1.17	1.40	4.11	5.85	6.55

Widely held firms are more important amongst financial and large firms, while families are more important for non financial and small firms. In some continental European countries, the State controls a significant number of larger firms. We also document the means whereby owners gain control rights in excess of their cash-flow rights. The use of multiple class voting shares contribute only marginally to this, except in just a few countries. The use of pyramids and holdings through multiple control chains is also marginal.

NOTES

* Corresponding author.
† We are grateful to Marco Bigelli, Lorenzo Caprio, Edith Ginglinger, Arun Khanna, John McConnell, Stefano Mengoli, Robert Pye, Gordon Roberts, Bill Schwert (the editor), George Tian, and especially Andrei Shleifer and an anonymous referee for providing helpful comments. We benefited from comments from workshop participants at the National University of Singapore, Washington University at St Louis, the Capacity Building Seminar in Manila (sponsored by the Asian Development Bank), the European Financial Management Association meeting (Athens), the European Finance Association meeting (London), the Financial Management Association meeting (Seattle), and the Scottish Institute for Research in Investment and Finance (Edinburgh). We also thank Bolsa de Valores de Lisboa, Commerzbank, Helsinki Media Blue Book, Hugin, the Union Bank of Switzerland, and the Vienna Stock Exchange for generously providing us with their data sets. Mara Faccio acknowledges research support from Università Cattolica, Milan, and MURST (research grant #MM13572931). Larry Lang acknowledges research support from a Hong Kong Earmarked Grant.

1 Japan stands apart from the rest of East Asia in this regard: the top Japanese family controls only 0.5% of total market capitalization.
2 In addition, Greek shares are often held in bearer form, masking the identities of their owners.
3 La Porta et al. (1999) use Hugin for Denmark. However, Hugin covers less than 20%

of all listed firms and we could not locate information from other official sources.

4   The Stichting Toezicht Effectenverkeer (STE, the Securities Board of the Netherlands), responded to our request for data as follows: "The implementation of the 1992 Act has resulted in the list of disclosed notifications being no more than an historical overview that has been overtaken by countless events and no longer provides the desired transparency of the (Dutch) stock market. Furthermore, the file corruption will become greater with the passage of time. Given the above and the fact that the 1996 Act does not empower the STE to take any measures in this regard which would lead to an up-to-date overview, the STE does not issue this list to third parties." See also De Jong et al. (1998).

5   Data are from 1996 for France, Germany, Italy, Switzerland, and the UK; from 1997 for Spain and Portugal; from 1998 for Sweden and Norway; and from 1999 for Austria, Belgium, Finland, and Ireland.

6   Becht and Boehmer (1998) for Germany; Bianchi et al. (1998) for Italy; Bloch and Kremp (1998) for France; Crespi-Cladera and Garcia-Cestona (1998) for Spain; De Jong et al. (1998) for the Netherlands; Renneboog (1998) for Belgium; Goergen and Renneboog (1998) for the UK.

7   Our sample coverage of countries is: Austria: 100.00 (%), Belgium: 89.04, Finland: 87.76, France: 89.26, Germany: 99.15, Ireland: 82.14, Italy: 100.00, Norway: 72.77, Portugal: 100.00, Spain: 100.00, Sweden: 94.96, Switzerland: 100.00, and the UK: 95.69. The low figure for Norway is due more to limited data coverage than to our screening.

8   AIDA is a private database provided by Bureau Van Dijk. The AIDA database provides accounting information for about 130,000 Italian firms and ownership information for 25,314 Italian firms. Firms with ownership data in the AIDA database are not ranked in any order. We traced ownership to ultimate owners starting from the first firm listed in the AIDA database using ownership information contained in that database. A firm was included if we could trace its ultimate owners. We stopped when our sample reached 15% of firms with ownership data.

9   Their results were based on data compiled by the French central bank (Fiben), that is unavailable to the public.

10   The figures are based on a sample of 12,600 unlisted firms from the Jordan's database, which is compiled by a private data vendor, Bureau Van Djik.

11   Voting caps are used, for example, by BASF (2.62%), Bayer (5%), Deutsche Bank (5%), Linde (10%), Mannesmann (5%), Phoenix (10%), Schering (3.51%), and Volkswagen (20%) in Germany; and Telefonica (10%) in Spain. In Italy, the law requires voting caps for cooperative banks; they are rather common in recently privatized firms such as Comit (3%) and Credit (3%). Voting caps also obtain in France, e.g., in Alcatel, Danone, and Pernod Ricard. In Switzerland, 12 out of the 50 largest firms have voting caps. Examples from the ten largest corporations include Novartis (2%), Nestlé (3%), UBS (5%), Swiss Bank Corporation (5%), and Zurich Insurance (3%).

12   As reported in Crespi-Cladera and Garcia-Cestona (1998), the State holds these golden shares in some recently privatized Spanish firms, such as Repsol, Telefonica, and Endesa. The use of golden shares is also popular among privatized firms in Italy, as emerged from the vicissitudes of Telecom Italia and Enel in the late 1990s.

13   Similar evidence is reported for Spain in Crespi-Cladera and Garcia-Cestona (1998) and for France in Muus (1998).

14   These figures are, respectively, 2.62% and 2.27% if we also include second ultimate owners (see Table 7.3).

15   Brioschi et al. (1989) show that, in the mid-1980s, more than a quarter of total market capitalization could be traced to the control of three single families.

REFERENCES

Barclay, M., Holderness, C., 1989. Private benefits from control of public corporations. Journal of Financial Economics 25, 371–395.

Barth, J.R., Caprio Jr., G., Levine, R., 2000. Banking systems around the globe: do regulation and ownership affect performance and stability? Unpublished working paper, World Bank, Washington DC.

Becht, M., Boehmer, E., 1998. Ownership and voting power in Germany. Unpublished working paper, European Corporate Governance Network.

Bennedsen, M., Wolfenzon, D., 2000. The balance of power in closely held corporations. Journal of Financial Economics 58, 113–139.

Bergström, C., Rydqvist, K., 1990. Ownership of equity in dual-class firms. Journal of Banking and Finance 14, 255–269.

Berle, A., Means, G., 1932. The Modern Corporation and Private Property. MacMillan, New York.

Bianchi, M., Bianco, M., Enriques, L., 1998. Pyramidal groups and the separation between ownership and control in Italy. Unpublished working paper, European Corporate Governance Network.

Bloch, L., Kremp, E., 1998. Ownership and control in France. Unpublished working paper, INSEAD Business School.

Bolsa de Valores de Lisboa, 1998. Sociedades Cotadas 1997. Lisbon Stock Exchange, Lisbon.

Brioschi, F., Buzzacchi, L., Colombo, M.G., 1989. Risk capital financing and the separation of ownership and control in business groups. Journal of Banking and Finance 13, 747–772.

Claessens, S., Djankov, S., Lang, L.H.P., 2000. The separation of ownership and control in East Asian corporations. Journal of Financial Economics 58, 81–112.

Claessens, S., Djankov, S., Fan, J., Lang, L.H.P., 2002. Disentangling the incentive and entrenchment effects of large shareholdings. Journal of Finance, forthcoming.

Comision Nacional del Mercado de Valores, 1998. Participaciones significativas en sociedades cotizadas. (Data file). CNMV, Madrid.

Commerzbank, 1997. Wer gehört zu wem, 19th Enlarged Edition. Commerzbank AG, Frankfurt-am-Main.

Commissione Nazionale per le Società e la Borsa, CONSOB, 1997. Bollettino - edizione speciale n. 4/97 - Compagine azionaria delle società quotate in borsa o ammesse alle negoziazioni nel mercato ristretto al 31 dicembre 1996. CONSOB, Milan.

Crespi-Cladera, R., Garcia-Cestona, M.A., 1998. Ownership and control: a Spanish survey. Unpublished working paper, European Corporate Governance Network.

De Jong, A., Kabir, R., Marra, T., Roell, A., 1998. Ownership and control in the Netherlands. Unpublished working paper, European Corporate Governance Network.

Financial Times, 1997. Extel Financial, Company Research CD-rom #36/1997. FT, London.

Gardiol, L., Gibson-Asner, R., Tuchschmid, N.S., 1997. Are liquidity and corporate control priced by shareholders? Empirical evidence from Swiss dual class shares. Journal of Corporate Finance 3, 299–323.

Goergen, M., Renneboog, L., 1998. Strong managers and passive institutional investors in the UK. Unpublished working paper, University of Reading.

Gomes, A., Novaes, W., 1999. Multiple large shareholders in corporate governance. Unpublished working paper, University of Pennsylvania, Wharton.

Holderness, C., Kroszner, R., Sheehan, D., 1999. Were the good old days that good? Changes in managerial stock ownership since the great depression. Journal of Finance 54, 435–470.

Horner, M.R., 1988. The value of the corporate voting right: evidence from Switzerland. Journal of Banking and Finance 12, 69–84.

Il Sole 24 ore, 1997. Il taccuino dell'azionista. Il Sole 24 Ore Radiocor, Milan.

Jensen, M., Meckling, W., 1976. Theory of the firm: managerial behavior, agency costs, and ownership structure. Journal of Financial Economics 11, 5–50.

Johnson, S., La Porta, R., Lopez-de-Silanes, F., Shleifer, A., 2000. Tunnelling. American Economic Review Papers and Proceedings 90, 22–27.

La Porta, R., Lopez-de-Silanes, F., Shleifer, A., Vishny, R.W., 1997. Legal determinants of external finance. Journal of Finance 52, 1131–1150.

La Porta, R., Lopez-de-Silanes, F., Shleifer, A., 1999. Corporate ownership around the world. Journal of Finance 54, 471–518.

La Porta, R., Lopez-de-Silanes, F., Shleifer, A., Vishny, R.W., 2002. Investor protection and corporate valuation. Journal of Finance 57, 1147–1170.

Lease, R.C., McConnell, J.J., Mikkelson, W.H., 1983. The market value of control in publicly traded corporations. Journal of Financial Economics 11, 439–471.

Lins, K., Servaes, H., 1999a. International evidence on the value of corporate diversification. Journal of Finance 54, 2215–2239.

Lins, K., Servaes, H., 1999b. Is corporate diversification beneficial in emerging markets? Unpublished working paper, London Business School.

London Stock Exchange, 1997. The London Stock Exchange Yearbook. LSE, London.

Megginson, W., 1990. Restricted voting stock, acquisition premiums, and the market value of corporate control. The Financial Review 25, 175–198.

Muus, C.K., 1998. Non-voting shares in France: an empirical analysis of the voting premium. Unpublished working paper, Johann Wolfgang Goethe-Universitat, Frankfurt-am-Main.

Muus, C.K., Tyrell, M., 1999. An empirical analysis of the voting premium in Germany. Unpublished working paper, Johann Wolfgang Goethe-Universitat, Frankfurt-am-Main.

Nenova, T., 2000. The value of corporate votes and control benefits: a cross-country analysis. Unpublished working paper, Harvard University.

Renneboog, L., 1998. Shareholding concentration and pyramidal ownership structures in Belgium: stylized facts. Unpublished working paper, European Corporate Governance Network.

Rydqvist, K., 1992. Dual-class shares: a review. Oxford Review of Economic Policy 8, 45–57.

Shleifer, A., Vishny, R., 1997. A survey of corporate governance. Journal of Finance 52, 737–783.

The Herald Tribune, 1997. French Firm Handbook 1997. SFB-Paris Bourse.

Union Bank of Switzerland, 1998. Swiss Stock Guide 96/97. UBS, Zurich.

Wiener Börse, 2000. Yearbook 1999. Vienna Stock Exchange, Vienna.

Zingales, L., 1994. The value of the voting right: a study of the Milan stock exchange experience. Review of Financial Studies 7, 125–148.

Chapter 8

Marc Goergen and Luc Renneboog

WHY ARE THE LEVELS OF CONTROLS (SO) DIFFERENT IN GERMAN AND UK COMPANIES? EVIDENCE FROM INITIAL PUBLIC OFFERINGS

Source: *Journal of Law, Economics and Organization*, 19(1) (2003): 141–175.

ABSTRACT

We analyze why the control of listed German and U.K. companies is so different. As shareholders in Germany are less protected and control is less expensive, German investors prefer controlling stakes. We also focus on economic factors such as profitability, risk, and growth to predict the probability of occurrence of different states of control six years after the flotation. Large U.K. companies become widely held, whereas in large German firms new shareholders control significantly larger stakes. Wealth constraints become binding for U.K. shareholders, whereas German shareholders can avoid this by using pyramids. We find substantial differences between a takeover by a concentrated shareholder and one by a widely held company. For the United Kingdom, the probability of the former increases when the company is risky, small, and poorly performing. Conversely, the latter is more likely when the target is large, fast growing, and profitable. Poor performance and high risk require control and monitoring by a concentrated shareholder. Conversely, high growth and profitability attract widely held companies. Founders are less inclined to dilute their stake to retain private benefits of control. When German firms are profitable and risky, control is likely to go to a concentrated shareholder, but growth and low profitability increase the probability of a control acquisition by a widely held firm.

1. INTRODUCTION

THERE IS A WELL DOCUMENTED—BUT SO FAR largely unexplained—discrepancy in the levels of control concentration between listed continental European and Anglo-American firms. For example, about 90% of companies listed on the London Stock Exchange do not have a major shareholder owning 25% or more of the voting rights, whereas 85% of the listed German companies have such a shareholder (La Porta et al., 1999;

Becht and Mayer, 2001). Not only does the concentration of control differ between these countries, but so does the nature of ownership: Germany is characterized by intercorporate equity relations and family control, whereas institutional shareholders hold most of the voting rights in the United Kingdom. Also, German firms are on average more than 50 years old when they are floated, whereas U.K. initial public offerings (IPOs) are only 12 years old. It comes as a surprise that such substantial differences are still observable, especially in the wake of high product-market competition and economic globalization. This study contributes to a better understanding of the reasons for the differences in control between Germany and the United Kingdom. To this aim, we analyze a unique database of recently floated German and U.K. firms containing detailed data on the control structure for a period of up to six years after the IPO.

We argue that the relative cost of holding large control stakes differs across countries. In countries with a low protection of shareholder rights, shareholders can prevent a violation of their rights by building up controlling stakes and by taking advantage of a higher level of private benefits of control (Dyck and Zingales, 2001). A thorough investigation of minority shareholder protection regulation, control disclosure, multiple-class shares, fiduciary duties and composition of the board of directors, ownership structure, voting rules and practice, the arm's length relation with large shareholders, and mandatory takeover thresholds reveals that investors in the United Kingdom are substantially better protected than the ones in Germany and that the relative cost of control is lower in Germany. This result is in line with the findings of La Porta et al. (2000). We pursue our analysis of the impact of the legal and regulatory aspects on control by investigating the role of inheritance tax and listing requirements on the stock exchanges.

After examining the legal and regulatory differences which may explain differences in the level of control concentration, we analyze the corporate characteristics (such as profitability, size, risk, and growth), that is, the economic determinants that may trigger changes in control. More specifically, we intend to predict whether or not the initial shareholders retain control or transfer control to a new widely held shareholder or to a concentrated bidder or to a large number of new diffuse shareholders. We also analyze whether or not U.K. and German control changes are subject to different economic factors. We find substantial differences between takeovers by concentrated shareholders and those by widely held companies. For the United Kingdom, the probability of a transfer of control to a concentrated shareholder increases when a company is risky, small, and poorly performing. A U.K. firm is more likely to be taken over by a widely held firm if the target firm is large, fast growing, and profitable. So, for the United Kingdom, poor performance and high risk necessitate a high level of control and tight monitoring by a concentrated shareholder. Conversely, high growth and profitability attract widely held companies whose management may well be driven by an "empire building" acquisition programme. We find that high growth also leads to more diffuse ownership in the United Kingdom. However, this is less likely when the founder family is still involved in the company. When German firms are profitable and risky, control is more likely to go to a concentrated shareholder, but growth and low profitability trigger a control acquisition by a widely held firm. If the founder of a German firm is still a shareholder at the IPO and if there are nonvoting shares outstanding, control is likely to remain with the initial shareholders. This is not surprising as founding families often extract (nonpecuniary) private benefits of control and nonvoting shares enable them to raise additional equity while maintaining control. Large U.K. companies evolve toward a more widely held equity structure, whereas in large German firms, new shareholders control significantly larger voting stakes. The reason is that wealth constraints may become binding for U.K. shareholders, whereas German shareholders can avoid this by using pyramidal ownership structures. These ensure control while allowing for a dispersion of cash flow rights. Age has the opposite impact on control concentration of German and U.K. firms: initial shareholders of older German firms tend to retain smaller voting stakes than those of relatively older U.K. firms.

The article proceeds as follows. In Section 2 we state some conjectures regarding the impact of the differences in inheritance tax, stock exchange regulation, and legal rules on German and U.K. control levels. In addition, we analyze the potential impact of regulation on the relative costs of holding large voting stakes. In Section 3 we formulate our propositions regarding the relation between specific corporate characteristics and the dynamics of control concentration in both countries. Section 4 describes our data sources and the methodology. In Section 5 we present some stylized facts on control which provide further empirical justification for the research objective of this article. The empirical results of the Tobit and multinomial logit models are presented in Section 6. Section 7 concludes.

2. REGULATORY DETERMINANTS OF THE LEVEL AND EVOLUTION OF CONTROL

In this section we compare the German and U.K. legal corporate governance rules, stock exchange regulations, and inheritance taxes and formulate conjectures about the impact of these on the level of control concentration in both countries. We analyze whether differences in regulation and legislation can explain the stronger concentration of control in German companies compared to U.K. firms.

2.1 Stock exchange listing requirements and inheritance tax

As reported in the introduction and detailed in Section 5, there are striking discrepancies in control concentration between Germany and the United Kingdom. The differences in control may depend on the initial differences at the float and such differences may disappear over time. At the IPO, large shareholders of German firms own on average a supermajority (76% of the voting stock) versus 63% in the United Kingdom. This may be caused by differences in listing requirements and inheritance taxes.

We expect that lower levels of control at the float are to be found in the country where the stock exchange imposes the highest minimal free float (conjecture 1). Hence, as the level of control held by the initial shareholders in U.K. firms is significantly lower than that in German companies, we expect that the London Stock Exchange requires that a higher percentage of the equity is offered to the public. However, this is not the case: Goergen (1998) shows that in the 1980s and 1990s the admission requirements were very similar in terms of minimum size, minimum ownership dispersion, and trading history. Consequently the listing requirements cannot account for differences in initial control. This refutes conjecture 1.

High inheritance taxes may force owners to float a company to be able to afford the taxes (Hay and Morris, 1984). Thus we expect that a lower degree of ownership retention will occur in the country with the higher tax and a higher average corporate age (conjecture 2). The higher initial control concentration in Germany could be partially explained by higher inheritance taxes in the United Kingdom and by a higher corporate age of U.K. firms. We find precisely the opposite: German firms at flotation are on average 50 years old, compared to a mere 12 years for U.K. firms (see infra). Furthermore, during the 1980s and 1990s the levels of inheritance tax in Germany exceeded those in the United Kingdom (Goergen, 1998). This evidence fails to support conjecture 2.

2.2 Protection of shareholder rights

When shareholder rights are not sufficiently protected or cannot be easily enforced in court, shareholders may increase their control to levels that make them no longer vulnerable to expropriation or to levels that ensure large private benefits of control. For example, a shareholder or coalition of shareholders who owns a (combined) stake of 20% and is afraid of minority shareholder expropriation by a majority shareholder has an interest to increase the stake to at least 25%. Such a minority stake enables blocking of changes to the statutes, including changes to voting rights and their distribution. We expect a higher control concentration in Germany given the lower degree of shareholder rights. Consequently, if the initial shareholders decide to sell out, new large shareholders arise and the free float will remain low (conjecture 3). To make this case we investigate legal origin, the threshold of compulsory tender offers, control disclosure, board representation, fiduciary duties of directors, complex shareholding structures, proxy voting, the arm's length clause between the major shareholder and the company, and the possibility to limit voting rights (see Table 8.1). More precisely, we show that the value attached to partial control is expected to be higher in Germany than in the United Kingdom.

2.2.1 Legal origin

La Porta et al. (1997, 1998, 2000) investigate the relation between legal origin (common law versus civil law), quality of investor protection, and quality of law enforcement, on the one hand, and company characteristics (among them, control concentration), on the other hand, for 49 countries. The authors find that the average company in civil law countries (such as Germany) has concentrated control. In contrast, the common law system of the United Kingdom corresponds to, on average, widely held firms. La Porta et al. (1998) also find a close correspondence between the legal origin and shareholder protection: the common law system provides higher guarantees for shareholder rights and the enforceability of such rights is also better. Consequently the findings of La Porta et al. (1998) provide empirical support for conjecture 3, which states that the lower degree of shareholder protection in Germany is related to a higher control concentration and to a lower occurrence of widely held firms, whereas a high quality of investor protection allows shareholders to hold smaller voting stakes in the United Kingdom.

2.2.2 Control-induced tender offers

The City Code on Takeovers and Mergers and the U.K. Company Law protect minority and dispersed shareholders by creating obstacles to building controlling stakes. When a stake of 30% or more has been acquired in a U.K. firm, a tender offer for all remaining shares is mandatory. Therefore some shareholders limit their control stake to just below the 30% level (Goergen and Renneboog, 2001). In Germany, a similar takeover code was introduced only as recently as 1995 (just after our sample period which ends in 1994), but minority protection is still weaker. A mandatory tender offer only has to take place when a large shareholder obtains a 75% control stake (Boehmer, 1999). Furthermore, Wenger, Hecker, and Knoesel (1996) show that in 60% of the offers to minority shareholders, the offer price is below the market value, whereas in the United Kingdom the tender price has to be at least as high as the price at which the bidder acquired the shares over the previous 12 months. To conclude, shareholders in the United Kingdom without the intention to acquire a company may consider a 29.9% stake as an upper limit. German shareholders only face a 75% tender threshold, but can make the tender offer unattractive by setting the offer price below the market value.

2.2.3 Board representation and directors' fiduciary duties

Another incentive for shareholders to build up large blocks in German firms but not in U.K. ones is created by board representation and the definition of directors' fiduciary duties. On the one-tier U.K. board, about 60% of the directors are nonexecutives (Franks et al., 2001), most of which are independent from management and are not direct representatives of specific (major) shareholders. The need for independent directors was emphasized by the Code of Best Practice of the Cadbury Commission in 1992, which the London Stock Exchange has endorsed for all listed firms

Table 8.1 Comparison of Regulatory Issues

	Germany	United Kingdom
Ownership disclosure		
Minimum disclosure level	5% of voting rights (25% prior to 1995)	3% (5% prior to 1989)
Minimum threshold of control to reveal strategic intent (takeover intentions)	None	15%
Dual-class shares	Nonvoting shares: common	No nonvoting shares
Voting caps	Common at 5–10%, but caps were abolished in 1998 with a grandfather clause for existing voting caps in by-laws	No
Control structure	Complex, multilayered cascades of ownership levels	Simple, one ownership tier
Takeover code	(since 1995)	
Minimum level of control for obligatory tender offer on all shares	75%	30%
Minimum price of tender	Can be lower than market value	Not lower than the highest share price during last 12 months
Using voting rights		
Casting votes	Presence at AGM required in person or representative	Allowed by mail, fax, or Internet. But, in practice, presence (in person or by representative) is required for show of hands. Proxy votes only matter in poll
Registration of votes	Deposit of shares with notary, depository bank, or company itself	Shares need to be registered
Degree of minority protection	Weak	Strong
Boards	Two-tier board with a large-shareholder dominated supervisory board	One-tier board with independent nonexecutive directors
Corporate aim of management	Pursuing stakeholder interest	Maximizing shareholder value

(*continued*)

Table 8.1 Continued

	Germany	United Kingdom
Fiduciary duty of directors	Duty of care and duty of loyalty (*Treuepflicht*)	Wider and more developed than in Germany
New equity issues	Via rights	Via rights
Listing requirements	Similar to the United Kingdom	Similar to Germany
Inheritance tax	Higher than in the United Kingdom	Lower than in Germany

since 1993. In Germany, in contrast, the *Aufsichtsrat* (supervisory board of the two-tier board system) is not independent: it represents shareholders and employees and is dominated by large shareholders.[1] Baums (2000) compares the fiduciary duties (duty of care and loyalty) in German and U.K. corporate law and concludes that "the range of fiduciary duties in the English law system seems wider and more developed than in its German counterpart" (p. 8). The relatively stronger independence of U.K. nonexecutive directors and their wider fiduciary duties enable shareholders to hold smaller stakes, as their rights are better safeguarded. This supports conjecture 3.

2.2.4 Relation with major shareholders: Arm's length?

In the United Kingdom, minority protection is based on the "property rule," which prevents any transaction from proceeding without the consent of the minority owners (Goshen, 1998). In addition, the rules of the London Stock Exchange prohibit controlling shareholders owning more than 50% of shares from having too large an impact on the firm: "a firm must be capable at all times of operating and making decisions independently of any controlling shareholder and all transactions and relationships in the future between the applicant and any controlling shareholder must be at arm's length and on a normal commercial basis."[2] A majority of the directors of the subsidiary must be independent from the parent firm and minority shareholders have the right to be consulted about, and approve, transactions with the parent firm (Franks et al., 2001).[3] The effect of these rules is to increase the costs of holding equity stakes. They explain why almost all bids are made conditional on being accepted by 90% or more of the target's shareholders. The remainder can be purchased at the original bid price using a squeeze-out rule under the 1948 Companies Act. German law also has an arm's length concept (para. 76, Stock Corporation Act): the management board of a subsidiary is not allowed to follow instructions or take measures which are not in the interest of the subsidiary and is not allowed to be compensated by the holding company. Still, it is doubtful how the relation between a company and its controlling shareholders can be at arm's length with a shareholder-dominated supervisory board. The efficiency of the arm's-length regulation in German firms is eroded by the fact that large shareholders nominate representatives to the supervisory boards. Such actions may ensure that large shareholders safeguard their private benefits of control. This is further support for conjecture 3.

2.2.5 Control through pyramids

The regulation discussed above encourages shareholders in Germany to hold a large control stake. To compensate for the cost of owning large equity stakes in terms of lost liquidity, an intricate web of multilayered tiers of shareholdings is often used by families or companies. The main reason for building such pyramids is control leverage.[4] As companies can issue up to 50% of the equity as nonvoting shares, a mere 25% of the cash flow rights (50% of the voting rights) at every tier of shareholdings is sufficient for a shareholder to retain control over a target company while the capital investment is minimized. In addition, a shareholder (e.g., a family) could also hide his identity prior to the introduction of the disclosure regulation.[5] While pyramids are not explicitly forbidden in U.K. corporate law, it is surprising that this control leverage technique is not used at all. The main reason is that ownership disclosure regulation in the United Kingdom not only applies to individuals or companies but also to individuals and companies with voting agreements. Such voting agreements consist of obligations or restrictions between shareholders with respect to the use, retention, or disposal of their stakes. A coalition of shareholders with a voting agreement will be considered by the regulatory authorities as a single shareholder. This implies, for instance, that if the combined direct and indirect shareholdings of a coalition amount to at least 3%, disclosure is compulsory.[6] Furthermore, a coalition controlling directly and indirectly 30% or more of the equity will be obliged to make a tender offer for all shares outstanding.[7] This section has shown that the costs of holding large share stakes are reduced by pyramids that allow the combination of strong control with limited investment.

2.2.6 Nonvoting shares and voting caps

By issuing nonvoting shares, initial owners can dilute their cash flow rights in the firm without relinquishing control. Although nonvoting shares are in principal admitted by the London Stock Exchange, issues of nonvoting shares have been actively discouraged (Brennan and Franks, 1997). Goergen and Renneboog (2001) report that the few listed U.K. companies that had

issued nonvoting shares converted them into voting shares under the pressure of the London Stock Exchange and institutional investors during the early 1990s. Whereas German corporate law (*Aktiengesetz*, para. 139) prohibits the issue of multiple voting rights, nonvoting shares up to the amount of ordinary shares outstanding are explicitly allowed.[8] As such, the issue of nonvoting shares increases the relative power of the initial shareholders and allows them to retain control with limited investment.[9]

The only regulatory element which discourages shareholders in Germany from holding large equity stakes is that voting limitations can be imposed by the by-laws. Usually the voting power of a shareholder is limited to 5% or 10%.[10] Only recently have voting caps been prohibited in Germany (Act on Control and Transparency of Enterprises of 1998 (KonTraG)), but a grandfather clause applies for existing voting caps. Voting caps in listed U.K. companies are not allowed. Hence, the one-share-one-vote principle is better upheld in the United Kingdom than in Germany.

2.2.7 Proxy voting and voting practice

Another important element of the protection of shareholder rights is the voting procedure. In both the United Kingdom and Germany, a person or legal entity can represent a shareholder at the AGM. At first sight there seems to be less need to resort to proxy voting in the United Kingdom because exercising one's voting rights seems substantially easier. However, the general voting practice requires that a shareholder of a U.K. firm or his representative is present at the general meeting in order to cast his votes. The U.K. voting practice is captured by this statement from the IPO prospectus of Compel plc. "At a general meeting every member *present in person* shall, on a show of hands, have one vote and every member present in person or by proxy shall, *on a poll*, have one vote for every ordinary share of which he is the holder." On uncontroversial issues, voting takes place by a show of hands, which requires that shareholders be present and all shareholders present in person have a vote regardless of their number of voting rights (see Stapledon, 1996; Goergen and Renneboog, 2001). However, every shareholder (present) can ask for a poll on any item of the agenda. Only then does the number of voting rights owned by every shareholder matter and the proxy votes are counted. In spite of the fact that legal rules seem to facilitate voting in U.K. firms, there is not much of a difference between Germany and the United Kingdom in terms of the requirement that shareholders or a representative be present at the AGM.[11] Both Baums and Schmitz (2000) and Boehmer (1999) point out that the German proxy voting system comprises significant deficiencies. Banks can receive proxy votes from the shareholders who have deposited the shares in the bank (Depotstimmrecht) such that these control rights substantially outweigh the banks' own control rights. Typically the amount of debt held by banks exceeds the amount of equity held in the firm by a factor greater than 10. Consequently banks have little incentive to act on behalf of other shareholders. Finally, banks virtually always vote in favor of management proposals (Baums and Fraune, 1995) and seem to have little impact on corporate performance (Chirinko and Elston, 1996). In the United Kingdom, the management can solicit proxy votes in support of managerial plans (Stapledon, 1996). Thus, although the regulation on voting procedures seems to plead more in favor of minority protection in the United Kingdom, the voting practice in Germany and the United Kingdom is not substantially different. This fails to support conjecture 3.[12]

To summarize, this section has discussed the many incentives for shareholders to hold relatively larger voting stakes in Germany than in the United Kingdom. First, we investigated whether the initial (and lasting) differences in equity concentration in German and U.K. IPOs can be explained by differences in stock exchange listing requirements and by inheritance tax law, which neither can. Second, the higher protection of shareholder rights in the United Kingdom makes holding blocks relatively more costly than in Germany. Third, owning large blocks in Germany is less costly than in the United Kingdom because (i) pyramids can be used in Germany, (ii) nonvoting shares can be issued, and (iii) supervisory board representatives can safeguard shareholders' private benefits of control. The only dissuasive factor against holding a high level of control in Germany is the possibility that voting rights are restricted in the corporate by-laws. Table 8.1 summarizes the results from this section.

3. ECONOMIC DETERMINANTS OF CONTROL CONCENTRATION AND EVOLUTION

Whereas the previous section has shown that legal rules and stock exchange regulations provide incentives for a stronger concentration of share ownership in Germany (compared to the United Kingdom), these rules do not explain how control evolves from the float onwards. Several years subsequent to the IPO, control concentration can result from a high retention rate by initial shareholders, from a transfer of a controlling block to a new shareholder, or from a full takeover. In the case of a transfer of control, the (potential) agency costs are different when control is acquired by either a widely held firm, or by a closely held firm, a family, or an individual (as the ultimate shareholder). In the former case, management has a lot of discretion, whereas in the latter, large shareholders may influence corporate actions, possibly even at the expense of minority shareholders. This section develops the relation between corporate characteristics and control, and formulates the expected differences between Germany and the United Kingdom. Specifically, these hypotheses will be tested on a sample of German and U.K. firms of which the level of and changes in control are collected for the six years after the float.

The first economic determinant of control concentration is firm size. Demsetz and Lehn (1985) argue that wealth limitations as well as portfolio diversification needs restrict the existence of substantial share stakes in large firms. Therefore we expect that the larger the firm, the higher is the probability that wealth and diversification constraints of the initial shareholders become binding. Thus the control retention by the initial shareholders will be lower in larger firms and these firms will evolve toward widely held control and have fewer new large shareholders. Whereas the negative relation between ownership and size may be equally valid for the United Kingdom and Germany, the relation between control and size may differ. In the United Kingdom, share ownership is equivalent to control as a result of the one-share-one-vote principle. Conversely this principle may be violated in German companies because nonvoting shares are frequently issued (in 38% of our sample firms). This enables the initial shareholders to retain control more easily, while the firm can at the same time attract additional capital without diluting the initial shareholders' control. In addition, pyramids (see above) also limit the direct investment needed to keep controlling stakes. Consequently the negative relation between size and control is expected to be weaker in German than in U.K. firms (Proposition 1).

We also expect that control retention by the initial shareholders decreases with rising corporate age. Over time, these initial shareholders (or their heirs) may face personal liquidity needs and hence decide to liquidate (part of) their stakes. As the average age of German firms at the float is substantially higher than the one of U.K. firms, we expect the control retention in U.K. firms to be higher than the one in German firms (Proposition 2). In the cases where control is reduced by the initial shareholders of German firms, we expect control stakes to be transferred and not dissipated, as blocks are valuable (Shleifer and Vishny, 1986). This implies that we expect to see a higher incidence of new large shareholders in German firms.

If the founder family is still involved in the firm (in terms of voting rights) at the float, the odds are higher that they will remain among the major shareholders in subsequent years. Morck, Shleifer, and Vishny (1988) argue that the founder of a firm may provide essential leadership skills, especially in younger firms, and should therefore retain control. Founder commitment at the time of the IPO is included in the model as a proxy for the private benefits (which may be nonpecuniary) that the founder extracts from controlling the firm (Johnson et al., 2000). Given that large shareholders are more likely to extract private benefits[13] in German firms, we expect higher control concentration in Germany (Proposition 3). Zingales (1995) and Mello and Parsons (1998) show that the optimal path of selling control to maximize the proceeds consists of two stages. First, the initial shareholders should take the firm public and sell some cash flow rights to a large number of investors in order to retain control.[14] Second, they should sell control to a new controlling shareholder at a premium. Morck, Strangeland, and Yeung (2000) distinguish between large shareholder stakes resulting from entrepreneurial investment and those resulting from inherited wealth. The authors find that heir-controlled Canadian firms have lower levels of financial performance, labor-capital ratios, and research and development (R&D). In contrast to entrepreneurial control, concentrated, inherited ownership impedes growth and shows signs of entrenchment and political rent seeking.

Bolton and von Thadden (1998) model the evolution of control from its initial level toward its optimal level and find that high-risk firms will end up being widely held. Their proposition has been supported by several empirical studies: for example, a negative relationship between control and risk is found by Demsetz and Lehn (1985) for the United States and Leech and Leahy (1991) for the United Kingdom. Alternatively, high risk may trigger a control transfer to a shareholder with a stronger ability to monitor the firm. Therefore we propose that the probability that the firm's original owners will reduce their control stake increases with risk and high risk triggers control transfers to large shareholders with strong monitoring skills (Proposition 4). As German firms are older at the float (and have more stable and less risky cash flows than their U.K. counterparts) and as shareholders can control a German firm with a lower percentage of voting rights, Proposition 4 is more likely to hold for U.K. firms.

Growth may also force changes in control: rapidly growing firms may have to resort to attracting more external equity than firms operating in mature industries. Thus the stronger the growth, the higher is the probability that control by the initial shareholders is diluted and that either a new shareholder emerges (by a partial or full takeover) or that the firm becomes widely held (Crespi, 1998) (Proposition 5). We expect this relation to hold more strongly for U.K. than for German firms because, in the latter, pyramids enable shareholders to attract external capital while limiting control dilution.

In line with DeAngelo and DeAngelo (1985) for the United States, voting shares in German IPOs are normally held by the initial owners, whereas nonvoting shares are issued to the outsiders in the IPO (Goergen, 1999). Immediately after the IPO, the family shareholder owns on average 57% of the voting rights, but only 47% of total equity (voting plus nonvoting shares). Thus, we expect that issuing non-voting shares at the IPO leads to higher control retention by initial shareholders and that control retention will be higher in Germany than in the United Kingdom (Proposition 6). For those cases where control is transferred, we expect new share-holders to be able to acquire control more easily in Germany than in the United Kingdom. For instance, suppose that there are two firms with a different equity structure but which are otherwise identical: one firm has only voting shares outstanding, while the other has issued 50% voting and 50% nonvoting shares. If the initial share-holders decide to sell a controlling stake, the new controlling shareholder will only need half of the capital to acquire control in the firm with the nonvoting equity.[15]

Profitable firms generating sufficient cash flow allow the initial shareholders to retain control for a longer period than poorly performing firms (Dennis and Sarin, 1999). Poor performance may reflect not only weak management but also poor monitoring, which may activate the market for corporate control or persuade another shareholder with superior monitoring skills to acquire control (Franks et al., 2001). Thus we expect poor performance to trigger changes in control (Proposition 7). Such changes in control are likely to occur differently in the United Kingdom than in Germany. In the former, the market for corporate control consists in full takeovers (Franks and Mayer, 1996), whereas in Germany it operates via partial takeovers or a transfer of a controlling stake to a new major shareholder (Jenkinson and Ljungqvist, 2001).

4. DATA SOURCES, DESCRIPTION OF VARIABLES, AND METHODOLOGY

4.1 Sample description and data sources

Even though the German economy is about 1.8 times larger in terms of gross domestic product (GDP) than the U.K. economy, its capitalization is substantially smaller, as the number of quoted companies on the German exchanges is less than one-third the number of listed firms on the London Stock Exchange (which is around 2,000 firms, including 550 financial institutions and investment funds). Similarly the number of IPOs on the London Stock Exchange is much larger. In the United Kingdom, 764 firms went public during the period 1981–1988, of which 284 were floated on the Official Market and 480 on the Unlisted Securities Market (USM), that is, the secondtier market. Over the same period, a total of only 96 German firms went to the stock exchange, 51 of which were listed on the Official Market and 45 chose a listing on the Regulated Market (the second-tier market). This study concentrates on domestic IPOs listed on the official and secondary markets, as data for lower market tiers[16] are usually not available.

To ensure comparability across the German and U.K. IPOs, in this study we only retain those IPOs controlled by an individual or a group of persons, such as a family or unrelated associates. Thus we do not include privatizations or equity carve-outs. Consequently this study analyzes more than 90% of all German IPOs with available data.[17]

The distribution of the population of 96 German and 764 U.K. IPOs across industries reveals significant differences.[18] Although the industry with the highest frequency of IPOs is the same for both countries (electricals, electronics, and office equipment), there are proportionally more German IPOs in mature industries (such as mechanical engineering with 15.5% of the total number of IPOs and motor components with 5.2%). Conversely, there is a higher proportion of U.K. IPOs in cyclical service industries with 29% of the sample (service agencies with 9.0%, property with 6.0%, leisure with 5.7%, chain stores with 3.6%, and construction with 4.9%). Within each industry, U.K. IPOs are also usually smaller than German IPOs.

Table 8.2 shows that there are also marked differences between the population of German and U.K. IPOs in terms of size, age, industry, and risk. The German IPOs are twice as large as the U.K. IPOs, with market capitalizations at the end of the first day of listing of £113 million and £56 million, respectively.[19] On average, the German IPOs were founded 51 years prior to the float whereas U.K. firms were set up only 14 years before the IPO. The age of the German and U.K. sample IPOs matched by size is similar to the population: German and U.K. firms are, respectively, 50 and 12 years old prior to the float. The Herfindahl index demonstrates that voting rights in the German firms at the IPO are more concentrated than in their U.K. counterparts (the difference is significant at the 1% level; see Table 8.2, panel B). German founder families own shares at the float in 92% of the firms, while this is the case in 85% of U.K. firms.

The U.K. firms are riskier (at the 1% level of significance), measured by the standard deviation of their monthly share returns. German firms also have a higher cash flow both as a proportion of their book value of assets (CF1) and as a proportion of the sum of the market value of equity and the book value of debt (CF2).

Information on the identity of initial shareholders and on pre- and post-IPO holdings was obtained from the IPO prospectuses. Substantial share stakes were traced over the period after the IPO through the company reports as well as the London Stock Exchange Yearbooks for the United Kingdom and the *Saling Aktienführer* for Germany. Information on both the direct and ultimate voting stakes was collected for the German firms. To identify the ultimate shareholder and his level of control, the ownership pyramids were reconstructed on a year-by-year basis. Higher tiers of ownership were traced for those large shareholders owning 25% or more of the voting rights as long as the control chain in the ownership cascade was not interrupted. The ultimate level of control is reached when the ultimate shareholder is either an individual or a family, or is a widely held company (i.e., a firm that does not have a shareholder owning at least 25% of its voting rights). Whereas ultimate control is only relevant for German companies, ownership in the United Kingdom is equivalent to control, as multiple or nonvoting shares are not used. Also, U.K. ownership structures are simple and pyramids are rare (Goergen and Renneboog, 2001).

Share prices were collected from the *Karlsruher Kapitalmarktdatenbank* (KKMDB) and the London Share Price Database (LSPD). IPO characteristics (age and industry) and the closing market capitalization for the first day of listing were obtained from the Deutsche Börse AG and the London Stock Exchange. Accounting information was collected from the IPO prospectuses, company reports, the Extel Financial Company Research and Global Vantage CD-ROMs for both countries, and from Datastream and the Extel Microfiches for the United Kingdom.

Table 8.2 Summary Statistics of Independent Variables

Variable	Age (years)	Size (£m)	Herfin-dahl	Founder	Risk (%)	CF1 (%)	CF2 (%)
Panel A: Mean, median, proportion = 1, minimum, maximum and sample size							
Germany							
Mean	49.4	56.4	0.92	—	9.1	17.7	11.0
Median	48.0	28.4	1.00	—	9.0	17.1	11.3
Proportion = 1	—	—	43	92.2	—	—	—
Min	0.0	5.3	0.22	—	4.8	−5.5	−6.2
Max	171.0	296.0	1.00	—	15.9	40.7	22.0
Sample size	55	55	53	51	54	48	48
United Kingdom							
Mean	11.8	58.4	0.44	—	12.8	15.8	9.2
Median	6.0	28.2	0.39	—	13.1	14.8	9.6
Proportion = 1	—	—	2.0	85.2	—	—	—
Min	0.0	5.3	0.03	—	4.8	−2.0	−4.0
Max	84.0	313.6	1.00	—	22.4	64.8	17.3
Sample size	55	55	50	54	54	46	43
Panel B: *t*-statistics for the difference in sample means							
	6.826***	−0.147	9.826***	1.122	−5.797***	0.954	1.885*

The table is based on a sample of German and U.K. IPOs matched by size (market capitalization). The Z-test in panel B is a two-tailed test for the equality between two proportions following a binomial distribution. Age is the firm's age since registration. Size is in million pounds sterling and is the market capitalization. Concentrated ownership is measured by a Herfindahl index of all pre-IPO stakes. Founder is a dummy variable set equal to one when the founder or his heirs still own a large equity stake in the firm at the float. Risk is the standard deviation of the monthly share price return over the five years following the IPO. CF1 is the annual cash flow defined as the published profit gross of depreciation, interest, taxes, and changes in provisions divided by the sum of the book values of equity and debt. CF2 is annual cash flow divided by the market value of equity and the book value of debt. ***, **, * represent the level of statistical significance at the 1%, 5%, and 10% level, respectively. Sources: IPO prospectuses, company reports, Datastream, Extel Financial, and London Stock Exchange.

4.2 Methodology and model description

The direct comparability of control in the two countries was enhanced by matching the German firms with U.K. IPOs by industry and size. This way we select twin companies whose control evolution we analyze while controlling for factors such as risk, profitability, and growth. The size-matched sample consists of 54 German and U.K. firms, whereas the industry-matched sample contains 58 IPOs from each country.[20] The average difference in size between a German IPO and its matched U.K. IPO is 2.7%, with a median of 0.5% and a standard deviation of 4.7%. For seven German firms, a close match, defined as a match within ±25% difference in size, could not be found, neither was it possible to find a U.K. industry match for three German IPOs. The two German samples have 52 firms in common.[21]

For the IPO samples, the following cross-sectional industry-fixed effects are estimated:

$$
\begin{aligned}
\text{Percent voting control}_i \\
= \delta &+ \gamma_1 Country_i + \gamma_2 Size_i \\
&+ \gamma_3 Founder_i + \gamma_4 Risk_i \\
&+ \gamma_5 Growth_i + \gamma_6 Nonvoting_i \\
&+ \gamma_7 Profit_i + \gamma_8 Age_i + \gamma_9 Country_i * Size_i \\
&+ \gamma_{10} Country_i * Founder_i \\
&+ \gamma_{11} Country_i * Risk_i \\
&+ \gamma_{12} Country_i * Growth_i \\
&+ \gamma_{13} Country_i * Profit_i \\
&+ \gamma_{14} Country_i * Age_i + \text{time dummies} \\
&+ \text{industry dummies} + \varepsilon_i.
\end{aligned}
$$

The *percent voting control* is the percentages of voting rights held six years after the float by (i) the initial shareholders, (ii) the new large shareholders, and (iii) small shareholders (the free float), respectively. As the dependent variable is censored (the variable is zero in 33%,

27.4%, and 22.2% of the cases in the models with initial shareholders, new shareholders, and the free float as dependent variables, respectively), we estimate Tobit models.

Firm size (*Size*) is the natural logarithm of the market capitalization at the closing price on the first day of trading, converted into 1985 pounds sterling. Founder involvement is captured by the dummy variable *Founder*, which equals one if the founder or his heirs hold a control stake in the firm at the IPO and zero otherwise. The level of a firm's risk (*Risk*) is measured by the standard deviation of monthly stock returns over the five-year period after the flotation. The growth rate (*Growth*) is defined as the average annual growth rate of total assets over the first five years after the float. Nonvoting shares (*Nonvoting*) is a dummy variable capturing the issue of nonvoting shares at the time of going public (dummy equals one). Twenty-three and 25 German firms issued nonvoting shares in the size- and industry-matched samples, respectively. The profit rate (*Profit*) is defined as the annual cash flow divided by the book value of total assets with annual cash flow measured as the profit gross of depreciation, interest, taxes, and changes in tax, pension, and special provisions. Age measures the age of the firm in years at the time of the IPO.

As both German and U.K. IPOs are included in the model, a dummy variable *Country* is used, which equals one for a German company and zero otherwise. The coefficient on this dummy registers a possible difference in the intercept between German and U.K. IPOs. In order to determine whether there is a country-specific effect for each of the variables described above, interactive terms consisting of the product of each of the above variables with the *Country* dummy is included in the model. The interactive terms pick up the differential effect (i.e., the differential slope coefficient) for the German firms.

Table 8.A1 in the appendix shows the Pearson correlation coefficients for the independent variables and the *p*-values for the coefficients. We find that (i) *Risk* is

correlated with *Age, Profit, Nonvoting*, and *Country*, and (ii) *Age* is related to *Country, Growth*, and *Nonvoting*. These seven correlation coefficients are statistically significant but are not large in absolute terms. As these correlations may cause multicollinearity problems, we subtract from the variables *Age* and *Risk* the country averages of these variables. Table 8.A1 in the appendix shows that the statistical significance of the correlations between the variables $Risk_{minuscountryavg}$ on the one side, and *Age, Country*, and *Nonvoting* on the other has disappeared, as well as the one between $Age_{minuscountryavg}$ on one side and *Country, Growth*, and *Nonvoting* on the other side. The high correlation between *Nonvoting* and *Country* cannot be eliminated, as nonvoting shares are only issued by German firms.

For the sake of robustness, we also use a set of alternative independent variables. *Size* is now measured by the book value of total assets at the end of the financial year covering the IPO date. *Founder* stands for founder involvement in the management of the firm: the dummy variable equals one if the founder or a member of the founder family is an executive director of the firm, and zero otherwise. *Risk* is the standard deviation of the cash flows at the IPO and during the five years subsequent to the IPO. *Nonvoting* is now a continuous variable measuring the proportion of nonvoting shares in the firm's total equity immediately after the IPO. For *Growth*, the same definition is used as for the first set of independent variables. The profit rate (*Profit*) is now the cash flow over the sum of the market value of equity and the book value of debt.

As the dependent variables of the three Tobit models are interrelated, we also estimate multinomial logit models. Here we distinguish between four states of control six years before the float: firm *i* is (i) controlled by the original owners (SC), (ii) widely held (WH), (iii) taken over by a closely held bidder (TC), or (iv) taken over by a widely held bidder (TW). Six years after the float, two-thirds of the German firms in the size-matched sample were still controlled by their initial owner.

This proportion is three times higher than for the U.K. sample. However, the number of (full and partial) takeovers is similar: 19 and 22 German and U.K. firms, respectively. As in most U.K. and German firms, the initial shareholder retains majority control at the float, we use this state as the benchmark case in the multinomial logit regressions.[22] The specifications include a differential intercept and interactive slope coefficients, which pick up possible differential effects for the German IPOs. For the size- and industry-matched samples, the following cross-sectional multinomial model is estimated by

$$U_{ij} = \beta' z_{ij} + \varepsilon_{ij} \text{ and for}$$
$$j = 1, 2, \ldots, J:$$

$$Pr(Y = 0) = \frac{1}{1 + \sum_{k=1}^{J} e^{\beta'_k x_i}}$$

$$Pr(Y = j) = \frac{e^{\beta'_k x_i}}{1 + \sum_{k=1}^{J} e^{\beta'_k x_k}}$$

More specifically, U_{ij} is the state of control j in company i:

State of control$_{ij}$
$$= \alpha + \beta_1 Country_i + \beta_2 Size_i$$
$$+ \beta_3 Founder_i + \beta_4 Risk_i$$
$$+ \beta_5 Growth_i + \beta_6 Nonvoting_i$$
$$+ \beta_7 Profit_i + \beta_8 Age_i$$
$$+ \beta_9 Country_i * Size_i$$
$$+ \beta_{10} Country_i * Founder_i$$
$$+ \beta_{11} Country_i * Risk_i$$
$$+ \beta_{12} Country_i * Growth_i$$
$$+ \beta_{13} Country_i * Profit_i$$
$$+ \beta_{14} Country_i * Age_i$$
$$+ \text{time dummies}$$
$$+ \text{industry dummies} + \varepsilon_{ij}.$$

5. CONTROL EVOLUTION AFTER THE FLOAT: STYLIZED FACTS

5.1 Control evolution by the initial and new large shareholders

The voting power held by the three categories of owners (initial, new large, and new small shareholders) over the six-year period after the IPO is recorded in Table 8.3 for the sample matched by size. Initial control is statistically different in the German and U.K. firms immediately after the IPO: the initial shareholders in German firms retain 76.4% versus only 62.8% in U.K. companies. Initial shareholder control is diluted much more rapidly in the United Kingdom than in Germany. The original shareholders of British IPOs lose majority control on average only two years after the float, whereas their German counterparts retain majority control up to five years. Although the reduction in control is slower in German IPOs, as much as 35% of these voting rights change hands during the six-year period. The differences in initial shareholder concentration in German and U.K. IPOs are statistically significant at the 1% level for each of the six years following the float.

At the float of U.K. firms, most of the shares are purchased by small shareholders, as the rationing schemes for share distribution in case of oversubscription often favor small shareholders for control reasons (Brennan and Franks, 1997). Consequently the free float is significantly higher (at the 1% level of significance) in U.K. firms (37.2%) than in German ones (22.2%), but remains relatively stable in both countries over the six-year period after the IPO. Over this period control is transferred from the initial shareholders to new large shareholders who, on average, control about 30% of the voting rights in both the German and U.K. samples six years subsequent to the float.

5.2 Changes of control and control states

Whereas Table 8.3 shows how control evolves over time, Table 8.4 reports the control state six years after the float. Panel A of Table 8.4 shows that full takeovers are uncommon in Germany, with only one case in our sample.[23, 24] In contrast, 35% of the U.K. companies were acquired in a full takeover within six years after the float. In Germany, control is less frequently transferred via a full takeover than via the sale of large voting blocks (which in fact constitutes a "partial" takeover). Such partial takeovers

Table 8.3 Proportion of Voting Rights Held by Initial Shareholders, by New Large Shareholders, and by Small Shareholders in Recent German and U.K. IPOs

	German sample				U.K. sample			
Time after IPO (years)	Initial shareholders (%)	Free float (%)	New large shareholders (%)	Sample size	Initial shareholders (%)	Free float (%)	New large shareholders (%)	Sample size
Immediately	76.4	22.2	1.5	54	62.8***	37.2***	0.1*	54
1	73.7	24.0	2.4	54	51.4***	43.1***	5.5	54
2	69.6	25.0	5.4	54	47.3***	39.5**	13.3**	54
3	64.9	25.3	9.8	54	37.7***	36.0**	26.4***	52
4	59.4	25.0	15.5	54	33.6***	37.6**	28.8**	52
5	50.7	26.3	23.1	54	31.4***	36.5**	32.1	52
6	45.0	24.8	30.2	54	30.0***	40.8***	29.2	48

The German IPOs are matched by size with the U.K. IPOs. If a company is taken over and delisted, it is classed as a case of 100% control by the new shareholder as of the year of the takeover. If a company is taken private by its original shareholders, it will be recorded as a company owned 100% by its original shareholders.
*** ** * indicate that the average stake in U.K. firms is statistically different from the stake in German firms at the 1%, 5%, and 10% significance level, respectively, of a t-test on the means. Sources: IPO prospectuses, Saling, company reports, Hoppenstedt, London Stock Exchange, and Extel.

Table 8.4 State of Control of IPOs Six Years After Flotation

	Size sample		Industry sample	
	Germany	*U.K.*	*Germany*	*U.K.*
Panel A: Number of firms by state of control				
Full takeover	1	19	1	18
Partial takeover	18	5	20	4
Widely held (<25%)	1	17	1	16
Still controlled by initial shareholders	34	13	36	20
Total	54	54	58	58
Panel B: Average number of years before reaching the new state of control				
Full takeover	6.0	3.7	6.0	3.5
Partial takeover	4.4	3.0	4.3	3.5
Widely held (25% def.)	—	1.8	—	1.7

Panel C: Ultimate shareholder in targets of full and partial takeovers (size-matched sample)

	Targets full takeover		Targets partial takeover		All full and partial takeovers	
	Germany	*U.K.*	*Germany*	*U.K.*	*Germany*	*U.K.*
Widely held	1	14	8	—	9	14
Closely held	—	5	10	5	10	9

For panels A and B, the disclosed state is the one six years after the IPO or the one the last year of listing if the firm was delisted before the sixth year after the float. A full takeover is a takeover of the entire voting rights of the firm, followed by the delisting of the firm. A partial takeover is a change of the major shareholder, the major shareholder being the largest shareholder holding at least 25% of the voting equity. A firm is widely held if no single shareholder owns more than 25% of the voting rights. A firm is still controlled by an initial shareholder if the initial shareholder is the largest shareholder and holds more than 25% of the votes. In panel C, a firm is classed as widely held if its ultimate largest shareholder is widely held, that is, is not controlled by a person or family holding more than 25% of the votes. A firm is classed as closely held if the ultimate largest shareholder is a person or a family. Sources: McCarthy microfiches, *Saling Aktienführer, Financial Times*, company reports.

are infrequent in the United Kingdom because of the legal requirement to make a tender offer for the entire equity of the firm as soon as an investor acquires 30% or more of a firm's equity.[25] Thus, if shareholders in a U.K. company do not want to end up with 100% control, they will deliberately remain below the 30% threshold (Goergen and Renneboog, 2001).

As a matter of fact, partial takeovers in Germany and full takeovers in the United Kingdom bring about similar results in terms of control change (Goergen, 1998). Panel A of Table 8.4 shows that, after amalgamating all control changes (both full and partial takeovers), the percentage (36% and 38%) is almost equal in German and U.K. IPOs. However, the distribution of

control across the remaining German and U.K. firms is still substantially different, as 62% of the German firms remain in the hands of their initial owners, compared to only 24% of the U.K. firms in the size-matched sample (and 35% in the industry-matched sample). Only one German company becomes widely held, whereas 32% of U.K. firms are already widely held six years after the IPO. The reason why we follow the control evolution for a six-year period subsequent to the float can be found in panel B of Table 8.4.[26] Control changes in U.K. IPOs take place three to four years after the float, whereas in German IPOs they happen within a four-to-six year period.

Even though the percentage of German and U.K. firms with a control change

Table 8.5 Voting Rights in Excess of 25%, Six Years After Flotation

	Germany	United Kingdom
A: companies without a large shareholder	1.85%	33.33%
B: companies with a large shareholder	98.15%	66.67%
1. Another domestic company	7.41%	29.63%
2. A foreign company	22.22%	5.56%
3. An insurance company	1.85%	0.00%
4. A trust/institutional investor	0.00%	3.70%
5. A family group	66.67%	27.78%
6. A bank	0.00%	0.00%
Total	100.00%	100.00%

This table is based on a sample of German and U.K. IPOs matched by market capitalization. The sample is unbalanced, that is, if a firm is delisted prior to its sixth year after going public, the largest shareholder in the last year prior to the delisting is reported.

(full and partial takeovers) may be roughly similar, the question whether the (ultimate) bidder is widely held or is concentrated remains important. The potential agency problems in widely held (and hence management-controlled) firms are different from those in closely held firms (Bratton and McCahery, 1995; Shleifer and Vishny, 1997). For the former, the target firm will be monitored by the bidder's management, which may have objectives in conflict with the maximization of shareholder value. For the latter, it is the *ultimate* large shareholder who is expected to monitor the target. Thus the objectives of the bidder may differ depending upon who ultimately controls the bidder. For example, the management of the bidder with dispersed ultimate control may be more interested in acquiring large, profitable, low-risk firms, whereas the bidder with a strong shareholder may prefer a more-risky, high-growth firm. Empirical evidence suggests that it is the ultimate shareholder at the top of the ownership pyramid who disciplines management rather than the shareholders at the first ownership tier (see Renneboog, 2000). Panel C of Table 8.4 differentiates between takeovers by an ultimately dispersed or concentrated bidder. The bidder in 52% of the German partial takeover targets in the size-matched sample is ultimately closely held. The remaining German companies are ultimately widely held. Out of the 24 U.K.

companies which are fully or partially taken over, 14 are taken over by a bidder with dispersed control.

Not only are there differences in the evolution of control between Germany and the United Kingdom, but there are also differences in terms of who owns the votes. Table 8.5 shows the identity of the major shareholder six years after the float for the size-matched sample. In German firms, families control two-thirds of the voting rights and other companies (mainly foreign ones) control about one-third. For U.K. firms, other firms (mainly domestic ones) and families control 35% and 28% of the voting rights, respectively.

6. PREDICTION OF CONTROL IN GERMAN AND U.K. FIRMS

6.1 Determinants of the evolution of control

Table 8.6 investigates the determinants of the evolution of control six years after the float. We not only analyze the dilution of stakes held by the initial shareholders, but also the evolution of the free float and the emergence of new large shareholders. All shareholdings which are directly or indirectly controlled by the same (ultimate) owner are aggregated. Large U.K. companies (measured by market capitalization) tend to evolve

Table 8.6 Determinants of the Evolution of Control Concentration in Recent German and U.K. IPOs (Tobit Regressions)

	Parameter estimates		
	(1) Initial shareholders	(2) Free float	(3) New shareholder
Constant	0.074	−0.058	1.016***
	(0.839)	(0.780)	(0.006)
Country	0.230	0.837***	−0.887
	(0.636)	(0.004)	(0.103)
Size	0.043	0.162***	−0.158**
	(0.542)	(0.000)	(0.024)
Size * Country	−0.111	−0.189***	0.240**
	(0.312)	(0.004)	(0.045)
$Age_{minuscountryavg}$	0.005	0.003	−0.007
	(0.175)	(0.125)	(0.102)
$Age_{minuscountryavg}$ * Country	−0.008*	−0.003	0.009**
	(0.065)	(0.180)	(0.045)
Founder	−0.189	−0.263***	0.279
	(0.269)	(0.008)	(0.115)
Founder * Country	0.550*	−0.230	−0.511*
	(0.055)	(0.180)	(0.098)
$Risk_{minuscountryavg}$	−1.281	−2.322***	2.387*
	(0.378)	(0.004)	(0.089)
$Risk_{minuscountryavg}$ * Country	3.334	10.950***	−6.752
	(0.417)	(0.000)	(0.152)
Growth	−0.351	0.006	0.204
	(0.112)	(0.958)	(0.315)
Growth * Country	−0.992**	0.116	1.117**
	(0.048)	(0.696)	(0.042)
Nonvoting	0.487***	−0.278***	−0.375**
	(0.000)	(0.001)	(0.013)
Profit rate	0.155	0.203	−0.618
	(0.820)	(0.574)	(0.327)
Profit rate * Country	−0.258	0.426	0.504
	(0.795)	(0.487)	(0.652)
Observations	84	84	84

This table shows the determinants of the concentration of voting equity 6 years after flotation for the size-matched sample of German and U.K. IPOs using Tobit regressions. The dependent variables Free float and New shareholder are the shares held by small shareholders and the proportion of shares held by new shareholders (large shareholders who did not hold shares prior to the IPO), respectively. Stakes below 25% are ignored. The dummy variable *Country* equals one for a German company and zero otherwise. *Size* is the natural logarithm of the market capitalization at the closing price on the first day of trading and converted into 1985 pounds sterling. *Founder* equals one if the founder or his heirs held an equity stake in the firm immediately prior to the IPO, and equals zero otherwise. *Risk* is measured by the standard deviation of monthly stock returns over a five-year period subsequent to the IPO. *Growth* is the average annual growth rate of total assets over the first five years after the float. *Nonvoting* is a dummy variable which is set to one if nonvoting shares were issued at the time of going public, and zero otherwise. *Profit* is the annual cash flow standardized by the book value of total assets. *Age* is the number of years since the registration of the firm. From the variables *Age* and *Risk*, the average by country was subtracted in order to avoid multicollinearity. The *p*-values are shown in parentheses. ***, **, * represent statistical significance at the 1%, 5%, and 10% level, respectively. Industry and time dummies are included.

toward a widely held equity structure as wealth constraints put a limit on holding large blocks of equity (column 2). However, these wealth constraints do not seem to be binding for German firms, as the market capitalization does not influence control concentration (the parameter estimates of 0.162 and −0.189 largely cancel out). Larger U.K. firms also have fewer new large blocks of equity, but this is not the case for larger German firms in which new shareholders control significantly larger equity stakes. Thus these findings support Proposition 1, stating that there is a stronger negative relation between control and corporate size for U.K. firms.

To control for the fact that the average German firm is substantially older, we have subtracted the country average from *Age*. Table 8.6 shows that the initial shareholders of German firms with an above-average age tend to retain smaller voting stakes than those of relatively older U.K. firms. This supports Proposition 2. The control relinquished by the initial shareholders in the relatively older German firms is not dissipated but is taken over by new large shareholders (column 3).

Table 8.6 also investigates the influence of the founder family on control six years after the float. The table reports different results for U.K. and German IPOs. If the founder of a German firm is still a shareholder at the IPO, control is likely to remain tight. Given that the initial shareholders retain large stakes, it is less likely for large new shareholders to acquire controlling stakes in German firms (column 3). In contrast, the presence of the founder family among the initial shareholders in the United Kingdom has little impact on the degree of control exerted by the initial and new shareholders, although the likelihood that the firm evolves toward widely held ownership decreases. These findings support Proposition 3.

Demsetz and Lehn (1985) found a negative relation between risk and ownership concentration for U.S. firms. Our findings support this picture for U.K. firms: in companies with risk above the average 12.8%, the control held by new large shareholders

is higher than in firms with below average risk. Moreover, the free float in risky U.K. firms is lower. High-risk German companies also require a strong new shareholder with potentially strong monitoring skills (column 3). Still, column 2 also shows that a high degree of risk also leads to a higher free float in German firms. Thus control concentration is related more strongly to risk in the United Kingdom than in Germany, and this partially supports Proposition 4.

Although we do not find any impact of growth on the control of U.K. firms, strong growth in German firms leads to a reduction in the initial shareholders' control and control is transferred to new large shareholders. The findings support Proposition 5 for the German firms, but not for the U.K. ones. None of the U.K. firms had issued nonvoting shares versus 38% of the German firms. (Nonvoting shares enable the initial shareholders to raise additional equity capital while maintaining control.) Table 8.6 confirms that the voting rights of the initial shareholders do not tend to be dissipated after the IPO when the company has nonvoting outstanding shares (column 1). Thus both a transfer of control to a new large shareholder and a dissipation of control are less likely (columns 2 and 3). This supports Proposition 6. Proposition 7 states that when sufficient cash flows are generated, there is a higher probability that the initial shareholder retains control. Unlike Heiss and Köke (2001), we do not find any such evidence in Table 8.6 and reject Proposition 7.[27]

To conclude: in fast-growing, older German firms, the initial shareholders substantially reduce their controlling share stakes over the six years after the float, provided they are not part of the founder family. In contrast, the initial shareholders of German firms tend to retain control in firms with nonvoting shares. New shareholders acquire control in larger, older, and strongly growing German firms in which the founder family is no longer involved and which have no nonvoting equity. A higher free float tends to occur in highrisk German firms. In U.K. firms, we find a strong relation between control and size: the larger the firm, the lower is the control by the new shareholders and hence the larger is the free float. When the founder does not sell out at the float, the probability that control is dissipated is low. High risk seems to necessitate high control by the new large shareholders.[28]

6.2 Multinomial logit prediction of the state of control

Whereas in the previous section we investigated the determinants of the control levels of initial and new shareholders, we now estimate the likelihood that six years after the float the following four different states of control arise: initial shareholder control (SC), diffuse control (WH), takeover by a closely held bidder (TC), or takeover by a widely held bidder (TW). This analysis is performed for two reasons. First, it sheds some light on how control concentration comes about (via different types of takeover, or via control retention). Second, the Tobit models estimated in the previous section (Table 8.6) assume that the dependent variables (control held by initial or new large shareholders or diffuse control) are independent, which is not the case. Therefore we estimate multinomial logits predicting the control state.[29] Table 8.7 confirms that there is a higher probability for large firms to end up with diffuse control (panel B). This supports Proposition 1. In addition, large firms are more likely to be taken over by a widely held firm than by a concentrated bidder. This is expected for two reasons. First, a concentrated bidder (a family or individual) is more likely to be wealth constrained than a widely held firm or may be less able to raise external funds to finance the control acquisition. Second, the reason for a takeover by a widely held firm may be agency related: the management of a widely held firm may be tempted to "build an empire" when it is insufficiently monitored (Berkovitch and Narayanan, 1993; Goergen and Renneboog, 2003).

Age does not seem to matter for either country's control levels such that we have

to reject Proposition 2. If the founder or his heirs are involved in the firm at the IPO, the likelihood that they retain control over the six-year period subsequent to the IPO is large and hence the likelihood that the firm evolves toward diffuse control is significantly reduced. This supports Proposition 3. The fact that founder involvement at the flotation does not influence the probability of being taken over provides some support for the predictions of the models by Zingales (1995) and Mello and Parsons (1998) and is also consistent with the empirical findings for the United States (Chung and Pruitt, 1996).

In companies with high risk, we expect the initial shareholders to reduce control in favor of new large, stable shareholders with good monitoring abilities. Table 8.7 reveals that high risk significantly increases the probability of full and partial takeovers relative to the possibility that the firm remains controlled by the initial shareholders (panel A) and relative to the state of diffuse ownership (panel B). Panel C also reveals an interesting result: high risk increases the likelihood of a takeover by a concentrated bidder rather than by a widely held firm. So it seems that tight control with increased monitoring is the best solution to high risk. This contradicts Proposition 4 and the predictions of Bolton and von Thadden's (1998) model. While we hypothesized that Proposition 4 would hold more strongly for the U.K. firms, we find no differences in the risk-control relation between the United Kingdom and Germany.

High growth could lead to control dilution resulting from the limited availability of internally generated funds and the implied need to attract external capital to finance investment opportunities.[30] Table 8.7 confirms Proposition 5: both diffuse control and a takeover by a widely held company are the more likely "equilibrium" states six years after the float for growth companies. This proposition is expected to hold more strongly for the U.K. firms than for the German ones. Panel C of Table 8.7 shows that this is the case: high growth triggers more partial takeovers, but not necessarily by widely held bidders. The reason is that pyramids enable shareholders to attract external capital while limiting control dilution.

For German firms, the consistently negative sign of the dummy variable *Nonvoting* indicates that firms with nonvoting shares are less likely to undergo a change in control. Still, in contrast to the results in Table 8.6, the parameter coefficients are not statistically significant, such that we fail to support Proposition 6.

Table 8.7 supports the proposition by Burkart, Gromb, and Pannunzi (1997) that different states of the world require specific control structures (Proposition 7). Some states of the world (such as the ones with a low profitability) require a large stable shareholder, while others cope well with dispersed control, allowing for sufficient managerial discretion. We find that a low profit rate increases the probability of a U.K. firm being acquired by a closely held bidder. Thus it seems that incumbent shareholders sell out to a concentrated bidder, if the former are not able to provide sufficient monitoring to improve the firm's performance. Indeed, poor performance not only results from poor managerial performance, but also from a breakdown of corporate governance. These findings support Proposition 7 for the United Kingdom. Conversely the higher the profitability, the higher the odds that the firm is taken over by a widely held bidder. The fact that widely held companies prefer profitable takeover targets can be explained in an agency-cost setting: managers of widely held firms may find it easier to boost financial performance by taking over profitable firms rather than by improving the financial results of their current businesses.[31] Alternatively, widely held bidders may not be able to provide the level of monitoring, which is required to turn around a badly performing target firm. For Germany we find a much weaker relation between control states and profitability. First, as in the United Kingdom, poor performance entails a higher likelihood that control is transferred than diluted. Second, unlike our findings for the United Kingdom, strong performance leads to a higher occurrence

of acquisitions by closely held bidders than by widely held bidders.

Finally, it should be noted that the dummy variable *Country* is not statistically significant. This strongly suggests that the country interaction terms are capturing all the economic determinants of the control states.

7. CONCLUSION

This article analyzes why the levels of control are so different in Germany and the United Kingdom. A first reason for shareholders to hold larger voting stakes in German firms is found in the differences in the regulatory and legal environment. A detailed analysis of the regulation of the German and U.K. stock exchanges, of the rules on minority shareholder protection, of informational transparency, and of the takeover codes shows that there is lower shareholder protection in Germany. The voting practice at annual meetings, the composition of the board of directors, and their fiduciary duties further reinforce this relative weakness of shareholder rights in Germany. As a consequence, control is more valuable to shareholders of German firms either to avoid expropriation of their investments or to take advantage of the higher levels of private benefits. Furthermore, holding large control stakes is less expensive in Germany relative to the United Kingdom because ownership pyramids, the possibility of issuing nonvoting stock, and the possibility of nominating one's representatives to the board of directors ensure that control can be maintained with relatively low levels of cash flow rights.

Although the legal environment predicts stronger levels of control in Germany, it does not explain how the difference in control concentration comes about. Both U.K. and German firms are floated on the stock exchange with high levels of initial control, and this raises the question as to what triggers subsequent changes in control. To answer this question we investigate the economic factors that determine control retention

Table 8.7 Prediction of State of Control for German and U.K. IPOs (Multinomial Logit)

	Panel A			Panel B		Panel C
	$Log\,(P_{WH}/P_{SC})$	$Log\,(P_{TC}/P_{SC})$	$Log\,(P_{TW}/P_{SC})$	$Log\,(P_{TC}/P_{WH})$	$Log\,(P_{TW}/P_{WH})$	$Log\,(P_{TW}/P_{TC})$
Constant	2.126	-25.323	-31.793	-27.974	-34.430	-6.678
	(0.417)	(1.000)	(1.000)	(1.000)	(1.000)	(1.000)
Country	-34.405	20.627	30.522	54.378	64.399	10.103
	(1.000)	(1.000)	(1.000)	(1.000)	(1.000)	(1.000)
Size	0.499	-1.753	0.314	-2.253*	-0.185	2.067*
	(0.328)	(0.131)	(0.607)	(0.062)	(0.758)	(0.100)
Size * Country	0.014	2.231	0.440	2.356	0.565	-1.791
	(1.000)	(0.221)	(0.672)	(1.000)	(1.000)	(0.373)
$Age_{minuscountryavg}$	0.004	-0.052	-0.016	-0.056	-0.020	0.036
	(0.879)	(0.638)	(0.577)	(0.616)	(0.464)	(0.746)
$Age_{minuscountryavg}$ * Country	0.017	0.070	0.043	0.057	0.030	-0.028
	(1.000)	(0.539)	(0.196)	(1.000)	(1.000)	(0.813)
Founder	-4.983**	31.804	26.097	37.311	31.730	-5.498
	(0.036)	(1.000)	(1.000)	(1.000)	(1.000)	(1.000)
Founder * Country	1.883	-35.509	-27.047	-38.187	-29.851	8.254
	(1.000)	(1.000)	(1.000)	(1.000)	(1.000)	(1.000)
$Risk_{minuscountryavg}$	-7.170	41.215*	-1.068	48.385*	6.102	-42.283*
	(0.658)	(0.059)	(0.954)	(0.051)	(0.744)	(0.100)
$Risk_{minuscountryavg}$ * Country	-11.056	13.176	-60.541	20.285	-53.431	-73.717
	(1.000)	(0.833)	(0.185)	(1.000)	(1.000)	(0.314)

	(1)	(2)	(3)	(4)	(5)	(6)
Growth	5.031*	0.919	7.671**	−4.112	2.640	6.753**
	(0.083)	(0.764)	(0.013)	(0.190)	(0.215)	(0.039)
Growth * Country	0.222	8.917	−7.080	9.945	−6.051	−15.996*
	(1.000)	(0.169)	(0.294)	(1.000)	(1.000)	(0.059)
Nonvoting	−1.215	−3.064	−1.546	−2.166	−0.648	1.518
	(1.000)	(0.230)	(0.250)	(1.000)	(1.000)	(0.589)
Profit rate	9.040	−21.144*	16.530*	−30.184**	−34.570	37.674**
	(0.226)	(0.096)	(0.053)	(0.031)	(1.000)	(0.010)
Profit rate * Country	−0.110	33.487**	−25.544*	35.207	−23.823	−59.030**
	(1.000)	(0.041)	(0.080)	(1.000)	(1.000)	(0.006)
Chi-squared (c.f., p-value)	111		111		111	
	(51,0.000)		(51,0.000)		(51,0.000)	
% of correct predictions	75.00		58.33		67.86	
Observations	84		84		84	

This table shows the probability of control for a size-matched sample of German and U.K. firms using a multinomial logit model with four possible states of control: SC (control remains in the hands of the initial [pre-IPO] shareholders), WH (the firm is widely held [no shareholder owns a stake of more than 25%]), TW (the firm is taken over by a widely held company), and TC (the firm is taken over by a concentrated shareholder). The dummy variable *Country* equals one for a German company and zero otherwise. *Size* is the natural logarithm of the market capitalization at the closing price on the first day of trading, converted into 1985 pounds sterling. *Founder* equals 1 if the founder or his heirs held an equity stake in the firm immediately prior to the IPO, and equals zero otherwise. *Risk* is measured by the standard deviation of monthly stock returns over a five-year period after the IPO. *Growth* is the average annual growth rate of total assets over the first five years after the float. *Nonvoting* is a dummy variable capturing the issue of nonvoting shares at the time of going public (dummy equals 1). *Profit* is the annual cash flow standardized by the book value of total assets. *Age* is the number of years since the registration of the firm. From the variables *Age* and *Risk*, the average by country was subtracted to avoid multicollinearity. The *p*-values are in parentheses. ***, **, * represent statistical significance at the 1%, 5%, and 10% level, respectively. Industry and time dummies are included in the model.

APPENDIX

Table 8.A1 Pearson Correlation Coefficients of Independent Variables

	Country	Size	Founder	Risk	Growth	Nonvoting	Profit	Age	$Risk_{minuscountryavg}$	$Growth_{minuscountryavg}$	$Age_{minuscountryavg}$
Country	1										
Size	0.026 (0.483)	1									
Founder	0.121 (0.133)	0.081 (0.139)	1								
Risk	−0.533 (0.000)	0.117 (0.135)	−0.016 (0.296)	1							
Growth	−0.154 (0.080)	−0.099 (0.286)	0.177 (0.053)	0.070 (0.244)	1						
Nonvoting	0.541 (0.000)	0.152 (0.172)	0.094 (0.123)	−0.281 (0.006)	−0.009 (0.478)	1					
Profit	0.191 (0.291)	−0.069 (0.367)	0.099 (0.277)	−0.250 (0.008)	0.056 (0.154)	0.180 (0.194)	1				
Age	0.342 (0.000)	0.003 (0.218)	0.176 (0.129)	−0.015 (0.000)	0.035 (0.080)	0.000 (0.015)	0.098 (0.273)	1			
$Risk_{minuscountryavg}$	0.009 (0.461)	0.086 (0.189)	0.090 (0.183)	0.875 (0.000)	−0.043 (0.403)	−0.024 (0.015)	−0.380 (0.000)	−0.107 (0.136)	1		
$Growth_{minuscountryavg}$	0.000 (0.500)	−0.061 (0.278)	0.191 (0.035)	−0.005 (0.480)	0.989 (0.000)	0.081 (0.217)	0.124 (0.121)	−0.067 (0.257)	−0.051 (0.311)	1	
$Age_{minuscountryavg}$	0.000 (0.500)	0.094 (0.168)	0.062 (0.267)	−0.118 (0.114)	−0.079 (0.221)	−0.093 (0.170)	0.038 (0.358)	0.833 (0.000)	−0.134 (0.083)	−0.080 (0.220)	1

This table shows the Pearson correlation coefficients of the determinants of the concentration of ownership six years after the float. The dummy variable *Country* equals one for a German company and zero otherwise. *Size* is the natural logarithm of the market capitalization at the closing price on the first day of trading and converted into 1985 pounds sterling. *Founder* equals one if the founder or his heirs held an equity stake in the firm immediately prior to the IPO and equals zero otherwise. *Risk* is measured by the standard deviation of monthly stock returns over a five-year period subsequent to the IPO. *Growth* is the average annual growth rate of total assets over the first five years after the float. *Nonvoting* is a dummy variable capturing the issue of nonvoting shares at the time of going public (dummy equals 1). *Profit* is the annual cash flow standardized by the book value of total assets. *Age* is the number of years at the IPO since the creation of the company. $Risk_{minuscountryavg}$ $Growth_{minuscountryavg}$ and $Age_{minuscountryavg}$ are the respective *Risk*, *Growth*, and *Age* variables of which the country average is subtracted. The statistical significance is in parentheses.

by large initial shareholders, dissipation of control among many small shareholders, and control transfers whereby we make a distinction between widely held and concentrated bidders. The article uses a unique database of IPOs with data over the period 1981–1994. Industry and size effects are controlled for by creating size- and industry-matched samples of "twin" German and U.K. firms whose evolution of control was followed over a six-year period. We find that not only do the initial shareholders in the average German company own much larger stakes than their U.K. counterparts, they also lose majority control only six years after the public offering. In contrast, initial owners in U.K. companies lose majority control two years after going public.

We have found strong evidence that corporate characteristics lead to differences in control evolution across companies but also between the United Kingdom and Germany. The Tobit models that estimate the percentage of control held by the initial and new large shareholders and the size of the free float six years subsequent to the float show that size is an important determinant of control concentration in the United Kingdom but not in Germany. Large U.K. companies evolve toward a more widely held equity structure, whereas in large German firms, new shareholders hold significantly larger voting stakes. The reason is that wealth constraints become binding for U.K. shareholders, whereas German ones can avoid this effect by leveraging control via pyramids. Age has an inverse impact on the control of German and U.K. firms: initial shareholders of older German firms tend to retain smaller voting stakes than those of relatively older U.K. firms.

If the founder of a German firm is still a shareholder at the IPO and if there are nonvoting shares outstanding, control is likely to remain tight in the hands of the initial shareholders. This is not surprising, as founding families often extract (nonpecuniary) private benefits of control and nonvoting shares enable them to raise additional equity capital while maintaining control. Whereas we do not find any impact

of growth on the control concentration of U.K. firms, strong growth in German firms leads to the initial shareholders transferring control to new large shareholders. The impact of risk on control is stronger in the United Kingdom than in Germany. In U.K. companies with above average risk, the degree of control held by new large shareholders is higher and the free float is lower.

The multinomial logit models, which predict the occurrence of different states of control (initial shareholders retain control, control is diluted, control is transferred to a concentrated shareholder or to a widely held firm), show that specific corporate characteristics lead to different "equilibrium" control states six years after the float. We find substantial differences between takeovers by a concentrated shareholder and takeovers by widely held companies. For the United Kingdom, the probability of a transfer of control to a concentrated shareholder increases when a company is risky, small, and poorly performing. A U.K. firm is more likely to be taken over by a widely held firm if it is large, fast-growing, and profitable. So, for the United Kingdom, poor performance and high risk necessitate a high level of control and tight monitoring by a concentrated shareholder. High growth and profitability attract widely held companies whose management may follow an "empire building" acquisition program. We found that high growth also leads to more diffuse control, which in turn is less likely when the founder family is still involved in the company. Founding families may be less inclined to dilute their stake in order to retain private benefits of control. When German firms are profitable and risky, control is more likely to be acquired by a concentrated shareholder, but growth and low profitability increase the likelihood of being acquired by a widely held firm.

NOTES

* We are deeply indebted to Alan Schwartz, the editor, as well as to two anonymous referees. Their comments and suggestions have substantially improved this article. We are also grateful to

Rafel Crespi, Julian Franks, Carles Gispert, Uli Hege, Alan Hughes, Jens Köke, Colin Mayer, Joe McCahery, Josep Tribo, Eddy Wymeersch, and the participants at the 2001 meeting of the European Finance Association in Barcelona, the participants at seminars at Oxford University, UMIST, Tilburg University, CUNEF (Madrid), and the participants at the conference on "Convergence and Diversity in Corporate Governance Regimes and Capital Markets" in Eindhoven for stimulating comments.

1.   Full-parity determination for the shareholders and employees only exists in the steel and coal sector. In small companies with more than 500 but less than 2,000 employees, one-third of the supervisory board consists of labor representatives. In larger firms with more than 2,000 employees, a system of quasi-parity codetermination exists as employee representatives make up half of the supervisory board, but the chairman who is a shareholder representative has a casting vote in case of stalemate.

2.   See sections 3.12 and 3.13 of Chapter 11 of the Listing Rules.

3.   See sections 11.4 and 11.5 of the Listing Rules.

4.   Correia da Silva, Goergen, and Renneboog (2003) argue that the taxation of dividends in Germany does not provide an incentive to construct shareholding pyramids.

5.   In the United Kingdom, the Company Act requires the identity of shareholders purchasing share blocks in excess of 3% (5% prior to 1989) to be disclosed to the target company. Germany was the last European country to introduce such a disclosure regulation (for stakes of 5% or more): the European Transparency Directive (88/627/EEC) was only implemented in Germany in 1995 (the *Wertpapierhandelsgesetz*). Prior to 1995, there was only compulsory disclosure of control at the level of 25%. In the United Kingdom, shareholders owning 15% or more of the equity of a U.K. firm must make public their intentions with regard to launching a takeover. There is no such requirement in Germany. Becht and Boehmer (2001) argue that the efficiency of the 1995 disclosure regulation is very low, as ultimate ownership cannot easily be inferred from published filings, there is no disclosure on who exercises proxy votes, and accumulated votes held by business groups cannot easily be determined. They conclude: "the low transparency of control is likely to increase the cost of capital to affected German corporations relative to their international competitors listed in markets that are more transparent. Full disclosure of control

is likely to reduce uncertainty with respect to expropriation and increase the value of affected firms."

6.   Section 204 of the Companies Act 1985.

7.   See the City Code on "concert parties." It should be noted that this regulation does not apply for "ad hoc" coalitions which are temporary and formed with one particular aim, for example, the removal of poorly performing management (Stapledon, 1996).

8.   Nonvoting shares have dormant voting rights that are triggered by two consecutive omitted dividend payments (*Aktiengesetz*, par. 140).

9.   It should be noted that in neither country can the control stakes be diluted by seasoned equity offerings. In the United Kingdom, seasoned new equity must be in the form of rights issues (Section 89(1) of the Companies Act 1985). These rights may only be waived if a supermajority (of at least 75%) votes to do so. Even where shareholders vote to drop their pre-emption rights, the discount of any new issue must not exceed 10% of the market price at the time of the issue's announcement (para. 4.26, Stock Exchange Rules, 1999). These rules ensure that the stakes of the initial shareholders cannot be diluted by the ones of new shareholders. They are reinforced by guidelines, issued by the National Association of Pension Funds and the Association of British Insurers, limiting companies to raise 5% of their share capital each year by any method apart from rights issues, and 7.5% in any rolling three-year period. German corporate law is similar: it requires seasoned equity issues expanding the equity by 10% or more to take place via rights issues.

10.   Voting caps in the by-laws do not apply to the proxies which banks have collected (Baums and Schmitz, 2000).

11.   The fact that bearer shares are common in German firms, whereas nominal shares are used in the United Kingdom, does not lead to differences in voting procedure. In both countries, shares need to be registered if one wants to exert voting rights (Baums, 1997).

12.   Given the competition in a globalized economy, it is surprising that corporate governance regulation has not converged more. Bebchuk and Roe (1999) claim that the rigidity to changes in control concentration hinges to a large extent on the structures with which the economy started (structure-driven path dependence). The efficient choice of a corporate control structure is influenced by sunk costs. Furthermore, there is an endowment effect, as there are advantages to using the dominant form in the economy, which is the one which

most players are familiar with. Internal rent seeking by parties who participate in corporate control may also explain why such parties would attempt to impede change toward a more efficient control structure. For example, the management of widely held companies may prefer to retain a diffuse control structure, as this enables them to maintain their private benefits at the expense of shareholders. Likewise, Bebchuk (1998) argues that concentrated ownership—and hence uncontested corporate control—prevails in continental Europe because the lax corporate-governance regulation allows large shareholders to reap substantial private benefits of control. Hence, as long as continental European regulation does not change, control concentration will resist change (Bratton and McCahery, 1999).

13. See the discussion on minority protection in Section 2. Evidence of the extraction of private benefits of control by large shareholders in Germany is given by Franks and Mayer (2001), and by Dyck and Zingales (2001) in an international comparison.

14. Brennan and Franks (1997) show that control retention is an important reason for underpricing: share-rationing schemes enable the original shareholders to disperse shares to atomistic subscribers.

15. This argument assumes that the voting share prices in both companies are equal.

16. During the period of the study, lower-tier markets were the Unregulated Unofficial Market and the OTC for Germany and the Third Market and OTC for the United Kingdom.

17. Control and ownership concentration of 61 of these 80 German firms could be traced reliably over time. For most of the other IPOs, the identity of the shareholders was available, but not the exact size of their holdings.

18. The industry classification is based on the two-digit U.K. SE groups, the industrial classification used by the London Stock Exchange to compile its quarterly lists of new issues. The groups are covered by the F.T. Actuaries Investment Index Classification with the amalgamation of certain related groups. For each German firm the industry description at the time of the IPO in the *Satling Aktienführer* was recorded. Subsequently German firms were reclassified into two-digit U.K. SE groups. We have merged specific groups which only had a small number of IPOs: for example, groups 27 (Misc. Mechanical Engineering) and 28 (Machine and Other Tools) were merged. Groups 19 (Electricals), 35 (Electronics), and 69 (Office Equipment) were also merged since groups 35 and 69 did not exist at the beginning

of the 1980s and computer and software manufacturers were first assigned to group 19, then to group 69, and only later to group 35.

19. Market capitalization is adjusted for U.K. inflation by the annual GDP deflator (base year 1985) of the International Monetary Fund (IMF). Several German firms in our sample have dual-class shares of which one class is not listed. The market capitalization for these firms was computed by multiplying the total number of shares by the market price of the listed class of shares.

20. It may be argued that a different type of matching based on firm age should also have been performed. However, a reasonable match (plus or minus two years of difference) could only be found for about 19 German firms. However, we control directly for age in the regressions. Similarly we tried to match firms simultaneously by size and industry. However, again for more than three-quarters of the firms, a satisfactory match within the 25% range could not be found.

21. The German size-matched sample includes two companies which are not included in the industry-matched sample, because there were no U.K. IPOs in these specific industries during the period of study. The German industry-matched sample comprises six firms not included in the size-matched sample.

22. As $\log P_{WH}/P_{SC} = -\log P_{SC}/P_{WH}$, we report results for (i) $\log(P_{WH}/P_{SC})$, $\log(P_{TC}/P_{SC})$, $\log(P_{TW}/P_{SC})$, (ii) $\log(P_{TC}/P_{WH})$, $\log(P_{TW}/P_{WH})$, and (iii) $\log(P_{TW}/P_{TC})$.

23. Franks and Mayer (1998) report that hostile takeovers have been a rare phenomenon in Germany. Since World War II and prior to 2000, there have only been three attempts, two of which failed. Since then there has been a fourth successful hostile takeover (the Mannesmann takeover by Vodaphone in 2000).

24. Whereas panel A considers only direct holdings, panel C takes both direct and indirect holdings into account.

25. The Takeover Panel may grant an exception to this rule, which makes a tender offer mandatory to a party which reaches the 30% threshold of equity (or voting rights), in the case where a shareholder takes a large stake in a financially distressed company.

26. Expanding the analyzed time period of six years subsequent to the IPO to eight years changes neither the data presented in Table 8.3 nor the results of this article.

27. As a robustness check, similar Tobit regressions but with alternative independent variables (for the definition, see Section 4.2) were estimated. The country-dummy variables

confirm that the share stakes of initial shareholders are higher in Germany, whereas the percentage controlled by new large shareholders is higher in the United Kingdom (as a result of the more frequent occurrence of full takeovers). Firm size (book value of total assets) is positively related to the control held by small shareholders and by new large shareholders, which confirms the findings of this section. We find that, if the founder is on the management board (*Vorstand*) of a German firm, control by the initial shareholders is less likely to be reduced over the six years after the IPO. These initial shareholders retain a higher percentage of the voting rights than those in firms without founder involvement. As expected, a higher retention rate goes hand in hand with a reduced presence of new shareholders. Growth, in contrast, is strongly related to control concentration. High growth in total assets leads to a reduction in the stakes of the initial shareholders in the United Kingdom and even more so in Germany. Furthermore, a higher proportion of nonvoting shares in Germany allows the initial shareholders to retain their control. In contrast to the findings presented in Table 8.6, we find different results for our risk and profitability measures. We do not find a relation between the risk measured as the standard deviation of cash flows over the five-year period after the IPO and control. This may be due to the fact that our original risk measure (based on the volatility of stock returns) is the better one. Whereas the profitability measure (cash flow/book value of total assets) was not related to ownership concentration in Table 8.6, the alternative profit rate (cash flow over market value of equity plus book value of debt) shows a statistically significant relation with control concentration. These results support the proposition by Burkart, Gromb, and Panunzi (1997) that different states of the world require different control structures. In some states of the world (such as the one with low profitability), a major, stable shareholder is needed, while in other cases a dispersed share structure provides the necessary managerial discretion. High profitability in the United Kingdom ensures that the initial shareholders retain control and consequently that the voting blocks held by new shareholders in the more profitable firms are smaller. For Germany, in contrast, we find the opposite result: initial shareholders seem to consider high profitability as an opportunity to transfer control stakes to new large shareholders. We conclude that the findings of Table 8.6

discussed above are robust to alternative variable specifications.

28.   All the results in this section—apart from the conclusions concerning corporate growth—are also valid for the industry-matched sample. These results are not reported in the article, but are available upon request. The only difference in results is that the *Growth* coefficient is not significantly different from zero at the 10% level for the industry sample. This is probably due to the fact that firms matched by industry have more comparable growth rates than those matched by size.

29.   It should be noted that the state of control is based on ultimate control. The predictive power of these models with control based on direct shareholding was lower than the one based on ultimate control. Statistical significance for the direct ownership models was always worse for the case of the size-matched sample, and worse or similar for the industry-matched sample.

30.   All results in this section—apart from the conclusions concerning corporate growth—are also valid for the industry-matched sample. These results are not reported in the article, but are available upon request. The only difference in results is that the *Growth* coefficient is not significantly different from zero at the 10% level for the industry sample. This is probably due to the fact that firms matched by industry have more comparable growth rates than those matched by size (see also Goergen, 1999).

31.   This finding is confirmed by a study on hostile takeovers in the United Kingdom by Franks and Mayer (1996).

REFERENCES

Baums, T. 1997. "Shareholder Representation and Proxy Voting in the European Union: A Comparative Study," working paper, University of Osnabrück.

——. 2000. "Corporate Governance in Germany—System and Current Developments," working paper, University of Osnabrück.

——, and C. Fraune. 1995. "Institutionelle Anleger und Publikumsgesellschaft: Eine Empirische Untersuchung," 40 *Die Aktiengesellschaft* 97–112.

——, and R. Schmitz. 2000. "Shareholder Voting in Germany," working paper 76, University of Osnabrück.

Bebchuk, L. 1998. "A Theory of the Choice Between Concentrated and Dispersed Ownership of Corporate Shares and Votes," working paper, Harvard Law School.

——, and M. Roe. 1999. "A Theory of Path Dependence in Corporate Governance and Ownership," 52 *Stanford Law Review* 127–70.

Becht, M., and E. Boehmer. 2001. "Ownership and Control in Germany," in F. Barca and M. Becht, eds., *The Control of Corporate Europe*. Oxford: Oxford University Press; 128–53.

Becht, M., and C. Mayer. 2001. "Introduction," in F. Barca and M. Becht, eds., *The Control of Corporate Europe*. Oxford: Oxford University Press; 1–45.

Berkovitch, E., and M. P. Narayanan. 1993. "Motives for Takeovers: An Empirical Investigation," 28 *Journal of Financial and Quantitative Analysis* 347–62.

Boehmer, E. 1999. "Corporate Governance in Germany: Institutional Background and Empirical Results," working paper, Humboldt University, Berlin.

Bolton, P., and E.-L. von Thadden. 1998. "Liquidity and Control: A Dynamic Theory of Corporate Ownership Structure," 154 *Journal of Institutional and Theoretical Economics* 177–211.

Bratton, W. W., and J. A. McCahery. 1995. "Regulatory Competition, Regulatory Capture, and Corporate Self-Regulation," 73 *North Carolina Law Review* 1861–948.

——. 1999. "Comparative Corporate Governance and the Value of the Firm: The Case Against Global Cross-Reference," 38 *Columbia Journal of Transnational Law* 213–237.

Brennan, M., and J. Franks. 1997. "Underpricing, Ownership and Control in Initial Public Offerings of Equity Securities in the UK," 45 *Journal of Financial Economics* 391–413.

Burkart, M., D. Gromb, and F. Panunzi. 1997. "Large Shareholders, Monitoring and the Value of the Firm," 112 *Quarterly Journal of Economics* 693–728.

Chirinko, R., and J. Elston. 1996. "Finance, Control and Profitability: The Role of West German Banks," working paper, WZB Berlin.

Chung, K., and S. Pruitt. 1996. "Executive Ownership, Corporate Value and Executive Compensation: A Unifying Framework," 20 *Journal of Banking and Finance* 1135–59.

Correia da Silva, L., M. Goergen, and L. Renneboog. 2002. *Corporate Governance and Dividend Policy*. Oxford: Oxford University Press.

Crespi, R. 1998. "Determinantes de la Estructura de Propiedad: Una Aproximacion al Caso Espanol con Datos de Panel," 206 *Moneda y Credito* 115–43.

DeAngelo, H., and L. DeAngelo. 1985. "Managerial Ownership of Voting Rights—A Study of Public Corporations with Dual Classes of Common Stock," 14 *Journal of Financial Economics* 33–69.

Demsetz, H., and K. Lehn. 1985. "The Structure of Corporate Ownership: Causes and Consequences," 93 *Journal of Political Economy* 1155–77.

Dennis, D., and A. Sarin. 1999. "Ownership and Board Structures in Publicly Traded Corporations," 52 *Journal of Financial Economics* 176–223.

Dyck, A., and L. Zingales. 2001. "Private Benefits of Control: An International Comparison," working paper, University of Chicago.

Franks, J., and C. Mayer. 1996. "Hostile Takeovers in the UK and the Correction of Managerial Failure," 40 *Journal of Financial Economics* 163–81.

——. 1998. "Bank Control, Takeovers and Corporate Governance in Germany," 22 *Journal of Banking and Finance* 1385–403.

——. 2001. "Ownership and Control of German Corporations," 14 *Review of Financial Studies* 943–77.

——, and L. Renneboog. 2001. "Who Disciplines Management of Poorly Performing Companies?," 10 *Journal of Financial Intermediation* 209–48.

Goergen, M. 1998. *Corporate Governance and Financial Performance: A Study of German and UK Initial Public Offerings*. Cheltenham: Edward Elgar.

——. 1999. "Insider Retention and Long-Run Performance in German and UK IPOs," working paper, UMIST.

——, and L. Renneboog. 2001. "Strong Managers and Passive Institutional Investors in the UK," in F. Barca and M. Becht, eds., *The Control of Corporate Europe*. Oxford: Oxford University Press; 258–84.

Goergen, M. and L. Renneboog. 2003. "Shareholder Wealth Effects of Large European Takeover Bids," in C. Cooper and A. Gregory, eds., *Advances in Mergers and Acquisitions*, vol. 2. Amsterdam: JAI Press.

Goshen, Z. 1998. "Liability Rule or Property Rule: Voting in Conflict of Interests in Corporate Law and Minority's Protection," mimeo. Jerusalem: Hebrew University of Jerusalem.

Hay, D., and D. Morris. 1984. *Unquoted Companies: Their Contribution to the United Kingdom Economy.* London: Macmillan.

Heiss, F., and J. Koke. 2001. "Dynamics of Ownership and Firm Survival: Evidence from Corporate Germany," Discussion Paper, 01-63, Center for European Economic Research (ZEW).

Jenkinson, T., and A. Ljungqvist. 2001. "The Role of Hostile Stakes in German Corporate Governance," 7 *Journal of Corporate Finance* 397–446.

Johnson, S., R. La Porta, F. Lopez-de-Silanes, and A. Shleifer. 2000. "Tunnelling," working paper 7523, NBER.

La Porta, R., F. Lopez-de-Silanes., A. Shleifer, and R. Vishny. 1997. "Legal Determinants of External Finance," 52 *Journal of Finance* 1131–50.

——. 1998. "Law and Finance," 106 *Journal of Political Economy* 1113–55.

——. 1999. "Ownership Around the World," 54 *Journal of Finance* 471–517.

——. 2000. "Investor Protection and Corporate Governance," 58 *Journal of Financial Economics* 3–27.

Leech, D., and J. Leahy. 1991. "Ownership Structure, Control Type Classifications and the Performance of Large British Companies," 101 *Economic Journal* 1418–37.

Mello, A., and J. Parsons. 1998. "Going Public and the Ownership Structure of the Firm," 49 *Journal of Financial Economics* 79–109.

Morck, R. K., A. Shleifer, and R. Vishny. 1988. "Management Ownership and Market Valuation. An Empirical Analysis," 20 *Journal of Financial Economics* 293–315.

Morck R. K., D. A. Strangeland, and B. Yeung. 2000. "Inherited Wealth, Corporate Control and Economic Growth: The Canadian Disease," in R. Morck, ed., *Concentrated Corporate Ownership.* Chicago: University of Chicago Press.

Renneboog, L. 2000. "Ownership, Managerial Control and the Disciplining of Poorly Performing Companies Listed on the Brussels Stock Exchange," 24 *Journal of Banking and Finance* 1959–95.

Shleifer, A., and R. W. Vishny. 1986. "Large Shareholders and Corporate Control," 95 *Journal of Political Economy* 461–88.

——. 1997. "A Survey of Corporate Governance," 52 *Journal of Finance* 737–83.

Stapledon, G. 1996. *Institutional Shareholders and Corporate Governance.* Oxford: Clarendon Press.

Wenger, E., R. Hecker, and J. Knoesel. 1996. "Abfindungsregeln and Minderheitenschutz bei Börsennotierten Kapitalgesellschaften," working paper, University of Würzburg.

Zingales, L. 1995. "Insider Ownership and the Decision to Go Public," 62 *Review of Economic Studies* 425–48.

Chapter 9

Mara Faccio[1] and M. Ameziane Lasfer[*]

DO OCCUPATIONAL PENSION FUNDS MONITOR COMPANIES IN WHICH THEY HOLD LARGE STAKES?

Source: *Journal of Corporate Finance,* 6(1) (2000): 71–110.

ABSTRACT

In this paper we analyze the monitoring role of occupational pension funds in the UK. We argue that because of their objectives, structure and overall share holding, occupational pension funds are likely to have more incentives to monitor companies in which they hold large stakes than other financial institutions. By comparing companies in which these funds hold large stakes with a control group of companies listed on the London Stock Exchange, we show that occupational pension funds hold large stakes over a long-time period mainly in small companies. However, the value added by these funds is negligible and their holdings do not lead companies to comply with the Code of Best Practice or outperform their industry counterparts. Overall, our results suggest that occupational pension funds are not effective monitors.

1. INTRODUCTION

IT IS NOW WIDELY RECOGNIZED THAT COMPANIES have to set a number of mechanisms to control the agency problems, which arise whenever managers have incentives to pursue their own interests at the expense of those of shareholders. In an extensive survey of corporate governance, Shleifer and Vishny (1997) show that legal protection alone is not sufficient to ensure investor protection and that other mechanisms, such as ownership concentration, could be the solution to these, so called, agency problems. However, the empirical evidence provided to date on the role and effectiveness of such alternative mechanisms is mixed. For example, Demsetz and Lehn (1985) find no cross-sectional relationship between the concentration of shareholdings and the accounting rates of return. Similarly,

Agrawal and Knoeber (1996) show that the relationship between large institutional shareholding or blockholding and corporate performance as measured by Tobins Q is weak.[2] In contrast, other studies show that large shareholders play a significant role in top management turnover (e.g., Franks and Mayer, 1994; Kaplan and Minton, 1994; Kang and Shivdasani, 1995), in take-overs (Shleifer and Vishny, 1986; Agrawal and Mandelker, 1990; Sudarsanam, 1996), in the certification of initial public offerings (Lin, 1996) and that block purchases by large shareholders are typically followed by an increase in value, in top management turnover, in financial performance and in asset sales (e.g., Mikkelson and Ruback, 1985; Shome and Singh, 1995; Bethel et al., 1998). Other studies that specifically analyze shareholder activism also yield mixed results.[3]

For example, while Strickland et al. (1996) show that monitoring by shareholders enhances firm value, Karpoff et al. (1996) do not find evidence that shareholder proposals increase firm value or influence firm policies.

The purpose of this paper is to extend previous research that documents the impact of large holdings on corporate performance by analyzing the monitoring role of occupational pension funds in the UK. We identify separately these funds from other financial intermediaries because of the large dimension of their overall stakes in the UK market, the particular structure of their portfolios and their investment objectives. As defined by Brickley et al. (1988; 1994), occupational pension funds are typical pressure-resistant institutions as opposed to other institutions, such as banks, investment and unit trusts and insurance companies, which are pressure-sensitive. Unlike previous studies (e.g., Strickland et al., 1996; Bethel et al., 1998) we do not analyze block purchases because of event date uncertainty and we do not concentrate on formal targeting by pension funds because we could not find any event where occupational pension funds in the UK target companies, i.e., make particular proposals at the company's annual meetings or negotiate privately some corporate governance issues (as in Carleton et al., 1998). Instead, we compare firms in which occupational pension funds hold large stakes against a control group of companies listed on the London Stock Exchange and test the hypotheses that monitoring increases with ownership concentration and, as a result, these funds reduce agency conflicts and lead companies to better performance.

Further research in this area is warranted for a number of reasons. First, the issue of involvement of pension funds in the running of companies is controversial. The popular belief is that pension funds are short-termists and impose their views on companies in which they invest. In particular, given their tax-exempt status, UK pension funds are criticized for making companies pay high cash dividends that could be used to finance growth opportunities (e.g., Hutton, 1995).[4] In contrast, other studies show that pension funds do not get involved in corporate monitoring because they find it easier and cheaper to sell their holdings, they do not want to sit on the board for fear of getting price sensitive information or because of the agency problems within the funds themselves.[5] At the same time, policy makers in the UK tend to rely on these institutions to promote corporate governance (e.g., Cadbury, 1992; Greenbury, 1995).[6] Second, previous studies were mainly undertaken under the US framework. Franks and Mayer (1997) show that, despite the fact that the US and the UK governance systems are both market-based, the two countries differ in two major respects: the US has more quoted companies than the UK and, while the largest category of shareholders in the UK is pension funds, most of the equity in the US is held by individuals (if each different type of institutional shareholder is treated as a different category). In addition, unlike US pension funds where investments and activism programs are developed and implemented by fund staff then overseen and approved by trustees (Del Guercio and Hawkins, 1999), the UK pension funds, despite the size of their holdings, are not known for their monitoring and hardly vote at the annual general meetings (NAPF, 1996b; Financial Times, 1999). Thus, testing of the empirical hypotheses in a pension fund dominated market such as the UK where corporate governance issues are debated and companies suffer from the same free cash flow problems as their US counterparts, will strengthen the evidence provided to-date.[7] Third, since our analysis is centered on pension funds that are tax exempt and hold large stakes, the evidence we provide should be of relevance to tax and market regulators and to policy makers involved in the growth of the UK economy.

We construct from the financial statements of all UK quoted non-financial companies a test sample of companies in which pension funds hold more than 3% of the issued share capital and a control sample by matching our test firms by industry and size.[8] We find that pension funds hold large stakes in 289 out of 1640 (18%) companies. These holdings are mainly in small companies and they did not change significantly over the 1992–1996 sample period. We show that our test companies are not more likely to restrain management compensation and/or adopt the Code of Best Practice, i.e., split the roles of chairman and CEO, have more non-executive directors and/or narrow the size of their board than our control firms. These results are not consistent with the recommendations of Cadbury (1992) and Greenbury (1995). In addition, we find that our test companies are not more profitable and do not pay higher dividends than the control firms despite the tax credit pension funds could claim during the sample period. We report weak and even negative relationship between occupational pension funds blockholdings and firm value, and, over a longer time period, our test firms do not overperform their peers. Our overall results are consistent with previous US evidence (e.g., Romano, 1994 and Wahal, 1996) and cast doubt on the effectiveness of UK occupational pension funds' monitoring role. At the same time, our results provide support to the proposition of Coffee (1991) and imply that pension funds do not follow an 'exit' policy which is increasingly more expensive because they must accept substantial discounts in order to liquidate their holdings. Thus, once "locked in", occupational pension funds avoid costly monitoring and refrain from selling their large stake for fear of losing from large discounts and/or conveying information to the market.

The rest of the paper is structured as follows. Section 2 presents the theoretical background. Section 3 describes the data. Section 4 presents the results. Conclusions are in Section 5.

2. THEORETICAL FRAMEWORK

In recent years, more than a third of all listed equities in the UK are held by pension funds. A large proportion of these holdings is concentrated in the portfolios of large funds. In this section we review the literature on the role of large shareholders, discuss the literature on pension funds activism, and analyze the structure of the UK occupational pension funds, the importance of equities in their portfolios, the relatively high concentration of their industry and the management approaches and objectives.

2.1. Review of the literature

Corporate governance deals with how companies are managed in the long-term interest of their shareholders. The literature has identified two main corporate governance systems that predominate in the developed economies: the *market-based* systems of the UK and the US characterized by liquid markets and unconcentrated company ownership, and the relationship-based systems of Japan and Germany where ownership is concentrated and markets are relatively illiquid.[9] The issue, although not trivial, has been considered in the literature only recently when agency theorists argue that public corporations suffer from excessive costs as managers pursue their own interests rather than the interests of shareholders (e.g., Jensen, 1986). As a result, there is a need for setting up mechanisms to make managers maximize shareholder wealth. These mechanisms include shareholding of managers, intermediaries and large blockholders (McConnell and Servaes, 1990; Morck et al., 1988), outside directors (Cotter et al., 1997), debt policy (Lasfer, 1995; McConnell and Servaes, 1995; Lang et al., 1996), the market for corporate control and incentive contracts (Hart and Holmstrom, 1987; Hart, 1995), large intermediaries (Diamond, 1984; Admati et al., 1994), and long-term relationships (Ayres and Cramton, 1993).

In theory, Diamond (1984) suggests that a large intermediary can represent a better solution to agency conflicts because of economies of scale and diversification. Admati et al. (1994) argue that when monitoring is costly, the intermediary will monitor only if this will result in a modification in firm's payoff structure and lead to net gains. When the intermediary does not hold all the firm's equity and the transaction costs are not excessive, the level of commitment will be sub-optimal even when optimal risk-sharing is attained. Maug (1998) extends this analysis and argues that liquid markets reduce large shareholders incentive to monitor because they can sell their holdings easily, but such markets make corporate governance more effective as it is cheaper and easier to acquire and hold large stakes. Kahn and Winton (1998) distinguish between liquidity, speculation and intervention and argue that intervention is a function of the size of the institution's stake, firm specific factors and institution's trading profit. Shleifer and Vishny (1997) and Agrawal and Knoeber (1996) suggest that large investors, because of the relevance of the resources invested, have all the interest and the power to monitor and promote better governance of companies.

Previous empirical studies show that institutions behave differently from individuals in sponsoring initiatives (Jarrell and Poulsen, 1987; Karpoff et al., 1996) and that the institutional behavior is not homogeneous as it depends on the sensitivity to managerial pressure (Brickley et al., 1988; Gordon and Pound, 1993). However, they disagree on the effectiveness of shareholder activism.[10] In particular, Wahal (1996) and Karpoff et al. (1996) find little evidence that operating performance of companies that are the target of pension funds proposals improves. These results are consistent, among other things, with the arguments of Murphy and Van Nuys (1994) and Romano (1994) that pension funds are not effective monitors because of the agency problems within the funds themselves. In contrast, Nesbitt (1994) and Smith (1996) find that companies targeted by large pension funds, such as CalPERS, increase significantly their performance. More recently, Del Guercio and Hawkins (1999) show that the monitoring effectiveness depends on the investment strategies

of pension funds. They find that, unlike proposals sponsored by externally-managed funds, those made by internally managed funds are not associated with general increases in governance-related events at target firms. Other studies that looked at the characteristics of companies in which institutions hold large stakes find that the relationship between such holdings and firm value or accounting rates of return is weak (e.g., Demsetz and Lehn, 1985; Agrawal and Knoeber, 1996).

In sum, the primarily US-based studies provide mixed results on the monitoring role of pension funds. The testing of these hypotheses under a different institutional framework is, thus, warranted.

2.2. Institutional settings

In this section we describe the pension funds industry and the corporate governance system in the UK and set up the hypotheses.

2.2.1. The UK pension fund system

The UK pension fund system includes, in addition to the public pension scheme, occupational pension schemes, which are organized and sponsored by employers, and individual pension schemes offered by financial institutions. The occupational pension schemes are usually defined-benefits (DB) where the amount of benefits relates to the final salary of the member while individual pension schemes are defined-contribution (DC) where pension benefits depend on the contributions paid during the working life of the members and the returns realized on the investment (Blake, 1995). This difference has significant implications on these two schemes' investment policies. With defined contribution plans, individuals bear the investment risk and require a more cautious investment strategy. As a result, the proportion of shares relative to total assets of occupational pension schemes ranges between 70% and 80% while defined contribution pension plans usually hold no more than 25–30% of shares (NAPF, 1996b). In 1997 the overall value of individual pension schemes assets was £190 billion (ABI, 1998) while occupational pension funds assets (including insured schemes) reached £635 billion.[11]

The proportion of UK pension funds assets invested in equities is the highest amongst OECD countries (Davis, 1995). For example, in 1993, 78% of assets were invested in equities, 12% in fixed income securities and the remaining in cash and property (Business Monitor, 1997). This trend is likely to reflect the overall investments of all pension funds as Blake (1995) shows that asset structure is not significantly associated with the size of pension funds assets. The preference of equities over fixed income securities can be related to the tax-exempt status of pension funds who, like charities, are not subject to capital gains tax and claim back the tax credit, referred to as the advanced corporation tax, when they receive dividends. Lasfer (1996) shows that this tax credit discriminates in favor of dividends relative to capital gains.

In contrast, US pension funds invest a lower proportion of their assets in equities. For example, in 1990, out of the total assets of $2,491 billion, 38.6% are invested in equities (Charkham, 1995). Davis (1995) shows that the proportion of assets invested in equities has not changed over the 1970–1990 period. However, these investments are not evenly distributed but concentrated mainly in large firms (Charkham, 1995; Stapledon, 1996; Brancato, 1997).

In managing these assets, the UK pension funds are subject to trust law and implicitly follow the prudent-man concept. There is no explicit prudent-man rule and the pension trust law is very flexible. However, the duty of prudence to trustees can be interpreted as requiring the pension funds money to be invested for the sole benefit of the beneficiaries. The recent legislation for pension fund management (e.g., the 1995 Pension Fund Act) is similar to the American Employee Retirement Scheme Act with a basic view towards prudence. The legal barriers against

institutional activism are weaker in the UK because active shareholders that hold a "block of shares" are not subject to any filing requirements, such as the 13D Form with the SEC in the US, and they cannot be sued for breaching any duty of disclosure of their plans or proposals. This rule applies in the US to shareholders who act together (e.g., in the case of co-ordinated activism), and to investors who, *individually* or *jointly* hold 5% or more of a firm's equity (Black, 1998). Moreover, unlike in the US, UK pension funds have no legal duty to vote.

The pension fund industry is highly concentrated. For example, in 1994, the largest five in-house managed occupational pension funds managed assets worth £65.8 billion, 14.8% of all occupational pension funds assets (NAPF, 1996a) and British Telecommunications, accounted for £17.2 billion. The largest 68 schemes, whose assets value exceeds £1 billion in 1995, accounted for 57.3% of all occupational pension funds assets (Pension Funds and their Advisers, 1996). The industry of fund managers is also highly concentrated. At the end of 1996, the top 20 segregated fund managers managed assets worth £285.7 billion on behalf of occupational pension funds and, as a whole, managed assets of some £1029.2 billion (Financial Times, 1997a).

Over the last three decades, the aggregate share ownership in the UK has changed substantially. While in 1963 individuals were the main shareholders with 58.7% of all UK listed equities and pension funds held only 7%, by 1993 pension funds stakes increased to 34.7% (London Stock Exchange, 1995). In contrast, in the US, individuals held 50% in 1990 followed by pension funds with 20.1%, increasing to 25.4% in 1995 (Prowse, 1994; Brancato, 1997).

We use our sample firms (detailed below) to analyze further the ownership structure of UK companies. The results, reported in Figure 9.1, show that managers and block shareholders (including occupational pension funds) own 53% of equity, implying a rather concentrated ownership structure. However, within these blocks, no

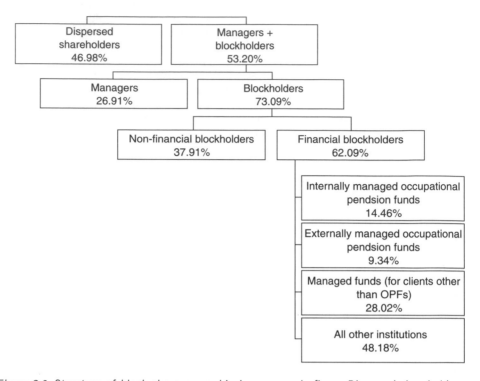

Figure 9.1 Structure of block share ownership in our sample firms. *Dispersed shareholders* are defined as those owners who individually own less than 3% of ordinary shares, excluding managers. *Blockholders* are owners who individually own at least 3% of ordinary shares (excluding managers). *Non-institutional blockholdings* are block shareholdings attributable to individuals and families, non-financial companies, public bodies, foreign investors and nominees. *Institutional blockholdings* refer to block shareholdings held by financial institutions. *Internally managed occupational pension funds* are those pension funds whose assets are, wholly or in part, managed directly by the fund's trustees. *Externally managed pension funds* holdings refer to block shareholdings attributable to the largest 20 segregated pension fund managers, times the incidence of pension fund assets to the total asset managed by the segregated fund. *Managed funds (for clients other than OPFs)* refer to the residual proportion of block shareholdings managed by the top 20 segregated pension fund managers, once accounted for the assets managed on behalf of occupational pension funds (previous variable). Finally, *all other institutional holdings* are computed as residual item, and refer to block shareholdings held by merchant banks, unit and investment trusts, insurance companies, venture capital firms, and all other financial institutions. All percentages reported are computed assuming the relative upper line to be equal to 100%.

single class of shareholders clearly dominates the others. Financial blockholders account for 62% of block shareholdings by holding 24% of our firms' equity, while the remaining 38% are attributable to individuals and families, non-financial companies, public authorities, foreign investors and nominees. Internally managed occupational pension funds account for 14% of all financial blockholdings as they hold an average of 3% of equity. Externally managed occupational pension funds account for 9% by holding 2% of equity. The assets managed by external pension fund managers on behalf of clients other than pension funds represent 28% of these stakes, i.e., 7% of equity. Finally, all other financial institutions (including merchant banks, insurance companies, unit and investment trusts) wholly account for 48% of institutional holdings as they hold about 12% of equity.

2.2.2. The UK corporate governance system

The importance of corporate governance in the UK has been emphasized by recent concerns about the way in which remuneration packages for senior executives have been determined, the spectacular collapse of a number of large companies and by the fraudulent use of the pension fund of Mirror Group Newspapers to finance an illegal scheme for supporting the share price of Maxwell Communications Corporation. These cases have highlighted instances where directors do not act in the best interest of shareholders.

In the train of these and other scandals, the Committee on the Financial Aspects of Corporate Governance (referred to as the Cadbury Committee after its chairman) was set up to look at the changes needed in corporate governance in the UK and published a report in December 1992 (Cadbury, 1992). The report is similar to the Statement on Corporate Governance released in September 1997 in the US by the Business Roundtable, an association of CEOs of large companies. At the heart of the report is the Code of Best Practice which details the role and composition of the board of directors, the appointment of non-executive directors, the disclosure of the remuneration of executive directors and the renewal of their contracts, and the way companies should report and audit their accounts. The main recommendation is that the offices of the chairman and the chief executive officer should be separated to prevent excessive concentration of power in boardrooms and that companies should appoint independent non-executive directors with high caliber so that their views will carry weight in board discussions.[12] The code defines the various roles non-executive directors should play. For example, they are to be in a majority on the nominating committee which is responsible for making recommendations for board membership, they should be the sole or majority members of the remuneration committee which makes recommendations to the board on the pay of executive directors, and of the audit committee whose function is to advise on the appointment of auditors, to insure the integrity of the company's financial statements and to discuss with the auditors any problems arising during the course of the audit.[13]

The report has also highlighted the responsibilities of institutional investors such as pension funds and suggests that such institutions should be encouraged to make greater use of their voting rights and to seek contacts with companies at a senior executive level. In particular, they should monitor boards where there is a concentration of power in the hands of the chief executive, seek to promote the influence of non-executive directors and they are expected to bring about changes in underperforming companies rather than dispose of their shares. Although the report recognizes that closer relations with managers can result in these investors gaining price sensitive information which makes them insiders, it does not go so far as to recommend the formation of shareholders' committees and the participation of shareholders in the appointment of directors and auditors.

This emphasis on institutions is driven by the size of their holdings but also by the fact that these institutions, such as pension funds, do not target companies and they rarely caste their vote at the annual general meetings, making them the object of public criticism (e.g., Mallin, 1997). This passive stance has not changed even after the advent of the Cadbury Report. More recently, commenting on the first major corporate governance action by pension funds, namely the ousting of the head of Mirror Group, a media company which has underperformed the market by 34% over the last 5 years, the Financial Times (1999) wrote:

Unlike in the US, investor mutinies in Britain are still a relatively rare event. Complacency, reflected in the dismal attendance at annual general meetings, is the norm. This state of affairs has its critics. The Treasury, for example, has let it be known that it regards funds managers as a breed of idle "fat cats" who are partly to blame for the nations economic ills.

The main reservation of the code centers on the issue of compliance and enforcement. The corporate governance system in the UK has traditionally stressed the importance of internal controls and the importance of financial reporting and accountability as opposed to a large amount of external legislation. In this spirit, the Code of Best Practice is voluntary and lacks effective sanctions. Nevertheless, as a continuing obligation of listing, the London Stock Exchange requires all companies registered in the UK to state, after June 1993, whether they are complying with the code and to give reasons for any areas of non-compliance.

2.2.3. Pension fund management style and corporate monitoring

Del Guercio and Hawkins (1999) show that the level of monitoring by pension funds depends significantly on the way their assets are managed. In the UK pension funds assets can be managed in three different ways: self-managed, externally managed and insured. Within self-managed schemes, the trustees of the scheme define asset allocation, portfolio selection policies and directly invest pension fund assets. Within externally managed schemes, the investment power is wholly or in part delegated to one or few external managers. In the case of insured schemes, the funds are invested in insurance policies or managed through fund contracts taken out with an insurance company.

We expect internally managed occupational pension funds to have a stronger incentive to monitor than externally managed pension funds for a number of reasons. First, internally managed pension funds are larger than externally-managed and insured schemes (e.g., Minns, 1980;

Blake, 1995; NAPF, 1996a). In addition, Stapledon (1996) reports that many large companies managed internally their pension schemes in the early 1990s. For example, in 1993, 14% of occupational pension schemes were managed wholly internally but these account for some 38% of the total assets invested.[14] Thus, following the arguments of Admati et al. (1994) and Diamond (1984), we would expect internally managed occupational pension funds to be more active in corporate monitoring because of their size and the magnitude of their holdings. Their size and expertise minimize the monitoring costs. They are likely to understand when activism is necessary and they are large enough to make monitoring effective. Their large holdings are expected to alleviate the free-rider problem that makes atomistic shareholders' action non-rational and inefficient.

Second, internally managed occupational pension funds are expected to monitor companies in which they hold large stakes because they control directly or indirectly the investment and the voting decisions. Their objective is likely to maximize the value of funds in order to minimize the company's contributions and, possibly, use any pension fund surplus to inflate company's profits (Short and Keasey, 1997). In contrast, funds that delegate their investment functions to external managers effectively disconnect their activism efforts from their investment actions (Del Guercio and Hawkins, 1999). As a result, given that they will not be able to trade profitably on any private information that results from their activism, they are not likely to monitor or to publicize their activism efforts. The level of monitoring role of externally managed pension funds will depend on the content of the contract with the trustees and the level of competition among fund managers. Given that we do not have data on these contracts and on the investments made on behalf of pension funds, we cannot expect all externally managed funds to monitor.

Internally managed occupational pension funds may not monitor individual companies if they find it easier to sell, if they do not want to gain access to price sensitive information or if they themselves are subject to agency problems. In addition, given that these funds are defined benefits schemes, they are likely to be indexed and passive to minimize their management risk, transaction costs and to fit the needs of long-term pension investors (Tomlinson, 1998). Del Guercio and Hawkins (1999) argue that such passive management style will lead pension funds to monitor by promoting spill-over effects that boost the performance of the stock market overall rather than specific stocks. In our analysis we focus on internally-managed pension funds to test whether size and passive management styles define the level of monitoring activity but we control also for the monitoring roles of external pension funds and other blockholders.

The monitoring activity can take the form of selecting the board structure and/or improving performance. The monitoring of the board relates to the size of the board and its composition so that it becomes more accountable to the shareholders (Cadbury, 1992).[15] Jensen (1993) argues that as the size of the board increases, its ability to control management decreases and the communication and co-ordination problems increase. Consistent with this proposition, Yermack (1996) and Eisenberg et al. (1998) find a negative correlation between board size and firm performance. Thus, if occupational pension funds are effective monitors, they are expected to mitigate this agency conflict by restricting the size of the board. At the same time, they will lead companies to adopt the Code of Best Practice defined by Cadbury (1992), i.e., to split the roles of chairman and chief executive officer, to have a high proportion of non-executive directors and to restrain executive pay.[16]

The monitoring of firm performance implies that companies in which occupational pension funds hold large stakes have a higher value than widely held companies and/or companies held by other blockholders. This level of monitoring is a function of the size of the pension funds and the relative importance of the amount of assets invested in these companies. We expect large pension funds and those with significant commitments to have a higher incentive to monitor companies in which they hold large stakes. In the long run, companies in which occupational pension fund carry on holding large stakes are expected to outperform their industry counterparts.

3. SAMPLE CONSTRUCTION AND DEFINITION OF PROXY VARIABLES

We search all the 1640 non-financial companies quoted in the London Stock Exchange In 1995–1996 for those where occupational pension funds hold large stakes. We exclude financial companies because of the specificity of some of their ratios such as leverage, which cannot be related to the level of their risk and/or resolution of their agency conflicts. To avoid survivorship bias, our sample includes all companies for which the relevant data is available even if they are currently extinct.[17]

We started by gathering information on shareholding by category from the annual reports but we find that only a handful of companies disclose this information in their Analysis of Ordinary Shareholdings section of their accounts. This data would have been ideal but it would have given us only the aggregate holding of pension funds without distinguishing between funds that are internally managed from those that are externally managed. Instead, we rely on any disclosed holding above 3% threshold in the accounts and reported in Extel Financial[18] and define these as occupational pension funds holdings or blockholders. All the holdings of directors are disclosed even if they are zero (Company Act 1985). Although this cut off point of 3% is constraining, it is the only data available. We, nevertheless, posit that the holding of 3% or above is significant to warrant monitoring and to allow us to test directly the Diamond (1984) and Admati et al. (1994) propositions. We searched for the keywords *pension, pension funds, retirement, superannuation and superannuation schemes* and for known pension funds, such as Hermes, to define the holdings of occupational pension funds. We identified 289 individual companies (18% of our total sample) with at least one occupational pension fund holding above 3%, and 356 large stakes held by 99 individual occupational pension funds. We split the other major disclosed holdings (other than managerial holdings) into externally managed pension funds, institutional and non-institutional blockholding depending on the identity of the shareholders. We compare the performance of our test firms against all other remaining companies and against a control group of companies with similar size and industry characteristics. We collect all the relevant accounting and financial data from Extel Financial and from each company's accounts.

Table 9.1 reports the proxy variables used to test our hypotheses. We use five definitions of pension fund holdings: (i) the first largest stake held by pension funds, LPF; (ii) the sum of all pension fund holdings, TPF, to analyze pension funds' individual and collective monitoring roles; (iii) the pension fund incidence, IPF, the ratio of pension fund investment in our test sample over their total assets to assess the magnitude of such investment in their portfolio;[19] (iv) the number of occupational pension funds in our test firms, NPF, and (v) the logged value of the largest pension fund's asset, LNPFA. Directors' ownership, Dir, is used to control for the managerial entrenchment hypothesis.[20] Any other large stake, Block, is used to control for the monitoring role of blockholders. This variable is split into institutional block shareholdings, IBlock, which includes all financial institutions' stakes (excluding internally- and externally-managed occupational pension funds' stakes), externally-managed pension funds, EPFM, i.e., the stakes held by the largest 20 external pension fund managers (either on behalf of occupational pension funds and other clients), and NIBlock, the holdings of individuals and families, non-financial companies, public bodies, foreign investors and nominees.[21]

As in Agrawal and Knoeber (1996), we compute Tobin's Q as the ratio of market value of equity *plus* book value of debt over total assets to measure firm value. The results are simulated using other measures of firm value such as market-to-book, *M/B*, and market-to-sales, *M/S*, ratios (Lins and Servaes, 1999). These variables are, however, ambiguous measures of value-added by pension funds investments, since they can also capture the value of future investment opportunities. As in Yermack (1996), we control for growth opportunities by using *P/E* ratio. In addition, we use various accounting rates of returns and a one year share price return, $R_{i, t - 12 \text{ to } t}$, to measure performance and market value of equity, ME, or total assets, TA, to control for size. We follow previous literature (e.g., Lang et al., 1996) and use both the market value of leverage, Mlev, defined as long-term debt over market value of equity *plus* long-term debt, and the book value of leverage, Blev, defined as long-term debt over shareholders funds *plus* long-term debt, to test for the monitoring role of debtholders. We use Split (a dummy variable equal to 1 if the role of chairman and CEO are differentiated), Nechair (a dummy equal to 1 if the position of chairman is covered by a non-executive director), number of directors, #DIR, the proportion of non-executive directors in the board, %NED, and the relative remuneration of directors, Dir rem./Sal, to assess the pension fund role in monitoring board composition and compensation policy. Finally, payout ratio is used to test the hypothesis that pension funds prefer to invest in companies that pay high dividends.

4. EMPIRICAL RESULTS

4.1. Characteristics of occupation pension funds holdings

Table 9.2, Panel A, reports the distribution of companies with pension funds holdings. Out of 289 test companies, 175 (61%) reported an overall holding of between 3% and 6%, and 70 (24%) had between 6 and 10%.

Table 9.1 Description of proxy variables. Expected signs (E_{sign}) are for the Logit regressions

Variables	Definition	Proxying for (Hypotheses)	E_{sign}
LPF	Proportion of outstanding equity owned by largest occupational pension funds	Pension fund commitment to monitoring	+
TPF	The proportion of outstanding equity owned by all occupational pension funds	Pension fund commitment to monitoring	+
IPF	Occupational pension funds' holdings in test companies relative to their assets	Pension fund commitment to monitoring	+
NPF	Number of occupational pension funds holding large stakes in our test companies	Pension fund commitment to monitoring	+
LNPFA	Log of the asset value of the pension fund with the largest stake	Pension fund commitment to monitoring	+
Dir	Proportion of outstanding equity owned by directors	Management entrenchment	−
Block	Proportion of outstanding equity owned by other large shareholders	Blockholders' incentive to monitor	+
EPFM	Proportion of outstanding equity owned by the top 20 external fund managers	External managers' incentive to monitor	+
IBlock	Proportion of outstanding equity owned by financial institutions, other than internally and externally managed pension funds	Incentive to monitor by other financial companies	+
NIBlock	Proportion of outstanding equity owned by non-financial shareholders	Blockholders' incentive to monitor	+
Q	Market value of equity *plus* book value of debt over total assets	Firm value	+
M/B	Market value of equity over shareholders' funds	Firm value	+
M/S	Market value of equity *plus* book value of debt over sales	Firm value	+
P/E	Year-end share price over earnings per share	Growth opportunities	+
ROA	Profit before interest and tax over total assets	Firm performance	+
ROE	Earnings over shareholders' funds	Firm performance	+
ROS	Profit before interest and tax over sales	Firm performance	+
$R_{i,t-12 \text{ to } t}$	1-year share price return, adjusted for stock issues and dividends	Firm performance	+
ME	Market value of equity at balance sheet date	Firm size	+
TA	Total assets	Firm size	−
Mlev	Long-term debt over long-term debt *plus* market value of equity	Monitoring role of debtholders	−
Blev	Long-term debt over long-term debt *plus* shareholders' funds	Monitoring role of debtholders	−
Dir rem./Sal	Directors' monetary pay (excl. options) over sales	Monitoring directors' pay	−
Nechair	Dummy = 1 if the Chairman is attributed to a non-executive director	Monitoring board composition	+
Split	Dummy = 1 if the role of Chairman is split from that of CEO	Monitoring board composition	+
#DIR	Number of directors (both executives and non-executives)	Monitoring board size	+
%NED	Proportion of non-executive directors	Monitoring board composition	+
Payout	Ordinary dividends over earnings	Monitoring of dividends	+

Table 9.2 Distribution of pension funds holdings in test companies

The sample includes 289 test companies where occupational pension funds hold 3% or more of ordinary shares and 356 individual pension fund block shareholdings. LPF is the proportion of outstanding equity owned by largest occupational pension funds; TPF is the proportion of outstanding equity owned by all identified pension funds; IPF is the ratio of occupational pension funds holdings over their total assets; NPF is the number of occupational pension funds; EPFM is the proportion of shares owned by the largest 20 external pension fund managers, either on behalf of occupational pension funds or other clients; N_C is number of companies; and N_{Stakes} is for number of stakes; $N_{Pension\ funds}$ is the total number of pension funds.

(Panel A) Distribution of companies by total pension funds holdings (N_C 5 289)

% holdings (TPF)	3–6%	6–10%	10–20%	+20%
Number of companies	175	70	36	8
% of total	60.6	24.2	12.5	2.8

(Panel B) Distribution of companies by *number of pension funds' stakes* ($N_C = 289; N_{Stakes} = 356$)

Number of pension funds' stakes (NPF)	1	2	3	4	5
Number of companies	238	40	8	1	2
% of total	82.3	13.8	2.8	0.3	1.0

(Panel C) Distribution of pension funds by number of stakes held ($N_{Stakes} = 356; N_{Pension\ funds} = 99$)

Number of stakes held	1	2–4	5–9	10–19	20–39	40+
Number of pension funds	68	18	4	4	3	2
% of total	68.7	18.2	4.0	4.0	3.0	2.0

(Panel D) Descriptive statistics of pension funds and block holdings %

	Mean	Median	Minimum	Maximum
LPF	6.01	4.70	3.00	56.90
TPF	6.96	5.06	3.00	56.90
NPF	1.23	1.00	1.00	5.00
IPF	0.15	0.03	0.01	14.75
EPFM	8.99	4.79	0.00	61.88

Thus, more than 84% of our test companies have pension funds holdings between 3 and 10%. In 36 companies (12%) pension funds hold between 10% and 20% and in 8 companies (3%) the holdings exceed 20%. Although the pension fund deeds often set up upper limits of the proportion of shares that a fund is allowed to hold in an individual company, the law in force does not establish any limitations. The only limit is that a pension fund cannot invest more than 10% of its assets value in the sponsoring company's shares.

Table 9.2, Panel B, shows that 238 companies (82%) have only one pension fund interest; 40 companies (14%) have two relevant pension funds, 8 (3%) have three pension funds, 1 company had four pension funds and 2 reported five relevant pension funds holdings, a total of 356 stakes.

Table 9.2, Panel C, reports the distribution of the 99 pension funds that hold these 356 stakes. The vast majority of these funds hold a small number of stakes: 68 pension funds hold just one large stake, and 18 pension funds hold less than five large stakes. These 86 pension funds hold a total of 115 large stakes. Although not reported in the table, we find that the magnitude of the holdings is positively correlated with the size of individual occupational pension funds. The nine occupational pension funds that hold at least 10 large stakes, hold a total of 211 stakes (59% of our sample of stakes) and, with the exception of Mars Pension, the market value of their managed assets exceeds £4 billion. British Telecommunications-Post Office Pensions, the largest occupational pension fund in the UK, holds 53 stakes.

Table 9.2, Panel D, reports the descriptive statistics of occupational pension funds holdings and their incidence. On average, occupational pension funds hold individually 6% and collectively 6.96% of our test firms equities. Although these holdings range between 3 and 57%, the vast majority of our companies reported holdings of between 3 and 6% (Panel A). These holdings are relatively large comparing to those used in previous studies. For example, the average stake of institutional investors in target firms is 0.3% in Wahal (1996) and between 0.4% and 2.3% in Del Guercio and Hawkins (1999).

To assess the impact of these stakes on each individual pension fund assets, we compute Incidence on Pension Funds (IPF), the ratio of these investments over total assets of each pension fund. As stated above, the data on the portfolio of the assets managed is not available for all pension funds. The denominator of this ratio which includes other investments in fixed income securities, property, overseas equity and cash, is likely to be larger than pension fund equity investment. Thus, this ratio will understate the actual incidence level.[22] Keeping this drawback in mind, Table 9.2, Panel D shows that, on average, the investment of pension funds in our test companies represents 0.15% of their total assets, ranging between 0.01 to 14.75%. These proportions are larger than those reported by Del Guercio and Hawkins (1999) who show that pension funds holdings represent between 0.17 and 0.34% of their invested portfolio. However, given that, in our sample, 211 blocks out of 356 are held by only nine funds, the combination of the pension fund incidence statistics with this high concentration of holdings implies that the

total, rather than the individual, incidence is likely to be high. In particular, the largest fund, British Telecommunications/Post Office pension fund, holds 53 large stakes, implying an average incidence of 7.95% (53 $\times$ 0.15%). Thus, while, the aggregate blocks may represent, individually, a small proportion of pension fund assets, for each pension fund the total stake may be substantial, suggesting that their monitoring role should be beneficial.

Overall, the results reported in Table 9.2 are striking and suggest that, despite their aggregate holdings, individually, internally-managed occupational pension funds hold large stakes in a small number of companies, most of these stakes are between 3 and 10%, the vast majority of our test firms report only one occupational pension fund holding and these holdings represent a relatively small proportion of pension funds' assets.

Table 9.2, Panel D, shows that external pension fund managers, EPFM, as a whole, hold, on average, 8.99% (median 4.79%) of our sample firms' equity, but these holdings are not statistically different from those of internally managed occupational pension funds (t-statistic of the difference in means = −1.07). However, Financial Times (1997a) reports that only about 25% of these funds' assets are managed on behalf of occupational pension funds. This implies that the large stakes held by these external managers on behalf of occupational pension funds represent on average roughly 2.25% (8.99% * 0.25) of firms' equity, assuming that these funds invest in the same way pension funds assets and other assets they manage. This suggests that the impact of these investors is likely to be marginal. Unfortunately, we do not have data on the way these stakes are allocated among the different clients, but we have included them in our analysis to assess the extent to which externally managed pension funds monitor companies.

In Table 9.3, Panel A and B, we report changes in the holdings of occupational pension funds in our test firms over the 1992–1996 period and the t-statistics of differences in means and medians. Data on

Table 9.3 Annual changes in occupational pension fund holdings and list of occupational pension funds investing in their own companies

(Panel A) Distribution of occupational pension funds annual holdings

	Mean	*Median*	*Minimum*	*Maximum*
1992	6.21	5.00	3.00	41.6
1995	5.93	4.70	3.00	41.6
1996	6.09	4.60	3.00	56.9

(Panel B) *t*-statistics of annual differences in means and medians

	t-statistics of differences in means (p-value in parentheses)	*Mann–Whitney p-value*
1992 vs. 1995	−0.80 (0.43)	0.193
1992 vs. 1996	−0.32 (0.75)	0.149
1995 vs. 1996	−0.44 (0.66)	0.844

(Panel C) The holdings of Pension fund in their parent company

Company	*Proportion of equity held (%)*
Ensor Holdings	4.70
Eve group	4.48
Fuller, Smith and Turner	3.30
Garton Engineering	3.09
Gibbs and Dandy Pension Trustees	10.86
LPA Industries	4.82
Lucas Industries	6.11
MS International	10.90
Oliver Group	4.26
Rexmore	3.60
Walker, Thomas	5.11

pension fund stock ownership in 1992 is taken from the Hambros Company Guide and from the London Stock Exchange Yearbook,[23] since Extel Financial provides data only for the latest year. The table shows that 241 companies (83% of our test companies) reported large pension funds holdings in 1992 and 1996. On average, occupational pension funds held individually 6.21% of shares in 1992, 5.93% in 1995 and 6.09% in 1996. The difference in means and in median across these years is not statistically significant. We repeat the exercise using total pension fund holdings and number of pension funds and the results (not reported in Table 9.3)

confirm that pension fund holding did not change over the 1992–1996 period. The results are consistent with WM (1996) findings and suggest that pension funds are long-term investors and that our analysis is not sample dependent.

We check whether pension funds invest in their own companies where they may have different objectives and monitoring roles than when they invest in other firms. Table 9.3, Panel C, lists the 11 companies (3.8% of our test firms) with such stakes. The number of these companies and the magnitude of their holdings are not substantial and the inclusion of these companies in our test sample did not alter our results.

4.2. Financial characteristics of our test companies

Table 9.4 reports the descriptive statistics of financial attributes of the test and control firms. We compute the t-statistics to test for differences in means and the Mann–Whitney p-value to test for differences in medians.[24] In Panel A, we test for a number of attribute differences between our test and all the remaining non-financial companies listed on the London Stock Exchange. Companies in which pension funds hold large stakes are, on average, very small. Their average (median) market value is £97 million (£28 million) compared to £534 million (£43 million) for the remaining sample. The test statistics of the differences in means and in medians are both significant at the 1% level, suggesting that, on average, our test firms are significantly smaller than all the remaining firms in the UK market. The results based on total assets as an alternative measure of size confirm that our test companies are substantially smaller than the control firms. However, our test companies are not all small. Out of the 289 test companies, 188 (65%) are part of the FTA All Share Index, the 800 most traded companies in the London Stock Exchange, with 8 companies (1.4% of our test sample) that are in the UK top 100 companies (FTSE 100 Index). The remaining 101 companies are from the mid-capitalization and the small companies indices. The findings that pension funds did not change their holdings over the 1992–1996 period reported above are not likely to be the result of illiquidity of our test companies. Bethel et al. (1998) report also a large number of small companies in their sample of firms in which large investor acquire large stakes. However, given that pension funds hold, at the aggregate, more than a third of the UK equity market and that our test companies are relatively small, we can tentatively conclude that the vast majority of companies in which pension funds invest (but without holding significant stakes) are large.

Panel A, Table 9.4, shows that our test companies have lower leverage but higher directors remuneration than other companies. Interestingly, the difference in payout ratios between our test and control firms is not statistically different. This comparison is, however, likely to be driven by size differences across the two samples. To overcome this bias we construct a control sample, by matching every test company with a similar company from the same industry and size, using year-end market value of equity.

Panel B, shows that compared to the industry and size-adjusted control group, the block and managerial holdings in our test firms are not statistically different. Blockholders hold an average of 34% in our test firms and 36.5% in our control sample. Insiders hold an average of 14.5% in our test firms and 14% in our control sample. The test statistics for differences in means and medians are not statistically significant at any confidence level. The results imply that our analysis is not affected by block or managerial ownership. However, compared to the results reported in Table 9.2, insiders and blockholders hold significantly larger stakes in our test firms than occupational pension funds, suggesting that these funds do not invest a large proportion of their assets in our test companies.

Table 9.4, Panel B, shows that the value of our test firms is significantly lower than that of our control group. The average Tobin's Q of our test firms is 1.16 while that of the control group is 1.62. The same conclusion is reached when we use market-to-book and market-to-sales as alternative measures of firm value. At the same time, our test companies have lower leverage than our control firms. However, in terms of accounting and market rates of return and P/E ratio, our test companies are not different from the control firms.

In terms of internal governance structure, our test and control companies have exactly the same number of directors of about 6, ranging between 2 and 15, and the same proportion of non-executive directors of about 40%. The proportion of our control companies that split the roles of chairman and CEO of 88% is higher than that of our test firms (84%). Finally, Table 9.4

Table 9.4 Descriptive statistics on means of selected data on the test and control firms

This table provides the descriptive statistics of the proxy variables. The test sample includes all companies that reported pension fund holding above 3% in 1995–1996. In Panel A, the control sample includes all other quoted companies in the London Stock Exchange. In Panel B, the control sample includes industry and size matched firms. Block is the proportion of outstanding equity owned by blockholders other than directors and occupational pension funds; Dir is the proportion of outstanding equity capital owned by directors; ME is market value of equity at balance sheet date; TA is total assets; Q is the ratio of market value of equity plus book value of debt over total assets; M/S is the market value of equity plus book value of debt over sales; M/B is the market value of equity over book value of equity; $R_{i,t-12\,to\,t}$ is a 1-year stock return; P/E is the price-earnings ratio at the balance sheet date; Blev is the ratio of long-term debt over long-term debt plus shareholders funds; Mlev is the ratio of long-term debt over long-term debt plus market value of equity; Dir rem./Sal is the ratio of directors' remuneration over sales; Split is a dummy variable equals to 1 if the roles of chairman and CEO are split; #DIR. is the number of directors in the board; %NED is the proportion of non-executive directors; Payout is the ratio of dividends over earnings.

Variables	Test sample		Control sample		t-statistics of difference in means	Mann–Whitney p-value
	Mean	Median	Mean	Median		
Panel A: Size and other variables relative to all companies in the UK (N_{Test} = 586; $N_{Control}$ = 2702)						
ME (£ million)	96.7***	28.1***	534.10***	42.87***	−3.38	0.000
TA (£ million)	125***	33.4***	571.61***	49.54***	−2.41	0.000
Q	1.16	0.87	1.48	0.87	−1.32	0.520
ROA (%)	6.13	8.9	6.73	8.93	1.15	0.304
ROE (%)	−1.10	11.30	−24.97	11.72	0.75	0.960
Blev (%)	14.58***	9.90***	19.10***	14.60***	−3.88	0.001
Dir rem./Sal (%)	2.40	1.00***	2.56	0.79***	0.25	0.000
Payout (%)	31.78	33.0	36.03	33.55	−1.41	0.120
Panel B: Size and other variables relative to industry and size matched control firms (N = 586)						
Block	34.00	32.48	36.54	34.82	−1.29	0.135
Dir	14.53	6.02	14.01	7.38	0.32	0.875
ME (£ million)	96.7	28.1	121.1	31.1	−1.26	0.875
TA (£ million)	125	33.4	122	32.0	0.12	0.519
Q	1.16***	0.87***	1.61***	0.94***	−2.21	0.005
M/S	1.33*	0.60*	2.65*	0.65*	−1.68	0.051
M/B	2.78*	1.68***	3.44*	1.87***	−1.68	0.004
ROA (%)	6.13	8.90	4.10	8.70	1.03	0.550
ROE (%)	−1.10	11.30	11.95	12.00	−1.16	0.113
ROS (%)	5.49	6.80	−0.00	6.50	1.11	0.758
$R_{i,t-12\,to\,t}$ %	23.57	15.40	20.04	5.75	0.74	0.133
P/E	9.68	8.25	9.33	8.36	0.48	0.101
Mlev (%)	11.34***	5.80**	17.90***	12.75**	−3.21	0.012
Blev (%)	14.58***	9.90	21.01***	13.30	−3.08	0.458
Dir rem./Sal (%)	2.4	1.00	2.30	0.90	0.10	0.469
Split	0.84	1.00	0.88	1.00	−1.61	0.121
#DIR	5.92	6.00	5.80	6.00	0.85	0.382
% NED	0.40	0.40	0.38	0.40	1.31	0.334
Payout (%)	31.78	33.00	33.10	30.70	−0.40	0.399

Notes: *** Significant at 0.01 levels. ** Significant at 0.05 levels. * Significant at 0.10 levels.

shows that, our test firms do not exhibit lower directors' remuneration than the control firms. These results are striking and suggest that pension funds large holdings do not increase the likelihood of compliance with the Cadbury (1992) and Greenbury (1995) recommendations.

Table 9.4, Panel B, shows that our test firms pay an average of 32% of their earnings as dividends. This is not statistically different from the average payout ratio of 33% of our control firms. The results are not consistent with the short-termism arguments and indicate that occupational pension funds do not necessarily demand high payouts from companies in which they hold large stakes. Following Jensen (1986) arguments, the results also imply that pension funds are not monitoring these companies as they do not make them disgorge the free cash flow. The results are, nevertheless, consistent with previous studies who do not find dividend tax clientele in the UK (e.g., Lasfer, 1996).

4.3. Do pension funds affect firm value and board structure?

Table 9.5 reports the results of the Logit regressions where the various agency variables are considered simultaneously. The dependent variable is equal to 1 if company *i* is in the test sample and 0 if it is part of the control sample. The table shows that, with the exception of the variables that proxy for firm value that are significantly lower for our test firms, there is no statistical difference between our test and control firms. As shown in Table 9.4, companies in which occupational pension funds hold large stakes are not more profitable and do not pay higher dividends than the control firms. In addition, our test firms are not more likely to split the roles of chairman and chief executive officer, have less directors or more non-executive directors than our control group. These two last issues were the main focus of the recommendations of Cadbury (1992), which relied on pension funds for their implementation.

Column (6), Table 9.5, controls for differences in other monitoring mechanisms to account for the fact that these various mechanisms may be substitutes. The results show that the main difference between our test and control firms is the measure of firm value, Q, suggesting that our test firms have lower value than the control firms.[25] The coefficient of block-holding is also negative and significant at the 10% confidence level, suggesting that, after controlling for all other differences between our test and control firms, the test companies have lower blockholding than our control firms. No single pension fund-monitoring variable is significant at any confidence level. These results cast doubt on the monitoring role of pension funds in the UK.[26]

In Table 9.6 we analyze the causality in the relationship between board structure and occupational pension funds holdings. We run a set of regressions where the various dependent variables which proxy for board structure are measured in the 1996–1997 financial year and the explanatory variables such as pension funds holdings are in 1995–1996 financial year. We hypothesize that pension funds require companies in which they hold large stakes in 1995–1996 to adopt the Cadbury's (1992) board structure in 1996–1997, i.e., to split the roles of chairman and chief executive officer, to appoint a non-executive director as a chairman and to have a large proportion of non-executive directors on the board. In addition, we follow McConnell and Servaes (1995) and focus separately on low and high growth firms using E/P ratio as a proxy for growth opportunities. Firms with E/P ratio above (equal or below) the median are classified as low (high) growth. We expect a positive relationship between pension funds holdings and the adoption of the Cadbury (1992) recommendations on the composition of the board of low growth companies, which are more likely to suffer from the free cash flow problem.

The first three columns of Table 9.6 report the results of the Logit regression where the dependent variable is equal to 1

Table 9.5 Logit regressions of the probability that pension fund holdings exceeds 3% of shares 95–96

The dependent variable is equal to 1 for companies that reported pension fund holding above 3% in 1995–1996 and to 0 for industry and size matched control firms. M/S is market value of equity plus book value of debt over total assets; Blev is the ratio of long-term debt over long-term debt plus shareholders funds; Q is the ratio of market value of equity plus book value of debt over sales; $R_{i,t-12\ \text{to}\ t}$ is a 1-year share price return; Dir rem./Sal is the ratio of directors remuneration over sales; Split is a dummy variable equals to 1 if the roles of chairman and CEO are split; #DIR is the number of directors on the board; %NED is the proportion of non-executive directors in the board; Payout is the ratio of dividends over earnings; Dir is the proportion of outstanding equity held by directors; Block is the proportion of outstanding equity capital held by blockholders other than directors and occupational pension funds; χ^2, the chi-squared, is used to test that all slopes of the Logit regression are zero by comparing the restricted and the unrestricted log likelihoods. *t*-values are in parentheses.

	(1)	(2)	(3)	(4)	(5)	(6)
Constant	0.71*** (6.64)	0.61*** (6.69)	0.52*** (31.91)	0.52*** (32.16)	0.47* (1.84)	0.79*** (6.93)
Split	−0.014 (−0.27)	−0.017 (−0.31)				−0.005 (−0.09)
#DIR	0.011 (1.18)	0.016 (1.58)				0.008 (0.70)
%NED	0.04 (0.37)	0.042 (0.36)				−0.02 (−0.19)
Dir	−0.003 (0.28)	0.005 (0.53)				−0.00 (−0.00)
Block	−0.002 (−1.55)				0.001 (0.10)	−0.002* (−1.85)
Dirrem./Sal		0.123 (0.56)				0.005 (0.01)
Q			−0.01*** (−2.14)	−0.01*** (−2.51)		−0.015*** (−2.20)
M/S					−0.108* (−1.72)	
ROA			0.04 (0.92)	0.013 (0.75)		0.05 (0.64)
ROS						
$R_{i,t-12\ \text{to}\ t}$					0.006 (0.03)	
Blev					−1.65*** (−3.48)	−0.025 (−0.95)
Payout			0.006 (1.10)	0.006 (1.10)	−0.041 (−0.16)	−0.019 (−0.63)
χ^2	1.05	0.66	2.33*	2.81*	16.53***	1.42

*** Significant at the 0.01 level.
** Significant at the 0.05 level.
* Significant at the 0.10 level.

if the roles of CEO and Chairman are split and zero otherwise. The results show that the coefficients of the pension fund variables are positive but not significant except for pension fund size (LNPFA). When we split our sample into high and low growth companies none of the pension funds variables is significant. We tested for possible multicollinearity problem by running the regressions with each single variable. We find (but do not report) that the holdings of directors, Dir, and the coefficient of non-institutional block shareholders, NIBlock, are negative and significant. None of the occupational pension funds variables is significant. We find that the coefficient of the external pension fund managers variable, EPFM, is positive and significant for the whole sample, though it is not when the sub-samples of high and low growth firms are separated.

Columns 4 to 6 provide the results of the Logit regressions where the dependent variable is equal to 1 if the company has appointed a non-executive director as chairman and zero otherwise. Here again none of the coefficients of the pension fund variables are significant. However, when we run the regressions with a single independent variable, we find that the coefficient of pension funds incidence, IPF, is positive and significant (1.36 with $t = 1.71$) for the whole sample. For the low-Q companies, we find that the coefficient of total pension funds, TPF, is positive and significant (0.06 and $t = 1.93$). The coefficients of directors ownership, Dir, and non-institutional blockholders, NIBlock, are negative and significant while those of institutional blockholders and external fund managers are positive and significant.

The last three columns present the results of the OLS regressions where the dependent variable is the proportion of non-executive directors in the board. The results show that none of the pension fund variables is significant. When the regressions are run separately, we find that only size, Ln(TA), and leverage, Blev, are positive and significant.

The overall results do not provide strong support for the occupational and externally-managed pension fund monitoring of the board structure. At the same time, board structure is unrelated to market performance, suggesting that the recent trend towards the adoption of the Cadbury's prescriptions was not related to the presence of agency conflicts, but rather dictated by some "need of visibility" by companies. Franks et al. (1998) also report a similar relationship. We do, however, report some evidence consistent with monitoring role of other than pension funds institutional shareholders and of debtholders, at least with regards to the appointment of non-executive directors within low growth firms. There is also some evidence that managerial ownership is used to entrench the position of incumbent managers as the coefficient of directors' ownership is, in most cases, negative and significant. Finally, our results are consistent with the hypothesis that institutional blockholders (other than pension funds) lead high growth firms to appoint a non-executive chairman. We simulated our results using growth in profits, market returns and Q as proxies for growth opportunities and/or presence of agency conflicts. The results are qualitatively similar to those reported in Table 9.6.

4.4. Pension funds investments and firm value

In this section we focus only on our test companies and test for the relationship between firm value and ownership structure. Table 9.7 reports the Pearson correlation matrix. The correlation between the various measures of occupational pension fund holdings and firm value is, in most cases, weak and negative. An exception is represented by the correlation between the market-to-sales ratio and the pension fund incidence variable. Similarly the correlation between firm value, blockholding and directors holdings is not significant. However, ownership variables are negatively correlated with size as measured by total assets, suggesting that occupational pension funds, directors, institutional blockholders (other than pension fund managers) and

Table 9.6 Determinants of board structure for low and high growth firms

In each regression the dependent variable is computed for the period 1996–1997, while all independent variables are 1-year lagged (i.e., 1995–1996). The regressions are run separately for all 250 companies, All, low-growth companies (119), and high growth companies (131). Growth opportunities are measured using the median E/P ratio. The first six columns are Logit regressions where Split or Nechair are equal to 1 if the company has split the roles of its chairman and chief executive officer or has a non-executive director as a chairman, and zero otherwise. In these regressions the Pseudo-R^2 measures the goodness of fit. In the last three columns we run OLS regression with the proportion of non-executive on the board %NED as the dependent variable. TPF is the proportion of outstanding equity owned by all identified pension funds; IPF is the ratio of occupational pension funds holdings over their total assets; LNPFA is the log of the asset value of the pension fund; Dir is the proportion of outstanding equity owned by the directors; EPFM is the proportion of equity held by external pension fund managers (either on behalf of pension funds or other clients); IBlock represents the proportion of equity overall held by institutional block shareholders other than (both internally and externally managed) pension funds; NIBlock is the proportion of equity held by non-institutional blockholders; $R_{i,t-12\ to\ t}$ is a 1-year stock return.

	Split			Nechair			%NED		
	All	Low growth	High growth	All	Low growth	High growth	All	Low growth	High growth
Constant	−2.974	0.611	−6.447	0.091	−0.165	0.121	0.163	0.213	0.048
	(−0.68)	(−1.11)	(−1.11)	(0.02)	(−0.03)	(0.02)	(0.60)	(0.50)	(0.13)
Dir	−0.004	−0.019	0.002	−0.024**	−0.020	−0.019	−0.0002	−0.0001	−0.0004
	(−0.44)	(−0.88)	(0.19)	(−2.17)	(−1.42)	(−1.28)	(−0.24)	(−0.09)	(−0.46)
IBlock	0.030	−0.010	0.028	0.039**	0.015	0.067**	0.0002	0.001	−0.002
	(1.13)	(−0.19)	(0.77)	(2.34)	(0.74)	(2.06)	(0.21)	(0.74)	(−1.25)
NIBlock	−0.011	−0.068*	0.000	−0.017	−0.025	−0.003	0.001	0.001	−0.00003
	(−0.96)	(−1.79)	(0.03)	(−1.46)	(−1.44)	(−0.18)	(0.73)	(1.00)	(−0.03)

TPF	0.02	0.10	0.03	0.05	0.03	0.05	0.002	−0.001	0.003
	(0.38)	(0.86)	(0.51)	(1.38)	(0.71)	(1.03)	(0.79)	(−0.36)	(1.9)
LNPFA	0.53**	0.06	0.26	−0.01	0.13	−0.05	−0.01	−0.001	0.005
	(2.15)	(0.12)	(0.94)	(−0.01)	(0.50)	(−0.17)	(−0.64)	(−0.01)	(0.27)
IPF	1.48	1.46	0.75	0.74	1.88	1.05	0.0005	−0.001	0.10
	(1.26)	(0.46)	(0.45)	(0.94)	(1.13)	(0.77)	(0.04)	(−0.10)	(1.55)
EPFM	0.016	0.259	0.002	−0.004	0.006	−0.001	−0.0002	−0.0001	−0.001
	(0.43)	(1.10)	(0.05)	(−0.25)	(0.28)	(−0.05)	(−0.23)	(−0.04)	(−0.35)
Blev	6.25**	0.63	1.54	1.56	0.11	1.18	0.10*	0.08	0.17
	(2.17)	(0.32)	(0.63)	(1.61)	(0.10)	(0.78)	(1.70)	(0.99)	(1.61)
$R_{i, t-12 \text{ to } t}$	0.03	0.83	0.11	−0.21	−0.02	−0.34	0.01	0.02	0.005
	(0.08)	(1.23)	(0.07)	(−0.82)	(−0.06)	(−0.94)	(0.76)	(0.83)	(0.18)
LN(TA)	−0.47	0.09	0.07	−0.02	−0.14	−0.004	0.02**	0.02	0.01
	(−1.56)	(0.24)	(0.18)	(−0.12)	(−0.68)	(−0.01)	(2.19)	(1.40)	(0.76)
Pseudo-R^2 or R^2	7.29%	15.92%	4.87%	15.27%	11.98%	19.82%	0.95%	0.00%	3.17%

*** Significant at the 0.01 level.
** Significant at the 0.05 level.
* Significant at the 0.10 level.

Table 9.7 Pearson correlation coefficients between the variables used

The sample includes all companies that reported occupational pension fund holding above 3%. The dependent variables Q and M/S are measured in 1996–1997 financial year. LPF is the proportion of outstanding equity owned by largest occupational pension funds. All the variables are measured in 1995–1996 financial year. TPF is the proportion of outstanding equity owned by all identified pension funds; IPF is the ratio of occupational pension funds holdings over their total assets; NPF is the number of occupational pension funds; Dir is the proportion of outstanding equity owned by the directors; EPFM is the proportion of equity held by external pension fund managers (either on behalf of pension funds or other clients); IBlock represents the proportion of equity overall held by institutional block shareholders other than (both internally and externally managed) pension funds; NIBlock is the proportion of equity held by non-institutional blockholders; ln(TA) is the log of total assets; Blev is the ratio of long-term debt over long-term debt plus shareholders funds; #DIR is the number of directors on the board; Split is a dummy variable equals to 1 if the roles of chairman and CEO are split; %NED is the proportion of non-executive directors in the board; P/E is the price–earnings ratio at the balance sheet date.

	Q	M/S	TPF	IPF	NPF	LNPFA	EPFM	Dir	Dir²	IBlock	NIBlock	ln(TA)	Blev	No.Dir	Split	%NED
M/S	0.59															
TPF	−0.18	−0.07														
IPF	0.02	0.31	−0.03													
NPF	−0.12	−0.11	0.69	−0.04												
LNPFA	0.04	−0.08	0.04	−0.28	0.01											
EPFM	−0.10	−0.04	−0.01	0.02	0.04	0.16										
Dir	0.11	0.00	−0.05	−0.04	−0.04	−0.25	−0.34									
Dir²	0.11	−0.02	−0.09	−0.04	−0.08	−0.21	−0.29	0.95								
IBlock	−0.04	0.10	0.15	−0.01	0.00	0.04	0.02	−0.25	−0.23							
NIBlock	−0.02	−0.10	−0.04	−0.09	−0.05	−0.05	−0.27	−0.02	−0.06	−0.27						
ln(TA)	−0.07	0.07	−0.18	0.29	−0.01	0.22	0.36	−0.32	−0.25	−0.17	−0.25					
Blev	−0.06	−0.05	−0.04	0.13	−0.02	0.11	0.30	−0.21	−0.20	−0.10	−0.05	0.46				
No.Dir	0.09	0.07	0.01	0.01	0.05	0.18	0.07	−0.13	−0.12	−0.13	0.03	0.38	0.21			
Split	−0.11	−0.16	−0.02	0.05	−0.08	0.15	0.07	−0.21	−0.15	0.10	0.06	0.13	0.13	0.07		
%NED	0.06	0.04	−0.07	0.04	−0.11	0.07	0.10	−0.26	−0.17	0.13	−0.01	0.20	0.13	0.03	0.17	
P/E	0.37	0.26	−0.02	−0.01	−0.02	0.07	−0.04	−0.03	−0.02	0.03	−0.12	−0.06	−0.06	0.03	−0.04	−0.05

non-institutional blockholders hold large stakes mainly in small firms. However, the fund manager variable is positively related to size. Consistent with previous evidence (e.g., Lasfer, 1995), leverage is positively related to firm size but negatively correlated with firm value. The number of directors is positively correlated with occupational pension fund, externally-managed pension funds, non-institutional blockholding, leverage and size, while it is negatively correlated with institutional blockholders and directors' ownership.

The split dummy variable is positively related to leverage, block ownership, size and proportion of non-executive directors in the board, but negatively related to directors' holdings. This suggests that the larger the company and the higher the debt–equity ratio, blockholding and the proportion of non-executive directors in the board, the higher its propensity to split the roles of chairman and CEO. However, none of the occupational pension fund measure is statistically related to the split dummy, implying that pension funds, individually or collectively, do not push companies to split the roles of chairman and chief executive officer. Finally, directors' holdings are negatively related to the proportion of non-executive directors in the board, suggesting that such holdings exacerbate the potential agency conflicts between the board and the management.

In Table 9.8, columns (1) to (3), we report the results of the regressions of firm value, as measured by Tobin's Q in 1996/97, against various measures of occupational pension funds holdings in the 1995/96 financial year. These results show that, with the exception of total pension funds stakes, TPF, none of the various measures of pension funds holdings explain firm value. The total pension funds stakes variable, TPF, is actually, negative and significant, suggesting that pension funds collectively destroy value. Even after controlling for other monitoring mechanisms documented in the previous literature (e.g., Agrawal and Knoeber, 1996; Yermack, 1996), such as size and P/E, firm value is still negatively related to total pension

funds holdings (3). Although the coefficient of pension fund incidence, IPF, and the size of pension fund, LNPFA, are positively related to firm value, they are not significant. The coefficient of external pension fund managers' stakes is negatively, though not significantly, related to firm value.

In contrast to previous studies (e.g., Yermack, 1996, and Eisenberg et al., 1998) we report a positive relationship between firm value and the number of directors. The difference in the results could be due to the fact that our companies are relatively middle-sized compared to the sample of small companies of Eisenberg et al. (1998) and that of large companies of Yermack (1996). Finally, the coefficients of the holdings of directors variable and its squared value are not significant suggesting that there is no linear or non-linear relationship between value and managerial ownership. These results are not consistent with the findings of McConnell and Servaes (1990; 1995).

We simulate these results using market value of the firm over sales as a proxy for firm value (Lins and Servaes, 1999). The results, reported in (4) and (5), show a positive relationship between value and pension fund incidence, but a negative relationship with the number of pension funds. The coefficient of externally-managed pension funds is negative but not significant while that of institutional block ownership is positive and significant. We also simulate our results by using sales as a measure of size and capital expenditure over total assets as a proxy for growth opportunities. The results, not reported for space reasons, are qualitatively similar to these reported in Table 9.8. Overall, our results suggest that pension funds do not add value to companies in which they hold large stakes.

4.5. Effects of pension fund holdings on firms' long-term performance

We analyze the long term performance of our test firms by comparing the changes in accounting and stock price performance over the sample periods 1994–1995 and 1996–1997. As in Karpoff et al. (1996)

EQUITY OWNERSHIP STRUCTURE AND CONTROL

Table 9.8 Relationship between firm value and pension fund holdings

The sample includes all companies that reported occupational pension fund holding above 3%. In columns (1) to (3) we use Q, the ratio of market value of equity plus book value of debt over total assets, as the dependent variable. In column (4) and (5) the results are simulated using the market value of equity to sales as dependent variable. The dependent variables are measured in 1996–1997 while the independent variables are measured in 1995–1996. TPF is the proportion of outstanding equity owned by all identified pension funds; IPF is the ratio of occupational pension funds holdings over their total assets; LNPFA is the log of the market value of the largest pension fund's asset; NPF is the number of occupational pension funds; EPFM is the proportion of equity held by external pension fund managers (either on behalf of pension funds or other clients); Dir is the proportion of outstanding equity owned by the directors; Dir² is its squared value; IBlock represents the proportion of equity overall held by institutional blockholders other than (both internally and externally managed) pension funds; NIBlock is the proportion of equity held by non-institutional blockholders; #DIR is the number of directors; Split is a dummy variable equals to 1 if the roles of chairman and CEO are split; %NED is the proportion of non-executive directors; P/E is the price–earnings ratio at the balance sheet date. *t*-values are in parentheses.

| | Q | | | M/S | |
	(1)	(2)	(3)	(4)	(5)
Constant	−0.97 (−0.64)	0.62 (0.39)	0.57 (0.36)	0.07 (0.04)	0.97*** (2.80)
TPF	−0.033*** (−2.60)	−0.042*** (−3.07)	−0.049** (−2.57)	0.001 (0.06)	
IPF	0.034 (−0.46)	0.083 (1.34)	0.086 (1.38)	0.36*** (4.50)	0.372*** (5.41)
LNPFA	0.110 (1.62)	0.092 (1.46)	0.095 (1.50)	0.007 (0.09)	
NPF			0.09 (0.56)	−0.29** (−1.41)	−0.28** (−2.01)
EPFM		−0.003 (−0.51)	−0.003 (−0.53)	−0.001 (−0.18)	
Dir		0.004 (1.28)	0.000 (0.42)	0.010 (0.80)	
Dir²			0.000 (0.03)	−0.000 (−0.79)	
IBlock		−0.002 (−0.37)	−0.002 (−0.33)	0.013* (1.66)	0.013** (2.00)
NIBlock		−0.002 (−0.36)	−0.002 (−0.36)	−0.001 (−0.13)	
ln(TA)		−0.11* (−1.79)	−0.12* (−1.83)	0.03 (0.41)	
Blev		0.002 (0.01)	0.020 (0.04)	−0.619 (−1.09)	−0.512 (−1.02)
No.Dir		0.062* (1.86)	0.061* (1.85)	0.056 (1.32)	0.066* (1.71)
Split		−0.23 (−1.53)	−0.22 (−1.47)	−0.56** (−2.92)	−0.57*** (−3.11)
%NED		0.67* (1.78)	0.69* (1.77)	0.40 (0.80)	
P/E		0.035*** (5.65)	0.035*** (5.62)	0.032*** (3.98)	0.031*** (4.08)
Adj. R^2%	2.21%	18.08%	17.43%	18.09%	20.63%
F	2.99**	4.84***	4.18***	4.31***	9.35***

Notes: * Significant at 10% level. ** Significant at 5% level. *** Significant at 1% level.

and Del Guercio and Hawkins (1999), we investigate whether companies in which pension funds hold large stakes rebound more quickly from poor performance or maintain their good performance over a longer time period. We use return on assets (ROA) as a proxy for accounting performance. We follow Wahal (1996) and compute the 2-year industry-adjusted Cumulative Abnormal Return On Assets (CAROA) as

$$CAROA_{i,t,T} = \prod_{n=t}^{T}(1 + ROA_{i,n}) - \prod_{n=t}^{T}(1 + ROA_{s,n})$$

where $ROA_{i,t}$ is company i return on assets in year t and computed as

$$ROA_{i,t} = \frac{\text{Profit Before Interest and Tax}}{\text{Book Value of Total Assets}}.$$

$ROA_{s,t}$ is the industry s median return on assets in year t.

We simulate our results by computing in the same way Cumulative Abnormal Return On Equity (CAROE) and Cumulative Abnormal Return On Sales (CAROS). All measures of performance are adjusted by subtracting the industry median.

The abnormal performance is also evaluated using stock market returns. We compute the Share Price Return (SPR) from a buy-and-hold strategy over the sub-periods 1994–1995 and 1996–1997 as follows:

$$SPR_{i,t,T} = \prod_{n=t}^{T}\{1 + r_{i,n}\} - \prod_{n=t}^{T}\{1 + r_{c^*,n}\}$$

where

$$r_{i,n} = \frac{P_{i,n}}{P_{i,n-1}} - 1.$$

We adopt the Barber and Lyon (1997) methodology, and control for size (market capitalization) and market-to-book. We match each test company with a control

company selected by identifying all firms with a market value of equity between 70% and 130% of that of the test company. Then, from this set of firms, we select the company with the market-to-book ratio closest to that of the test firm. We use the return of this company, $r_{c^*,n}$, as a benchmark.

This measure of performance accounts for the fact that occupational pension funds are long-term investors, as reported in Table 9.3, and does not suffer from cumulating biases observed in arithmetic mean returns (Conrad and Kaul, 1993; Wahal, 1996; Barber and Lyon, 1997). We eliminate survivorship bias by including dead companies in our sample. Out of our 289 test companies, 34 firms (11.76%) are excluded because they went public after 1995 and we could not compute the market performance for the first period.

The results reported in Table 9.9 show that the industry-adjusted return on assets (CAROA) has not changed significantly over the two sub-periods. Companies in which occupational pension funds hold large stakes underperform the industry average (though not significantly) by 3.38% in 1994–1995 and by 1.50% in 1996–1997. As in Wahal (1996), we split the sample into overperformers and underperformers. Companies with CAROA below (above) the median are classified as underperformers (overperformers).[27] The abnormal performance of the overperforming companies decreased from 11.62% to 6.44% and that of the underperformers has increased from −18.5% to −9.51%. The results are consistent with Wahal (1996) and indicate that both the under-and overperformers experience a convergence to industry means. The results are not qualitatively affected by the use of other measures of performance such as industry-adjusted return on equity (Panel B) or industry-adjusted return on sales (Panel C).

Panel D and E report the changes in firm value as measured by (the industry-adjusted) Tobin's Q and changes in abnormal returns. For the full sample, the industry-adjusted Q has decreased from 0.163 to

Table 9.9 Pension fund holdings and long term accounting and stock price performance

The sample includes all companies that displayed (at least) one relevant pension fund holding. Industry-adjusted return on assets (CAROA) is the return on assets of each company in the sample less the median return on asset of the industry. Industry-adjusted return on equity and return on sales and *Q* are computed in a similar way. The control sample includes firms taken from the same SEC industry whose 1994–1995 performance is the closest to our test firm. Panel E reports the results based on the size and market-to-book adjusted share price returns using the Barber and Lyons (1997) methodology. The sample is dividend into a sample of underperformers and overperformers based on the median performance of the firm in 1994–1995. For example, if the industry-adjusted return on assets for a firm is lower (higher) than the median, the firm is classified as an underperformer (overperformer).

	N	1994–1995		1996–1997		t-statistic difference in means	Mann–Whitney p-value
		Mean	Median	Mean	Median		
(Panel A) Industry-adjusted return on assets CAROA%							
Full sample	255	−3.38	−0.584	−1.50	−0.31	−1.24	0.344
Overperformers	128	11.62***	6.48***	6.44***	3.56***	3.56	0.000
Underperformers	127	−18.50***	−10.30***	−9.51***	−4.76***	−3.59	0.000
(Panel B) Industry-adjusted return on equity CAROE%							
Full sample	255	−4.96	−1.412	−3.89	−0.53	−0.36	0.906
Overperformers	128	20.79***	10.31***	5.72***	2.13***	4.48	0.000
Underperformers	127	−30.90***	−16.50***	−13.56***	−6.91***	−3.94	0.000
(Panel C) Industry-adjusted return on sales CAROS%							
Full sample	255	−0.08	−0.67	0.33	0.00	−0.24	0.811
Overperformers	128	14.99***	7.13***	7.78***	4.92***	3.32	0.000
Underperformers	127	−15.27***	−7.57***	−7.19***	−4.75***	−3.35	0.000
(Panel D) Industry-adjusted firm value Q							
Full sample	255	0.163***	−0.082***	0.072***	−0.095***	2.72	0.009
Overperformers	128	0.674***	0.346***	0.480***	0.15***	3.22	0.000
Underperformers	127	−0.353	−0.322	−0.339	−0.306	−0.58	0.237
(Panel E) Size and market-to-book adjusted share price return SPR%							
Full sample	255	0.49	−3.85	−3.20	−8.76	0.42	0.916
Overperformers	128	68.22***	43.64***	−6.83***	−13.05***	6.62	0.000
Underperformers	127	−67.76***	−57.19***	0.45***	−2.09***	−7.01	0.000

* Significant at 10%, 5% and 1% respectively.
** Significant at 10%, 5% and 1% respectively.
*** Significant at 10%, 5% and 1% respectively.

0.072.[28] The decrease in both the average and median firm value is statistically significant. The results suggest that, over time, the value of companies in which occupational pension funds hold large stakes decreases. As in the above panels, we split the sample into overperformers and underperformers. Overperforming (underperforming) companies are companies with Tobin's *Q* higher (lower) than the median. The overperforming companies have done worst over the two sample periods. Their average value has decreased from 0.67 to 0.48. The decrease in the mean median are statistically significant. In contrast, the average and the median Tobin's *Q* of the underperforming companies did not change significantly. These companies have underperformed in 1994–1995 period and carried on underperforming in the 1996–1997 period. These results are striking as they imply that companies in which occupational pension funds hold large stakes decrease in value through time, and those that are already underperforming do not improve. In sum, it appears that pension funds are passive investors: they do not make companies in which they hold large stakes improve their performance and they do not sell their holdings in companies that are underperforming.

Panel E reports the results based on the size and market-to-book adjusted share price returns using the Barber and Lyon (1997) methodology. For the full sample, companies have decreased their average performance from 0.49% to −3.2% and the median performance from −3.85% to −8.76%. However, this decrease is not statistically significant. The stock price performance of the sub-sample of the overperforming firms declined significantly from 68.22% to −6.83% (t-statistic of the difference in means = 6.62), while underperforming companies increased their performance from −67.76% to 0.45% (t-statistic of the difference in means = −7.01). As in Wahal (1996), our results are consistent with mean reversion hypothesis and cannot be attributed to pension funds investments.[29]

5. DISCUSSION AND CONCLUSIONS

In this paper we analyze the performance of companies in which occupational pension funds hold large stakes and test the hypotheses that, because of their size, structure and objectives, these funds should be effective monitors of UK companies.

We compare the financial performance of companies in which occupation pension funds hold more than 3% of the issued share capital against all other non-financial and industry and size-adjusted control groups. We show that our test firms are small and have low value. These companies are also not likely to be more efficient and/or to pay higher dividends than the control group. However, our results show that these holdings constitute a small proportion of the occupational pension funds assets, suggesting that most of their funds are invested in large companies where they do not hold large stakes. We report that pension funds do not add value to the

companies in which they hold large stakes. Our results cast doubt on the monitoring role of pension funds which are considered theoretically, on the one hand, to be the main promoters of corporate governance in the UK, and, on the other hand, to be short-termist and dictate their rules to companies. At the same time, we show that, despite the relatively poor performance of the companies in which they invest, occupational pension funds do not opt for the 'exit' strategy. We show that there is no apparent specific relationship between the funds and the companies in which they invest and these companies are not illiquid to make it impossible to exit. One possibility is that pension funds choose to invest in low Q firms to benefit from return reversals on these securities. However, the lack of data on the investment styles of these funds does not allow us to explore this issue further. At this stage, our results suggest that, once 'locked in' pension funds find it difficult and costly to monitor or to sell their holdings for fear of selling at a discount or to convey information to the market.

Our results may not come as a surprise. There is a large debate in the UK about the lack of monitoring by pension funds and it is only recently that the National Association of Pension Funds considered seriously this issue (NAPF, 1996b). In addition, occupational pension funds may not have a material effect on the performance of companies in which they hold large stakes because these blocks tend to represent relatively small fractions of the total values of the funds' assets. The mean (median) block represents only 0.15% (0.03%) of the typical funds assets, and with such a small fraction, it is not clear that the gains to the funds of expending effort monitoring the sample firms would justify the costs. Thus, our results are consistent with Admati et al. (1994) proposition that, given that monitoring is costly, these funds will not monitor as this is not likely to result in a modification in the firms payoff structure and will not lead to net gains. They may also refrain from intervening publicly for fear of drawing to public attention the difficulties the company is facing and/or trading on insider information. However, our results could also imply that pension funds are passive investors, investing most of their funds in the index and these investments we analyzed in this paper are peripheral.

While our results are not consistent with the monitoring role of occupational pension funds, our study does not fill all the gaps in the literature. Our sample includes only companies in which occupational pension funds hold more than 3% of the issued share capital. A more desegregated and comprehensive data is not available. Similarly, because of data unavailability, we have not addressed the question of whether occupational pension funds sponsor initiatives, whether they meet with companies and whether there is a co-operation between various funds. The extent to which these additional factors will strengthen or alter our analysis is a matter of further investigation.

ACKNOWLEDGEMENTS

We are grateful to Yakov Amihud, Francesco Cesarini, John McConnell, Annette Poulsen (the editor), Jonathan Sokobin, Geof Stapledon, Sudi Sudarsanam, an anonymous referee, and seminar participants at Brunel University and the 1998 European Financial Management Association meeting in Lisbon for valuable insights and helpful comments. Faccio acknowledges a research grant from City University Business School. All errors are our responsibility.

NOTES

* Corresponding author. Tel.: +44-0-171-477-8634; fax: +44-0-171-477-8648; e-mail: m.a.lasfer@city.ac.uk
1   Tel.: +39-02-7234-2436; e-mail: m.faccio@iol.it.
2   Other studies suggest that the relationship between ownership, such as the fraction of shares held by insiders and performance is not linear but roof-shaped (e.g., Morek et al., 1988; Stulz, 1988; McConnell and Servaes, 1990).

3   See Black (1998) and Karpoff (1998) for a survey of the shareholder activism literature.
4   Hutton (1995) argues that "pension funds . . . have become classic absentee landlords, exerting power without responsibility and making exacting demands upon companies without recognizing their reciprocal obligations as owners" (p. 304).
5   For example, Drucker (1976) stipulates that "pension funds are not 'owners', they are investors. They do not want control . . . If they do not like a company or its management, their duty is to sell the stock" (p. 82). More recently, Porter (1997) argues that institutional investors, despite their substantial aggregate holdings, do not sit on corporate boards and have virtually no real influence on managements behavior because they invest nearly all their assets in index funds rather than directly in companies. Short and Keasey (1997) suggest that once pension funds are locked in, it is costly to get involved in monitoring and they cannot exit in case they are considered to trade on insider information. Murphy and Van Nuys (1994) argue that pension funds are run by individuals who do not have the proper incentives to maximize fund value.
6   Cadbury (1992) notes that "Because of their collective stake, we look to the institutions in particular, with the backing on Institutional Shareholders' Committee, to use their influence as owners to ensure that the companies in which they have invested comply with the Code" (para. 6.16). The National Associate of Pension Funds also endorses such recommendations (NAPF, 1996b).
7   A number of studies document the free cash flow problem in the UK. For example, Franks and Mayer (1994) find that UK companies pay high dividends relative to German companies; Lasfer (1995) shows that debt mitigates the free cash flow problem; Lasfer (1997) provides evidence that firms with free cash flow problems pay scrip, rather than cash, dividends. The reports of Cadbury (1992) and Greenbury (1995) are a manifestation of the previous debate on the various wider corporate governance issues detailed in Charkham (1995), Stapledon (1996) and Keasey et al. (1997).
8   Companies Act 1995, Sections 198 and 199 requires UK companies to disclose in their accounts the name of any investor who holds 3% or more of the issued share capital.
9   See Chew (1997) for a collection of papers dealing with these two corporate governance systems.
10 See Black (1998) and Karpoff (1998) for a survey.

11 Similarly, in the US, the value of DC plans in 1993 was $1068 billion compared to $1248 billion for DB plans. However, DC schemes are growing at much faster rates of 19% per year, compared to 14% for DB plans (Jepson, 1998).
12 The report states that no "one individual has unfetted powers of decision. Where the chairman is also chief executive, it is essential that there should be a strong and independent element on the board, with a recognised senior member".
13 The Code of Best Practice No 4.3 recommended an audit committee of at least three non-executive directors with written terms of reference and No 4.30 recommends the institution of a nomination committee as an internal committee within the board. This committee should be composed of majority of non-executive directors and chaired by the chairman of the board.
14 The 99 in-house managed pension funds included in our study manage assets for some £150 billion, which correspond to 26.8% of all occupational pension funds' assets.
15 The report summarizes the functions of the board as follows: "The responsibilities of the board include setting up the companys strategic aims, providing the leadership to put them into effect, supervising the management of the business and reporting to shareholders on their stewardship". As to the financial aspects of corporate governance, the report mentions: "The way in which boards set financial policy and oversee its implementation, including the use of financial controls, and the process whereby they report on the activities and progress of the company to the shareholders".
16 See John and Senbet (1998) for an extensive survey of the monitoring role of corporate board of directors and Stapledon (1996, pp. 138–153), for the monitoring role of non-executive directors.
17 The choice of 1995–1996 sample period is driven by data availability. The data on shareholding is inserted manually because Extel Financial provides only the latest data on shareholding in text format and this data is not available in machine-readable form. Other similar studies use also short time period (see Karpoff, 1998, for a review). We report below that the vast majority of companies (83% of our test firms) had large pension funds holdings in both 1992 and 1996 periods and the magnitude of their holdings has not changed significantly. Thus, our results are not likely to be sample-period dependent.
18 Extel Financial is a financial database microsystem. The database provides accounting as well as financial and reference data for all UK companies and many international companies.

19 The ideal would be to exclude from the denominator of this ration other assets such as property, cash and fixed income securities, but the desegregated data on equity investment is not available.
20 This variable includes directors holdings but excludes those of officers. UK quoted companies are required to disclose in their financial statements the proportion of shares held directly and indirectly by executive and non-executive directors (Companies Act 1985). However, no similar disclosure applies to officers. This legal disclosure requirement means that we had to define managerial ownership as ownership by members of the board of directors. Although this definition is consistent with that of Morck et al. (1988), it differs from that of McConnell and Servaes (1990) and Denis and Sarin (1999) as we do not include shares owned by corporate officers not members of the board.
21 Denis and Kruse (1999) and Denis and Sarin (1999) distinguish between unaffiliated and affiliated block shareholdings. Unaffiliated blockholders would be expected to perform an important monitoring role and make firms comply with the Code of Best Practice, while affiliated blockholders are more likely to be sensitive to managerial pressure or pursue goals other than share price maximization (Brickley et al., 1988, 1994). In this perspective, our internally managed occupational pension funds are clearly "unaffiliated shareholders". Since our data does not generally allow us to check for the intensity of the relationships between firms and shareholders, we consider together affiliated and unaffiliated shareholders in the category of blockholders. However, we distinguish between institutional and non-institutional blockholders, because these two categories of investors were shown to behave differently, i.e., when sponsoring initiatives (Jarrell and Poulsen, 1987; Karpoff et al., 1996).
22 One possibility of overcoming this problem of lack of data of pension fund assets invested in UK equities would be to assume that all pension funds are homogeneous in their investment styles, i.e., the aggregate distribution of pension fund assets would apply to each fund. They would therefore hold an average of 53% of their assets in UK equities and the remaining 47% in fixed income securities, overseas equities, property and cash, as reported in NAPF (1996a). However, we consider that this assumption is not likely to hold as the average holding is not constant through time.
23 Hambros Company Guide is a quarterly publication, which gives a summary financial

data and shareholdings above 3% of UK companies. The Stock Exchange Yearbook is an annual publication of the London Stock Exchange. It provides a summary data of the activities, shareholdings and performance of UK listed companies.
24   We exclude 58 companies with negative book value of equity due to goodwill write-offs when we use the market-to-book ratio, book leverage and return on equity. The inclusion of these companies did not, however, alter our reported results.
25   The negative relationship between pension fund investments and Q has been widely documented in the investment literature. For example, Lakonishok et al. (1994) show that pension funds invest in glamour stocks (low book-to-market firms), which generally underperform value stocks (high book-to-market firms) because the previous success of the glamour stocks helps institutions justify their portfolio selection to their investors.
26   The issue of director's pay system has just been considered by the National Association of Pension Funds through their call to vote on boardroom pay (Financial Times, 1997b).
27   We have also split the sample into over- and underperformers on the basis of positive and negative CAROA or other variables used below but the results did not change.
28   For both 1994–1995 and 1996–1997, the Q ratio is computed as arithmetic average.
29   We obtained similar results either by using the industry median return as benchmark and, by matching our test firms by industry and prior performance. Also, for all accounting measures of performance, as well as firm value, the results were qualitatively similar when we compared the industry adjusted performance of 1990–92 to that of 1993–95. Similar results are obtained when we concentrate on survived companies, and exclude IPO firms.

REFERENCES

ABI, 1998. Research update: How much in funded pensions in 1996? Insurance Trends 16, 27–29.
Admati, A.R., Pfleiderer, P., Zechner, J., 1994. Large shareholder activism, risk sharing, and financial market equilibrium. Journal of Political Economy 102, 1097–1130.
Agrawal, A., Knoeber, C.R., 1996. Firm performance and mechanisms to control agency problems between managers and shareholders. Journal of Financial and Quantitative Analysis 31, 377–397.
Agrawal, A., Mandelker, G.N., 1990. Large shareholders and the monitoring of managers: The case of antitakeover charter amendments. Journal of Financial and Quantitative Analysis 25, 143–162.
Ayres, I., Cramton, P., 1993. An agency perspective on relational investing. Working Paper, Stanford University, Stanford, CA.
Barber, B.M., Lyon, J.D., 1997. Detecting long run abnormal stock returns: The empirical power and specification of test-statistics. Journal of Financial Economics 43, 341–372.
Bethel, J.E., Liebeskind, J.P., Opler, T., 1998. Block share repurchases and corporate performance. Journal of Finance 53, 605–635.
Black, B.S., 1998. Shareholder activism and corporate governance in the United States. In: Newman, P. (Ed.), The Palgrave Dictionary of Economics and the Law.
Blake, D., 1995. Pension Schemes and Pension Funds in the United Kingdom. Clarendon Press, Oxford.
Brancato, C.K., 1997. Institutional Investors and Corporate Governance: Best Practice for Increasing Corporate Value. McGraw Hill, Chicago.
Brickley, J.A., Lease, R.C., Smith, C.W. Jr., 1988. Ownership structure and voting on antitakeover amendments. Journal of Financial Economics 20, 267–291.
Brickley, J.A., Lease, R.C., Smith, C.W. Jr., 1994. Corporate voting: Evidence from charter amendment proposals. Journal of Corporate Finance 1, 5–30.
Business Monitor, 1997. Central Statistical Office, London.
Cadbury, A., 1992. Report of the Committee on the Financial Aspects of Corporate Governance. Gee, London.
Carleton, W.T., Nelson, J.M., Weisbach, M.S., 1998. The influence of institutions on corporate governance through private negotiations: Evidence from TIAA-CREF. The Journal of Finance 53, 1335–1362.
Charkham, J., 1995. Keeping Good Company: A Study of Corporate Governance in Five Countries. Oxford University Press, Oxford.
Chew, D.H. (Ed.), 1997. Studies in International Corporate Finance and Governance Systems: A Comparison of the US, Japan and Europe. Oxford University Press, New York.

Coffee, J., 1991. Liquidity versus control: The institutional investor as corporate monitor. Columbia Law Review 91, 1277–1368.

Conrad, J., Kaul, G., 1993. Long-term market overreaction or biases in computed returns? Journal of Finance 48, 39–64.

Cotter, J.F., Shivdasani, A., Zenner, M., 1997. Do independent directors enhance target shareholder wealth during tender offers? Journal of Financial Economics 43, 195–218.

Davis, E.P., 1995. Pension Funds. Retirement-Income, Security and Capital Markets. An International Perspective. Clarendon Press, Oxford.

Del Guercio, D., Hawkins, J., 1999. The motivation and impact of pension fund activism. Journal of Financial Economics 52, 293–340.

Demsetz, H., Lehn, K., 1985. The structure of corporate ownership: causes and consequences. Journal of Political Economy 93, 1155–1177.

Denis, D.J., Kruse, T.A., 1999. Managerial discipline and corporate restructuring following performance declines. Working Paper, Purdue University, West Lafayette, IN.

Denis, D.J., Sarin, A., 1999. Ownership and board structures in publicly traded corporations. Journal of Financial Economics 52, 187–223.

Diamond, D.W., 1984. Financial intermediation and delegated monitoring. Review of Economic Studies 51, 393–414.

Drucker, P.F., 1976. The Unseen Revolution: How Pension Fund Socialism Came to America. Heinemann, London.

Eisenberg, T., Sundgren, S., Wells, M.T., 1998. Large board size and decreasing firm value in small firms. Journal of Financial Economics 48, 35–54.

Financial Times, 1997. FT Survey on Pension Fund Investment. May 9, 1997.

Financial Times, 1997. Pension Funds to Call for Votes on Boardroom Pay: NAPF Will Oppose Hampel Committees Findings. September 29, 1997, p. 20.

Financial Times, 1999. Fighting Fit. January 29, 1999, p. 17.

Franks, J.R., Mayer, C., 1994. The ownership and control of German corporations. Working Paper, London Business School, London.

Franks, J.R., Mayer, C., 1997. Corporate ownership and control in the UK, Germany, and

France. Journal of Applied Corporate Finance 9, 30–45.

Franks, J.R., Mayer, C., Renneboog, L., 1998. Who disciplines bad managers? Working Paper, London Business School, London.

Gordon, L.A., Pound, J., 1993. Information, ownership structure, and shareholder voting: Evidence from shareholder-sponsored corporate governance proposals. Journal of Finance 48, 697–718.

Greenbury, R., 1995. Directors Remuneration: Report of a Study Group Chaired by Sir Richard Greenbury. Gee, London.

Hart, O., Holmstrom, B., 1987. The theory of contracts. In: Bewley, T. (Ed.), Advances in Economic Theory. Cambridge University Press, Cambridge, pp. 71–155.

Hart, O., 1995. Firms, Contracts, and Financial Structure. Oxford University Press, Oxford.

Hutton, W., 1995. The State We Are In. Vintage Press, London.

Jarrell, G.A., Poulsen, A.B., 1987. Shark repellents and stock prices: The effects of antitakeover amendments since 1980. Journal of Financial Economics 19, 127–168.

Jensen, M.C., 1986. Agency costs of free cash flow, corporate finance, and takeovers. American Economic Review 76, 323–329.

Jensen, M.C., 1993. The modern industrial revolution, exit, and the failure of internal control systems. Journal of Finance 48, 831–880.

Jepson, J., 1998. US Defined Benefits and Defined Contribution: Comparison and Implications. Paper presented at the 1998 NAPF Conference, Eastbourne, UK.

John, K., Senbet, L.W., 1998. Corporate governance and board effectiveness. Journal of Banking and Finance 22, 371–403.

Kahn, C., Winton, A., 1998. Ownership structure, speculation and shareholder intervention. Journal of Finance 53, 99–129.

Kang, J.K., Shivdasani, A., 1995. Firm performance, corporate governance, and top executive turnover in Japan. Journal of Financial Economics 38, 29–58.

Kaplan, S.N., Minton, B.A., 1994. Appointments of outsiders to Japanese Boards: Determinants and implications for managers. Journal of Financial Economics 36, 225–258.

Karpoff, J.M., 1998. Does Shareholder Activism Work? A Survey of Empirical

Findings. Working Paper, University of Washington, Seattle, WA.

Karpoff, J.M., Malatesta, P.H., Walkling, R.A., 1996. Corporate governance and shareholder initiatives: empirical evidence. Journal of Financial Economics 42, 365–395.

Keasey, K.S., Thompson, S., Wright, M., 1997. Corporate Governance: Economic, Management, and Financial Issues. Oxford University Press, Oxford.

Lakonishok, J., Shleifer, A., Vishny, R.W., 1994. Contrarian investment, extrapolation, and risk. Journal of Finance 49, 1541–1578.

Lang, L.H.P., Ofek, E., Stulz, R.M., 1996. Leverage, investment, and firm growth. Journal of Financial Economics 40, 3–29.

Lasfer, M.A., 1995. Agency costs, taxes and debt: The UK evidence. European Financial Management 1, 265–285.

Lasfer, M.A., 1996. Taxes and dividends: The UK evidence. Journal of Banking and Finance 20, 455–472.

Lasfer, M.A., 1997. On the motivation for paying script dividends. Financial Management 26, 62–80.

Lin, T.H., 1996. The certification of large block shareholders in initial public offerings: The case of venture capitalists. Quarterly Journal of Business and Economics 35, 55–65.

Lins, K., Servaes, H., 1999. International evidence on the value of corporate diversification. Journal of Finance 54, 2215–2239.

London Stock Exchange, 1995. Survey on Share Ownership, Stock Exchange, London.

Mallin, C.A., 1997. Investors voting rights. In: Keasey, K., Wright, M. (Eds.), Corporate Governance: Responsibilities, Risks and Remuneration. Wiley: West Sussex.

Maug, E., 1998. Large shareholders as monitors: is there a trade-off between liquidity and control? Journal of Finance 53, 65–98.

McConnell, J.J., Servaes, H., 1990. Additional evidence on equity ownership and corporate value. Journal of Financial Economics 27, 595–612.

McConnell, J.J., Servaes, H., 1995. Equity ownership and the two faces of debt. Journal of Financial Economics 39, 131–157.

Mikkelson, W.H., Ruback, R.S., 1985. An empirical analysis of the interfirm equity investment process. Journal of Financial Economics 14, 523–553.

Minns, R., 1980. Pension Funds and British Capitalism: The Ownership and Control of Shareholders. Heinemann, London.

Morck, R., Shleifer, A., Vishny, R.W., 1988. Management ownership and market valuation: An empirical analysis. Journal of Financial Economics 20, 293–316.

Murphy, K., Van Nuys, K., 1994. State pension fund shareholder activism. Working Paper, Harvard Business School, Boston, MA.

NAPF, 1996. Year Book. National Association of Pension Funds, London.

NAPF, 1996. Good Corporate Governance. National Association of Pension Funds, London.

Nesbitt, S.L., 1994. Long-term rewards from shareholder activism: a study of the 'CalPERS effect'. Journal of Applied Corporate Finance 6, 75–80.

Pension Funds and their Advisers, 1996. London.

Porter, M.E., 1997. Capital choices: Changing the way American invests in industry. In: Chew, D.H. (Ed.), Studies in International Corporate Finance and Governance Systems: A Comparison of the US, Japan and Europe. Oxford University Press, New York, pp. 5–17.

Prowse, S., 1994. Corporate governance in and international perspective: A survey of corporate control mechanisms amongst large firms in the United States, the United Kingdom, Japan and Germany. BIS Economic Papers, No. 41, Bank of International Settlements, Basel.

Romano, R., 1994. Public pension fund activism in corporate governance reconsidered. Columbia Law Review 93, 795–853.

Shleifer, A., Vishny, R.W., 1986. Large shareholders and corporate control. Journal of Political Economy 94, 461–488.

Shleifer, A., Vishny, R.W., 1997. A survey of corporate governance. Journal of Finance 52, 737–783.

Shome, D.K., Singh, S., 1995. Firm value and external blockholdings. Financial Management 24, 3–14.

Short, H., Keasey, K., 1997. Institutional shareholders and corporate governance in the United Kingdom. In: Keasey, K.S., Thompson, S., Wright, M. (Eds.), Corporate Governance: Economic, Management, and Financial

Issues. Oxford University Press, Oxford, 18–53.

Smith, M.P., 1996. Shareholder activism by institutional investors: evidence from CalPERS. Journal of Finance 51, 227–252.

Stapledon, G.P., 1996. Institutional Shareholders and Corporate Governance. Clarendon Press, Oxford.

Strickland, D., Wiles, K.W., Zenner, M., 1996. A requiem for the USA: Is small shareholder monitoring effective? Journal of Financial Economics 40, 319–338.

Stulz, R.M., 1988. Managerial control of voting rights: Financing policies and the market for corporate control. Journal of Financial Economics 20, 25–54.

Sudarsanam, S., 1996. Large shareholders, takeovers and target valuation. Journal of Business Finance and Accounting 23, 295–314.

Tomlinson, L., 1998. Should the Future Be All Passive? Paper presented at the 1998 NAPF Conference, Eastbourne, UK.

Wahal, S., 1996. Pension fund activism and firm performance. Journal of Financial and Quantitative Analysis 31, 1–23.

WM, 1996. UK Pension Fund Industry Results. WM, Edinburgh (various issues 1994–1996).

Yermack, D., 1996. Higher market valuation of companies with a small board of directors. Journal of Financial Economics 40, 185–211.

Part 3

Corporate governance, underperformance and management turnover

INTRODUCTION

PART 3 COMPRISES PAPERS THAT DEAL WITH THE effectiveness of corporate governance mechanisms in disciplining top managers. A measure of such discipline is the removal or turnover of such managers in response to poor corporate performance. Where such managers are entrenched owing to their ownership of the company's voting shares, connections to controlling shareholders or both, this form of disciplining is unlikely and the corporate governance mechanism is rendered ineffective. The controlling large block shareholder may in theory have an incentive to improve corporate performance, if necessary by disciplining top managers of underperformers but this concern may be overridden by their enjoyment of private benefits of control. Minority shareholders, however, do not enjoy such countervailing private benefits. Large shareholding thus may align the interests of managers and large shareholders but create another agency problem (i.e. between large, controlling shareholders and minority shareholders). The phenomenon whereby controlling shareholders manage to receive private benefits at the expense of minority shareholders is called 'tunnelling'.

In the first of the papers in this part, Volpin (Ch.10) uses the interesting Italian setting to test the disciplinary effect of ownership structure on management turnover. Italy features low on the ranking of shareholder rights as noted by La Porta et al. in their paper (see Part 1, Ch.3). Corporate ownership structure in Italy is characterised by large controlling, often family, shareholders, voting syndicates binding significant shareholders to vote together, thereby achieving joint control, and pyramidal ownership in which a controlling block of voting rights allow control of a hierarchy of group companies with less than majority ownership. Italy also has a substantial incidence of voting versus non-voting shares separating voting rights from mere cash-flow rights to dividends.

Volpin explores the impact of controlling shareholders, voting syndicates and pyramidal controls on the sensitivity of management turnover to underperformance with a large sample of firms listed in Milan and over a long sample period. His results suggest that there is poor governance, as measured by a low sensitivity of turnover to performance and a low Q ratio, when (i) the controlling shareholders are also top executives, (ii) the control is fully in the hands of one shareholder and is not shared by a set of core shareholders, and (iii) the controlling shareholders own less than 50 percent of the firm's cash-flow rights. He also reports further interesting insights. Large cash-flow rights are important even for controlling shareholders and help to align controlling and minority shareholder interests. Furthermore, where control is contestable, as in a syndicate of significant shareholders, management turnover becomes sensitive to underperformance.

Normally corporate governance is made up of more than a single mechanism with extant mechanisms working in tandem (complementary mode) or as substitutes (substitutory mode).

In the latter case, some of the mechanisms may be redundant although, *ex ante*, determining which ones are redundant may be difficult. In the second paper in this part, Luc Renneboog (Ch.11) examines how corporate control is exerted in companies listed on the Brussels Stock Exchange. There are several alternative corporate governance mechanisms, which may play a role in disciplining poorly performing management: block-holders (holding companies, industrial companies, families and institutions), the market for partial control, creditors, and board composition. Even if there is redundancy of substitute forms of discipline, some mechanisms may dominate. It is found that top managerial turnover is strongly related to poor performance measured by stock returns, accounting earnings in relation to industry peers and dividend cuts and omissions. Tobit models reveal that there is little relation between ownership and managerial replacement, although industrial companies resort to disciplinary actions when performance is poor. When industrial companies increase their share stake or acquire a new stake in a poorly performing company, there is evidence of an increase in executive board turnover, which suggests a partial market for control. There is little relation between changes in ownership concentration held by institutions and holding companies, and disciplining. Still, increased disciplining also follows high leverage and decreasing solvency and liquidity variables, as are a high proportion of non-executive directors and the separation of the functions of CEO and chairman.

The third paper by Julian Franks, Colin Mayer and Luc Renneboog (Ch.12) follows a similar line of empirical enquiry into the relative effectiveness of different disciplinary devices but this time in the UK context and the focus is on financially distressed firms. Economic theory points to five parties disciplining management of poorly performing firms: holders of large share blocks, acquirers of new blocks, bidders in takeovers, non-executive directors, and investors during periods of financial distress. This paper reports a comparative evaluation of the role of these different parties in disciplining management. The authors find that, in the United Kingdom, most parties, including holders of substantial share blocks, exert little disciplining and that some, for example, inside holders of share blocks and boards dominated by non-executive directors, actually impede it.

Bidders replace a high proportion of management of companies acquired in takeovers but do not target poorly performing management. In contrast, during periods of financial constraints prompting distressed rights issues and capital restructuring, investors focus control on poorly performing companies. These results stand in contrast to the United States, where there is little evidence of a role for new equity issues but non-executive directors and acquirers of share blocks perform a disciplinary function. The different governance outcomes are attributed to differences in minority investor protection in two countries with supposedly similar common law systems. This paper makes the interesting link between the relative effectiveness of different corporate control mechanisms and the larger legal environment in which these mechanisms operate.

In 1992, the Cadbury Committee issued the Code of Best Practice (the Code). It recommends that boards of UK corporations include at least three outside (i.e. independent) directors and that the positions of chairman and CEO be held by different individuals (the non-duality principle). The underlying presumption is that these recommendations would lead to improved board oversight. Jay Dahya, John McConnel and Nick Travlos (Ch.13) empirically investigate the impact of the Code by comparing the relationship between CEO turnover and corporate performance before and after the Code. CEO turnover increased following issuance of the Code; the negative relationship between CEO turnover and performance became stronger following the Code's issuance; and the increase in sensitivity of turnover to performance was concentrated among firms that adopted the Code. This Code is now part of the listing requirements on the London Stock Exchange on the 'comply or explain' (non-compliance) basis. Dahya et al.'s study is an interesting example of empirical methodology for evaluating externally imposed corporate governance regimes in their impact on corporate behaviour and performance.

## Chapter 10

Paolo F. Volpin

GOVERNANCE WITH POOR INVESTOR PROTECTION: EVIDENCE FROM TOP EXECUTIVE TURNOVER IN ITALY[*]

Source: *Journal of Financial Economics,* 64(1) (2002): 61–90.

ABSTRACT

This paper studies the determinants of executive turnover and firm valuation as a function of ownership and control structure in Italy, a country that features low legal protection for investors, firms with controlling shareholders, and pyramidal groups. The results suggest that there is poor governance, as measured by a low sensitivity of turnover to performance and a low Q ratio, when (i) the controlling shareholders are also top executives, (ii) the control is fully in the hands of one shareholder and is not shared by a set of core shareholders, and (iii) the controlling shareholders own less than 50% of the firm's cash-flow rights.

1. INTRODUCTION

THE "LAW AND FINANCE" APPROACH, RECENTLY advocated by La Porta et al. (1998, 2000), emphasizes the important role of laws and institutions protecting investors for the development of a country. These authors argue that a firm's ability to raise external capital and grow is limited by the extent to which control can be effectively separated from ownership without increasing the risk that investors are expropriated by management. Better legal protection for investors reduces the risk of expropriation, allows more separation between ownership and control, and increases growth.

As shown in La Porta et al. (1999a), in several countries "plagued" by low investor protection some separation of ownership from control is obtained via pyramidal groups and nonvoting shares. On the one hand, these institutions preserve sufficiently high ownership concentration to help solve the managerial agency problem because controlling shareholders have the incentives and the power to discipline management. On the other hand, they create the conditions for a new agency problem because the interests of controlling and minority shareholders are not perfectly aligned. For instance, the controlling shareholders can expropriate minority ones via targeted issues and repurchases of securities, transfers of assets, entrenchment, and exploitation of a business relationship with affiliated companies through transfer pricing. Johnson et al. (2000) call this form of agency problem "tunneling".

From a theoretical point of view, Bebchuk (1999), Wolfenzon (1998), and Bebchuk et al. (1998) argue that the balance between the two forces (namely, the reduction in managerial discretion due to the presence of a controlling shareholder and the potential conflict of interest between controlling and minority shareholders) is likely resolved in favor of the second one, leading to a magnification rather than a reduction of the agency problem. This paper provides direct evidence on the potential costs of pyramidal groups and nonvoting shares by analyzing executive turnover and market valuation in Italian listed companies.

Italy represents an ideal setting to address these issues because it features weak legal protection of creditors and shareholders, inefficient law enforcement, high ownership concentration, and an abundance of pyramidal groups and nonvoting shares. There is suggestive evidence that the size of the private benefits of control is particularly large in Italy. Zingales (1994) finds an average voting premium of 82% in Italian companies with dual-class shares, while the average voting premium in the US is 10%, in the UK is 13%, in Canada 23%, and in Switzerland is 27%.

The existing literature indicates two strategies to assess the effectiveness of a corporate governance system. The first one, following Kaplan (1994a) and Coffee (1999), is to test whether executive turnover increases as a firm's performance declines. The second one, derived from Morck et al. (1988) and McConnell and Servaes (1990), is to analyze the firm's valuation in relation with similar companies.

Accordingly, this paper will first study the determinants of executive turnover in Italian publicly traded companies, by focusing on how the ownership and control structure of a firm affects the sensitivity of the firm's executive turnover to performance. Then, it will evaluate the effect of these same factors on the firm's Q ratio. Both analyses are based on a large data set, which covers all traded companies in Italy (banks and insurance companies excluded) during the period 1986–1997 and contains information on ownership, board, and capital structures. For all companies in the sample, I was able to trace back the control chain, identify the ultimate owner, and determine his ownership stake in the company, distinguishing between voting and cash flow rights (for an example of pyramid, see Figure 1).

The first finding in the analysis is that controlling shareholders are entrenched. Indeed, the probability of turnover and its sensitivity to performance are significantly lower for top executives who belong to the family of the controlling shareholder than for other executives. Second, the larger the fraction of cash-flow rights owned by the controlling shareholder, the more sensitive turnover is to performance. This result suggests that incentives matter and that governance improves when the controlling shareholder internalizes the consequences of his actions. The third finding is that turnover is more sensitive to performance when a voting syndicate controls the firm. A voting syndicate is a coalition of relevant shareholders who sign a binding agreement to vote together for a few years. About 15% of the companies in the sample have a voting syndicate. These coalitions help the largest shareholder to control a company when his stake would not be large enough to do so by himself. This result suggests that turnover becomes more sensitive to performance when control is, to some extent, contestable, as in the case of a voting syndicate.

These findings are confirmed by the analysis of the firm's Q ratio: Q is significantly smaller in firms where the controlling shareholders are among the top executives, is significantly larger when control is partially contestable as in the case of a voting syndicate controlling the firm, and increases with the fraction of cash-flow rights owned by the controlling shareholder.

Within pyramidal groups, I find a significant lower Q ratio (between 13% and 27%) in firms at the bottom of a pyramid. This result is consistent with the argument that pyramids increase agency problems by creating a wedge between voting and cash-flow rights. A possible explanation is that good managers are promoted to a higher layer of the pyramidal group against the interests of investors in the firms at the bottom of the pyramid. Indeed, the relationship between turnover and performance is weaker in pyramidal groups although the difference is not statistically significant.

Regarding the role of large minority shareholders, they do not seem to play an important monitoring role within the firm. Specifically, the results in this paper suggest that minority shareholders have a governance role only if their votes are necessary to the controlling shareholder to control the firm, as is the case in voting syndicates. Except for their role in a voting syndicate, large minority shareholders do not improve the firm governance since they do not increase the sensitivity of turnover to performance nor the firm's valuation.

Finally, turnover is much lower in the company at the top of a pyramid (6%) than in its subsidiaries (16%). This result may be explained by the fact that the controlling shareholders of the group sit as executives of their holding companies and they are entrenched in control. They do so because the benefits of control are larger in the holding company, as suggested by the finding that the voting premium in the holding companies is significantly higher than in the subsidiaries.

The structure of the paper is as follows. Section 2 formulates the hypothesis to test by overviewing the literature and describing the Italian corporate governance system. Section 3 describes the data set. Section 4 contains and discusses the results on the determinants of top executive turnover and firm valuation. Section 5 extends the analysis to pyramidal groups and evaluates the role of the market for corporate control. The conclusion is in Section 6.

2. EXISTING LITERATURE AND TESTABLE HYPOTHESES

Studying top executive turnover and the sensitivity of turnover to performance is one way to assess the quality of the corporate governance standards within a firm or within a country. The reason is, as argued by Coffee (1999), that successful governance systems penalize managers of firms with poor stock performance and with low cash flows. This statement is supported by large international evidence.[1]

Hence, the basic empirical hypothesis to be tested in this paper is the following.

Basic Hypothesis. Top executive turnover is negatively related to performance.

If the basic hypothesis is verified on the whole sample, the second step is to study whether there are significant differences across firms. An important factor that may affect turnover is the ownership structure of a firm.

Firms on the Italian stock market typically have a clearly identifiable controlling shareholder who controls at least 20% of the voting rights. Exceptions are banks and insurance companies. However, these are excluded from the sample because their accounting measures of performance are not directly comparable with the other firms.

Hence, Italian traded companies can be classified into four large categories according to their ultimate owner: the state, a foreign company, a set of banks, and one or more Italian individuals (I define this last category as family-controlled firms). One may expect to find differences across these groups in the sensitivity of turnover to performance. For example, in state-controlled companies management turnover can be more affected by political than economic factors. Therefore, I first check whether there are differences across these categories. However, in order to use a homogeneous and large set of observations, I focus the remainder of the analysis on the set of firms that are controlled by Italian individuals.

2.1. Ownership structure and executive turnover

Within family-controlled firms, there may be significant differences across firms depending on the relationship between the management and the controlling shareholder of the firm. Denis and Denis (1994) find that in the US, majority-owned firms experience significantly lower turnover for given performance than widely held ones. Also, they find that in majority-owned firms the controlling shareholder typically sits as top executive of the firm.

Consistent with the result above, Denis et al. (1997) show that the probability of top executive turnover (and the sensitivity of turnover to performance) is negatively correlated with the ownership stake held by officers. Most Italian traded companies are majority owned. Moreover, the size of the private benefits of control is extremely large in Italy, as shown by Zingales (1994). It is possible that the controlling shareholder is entrenched as a top executive against the interest of the other shareholders, in order to preserve his ability to extract those benefits. Hence, the first main hypothesis to test is the entrenchment hypothesis.

Entrenchment Hypothesis. Top executive turnover is lower and less sensitive to performance if the controlling shareholder is an executive.

In Italy, the separation between ownership and control is enhanced by the widespread use of traded pyramids and nonvoting shares. The sensitivity of turnover to performance can be proportionate to the fraction of cash-flow rights owned by the controlling shareholder. One immediate rationale for this hypothesis is that monitoring the management may come at a cost. Hence, the higher the fraction of cash-flow rights owned by the controlling shareholder, the larger the controlling shareholder's incentive to monitor the management.

Incentive Hypothesis. Top executive turnover is more sensitive to performance if the controlling shareholder owns a larger fraction of cash-flow rights.

In about 15% of Italian traded companies, a coalition of important shareholders helps the controlling party control the company. These shareholders are kept together by explicit agreements to vote together, which are called voting syndicates ("sindacati di voto"). These agreements are publicly announced on national newspapers, last for a fixed number of years (usually three) and can be renewed. A voting syndicate can decide on its actions either unanimously or by majority rule. According to law experts (see Galgano, 1997), these agreements are legally binding only in the former case. It is important to notice that the degree of entrenchment of the controlling shareholder could be much lower if he or she needs a voting syndicate to control the firm. With a voting syndicate, the controlling shareholder does not have a lock on control and control is partially contestable.

An example is given by the turnover in Olivetti in 1996 (*Il Sole 24 Ore*, September 4, 1996). Carlo De Benedetti, the long-time Chairman and President of the Board, was the relative majority shareholder in Olivetti with 15% of the voting rights. Thanks to a voting syndicate he controlled another 25% of the votes. In January 1996, after several years of very poor performance at Olivetti, the voting syndicate broke down, and in September of the same year De Benedetti was forced to step down from all executive roles in the company. This case suggests that executive turnover is more sensitive to performance if the controlling shareholder does not have absolute control over the company, that is, in the instances where there exists a voting syndicate. However, it is also conceivable that voting syndicates sustain collusive agreements among large families aiming at preserving the stability of control. In this second case, voting syndicates do not necessarily increase turnover or the sensitivity of turnover to performance.

Pagano and Roell (1998) argue from a theoretical viewpoint that large minority shareholders play a role in monitoring the controlling shareholder. For the US, Denis et al. (1997) show that the probability of top executive turnover is positively correlated to the presence of an outside blockholder.

Outside Monitoring Hypothesis. Top executive turnover is higher and more sensitive to performance in companies with a large minority shareholder and/or a voting syndicate.

An alternative way to test the quality of the corporate governance within a firm is to look at the valuation of the firm. For the US, Morck et al. (1988) and McConnell and Servaes (1990) find a nonlinear relationship between Q ratio and managerial ownership. A similar approach is employed also in Yermack (1996) and in La Porta et al. (1999b).

If the absence of sensitivity of turnover to performance is an indicator of bad governance, this should be reflected in the firm's valuation. Hence, I will test the following hypotheses on the Q ratio.

Entrenchment Hypothesis. Q is lower if the executives are controlling shareholders.

Incentive Hypothesis. Q is higher if the controlling shareholder owns a larger fraction of the cash-flow rights.

Outside Monitoring Hypothesis. Q is higher in firms where there are outside blockholders and/or a voting syndicate.

2.2. Pyramidal groups

The above hypotheses will be tested in Section 4 of this paper and will help characterize the relationship between executive turnover and ownership structure in Italian firms. However, as mentioned before, many firms in Italy (more than half of the firms traded on the Milan stock exchange) are organized in pyramidal groups. Pyramids of traded firms magnify the separation between ownership and control because they allow the controlling shareholder of the holding company at the top of the pyramid to control the companies in the pyramid by owning a small fraction of their capital. By the same token, they magnify the potential conflict of interest between controlling and minority shareholders. The impact of pyramidal groups on executive turnover and firm valuation is studied in Section 5.1.

2.3. Transfer of corporate control

Finally, the paper will try to evaluate the relative role of external and internal governance forces. Martin and McConnell (1991), for the US, and Franks and Mayer (1996), for the UK, find that turnover increases following takeovers. Barclay and Holderness (1991), for the US, and Franks et al. (2001), for the UK, find a similar increase in turnover following block trades.

Since Italian firms typically have a controlling shareholder, a sale of the controlling stake is a simple proxy for a change in the firm's ownership structure and should be associated with an increase in top executive turnover. However, since the sale can only happen with the consent of the controlling shareholder, control is not contestable, and takeovers in Italy can have a more limited disciplinary role than in the US or UK.

Gilson (1989), for the US, and Franks et al. (2001), for the UK, find that turnover is higher in firms at the onset of a financial crisis, when the firm's creditors increase their pressure on the management and seize control. Transfer of the control to creditors should then be associated with an increase in top executive turnover in the Italian sample.

The impact of transfers of control as a determinant of executive turnover will be evaluated in Section 5.2.

3. DESCRIPTION OF THE DATA SET

The sample is collected from several issues of "Il Taccuino dell'Azionista", an annual publication edited by Il Sole 24 Ore. This source provides basic balance sheet data, information about the ownership structure, and the names of the individuals sitting on the Board of Directors ("Consiglio di Amministrazione") of all companies traded on the Italian stock market. Data cover a period of 12 years, from 1986 to 1997. From the set of all companies traded on the Milan stock exchange over that period, I exclude banks, insurance companies, and foreign companies because of different accounting rules. Foreign companies are firms incorporated abroad, while foreign-controlled companies are firms incorporated in Italy even though owned by foreigners. The latter ones are included in the sample. I exclude all companies that were traded on the Milan stock exchange for less than three years because I need at least three years of data to compute the measures of performance and turnover.

Hence, the sample used in the regressions covers 205 firms and contains a total

Table 10.1 Descriptive statistics: sample of all firms traded on the Milan Stock Exchange

The table reports the number of observations, the mean, median, standard deviation, minimum, and maximum for some of the variables used in the analysis. *Top executive turnover* is a dummy variable that takes value 1 in year *t* if at least half of the top executives are replaced between *t* and *t* + 1. The sample includes all companies traded on the Milan Stock Exchange, excluding banks, insurance, and pure financial companies, in the years 1987 through 1996. The number of observations is 1,611.

Variable	Mean	Median	Std. Dev.	Min.	Max.
Ownership structure					
Fraction of cash-flow rights owned by controlling shareholder (%)	38.0	40.5	25.0	0.3	99.4
Fraction of voting rights controlled by controlling shareholder (%)	56.4	53.8	14.7	20.1	100
Board composition					
Number of directors	10.4	10	3.3	3	25
Number of top executives	3.34	3	0.68	1	6
Turnover data					
Fraction of top executives replaced in a year (%)	16.9	0	25.3	0	100
Top executive turnover	0.14	0	0.35	0	1

of 1,611 observations. Table 10.1 reports summary statistics on ownership structure, board composition, and executive turnover for this sample. All variables used in the analysis are defined in Appendix A.

Italian law limits the extent of cross-holdings to 2% of voting rights among traded companies. Moreover, controlled firms cannot exercise the voting rights eventually owned in their parent company. Hence, it is simple to identify the control chain once ownership data are available for all companies. An example of a common control structure is represented in Figure 10.1. The figure shows the structure of the Pesenti group at the end of 1995. The Pesenti family is defined as the controlling shareholder because an individual, Rosalia Radici Pesenti, owns the controlling stake in the holding company (44.87%).

The observations have been classified into four categories according to the information available on the controlling shareholder. A firm is classified as foreign-controlled in a given year if the ultimate owner is a foreign company (106 observations); and is defined as state-controlled if the ultimate owner is the state or a government agency (216 observations). In 55 observations the controlling party is a group of banks, since the company defaulted and the banks took control. The rest of the observations (1,234) have one or more private Italian citizens or an Italian family as the ultimate owner (I will call this last set family-controlled firms).

In Table 10.1, two variables describe the firm ownership structure. *The fraction of cash-flow rights owned by the largest shareholder* is defined as the product of the fraction of voting rights along the controlling path. This number is corrected for nonvoting shares by assuming that the ultimate owner owns none of them. For example in Figure. 10.1, the fraction of cash-flow rights owned by the Pesenti family in Italmobiliare is 29.4%, while the fraction of voting rights is 44.8% because about a third of Italmobiliare's equity is made up of nonvoting shares. The fraction of cash-flow rights owned by the Pesenti family in Italcementi is 9.5%, which is the product of 29.4% (the fraction of cash-flow rights directly owned by the family in the holding company

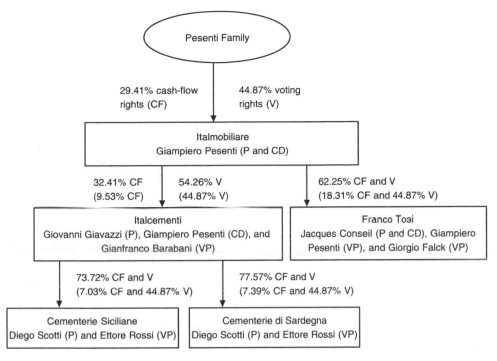

Figure 10.1 Structure of the Pesenti's group as of 12/31/1995. The figure shows the ownership and control structure of the traded companies controlled by the Pesenti family. Each box represents a traded company. Inside each box are the name of the company and the names of the top executives with their role on the board of directors: P = President, CD = CEO ("Consigliere Delegato"), VP = Vice-President. The arrow indicates the direction of control. The numbers above each box represent the percentages of cash-flow (CF) and voting (V) rights directly owned by the controlling party (individual or company). In parenthesis are the fractions of cash-flow and voting rights directly or indirectly owned by the ultimate owner (the Pesenti family). These are computed according to the definitions reported in Appendix A.

Italmobiliare) and 32.4% (the fraction of cash-flow rights owned by Italmobiliare in Italcementi). *The fraction of voting rights controlled by the controlling shareholder* is computed as the minimum share of voting rights controlled by the controlling shareholder along the control path.

The rationale for this definition is explained as follows with the help of Figure 10.1. Let us consider the second layer firm Italcementi and try to evaluate the voting rights of the Pesenti family in this company. The Pesenti family controls Italcementi through the holding company Italmobiliare. In order to exercise the voting rights that Italmobiliare owns in Italcementi, the Pesenti family needs to

exercise its voting rights on Italmobiliare. This represents the burden of having an extra layer of control. Even if Italmobiliare owns 54.26% of the voting rights in Italcementi, the Pesenti family owns only 44.87% of the voting rights in Italmobiliare. Hence, the effective voting power of the Pesenti family in Italcementi is equal to 44.87%. The logic of this example simply generalizes to more complex control structures. In the case of a syndicate among shareholders, the controlling party is assumed to control all the voting rights that belong to the syndicate.

As measure of executive turnover, I use the fraction of top executives replaced within a year. This is preferable to the CEO turnover because in Italian firms all top executives (*Presidente, Vice-Presidente, and Amministratore delegato*) have similar executive power and there is no clear ranking in authority among them (especially between *Presidente and Amministratore delegato*). Also, some firms do not have a CEO; others have many CEOs. The data have been cleaned of the cases of retirement identifiable through LEXIS-NEXIS (42 observations are relabeled as non-turnover in this way). However, Italian companies do not provide information about the age and tenure of their executives in the annual report. Since I was able to collect data on age and tenure for only a subset of the executives, I exclude these two variables from the regressions.[2] In order to reduce the biases due to potential mislabeling of individual cases of turnover, in the regressions I use as dependent variable a dummy variable (*Top executive turnover*) that takes value one in year t when at least half of the top executives are replaced between t and $t + 1$.

Two alternative measures of performance are used in the analysis: the change in the ratio of earnings before interest and taxes (EBIT) and total assets between $t - 1$ and t and the annual stock return between $t - 1$ and t. The former is the measure of performance used in Denis and Kruse (2000). The latter one, the stock return, is the standard measure of performance used in studies of executive turnover since the contributions by Warner et al. (1988) and Weisbach (1988). In unreported regressions I performed the analysis with the addition of lagged measures of performance without finding any difference.

As illustrated in Table 10.1, all companies in the sample have a controlling shareholder, that is a shareholder who controls a fraction of voting rights larger than 20%. The fraction of voting rights held by the controlling shareholder is on average 56%, while it ranges between 20.1% and 100%. There is a large variability in the fraction of cash-flow rights owned by the controlling shareholder. The average is 40%, while the minimum is 0.3% and the maximum

99.4%. Disciplinary turnover (measured as top executive turnover) happens in 14% of the observations. The median number of top executives in the sample is three, while the median size of the board is ten directors.

4. EMPIRICAL ANALYSIS

In this section, I will test each of the hypotheses discussed in Section 2, starting with the relationship between turnover and performance in the whole sample.

4.1. Turnover and performance

In Table 10.2, the observations are classified according to the ultimate owner in family-, state-, foreign-, and bank-controlled firms. The table shows that turnover is negatively related to performance in the sample as a whole. More precisely, the observations are sorted into quintiles according to the firm's past performance. I then compare turnover between the worst quintile and the best one. In Panel A, performance is proxied by the change in the ratio of EBIT over assets, while in Panel B is measured by the stock return.

In the whole sample, the probability of top executive turnover is significantly lower if performance is good than if is bad. In Panel A, the average turnover increases from 14.5% in best performing firms to 22.5% in worst performing ones. Similarly, in Panel B, turnover increases from 14.5% in best performing firms to 19.3% in worst performing ones. In Panel A, the average turnover decreases monotonically as performance improves across quintiles with the significant jump being the one between the first and second quintiles. In Panel B, the average turnover is not monotonic and the third and fourth quintiles are not significantly different from the first one, as far as turnover is concerned.

When examining turnover across types of ultimate owner, one finds a negative and significant relationship between turnover and performance according to either performance measure only for family-controlled firms. It is interesting to notice that in

Table 10.2 Turnover and performance: family-, state-, foreign-, and bank-controlled firms

The table reports the average fraction of top executives replaced by quintiles of performance. The observations are sorted in five classes according to their past performance (1 = low, 2–5 = high). The average turnover is compared between the firms with low performance and those with high performance using a two-tailed *t*-test. The observations are also classified according to the type of ultimate owner (a family, the state, a foreign company, a bank).

Average fraction of top executives replaced	1 = Low performance	2	3	4	5 = High performance	Test: (1) = (5)
Panel A: Observations are sorted according to change in EBIT/total assets						
All firms	22.5	16.6	15.4	15.3	14.5	***
	[323]	[322]	[322]	[322]	[322]	
Family-controlled firms	21.6	13.5	13.5	13.9	12.6	***
	[259]	[250]	[222]	[243]	[260]	
State-controlled firms	34.6	34.1	19.8	17.2	22.4	0
	[26]	[46]	[74]	[44]	[26]	
Foreign-controlled firms	20.0	14.9	20.6	22.3	19.9	0
	[30]	[14]	[17]	[22]	[23]	
Bank-controlled firms	21.9	18.1	16.7	23.1	28.2	0
	[8]	[12]	[9]	[13]	[13]	
Panel B: Observations are sorted according to stock return						
All firms	19.3	15.3	18.0	17.6	14.4	**
	[320]	[320]	[319]	[320]	[319]	
Family-controlled firms	19.1	13.7	15.2	15.4	12.0	***
	[238]	[245]	[246]	[254]	[239]	
State-controlled firms	22.9	21.4	31.5	22.4	22.0	0
	[35]	[37]	[54]	[42]	[47]	
Foreign-controlled firms	19.6	16.3	13.9	31.9	17.6	0
	[28]	[21]	[12]	[18]	[25]	
Bank-controlled firms	14.0	23.0	17.9	33.3	37.5	**
	[19]	[17]	[7]	[6]	[8]	

*, **, and *** denote significance at the 10%, 5%, and 1% level, respectively. Zero denotes no significant difference. In the first panel performance is measured by the change in EBIT/total assets between $t - 1$ and t; in the second panel performance is measured by the excess stock return between $t - 1$ and t.

bank-controlled firms turnover is significantly higher after a good performance than otherwise (when stock return is the measure of performance). This result can be explained by noticing that bank-controlled firms are firms that recently defaulted. For troubled companies, the replacement of the management could be a positive signal that liquidation can be avoided and the firm can emerge from reorganization (see, e.g., Gilson et al., 1990).

Table 10.3 presents the results of two regressions that characterize the relationship between turnover and performance after controlling for year and industry dummies and firm size. Interactive dummies allow for different coefficients across the types of ultimate ownership. In family-controlled firms, the relationship between turnover and performance is strongly significant and negative. For the remaining firms, the results in Table 10.2 are confirmed, although in a weaker sense. While the relationship between turnover and performance is weak in all but family-controlled firms, the regression fails to find significant differences across ultimate owners. The only exception is the case of bank-controlled firms for which the sensitivity of turnover to performance is significantly different from family-controlled firms when performance is proxied by the stock return.

In Table 10.3, the coefficients of the probit model are transformed to simplify their

Table 10.3 Turnover and performance: regression analysis of the whole sample

Probit regressions. The dependent variable (*Top executive turnover*) is a dummy variable that takes value 1 in year t if at least half of the top executives are replaced between t and $t + 1$. *Size* is the logarithm of total assets (in millions of Liras). *Performance* is the change in the ratio of EBIT and total assets between year $t − 1$ and year t in regression (1) and the stock return between $t − 1$ and t in regression (2). Robust standard errors (in parentheses) control for correlation and clustering at firm level. Year and industry dummies are included but their coefficients are not reported.

	Performance = change in EBIT/TA (1)	Performance = stock return (2)
Performance	−0.646***	−0.063**
	(0.188)	(0.026)
Performance ∗ State ownership dummy	−0.158	0.008
	(0.467)	(0.070)
Performance ∗ Foreign ownership dummy	0.447	0.055
	(0.422)	(0.058)
Performance ∗ Bank ownership dummy	0.834*	0.394***
	(0.481)	(0.153)
State ownership dummy	0.098***	0.103***
	(0.034)	(0.034)
Foreign ownership dummy	0.038	0.034
	(0.040)	(0.040)
Bank ownership dummy	0.010	0.051
	(0.038)	(0.054)
Size	−0.002	−0.004
	(0.008)	(0.006)
Pseudo R^2	0.050	0.044
No. of observations	1,611	1,598

*, **, and *** denote significance at the 10%, 5%, and 1% level, respectively. The reported coefficients are transformed to represent the change in probability for an infinitesimal change in each independent variable evaluated at the mean values.

economic interpretation. The reported coefficients represent the change in probability for an infinitesimal change in each independent variable evaluated at the mean values of the regressors. All probit regressions throughout the paper will be reported with this transformation. Hence, in Table 10.3 the coefficient on the independent variable "Performance" in regression (1) indicates that a decrease in earnings over assets by 10% (or 0.1) increases the probability of turnover in an average firm by 6.5%. The sensitivity of turnover to performance is much weaker in regression (2): a past stock return equal to −10% increases turnover only by 0.6%.

In the rest of the paper I restrict the analysis to the set of family-controlled firms in order to study a large and homogeneous sample.

4.2. Turnover and control

Table 10.4 evaluates the impact of the separation of ownership and control on turnover. For these purposes, I have created four dummy variables.

The first one (*owner-manager*) identifies the cases in which a member of the family of the controlling shareholder sits as top executive of the firm. I classify the top executives depending on whether they belong to the family of the controlling shareholder. To do so, I searched all available sources for each executive in the sample to find his/her relationship with the controlling shareholder. For example, in Figure 10.1, only one of the Pesenti's executives belongs to the Pesenti family: Giampiero Pesenti, son of the controlling shareholder, Rosalia Radici Pesenti. To be

Table 10.4 Turnover and performance in family-controlled firms

Probit regressions. The dependent variable (*Top executive turnover*) is a dummy variable that takes value 1 in year t if at least half of the top executives are replaced between t and $t + 1$. *Size* is the logarithm of total assets (in millions of Liras). *Performance* is the change in the ratio of EBIT and total assets between year $t - 1$ and year t in regressions (1) and (2), and the stock return between $t - 1$ and t in regressions (3) and (4). *Owner-manager* is a dummy variable that identifies the cases when at least half of the top executives belong to the family of the controlling shareholder. *Owner with high incentives* is a dummy variable that identifies the cases when the controlling shareholder owns more than 50% of the cash-flow rights. *Voting syndicate* is a dummy variable that takes value 1 when the firm is controlled by a voting syndicate. *Large minority shareholders* is a dummy variable that takes value 1 when the second largest shareholder owns a fraction larger than 5% of the firm's voting rights. Robust standard errors (in parentheses) control for correlation and clustering at firm level. Year and industry dummies are included but the coefficients are not reported.

	Performance 5 change in EBIT/TA		Performance 5 stock return	
	(1)	(2)	(3)	(4)
Performance	-0.581^{***}	-0.283	-0.107^{***}	-0.097^{***}
	(0.211)	(0.201)	(0.032)	(0.032)
Performance * Owner-manager dummy	0.387	0.279	-0.011	-0.007
	(0.395)	(0.413)	(0.058)	(0.058)
Performance * Owner with high incentives dummy	-0.505^{*}	-0.702^{**}	0.059	0.051
	(0.280)	(0.295)	(0.044)	(0.045)
Performance * Large minority shareholders dummy	0.136		0.003	
	(0.361)		(0.055)	
Performance * Voting syndicate dummy		-0.741^{**}		-0.062
		(0.357)		(0.060)
Owner-manager dummy	-0.065^{***}	-0.065^{***}	-0.069^{***}	-0.069^{***}
	(0.018)	(0.019)	(0.018)	(0.018)
Owner with high incentives dummy	-0.002	-0.000	0.013	0.012
	(0.019)	(0.021)	(0.021)	(0.021)
Large minority shareholders dummy	-0.018		-0.019	
	(0.020)		(0.019)	
Voting syndicate dummy		-0.028		-0.012
		(0.024)		(0.028)
Size	-0.008	-0.007	-0.010	-0.009
	(0.007)	(0.007)	(0.007)	(0.007)
Pseudo R^2	0.071	0.074	0.056	0.056
No. of observations	1,234	1,234	1,222	1,222

*, **, and *** denote significance at the 10%, 5%, and 1% level, respectively. The reported coefficients are transformed to represent the change in probability for an infinitesimal change in each independent variable evaluated at the mean values.

consistent with the definition of turnover, the *owner-manager* dummy variable is set equal to one when at least half of the top executives belong to the family of the controlling shareholder. This happens in about 30% of the observations. The purpose of this first dummy variable is to address the Entrenchment Hypothesis described in Section 2.

The second dummy variable (*owner with high incentives*) identifies the companies in which the controlling shareholder owns a large fraction of the cash-flow rights. More specifically, I define as such all companies in which the controlling shareholder owns more than 50% of the cash-flow rights, a requirement that roughly selects 30% of the observations. The purpose of this second dummy variable is to address the Incentive Hypothesis.

According to the Outside Monitoring Hypothesis discussed in Section 2, turnover should be more sensitive to performance when the company has large minority shareholders. The intuition is that large minority shareholders can play an active role in corporate governance. This hypothesis is tested in Table 10.4 by using two alternative proxies for minority share-holders. The first is an indicator of whether the second largest shareholder owns a fraction larger than 5% of the voting rights (*large minority shareholder*). This happens in about 40% of the observations. The second one identifies cases where the firm is controlled by a voting syndicate, as happens in 15% of the observations (*voting syndicate*).

The methodology I use to address the hypotheses above is to run a probit regression with the dummies just described entering both additively and in interaction with the measure of performance. Eq. (1) describes the probit model estimated in Table 10.4:

$$Pr(Turover_{it} = 1) = \Phi(\alpha_t + \beta_0\, Performance_{it}$$
$$+ \sum_{j=1}^{4} (\beta_j\, Performance_{it}$$
$$+ \gamma_j) D_{it}^j + \delta\, Size_{it}$$
$$+ \Phi\, Industury\, dummy_{it}$$
$$+ \varepsilon_{it}), \qquad (1)$$

where $\Phi(.)$ is the cumulative gaussian distribution, α_t is the year dummy, and firm's size and an industry dummy (firms are classified in nine industries according to the official classification on the Milan stock exchange) are introduced as control variables.[3]

In the regression, I cannot control for firm effects, as with traditional linear models, because a fixed-effect estimator is not available in a probit model. Since the obser-vations are likely not to be independent, the standard errors are corrected for correlation and clustering at the firm level. In an unreported regression, I estimated a linear OLS model with fixed effects at firm level, finding similar results to the ones reported.

The results in Table 10.4 are as follows. Regressions (1) and (2) show that turnover does not always decrease with performance when the latter is proxied by the change in earnings. Specifically, in regression (1), a 10% decrease in earnings over assets increases the probability of executive turnover by 5.8%. However, in regression (2), the increase in the probability of exec-utive turnover for a similar change is only 2.8% and is not statistically significant.

When the controlling shareholder sits as top executive of the firm, the relationship between turnover and performance becomes even weaker, as shown by the pos-itive (although not significant) coefficient on the first interactive term. The level of turnover is also significantly lower when a member of the family of the controlling shareholder sits among the top executives. The probability of executive turnover decreases with 6.5% when the controlling shareholder is a top executive. These results are weakly in favor of the Entrenchment Hypothesis.

The first two regressions also show that the sensitivity of turnover to performance increases significantly when the controlling shareholder owns a large stake in the firm. If the largest shareholder owns more than 50% of the cash-flow rights, a 10% decrease in earnings over assets increases turnover by 10%. This result is in favor of the Incentive Hypothesis.

Regarding the Outside Monitoring Hypothesis, regression (1) suggests that the presence of a large minority share-holder does not increase the sensitivity of turnover to performance. However, regres-sion (2) shows that a voting syndicate does indeed increase the sensitivity of turnover to performance. After a 10% decrease in earnings, executive turnover is 7% more likely if the firm is controlled via a voting syndicate than otherwise. The intuitive explanation for these results is that minority shareholders have the power to play a governance role (and they do so) only when control is not locked in the hands of the controlling shareholder. That is, only if the controlling shareholder needs a voting syndicate to control the firm.

Regressions (3) and (4), in which performance is proxied by the stock return, do not produce any significant coefficient on the interactive terms. The signs on the coefficients are consistent with the Outside Monitoring Hypotheses, but against the Entrenchment and the Incentive Hypothesis. The results in these two regressions can be explained by the fact that the stock return is not likely an ideal measure of performance in the sample of Italian firms. The stock return is a noisy measure of performance for many companies in the sample because many stocks suffer a lack of liquidity and infrequent trades.

4.3. Valuation

An alternative procedure to assess the efficiency of a governance regime is to evaluate the impact of ownership structure on firm valuation, as done by Morck et al. (1988) and McConnell and Servaes (1990). This analysis is performed in Table 10.5. The results of four fixed-effect regressions are represented in the table: regressions (1) and (2) include firm effects; regressions (3) and (4) include only industry effects but report standard errors corrected for clustering at the firm level. The rationale to present the second pair of regression together with the first one is that controlling for firm effects, as in (1) or (2), may reduce the significance of the coefficients because it eliminates most of the variability in the firm ownership structure, which is relatively constant across years. As done in Table 10.4, in regressions (1) and (3) the power of minority shareholders is measured by the dummy variable *large minority shareholders;* in regressions (2) and (4) minority shareholders' power is proxied by the dummy variable *voting syndicate.*

Table 10.5 Analysis of the firm's Q ratio

The dependent variable is the firm's Q ratio. *Size* is the logarithm of total assets (in millions of Liras). *Owner-manager* is a dummy variable that identifies the cases when at least half of the top executives belong to the family of the controlling shareholder. *Owner with high incentives* is a dummy variable that identifies the cases when the controlling shareholder owns more than 50% of the cash-flow rights. *Voting syndicate* is a dummy variable that takes value 1 when the firm is controlled by a voting syndicate. *Large minority shareholders* is a dummy variable that takes value 1 when the second largest shareholder owns a fraction larger than 5% of the firm's voting rights. Robust standard errors (in parentheses) control for correlation and heteroskedasticity. Year dummies are included but the coefficients are not reported.

	(1)	(2)	(3)	(4)
Owner-manager dummy	−0.067*	−0.116***	−0.092***	−0.083***
	(0.036)	(0.044)	(0.027)	(0.028)
Large minority shareholders dummy	−0.072		0.000	
	(0.048)		(0.027)	
Voting syndicate dummy		−0.400***		−0.141*
		(0.117)		(0.083)
Owner with high incentives dummy	0.026	0.080*	0.015	−0.006
	(0.052)	(0.048)	(0.031)	(0.032)
Size	−0.059**	−0.068***	−0.092***	−0.092***
	(0.025)	(0.024)	(0.027)	(0.027)
Fixed effects	Industry	Industry	Firm	Firm
Adjusted R^2	0.199	0.273	0.654	0.656
No. of observations	1,234	1,234	1,234	1,234

*, **, and *** denote significance at the 10%, 5%, and 1% level, respectively.

The results on Q match one-to-one those obtained in the analysis of turnover: firms where turnover is unaffected by performance are discounted by the market. Indeed, Table 10.5 shows that Q is significantly smaller (between 8% and 11% discount) for firms in which relatives of the controlling shareholder are among the top executives. This is consistent with the results in Table 10.4 and with the Entrenchment Hypothesis. Table 10.5 also shows that Q is significantly larger when control is partially contestable as in the case in which a voting syndicate controls the firm (between 14% and 40% premium). This result is consistent with the findings in Table 10.4 and with the Outside Monitoring Hypothesis. Finally, the table shows that Q increases only weakly with the fraction of cash-flow rights owned by the controlling shareholder: if the controlling shareholder owns more than 50% of the cash-flow rights, the firms trades at a premium estimated between 0% and 8%. This final result supports the Incentive Hypothesis. Consistent with the finding in Table 10.4, the dummy for large minority shareholder does not affect the Q ratio, as shown by regressions (1) and (3) of Table 10.5.

4.4. More on the Entrenchment Hypothesis

An alternative test of the Entrenchment Hypothesis is to measure directly the probability of turnover and its sensitivity to performance (for executives who belong to the family of the controlling shareholder and those who do not), and compare them. This is done in Table 10.6.

The executives in the sample are classified into two groups: *family-executives* (that is, firm's executives who belong to the family of the controlling shareholder of the firm) and *other executives* (that is, executives who do not belong to the family of the controlling shareholder). For each group, year, and company, I compute the fraction of executives replaced in one year. The average turnover is reported in the third column of Table 10.6, Panel A, which states

that turnover is significantly higher for other managers (18.4%) than for owner-managers (6.5%). Similarly, the sensitivity of turnover to past performance is significantly higher for other managers than for owner-managers. In Panel B, the turnover of family and non-family executives is compared by running a regression on both sets of data with a dummy variable (entering both additively and in interaction with performance) identifying whether the data on turnover refers to family or other executives. The findings are that both the level of turnover and its sensitivity to performance is significantly lower for family managers. In regression (1), a 10% decrease in earnings over assets implies a 6% increase in the probability of turnover for a non-family executive and only a 2% increase for a family executive. In regression (2), a realization of the stock return equal to -10% causes the probability of turnover to increase by 0.6% for non-family managers and only by 0.3% for family ones. These results suggest that, when a company is in trouble, non-family managers are likely to be replaced, but family managers are likely to stay, that is, family managers are entrenched.

4.5. International comparison

This section compares the findings on Italy with evidence available on other countries. Few studies have produced results that are directly comparable across countries because of differences in the econometric procedures and in the performance and turnover measures used. A partially comparable set of coefficients can be obtained from Kaplan (1994a, b) for Germany, Japan, and the US. In Table 10.7, I reproduce the results in these two papers and add comparable results obtained from the sample of (family-owned) Italian firms.

The coefficients on Germany are extracted from Kaplan (1994b), Table 10.2. The measure of turnover is the fraction of members of the management board replaced in one year. Similarly, turnover in the Italian sample is measured by the fraction of top executive replaced in one year.

Table 10.6 Family executives versus other executives

Panel A reports the average turnover and the sensitivity of turnover to performance for owner-managers (executives who belong to the family of the controlling shareholder) and other managers. Standard deviations are in parentheses. Performance is measured by the change in EBIT/total assets and by the stock return. Panel B presents the result of an OLS regression with the fraction of executives replaced in a year as dependent variable. Size is the logarithm of total assets (in millions of Liras). *Family-executive* is a dummy variable that identifies the executives belonging to the family of the controlling shareholder. Robust standard errors (in parentheses) control for correlation and clustering at firm level. Year and industry dummies are included but the coefficients are not reported.

Panel A: Descriptive statistics

	Number of observations	Average turnover (%)	Correlation between turnover and performance	
			Change in EBIT	stock return
Family-executives	805	6.5 (23.4)	20.061[*]	20.015
Other executives	1,184	18.4 (29.6)	20.119[***]	20.053[*]

Panel B: Regression analysis

	Performance = change in EBIT/TA (1)	Performance = stock return (2)
Performance	−0.572[***] (0.174)	−0.060[***] (0.021)
Performance * Family executive dummy	0.316[*] (0.171)	0.033[*] (0.020)
Family executive dummy	−0.112[***] (0.011)	−0.111[***] (0.012)
Size	−0.007 (0.006)	−0.009 (0.006)
Adjusted R^2	0.060	0.051
No. of observations	1,989	1,977

[*], [**], and [***] denote significance at the 10%, 5%, and 1% level, respectively.

The results on Japan and US are from Kaplan (1994a), Table 10.2, where turnover is measured over a two-year period and refers to representative directors in Japan and executive directors in the US. Due to the difference in the time horizon of the two turnover measures, the results are only partially comparable. Indeed, both turnover and performance are computed over a two-year period for Japan and the US, and over a one-year period for Germany and Italy.

The results in Table 10.7 show that turnover is correlated with performance in Italy as much as in the other countries. This finding holds across all performance measures. Also, the magnitude of the coefficients is not significantly different across countries. However, in the Italian sample performance explains a much smaller fraction of the variability in turnover than in Germany, Japan and US. The R^2 ranges between 2% and 4% in Italy, between 12% and 15% in Japan and the US, and between 5% and 10% in Germany. This suggests that, with respect of the other countries, executive turnover in Italy is

Table 10.7 International comparison

OLS regressions. The dependent variable is the fraction of top executives replaced in a year for Italy and the fraction of members of the management board replaced for Germany. For Japan the dependent variable is the fraction of representative directors replaced in a two-year period and for the US the fraction of executive directors replaced over the same horizon. Stock returns, sales growth, earnings growth, and negative net income dummies are used as performance measures. A separate regression is run for each performance measure where the latter enters contemporaneously and once lagged. For Italy and Germany, one lag is one year; for Japan and the US, one lag is two years. In Panel D for Japan and US, the regression does not contain the lagged negative income dummy. Robust standard errors are in parentheses. Year dummies are included but the coefficients are not reported.

	Italy	*Germany*	*Japan*	*US*
A. Stock return				
Contemporaneous	−0.034	−0.080*	−0.056	−0.072**
	(0.026)	(0.046)	(0.038)	(0.029)
Once lagged	−0.043**	−0.103**	−0.100***	−0.081***
	(0.022)	(0.046)	(0.037)	(0.030)
R^2	0.020	0.102	0.139	0.148
B. Sales growth				
Contemporaneous	−0.063***	−0.066	−0.177**	−0.171***
	(0.015)	(0.083)	(0.076)	(0.083)
Once lagged	−0.064**	0.057	−0.064	0.031
	(0.022)	(0.086)	(0.076)	(0.050)
R^2	0.040	0.054	0.133	0.150
C. Change in earnings/assets				
Contemporaneous	−0.160	0.494	−0.121	−0.208
	(0.197)	(0.376)	(0.460)	(0.147)
Once lagged	−0.636***	0.205	−0.707*	−0.219
	(0.173)	(0.485)	(0.447)	(0.152)
R^2	0.030	0.058	0.127	0.130
D. Negative net income				
Contemporaneous	−0.035*	0.095***	0.148***	0.074***
	(0.020)	(0.034)	(0.035)	(0.028)
Once lagged	0.066***	−0.042		
	(0.022)	(0.028)		
R^2	0.026	0.059	0.155	0.137
Mean dependent variable	0.152	0.099	0.285	0.234

*, **, and *** denote significance at the 10%, 5%, and 1% level, respectively. The results on Germany are from Kaplan (1994b, Table 2, p. 150); the results for Japan and the US are from Kaplan (1994a, Table 2, pp. 526–527).

explained by other factors than performance, such as ownership and control structure, personal relationships, family ties, and nonobservable performance measures.

5. EXTENSIONS

So far, the paper has evaluated the impact of the firm's ownership structure on top executive turnover. This section considers two extensions. First, more than half of the companies traded on the Milan stock exchange belong to pyramidal groups. It is interesting to see whether the pyramidal structure affects the dynamics of the executive turnover in specific ways not captured by the analysis in Section 4. The second extension explores whether the sensitivity of turnover to performance is due to internal or external governance forces.

5.1. Turnover in pyramidal groups

This section evaluates the impact on turnover and valuation of the firm organizational structure distinguishing between stand-alone firms and companies that belong to pyramidal groups.

Table 10.8 provides detailed information on the organizational structure of family-controlled firms. The observations are divided into four categories: (1) stand-alone firms and firms that belong to horizontal groups (that is, firms that are not controlled by any other traded company and do not own a controlling stake in any other traded company); (2) firms that are at the top of a pyramidal group (that is, firms that are not controlled by any other traded company and do control at least one other traded company); (3) firms that are at level 2 of a pyramidal group (that is, firms that are directly controlled by a company of type 2); and (4) firms that are at level 3 or higher of a pyramidal group (that is, firms that are controlled directly or indirectly by a company of type 3). The table presents the mean of a selection of variables conditional on the type of ownership structure.

About 55% of the observations in the sample come from pyramidal groups. The remaining firms in the sample belong to horizontal groups (42 observations only) or are stand-alone firms (all the rest). The first impact of the pyramidal structure is to create a wedge between the fraction of cash-flow and voting rights owned by the controlling shareholder. As shown in Table 10.8, the separation of voting and cash flow rights (as measured by the ratio of voting to cash-flow rights) increases from 1.4 at the top of the pyramid to seven at the bottom of it. The difference between voting and cash-flow rights in categories (1) and (2) is due to nonvoting shares (*azioni di risparmio*) and voting syndicates.

Table 10.8 Separation of ownership from control in family-controlled firms

The table reports conditional means. The observations are classified into four categories according to the structure of control. The first category comprises stand-alone firms and firms that belong to horizontal groups, the other three categories are for firms that belong to vertical (or pyramidal) groups. Companies belonging to pyramidal groups are divided in three groups depending on their position in the pyramid. Level 1 are the holding companies, Level 2 are the companies controlled by Level 1 firms, and Level 3 and higher are all the others. *Top executive turnover* is a dummy variable that takes value 1 in year t if at least half of the top executives are replaced between t and $t + 1$. *Modified top executive* turnover is a dummy variable that takes value 1 in year t if at least half of the top executives are replaced between t and $t + 1$ and leave all traded companies of the group to which the firm belongs.

	Horizontal groups and stand alone	Pyramidal group: Level 1	Pyramidal group: Level 2	Pyramidal group: Level 3+
Number of observations	541	173	243	277
Fraction of cash-flow rights owned by controlling shareholder (%)	49.4	42.2	22.5	6.0
Fraction of voting rights controlled by controlling shareholder (%)	58.2	59.8	52.5	42.6
Percentage of relatives of the controlling shareholder among the top executives (%)	38.2	50.1	26.6	7.4
Top executive turnover (%)	12.0	5.8	14.0	15.5
Modified top executive turnover (%)	7.9	4.0	9.5	10.1
Q ratio	1.13	1.01	1.09	1.00
Voting premium (%)	77.2	70.2	59.5	32.5
[Number of observations]	[184]	[118]	[108]	[127]

Regarding the top executives, turnover is significantly lower at the top of pyramidal groups than in all other firms. At the top of a pyramid, the probability that at least half of the executives are replaced in one year is less than 6%. This suggests the possibility of entrenchment. Moreover, the table shows that members of the family of the controlling shareholder are more likely to sit as top executives in firms at the top of a pyramid. Turnover at the bottom of a pyramid is significantly higher (about 16%) than at the top. One possible explanation is that the management of subsidiaries is replaced after good performance and promoted to higher layers of the pyramidal group. In order to address this concern, I relabeled as nonturnover all cases in which an executive leaves a company to move to another traded company within the same group. I will refer to this variable as *modified top executive turnover*. Table 10.8 suggests that turnover according to this measure is significantly lower. Hence, I find some support of the hypothesis that the higher turnover at the bottom of the pyramid is due to the dynamics in the internal managerial market in that well-performing managers are promoted to higher level of the pyramid while poor-performing ones are replaced. In the internal managerial market, the firms at the bottom of the pyramid work as a screening device for managers. They help the controlling shareholder select the best managers and discard the bad ones. An important caveat of this result is that I cannot control for cases in which the manager moves to a privately held company that belongs to a group, because I do not have data on nonlisted firms.

Table 10.8 also reports the average Q ratio for each type of ownership structure. Q is significantly lower at the bottom and at the top of pyramidal groups than in stand-alone firms. Interestingly, the Q ratio does not decrease monotonically as one proceeds down the pyramid. On the other hand, the voting premium is higher at the top than at lower layers of the pyramid (as also shown by Nicodano, 1998). This suggests that the reason why controlling shareholders entrench themselves as executives of the holding companies is to enjoy higher private benefits of control.

Each of the hypotheses suggested by the discussion of Table 10.8 is addressed more carefully in Tables 10.9 and 10.10. Table 10.9 tests whether turnover follows different dynamics in firms that belong to pyramidal groups than in stand-alone ones. Table 10.10 does the same for the Q ratio.

The regressions reported in Table 10.9 show that the sensitivity of turnover to performance is not significantly different in pyramidal groups and in stand-alone firms. This result holds independently of the measure of performance (change in earnings or stock return) and turnover (top executive turnover or modified top executive turnover) used. When looking at the sensitivity of turnover to performance within pyramids (by testing the hypothesis that the sum of the coefficients on the regressors *Performance* and *Performance * Pyramidal level* is equal to zero), turnover is unaffected by performance at the top of a pyramid and at the bottom of it, when the accounting measure of performance (change in EBIT) is used.

The weak results found in Table 10.9 suggest that the firm's organizational structure does not affect the sensitivity of turnover to performance directly. As shown in Section 4, the latter is affected directly by the firm ownership and control structure as measured by the fraction of cash-flow rights owned by the controlling shareholder, by the presence of a voting syndicate, and by whether the controlling shareholder is also a top executive in the firm. In an unreported regression, I added these three indicators to the regressions presented in Table 10.9. The result is that the coefficients on the variables describing the organizational structure (namely, the pyramidal level) are not significant, while those capturing directly the firm's ownership and control structure are.

Table 10.10 shows that there is a significant discount (between 13% and 27%)

Table 10.9 Executive turnover and pyramidal groups

Probit regressions. The dependent variable is *Top executive turnover* in regressions (1) and (2) and *modified top executive turnover in regressions* (3) and (4). *Size* is the logarithm of total assets (in millions of Liras). *Performance* is the change in the ratio of EBIT and total assets between year $t - 1$ and year t in regressions (1) and (3) and the stock return between $t - 1$ and t in regressions (2) and (4). *Pyramidal level* 1 is a dummy variable that identifies the firms that belong to a pyramidal group and are not controlled by any other traded company. *Pyramidal level* 2 is a dummy variable that identifies the firms that are directly controlled by a pyramidal level 1 company. *Pyramidal* level 3+ is a dummy variable that identifies the firms that are indirectly controlled by a pyramidal level 1 company. Robust standard errors (in parentheses) control for correlation and clustering at firm level. Year and industry dummies are included but the coefficients are not reported.

	Dependent variable: top executive turnover		Dependent variable: modified top executive turnover	
	Performance = change in EBIT/TA (1)	Performance = stock return (2)	Performance = change in EBIT/TA (3)	Performance = stock return (4)
Performance	-0.759^{***}	-0.070^{**}	-0.491^{***}	-0.030
	(0.201)	(0.032)	(0.144)	(0.020)
Performance * Pyramidal level 1 dummy	0.602	-0.047	0.479	-0.066
	(0.550)	(0.063)	(0.393)	(0.044)
Performance * Pyramidal level 2 dummy	0.056	0.023	-0.263	0.026
	(0.395)	(0.055)	(0.355)	(0.037)
Performance * Pyramidal level 3+ dummy	0.441	-0.025	0.221	-0.056
	(0.537)	(0.053)	(0.429)	(0.039)
Pyramidal level 1 dummy	-0.055^{*}	-0.061^{**}	-0.025	-0.032
	(0.025)	(0.025)	(0.022)	(0.022)
Pyramidal level 2 dummy	0.034	0.028	0.027	0.031
	(0.028)	(0.026)	(0.021)	(0.021)
Pyramidal level 3+ dummy	-0.050^{*}	0.040	-0.040^{*}	0.031
	(0.030)	(0.030)	(0.026)	(0.025)
Size	-0.009	-0.013^{*}	-0.009	-0.013^{**}
	(0.006)	(0.007)	(0.006)	(0.006)
Pseudo R^2	0.065	0.049	0.063	0.044
No. of observations	1,234	1,222	1,234	1,222

*, **, and *** denote significance at the 10%, 5%, and 1% level, respectively. The reported coefficients are transformed to represent the change in probability for an infinitesimal change in each independent variable evaluated at the mean values.

in firms at the bottom of a pyramid (those in the category "Pyramidal level 3+ "). This is consistent with the recent theoretical literature on pyramidal groups (see, e.g., Wolfenzon, 1998; Bebchuk et al., 1998). Since this difference does not show up in the analysis of the determinants of the executive turnover, the source of the agency costs created by the separation of ownership and control is to be found in other areas (like, for example, the firm's investment policy).

5.2. The market for corporate control

This section evaluates the importance of the external forces in the Italian corporate governance system. To do so, I run a simple regression of turnover on past performance where the changes of the controlling shareholder are identified by a dummy variable that is introduced both additively and in interaction with performance. If the market for corporate control plays a role in the corporate governance regime, we expect the interactive variable to be negative and significant, as the sensitivity of turnover to performance should increase when there is change of control.

The results are presented in Table 10.11. As in previous tables, I use the change in earnings over assets and the stock return as alternative measures of performance. In both regressions, I find that changes of control increase the level of turnover by more than 50%. However, the increase in executive turnover due to changes of control is largely independent of past performance. Indeed, the sensitivity of turnover to performance increases with a change in control. For example, in regression (1) the interaction term of performance and change of control is negative and significant. A 10% decrease in earnings over assets implies a 13% increase in the probability of executive turnover if there is a change of control. By contrast, the increase in the probability of executive turnover equals only 4% if there is no change of control. In regression (2), where performance is measured by the stock return, the coefficient on the interaction term is non significantly different from zero.

In a regression that is not reported, I find a higher probability of executive turnover and sensitivity of turnover to performance in forced changes of control (i.e., those changes of control due to the firm's default) than in voluntary ones (i.e., those due to the sale of the controlling stake). However, the difference between forced and voluntary changes of control is not significantly different from zero. This latter finding can be due to the relatively smaller number of cases of forced changes of control. Since

Table 10.10 Internal and external governance forces

Probit regressions. The dependent variable (*Top executive turnover*) is a dummy variable that takes value 1 in year *t* if at least half of the top executives are replaced between *t* and *t* + 1. Size is the logarithm of total assets (in millions of Liras). *Performance* is the change in the ratio of EBIT and total assets in regression (1) and the stock return in regression (2). *Change of control* is a dummy variable that takes value 1 in year *t* when the firm changes controlling shareholder between *t* and *t* + 1. Robust standard errors (in parentheses) control for correlation and clustering at firm level. Year and industry dummies are included but the coefficients are not reported.

	Performance = change in EBIT/TA (1)	Performance = stock return (2)
Performance	−0.426***	−0.080***
	(0.152)	(0.024)
Performance * Change of control dummy	−0.882**	0.104
	(0.446)	(0.076)
Change of control dummy	0.547***	0.592***
	(0.064)	(0.060)
Size	−0.004	−0.006
	(0.006)	(0.006)
Pseudo R^2	0.170	0.161
No. of observations	1,234	1,222

*, **, and *** denote significance at the 10%, 5%, and 1% level, respectively. The reported coefficients are transformed to represent the change in probability for an infinitesimal change in each independent variable evaluated at the mean values.

Table 10.11 Q ratio and pyramidal groups

OLS regression with fixed-effects. The dependent variable is the firm's Q. *Size* is the logarithm of total assets (in millions of Liras). *Pyramidal level* 1 is a dummy variable that identifies the firms that belong to a pyramidal group and are not controlled by any other traded company. *Pyramidal level* 2 is a dummy variable that identifies the firms that are directly controlled by a pyramidal level 1 company. *Pyramidal* level 3+ is a dummy variable that identifies the firms that are indirectly controlled by a pyramidal level 1 company. Robust standard errors (in parentheses) control for correlation and heteroskedasticity. Year dummies are included but the coefficients are not reported.

	(1)	*(2)*
Pyramidal level 1 dummy	−0.086	−0.013
	(0.065)	(0.075)
Pyramidal level 2 dummy	0.030	−0.010
	(0.097)	(0.114)
Pyramidal level 3+ dummy	−0.268*	−0.129*
	(0.156)	(0.070)
Size	−0.085***	−0.058***
	(0.028)	(0.027)
Fixed effects	Firm	Industry
Adjusted R^2	0.656	0.201
No. of observations	1,234	1,234

*, **, and *** denote significance at the 10%, 5%, and 1% level, respectively.

out of the 65 cases of changes of control, 16 qualify as forced and 49 as voluntary.

Overall, the results in this section suggest that the market for corporate control does not play an important role in the corporate governance regime operating in Italy. The main reason is probably that control is not really contestable, since all firms in the sample have a controlling shareholder.

6. CONCLUSION

This paper provides direct evidence on the performance of the corporate governance regime operating in countries characterized by low legal protection for investors, firms with large controlling shareholders, and some separation of ownership and control created via pyramidal groups and nonvoting shares. Studying Italy, a country that shares all these features, I find that the probability of turnover and its sensitivity to performance are significantly lower for top executives who belong to the family of the controlling shareholder than for other executives. This result is evidence that controlling shareholders are entrenched. Second, turnover is more sensitive to performance the larger the fraction of cash-flow rights owned by the controlling

shareholder. This result suggests that governance improves when the controlling shareholder's objectives are more aligned with those of minority share-holders. Third, turnover is more sensitive to performance when control is, to some extent, contestable, as in the case of a voting syndicate. Fourth, aside from the role of a voting syndicate, large minority shareholders do not seem to improve governance.

These findings are confirmed by an analysis of the firms' Q ratio. I find that Q increases with the fraction of cash-flow rights owned by the controlling shareholder, is significantly smaller for firms in which controlling shareholders are among the top executives, is significantly larger when a voting syndicate controls the firm, and is unaffected by the presence of large minority shareholders. The combined results on executive turnover and Q suggest a one-to-one correspondence between bad governance (that is, low sensitivity of turnover to performance) and low valuation (that is, low Q).

The paper also provides evidence on pyramidal groups. I find that executive turnover is not significantly affected by the firm's organizational structure. Indeed, the sensitivity of turnover to performance is not significantly different in stand-alone firms and in firms that belong to pyramidal groups.

Within pyramidal groups, turnover is very low in the holding company, while it is relatively high in the subsidiaries. This result suggests that pyramidal groups help the controlling shareholder select the best managers whereby well-performing managers are promoted to higher level of the pyramid while poor-performing ones are replaced. Finally, there is a significant discount in firms at the bottom of a pyramid since the Q ratio is between 13% and 27% lower in those firms if compared to similar standalone companies. This is consistent with the recent theoretical literature on pyramidal groups, suggesting that the separation of ownership and control created by these organizational structures is likely to generate large agency problems because of the conflict of interests between controlling and minority shareholders.

What can be done to improve corporate governance in a country like Italy? The finding that voting syndicates increase the sensitivity of turnover to performance and increase the firm's Q suggests that the creation of a more competitive and active market for corporate control may be the answer. However, an effective market for corporate control requires control to be contestable, otherwise control can be transferred only with the consent of the controlling shareholder or if the company defaults. Consistent with this view, the results in this paper

suggest that the market for corporate control still plays a very limited corporate governance role. According to Bebchuk (1999), large shareholders stay firmly in control wherever control is extremely valuable. Ultimately, as argued by La Porta et al. (1999a), control is valuable because low legal protection for investors enables the controlling shareholder to enjoy large private benefits. This suggests that the solution lies at a political level in new legislation to improve the quality and the enforcement of investor protection. The so-called Draghi Reform introduced in Italy in 1998 effectively increased the protection of minority shareholders and may be one step in this direction.

The diffusion among firms of codes of best practice is another way to improve corporate governance. Their effectiveness has been testified by a recent paper on the UK. Employing a methodology similar to the one in this paper, Dahya et al. (2000) show that the Cadbury report in the United Kingdom improved corporate governance by increasing executive turnover and its sensitivity to performance, especially in the firms that adopted the code. A similar phenomenon could take place in Italy and other countries, given the increasing attention to corporate governance throughout the world and the growing pressure from the international capital markets.

APPENDIX A

Definition of the variables used in the analysis.

Size	Logarithm of total assets expressed in billions Liras. $Size_{it} = 0.5TA_{it} + 0.5TA_{it-1}$
Change in EBIT	Change in earnings before interest and taxes normalized by size: $Change\ in\ EBIT_{it} = (EBIT_{it} - EBIT_{it-1})/Size_{it}$
Stock return	Stock return between year-end t-1 and t $Stock\ return_{it} = (P_{it} - P_{it-1})/(0.5P_{it} + 0.5P_{it-1}) + Dividend\ yield_{it}$. To reduce the impact of outliers, I have set the excess return equal to -1 when smaller than -1 and equal to 2 when larger than 2, for a total of 23 changes
Cash-flow rights of the controlling shareholder	Fraction of the firm's equity (voting and nonvoting shares) owned by the ultimate owner of the firm. If a firm A is controlled indirectly via another traded firm B, the fraction of cash-flow rights of A owned by the controlling shareholder is equal to the product of the cash-flow rights owned by the controlling shareholder in B times the

	fraction of cash-flow rights owned by firm B in firm A. This algorithm can be generalized to more layers of controls and more complex control structures
Voting rights of the controlling shareholder	Fraction of the shares with voting rights of a company controlled by its ultimate owner. If a firm A is controlled indirectly via another traded firm B, the fraction of voting rights of A in the hands of the controlling shareholder is equal to the minimum between the voting rights owned by the controlling shareholder in B and the voting rights owned by firm B in firm A. This algorithm can be generalized to more layers of controls and to more complex control structures
Ultimate owner indicator	Indicator that classifies the firm in four groups: family-controlled firms, state-controlled firms, foreign-controlled firms, and bank-controlled firms
Fraction of top executives replaced	Fraction of top executives of the firm at year t who are not executives of the firm any more at year $t + 1$. All discovered cases of retirement have been excluded
Top executive turnover	Dummy variable that takes value 1 in year t if the fraction of top executives replaced is at least one half
Modified executive turnover	Dummy variable that takes value 1 in year t if at least half of the top executives are replaced between t and $t + 1$ and at $t + 1$ do not hold any executive position in any traded companies of the group to which the firm belongs
Family-executives	Firm's top executives who belong to the same family of the controlling shareholder of the firm
Owner-manager	Dummy variable that takes value 1 if the fraction of relatives of the controlling shareholder among the top executives is at least 0.5
Owner with high incentives	Dummy variable that takes value 1 if the controlling shareholder owns a fraction of cash-flow rights in the firm larger than 50%
Large minority shareholder	Dummy variable that takes value 1 if there is a minority shareholder with at least 5% of the voting shares
Voting syndicate	Dummy variable that takes value 1 if a coalition of relevant shareholders is held together in a voting syndicate
Pyramidal level 1	Dummy variable that takes value 1 if the firm belongs to a pyramidal group and is not controlled by any other traded company
Pyramidal level 2	Dummy variable that takes value 1 if the firm is directly controlled by a "Pyramidal level 1" company
Pyramidal level 3+	Dummy variable that takes value 1 if the firm is directly or indirectly controlled by a "Pyramidal level 2" company
Q ratio	The ratio of market value of the firm (= market value of equity + book value of debt) over book value of total assets
Change of control	Dummy variable that takes value 1 if the firm's controlling shareholder changes between t and $t + 1$
Voting premium	It is defined only for firms with both voting and nonvoting shares: the percentage difference in the price of a voting share with respect to a nonvoting one

APPENDIX B

The matrix of correlations is given in Table 10.12.

Table 10.12 Matrix of correlations

	Top executive turnover	Size	Change in EBIT/ TA	Stock return	Owner-manager dummy	High-incentive dummy	Voting syndicate dummy
Size	−0.043						
Change in EBIT/TA	−0.135***	−0.002					
Stock return	−0.049*	−0.102***	0.163***				
Owner-manager dummy	−0.104***	0.041	0.019	−0.015			
High-incentive dummy	0.006	−0.202***	−0.001	0.068**	0.145***		
Voting syndicate dummy	−0.021	0.073**	−0.018	−0.004	0.116***	−0.219***	
Large minority dummy	−0.030	−0.118***	−0.012	−0.030	0.043	−0.089***	0.306***

*, **, and *** denote significance at the 10%, 5%, and 1% level, respectively. The number of observations is 1,611.

NOTES

* I thank an anonymous referee, Julian Franks, Rafael La Porta, Marco Pagano, Henri Servaes, Andrei Shleifer, and participants at seminars at Harvard University, London Business School, and London School of Economics for helpful comments. I also thank Richard Frost and Samanta Padalino for editing suggestions, and Marcello Bianchi for providing some of the data. I acknowledge financial support from a National Science Foundation and a Luciano Jona graduate fellowships, and the JP Morgan Chase research fellowship at London Business School.

1 The first studies on US data are Coughlan and Schmidt (1985), and Warner et al. (1988); on Japan, Kaplan and Minton (1994) and Kang and Shivdasani (1995); on Germany, Kaplan (1994b), and Franks and Mayer (2001); on the UK, Franks and Mayer (1996), and Franks et al. (2001); on Belgium, Renneboog (2000); on eight developing countries, Gibson (1999).

2 When the econometric analysis is performed on the subset of observations with complete data on age and tenure, representing about a third of the total sample, I find no change in the main results and I find that the coefficients on age and tenure are not significantly different from zero.

3 As already mentioned, the coefficients reported in the tables are not the α, β, γ, δ and $\emptyset$ in Eq. (1) because they have been transformed to represent the change in probability for an infinitesimal change of each independent variable evaluated at the mean values of the data.

REFERENCES

Barclay, M., Holderness, C., 1991. Negotiated block trades and corporate control. Journal of Finance 46, 861–878.

Bebchuk, L., 1999. A rent-protection theory of corporate ownership and control. NBER working paper, No. 7203.

Bebchuk, L., Kraakman, R., Triantis, G., 1998. Stock pyramids, cross-ownership, and dual class: the creation and agency costs of separation between control and cash flows rights. NBER working paper, No. 6951.

Coffee, J., 1999. The future as history: the prospects for global convergence in corporate governance and its implications. Northwestern University Law Review 93, 641–708.

Coughlan, A., Schmidt, R., 1985. Executive compensation, managerial turnover, and firm performance: an empirical investigation. Journal of Accounting and Economics 7, 43–66.

Dahya, J., McConnell, J., Travlos, N., 2000. The Cadbury committee, corporate performance and top management turnover.

Unpublished working paper, Cardiff University, Cardiff, UK.

Denis, D., Denis, D., 1994. Majority owner-manager and organizational efficiency. Journal of Corporate Finance 1, 91–118.

Denis, D., Kruse, T., 2000. Managerial discipline and corporate restructuring following performance declines. Journal of Financial Economics 55, 391–424.

Denis, D., Denis, D., Sarin, A., 1997. Ownership structure and top executive turnover. Journal of Financial Economics 45, 193–221.

Franks, J., Mayer, C., 1996. Hostile takeovers in the UK and the correction of managerial failure. Journal of Financial Economics 40, 163–181.

Franks, J., Mayer, C., 2001. Ownership and control of German corporations. Review of Financial Studies 14, 943–977.

Franks, J., Mayer, C., Renneboog, L., 2001. Who disciplines management in poorly performing companies? Journal of Financial Intermediation 10, 209–248.

Galgano, F., 1997. Diritto Commerciale. Zanichelli, Bologna, Italy.

Gibson, M., 1999. Is corporate governance effective in emerging markets? Unpublished working paper, Federal Reserve Board, Washington, DC.

Gilson, S., 1989. Management turnover and financial distress. Journal of Financial Economics 25, 241–262.

Gilson, S., Kose, J., Lang, L., 1990. Troubled debt restructurings: an empirical study of private reorganizations of firms in default. Journal of Financial Economics 27, 315–353.

Johnson, S., La Porta, R., Lopez-de-Silanes, F., Shleifer, A., 2000. Tunneling. American Economic Review Papers and Proceedings 90, 22–27.

Kang, J., Shivdasani, A., 1995. Firm perform-ance, corporate governance, and top executive turnover in Japan. Journal of Financial Economics 38, 29–58.

Kaplan, S., 1994a. Top executive rewards and firm performance: a comparison of Japan and the United States. Journal of Political Economy 102, 510–546.

Kaplan, S., 1994b. Top executives, turnover, and firm performance in Germany. Journal of Law, Economics and Organization 10, 142–159.

Kaplan, S., Minton, B., 1994. Appointments of outsiders to Japanese boards: determinants and implications for managers. Journal of Financial Economics 36, 225–258.

La Porta, R., Lopez-de-Silanes, F., Shleifer, A., Vishny, R., 1998. Law and finance. Journal of Political Economy 101, 678–709.

La Porta, R., Lopez-de-Silanes, F., Shleifer, A., 1999a. Corporate ownership around the world. Journal of Finance 54, 471–517.

La Porta, R., Lopez-de-Silanes, F., Shleifer, A., Vishny, R., 1999b. Investor protection and corporate valuation. Unpublished working paper, Harvard University, Cambridge, MA.

La Porta, R., Lopez-de-Silanes, F., Shleifer, A., Vishny, R., 2000. Investor protection and corporate governance. Journal of Financial Economics 58, 3–27.

Martin, J., McConnell, J., 1991. Corporate performance, corporate takeovers and management turnover. Journal of Finance 46, 671–687.

McConnell, J., Servaes, H., 1990. Additional evidence on equity ownership and corporate value. Journal of Financial Economics 26, 595–612.

Morck, R., Shleifer, A., Vishny, R., 1988. Management ownership and market valua-tion. Journal of Financial Economics 20, 293–315.

Nicodano, G., 1998. Corporate groups, dual-class shares and the value of voting rights. Journal of Banking and Finance 22, 1117–1137.

Pagano, M., Roell, A., 1998. The choice of stock ownership structure: agency costs, monitor-ing, and the decision to go public. Quarterly Journal of Economics 113, 187–275.

Renneboog, L., 2000. Ownership, managerial control and the governance of companies listed on the Brussels stock exchange. Journal of Banking and Finance 24, 1959–1995.

Warner, J., Watts, R., Wruck, K., 1988. Stock prices, event prediction, and event studies: an examination of top management restructur-ing. Journal of Financial Economics 20, 461–492.

Weisbach, M., 1988. Outside directors and CEO turnover. Journal of Financial Economics 20, 431–460.

Wolfenzon, D., 1998. A theory of pyramidal ownership. Unpublished working paper, Harvard University, Cambridge, MA.

Yermack, D., 1996. Higher market valuation of companies with a small board of directors. Journal of Financial Economics 40, 185–211.

Zingales, L., 1994. The value of the voting right: a study of the Milan stock exchange experience. Review of Financial Studies 7, 125–148.

Erratum

Paolo F. Volpin*

Erratum to 'Governance with poor investor protection: evidence from top executive turnover in Italy'
[Journal of Financial Economics
64 (2002) 61–90[†]]

Due to a mistake an error was made in Table 10.5 on p. 269. Two minus-signs were accidentally put in the row of "Voting syndicate dummy".

The corrected Table 10.5 is on the following page.

The Publisher apologizes for the inconvenience caused.

* Tel.: +44-20-72625050; fax:+44-20-77243317.
  E-mail address: pvolpin@london.edu (P.F. Volpin).
† PII of the original article S0304-405X(02)00071-5

Table 10.5 Analysis of the firm's *Q* ratio

The dependent variable is the firm's *Q* ratio. *Size* is the logarithm of total assists (in millions of Liras). *Owner-manager* is a dummy variable that identifies the cases when at least half of the top executives belong to the family of the controlling shareholder. *Owner with high incentives* is a dummy variable that identifies the cases when the controlling shareholder owns more than 50% of the cash-flow rights. *Voting syndicate* is a dummy variable that takes value 1 when the firm is controlled by a voting syndicate. *Large minority shareholders* is a dummy variable that takes value 1 when the second largest shareholder owns a fraction larger than 5% of the firm's voting rights. Robust standard errors (in parentheses) control for correlation and heteroskedasticity. Year dummies are included but the coefficients are not reported.

	(1)	(2)	(3)	(4)
Owner-manager dummy	−0.067*	−0.116***	−0.092***	−0.083***
	(0.036)	(0.044)	(0.027)	(0.028)
Large minority shareholders dummy	−0.072		0.000	
	(0.048)		(0.027)	
Voting syndicate dummy		0.400***		0.141*
		(0.177)		(0.083)
Owner with high incentives dummy	0.026	0.080*	0.015	−0.006
	(0.052)	(0.048)	(0.031)	(0.032)
Size	−0.059**	−0.068***	−0.092***	−0.092***
	(0.025)	(0.024)	(0.027)	(0.027)
Fixed effects	Industry	Industry	Firm	Firm
Adjuster R^2	0.199	0.273	0.654	0.656
No. of observations	1,234	1,234	1,234	1,234

*, **, and ***, denote significance at the 10%, 5%, and 1% level, respectively.

## Chapter 11

Luc Renneboog

OWNERSHIP, MANAGERIAL CONTROL AND THE GOVERNANCE OF COMPANIES LISTED ON THE BRUSSELS STOCK EXCHANGE

Source: *Journal of Banking & Finance*, 24(12) (2000): 1959–1995.

ABSTRACT

This paper examines how corporate control is exerted in companies listed on the Brussels Stock Exchange. There are several alternative corporate governance mechanisms which may play a role in disciplining poorly performing management: blockholders (holding companies, industrial companies, families and institutions), the market for partial control, debt policy, and board composition. Even if there is redundancy of substitute forms of discipline, some mechanisms may dominate. We find that top managerial turnover is strongly related to poor performance measured by stock returns, accounting earnings in relation to industry peers and dividend cuts and omissions. Tobit models reveal that there is little relation between ownership and managerial replacement, although industrial companies resort to disciplinary actions when performance is poor. When industrial companies increase their share stake or acquire a new stake in a poorly performing company, there is evidence of an increase in executive board turnover, which suggests a partial market for control. There is little relation between changes in ownership concentration held by institutions and holding companies, and disciplining. Still, high leverage and decreasing solvency and liquidity variables are also followed by increased disciplining, as are a high proportion of non-executive directors and the separation of the functions of CEO and chairman.

1. INTRODUCTION

WHEREAS IN ANGLO-AMERICAN COUNTRIES, managerial performance is maintained by the complementary intervention of both internal and external control mechanisms (see Shleifer and Vishny, 1997, for an overview), the disciplinary function of the (hostile) take-over market in Belgium, and most other Continental European countries, is limited. Recent Belgian legislative changes with regard to ownership disclosure laws and anti-take-over procedures have further reduced the likelihood of take-overs as a corporate control mechanism. Consequently, as in recent codes of good corporate governance – the Dutch Peeters report (1997), the French Viénot report (1995) and UK Cadbury report (1992) – the Belgian policy recommendations of 1998 by the Stock Exchange Commission, the Association of Employers (VBO) and the Commission for Banking and Finance focus on the effectiveness of internal corporate control mechanisms.[1]

This paper investigates whether or not poor corporate performance triggers board restructuring and whether disciplinary actions are initiated by internal governance. This paper also examines whether the accumulation of shares into large blocks of shares mitigates the problems of free riding in corporate control, permitting control to be exerted more effectively. The relation between the nature of ownership and incidence of disciplinary turnover when corporate performance is poor is also studied.

Besides ownership concentration, capital structure choice may be an instrumental monitoring variable as it can be a bonding device triggering corporate control actions. Such creditor monitoring is expected to be intensified in case of low interest coverage and low liquidity.

We also analyse whether a market for share stakes arises. In Continental Europe, such a market might play a role equivalent to the role of external markets in the UK and the US. If a company underperforms, able monitors can increase their voting rights to reach a control level allowing them to nominate a new management team.

We find that poor company performance precedes increased board restructuring (turnover of executives, of the management committee and of CEO and executive chairman). This is consistent with findings reported by, among others, Denis and Denis (1995) and Warner et al. (1988) for the US, by Franks and Mayer (1998) and Kaplan (1994) for Germany and by Franks et al. (1998) for the UK.

The composition of the board also has an important impact on the internal corporate control system. A high fraction of non-executives on the board and the separation of the functions of CEO and (non-executive) chairman increases the turnover of executive directors of underperforming companies. Weisbach (1988) also reports that outside directors of US firms play a larger role in monitoring management than inside directors. Franks and Mayer (1998) show that, in German companies with concentrated ownership, supervisory board representation goes hand in hand with ownership or large shareholdings. For Japan, Kaplan and Minton (1994) show that board appointments of directors representing banks and corporations are followed by increases in top management turnover. In contrast, Franks et al. (1998) report that non-executive directors seem to support

incumbent management in the UK even in the wake of poor performance.

Consistent with Shleifer and Vishny (1986) and Grossman and Hart (1980), we find that higher board turnover is positively correlated with strong concentration in ownership which limits free riding on control. Still, this relation is limited to industrial and commercial companies and family shareholders. Considering that the ownership structure is typically complex with stakes held through multiple tiers of ownership, we find that the decision to substitute top management of poorly performing companies is taken by ultimate shareholders (industrial companies and families) who control either directly or indirectly, via affiliated companies, a large percentage of the voting rights. However, neither large institutional investors nor holding companies seem to be involved in active corporate monitoring, which further questions the role and need for ownership cascades involving holding companies.

Although, an active market in share stakes exists, it is only weakly related to performance. Specific shareholder classes (industrial and commercial companies) with superior monitoring abilities or with private benefits of control, increase their voting stake to better position themselves to replace management. Such a market for blocks of control also exists in the UK and in Germany, as detailed in Franks et al. (1998) and Franks and Mayer (1998). Shareholders who increase their holdings do so with a clear intention to assume an active monitoring role since management turnover significantly increases in subsequent periods.

We also find that high leverage and low interest coverage are related to increased board restructuring which suggests that creditors intervene as the risk of financial distress increases. However, because this interpretation is not corroborated in interviews with monitors; liquidity and solvency-related indicators may act as monitoring triggers for directors or shareholders.

Finally, management replacement is followed by modest improvements in growth of dividends per share over a period of two years after turnover. However, board turnover is followed by decreases in earnings. The earnings decline may result from new management's decision to expense large costs while earnings reductions can still be attributed to predecessors, thus lowering the benchmark and allowing for substantial improvements in subsequent years (Murphy and Zimmerman, 1993).

The remainder of this paper is organised as follows. Section 2 explains the hypotheses. Section 3 presents the data and methodology. Section 4 provides stylised facts about the ownership structure in Belgian listed companies and Section 5 discusses the main results of the governance models. Finally, Section 6 summarises the findings.

2. RELATIONSHIP BETWEEN DISCIPLINING AND ALTERNATIVE GOVERNANCE MECHANISMS

Few of the tasks which good corporate governance consists of, like strategy development or control, are visible to non-insiders to the corporation. Minutes of board or committee meetings or the outcome of shareholder-management meetings are not disclosed. Hence, one of the few occasions to study corporate control actions (or the lack of them) is poor corporate performance or a financial crisis. The paper studies several substitute forms of discipline and, where there is redundancy, whether some forms dominate others consistently.[2] This section provides an overview of the hypotheses after which each of these are further expanded.

Hypothesis 1. Disciplining of top management is triggered by poor company performance: directors, CEOs, top managers and executive chairmen are replaced following poor share price performance and/or low accounting earnings and dividend cuts and omissions.

Hypothesis 2. The greater the proportion of non-executive directors, the lower potential board domination by management and the higher the monitoring ability of the non-executive directors. This is reflected in increased turnover of executive directors,

of the CEO and of the management committee when performance is poor. Separating the functions of CEO and chairman facilitates disciplining of underperforming management, and such dual control should lead to higher turnover.

Hypothesis 3. (a) When performance is poor, the presence of large shareholdings is followed by higher board turnover. (b) However, disciplining of underperforming management is accomplished by those large shareholders with superior monitoring abilities. Conflicts of interest dissuade institutions to monitor whereas holding companies, industrial companies, and families and individuals discipline management.

Hypothesis 4. Managerial disciplining decisions are taken by the decision maker at the top of an investor group pyramid, called 'ultimate or reference' shareholder.

Hypothesis 5. In companies without sufficiently large shareholders or with shareholders who take a passive stance concerning monitoring, poor performance gives rise to changes in the ownership structure. Hence, increases in shareholdings are associated with higher managerial turnover in the same year or the year following the monitors' disciplinary actions.

Hypothesis 6. Management of poorly performing companies with high leverage and poor liquidity and solvency face increased monitoring.

Hypothesis 7. Management and board restructuring, triggered by poor performance, results in improvements of company performance, but performance improvements are not expected in the year of management substitution but are expected in later years.

2.1. Corporate performance and disciplinary corporate governance actions

To the extent that share price and accounting returns are influenced by the quality of managerial inputs and actions, corporate performance provides useful information on managerial performance (Joskow and Rose, 1994). However, both market prices and accounting data present measurement problems of managerial quality. On one hand, the relation between (executive) board restructuring and share price performance may be weaker because share prices already incorporate market expectations regarding managerial replacement. On the other hand, accounting data can (temporarily) be manipulated by the choice of accounting policies (see e.g. Moses, 1987; Teoh et al., 1998). Therefore, the impact of both share price returns, and levels of and changes in operating and net accounting earnings, on turnover are included in testing Hypothesis 1. Besides share price and earnings performance, we also examine dividend changes. Such changes may be an important critical performance measure as management is generally reluctant to reduce dividends unless a reduction is unavoidable (Michaely et al., 1995). Consequently, dividend cuts or omissions are associated with unusually poor stock price and earnings performance (Healey and Palepu, 1988) and are expected to be negatively related to turnover.

2.2. The impact of board composition and structure on the board's ability to monitor performance

A balanced board including both executives and non-executives reduces the potential conflicts of interest among decision makers and residual risk bearers. It also reduces the transaction or agency costs associated with the separation of ownership and control (Williamson, 1983). There are several reasons why non-executives are (ex ante) expected to exert a control task. Non-executives are legally bound to monitor due to their fiduciary duty. Moreover, in an equity market with strong ownership concentration, many non-executives are appointed by and represent large shareholders. Thus, non-executives have

incentives to develop reputations as decision control experts whose human capital depends on performance (Fama and Jensen, 1983). Consequently, directors themselves face an external labour market which provides some form of disciplining for passive leadership, as reported for the US by Kaplan and Reishus (1990) and Gilson (1990). Separating the role of CEO and of non-executive chairman is also supposed to strengthen the board's monitoring ability since a non-executive chairman could ensure more independence from management.[3] Consequently, we expect both a high proportion of non-executive directors and the separation of the functions of CEO and chairman to be positively correlated with turnover (Hypothesis 2).

2.3. Ownership concentration, the costs of free riding on control and superior monitoring abilities

Monitoring management may be prohibitively expensive for small shareholders as a monitor pays all the costs related to his control efforts but only benefits in proportion to his shareholding (Grossman and Hart, 1980, 1988; Demsetz, 1983). In contrast, the costs of shirking are shared by all the shareholders. Therefore, monitoring will only be cost effective if a single party becomes large enough to internalise the costs of corporate control (Hypothesis 3a).

The incentives to monitor and correct managerial failure depend not only on the concentration of ownership, but also on its nature (category of shareholder). Specific classes of owners may value control differently as the source of the control premium is the additional compensation and perquisites the controlling security holders can accord themselves (Jensen and Meckling, 1976). Barclay and Holderness (1989) argue: "In absence of private gains, blocks of shares ought to be sold at a discount due to the greater risk exposure and due to the monitoring costs. However, blocks are usually sold at a premium which suggests the presence of private gains".

That different classes of owner have different abilities to extract control rents is empirically supported for the US by Demsetz and Lehn (1985), Barclay and Holderness (1991) and Holderness and Sheehan (1988). Holding companies are prevalent in Belgium and their private benefits and reasons for control accumulation are manifold: capturing tax reductions by facilitating intercompany transfers, reducing transaction costs by offering economies of scale or by supplying internal sources of funds (Banerjee et al., 1997). Likewise, corporate shareholders may hold substantial share stakes in a target that may be a supplier or customer, in order to influence and/or capitalise on the target's strategic decisions. In contrast, there is little or no systematic evidence of monitoring actions by institutions (investment funds, banks, insurance companies . . .). In Belgium, many institutions are affiliated with financial institutions and are legally obliged to avoid conflicts of interest (Renneboog, 1997). No such impediments hinder monitoring by holding companies, industrial and commercial companies, individual investors or families. We therefore expect a positive relation between turnover and ownership concentration held by holding companies, industrial and commercial firms, individuals and families and no relation between turnover and institutional shareholder share concentration (Hypothesis 3b).

2.4. Ultimate ownership and dilution of control

Ownership structures are frequently complex and pyramidal, and are constructed for reasons of control leverage (Wymeersch, 1994). Therefore, decisions about disciplining management may not be taken by direct investors but rather by the ultimate shareholders[4] who control these direct shareholders directly or through multiple tiers of ownership. Monitoring is not performed by intermediate holding companies which are investment vehicles of controlling industrial companies or individuals and families, but by these industrial companies and families themselves

(Hypothesis 4). Hence, the relation between turnover and direct ownership (voting rights) by category of owner is expected to be less statistically significant than the one between turnover and ownership concentration whereby the direct equity stakes (voting rights) are reclassified based on the shareholder category of the ultimate owner.

2.5. The disciplining role of the market for share stakes

Burkart et al. (1997) argue that the degree of voting right concentration acts as a commitment device to delegate a certain degree of authority from shareholders to management. They show that the use of equity implements state-contingent control: in states of the world with decreasing corporate profitability, close monitoring resulting from strong ownership concentration is desirable. In other states of the world, it may not be optimal to have close monitoring as this may reduce managerial discretion and hence management's effort (also in Bolton et al., 1998). Hence, when performance is poor, a partial corporate control market may arise, consisting of large (controlling) blocks. Furthermore, poor performance may reflect not simply poor management but also ineffective monitoring and control. If this is the case, poor performance may lead low quality monitors to sell their stakes and new (controlling) shareholders could improve future corporate performance by substituting incumbent management (Hypothesis 5). Shleifer and Vishny (1986) show that once a block of shares is assembled, the position is unlikely to be dissipated. It is in the large shareholder's interest to wait until someone who values control expresses interest in this block because if the block is broken up and sold on the open market, part of the firm's value arising from the possibility of value-increasing monitoring is lost.

2.6. Leverage as a bonding device

Creditor intervention may be expected when the probability of defaulting on debt covenants increases or when the company needs to be refinanced. The choice of gearing can be considered as a bonding mechanism for management (e.g. in Aghion and Bolton, 1992; Berkovitch et al., 1997) such that high turnover is positively related to high gearing (Hypothesis 6). Dennis and Dennis (1993) infer creditor monitoring from the fact that high leverage combined with managerial ownership improves shareholder returns.

2.7. Post-disciplining corporate performance

For internal and external control mechanisms to be effective, the replacement of underperforming top management should be followed by performance improvements (Dennis and Dennis, 1995) (Hypothesis 7). However, it is unclear which performance variables are expected to improve. As anticipations about future performance of a new management team will be reflected in share price returns at the latest at the announcement of the replacement, abnormal returns over periods subsequent to the announcement effect are not expected to be significantly positive. Furthermore, Murphy and Zimmerman (1993) conclude that 'earnings management'[5] is more likely to occur if the outgoing CEO is terminated following poor performance since it is more credible for the new CEO to blame the previous CEO for past mistakes. Moreover, by constantly overstating losses attributable to predecessors, management improves accounting expectations about the future and lowers the benchmark against which its own accounting performance will be measured (Elliott and Shaw, 1988). Hence, performance improvements are not expected in the year of management substitution but potentially only in later time periods. A competing hypothesis states that if performance leading to management replacement is poor, the success of managerial disciplining may not just be inferred from performance improvements but rather from the avoidance of bankruptcy.

3. DATA AND METHODOLOGY

3.1. Data sources

3.1.1. Sample description

The sample consists of all Belgian companies listed on the Brussels Stock Exchange during the period 1989–1994. In 1989 and 1994, respectively, 186 and 165 companies were listed.[6] Bankrupt companies and IPOs over the period 1989–94 were included until the year of bankruptcy and from the year of floatation.[7] About 40% of the Belgian listed companies are holding companies with multi-industry investments, 13 percent are in the financial sector (banking, insurance and real estate) and 47% are industrial or commercial companies.

3.1.2. Ownership data

Data on the ownership structure over the period 1989–1994 were collected from the Documentation and Statistics Department of the Brussels Stock Exchange. Ownership data are only available since 1989, following the introduction of the Ownership Disclosure Legislation (of 2 March 1989). To capture a company's ownership position at the end of its fiscal year and the yearly changes in shareholdings, about 5000 hardcopy Notifications of Ownership Change from 1989 till 1994 were consulted. With this information about major direct shareholdings and about indirect control which is complemented with details from annual reports, the multi-layered (pyramidal) ownership structures were reconstructed for each company over the period 1989–1994. As different classes of shareholders may have different information, monitoring competencies and incentives, all shareholders with stakes of 5 percent or more are categorised into 8 classes: (i) holding companies, (ii) banks, (iii) investment companies (pension funds, investment funds), (iv) insurance companies, (v) industrial and commercial companies, (vi) families and individual investors, (vii) federal or regional authorities, (viii) realty investment companies. The yearbooks of *Trends*

20,000, which comprise industry sector classification and financial data for most listed and non-listed Belgian companies, were used to classify all Belgian investors into ownership categories. Foreign investors were classified with information from *Kompass*.

3.1.3. Share price and accounting data

Monthly (from 1980) and weekly (from 1986) share price returns, corrected for stock splits and dividend pay-outs, and a value-weighted index of all companies listed on the Brussels Stock Exchange were provided by the *Generale Bank*. Accounting data (total assets, equity, operating income, earnings after tax, dividends per share, debt–equity structure) were collected from annual reports and from the database of Central Depository of Balance Sheets at the National Bank of Belgium.

3.1.4. Data on the board of directors and the management committee

The database of the National Bank of Belgium also contains data on the board of directors. Turnover data were compiled and reasons for directors to leave the company were collected from the notes in the annual reports. Natural turnover due to retirement, death or illness is usually reported and is used to correct the turnover data. Other reasons for turnover are rarely mentioned in either the annual reports or the financial press. When no grounds or non-informative reasons[8] were given for turnover, forced turnover due to disciplining actions or due to company policy disputes was assumed. Data on size and turnover of the management committee were gathered from the annual reports. When the annual report did not explicitly mention the existence of a management committee, the yearbooks *Memento der Effecten* and the *Jaarboek der Bestuurders* (Yearbook of Directors) were consulted to determine whether or not directors had executive functions. If the annual reports or other public sources did not reveal the data needed, companies were contacted by fax and phone to supplement lacking data.

3.2. Methodology

A panel of data is formed for the six year period 1989–94 with each firm-year representing a separate observation. The relation between board restructuring, performance, ownership, leverage, board structure is examined in the following model:

$$RESTRUC_{i,t} = \alpha_{i,t} + \sum_{k=1}^{3} \beta_{i,k} PERF_{i,t-k}$$

Performance (lagged)

$$+ \sum_{l=1}^{8} \gamma_{i,l} CONC_{i,l,t-1}$$

$$+ \sum_{l=1}^{8} \delta_{i,l} CONC_{i,l,t-1} PERF_{i,l,t-1}$$

Ownership concentration and interaction

$$+ \sum_{l=1}^{8} \gamma_{i,l} INCCONC_{i,l,t-1}$$

$$+ \sum_{l=1}^{8} \delta_{i,l} INCCONC_{i,l,t-1} PERF_{i,l,t-1}$$

Market in share stakes and interaction

$$+ \sum_{m=1}^{2} \phi_{im,l} DEBT_{i,m,t-1}$$

$$+ \sum_{m=1}^{2} \eta_{i,l} DEBT_{i,m,t-1} PERF_{i,m,t-1}$$

Debt policy and interaction

$$+ \sum_{n=1}^{2} \varphi_{im,l} BOARD_{i,n,t}$$

$$+ \sum_{n=1}^{2} \lambda_{i,l} BOARD_{i,n,t} PERF_{i,n,t-1}$$

Board composition and interaction

$$+ \log(SIZE_{i,t}) + \sum_{p=1}^{15} \tau_{i,p} \text{ industry}$$

$$+ \sum_{q=1}^{5} \tau_{i,q} \text{ year} + \varepsilon_{i,t}$$

Size, industry and time dummies

i = company, t = year, l = classes of owner, m = number of debt policy variables, n = number of board composition variables.

RESTRUC = Board restructuring, measured by (1) executive board turnover, (2) CEO or executive chairman turnover, (3) management committee turnover.

PERF = performance variable measured by lagged (1) market adjusted returns, (2) changes in earnings after tax, (3) earnings losses, (4) ROE, (5) ROE − industry median ROE (with earnings after tax), (6) ROA, (7) ROA − industry median ROA (with earnings from operations before interest and taxes), (8) changes in dividends, (9) changes in ROE, (10) changes in ROE − industry median of ROE changes, (11) changes in cash flow on equity, (12) changes in cash flow on equity − industry median of changes, (13) changes in cash flow margin, (14) changes in cash flow margin equity − industry median of changes.

CONC = ownership concentration (%) by class of owner: (i) holding companies, (ii) banks, (iii) investment companies (pension funds, investment funds), (iv) insurance companies, (v) industrial and commercial companies, (vi) families and individual investors, (vii) federal or regional authorities, (viii) realty investment companies. Both the percentages of ownership by category of owner and the percentage held by the largest shareholder are included (in separate regressions). Both direct shareholdings by category of owner are included as are the direct shareholdings reclassified into the categories of owner based on the category of the ultimate (reference) shareholder (in separate regressions). Herfindahl indices of the largest 3 shareholders by category of owner are also used as concentration measures.

INCCONC = purchases of share stakes (in %) by category of owner. Both direct shareholdings and reclassified ones based on ultimate shareholder are included, see CONC.

DEBT = debt policy and debt structure variables: debt/equity ratio, current ratio, quick ratio, interest coverage (EBIT/interest expenses). In each model, gearing was only included along with one of the other variables in order to avoid multicollinearity.

BOARD = board composition (% of non-executive directors), separation of the functions of CEO and chairman (1 = no separation), board size, tenure of CEO.

SIZE = logarithm of total assets or of total employees.

Logit models are used if the dependent variable is a dummy (in the case of CEO turnover). For executive director and management committee turnover, GLS models and OLS models with a logarithmic transformation of the dependent variable are used and the estimation is conducted with heteroscedasticity consistent covariance matrix estimator (White, 1980). Tobit models are also used to address that fact that the dependent variable (executive and committee turnover) is censored. Industry and time effects are accounted for by including industry and time dummies, respectively. Corporate board size and firm size are included as control variables.[9] The relations are also tested including corporate dummies and taking innovations to remove firm-specific effects. In order to address the endogeneity problems lagged data for ownership, performance and debt policy were utilised in the models. Over- or underperformance in relation to industry peers was measured by correcting performance variables for the median industry performance. In Section 5, Tobit models are shown, but tables with other estimation methods are available and the robustness of the results across estimation techniques is discussed.

4. OWNERSHIP STRUCTURE AND CONTROL OF BELGIAN LISTED COMPANIES: STYLISED FACTS

4.1. Ownership concentration

In a nutshell, the characteristics of Belgian corporate ownership can be summarised as follows: (i) few—only 165—Belgian companies are listed, (ii) there is a high degree of ownership concentration, (iii) holding companies and families, and to a lesser extent industrial companies, are the main investor categories, (iv) control is levered by pyramidal and complex ownership structures and (v) there is a market for share stakes. Properties (i) to (iv) imply that Belgium can be portrayed as a Continental European blockholder system rather than a market based system (Bratton and McCahery, 1999). However, typical for

Belgium is the importance of holding companies which are often part of pyramidal ownership chains and are used to lever control (Renneboog, 1997; Daems, 1998).

The sum of the share stakes held by large shareholders (owning at least 5% of outstanding shares) amounts to, on average, more than 65%. The largest direct shareholder controls 43% in the average listed company. The three most important direct investor classes are holding companies, industrial and commercial companies, and families and individual investors. They own, respectively, 33%, 15% and 4% of the voting rights. However, taking into account ownership cascades to reclassify the direct share stakes according to the shareholder category of the ultimate owner[10] reveals that holding companies control directly and indirectly an average of 26.7% of direct voting rights in listed Belgian companies whereas the category of industrial and commercial companies controls an average stake of 11%. Individual and family investors do not generally hold shares directly in Belgian companies, but use intermediate companies[11] as investment vehicles with which they control an average shareholding of 16%.

Table 11.1 illustrates the high level of ownership concentration and gives the percentage of Belgian listed companies with voting rights concentration of at least a blocking minority (25%), an absolute majority and a supermajority (75% and more). Panel A reveals that a voting rights majority exists in more than half (56%) of the listed companies. In 18% of the Belgian companies, a supermajority gives absolute control to one shareholder(group) since blocking minorities cannot be formed. Shareholdings of 25% or more are present in 85% of all companies. The concentrated ownership pattern is similar in the subsamples of listed holdings companies, financial and institutional companies, and industrial and commercial corporations.

4.2. Ownership cascades and the violation of one share-one vote rule

Table 11.2 shows that the ultimate ownership tier averages 2.2 (where direct share stakes are level 1-shareholdings). Ownership cascades are usually used to dilute the one-share-one-vote rule: a chain with intermediate holdings of e.g. 50% allows de facto majority control with limited cash flow rights. As a proxy for control leverage via ownership cascades, the ratio of the direct largest shareholding and its levered shareholding (the multiplication of the shareholdings on consecutive ownership tiers) is used. For instance, company A, whose shares are widely held, owns 40% of company B which, in turn, owns 40% of company C. In this example, the ultimate shareholder level is 2, the direct largest shareholding (of B in C) is 40%, the ultimate shareholding amounts to 16% (40% × 40%), and the leverage factor (largest direct shareholding/levered share stake) is 2.5 (40/16). For our sample companies, the average largest direct share stake amounts to about 55%, whereas the levered shareholding is 39%. The smaller the shareholdings with which control is maintained through intermediate levels and the larger the number of intermediate ownership tiers, the higher the control leverage factor or the more considerable the violation of the one-share-one-vote rule. Table 11.2 discloses that since 1989 the control leverage factor decreased from 3.6 to 2.7. Since the average ultimate ownership level and the ultimate levered shareholding do not change significantly over this time, the decline of the control leverage factor indicates that control on intermediate levels has become more concentrated.

4.3. The market for corporate control

Although a market for corporate control (commonly defined as a (hostile) take over market) is usually associated with the US and the UK, Table 11.3 shows that a partial control market or a market in substantial share blocks exists in Belgium. In more than 22% of the listed companies, substantial changes (of more than 5%) in ownership concentration take place and in 7.6% of firms blocking minorities are sold.

Table 11.1 Blocking minority, majority and supermajority shareholdings[a]

1994	All investors			Holding co's			Families			Indus. co's			Belgian investors			Foreign investors		
	MIN	MAJ	SUP	MIN	MAJ	SUP	MIN	MAJ	SUP	MIN	MAJ	SUP	MIN	MAJ	SUP	MIN	MAJ	SUP
Panel A: All sample companies (N = 157)																		
Direct	82	45	14	48	23	5	2	1	1	21	12	5	63	36	9	19	9	5
Dir. and indirect	85	56	18	41	26	6	23	14	3	15	8	5	51	33	9	34	23	10
Panel B: Holding companies (N = 64)																		
Direct	79	39	14	50	23	8	5	2	2	17	9	2	59	31	11	20	8	3
Dir. and indirect	83	59	20	50	36	13	22	13	2	9	6	3	45	30	11	38	30	13
Panel C: Financial sector (banking, insurance, real estate) (N = 20)																		
Direct	75	50	10	35	15	0	0	0	0	5	5	5	62	40	10	13	10	0
Dir. and indirect	80	55	15	40	15	5	5	5	0	5	5	5	48	33	10	32	22	5
Panel D: Industrial and commercial companies (N = 73)																		
Direct	86	47	15	48	25	4	0	0	0	28	15	8	66	37	7	20	10	8
Dir. and indirect	93	55	16	34	19	3	29	18	4	24	11	7	61	37	8	32	18	8

a Percentage of the sample companies with a minority, majority or supermajority shareholdings held by the main shareholder categories. MIN = % of companies with a stake of 25% or larger, MAJ = % of companies with a stake of 50% or larger, SUP = % of companies with a stake of 75% or larger. Direct stands for the direct shareholdings. Dir. and indirect refers to the fact that the direct shareholdings are classified according to the shareholder class of the ultimate investor: direct shareholdings belonging to the same ultimate; investor group were subsequently summed. Ultimate control (direct and indirect) is control based on (i) a majority control (minimal 50% of the voting rights) on every ownership tier of the ownership pyramid or (ii) shareholdings; of at least 25% on every tier in the absence of other shareholders holding stakes of 25% or more. A chain of fully owned subsidiaries are considered as one single shareholder.
Source: Own calculations based on BDPart and Ownership Notifications.

Table 11.2 Largest direct and ultimate (direct and indirect) levered shareholdings, and the control leverage factor[a]

	1989	1990	1991	1992	1993	1994
Sample size	160	156	156	156	156	158
Ultimate ownership level	2.2	2.2	2.1	2.1	2.0	2.0
	(1.364)	(1.290)	(1.188)	(1.159)	(1.098)	(1.020)
Direct largest shareholding	55.1	56.4	57.2	57.8	56.3	55.6
	(19.737)	(19.509)	(19.923)	(20.632)	(20.341)	(19.987)
Levered shareholding	38.0	38.5	40.3	41.7	42.0	39.4
	(22.524)	(22.906)	(23.988)	(24.600)	(23.657)	(21.454)
Control leverage factor	3.6	3.6	3.0	2.9	2.8	2.7
(direct/levered shareholding)	(8.391)	(8.650)	(6.756)	(6.710)	(6.432)	(6.356)

a This table presents the ultimate ownership level, defined as the highest level of ownership in an uninterrupted control chain (direct shareholdings are level 1). Ultimate control is control based on (i) a majority control (minimal 50% of the voting rights) on every ownership tier of the ownership pyramid or (ii) shareholdings of at least 25% on every tier in the absence of other shareholders holding stakes of 25% or more. A chain of fully owned subsidiaries are considered as one single shareholder. The direct largest shareholding is the average direct largest share stake of at least 25%. The levered shareholding is calculated by multiplying the share stakes of subsequent ownership tiers. The control leverage factor is the ratio of the direct shareholding divided by the ultimate levered shareholding. For instance, company A, whose shares are widely held, owns 40% of company B which, in turn, owns 40% of company C. The ultimate shareholder level is 2, the direct largest shareholding (of B in C) is 40%, the ultimate shareholding is 16% (40% ×40%), and the leverage factor is 2.5 (40/16). There was no direct shareholding of at least 25% in 17 sample companies, which were not included in this table. Standard deviation in parentheses.
Source: Own calculations based on data from the BDPart database and the Notifications of Ownership.

Twenty-eight majority stakes changed hands.[12] These findings suggest that this market for share stakes is not insignificant. Table 11.3 also discloses that the holding companies are the main sellers and purchasers of share stakes. Institutional investors, mainly banks and insurance companies, acquire 49 shareholdings of more than 5% and sell 43 stakes of similar size. Families and individuals sell 17 stakes of blocking minority size and more, while 10 such stakes are purchased. Most of the exchanges of the largest blocks of shares are negotiated deals and take place ex exchange.[13]

4.4. Capital structure

Belgian listed companies are relying to a large extent on short term debt: long term debt on equity amounts to 28% whereas short term debt (including trade credit) on equity is 53%. Holding companies carry more long term debt (39% on equity) than industrial and commercial firms (with only 12%). Average current ratios are 4.1 for industrial companies and 5.4 for holding companies.

5. RESULTS

Belgian companies have a one-tier board system with average board size amounting to 10 directors for the period 1989–1994 and with a median of 9. Yearly, between 9% and 12% of the directors leave the board. Annual turnover among executive directors in this period is high: between 27% and 41%, whereas only about 7% of the non-executive directors is replaced. The yearly replacement of the CEO (called 'delegated' or managing director) amounts to 18%. A third measure of top management restructuring consists of replacement in the management committee. Although such a management committee is no legal requirement, 65% of the companies mention in their annual reports such committees, which count on average 3.6 members (median of 4). The executive directors are always members of this committee and have an average of 2.4 members (median of 2). Annual turnover of the management committee totals 17%. Although managerial turnover is corrected for natural turnover related to

Table 11.3 The market in share stakes over the period 1989–1994[a]

1989–1994	Number of increases and decreases stakes					
	[1–5%]	[5–10%]	[10–25%]	[25–50%]	[50–100%]	Total
Panel A: Purchases for all sample companies						
Purchases: all shareholders	113	103	66	40	21	343
Purchases: holding companies	50	51	26	22	4	153
Purchases: institutional investors	39	25	13	5	6	88
Purchases: industr. and commerc. co's	10	14	13	7	7	51
Purchases: families and individuals	14	13	14	6	4	51
Panel B: Sales for all sample companies						
Sales: all shareholders	119	78	81	45	33	356
Sales: holding companies	40	47	46	17	20	170
Sales: institutional investors	49	13	15	12	3	92
Sales: industr. and commerc. Co's	5	4	7	3	6	25
Sales: families and individuals	25	14	13	13	4	69

a This table gives the size distribution of purchases and sales of large shareholdings by category of owner over the period 1989–1994. All changes are given excluding changes in government stakes and real estate as these categories are minor. Purchases and sales are calculated by comparing the share stakes of a shareholder category of a fiscal year to the shareholdings of previous year. Institutional investors consists of banks, investment and pension funds and insurance companies. Total number of firm-years over the period is 1024.
Source: Own calculations based on BDPart and Ownership Notifications.

retirement age, death or illness of directors, the turnover data may still contain some non-conflictual turnover since corporations do not generally release information regarding management replacement or do so in euphemistic terms.

5.1. Board restructuring in industrial and commercial companies

5.1.1. Executive board turnover

5.1.1.1. Corporate performance and disciplining of management.

A first question is whether or not turnover, corrected for natural turnover, is related to poor corporate performance and results from disciplinary actions. We also investigate when such corporate governance actions are undertaken and whether disciplining takes place at an early stage, i.e. rapidly after earnings, cash flows or share price declines or, rather late when the company is no longer able to generate profits or has to cut dividends? Including lagged performance up to three years prior to turnover allows us to investigate the reaction time of board restructuring.14 Warner et al. (1988) and Coughlan and Schmidt (1985) report that US boards react quickly to poor performance in their decision to replace management because share performance lagged up to two calendar years helps predict current-calendar-year management changes. Share price performance may underestimate the true relation between performance and executive turnover given that share prices reflect current profitability as well as expected future opportunities including the potential performance improvements under new management (Weisbach, 1988). As accounting earnings depend on discretionary managerial accounting choices, we use a combination of accounting, dividend, cash flow measures and market adjusted share returns as performance benchmarks in the Tobit models of Tables 11.4 and 11.5. Operating earnings before interest and taxes (standardised by total assets) are used as they are not sensitive to financing policy, tax regime, windfall profits or extra-ordinary losses. The use of operating income rather than net earnings after tax reduces the impact of the described 'earnings management' (Dennis and Dennis, 1994). ROE is taken after interest, extraordinary results and taxes. The industry medians are substracted from both the levels of and the changes in ROE and cash flow on equity.[15]

Table 11.4 (lines 2–4) shows that, for listed industrial and commercial companies, there is a negative significant relation between executive director replacement and market adjusted performance in the three years prior to management substitution. Earnings losses over the fiscal year prior to turnover are followed by increased levels of executive board turnover. Warner et al. (1988), amongst others, confirm for the US that unless performance is extremely good or bad, their management turnover models have little predictive value. Another critical performance benchmark, substantial cuts in dividends (of at least 25%) or omissions, also precede board restructuring. Given that deviations from expectations about dividend policy usually contain signalling information, management is generally reluctant to reduce dividends unless such a reduction is unavoidable. Hence, dividend cuts are associated with unusually poor stock-price and earnings performance (Healey and Palepu, 1988; Ofer and Siegel, 1987; Marsh and Merton, 1987). Including changes in earnings or dividends into the monitoring models yields weaker correlations with board restructuring.

Levels of performance as well as changes in performance, corrected by industry medians, are analysed as it may well be that it is not just low earnings which trigger managerial disciplining but peer group (industry) underperformance. Morck et al. (1989) find that when a firm significantly underperforms its industry, the probability of complete turnover of the top management team rises. Table 11.4 shows that both industry adjusted levels and changes in ROE and in cash flow are negatively correlated to management changes prior to turnover, but more so for changes than for levels.

All in all, the evidence of Table 11.4 fails to reject Hypothesis 1: it shows that the poorer the performance, the higher is the turnover of the executive board. These results are consistent through different estimation techniques (Tobit and OLS with and without fixed effects). Companies only resort to substituting executive directors when accounting returns are very weak: when the company was not able to generate profits or was forced to cut dividends in prior periods. Furthermore, disciplinary actions are undertaken when the company under-performs its industry peers and when market adjusted returns are negative in the period prior to board restructuring.

5.1.1.2. Ownership concentration.

As a single shareholder(group) controls a voting rights majority in more than half of Belgian listed companies, and as a blocking minority exists in 85% of firms, the control percentage of the largest block is included as an explanatory variable.[16] The free riding control-hypothesis predicts that large share blocks facilitate disciplining of management. However, Table 11.4 (lines 5–8) shows that that the presence of large share blocks held by holding companies and institutions (banks, investment funds or insurance companies) is not related to board restructuring. In contrast, management replacement is influenced by large

Table 11.4 Tobit model of the determinants of executive board restructuring in listed industrial and commercial companies[a]

Performance =	Market adj.return (%) Par.Estim	P(Chi)	Operating earnings losses (−1 = yes) Par.Estim	P(Chi)	Dividend cuts (−1 = yes) Par.Estim	P(Chi)	ROE-indus. median (%) Par.Estim	P(Chi)	Δ in ROE-Δ in industry median Par.Estim	P(Chi)	Cash flow on eq. − industry median (%) Par.Estim	P(Chi)	Δ in CF/Eq-Δ in industry median Par.Estim	P(Chi)
1 Intercept	−1.59057*	0.09	−1.27277**	0.04	−2.59715**	0.03	−5.26084***	0.00	−2.24604**	0.02	−2.35075**	0.01	−4.40507***	0.00
2 Perf. t−1	−0.78401***	0.00	−0.31887*	0.09	−0.29769*	0.09	−0.00470	0.23	−0.05700*	0.09	−0.01383	0.61	−0.08407*	0.10
3 Perf. t−2	−0.35742*	0.08					−0.09706*	0.08			0.00136	0.70		
4 Perf. t−3	−0.56100*	0.07												
Share stake held by the largest shareholder by category of owner at t−1:														
5 Hold. co's	0.00346	0.60	−0.01271***	0.00	0.00457	0.51	0.01330	0.07	0.00180	0.75	0.00123	0.85	0.00668	0.11
6 Institutions	0.00549	0.44	−0.01753***	0.00	0.00246	0.72	0.00006	0.99	0.00590*	0.09	−0.00143	0.85	0.00344*	0.10
7 Indus. co's	0.02212*	0.06	0.00347	0.26	0.01100**	0.02	0.01164**	0.01	0.01087***	0.00	0.00987**	0.04	0.02046***	0.00
8 Fam/Ind.	0.02297*	0.08	0.01192*	0.09	0.02706	0.17	0.01456*	0.17	0.01491**	0.07	0.00087	0.90	0.01169**	0.03
Interaction between share stake held by the largest shareholder by category of owner at t−1 and performance at t−1:														
9 Hold. co's	0.05232	0.11	0.00001	0.77	0.00016	0.77	−0.00015	0.37	0.00019	0.68	−0.00007	0.85	0.00037	0.11
10 Institutions	−0.00696	0.81	0.00016***	0.00	0.00000	0.00	−0.00097	0.98	0.00058	0.16	0.00011	0.64	−0.00018	0.35
11 Indus. co's	−0.06148**	0.05	−0.00002	0.32	−0.00007	0.32	−0.00042*	0.44	0.00037	0.08	−0.00034	0.15	0.00035*	0.10
12 Fam/Ind.	0.11505**	0.03	−0.00007	0.31	−0.00066*	0.31	0.00061	0.10	0.00100*	0.36	−0.00047	0.32	−0.00043	0.43
Increases in ownership concentration by category of owner within (t−1, t):														
13 Hold. co's	0.01521	0.28	−0.00259	0.63	0.00224	0.76	0.00971	0.18	0.02284**	0.01	0.00863	0.17	0.01869***	0.00
14 Institutions	1.61149	0.23	0.01714	0.82	0.02262**	0.03	−0.02440	0.77	−0.03032	0.73	−0.05295	0.65	0.03464	0.59

	Coef.	p	Coef.	p	Coef.	p	Coef.	p	Coef.	p	Coef.	p	Coef.	p
15 Indus. co's	0.05496*	0.06	0.02296**	0.02	0.04032***	0.00	0.02014**	0.02	0.01267**	0.04	0.31573**	0.01	0.01007***	0.00
16 Fam/Ind.	0.04521**	0.04	−0.03342	0.31	0.00648	0.56	0.01877	0.30	0.00968	0.77	−0.35741	0.26	−0.00367	0.92
Interaction between increases in ownership concentration by category of owner within (t−1, t) and performance at t−1:														
17 Hold. co's	0.07118	0.11	−0.00007	0.16	−0.00056	0.15	−0.00123	0.22	−0.00181**	0.03	−0.00098*	0.07	0.00059*	0.08
18 Institutions	15.90586	0.23	−0.00002	0.98	−0.03886	0.35	0.00054	0.55	−0.00088	0.41	0.00067	0.38	−0.00063	0.23
19 Indus. co's	−0.15233**	0.02	−0.00024**	0.01	−0.00071***	0.00	−0.00086**	0.03	−0.00148***	0.01	−0.00093*	0.09	−0.00144***	0.00
20 Fam/Ind.	−0.13707**	0.01	−0.00019*	0.08	0.04401	0.43	−0.00075	0.35	−0.00023	0.80	−0.00640*	0.10	0.00336	0.33
21 D/E t−1	0.00890**	0.04	0.01401***	0.00	0.00681**	0.03	0.02231***	0.00	0.00533	0.24	0.01118**	0.01	0.02212***	0.00
22 Intcov. t−1	−0.00056**	0.01	−0.00034**	0.01	−0.00016	0.60	−0.00074***	0.00	−0.00011	0.54	−0.00019*	0.06	−0.00098***	0.00
Interaction between debt variables and performance at t−1														
23 D/E t−1	−0.09332***	0.00	−0.00059*	0.07	0.00002	0.91	−0.00059*	0.10	−0.00100**	0.02	−0.00735**	0.05	−0.00066*	0.06
24 Intcov. t−1	0.00354***	0.00	0.00000	0.32	0.00000	0.62	0.00007*	0.08	0.00004	0.22	0.00002	0.23	−0.00001	0.39
25 Ch≠CEO	0.29686*	0.10	0.14492	0.34	0.08951	0.64	0.18795	0.31	0.14951	0.38	0.04767	0.80	−0.14957	0.20
26 % nonex.	5.31115***	0.00	3.80638***	0.00	3.44586***	0.00	5.20913***	0.00	3.85480***	0.00	4.17495***	0.00	4.46604***	0.00
Interaction between board variables and performance at t−1														
27 Ch≠CEO	−0.30067	0.14	0.00118	0.42	−0.00401	0.58	0.02899	0.19	−0.02100	0.19	0.01779	0.19	−0.03277***	0.00
28 % nonex.	4.66856**	0.01	0.00133	0.28	−0.00414	0.81	0.02346	0.38	0.00236	0.89	0.04264	0.28	0.00260	0.82
29 Num. dir.	0.00453	0.87	0.00057	0.67	0.00650	0.55	0.00046	0.61	−0.00851	0.88	0.00032	0.30	0.00152	0.64
30 Size (Log of tot. assets)	−0.21246***	0.00	−0.15899***	0.00	−0.05734	0.35	−0.04384	0.32	−0.10365**	0.01	−0.11967***	0.00	−0.04889*	0.08
Zero or neg. response	195		192		197		197		197		197		197	
Log likelihood Weibull	−16.773		−20.874		−28.567		−27.947		−24.859		−26.924		−26.924	

a Perf. = Performance, Hold. co's = Holding co's, Indus. co's = Indus. and comm. co's, Fam/Ind. = Families and Individuals, D/E = Debt/Equity, Intcov = Interest coverage, % non-ex. = Percentage non-executive directors, Num. dir. = Total number of directors. A dummy variable equal to 1 is included if the functions of CEO and chairman are combined by one person.

Table 11.5 Tobit model of the determinants of executive board restructuring in listed holding companies[a]

Performance =	Market adj.return (%)		Operating earn. losses (−1 = yes)		Dividend cuts (−1 = yes)		ROE − indus. median (%)		Δ in ROE − Δ in industry median		Cash flow on eq. − industry median (%)		Δ in CF/Eq − Δ in industry median	
	Par.Estim	P(Chi)	Par.Estim	P(Chi)	Par.Estim	P(Chi)	Par.Estim	P(Chi)	Par.Estim	P(Chi)	Par.Estim	P(Chi)	Par.Estim	P(Chi)
1 Intercept	−2.37284*	0.09	−3.68603	0.12	−0.34073	0.97	−1.36375	0.54	−0.42521	0.83	−1.51379	0.31	−1.85787	0.31
2 Perf. t−1	−1.30870	0.38	−0.30066*	0.09	−0.74106***	0.00	−0.00229	0.48	−0.30803**	0.01	−0.10645	0.32	0.01220	0.20
3 Perf. t−2	−0.02472	0.75					−0.14491*	0.10			−0.20236*	0.02		
4 Perf. t−3	−1.08528**	0.01												
Share stake held by the largest shareholder by category of owner at t − 1:														
5 Hold. co's	0.00067	0.93	−0.01075	0.24	−0.00906**	0.01	−0.02882***	0.00	−0.01048	0.14	0.03187**	0.00	−0.01475	0.12
6 Institutions	0.00973	0.41	0.01048	0.68	0.00248	0.82	−0.02129*	0.10	−0.03376	0.17	−0.02671*	0.06	−0.00557	0.59
7 Indus. co's	0.02852**	0.01	0.12457	0.24	−0.02773	0.50	−0.06358**	0.01	0.01492	0.56	−0.22205**	0.01	−0.02355	0.52
8 Fam/Ind.	0.00109	0.89	0.01489	0.16	−0.01479***	0.00	−0.03182***	0.00	−0.00506	0.67	0.03388**	0.01	0.01417	0.47
Interaction between share stake held by the largest shareholder by category of owner at t − 1 and performance at t − 1:														
9 Hold. co's	0.03150	0.20	0.00007	0.38	−0.00094***	0.00	0.00395***	0.00	0.00059	0.38	0.00325***	0.00	−0.00007	0.94
10 Institutions	0.01317	0.19	0.00017	0.41	−0.00048	0.45	0.00287*	0.45	−0.00035	0.50	0.00329***	0.00	−0.00053	0.54
11 Indus. co's	0.07345*	0.10	0.00160	0.24	−0.00028	0.80	−0.00570**	0.03	0.00761***	0.00	−0.01645	0.27	−0.03967*	0.06
12 Fam/Ind.	−0.03263*	0.07	0.00001	0.71	−0.00024**	0.05	0.00464**	0.05	0.00071	0.33	0.00890**	0.00	−0.00132	0.72
Increases in ownership concentration by category of owner within (t − 1, t):														
13 Hold. co's	0.00455	0.87	−0.01338	0.44	−0.06775***	0.00	0.01735	0.34	−0.00591	0.74	−0.02383	0.39	−0.04158*	0.06
14 Institutions	−11.49972	0.16	24.25648	0.29	−1.68032	0.59	22.30041	0.35	−7.97964	0.14	−4.48663*	0.08	6.95358	0.41
15 Fam/Ind.	1.34751*	0.07	−5.21520	0.29	−0.00545	0.82	−1.53244	0.29	1.01566	0.16	−1.77376**	0.04	−1.52486	0.40

Interaction between increases in ownership concentration by category of owner within $(t-1, t)$ and performance at $t-1$:

16 Hold. co's	0.16037**	0.01	0.00042**	0.02	0.00170***	0.00	-0.00395**	0.04	-0.00231*	0.09	-0.00046	0.93	0.00461	0.38
17 Fam/Ind.	16.25936	0.16	-0.06893	0.30	0.05833	0.56	-0.67105	0.36	-0.16702	0.12	0.37400*	0.06	-0.17474	0.44
18 D/E t−1	0.00981*	0.08	0.00974**	0.04	0.01531**	0.01	0.00096	0.76	0.00772**	0.01	0.02260**	0.01	0.00022	0.94
19 Intcov. t−1	0.00014	0.84	-0.00239**	0.04	0.00113	0.21	-0.00214**	0.04	-0.00419**	0.03	0.00519	0.12	-0.00307	0.25

Interaction between debt variables and performance at $t-1$

20 D/E t−1	0.02230	0.11	-0.00008**	0.05	-0.00092***	0.00	0.00001	0.97	-0.00058***	0.00	0.00232**	0.01	-0.00075**	0.04
21 Intcov. t−1	-0.00211	0.59	-0.00001	0.11	-0.00011	0.56	0.00019	0.51	0.00018**	0.03	-0.00096***	0.00	0.00012	0.39
22 Ch ≠ CEO	-0.07816	0.73	-0.88579**	0.00	-0.79457***	0.00	-0.08235	0.75	-0.93319**	0.04	-0.45780*	0.06	-0.61100	0.32
23 % nonex.	5.97179***	0.0	6.03862***	0.00	4.05689***	0.00	4.44313***	0.00	6.79918***	0.00	6.28175***	0.00	5.72372***	0.00

Interaction between board variables and performance at $t-1$

24 Ch ≠ CEO	0.65725	0.40	-0.00131	0.46	-0.02154***	0.00	-0.07418	0.11	-0.03945	0.11	-3.02876	0.26	0.03356	0.37
25 % nonex.	-7.71821**	0.04	-0.01051**	0.02	-0.01853	0.19	0.03948	0.74	0.34014	0.11	-3.14793	0.38	-0.10907**	0.05
26 Num. dir.	0.00042	0.77	-0.00073	0.59	0.00079	0.71	0.00110	0.47	-0.00361	0.61	0.00235	0.32	0.00079	0.91
27 Size (Log of tot. assets)	-0.20213*	0.05	-0.07609	0.63	-0.27650***	0.00	0.00408	0.97	-0.25987*	0.07	-0.26303***	0.00	-0.12670	0.33
Zero or neg. response	150		148		143		160		160		160		160	
Log likelihood	-12.297		-22.042		15.165		-10.436		-20.635		-12.893		-19.897	
Weibull														

a Perf. = Performance, Hold. co's = Holding co's, Indus. co's = Indus. and comm. co's, Fam/Ind. = Families and Individuals, D/E = Debt/Equity, Intcov = Interest coverage, % non-ex. = Percentage non-executive directors, Num. dir. = Total number of directors. A dummy variable equal to I is included if the functions of CEO and chairman are combined by one person.

industrial investor shareholdings (in 6 out of 7 models) and by blocks held by families (5 models). Piecewise regressions – with dummies indicating whether or not the largest owner holds a blocking minority, majority or supermajority (as in Hermalin and Weisbach, 1991) – reveal that minority stakes held by industrial companies are sufficiently large to exert control and to restructure the board.[17]

Table 11.4 (lines 9–12) also investigates whether the ownership structure plays a performance-induced disciplining role. None of the categories of large blockholders seem to be involved in disciplinary actions against management when performance is poor. The lack of institutional investor involvement is in line with Hypothesis 3 which states that they abstain from monitoring to avoid conflicts of interest. In contrast, the fact that the large holding companies do not seem to monitor is surprising as these often cite superior corporate governance as one of the core contributions of their stable ownership stakes as 'reference shareholders'.[18] The lack of significance of the interaction terms between large industrial and family owners, and performance, raises doubt about the fact whether board restructuring is initiated by families or industrial companies as a result of poor performance.[19] All in all, there is little evidence about the corporate control role of existing large shareholders.

5.1.1.3. The market in share stakes

When performance is poor, shareholders without a distinct interest in monitoring sell stakes, while those with strong monitoring abilities increase their stakes in order to reinforce their position as (major) shareholder. If this were true, we would expect positive signs for the increases in shareholdings (Hypothesis 3). In spite of the fact that institutions and holding companies actively trade in share stakes over 1989–1994 (Table 11.3), ownership increases by these categories are not correlated with changes in board structure (lines 13–16 of Table 11.4). However, there is one

exception: when industrial companies and families obtain substantial share stakes, changes in management are implemented. Such board restructuring takes place (lines 19–20) when prior performance was poor (negative market adjusted returns, negative changes or levels of performance), which suggests a partial corporate control market (Hypothesis 5). It can be observed that disciplining underperforming management happens in the year of turnover or in the subsequent fiscal year.[20]

Concerning the role of ownership concentration and the partial market for control, it is important to realise that above results were obtained after classifying all blocks of voting rights into ownership categories based on the identity of the ultimate or reference owners of each of these blocks. No significant results were attained in a first set of regressions where all ownership variables (levels and increases) were included by category of shareholder owner on the direct ownership level. For example, if a holding company holds 10% of the voting rights in a listed company, this 10% stake is classified as a stake owned by a holding company. The fact that the intermediate holding company may be directly or indirectly controlled by e.g. a family is ignored in this first set of regressions. However, when we reclassify all direct shareholdings (voting rights) in ownership categories based on the identity of the true (i.e. ultimate) owner – in the example above the 10% stake is a family controlled stake – we find the conclusions discussed above: significant results for the presence of industrial co's and families versus insignificant ones for institutions and holding companies. This suggests support for Hypothesis 4 and implies that the ultimate or 'reference' shareholder, who controls the voting rights of a listed target company by ways of a cascade of intermediate holdings, exerts corporate control.[21]

5.1.1.4. Gearing as a bonding mechanism

High leverage encourages management to generate sufficient funds to service the debt commitments. Consequently, a high debt–equity ratio is expected to reduce management's discretion and summon more intensive creditor monitoring, as is suggested in Table 11.4 (line 21) where executive director replacement is positively correlated with a high gearing (6 out of 7 regressions). Executive monitoring increases especially when corporate performance is negative (negative market adjusted returns, earnings losses, level and changes in ROE and cash flow adjusted for industry medians).[22] Low interest coverage is an important indicator of financial distress; when the interest cover decreases below 2, a company typically loses investment grade. Table 11.4 also shows that executive board restructuring also coincides with low interest coverage (line 22), but that the interaction of poor share price and accounting performance is not correlated to executive board turnover (line 24). This implies that interest coverage may be considered as another monitoring performance benchmark and important trigger for monitoring actions.[23] The strong correlation between gearing and interest cover, and performance (Hypothesis 6) suggests enhanced creditor monitoring when performance is poor. Interviews with executive and non-executive directors revealed that the monitoring role by creditors is considered limited (unless there is a danger of bond covenant violation).[24]

5.1.1.5. Board composition and separation of control

Table 11.4 supports the hypothesis that the board structure is instrumental for the monitoring efficiency of the internal governance mechanism (Hypothesis 2). The more independent the non-executive board from management, proxied by the proportion of non-executive directors, the easier it is to replace management when managerial performance is inadequate (lines 26 and 28). The fact that the role of large ownership stakes was not supported by our model (apart from for industrial companies) may be explained to some extent by the importance of the proportion of non-executives. It may well be that the number of non-executive

directors on board is a proxy for the control power of a share block and that these large shareholder representatives are performing their roles as monitors and are executing their disciplining part well. As only a few companies could (or were willing) to disclose the representative function of its board members, this hypothesis could not be tested further. Board size differs substantially across firms; some have small boards with 6 directors, while others count 15 or more. In spite of the fact that large boards may reduce efficiency, board size does not seem to influence managerial disciplining (line 29).

For the US, Weisbach (1988) finds that CEO turnover is more sensitive to performance in firms whose boards are dominated by outsiders. Outsiders are carefully defined as directors who work neither for the corporation nor have extensive dealings with that company. In a study on the performance effects of the composition of the board of directors in the US, Baysinger and Butler (1985) conclude that those firms with stronger independent boards ended up with superior performance records, in the form of superior relative financial performance (an industry corrected return on equity). It should be emphasised that research about the impact of US board composition on CEO turnover is not directly comparable with research on Belgian boards. The emphasis in the US has been put on the independence of 'outside' directors, whereas some non-executives in Belgium are large shareholder representatives and 'independent or expert' non-executive directors' appointment to the board might be subject to large shareholder approval.

Next to the strengthening of the independence of non-executive board members, another recommendation in the recent Guidelines for Good Corporate Governance (of the Cardon Commission, Stock Exchange Commission, Commission for Banking and Finance) is the separation of the functions of managing director and of chairman of the board, but this necessity is not upheld by the findings of this model (lines 25 and 27 of Table 11.4).

Although larger companies may have a bigger internal managerial labour market and have better access to the external managerial labour market, corporate size is negatively related to executive board replacement (line 30).[25] Are these disciplinary actions only directed at top managers who are on the board or do these actions extend to other managers, c.q. the members of the direction committee? The results with management committee turnover (executive directors and other top managers) as dependent variable gives weaker results than with executive turnover. This implies that performance related turnover is targeting the very top management, namely predominantly those three managers appointed to the board.

5.1.2. Disciplinary actions against CEO[26]

CEO replacement in industrial and commercial companies (corrected for natural turnover) is correlated with the presence of large shareholdings held by families and individuals, institutional investors and industrial companies. The fact that the interaction terms of ownership and performance are significant (10% level) suggests that these replacements are the result of corporate governance actions (Hypotheses 3 and 4). Furthermore, CEO substitution also follows increases in share stakes held by holding companies and industrial firms, but due to lack of significance in interaction terms it is questionable whether this stake accumulation is induced by poor performance (Hypothesis 5). Internal governance structure like separation of the functions of CEO and chairman, and the presence of a high proportion of non-executives facilitates disciplining of the CEO when the companies results are bad (Hypothesis 2).[27] Finally, there is evidence that low interest coverage leads to higher CEO turnover (Hypothesis 6).

5.2. Listed Belgian holding companies

Table 11.5 investigates whether executive director replacement takes place in holding

companies and which internal and external control mechanisms trigger such governance actions. Support for Hypothesis 1 is presented in Table 11.5: past poor share price and accounting performance in holding companies lead to executive board restructuring, although this relation is weaker than for listed industrial companies. Over the period 1988–1994, dividend cuts, earnings losses, low industry corrected ROE and cash flows precede executive director replacement (lines 2–4). There is evidence of leverage related monitoring (lines 18–21; Hypothesis 6) as high gearing ratios result in increased managerial removal when performance is poor. In addition, board composition does also seem to influence corporate control as high executive board turnover is positively related to a high percentage of non-executive directors on board (Hypothesis 2).

Although some holding companies are widely held, most of the others are controlled by families or other holding companies. Contrary to Hypothesis 3, there is no consistent relation between the presence of large share blocks and executive board restructuring of listed holding companies. The evidence in Table 11.5 even hints (in 3 out of 7 models) that less monitoring is expected in the presence of a controlling holding company (negative correlation in line 5).[28] Furthermore, the negative parameter coefficient in line 13 reveals that when there is poor performance and increases in share stakes controlled by holding companies, there is a reduced managerial disciplining. This raises the question why holding companies with controlling stakes or holding companies acquiring large stakes do not monitor. Like in France (Banerjee et al., 1997, hence BLV), holding companies in Belgium may enhance wealth creation by offering a internal capital market to the companies they control, by offering the possibility to invest indirectly in non-listed companies to individual investors, by smoothing tax liabilities of the group or by lowering bankruptcy costs by facilitating workouts. However, both the BLV study (1997) for France and Daems (1998) for Belgium fail to find wealth creation by holding companies. The share price of Belgian holding companies is even estimated to be 35–39% lower than the market value of all their equity participations.[29]

The potential corporate governance benefits by holding companies consist of the supply of strategic advice and a reduction in agency costs due to economies of scale in monitoring. Still, BLV state that "holding companies can create agency problems of their own and, with well-diversified portfolios, it is unclear why they would be willing or be able to engage in costly monitoring activities for each of the companies they control. The quality of their monitoring activities has never been ascertained, not has it ever been compared to that provided by other large shareholders, the external market for corporate control, . . . ". The findings in this paper corroborate this statement as controlling holding companies or holding companies which acquire large share stakes in listed Belgian industrial companies (Table 11.4)[30] and in listed Belgian holding companies (Table 11.5)[31] do not seem to be involved with performance correcting governance actions. Furthermore, listed Belgian holding companies may suffer from the very agency problems they pretend to solve for the companies they control because the controlling shareholders in holding companies do not seem to discipline holding companies' underperformance.

This conclusion about holding companies can be extended to the quoted financial institutions – in this paper defined as a rather heterogeneous sample of banks, insurance companies and real estate firms.[32] Most of these institutions are part of a holding group of which the monitoring abilities have been questioned. Bank Brussels Lambert (BBL) is often mentioned as an example of the break down of 'reference' or ultimate shareholder monitoring. Over whole time period of the paper (1989–94), BBL is controlled by the Group Brussels Lambert who holds a direct stake of 13% (the largest stake) and controls indirectly via the Royal Belge insurance group another 9.3%. In spite of the need for the development of an international

expansion strategy and the call to form one large Belgian commercial bank (merger with the Generale Bank), GBL has not favored such strategies.[33] All in all, the system with strong ownership concentration comprises important drawbacks (see also Daems, 1998; De Wulf et al., 1998).

5.3. Post-disciplining performance

The effectiveness of the corporate control mechanism could be assessed by analysing performance following the installation of new management (Hypothesis 7). Improved performance after executive board restructuring would confirm that the ousted directors and management had underperformed and that the monitors were able to attract a management better suited to reorganise the company. The post-disciplining earnings evolution is analysed by industry:[34] for the companies in which more than 25% of the executive board or the CEO resigned, the returns on equity two years prior and two years subsequent to executive board restructuring are compared. Prior and subsequent ROE are calculated as deviations from the ROE of companies which did not experience executive board restructuring of 25% or CEO replacement. Even after the executive board restructuring, the level of ROE in most industries subsequent to the board restructuring is still lagging the ROE of companies without board restructuring. There is little evidence of ROE improvements in time windows subsequent to board restructuring with exception of the industry of consumer goods/health/pharma. This finding may not come as a surprise as it is a well documented fact that in US and UK companies, a decrease in earnings often follows the departure of the CEO because new CEOs often write off as many expenses as possible during their first year (Murphy and Zimmerman, 1993). Moreover, the success of corporate governance actions, may not be visible in subsequent performance because, in specific cases, earnings stabilisation at a low level or avoidance of further financial distress or even bankruptcy may be considerable achievements.

Dividend policy (changes in dividends per share) are also compared for periods two years prior and two years subsequent to board restructuring. Similarly, changes in dividends are defined as the difference in changes of high turnover companies from the benchmark, namely dividend changes of companies with low board restructuring (less than 25% of executive board turnover and no CEO turnover). For the sectors of electrical equipment and electronics, and services, there is a significantly higher growth in dividends per share after board restructuring than prior. For holding companies, and the sector chemicals and materials, this effect is only marginally significant. This result may indicate that, as changes in dividends tend to have a permanent character, increases in dividends reflect some more confidence in future profitability after managerial disciplining.

6. CONCLUSION

In this paper the importance of several internal and external mechanisms of corporate governance was analysed in terms of disciplining management of poorly performing companies. There may be substitute forms of discipline, and even if there is redundancy, one form may dominate the other consistently. Disciplinary actions against management are taken when market adjusted share returns are negative and when the company generates operating earnings' losses or resorts to substantial cuts in dividends in the years prior to the restructuring. There is also evidence that companies with levels of and changes in ROE and cash flows below those of industry peers are subjected to increased monitoring. These performance–turnover relations are much stronger for listed industrial and commercial companies than for listed holding companies and financial institutions.

Belgian equity markets are characterised by few listings, a high degree of ownership concentration held by holding companies and families, and to a lesser extent industrial companies. Furthermore, control is levered by pyramidal and complex ownership structures and there is an important market for share stakes. Little relation was uncovered between ownership structures and the disciplining of top management in listed industrial and commercial companies. However, the presence of large industrial shareholders (and to a lesser extent of family shareholdings) is related to high executive board turnover when performance is poor, whereas no evidence was found for a monitoring role by institutions or holding companies.

A fraction of the market for share stakes may be considered as a corporate control market because industrial and commercial companies increase their shareholdings (or purchase large share blocks) in listed poorly performing industrial companies in which there is, subsequently, increased conflictual management replacement. In the light of disciplining actions undertaken by industrial companies (who are often in the same industry as the target company), the lack of active corporate control in the wake of poor performance by holding companies is striking. High ownership concentration held by a holding company group can lead to strategic deadlocks for quoted companies, as illustrated by the BBL case with the Group Brussels Lambert as reference shareholder. Daems (1998, p. 65) illustrates this deadlock with another example: 'A reference shareholder [belonging to a holding group] will tend to concentrate on the interests of the group as a whole. He might be tempted to divide its markets over its subsidiaries such that they do not compete too intensively with each other. Hence, [the French holding group] Suez, could have an interest in dividing the international [utility] markets over its subsidiaries, [the French] Lyonnaise des Eaux and [the Belgian] Tractebel. This limitation of strategic freedom of the subsidiaries is not in the interest of minority shareholders and investors who are participating in the group via the stock exchange.'

Although high leverage also seems instrumental to replace poorly performing management, there is no direct evidence that it is bondholders or banks who force underperforming management out. Interviews with non-executive directors disclosed that high leverage or low interest coverage stimulate actions by the (non-executive) board (and as such the share-holders) rather than creditor intervention. We find that the role of the non-executive directors is important in the disciplining process: a high proportion of non-executive directors leads to increased executive board turnover. Given that companies usually do not reveal the representation of the share-holders of the board of the directors, the percentage of non-executive directors was used as a proxy for independence of the board from management, but the board structure may very well be influenced by ownership concentration. Furthermore, a higher proba-bility of CEO replacement was found when the tasks of CEO ('delegated' director) and (non-executive) chairman are separated.

Corporate governance relations in holding companies and especially financial institutions are much weaker than in listed industrial companies. Board composition and leverage have a substantial impact on board restructuring, but neither ownership concentration nor a partial market for share stakes leads to increased disciplining in holding companies. Belgian listed holding companies may to a large extent suffer from a lack of corporate control and seem to have discharged themselves from efficient monitoring of the companies they control, as seems also be the case for French holding companies (Banerjee et al., 1997). In spite of the presence of a large shareholder in a vast majority of Belgian listed companies and of the breakdown – both in terms of performance and governance – of the ownership cascade system involving holding companies, it is problematic that the recent codes for good corporate governance do not encompass any recommendation with regard to large shareholder monitoring.[35]

ACKNOWLEDGEMENTS

I am indebted to Julian Franks for stimulat-ing discussions as well to Colin Mayer, Theo Vermaelen, Michel Habib, Ian Cooper, Lorenzo Caprio, Marc Goergen, Rafel Crespi, Rez Kabir, Marco Becht, Piet Moerland and Joe McCahery. Helpful advice was given by two anonymous referees, by the participants to the finance seminars at the universities of Tilburg, Antwerp (UFSIA), Barcelona (Autonoma), Venice, Oxford and by discussants at several conferences (EFA, EEA, Financial Markets Symposium of the CEPR in Gerzensee). I am grateful to Mr. Maertens of the Department of Information and Statistics of the Brussels Stock Exchange for allowing access to some of the data used in this study. Financial support was provided by the European Commission and the Netherlands Organisation for Scientific Research (NWO).

NOTES

* Present address: Department of Finance and CentER, Tilburg University, Warandelaan 2, 5000 Tilburg, Netherlands. Tel.: +31-13-466-8210; fax: +31-13-466-2875. *E-mail address:* Luc.Renneboog@kub.nl (L. Renneboog).
1 The recent changes in legislation on disclosure of voting rights now allow detailed corporate governance studies in Europe. Description of ownership and voting rights in Europe can be found in Barca and Becht (2000, forthcoming. Who Controls Corporate Europe?, Oxford University Press). The countries covered are Austria (Gugler, Kalss, Stomper and Zechner), Belgium (Becht, Chapelle and Renneboog), France (Bloch and Kremp), Germany (Becht and Bohmer), Italy (Bianchi, Bianco and Enriques), Netherlands (De Jong, Kabir, Mara and Roëll), Spain (Crespi and Garcia-Cestona), Sweden (Agnblad, Berglof, Hogfeldt and Svancar), UK (Goergen and Renneboog, 2000a,b), US (Becht).
2 Still, a priori, it is not certain whether one specific corporate governance mechanism is positively related to performance as, even if one mechanism may be used more frequently, the existence of other corporate governance devices and their interdependence may result in compa-rable equilibrium performance (Agrawal and Knoeber, 1996).
3 Such recommendations have been formu-lated in the US Bacon report (1993), the UK Cadbury Committee report (1992), the French

Viénot report (1995), the Dutch Peeters Commission report (1997), the Belgian corporate governance guidelines by the Stock Exchange Commission, the Association of Employers and the Commission for Banking and Finance (all in 1998).

4   An investor is considered to be the 'ultimate or reference shareholder' in an ownership–control chain if control is maintained through multiple tiers of ownership. Interlocking ownership via a holding company or through a more elaborate stock pyramid enables a given investor to own different quantities of voting and cash flow rights. For instance, 50.1% of ownership (and voting rights) held by the ultimate shareholder in an intermediary holding company which, in turn, owns 50.1% of an operating subsidiary could guarantee majority control on the subsidiary's board with only a 25.1% interest in its common stock cash flow.

5   Following management changes, asset write-offs (Strong and Meyer, 1987), changes to income reducing accounting methods (Moore, 1973) or income reducing accounting accruals (Pourciau, 1993) frequently occur.

6   The sample size was reduced by 9 companies in 1989 and by 10 in 1994 as these listed firms, all in coal mining and steel production, were involved in a long liquidation process but were still listed.

7   The results do not change when we exclude from the sample recent IPOs or companies that went bankrupt. Sector codes, dates of introduction and of delisting are provided by the Documentation and Statistics Department of the Brussels Stock Exchange. Companies disappearing as a separate entity following absorption by another company as a result of a merger are included until the year prior to the merger.

8   Warner et al. (1988) and Weisbach (1988) also mention that reasons for turnover are often lacking. Weisbach also only excludes retirements if they are age related (63 years or older) which eliminates most of the non-linearity in the turnover–age relationship: " . . . companies do not announce the true reason behind their CEOs' resignations. Therefore, I ignore the stated reasons for resignation in constructing my sample. I do, however, eliminate the resignations for which I am able to corroborate the cause independently. Changes in CEOs caused by death and preceding a takeover are excluded because these 'resignations' are totally verifiable." (p. 438). This bias is also mentioned by, among others, Dennis and Dennis (1995) and Hermalin and Weisbach (1991). Non-informative reasons found for leaving the company are of

the kind: "pursuing other interests", "spending more time with the family" or "retirements" at an age of 62 or below.

9   Including board size controls for the fact that different governance mechanisms may prevail in large versus small companies. Large companies may have a larger internal managerial labour market and have better access to an external managerial labour market.

10   We define a control relation between an ultimate shareholder and a target company if (i) there is a series of uninterrupted majority shareholdings on every ownership tier throughout the pyramid or (ii) if there is a large shareholding of at least 25% on every ownership level in the absence of other shareholders with stakes of blocking minority size or larger.

11   Often, Luxembourgian intermediate investment companies are used.

12   These changes exclude shareholding restructuring within investor groups, as these changes do not have any impact on control.

13   We find a negative correlation (significant at the 1% level) between past corporate performance and increases in ownership; the lower the performance, the larger the increases in ownership. Note that all increases, regardless of their size, are taken into consideration because some shareholders only need a small increase in the percentage of their voting rights to reach a blocking minority or a majority.

14   If the fiscal year end is e.g. March 1994, the data of this fiscal year are included in the regressions as 1993 as most of the fiscal year is in 1993. If the fiscal year end is 30 June 1994 or later in 1994, the data of the year are included in the regressions as 1994. The yearly market adjusted returns are calculated such that they coincide with the fiscal years of the corporations. Only lagged performance variables are included because a performance variable of the year coinciding with the year of turnover may be a (partial) lead variable especially if the turnover takes place early in the fiscal year.

15   Apart from the performance measures given in Tables 11.4 and 11.5, models with levels and changes of return (after interest, taxes and extraordinary) on assets (both with and without industry median correction) and cash flow margin were estimated. The results of these models are in line with the ones discussed.

16   Including the total share concentration by class of owner or Herfindahl indices, yields – expectedly – similar results. Including squared ownership does not yield robust results across models.

17   Piecewise regressions are not shown, but tables are available.

18   In the years following the take over battle between the French Suez group and the Italian group of de Benedetti in 1989, the Generale Maatschappÿ van België or the Société Générale de Belgique, was restructured using a focus strategy on 8 industrial and financial sectors. The Group Brussels Lambert, another large holding company, has often been criticized for failing to establish a strategic plan for the companies it controlled and is often given as an example of a stalemate situation brought about by the reference shareholder model. The fact that some of these large holding companies, which control several listed (and many unlisted) companies, may fail in their monitoring role has an important impact on our conclusions regarding the governance ability of holding companies. For a discussion, see Daems (1998) and Dewulf et al. (1998).

19   The findings described are robust across estimation methods. OLS with fixed effects yield somewhat stronger significance for the presence of large shareholdings held by industrial and commercial companies and by families: in three regressions, industrial and performance effects are significant.

20   Unlike the models with executive and CEO turnover, regressions with management committee turnover only yielded weakly significant results. This implies that only those top managers who hold a board seat are held responsible and subject to disciplinary corporate control.

21   Although control is exerted by the ultimate shareholder, there is evidence that when controlling stakes are held through multiple tiers of ownership and when intermediate shareholdings deviate from full ownership, ultimate investor control is diluted. For instance, sequences of majority control in the form of e.g. stakes of 50.1% throughout the pyramid might not guarantee the same degree of control a first tier majority holding would give, unless there is strong board representation on each ownership tier. Consequently, the larger the number of ownership tiers and the larger the deviation from full ownership, the weaker the relation between turnover and ownership concentration. Including levered shareholdings (see Section 4) by category of owner gives similar results but reduces significance.

22   Including changes in gearing did not give any significant results. Changes in capital structure in the form of new equity issues which took place in 40 firm-years was also included in the models but are not correlated to board turnover.

23   Current and acid ratios were significant but were not included in the model of Table 11.4

along with gearing and interest coverage in order to avoid multicollinearity.

24   Several directors (among others, M. Davignon (Generale Maatschappij van België/Société Générale de Belgique), M. Bodson (Tractebel), M. Samyn (NPM/SNP)) were interviewed and asked to comment on the results of this study. They confirmed the limited role of creditor monitoring unless a large refinancing takes place and emphasized the role of the large shareholders (for which we only found limited support) and of the board of directors (for which we found strong support).

25   Using the logarithm of the total number of employees as size variable, yields less significance (only 3 regressions out of 7 in Table 11.4).

26   Tables with logit models on CEO turnover are available upon request.

27   CEOs with long tenure are less easily removed when performance is poor as they may have a good track record. However, this conclusion is only based on one fourth of the sample companies as these data were only disclosed for a limited number of companies.

28   The probability that the CEO of listed holding companies is replaced increases with the degree of family control. This is especially the case when the market adjusted return is low and when the company faces losses and has to reduce dividends. In contrast to the capital structure, board composition is again a determining factor. Both a large percentage of non-executive directors and the separation of the functions of CEO and non-executive chairman increases the probability of CEO substitution.

29   De Standaard of 7, 8 August 1999.

30   See lines 5, 9, 13, and 17.

31   See lines 5, 9, 13, and 16.

32   Note that the reason why the proposed governance model does not fit the financial companies is not due to lack of turnover. The dependent variable executive turnover is between 22% and 37% depending on the year, which is similar to turnover in industrial and commercial companies.

33   A similar example of a reference shareholder hampering a fair M&A competition between Fortis and ABN Amro for control of the Generale Bank in 1997 has been detailed extensively in the financial press.

34   Due to sample size limitations, several sectors are added (based on NACE industry classifications) to form industry subsamples: holdings companies, energy and utilities, chemical and materials (metal and non-ferro), electrical and electronics, consumer products and health care/pharma. services (transport, leasing,

hotel, . . .). The utility sector was subsequently deleted due to small sample size.

35   See also Meeus (1998) and Wymeersch (1998) for a discussion of the content of the codes of good corporate governance.

REFERENCES

Aghion, Bolton, 1992. An incomplete contracts approach to financial contracting. Review of Economic Studies 59, 473–494.

Agrawal, A., Knoeber, C., 1996. Firm performance and mechanisms to control agency problems between managers and shareholders. Journal of Financial and Quantitative Analysis 31, 377–397.

Bacon, J., 1993. Corporate Boards and Corporate Governance, published by The Conference Board in co-operation with Booz Allen & Hamilton Inc.

Banerjee, S., Leleux, B., Vermaelen, T., 1997. Large shareholdings and corporate control: An anlysis of stake purchases by French holding companies. European Financial Management 3, 23–43.

Barca, F., Becht, M., 2000. Who Controls Corporate Europe. Oxford University Press, Oxford.

Barclay, M.J., Holderness, C.G., 1989. Private benefits from control of public corporations. Journal of Financial Economics 25, 371–395.

Barclay, M.J., Holderness, C.G., 1991. Negotiated block trades and corporate control. Journal of Finance 46, 861–878.

Baysinger, B.D., Butler, H.N., 1985. Corporate governance and the board of directors: Performance effects of changes in board composition. Journal of Law, Economics and Organization 1, 101–124.

Berkovitch, W., Israel, R., Spiegel, Y., 1997. Managerial compensation and capital structure, Working paper.

Bolton, P., von Thadden, E., 1998. Blocks, liquidity and corporate control. Journal of Finance 53(1), 1–25.

Bratton, W., McCahery, J., 1999. Comparative corporate governance and the theory of the firm: The case against global cross reference, Working paper, Law faculty, Tilburg University.

Burkart, M., Gromb, D., Panunzi, F., 1997. Large shareholders, monitoring and the value of the firm. Quarterly Journal of Economics, 693–728.

Cadbury, A., 1992. Report of the committee on the financial aspects of corporate governance, Gee & Co Ltd, London, December.

Coughlan, A.T., Schmidt, R.M., 1985. Executive compensation, managerial turnover, and firm performance: An empirical investigation. Journal of Accounting and Economics 7, 42–66.

Daems, H., 1998. De paradox van het Belgisch kapitalisme, Lannoo, Brussels.

Demsetz, H., 1983. The structure of ownership and the theory of the firm. Journal of Law and Economics 26, 375–390.

Demsetz, H., Lehn, K., 1985. The structure of corporate ownership: Causes and consequences. Journal of Political Economy 93, 1155–1177.

Denis, D.J., Denis, D.K., 1993. Managerial discretion, managerial structure, and corporate performance: A study of leveraged recapitalizations. Journal of Accounting and Economics 16, 209–236.

Denis, D.J., Denis, D.K., 1995. Performance changes following top management dismissals. Journal of Finance 50, 1029–1057.

DeWulf, H. et al., 1998. Corporate Governance: Het Belgische Perspectief, Intersentia Rechtswetenschappen, Antwerpen-Groningen, 245 p.

Elliott, J. and Shaw, W. 1988. Write-offs as accounting procedures to manage perceptions. Journal of Accounting Research Supplement to vol. 26, 32–40.

Fama, E., Jensen, M., 1983. Separation of ownership and control. Journal of Law and Economics 26, 301–325.

Franks, J., Mayer, C., 1998. Ownership and control of German corporations. Working paper, London Business School.

Franks, J., Mayer, C., Renneboog, L., 1998. Who disciplines bad management? Discussion paper, CentER, Tilburg University.

Goergen, M., Renneboog, L., 2000a. Insider control by large investor groups and managerial disciplining in listed Belgian companies. Managerial Finance, forthcoming.

Goergen, M., Renneboog, L., 2000b. Prediction of ownership and control concentration subsequent to initial public offerings in Germany and the UK. In: Renneboog, L., McCahery, J., Moerland, P., Raaijmakers, T. (Eds.), Convergence and Diversity of Corporate Governance Regimes and Capital Markets. Oxford University Press, Oxford.

Gilson, S.C., 1990. Bankruptcy, boards, banks, and blockholders. Journal of Financial Economics 27, 55–387.

Grossman, S.J., Hart, O., 1980. Takeover bids, the free-rider problem, and the theory of the corporation. Bell Journal of Economics 11, 42–64.

Grossman, S.J., Hart, O., 1988. One share-one vote and the market for corporate control. Journal of Financial Economics 20, 175–202.

Healey, P., Palepu, K., 1988. Dividend initiations and omissions as earnings signals. Journal of Financial Economics 21, 149–176.

Hermalin, B.E., Weisbach, M.S., 1991. The effects of board composition and direct incentives on firm performance. Financial Management 20, 101–112.

Holderness, Sheehan, 1988. The role of majority shareholders in publicly held corporations: An exploratory analysis. Journal of Financial Economics 20, 317–346.

Jensen, M.C., Meckling, W.H., 1976. Theory of the firm: Managerial behaviour, agency costs and ownership structure. Journal of Financial Economics 3, 305–360.

Joskow, P.L., Rose, M.L., 1994. CEO pay and firm performance: Dynamics, asymmetries, and alternative performance measures. Working paper Massachusetts Institute of Technology, Cambridge, MA.

Kaplan, S.N., 1994. Top executives, turnover and firm performance in Germany. Journal of Law, Economics and Organization 10, 142–159.

Kaplan, S.N., Minton, B.A., 1994. Appointments of outsiders to Japanese boards: Determinants and implications for managers. Journal of Financial Economics 36(2), 225–258.

Kaplan, S.N., Reishus, D., 1990. Outside directorships and corporate performance. Journal of Financial Economics 27, 389–410.

Meeus, D., 1998. De recente Belgische aanbevelingen inzake corporate governance. In: De Wulf, H. et al., Corporate Governance: Het Belgische Perspectief, Intersentia

Rechtswetenschappen, Antwerpen-Groningen, 245 p.

Michaely, R., Thaler, R., Womack, K., 1995. Price reactions to dividend initiations and omissions: Overreaction or drift? Journal of Finance 50(2), 573–608.

Moore, M., 1973. Management changes and discretionary accounting decisions. Journal of Accounting Research 11, 100–107.

Morck, R., Shleifer, A., Vishny, R.W., 1989. Alternative mechanisms for corporate control. American Economic Review 79, 842–852.

Moses, D., 1987. Income smoothing and incentives: Empirical tests using accounting changes. The Accounting Review 62, 358–377.

Murphy, K.J., Zimmerman, J.L., 1993. Financial performance surrounding CEO turnover. Journal of Accounting and Economics 16, 273–315.

Ofer, A., Siegel, D., 1987. Corporate financial policy, information and market expectations: An empirical investigation of dividends. Journal of Finance 42, 889–912.

Pourciau, S., 1993. Earnings management and nonroutine executive changes. Journal of Accounting and Economics 16, 317–336.

Renneboog, L., 1997. Shareholding concentration and pyramidal ownership structures in Belgium. In: Balling, M., Hennessy, E., O'Brien, R. (Eds.), Corporate Governance, Financial Markets and Global Convergence. Kluwer Academic Publishers, Dordrecht, December.

Shleifer, A., Vishny, R.W., 1986. Large shareholders and corporate control. Journal of Political Economy 95, 461–488.

Shleifer, A., Vishny, R.W., 1997. A survey of corporate governance. Journal of Finance 52(2), 737–783.

Strong, J., Meyer, J., 1987. Asset writedowns: Managerial incentives and security returns. Journal of Finance 20, 643–663.

Teoh, S., Welch, I., Wong, T., 1998. Earnings management and the underperformance of seasoned equity offering. Journal of Financial Economics 50(1), 63–99.

Viénot, M., 1995. The Board of Directors of Listed Companies in France, published by Conseil National du Patronat Français and the Association Française des Enterprises Privées, Paris, July 10.

Warner, J.B., Watts, R.L., Wruck, K.H., 1988. Stock prices and top management changes. Journal of Financial Economics 20, 431–460.

Weisbach, M., 1988. Outside directors and CEO turnover. Journal of Financial Economics 20, 431–460.

White, H., 1980. A heteroscedasticity-consistent covariance matrix estimator and a direct test for heteroscedasticity. Econometrica 48(2), 3–20.

Williamson, O.E., 1983. Organizational form, residual claimants, and corporate control. Journal of Law and Economics 26, 351–380.

Wymeersch, E., 1994. Aspects of Corporate Governance. Journal of Corporate Governance 2, 138–149.

Wymeersch, E., 1998. De Belgische initiatieven inzake corporate governance. In: De Wulf, H. et al., Corporate Governance: Het Belgische Perspectief, Intersentia Rechtswetens chappen, Antwerpen-Groningen, 245 p.

Chapter 12

Julian Franks, Colin Mayer and Luc Renneboog[2]

WHO DISCIPLINES MANAGEMENT IN POORLY PERFORMING COMPANIES?[1]

Source: *Journal of Financial Intermediation*, 10(3–4) (2001): 209–248.

ABSTRACT

Economic theory points to five parties disciplining management of poorly performing firms: holders of large share blocks, acquirers of new blocks, bidders in takeovers, nonexecutive directors, and investors during periods of financial distress. This paper reports the first comparative evaluation of the role of these different parties in disciplining management. We find that, in the United Kingdom, most parties, including holders of substantial share blocks, exert little disciplining and that some, for example, inside holders of share blocks and boards dominated by nonexecutive directors, actually impede it. Bidders replace a high proportion of management of companies acquired in takeovers but do not target poorly performing management. In contrast, during periods of financial constraints prompting distressed rights issues and capital restructuring, investors focus control on poorly performing companies. These results stand in contrast to the United States, where there is little evidence of a role for new equity issues but nonexecutive directors and acquirers of share blocks perform a disciplinary function. The different governance outcomes are attributed to differences in minority investor protection in two countries with supposedly similar common law systems.
Journal of Economic Literature Classification Number: G3. © 2001 Academic Press
 Key Words: corporate governance; control; restructuring; board turnover; regulation.

1. INTRODUCTION

HOW DO CAPITAL MARKETS DISCIPLINE THE management of poorly performing firms? We attempt to answer this question in the context of the UK capital market by running a "horse race" between the five principal competing parties suggested in the literature. First, shareholders, and in particular large shareholders, may intervene directly and replace management when performance is poor. Second, management replacement may follow the acquisition of a large block of shares. Third, bidders may discipline the management of the acquired company. Fourth, nonexecutive directors, i.e., outside directors,

may act on behalf of shareholders and replace management when they are thought to perform poorly. Finally, financial crises may trigger interventions by shareholders when new equity is issued.

This paper provides the first comparative assessment of the degree of managerial disciplining provided by the five parties. The assessment evaluates the relation between disciplining and the performance of firms. We examine the extent to which the parties provide significant disciplining of poorly performing management and consider whether that disciplining is focused. We measure *focus* by whether disciplining is concentrated exclusively on poorly performing firms. We measure *significance* by the extent to which different interventions contribute to high board turnover in poorly performing companies. A governance mechanism can be focused on poorly performing companies but have an insignificant effect on overall board turnover in these firms, i.e., have a high level of Type 1 errors. A governance mechanism can be significant in dismissing a large number of managers in poorly performing companies but be unfocused in also dismissing a large number of other managers in well performing firms, i.e., have a high level of Type 2 errors.

The evidence reported in Franks and Mayer (1996) illustrates this distinction. They report that, on average, target firms are not poorly performing companies. Bidders do not therefore provide a focused form of corporate control. Nevertheless, they could still perform a significant disciplinary function if they give rise to a high level of managerial replacement in poorly performing firms.

The horse race evaluates both the focus and significance of disciplining by different parties. The results are quite striking. We find that at least two parties—nonexecutive directors and directors with large share stakes—tend to entrench management by reducing board turnover in poorly performing firms. Neither existing holders nor new purchasers of large share blocks exert much disciplining and, as noted above, bidders impose high board turnover after takeovers but in an unfocused way. It is only when there is financial distress, requiring equity issues and capital restructuring, that disciplining is both significant and focused on the management of poorly performing firms.

Some of the results reported for the United Kingdom are similar to those recorded for the United States, most notably entrenchment by insiders. However, others are quite different. In the United States, nonexecutives perform a disciplinary function (see Hermalin and Weisbach, 1991); active outside shareholders discipline management when share blocks change hands (see Bethel et al., 1998); and there is no reported role for new share offerings in disciplining management. All these results stand in marked contrast to what was described above for the United Kingdom.

We believe that these differences are at least in part a consequence of regulation. At first sight, this is surprising since the United Kingdom and United States are countries usually characterized as having similar "common law" regulatory systems (see La Porta et al., 1998). Four examples will illustrate significant differences in regulation and how these lead to different governance outcomes in the two countries. First, the United Kingdom has a Takeover Code that makes accumulation of controlling blocks expensive; the United States does not. Second, the United Kingdom has stronger minority protection laws making the acquisition of partial controlling blocks as well as takeovers expensive. For example, in the United Kingdom a transaction between a large shareholder and its connected company must be undertaken at arms length and requires the consent of noncontrolling shareholders; in the United States, shareholder protection is limited to seeking redress in the courts for unfairly priced transactions. Third, in the United Kingdom all seasoned equity issues, above 5% of share capital, have to be in the form of rights issues and rights requirements can only be waived with considerable difficulty. These requirements provide dispersed shareholders with significant control when firms need to raise new equity financing. In the United States, shareholders can and do waive rights issue requirements for almost all seasoned offerings. Finally, in the United States there are significant fiduciary obligations on directors, breaches of which create high management turnover (Romano, 1991). There are few such obligations in the United Kingdom where "actions to enforce the duties of directors of quoted companies have been almost nonexistent" (see Stapledon, 1996, pp. 13–14). Where the role of nonexecutives is strengthened in the United Kingdom, through, for example, the adoption of the Cadbury Code (see Cadbury, 1992), it has been shown that the disciplinary function of boards increases (see Dahya et al., 2000).

In summary, we find that there are differences in regulation, even within two common law countries, and that these differences are associated with significantly different governance outcomes. The results of this paper therefore enrich the La Porta et al., (1998) view of regulation as an important influence on the operation of capital markets.

Section 2 of the paper describes the methodology employed in this paper. Section 3 examines the relation between board turnover and performance and the role of each of the five parties in disciplining poor management in the United Kingdom. Section 4 reports regressions of board turnover on performance: Section 4.1 reports the results for the total sample and Section 4.2 for poorly performing firms. Section 5 contrasts the UK results in this paper with those reported for the United States and shows how regulation may account for these differences. Section 6 summarizes the paper.

2. METHODOLOGY

This paper is concerned with identifying who precipitates board restructuring in poorly performing firms. The literature on managerial disciplining points to five parties: (i) Shleifer and Vishny (1986) show that large shareholdings mitigate free rider problems of corporate control; (ii) Scharfstein (1988) models the way in which takeovers perform a disciplinary function; (iii) Burkart et al. (1997, 1998) argue that trades in share blocks may be more cost effective than full takeovers; (iv) Fama (1980) and Fama and Jensen (1983) describe how managerial labor markets and nonexecutive directors assist in the governance of firms; and (v) Jensen (1986) and Aghion and Bolton (1992) discuss the role that capital structure plays in reducing agency costs.

This paper examines the role of all 5 forms of interventions in disciplining management. A sample of 250 companies, excluding financial institutions, real estate companies, and insurance companies, was randomly selected from all companies quoted on the London Stock Exchange in 1988. We collected data on their performance and board turnover over the period 1988 to 1993 and combined these with information on ownership, sales of share blocks, takeovers, board structure, and capital structure.

To be included in the sample, companies were required to have data on boards and ownership for at least 3 of the first 6 years of the sample period to allow panel data analyses to be performed. Companies delisted through takeovers or insolvencies for the first 3 years, between 1988 through to 1990, were therefore excluded. In addition, 7 of the original 250 companies were dropped because of lack of performance data.

Data on the composition of the board of directors were compiled for each year from 1988 to 1993 from annual reports, Datastream, the Financial Times, and Nexus databases. They include the names, tenure, and age of the CEO, Chairmen, and all directors, both executive and nonexecutive.

We measured annual executive turnover of the board from 1988 to 1993. Board turnover is calculated by dividing the total number of directors who leave the company by total board size. Executive and nonexecutive turnover is calculated in the same way, except that the denominator is the number of executive and nonexecutive directors, respectively. CEO and Chairman turnover represents the proportion of sample companies where the CEO and Chairman, respectively, leave the company. All turnover figures are corrected for natural turnover. We distinguish between natural and forced turnover, classifying a resignation as "natural" if the director was described as having left the board for reasons of retirement, death, or illness. Otherwise the resignation was classified as being forced. The normal retirement age is between 62 and 65 but some voluntary retirement does occur before that; we took 62 as the minimum retirement age and viewed any earlier retirement as forced.[3] This reflects the difficulty of establishing whether public announcements of resignations result from forced retirements or reflect the natural career progression of good managers. Where a company was taken over after 1990, board turnover was collected for two years after the acquisition to determine the survival rate of the pre-takeover directors of the target firm.

In the regressions, we examine the relation of executive board and CEO turnover to five different measures of performance: abnormal share price returns, dividend cuts and omissions measured as a dummy variable (equal to minus one where there is a cut or omission), after tax cash flow margins (cash flows divided by total sales), after tax rates of return on book equity, and earnings losses measured as a dummy variable (equal to minus one where there is a loss). Abnormal share price returns were taken from the London Share Price Database (LSPD).[4] We employed two measures of leverage, the ratio of pre-tax earnings to interest charges, and a debt to book (and market) value of assets ratio.

Different performance measures were used because it is not always clear what constitutes poor performance and because governance may be more sensitive to one performance measure than another. Marsh (1992) examines 6000 UK dividend announcements over the period 1989 to 1992. His evidence, which is consistent with that in the United States, shows that "dividend cuts are interpreted by the market as powerful signals of bad news both about the current situation and about future prospects" (p. 50). Ball et al. (1997) examine the discretion that managers have in different countries to smooth earnings; for example, UK managers have little discretion while German managers have considerable discretion and as a result, tend to use hidden reserves to smooth earnings and hide earnings losses. The three measures (abnormal returns, dividend cuts and omissions, and earnings losses) yield different incidence of poor performance in our data set; for example, 17.0% reported dividend cuts or omissions on average each year, compared with 10.4% that reported earnings losses. We

also examine performance measured relative to industry benchmarks, namely abnormal returns and return on equity relative to industry averages.

Since the focus of this paper is on the disciplining of management of poorly performing companies, we investigated the relation between very poor performance and executive board turnover in greater detail. Our sample of 243 companies has about 24 companies in the lowest decile in any one year, but across the entire sample the number of different companies in the lowest decile totals 90.[5] To expand the set of poorly performing companies, we collected a second sample of 50 companies in the lowest decile of abnormal share price returns in any one of the three years from 1988 to 1990. For the sample of all poorly performing companies, we used two further measures of poor performance: earnings losses combined with dividend cuts and omissions, and abnormal returns of less than minus 50% combined with earnings losses and dividends cuts and omissions.

In Section 3, we provide a univariate analysis of the relation between board turnover and performance, and the parties organizing interventions. We report either individual year data for the whole sample period, or we choose the sample of companies from 1990 and aggregate data over three years from 1990 to 1992.

In Section 4 we report the results of panel regressions of executive board turnover on performance, ownership, and capital structure over the period 1988 to 1993. We relate executive board turnover to performance in the current year, and with lags, to five classes of variables:

(i) Ownership for the different categories of investors described below,
(ii) Changes in share stakes of different categories of investors,
(iii) Takeovers,
(iv) Board structure: the proportion of nonexecutives on the board and separation of the position of chairman and CEO,
(v) Capital structure and the incidence of new equity issues.

In addition we include interactive terms between performance and the above five categories. The results reported below refer to interactive terms with performance lagged one year; regressions using interactive terms with contemporaneous performance were also performed.

We report executive board turnover panel regressions estimated using a Tobit regression to take account of fact that there are frequently no changes to boards. We also undertook OLS regressions with logistic transformations of the dependent variable. Within (fixed effect) regressions were also performed and time dummies for individual years were used. Since high board turnover in one year might lead to low turnover in a subsequent year, we investigated the robustness of the results using a cross-sectional OLS regression where the dependent variable is accumulated board turnover for the year of poor performance and two subsequent years. The results reported below refer to the panel regressions that include time as well as cross-sectional effects.

In Section 4.1 we report the results for the complete randomly selected sample of firms. Although the potential size of our sample is 1458 firm years (number of companies × 6 years), it is reduced to 1193 firm years as a result of takeovers (180), bankruptcies (10), and missing data (75), and if the independent variable is lagged then there is a further loss of 243 firm years. In Section 4.2 we report regressions for a sample of poorly performing firms drawn from the lowest decile of abnormal returns in any one of the years 1988 to 1990.

The results in Section 4.1 provide a measure of *focus*—To what extent are different interventions focused exclusively on high executive board turnover in poorly performing firms? The results in Section 4.2 provide an indication of *significance*—To what extent do different interventions contribute significantly to high board turnover in badly performing companies? A governance mechanism can be focused, in the sense of being well targeted on just poorly performing companies but insignificant in

its effect on board turnover of the worst performing companies, in other words in having a high level of Type-1 errors. A governance mechanism can be significant in dismissing a large number of managers in poorly performing companies but unfocused in dismissing a large number of other managers as well; i.e., it has a high level of Type-2 errors.

To rank the contribution of different governance mechanisms to board turnover, we report their economic as well as statistical significance. Economic significance is measured as the effect on board turnover of moving from the mean to the extreme (upper or lowest) decile value of the relevant independent variable. The economic significance of events, such as takeovers and new equity issues, are measured by their marginal impact on board turnover, i.e., the coefficient on the relevant dummy variable.

3. DATA ON BOARD TURNOVER AND PERFORMANCE AND PARTIES INITIATING INTERVENTIONS

This section investigates the relation between board turnover, performance, and the five different parties initiating interventions.

3.1. Board turnover and performance

Table 12.1 provides a snapshot of the relation between board turnover and performance. Panel A of the table partitions the sample into deciles of performance using abnormal returns. We choose the sample of companies from 1990 and aggregate data over three years from 1990 to 1992. The period 1990 to 1992 is chosen because 1990 is the first year when the threshold for disclosing share stakes held by outsiders was reduced from 5 to 3%, and subsequent regressions demonstrate that performance has an impact on executive board turnover in the current and following two years.

Table 12.1 Annual Board Turnover in 1990–1992 Partitioned by Decile of Abnormal Share Price Performance Calculated in 1990 for a Sample of 243 UK Quoted Companies

Panel A: Annual Board turnover over 1990–1992 partitioned by decile of abnormal share price performance in 1990

Decile of abnormal returns	Worst 1	2	3	5	9	Best 10	Average	t-test on decile difference	
Annual board turnover of:	<−45%	−45% to −27%	−27% to −19%	−13% to 5%	12% to 23%	>23%	Average	1 vs 5	1 vs 10
Total board	15.5%	7.0%	7.7%	6.8%	6.0%	6.4%	7.3%	2.122	2.085
Executive directors	21.1%	10.0%	9.9%	8.1%	8.0%	6.9%	9.2%	2.300	2.388
Nonexecutive directors	7.4%	1.7%	4.9%	4.2%	3.6%	4.8%	4.2%	0.758	0.511
CEOs	28.8%	19.2%	11.4%	11.6%	14.5%	10.4%	13.6%	1.815	1.953
Chairmen	15.8%	6.9%	5.8%	7.2%	2.9%	5.9%	7.0%	0.862	1.007
Sample size	24	24	24	23	23	23	23		

Panel B: Board turnover over 1990–1992 partitioned by dividends changes and by earnings, respectively during 1989–1990

Annual board turnover of:	Dividend cuts and omissions	Constant or increased dividends	t-test on differences in means	Earnings losses	Positive earnings	t-test on differences in means
Total board turnover	11.5%	6.2%	2.640	14.7%	6.4%	3.303
Executive directors	14.9%	7.0%	2.776	17.5%	8.0%	2.754
Nonexecutive directors	6.0%	5.8%	0.077	9.8%	3.7%	1.965
CEOs	25.9%	7.0%	2.795	26.0%	11.2%	1.846
Chairmen	15.9%	8.4%	1.464	19.1%	5.1%	2.302
Sample size (average)	36	181		18	190	

Note. This table reports the turnover of the total board, the executive and nonexecutive directors, the CEO and chairmen for the three-year period 1990–1992. Board turnover is calculated by dividing the total number of directors who leave the company (excluding those leaving as a result of retirement, death, or illness) by total board size. Executive and nonexecutive director turnover is calculated in the same way, except that the denominator is the number of executive and nonexecutive members, respectively. CEO and chairman turnover represents the proportion of sample companies where the CEO and the chairman, respectively, leave the company (corrected for natural turnover). Board turnover data for the sample of 243 companies are categorized by performance: panel A categorizes companies by abnormal share price performance in 1990 for six deciles; panel B categorizes companies by dividend cuts and omissions, and earnings losses in 1990.
Source: Annual reports, Datastream and London Share Price Database.

Table 12.1 records that there is a high level of board turnover in poorly performing companies. It also shows that the relation between board turnover and performance is highly nonlinear. Annual board turnover is substantially higher in decile one than in any of the other deciles, for example, 15.5% compared with 6.8 and 6.4% for deciles five and ten, respectively. Executive board turnover is much higher than nonexecutive turnover because nonexecutives perform both a monitoring and advisory function. CEO turnover is also much higher in decile 1 (at almost 28.8%) than in other deciles (for example, 11.6% in decile 5). Turnover of chairmen is relatively high in decile one, although the level is lower than for CEOs, reflecting the fact that some chairmen are nonexecutive and perform a monitoring role. When the sample was partitioned using abnormal returns accumulated over two years, 1989–1990, the relation between performance and turnover was very similar to that in panel A.[6]

Panel B reports that companies with losses and companies with dividend cuts or omissions have more than twice the executive board turnover of better performing companies. Companies with dividend cuts have 3.7 times the CEO turnover of those with increasing or stable dividends, and companies with earnings losses have 2.3 times those without. We therefore find that there is a strong, nonlinear relation between board turnover and performance.

3.2. Ownership concentrations

We collected data on the size of shareholdings over the period 1988–1993. All directors' holdings greater than 0.1% are included as well as outside share stakes greater than 5% until 1989. From 1990, the statutory disclosure threshold for outside shareholders was reduced to 3%.[7]

Shareholdings were classified according to 7 categories: (i) banks, (ii) insurance companies, (iii) institutional shareholders including investment trusts, unit trusts, and pension funds, (iv) industrial and commercial companies, (v) families and individuals, not directly related to any director,

(vi) executive directors and their immediate family and trusts, and (vii) nonexecutive directors and their immediate family and trusts.[8] We will refer to directors and their families as "insiders" and financial institutions, industrial and commercial companies, and other major shareholders as "outsiders."[9] The sizes of share stakes held by government and real estate companies were collected but not reported because they are so small.

The distinction between different outside holdings is important because some may be passive in the face of poor management performance while others are active. For example, institutional shareholders are often regarded as passive, and industrial companies and individuals/families as active. Corporate investors may have more knowledge about the industry than other investors, and individuals and families may have more incentive to intervene as principals rather than agents.

This section reports the pattern of ownership for the sample companies. Panel A of Table 12.2 records the largest individual share holding for all companies in each year from 1988 to 1993 with the average for all years being 15.3%. The largest five shareholders accounted for between 29.7 and 36.7% of the company's shares depending on the year. There is a large increase in reported blocks from 31.4 to 41.0% between 1989 and 1990, which we attribute to the change in the disclosure rule on block ownership, referred to earlier.

Panel B of Table 12.2 reports that the median size of the largest stake lies in the range 5–15% for all individual years, but there are a significant number of blocking minorities, defined as a stake of at least 25%. For example, in 1988 almost 24% of stakes are in excess of 25%.[10] Panel C disaggregates large shareholders by their type and size of holding in 1991. Institutional investors hold the highest proportion (52.6%). Insiders, directors, and their families are the next most significant holders. The difference between outsider and insider blocks is important because the latter may entrench poor management. Although not shown in the table, insider

Table 12.2 Size and Category of the Largest Shareholder in the Sample of UK Quoted Companies, 1988 to 1993

Panel A: Size of largest shareholding, sum of ownership of largest 5 share stakes and all reported large shareholdings respectively[a]

Year	Largest shareholding	Largest 5 shareholdings[b]	All reported large shareholdings[b]
1988	15.3%	29.7%	30.6%
1989	15.6%	30.7%	31.4%
1990	16.5%	36.4%	41.0%
1991	15.6%	36.7%	42.7%
1992	15.0%	35.2%	40.7%
1993	13.7%	30.4%	33.5%

Panel B: Percentage of firms with largest shareholding by size of holding

Year	[0–5%]	[5–15%]	[15–25%]	[25–50%]	[50–100%]
1988	23.0%	34.7%	18.4%	20.9%	2.9%
1989	17.0%	39.8%	20.7%	19.1%	3.3%
1990	11.6%	44.2%	21.9%	18.2%	4.1%
1991	10.0%	52.1%	19.6%	14.6%	3.8%
1992	10.6%	56.0%	17.4%	13.5%	2.4%
1993	15.5%	58.1%	13.5%	11.6%	1.3%

Panel C: Proportion of firms with the largest shareholder by type and size of holding for 1991

Category of shareholder	Total	[0–5%]	[5–15%]	[15–25%]	[25–50%]	[50–100%]
Institutional investors	52.6%	6.3%	37.9%	6.3%	1.7%	0.4%
Industrial companies	13.0%	0.8%	3.8%	4.2%	3.8%	0.4%
Families, individuals	3.8%	0.0%	1.3%	0.8%	1.7%	0.0%
Insiders (directors)	28.0%	2.1%	8.8%	7.9%	7.1%	2.1%
All[c]	97.4%	9.2%	51.8%	19.2%	14.3%	2.9%

Note. Panel A shows the average largest shareholding, the sum of the largest 5 shareholdings, and the sum of all reported large shareholdings over the period 1988 to 1993. Panel B shows the percentage of companies with a large shareholding in five size ranges over the period 1988 to 1993. Panel C reports the size distribution of the largest shareholding by type of shareholder in 240 companies in 1991. All holdings by directors greater than 0.1% are included; shareholdings by outsiders in excess of 5% are reported in 1988 and 1989 and in excess of 3% thereafter. Source: Annual reports.

a Sample sizes were 239, 241, 241, 240, 207, and 205 in each of the six years 1988 to 1993, respectively.
b The increase in 1990 reflects the reduction in the disclosure threshold from 5 to 3% in 1989.
c The sum is less than 100% because small shareholdings held by the government and real estate companies are not included.

holdings are roughly split two-thirds executive and one-third nonexecutive directors. The size distributions of institutional investors and insider holdings are very different. Insiders have a greater number of blocking minority stakes than financial institutions, for example, 9.2% of their stakes are greater than 25% compared with 2.1% for institutional investors.

Levels of concentration in the United Kingdom are similar to those reported in the United States. Holderness and Sheehan (1988) find that 13% of all publicly traded corporations and 5% of companies traded on the NYSE and AMEX exchanges have a single shareholder (family or another firm) holding a majority of the shares. In our UK sample, the figure is 3%. Measuring concentration by cumulating the largest five holdings, Demsetz and Lehn (1985) report a mean of 24.8% in the United States compared with 33% in our UK sample. Denis and Denis (1995) record insider ownership of 11.7% for the United States, as against 11.8% for our UK sample.[11]

By Continental standards, these are low levels of concentrations. In Italy, 84% of Italian companies have a single shareholder owning majority stakes (see Bianco et al., 1996). In Belgium, 93% of quoted industrial companies have a single shareholder who owns a block of at least 25% of voting rights (Renneboog, 2000), and in Germany, there is a single shareholder with at least 25% of shares in 85% of large quoted companies (see Franks and Mayer, 2000).

Table 12.3 disaggregates the UK sample by both size and performance measured by abnormal returns for three years 1990–1992. There is little relation between concentration of ownership and performance; for example, largest shareholdings are similar in the worst and best performing firms. However, concentration is related to the size of equity capitalization; for example, the sum of institutional shares is significantly greater in below-median-capitalization than in above-median-capitalization firms, 31.3% compared with 20.5% (for the worst performing sample).

In contrast, board turnover is closely related to performance (as noted above) but not to the size of firms: differences in board turnover are not economically large or statistically significant across the two groups of firms, those below and those above the median capitalization.

In summary, although the United Kingdom is described as a relatively dispersed capital market, coalitions of shareholders can potentially exert significant voting power, insiders have substantial blocks, and there is a strong relation between concentration of ownership and size, but not performance of firms. Since we have observed in the previous section a strong association between board turnover and performance but not to the size of firms, this suggests that concentrations of ownership may not bear a close relation to board turnover. We find confirmation for this in the regression results in Section 4.

3.3. Takeovers and trades in share blocks

In this section we report the incidence of full acquisition of firms and trades in share blocks. The rate of takeovers in the original sample of 243 companies, for the period up to 1993, is 6%.[12] If those same companies are tracked to 1997, the rate of acquisition increases to 13%. The rate of takeover for the second sample, of poorly performing firms, is substantially higher. Over the period 1988–1993, the rate of acquisition was 22%.[13] If those same companies are tracked to 1997, the rate of acquisition increases to 28%. This suggests that there is a higher acquisition rate among the worst performing companies but this only occurs after considerable lag from the year of poor performance.[14]

Data on board turnover were collected in companies subject to takeover both before and after the acquisition. They suggest relatively low rates of turnover prior to the takeover, but very high turnover post-takeover. For example, during the two years pre-takeover, total annual board turnover is 15.6% and annual CEO turnover is 17.4%, whereas for the two years

322 CORPORATE GOVERNANCE, UNDERPERFORMANCE AND MANAGEMENT TURNOVER

Table 12.3 Concentration of Ownership in Worst and Best Performing Companies, Partitioned by Size of Equity Market Capitalization

Average for 1990–1992	Smallest Below median of market capitalization	Large Above median of market capitalization	t-tests on differences in means
Worst performing quintile of annual abnormal returns 1990			
Largest shareholding (%)	16.2%	11.9%	1.029
Sum of institutional investor shares (%)	31.3%	20.5%	3.030
Sum of companies and family shares (%)	7.3%	5.9%	0.485
Sum of insiders' shares (%)	13.1%	6.4%	1.753
Executive board turnover	17.5%	14.7%	0.382
CEO turnover	28.6%	28.0%	0.030
Sample size	23	8	
Best performing quintile of annual abnormal returns 1990			
Largest shareholding (%)	14.0%	13.0%	0.266
Sum of institutional investor shares (%)	29.9%	12.5%	6.627
Sum of companies and family shares (%)	3.5%	6.6%	-1.364
Sum of insiders' shares (%)	11.3%	9.9%	0.684
Executive board turnover	6.5%	7.7%	-0.267
CEO turnover	6.7%	14.8%	-0.847
Sample size	15	27	

Note. The table reports average ownership concentration over the period 1990 to 1992 for firms with below median and above median market capitalization in 1990. Ownership concentration is reported for the largest shareholding and the sum of all disclosed shares held by investment institutions, industrial companies, families and individuals, and insiders. Board turnover is calculated by dividing the total number of directors who leave the company (excluding those leaving as a result of retirement, death, or illness), by total board size. Executive and nonexecutive director turnover is calculated in the same way, except that the denominator is the number of executive and nonexecutive members, respectively. CEO and chairman turnover represents the proportion of sample companies where the CEO and the chairman, respectively, leave the company (corrected for natural turnover).
Source: Annual reports, London Share Price Database.

post takeover they are 88 and 94%, respectively.[15] Moreover, there is little difference in turnover between poorly performing companies and better performing companies, suggesting that takeovers provide relatively unfocused disciplining. For example, if we define poorly performing companies as those in the bottom decile of abnormal share price performance in one of the two years prior to takeover, total board turnover is identical at 88% post takeover in both samples of poorly performing and better-performing firms.

In the United States, Bethel et al. (1998) examine the relation between block purchases of 5% or more and firm performance. They find that activist blockholders acquired stakes in highly diversified firms with poor profitability. They also find that the target firm's profitability increased after the block purchase, and as a result, they conclude that this market works as a market for corporate control. We investigate the size of this market in share blocks in the United Kingdom and the extent to which it is motivated by poor performance leading to the disciplining of management. We also distinguish between active and passive blockholders.

In Panel A of Table 12.4 we show the total number of purchases of share blocks by new shareholders in excess of 5% for the three-year period, 1991 to 1993.[16] We choose this subperiod because the disclosure threshold changed to 3% in 1990. There are a total of 303 purchases of stakes greater than 5% and 82 greater than 10%; the latter represents an annual rate of 9% per year compared with 6.7% for the United States cited in Bethel et al.[17] Almost one-half of block sales greater than 10% are made by companies, families, and insiders, suggesting greater scope for more active investing. In Panel B of the table we examine changes in the level of concentration by both existing and new shareholders. We accumulate share blocks by adding together individual purchases in each company greater than 5% in any one year. The panel reports that in 89 companies more than 10% of the equity was purchased by existing and new shareholders over the 3-year period. Panel B also shows that a single investor or a coalition of blockholders purchases an equity stake of 25% or more in 19 companies. The acquisition of blocking minority stakes takes place on average in 3.1% of listed firms per year, similar to the

Table 12.4 Purchases of Share Blocks for 243 Companies for the Period 1991 to 1993

Panel A: Number of share blocks purchased by new shareholders exceeding 5% for the period 1991 to 1993

	[5–10%]	[10–25%]	[25–50%]	≥50%	Total
Institutions	168	38	5	0	211
Companies	24	15	5	0	44
Families	19	6	2	0	27
Directors	10	11	0	0	21
Total	221	70	12	0	303

Panel B: Number of companies with increases in concentration greater than 5% over the period 1991 to 1993

Year	[5–10%]	[10–25%]	[25–50%]	≥50%	Total
1991	37	36	4	2	79
1992	16	25	5	2	48
1993	14	9	4	2	29
Total	67	70	13	6	156

Note. Panel A reports purchases of share blocks of between 5 and 10%, 10 and 25%, 25 and 50%, and more than 50% over the period 1991 to 1993 by type of purchaser. Panel B reports the number of companies with increases in concentration of more than 5% by new and existing shareholders over the period 1991 to 1993. Source: Annual reports.

annual rate of takeover activity in the United Kingdom of 3–4%, where control passes when a majority of shares are acquired by the bidder, usually via a tender offer.

Although not reported in the table, we examined the relation between purchases of share blocks and performance, measured over two years prior to, and the year of, the purchase. The number of share blocks is virtually identical in the worst and best deciles of performance and similar to the average for the complete sample.

In summary, there is a high level of both takeovers and trades in share blocks in the United Kingdom. There is some evidence of a relation between the incidence of takeovers and poor performance but not between trades in blocks and performance. This suggests that takeovers may be performing a disciplinary function but trades in blocks do not. We investigate this further in Section 4.

3.4. Board structure

Panel A of Table 12.5 reports the board structure of the sample of firms partitioned by decile of abnormal share price performance in 1990. There is evidence that the proportion of companies in which the roles of CEO and chairman are combined is lower in the worst performing decile of firms than in other deciles. However, in other respects there is very little relation between board structure and performance; for example, the proportion of nonexecutive directors is almost identical in the best and worst performing companies.

Panel B examines how the structure of the board alters after a change in CEO. The purpose is to analyze the extent to which a change in CEO is used to strengthen corporate governance by altering the composition of the board. It partitions the sample of firms into those where there was a change in CEO and those where there was no change using data from 1990. It reports the average board structure two years before and two years after 1990 for the two samples of firms. The proportion of non executive directors on the board increased in both sets of firms over the period, reflecting the increasing emphasis on nonexecutives in corporate governance in the United Kingdom.[18] More strikingly, in those companies where there is a change in CEO, there is a significant reduction in the proportion of companies with combined roles of CEO and chairman from 42.9%, before 1990, to 14.3% after. Subsequent regressions suggest that separation of CEO and chairman plays an important role in disciplining of management of poorly performing firms.

In summary, there is little relation between the proportion of nonexecutives on the boards of firms and corporate performance suggesting little disciplinary role associated with nonexecutive directors. However, there is evidence that the role of CEO and chairman is more frequently separated after changes in CEOs. We examine these observations further in the regressions in Section 4.

3.5. Capital structure

Jensen (1989) suggests that creditors may have greater incentives than shareholders to monitor and change management in exchange for new loans or the restructuring of existing loans. This suggests that board turnover may be particularly high where poor performance is combined with high leverage (or low interest cover). Alternatively, shareholders may be able to exert greater control over management where poor performance forces companies to seek outside equity finance. In this section we examine interventions by shareholders in companies facing financial constraints.

An analysis of our entire sample of 243 companies shows that leverage increases as performance declines. Although not shown in a table, for the period 1990 to 1992, there are significantly higher levels of capital leverage in the lowest decile of performance than in higher deciles—a median of 39.3% in the lowest decile compared with 34.9 and 23.9% in the 5th and 10th deciles, respectively. Similarly, interest coverage is significantly lower in decile 1 than

Table 12.5 Board Characteristics and Firm Performance for 243 Companies

Panel A: Board characteristics by decile of abnormal share price performance in 1990

Average 1990–1992	Worst Decile 1 <−45%	Decile 2 [−45, −27.9%]	Decile 3 [−27.9, −8.85%]	Decile 5 [−13.12, −5.0%]	Decile 9 [12.0, −22.5%]	Best Decile 10 >22.5%	Average
Total number of directors	8.7	8.7	8.4	9.6	10.9	8.4	9.3
Proportion of nonexec. dir. (%)	37.5%	37.3%	38.2%	42.4%	43.5%	40.7%	39.8%
Combined CEO/Chairman	27.1%	43.1%	31.0%	42.0%	34.8%	28.4%	32.9%
CEO age (years)	49.7	53.2	51.5	55.9	54.4	54.5	52.6
CEO tenure (years)	4.1	5.1	5.1	8.2	5.2	5.7	5.3
Chairman age (years)	55.0	60.3	59.8	59.6	60.3	58.5	59.0
Chairman tenure (years)	5.5	5.1	5.9	6.5	7.1	6.1	6.1

Panel B: Board characteristics of companies with and without CEO turnover in 1990 two years prior and two years post 1990

Companies with CEO turnover	Sample size	Two years prior (Average 1988–1989)	Two years after (Average 1991–1992)	t-test on difference in means
Proportion nonexec. dir. (%)	28	36.4%	41.5%	1.464
Combined CEO/Chairman	28	42.9%	14.3%	−2.449
CEO age (years)	19	51.9	52.6	0.329
Chairman age (years)	19	59.4	59.4	−0.032

Companies without CEO turnover	Sample size	Two years prior (Average 1988–1989)	Two years after (Average 1991–1992)	t-test on difference in means
Proportion nonexec. dir. (%)	180	36.2%	40.8%	2.483
Combined CEO/Chairman	180	42.2%	38.9%	−0.643
CEO age (years)	110	51.6	53.1	1.801
Chairman age (years)	121	57.8	59.1	1.419

t-statistics of differences between companies with and without CEO turnover in 1990

Proportion nonexecutive directors	0.068	0.305	
Combined CEO/Chairman	0.062	−3.213	
CEO age (years)	0.130	−0.332	
Chairman age (years)	1.144	0.221	

Note. Panel A shows board size, the proportion of nonexecutives on the board, the proportion of companies with combined CEO and Chairman, the age and tenure of the CEO and Chairman averaged annually over the period 1990 to 1992 for 6 deciles of abnormal share price performance in 1988. Panel B reports the proportion of nonexecutives, combined CEO and chairman, and age of CEO and chairman averaged over two years either side of 1990 for companies in which there was a change in CEO in 1990 and for companies in which there was no change in CEO in 1990.

in decile 5: a median of 1.8 compared with 4.0 in the worst performing decile.[19]

Table 12.6 shows that high leverage, combined with poor performance, is related to increased executive board turnover. Companies in the lowest decile of share price performance and the lowest quartile of interest coverage had significantly higher executive board and CEO turnover in the year of poor performance and the two years subsequently than those in the highest quartile of interest coverage, 69.6 and 24.2%, respectively. Companies in the lowest decile of share price performance and the highest quartile of capital leverage had higher executive board and CEO turnover than those in the lowest quartile of capital leverage (though only the latter was significant).

The annual rate of new equity issues in the sample of poorly performing firms used in the subsequent regressions at 11.5% is almost identical to that of the total sample at 11.6%. This suggests an important role for new equity issues in distressed companies. We investigated this further by undertaking press searches on 34 firms that were both below average performers and had high levels of debt. The criteria for selection were that firms both had interest coverage less than two and were in the bottom three deciles of performance in at least one year during the period 1990–1993.[20] In 28 firms the CEO or chairman resigned, or both resigned. Eighteen firms or about 54% of the sample raised new equity finance. Of these, 15 were rights issues or open offers, while the remaining three were offered to new shareholders in the form of placings.[21] In three cases the offer took the form of convertible preference shares, otherwise it was for straight equity.

There was a substantial number of other ownership changes. In 24 companies, or 72% of the sample, there was at least one of the following: a new issue, a takeover, or the emergence of a large shareholder. In some cases board changes coincided with one of these events, but in many cases capital or ownership changes preceded board changes by a matter of several months.

Debt restructuring is also important. There were five cases of a public debt issue and another five of a capital reconstruction or public recontracting of existing debt. In one case the bank stated at an Extraordinary General Meeting that a renewal of loan facilities was conditional on a resolution to approve the sale of assets. Since much of UK debt is in the form of private bank debt, the actual level of bank restructuring is much greater than that which is publicly revealed.

It is clear from the descriptions in The Financial Times (FT) that the party initiating the boardroom changes is not necessarily creditors. For example, in the departure of the CEO of Burton the FT reported "that he had not performed with sufficient vigor to impress [the board's] non-executive directors" (November 30, 1990). In another company, Cookson's, the FT stated that "the CEO/Chairman resigned after it became clear that he had lost the confidence of the company's own senior executives." (November 30, 1990). For Platon, "a series of boardroom changes was foreshadowed when the company detailed plans for a sterling open [equity] offer." The chairman of Era resigned a week after "a long and angry shareholders' meeting." Finally, in the case of Caledonian Newspapers, a large shareholder when approached about subscribing for new equity responded that "they would put more money up, but if so, it was good-bye management."

An important question is why large institutional shareholders are active only when poorly performing firms make distressed rights issues. Senior management at the largest fund managers in the United Kingdom informed us that although they might intervene where there was very poor performance, in the face of management opposition, they were likely to avoid confrontation because they disliked the consequent publicity and the costs of organizing other shareholders. However, it was a different story when the poorly performing company required new financing: "it comes to a crunch when companies raise additional finance" or "it all unpicks when a company needs money."

Table 12.6 The Relation between Board Turnover and Leverage for Companies in the Lowest Decile of Performance

	Cumulative executive turnover: Interest cover			Cumulative CEO turnover: Interest cover			Cumulative executive turnover: Capital leverage			Cumulative CEO turnover: Capital leverage		
Leverage	Sample	Mean	Stdev.	Sample	Mean	Stdev.	Sample	Mean	Stdev.	Sample	Mean	Stdev.
Quartile 1 (Highest)	21	67.2%	38.4%	23	69.6%	76.5%	22	56.4%	31.5%	24	79.2%	72.1%
Quartile 2	25	44.6%	27.7%	27	59.3%	63.6%	25	39.5%	27.8%	27	59.3%	63.6%
Quartile 3	34	45.4%	28.2%	34	55.9%	66.0%	35	45.0%	30.9%	36	47.2%	69.6%
Quartile 4 (Lowest)	32	34.3%	27.0%	33	24.2%	50.2%	31	44.7%	34.6%	31	22.6%	42.5%
t-statistics or differences in means												
Quartile 1 Minus Quartile 2	2.25	**		0.51			1.94	*		1.04		
Quartile 1 Minus Quartile 4	3.4	***		2.49	**		1.27			3.41	***	

Note. This table reports the cumulative turnover in poorly performing companies by quartile of interest coverage and capital leverage. Quartile 1 represents the lowest interest cover and the highest book leverage. Poorly performing companies are defined as in the lowest decile of annual abnormal return in at least one of the years in the period 1988–1993. For each of the poorly performing sample companies, the year of poor performance was identified and the cumulative executive board turnover and CEO turnover was calculated over the year of poor performance and two years subsequent. Differences in turnover are then studied based on quartiles of interest coverage and capital leverage.

   * Significant differences in sample means at better than the 10% level.
  ** Significant at better than 5% level.
 *** Significant at better than 1% level.
Source: Own calculations based on annual reports, Datastream, London Business School's Risk Measurement Service.

In summary, the financial structure of poorly performing companies is worse than that of other firms and there is a higher incidence of board turnover where leverage is very high (or interest cover is low) and new finance is raised. In a significant number of cases new financing includes equity. The regression results in the next section will shed further light on these observations.

3.6. Summary

The univariate analysis of this section reveals significant potential for coalition formation, a large market in acquisitions and share block sales, and a high incidence of new finance raised by poorly performing firms. However, we find little relation between poor performance and concentration of ownership, share block transactions, takeovers, and the proportion of nonexecutive directors on boards of firms. This suggests that holders of large share blocks, purchasers of share blocks, acquirers, and nonexecutive directors do not perform a strong disciplining function. In contrast, there is a large amount of new equity raised by poorly performing companies, which is associated with board changes, indicating that shareholders intervene when new equity is raised.

4. REGRESSION RESULTS FOR BOARD TURNOVER ON GOVERNANCE AND PERFORMANCE

This section reports the results of regressions of executive board turnover on performance and the five sets of governance variables described above over the period 1988 to 1993. Section 4.1 discusses the results for the total sample and Section 4.2 for the worst performing companies.

4.1. The total random sample

Table 12.7 records the results of a Tobit panel regression on executive board turnover; although not formally reported in the tables, comparisons were undertaken with different estimation techniques including industry and time dummies, OLS regressions, and fixed effect regressions.[22] Five different measures of performance are reported: annual abnormal returns, industry corrected annual abnormal returns, an earnings loss dummy, industry corrected return on equity, and a dummy for dividend decreases and omissions. The best explanatory power is found in the earnings loss equation. Consistent with Ball et al. (1997), earnings losses may therefore be the most relevant signal of managerial failure. Size, as measured by sales, was included as a control variable but is not significant in any of the regressions.

To rank the contribution of different parties to board turnover, we report the economic as well as statistical significance of the independent variables. These reflect the effect on executive board turnover of moving from their mean to their extreme (upper or lowest) decile value. For example, the highest decile ownership of executives is 43.5% as against a mean holding of 7.6%. The difference of 35.9% has been multiplied by the coefficient of -0.3576 (line 9) to yield a marginal effect on board turnover of moving from the average to the highest decile executive ownership of -12.8%.[23]

Performance

Lines 3 to 5 of Table 12.7 show a strong negative relation between board turnover for four out of five measures of performance either concurrently or with lags (the exception being industry corrected return on equity). The economic effect of abnormal returns in the lowest decile is to raise board turnover by 7.0% two years later. The economic effect of earnings losses is much larger in raising board turnover by 24.6% over a three-year period. This suggests that board turnover is more sensitive to earnings losses than contemporaneous abnormal share price returns.[24] It may be that management and shareholders regard earnings losses as a more serious sign of managerial failure than abnormal returns.

We report below the regression results describing the influence of existing shareholders, changes in shareholdings, takeovers, leverage, and board structure on board turnover.

Existing shareholders

If concentration of ownership overcomes a free rider problem of corporate control, we would expect there to be higher board turnover in poorly performing firms where concentration of ownership is high. The signs of the coefficients on the interactive terms between ownership and performance should therefore be negative in lines 11 to 15. In fact, there are few significant terms in lines 6–15, indicating that ownership concentration on its own or with interaction terms does not play a significant role in disciplining management. An exception is holdings of executive directors, which are consistently negatively related to board turnover for four performance measures. The economic effect of executive ownership (which has a mean value of 7.6%) is to lower board turnover by between 12.2 and 15.1%, depending on the performance measure, but it is generally unrelated to performance (line 14 in Table 12.7). This suggests that large ownership gives executives modest protection against outside intervention, irrespective of company performance. This is robust to different estimation techniques.

Increases in shareholdings

Significant changes in shareholdings are likely to give rise to changes in management irrespective of corporate performance. However, if these changes are performing a disciplinary function then there should be higher board turnover with poor performance and with changes in shareholdings. We would therefore expect to observe positive coefficients on lines 16 to 20 and negative coefficients in lines 21 to 25.

Table 12.7 shows a strong positive relation between increases in share holdings by both families and executive directors, and executive board turnover (lines 18 and 19).

This is consistently observed across different estimation techniques. Purchases of share stakes are for the most part new holdings rather than increases in existing holdings. The economic effect of increases in holdings by families and individuals (on average 0.7%) is to increase board turnover by between 5.4 and 7.7%, depending on the performance measure used. The economic effect of increase in holdings by executives (on average 0.7%) is between 10.5 and 12.5% increases in board turnover. However, the interaction terms do not support the view that changes in family and executive holdings are performing a disciplinary function (lines 23 and 24). We do not observe a relation of executive board turnover to industrial companies shareholdings either on their own (line 17) or interactively with performance (line 22). There is therefore little difference in impact of active and passive shareholders on corporate governance.[25]

Takeovers

We included a dummy variable in the regression for whether the firm was taken over and an interactive dummy variable with performance. The takeover variable was significant in every regression but the interactive term with performance was significant in none. The economic effect of takeovers on board turnover is in the range 89.5 to 113.2% depending on the measure of performance used. This confirms the result in Franks and Mayer (1996) that there is a very high level of board turnover associated with takeovers but it is unrelated to poor performance. In Section 3.3, we observed that over an extended period of time, the incidence of takeovers is higher in poorly performing than other firms. This suggests that the disciplinary effect of takeovers may be delayed beyond the one- or two-year lags in these regressions.

Board structure

If nonexecutive directors perform a corporate governance function then we would

Table 12.7 Regressions of Executive Board Turnover on Governance and Performance for the Total Sample, 1988–1993

Pooled Tobit regression: dependent variable is executive board turnover

Performance 1988–1993 / Independent variable	Ann. abn. Return		Industry corrected ann. abn. Return		Earnings losses (dummy = −1)		Industry corrected ROE		Dividend decreases/ omissions (dum = −1)	
	Par. Est.	p-value	Par. Est.	p-value	Par. Est.	p-value	Par. Est.	p-value	Par. Est.	p-value
1. Sample size	905		905		938		948		948	
Noncensored	337		337		349		352		352	
Left censored	568		568		589		596		596	
2. Intercept	6.4890	0.16	4.1165	0.36	5.3199	0.23	1.0762	0.81	4.6022	0.33
Performance										
3. Performance T-2	−0.1041	0.00	−0.1057	0.00	−10.2785	0.04	−0.0085	0.53	−10.4561	0.00
4. Performance T-1	0.0928	0.45	0.0536	0.68	−28.3968	0.16	−0.0761	0.31	−5.8946	0.59
5. Performance T	−0.0367	0.18	−0.0278	0.34	−14.3359	0.00	−0.0124	0.20		
Existing shareholders										
6. institutions	−0.0019	0.98	0.0038	0.97	−0.0206	0.82	0.0141	0.87	−0.0532	0.59
7. industrial cos	0.0713	0.51	0.1010	0.33	0.0801	0.45	0.1179	0.27	0.1395	0.21
8. families and indiv.	−0.2040	0.25	−0.2512	0.16	−0.3520	0.06	−0.4198	0.04	−0.2151	0.26
9. executive directors	−0.3576	0.00	−0.3397	0.00	−0.3433	0.00	−0.3671	0.00	−0.4200	0.00
10. non-executive dir.	−0.1022	0.51	−0.0655	0.66	−0.0321	0.82	0.0475	0.74	0.0852	0.57
Interaction terms : cum ownership per category* performance T-1										
11. institutions	−0.0027	0.37	−0.0043	0.19	0.8986	0.03	0.0006	0.80	−0.0470	0.32
12. industrial cos	−0.0016	0.60	−0.0015	0.67	0.2851	0.42	0.0026	0.40	0.1131	0.58
13. families and indiv.	0.0004	0.94	−0.0010	0.85	0.1298	0.84	−0.0191	0.02	0.6004	0.21
14. executive directors	−0.0018	0.55	0.0003	0.92	0.9214	0.02	0.0007	0.75	0.0603	0.79
15. nonexecutive dir.	−0.0007	0.88	−0.0006	0.89	0.2432	0.65	−0.0017	0.64	0.6443	0.06

Increases in shareholding

16. institutions	0.1607	0.28	0.1774	0.22	0.2059	0.16	0.1029	0.48	0.2616	0.09
17. industrial cos	0.1111	0.71	0.0650	0.82	-0.0535	0.85	0.3865	0.14	-0.0041	0.99
18. families and indiv.	0.9933	0.01	1.1462	0.00	1.2302	0.00	1.4283	0.00	1.1242	0.00
19. executive directors	1.3076	0.00	1.1639	0.00	1.1922	0.00	1.2396	0.00	1.3886	0.00
20. nonexecutive dir.	0.5908	0.28	0.6350	0.21	0.6241	0.13	0.4658	0.28	0.5673	0.21

Interaction terms : increases in shareholdings per category * performance T-1

21. institutions	0.0042	0.29	0.0051	0.23	0.4138	0.44	0.0016	0.67	0.6734	0.07
22. industrial cos	-0.0072	0.35	-0.0126	0.15	-1.4877	0.05	-0.0048	0.49	-0.9204	0.13
23. families and indiv.	-0.0105	0.29	-0.0086	0.45	0.7496	0.66	0.0223	0.14	-0.9359	0.29
24. executive directors	0.0171	0.14	0.0064	0.59	-0.9735	0.33	-0.0031	0.84	0.6782	0.41
25. non-executive dir	-0.0113	0.56	-0.0090	0.64	1.0021	0.66	0.0030	0.69	-0.5732	0.58

Board structure, leverage and takeovers

26. % nonexec dir.	-0.3185	0.00	-0.3022	0.00	-0.3263	0.00	-0.3006	0.00	-0.3855	0.00
27. Separ. CEO-chair	1.9722	0.41	1.7487	0.45	0.4776	0.84	1.5695	0.50	0.8427	0.73
28. Cap. Lev. (book)	0.0481	0.37	0.0440	0.40	0.0567	0.25	0.1656	0.00	0.0977	0.08
29. New equity issue	9.4970	0.00	9.9686	0.00	4.9607	0.12	6.6196	0.04	7.1537	0.03
30. Merger/Acquis	113.2149	0.00	96.2547	0.00	98.4948	0.00	89.4849	0.00	96.7921	0.00

Interaction terms: board structure, leverage, takeovers, and performance at T-1:

31. % nonexec dir.	-0.3300	0.16	-0.2614	0.29	2.8602	0.93	0.0152	0.94	-0.3294	0.09
32. Separ. CEO-chair	-0.0024	0.97	-0.0420	0.59	9.9548	0.35	0.0285	0.62	-0.1324	0.98
33. Leverage	-0.0026	0.05	-0.0026	0.06	-0.0574	0.50	0.0011	0.11	0.0151	0.85
34. Equity issues	0.0299	0.75	-0.0320	0.75	-36.2614	0.00	-0.0890	0.19	-2.9039	0.77

(Table 12.7 continued)

Table 12.7 Continued

Pooled Tobit regression: dependent variable is executive board turnover

Performance 1988–1993	Ann. abn. Return		Industry corrected ann. abn. Return		Earnings losses (dummy = −1)		Industry corrected ROE		Dividend decreases/ omissions (dum = −1)	
	Par. Est.	Pr>Chi	Par. Est.	p-value	Par. Est.	Pr>Chi	Par. Est.	p-value	Par. Est.	Pr>Chi
35. Merger/Acquis	0.9832	0.17	0.6005	0.17	−6.8505	0.79	−0.1227	0.53	27.4024	0.16
36. Disclosure dum	−6.8984	0.02	−3.6863	0.17	−5.7543	0.03	−4.5981	0.09	−5.1204	0.05
37. Total sales (log)	1.56E-07	5.79E-01	1.42E-07	6.14E-01	4.47E-08	8.72E-01	6.69E-08	8.20E-01	5.76E-09	9.84E-01
p-value of F-test	0.001		0.0001		0.001		0.0001		0.001	
Rsq adj	0.1957		0.1962		0.2119		0.1512		0.1913	

Note. The table records a Tobit regression of annual board turnover on performance, ownership, increases in shareholdings, board composition, and takeovers for the period 1988 to 1993. The measures of performance include annual abnormal returns, both with and without a correction for industry abnormal returns, earnings losses (dummy, loss = −1), return on equity corrected for average industry performance, dividend decreases and omissions (dummy, dividend cuts or omissions = −1). Nine blocks of independent variables are reported. The first relates to performance with up to two-year lags. The second relates to concentration of ownership by five classes of investors. The third relates to the interaction of concentration of ownership with prior year performance for the different classes of investors. The fourth relates to increases in concentrations of share holdings. The fifth relates to the interaction between these increases and performance in the prior year. The sixth relates to the structure of the board (separation of CEO-Chairman = 1 if there is separation, %nonexec. directors is the proportion of nonexecutives on the board), leverage, new equity issues = 1 if there is a new issue and takeovers = 1 if the firm is acquired. The seventh relates to the interaction of the board, financial structure, and takeover variables with prior year performance. The eighth relates to a dummy variable which equals zero in the years 1988–1989 and 1 in the other years (1990–1993) reflecting the reduction in ownership disclosure from 5 to 3% over the period 1989–1990. The ninth relates to size of firm measured by log of total sales. Ownership variables, capital leverage, and % of nonexecutives are all in percentages.

*   Significant at better than the 10% level.
**   Significant at better than 5% level.
***   Significant at better than 1% level.
Source: own calculations based on annual reports, Datastream, London Business School's Risk Measurement Service.

expect to observe more board turnover in poorly performing companies with separate chairmen and chief executives and with a high proportion of nonexecutive directors (negative signs on the interactive terms in lines 31 and 32, respectively). If, however, nonexecutives perform more of an advisory than a monitoring role then we would expect nonexecutives and separate chairmen to reduce executive board turnover irrespective of performance (i.e., negative signs in lines 26 and 27) and the interactive terms in lines 31 and 32 to be insignificantly different from zero. What we observe is more consistent with the latter than the former. For all five measures of performance, the relation with proportion of nonexecutives (line 26) is negative and the interactive terms (lines 31 and 32) are not significantly different from zero (weakly so in the presence of dividend cuts). The economic effect of an increase in nonexecutives to the upper decile average of 63.6% from a mean of 38.9% is associated with a decline in board turnover of between 7.4% and 9.5%, depending upon the performance measure. The proportion of nonexecutives therefore has a substantial negative influence on board turnover.

Financial structure

If capital structure influences executive board turnover, we expect a high level of executive board turnover to be related to high levels of capital leverage (a positive coefficient in line 28), and low levels of interest coverage combined with poor performance (a negative coefficient in line 33). In addition, we examine whether board turnover is associated with new equity issues (a positive coefficient in line 29 and a negative coefficient in line 34 with an interaction with performance). We find that high leverage is significantly related to turnover in two of the five regressions, and it is negatively related to the interaction of leverage with performance in two of the remaining regressions. The economic effect of leverage increasing to the upper decile level of 72.2% from a mean of 32.7% is

an increase in board turnover of between 3.9 and 6.9% depending on which performance measure is used. We also reran our regressions using interest coverage. We expect a high level of board turnover to be related to low levels of interest coverage particularly when combined with poor performance. We find a strong relation between turnover and interest coverage, including interactions with lagged performance. The significance of leverage and interest coverage is consistently observed using different estimation techniques.[26]

There is a strong correlation between new equity issues and board turnover (four significant positive coefficients in line 29 and the remaining one has a significant negative interactive coefficient with performance). When new equity is issued then board turnover increases by between 6.6 and 10.0%. The significant interaction between new equity issues and performance in the earnings loss regression is consistent with the case study observation of Section 3.5 that corporate refinancing in the wake of poor performance provides an opportunity to restructure the board.

Overview

The results to date suggest that neither owners nor purchasers of share blocks perform a disciplinary function. The only significant effect of large block holdings is associated with those in the hands of executives and these are used to entrench rather than discipline management. Share sales by families and executives are associated with board turnover but not interactively with performance. Takeovers have a very large impact on board turnover but again not interactively with performance. Share block sales and takeovers therefore have a significant effect on board turnover but they are not focused on the worst-performing companies. Nonexecutives appear to perform more of an advisory and supportive than a disciplinary role. In contrast, financial variables (leverage and new equity issues taken together) are economically and significantly related to board turnover and performance. They are therefore both significant and focused and are thus far ahead in the horse race.

4.2. Poor performance

The results in the previous section were based upon all firms in the sample. In this section, we examine only poorly performing firms. We look at how board turnover is related to the five governance mechanisms in the presence of five definitions of poor performance. The first is annual abnormal returns of less than −50%. The second is incidence of earnings losses. The third is dividend cuts and omissions. The other two definitions take even more extreme measures of poor performance: earnings losses combined with dividend cuts and omissions, and abnormal returns of less than 50% combined with earnings losses and dividends cuts and omissions. Clearly, the sample sizes for the fourth and fifth definitions are appreciably smaller than for the other three.

Table 12.8 reports regression results for our sample of poorly performing firms with the same variables as in Table 12.7, excluding the interactive terms with performance.

Existing shareholders

The results for the worst performing firms are almost identical to those of the complete sample. There is no evidence of share concentrations affecting turnover, except for holdings by executive directors. Again there is strong evidence of entrenchment. The economic effect of moving from average to upper decile executive ownership is a decrease of between 10.4 and 17.9% in executive board turnover in the worst performing firms depending on what measure of poor performance is used.

Increases in shareholdings

As in the complete sample, increases in shareholdings by families and executive directors are associated with significant increases in board turnover. The economic effects of moving from average to upper decile ownership by families and executive directors are between 5.8 and 8.2%, and

4.4 and 6.8% increases in board turnover, respectively. Increases in institutional ownership are associated with significant decreases in board turnover, suggesting that institutions sell to other investors to accomplish board replacements in poorly performing companies. The economic effect of such institutional sales is between 3.5 and 7.2% increases in board turnover for a reduction in holdings from upper decile to average levels.

Board structure

The proportion of nonexecutives on the board of poorly performing companies is not significantly related to board turnover. The number of nonexecutives does not therefore affect managerial disciplining. However, separation of the roles of chairman and chief executive is associated with significantly higher board turnover — between 8.5 and 12.0% more turnover.

Financial structure

Capital leverage is associated with significantly higher board turnover. An increase from average to upper decile levels of leverage raises board turnover by between 2.5 and 3.9%. Firms with earnings losses that make rights issues have a 13.8% higher level of board turnover than those that do not.

Takeovers

Takeovers are a highly significant influence on board turnover in the worst performing companies and are associated with a 64.1 to 78.7% increase in executive board turnover. This is, however, appreciably lower than the board turnover of firms in the complete sample that are targets of takeovers.

Summary

The results for the worst-performing companies are very similar to those for the complete sample. There is evidence of managerial entrenchment through executive share ownership while block holdings in the hands of other investors are not associated with managerial disciplining. Purchases of share blocks by families and executives, and financial constraints are associated with increases in board turnover and takeovers have an even more significant impact.

While the previous tests established the focus of different governance mechanisms, these results shed light on significance. Takeovers emerge as being the most significant governance mechanism but are unfocused. Purchases of share blocks by families and executives are also significant but unfocused. Only financial constraints are both focused and significant, in the case of new equity finance in particular when poor performance is measured by earnings losses.

4.3. Other tests

We performed several tests of the robustness of the results to alternative specification and different definitions of variables.

CEO in place of executive board turnover

We examined the effect of using CEO replacement in place of board turnover and related CEO replacement in a logistic regression on the same performance governance measures. We find that there is a significant relation between CEO replacement and performance when companies made losses, when dividends were cut or omitted, and when past abnormal returns were negative. Ownership variables are not generally significant, except for holdings by executive directors, with the sign suggesting managerial entrenchment. For four performance measures, changes in share holdings of nonexecutive directors are significant implying that greater ownership by this group is related to higher CEO replacement. This effect is independent of performance, suggesting a nondisciplinary reason for replacement.

The structure of the board is important for all five measures of performance; in particular, the separation of the CEO and chairman leads to greater CEO replacement.[27] This suggests that the presence of a nonexecutive chairman is of considerable importance in governance when firms

perform poorly. However, there is some evidence that a higher proportion of nonexecutive directors is negatively related to CEO turnover, the same result as reported above for board turnover using the complete sample. Both financial ratios— capital leverage and interest coverage[28]— lead to increased CEO changes for two measures of performance.

Overall, board structure is more important in the CEO than the board regressions with separation of the position of CEO and chairman leading to higher CEO turnover. Boards are therefore instrumental in dismissing CEOs in response to earnings losses or dividend cuts. To achieve wider board restructuring, investors require the leverage of external finance provided by high debt levels.

Serial correlation tests

If there is high annual board turnover in one year it may be followed by low board turnover, thus inducing serial correlation in the panel data. To check for this we performed a cross sectional regression where the dependent variable was the annual average board turnover for each company in the three-year period including the year of poor performance. The independent variables were measured in the year of poor performance in one set of regressions and with a lag of one year in another set of regressions. These cross-sectional regressions were performed using data from firms in two years, 1990 and 1991. We find that the results are consistent with the panel data, although the level of significance is different in a number of cases. We find statistical support for the entrenchment effect of insider holdings by directors, for the relation between leverage (and interest cover) and performance, rights issues, and executive board turnover, and that nonexecutive directors support incumbent management.

Exogeneity tests

An important assumption in the previous specification is that all the independent

Table 12.8 Regressions of Executive Board Turnover on Governance and Performance for the Worst Performing Companies, 1988–1993

Pooled Tobit regression: dependent variable is executive board turnover

Sample selection criterion 1988–1993	Ann. abn return ≤ 50%		Earnings losses		Dividend cuts and omissions		Earnings losses and dividend cuts and omissions		Abn. return ≤50% and losses and dividend cuts	
	Par. Est.	p-val.	Par. Est.	p-val.	Par. Est.	p-val.	Par. Est.	p-val.	Par. Est.	p-val.
Independent variable										
Sample size	228		171		248		138		73	
Noncensored data	125		100		131		82		52	
Censored data	103		71		117		56		21	
Intercept	14.2893	0.11	19.6005	0.08	14.9767	0.12	24.6063	0.04	37.1205	0.02
Existing shareholders										
Institutions	0.1201	0.42	0.1422	0.41	0.0405	0.78	0.1210	0.53	0.3211	0.19
Industrial cos	0.1302	0.46	0.0303	0.88	0.0297	0.86	0.0050	0.98	−0.0112	0.96
Families and indiv.	−0.5044	0.21	−0.5132	0.20	−0.7840	0.05	−0.6628	0.17	−0.5507	0.48
Executive directors	−0.2886	0.06	−0.4011	0.02	−0.5000	0.00	−0.5870	0.00	−0.4588	0.08
Nonexecutive dir.	−0.0714	0.78	−0.1717	0.59	−0.3390	0.19	−0.1778	0.58	0.5312	0.25
Increases in shareholding										
Institutions	−0.5499	0.03	−0.7006	0.01	−0.4166	0.08	−0.6495	0.03	−0.3431	0.30
Industrial cos	0.4391	0.25	0.4388	0.28	0.7214	0.03	0.5559	0.24	0.5183	0.39
Families and indiv.	1.0760	0.08	1.1109	0.06	1.5230	0.01	1.2999	0.06	1.0070	0.33
Executive directors	0.4983	0.06	0.4874	0.11	0.7542	0.01	0.7155	0.02	0.4494	0.16
Nonexecutive dir.	0.1054	0.87	0.1597	0.82	0.3288	0.69	−1.2174	0.34	−2.6717	0.06

Board structure, leverage, and takeovers

% nonexec. dir.	−0.0870	0.54	−0.0625	0.70	−0.1074	0.45	−0.0903	0.61	−0.2975	0.22
Separ. CEO-chair	8.4895	0.09	9.8290	0.09	2.3962	0.63	12.0251	0.06	5.4033	0.51
Cap. Leverage (book)	0.0751	0.03	0.0707	0.04	0.0982	0.00	0.0835	0.02	0.0635	0.07
New equity issue	11.0971	0.12	13.6903	0.08	5.3056	0.49	11.7129	0.20	15.7946	0.18
Mergers/acquisitions	78.7200	0.00	76.0784	0.00	76.5755	0.00	69.1113	0.00	64.0700	0.00
Disclosure dummy	−5.4827	0.33	−5.3182	0.51	−4.3605	0.48	−6.5226	0.45	−13.9756	0.16
Total sales (log)	1.19E-07	0.85	3.12E-08	0.96	−3.08E-07	0.55	−1.80E-08	0.98	−2.60E-06	0.65
F-test	0.001		0.001		0.001		0.001		0.1	
Rsq adj	15.4		17.6		20.8		20.9		11.9	

Note. The worst performing companies include those in the original random sample of 243 companies supplemented with a further 50 companies from the worst performing decile. The samples were selected on one of five criteria: annual abnormal returns of less than −50%, earnings losses, dividend cuts and omissions, earnings losses and dividend cuts, and omissions and annual abnormal returns of less than 50% together with earnings losses and dividend cuts and omissions. The table reports a Tobit regression of annual board turnover on levels and increases in concentration of ownership by five classes of investors, the structure of the board (separation of CEO-Chairman = 1 if there is separation, %nonexec. directors is the proportion of nonexecutives on the board), leverage, new equity issues = 1 if there is a new issue and takeovers = 1 if the firm is acquired. A dummy variable which equals zero in the years 1988–1989 and 1 in the other years (1990–1993) reflecting the reduction in ownership disclosure from 5 to 3% over the period 1989–1990 is included as is the size of the firm measured by log of total sales. Ownership variables, capital leverage, and % of nonexecutives are all in percentages.

* Significant at better than the 10% level.
** Significant at better than 5% level.
*** Significant at better than 1% level.

Source: own calculations based on annual reports, Datastream, London Business School's Risk Measurement Service.

variables are exogenous. To investigate this question we lagged all independent variables by one year in a panel OLS regression with fixed effects. We find that most of the results in the previous regressions are supported: board turnover increases with past poor performance and it decreases with high concentration of ownership when held by executive directors (entrenchment). Book leverage is positively correlated with executive turnover, but interest coverage is not. A Tobit with lags produced some significance on rights issues with board turnover.

Demsetz and Lehn (1985) and Himmelberg et al. (1999) argue that ownership is endogenous to performance. We investigated this by running reversed regressions of performance on ownership and changes in ownership, disaggregated by different classes of investor. We ran six regressions using abnormal returns, earnings losses, changes in earnings per share, return on equity, cash flow margins, and changes in dividends per share as dependent variables. No consistent relation was found between these measures of performance and either ownership or changes in ownership.

Summary

We have investigated the robustness of the results reported in the previous sections to replacing board turnover with CEO turnover and to tests of serial correlation and exogeneity of the independent variables. We have found that the conclusions of the previous section are robust to these changes and that there is some evidence that board structure has more of an influence on CEO replacement than on executive board turnover.

5. INFLUENCE OF REGULATION ON GOVERNANCE

In Section 5.1 we discuss how UK regulation may have affected the above results on governance. In Section 5.2, we compare the results that we have found in the United Kingdom with those reported in the United States. In Section 5.3, we describe how regulatory differences between the United Kingdom and United States might explain differences in outcomes between two seemingly similar capital markets.

5.1. Influence of UK regulation

5.1.1. Protection of minorities

Minority and dispersed shareholders are protected in the United Kingdom by The City Code on Takeovers and Mergers (called "The Code") and by UK company law. These create obstacles to building controlling stakes. For example, an outside blockholder who owns 15% or more of the equity of a firm must make public their intentions of launching a takeover. Where a stake of 30% or more has been acquired, there is a compulsory tender provision for all remaining shares and the tender price must be at least that paid for any shares acquired over the previous 12 months. Purchases of share blocks in excess of 3% together with the identity of the buyer must be disclosed to the market. These rules are designed to establish "fair play" in takeovers and to reduce the potential for predators to purchase stakes cheaply. However, they have the effect of raising acquisition costs.

Other rules affect incentives to acquire less than 100% of the shares of a target. The Stock Exchange lays down specific rules concerning transactions between controlling blockholders, who own more than 50% of shares, and related parties. These state that the firm "must be capable at all times of operating and making decisions independently of any controlling shareholder and all transactions and relationships in the future between the applicant and any controlling shareholder must be at arm's length and on a normal commercial basis."[29] A majority of the directors of the board of the subsidiary must be independent of the parent firm and minority shareholders have the right to be consulted about, and approve, transactions with the parent firm (Sections 11.4 and 11.5 of The Stock Exchange rules). The effect of these rules is to increase the costs of partial stakes. They explain why almost all bids are made conditional on acceptance by 90% or more of target shareholders. The remainder can be purchased compulsorily at the original bid price using a squeeze out rule under the 1948 Companies Act. In a recent bid by Capital Shopping Centres (CSC) for 25% of shares of Liberty International that they did not already own, the independent directors of Liberty advised minority shareholders not to accept the offer. They argued that "it does not give any premium for full control of the company" (The Financial Times, October 19, 2000).

5.1.2. Fiduciary duties of directors

Can regulation explain the results reported earlier about the role of nonexecutive directors in poorly performing companies? One important characteristic of UK regulation is the lack of fiduciary responsibilities of directors. Stapledon (1996) finds that although directors in the United Kingdom owe their companies "fiduciary duties of honesty and loyalty, and a duty of care and skill," in practice "actions to enforce the duties of directors of quoted companies have been almost non-existent" (pp. 13–14).[30] Problems of mounting such actions may have been exacerbated by free rider problems, the difficulty of recovering costs of the action from the firm, and the illegality of contingent fees (Miller, 1998).[31] In the absence of a duty of care, we would expect nonexecutive directors to perform an advisory role.

5.1.3. Rights issues

Another significant mechanism in the horse race was equity issues. Section 89(1) of the Companies Act 1985 states that seasoned new equity issues by companies must be in the form of rights issues.[32] Section 95 of the same Companies Act describes the circumstances under which pre-emption rights may be waived. It requires a super-majority vote by shareholders of 75% or more on each and every occasion an equity issue is to be made. In a recent case, involving the

Olivier Company, shareholders controlling 30% of the shares prevented a waiver of a rights issue.[33] Even where shareholders vote to drop pre-emption rights the discount of any new issue must not exceed 10% of the market price at the time of the issue's announcement (paragraph 4.26, Stock Exchange Rules, 1999). These rules ensure that old shareholders cannot be diluted by new shareholders.[34] They are reinforced by guidelines, authorized by the National Association of Pension Funds and the Association of British Insurers, limiting companies to raising 5% of their share capital each year by any method apart from rights issues—and 7.5% in any rolling three-year period.

5.2. Comparison of UK and U.S. empirical results

In some respects, the determinants of board turnover in the United Kingdom and United States are similar. We find a significant negative relation between board turnover and performance, similar to results reported for the United States (see Weisbach, 1988; Warner et al., 1988; and Coughlan and Schmidt, 1985). There is strong evidence of entrenchment by insiders in both countries in the form of a negative relation between board turnover and insider holdings (see Hermalin and Weisbach, 1991; and McConnell and Servaes, 1990, for results in the United States).[35,36]

We have found little evidence in our UK sample of a relation between concentration of outside shareholdings and board turnover. The U.S. results are similar. For example, Holderness and Sheehan (1988) report that the identity of large outside block owners is important, and that firms with majority outside blockholders have better performance than those with diffuse ownership, but the differences are not statistically significant. Denis and Kruse (2000) find that the presence of large blockholders, other than directors and their families, does not have an impact on industry-adjusted operating performance and they find no evidence of ownership structure influencing nonroutine board turnover.

However, in other respects UK and U.S. results differ significantly. There is more evidence in the United States than in the United Kingdom of disciplining associated with sales of share blocks. In the United States, Bethel *et al.* (1998) report that purchases of share blocks by active investors are targeted on poorly performing companies. Holderness and Sheehan (1988) find that when their majority blocks trade, there is substantial management turnover and stock prices increase. In the United Kingdom, we have found little evidence that changes in share blocks by potentially active investors perform a disciplinary function.

There are two still more pronounced differences between the United Kingdom and United States. First, in the United States, Weisbach (1988) reports a closer relation of CEO turnover to performance in firms where nonexecutive directors dominate the board. Also, Gilson (1990) and Kaplan and Reishus (1990) find that nonexecutive directors of poorly performing companies lose reputation and are frequently unable to find replacement positions. In the United Kingdom, we found no evidence of disciplining by nonexecutive directors; indeed, the relation is negative between the proportion of nonexecutives and board turnover. Second, we find that capital structure and new equity financing are particularly significant influences on board turnover in the United Kingdom. We are not aware of any U.S. study reporting this relation. The Table below summarizes evidence on the parties performing disciplining in the United Kingdom and United States. It shows the effect on disciplining of different parties' interventions in the two countries.

Effect on disciplining	United Kingdom	United States
Negative	Executive block holders Nonexecutive directors	Executive block holders
Neutral	Other block holders Purchasers of blocks	Other block holders Providers of new finance
Positive	Bidders Providers of new finance	Some purchasers of blocks Bidders Nonexecutive directors

5.3. Regulatory differences between the United Kingdom and United States

5.3.1. Protection of minorities

We have already reported that protection of minorities is extensive in the United Kingdom. In terms of Goshen's characterization (1998) of systems of minority protection, the United Kingdom has a "property rule" which prevents any transaction from proceeding without the minority owner's consent. In contrast, the United States has a "liability rule" which allows transactions to be imposed on an unwilling minority but ensures that the minority is adequately protected in objective market value terms.[37, 38] Protection of investors, especially minorities, is primarily the concern of the courts. Until this year, there was no U.S. equivalent of the UK Takeover Code requiring full bids for companies to be made but there are much more extensive takeover defences in state legislation and company charters than in the United Kingdom (Miller, 1998).[39, 40]

The impediments to the exercise of control by dominant shareholders in the United Kingdom and the more liberal view of takeovers encourage full acquisitions of companies rather than control through partial share blocks. This may explain why, in contrast to the United States, trades in share blocks in the United Kingdom do not involve active shareholders and are not disciplinary in nature.

5.3.2. Fiduciary duties of directors

While powers to enforce fiduciary responsibilities on directors in the United Kingdom are weak, in the United States, directors (both executive and nonexecutive) have a duty of care to shareholders and can be sued for failing to fulfil their fiduciary responsibilities.[41] This may explain why nonexecutives play quite different roles in the United Kingdom and United States— an active governance function in the United States as against an advisory role in the United Kingdom. There is evidence to support the view that litigation encourages boards to be active in the United States (see Millstein and MacAvoy, 1998). This is strengthened by the high proportion of nonexecutive directors in the United States—an average of 75% of the total board compared with only 33% in our UK sample (see Kini et al., 2000).

5.3.3. Rights issues

As noted above, in the United Kingdom new equity issues generally take the form of rights issues. In the United States, companies frequently obtain shareholders' agreement to drop pre-emption rights. Brealey and Myers (1996) suggest that "the arguments [by management] for dropping pre-emption rights do not make sense" (p. 405). Our results imply that managers have incentives to drop pre-emption rights to allow equity issues to be made to new shareholders at a discount to the equilibrium price, thereby diluting existing shareholder wealth. The discount would be in exchange for implicit or explicit agreements to new shareholders to leave existing management in place. The U.S. evidence provided by Loderer et al. (1991) suggests that a significant minority of new seasoned equity issues are made at a discount from the market price, although not necessarily below their equilibrium price. Stronger rights requirements in the United Kingdom may therefore have allowed investors to exert greater control over management as a pre-condition for the provision of new finance.

In summary, while La Porta et al. (1998) suggest that the rights of shareholders in the United Kingdom and United States are similar, we find significant differences in minority investor protection,

fiduciary responsibilities of nonexecutives, and rules relating to new equity issues.[42] These differences in protection appear to be related to the more active role of share block purchasers and nonexecutive directors in the United States and the more active role for providers of new finance in the United Kingdom.

6. CONCLUSIONS

The question posed at the beginning of the paper was: Who initiates control changes in poorly performing companies? Five parties were suggested: existing large shareholders, purchasers of blocks, bidders in takeovers, nonexecutive directors, and shareholders supplying new equity finance.

Coalitions of five shareholders can on average control more than 30% of shares in the United Kingdom. However, there is little evidence that they do. On the contrary, the main source of block holder control comes from those in the hands of insiders and these are used to entrench rather than to discipline management.

An as yet undocumented characteristic of the UK capital market is an active market in share blocks. Markets in share blocks could be used to discipline poorly performing management, and in the United States there is some evidence that they do. But in the United Kingdom they do not; instead, board turnover is primarily associated with full acquisitions in takeovers.

The role of boards in exercising governance is also weak as evidenced by the fact that nonexecutive directors do not perform a disciplinary function. In this respect, the United Kingdom is quite different from the United States. In the United Kingdom, ineffective implementation of fiduciary responsibilities results in nonexecutive directors regarding their role as being primarily advisory rather than disciplinary.

If neither holders of share blocks nor boards discipline management in poorly performing companies in the United Kingdom, who does? We find that capital structure is a significant determinant of board changes and high levels of leverage and low interest coverage are associated with high levels of board turnover in poorly performing companies. At first sight, this suggests that creditor intervention is the main source of corporate reorganization. However, evidence from 34 case studies and from the regression analyses revealed an important role for new equity issues in board restructurings.

Regulation appears to be a significant influence on this pattern of governance in the United Kingdom. Strong minority protection has discouraged partial accumulation of share blocks in favor of full acquisitions in takeovers. Weak fiduciary obligations on directors have resulted in nonexecutives playing more of an advisory than a disciplinary role. Rights issue requirements protect existing shareholders against wealth transfers initiated by the management of poorly performing firms and allow outside shareholders to impose board changes as a condition for the provision of new equity finance.

Thus, despite the frequent categorization of UK regulation under the same "common law" classification as the United States, there are significant differences — more minority investor protection in the United Kingdom than in the United States, less fiduciary obligations on directors in the United Kingdom but stricter rights issue requirements. These differences appear to be associated with more governance through partial acquisitions of share blocks and by nonexecutive directors in the United States, but less governance through the provision of new financing than in the United Kingdom. Subtle differences in regulatory systems may therefore be associated with pronounced difference in governance outcomes.

What is the significance of these differences for corporate performance? We have not attempted to answer this question directly in this paper; however, it might be argued that greater reliance on financial constraints and less reliance on boards in the United Kingdom leads to a greater concentration of disciplining on the worst-performing firms. This is consistent with the observation that higher board turnover is restricted to the very worst performing firms. The greater reliance on "unfocused" takeovers may to some extent have compensated for this but, if regulation makes this an expensive form of intervention, then there may still be inadequate restructuring in the United Kingdom prior to the emergence of financial distress.

NOTES

1   We are grateful for comments from participants at conferences at the London School of Economics, Fondazione ENI Enrico Mattei in Milan, Wissenschaftszentrum Berlin fur Sozialforschung, the University of Amsterdam, the University of Venice, the Autonoma University of Barcelona, the conference of the ESRC Network for Industrial Economics, the European Corporate Governance Network, the European Finance Association Meeting in Milan, the CEPR European Summer Symposium in Financial Markets in Gerzensee, the CEPR workshop on corporate finance in Toulouse, the SUERF meeting in Budapest, the TMR Meeting in Florence, the EFMA Meeting in Lisbon, and the Annual Meetings of the American Finance Association. We are particularly grateful to our discussants Fabrizio Barca, Alan Hughes, Alexander Ljungqvist, Marco Pagano, Sigurt Vitols, and Jozef Zechner. We received useful suggestions from Margaret Bray, Luis Correia da Silva, Rafel Crespi, Jay Dahya, Carles Gispert, Marc Goergen, Michel Habib, Uli Hege, Joe McCahery, Piet Moerland, Anthony Neuberger, Kjell Nyborg, Enrico Perotti, Christian Rydqvist, Henri Servaes, James Tomkins, David Webb, and Michael Weisbach. We thank Matthew Beardmore-Gray and Huw Jones of Prudential for very helpful discussions. We are grateful to the referees of our paper and to the editor of the *Journal of Financial Intermediation* for very helpful comments. Julian Franks and Colin Mayer acknowledge financial support from the European Union's Training and Mobility of Researchers Network (Contract FRMXCT960054) and Luc Renneboog is grateful for financial support from the Netherlands Organization of Scientific Research.
2   To whom correspondence should be addressed.
3   Weisbach (1988) also assumes that any resignation over 62 is natural turnover, unless there is evidence of conflict.

4   This uses a Capital Asset Pricing Model with Bayesian updating and a thin trading correction. Further details can be found in LSPD, London Business School, 1997.

5   This is after adjusting for bankruptcies, acquisitions, and double counting of those companies appearing in the bottom decile in more than one year.

6   Lai and Sudarsanam (1998) also report declines in board turnover after performance declines.

7   The disclosure threshold in the United States is 5%.

8   As well as direct (or beneficial) holdings, we included all nonbeneficial holdings held by directors on behalf of families and charitable trusts. Directors do not obtain cash flow benefits from these holdings but they have control rights. We also investigated nominee holdings and found that in 95% of the cases, institutional investors used the nominee registration to reduce administrative costs. The nominee shareholdings were classified according to category of shareholder using nominee accounts.

9   Recent IPOs may particularly affect the pattern of ownership; however, the large majority of our companies, 71%, have been listed for at least eight years.

10   Individual stakes of 30% or greater were almost always built up prior to the company's IPO. In other cases they resulted from acquisitions in which target shareholders did not tender all their shares.

11   Bristow's data (1995) show that for 3963 firms median insider ownership is 12.5% and for other much smaller samples the median rises to about 16%.

12   The quotation of 3 was suspended or cancelled, 1 company was taken private and the equity of 3 other firms was converted into a different security.

13   A total of 14% of companies had quotations suspended or cancelled.

14   The bankruptcy rate is low. For the original sample of 243 companies it is zero. For the additional sample of poorly performing companies it is 4% for the period 1988–1993. It increases to 6% if we follow the sample to 1997.

15   Martin and McConnell (1991) also report high board turnover post takeover, between 58 and 64%, depending upon whether the takeover was hostile or friendly.

16   If we included increases in existing shareholdings, the totals would increase by 22 for [5, 10%], 15 for [10, 25%], and 3 for [25, 50%].

17   The lower rate of block sales in the United States may be due to their sample being confined to the Fortune 500 companies, whereas our sample is drawn from all quoted companies.

18   Hermalin and Weisbach (1998) predict that the "probability that independent directors are added to the board increases following poor corporate performance."

19   Similar relations between interest coverage and other measures of performance are found. For example, median interest cover for companies with dividend cuts is 0.6 compared with 4.5 for those with stable or increasing dividends.

20   A level of two is chosen because investment grade companies "typically have coverage ratios exceeding two times interest expense" (Copeland et al., 1995, p. 178).

21   Rights issues are offered to existing shareholders and any rights not taken up may be sold for the benefit of the shareholder; in open offers, rights not taken up may not be sold by the original holder and can be sold by the company to other shareholders.

22   We controlled for the change in the disclosure threshold from 5 to 3% in 1989 by including a dummy variable which equals 0 for 1988–1989 and 1 afterwards. We also verified the robustness of our results, by including dummy variables for the years and by running the regression on subsamples which excluded the years 1989 and 1990. This did not significantly alter the results reported below.

23   In the case of zero-one (or minus one) dummy variables (earnings losses, dividend cuts and omissions, takeovers, and new equity issues), economic effects relate to the effect of switching from zero to one (or minus one). The tables with the means and percentiles of independent variables are available on request.

24   We examined the effect of interactions between dividend cuts/omissions and negative share price performance on board turnover by restricting the regression to the sample of companies that incurred abnormal losses. The regression results were little affected.

25   The results were rerun assuming coalitions of shareholders, for example, all outside shareholders were grouped together, with executive and nonexecutives forming two other groups. The results are similar to those in Tables 12.7 and 12.8. These results are available on request.

26   Results remained unaltered when leverage and interest cover were included with a lag of a year, rejecting a reversed causation explanation for their significance.

27   Including a variable for the length of tenure of the CEO eliminated the significance of the separation variable. However, length of

tenure was only available for a subsample of firms (130 observations were lost) and has not therefore been shown in the table. There is likely to be less CEO–chairman separation in companies where CEOs have been in place for long periods of time and a nonexecutive chairman may be able to exert less influence where CEOs are firmly entrenched. As a consequence, tenure extinguishes the significance of separation.

28 Interest coverage was substituted for leverage in separate regressions.

29 See Sections 3.12 and 3.13 of Chapter 11 of the Stock Exchange rules.

30 See also Parkinson (1993).

31 In Germany there are particular lawsuits by shareholders that must be funded by the company, for example, where shareholders object to being "squeezed out" when a blockholder has at least 95% of the target's shares. The minority may demand a court hearing at the company's expense.

32 If shareholders fail to take up their rights, the rights may be sold for the shareholder's benefit. These pre-emption rights are recognised in European Community law.

33 Financial Times, May 29, 1998.

34 The Exchange may relax these rules if the company is in severe financial difficulties.

35 Morck et al. (1988), and McConnell and Servaes (1990) find that corporate performance as measured by Tobin's Q initially rises with low levels of insider ownership (for example, up to 5% in the Morck et al. study) and then declines.

36 Our results are also consistent with the use of anti-takeover amendments, recorded by Borokhovich et al. (1997), to entrench management, and Stultz's argument (1988) that anti-takeover amendments substitute for insider ownership as an entrenchment mechanism.

37 The difference that is drawn here between UK and U.S. minority protection conforms with the more general distinction which Atiyah and Summers (1987) and Posner (1996) draw between reliance on substantive reasoning under U.S. law and formal reasoning in UK law.

38 The United States does have the Williams Act of 1968 which introduced rules on block disclosure (10% later amended to 5%), a minimum period for which a tender offer must be left open, and a provision explicitly allowing targets to sue bidding firms.

39 Protection may even fall short of that provided by the application of a fair price rule. Gilson (1995) argues that in Sinclair Oil Corp v. Levien business judgment rather than intrinsic fairness tests should have been applied. It is debatable whether minority protection in the United States interferes with business judgments

of parents. Eisenberg (1976) states that "the checks on unfair dealing by the parent are few. In theory, of course, the fairness of the parent's behaviour is subject to the check of judicial review; but in practice such review is difficult even where the courts have the will to engage in it, and they often lack the will."

40 La Porta et al. (1997, 1999) measure anti-director rights in the United Kingdom and United States and find greater protection for minorities in the United States. However, they focus on the rights under commercial law and do not consider the influence of the nonstatutory, but highly effective, Takeover Code and Stock Exchange rules.

41 Clark (1986) describes the circumstances under which shareholders can be sued in the United States. For example, in Smith v. Van Gorkum, shareholders successfully sued directors for a breach of duty of care with respect to a merger. However, Clark also notes the paucity of such successful cases.

42 An example in differing interpretations is Preemptive Right to New Issues. The evidence is clear that in the United Kingdom waiver of rights issues is very difficult unless the company is in distress, whereas in the United States waivers are the norm. Nevertheless, La Porta et al. (1997) give the two countries the same score.

REFERENCES

Aghion, P., and Bolton, P. (1992). An incomplete contracts approach to financial contracting, Rev. Econ. Stud. 59, 473–494.

Atiyah, P., and Summers, R. (1987). "Form and Substance in Anglo-American Law," Clarendon, Oxford.

Ball, R., Kothari, S. P., and Robin, A. (1997). "The Effect of Institutional Factors on Properties of Accounting Earnings: International Evidence," working paper, University of Rochester, May.

Bethel, J. E., Liebeskind, J. P., and Opler, T. (1998). Block share purchases and corporate performance, J. Finance 53, 605–634.

Bianco, M., Gola C., and Signorini, L. F. (1996). Dealing with separation between ownership and control: State, family, coalitions and pyramidal groups in Italian corporate governance, Fondazione Eni Enrico Mattei Note di Lavoro: 05/96, February.

Borokhovich, K. A., Brunarski, K. R., and Parrino, R. (1997). CEO contracting and anti-takeover amendments, *J. Finance* **52**, 1495–1517.

Brealey, R., and Myers, S. (1996). "Principles of Corporate Finance," McGraw–Hill, New York.

Bristow, D. K. (1995). The time series and cross sectional properties of directors and officers' stock holdings, mimeo, UCLA.

Burkart, M., Gromb, D., and Panunzi, F. (1997). Large shareholders monitoring, and the value of the firm, *Quart. J. Econ.* **112**, 693–728.

Burkart, M., Gromb, D., and Panunzi, F. (1998). Why higher takeover premia protect minority shareholders, *J. Polit. Econ.* **196**, 176–204.

Cadbury, A. (1992). "Report of the Committee on the Financial Aspects of Corporate Governance," Gee & Co, London.

Clark, R. C. (1986). "Corporate Law," Little, Brown & Co., Boston.

Copeland, T., Koller, T., and Murrin, J. (1995). "Valuation: Measuring and Managing the Value of Companies," Wiley, New York.

Coughlan, A. T., and Schmidt, R. M. (1985). Executive compensation, managerial turnover and firm performance: An empirical investigation, *J. Acc. Econ.* 7, 42–46.

Dahya, J., McConnell, J., and Travlos, N. (2000). "The Cadbury Committee, Corporate Performance and Top Management Turnover," working paper, Cardiff Business School.

Demsetz, H., and Lehn, K. (1985). The structure of corporate ownership: Causes and consequences, *J. Polit. Econ.* **93**, 1155–1177.

Denis, D., and Denis, D. K. (1995). Performance changes following top management turnover, *J. Finance* **50**, 1029–1057.

Denis, D., and Kruse, T. (2000). Managerial discipline and corporate restructuring following performance declines, *J. Finan. Econ.* **55**, 391–424.

Eisenberg, M. (1976). "The Structure of the Corporation," Little, Brown & Co, Boston.

Fama, E. (1980). Agency problems and the theory of the firm, *J. Polit. Econ.* **88**, 288–307.

Fama, E., and Jensen, M. (1983). Separation of ownership and control, *J. Law Econ.* **26**, 301–325.

Franks, J., and Mayer, C. (1996). Hostile takeovers in the UK and the correction of managerial failure, *J. Finan. Econ.* **40**, 163–181.

Franks J., and Mayer, C. (2000). The ownership and control of German corporations, *Rev. Finan. Stud*, in press.

Gilson, R. J. (1995). "The Law and Finance of Corporate Acquisitions," Foundation Press, Westbury, New York.

Gilson, S. C. (1990). Bankruptcy, boards, banks and blockholders, *J. Finan. Econ.* **27**, 355–387.

Goshen, Z. (1998). Liability rule or property rule: Voting in conflict of interests in corporate law and minority's protection, mimeo.

Hermalin, B., and Weisbach, M. (1991). The effects of board composition and direct incentives on firm performance, *Finan. Manage.* **20**, 101–112.

Hermalin, B., and Weisbach, M. (1998). Endogenously chosen boards of directors and their monitoring of the CEO, *Amer. Econ. Rev.* **88**, 96–118.

Himmelberg, C. P., Hubbard, R. G., and Palia, D. (1999). Understanding the determinants of managerial ownership and ownership, *J. Finan. Econ.* **53**, 353–384.

Holderness, C. G., and Sheehan, D. P. (1988). The role of majority shareholders in publicly held corporations: An exploratory analysis, *J. Finan. Econ.* **20**, 317–346.

Jensen, M. (1986). Agency costs of free cash flow, corporate finance and takeovers, *Amer. Econ. Rev.* **76**, 323–339.

Jensen, M. (1989). The eclipse of the public corporation, *Harvard Bus. Rev.* 61–74.

Kaplan, S., and Reishus, D. (1990). Outside directorships and corporate performance, *J. Finan. Econ.* **27**, 389–410.

Kini, O., Kracaw, W., and Mian, S. (2000). The nature of discipline by corporate takeovers in an active takeover market, mimeo, Georgia State University.

La Porta, R., Lopez-de-Silanes, F., Shleifer, A., and Vishny, R. (1997). Legal determinants of external finance, *J. Finance* **52**, 1131–1150.

La Porta, R., Lopez-de-Silanes, F., Shleifer, A., and Vishny, R. (1998). Law and finance, *J. Polit. Econ.* **106**, 1113–1155.

La Porta, R., Lopez-de-Silanes, F. Shleifer, A., and Vishny, R. (1999). Ownership around the world, *J. Finance* **54**, 471–517.

Lai, J., and Sudarsanam, S. (1998). Corporate restructuring in response to performance decline: Impact of ownership, governance and lenders, *Europ. Finance Rev.* **1**, 197–233.

Loderer, C., Sheehan, D. P., and Kadlec, G. (1991). The pricing of equity offerings, *J. Finan. Econ.* **29**, 35–58.

Marsh, P. (1992). Dividend announcements and stock price performance, unpublished manuscript, London Business School.

Martin, K., and McConnell, J. J. (1991). Corporate performance, corporate takeovers, and management turnover, *J. Finance* **46**, 671–687.

McConnell, J. J., and Servaes, H. (1990). Additional evidence on equity ownership and corporate value, *J. Finan. Econ.* **27**, 595–612.

Miller, G. (1998). Political structure and corporate governance: Some points of contrast between the United States and England, *in* "The Sloan Project on Corporate Governance," pp. 629–648. *Corporate Governance Today*, Columbia Law School.

Millstein, I., and MacAvoy, P. (1998). The active board of directors and performance of the large publicly traded corporation, *Columbia Law Rev.* **98**, 1283–1321.

Morck, R., Shleifer, A., and Vishny, R. (1988). Management ownership and market valuation: An empirical analysis, *J. Finan. Econ.* **20**, 293–316.

Parkinson, J. (1993). "Corporate Power and Responsibility: Issues in the Theory of Company Law," Oxford Univ. Press, Oxford.

Posner, R. (1996). "Law and Legal Theory in the UK and USA," Clarendon, Oxford.

Renneboog, L. (2000). Ownership, managerial control and the governance of poorly performing companies listed on the Brussels Stock Exchange, *J. Banking Finance* **24**, 1959–1995.

Romano, R. (1991). The shareholder suit and litigation without foundation, *J. Law Econ., Organ.* **7**, 55–87.

Scharfstein, D. (1988). The disciplinary role of takeovers, *Rev. Econ. Stud.* **55**, 185–199.

Shleifer, A., and Vishny, R. (1986). Large shareholders and corporate control, *J. Polit. Econ.* **94**, 461–488.

Stapledon, G. (1996). "Institutional Shareholders and Corporate Governance," Clarendon, Oxford.

Stulz, R. (1988). Managerial control of voting rights: Financing policies and the market for corporate control, *J. Finan. Econ.* **20**, 25–54.

Warner, J. B., Watts, R. L., and Wruck, K. H. (1988). Stock prices and top management changes, *J. Finan. Econ.* **20**, 431–460.

Weisbach, M. S. (1988). Outside directors and CEO turnover, *J. Finan. Econ.* **20**, 431–446.

Chapter 13

Jay Dahya, John J. McConnell and Nickolaos Travlos[*]

THE CADBURY COMMITTEE, CORPORATE PERFORMANCE, AND MANAGEMENT TURNOVER

Source: *Journal of Finance*, 57(1) (2002): 461–483.

ABSTRACT

In 1992, the Cadbury Committee issued the *Code of Best Practice* which recommends that boards of U.K. corporations include at least three outside directors and that the positions of chairman and CEO be held by different individuals. The underlying presumption was that these recommendations would lead to improved board oversight. We empirically analyze the relationship between CEO turnover and corporate performance. CEO turnover increased following issuance of the *Code*; the negative relationship between CEO turnover and performance became stronger following the *Code*'s issuance; and the increase in sensitivity of turnover to performance was concentrated among firms that adopted the *Code*.

THE CADBURY COMMITTEE WAS APPOINTED by the Conservative Government of the United Kingdom in May 1991 with a broad mandate to "...address the financial aspects of corporate governance" (*Report of the Committee on the Financial Aspects of Corporate Governance*, 1992, Section 1.8). The Committee was chaired by Sir Adrian Cadbury, CEO of the Cadbury confectionery empire, and included other senior industry executives, finance specialists, and academics. In December 1992, the Committee issued its report, the cornerstone of which was *The Code of Best Practice*, which presents the Committee's recommendations on the structure and responsibilities of corporate boards of directors. The two key recommendations of the *Code* are that boards of publicly traded companies include at least three nonexecutive (i.e., outside) directors and that the positions of chief executive officer (CEO) and chairman of the board (COB) of these companies be held by two different individuals.[1]

The apparent reasoning underlying the Committee's recommendations is that greater independence of a corporate board improves the quality of board oversight.

As of 2001, the *Code* has not been enshrined into U.K. law and compliance with its key provisions is entirely voluntary. Nevertheless, the *Code* is not without "teeth." First, the Cadbury Committee's report explicitly recognizes that legislation would very likely follow if companies did not comply with the guidelines of the *Code* (*Report of the Committee on the Financial Aspects of Corporate Governance*, 1992, Section 1.1). Second, the report has been given further bite by the London Stock Exchange (LSE), which, since June 1993, has required a statement from each listed company that spells out whether the company is in compliance with the *Code* and, if not, requires an explanation as to why the company is not in compliance.

To appreciate the significance of the Cadbury Committee and its recommendations, it is important to appreciate the environment surrounding the establishment of the Committee. First, the Committee was appointed in the aftermath of the "scandalous" collapse of several prominent U.K. companies during the later 1980s and early 1990s, including Ferranti, Colorol Group, Pollypeck, Bank of Credit and Commerce International, and Maxwell Communication. The broadsheet press popularly attributed these failures and others to weak governance systems, lax board oversight, and the vesting of control in the hands of a single top executive.

The Cadbury Committee was set up in response to a number of corporate scandals that cast doubt on the systems for controlling the ways companies are run. The downfall of powerful figures such as Asil Nadir or the late Robert Maxwell, whose personal control over their companies was complete, raised fears about the concentration of power. (Self-regulation seen as the way forward, 1992)

Second, historically, executive (i.e., inside) directors have heavily dominated U.K. boards. For example, during 1988, for only 21 companies of the *Financial Times* (FT) 500 did outside directors comprise a majority of the board and, when boards are ranked according to the fraction of outside board members, outsiders comprised only 27 percent of the median board's membership (The Corporate Register, 1989). In comparison, outsiders comprised a majority of the board for 387 of the Fortune 500 companies. Furthermore, for the median board of the Fortune 500 companies, outside directors comprised 81 percent of the membership (Annual Corporate Proxy Statements). With respect to the joint position of CEO and COB, the United Kingdom and United States historically are similar. For example, during 1988, a single individual jointly held the positions of CEO and COB for 349 of the Fortune 500 and for 328 of the FT 500.

At its issuance, the Cadbury Report was greeted with skepticism both by those who felt that it went too far and by those who felt that it did not go far enough. The general unease of those who felt it went too far can be summarized as a concern that the delicate balance between shareholders and managers is better left to the forces of competition. A less generous interpretation of this perspective, which was most frequently espoused by corporate managers, might be characterized as "leave us alone—we know best."

There is danger in an over emphasis on monitoring; on non-executive directors independence...[and] on controls over decision making activities of companies. (Green, 1994)

The general concern of those who thought that the report did not go far enough centered on the "voluntary" nature of the Report's recommendations.

The Committee's recommendations are steps in the right direction. But...[s]hareholders, investors and creditors will have been disappointed that just when the corporate failures of recent years cried out for bold and imaginative legal reform, the body from which so much had been expected came up with a little tinkering and a voluntary code (Cadbury Committee Draft Orders Mixed News for Shareholders, 1992).

Against this background, this study empirically investigates the impact of the key Cadbury recommendations on the quality of board oversight in U.K. firms over the period 1989 through 1996.

We begin our investigation with the presumption that an important oversight role of boards of directors is the hiring and firing of top corporate management. We further presume that one indicator of effective board oversight is that the board replaces ineffective or poorly performing top management. Finally, we presume that corporate performance is a reliable proxy for the effectiveness of top management. With those presumptions in place, we empirically investigate the relationship between top management turnover and corporate performance before and after the Cadbury Committee issued its recommendations.

We assemble a sample of 460 U.K. industrial companies listed on the LSE as of December 1988. For each company, we collect data on management turnover, board composition, and corporate performance for up to seven years before and four years after the issuance of the Cadbury Report. With these data, we determine that the relationship between top management turnover and corporate performance is statistically significant both before and after adoption of the Cadbury Committee's recommendations, that is, poorer performance is associated with higher turnover. Importantly, for our purposes, this relationship is significantly stronger following adoption of the Committee's recommendations. Upon further exploration, the increased sensitivity of turnover to performance is due to an increase in outside board members among firms that complied with the key provisions of the *Code*.

The next section describes our sample selection procedure. Section II presents descriptive statistics for the sample. Section III presents the results of our empirical analysis. We reserve our literature review until Section IV, in which we present our conclusions in the context of prior related empirical studies.

I. SAMPLE SELECTION

Our investigation focuses on top management turnover during the eight-year interval surrounding publication of the Cadbury Report in December 1992 (i.e., December 1988 through December 1996). To begin, we randomly selected 650 out of a total of 1,828 industrial firms on the *Official List* of the LSE as of year-end 1988 (Stock Exchange Yearbook, 1988–1996). For each of the 650 firms for which data are available in the *Corporate Register* for 1988, we determine the names of board members, the outside directors, the total shares held by the board, the total shares held by institutions, and the number of

block shareholders, where a block shareholder is defined as any shareholder owning greater than three percent of the company's stock. Such data are available for 548 of the firms in the initial sample. Stock price and accounting data are taken from Datastream for the years 1985 through 1988. If such data are not available for the years 1985 through 1988, the firm is dropped from the sample. Forty-seven of the 548 firms were dropped because of insufficient stock price data; 41 were dropped due to insufficient accounting data. The resulting sample contains 460 firms. These firms are then identified according to their Financial Times Industry Classification (FTIC). The sample includes at least one firm from each of the 33 FTIC categories.

To keep the sample at 460 firms at all times, when a firm ceases to be listed, we search chronologically among newly listed industrial firms until we identify the first firm with book value of assets within plus or minus 20 percent of the book value of assets of the firm that ceased to be listed. For this firm to be eligible for our sample, we require that data be available on management identity, board composition, share ownership, and financial performance. Finally, we require that if the existing firm was (was not) in compliance with the *Code*, the replacement firm must (must not) be in compliance. In this way, a replacement firm was identified for each firm that ceased to be listed within at most four months of delisting. We continue this procedure each year from December 1988 onward, replacing firms that are no longer listed on the LSE, through the end of 1996.

For each firm in the sample, for each year, we collect the names of board members, the number of outsiders, the number of shares held by the board and by institutions, and the number of block holders from the *Corporate Register*. We take stock returns and accounting data from Datastream. For new firms, accounting data for three years prior to LSE listing are taken from filings with the LSE at the time of listing. The shares of some newly listed firms traded elsewhere prior to entering the LSE *Official List*. For these firms, stock price data are collected for up to three years preceding their listing dates. For other firms, we use price data beginning with their entry onto the *Official List*.

To determine top management turnover, we compare the names of top management from year to year over the time period December 1988 through December 1996. For each company, we identify the top executive as the individual with the title of CEO or Executive Chairman. In addition, we identify other board members as members of the top management team if the board member is an employee of the firm and holds the title of Chief of Operations or Managing Director. If the name of the top executive changes between successive years, we classify that as turnover in the top executive. For other members of the top management team, if a name disappears from the top management list, that event is deemed to be a turnover in the top management team excluding the top executive. If the top executive exits the list of top management and is replaced by another member of the top team, that event is considered turnover in the top executive position, but not turnover in the top management team. We do not count as turnover the event in which the position of Executive Chairman is split into the positions of CEO and COB. (Henceforth, we refer to the top executive position as the CEO.)

We further identify turnover as "forced" by examining articles in the *Extel Weekly News Summaries*, the *Financial Times*, and *McCarthy's News Information Service*. Turnover is labeled forced when (a) a news article states that the executive was "fired"; (b) an article states that the executive "resigned"; or (c) an article indicates that the company was experiencing poor performance. In addition, for criteria (b) and (c), the executive must be less than 60 years old and no other article can indicate that the executive took a position elsewhere or cite health or death as the reason for the executive's departure. All other turnover is labeled "normal."

In our tests, we employ both accounting earnings and stock returns to measure corporate performance. Specifically, as our measure of accounting earnings, we use three-year average industry-adjusted return on assets (IAROA). For each firm in the sample and for each year, we calculate return on assets (ROA) as earnings before depreciation, interest, and taxes (EBDIT) divided by beginning-of-the-year total assets. Then, for each firm with the same FTIC as the sample firm, we calculate ROA in the same way. Next, for each FTIC group for each year, we determine the median ROA. IAROA is calculated by subtracting the industry median ROA from the sample firm's ROA for each of the three years prior to a turnover event. The average of these three IAROAs is in our measure of accounting performance.

For measuring stock price performance, we use industry- and size-adjusted stock returns (ISARs), where ISARs are calculated by subtracting the daily stock returns of an industry- and size-matched portfolio from the return of the sample firm beginning 36 calendar months prior to, and ending 2 days prior to, the announcement of the management change. To construct the industry- and size-matched portfolio, for each sample firm, all other firms with the same FTIC code are ranked from largest to smallest according to their equity market values. The firms are then divided into four size portfolios. The differences between the return on the stock in our sample and the equal-weighted average return of the industry- and size-matched portfolio are calculated. The sum of these differences is the ISAR for that firm.

II. CHARACTERISTICS OF THE SAMPLE

To conduct our analysis, we split management turnover along two dimensions. First, we split turnover events into a pre-Cadbury time period (1989 through 1992) and a post-Cadbury time period (1993 through 1996). Descriptive data for these two samples are presented in the first set of columns in Table 13.1.

Table 13.1 Financial, Ownership, and Board Characteristics for 460 U.K. Industrial Firms over the Period 1989 through 1996

Descriptive statistics for a random sample of 460 publicly traded U.K. industrial firms over the period 1989 through 1996. The sample firms are classified into three sets based on whether they were (a) always in compliance with the Cadbury recommendations, (b) never in compliance with the Cadbury recommendations, or (c) adopted Cadbury recommendations. Sample firms in (a) and (b) are analyzed over two four-year periods, pre- and postpublication of the Cadbury Report (1989 through 1992 and 1993 through 1996). Sample firms in (c) are analyzed over two four-year periods, pre- and postadoption of the Cadbury recommendations ($y - 4$ through $y - 1$ and $y + 1$ through $y + 4$). The sample is taken from industrial companies included in the *Stock Exchange Yearbook*, the *Corporate Register*, and listed on the LSE. Firms that leave the sample between 1989 and 1996 are replaced by firms entering the LSE on the date closest to departure. Management and board characteristics are from the *Corporate Register*. Accounting information and share prices are from Datastream.

	Years	Full Sample N = 460 Mean	(Median)	Always in Compliance N = 150 Mean	(Median)	Never in Compliance N = 22 Mean	(Median)	Adopted Cadbury N = 288 Years	Mean	(Median)
Book value of assets (£ million)	1989–1992	149.2*	(50.8)	148.8*	(48.8)	146.8	(45.3)	$y-4$ to $y-1$	150.1*	(50.7)
	1993–1996	156.8	(56.7)	155.6	(53.2)	150.7	(49.2)	$y+1$ to $y+4$	158.6	(58.7)
Top executive ownership	1989–1992	2.23	(2.39)	2.22	(2.23)	9.93	(10.11)	$y-4$ to $y-1$	2.23	(2.44)
	1993–1996	2.24	(2.34)	2.09	(1.96)	8.34	(9.27)	$y+1$ to $y+4$	2.25	(2.43)
Board ownership	1989–1992	10.70	(10.96)	12.83	(12.60)	16.45	(15.93)	$y-4$ to $y-1$	9.79	(9.99)
	1993–1996	11.35	(10.83)	13.32	(13.01)	16.09	(15.99)	$y+1$ to $y+4$	11.09	(10.44)
Institutional ownership	1989–1992	21.39	(20.84)	22.55	(20.60)	16.37	(15.93)	$y-4$ to $y-1$	19.88	(19.82)
	1993–1996	20.04	(19.05)	22.09	(19.51)	16.29	(16.22)	$y+1$ to $y+4$	20.09	(20.44)
Number of block holders	1989–1992	2	(2)	3	(2.04)	1	(1)	$y-4$ to $y-1$	2*	(2)*
	1993–1996	3	(3)	3	(3.05)	1	(1)	$y+1$ to $y+4$	3	(3)
Board size	1989–1992	5.71	(5.00)*	6.69	(6.00)	4.53	(4.00)	$y-4$ to $y-1$	5.49*	(5.00)*
	1993–1996	7.29	(7.00)	7.41	(7.00)	5.02	(5.00)	$y+1$ to $y+4$	7.13	(7.00)
Percent outside directors	1989–1992	35.3**	(36.9)**	48.6	(43.4)	17.9	(15.4)	$y-4$ to $y-1$	26.1**	(25.7)**
	1993–1996	46.0	(43.1)	48.5	(45.8)	21.5	(20.9)	$y+1$ to $y+4$	46.6	(40.6)

** and * denote significance at the one and five percent levels, respectively, for both the t-statistic and Wilcoxon statistic. Tests are comparisons of before and after Cadbury values.

Second, we classify the observations according to whether the firm that experienced the turnover was (or was not) in compliance with the two key provisions of the *Code*. This second classification scheme gives rise to three sets of firms. The first set includes 150 firms that were in compliance with the *Code* for each year that the firm is in our sample (hereafter, the "always-in-compliance" set). The second set includes 22 firms that were never in compliance with the *Code* during any year in which the firm is in our sample (hereafter, the "never-in-compliance" set). The third set includes those firms that came into compliance with the *Code* during a year in which the firm is in our sample (hereafter, the "adopted-Cadbury" set; 288 firms). Descriptive data for the first and second sets are split into pre- and post-Cadbury time periods. These data are presented in the second and third sets of columns in Table 13.1. Descriptive data for the third set of firms (i.e., the adopted-Cadbury set) are split into pre- and post-Cadbury adoption time periods (i.e., $y - 4$ through $y - 1$ and $y + 1$ through $y + 4$, where y equals the year in which the firm came into compliance with the *Code*). These data are presented in the fourth set of columns in Table 13.1.

The descriptive data include the mean and median of book value of assets, share ownership by the CEO, share ownership by the board, share ownership by institutions, number of block holders, board size, and number of outside directors. In terms of book value of assets, the three sets of firms are remarkably similar before and after Cadbury and to each other. (Other financial data [not shown] also exhibit little variation across the three sets of firms.)

In terms of share ownership, regardless of the category of investor, the fraction of shares held by that category is essentially unchanged from before to after Cadbury. Additionally, on this dimension, the always-in-compliance set and the adopted-Cadbury set are similar to the full sample and to each other. However, the never-in-compliance set has significantly more ownership by the CEO, significantly greater board ownership,

significantly lower institutional ownership, and fewer outside block holders than the other two sets. Apparently, firms with greater "inside" ownership of shares are less likely to adopt the *Code*.

As regards board composition, for the full sample prior to Cadbury, 35.3 percent of directors are outsiders; after Cadbury, this figure is 46.0 percent. Almost all of this increase occurs in companies that came into compliance with the *Code*. For this set, the fraction of outsiders increases from 26.1 percent before adoption to 46.6 percent afterward. For the always-in-compliance set, the percentage of outside directors prior to Cadbury (48.6 percent) is nearly identical to the percentage afterward (48.5 percent). Finally, most of the increase in outside directors came about through an increase in board size as opposed to the replacement of inside directors with outside directors. The median board increases by two members, from five to seven for the full sample, and most of this increase occurs among the adopted-Cadbury set.

As regards the positions of CEO and COB (not shown), not surprisingly, there is considerable variation before and after Cadbury and across the various sets of firms. For the full sample prior to Cadbury, the CEO is also the COB in 36.5 percent of the companies; after Cadbury, that fraction drops to 15.4 percent. Of course, most of this change is due to the set of companies that became compliant with the *Code*. For this set, prior to Cadbury, a single individual held the position of CEO and COB in 39 percent of the firms; after adoption of Cadbury, in none of these companies did a single individual hold both positions.

A related question is when did firms become compliant with the key recommendations of the *Code*. At least some firms came into compliance every year throughout the interval 1989 through 1996, but the bulk of these firms, 202 out of 288, became compliant after 1992. Of these 202, 82 were in compliance with one or the other of the two key Cadbury provisions prior to becoming fully compliant. However, 160 were not in compliance with either recommendation prior to simultaneously adopting both provisions, and, again, most of these occurred after 1992.

III. MANAGEMENT TURNOVER

What our analysis shows thus far is that the informal arm-twisting associated with the Cadbury recommendations appears to have had considerable impact on the size and composition of boards of directors, and on the number of firms in which one individual holds the titles of CEO and COB. Indeed, as of 1998, 96 of the FT 100 and 90 percent of all LSE firms were Cadbury-compliant (The Corporate Register, 1998). The key questions to which we now turn are: What impact have these changes had on top management turnover and on the sensitivity of turnover to corporate performance?

A. Incidence and rate of top management turnover

Table 13.2 shows the incidence and rates of CEO turnover for the full sample and the three subsets. As in Table 13.1, the data are arrayed into pre- and post-Cadbury time periods (1989 through 1992 and 1993 through 1996) and pre- and post-Cadbury adoption time periods ($y - 4$ through $y - 1$ and $y + 1$ through $y + 4$). The incidence of turnover is the number of instances in which we identify a change in the CEO. The rate of turnover is the annualized rate calculated as the incidence of turnover divided by 460 firms divided by four years. The first two rows present data on all CEO turnover and the second two rows present data on forced CEO turnover.

For the full sample, the incidence and rate of CEO turnover increase significantly from before to after issuance of the Cadbury Report. The increase in turnover is due to an increase in what we have classified as forced turnover. For example, for the full sample, the rate of all CEO turnover increased from 6.48 percent to 7.71 percent (p-value = 0.02), and the rate of forced CEO turnover increased from 3.10 percent

to 4.30 percent (p-value = 0.04). Furthermore, the increase in CEO turnover is concentrated in the adopted-Cadbury set of firms. For this set of firms, the rate of all CEO turnover increased from 7.24 percent to 8.87 percent (p-value = 0.01), and the rate of forced CEO turnover nearly doubled, from 2.71 percent to 4.98 percent (p-value = 0.01). For the always-in-compliance set, the rate of CEO turnover is essentially unchanged from before to after Cadbury. For the never-in-compliance set, the rate of turnover declined modestly from before to after Cadbury, but, given the small sample size, we are inclined not to place much weight on this result. Thus, the increase in CEO turnover following Cadbury is primarily attributable to those firms that adopted the key provisions of the *Code of Best Practice*.

CEO turnover data are consistent with an argument that the Cadbury Committees' recommendations increased the quality of board oversight. That is, turnover, especially forced turnover, in the CEO position has increased and this increase is concentrated in the set of firms that adopted the key provisions of the *Code of Best Practice*. Of course, it could be that the increased management turnover that we document following Cadbury is random across firms. The pertinent issue for our purposes is whether turnover is correlated with corporate performance. That is, are the "right" managers being replaced? That is the key question to which we now turn.

B. Relationship between top management turnover and corporate performance

Table 13.3 presents a preliminary look at the connection between forced CEO turnover and corporate performance, where performance is measured as three-year average IAROA as described in Section I. For each calendar year, firms are ranked from lowest to highest on the basis of their prior three-year average IAROA. For each year, observations are then sorted into quartiles with quartile one containing the 115 firms with the lowest IAROA and

Table 13.2 Incidence and Rates of CEO Turnover in 460 U.K. Industrial Firms, 1989 through 1996

CEO turnover for a random sample of 460 publicly traded U.K. industrial firms over the period 1989 through 1996. The sample firms are classified into three sets based on whether they were (a) always in compliance with the Cadbury recommendations, (b) never in compliance with the Cadbury recommendations, or (c) adopted Cadbury recommendations. Sample firms in (a) and (b) are analyzed over two four-year periods, pre- and postpublication of the Cadbury Report (1989 through 1992 and 1993 through 1996). Sample firms in (c) are analyzed over two four-year periods, pre- and postadoption of the Cadbury recommendations ($y - 4$ through $y - 1$ and $y + 1$ through $y + 4$). For each firm, the name of the CEO in the *Corporate Register* is compared from 1988 through 1996 to determine turnover. Turnover is classified as forced by examining news articles in the *Extel Weekly News Summaries*, the *Financial Times*, and *McCarthy's News Information Service*.

	Years	Full Sample N = 460		Always in Compliance N = 150		Never in Compliance N = 22		Adopted Cadbury N = 288		
		Incidence	Rate	Incidence	Rate	Incidence	Rate	Years	Incidence	Rate
All CEO Turnover	1989–1992	119*	6.48*	35	5.44	4	4.55	$y - 4$ to $y - 1$	80**	7.24**
	1993–1996	138	7.71	37	5.75	3	3.41	$y + 1$ to $y + 4$	98	8.87
Forced CEO Turnover	1989–1992	57*	3.10*	24	3.76	3	3.26	$y - 4$ to $y - 1$	30**	2.71**
	1993–1996	79	4.30	20	3.14	1	1.09	$y + 1$ to $y + 4$	58	4.98

** and * denote significance at the one and five percent levels, respectively, for both the *t*-statistic and Wilcoxon statistic. Tests are comparisons of before and after Cadbury values.

Table 13.3 Forced CEO Turnover in 460 U.K. Industrial Firms Grouped by Quartiles of Performance, 1989 through 1996

Forced CEO turnover for a random sample of 460 publicly traded nonfinancial U.K. firms grouped into quartiles based on IAROA in the two four-year periods during the interval 1989 through 1996. IAROA is calculated as earnings before interest, taxes and depreciation divided by the total book value of assets less the median performance of firms in the same FTIC grouping. Three years of IAROA are averaged. Turnover is classified as forced by examining news articles in the *Extel Weekly News Summaries*, the *Financial Times*, and *McCarthy's News Information Service*. The sample firms are classified into three sets based on whether they were (a) always in compliance with the Cadbury recommendations, (b) never in compliance with the Cadbury recommendations, or (c) adopted Cadbury recommendations. Sample firms in (a) and (b) are analyzed over two four-year periods, pre- and postpublication of the Cadbury Report (1989 through 1992 and 1993 through 1996). Sample firms in (c) are analyzed over two four-year periods, pre- and postadoption of the Cadbury recommendations ($y - 4$ through $y - 1$ and $y + 1$ through $y + 4$).

| | | Interval | | | | | | | |
| | | Quartile 1 (Lowest IAROA) | | Quartile 2 | | Quartile 3 | | Quartile 4 (Highest IAROA) | |
	Years	Incidence	Rate (%)	Incidence	Rate (%)	Incidence	Rate (%)	Incidence	Rate (%)
Full sample	1989–1992	33*	7.2*	15	3.3	9	2.0	0	0.0
	1993–1996	47	10.2	25	5.4	7	1.5	0	0.0
(a) Always in compliance	1989–1992	15	10.0	6	4.0	3	2.0	0	0.0
	1993–1996	15	10.0	5	3.3	0	0.0	0	0.0
(b) Never in compliance	1989–1992	2	9.1	1	4.5	0	0.0	0	0.0
	1993–1996	1	4.5	0	0.0	0	0.0	0	0.0
(c) Adopted Cadbury	$y - 4$ to $y - 1$	16**	5.5**	8	2.3*	6	2.1	0	0.0
	$y + 1$ to $y + 4$	31	10.8	20	6.9	7	2.8	0	0.0

** and * denote significance at the one and five percent levels, respectively, for both the *t*-statistic and Wilcoxon statistic. Tests are comparisons of before and after Cadbury values.

quartile four containing the 115 firms with the highest IAROA.

For the full sample, both before and after Cadbury, the incidence and rate of forced CEO turnover increases as we move from the best to the poorest performing firms. Additionally, the data indicate that the increase in CEO turnover from before to after Cadbury that we document in Table 13.3 is due to an increase in turnover in the lowest two performance quartiles in the adopted-Cadbury set of firms. For example, for this set of firms, the rate of turnover in quartiles one and two increased by nearly 100 percent, from 5.5 percent to 10.8 percent (p-value = 0.01) and by almost 300 percent, from 2.3 percent to 6.9 percent (p-value = 0.04), respectively, from before to after adoption of Cadbury. In comparison, for the always-in-compliance set, in the same bottom two quartiles, the rate of turnover is essentially unchanged from before to after Cadbury.

The data in Table 13.3 are representative of the pattern of turnover (not shown) that emerges when we consider *all* CEO turnover and when we evaluate performance based on ISARs. That is, turnover is concentrated in the poorest performing quartiles of firms, and the increase in turnover is concentrated in the adopted-Cadbury set of firms.

C. Multivariate analysis of the relationship between top management turnover and corporate performance

The final questions, to which we now turn, are whether the relationship between turnover and performance is statistically significant and whether the sensitivity of turnover to performance is greater following Cadbury. To answer those questions and to control for other factors that may influence managerial turnover, we estimate logit regressions with pooled time series, cross section data. Initially, we estimate regressions in which the dependent variable is 1 if a firm experiences CEO turnover during a calendar year and 0 otherwise. We estimate separate regressions for all turnover and

for forced turnover. We estimate separate regressions using three-year prior IAROAs and three-year ISARs as our performance measures. We include yearly observations of four control variables: fraction of shares owned by directors, fraction of shares owned by institutions, number of block shareholders, and log of total assets.

The results of our regressions are presented in Tables 13.4 and 13.5. In Table 13.4, the performance variable is *logIAROA*. In Table 13.5, performance is *logISAR*.[2] Panel A of each table presents regressions with all CEO turnover as the dependent variable and Panel B presents regressions with forced turnover as the dependent variable. In total, we have 20 regressions that have either *logIAROA* or *logISAR* as an independent performance variable. In each regression, the coefficient of the performance variable is negative and, with two exceptions, each has a p-value of less than 0.05. Thus, CEO turnover is significantly negatively correlated with corporate performance: the poorer the firm's performance, the greater the likelihood that the CEO will depart his position. (We also estimate regressions separately for the pre- and post-Cadbury time periods [not shown]. In every regression, the coefficient of the performance variable is negative with a p-value less than 0.05. Thus, turnover is significantly negatively correlated with performance both before and after Cadbury.)

Of the four control variables, only the fraction of shares owned by directors regularly has a p-value less than 0.10. The coefficient of this variable is always negative, which indicates that, after controlling for performance, increased share ownership by the board reduces the likelihood that the CEO will depart his position.

We now turn to the effect of Cadbury on CEO turnover and the effect of Cadbury on the relationship between CEO turnover and corporate performance. The five regressions in each panel explore that question from different perspectives. The first regression in each panel is estimated for the full sample of firms and includes an indicator variable (*Dum for 1993–1996*) which takes a value of 0 for all observations before January 1993 (the pre-Cadbury period) and a value of 1 for all observations after that date (the post-Cadbury period) along with a performance variable, either *logIAROA* or *logISAR*, and the four control variables. In each panel, in the first regression, the coefficient of the indicator variable *Dum for 1993–1996* is positive with p-values ranging from 0.04 to 0.11. Thus, even after controlling for corporate performance, turnover is higher in the post-Cadbury period. However, as we observed in Table 13.4, increased turnover appears to be attributable to the set of firms that came into compliance with the Cadbury Committees' recommendations (the adopted-Cadbury set) as opposed to those firms that were always in compliance.

To determine whether the Cadbury/turnover relationship is due to a general phenomenon affecting all firms or whether it is due specifically to a change in board structures traceable to the Cadbury recommendations, we next estimate the regressions separately for the always-in-compliance set of firms and for the adopted-Cadbury set. The only difference in the regressions is that for the adopted-Cadbury set, the indicator variable (*Dum-for-Adopt*) takes on a value of 0 in all years prior to the year in which the firm came into compliance with the *Code* and a value of 1 for all subsequent years. These are the second and third regressions in each panel.

For the always-in-compliance set, the coefficient of the Cadbury dummy variable (*Dum for 1993–1996*) is always positive, but the p-values range from 0.79 to 0.92. Thus, publication of the Cadbury Report had a trivial impact, if any, on the rate of turnover among CEOs in firms that were already in compliance with the key provisions of the *Code*. For the adopted-Cadbury set, the coefficient of the indicator variable *Dum-for-Adopt* is always positive with p values ranging from 0.06 to 0.08. Additionally, the magnitude of the coefficient is at least four times the magnitude of the coefficient of the Cadbury dummy (*Dum for 1993–1996*) for the always-in-

compliance set. Thus, publication of the *Code of Best Practice* did not have an impact, per se, on the rate of turnover among top U.K. executives; rather, the effect was concentrated among those firms that altered their board structures to comply with the *Code*. This is not to say that the rate of turnover among top executives in firms that were always-in-compliance was "too low" either before or after Cadbury. The data only show that the rate of turnover for these firms did not change between the pre- and post-Cadbury periods. In comparison, the rate of turnover increased significantly among firms that came into compliance with the Cadbury recommendations during the period of this study.

To determine whether the increase in turnover is correlated with performance, we estimate a regression with only the adopted-Cadbury set of firms that includes the adopted Cadbury dummy (*Dum-for-Adopt*) and the adopted Cadbury dummy interacted with our measures of performance (either *Dum-for-Adopt* × *logIAROA* or *Dum-for-Adopt* × *logISAR*) along with our measures of performance (either *logIAROA* or *logISAR*) and our four control variables. These are the key regressions of our analysis and are given as the fourth regression in each panel.

The coefficient of the interaction variable indicates whether the increase in turnover among firms that adopted Cadbury is randomly distributed across those firms or is concentrated among the poorest performing firms. In each regression, the coefficient of the interaction variable is negative with p-values ranging from 0.02 to 0.07. Additionally, the coefficient of the adopted Cadbury dummy (*Dum-for-Adopt*) is reduced by 60 percent and now has p-values ranging from 0.60 to 0.77. These results indicate that the increase in CEO turnover is not random; rather it is (inversely) correlated with performance: After controlling for performance, the likelihood that the CEO will depart his position is greater once a poorly performing firm comes into compliance with the key provisions of the *Code*. The answer to the

Table 13.4 Logit Regressions of CEO Turnover on IAROA and Status of Cadbury Compliance, 1989 through 1996

CEO turnover for a random sample of 460 publicly traded U.K. industrial firms in two four-year periods during the interval 1989 through 1996. IAROA is calculated as earnings before interest, taxes, and depreciation divided by the total book value of assets less the median performance of firms in the same FTIC grouping. Three years of IAROA are averaged. CEO turnover is classified as normal or forced by examining news articles in the *Extel Weekly News Summaries*, the *Financial Times*, and *McCarthy's News Information Service*. The sample firms are classified into three sets based on whether they were (a) always in compliance with the Cadbury recommendations, (b) never in compliance with the Cadbury recommendations, or (c) adopted Cadbury recommendations. Sample firms in (a) and (b) are analyzed over two four-year periods, pre- and postpublication of the Cadbury Report (1989 through 1992 and 1993 through 1996). Sample firms in (c) are analyzed over two four-year periods, pre- and postadoption of the Cadbury recommendations ($y - 4$ through $y - 1$ and $y + 1$ through $y + 4$). Accounting information and share prices are from Datastream. The dependent variable equals one when turnover occurs. *Dum for 1993–1996* equals one for the period 1993 through 1996. *Dum-for-adopt* equals one for the period following the adoption of the key recommendations of the Cadbury Report. The interactive dummy is *Dum-for-adopt* multiplied by logIAROA. *P*-values are in parentheses.

Variable	Total Sample N = 460	Always in Compliance N = 150	Adopted Cadbury N = 288	Adopted Cadbury N = 288	Adopted Cadbury N = 288
Panel A: Logit Regressions of All CEO Turnover on Log IAROA and Cadbury Status					
Intercept	−1.866 (0.08)	−1.849 (0.09)	−2.570 (0.00)	−2.799 (0.00)	−2.583 (0.00)
Performance variable					
Log IAROA	−2.034 (0.02)	−1.859 (0.10)	−3.180 (0.00)	−3.228 (0.00)	−3.019 (0.00)
Cadbury variable					
Dum for 1993–1996	0.457 (0.11)	0.055 (0.92)			
Dum-for-adopt			0.593 (0.06)	0.148 (0.66)	0.112 (0.72)
Dum-for-adopt × logIAROA				−0.739 (0.02)	0.038 (0.96)
Board variables					
Prop outsiders					0.331 (0.30)
Prop outsiders × logIAROA					−0.566 (0.08)
Dum for single CEO/COB					−0.062 (0.86)
Dum for single CEO/COB × logIAROA					−0.052 (0.89)
Board size					−0.039 (0.20)
Board size × logIAROA					−0.064 (0.08)

Control variables	(1)	(2)	(3)	(4)	(5)
Board share ownership	−0.984 (0.04)	−1.092 (0.05)	−0.812 (0.08)	−0.844 (0.09)	−0.762 (0.12)
Institutional share ownership	1.294 (0.08)	1.027 (0.21)	0.985 (0.28)	1.032 (0.21)	0.597 (0.65)
Block holders	0.039 (0.60)	0.045 (0.48)	0.028 (0.72)	0.031 (0.68)	0.044 (0.46)
Log assets	−0.159 (0.02)	−0.122 (0.06)	−0.142 (0.05)	−0.139 (0.05)	−0.105 (0.12)
Observations	3,680	1,200	2,304	2,304	2,304
Log-likelihood	−572.89	−387.66	−454.11	−499.20	−501.58
Chi-square	86.45 (0.00)	37.10 (0.00)	60.84 (0.00)	70.36 (0.00)	70.93 (0.00)

Panel B: Logit Regressions of Forced CEO Turnover on Log IAROA and Cadbury Status

	(1)	(2)	(3)	(4)	(5)
Intercept					
Performance variable	−1.745 (0.16)	−1.887 (0.10)	−2.995 (0.00)	−2.819 (0.00)	−2.493 (0.00)
Log IAROA	−2.932 (0.00)	−2.293 (0.00)	−4.882 (0.00)	−4.659 (0.00)	−3.921 (0.00)
Cadbury variables					
Dum for 1993–1996	0.531 (0.08)	0.151 (0.79)			
Dum-for-adopt			0.631 (0.07)	0.164 (0.61)	0.132 (0.68)
Dum-for-adopt × logIAROA				−0.659 (0.06)	0.129 (0.68)
Board variables					
Prop outsiders					0.364 (0.30)
Prop outsiders × logIAROA					−0.618 (0.07)
Dum for single CEO/COB					−0.053 (0.87)
Dum for single CEO/COB × logIAROA					−0.103 (0.69)
Board size					−0.031 (0.25)
Board size × logIAROA					−0.058 (0.08)
Control variables:					
Board share ownership	−1.190 (0.01)	−1.114 (0.05)	−0.820 (0.10)	−0.854 (0.08)	−0.852 (0.08)
Institutional ownership	1.260 (0.10)	1.039 (0.22)	1.140 (0.15)	1.176 (0.15)	1.144 (0.15)
Block holders	0.051 (0.48)	0.076 (0.38)	0.044 (0.46)	0.049 (0.45)	0.043 (0.46)
Log assets	−0.131 (0.05)	−0.129 (0.06)	−0.166 (0.04)	−0.170 (0.04)	−0.189 (0.03)
Observations	3,680	1,200	2,304	2,304	2,304
Log-likelihood	−621.87	−485.07	−569.29	−588.65	−603.03
Chi-square	89.35 (0.00)	53.58 (0.00)	88.66 (0.00)	87.69 (0.00)	88.21 (0.00)

Table 13.5 Logit Regressions of CEO Turnover on ISAR and Status of Cadbury Compliance, 1989 through 1996

CEO turnover for a random sample of 460 publicly traded U.K. industrial firms in the two four-year periods during the interval 1989 through 1996. ISARs are industry- and size-adjusted cumulative excess stock returns computed using daily stock returns beginning 36 calendar months prior to, and ending 2 days prior to the announcement of the top executive change. CEO turnover is classified as normal or forced by examining news articles in the *Extel Weekly News Summaries*, the *Financial Times*, and *McCarthy's News Information Service*. The sample firms are classified into three sets based on whether they were (a) always in compliance with the Cadbury recommendations, (b) never in compliance with the Cadbury recommendations, and (c) adopted Cadbury recommendations. Sample firms in (a) and (b) are analyzed over two four-year periods, pre- and postpublication of the Cadbury Report (1989 through 1992 and 1993 through 1996). Sample firms in (c) are analyzed over two four-year periods, pre- and postadoption of the Cadbury recommendations ($y − 4$ through $y − 1$ and $y + 1$ through $y + 4$). Accounting information and share prices come from Datastream. The dependent variable equals one when turnover occurs. *Dum for 1993–1996* equals one for the period 1993 through 1996. *Dum-for-adopt* equals one for the period following the adoption of the key recommendations of the Cadbury Report. The interactive dummy is *Dum-for-adopt* multiplied by logISAR. *P*-values are in parentheses.

Variable	Total Sample N = 460	Always in Compliance N = 150	Adopted Cadbury N = 288	Adopted Cadbury N = 288	Adopted Cadbury N = 288
Panel A: Logit Regressions of All CEO Turnover on Log ISAR and Cadbury Status					
Intercept	−3.194 (0.00)	−2.925 (0.00)	−2.639 (0.00)	−2.612 (0.00)	−2.495 (0.00)
Performance variable					
LogISAR	−0.019 (0.00)	−0.012 (0.03)	−0.022 (0.00)	−0.023 (0.00)	−0.019 (0.00)
Cadbury variables					
Dum for 1993–1996	0.519 (0.09)	0.066 (0.87)			
Dum-for-adopt			0.572 (0.08)	0.119 (0.77)	0.090 (0.85)
Dum-for-adopt × logISAR				−0.680 (0.05)	−0.144 (0.60)
Board variables					
Prop outsiders					0.262 (0.43)
Prop outsiders × logISAR					−0.573 (0.08)
Dum for single CEO/COB					−0.064 (0.82)
Dum for single CEO/COB × logISAR					−0.055 (0.85)
Board size					−0.037 (0.37)
Board size × logISAR					−0.050 (0.10)

Control variables					
Board share ownership	-0.930 (0.04)	-1.190 (0.02)	-0.804 (0.08)	-0.810 (0.08)	-0.850 (0.07)
Institutional share ownership	1.187 (0.13)	1.062 (0.16)	0.817 (0.40)	0.837 (0.34)	0.936 (0.22)
Block holders	0.059 (0.39)	0.072 (0.29)	0.039 (0.51)	0.031 (0.68)	0.039 (0.51)
Log assets	-0.087 (0.15)	-0.126 (0.04)	-0.077 (0.17)	-0.085 (0.16)	-0.087 (0.15)
Observations	3,680	1,200	2,304	2,304	2,304
Log-likelihood	-598.19	-491.39	-509.66	-584.02	-590.73
Chi-square	86.69 (0.00)	49.76 (0.00)	75.93 (0.00)	80.80 (0.00)	81.40 (0.00)

Panel B: Logit Regression of Forced CEO Turnover on Log ISAR and Cadbury Status

Intercept					
Performance variable					
LogISAR	-4.892 (0.00)	-3.023 (0.00)	-4.538 (0.00)	-4.624 (0.00)	-4.291 (0.00)
	-0.030 (0.00)	-0.009 (0.07)	-0.049 (0.00)	-0.040 (0.00)	-0.039 (0.00)
Cadbury variables					
Dum for 1993–1996	0.598 (0.04)	0.050 (0.86)	0.538 (0.08)		
Dum-for-adopt				0.227 (0.60)	0.030 (0.92)
Dum-for-adopt × logISAR				-0.590 (0.07)	-0.134 (0.65)
Board variables					
Prop outsiders					0.272 (0.39)
Prop outsiders × logISAR					-0.564 (0.08)
Dum for single CEO/COB					-0.060 (0.83)
Dum for single CEO/COB × logISAR					-0.039 (0.93)
Board size					-0.042 (0.34)
Board size × logISAR					-0.045 (0.10)
Control variables					
Board share ownership	-0.921 (0.05)	-0.925 (0.05)	-0.807 (0.09)	-0.840 (0.07)	-0.763 (0.13)
Institutional share ownership	1.040 (0.21)	1.100 (0.19)	0.638 (0.58)	0.635 (0.58)	0.567 (0.67)
Block holders	0.078 (0.25)	0.101 (0.07)	0.044 (0.48)	0.048 (0.47)	0.043 (0.47)
Log assets	-0.119 (0.07)	-0.142 (0.03)	-0.066 (0.26)	-0.061 (0.27)	-0.049 (0.31)
Observations	3,680	1,200	2,304	2,304	2,304
Log-likelihood	-629.65	-555.36	-581.41	-584.07	-588.82
Chi-square	117.41 (0.00)	48.37 (0.00)	50.21 (0.00)	50.46 (0.00)	50.61 (0.00)

question of whether the "right" managers are leaving the firms appears to be yes, assuming, of course, that our measures of performance properly identify the right managers.

Thus far, we have employed an indicator variable to capture the key provisions of the *Code of Best Practice*. A further question is: Which of the key provisions is responsible for the increased sensitivity of turnover to corporate performance? To address that question, we estimate a final regression with the adopted-Cadbury set of firms in which we include annual observations on the fraction of outside directors (*Prop Outsiders*), an interaction between the fraction of outsiders and our measures of corporate performance (either *Prop Outsiders* × *logIAROA* or *Prop Outsiders* × *logISAR*), an indicator variable to identify observations in which the positions of CEO and COB are held by a single individual (equal to 1) or by two individuals (equal to 0) and an interaction between this indicator variable and our measures of corporate performance (either *Dum for Single CEO/COB* × *logIAROA* or *Dum for Single CEO/COB* × *logISAR*). These variables are designed to capture the changes brought about by the *Code of Best Practice*. Because adoption of the *Code* led to a general increase in board size, we also include the number of directors and an interaction between the number of directors and our measure of performance. These regressions, which also include a performance measure, *Dum-for-Adopt*, and the four control variables, are shown as the fifth regression in each panel.

According to the regressions, when the board composition and CEO/COB variables are included, the coefficients of the interaction of the *Dum-for-Adopt* and our measures of performance are not significant (*p*-values range from 0.60 to 0.96). Additionally, the coefficient of the fraction of outsiders on the board is positive, albeit not significant, in each regression (*p*-values range from 0.30 to 0.43). More interestingly, the coefficients of the interaction between the fraction of outsiders and our measures of performance are always negative, with

p-values that range from 0.07 to 0.08. In contrast, in none of the regressions does the coefficient of the dummy for the CEO/COB or the coefficient of the interaction of this variable with our measures of performance begin to approach statistical significance (*p*-values range from 0.69 to 0.93).

Apparently, the increased sensitivity of turnover to corporate performance for the adopted-Cadbury set of firms (and the contemporaneous loss in significance of the interaction of *Dum-for-Adopt* with performance) is attributable to the increase in the fraction of outside directors. Splitting the responsibilities of the CEO and COB between two individuals appears to have had no effect on the rate of CEO turnover.

D. Spurious correlation?

A question that may arise is whether the correlation between management turnover and corporate performance interacted with Cadbury compliance is spurious. More specifically, is it possible that both turnover and Cadbury compliance are caused by poor performance, perhaps because poorly performing firms adopt Cadbury to placate shareholders and, concurrently, dismiss top managers—a change in management that would have occurred even in the absence of Cadbury? Several analyses seem to indicate that this is not the case.

First, by construction, for the adopted-Cadbury set of firms, all post-adoption CEO turnover follows compliance with the *Code*. This occurs because we use year-end data to determine whether a firm is in compliance. Only after the year-end in which the firm becomes compliant with the *Code* do we consider turnover to be postadoption. Thus, all post-Cadbury CEO turnover is postadoption. Related to this point, most postadoption turnover does not follow closely after Cadbury compliance. For example, for the 58 instances of postadoption *forced* CEO turnover, 18 occur within 12 months after the year-end of adoption, 23 occur in months 13 through 24, and

17 occur in months 25 through 36. Thus, forced CEO turnover is not clustered in the months immediately following adoption. The same is true for *all* CEO turnover. Second, corporate performance prior to adoption for those 288 firms that became Cadbury-compliant is not poor. For example, over the three years prior to adoption, both the mean IAROA and the mean ISAR are positive: They are +0.057 and +0.039, respectively, but neither is statistically significantly different from zero (*p*-values = 0.24 and 0.40). Thus, it is not just poorly performing firms that adopt Cadbury. Third, even for the set of 57 firms that came into compliance and then experienced forced CEO turnover, the three-year preadoption mean IAROA and ISAR are positive (+0.027 and +0.014), but not significantly different from zero (*p*-values = 0.55 and 0.69).

In sum, adoption of Cadbury and CEO turnover are not simultaneous, adoption of Cadbury is not concentrated among poorly performing firms, and firms that adopt Cadbury and have CEO turnover are not performing poorly prior to adoption. These analyses argue against spurious correlation.

E. How much additional turnover?

To give some indication of the economic significance of the statistical relationship we document, we use the last regression in Panel A and Panel B of Table 13.5 to calculate the implied increase in the instances of total CEO turnover and forced CEO turnover for the adopted-Cadbury set of firms during years $y - 4$ through $y - 1$. The predicted instances of total CEO turnover are 95 and the predicted instances of forced CEO turnover are 54. These compare with actual total turnover of 80 and actual forced turnover of 30. Thus, the regressions imply all CEO turnover would be 20 percent higher and forced turnover would be 80 percent higher had these firms been in compliance with the *Code* over the four years prior to adoption.[3]

F. Corporate performance and turnover in the top team

As noted at the outset, we focus our discussion on turnover in the CEO position. However, we also gathered turnover data for the entire top team of managers. For the top team of managers, excluding the CEO, we conduct each of the same analyses as undertaken for the CEO. In general, the results for the top team (excluding the CEO) are similar to, albeit weaker than, those for the CEO. For example, the regressions reported in Tables 13.4 and 13.5 for CEO turnover are also estimated for turnover in the top management team (excluding the CEO). The signs of the coefficients for these regressions (not shown) are identical to those of Tables 13.4 and 13.5; however, the *p*-values of the variables are not significant at traditional levels. For example, the sign of the Cadbury 1993 through 1996 dummy variable is positive with *p*-values that range from 0.16 to 0.20. Similarly, the sign on the *Dum-for-Adopt* variable is also positive in each regression, but has *p*-values that range from 0.17 to 0.24. The coefficient for the interaction of *Dum-for-Adopt* and our measures of performance in the same regression is always negative with *p*-values that range from 0.15 to 0.26.[4] In short, the regressions for turnover in the top management team (excluding the CEO) are consistent with those of turnover in the CEO, but the levels of statistical significance are weaker.

IV. COMMENTARY AND CONCLUSIONS

We initiated this study with a degree of skepticism. Given the potential bite associated with the recommendations of the Cadbury Committee, we are not surprised to observe a significant increase in board sizes, a significant increase in the number and fraction of outside board members, and a significant reduction in the number and fraction of firms with a single individual as CEO and COB. Further, because of prior studies on the relationship between corporate performance and CEO turnover, we also are not surprised to find a significant (negative) correlation between corporate performance and top management turnover both before and after Cadbury (Coughlan and Schmidt (1985), Warner, Watts, and Wruck (1988), Weisbach (1988), Gilson (1989), Martin and McConnell (1991), Murphy and Zimmerman (1993), Kaplan (1994), Kang and Shivdasani (1995), Franks and Mayer (1996), Huson, Parrino, and Starks (1998), Mikkelson and Partch (1997), and Denis and Sarin (1999)). We were, however, skeptical as to whether the observed changes in board composition would lead to changes in corporate decision making or to a change in the relationship between corporate performance and top management turnover.

Part of our skepticism may stem from the mixed results of prior studies on board composition and management turnover. For example, for 367 publicly traded U.S. companies, Weisbach (1988) determines that CEO turnover is more highly negatively correlated with performance in firms with outsider-dominated boards. Contrarily, for 270 publicly traded Japanese companies, Kang and Shivdasani (1995) find that the sensitivity of CEO turnover to performance is unrelated to the fraction of outside directors. Finally, Franks, Mayer and Renneboog (2000) examine CEO turnover for a sample of poorly performing U.K. firms for the period 1988 through 1993. They are unable to draw definitive conclusions as to whether or not CEO turnover is more sensitive to performance when the board comprises more outside directors.

The other part of our skepticism largely stems from our general expectation that, prior to Cadbury, market forces were likely to have propelled boards toward efficient structures. Thus, we are surprised to observe a significant increase in management turnover following Cadbury adoption, to find an increase in the sensitivity of management turnover to corporate performance following Cadbury adoption, and, especially, to find that the increase in

sensitivity of turnover to performance is due to an increase in outside board members. These results are consistent with, and support, the argument that the Cadbury recommendations have improved the quality of board oversight in the United Kingdom. However, a caveat is in order: Increased management turnover and increased sensitivity of turnover to our measures of performance do not necessarily mean an improvement in corporate performance. As observed by Bhagat and Black (1999), prior research on board composition and corporate performance generally appears to show that board composition does affect the way in which boards accomplish discrete tasks, such as hiring and firing top management, responding to hostile takeovers, setting CEO compensation and so forth (Klein and Rosenfeld (1988), Kaplan and Reishus (1990), Rosenstein and Wyatt (1990), Byrd and Hickman (1992), Shivdasani (1993), Denis and Denis (1995), Kini, Kracaw, and Mian (1995), Agrawal and Knoeber (1996), Cotter, Shivdasani, and Zenner (1997), Hermalin and Weisbach (1998), and Bhagat and Black (2000)). However, such studies generally show less (or no) connection between board composition and corporate profitability. Our study analyzes the effect of the Cadbury recommendations on a discrete board task. In a subsequent study, we intend to investigate whether the Cadbury recommendations have influenced corporate performance more generally.

NOTES

* Dahya and McConnell are from Krannert Graduate School of Management, Purdue University, and Travlos is from Athens Laboratory of Business Administration and Cardiff Business School, Cardiff University. This paper has benefited from the helpful comments and suggestions of George Benston, David Denis, Diane Denis, Julian Franks, Paul Marsh, Robert Parrino, Ronan Powell, David Power, Raghu Rau, Andrew Stark, Jason Xiao, and seminar participants at Emory University, Purdue University, the University of Iowa, the University of Oklahoma, the EFMA (Paris) and

the FMA (Orlando). McConnell acknowledges financial support from the Center for International Business Education and Research (CIBER) at Purdue University. Dahya acknowledges financial support received from the Nuffield Foundation. Travlos acknowledges financial support received from the Kitty Kyriacopoulos Chair in Finance.

1 The report also recommended: (a) full disclosure of the pay of the chairman and the highest paid director; (b) shareholders' approval on executive directors contracts exceeding three years; (c) executive directors pay be set by a board subcommittee composed primarily of outsiders; and (d) directors establish a subcommittee of the board, comprised mainly of outside directors, to report on the effectiveness of the company's system of internal control.

2 We also estimated the regressions with market model excess returns and CAPM excess returns as our measure of performance. The p-values of the coefficients are essentially unchanged.

3 As a benchmark, we calculated the implied instances of total CEO turnover during years $y + 1$ through $y + 4$ to be 96 versus actual turnover of 98 and forced turnover to be 56 versus actual forced turnover of 58.

4 The results of our analyses of the top team excluding the CEO are available from the authors.

REFERENCES

Agrawal, Anup, and Charles R. Knoeber, 1996, Firm performance and mechanisms to control agency problems between managers and shareholders, *Journal of Financial and Quantitative Analysis* 31, 377–397.

Bhagat, Sanjai, and Bernard S. Black, 1999, The uncertain relationship between board composition and firm performance, *Business Lawyer* 54, 921–964.

Bhagat, Sanjai, and Bernard S. Black, 2000, Board independence and long-term performance, Working paper, University of Colorado and Columbia Law School.

Byrd, John W., and Kent A. Hickman, 1992, Do outside directors monitor managers? Evidence from tender offer bids, *Journal of Financial Economics* 32, 195–221.

Cadbury committee draft orders mixed news for shareholders, 1992, *Financial Times*, June 2, p. 16.

The Corporate Register, 1989 to 1996, 1998 (Hemmington Scott Publications, London).

Cotter, James F., Anil Shivdasani, and Marc Zenner, 1997, Do independent directors enhance target shareholder wealth during tender offers? *Journal of Financial Economics* 43, 195–218.

Coughlan, Anne T., and Ronald M. Schmidt, 1985, Executive compensation, management turnover, and firm performance, *Journal of Accounting and Economics* 7, 43–66.

Denis, David J., and Diane K. Denis, 1995, Performance changes following top management dismissals, *Journal of Finance* 50, 1029–1057.

Denis, David J., and Atulya Sarin, 1999, Ownership and board structures in publicly traded corporations, *Journal of Financial Economics* 52, 187–224.

Franks, Julian, and Colin Mayer, 1996, Hostile takeovers and the correction of managerial failure, *Journal of Financial Economics* 40, 163–181.

Franks, Julian, Colin Mayer, and Luc Renneboog, 2000, Who disciplines managers in poorly performing companies? Working paper, London Business School.

Gilson, Stuart, 1989, Management turnover and financial distress, *Journal of Financial Economics* 25, 241–262.

Green, Sir Owen, 1994, Pall Mall Lecture on U.K. Corporate Governance, February 24.

Hermalin, Benjamin E., and Michael S. Weisbach, 1998, Endogenously chosen boards of directors and their monitoring of the CEO, *American Economic Review* 88, 96–118.

Huson, Mark R., Robert Parrino, and Laura T. Starks, 1998, Internal monitoring mechanisms and CEO turnover: A long term perspective, Unpublished manuscript, University of Alberta.

Kang, Jun-Koo, and Anil Shivdasani, 1995, Firm performance, corporate governance, and top executive turnover in Japan, *Journal of Financial Economics* 38, 29–58.

Kaplan, Steven N., 1994, Top executives, turnover and firm performance in Germany, *Journal of Law, Economics and Organization* 10, 142–159.

Kaplan, Steven N., and David Reishus, 1990, Outside directorships and corporate performance, *Journal of Financial Economics* 27, 389–410.

Kinl, Omesh, William A. Kracaw, and Shehzad Mian, 1995, Corporate takeovers, firm performance, and board composition, *Journal of Corporate Finance* 1, 383–412.

Klein, April, and James Rosenfeld, 1988, Targeted share repurchases and top management changes, *Journal of Financial Economics* 20, 493–506.

Martin, Kenneth J., and John J. McConnell, 1991, Corporate performance, corporate takeovers, and top management turnover, *Journal of Finance* 46, 671–687.

Mikkelson, Wayne, and Megan Partch, 1997, The decline of takeovers and disciplinary management turnover, *Journal of Financial Economics* 44, 205–228.

Murphy, Kevin J., and Jerold L. Zimmerman, 1993, Financial performance surrounding CEO turnover, *Journal of Accounting and Economics* 16, 273–315.

Report on the Financial Aspects of Corporate Governance (*With the Code of Best Practice*), 1992 (Gee and Co. Ltd., London).

Rosenstein, Stuart, and Jeffrey G. Wyatt, 1990, Outside directors, board independence, and shareholder wealth, *Journal of Financial Economics* 26, 175–191.

Self-regulation seen as the way forward, 1992, *The Financial Times*, May 28, p. 17.

Shivdasani, Anil, 1993, Board composition, ownership structure, and hostile takeovers, *Journal of Accounting and Economics* 16, 167–198.

Stock Exchange Yearbook, 1989–1996 (London Stock Exchange, London).

Warner, Jerold B., Ross L. Watts, and Karen H. Wruck, 1988, Stock prices and top management changes, *Journal of Financial Economics* 20, 461–492.

Weisbach, Michael S., 1988, Outside directors and CEO turnover, *Journal of Financial Economics* 20, 431–460.

Part 4

Directors' remuneration

INTRODUCTION

ONE OF THE IMPORTANT TOOLS IN THE ARMOURY of the board of directors to align the interests of shareholders and managers is the executive compensation contract for the CEO and other executive managers. In theory, a properly written contract should achieve such alignment by making level of compensation conditional upon performance. However, in practice, there are problems in both contract writing and enforcement and in specifying the appropriate performance measures and the time horizon for the award of compensation. Many scholars (e.g. Bebchuk and Fried, 2004) have argued that entrenched top managers capture the pay setting process and manipulate the boards into awarding them excessive pay. They argue that such managers often get rewarded for failure rather than success in delivering performance and shareholder value. Thus, far from being a solution to the agency problem, executive compensation may itself be a manifestation of an agency problem and reflect failure of the governance arrangements in firms. The sensitivity of pay to performance is therefore an important test of governance effectiveness. Executive compensation arrangements may vary from country to country depending on governmental and public attitudes to 'high' managerial remuneration. The papers in this part deal with many of these issues and provide empirical evidence.

Martin Conyon and Kevin Murphy (Ch.14) document differences in CEO pay and incentives in the United States and the United Kingdom for 1997. After controlling for size, sector and other firm and executive characteristics, they find that CEOs in the US earn 45 percent higher cash compensation and 190 percent higher total compensation. The calculated effective ownership percentage in the US implies that the median CEO receives 1.48 percent of any increase in shareholder wealth compared to 0.25 percent in the UK. The differences can be largely attributed to greater share option awards in the US arising from institutional and cultural differences between the two countries.

In the next paper, Wayne Guay (Ch.15) deals with the problem of appropriate measures of compensation incentives for performance. An important determinant of performance is the level of risk taken by managers in their corporate decisions. It is in the interest of shareholders that managers are incentivised to accept high risk if that avoids the problem of under-investment in risky projects by risk adverse managers. On the other hand, excessive risk incentive can lead to value destroying, speculative investments. To control risk-related incentive problems, equity holders are expected to manage both the convexity and slope of the relation between firm performance and managers' wealth. The author finds stock options, but not common stockholdings, significantly increase the sensitivity of CEOs' wealth to equity risk. Cross-sectionally, this sensitivity is positively related to firms' investment opportunities. This result is consistent with managers receiving incentives to invest in risky projects when the potential loss from under-investment in valuable risk-increasing projects is greatest. Firms' stock-return volatility is positively related to the convexity provided to managers, suggesting convex incentive schemes influence investing and financing decisions. This paper has pioneered the literature on not only how different compensation components influence corporate risk taking and performance but also how to measure risk taking and performance incentives.

An interesting manifestation of the managerial capture of the pay setting process referred to above is when executive stock options are repriced. Following the stock market crash and the dotcom collapse of the late 1990s, stock options with exercise prices set in relation to pre-crash levels lost their incentive character since they had fallen too 'deep in the water'. In response to this development many firms re-set the exercise price at much lower levels. This retrospective 'manipulation' of compensation incentive was, in the eyes of many scholars and observers (e.g. Bebchuk and Fried, 2004), a case of top managers' 'having their cake and eating it too' or enjoying a 'heads, I win and tails, you lose' gamble. Chidambaran and Prabhala (Ch.16) test the management capture view and examine firms that reprice their executive stock options and find little evidence that repricing reflects managerial entrenchment or ineffective governance. Repricing grants are economically significant, but there is little else unusual about compensation in repricing firms. Repricers tend to be smaller, younger, rapidly growing firms that experience a deep, sudden shock to growth and profitability. They are also more concentrated in the technology, trade, and service sectors and have smaller boards of directors. Repricers have abnormally high CEO turnover rates, which is inconsistent with the entrenchment hypothesis. Over 40 percent of repricers exclude the CEOs' options when they reprice.

Julie Ann Elston and Lawrence G. Goldberg (Ch.17) focus on executive compensation arrangements in Germany with a different corporate governance system from that in many other countries including the US, UK and France. The presence of workers on German supervisory boards under the co-determination system also means that the pay setting process has a different political dynamic in Germany than in countries without such representation. However, with the growth of international mergers like DaimlerChrysler, which dramatically illustrated the compensation differentials between US and German top managers, interest in executive compensation practices in different countries, partic-ularly in Germany, has increased. Using unique data sources for Germany, the authors find that, similar to US firms, German firms also have agency problems caused by the separation of ownership from control, with ownership dispersion leading to higher compensation. Compensation is also positively related to firm size but there is evidence that bank influence has a negative impact on compensation. Large shareholdings also restrain managerial compensation suggesting greater monitoring by block shareholders and bank creditors.

Does stock ownership by managers necessarily align shareholder and managerial interests and lead to better corporate performance and shareholder value creation? John Core and David Larcker (Ch.18) provide evidence by examining a sample of US firms that adopt 'target ownership plans', under which managers are required to own a minimum amount of stock. They find that, prior to plan adoption, such firms exhibit low managerial equity ownership and low stock price performance. Managerial equity ownership increases significantly in the two years following plan adoption. The authors also observe that excess accounting returns and stock returns are higher after the plan is adopted. Thus, for the sample of firms, the required increases in the level of managerial equity ownership result in improvements in firm performance. This study highlights the importance of executive stock ownership as an effective corporate governance tool.

REFERENCE

Bebchuk L. and Fried J. (2004), *Pay without performance*, Cambridge, Mass: Harvard University Press.

Chapter 14

Martin J. Conyon and
Kevin J. Murphy*

THE PRINCE AND THE PAUPER?
CEO PAY IN THE UNITED STATES
AND UNITED KINGDOM

Source: *The Economic Journal*, 110 (2000): 640–671.

ABSTRACT

We document differences in CEO pay and incentives in the United States and the United Kingdom for 1997. After controlling for size, sector and other firm and executive characteristics, CEOs in the US earn 45% higher cash compensation and 190% higher total compensation. The calculated effective ownership percentage in the US implies that the median CEO receives 1.48% of any increase in shareholder wealth compared to 0.25% in the UK. The differences, can be largely attributed to greater share option awards in the US arising from institutional and cultural differences between the two countries.

CORPORATE GOVERNANCE PRACTICES IN THE United Kingdom received increased attention in the 1990s, culminating in influential reports issued by the Cadbury (1992), Greenbury (1995) and Hampel (1998) committees. Among other recommendations, the reports outlined a best-practice framework for setting executive pay, and significantly expanded disclosure rules for UK executive compensation. The Greenbury and Hampel reports were, in part, a response to a growing controversy over chief executive officer (CEO) pay levels triggered when executives in several recently privatised electric utilities exercised share options worth millions of pounds. However, in spite of these reports, CEO pay levels rose more than 18% in 1997 alone, even as public-sector workers were being asked to accept raises of less than 3% (Buckingham and Cowe, 1998 *a*, *b*). The continuing controversy, coupled with enhanced data availability through the new disclosure requirements, has sparked considerable academic interest in UK executive pay practices.

Although CEO pay levels in the United Kingdom have grown in recent years, they remain far behind pay levels enjoyed by CEOs in the United States. The international pay gap is especially pronounced after including gains realised from exercising share options. Chief executives in the 500 largest UK companies in aggregate made £330 million (or £660,000 each) in 1997, including £74 million from exercising options. In contrast, the top 500 US CEOs made in aggregate £3.2 *billion* (or £6.3 million each), including £2.0 billion from option exercises.[1] Indeed, Disney's Michael Eisner, dubbed by pay-critic Graef Crystal (1991) as the 'Prince of Pay', exercised options worth £348 million in December 1997, thus single-handedly out-earning the aggregate paycheques of the top 500 CEOs in the United Kingdom. British Sky Broadcasting's Sam Chisolm, the highest-paid UK executive, is a mere pauper by American standards: his £6.8 million pay package would only rank as the 97th highest among US chief executives.

These anecdotal comparisons, while driven by option gains in the robust US stock market, hint at important differences in CEO pay practices in the United Kingdom and the United States. The purpose of this article is to provide a comprehensive comparison of pay practices in the two countries, and to generate stylised facts to stimulate future research. Existing international comparisons of pay practices have typically relied on non-comparable survey data, or have focused on narrow definitions of compensation that usually exclude the grant-date value of share options.[2] In contrast, our results are based on comparable and complete measures of CEO pay and stock-based incentives, utilising detailed data made available through enhanced disclosure requirements in the United States and (more recently) the United Kingdom. Our use of micro data allows us to analyse differences in compensation and incentives while controlling for factors such as company size, industry, human capital, growth opportunities, and performance.

We begin in Section 1 by offering an introduction to executive compensation, aimed at academic economists new to the area. In this section, we identify available data sources for CEO pay in the two countries, describe our sample, and discuss how to measure and value share options and other pay components.[3] Section 2 analyses the level and structure of executive compensation, based primarily on data from 510 UK and 1,666 US corporations. We show that, while company size is an important determinant of pay in both countries, the rewards for scale are more pronounced in the United States than in the United Kingdom. We document that share option grants, valued at grant date, comprise a fairly small percentage of total pay for the typical British CEO, but are much more important for American CEOs. In addition, we document that American CEOs indeed out-earn their British counterpart, earning 45% more in cash pay and 190% more in total pay, even after controlling for size, industry, growth opportunities, CEO human capital, and other observable characteristics.

Also, Section 2 offers some cross-country time-series evidence on the levels of cash compensation from 1989–97, and on the prevalence of stock option plans from 1979–97. We show that, although cash compensation has been growing at about the same rate in both countries since the mid-1990s, the prevalence of option plans has been growing in the United States while declining in the United Kingdom.

Section 3 explores stock-based financial incentives for CEOs in the two countries. CEO wealth is linked directly to company share-price performance through their share holdings, their option holdings, and through shares awarded through long-term incentive plans (LTIPs). We show that these various holdings can be aggregated to form an 'effective' ownership percentage (or, following Jensen and Murphy (1990 a,b), the 'Pay-Performance Sensitivity'). Similar to our analysis of CEO pay levels, we compute the effective ownership percentage for each CEO and analyse how it varies across countries and with different firm and executive characteristics. We find that American CEOs, on average, own much larger fractions of their firms' stock than do British CEOs. For example, the median holding for US CEOs is 0.29%, while the median holding for UK CEOs is only 0.05%. The median *effective* ownership (including options and LTIP grants) is more disparate: 1.48% for US CEOs vs. only 0.25% for UK CEOs.

Section 3 also explores how CEO cash compensation varies with share-price performance. We show that the elasticity of cash compensation to performance is higher in the United States than in the United Kingdom for all industries, although the difference is only statistically significant for the financial services industry. In addition, we examine the relation between CEO turnover and company performance. We find that CEO turnover is negatively correlated with shareholder returns in both the United Kingdom and United States, indicating that CEOs in both countries are more likely to lose their jobs following poor performance. The cross-country difference in the turnover-performance relationship is not statistically significant.

Section 4 considers a variety of explanations for the observed Anglo-American differences in compensation and incentives, including agency theory, taxes, and culture. Our objective is not to reconcile completely the differences in pay practices, but rather to identify potential explanations as opportunities for future research. We argue that traditional agency-theoretic considerations offer little insight in explaining the differences, unless US and UK executives differ systematically in their ability, productivity, or risk aversion. We document that, while personal income tax rates and rules in the United States and United Kingdom are generally quite similar, there are differences in corporate tax rules that may explain at least some of the observed differences in compensation and incentives. Finally, we consider a variety of economic, political, and cultural factors that help explain why share option compensation has increased dramatically in the United States, but not in the United Kingdom. Section 5 summarises our results, and explores implications of our results to broader multi-country comparisons of international pay practices.

1. AN INTRODUCTION TO EXECUTIVE COMPENSATION

1.1. Data sources

The United States, United Kingdom, and Canada are currently the only countries that require detailed disclosure on the compensation practices for individual top corporate executives.[4] Disclosure rules for US executives were standardised and expanded in 1992 by the US Securities and Exchange Commission (SEC), and require details on share ownership, share options, and all components of compensation for the top five corporate executives. Disclosure rules in the United Kingdom were significantly expanded in recent years following the Greenbury (1995) and Hampel (1998) reports, and require disclosure of data comparable to those available for US executives (including previously unavailable details on share option grants and holdings).[5] Although there are a variety of 'secondary sources' for compensation data in the two countries, the primary data source is the annual report

in the United Kingdom, and the proxy statement in the United States.[6]

Although we offer some longitudinal comparisons, our analysis is based primarily on 1997 fiscal-year data, since this was the first year covered by the new UK disclosure requirements. The UK data analysed in this paper are drawn directly from the annual reports for the 510 largest companies (ranked by market capitalisation). The pay and ownership data are matched to Datastream data on company size, industry, and performance. Together, these companies account for virtually all (98%) of the market capitalisation of the entire UK stock market. The fiscal 1997 US compensation and company data are extracted from Standard and Poor's (S&P's) Compustat's 'ExecuComp' database, which includes proxy-statement data for 1,666 top executives in the S&P 500, the S&P Mid-Cap 400, the S&P Small-Cap 600, and other supplemental S&P indices. For each country and company, we identified the CEO (or most senior executive officer), and collected information on share ownership, current and prior option grants, salaries, annual bonuses, benefits, and LTIP cash and share awards.

The largest US companies are considerably larger than the largest UK companies, and our combination of large, mid, and small-cap US companies is meant to provide a distribution of US firms similar to the UK distribution. Nonetheless, our sample of US firms remains somewhat larger, with mean (median) 1997 market capitalisation of £3.4 billion (£790 million) in the United States, compared to £2.2 billion (£480 million) in the United Kingdom. Our results below include company size controls to adjust for systematic differences in size.

1.2. Measuring and valuing the components of pay

Compensation arrangements in both the United Kingdom and the United States contain the same basic components. CEOs in both countries receive base salaries and are eligible to receive annual bonuses paid based on accounting performance. CEOs in both countries also typically receive share options, which are rights to purchase shares of stock at a pre-specified 'exercise' price for a pre-specified term. CEOs also often participate in long-term incentive plans (LTIPs). In the United Kingdom, LTIPs are typically grants of shares of stock that become 'vested' (i.e., ownership is trans-ferred to the CEO) only upon attainment of certain performance objectives. LTIPs in the United States take two primary forms: (1) 'restricted stock' grants that vest with the passage of time (but not with perform-ance criteria); and (2) multi-year bonus plans typically based on rolling-average three or five-year cumulative accounting performance.

We define total compensation as the sum of base salary, annual bonus, LTIP awards, and share options valued at grant date. We measure LTIP share grants at the face value of the shares on the grant date, and impose 20% discounts for performance-contingent UK grants. LTIP cash awards are valued as the amount actually paid during the fiscal year. In valuing share options, we follow the approach used by both practitioners and academic researchers by measuring the grant-date expected value using the Black and Scholes (1973) formula, adjusted for continuously paid dividends:

$$Option\ Value\ =\ Pe^{-\ln(1+d)T}N(z)$$
$$-\ Xe^{-\ln(1+r)T}N(z\ -\ \sigma\sqrt{T}), \qquad (1)$$

where P is the grant-date share price, X is the exercise price, T is the time remaining until expiration, d is the annualised dividend yield, σ is the stock-price volatility, r is the risk-free discount rate, $N(\ )$ is the cumulative normal distribution function, and

$$z = \frac{\ln(P/X) + [\ln(1+r) - \ln(1+d) + \sigma^2/2]T}{\sigma\sqrt{T}}$$
$$(2)$$

We measure the risk-free rates for the two countries as the average yield on 7-year UK and US Treasury bills.[7] Volatilities are defined as the standard deviation of monthly continuously compounded returns over the prior 48 months, multiplied by $\sqrt{12}$. Dividend yields are computed as the average

of the prior 48 monthly observations on cash dividend per share.[8]

In spite of its prevalence in both practice and academia, there are many drawbacks to using the Black-Scholes formula for calculating the value of an executive share option. First, the Black-Scholes value is, at best, a measure of the company's opportunity cost of granting the option, and will typically overstate the value to the executive-recipient (Hall and Murphy, 2000). Second, executive share options are subject to forfeiture if the executive leaves the firm prior to vesting; this probability of forfeiture reduces the cost of granting the option and thus implies that the Black-Scholes formula overstates option values. Third, the Black-Scholes formula assumes that options can only be exercised at the expiration date, but executive options can be exercised immediately upon vesting, which typically occurs relatively early in the option's term.[9] Finally, following recom-mendations in the Greenbury (1995) report, share options granted in the United Kingdom typically vest only upon attain-ment of some performance criteria, often based on earnings-per-share growth. Although the existence of performance criteria will naturally reduce the company's cost of granting an option, the expected discount is fairly modest, because the crite-ria are seldom binding.[10] Moreover, to the extent that the performance criteria are correlated with share prices, the criteria will be binding only when the intrinsic value of an unrestricted share option is low. Subject to these caveats, we present Black-Scholes values of stock options in our analyses below.

2. THE LEVEL AND COMPOSITION OF CEO PAY

2.1. Summary statistics

Table 14.1 provides summary statistics for the level and composition of fiscal 1997 CEO pay, by company size, and industry, and country. Total pay is defined as the sum of salaries, bonuses, benefits, other cash pay, grant-date values of share options, and grant-date value of LTIP shares (discounted, where appropriate, for performance contingencies). Dollar-denominated data for each US executive are converted to UK pounds using the average exchange rate during the company's fiscal year; this rate varied between 1.61 $/£ and 1.65 $/£ during our sample period.

As reported in the top panel of Table 14.1, the average total compensation for the 510 UK CEOs is £589,000, while the median pay is £414,000. Total pay increases with firm size: the median pay for companies with 1997 revenues in excess of £1,500 million is £811,000, far larger than the £287,000 median pay for companies with revenues below £200 million. Median and average total pay is somewhat less in utilities than in other industries. The bottom panel shows that American CEOs earn substantially more than their British counterparts, for every size and industry group. The average total compensation for the 1,666 US CEOs is £3.6 million, or 500% more than the average pay for UK executives. Similarly, the US median pay of £1.5 million is 260% more than the

Table 14.1 Summary statistics for 1997 CEO total compensation, by company size and industry

| Group | Sample firms | Total pay | | Average composition of total pay (%) | | | | |
		Average (£000s)	Median (£000s)	Base salary	Annual bonus	Option grant	LTIP shares	Other pay
United Kingdom								
All companies	510	589	414	59	18	10	9	5
By firm sales (millions)								
Less than £200	152	452	287	64	17	10	4	5
£200 to £500	119	403	335	61	19	8	6	6
£500 to £1,500	116	601	507	54	20	10	12	4
Above £1,500	123	927	811	55	16	10	15	4
By industry								
Mining/manufacturing	217	564	436	59	17	9	9	5
Financial services	84	559	411	60	22	6	7	4
Utilities	19	448	382	58	15	6	14	8
Other	190	645	397	58	17	11	8	5
United States								
All companies	1,666	3,565	1,508	29	17	42	4	8
By firm sales (millions)								
Less than £200	339	1,166	686	38	14	43	1	4
£200 to £500	379	1,833	926	36	18	36	3	7
£500 to £1,500	458	3,038	1,604	28	18	40	5	9
Above £1,500	490	7,056	3,552	20	17	48	5	10
By industry								
Mining/manufacturing	842	3,388	1,540	28	17	43	3	8
Financial services	198	6,277	2,787	19	20	47	5	8
Utilities	120	1,333	707	43	15	23	6	13
Other	506	3,326	1,438	32	16	43	3	6

Note: UK data from the largest companies in fiscal 1997, ranked by market capitalisation. US data include firms in the S&P 500, the S&P MidCap 400, the S&P SmallCap 600, and companies in S&P supplemental indices. Revenues for financial firms defined as net interest income (banks) and total income (insurance companies). Total compensation defined as the sum of salaries, bonuses, benefits, share options (valued on date of grant using the Black-Scholes formula), LTIP-related stock grants (valued at 80% of face value for performance-contingent awards), and other compensation. US dollar-denominated data are converted to UK pounds using the average $/£ exchange rate during the fiscal year.

median UK pay. The US premium is especially pronounced for large firms (where the median US CEOs earns 340% more) and financial firms (where the average US CEOs earns 580% more).

The right-hand portion of Table 14.1 describes the average composition of CEO pay in the two countries. On average, CEOs in the United Kingdom receive 59% of their total pay in the form of base salaries, 18% in bonuses, 10% in share options (valued at grant-date), and 9% in LTIP shares (valued at grant-date, with a 20% discount for performance contingencies). In contrast, base salaries comprise a much smaller percentage of total pay for US executives (only 29%), while share option

grants comprise a much larger percentage (42%). The divergence between UK and US pay practices is, again, especially pronounced for companies with revenues exceeding £1,500 million. Within this group, salaries account for more than half of pay for UK CEOs, but account for only one fifth of pay for US CEOs. Similarly, share option grants account for nearly 50% of pay for CEOs in large US firms, but only account for 10% of pay in large British firms.

Table 14.2 compares base salaries and the prevalence of contingent-pay practices in the two countries. The median United States base salary of £317,000 is more than 30% higher than the median United

Table 14.2 Summary statistics for components of CEO pay, by company size and industry

Group	Base salary median (£000s)	Annual bonus received		Value of option grant		Value of LTIP shares	
		% with bonus	Median (£) (for >£0)	% with grants	Median (£) (for >£0)	% with grants	Median (£) (for >£0)
United Kingdom							
All Companies	240	81	91	50	69	32	161
By firm sales (millions)							
Less than £200	175	76	59	40	70	14	58
£200 to £500	200	82	69	44	45	25	94
£500 to £1,500	264	87	104	59	73	44	148
Above £1,500	410	80	146	59	108	50	294
By industry							
Mining/manufacturing	254	84	90	53	67	34	165
Financial services	222	83	115	45	50	29	132
Utilities	240	84	86	47	43	58	120
Other	221	77	83	48	110	29	177
United States							
All companies	317	83	270	72	1,142	19	325
By firm sales (millions)							
Less than £200	195	74	99	69	592	6	107
£200 to £500	256	82	180	64	787	15	180
£500 to £1,500	335	85	299	71	1,053	22	315
Above £1,500	487	89	518	80	2,505	30	579
By industry							
Mining/manufacturing	318	85	280	74	1,111	18	318
Financial services	395	92	437	81	1,713	31	611
Utilities	291	81	157	53	392	25	177
Other	301	78	239	68	1,232	15	336

Note: Median data for bonuses, options, and LTIP represent the median value of award/grant (in £000s) for the subsample of CEOs actually receiving awards/grants during the 1997 fiscal year. Revenues for financial firms defined as net interest income (banks) and total income (insurance companies). Share options (valued on date of grant using the Black-Scholes formula), LTIP-related stock grants (valued at 80% of face value for performance-contingent awards), and other compensation. US dollar-denominated data are converted to UK pounds using the average $/£ exchange rate during the fiscal year.

Kingdom salary of £240,000; median salaries are higher in the United States for each size and industry group. The percentage of CEOs receiving bonuses is roughly the same in the two countries (81% in the UK compared to 83% in the US). However, conditional on receiving a bonus, US bonuses are much higher: the median bonus paid in the United States of £270,000 is triple the median bonus paid in the United Kingdom. American CEOs are more likely to receive option grants than their UK counterparts (72% in the United States versus only 50% in the United Kingdom). In addition, they are likely to receive much larger grants: the median option grant in the United States (for CEOs receiving options) of £1,142,000 is nearly *twenty times* the median grant value for UK CEOs (who receive only £69,000). Finally, Table 14.2 shows that 32% of UK CEOs receive LTIP share grants, while only 19% of US CEOs receive similar grants. However, although fewer US executives receive LTIP share grants (primarily restricted stock), the value of the grant (for those receiving grants) is higher in the US.

2.2. Time-series comparisons

Although longitudinal comparisons of total compensation are not possible because of UK disclosure requirements prior to 1997, time-series data on cash compensation (salaries and bonuses) are available for the sample companies. Figure 14.1 shows the median cash compensation received from 1989–97 for UK CEOs and US CEOs in the S&P 500, and from 1992–97 for US CEOs in the MidCap 400 and SmallCap 600. The figure includes data from firms in our 1997 sample of 510 UK and 1,666 US firms.[11] As shown in the figure, the median cash pay for UK CEOs has grown from £158,000 in 1989 to £340,000 in 1997 (representing a 10% average annual growth). In the United States, median pay among S&P 500 CEOs has grown 6.4% annually, from £574,000 in 1989 to £945,000 in 1997. Since 1992, UK CEO cash compensation

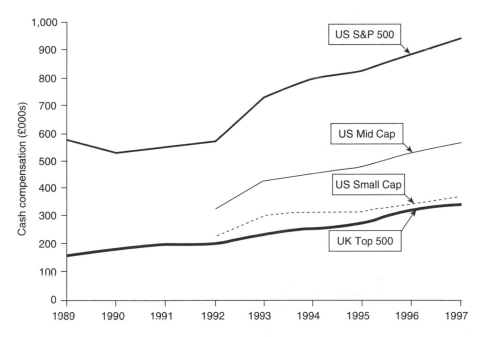

Figure 14.1 Median Cash Compensation of US and UK CEOs, 1989–97.

Note: Cash compensation includes salaries and bonuses. UK data from the largest 510 companies in fiscal 1997, ranked by market capitalisation. US data include firms in the firms in the 1997 S&P 500, the S&P MidCap 400, and S&P SmallCap 600. US dollar-denominated data are converted to UK pounds using the average $/£ exchange rate during each calender year.

has increased on average 11.2% per year, compared to growth rates of 10.7%, 11.9%, and 10.2% for CEOs in the S&P 500, MidCap, and SmallCap companies, respectively.

The results in Figure 14.1 suggest that cash compensation in UK firms is roughly 'on par' with median pay among CEOs in Small-Cap US firms, but still lies significantly below pay in larger US firms.[12] Moreover, as documented by Hall and Liebman (1998) and Murphy (1999), the value of share options granted to US CEOs has grown much faster than their cash compensation since the early 1990s. Indeed, as indicated in Table 14.1, share options have emerged as the single largest component of compensation for CEOs in the largest US companies. Although comparable longitudinal data on share-option grants in the United Kingdom are not systematically available, time-series data on the prevalence of option plans among UK and US companies are available and are reported

in Figure 14.2. The UK data are from Main (1999), and are based on data provided by a large compensation consulting firm. The US data for 1979–96 are from the Conference Board 'Top Executive Compensation' reports, which cover predominately S&P 500 companies.[13] The data for 'US Small and MidCap' firms are extracted from ExecuComp, and defined as the fraction of MidCap and SmallCap companies in which the top five executives hold any options during the year.

As reported by Main (1999) and replicated in Figure 14.2, option grants in the United Kingdom grew dramatically in popularity from the mid-1980s to the early-1990s. In particular, in 1978 only 10% of UK companies offered options to their top executives, by 1983 over 30% of companies offered options, and by 1986 nearly 100% offered options. However, the use of share options in the UK fell substantially in the mid-1990s; by 1997 only 68% of companies offered options to their top

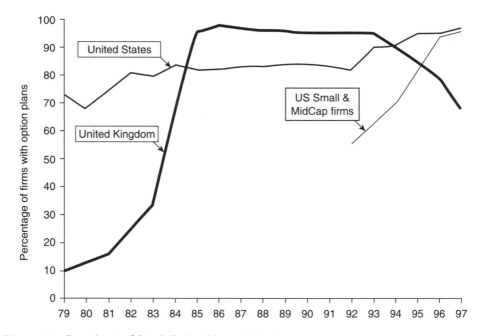

Figure 14.2 Prevalence of Stock Option Plans, 1979–97.

Note: UK data from Main (1999). US data 1979–96 from the Conference Board 'Top Executive Compensation' reports (various issues). US data for 1997 include percentage of S&P 500 companies that have executives holdings options (these data closely track the Conference Board data from 1992–96). US Small and MidCap data include percentage of companies in the S&P MidCap 400 and SmallCap 600 that have executives holding options.

executives. In contrast to the UK experience, Figure 14.2 shows that the prevalence of option plans in the US has increased rather than decreased in recent years. In particular, the percentage of large firms with option plans grew from 82% in 1992 to 97% in 1997. The growth in prevalence is more pronounced in smaller firms: in 1992 only 55% of all small and midcap firms offered options to its top executives; 96% of the companies had plans in place by 1997.

Figure 14.2 shows the percentage of companies that have option plans, but does not provide information on the magnitude of the grants to executives. Although UK option data prior to 1997 are not publicly available, Hemmington Scott estimate the total number of option shares held by the CEO in both 1991 and 1997. For 395 UK companies with share option data in both years the Hemmington Scott reports that the mean CEO option holdings (measured as a percentage of common equity) fell from 0.26% in 1991 to 0.22% in 1997; median holdings over the same time period increased slightly from 0.09% to 0.11%. In contrast, mean option holdings among US CEOs in 1,128 Execu-Comp firms with share option data in both 1997 and 1992 (the first year such shares were publicly disclosed) grew from 0.87% in 1992 to 1.1% in 1997; median holdings grew from 0.16% to 0.64% over the same time period.

Overall, Fig 14.1 and 14.2 and our results on option shareholdings suggest that UK and US pay levels are diverging rather than converging in recent years. While CEO cash compensation is growing at roughly the same rate in both countries, the use of share options has increased in the United States while declining in the United Kingdom. In Section 5 below, we analyse the political and economic factors contributing to the divergence of option-granting practices in the two countries.

2.3. Regression results

The best-documented empirical finding in the executive compensation literature is the consistency of the relation between CEO pay and company size, typically measured as the elasticity of cash compensation to company revenues. Rosen (1992) summarises academic research covering a variety of industries and a variety of time periods in both the United States and the United Kingdom. Even though there is some variation in wage-size elasticities, his general conclusion is that the 'relative uniformity [of estimates] across firms, industries, countries, and periods of time is notable and puzzling because the technology that sustains control and scale should vary across these disparate units of comparison.' Table 14.3 replicates these earlier findings for 1997 CEO pay data, with pay-size elasticities η estimated from the regression:

$$\ln (1997 \; CEO \; Pay) = \alpha + \eta \ln(1997 \; Sales). \tag{3}$$

Consistent with prior findings (see Murphy, 1999), the estimated elasticities for US cash compensation (salary plus bonus) are not significantly different from $\eta \approx 0.3$ for all companies or for each of the four industry groups. The US elasticities for total compensation (including salaries, bonuses, benefits, share options, LTIP-shares, and other compensation) are somewhat higher than the elasticities for cash compensation, reflecting primarily that option grants are increasingly larger in bigger firms.

Interestingly, the estimated pay-size elasticities for UK firms in Table 14.3, while positive and statistically significant for all industries, are uniformly and significantly smaller for UK firms than for US firms. For example, an elasticity of cash pay to sales of 0.316 in the United States and 0.197 in the United Kingdom indicates that doubling size increases cash pay by 32% in the United States but only by 20% in the United Kindgom. Similarly, doubling size increases total pay by 41% in the United States, but only by 22% in the United Kingdom.[14]

Table 14.4 reports coefficients of regressions estimating the US pay premium after controlling for company size and industry. We use revenues as our measure of company size, and classify companies into four broad industry groups; our results are not changed using alternative size definitions (assets,

Table 14.3 Estimated elasticities of CEO compensation with respect to firm revenues

Industry	United States		United Kingdom	
	Salary + bonus	Total pay	Salary + bonus	Total pay
All companies	0.316 [0.24]	0.413 [0.28]	0.197* [0.31]	0.217* [0.26]
Mining & manufacturing	0.294 [0.20]	0.423 [0.35]	0.189* [0.31]	0.157* [0.23]
Financial services	0.342 [0.42]	0.465 [0.34]	0.177* [0.26]	0.205* [0.30]
Utilities	0.334 [0.36]	0.459 [0.30]	0.209 [0.17]	0.314 [0.32]
Other	0.329 [0.28]	0.366 [0.20]	0.270 [0.45]	0.296 [0.33]

Note: Elasticities computed from regressions of ln(*Pay*) on ln(*Sales*) for 510 UK and 1,666 US companies. R^2 in brackets. Revenues for financial firms defined as net interest income (banks) and total income (insurance companies).
* indicates that the estimated elasticity in the United Kingdom is significantly different from the US elasticity at the 1% level.

market capitalisation) or more narrowly defined industries. The dependent variable in columns (1) and (2) is ln(*Salary + Bonus*), while the dependent variable in columns (3) and (4) is ln(*Total Pay*). The coefficient on the US dummy in column (1) of 0.3861 indicates that, after controlling for size and industry, CEOs in the United States earn approximately 47% more than their British counterparts.[15] Similarly, the US dummy in column (3) of 1.142 indicates that total expected pay is 215% higher in the United States after controlling for size and industry.

Existing empirical studies of executive compensation have consistently documented that company size and industry are the two most important factors determining levels of CEO pay. However, researchers routinely include additional controls for risk (because CEOs will demand higher expected pay levels if compensation is risky), investment opportunities (because firms with growth options need better managers), and human capital. The regressions in columns (2) and (4) of Table 14.4 include as additional explanatory variables the volatility of shareholder returns (as a proxy for risk), the book-to-market ratio (the inverse of a proxy for investment opportunities), and CEO age and age-squared (traditional human capital variables to allow concave age-earnings profiles). In addition, the regressions include a dummy variable set to unity if the CEO and board chairman position are combined, and zero if the corporation has a separate non-executive

chairman. Combining the CEO and chairman position is expected to increase pay for two reasons. First, the combination is a proxy for added responsibility and/or ability of the incumbent CEO. Second, the combination is a proxy for the CEO's influence over the board and the remuneration committee. In the United Kingdom, such combinations are the exception: only 18% of the sample companies have CEOs who also serve as board chairmen. However, in the United States such combinations are the rule: nearly two-thirds (66%) of the sample have combined CEO/chairmen.

Columns (2) and (4) of Table 14.4 report coefficients for cash and total compensation. The control for risk is insignificant in the cash compensation regression, but significant for total compensation, while the control for investment options is insignificant in both regressions.[16] The human capital controls are significant, and suggest that CEO age-earnings profiles for cash (total) compensation turn downward after age 55 (age 43).[17] The coefficients on the CEO/chairman dummy variables are positive and significant, indicating that the combination increases cash and total compensation by 11% and 19%, respectively. Including the control for CEO/chairman combinations reduces the estimated US premium slightly, from 47% to 45% for salary and bonus, and from 215% to 190% for total compensation.

Several stylised facts emerge from the results of Tables 14.1–14.4 and

Table 14.7 Explanatory regressions for 1997 CEO compensation

Independent variable	Dependent variable			
	ln (Salary and Bonus)		ln (Total Pay)	
	(1)	(2)	(3)	(4)
Intercept	4.023 (52.6)	2.293 (3.7)	3.839 (42.6)	1.435 (2.0)
ln(Sales)	0.2873 (26.9)	0.2693 (20.8)	0.3689 (29.3)	0.3883 (25.7)
Finance (Dummy)	0.3236 (6.1)	0.3278 (5.7)	0.3553 (5.7)	0.4083 (6.1)
Utility (Dummy)	-0.3848 (-5.4)	-0.3902 (-5.0)	-0.7891 (-9.3)	-0.7146 (-7.8)
Other Industry (Dummy)	-0.1130 (-2.9)	-0.0625 (-1.5)	-0.0956 (-2.1)	-0.1248 (-2.6)
Volatility of Shareholder Returns	—	-0.0609 (-0.3)	—	0.8702 (4.0)
Book to Market Ratio	—	-0.0007 (-0.2)	—	0.0006 (0.1)
CEO/Chairman Combined (Dummy)	—	0.1038 (2.5)	—	0.1771 (3.7)
CEO Age	—	0.0663 (3.0)	—	0.0779 (3.3)
CEO Age-Squared	—	-0.0006 (-3.1)	—	-0.0009 (-4.0)
US Firm (Dummy)	0.3861 (9.5)	0.3747 (7.7)	1.142 (23.9)	1.072 (18.8)
Sample Size	2,165	1,805	2,165	1,805
R^2	0.306	0.315	0.437	0.474

Note: t-statistics in parentheses. Total compensation defined as the sum of salaries, bonuses, benefits, share options (valued on date of grant using the Black-Scholes formula), LTIP-related stock grants (valued at 80% of face value for performance-contingent awards), and other compensation. Book to market defined as the book value of tangible equity divided by the end-of-year market capitalisation. US dollar-denominated data are converted to UK pounds using the average $/£ exchange rate during the fiscal year.

Figs 14.1–14.2. First, American chief executives are paid significantly more than British chief executives, even after controlling for company size, industry, and other firm and executive characteristics. Second, although CEO pay increases with company size in both countries, the pay-size gradient is significantly higher in the United States than in the United Kingdom. Third, the US pay premium can be traced largely, but not entirely, to the prevalence and magnitude of share option grants, which have increased in the United States since the mid-1990s, while declining in the United Kingdom.

3. THE RELATION BETWEEN CEO PAY AND CORPORATE PERFORMANCE

Empirical investigations of executive incentives have typically focused on the relation between the CEO's wealth and the wealth of the company's shareholders. CEO wealth is *directly* related to shareholder wealth through the CEO's holdings of shares, share options, and LTIP shares. In addition, CEO wealth can be *indirectly* related to shareholder wealth through accounting-based bonuses (reflecting the correlation between accounting returns and share-price performance) and through year-to-year adjustments in salary levels, target bonuses, and option and LTIP grant sizes. Finally, CEO wealth (and reputation) is affected by performance if CEOs lose their jobs when their firms are performing poorly.

3.1. The direct relation between CEO and shareholder wealth

The most obvious linkage between CEO and shareholder wealth comes from the CEO's holdings of company shares. As reported in Table 14.5, the share ownership for UK CEOs is worth an average of £7 million, sub-stantially smaller than the average holdings among US CEOs of over £60 million. The ownership distribution is significantly skewed: the median holdings for UK and US executives are £460,000 and £3.3 million, respectively. Interestingly, the value of

shares held by the CEO declines with company size in the United Kingdom, but *increases* with company size in the United States. In the largest firms, US CEOs hold on average shares worth £145 million (median £5 million), while UK CEOs hold shares worth only £3.4 million (median £330,000).

Since agency costs arise when agents receive less than 100% of the value of output, the CEO's share of ownership is a natural measure of the severity of the agency problem. As reported in Table 14.5, the average and median shareholdings for UK CEOs (expressed as a percentage of outstanding shares) are 2.13% and 0.05%, respectively, significantly smaller than the average and median holdings among US CEOs of 3.10% and 0.29%, respectively. In the largest firms, US CEOs hold on average 1.61% of their company's shares (median 0.09%), while UK CEOs hold only 0.21% (median 0.01%). In fact, whether measured in pounds or percentages, or at averages or medians, share ownership among US CEOs is substantially higher than ownership among UK CEOs for each size and industry group in Table 14.5. Consequently, share ownership mitigates more of the agency problem in the United States than in the United Kingdom.

Holdings of unexercised share options also provide a direct link between CEO and shareholder wealth, because the value of the options held increases with increases in the share price. Table 14.5 shows that the average US executive holds options to purchase 1.18% of the company's outstanding shares (median 0.72%), while the average UK executive holds options to purchase only 0.24% (median 0.11%) of his company's shares. Again, pair-wise comparisons from the top and bottom panels of Table 14.5 reveal that holdings of previously granted but unexercised share options are substantially higher in the United States than in the United Kingdom for every size and industry group.

Finally, holdings of unvested LTIP shares provide an additional direct link between CEO and shareholder wealth. First, the value of the underlying shares naturally increases penny-for-penny with increases in the share

Table 14.5 Summary statistics for stock-based CEO incentives, by company size and industry

Group	Share holdings (£ millions)		Share holdings (% of common)		Option holdings (% of common)		Pay-performance sensitivity (%)	
	Average	Median	Average	Median	Average	Median	Average	Median
United Kingdom								
All companies	7.01	0.46	2.13	0.05	0.24	0.11	2.33	0.25
By firm sales (millions)								
Less than £200	9.86	1.41	4.38	0.63	0.38	0.21	4.72	1.09
£200 to £500	9.50	0.70	2.55	0.14	0.24	0.14	2.75	0.42
£500 to £1,500	4.55	0.13	0.76	0.02	0.19	0.12	0.91	0.16
Above £1,500	3.40	0.33	0.21	0.01	0.10	0.04	0.31	0.05
By industry								
Mining/ manufacturing	6.01	0.26	1.91	0.04	0.24	0.14	2.11	0.23
Financial services	5.95	0.84	1.98	0.07	0.19	0.05	2.14	0.31
Utilities	0.16	0.11	0.01	0.00	0.03	0.02	0.05	0.02
Other	9.31	0.71	2.64	0.10	0.28	0.11	2.89	0.37
United States								
All companies	60.37	3.26	3.10	0.29	1.18	0.72	4.18	1.48
By firm sales (millions)								
Less than £200	16.63	2.07	5.32	0.96	1.84	1.37	6.98	3.65
£200 to £500	23.84	2.93	3.94	0.58	1.39	0.94	5.20	2.05
£500 to £1,500	32.25	2.64	2.36	0.25	1.12	0.70	3.43	1.26
Above £1,500	145.26	4.96	1.61	0.09	0.62	0.40	2.17	0.56
By industry								
Mining/ manufacturing	33.77	3.14	2.78	0.31	1.22	0.76	3.87	1.53
Financial services	127.46	7.58	2.25	0.31	0.98	0.52	3.17	1.01
Utilities	6.19	0.58	0.25	0.05	0.35	0.12	0.53	0.16
Other	91.34	4.22	4.63	0.38	1.40	0.95	5.96	2.01

Note: UK data from the largest companies in fiscal 1997, ranked by market capitalisation. US data include firms in the S&P 500, the S&P MidCap 400, the S&P SmallCap 600, and companies in S&P supplemental indices. Revenues for financial firms defined as net interest income (banks) and total income (insurance companies).

The Pay-Performance Sensitivity is defined as:

$$\left(\begin{array}{c}\text{Shares held as}\\ \text{\% of firm shares}\end{array}\right) + \left(\begin{array}{c}\text{Options held as}\\ \text{\% of firm shares}\end{array}\right) \times \left(\begin{array}{c}\text{Options}\\ \text{Delta}\end{array}\right) + \left(\begin{array}{c}\text{LTIP shares as}\\ \text{\% of firm shares}\end{array}\right) \times \left(\begin{array}{c}\text{LTIP}\\ \text{Delta}\end{array}\right)$$

where $0 <$ Option Delta < 1 is the share-weighted-average slope of the Black-Scholes function at the year-end stock price, for options outstanding at the fiscal year end, and (LTIP Delta) = 1.

price. Second, there is an additional link to the extent that the shares vest only upon meeting share-based performance criteria. The average US executive holds LTIP shares (primarily restricted stock) on 0.09% of the company's outstanding shares, while the average UK executive holds LTIP shares on 0.03%; the median LTIP shareholdings is zero in both countries.

One way to aggregate the various components of the direct link between CEO and shareholder wealth is to simply sum the various ownership percentages. However, a share option provides the same incentives as a share of stock only if the option is deep 'in the money' (that is, the share price is far in excess of the exercise price). Therefore, each share option should count somewhat less than one share of stock when adding the holdings to form an aggregate measure of CEO incentives. In constructing our aggregate measure of CEO incentives, we weight each option by the 'Option Delta', which ranges from near zero (for deep out-of-the-money options) to near one (for deep in-the-money options on non-dividend paying stock).[18] The option delta is a well-known concept from option pricing theory, and equals the 'slope' of the Black-Scholes function (that is, the change in the Black-Scholes value for an incremental change in the share price). Formally,

$$Option\ Delta = e^{-\ln(1 + d)T}\ N(z), \qquad (4)$$

where d, T, and z are as defined in (1). Option deltas for ten-year 'at the money' options are ≈ 0.9 for options on non-dividend paying shares, and ≈ 0.6 for options on shares with a 3% dividend yield.

Calculating the option delta for each option held at the end of the fiscal year requires exercise price and expiration-term information for each outstanding option grant. The information required to calculate option deltas for 1997 grants is publicly disclosed (and hence available) for companies in both the United Kingdom and United States. The required data are not uniformly available, however, for grants made prior to 1997, but unexercised at the end of the 1997 fiscal year. In particular, although most UK companies provide detailed data on each grant held at the fiscal year closing, some UK companies and all US companies only provide data on (1) the number of share options held, and (2) the average exercise price for unexercised options granted in prior years.[19] In cases where complete data were not available, we calculated deltas for an aggregated prior grant, with an exercise price equal to the average exercise price and a term assumed to be five years.[20]

LTIP shares are also not equivalent to unrestricted shares owned, because they may be forfeited if certain employment and performance objectives are not achieved. Analogous to our treatment of stock options, we weight each LTIP share by an 'LTIP Delta', which is a measure of the change in value of each LTIP share for an incremental change in the share price. We assume that LTIP recipients will remain employed long enough for all time-related restrictions to lapse. Under this assumption,

American-style restricted shares (which vest with the passage of time, without a performance contingency) have an LTIP delta of one, because a £1 increase in the share price results in a £1 increase in the LTIP share. Calculating LTIP deltas for performance-contingent grants is more complicated. The delta is near zero when there is little chance of achieving threshold performance, near one when the LTIP shares are highly likely to become vested, and above one in the range where small changes in share prices have a large effect on the likelihood of vesting. As a simplification, we assume that LTIP deltas for all LTIP shares are one, independent of performance-vesting contingencies.

Our aggregate measure of direct incentives is the CEO's 'effective' ownership percentage, computed as the following delta-weighted average:

$$\begin{pmatrix} Shares\ held\ as \\ \%\ of\ firm\ shares \end{pmatrix}$$

$$+ \begin{pmatrix} Options\ held\ as \\ \%\ of\ firm\ shares \end{pmatrix} \times \begin{pmatrix} Options \\ Delta \end{pmatrix}$$

$$+ \begin{pmatrix} LTIP\ shares\ as \\ \%\ of\ firm\ shares \end{pmatrix} \times \begin{pmatrix} LTIP \\ Delta \end{pmatrix} \quad (5)$$

Our measure of effective CEO ownership is essentially the 'Pay-Performance Sensitivity' introduced by Jensen and Murphy (1990a). The difference is that we have measured the effective ownership percentage, while Jensen and Murphy measured the change in CEO wealth per $1,000 change in shareholder wealth, which equals the effective ownership percentage multiplied by ten. Also, our effective CEO ownership statistic yields a distribution of CEO incentives. That is we calculate directly the incentive (pay-performance term) for each CEO separately. This differs from much of the prior compensation literature which relies on regression techniques to derive a single average estimate of the pay-performance link.[21]

The final two columns of Table 14.5 show the average and median pay-performance sensitivity for CEOs grouped by country,

Table 14.6 Explanatory regressions for stock-based pay-performance sensitivity

Independent variable	OLS regressions		Median regressions	
	(1)	(2)	(3)	(4)
Intercept	8.181 (12.1)	32.191 (5.8)	3.052 (21.3)	9.545 (9.3)
ln (Sales)	−1.038 (−11.0)	−1.103 (−9.5)	−0.414 (−20.6)	−0.320 (−15.1)
Finance (Dummy)	−0.324 (−0.7)	−0.645 (−1.3)	−0.188 (−1.9)	−0.037 (−0.4)
Utility (Dummy)	−2.724 (−4.3)	−2.533 (−3.6)	−0.946 (−7.0)	−0.557 (−4.4)
Other Industry (Dummy)	1.764 (5.2)	2.026 (5.4)	0.304 (4.2)	0.360 (5.2)
Volatility of Shareholder Returns		2.303 (1.4)		4.384 (14.3)
Book to Market Ratio		0.018 (0.4)		0.003 (3.9)
CEO/Chairman Combined (Dummy)		2.898 (7.9)		0.394 (5.8)
CEO Age		−0.967 (−5.0)		−0.320 (−8.9)
CEO Age-Squared		0.009 (5.5)		0.003 (9.8)
US Firm (Dummy)	2.467 (6.9)	0.963 (2.2)	1.225 (16.1)	0.652 (8.2)
Sample Size	2,174	1,812	2,174	1,812
R^2	0.092	0.157	0.080	0.102

Note: t-statistics (for OLS) and asymptotic t-statistics (for median regressions) in parentheses. Sales for financial firms defined as net interest income banks) and total income (insurance companies).
See the footnote on the prior table for our definition of the Pay-Performance Sensitivity.

company size, and industry. The average and median pay-performance sensitivities for US CEOs are 4.18% and 1.48%, respectively, significantly higher that the average (2.33%) and median (0.25%) sensitivities for UK CEOs. In the largest firms, the median US CEO has a sensitivity, or effective ownership, of 0.56%, more than ten times the effective ownership of their British counterparts.

Table 14.6 presents coefficients from OLS and median regressions where the dependent variable is the stock-based pay-performance sensitivity from (5). The coefficient on the US dummy in column (1) of 2.467 indicates that the average effective ownership is 2.5 percentage points higher in the United States than the United Kingdom, after controlling for company size and industry. The regression in column (2) includes controls for risk, investment opportunities, and human capital introduced in Table 14.4: the volatility of returns, the book-to-market ratio, CEO age and age-squared, and a dummy variable indicating that the CEO and board chairman position are combined. The volatility and book-to-market variables are insignificant, while the age variables are significant and indicate that pay-performance sensitivities are monotonically increasing after age 52. The coefficient of the CEO/chairman dummy variable is positive and significant, indicating that pay-performance sensitivities are higher for combined CEO/chairmen. So, although the level of pay is higher when the posts are combined (and corporate governance reformers typically argue for these posts to be separated for this reason) the link between pay and performance (effective ownership percentage) is also higher. Including the control for CEO/chairman combinations reduces the coefficient on the US dummy variable to 0.9632, but the coefficient remains significantly positive. Columns (3) and (4) present coefficients from median regressions. The book to market and volatility measures are now significant. Importantly, the US dummy variables in both columns (3) and (4) are positive and significant (although quantitatively smaller than in the mean regressions), indicating that median pay-performance sensitivities are substantially higher in the United States, even after including our control variables.

3.2. The indirect relation between CEO and shareholder wealth

In addition to the *direct* relation through ownership, LTIP shares, and options, CEO wealth is *indirectly* related to company stock-price performance through performance-based bonuses, raises, and LTIP and option grant sizes. The CEO pay literature has yet to reach a consensus on the appropriate methodologies and metrics to use in evaluating the indirect relation between CEO pay and company stock-price performance.[22] However, the most common approach has involved estimating some variant of the following first-difference regression:

$$\Delta\ln(Salary + Bonus)_{it} = \alpha + \beta\Delta\ln(Shareholder\ Value)_{it}, \quad (6)$$

where the change in shareholder value, $\Delta\ln$ (*Shareholder Value*)$_t$ ignores share issues or repurchases and therefore equals the continuously accrued rate of return on common stock, r_t. The estimated coefficient β is the elasticity of cash compensation with respect to shareholder value (or, following Rosen (1992), the 'semi-elasticity' of pay with respect to the rate of return).[23]

Table 14.7 reports coefficients from estimating (6) with US interactions. The pay-performance elasticity for UK CEOs in column (1) is 0.1213, indicating that an additional ten percentage point shareholder return corresponds to an additional 1.2% pay raise. The pay-performance elasticity for US CEOs in column (1) is 0.27 ($\approx$0.1213 + 0.1488), or more than double the elasticity for UK CEOs. The difference in elasticities is statistically significant at the 10% level. The remaining columns in Table 14.7 report estimated elasticities for the industrial groups. The estimated US elasticity is higher than the corresponding UK elasticity for all industries, although the difference is only statistically significant for the financial services industry.

Table 14.7 CEO pay-performance elasticities for salary and bonus, by industry

Independent variable	Dependent variable: Δln (Salary + Bonus)				
	All industries	Mining & manufacturing	Financial services	Utilities	Other industries
	(1)	(2)	(3)	(4)	(5)
Intercept	0.1448 (7.1)	0.1552 (6.6)	0.2298 (3.4)	0.5689 (1.3)	0.1158 (3.0)
ln(1 + Shareholder Return)	0.1213 (2.0)	0.1569 (2.2)	−0.1809 (−1.0)	−0.6359 (−0.6)	0.1348 (1.3)
(Dummy) US Firm	−0.0861 (−2.8)	−0.0883 (−2.8)	−0.3273 (−2.8)	−0.6182 (−1.4)	−0.0350 (−0.5)
(Return) × (US Dummy)	0.1558 (1.9)	0.1268 (1.5)	0.7567 (2.9)	1.062 (1.0)	0.1101 (0.7)
R^2	0.038	0.050	0.107	0.065	0.026
Sample Size	2,069	1,009	273	135	652

Note: White asymptotic t-statistics in parentheses. UK data from the largest 510 companies in fiscal 1997, ranked by market capitalisation. US data include firms in the S&P 500, the S&P MidCap 400, and the S&P SmallCap 600. Shareholder return from Datastream (UK) and Compustat (US).

Table 14.8 CEO turnover-performance regressions, by industry

Independent variable	Dependent variable: CEO Turnover in 1996				
	All industries	Mining & manufacturing	Financial services	Utilities	Other industries
	(1)	(2)	(3)	(4)	(5)
Intercept	-1.71 (-10.7)	-1.70 (-7.8)	-2.34 (-3.9)	-0.78 (-1.0)	-1.63 (-5.8)
ln(1 + Shareholder Return)	-1.65 (-2.8)	-1.56 (-1.7)	-0.20 (-0.1)	-12.54 (-1.8)	-1.81 (-2.2)
(Dummy) US Firm	-0.26 (-1.4)	-0.40 (-1.6)	-0.78 (-1.0)	-1.15 (-1.4)	-0.12 (-0.4)
(Return) × (US Dummy)	0.43 (0.7)	0.29 (0.3)	2.66 (1.1)	11.37 (1.6)	0.50 (0.5)
Sample Size	1,942	984	241	135	582
Pseudo R^2	0.030	0.037	0.023	0.034	0.042

Note: Dependent variable = 1 if CEO is in last year of office in 1996. Mean of the dependent variable is 0.119. Shareholder return is measured in 1996. z-statistics in parentheses. UK data from the largest 510 companies in fiscal 1997, ranked by market capitalisation. US data include firms in the S&P 500, the S&P MidCap 400, the S&P SmallCap 600, and companies in supplemental S&P indices. Shareholder return from Datastream (UK) and Compustat (US).

3.3. CEO turnover and corporate performance

Another important potential source of managerial incentives is the threat of being fired for poor performance. Several researchers, beginning with Coughlan and Schmidt (1985), Warner *et al.* (1988), and Weisbach (1988) have documented an inverse relation between CEO turnover and shareholder returns for US companies; Conyon (1998) has shown that the inverse relation holds for UK data as well, and Kaplan (1994 *a, b*) reports similar findings for Japan and Germany.

Table 14.8 reports the coefficient estimates from logistic regressions of CEO turnover on shareholder returns by industry. The dependent variable is equal to one if the CEO is in his last full year of office in fiscal year 1996. The independent variables include 1996 fiscal-year performance, a US dummy, and the US dummy interacted with the performance variable to identify crosscountry differences in the turnover-performance relation. The coefficient on the performance variable is negative in all regressions (and significant in all but financial services), indicating that CEOs in the United Kingdom are indeed more likely to depart following poor performance. The interaction variable is positive but insignificant in all regressions, suggesting that there are no systematic US-UK differences in the CEO turnover-performance relation in our data.[24]

Our conclusion that the turnover-performance relation in the United Kingdom is not significantly different from that in the United States is robust to alternative definitions of performance (using various lagged performance measures, and allowing performance-size interactions). In addition, our conclusion is consistent with Kaplan (1994a,b), who finds no systematic differences in turnover-performance relations in the United States vs. Japan or the United States vs. Germany. However, we view our results here as preliminary because (i) they are based on only a single year of turnover data; (ii) we are not controlling for turnover related to normal retirement; and (iii) we are not controlling for corporate governance variables, including the composition of the board. We leave a comprehensive investigation to future research.

4. DISCUSSION

Consistent with our objective of generating stylised facts to stimulate future research, our paper to this point has been primarily descriptive. That is, although we have documented that American CEOs are higher paid and have better stock-based incentives than British CEOs, we have offered little in the way of theory or conjecture to help explain these interesting differences. In this section, we will briefly discuss a variety of factors that may explain the crosscountry differences. As noted earlier, our objective is not to reconcile completely the differences in pay practices, but rather to identify potential explanations, leaving formal hypothesis development and testing to future research.

4.1. Agency-theoretic considerations

The traditional principal-agent model highlights the trade-off between risk and incentives. Increasing the pay-performance sensitivity imposes more risk on CEOs, who in turn demand higher levels of expected compensation to compensate for the additional risk. Therefore, the facts that US CEOs are better paid and have stronger incentives than UK CEOs may both reflect equilibrium incentive contracts.

To illustrate, suppose that firm value is given by $x = e + \varepsilon$, where e is executive effort, and ε is (normally distributed) uncontrollable noise, $\varepsilon \approx N(0, \sigma^2)$. Moreover, suppose that managerial contracts take the simple linear form $\omega(x) = s + bx$, where s is a fixed salary and b is the sharing rate (or 'pay-performance sensitivity'). Assuming that the executive has exponential utility, $U(x) = -e^{r[W-c(e)]}$, where r is the executive's absolute risk aversion and $c(e)$

is the convex disutility of effort, the optimal sharing rate is given by:[25]

$$b = \frac{1}{1 + r\sigma^2 c''}.\qquad(7)$$

Equation (7) implies that the optimal pay-performance sensitivity b will equal 1 when output is certain ($\sigma^2 = 0$) or executives are risk-neutral ($r = 0$). Incentives will be weaker for more risk-averse executives ($\partial b / \partial r < 0$), and will also be weaker the greater the uncontrollable noise in firm value ($\partial b / \partial \sigma^2 < 0$). Moreover, expected compensation E (w) = $s + b$E (x) will increase monotonically with b to compensate for both the increased risk imposed, and the increased effort induced, by higher pay-performance sensitivities.

Equation (7) suggests a finite number of factors that might explain higher pay and incentives among US executives. First, American CEOs may be less risk averse or have steeper marginal costs of effort than their British counterparts, but to our knowledge there is no theory or empirical work suggesting such international differences in risk-aversion coefficients. Second, UK performance might be measured with substantially more noise than in the United States, leading to lower pay-performance sensitivities and lower expected levels of pay. However, we find no evidence that cash flows or shareholder returns are systematically more variable in the United Kingdom than in the United States.

Overall, the traditional principal-agent model encapsulated in (7) does not offer promising explanations for the difference in pay levels and incentives in the two countries. Extensions of the model to incorporate differences in both ability and in the marginal productivity of CEO effort might help reconcile the data, but only given the additional assumptions that executives are more able and more productive in the United States.[26] For example, Granick (1972) shows that US managers have greater exposure to different functions and operating divisions and that such diversity is rewarded at the top of the hierarchy. The complexity of the filtering and training processes, and differences in each country, may explain divergences in pay between the United States and United Kingdom. Similarly, American CEOs may have more decision rights and influence over corporate results than do British executives.

Unfortunately, traditional agency theory gives little guidance on why the career paths, production functions, or hierarchical structures should vary across international boundaries.

4.2. Taxes

As emphasised by Miller and Scholes (1982) and Abowd and Bognanno (1995), corporate and personal tax regimes affect the optimal structure of executive compensation contracts. Overall, the personal income tax rules and rates affecting executive pay are quite similar in the United States and United Kingdom. Cash compensation and gains from 'unapproved' (or 'nonqualified') share options are taxed as personal income in both countries, at comparable rates.[27] 'Approved' share options, granted infrequently to top executives because of institutional restrictions, are taxed at capital gains rates in both countries. In recent years, the capital gains rate in the UK has increased from 30% to 40%, while falling from 28% to 20% in the US.

Apart from the difference in capital gains tax rates, which is both relatively recent and fairly benign (given the paucity of approved share grants), there are no major differences in the personal tax regimes in the United Kingdom and the United States related to executive compensation. However, there are two significant differences in the extent to which compensation is deductible from corporate profits as an ordinary business expense. First, the exercise-date spread between the market and exercise price on unapproved options is treated as a deductible compensation expense in the United States, but not in the United Kingdom. Second, under rules passed in 1993, the United States limits the deductibility of 'non-performance-based' compensation (including salaries, restricted stock, and discretionary bonuses) to $1 million.[28] Thus, UK rules allow deductions for cash compensation but not for exercised options, while US rules allow deductions for exercised options but limit deductions for cash compensation. As discussed in the next sub-section, we believe that these differences have played at least some role in the relative prevalence of share options in US pay packages.

4.3. The rise (US) and fall (UK) of share options

The fact that US CEOs are better paid with stronger pay-performance sensitivities is largely attributable to the relative prevalence and magnitude of share options in the US. As documented by Hall and Liebman (1998) and Murphy (1999) and suggested by Figure 14.2, the importance of share options in US compensation packages is a relatively recent phenomenon, reflecting an explosion in option granting practices since the mid-1980s. Over the same period, many UK companies have rejected share option plans in favour of performance share plans such as LTIPs (Main, 1999). Understanding the factors that have led to the rise in share options in the United States, and the fall of share options in the United Kingdom, is critical in understanding the differences in compensation and incentives in the two countries.

The increased popularity of share option grants for US executives can be traced, in large part, to a combination of economic, political, and cultural factors. Shareholder groups and academics in the early 1990s called for more stock-based compensation in CEO pay packages, citing the lack of meaningful rewards and penalties in the typical package. The deductibility limitations on non-performance-related pay introduced by the Clinton Administration in 1993 further fuelled the popularity of stock options. The trend was nearly reversed in the mid-1990s, however, when the Financial Accounting Standards Board (FASB) announced plans to institute a grant-date accounting charge for companies granting share options. Ultimately, FASB yielded to pressure from the business community, accounting firms, and the hi-tech ('Silicon Valley') sector,

and opted against requiring an accounting change, adopting instead enhanced footnote disclosure of granting practices. The October 1995 FASB retreat ensured the continued trend in option awards, since the grants remained invisible from an accounting perspective, but fully deductible from a tax perspective.

The S&P500 Index (a broad measure of US stock-market performance) increased by 300% in the 1990s; the UK FTSE Index increased by only 150% during the same period. Proponents of large share option grants have pointed to the US stock-market performance as evidence that options provide incentives for executives to increase shareholder wealth. But, the robust stock market has also been a contributing factor to the growing demand for option compensation among US executives. The current cohort of executives has not experienced a major market downturn, and the overwhelming majority of US share options issued since 1980 have been exercised well in-the-money. As a result of these past successes, both executives and employees have embraced share options as the quickest, and (by their perception) the surest, route to obtaining substantial wealth.

Economic, political and cultural factors have also shaped option granting policies in the United Kingdom. In contrast to the United States, where these factors have encouraged the use of share option compensation, a variety of recent statutory and non-statutory arrangements in the United Kingdom have *discouraged* share option grants. Options in the United Kingdom became controversial in 1995, after executives in several recently privatised electric utilities exercised options worth millions of pounds. The influential Greenbury report (1995) encouraged companies to replace their option plans with LTIP share plans which 'may be as effective, or more so, than improved share option schemes in linking rewards to performance' Greenbury (1995, paragraph 6.32). In response to the Greenbury report and the ongoing controversy, the government tightened the restrictions on approved option awards, reducing the amount that could be awarded (expressed as the aggregate exercise price) from the greater of £100,000 or four times cash emoluments to only £30,000.

An important non-statutory consideration for UK companies is the codes of conduct issued by institutional investors and their representatives. Although not legally binding, policy guidelines from the Association of British Insurers (ABI) and other investor groups are highly influential and closely followed. The ABI guidelines (1994, 1995), for example, effectively constrain the issuing of share options—approved and unapproved—to four times cash compensation.[29] More recently, the Pension Investment Research Consultants (PIRC, 1998) called on companies to toughen performance targets for executive option schemes and other incentive plans.

In sum, executive pay has been highly controversial in both the United States and the United Kingdom, and has generated a variety of responses from the government and tax authorities, the accounting boards, the media, and institutional investors. Although the root causes of the controversy in the two countries are basically similar, the responses have been markedly different: while the net effect of these factors has been to greatly increase option grants in the United States, the net effect has discouraged the use of option grants in the United Kingdom in favour of LTIPs.

4.4. Culture

We have documented that US CEOs have higher pay and stock-based incentives than CEOs in the United Kingdom, and shown that these results are driven, in large part, by the recent divergence in share option practices. Although it is difficult for us to explain why a similar controversy over CEO pay has led to increased option grants in the United States but decreased grants in the United Kingdom, it is tempting to attribute at least part of the divergence to cultural differences between the two countries. The United States, as a society, has historically been more tolerant of income inequality, especially if the inequality is driven by differences in effort, talent, or entrepreneurial risk taking. In this light,

perhaps it is natural that the United States reacts to claims of excessive CEO pay by increasing the link between pay and performance, thus exacerbating income inequality, while the United Kingdom reacts through wage compression and reducing the pay-performance link.

The divergence in top wages in the UK vs. US is not, of course, limited to top executives. The best doctors, engineers, professors, athletes, lawyers, investment bankers, and entertainers all earn substantially more in the United States than in the United Kingdom. The US wage premiums for 'superstars' in all occupations persist in spite of the similarities in language, culture, tax regimes, and institutions. These premiums may be evidence that the US market for superstars (Rosen, 1981) is more competitive than the UK market, with 'winner-take-all' rents flowing to the producers (Frank and Cook, 1995). Thus, perhaps the CEO-pay differentials should be examined in the context of broader competitive and culture factors.

5. CONCLUSION

The recent wave of international corporate mergers, such as Daimler-Chrysler and British Petroleum-Amoco, has sparked academic and practitioner interest in understanding international differences in executive pay policies. International comparisons are inherently difficult, because of fundamental differences in data availability, tax regimes, corporate governance and the organisation of business. For a variety of reasons, the United States and United Kingdom offer a natural laboratory to examine in detail differences in compensation and incentives practices. First, the United Kingdom and United States (along with Canada) are currently the only countries that require detailed disclosure on the compensation practices for individual top corporate executives. Second, the United Kingdom and United States share a common language and have similar capital markets and underlying economies. Third, the United States and United Kingdom employ similar corporate governance structures, especially when compared to those in Japan, Germany, and other economic powers. These important similarities, in a sense, stack the deck against finding significant differences in pay practices.

Nonetheless, several stylised facts have emerged from our comprehensive comparison of CEO incentives and pay practices in the United Kingdom and the United States. Expected pay levels, after controlling for company size and industry, are significantly higher in the United States than in the United Kingdom. Although base salaries are modestly higher in the United States, and annual bonuses substantially higher, the driving force behind the US premium is the prevalence and sheer magnitude of share option grants to US executives. The divergence between UK and US pay practices is especially pronounced in large firms and financial firms.

The link between CEO wealth and shareholder wealth is also much stronger in the United States than in the United Kingdom. Jensen and Murphy (1990 a) argued that US CEOs have insufficient incentives to increase shareholder wealth, but incentives among British CEOs pale compared to their American counterparts. CEOs in the US hold more shares of stock (measured both in value and as a percentage of outstanding shares), hold more share options, and hold at least as many LTIP shares as do UK CEOs. Overall, the pay-performance sensitivity is substantially higher in the United States than the United Kingdom, for every size and industry group. Moreover, the indirect relation between cash compensation and stock-price performance is also more strongly positive in the United States than the United Kingdom. In short, CEOs in the United States have more incentives to improve shareholder wealth than do CEOs in the United Kingdom.

The differences between pay and incentive practices in the United States and United Kingdom are somewhat surprising, given the similarities in corporate governance and the managerial labour markets. The differences are especially surprising since executive pay has been highly controversial in both countries, for similar underlying reasons. We believe that corporate tax deductibility rules—which encourage option compensation in the United States while discouraging option compensation in the United Kingdom—help explain the observed differences in pay structures. Ultimately, however, the differences largely reflect subtle political and cultural differences in the two countries. In the US, the controversy over CEO pay has led to tighter links between executive pay and performance (primarily through an explosion in option grants), exacerbating wage inequality given the robust US stock market. In the United Kingdom, the pay controversy has led to statutory and non-statutory policies that discourage large share option grants, lessening the pay-performance link and leading to a relatively compressed wage structure.

The differences in pay practices between the United States and the United Kingdom (or, more generally among any countries) would have few consequences on supply and demand relations if the managerial labour markets were truly isolated within country boundaries. But, large companies are increasingly multinational, and must continuously deal with expatriate compensation and horizontal wage inequities caused by heterogeneous local labour market conditions. Moreover, top-level managers are increasingly mobile and will naturally flow to higher-paid markets: 62 of the top 800 CEOs in the United States are foreign born, 30 are originally European.[30] Understanding the magnitude, causes, and consequences of international differences in executive pay practices has important implications for our understanding of the globalisation of world commerce.

NOTES

* We would like to thank John Core, Harry DeAngelo, Linda DeAngelo, Wayne Guay, Brian Hall, Steve Machin, Brian Main, Simon Peck and Andrew Samwick for comments on this paper and its predecessors. Advice from practitioner-colleagues at PriceWaterhouseCoopers (especially Stephen Clements) is appreciated. We would like to thank Graham Sadler for excellent research assistance in assembling the UK data. Financial support provided by the Economic and Social

Research Council (Award number R000237246) and the USC Marshall School is gratefully acknowledged.

1   The US dollar-denominated data in this paper are converted to UK pounds by the contemporaneous exchange rate, which ranged from 1.61$/£ to 1.65$/£ over the 1997 fiscal year.

2   Abowd and Bognanno (1995) use survey data from compensation consultants to show that CEO pay differs internationally in both level and structure but little attempt is made to ensure commensurability between economies and control for scale, etc. Conyon and Schwalbach (1999) show differences in executive cash compensation across European economies after controlling for company size and job position. Main et al. (1994) compare cash compensation in 1990 between the United States and United Kingdom but exclude any comparison of the structure of pay.

3   Murphy (1999) provides a comprehensive review of the executive compensation literature, with an emphasis on US data. Recent UK research includes Main et al. (1996), Cosh and Hughes (1997), Conyon (1998), Conyon and Peck (1998b), and Ezzamel and Watson (1998). With the exception of Main et al., these studies exclude share options and focus only on cash compensation.

4   Other countries, including Japan and Germany, require disclosures of the aggregate amount paid to the group of top directors or executives, but do not identify individuals. Disclosure in Canada was mandated in 1993 by the Ontario Securities Regulation, and covers all publicly traded companies in the province of Ontario (including all companies on the Toronto Stock Exchange). See Zhou (1999) for an extensive analysis of CEO pay and incentives in Canada.

5   Although the US reporting requirements are generally more stringent than the UK requirements, data on prior share option grants are more detailed in the United Kingdom.

6   Secondary sources in the United Kingdom include Datastream and PriceWaterhouse-Coopers' Corporate Register published by Hemmington Scott. These sources typically ignore share options, combine other pay components into a single number, and focus on the highest-paid executive rather than the CEO. Information about options can be obtained from the Register of Directors' Interests. In practice it can be difficult to access this source (see Main et al., 1996, p. 1632). Secondary sources in the United States include the comprehensive Compustat ExecuComp data, and the less-comprehensive surveys published by Forbes, Business Week, and the Wall Street Journal.

7   Options typically expire after either 5 or 10 years; our results are not sensitive to whether we use the 5, 7, or 10-year risk-free rates. The US risk-free rate is estimated at 6.3% for all fiscal 1997 data. The risk-free rate is set to 6.0% for UK firms with fiscal closings prior to July 31, 1997, and 7.0% for firms with later closings.

8   Dividend yields above 5% are 'trimmed' to 5%, and volatilities are trimmed to lie in the range 20% to 60%. We imposed these constraints because abnormal historical dividend yields and volatilities are poor predictors of yields and volatilities over the term of the option. These constraints do not, however, change any of our qualitative results.

9   Early exercise has ambiguous implications for the cost of granting options. On one hand, the right to exercise early increases the amount an outside investor would pay for the option, and hence increases the option's cost. On the other hand, risk-averse undiversified executives tend to exercise much earlier than would a rational outside investor, and these early exercise decisions reduce the company's cost of granting options (Carpenter, 1998).

10   The most common criterion requires earnings-per-share growth exceeding 2% in any three years of the options' term. The Pension Investment Research Consultants (PIRC, 1998) argue that most requirements are non-demanding as their index of large companies has achieved real EPS growth rates in excess of 3%. Similarly, we calculated in our data set of UK companies that average (median) real earnings per share growth between 1992 and 1997 was 11.04% (13.32%). Even the company at the 20th percentile achieved average real EPS growth over the period of 2%.

11   The full time-series is not available for all of our 1997 sample firms, and the medians in Figure 14.1 are therefore based on smaller samples in earlier years. The results are unchanged when we restrict the analysis to only firms with complete time-series data.

12   The firms in the Small-Cap sample are considerably smaller than the firms in the UK sample, with mean (median) 1997 market capitalisation of only £344 million (£247 million) in the US Small-Cap sample compared to £2.2 billion (£484 million) in the UK sample.

13   The Conference Board discontinued their plan-prevalence data series in 1997. For this year, we use ExecuComp data on the fraction of

S&P 500 companies in which the top five executives hold any share options. This definition of prevalence closely tracks the Conference Board's survey responses for the 1992–6 period where both sources of prevalence data are available.

14 Guy (1999) documents empirical evidence that the annually estimated CEO pay-size elasticity varies positively with annual median pay. This is consistent with our results since median US pay is higher than in the United Kingdom.

15 Calculated as $e^{0.3861} - 1 \approx 0.47$.

16 However, in unreported regressions on only UK data, cash compensation is positively and significantly related to volatility, and negatively and significantly related to book-to-market ratios. Since our primary objective here is to identify cross-country differences in pay levels, we leave further examination of cross-country differences in slope coefficients to future research.

17 For example, $0.0663 \times Age - 0.0006 \times Age^2$ reaches a maximum at age $0.0663/(2 \times 0.0006) = 55.25$.

18 The percentage option holdings multiplied by the option delta is a measure of the change in CEO option-related wealth corresponding to a change in shareholder wealth. More formally, suppose that the CEO holds N share options, and suppose that shareholder wealth increases by £1. If there are S total shares outstanding, the share price P will increase by $\Delta P = £1/S$, and the value of the CEO's options will increase by $N\Delta P(\partial V/\partial P)$, where V is the Black-Scholes value of each option. Substituting for ΔP, the CEO's share of the value increase is given by $(N/S)(\Delta V/\partial P)$, or the CEO's options held as a fraction of total shares outstanding multiplied by the 'slope' of the Black-Scholes valuation. For examples of this approach which yield a distribution of CEO incentives, see Jensen and Murphy (1990b), Yermack (1995), and Murphy (1999). Hall and Murphy (2000) offer a modified approach to measure the pay-for-performance incentives of risk-averse undiversified executives. An alternative approach, adopted by Jensen and Murphy (1990a) for the United States and Main, et al. (1996) for the United Kingdom, involves estimating the option pay-performance sensitivity as the coefficient from a regression of the change in option value on the change in shareholder wealth. The procedure is similar to how we identify the 'indirect' relation between pay and performance below.

19 Although the Greenbury report generally required detailed disclosure of prior grants, it recognised that 'in the disclosure of share option

details there is some risk that the abundance of information will mask rather than highlight the nature and scale of option schemes', and allowed less-than-complete option information when remuneration committees are 'satisfied that this will not result in failure to disclose information of material importance'. Greenbury (1995, p. 29).

20 About 80% of UK annual reports provided full information (i.e. the exercise price and expiration date) on every prior grant of options still outstanding. In the remaining 20% of cases an exercise price is almost always given although it is weighted exercise price of all options held (see Conyon and Sadler, 1999). The expiration date is given in only 50% of cases and is typically the expiration date of the longest-dated option. US proxy statements provide information on the number and intrinsic value of options held at the end of the fiscal year (based on the fiscal year-end stock price, P). The number (N) and intrinsic value (Y) of previously granted options is calculated by subtracting new grants from total outstanding options, and adjusting the year-end intrinsic value of the new grants from the total intrinsic value. We treat the previously granted options as a single prior grant with exercise price X, where $N(P - X) = Y$, or $X = P - (Y/N)$.

21 See, for example, Conyon and Peck (1998 a).

22 See Murphy (1999) for a discussion and comparison of the various approaches.

23 Most of the UK literature has been concerned with estimating this type of equation and ignoring the importance of the direct relation between CEO pay and shareholder wealth (as reviewed in Conyon et al., 1995). Moreover, Gregg et al. (1993) show that the 'implicit' link between CEO pay and shareholder returns became de-coupled in the 1990s. In fact, this may simply be attributable to the restructuring of CEO pay packages and the importance of non-cash forms of compensation.

24 Estimating logit regressions for each country separately yielded negative and significant correlations between CEO turnover on shareholder returns in both the US and UK data.

25 For similar derivations of the optimal pay-performance sharing rate, see Lazear and Rosen (1981), Holmstrom and Milgrom (1991), Gibbons and Murphy (1992), and Milgrom and Roberts (1992).

26 Half of us are unwilling to concede to such assumptions.

27 The highest marginal tax rate is approximately 40% in both countries. The top UK rate affects incomes above £28,000, while the top US

bracket is indexed for inflation and is currently about £175,000 for married taxpayers.

28   Research on the effects of the deductibility limitation, which apply only to the top five executives in publicly traded corporations, has concluded that the rule has had a modest influence on both the level and structure of US pay plans (Perry and Zenner, 1999; Rose and Wolfram, 1997).

29   Conyon and Sadler (1999) and Main (1999) consider the implications of this rule.

30   Based on data from *Forbes'* Annual Survey of Executive Compensation, May 19, 1997.

REFERENCES

Abowd, J. and Bognanno, M. (1995). 'International differences in executive and managerial compensation.' In (R. Freeman and L. Katz, eds.) *Differences and Changes in Wage Structures*, pp. 67–103. Chicago: University of Chicago Press.

Association of British Insurers (1995) 'Share options and profit sharing incentive schemes.' ABI, London.

Association of British Insurers (1994) 'Long term remuneration for senior executives.' ABI, London.

Black, F. and Scholes, M. (1973). 'The pricing of options and corporate liabilities.' *Journal of Political Economy*, vol. 81, pp. 637–59.

Buckingham, L. and Cowe, R. (1998a). 'Boardroom pay 98: Pleas for restraint fail to curb executive excess.' *The Guardian*, 22 July.

Buckingham, L. and Cowe, R. (1998b). 'The boardroom bonanza: exclusive survey reveals top directors' pay soaring by 18%.' *The Guardian*, 22 July.

Cadbury, A. (1992). 'Code of best practice.' Report from the Committee on Financial Aspects of Corporate Governance. London: Gee Publishing.

Carpenter, J. (1998). 'The exercise and valuation of executive stock options.' *Journal of Financial Economics*, vol. 48(2), pp. 127–58.

Conyon, M. J. (1998). 'Directors' pay and turnover: an application to a sample of large UK firms.' *Oxford Bulletin of Economics and Statistics*, vol. 60, pp. 485–507.

Conyon, M. J. and Peck, S. I. (1998a). 'Recent developments in UK corporate governance.' In (T. Buxton, P. Chapman and P. Temple, eds.) *Britain's Economic Performance*. London: Routledge.

Conyon, M. J. and Peck, S. I. (1998b). 'Board control, remuneration committees and top management compensation.' *Academy Management Journal*, vol. 41, pp. 146–57.

Conyon, M. J. and Sadler, G. V. (1999). 'CEO compensation, option incentives and information disclosure.' Warwick University mimeograph.

Conyon, M. J. and Schwalbach, J. (1999). 'Corporate governance, executive pay and performance in Europe.' In (J. Carpenter and D. Yermack, eds.) *Executive Compensation and Shareholder Value: Theory and Evidence*, pp. 13–34. Dordrecht: Kluwer Academic Press.

Conyon, M. J., Gregg, P. and Machin, S. (1995). 'Taking care of business: executive compensation in the UK.' ECONOMIC JOURNAL, vol. 105 (May), pp. 704–15.

Cosh, A. and Hughes, A. (1997). 'Executive remuneration, executive dismissals and institutional shareholdings.' *International Journal of Industrial Organization*, vol. 15, pp. 469–92.

Coughlan, A. T. and Schmidt, R. M. (1985). 'Executive compensation, managerial turnover and firm performance.' *Journal of Accounting and Economics*, vol. 7, pp. 43–66.

Crystal, G. (1991). *In Search of Excess: The Overcompensation of American Executives*. New York: Norton & Company.

Ezzamel, M. and Watson, R. (1998). 'Market comparison earnings and the bidding-up of executive cash compensation: evidence from the United Kingdom.' *Academy Management Journal*, vol. 41, pp. 221–31.

Frank, R. H. and Cook, P. J. (1995). *Winner-Take-All Society*. New York: Free Press.

Gibbons, R. and Murphy, K. J. (1992). 'Optimal incentive contracting in the presence of career concerns: theory and evidence.' *Journal of Political Economy*, vol. 100, pp. 468–505.

Granick, D. (1972). '*Managerial Comparisons of Four Developed Countries: France, Britain, United States and Russia.*' Cambridge MA: MIT Press.

Greenbury, R. (1995). '*Directors' Remuneration: Report of a study group chaired by Sir Richard Greenbury.*' London: Gee Publishing.

Gregg, P., Machin, S. and Szymanski, S. (1993). 'The disappearing relationship between directors' pay and corporate performance.'

British Journal of Industrial Relations, vol. 31, pp. 1–10.

Guy, F. (1999). 'Earnings distribution, corporate governance and CEO pay.' ESRC Centre for Business Research, University of Cambridge. Working Paper No. 126.

Hall, B. J. and Leibman, J. B. (1998). 'Are CEOs really paid like bureaucrats?' *Quarterly Journal of Economics*, vol. 113 (3), pp. 653–91.

Hall, B. J. and Murphy, K. J. (2000). 'Optimal exercise prices for executive stock options.' *American Economic Review*, Volume 20, No 2, May, pp. 209–214.

Hampel, R. (1998). 'Committee on Corporate Governance: Final Report.' London: Gee Publishing.

Holmstrom, B. and Milgrom, P. (1991). 'Multi-task principal-agent analyses: incentive contracts, asset ownership and job design.' *Journal of Law, Economics and Organization*, vol. 7, pp. 24–52.

Jensen, M. and Murphy, K J. (1990a). 'Performance pay and top-management incentives.' *Journal of Political Economy*, vol. 98(2), pp. 225–64.

Jensen, M. and Murphy, K. J. (1990b). 'CEO incentives: it's not how much you pay, but how.' *Harvard Business Review*, vol. 68 (May/June), pp. 138–49.

Kaplan, S. (1994a). 'Top executive rewards and firm performance: a comparison of Japan and the United States.' *Journal of Political Economy*, vol. 102(3), pp. 510–46.

Kaplan, S. (1994b). 'Top executives, turnover, and firm performance in Germany.' *Journal of Law, Economics and Organization*, vol. 10(1), pp. 142–59.

Lazear, E. and Rosen, S. (1981). 'Rank order tournaments as optimum labour contracts.' *Journal of Political Economy*, vol. 89, pp. 841–64.

Main, B. G. (1999). 'The rise and fall of executive share options in Britain.' In (J. Carpenter and D. Yermack, eds.) *Executive Compensation and Shareholder Value: Theory and Evidence*, pp. 83–113.

Dordrecht, Kluwer Academic Press.

Main, B. G., Bruce, A. and Buck, T. (1996). 'Total board remuneration and company performance.' Economic Journal, vol. 106, pp. 1627–44.

Main, B. G., O'Reilly, C. and Crystal, G. (1994). 'Over here and over there: a comparison of top executive pay in the UK and the USA.' *Contributions to Labour Studies*, vol. 4, pp. 115–27.

Milgrom, P. and Roberts, J. (1992). *Economics, Organizations, and Management*. New Jersey: Prentice Hall.

Miller, M. and Scholes, M. (1982). 'Executive compensation, taxes and incentives.' In (W. Sharpe and C. Cootner, eds.) *Financial Economics: Essays in Honor of Paul Cootner*, pp. 179–201. Englewood Cliffs NJ: Prentice Hall.

Murphy, K. J. (1999). 'Executive compensation.' In (O. Ashenfelter and D. Card, eds.) *Handbook of Labor Economics*, vol. 3. Amsterdam: North Holland.

PIRC (1998). *Executive Share Schemes: Trends in 1998*. London, Pension Investment Research Consultants.

Perry, T. and Zenner, M. (1999). 'Pay for performance? Government regulation and the structure of compensation contracts.' University of North Carolina mimeograph.

PriceWaterhouseCoopers Corporate Register, various years, published Hemmington Scott.

Rose, N. and Wolfram, C. (1997). 'Regulating CEO pay: assessing the impact of the tax-deductibility cap on executive compensation.' MIT.

Rosen, S. (1981). 'The economics of superstars.' *American Economic Review*, vol. 71 (5), pp. 845–58.

Rosen, S. (1992). 'Contracts and the market for executives.' In (L. Werin and H. Wijkander, eds.) *Contract Economics*, pp. 181–211. Oxford: Blackwell.

Warner, J., Watts, R. and Wruck, K. (1988). 'Stock prices and top management changes.' *Journal of Financial Economics*, vol. 20, pp. 461–92.

Weisbach, M. (1988). 'Outside directors and CEO turnover.' *Journal of Financial Economics*, vol. 20, pp. 431–60.

Yermack, D. (1995). 'Do corporations award CEO stock options effectively?' *Journal of Financial Economics*, vol. 39, pp. 237–69.

Zhou, X. (1999). 'CEO pay, firm size and corporate performance: evidence from Canada.' *Canadian Journal of Economics*, (forthcoming).

Chapter 15

Wayne R. Guay*

THE SENSITIVITY OF CEO WEALTH TO EQUITY RISK: AN ANALYSIS OF THE MAGNITUDE AND DETERMINANTS

Source: *Journal of Financial Economics*, 53(1) (1999): 43–71.

ABSTRACT

To control risk-related incentive problems, equity holders are expected to manage both the convexity and slope of the relation between firm performance and managers' wealth. I find stock options, but not common stockholdings, significantly increase the sensitivity of CEOs' wealth to equity risk. Cross-sectionally, this sensitivity is positively related to firms' investment opportunities. This result is consistent with managers receiving incentives to invest in risky projects when the potential loss from underinvestment in valuable risk-increasing projects is greatest. Firms' stock-return volatility is positively related to the convexity provided to managers, suggesting convex incentive schemes influence investing and financing decisions.

1. INTRODUCTION

JENSEN AND MECKLING (1976) ILLUSTRATE that, to reduce agency conflicts with managers, shareholders are expected to tie managers' wealth to firm, or stock price, performance. By using compensation policy to manage the slope of the relation between managers' wealth and stock price, shareholders can induce managers to take actions that increase equity value. Managing this slope, however, is not sufficient to control agency conflicts arising between stockholders and managers. As is well-recognized in studies by Jensen and Meckling (1976), Haugen and Senbet (1981), and Smith and Stulz (1985), the convexity of the relation between stock price and managers' wealth, in addition to the slope, must be managed to induce managers to make optimal investment and financing decisions.

The convexity, or curvature, of the wealth-performance relation refers to the sensitivity of managers' wealth to the volatility of equity value. To date, no empirical evidence exists on the importance of convexity in the design of executives' incentives. This study quantifies the impact of equity risk, or stock-return volatility, on the value of stock options and common stock held by corporate CEOs, and provides evidence on cross-sectional determinants of convexity in executives' incentive schemes.

Smith and Stulz (1985) show that when managers' wealth is dependent upon firm performance, risk-aversion can cause managers to pass up risk-increasing, positive net-present-value projects. They illustrate how shareholders can reduce this risk-related agency problem by using stock options or common stock to structure managers' wealth as a convex function of firm performance. Since risk-related investment problems are expected to be greatest for firms with substantial investment opportunities, the magnitude of convexity in executives' wealth-performance relation is predicted to be positively related to the proportion of assets that are growth options. Smith and Watts (1992) also hypothesize that growth options are a determinant of executives' incentives. However, their argument focuses primarily on the slope of the wealth–performance relation. Theory suggests that, in addition to influencing the slope, the investment opportunity set is also a determinant of the convexity in the wealth–performance relation.

To illustrate differences between the slope and convexity of the wealth–performance relation, consider the options and common stock held by the following two CEOs. As of December 31, 1993, the CEO of Conrail Inc. held 94,400 shares of stock, worth $6.3 million, and 102,500 stock options, worth approximately $3.9 million. At that time, the CEO of GTE Corp. held 61,100 shares of stock worth $2.1 million and 539,900 stock options worth approximately $4.3 million. Using a Black and Scholes (1973) option-pricing framework (its application in this study is discussed in Section 4), and parameter values as of December 31, 1993, the securities held by each of the CEOs would increase in value by about $600,000 for a 5% increase in their firm's stock price. That is, the slope of the wealth–performance relation is approximately the same for both CEOs on this date. However, the convexity in their wealth–performance relation differs considerably. The GTE CEO's securities would increase in value by about $505,000 for a 5 percentage point increase in the annualized standard deviation of GTE's stock returns. This figure compares to a $55,000 increase in the value of the Conrail CEO's securities for the same increase in stock-return volatility. Therefore, the GTE CEO appears to have significantly greater risk-taking incentives than the CEO of Conrail Inc.

Using compensation data for 278 corporate CEOs, I present evidence that stock options, but not common stockholdings, play an economically significant role in increasing the convexity of the relation between managers' wealth and stock price. I measure convexity as the change in the value of managers' stock options and stockholdings for a given change in stock-return volatility. The median change in the value of CEOs' option portfolios for a 10 percentage point change in the standard deviation of stock returns is approximately $300,000, with an interquartile range of $425,000.[1] Convexity provided by common stock, on the other hand, is several orders of magnitude lower than that of stock options, and is of little economic importance for most CEOs in the sample. The median change in the value of CEOs' common stockholdings for a 10 percentage point change in return volatility is only $22, with an interquartile range of $2400. Since most firms are financially healthy, common stock, when viewed as an option on the firm's asset value, is generally so deep 'in the money' that the payoff to shareholders is effectively a linear function of firm value.

I also find that the convexity in CEOs' incentive schemes is positively related to the proportion of a firm's assets that are growth options. Thus, firms appear to provide managers with incentives to invest in risky projects when the potential loss from forgoing valuable risk-increasing projects is greatest. Finally, equity risk is shown to be positively related to the convexity provided to CEOs, suggesting that managers' investment and financing decisions are influenced by their risk-taking incentives.

Section 2 briefly highlights the relation between convexity, managers' preferences toward firm risk, and risk-related agency costs. The data are summarized in Section 3. Section 4 describes the procedure used to estimate the slope and convexity of the wealth–performance relation, and provides descriptive findings. The cross-sectional relation between firms' investment opportunities and the convexity provided to managers is explored in Section 5. Section 6 examines whether firms' stock-return volatility is related to the convexity of managers' wealth–performance relation. I conclude with Section 7.

2. MANAGERS' PREFERENCES TOWARD FIRM RISK AND RISK-RELATED AGENCY COSTS

The relation between firm risk and managers' incentives is well-developed in the literature. When a manager holds common stock and stock options, a dependence exists between his wealth and the firm's stock-price performance (see Jensen and Meckling, 1976; Jensen and Murphy, 1990). This dependence is commonly referred to as the wealth–performance relation. Since stock price varies over time, the payoffs to this incentive scheme are uncertain, and risk is imposed on the manager. In Pratt (1964), a risk-averse manager is shown to be indifferent between a risky payoff and the following payoff with certainty:

$$\text{Certainty equivalent} = E(\text{wealth}) - \text{risk premium}. \quad (1)$$

Differentiating this expression with respect to firm risk yields the following:

$$\partial CE/\partial\sigma = \partial E(\text{wealth})/\partial\sigma - \partial(\text{risk premium})/\partial\sigma. \quad (2)$$

Smith and Stulz (1985) and Lambert et al. (1991) illustrate how this expression partitions the effect of firm risk on managers' preferences into two components. The first component, $\partial E(\text{wealth})/\partial\sigma$, which I will refer to as the wealth effect, represents the change in expected wealth experienced by a manager when firm risk changes. When the payoffs of an incentive scheme are a linear function of firm performance, the wealth effect is zero, since changes in the distribution of firm performance do not affect managers' expected wealth. Expected wealth is an increasing function of risk when managers own securities with convex payoffs, such as stock options or common stock, that increase in value as firm risk increases. Bonus plans and other incentive schemes can also contribute to the wealth effect when their payoffs are concave or convex functions of firm performance (see Section 5.2 for further discussion).

The presence of convex, or option-like, payoffs in the structure of executives' incentives is well-recognized by both academics and practitioners. For example, Jensen and Meckling (1976) point out that equity holders in a levered firm essentially hold a European call option to buy the firm at an exercise price equal to the face value of debt. As such, the value of common stock increases with the volatility of the firm's cash flows. Haugen and Senbet (1981) analyze the incentive effects of convex payoffs from employee stock options. Several empirical studies, such as Agrawal and Mandelker (1987), DeFusco et al. (1990), and Tufano (1996), have also examined the convexity implications of managers' stock-based wealth. However, none of these studies has quantified the magnitude of this convexity for common stock or stock options, or explored its determinants. The following excerpt from the *Committee Report on Executive Compensation* in BellSouth's 1993 proxy statement (p. 11) illustrates that corporate compensation committees also recognize the need to structure compensation plans to give executives appropriate risktaking incentives:

> BellSouth's long term [incentive] program is intended to focus the executive group on the achievement of corporate goals .... Recognizing the dynamic convergence of industries such as telecommunications, entertainment, and cable which will continue throughout the next decade, the Committee wants to motivate BellSouth executives to take the risks necessary to secure a strong foothold for BellSouth in this extremely competitive new marketplace.

The second component in Eq. (2), $\partial(\text{risk premium})/\partial\sigma$, which I will refer to as the risk-aversion effect, captures the influence of risk-aversion on managers' utility. If managers are risk-averse and poorly diversified with respect to firm-specific wealth, an increase in firm risk decreases managers' expected utility. The magnitude of the risk-aversion effect is expected to depend upon the degree of diversification in a manager's portfolio of wealth, the level of a manager's wealth, and manager-specific risk-aversion parameters.

A manager's overall preference toward firm risk will depend upon the relative magnitudes of the wealth effect and the risk-aversion effect. If the risk-aversion effect dominates, the manager will prefer to decrease firm risk. This condition can give rise to risk-related agency problems. When shareholders hold well-diversified portfolios, they would like managers to invest in all positive net-present-value projects, irrespective of the risk associated with those projects. However, due to a lack of diversification, risk-averse managers may choose to forgo some positive net-present-value projects that would increase firm risk. Smith and Stulz (1985) and Milgrom and Roberts (1992) argue that by making adjustments to the slope and convexity of the wealth-performance relation, shareholders can reduce the likelihood that managers pass up valuable risky projects. Holding the slope constant, greater convexity in the wealth-performance relation is expected to shrink the gap between the risk-aversion effect and the wealth effect. Though, in principle, the wealth effect could dominate the risk-aversion effect, Lambert et al. (1991) find that, for most plausible incentive schemes, managers are likely to remain averse to firm risk.

Unlike the wealth effect, which can be estimated with option pricing techniques and readily available data about managers' stock options and common stockholdings, a measure of the risk-aversion effect requires manager-specific data that is much more difficult, if not impossible, to obtain. For example, the risk-aversion effect is expected to be a function of a manager's total wealth, the degree of diversification in a manager's portfolio of wealth, and a manager's utility function. Given these measurement problems, this study focuses primarily on developing

a better understanding of the magnitude and cross-sectional variation in the wealth effect.[2] However, I do not ignore the risk-aversion effect in the empirical tests. Since securities that induce convexity in the wealth-performance relation, such as stock options and common stock, are also likely to influence managers' aversion toward firm risk, the wealth effect and risk-aversion effect are expected to be correlated. Section 5 addresses the implications of this correlation and how the research design is structured to control for these effects.

3. DATA AND DESCRIPTIVE STATISTICS

I compile compensation and stock-based wealth data for 278 corporate CEOs as of December 31, 1993. To obtain the sample, I first rank the largest 1000 firms included in the Compustat database by market value as of December 31, 1988. By allowing a five-year period between the ranking date and the compensation measurement period, I reduce the potential bias of including only successful firms in the sample, and increase the probability of finding cross-sectional variation in the firms' financial characteristics. However, because firms are required to have survived from 1988 until 1993, a survival bias could be present, as some firms are likely to have been eliminated due to bankruptcy or being acquired. From this initial sample, 500 firms are chosen for inclusion in the final sample using a uniform selection method where every other firm is selected.

I delete firms without a December-end fiscal year from the sample. Firms are also removed if data are not available from the Center for Research in Security Prices (CRSP) or Compustat. These selection criteria result in a sample of 315 firms. For 20 of these firms, either the time series of proxy statements is incomplete, or sufficient proxy data are not available to construct the CEO's option portfolio. To check for errors in the procedure used to construct option portfolios, I compute the cash value each CEO would obtain if all options in the constructed portfolios were exercised on December 31, 1993, and compare this amount to the cash value of the CEOs' options if exercised immediately. This cash value disclosure is required for all named executive officers. CEOs are excluded from the sample if these two cash value measures differ by more than 25% and $200,000, resulting in the removal of 14 CEOs. Finally, CEOs are excluded if they own more than one-third of their corporation's common stock, since it is doubtful that these managers' compensation schemes are designed for contracting purposes. This criteria reduces the sample by three CEOs. The results are not sensitive to using a lower ownership threshold, such as five or ten percent stockholdings. The final sample contains 278 CEOs.

3.1. Summary of compensation and stock-based wealth data

For each CEO, I compile data on common stock, restricted stock, and outstanding stock options held as of December 31, 1993, as well as salary and bonus received during 1993. With the exception of the composition of the CEOs' option portfolios, this data is readily available from the firms' 1993 proxy statements. To reduce the influence of a few CEOs that hold extremely large quantities of common stock, the uppermost percentile of aggregate stockholdings and sensitivities of these stockholdings to stock price and equity risk are set equal to the stockholdings and sensitivities of the CEOs at the 99th percentiles.

I construct the CEO's option portfolios using the past time-series of proxy statements. For each CEO, I collect data on the number of options granted in each fiscal period, the average exercise price per option granted, and the actual or maximum allowable time-to-maturity for the options granted. In approximately 5% of the fiscal periods, it was necessary to average option grants over a multi-year period. Beginning in 1992, proxy statements report the total number of stock options held by each named executive officer. I use the number of options held at the end of 1993,

combined with the time series of options granted, to construct an estimate of the composition of each CEO's option portfolio as of December 31, 1993. Detailed information on option exercises is not readily available from proxy statements prior to 1992. I assume that, unless otherwise noted, options with the shortest remaining time-to-maturity are exercised first. Since this exercise strategy is expected to simulate the true exercise strategies with error, it is important to remove CEOs with constructed option portfolios that differ significantly from the option portfolio characteristics disclosed in the 1993 proxy statements, as described in Section 3.

Table 15.1 indicates that common stock and options are significant components of CEOs' incentive schemes. Using the Black and Scholes (1973) model, the median stock option portfolio has a value of $1.78 million. Furthermore, the substantial standard deviation and interquartile range (not reported) suggest there is considerable variation in the extent to which firms use options to provide managers with incentives. The median value of CEOs' common stock-holdings is $2.74 million, which is about 50% larger than the median value of option holdings. Though restricted stock is held by less than half of the CEOs, nearly 25% of the CEOs hold restricted stock valued at $1 million or more. The median value of total stock-based wealth, including stock options, common stockholdings, and restricted stock, is $6.79 million, and several times larger than the median annual cash compensation of $866,700.

4. ESTIMATING CONVEXITY IN THE WEALTH–PERFORMANCE RELATION

As discussed above, the focus of this study is not on the slope of CEOs' wealth–performance relation, but instead on the convexity of this relation. I measure the convexity contributed by a stock option or share of common stock as the change in the security's value for a 0.01 change in the annualized standard deviation of stock

Table 15.1 Summary statistics for CEOs' stock option portfolios, common stockholdings, and cash compensation

The sample consists of 278 CEOs selected uniformly from the 1000 largest firms on Compustat, ranked by market value of equity on December 31, 1988. The CEOs' salary and bonus are for the fiscal year ending December 31, 1993. The number of options held by the CEOs and their stock-based wealth are as of December 31, 1993. Option values are based on the Black-Scholes formula for valuing European call options, as modified to account for dividend payouts by Merton (1973). Option value is calculated as $[Se^{-dT}N(Z) - Xe^{-rT}N(Z - \sigma T^{(1/2)})]$, where Z is equal to $[\ln(S/X) + T(r - d + \sigma/2)]/\sigma T^{(1/2)}$. The parameters in the Black-Scholes model are set as follows: S = price of the underlying stock at December 31st, 1993, E = exercise price of the option, σ = annualized volatility, estimated as standard deviation of daily logarithmic stock returns over the last 120 trading days in 1993, multiplied by $252^{(1/2)}$, $r = \ln(1 + \text{risk-free interest rate})$, where the risk-free interest rate is the yield, as of December 31, 1993, on a U.S. Treasury strip with the same time to maturity as the remaining life of the stock option, T = remaining time to maturity of the option in years, as of December 31, 1993, and $d = \ln(1 + \text{expected dividend rate})$, where the expected dividend rate is set equal to the dividends paid during 1993 divided by the year-end stock price. Total stock-based wealth is the sum of the value of the CEO's options, stockholdings, and restricted stock.

Compensation component (in $ millions)	Mean	Standard deviation	Minimum	Median	Maximum
Salary + bonus	1.10	0.93	0.00	0.87	8.87
Number of options held (000s)	257.89	329.69	0.00	170.55	2500.00
Value of option portfolio	4.23	6.83	0.00	1.78	42.53
Value of common stockholdings	24.23	88.75	0.00	2.74	600.90
Value of restricted stock	0.97	2.46	0.00	0.00	25.17
Total stock-based wealth	29.43	89.80	0.04	6.79	600.90

returns. The contribution of stock options and common stock to the convexity in the wealth-performance relation can vary widely across CEOs, and is a function of firms' financial characteristics, the quantities of each security held, and the specific parameters that underlie the stock-based components, such as the exercise prices and times to maturity of the options in a manager's portfolio.

I estimate the incentive effects of employee stock options using the Black-Scholes formula for valuing European call options, as modified to account for dividend payouts by Merton (1973). The details of this procedure are presented in Section A.1 of the appendix. Huddart (1994) and Cuny and Jorion (1995) point out that the optimal exercise policy is likely to deviate from the assumptions underlying the Black-Scholes framework, due to managers' risk-aversion and the non-transferability of employee stock options.[3] However, adjusting the Black-Scholes model to

accommodate these differences is not straightforward. First, there is no clear method of determining the value of an employee stock option from the employee's perspective, as opposed to the firm's perspective. Second, since there is considerable variation in the remaining time-to-maturity for the options held by the CEOs, it is difficult to estimate the expected time until these options will be exercised.

I estimate the sensitivity of an option portfolio's value to equity risk as follows. First, for each option in a CEO's portfolio, I compute the Black-Scholes partial derivative of option value with respect to a 0.01 change in the annualized standard deviation of stock returns. Next, the partial derivatives are weighted by the number of options in the portfolio. The procedure and parameters used to compute the Black-Scholes partial derivatives are described in Section A.1. of the appendix.

To check the sensitivity of the reported results to alternative option valuation techniques, all tests are reproduced using the methods suggested in Hemmer et al. (1994) and in Statement of Financial Accounting Standards No. 123, 'Accounting for stock-based compensation' (FASB, 1995). To implement the Hemmer et al. and FASB techniques, I assume that the expected time to exercise for all options held is equal to 60% of the remaining time-to-maturity, though the cross-sectional results are not sensitive to varying this percentage. With respect to the Hemmer et al. method, I also assume that all options have a three-year vesting period at the grant date. The option values and convexity measures using these procedures are generally about 10–25% lower than those using the Black-Scholes formula. However, all cross-sectional results are qualitatively unchanged.

As illustrated by Black and Scholes (1973) and Smith (1976), the payoff to a share of common stock in a levered firm can also be viewed as a call option, where the option's underlying asset is the value of the firm and the exercise price is the face value of the firm's liabilities. Unlike stock options, the Black-Scholes parameters for common stock are not all readily available. However, an estimate of the value of the option component is readily observable in the stock price. Knowledge of this option value reduces, by one, the number of Black–Scholes parameters that must be estimated. I estimate parameters for the exercise price, time to maturity, interest rate, dividend yield, and volatility of firm value as described in Section A.2. of the appendix. Firm value, the sum of market value of equity and market value of debt, and the underlying asset in this option pricing application, is left as the free parameter. Using the Black–Scholes model, I compute the implied per-share value of each sample firm. As reported in Table 15.6 of the appendix, the implied per-share firm values are slightly smaller than the sum of per-share book value of debt plus stock price for nearly all firms. This relation is not surprising given that the value of an option is strictly greater than the price of the underlying asset less the exercise price. The correlation between the implied firm value and the

sum of book debt plus market value of equity is 0.99.

Together with the other parameters, I use the implied firm value to estimate the Black–Scholes partial derivative of each firm's stock price with respect to volatility. Note that because common stock is an option on firm value, its value is sensitive to the volatility of firm value. In contrast, a stock option's value is sensitive to stock-return volatility. To make the two convexity measures comparable, I compute the change in common stock value with respect to a 0.01 change in the annualized standard deviation of stock-returns. Since firm value is the sum of debt value plus equity value, portfolio theory suggests that the volatility of firm value can be estimated using measures of debt volatility and equity volatility, and an assumption about the correlation between debt value and equity value. For simplicity, I set this correlation equal to one, though the results are not sensitive to this assumption. The sensitivity of common stock value to equity volatility is then estimated, at the margin, by holding debt volatility constant while stock-return volatility is allowed to vary by 0.01 (see Section A.2. for further details). Finally, I estimate the aggregate sensitivity of a CEO's common stock to equity risk as the partial derivative of stock price with respect to stock-return volatility, multiplied by the number of shares of stock held by the CEO.

To gain some insight for the source of convexity inherent in common stock, consider how the value of common stock varies as a function of firm value. In an unlevered firm, the payoff to common stock is a linear function of firm value, and the value of common stock increases by $1 for every $1 increase in firm value. For a levered firm, an increase in firm value will not accrue entirely to common stockholders, but will instead be shared between the debtholders and shareholders, assuming the probability of financial distress is greater than zero. Confirming this notion, a $1 change in firm value translates into a median change in common stock value of only $0.97, with $0.03 accruing to the firms' debtholders (see Table 15.6 in the appendix).

4.1. Descriptive statistics on convexity in the wealth–performance relation

Table 15.2 presents the characteristics of the stock option portfolios held by the CEOs in the sample. Panel A indicates that the characteristics of the CEOs' options vary considerably. For each CEO, I compute the mean price-to-strike ratio and mean time-to-maturity of the options in their portfolio. The price-to-strike ratio is the stock price divided by the option's exercise price. The mean price-to-strike ratio indicates, on average, the extent to which the CEO's options are in the money. The value of an option with a price-to-strike ratio much greater than one increases almost linearly with stock price, and as such, will be quite insensitive to changes in stock-return volatility. By comparison, an "at the money" option has a price-to-strike ratio of one, and will be more sensitive to equity risk. The mean price-to-strike ratio has a median value of 1.3, and ranges from about 0.4 to 9.0. The mean time-to-maturity is the number of years remaining to expiration, on average, for a CEO's options. The mean time-to-maturity has a median value of 7.2 years, and ranges from 1.5 to 16.5 years. This variation suggests that per-option incentive effects are expected to vary widely across CEOs.

Estimates of the sensitivity of CEOs' options and stock to equity risk are presented in Panel B of Table 15.2. In the first row, the sensitivity of option value to equity risk is averaged over the options in each CEO's portfolio. For the 228 CEOs with options, the median change in value, per option, for a 0.01 change in the standard deviation of stock returns is $0.156, and ranges from $0.001 to $0.748. The considerable variation in these per-share statistics indicates that the incentive effects of stock options are heavily dependent on security-specific parameters. Measures that ignore this variation are likely to estimate the incentive effects of these instruments with

considerable error. The median aggregate sensitivity of CEOs' wealth to equity risk due to options is $29,893. These sensitivities range from a minimum of $0 for the 50 CEOs that do not hold options, up to a maximum of $347,256 for the CEO holding the option portfolio most sensitive to equity risk.

The sensitivity of common stock to equity risk is much smaller than that of options. The median change in per-share stock price for a 0.01 change in stock-return volatility is $0.00005, compared to $0.156 per option. This result is not surprising, given that the median price-to-strike ratio for a share of common stock is 1.9, which is much larger than the price-to-strike ratio of most CEOs' stock options (see Table 15.6 of the appendix). Even when multiplied by the quantity of stock held, the total sensitivity of common stock value to equity risk is very small for most CEOs, with a median sensitivity of $2. As a result, for most firms, the aggregate sensitivity of CEOs' stock-based wealth to equity risk due to options plus stock is driven primarily by stock options. However, the sensitivity of stock value to equity risk is significant for a small number of CEOs. For approximately 3% of the CEOs, the change in stock value for a 0.01 change in stock-return volatility exceeds $25,000. Thus, while the sensitivity of stock value to equity risk can potentially provide managers with incentives to shift wealth from bond-holders, this effect is expected to be extremely isolated, and relevant only for firms experiencing severe financial distress.

To interpret the economic significance of these sensitivities, one must consider both the sensitivity of a CEO's wealth to equity risk and his ability to alter the risk of the firm. I estimate the latter component for each sample firm by first computing the difference between 1993 stock-return volatility and the 1990 volatility of a control sample obtained from the CRSP tapes, and matched on two-digit SIC code and market value of equity. Each sample firm is then assumed to experience a change in equity volatility that brings it in line with its industry and size-matched control portfolio.

Table 15.2 The sensitivity of CEOs' wealth to equity risk and stock price

The data consist of option portfolios and common stockholdings for 278 CEOs selected uniformly from the 1000 largest firms on Compustat, ranked by market value of equity on December 31, 1988. Price-to-strike ratio is the December 1993 stock price divided by the exercise price of an option. The mean price-to-strike ratio is the simple average of the price-to-strike ratios for all options in a CEO's option portfolio. Time-to-maturity is the remaining time to expiration for an option as of December 31, 1993. The mean time-to-maturity is the simple average of the time-to-maturity for all options in a CEO's option portfolio. Sensitivity of wealth to equity risk due to options and stock is the change in the dividend-adjusted Black–Scholes value of a CEO's stock option portfolio and common stockholdings for a 0.01 change in the annualized standard deviation of the firm's stock returns (see the appendix). The average sensitivity of an option's value to equity risk is the sensitivity of wealth to equity risk averaged over all options in a CEO's option portfolio. Total sensitivity of wealth to equity risk aggregates the per option and per-share sensitivities weighted by the number of securities held. Sensitivity of wealth to a 1% change in stock price is the change in the dividend-adjusted Black–Scholes value of stock options or common stockholdings for a 1% change in the value of the firm's stock price (see the appendix). The average sensitivity of an option's value for a 1% change in stock price is the sensitivity of wealth to stock price averaged over all options in a CEO's option portfolio.

Option portfolio characteristic	Mean	Standard deviation	Minimum	Q1	Median	Q3	Maximum
Panel A:							
Mean price-to-strike ratio[a]	1.50	0.86	0.38	1.07	1.30	1.67	9.00
Mean time-to-maturity per option[a]	7.18	1.68	1.50	6.25	7.23	8.17	16.53
Panel B:							
Average sensitivity of an option's value to equity risk ($)[a]	0.167	0.105	0.001	0.097	0.156	0.212	0.748
Total sensitivity of wealth to equity risk: options ($)[a]	45,967	51,641	82	14,108	29,893	56,590	347,256
Total sensitivity of wealth to equity risk: options – all CEOs ($)	37,700	49,982	0	4614	20,915	48,164	347,256
Per-share sensitivity of stock price to equity risk: ($)	0.005	0.016	0.000	0.000	0.000	0.002	0.225
Total sensitivity of wealth to equity risk: stock ($)	2857	12,654	0	0	2	240	98,232
Total sensitivity of wealth to equity risk: stock + options ($)	40,557	50,777	0	6489	22,664	55,770	347,292
Panel C:							
Average sensitivity of an option's value to a 1% change in stock price ($)[a]	0.272	0.173	0.006	0.147	0.231	0.366	1.160
Per-share sensitivity of stock price to a 1% change in stock price: options ($)	0.393	0.247	0.029	0.248	0.336	0.490	2.548
Total sensitivity of wealth to a 1% change in stock price: options ($)	72,169	104,844	0	3997	36,407	96,250	687,350
Total sensitivity of wealth to a 1% change in stock price: stock ($)	251,995	886,860	0	10,571	37,307	108,341	6,008,957
Total sensitivity of wealth to a 1% change in stock price: stock + options ($)	324,164	904,534	353	38,784	90,685	222,387	6,300,594

a Excludes 50 CEOs that do not hold stock options.

The mean change in CEOs' stock-based wealth from this change in volatility would be $324,000, with a standard deviation of $562,000. This mean change in wealth is about 20% larger, at $391,000, when considering only CEOs with option portfolios. The magnitude of these wealth effects suggests that the convexity generated by stock options is potentially large enough to influence managers' behavior.

The maintained hypothesis in this paper is that firms add convexity to a manager's incentive scheme to encourage investment in valuable risk-increasing projects, that is, to help overcome the risk-aversion effect. However, note that even in the absence of convexity in the wealth–performance relation, managers have incentives to undertake positive NPV projects when the slope of the wealth–performance relation is greater than zero. Therefore, it is difficult to precisely determine how much convexity, at the margin, is necessary to induce managers to invest in risk-increasing, positive NPV projects.

To illustrate the differences between the slope and convexity of the wealth–performance relation, Panel C of Table 15.2 reports descriptive statistics on the sensitivity of CEOs' wealth to stock price. On average, a stock option changes in value by $0.27 for a 1% change in stock price, compared to $0.39 for a share of common stock. Thus, in contrast to the convexity induced by each of these securities, a share of stock increases the slope of the wealth–performance relation by about 40% more than a stock option does, on average. On an aggregate basis, both stock options and common stock make a substantial contribution to the wealth–performance slope. The median change in option portfolio value for a 1% change in stock price is $36,400, compared to a median change of $37,300 for common stockholdings.

5. CONVEXITY AND THE INVESTMENT OPPORTUNITY SET

As illustrated in Section 2, risk-related agency problems can cause managers to pass up risky, positive NPV projects. This problem is likely to be most severe in firms with substantial investment opportunities (see Milgrom and Roberts, 1992, Chapter 13, for a discussion of potential risk-related agency costs in firms with valuable growth opportunities).[4] As such, the expected loss from valuable projects bypassed by managers is hypothesized to be positively related to the proportion of assets that represent growth options. By providing managers with incentive schemes that have convex payoffs, equity holders can reduce these risk-related agency costs. The following hypothesis follows directly: Convexity in the relation between managers' wealth and stock price is positively related to the proportion of assets that are growth options.

I use three proxies to capture variation in firms' investment opportunities. These are: (i) the book-to-market ratio, (ii) expenditures on research and development, scaled by market value of assets, and (iii) a measure of investment expenditures defined as the sum of capital expenditures plus acquisitions over the most recent three years, divided by market value of assets. Though these variables are expected to contain information about investment opportunities, each has unique limitations as a measure of this unobservable underlying construct. Therefore, as in Baber et al. (1996) and Gaver and Gaver (1993), I employ common factor analysis to construct a single variable that captures variation common to these observable proxies. Separate results are presented using the common factor as an alternative to the above three proxies.

Table 15.3 summarizes the proxies for investment opportunities and the financial characteristics of the 278 sample firms. In general, the sample firms are large, with median market value of assets equal to $5.4 billion. The range in values for book-to-market, R&D, and investment expenditures is quite large, suggesting that there is considerable variation in investment opportunities across the sample firms. The factor score for investment opportunities has a mean of zero, by construction, and varies from −0.85 to 2.27.

Table 15.3 Summary firm characteristics

The sample consists of 278 CEOs selected uniformly from the 1000 largest firms on Compustat, ranked by market value of equity on December 31, 1988. All financial variables are computed for fiscal year ending December 31, 1993. Book-to-market ratio is the book value of assets divided by the sum of book value of liabilities and market value of equity. R&D expenditures is R&D expense divided by the market value of assets (in %). Investment expenditures is the sum of capital expenditures plus acquisitions over the period 1991 through 1993, divided by market value of assets. Factor score is obtained using common factor analysis on the variables Book-to-market, R&D expenditures, and Investment expenditures. Market value of assets is book value of debt plus market value of equity. Leverage is calculated as [(book value of assets − book value of equity)/ market value of equity].

Firm characteristics	Mean	Standard deviation	Minimum	Median	Maximum
Book-to-market ratio	0.74	0.21	0.24	0.78	1.20
R&D expenditures	0.80	1.78	0.00	0.00	13.80
Investment expenditures	0.13	0.10	−0.01	0.12	0.71
Factor score (investment opportunities)	0.00	0.54	−0.85	−0.05	2.27
Market value of assets($billion)	16.59	34.15	0.20	5.42	315.21
Leverage	2.74	4.13	0.06	1.10	34.28

5.1. Empirical results: convexity and the investment opportunity set

To explore the relation between convexity and the investment opportunity set, I regress the sensitivity of CEOs' wealth to equity risk on the proxies for growth options described in the previous section. I use two alternative measures of the sensitivity of CEOs' wealth to equity risk: (i) the sensitivity of CEOs' option portfolios to equity risk, and (ii) the combined sensitivity of stock options and common stockholdings to equity risk.

Though stock options and common stockholdings add convexity to the relation between managers' wealth and stock price, both securities also increase the slope of this relation. Smith and Watts (1992) argue that because the management of investment opportunities is difficult to monitor, firms with greater investment opportunities are expected to tie managers' wealth more closely to firm performance.[5] To control for a relation between the wealth– performance slope and investment opportunities, the

sensitivity of CEOs' wealth to stock price is included in all regressions. The market value of assets is also included in the regressions to control for a relation between firm size and both the probability of having a formal incentive compensation plan, such as a stock option plan, and the level of compensation (see Smith and Watts, 1992; Gaver and Gaver, 1993). All *t*-statistics are calculated using heteroskedasticity-consistent standard errors.

The regression results are reported in Table 15.4. The negative coefficient on book-to-market and positive coefficients on R&D and investment expenditures are consistent with the hypothesis that the investment opportunity set is positively related to convexity in the relation between CEOs' wealth and stock price. In Columns (2) and (5), book-to-market ratio, R&D expenditures, and investment expenditures are replaced with the factor variable that captures variation common to these observable proxies for investment opportunities. In both columns, the coefficient on this factor is positive and significant at the 1% level.

Table 15.4 The relation between investment opportunities and the sensitivity of CEOs' wealth to equity risk

Sensitivity of wealth to equity risk $= a + b_1$(Book-to-market) $+ b_2$(R&D) $+ b_3$(Investment expenditures) $+ c_1$ Log(market value of assets) $+ c_2$(Sensitivity of wealth to stock price) $+ c_3$(Cash compensation) $+ c_4$ Log(sensitivity of wealth to stock price) $+ c_5$ Age $+$ error.

All variables are measured as of December 31, 1993. Sensitivity of wealth to equity risk from options is the change in the dividend-adjusted Black-Scholes value of a CEO's stock option portfolio for a 0.01 change in the annualized standard deviation of the firm's stock returns (in $ thousands). Sensitivity of wealth to equity risk from options and stock is the change in the dividend-adjusted Black-Scholes value of a CEO's stock option portfolio and common stockholdings for a 0.01 change in the annualized standard deviation of the firm's stock returns (in %). Book-to-market ratio is (book value of assets/market vlaue of assets). R&D expenditures is R&D expense divided by market value of assets (in %). Investment expenditures is the sum of capital expenditures plus acquisitions over the period 1991 through 1993, divided by market value of assets at December 31, 1993. Factor score is obtained using common factor analysis on the variables Book-to-market ratio, R&D expenditures, and Investment expenditures. Log[market value of assets] is the natural logarithm of [book value of liabilities + market value of equity]. Sensitivity of wealth to stock price is the change in the dividend-adjusted Black-Scholes value of a CEO's stock option portfolio and common stockholdings for a 1% change in the value of the firm's stock price (in $ thousands). Cash compensation is the sum of salary plus cash bonus for 1993 (in $ millions). Age is the CEO's age in years. T-statistics in parentheses are computed using White's heteroskedasticity-consistent standard errors.

	Predicted sign	Sensitivity of wealth to equity risk: options (000's)			Sensitivity of wealth to equity risk: options & stock (000's)		
		(1)	(2)	(3)	(4)	(5)	(6)
Intercept	(?)	-82.62 (-3.67)	-112.37 (-5.18)	$-71.05^a(-2.03)$	$-77.29^a(-3.40)$	$-103.04^a(-4.64)$	$-80.80^a(-2.28)$
Book-to-market ratio	$(-)$	$-63.72^a(-4.61)$			$-55.79^a(-3.76)$		
R&D expenditures	$(+)$	$3.10^a(2.44)$			$3.29^a(2.51)$		
Investment expenditures	$(+)$	$48.29\ (1.63)$			$46.81\ (1.54)$		
Factor score (investment opportunities)	$(+)$		$27.76^a(5.32)$	$19.46^a(3.96)$		$26.44^a(4.92)$	$17.12^a(3.44)$
log(market value of assets)	$(+)$	$18.19^a(6.59)$	$17.13^a(6.44)$	$11.00^a(3.54)$	$17.10^a(6.01)$	$16.26^a(6.01)$	$9.61^a(3.08)$
Sensitivity of wealth to stock price	$(+)$	$-0.00\ (-0.02)$	$0.00\ (0.18)$	$-0.01^a(-2.08)$	$0.00\ (0.74)$	$0.00\ (0.85)$	$-0.01^b(-1.70)$
Cash compensation	$(\pm)$			$7.06\ (1.48)$			$6.71\ (1.44)$
Log (sensitivity of wealth to stock price)	$(+)$			$10.96^a(6.11)$			$12.79^a(6.84)$
Age	$(\pm)$			$-0.70\ (-1.57)$			$-0.41\ (-0.87)$
Adjusted R^2		22.47	20.76	31.77	20.12	19.25	32.59

a Statistical significance at the 5% level.
b Statistical significance at the 10% level.

To interpret the magnitude of the factor score coefficient, consider two CEOs with factor scores that differ by the standard deviation of the sample firms' factor scores. The coefficient on the factor score in Column (5) implies that the compensation schemes for these two CEOs are expected to be set so that a ten percentage point rise in stock-return volatility increases the stock-based wealth of the CEO managing the high growth options firm by about $143,000 more than the CEO managing the low growth option firm.

As noted in Section 2, the sensitivity of CEOs' wealth to equity risk, or the wealth effect, is expected to measure the impact of risk on managers' utility with error. Missing from this estimate is the risk-aversion effect, or the reduction in utility that risk-averse, poorly diversified managers experience when the volatility of their wealth increases. To examine whether this omitted variable is influencing the results, I include proxies for the risk-aversion effect in the regressions.

The dollar value of 1993 cash compensation, salary plus bonus, is included to control for the level of CEOs' outside wealth. The greater the cash compensation that can be invested outside the firm, the better diversified the CEO is likely to be, and the lower the expected risk-aversion effect. CEO age is included to control for manager-specific variation in diversification of wealth and degree of risk-aversion. The results are robust to the following alternative treatments of the age variable: (i) including dummy variables for various age categories, (ii) interacting age with the other independent variables, and (iii) re-estimating the regressions on subsamples of the CEOs formed by age. The signs of the coefficients on cash compensation and age are difficult to predict since it is unclear how the wealth and risk-aversion effects are likely to be correlated for these variables. The log of the sensitivity of CEOs' wealth to stock price is also added as a proxy for the CEOs' degree of diversification. The more sensitive the CEO's wealth is to firm performance, the less well-diversified the CEO is likely to be, and

the greater the expected risk-aversion effect. Though logarithm is the reported functional form of this variable, the regressions are not sensitive to using other concave functional forms, such as the square root. Since the same stock-based securities drive both the sensitivity of CEOs' wealth to equity risk and to equity value, a positive coefficient is predicted.

When these variables are included, as shown in Columns (3) and (6), the coefficient on log[sensitivity of wealth to stock price] is significantly positive, indicating that securities that increase the risk-aversion effect also increase the wealth effect. However, the coefficient on the investment opportunities factor remains significantly positive in both columns, providing further support for the hypothesis that firms provide managers with incentives to invest in risky projects when the potential loss from underinvestment in valuable risk-increasing projects is greatest.

Yermack (1995) concludes that investment opportunities are not an important determinant for grants of CEO stock options. However, the sensitivity of wealth to stock price is used as the dependent variable in his tests. The results in Table 15.4 suggest that firms are expected to consider the sensitivity of wealth to equity risk, in addition to sensitivity of wealth to stock price, when granting stock options.

5.2. Specification checks

Corporate hedging theory identifies circumstances where firm value can be increased through reductions in risk (e.g., Myers, 1977; Smith and Stulz, 1985; Smith and Mayers, 1987, 1990; Froot et al., 1993). All else being equal, firms with strong incentives to hedge are expected to provide managers with weaker incentives to increase firm risk. To examine the sensitivity of the reported results to these factors, I include measures of financial leverage, operating performance, cash flow volatility, and tax-loss-carryforwards in the Table 15.4 regressions as proxies for firms' incentives to hedge. The coefficients and significance levels on the growth option variables (not reported) are qualitatively similar to those reported previously. The coefficient on leverage is in the predicted direction, negative, and is significantly different from zero. The coefficients on the other hedging variables are not significantly different from zero.[6]

Yermack (1995) and Dechow et al. (1996) hypothesize that liquidity constraints can induce firms to use stock options in lieu of cash compensation. If firms with substantial growth options tend to be cash constrained, the inferences drawn in this section could be spurious. The results reported in Table 15.4 are robust to including free cash flow, measured as cash flow from operations less capital expenditures, and financial leverage, as proxies for cash constraints.

The preceding analysis focuses exclusively on the convexity of payoffs in CEOs' stock-based wealth. However, it is possible that firms make adjustments to other forms of compensation, such as salary and bonuses, to offset changes in stock-based wealth that CEOs' experience when equity risk changes. To explore this possibility, I examine the relation between changes in the CEOs' salary and bonuses from 1993 to 1994, and both changes in firms' stock-return volatility and estimates of realized changes in CEOs' stock-based wealth due to changes in equity risk. To estimate the CEOs' realized change in stock-based wealth due to equity risk, the sensitivity of the CEOs' wealth to equity risk at December 31, 1993, is multiplied by the change in stock-return volatility from 1993 to 1994. The change in stock-return volatility is computed as the standard deviation of daily stock returns over the last 120 trading days in 1994 minus the standard deviation of stock returns over the last 120 trading days in 1993. Note that this method measures the true changes in wealth during 1994 with error due to new grants/exercises of options, changes in stockholdings, and changes in the Black/Scholes parameters used to estimate the 1993 sensitivities. I find no significant correlations between these variables.

6. THE RELATION BETWEEN STOCK-RETURN VOLATILITY AND THE SENSITIVITY OF CEOS' WEALTH TO EQUITY RISK

The analysis in Section 2 suggests that managers are more willing to invest in risk-increasing projects as the convexity of payoffs in the relation between their wealth and stock price increases. This relation between convexity and investment choice also underlies the hypothesis tested in Section 5, that the sensitivity of CEOs' wealth to equity risk is directly related to firms' investment opportunities. Therefore, it is of interest to examine whether firms' stock-return volatility, as a measure of the riskiness of a firm's projects, is positively related to the sensitivity of managers' wealth to equity risk.

To explore the relation between equity risk and the convexity of payoffs to managers, I regress contemporaneous stock-return volatility on the sensitivity of CEOs' wealth to equity risk.[7] The dependent variable, stock-return volatility, is computed over 240 trading days, from 120 days before through 120 days after the compensation measurement date of December 31, 1993. The results are not sensitive to alternatively measuring volatility over 120 or 240-day periods starting at the compensation measurement date. To control for other determinants of equity risk, the log of market value of assets and financial leverage are included in all regressions. All t-statistics are calculated using heteroskedasticity-consistent standard errors.

Column (1) of Table 15.5 indicates that firms' stock-return volatility is positively related to the sensitivity of CEOs' wealth to equity risk. However, given the findings in Table 15.4, and the likelihood of a positive correlation between investment opportunities and equity risk, there is a concern that these inferences are spurious. When the factor score for investment opportunities is added to the regression, the coefficient on the sensitivity of wealth to equity risk is about 25% lower, but remains significantly

Table 15.5 The relation between stock-return volatility and the sensitivity of CEOs' wealth to equity risk

$$\text{Stock-return volatility} = a + b_1(\text{Sensitivity of wealth to equity risk})$$
$$+ c_1(\text{market value of assets}) + c_2(\text{Leverage})$$
$$+ c_3(\text{Factor score for investment opportunities}) + \text{error.}$$

Stock-return volatility is the annualized standard deviation of daily logarithmic stock returns (in %) over 240 trading days, starting with the last 120 trading days in 1993 and ending with the first 120 trading days in 1994, multiplied by $252^{(1/2)}$. Sensitivity of wealth to equity risk from options and stock is the change in the dividend-adjusted Black-Scholes value of a CEO's stock option portfolio and common stockholdings (in $ thousands) for a 0.01 change in the annualized standard deviation of the firm's stock returns. Adjusted sensitivity of wealth to equity risk due to options and stock removes the influence of firm-specific stock-return volatility by using the sample mean standard deviation of stock returns in all Black-Scholes computations, instead of using the equity risk specific to each firm. Log[market value of assets] is the natural logarithm of [book value of liabilities + market value of equity] at December-end 1993. Leverage is [(Book value of assets − book value of equity)/market value of equity]. Factor score is obtained using common factor analysis on the variables Book-to-market ratio, R&D expenditures, and Investment expenditures as described in Section 5.

| | Annualized standard deviation of stock returns (%) | | | |
	(1)	(2)	(3)	(4)
Intercept	55.37[a]	51.84[a]	53.91[a]	50.07[a]
	(10.47)	(10.97)	(9.68)	(10.21)
Sensitivity of wealth to equity risk:	0.047[a]	0.035[a]		
options + stock	(4.69)	(3.90)		
Adjusted sensitivity of wealth to equity risk:			0.026[a]	0.016[b]
options + stock			(2.97)	(1.88)
Control variables:				
log(market value of assets)	−3.85[a]	−3.51[a]	−3.57[a]	−3.21[a]
	(−6.03)	(−6.20)	(−5.33)	(−5.41)
Leverage	0.67[a]	1.04[a]	0.62[a]	1.02[a]
	(3.83)	(4.53)	(3.44)	(4.31)
Factor score: investment opportunities		6.20[a]		6.63[a]
		(5.12)		(5.28)
Adjusted R^2	19.63	27.88	15.91	25.48

T-statistics are in parentheses and are computed using White's heteroskedasticity-consistent standard errors.
a Statistical significance at the 5% level.
b Statistical significance at the 10% level.

positive. The regression results are robust to including the book-to-market ratio, R&D expenditures, and investment expenditures in place of the factor score as proxies for investment opportunities.

Since the standard deviation of stock returns is an input in the Black-Scholes model, it is possible that the regression coefficients are influenced by a mechanical relation between stock-return volatility and the Black-Scholes partial derivatives used to estimate the sensitivity of CEOs' wealth to equity risk. To address this concern, I recompute all Black–Scholes partial derivatives using the sample mean standard deviation of stock returns, instead of the volatility specific to each firm. Though this adjusted measure of sensitivity of wealth to equity risk is not expected to fully reflect the incentive effects of managers' compensation schemes, it is free from a mechanical relation with firm-specific stock- return volatility. As indicated in Columns (3) and (4) of Table 15.5, the coefficients on this adjusted measure of convexity are about 50% smaller than in the previous regressions. However, they remain significantly positive.

These findings support the hypothesis that firms' stock-return volatility is positively related to the convexity of payoffs in managers' incentive schemes. The coefficient on the sensitivity of CEOs' wealth to equity risk in Column (2) of Table 15.5 indicates that a difference of one sample standard deviation in the sensitivities of two CEOs' wealth to equity risk is expected to be associated with a two percentage point difference in the annualized standard deviation of their firms' stock returns. For a firm with the sample median standard deviation of stock returns, this difference amounts to nearly 10% of the firm's equity risk.

7. CONCLUSION

The determinants of executive compensation practices, and in particular the relation between managers' wealth and firm performance, is a topic of importance to both academics and practitioners. Though the slope of this relation has been examined in considerable detail, no study has quantified or explored the determinants of curvature, or convexity, in this relation. I argue that to effectively control agency conflicts between stockholders and managers, shareholders are expected to manage the convexity, in addition to the slope, of the relation between firm performance and managers' wealth. Since convexity in an incentive scheme generates a positive relation between a manager's wealth and firm risk, compensation components with convex payoffs, such as stock options and common stock, can induce risk-averse managers to invest in valuable risk-increasing projects that they may otherwise forgo.

My evidence indicates that the convexity of payoffs in managers' stock-based wealth

is potentially large enough to influence investing behavior. In a sample of 278 corporate CEOs, I find stock options play an economically significant role in increasing the convexity of the relation between managers' wealth and stock price. The magnitude of the convexity provided by common stock is much lower than that of stock options, and of little economic importance for most CEOs in the sample.

In cross-sectional tests, after controlling for the slope of the wealth-performance relation, convexity is positively related to proxies for the importance of growth options in firms' assets. This finding supports the hypothesis that firms provide managers with incentives to invest in risky projects when the potential loss from underinvestment in valuable risk-increasing projects is greatest. Finally, consistent with managers making investment and financing decisions in accordance with their risk-taking incentives, I find that firms' equity risk is positively related to the convexity provided to CEOs.

This study makes two important contributions to the literature. First, I emphasize that the incentive effects of stock-based compensation encompass more than simply encouraging managers to increase stock price. Specifically, I consider firms' use of stock-based compensation to manage the sensitivity of managers' wealth to firm risk, and find evidence consistent with firms using stock options to control risk-related agency problems. Second, I stress the importance of considering an executive's complete portfolio of stock options and common stock when analyzing firms' compensation practices. Yermack (1995) observes that the absence of complete data on managers' option portfolios can hinder researchers' ability to find a strong link between extant agency and financial contracting theory, and firms' use of stock options. Since managers' incentives derive from both newly awarded and previously issued options and stock, firms are expected to consider the incentive effects of outstanding options and stock when choosing the size and characteristics of the current year's options grant.

APPENDIX A

A.1. Estimating the sensitivity of stock option portfolios to stock-return volatility

Estimates of the sensitivity of stock options and common stock to equity risk at December 31, 1993, are based on the Black-Scholes formula for valuing European call options, as modified to account for dividend payouts by Merton (1973), as follows:

$$\text{Option value} = [Se^{-dT}N(Z) - Xe^{-rT}N(Z - \sigma T^{(1/2)})],$$

where

Z is the $[\ln(S/X) + T(r - d + \sigma^2/2)]/\sigma T^{(1/2)}$, N the cumulative probability function for the normal distribution, S the price of the underlying stock, X the exercise price of the option, σ the expected stock-return volatility over the life of the option, r the risk-free interest rate, T the time to maturity of the option in years, and d the expected dividend rate over the life of the option.

The partial derivative with respect to stock-return volatility is defined as

$$\partial(\text{option value})/\partial(\text{stock volatility}) = e^{-dT}N'(Z)ST^{(1/2)},$$

where N' is the normal density function.

The parameters of the Black–Scholes model are estimated for stock options as follows:

S = price of the underlying stock on December 31, 1993.

X = exercise price of the option. The exercise price could not be obtained for approximately 2% of the options. For these options, the exercise price is set equal to the simple average of the stock prices prevailing at the beginning and end of the year in which the option was granted.

σ = annualized volatility, estimated as the standard deviation of daily logarithmic stock returns over the last 120 trading days in 1993, multiplied by $252^{(1/2)}$. There were 252 trading days in 1993.

r = $\ln(1 + \text{risk-free interest rate})$, where the risk-free interest rate is the yield, on December 31, 1993, on a U.S. Treasury strip with the same time to maturity as the remaining life of the stock option.

T = remaining time to maturity of the option, in years, as of December 31, 1993. I use the grant date and duration of the option when granted to compute the remaining time to maturity. If the grant date is unavailable, I set it equal to July 1st in the year the option is issued. If the duration of the option is not specified, I set it equal to ten years at the grant date, since over 90% of newly issued options in the sample have a ten-year duration.

d = $\ln(1 + \text{expected dividend rate})$, where the expected dividend rate is the per-share dividends paid during 1993 divided by the year-end stock price.

A.2. Estimating the sensitivity of common stock value to stock-return volatility

I estimate the per-share sensitivity of common stock value to equity risk at December 31, 1993, in two steps: i) Compute the implied, per-share firm value using the Black–Scholes model. ii) Use the implied firm value to estimate the Black–Scholes partial derivative of stock price with respect to a 0.01 change in the annualized standard deviation of stock returns.[8]

Descriptive statistics for the parameters used to estimate the sensitivity of common stock to stock-return volatility appear in Table 15.6. These parameters are defined as follows:

Option value = per-share price of common stock

X = the per-share book value of debt, estimated as the book value of total liabilities divided by common shares outstanding.

Table 15.6 Description of parameters used in Black–Scholes computations for common stock

The sample consists of 278 CEOs selected uniformly from the 1000 largest firms on Compustat, ranked by market value of equity on December 31, 1988. All data are for 1993. Per-share stock price is the stock price on December 31. 1993. Per-share book value of debt is the book value of liabilities as of December 31, 1993. Per-share market value of assets is per-share stock price plus per-share book value of debt. Implied per-share market value of assets is computed using the Black–Scholes model (see Section A.2 of the appendix). The standard deviation of equity returns is the standard deviation of daily logarithmic stock returns over the last 120 trading days in 1993, multiplied by $252^{(1/2)}$. The standard deviation of debt is the standard deviation of monthly logarithmic returns on the Merrill Lynch corporate bond index that matches the firm's S&P senior debt rating, multiplied by $12^{(1/2)}$. The standard deviation of bond index returns is estimated over the five-year period ending December 1993. The standard deviation of equity and debt returns are used to compute the estimated standard deviation of returns on firm value (σ) (see Section A.2 of the appendix). The risk-free interest rate is the yield, as of December 31st, 1993, on a U.S. Treasury strip with the same time to maturity as the weighted average maturity of the firm's liabilities. The weighted average maturity of liabilities is estimated as described in Section A.2 of the appendix. Dividend yield is dividends per share paid during 1993, divided by the implied per-share market value of assets. Price-to-strike ratio is the implied per-share market value/per-share book value of debt. Sensitivity of stock price to a $1 change in firm value is the change in the dividend-adjusted Black-Scholes value of common stock for a $1 change in the value of the firm (see Section A.2 of the appendix).

Firm characteristics	Minimum	Median	Maximum
Per-share stock price ($)	2.88	33.56	254.75
Per-share book value of debt ($)	0.84	38.90	1632.73
Per-share market value of assets ($)	9.78	76.75	1680.35
Implied per-share market value of assets ($)	9.51	75.04	1617.96
Standard deviation of equity returns (%)	11.82	22.22	62.06
Standard deviation of debt returns (%)	3.48	4.15	12.24
Est. std. dev. of returns on firm value (%)	3.89	10.70	52.20
Risk-free interest rate (%)	3.22	4.33	5.57
Weighted average maturity of liabilities (yrs.)	0.50	2.57	7.60
Dividend yield (%)	0.00	1.11	5.06
Price-to-strike ratio	0.82	1.88	18.56
Sensitivity of stock price to a $1 change in firm value ($)	0.68	0.97	1.00

σ = annualized volatility of firm value, estimated as the annualized standard deviation of the rate of return on a portfolio that includes the firm's debt and equity. Portfolio theory implies that the variance of firm value is equal to $X^2_{debt}\, \sigma^2_{debt} + X^2_{equity}\, \sigma^2_{equity} + 2X_{debt}X_{equity}\, \text{Cov}\,(\sigma_{debt}\sigma_{equity})$. X_{debt} and X_{equity} are the weights on equity and debt in the firm's capital structure. σ_{equity} is estimated as the standard deviation of daily logarithmic stock returns over the last 120 trading days in 1993, multiplied by $252^{(1/2)}$. σ_{debt} is estimated as the standard deviation of monthly logarithmic returns on the Merrill Lynch corporate bond index that matches the firm's S&P senior debt rating, multiplied by $12^{(1/2)}$. The standard deviation of bond index returns is estimated over the five-year period ending December 1993. The correlation between equity and debt returns is set equal to one, which assumes that shocks to firm value affect equity and debt values similarly Though this assumption is not expected to hold empirically (e.g., the value of debt may be much more dependent upon interest rates than the value of equity), the results are not sensitive to varying this correlation.

T = the weighted average maturity of the firm's liabilities estimated using Compustat data on corporate liabilities maturing in less than 1 year, 2 years, 3 years, 4 years, 5 years, and more than five years. When the firm has outstanding debt with different times to maturity, common stock is technically a compound option. That is, when a portion of the debt matures, the stockholders have the option to pay off that portion of debt and purchase an option to buy the firm for the remaining book value of debt. To approximate the sensitivity of wealth to firm risk for this compound option, I make the simplifying assumption that the firm has a single debt obligation with time to maturity equal to the weighted average time to maturity of the firm's debt. I assume a maturity of ten years for the portion of debt maturing in more than five years. For most banks, utilities, and insurance firms, maturity data for years two and over is unavailable. I assume these firms have an average maturity on long-term debt of 7.5 years, though the results are not sensitive to alternative maturity assumptions.

r = $\ln(1 + \text{risk-free interest rate})$, where the risk-free interest rate is the yield, as of December 31, 1993, on a U.S. Treasury strip with the same time to maturity as the weighted average maturity of the firm's liabilities.

d = $\ln(1 + \text{expected dividend rate on firm value})$, where the expected dividend rate is set equal to dividends paid during 1993 divided by the implied market value of the firm. Note that the dividend rate on firm value is not known ex ante. It is obtained in step (i) when the implied total market value of the firm is computed.

NOTES

* I thank Ray Ball, Michael Barclay, John Core, Paul Fischer, Dan Gode, Jarrad Harford, Christian Leuz, Jon Lewellen, John Long, Wayne Mikkelson (the referee), Cathy Schrand, Clifford Smith, Philip Stocken, Jerry Warner, Ross Watts, Jerry Zimmerman, workshop participants at Baruch College, University of Chicago, Columbia University, Northwestern University, and The Wharton School, and especially S.P. Kothari for helpful comments. I gratefully acknowledge financial support from the American Compensation Association. Earlier drafts of this work were titled 'Compensation, Convexity, and the Incentives to Manage Risk'.

1 A 10 percentage point change represents the standard deviation of the sample firms' stock-return volatility, adjusted for industry and firm size. Stock-return volatility is measured as the annualized standard deviation of daily stock returns.

2 Ofek and Yermack (1997) provide evidence that managers can influence the magnitude of their own stock-based wealth and degree of diversification. This suggests a less important role for the risk-aversion effect. However, to the extent that convexity in managers' incentive schemes comes largely from non-portable employee stock options, managers are less likely to be able to influence the wealth effect.

3 Cuny and Jorion (1995) and Statement of Financial Accounting Standards No. 123, 'Accounting for stock-based compensation', address valuation issues resulting from vesting and portability restrictions. The difference between Cuny and Jorion's 'corrected' option value and Black/Scholes' value is smallest when options do not have vesting restrictions. Since most of the options valued in this study are not newly granted options, measurement error due to vesting issues is not likely to be a serious problem. Failure to consider portability restrictions is likely to lead to upward biased estimates of option values and convexity. However, it is much more difficult to determine how portability restrictions affect cross-sectional variation in option values and convexity.

4 Note that this risk-related agency problem is somewhat different than the well-known underinvestment problem described by Myers (1977). He demonstrates that when fixed claims are present in the capital structure, equity holders may forgo positive net-present-value projects if the gains accrue primarily to fixed claim holders. The risk-related agency problem described here does not require debt in the capital structure, but instead derives from risk-averse managers that are poorly diversified with respect to their firm-specific wealth.

5 Gaver and Gaver (1993) and Baber et al. (1996) provide further empirical support for this hypothesis. Yermack (1995) finds that the

investment opportunity set does not help in explaining the wealth-performance slope when examining new grants of stock options.

6   In addition to the determinants posited here, Jensen and Meckling (1976) explain how fixed claims in the capital structure can create incentives for equity holders to transfer wealth from bondholders by increasing the firm's risk. This incentive to shift wealth from bondholders may increase the desire of equity holders to motivate managers to invest in risky projects. However, this argument is only relevant ex-post with respect to the issuance of debt. Prior to issuing debt, equity holders, as the residual claimants, are expected to structure incentive schemes that discourage wealth transfer from fixed claim holders.

7   Theories of risk management hypothesize that the benefits from hedging are increasing in cashflow volatility. Therefore, other things equal, managers of firms with highly volatile cashflows are expected to be provided with weaker incentives to increase equity risk than managers' of firms with steady cashflows. Since cashflow volatility and stock-return volatility are positively correlated, the alignment of managers' incentives with optimal hedging strategies can induce a bias against finding the positive relation hypothesized between equity risk and the sensitivity of managers' wealth to equity risk. Though this issue clouds the interpretation of the results if the null hypothesis cannot be rejected, it does not create interpretive difficulties when the null hypothesis can be rejected.

8   In contrast to stock options, where the price of the underlying asset is allowed to vary freely above or below the exercise price during the option's life, the option value of common stock may be reduced by the existence of bond covenants that generally do not allow the value of the firm to drop below a certain point without triggering technical default and forced renegotiation. To incorporate this feature into the Black–Scholes computations requires detailed assumptions about the constraints placed upon equity holders by firms' creditors. Since there is no theoretical or empirical guidance in making these assumptions, I use the standard Black–Scholes model to compute the sensitivity of common stock value to firm risk. Failure to incorporate this feature results in an upward-biased estimate of the option component and convexity contributed by common stock (see Core and Schrand (1998) for a detailed discussion of the impact of covenants on the option component of common stock).

REFERENCES

Agrawal, A., Mandelker, G., 1987. Managerial incentives and corporate investment and financing decisions. Journal of Finance 42, 823–837.

Baber, W., Janakiraman, S., Kang, S., 1996. Investment opportunities and the structure of executive compensation. Journal of Accounting and Economics 21, 297–318.

Black, F., Scholes, M., 1973. The pricing of options and corporate liabilities. Journal of Political Economy 81, 637–659.

Core, J., Schrand, C., 1998. The effect of accounting–based debt covenants on equity valuation. Journal of Accounting and Economics, forthcoming.

Cuny, C., Jorion, P., 1995. Valuing executive stock options with a departure decision. Journal of Accounting and Economics 20, 193–205.

Dechow, P., Hutton, A., Sloan, R., 1996. Economic consequences of accounting for stock-based compensation. Journal of Accounting Research 34 (Suppl.), 1–20.

DeFusco, R., Johnson, R., Zorn, T., 1990. The effect of executive stock option plans on stockholders and bondholders. Journal of Finance 45, 617–627.

Financial Accounting Standards Board, 1995. Accounting for stock-based compensation. SFAS No. 123, Norwalk, CT.

Froot, K., Scharfstein, D., Stein, J., 1993. Risk management: coordinating corporate investment and financing policies. Journal of Finance 48, 1629–1648.

Gaver, J., Gaver, K., 1993. Additional evidence on the association between the investment opportunity set and corporate financing, dividend, and compensation policies. Journal of Accounting and Economics 16, 125–160.

Haugen, R., Senbet, L., 1981. Resolving the agency problems of external capital through options. Journal of Finance 36, 629–648.

Hemmer, T., Matsunaga, S., Shevlin, T., 1994. Estimating the "fair value" of employee stock options with expected early exercise. Accounting Horizons 8, 23–42.

Huddart, S., 1994. Employee stock options. Journal of Accounting and Economics 18, 207–231.

Jensen, M., Meckling, W., 1976. Theory of the firm: managerial behavior, agency costs, and ownership structure. Journal of Financial Economics 3, 305–360.

Jensen, M., Murphy, K., 1990. Performance pay and top-management incentives. Journal of Political Economy 98, 225–264.

Lambert, R., Larcker, D., Verrecchia, R., 1991. Portfolio considerations in valuing executive compensation. Journal of Accounting Research 29, 129–149.

Mayers, D., Smith, C., 1987. Corporate insurance and the underinvestment problem. Journal of Risk and Insurance 54, 45–54.

Mayers, D., Smith, C., 1990. On the corporate demand for insurance: evidence from the reinsurance market. Journal of Business 63, 19–40.

Merton, R., 1973. Theory of rational option pricing. Bell Journal of Economics and Management Science 4, 141–183.

Milgrom, P., Roberts, J., 1992. Economics, Organization, and Management. Prentice-Hall Inc., Englewood Cliffs, NJ.

Myers, S., 1977. The determinants of corporate borrowing. Journal of Financial Economics 5, 147–175.

Ofek, E., Yermack, D., 1997. Taking stock: does equity-based compensation increase managers' ownership. Unpublished working paper. New York University.

Pratt, J., 1964. Risk aversion in the small and in the large. Econometrica (January), 122–136.

Smith, C., 1976. Option pricing. Journal of Financial Economics 3, 3–51.

Smith, C., Stulz, R., 1985. The determinants of firm's hedging policies. Journal of Financial and Quantitative Analysis 20, 391–405.

Smith, C., Watts, R., 1992. The investment opportunity set and corporate financing, dividends, and compensation policies. Journal of Financial Economics 32, 263–292.

Tufano, P., 1996. Who manages risk? An empirical examination of risk management practices in the gold mining industry. Journal of Finance 51, 1097–1137.

Yermack, D., 1995. Do corporations award CEO stock options effectively? Journal of Financial Economics 39, 237–269.

## Chapter 16

N. K. Chidambaran* and Nagpurnanand R. Prabhala

EXECUTIVE STOCK OPTION REPRICING, INTERNAL GOVERNANCE MECHANISMS, AND MANAGEMENT TURNOVER[†]

Source: *Journal of Financial Economics*, 69(1) (2003): 53–89.

ABSTRACT

We examine firms that reprice their executive stock options and find little evidence that repricing reflects managerial entrenchment or ineffective governance. Repricing grants are economically significant, but there is little else unusual about compensation in repricing firms. Repricers tend to be smaller, younger, rapidly growing firms that experience a deep, sudden shock to growth and profitability. They are also more concentrated in the technology, trade, and service sectors and have smaller boards of directors. Repricers have abnormally high CEO turnover rates, which is inconsistent with the entrenchment hypothesis. Over 40% of repricers exclude the CEO's options when they reprice.

1. INTRODUCTION

STOCK OPTIONS HAVE BECOME AN increasingly important component of executive compensation, and are used by most Fortune 500 firms to compensate their senior executives. In an extensive review, Murphy (1998, p. 21) states that "The most pronounced trend in executive compensation in the 1980s and 1990s has been the explosion of stock option grants, which on a Black–Scholes basis now constitute the single largest component of executive pay." The most frequently cited explanation for granting options is their incentive effect. Options create a direct link between management compensation and shareholder wealth and thereby align the interests of a firm's managers with those of its shareholders.

The parameters of executive stock options (ESOs) are fixed at the time of the grant. Most ESOs have three-to-four-year vesting schedule, final maturities of five to ten years, and strike prices that are almost always equal to the company's share price on the grant date. The parameters of option grants are, however, sometimes reset before the options expire. The most common instance of such resetting is the "repricing" of executive stock options, in which firms lower the strike prices of ESOs following a decline in a firm's share price. The new strikes are often 30–40% lower than the old strike prices, and the strike reset is often accompanied by an extension of the option maturity. The net effect is to transform options that are worth little into options with considerable value to the repriced executive.

Repricing is formally executed either by canceling the old options and replacing them with new grants at more favorable terms, or by simply rewriting the terms of the existing option contracts. The Financial Accounting Standards Board (FASB) recognizes both types of transactions as being equivalent.

ESO repricing has received considerable attention in the popular press. For instance, a LEXIS–NEXIS search for "option repricing" reveals over 50 published stories from January to December 1999. Most articles harshly criticize repricing. Critics appear to be perturbed by two aspects of repricing. First, repricing typically follows a period of poor stock price performance and decline in firm value. Thus, it seems to reward managers for underperformance; in fact, it has the perverse effect of increasing managers' wealth when they ought perhaps to be fired. Repricing is, therefore, seen as a signal that the managers of the firm are entrenched and shareholders are unable to replace them. Additionally, repricing seems to undermine the role of options as a link between management and shareholder wealth. With repricing, executives profit both when stock prices increase (when options become in-the-money) and when stock prices fall precipitously (when out-of-the-money options are repriced).

Active institutional investors have been particularly strident in their criticism of ESO repricing. These investors argue that repricing is an example of managerial entrenchment, and that it illustrates the inability of existing governance mechanisms to curb self-serving behavior by managers. Some institutions suggest that repricing should not be permitted without prior shareholder approval. These attempts at redrafting company charters have met with mixed results.[1] The Financial Accounting Standards Board also appears to have taken a dim view of repricing. On August 12, 1998, the FASB decided to reconsider stock option accounting policies in light of the repricing phenomenon. The FASB argues that repriced options cannot be regarded as being "fixed" and that firms must use the variable accounting method if options are

repriced. This method is unpopular because it requires that repricing costs be explicitly expensed in income statements and not merely reported in footnotes. In October 1999, the FASB ruled that repricings conducted after December 15, 1998 should be accounted for using the variable method (Carter and Lynch, 2000).

Proponents of repricing offer two major explanations for repricing. One argument is that deep-out-of-the-money options no longer provide any meaningful incentives to executives (Hall and Murphy, 2000), so it is necessary to revise the strike price downward. A second argument, often cited by high-technology companies, is that repricing is needed to retain key executives. Executives will leave if options are so underwater that they are no longer a material part of the compensation contract. This explanation is especially prominent in Silicon Valley companies such as Symantec Corporation and Apple Computers, who indicate that they have repriced their executive stock options to retain talented executives.

The academic literature on repricing is somewhat sparse. A major impediment to empirical research has been the lack of adequate disclosure on repricing. Starting in 1992, the SEC has required firms that reprice executive stock options to disclose in their annual financial statements, all instances of repricing over the preceding ten fiscal years. Gilson and Vetsuypens (1993) report instances of repricing in a small sample of financially distressed firms that file for bankruptcy. Saly (1994) and Acharya, John, and Sundaram (2000) provide theoretical models of the incentive effects of repricing. Brenner, Sundaram, and Yermach (2000) develop models for valuing options subject to repricing features, by analogy to barrier options, and like Chance, Kumar, and Todd (2000), find that size is about the only variable that explains the repricing decision. The typical repricer is small relative to the population of the S&P 500 firm.

In this paper, we analyze over 200 repricing announcements between 1992 and 1997 reported in Standard & Poor's executive compensation database (EXECUCOMP).

We present new evidence on cross-sectional determinants of repricing and on top management turnover in repricing firms. In doing so, we shed new light on the relevance of the agency and poor governance explanations underlying much of the public criticism of repricing. We begin by characterizing the negative shock that leads to repricing. Repricers experience negative returns over the two years before the repricing fiscal year. The return shock is accompanied by a steep decline in profitability and sales growth that is not reversed in the next two years. The evidence provides a clear picture of the typical repricer: it is a young and rapidly growing firm that experiences an abrupt and relatively permanent shock to growth and profitability.

We analyze repricing in the context of overall executive compensation, focusing on top management. We examine whether repricings are economically significant compensation events by analyzing the levels of compensation in repricers and the compensation changes that accompany repricing. We find that repricing grants are economically significant in relation to both overall pay levels and previous-year option grants, and they also significantly exceed option grants in matched peers of repricers. However, compensation adjustments accompanying repricing tend to be small, and compensation levels in repricers are similar to those in matched peers. Thus, repricings are themselves economically significant compensation events, but there is little else unusual about the compensation levels or changes in compensation that accompany repricing.

We then investigate cross-sectional determinants of a firm's repricing decision. Given a shock to firm value, some firms choose to reprice their executive stock options while others do not. What industry, financial, and governance characteristics differentiate the two sets of firms? Our cross-sectional analysis adds to the literature in two ways. One contribution is methodological. A key difficulty in comparing repricers to control firms that do not reprice despite similar stock price drops is that the control firms are never explicitly identified in the data. We use statistical methods to account for imperfectly observed control samples. Our approach exploits the information in variables such as past returns or option grant prices that point to plausible control firms, recognizes that the instruments are imperfect, and produces a statistical comparison of repricers with (never observed) control firms. We further implement the methodology by conditioning directly on the "underwater" nature of options.

Second, our analysis contributes to the literature by introducing several new findings on the cross-sectional determinants of firms' repricing decisions. While previous work (Brenner et al., 2000; Chance et al., 2000) finds that firm size is about the only variable that explains why firms reprice, we uncover evidence that other industry and firm-specific variables matter. Younger firms, rapidly growing firms, firms belonging to the technology, trade, and service sectors, and firms with smaller boards are more likely to reprice. We also find no evidence that repricers have longer-serving managers, more diffuse stock ownership, or especially low institutional ownership. Overall, the evidence provides little support for the notion that repricing primarily manifests agency problems or ineffective governance of firms.

We also develop evidence on top management turnover in repricers. One criticism of repricing is that it reflects the inability of shareholders to fire poorly performing managers because these managers are entrenched. The entrenchment hypothesis predicts that top management turnover rates in repricers are abnormally low. However, we find the opposite result: repricers have abnormally high CEO attrition rates. There is little evidence that repricers are unable to effect changes in management, as an entrenchment hypothesis might suggest.

The last part of our paper documents and analyzes an interesting heterogeneity in executives included in firms' repricing announcements. In over 40% of all repricing announcements, the CEO is not included in the list of executives repriced.

We find a pronounced imbalance in compensation structures in these "non-CEO" repricers. Specifically, the CEO has fewer options and more direct shareholdings, while non-CEO executives have relatively more options than shares in these firms. Thus, a negative return shock in non-CEO repricers weakens incentives of non-CEO executives far more than those of the CEO. Here, repricing seems to play the role of mitigating the intra-management incentive imbalances created by negative return shocks.

We proceed as follows. Section 2 describes the repricing sample. We characterize the industry and time trends in repricing and the nature of the return and operating shocks that precede repricing. Section 3 describes repricing grants in the context of overall compensation policy. Section 4 conducts a cross-sectional analysis of firms' decisions to reprice. Section 5 analyzes CEO and non-CEO repricing. Section 6 offers conclusions.

2. DATA

Our repricing sample is based on Standard & Poor's, 1998 EXECUCOMP database, which contains information for 51,555 executives for 1,836 firms for fiscal year 1992 to fiscal year 1997. In this six-year period, EXECUCOMP identifies a total of 864 executives who are repriced, which translates into 240 separate firm-level repricing announcements. Following Brenner et al. (2000), we read the proxy statements, 10-K filings, or annual reports to cross-verify the repricing event. For some years, repricing is disclosed only in the filings in subsequent years. In general, repricing-related reporting has become both more uniform and more comprehensive in recent years.

From the initial sample of 240 instances of repricing in EXECUCOMP, we discard 27 cases; 14 of these contain reporting errors. EXECUCOMP sometimes classifies an ESO repricing that occurred in a prior year as belonging to the current year. The database, for example, misclassifies

a repricing that took place after the fiscal year but before the annual proxy filing as an event pertaining to the proxy's fiscal year. We discard seven cases because the repricing is caused by a merger, spinoff, or regrant of options in a division instead of options in a parent company. In four cases, the repricing does not relate to named executives of the firm but to lower employees. In one case, option strike prices are actually increased to the current market price and the maturity is extended, perhaps motivated by tax considerations. In another case, the executive bought options at the Black–Scholes value from the company.

Our final repricer sample has 213 instances of repricing. The sample is larger than that used by Brenner et al., who analyze 133 repricings in EXECUCOMP between 1992 and 1995. Our sample size also significantly exceeds that used in Chance et al. (2000), who analyze 53 announcements between 1985 and 1994 identified through a LEXIS–NEXIS search. For each year in which a firm reprices executive stock options, we identify the executives whose options are repriced and, in particular, note whether the CEO's options are repriced. To identify whether a repriced executive is a CEO or not, we match executive names to CEO titles determined as described below, and also verify the data manually in the proxy. We also count the number of executives for whom stock options are repriced for each repricing event.

For each firm in EXECUCOMP, we obtain dates when an executive assumes the CEO title and when the executive leaves the CEO position. This allows us to identify the CEO in charge at the beginning of each year. When the dates are not reported, we use EXECUCOMP's classification of CEO for that fiscal year. This procedure identifies CEOs for 10,042 firm-years. For each CEO, we obtain the compensation package and the number of options and shares held. We also obtain the aggregate number of options and shares held by all other executives named in the proxy. If the CEO of a firm changes during a fiscal year, we classify the firm-year as having a turnover event. Some observations for the 1997 fiscal year are missing from the 1998 EXECUCOMP data. We fill these in from the 1999 EXECUCOMP database.

For the entire sample of firms, we obtain return data from the Center for Research in Security Prices (CRSP) and cross-sectional data on firm characteristics from the annual COMPUSTAT tapes. We obtain data on the number of members serving on a company's board of directors from Investor Responsibility Research Center (IRRC). Board-related observations are available for about 75% of the sample of 11,016 firm-years. Additionally, we obtain two measures of the fragmentation of firm ownership reported in the SPECTRUM Disclosure database: institutional owner ship and aggregate shareholdings of 5% block-holders of the firm. Both variables are available for slightly more than two-thirds of the sample. We merge the return, firm characteristics, and governance data with the repricing data set.

2.1. The repricing sample: industry and time trends

Table 16.1 presents an annual breakdown of the repricers in our sample and the number of executives repriced at each announcement. Repricing seems to have become more popular over time. There are 15 repricing events in fiscal 1992, a peak

of 55 events in fiscal 1996, and 36 events in fiscal 1997. The number of executives repriced is relatively stable at a median value of four. Table 16.1 also shows that repricings not involving the CEO have become more common over time, starting from only one non-CEO repricing in 1992 to 22 in 1996.

Table 16.2 presents the number of repricing announcements classified by industry. We classify all firms in EXECUCOMP into 18 industry categories. Our primary classification is according to two-digit SIC codes, but in some instances, we use four-digit SIC codes, as this is more informative about the types of companies that engage in repricing. Unlike Brenner et al. and Chance et al., we find evidence of industry patterns in repricing. Firms in the computers and electronic parts, software and high-technology, and biotechnology industries account for 80 of 213, or about 37.5%, of all repricing events. Other industry segments with some concentration of repricers are the trade (wholesale and retail) and service segments. The technology, trade, and service sectors together account for over two-thirds of all repricing announcements. On the other hand, repricing is rare in the heavy industries such as utilities and mining.

The more detailed industry classifications appear to be helpful in identifying industry patterns in repricing. Part of the gain in

Table 16.1 Repricing announcements by year

Table 16.1 presents annual distribution of all repricing events reported in EXECUCOMP. Column 1 shows the total number of repricing events. Columns 2 and 3 show the number of repricing events when the CEO is repriced and the number of repricing events when the CEO is not repriced, respectively. Column 4 shows the median (mean) number of repriced executives named in the proxy statements of the firm.

Year	Number of Repricers	CEO repricers	Non-CEO repricers	Named executives
1992	15	14	1	4 (3.36)
1993	31	21	10	4 (3.59)
1994	33	17	16	4 (3.24)
1995	43	24	19	3 (4.02)
1996	55	33	22	4 (3.91)
1997	36	18	18	4 (3.87)
TOTAL	213	127	86	4 (3.74)

Table 16.2 Repricing announcements by industry

Table 16.2 reports the distribution of repricing and non-repricing firms across industry segments. We classify firms into 18 industry segments based on SIC codes, as detailed in the table.

Industry number	Industry name	Full sample	Number of repricers	% Repricing	CEO repricers	Non-CEO repricers
1	Agriculture & food 100, 200, 2000–2090	330	6	1.81	5	1
2	Mining 1000–1090, 1400	126	0	0	0	0
3	Construction 1500–1700	120	2	0	1	1
4	Oil & petroleum 1300–1389, 2900–2990	444	4	0.90	4	0
5	Small scale manufact. 2100–2690, 2830–2832, 2837–2839	576	10	1.74	6	4
6	Chemicals/related manufact. 2800–2899, 3000–3569	1,392	6	0.43	3	3
7	Industrial manufact. 3680–3990	942	19	2.02	12	7
8	Computers & electronic parts 3570–3679	1,008	40	3.97	21	19
9	Printing & publishing 2700–2799	234	1	0.43	1	0
10	Transportation 4000–4790	312	0	0	0	0
11	Telecommunication 4800–4899	270	2	0.74	1	1
12	Utilities 4900–4999	822	5	0.60	3	2
13	Wholesale 5000–5190	372	11	2.96	9	2
14	Retail 5200–5799, 5900–5990	756	20	2.65	10	10
15	Services 5800–5820, 7000–7363, 7389–9999	1,002	43	4.29	24	19
16	Financials 6000–6999	1,476	4	0.20	4	0
17	Software & technology 7370–7377	414	21	5.08	12	9
18	Biotech 2833–2836	366	19	5.46	12	7

power comes from working with four-digit SIC codes rather than two-digit SIC codes. This allows us, for instance, to separate out biotech companies within the small manufacturing sector and software companies from non-software firms in the services sector. The detailed classifications, however, do not eliminate all problems. For instance, firms in the retail sector concentrating on software and computers might be better classified as computer-related industries, but these firms are classified as retailers and share SIC codes all the way down to four-digit levels with other retailers not in computer-related businesses. Without adhoc choices on our part, we cannot reclassify these firms.

2.2. The repricing sample: pre-repricing returns

Repricing firms usually experience a significant decline in stock prices over some period of time prior to repricing. For instance, Brenner et al. find that three-year returns prior to repricing are significantly negative. We characterize this price drop in six-month intervals over the three years before the repricing fiscal year-end. These findings help define control firms that experience large negative price drops yet do not reprice their ESOs. Table 16.3 reports the distributional features of six-month buy-and-hold returns covering three years going back from time zero for repricers and all non-repricers, where year zero is the repricing fiscal year-end for repricers and every fiscal year-end for every firm is a time zero for non-repricers.

Repricers experience lower returns than non-repricers in all six-month periods

starting from month -24 but not before. Wilcoxon z (p) values for differences between repricers and non-repricers for the periods $[-24, -18]$, $[-18, -12]$, $[-12, -6]$, and $[-6, 0]$ are -5.41, -10.12, -11.68, and -6.59, respectively, all significant at 1%, while Wilcoxon z (p) values for differences in periods $[-30, -24]$ and $[-36, -30]$ are 0.96 $(p = 0.34)$ and 1.21 $(p = 0.23)$, both insignificant.[2] Dissimilarities in returns between repricers and non-repricers evidently surface about two years prior to the repricing fiscal year-end and persist through the year of repricing. Negative returns are dispersed over the two-year period even for the repricing sample, so the data provide less guidance on the magnitude of negative returns or their timing within the two-year period to qualify a non-repricer as a valid control firm. We choose firms with returns of less than -15% in months $[-24, -6]$ or -30% in $[-6, 0]$ as our control sample. The former group of firms experience a relatively permanent shock to prices, while the latter group represents firms with large negative shocks in a recent period. We recognize that the definition is adhoc so the control sample is probably imperfect with errors of both inclusion and exclusion. (We address this issue through econometric methods in Section 3.)

Table 16.3 Prior returns of repricers

Table 16.3 presents data on the distribution of stock returns for repricing and non-repricing firms. A repricer is a firm on the EXECUCOMP database that makes a repricing announcement in a fiscal year, and a non-repricer is a firm on the EXECUCOMP database that does not make such an announcement. Each row reports buy-and-hold returns (in percent) for several six-month periods prior to the fiscal year-end of the repricing year, which is month zero. For each period, we report the first quartile, median, third quartile, and the mean of the returns distribution.

Period	Repricers				All other firms			
	1st Q	Med	3rd Q	Mean	1st Q	Med	3rd Q	Mean
$[-6, 0]$	-27.72	-6.14	19.37	-1.59	-5.39	8.07	23.53	11.17
$[-12, -6]$	-36.1	-16.67	5.61	-11.71	-3.13	10.59	25.71	13.86
$[-18, -12]$	-33.33	-14.75	5.69	-9.31	-7.63	5.79	20.98	9.20
$[-24, -18]$	-20.6	-1.18	26.37	8.31	-2.5	11.14	27.79	16.03
$[-30, -24]$	-22.48	7.73	31.61	15.61	-11.11	3.09	19	6.75
$[-36, -30]$	-6.35	13.46	43.17	21.94	-3.37	11.47	28.98	16.54

2.3. The repricing sample: operating performance

Panels A and B of Table 16.4 present data on the operating performance of repricers from year −2 through year +2, where year zero is the repricing fiscal year-end for repricers and every fiscal year end for every firm is a year zero for non-repricers. Our metric for judging operating performance is the "EBITDA" ratio, i.e., earnings before interest, taxes, and depreciation in year t (COMPUSTAT item # 13) divided by the average book value of assets (COMPUSTAT item # 6) in years t and $t − 1$ (Barber and Lyon, 1996). Following Barber and Lyon, we compute the abnormal EBITDA ratio as the raw number less the median

EBITDA ratio for all firms in the same industry group and fiscal year. As recommended by Barber and Lyon, our analysis focuses on median rather than mean abnormal performance, as mean ratios can be distorted by outliers.

Repricers perform at industry levels in year −2, when the median abnormal EBITDA ratio equals −0.52%, not significantly different from zero; the Wilcoxon $z(p) = −0.44$ (0.65). However, the operating performance of repricers tails off rather sharply in the next two years. The abnormal EBITDA ratio in year zero is negative (median = −6.71%) and significant at 1% (Wilcoxon $z(p) = −7.77$ (0.00)) and the performance decline is not reversed in the next two years. The decline in repricer

Table 16.4 Operating performance of repricers, non-repricers and control firms

Table 16.4 reports data on operating performance of three groups of firms. Repricers are firms on the EXECUCOMP database that make a repricing announcement during a fiscal year. Non-repricers are firms that do not make such an announcement during the fiscal year. Control firms are firms with a return not exceeding −15% in months −24 through −6 or −6 through zero, where zero denotes the fiscal year-end month. The columns in Table 16.4 report characteristics for the fiscal year and a window of two years preceding and following the fiscal year. For each group of firms, we report EBITDA, defined as earnings before interest, taxes, and depreciation (COMPUSTAT item # 13) as a percentage of the average book value of assets (COMPUSTAT item # 6) in the fiscal year and the year preceding, abnormal EBITDA, which equals EBITDA minus industry median EBITDA, sales, percentage sales growth, and industry-adjusted sales growth (sales growth minus industry median sales growth). In each case, we report the median (mean) of the relevant characteristic.

	Year −2	Year −1	Repricing year	Year +1	Year +2
A: EBITDA					
Repricers	15.79 (15.16)	13.02 (11.35)	9.58 (7.53)	11.31 (7.79)	11.35 (7.70)
Non-repricers	14.45 (14.78)	14.53 (14.84)	14.74 (15.05)	14.67 (14.93)	14.68 (14.85)
Control firms	15.42 (14.67)	12.47 (11.76)	11.41 (9.81)	11.67 (9.88)	12.78 (11.08)
B: Abnormal EBITDA					
Repricers	−0.58 (−0.91)	−3.49 (−4.82)	−6.71 (−8.53)	−5.20 (−8.43)	−4.88 (−7.90)
Non-repricers	0.00 (0.56)	0.00 (0.58)	0.02 (0.57)	0.01 (0.46)	0.01 (0.32)
Control firms	−0.20 (−0.77)	−2.29 (−3.63)	−3.60 (−5.64)	−3.29 (−5.54)	−2.20 (−4.37)
C: Sales					
Repricers	222 (639)	276 (723)	320 (717)	334 (709)	355 (796)
Non-repricers	652 (2627)	708 (2768)	803 (2994)	923 (3265)	984 (3417)
Control firms	380 (1475)	417 (1544)	462 (1652)	500 (1814)	540 (1954)
D: Sales growth					
Repricers	28.16 (47.12)	22.22 (53.7)	3.61 (13.26)	5.85 (13.73)	8.06 (27.28)
Non-repricers	8.93 (17.30)	9.13 (17.43)	10.07 (18.71)	10.15 (18.15)	10.39 (17.52)
Control firms	14.77 (33.91)	9.38 (20.06)	6.57 (16.24)	6.87 (15.04)	8.36 (16.53)
E: Industry-adjusted sales growth					
Repricers	13.78 (34.43)	7.60 (40.89)	−7.26 (0.82)	−5.14 (2.09)	−1.11 (15.84)
Non-repricers	−0.07 (7.40)	−0.00 (7.35)	0.02 (7.86)	0.00 (7.38)	0.00 (6.51)
Control firms	4.17 (22.31)	−1.17 (8.76)	−4.33 (4.38)	−3.5 (3.29)	−2.48 (5.07)

operating performance is economically significant, amounting to a decline of over $6 in pre-tax cashflows for every $100 of the book value of assets, or a quarter to a third of the pre-repricing EBITDA ratio. Patterns for control firms are similar, though the troughs are not as pronounced.

To obtain additional insight into the operating shocks that cause repricing, we examine the pattern of sales and sales growth surrounding the fiscal year of repricing. Panels C, D, and E of Table 16.4 report sales, sales growth, and industry-adjusted sales growth for repricers, control firms, and all non-repricers, respectively. Repricers are rapidly growing in year −2. Their median raw and industry-adjusted sales growth are 28% and 13.78%, respectively, and both are significant at 1%. However, sales growth drops dramatically in the next two years. The year zero sales growth rate is only 3.6% and the industry-adjusted growth rate is −7.82%, indicating that growth in repricers essentially stalls and is well below industry levels. Sales growth remains mired in single digits after the repricing year, well below the historically high growth of repricers. Patterns for control firms are similar except that the troughs are again less steep than for repricers.[3]

The empirical evidence provides a clear picture of the typical repricing event. A firm that initiates repricing is likely to have enjoyed rapid, above-industry growth rates and industry-level profitability two years before repricing. The growth rate of repricers experiences a steep and somewhat abrupt drop to well below industry levels in the repricing year. Repricers never regain their historical profitability levels or growth rates, which suggests that the shock that precipitates repricing is lasting.

3. REPRICING IN THE CONTEXT OF COMPENSATION POLICY[4]

The decision to reprice an executive's stock options is only one part of the overall compensation decision concerning the executive. To assess whether repricing is an economically significant compensation event, it is necessary to understand repricing in the context of overall executive compensation as well as changes in other compensation variables such as salaries, bonuses, or new option grants. In this section, we characterize the levels of compensation and the adjustments in other pay components when an executive is repriced, focusing on the top management level.

We begin by determining whether the CEO in charge at the beginning of the repricing fiscal year is included in the repricing announcement for each repricing firm. For this purpose, we match the list of CEO titles with the list of repriced executives that EXECUCOMP reports. We cross-verify the repricing information with the actual proxy statements and/or annual 10-K filings. Our sample has 127 repriced CEOs. We first report the level of compensation and its structure for these repriced CEOs and then analyze compensation variable changes in the fiscal year of repricing. We also examine CEO pay changes in the subsample of firms that reprice other executives but not the CEO.

3.1. Exante compensation level

We start by analyzing compensation levels in the fiscal year prior to repricing. Focusing on the prior year ensures that our analysis is exante. Thus, we only incorporate information available to the board and compensation committee at the time of the repricing and do not confound exante compensation with adjustments that occur in the repricing fiscal year. Panel A in Table 16.5 reports the total dollar compensation (field TDC1 in the EXECUCOMP database) and its three major components, i.e., salary, bonus, and option grants, for all repriced CEOs. The three components account for a median of 87% of total CEO pay in our sample.

Median previous-year salary, bonus, option grants, and total pay for the repriced CEOs are $375,000, $71,030, $247,400, and $941,700, respectively. To benchmark these results, the corresponding median compensation variables across all firms in EXECUCOMP are $450,000, $234,600,

Table 16.5 Compensation level, structure, and changes

Table 16.5 reports compensation levels and changes for a sample of 126 CEOs whose stock options are repriced between 1992 and 1997 and corresponding compensation variables for firms matched by size decile, industry, and fiscal year. Panel A reports salary, bonus, the Black–Scholes value of option grants, and total dollar compensation in the fiscal year prior to repricing. Panel B reports the dollar changes in salary and bonus between the repricing and prior year. Panel C reports the Black–Scholes value of (a) the total repricing-year grants, (b) fresh replacement options granted in lieu of the options canceled in repricing, and (c) new option grants. Panel C also gives the change in the Black–Scholes value of the new option grants relative to the previous-year grants. Columns 1 and 2 report data for repricers and matched firms, respectively, while Column 3 gives Wilcoxon *z* (*p*) values for testing differences between the two. For each characteristic, we report the median (mean).

Variable	Repriced CEO	Matched firm	Wilcoxon z (p)
Panel A: Compensation levels ($000)			
Salary	375.00 (417.70)	369.50 (385.00)	0.30 (0.77)
Bonus	71.03 (192.70)	159.20 (180.20)	−3.42 (0.00)
Option grants	247.40 (1356.00)	151.00 (323.10)	1.67 (0.09)
Total compensation	941.70 (2028.00)	916.50 (1164.00)	0.49 (0.62)
Panel B: Salary & bonus changes ($000)			
Δ Salary	11.85 (10.15)	18.34 (19.82)	−2.00 (0.05)
Δ Bonus	0.00 (16.68)	7.60 (24.97)	−2.11 (0.04)
Panel C: Options in repricing year ($000)			
Total grants	1222.00 (2931.00)	218.70 (345.70)	9.21 (0.00)
Repriced options	870.10 (2307.00)	—	—
New grants	123.10 (612.20)	218.70 (345.70)	−1.61 (0.10)
Δ option grants	−17.56 (−240.6)	73.50 (67.71)	−3.90 (0.00)

$181,900, and $1,197,000, respectively. Three of the four compensation variables — salary, bonus, and total compensation are lower in repricers at significance levels of 1% or better, while the fourth (option grants) is higher but only marginally significant at 10%. This suggests that options are a relatively more important part of pay in repricers. Indeed, options represent a median (mean) proportion of 31.8% (36.5%) of total compensation in repricers versus 17.5% (22.8%) for all other firm-years and the difference is significant at 1% (Wilcoxon *z* = 3.96) (Figure 16.1).

The straight differences between repricers and non-repricers could well reflect compensation patterns peculiar to repricers. However, the compensation differences could also reflect systematic variation due to the characteristics of repricers, such as the industries in which repricers are concentrated or perhaps time periods in which repricing is more prevalent. We find

three sources of systematic variation in compensation: time period, firm size, and industry sector.

Time: Figure 16.2, which plots median annual compensation variables across all firms in EXECUCOMP, illustrates the time trend in compensation levels. Median prior-year CEO salaries, bonuses, and option grants across all firms in EXECUCOMP increase from $420,000, $87,000, and $144,000 in fiscal 1993 to $500,000, $300,300, and $352,000, respectively, in fiscal 1997, while total pay rises from $1 million to $1.6 million over the same period.

Size: Executive compensation tends to be lower in small firms (see, e.g., the recent work of Himmelberg and Hubbard, 2000). Figure 16.3, which plots median compensation for ten size deciles (based on book value of assets) of firms, illustrates this strong relation. Median total dollar CEO pay, for instance, amounts to $3.3 million

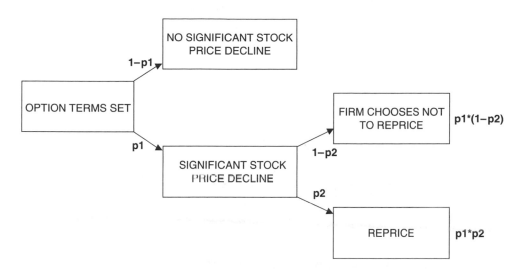

Figure 16.1 Model of the repricing decision as a sequential two-stage process, where p_1 is the probability that firms experience a significant stock price decline and p_2 is the probability that firms choose to reprice conditional on such a decline. Non-repricers either do not experience a significant price decline [probability $(1 - p_1)$] or choose not to reprice despite such a price decline [probability $(p_1 * (1 - p_2))$].

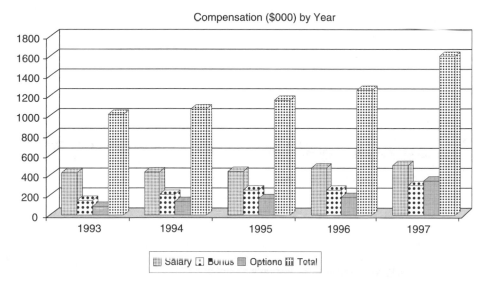

Figure 16.2 Median annual values by year for salary, bonus, option grants, and total compensation, across all firms in EXECUCOMP.

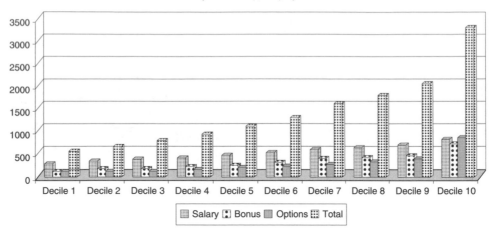

Figure 16.3 Median annual values by size decile for salary, bonus, option grants, and total compensation, across all firms in EXECUCOMP. Firms are classified into ten size deciles (based on the book value of assets) of firms. Decile 1 and Decile 10 consist of the smallest and the largest firms, respectively.

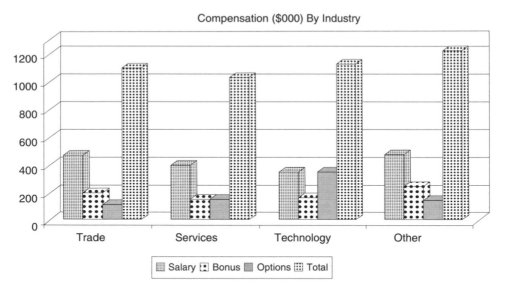

Figure 16.4 Median annual values by industry for salary, bonus, option grants, and total compensation, across all firms in EXECUCOMP. Firms are classified into four industries: trade, services, technology, and other.

for the top-decile firms versus $503,800 for the lowest-decile firms. Similar trends are also apparent in all components of CEO compensation.

Industry: The data in Section 2.1 and Section 3 show that repricers tend to concentrate in specific industries, particularly trade, services, and technology. Figure 16.4

depicts total compensation and its elements in these three sectors and corresponding compensation variables in all other industries taken together. Salary, bonus, and total compensation are lower in the technology, services, and trade sectors compared to other sectors, and the differences are significant at 1% or better (z and p values not reported here). Additionally, option grants are significantly more dominant forms of compensation in the technology sector, where options constitute a median of 31% of pay versus 14–20% for other industry sectors.

The mechanics of adjusting for size, industry, and time are as follows. We divide all firms in EXECUCOMP, year by year, into ten size deciles formed on the basis of the book value of assets (from COMPUSTAT) at the beginning of the fiscal year. We also classify firms as belonging to technology, trade, services, or other industry sectors. For each firm, we then compute matched peer salary, bonus, option grant, and total compensation as the median of the relevant CEO compensation variable for all firms in the same size decile, industry group, and fiscal year. Panel A in Table 16.5 reports compensation variables for repriced CEOs and matched peers. It also reports Wilcoxon z (p) values for testing differences between repriced CEOs and their matched peers.

The matching procedure does attenuate some of the differences between repricers and all non-repricers. Median total dollar compensation (TDC) of repriced CEOs ($941,700) is closer to the TDC of the peer-matched sample ($916,500) than that of all non-repricers ($1,197,000) and TDC differences are no longer significant. Likewise, salaries (median = $375,000) are closer to and not significantly different from peer-matched salaries (median = $369,500), while they are significantly lower than salaries in all non-repricers (median = $450,000). Previous-year stock grants (median = $247,400) tend to be somewhat higher than those in matched firms (median = $151,000), but as before, the difference is only significant at 10% (Wilcoxon z (p) = 1.67 (0.09)). Bonuses

remain somewhat lower for repriced CEOs (median = $71,030) than in matched firms (median = $159,200). This finding is not surprising, following Core and Guay (2001) and Yermack (1995), who argue that firms facing high cash needs and with costly external finance reduce their use of cash compensation. Repricers are small and rapidly growing firms that have experienced severe, permanent operating shocks, and plausibly need to conserve resources to recoup. Finally, repriced CEOs have about the same levels of overall compensation as in firms matched by industry, size, and fiscal year.

3.2. Compensation changes

In this section, we examine adjustments in compensation variables that tend to accompany repricing. Panel B in Table 16.5 reports median and mean salary and bonus changes for repriced CEOs in the fiscal year of repricing and corresponding statistics for industry-, size-, and year-matched firms. The median salary change accompanying repricing is $11,850 versus $18,340 for matched non-repricing peers, and a similar difference exists for the means. The difference is economically small but significant at 5% (Wilcoxon z (p) = −2.00 (0.05)). The median bonus change is zero versus $7,600 for matched peers. Again, the differences are economically small but statistically significant at 5% (Wilcoxon z (p) = −2.11 (0.04)). The low levels of bonuses and their apparent downward rigidity suggest that repriced CEOs have bonuses that amount to floor amounts and are probably not a significant component of discretionary annual performance-linked incentive pay.

Dealing with the third element of compensation, option grants, is more intricate. Option grants in the repricing year consist of two distinct components: (a) options granted *in lieu* of the canceled (repriced) options; and (b) additional *new* grants over and above the repriced options. The two components must be disentangled to assess the magnitude of the repricing grant and the size of new grants that accompany repricing.

This breakup, however, faces two obstacles. First, option grants reported in proxy statements (and EXECUCOMP) do not separately identify the number of repriced options. A second issue is the lack of uniformity in reporting practices. Some firms seem to regard repricing as just an alteration of existing options. These firms do not include repriced options in the repricing-year options grant. Other firms view repricing as a cancelation of old options and regrant of fresh replacement options. These firms do include the replacement options as part of the repricing-year option grants. Thus, straight grant numbers reported in EXECUCOMP and proxies are not comparable across firms.

We read proxies or annual reports of repricers to obtain the number of repriced options and also use these proxies to ascertain whether repriced options are included in the grants table. Sufficient information is available for 109 out of 127 cases, mostly in footnotes to the option grants table. In about 75% of the sample, repricing-year grants include repriced options. Here, we deflate the total repricing-year grant by the number of repriced options included in the grant to obtain new option grants. In other cases (about two dozen), repricing-year option grants explicitly exclude repriced options. Here, new options directly equal grant figures reported in EXECUCOMP and we obtain the number of repriced options separately by reading proxy statements.

Panel C in Table 16.5 reports the value of total grants, repriced options, and new options, and the change in option grant relative to the previous year's option grant. The median Black–Scholes value of the total repricing-year grant, which incorporates both repriced options and new grants, is $1,222,000. This far exceeds both matched grant values (median = $218,700) and previous-year grants (median = $247,400). Our findings are consistent with those of Brenner et al., who also find that the EXECUCOMP reported Black–Scholes value of repricing-year grants is unusually high for repriced executives.

Turning to the components of the total repricing-year grants, the median value of the new grants accompanying repricing is $123,100. This is somewhat lower than matched firm grants, as seen in Table 16.5, and also lower than previous-year grants (median = $247, 400), although the differences are only significant at about 10%. The median ratio of current-year to previous-year grants is 67% and is not significantly different from 100% (Wilcoxon z $(p) = -1.38$ (0.19)). Thus, firms appear to maintain or reduce the number of new options granted in the fiscal year of repricing. The value of *repriced* options (median = $870, 100) significantly exceeds the value of the previous-year grant (median = $247, 400) with Wilcoxon z $(p) = 4.36$ (0.00). Likewise, the ratio of the number of repriced options to previous-year grants has a median of 182% (mean = 284%) and significantly exceeds 100% (Wilcoxon z $(p) = 5.11$ (0.00)). The evidence suggests that repricing is in fact a significant addition rather than an alternative to options granted in the normal course by firms.

A related question of some interest is whether large option grants are associated with poorly performing firms in general, in which case we should not view repricing as a special event. To address this issue, we examine option grants for the control firms with negative returns used in Section 2 and Table 16.3. The median (mean) current-year grants for this sample equal $247,600 ($807,600). These are slightly below the previous-year grants for the same firms (median (mean) equal to $264,300 ($889,400)), and also significantly below the value of options repriced.[5] Repricing is therefore special; it is not the case that poorly performing firms that do not reprice instead give large option grants in lieu of repricing.

An alternative to repricing is to issue new options but leave the old, out-of-the-money options untouched. Firms might be reluctant to use this alternative because the total number of options are capped at levels pre-authorized by shareholders. It can be difficult for firms to make large grants similar to those involved in ESO repricing without seeking specific shareholder approval for increasing the cap, whereas repricing preserves decision-making at the board level without having to get shareholder approval.[6] Leaving old options untouched also has the disadvantage that it could adversely affect the future diluted EPS of the firm. This alternative can be more attractive, however, following the October 1999 FASB ruling that companies must expense costs of repricing because repriced options are deemed to have "variable" strike prices. Taxes are unlikely to play a role in this choice, as tax events in ESOs are triggered only at eventual option exercise.

Finally, the above analysis focuses on compensation changes of repriced CEOs. However, several firms reprice other members of the top management team but not the CEO. We check whether CEOs in these firms receive backdoor compensation through unusual salary, bonus, or grant changes. The data do not support this hypothesis. For non-CEO repricers, the median (mean) change in CEO salary, bonus, and option grants is $12,290 ($13,600), $0 (−$72, 370), and −$22,270 (−$1, 050, 000), respectively, versus $17,570 ($20,340), $8,000 ($16,460), and $57,690 ($232,600), respectively, for matched peers, with Wilcoxon z (p) values for differences equal to −1.66 (0.10), −3.52 (0.00), and −0.36 (0.72), respectively. There is little evidence that firms give backdoor compensation through other means as a substitute for a conventional strike reset repricing.

In sum, compensation levels in repricers match those in peers, and changes in compensation variables accompanying repricing are economically small. The repricing grant, however, is large and comparable to annual total compensation levels. Thus, the repricing grant itself is significant to the repriced executive but there is little else unusual in the accompanying compensation changes.

4. CROSS-SECTIONAL CHARACTERISTICS OF REPRICING FIRMS

This section analyzes factors that explain firms' repricing decisions. We expand the repricing literature through new methodology

and by introducing new variables into the cross-sectional analysis. The expanded analysis permits, in particular, a more detailed investigation of alternative explanations for repricing, particularly the agency explanation that underlies much of the public criticism of repricing.

Section 4.1 discusses univariate comparisons of repricers with non-repricers and with control firms that experience negative returns but do not reprice. Section 4.2 reports estimates of multivariate specifications in which repricers are compared to control firms, accounting for the unobservability of control firms. Section 4.3 discusses an alternate definition of control firms that conditions directly on the underwater nature of outstanding options. Section 4.4 offers a summary of the results in relation to alternative explanations for ESO repricing.

4.1. Univariate comparisons

Table 16.6 presents cross-sectional data for repricers, all non-repricers, and control firms. Column 1 reports the data for repricers, Column 2 reports data for all non repricers, and Column 3 reports data for control firms. Column 4 reports the nonparametric Wilcoxon (or Mann–Whitney) z-statistics and p-values for testing differences between repricers and the control sample. The variables in Table 16.6 are organized into four categories: (i) CEO turnover in repricers; (ii) three proxies for firm size, a focus of much previous work; (iii) data on several other firm and governance characteristics including firm age, ownership, and board size; and (iv) data on executive equity and option holdings.

4.1.1. CEO turnover

One of the main criticisms of repricing is that it reflects the agency problems of managerial entrenchment in firms. According to this argument, entrenched under-performing managers are able to reward themselves via repricing instead of being fired by shareholders for poor

Table 16.6 Cross-sectional characteristics of repricers

Table 16.6 reports the number of CEO turnovers and several firm-specific characteristics of three groups of firms. Repricers are firms on the EXECUCOMP database that make a repricing announcement during a fiscal year. Non-repricers do not make such an announcement during the fiscal year. Control firms are firms with returns not exceeding −15% in months −24 through −6 or −6 through zero, where zero denotes the fiscal year-end month. The last column reports z and p values for Wilcoxon tests that compare characteristics of repricers with those of control firms. The firm-specific characteristics are the annual sales, book value of assets, market value of equity, shares and executive stock options held by all executives named in the firm's proxy statement, the firm's age (defined as the time in months since listing), the tenure of the CEO (in years), the aggregate institutional ownership and aggregate ownership of 5% block-holders in a firm, and the number of members in a firm's board of directors. For each characteristic, we report the median (mean).

Variable	Repricing firms	All non-repricers	Control firms	Wilcoxon z (p-value)
# of Firms	213	10,072	1471	
# CEO turnovers				
Year [0]	41 (19.25%)	634 (6.29%)	151 (10.26%)	2.19 (0.03)
Years [0, 1]	55 (25.82%)	1,266 (12.57%)	268 (18.21%)	2.21 (0.03)
Firm size				
Sales	276 (723)	708 (2,768)	417 (1,544)	−3.71 (0.00)
Total assets	309 (647)	814 (5,809)	383 (1,829)	−3.20 (0.00)
Equity value	332 (647)	718 (2,830)	353 (1,360)	−1.85 (0.06)
Other characteristics				
Firm age (months)	83 (112)	237 (214)	126 (196)	−6.14 (0.00)
CEO tenure	6.74 (7.83)	5.89 (8.17)	6.56 (8.13)	−0.20 (0.83)
Institutional ownership	49.05 (47.82)	50.76 (49.51)	47.34 (46.29)	0.79 (0.43)
5% block owners	26.12 (28.73)	20.56 (25.37)	23.69 (27.87)	0.32 (0.75)
Board size	7 (7.41)	9 (9.84)	8 (8.60)	−5.74 (0.00)
Equity and option holdings				
Shares (all executives)	461 (2,625)	707 (7,308)	437 (3,855)	0.16 (0.87)
Options (all executives)	444 (874)	691 (1,800)	385 (956)	2.38 (0.02)

performance. A directly testable implication of this entrenchment explanation for repricing and the related contention by Chance et al. (p. 129) that "firms with greater agency costs are more likely to reprice" is that repricers should have abnormally low top management turnover. We contribute to this debate by presenting evidence on rates of top management turnover in repricers.

Row 1 of Table 16.6 reports the number of firms that experience a CEO change in the year of repricing, while Row 2 reports a two-year turnover rate, i.e., the number of CEO changes in the year of the repricing or the next year. The two-year window is useful to account for a potential lag between the time a CEO change is initiated and its actual implementation, and for

repricing announcements that occur towards fiscal year-ends. By either metric, repricers show surprisingly high CEO turnover rates. About 19% of repricers experience a CEO turnover in the year of repricing and 25% of repricers experience turnover in the repricing year or the next. Both the one-and two-year attrition rates are significantly higher than those for non-repricers and for control firms. The turnover data in Table 16.6 provide little support for the notion that ESO repricers are especially reluctant to undertake a CEO change, as an entrenchment hypothesis might suggest. On the contrary, firms that announce a stock option repricing are also more likely to experience an accompanying CEO turnover.

Besides providing a test of the entrenchment-agency explanation for repricing, the turnover findings also have interesting implications for contingent-claims style valuation models of executive stock options (see, e.g., Carpenter, 1998). ESO valuation models attempt to incorporate features of executive stock options that are not present in standard option valuation models. One stream of this literature accounts for the repricing feature of executive stock options (e.g., Brenner et al.). A different set of papers deals with turnover and its effect on ESO valuation (e.g., Cuny and Jorion, 1995). Our evidence suggests that ESO valuation models should incorporate both repricing and turnover features simultaneously, because conditions that lead firms to reprice also appear to increase the probability of CEO turnover. Valuation models that ignore the probability of higher turnover while incorporating the repricing feature can overstate the value of the reset feature in executive stock options.

4.1.2. Firm size

We report three proxies for firm size — the book value of all assets of a firm, the firm's sales, and the market value of a firm's equity. We measure all variables as of the beginning of the fiscal year. By all three metrics of size, repricers are smaller than non-repricers and control firms. For instance, the median sales of all non-repricers are about 2.0–2.5 times the median repricer sales, as in Brenner et al.

It is difficult to unambiguously interpret why small firms are more likely to reprice. One possibility is that repricing reflects agency problems. Small firms perhaps face less scrutiny from the financial community and institutional ownership, which could curb rent-seeking behavior, is perhaps lower in small firms. On the other hand, agency problems are more pronounced in larger, mature firms that have more diffuse ownership and greater separation between ownership and control. A finding that small firms reprice more often is actually inconsistent with the idea that repricing reflects shareholder–manager agency problems.

Other explanations for small firm repricing do not rely on agency hypotheses. Small firms tend to be younger firms with less well developed lines of management, so the costs of replacing managers could be higher for these firms. Renegotiation of compensation contracts might also be easier in small firms because these firms are organizationally less complex, which makes for faster decision-making.

It is not clear which of the above explanations accounts for the size effect, but the data certainly suggest that we should control for size in the multivariate analysis. Following Brenner et al., we use sales as a proxy for firm size. As the empirical distribution of firm size is skewed, we use the natural logarithm of firm size in regression specifications.

4.1.3. Firm age

We measure the age of the firm as the number of months since the first price for the firm is reported in the CRSP tapes. Younger firms are less likely to have well developed lines of succession, so management turnover is likely to be costly for young firms. If executive retention motivates repricing, young firms might be more likely to reprice. The evidence in Table 16.6 is consistent with this explanation. Repricers tend to be younger, with a median time since listing of about seven years versus about 19 years for all non-repricers and 11 years for control firms.

4.1.4. CEO tenure

Long-serving CEOs are perhaps more entrenched and have more pliable boards of directors in place. If an entrenchment-expropriation hypothesis explains repricing, repricers should have high CEO tenure. The data in Table 16.6 provide little support for such a hypothesis. CEO tenure is not statistically different between repricers and control firms, or between repricers and the universe of non-repricers. In each case, the median CEO tenure is about seven years. This result is also invariant to alternate definitions of long-serving

CEOs, such as CEOs who have served for at least five years.

4.1.5. Institutional and block ownership

We examine the aggregate level of institutional ownership in a firm. Firms with low institutional ownership are perhaps subject to less intense monitoring, so the balance of power between shareholders and managers may tilt more towards management in these firms. If poor monitoring explains repricing, repricing will be more concentrated in firms with low institutional holdings. We find no evidence to support this contention. Repricers have median institutional ownership of about 49.05%, which is slightly but not significantly higher than the 47.34% institutional ownership in control firms. Institutional ownership is somewhat higher in the universe of all non-repricers, consistent with higher institutional involvement in large firms.

In addition to institutional ownership, we also obtain one other proxy for ownership fragmentation available in the CD SPECTRUM database—the aggregate shareholdings of all 5% block-holders in a company. This variable is inversely related to the fragmentation in a firm's ownership. If shareholder expropriation explains repricing, firms with more diffuse and fragmented ownership should be more likely to reprice. We find little support for this hypothesis. The median aggregate block holding in repricers (26.12%) is not significantly different from that in control firms (23.69%).

4.1.6. Board size

The number of members in a firm's board of directors can be viewed in two ways in relation to repricing. One is that smaller boards offer greater flexibility and speed in renegotiating contracts with managers. This suggests that smaller boards should be more likely to reprice. A different perspective of board size is offered by Yermack (1996), who finds that small boards are associated with greater market valuation of firms, suggesting that smaller boards are more shareholder value oriented. If repricing reflects shareholder–manager agency problems, repricers should have greater board sizes, to the extent that board size is symptomatic of the existence of such agency problems.

The last row in Table 16.6 reports median and mean board sizes of repricers, non-repricers, and control firms. We find little evidence that repricers have larger boards: in fact, the evidence suggests exactly the opposite. The median board in repricers has seven members compared to nine members for all non-repricers and eight for control firms. The differences in board size are significant at 1%. To the extent that small boards reflect greater orientation towards shareholder value maximization, repricing is unlikely to be an outcome of ineffective governance.

4.1.7. Equity and option holdings of executives

Firms in which executives have large option holdings as compared to direct equity ownership are probably more likely to reprice. One explanation is that negative return shocks cause greater misalignment in managerial incentives when executives have more options rather than straight equity. Another explanation is that, whatever be the reason for ESO repricing, it is worth the effort only when option holdings are sufficiently large.

Table 16.6 reports the number of options and shares held by all named executives appearing in company proxy statements. We normalize all share prices to $25 so firms with beginning-of-year share prices greater than $25 have the number of share and options scaled up, while those with share prices below $25 are scaled down, to make share and option holdings more comparable across firms. The data in Table 16.6 show no significant difference between the shares held by all executives in repricing firms from those held by all executives in control firms. The data do indicate that repricers have more options outstanding relative to control firms. Therefore, stock options are not lower when executive shareholdings are high, as in Yermack (1995). Options seem to be important elements of compensation and incentives in repricers regardless of executive shareholdings in these firms.

Are repricers the types of firms in which one might expect greater use of options in executive compensation? The characteristics of repricers in Table 16.6 fit the profile of firms in which we expect options to be used more extensively. Repricers are small, young, and rapidly growing firms that have high internal demands for cash, and non-cash compensation (such as stock options) is more likely to be used in such firms. Further, since repricers are young firms, executives are less likely to have exercised their option grants. An industry effect in repricers—specifically, their concentration in the technology industry—also explains the more widespread use of options. In the 1990s, technology firms simultaneously witnessed rapid growth and a short supply of management talent, and used options widely as "golden handcuffs" to facilitate management retention since options almost always vest over periods of three to four years. For instance, Auspex Systems Inc. writes in its proxy statement dated November 20, 1997 that "...competition for qualified employees in the technology market is extremely intense, and, due to the rapid growth of many successful companies in this sector, such competition is increasing..." and "...the Board of Directors believes that having a stock [option] plan in place is vital to retaining, motivating, and rewarding employees, executives and consultants, by providing them with long-term equity participation in the company relating directly to the financial performance and long-term growth of the company."

The evidence developed thus far emphasize two main issues. First, there are several systematic differences between repricers and both the universe of all non-repricers and control firms. The evidence also underlines the value of comparisons with control firms. For instance, the median market value of all non-repricers is 216% of median repricer market value but control firms are only 5% larger than repricers. Absent control firm comparisons, it is hard to say whether repricer versus non-repricer differences reflects characteristics peculiar to repricers or those generally associated with firms that experience large price drops.

4.2. Multivariate tests

In this section, we report evidence from multivariate tests to simultaneously assess the role of industry- and firm-specific factors in differentiating repricers from firms that experience negative return shocks but elect not to reprice.

Implementing such a comparison is afflicted by an identification problem. Figure 16.1 illustrates this issue. While we can observe firms that make a repricing announcement, non-repricers could either be firms that never experience significant price declines or control firms that experience such declines but choose not to reprice. We could identify the latter by specifying that control firms should have experienced past returns below a negative return cutoff, say $-r^*$, as in Table 16.6. However, such control samples would probably be imperfect because the cutoff return and the period over which it is defined are essentially arbitrary choices. The control sample could also require more complex definitions involving multiple return cutoffs over several prior periods. Finally, including some firms as controls while altogether ignoring others ignores variation *within* a selected control sample. For instance, a firm with a return of -40% is probably more likely to belong to the control sample than a firm with a "borderline" return of -15%. However, this differential is not reflected in the standard control sample procedure, whereby both firms receive equal weights as members of the selected control sample.

We use statistical methods based on "partial observability" probit models (e.g., Abowd and Farber, 1982) to address unobservability of control samples. Roughly speaking, the technique compares repricers to a "weighted average" of non-repricers, with higher weights assigned to firms that are more likely to be appropriate control firms, i.e., firms with more negative histories of past returns. The weights, however, need not be specified by the researcher; the technique estimates the weighting function endogenously as part of the likelihood function and produces a statistical comparisons of repricers with the (never observed) control firms.

Formally, the procedure takes as input two sets of variables. In the first stage, the input is a vector of instruments, say x_{1i} (e.g., past six-month returns), that help determine whether firm i belongs to the appropriate control sample of firms that have negative returns but choose not to reprice. In the second stage, the input is a second set of variables, say x_{2i} (such as firm size, age, board size, etc.) that potentially differentiate repricers from non-repricers, conditional on a negative shock. The likelihood function for the model can be written as

$$L(x_1, x_2) = \Pi_{\text{Repricers}}[p_1(x_1)^*p_2(x_2)]$$
$$\Pi_{\text{Non-Repricers}}[1 - p_1(x_1)^*p_2(x_2)] \qquad (1)$$

The likelihood function is derived by noting that repricers have received a negative return shock large enough to precipitate consideration of repricing (probability p_1) and have chosen to reprice (probability p_2) in response to this shock, to give a compound probability of $p_1{}^*p_2$, the first term in Eq. (1). Firms that have not announced a repricing either do not receive a large negative return shock (probability $1 - p_1$), or receive such a shock but choose not to reprice (probability $P_1{}^*(1 - p_2)$). The total probability of these two possibilities is $1 - p_1 + p_1{}^*(1 - p_2) = 1 - p_1{}^*p_2$. The likelihood function follows.

Table 16.7 provides estimates of several two-stage models fitted to the repricing firms. The first-stage estimates determine what types of firms are likely to be in the control sample. As expected, the procedure weights returns in six-month periods between $t = -24$ and $t = 0$ negatively. Returns in the time interval $[-12, -6]$ and $[-18, -12]$ have the largest (absolute)

weights, while returns in $[-24, -18]$ and $[-6, 0]$ are less important in precipitating a repricing decision. Weights on returns in periods prior to $t = -24$ are not significant, so we do not include these in the final specifications.

The second-stage estimates identify what types of firms are more likely to respond to negative return shocks by repricing their executive stock options. In the baseline specification, Model 1, we include four industry dummies consisting of a technology group (our industry groups 8, 17, and 18), services (group 15), trade (groups 13 and 14), and industrial manufacturing (group 7). To the industry dummies, we add firm size, proxied by the natural logarithm of sales. We also include firm age (our proxy being the time since first listing on the CRSP tapes), which is negatively related to management turnover costs. Finally, we add the number of options held by all executives listed in EXECUCOMP for the firm, as a proxy for the demand for repricing. The baseline specification estimates confirm that repricing concentrates in technology, services, trade, and manufacturing relative to all other sectors such as construction and utilities. Dummies for technology, services, and trade are 2.5–3.5 times the dummy for manufacturing, indicating a greater preponderance of repricing in the first three sectors relative to the latter. As in Brenner et al., firm size is important: small firms are more likely to reprice conditional on a negative return shock. Firm age is also significant and remains so across all specifications. The number of options is positively related to the conditional probability of repricing.

Models 2–4 sequentially add other explanatory variables to the baseline specification. Model 2 adds the change in the industry-adjusted EBITDA ratio (similar results obtain with differences in unadjusted EBITDA ratios) from year -2 to the year of repricing, and the change in sales growth from year -2 through the repricing year. As indicated in Table 16.4, profitability and sales growth shocks are more severe for repricers compared to control firms, and we test this proposition

Table 16.7 Multivariate analysis of repricing firms

Table 16.7 reports estimates of a two-stage probit model fitted to firms on the 1998 EXECUCOMP database, to compare repricers with firms that face similar return shocks but choose not to reprice. The dependent variable is one if a firm announces a repricing in a fiscal year and zero otherwise. Independent variables for the first stage include six-month returns over four periods beginning in month -24, where month zero denotes the fiscal year-end. Independent variables for the second stage are dummies for membership in the technology, services, trade, and manufacturing sectors, the natural logarithm of annual sales, the natural logarithm of the number of options held by all named executives, firm age (years since first listing), the change in the EBITDA ratio and annual sales growth over the last two fiscal years, and the number of members in a firm's board of directors. Numbers in parentheses denote *t*-statistics.

Variables	Model 1	Model 2	Model 3	Model 4
First stage				
Intercept	-1.28 (-12.86)	-1.15 (-11.19)	-1.33 (-14.11)	-1.23 (-10.84)
Return $[-24, -18]$	-0.38 (-4.36)	-0.37 (-3.91)	-0.41 (-4.17)	-0.44 (-10.84)
Return $[-18, -12]$	-0.97 (-13.37)	-0.88 (-11.72)	-1.14 (-9.31)	-1.08 (-9.10)
Return $[-12, -6]$	-1.33 (-14.10)	-1.24 (-11.44)	-1.43 (-9.86)	-1.36 (-8.41)
Return $[-6, 0]$	-0.49 (-4.51)	-0.40 (-3.47)	-0.49 (-3.14)	-0.42 (-3.14)
Second stage				
Intercept	1.36 (2.13)	1.34 (2.23)	1.62 (1.77)	1.28 (1.46)
Technology	1.71 (4.14)	1.49 (4.46)	1.88 (3.30)	1.69 (3.58)
Services	1.45 (3.85)	1.23 (3.70)	2.15 (3.72)	1.55 (3.22)
Trade	1.45 (4.51)	1.42 (4.66)	1.58 (3.59)	1.44 (3.59)
Manufacturing	0.45 (1.97)	0.44 (1.86)	0.61 (1.76)	0.58 (1.79)
Log (sales)	-0.34 (-3.61)	-0.40 (-4.17)	-0.14 (-1.14)	-0.21 (-1.67)
Firm age (years)	-0.05 (-5.06)	-0.05 (-4.82)	-0.06 (-4.26)	-0.05 (-4.21)
Log (#options)	0.07 (2.36)	0.06 (2.32)	0.05 (1.14)	0.04 (1.10)
Δ EBITDA		-2.25 (-1.98)		-1.22 (-0.71)
Δ Sales growth		-0.64 (-2.67)		-0.72 (-2.05)
Board size			-0.16 (-2.91)	-0.10 (-1.94)
Model significance				
χ^2 (d.f.)	434 (12)	491 (13)	392 (13)	394 (15)

in a multivariate context. Both the change in profitability and the change in sales growth are significant, indicating that repricers are likely to have experienced steeper declines in profitability and a greater shock to sales growth compared to control firms. Model 3 adds in the board size to the baseline specification. Board size appears to subsume the explanatory power of firm size in explaining firms' repricing responses to negative return shocks. The coefficient for firm size falls in statistical significance, and also drops by about half.

Model 4 reports the complete multivariate specification. Some variables drop in significance in the multivariate specification. The major drops in coefficient magnitudes are for firm size and the change in the EBITDA ratio. Neither variable is significant in the full specification even at 10%. The coefficient for firm size is sensitive to inclusion of board size: individually, when only one of the two is included as a regressor, it matters. However, when both firm size and board size are included jointly, firm size loses significance. In the multivariate specification, coefficients for both the manufacturing industry dummy and sales growth do not drop by much, though significance levels are reduced. Finally, the industry dummy variables for technology, services, and trade continue to be significant, as does firm age. Variables other than firm size, notably industry membership and firm age, do matter in explaining the conditional probability of repricing given a negative return shock.

4.3. Control sample based on approximate moneyness[7]

Section 4.2 uses prior stock returns to identify control firms that do not reprice despite negative return shocks that plausibly cause their options to go underwater. This section attempts to further refine control sample comparisons by conditioning more directly on the underwater nature of outstanding ESOs.

The key obstacle in assessing the moneyness of outstanding ESOs is that disclosures do not report data on strike prices of outstanding options. This is, of course, a well known issue afflicting all empirical research on executive stock options. However, an approximation is possible based on option grant prices reported in proxies (see also Carter and Lynch, 2001). Since options are normally granted at-the-money, the difference between strikes of current grants and lagged grants is a plausible proxy for the moneyness of previously granted options.

Accordingly, for each firm-year we compute the weighted average of strike prices of option grants, with weights for a given strike price proportional to the number of options granted at that price. From Table 16.3, return shocks to repricers are spread over 24 months prior to the repricing fiscal year-end. Hence, the ratio of the current-year strike to the two-year-back lagged strike is a rough measure of the moneyness of previously granted options. For our sample of repricers, median and mean strike price ratios equal 56.27% and 69.20%, respectively, suggesting that the median repricer has options that are about 40% out-of-the-money. This accords well with the 40% figure reported in both Brenner et al. and Chance et al., and

provides additional justification for the 40% out-of-moneyness underlying the Appendix A computations.[8]

We reestimate the two-step probit specification of Section 4.2, using the strike price ratio instead of past returns as the first-step instrument pointing towards plausible control firms. The results are qualitatively similar to those in Table 16.7 and are not reported here. As expected, we find that the strike price ratio has a negative coefficient and is significant at better than 1%. This indicates that firms with lower strike price ratios, i.e., those with more out of money options, are more likely to be at the node at which a repricing decision must be made. With regard to the second-step estimates, the significant changes are in firm size and the change in the EBITDA ratio in the full specification. While firm size altogether loses its marginal (10%) significance, the change in the EBITDA ratio now becomes significant at better than 1%. (The results are available upon request.)

4.4. Summary of cross-sectional results

Our cross-sectional analysis provides an extensive investigation into factors that explain repricing. We contribute several new results to the repricing literature by examining a richer slate of variables. Two aspects of our results deserve special comment. First, we show that several variables other than firm size explain why firms reprice. Our results also provide a more thorough evaluation of agency-based criticisms of repricing, and they cast some doubt on the notion that repricing primarily manifests shareholder–manager agency problems or ineffective governance of firms. Specifically,

- Repricers are young and rapidly growing firms concentrated in the technology, services, and trade sectors (together accounting for over 70% of all repricings). These are not traditionally viewed as the types of firms in which shareholder – manager agency problems are especially significant.

- Institutional ownership is not lower in repricers nor is the ownership of repricers more fragmented. Repricers have significantly smaller boards, while large boards are more likely symptomatic of ineffective governance or non-value maximizing behavior (e.g., Yermack, 1996).
- Repricers experience abnormally *high* CEO attrition rates. This is inconsistent with the entrenchment view of repricing, which holds that shareholders are unable to fire executives in repricers despite their displeasure with management's poor performance, because managers are entrenched.

These findings suggest that it is premature, and probably incorrect, to conclude as do Chance et al. (p. 129), based on a more limited analysis of an earlier sample, that "firms with greater agency costs are more likely to reprice."

While the cross-sectional analysis comes down somewhat against the agency-expropriation explanation for repricing, it is also useful to consider whether it supports a view of repricing as optimal recontracting by shareholders with managers. Devising a test for optimality is difficult because contract theory provides few concrete guidelines for such tests and theoretical work on repricing is relatively sparse. The analysis in Acharya et al. provides some initial pointers. We explore whether our results, particularly some of the newer ones, are consistent with their optimal recontracting framework.

According to Acharya et al., the key consideration in determining optimality of repricing is the impact of managerial control on the returns distribution of the firm. Repricing is more likely to be optimal when managers have more control over future return distributions. They suggest two testable implications. First, they refute the notion that repricing is initiated due to

"factors beyond the manager's control" because systematic factors constitute background risk that makes it harder to fine tune incentives in repriced options. They argue on this basis that repricing is unlikely to be associated with systematic or industry-wide shocks to firms. Consistently, we find that negative returns leading to repricing are associated with firm-specific operating shocks to growth and EBITDA.

In the same vein, Acharya et al. also argue that repricing should be more prevalent in firms where managerial input exerts more influence on future return distributions. We also find empirical support for this implication. Repricers tend to be young, rapidly growing firms. Managers probably have more influence over the return distributions of such firms rather than of older firms in mature businesses. We also find that the technology dummy is positively related to repricing. Close to 40% of all repricings are concentrated in this sector, which together with the services and trade sectors accounts for over 70% of all repricings. The technology and service sectors, and perhaps to a lesser extent the trade sector, are plausibly industries in which managerial input, as opposed to other competitive advantages in the product market, is key in influencing future returns of firms.

5. TOP MANAGEMENT REPRICING AND TURNOVER

Our earlier analysis compares the sample of repricers with firms that do not reprice. In this section, we examine variation within the sample of firms that reprice their ESOs. We document that while the CEO is often included among the executives repriced by a firm, several firms reprice other executives but not the CEO. The phenomenon of "non-CEO repricing" is an interesting facet of the data not noted in previous literature.

Section 5.1 reports characteristics of CEO repricers and non-CEO repricers and also examines these firms relative to control firms, evaluating whether either of the two subsamples displays support for the agency, governance, or entrenchment explanations for repricing. Section 5.2 analyzes CEO turnover in non-CEO and CEO repricers.

5.1. Do repricers reprice their CEOs?

We begin our analysis of CEO and non-CEO repricing by identifying the CEO in charge at the beginning of the repricing fiscal year. For each repricing announcement, EXECUCOMP reports names of repriced executives. We match this list of repriced executives with the list of CEO titles to determine whether the CEO in charge at the beginning of the repricing fiscal year is included in the repricing announcement. We cross-verify the repricing information with the actual proxy statements in the repricing year where available, and otherwise verify it in ten-year repricing tables provided in subsequent proxy statements or annual 10-K filings. If the CEO is repriced, we define the repricing event as a "CEO repricing," and if not, we call it a "non-CEO repricing."

Table 16.8 reports the number of CEO and non-CEO repricings. Non-CEO repricings constitute 86 out of 213, or about 40% of all repricings. Table 16.8 also reports cross-sectional characteristics of both sets of firms. All CEO-related data pertain to the CEO in charge at the beginning of the

Table 16.8 Characteristics of CEO repricers and non-CEO repricers

Table 16.8 reports data on turnovers and several characteristics of firms in the 1998 EXECUCOMP database that announce a repricing between 1992 and 1997. Column 1 reports data for firms that reprice their CEO, while Column 2 gives data for firms that reprice executives other than CEOs. Column 3 reports z and p values for Wilcoxon tests that compare the two sets of firms. Characteristics reported here include annual sales, book value of assets, market value of equity, shares and options held by the CEO and other executives in the proxy statement, the difference between the options (as a fraction of option plus equity) of the CEO and other executives, the firm's age (months since first listing), CEO tenure in years, the aggregate ownership of institutions and 5% block-holders, and the number of members in a firm's board of directors. For each characteristic, we report the median (mean).

Variable	CEO repricers	Non-CEO repricers	Wilcoxon z (p-value)
Number of firms	127	86	
# CEO turnovers			
Year [0]	15 (11.81%)	26 (30.23%)	−2.35 (0.02)
Years [0, 1]	24 (18.89%)	31 (36.05%)	−2.59 (0.01)
Firm size			
Sales	291 (680)	265 (789)	0.07 (0.94)
Total assets	341 (582)	271 (744)	0.84 (0.40)
Market value of equity	296 (672)	363 (611)	−0.78 (0.43)
Other characteristics			
Firm age (months)	87 (121)	78 (97)	2.02 (0.04)
CEO tenure	6.32 (7.63)	7.48 (8.14)	−0.47 (0.64)
Institutional owners	53.58 (49.29)	45.63 (45.37)	1.10 (0.27)
5% block owners	23.01 (25.89)	30.41 (33.51)	−1.79 (0.07)
Board size	7 (7.54)	7 (7.23)	1.08 (0.28)
Equity and option holdings			
CEO options	131 (311)	81 (209)	2.61 (0.01)
CEO shares	70 (341)	278 (908)	−2.79 (0.01)
Non−CEO executive options	366 (661)	267 (508)	1.57 (0.12)
Non−CEO executive shares	77 (2,911)	74 (9,635)	−0.22 (0.83)
% Options (non−CEO) −% Options (CEO)	4.78 (8.40)	21.99 (27.27)	−2.80 (0.00)

repricing fiscal year, with respect to whom firms must make repricing and turnover decisions. Columns 1 and 2 give characteristics of CEO repricers and non-CEO repricers, respectively. Column 3 reports Wilcoxon z and p values for testing differences in characteristics of CEO repricers and non-CEO repricers. As in Section 4, the cross-sectional data in Table 16.8 are organized into four categories: CEO turnover, firm size, other firm characteristics, and equity and options holdings.

The CEO turnover data emphasize that on average, both CEO repricers and non-CEO repricers are not particularly averse to initiating CEO changes. In neither CEO repricers nor non-CEO repricers do we find evidence of abnormally low turnover rates. For non-CEO repricers, the one- and two-year attrition rates are 30% and 36%, respectively. The one- and two-year attrition rates for CEO repricers are 11.81% and 18.89%, respectively. The one- and two-year turnover rates for these firms significantly exceed turnover rates for all non-repricers, which are 6.29% and 12.57%, respectively (from Table 16.6). For both samples, CEO turnover rates are also at least as high as the rates for control firms, which are 10.26% and 18.21%, respectively. There is little evidence that turnover rates in either sample are abnormally low, as an entrenchment hypothesis would suggest.

Other cross-sectional characteristics of CEO repricers and non-CEO repricers also reveal no evidence of expropriation or poor governance. We find no significant differences in size, as measured by sales, assets, or market value of equity, between CEO repricers and non-CEO repricers. CEO repricers tend to be older (87 months) than non-CEO repricers (78 months), but both sets of firms are much younger than the control group of firms (126 months, from Table 16.6). We also detect no statistically significant differences in CEO tenure: CEO repricers have a median tenure of 6.32 years versus 7.48 years for non-CEO repricers and 6.56 years for control firms. Board sizes in both samples are roughly equal, with a median board size of seven members; both types of firms have small boards.

Institutional ownership is actually higher in CEO repricers, though not significantly so, while block ownership is comparable to control firms. There is no compelling evidence of poor governance in either sample.

The data do, however, show pronounced asymmetries in the structure of the equity holdings of CEOs relative to other executives in CEO versus non-CEO repricers. In non-CEO repricers, CEOs have more straight equity compared to options, while other executives have relatively more options compared to equity. In CEO repricers, the tilt of equity versus options for CEOs compared to other executives is not as pronounced. The asymmetry in CEO and other executives' equity holdings relative to options is captured by the variable "% Options (non-CEO) − % Options (CEO)" in Table 16.8. To compute this variable, we first calculate the aggregate number of options held by executives other than the CEO, and express this as a percentage of the total number of options and shares they hold. We then compute the same measure for the CEO, and subtract the option percentage for the CEO from the option percentage for non-CEO executives. As Table 16.8 shows, the difference in the option percentage is positive for both CEO repricers and non-CEO repricers, which indicates that executives have greater proportions of their equitylinked compensation in options compared to CEOs. However, the variable is significantly larger for non-CEO repricers (median = 21.99%) than for CEO repricers (median = 4.78%). This indicates that for the sample of non-CEO repricers, executives other than the CEO have more options relative to straight equity holdings, while CEO repricers have more equity relative to options.

The imbalance in options relative to equity between the CEO and other executives provides one possible explanation for the incidence of non-CEO repricing. A price decline has a differential impact on the value of options and the value of shares. Further, when the price decline is such that the options end up out-of-the-money, executives may place very little value on them (Hall and Murphy, 2000). Therefore, if executives have more options compared to equity, a negative return shock misaligns incentives for non-CEO executives more than it does for the CEO. The CEO's incentives are less adversely affected because the CEO has relatively more equity compared to options. Non-CEO repricing should, therefore, be more common when equity-linked compensation is option-oriented for executives but straight equity-oriented for CEOs, which is what we find. This would suggest that repricing has a "re-incentivizing" role, in which it corrects incentive imbalances *within* the top management team that arise from a negative return shock.

In computing the variable "options," we normalize the current stock price level to $25. This accounts for differences in stock price levels across firms, so options on a stock trading at $30 are counted as being three times as valuable as options on a stock trading at $10. However, the normalization does not account for other differences such as differences in option maturities across firms or across-firm variation in stock return volatilities. These differences could be important and result in variation in option values across firms (see, e.g., Guay, 1999). Appendix A presents two alternate approaches to calculating the dollar value of option holdings and recalculates the variable "% Options (non-CEO) − % Options (CEO)" under these measures. The option-equity asymmetry between CEOs and non-CEO executives in CEO repricers and non-CEO repricers persists under the alternate measures of compensation asymmetry as well.

5.2. CEO repricing and turnover in ESO repricers

As Table 16.8 shows, the rates of CEO turnover for non-CEO repricers is higher than the rates of CEO turnover for CEO repricers. The difference in CEO attrition rates suggest that *within* firms that reprice their ESOs, the decision to reprice a CEO is related to the incidence of CEO turnover. Specifically, repricers that include the CEO among repriced executives are less likely to witness CEO turnover, while ESO repricers

that exclude the CEO from repricing are more likely to experience CEO turnover.

Table 16.9 reports probit estimates in which the incidence of CEO turnover in repricers is modeled as a function of a firm's decision to include the CEO in the list of executives repriced. Controls include firm size, industry dummies for technology, service, trade, and manufacturing, and the number of shares held by the CEO, since firms with high CEO shareholdings are less likely to experience CEO turnover (see, e.g., Denis et al., 1997). Column 1 reports estimates of a specification that includes a zero/one CEO repricing dummy as an explanatory variable. The coefficient for CEO repricing is negative and significant at 5%.

The dummy variable specification we report in the first column of Table 9 ignores the endogeneity of the CEO repricing decision. Ignoring selection-bias potentially leads to inconsistent parameter estimates (see, e.g., Greene, 1993, Chapter 22). We correct for the selection-bias using the two-step procedure suggested in Heckman (1979). In the first step, we estimate a probit model for the CEO repricing decision. In the second step, the inverse Mills ratio from the probit estimate replaces the CEO repricing dummy in the turnover regression. Columns 2 and 3 report the results from the two-step procedure. Column 2 reports the turnover probit estimates with the selection-bias correction. Column 3 reports estimates of the first-step probit model for whether the CEO is repriced with past returns, industry, firm age, and size, and the difference between the option percentage of the CEO and other executives as explanatory variables. The negative sign for repricing persists in this selection-bias corrected specification as well. Thus, ESO repricers that reprice their CEOs are less likely to witness CEO turnover.

6. CONCLUSION

The repricing of executive stock options has received considerable attention recently, much of it unflattering. Institutional

Table 16.9 Relation between CEO repricing and turnover

Table 16.9 reports estimates of probit models fitted to 213 firms on the 1998 EXECUCOMP database that reprice their executive stock options. The dependent variable is one if there is CEO turnover in the repricing year and zero otherwise. Independent variables include six-month returns for four non-overlapping periods beginning in month −24 where month zero is the repricing fiscal year-end, industry dummies for technology, services, trade, and manufacturing sectors, the natural logarithm of sales, firm age (years since listing), the natural logarithm of the shares held by the beginning-of-year CEO, a zero/one dummy variable for CEO repricing, and the inverse Mills ratio based on probit estimates in Column 3. The dependent variable in Column 3 is one for a CEO repricing and zero otherwise, and independent variables include, additionally, the option percentage (the number of executive options divided by the options plus the number of shares) for the non-CEO executives minus that for the CEO. Numbers in parentheses denote *t*-statistics.

		Model 2	
Dependent variable	Model 1 CEO turnover	CEO turnover	CEO repricing
Independent variables			
Intercept	−1.99 (−2.51)	−2.46 (−3.19)	0.85 (1.83)
Return [−6, 0]	0.27 (0.92)	0.19 (0.63)	0.08 (0.32)
Return [−12, −6]	−0.81 (−1.78)	−0.89 (−1.97)	0.35 (1.17)
Return [−18, −12]	−0.70 (−1.71)	−0.63 (−1.53)	−0.15 (−0.61)
Return [−24, −18]	−0.02 (−0.10)	−0.02 (−0.07)	−0.32 (−1.39)
Technology	0.86 (1.34)	0.89 (1.37)	−0.55 (−1.57)
Services	0.66 (0.94)	0.66 (0.93)	−0.06 (−0.16)
Trade	1.43 (2.12)	1.36 (2.01)	−0.31 (−0.74)
Manufacturing	0.43 (0.63)	0.34 (0.49)	−0.38 (−1.00)
Log (sales)	0.14 (1.42)	0.15 (1.56)	−0.05 (−0.65)
Log (# CEO shares)	−0.11 (−3.77)	−0.10 (−3.03)	
Age firm			0.04 (1.39)
% Options (non-CEO)−			
% Options (CEO)			−0.64 (−2.65)
CEO repriced	−0.66 (−2.69)		
Inverse Mills ratio		−0.40 (−2.56)	
Model significance			
χ^2_{11} (*p*-value)	38.41 (0.00)	35 (0.00)	22.88 (0.02)

investors, in particular, often frown upon this practice, as it seems to reward managers despite poor performance, precisely when they perhaps ought to be fired instead. It is therefore natural to inquire whether repricing represents an indictment of poor shareholder governance systems, reflecting entrenched and possibly over-compensated managers expropriating shareholder wealth.

We contribute to the repricing debate by developing new and extensive empirical evidence on over 200 repricing events between 1992 and 1997. Besides a larger sample of repricings, our paper adds to

the literature in three ways. First, we present evidence on whether repricings are economically significant compensation events. We find that while repricing grants are large, and in fact, comparable to total annual compensation levels, compensation changes accompanying repricing tend to be small, and compensation levels in repricers are not abnormally high. Thus, repricing is itself significant to the repriced executive, but there is little else unusual in the compensation patterns in repricers.

Our second contribution is methodological. In comparing repricers with control firms that do not reprice despite negative returns, a key issue is that control firms are not explicitly identified in the data except through imperfect conditioning instruments such as past returns or option grant prices. We implement statistical methods to account for unobserved control firms. The technique exploits information in the conditioning instruments but recognizes that the instruments are imperfect pointers and produces a comparison between repricers and (never observed) control firms. We also implement the technique by conditioning directly on the underwater nature of options rather than through poor past returns.

Finally, we expand the literature through a richer cross-sectional analysis of the repricing decision. We present several new findings that shed light on alternative explanations for repricing. In particular, we offer an extensive evaluation of the agency and ineffective governance explanations that underlie much of the public criticism of repricing. We find, as in previous work, that repricers are small firms. However, unlike previous work, we find that other variables matter in explaining the repricing decision, even after controlling for firm size.

We find that the typical repricer is a young, rapidly growing firm that experiences a steep and somewhat abrupt shock to its growth that is not reversed in the following two years. Repricers are more likely to belong to the technology sector, which accounts for close to 40% of all repricings in our sample. Repricers are also more likely to come from the services and trade sectors, and together the three sectors account for over two-thirds of all repricing announcements. There is no evidence that institutional ownership in repricers is low or that the ownership structure is especially fragmented in repricers, or that CEOs in repricers are entrenched by virtue of being long-tenured. Finally, repricers tend to have smaller boards of directors. Collectively, our cross-sectional results reveal no evidence that repricing is concentrated in firms whose shareholder–manager agency problems are especially prominent, nor do the results reveal any compelling evidence that repricers are poorly governed. In fact, by at least one metric, board size, repricers appear to be better governed firms.

We develop some first evidence on CEO turnover in repricers, in perhaps the most direct examination of the entrenchment explanation for repricing. If repricing reflects the inability of shareholders to fire poorly performing managers because managers are entrenched, top management turnover in repricers should be abnormally low. In fact, repricers have abnormally *high* rates of top management turnover. Over 25% of firms making a repricing announcement experience a CEO change either in the year of repricing or the year after. This attrition rate exceeds that in both the universe of non-repricers and control firms of non-repricers with poor past returns. We thus find no evidence that repricers are especially reluctant to initiate top management changes, as an entrenchment hypothesis suggests.

Finally, our paper presents some new evidence on within-sample variation in repricers. We find that a significant 40% proportion of repricings are "non-CEO" repricings, in which repricers do not include their CEOs in the list of executives repriced. In these instances, repricing may redress *within*-management incentive distortions created by negative return shocks. We also document that within repricers, CEO turnover is lower at firms that include the CEO in their repricing. Thus, the inclusion of the CEO in a repricing lowers the probability of turnover while exclusion of the CEO is likely to be associated with CEO departure.

Repricing is a key governance issue for institutional investors, who must decide whether to support this compensation practice. Much of the controversy surrounding repricing arises because repricing appears to confer rewards upon poorly performing executives, perhaps symptomatic of agency problems, entrenchment, or poor governance of firms. The broader picture, however, tells a different story. Cross-sectional characteristics of repricers, their compensation policies, the incidence of non-CEO repricing, and the high rate of top management turnover in repricers do not support the idea that repricing is primarily a manifestation of poor governance or managerial entrenchment.

APPENDIX A. VALUE OF OPTION HOLDINGS

In computing the variable "options" held for each executive, we normalize the current stock price level to $25. This accounts for differences in stock price levels across firms, but does not account for other differences such as differences in option maturities across firms or across-firm variation in stock return volatilities. In this appendix, we consider two alternate measures that attempt to capture the dollar value of outstanding options for each executive.

Estimating outstanding option values is not straightforward because of insufficient disclosure in proxy statements. This is a well known problem that plagues empirical research on executive stock options. Proxies do not report the value of outstanding options for executives, nor do they report even basic inputs necessary for option valuation such as strike prices and maturities of outstanding options. Proxy statements report two pieces of information regarding outstanding options of executives: the total number of exercisable and unexercisable options outstanding (but not a breakup of these by strikes or moneyness) and the immediate payoff from exercising in-the-money options but little on out-of-the-money options. Some approximation of option values is required using what is available in proxy statements.

Our first measure, *PAYOFF*, uses only information that is available in proxy statements and coded by EXECUCOMP. *PAYOFF* is equal to the intrinsic value of exercisable and unexercisable options that are in-the-money on the reporting date, or $\Sigma_i\ max(S - X_i, 0)$, where S denotes the stock price on the reporting date and X_i denotes the strike price of the ith stock option outstanding. We recompute "% Options (non-CEO) − % Options (CEO)" by setting the value of the options portfolio equal to *PAYOFF* and using the market value of equity held by executives. Doing so gives the median (mean) difference in option percentage between CEOs and non-CEOs equal to 0.08% (8.65%) for CEO repricers and equal to 11.79% (23.47%) for non-CEO repricers, and the difference is

significant (Wilcoxon $z\ (p) = -2.69\ (0.00)$). The asymmetry in compensation between CEOs and non CEO executives across CEO repricers and non-CEO repricers persists under this second measure of compensation asymmetry, too.

PAYOFF gives the intrinsic value of options but ignores the time value of options, and in particular, assigns zero value to all options that are out-of-the-money on the reporting date. Our second measure attempts to correct for this by exploiting information disclosed in repricing-year proxies in addition to that available through EXECUCOMP. EXECUCOMP identifies a list of repriced executives. For each executive in the list, we obtain the total number of outstanding options at the beginning of the repricing year as the sum of exercisable and unexercisable options. We next read individual repricer proxies to ascertain the number of options repriced for each executive and obtain the number of non-repriced options as the difference between the beginning of year outstanding options and the repriced options.

We calculate the value of the repriced and non-repriced options separately and sum to compute the value of total options holdings. We compute the Black–Scholes value of repriced options assuming they are 40% out of the money (Brenner et al. and Chance et al. report similar moneyness levels for repricing), using the maturity of the replacement options, risk-free interest rates of 8% per annum, and volatilities based on 120-day daily returns prior to the fiscal year-end of repricing following Guay (1999). The value of non-repriced options is computed as the value of an at the-money option with the same parameters plus the intrinsic value of exercisable plus unexercisable options, i.e., *PAYOFF*.

The additional data requirement for developing this proxy shrinks our sample to 137 repricing announcements (84 CEO repricers and 53 non-CEO repricers). The drop in sample size occurs because of missing repricing-year proxy statements and incomplete information in repricing or subsequent-year proxy statements.

We use the second value measure to recalculate the variable "% Options (non-CEO) − % Options (CEO)." The median (mean) difference in option percentage between CEOs and non-CEOs is equal to −2.31% (−5.04%) for CEO repricers, which is not significantly different from zero (Wilcoxon z (p) = −0.71 (0.41)), while the difference for non-CEO repricers has a median (mean) value of 15.97% (14.02%) and is significant at 5% (Wilcoxon z (p) = 2.09 (0.04)). The ratio difference between CEOs and non-CEOs is significant at 5% (Wilcoxon z (p) = 2.17 (0.03)). The option-equity asymmetry between CEOs and non-CEO executives in CEO repricers and non-CEO repricers remains under this third measure of compensation asymmetry as well.

NOTES

† We are grateful to G. William Schwert (the editor) and two anonymous referees for very helpful comments. We also thank Mary Ellen Carter, Jonathan Karpoff, Scott Lee, Kai Li, Arvind Mahajan, Vojislav Maksimovic, Thomas Noe, Gordon Phillips, S. Abraham Ravid, K. Geert Rouwenhorst, and seminar participants at the Tuck/JFE Contemporaneous Corporate Governance Conference, the 2000 AFA and 2001 AFE meetings, Louisiana State University, Texas A&M University, Tulane University, University of Massachusetts, Amherst, University of Virginia, and Yale University for their comments. Kristina Minnick and Subhankar Nayak provided excellent research assistance. Special thanks to Kose John and David Yermack for extensive feedback on an earlier draft.

* Corresponding author. Rutgers Business School-Newark and New Brunswick, Rutgers University, 94 Rockafeller Road, Piscataway, NJ 70118, USA. Tel.: +1-732-445-4446; fax: +1-732-445-2333. E-mail address: chiddi@rci.rutgers.edu (N.K. Chidambaran), nprabhal@rhsmith.umd.edu (N.R. Prabhala).

1   In one unsuccessful instance, the State of Wisconsin Investment Board (SWIB) attempted to force a computer networking company, Shiva Corporation, to include such a proposal in the annual proxy statement, but failed to do so. More recently, however, SWIB has successfully pushed through binding bylaw resolutions that block repricing without shareholder

approval (see, e.g., the case of General Data Comm Industries, Investor Relations Business, February 15, 1999).

2   Prior returns of repricers and non-repricers overlap in calendar time. Positive correlation across two samples tends to understate significance, but correlation within samples can overstate significance levels. To mitigate within-sample correlation, we also compute returns as an excess over median industry, time period, and size decile matched portfolio returns. Patterns in these excess returns are similar to those in raw returns. Differences between repricer and matched returns for the six prior periods going back from [−6, 0] have z statistics of −4.38, −10.05, −8.30, −3.51, −0.25, and −0.99, respectively; the first four are significant at 1% but not the last two (p = 0.80 and 0.32, respectively).

3   The abnormal EBITDA and sales growth statistics for non-repricers show that industry adjustment on the lines of Barber and Lyon (1996) produces well-behaved statistics. The median abnormal operating performance (Panel B) and abnormal sales growth (Panel E) are close to zero and economically and statistically insignificant. The mean statistics are positive, suggesting that the metrics are positively skewed, as in Barber and Lyon (1996).

4   We are grateful to an anonymous referee for motivating and developing this section

5   While current-year grants in these control firms are lower than the repriced option grants, they exceed the new option grants in repricers; median (mean) = $123, 100 ($612, 200). This can be attributed to the fact that repricers scale back grants of new options in the repricing fiscal year.

6   For example, the board in Bell Sports Corp. sought ways to stay within the cap. The company writes in its November 1996 proxy that senior managers with long tenure were asked to cancel 40% of existing stock options to increase stock options available for grants to other employees.

7   We are grateful to an anonymous referee for suggestions on developing and implementing this analysis.

8   The requirement of lagged strike prices means that we lose data for fiscal 1992 and 1993, the first two years of data in EXECU-COMP. We develop a second strike price proxy by augmenting the data with the two-year back market price of the stock from CRSP whenever lagged strikes are missing. Repricers have similar median and mean strike price ratios (58.61% and 72.05%, respectively) under this alternative measure.

REFERENCES

Abowd, J., Farber, H., 1982. Job queues and union status of workers. Industrial and Labor Relations Review 35, 354–367.

Acharya, V., John, K., Sundaram, R., 2000. Contract renegotiation and the optimality of resetting executive stock options. Journal of Financial Economics 57, 65–101.

Barber, B.M., Lyon, J.D., 1996. Detecting abnormal operating performance: the empirical power and specification of test statistics. Journal of Financial Economics 41, 359–399.

Brenner, M., Sundaram, R.K., Yermack, D., 2000. Altering the terms of executive stock options. Journal of Financial Economics 57, 103–128.

Carpenter, J.N., 1998. The exercise and valuation of executive stock options. Journal of Financial Economics 48, 127–158.

Carter, M.E., Lynch, L.J., 2000. Does accounting affect economic behavior? Evidence from stock option repricing. Unpublished working paper, Columbia University, New York, NY.

Carter, M.E., Lynch, L.J., 2001. An examination of executive stock option repricing. Journal of Financial Economics 61, 207–225.

Chance, D.M., Kumar, R., Todd, R.B., 2000. The 'repricing' of executive stock options. Journal of Financial Economics 57, 129–154.

Core, J.E., Guay, W., 2001. Stock option plans for non-executive employees. Journal of Financial Economics 61, 253–287.

Cuny, C., Jorion, P., 1995. Valuing executive stock options with an endogenous departure decision. Journal of Accounting and Economics 20, 193–205.

Denis, D.J., Denis, D.K., Sarin, A., 1997. Ownership structure and top executive turnover. Journal of Financial Economics 45, 193–221.

Gilson, S.C., Vetsuypens, M.R., 1993. CEO compensation in financially distressed firms: an empirical analysis. Journal of Finance 48, 425–458.

Greene, W., 1993. Econometric Analysis. Macmillan, New York.

Guay, W., 1999. The sensitivity of CEO wealth to equity risk: an analysis of magnitudes and determinants. Journal of Financial Economics 53, 43–71.

Hall, B.J., Murphy, K.J., 2000. Optimal exercise prices for executive stock options. Unpublished working paper, National Bureau of Economic Research, Cambridge, MA.

Heckman, J.J., 1979. Sample selection bias as a specification error. Econometrica 47, 153–161.

Himmelberg, C.P., Hubbard, R.G., 2000. Incentive pay and the market for CEOs: an analysis of pay-for-performance sensitivity. Unpublished working paper, Columbia University, New York, NY.

Murphy, K.J., 1998. Executive compensation. Unpublished working paper, University of Southern California, Los Angeles, CA.

Saly, P.J., 1994. Repricing of executive stock options in a down market. Journal of Accounting and Economics 18, 325–356.

Yermack, D., 1995. Do corporations award CEO stock options effectively? Journal of Financial Economics 39, 237–269.

Yermack, D., 1996. Higher market valuation of companies with a small board of directors. Journal of Financial Economics 40, 185–211.

## Chapter 17

Julie Ann Elston[1] and Lawrence G. Goldberg*

EXECUTIVE COMPENSATION AND AGENCY COSTS IN GERMANY

Source: *Journal of Banking & Finance*, 27(7) (2003): 1391–1410.

ABSTRACT

With the growth of international mergers like DaimlerChrysler, interest in executive compensation practices abroad, particularly in Germany, has increased. Using unique data sources for Germany, we find that similar to US firms, German firms also have agency problems caused by the separation of ownership from control, with ownership dispersion leading to higher compensation. In addition, there is evidence that bank influence has a negative impact on compensation.

1. INTRODUCTION

THE DIFFERING LEVELS OF EXECUTIVE compensation across countries have recently aroused significant public interest as cross-country mergers have increased. While the academic literature has focused mostly on compensation behavior in the US, recent studies have begun to explore compensation practices in other countries, particularly in Germany. Mergers between firms in different countries naturally raise issues of comparability of pay and incentives-for-performance practices between countries. Numerous studies have tried to identify the most important factors impacting executive compensation. Recently several studies have examined the agency problems of firms by relating the level of executive compensation to corporate control measures. Germany is a country of particular interest not only because it has considerably lower levels of compensation than the US, but also because it has a very different corporate governance structure, characterized by concentrated firm ownership and a strong bank presence. In this paper we examine the factors affecting the level of executive compensation in Germany, with particular emphasis on the agency problem created by the separation of management and ownership.

Agency problems caused by the separation of ownership from control in large corporations were first popularized by Berle and Means (1932) and have since been examined extensively in both the popular and academic literature. Jensen and Meckling (1976) formalized the agency problem and stimulated interest in executive compensation, the most easily measured way that managers could take advantage of lack of control by owners.

Top executive compensation has grown dramatically in the United States, and consequently, public interest in compensation levels has increased. Popular publications regularly reveal the compensation of the top executives and particularly the chief executive officers (CEO) of the large corporations. The Securities and Exchange Commission (SEC) requires companies to reveal compensation components for top executives. Since US executives are the highest paid in the world, the US has the largest economy, and data are readily available in the US, most popular and academic attention has focused almost exclusively on the United States. However, there has been increased interest in executive compensation in other countries, and particularly in Germany.[2]

Several bodies of literature have developed in order to determine whether management is taking advantage of the lack of ownership control. The first body of literature examines the relationship between executive compensation and corporate performance, while the second relates corporate performance to the degree of control that owners have over managers. Our study contributes to the relatively smaller third body of literature relating corporate control directly to executive compensation and thus directly tests the agency issue. Section 2 reviews some of the most relevant studies to date.

Though we know less about executive compensation in countries other than the US, researchers are currently investigating very similar issues in some of these countries, although data availability has impeded this process. Germany has the third largest economy in the world and consequently is of considerable interest. Internationalization has progressed recently at a rapid pace and German firms are more commonly merging with firms from other countries. Executive compensation becomes a particularly important issue when a German firm merges with an American firm, such as in the case of the Daimler–Benz merger with Chrysler. Corporate structure differs greatly between the two countries. Do American CEOs get paid more than their German counterparts? If so, can this be justified? A recent article in the German magazine *Focus* has claimed that German executives are underpaid

despite high performance. The article cites 1997 German salaries of top executives including:

- Jurgen Schremp of DaimlerChrysler at 3 million DM;
- Bernd Pischetsrieder of BMW at 3.5 million DM;
- Ulrich Hartmann of VEBA at 2.9 million DM; and
- Heinrich Von Pierer of Siemens at 2 million DM.

These compensation levels seem low compared to equivalent executives in the US such as:

- Bob Eaton of DaimlerChrysler at 20 million DM;
- John Welch of GE at 69 million DM;
- Andrew Grove of Intel at 89 million DM; and
- Richard Scrushy of Healthsouth at 181 million DM.

Although this difference between the two countries has been narrowing recently as German firms have increasingly turned to granting stock options to top executives (Kroll, 1999), corporate control systems remain quite different in the two countries.[3] One main difference is that many German firms have a 2-tiered board system and also many firms have representation of banks on the supervisory board (SB) of the firm. All the firms in our sample do in fact have a 2-tiered board system. For many reasons then, it is quite important to identify the factors affecting executive compensation in Germany and to assess the effect of corporate control mechanisms on executive compensation.

In order to analyze this issue we have compiled a unique and comprehensive data set in order to analyze German executive compensation. This data set is more extensive than data used in previous studies of German compensation. This enables us to contribute to the literature, based largely on American data, by analyzing the factors affecting executive compensation and the effects of ownership control on executive compensation in Germany. The results for German executives are strikingly similar to those found previously for American executives. We find evidence that both sales and ROE are positively correlated with compensation, and that greater ownership dispersion leads to higher levels of executive compensation holding other factors constant. Thus, agency problems appear to exist in Germany as well as in the United States. Further there is evidence that bank influence reduces compensation, and that large block ownership of stock by various groups also has a negative effect on compensation.

Section 2 of the paper reviews the previous relevant literature. Section 3 describes the German corporate governance structure, including the two types of boards and the role of banks in corporate control. Section 4 presents the empirical model and the refutable hypotheses. Section 5 describes the data employed. The empirical results are presented and discussed in Section 6. Section 7 concludes with implications for corporate control.

2. LITERATURE REVIEW

Berle and Means (1932) raised a number of issues about the operation of the modern corporation and noted the problems that arise with the separation of ownership and management. When owners do not control the corporation, managers are able to pursue their own economic interests. Dispersion of ownership reduces the ability of shareholders to remove bad managers and also reduces the incentive for and the ability of shareholders to monitor managerial activity. Ownership dispersion also provides managers incentives to exploit their protected positions and extract benefits for themselves. The most direct benefit managers could obtain is increased monetary compensation, and this benefit is also the easiest one to measure. Non-monetary benefits, such as the size and quality of the support staff, the character of the work environment, and access to corporate assets for personal use, are difficult to measure or compare across companies. Consequently, in this study we follow the practice of previous studies and compare monetary compensation.

The earliest empirical studies of executive compensation in the United States used simple correlation coefficients to identify the factors related to the level of compensation. Patton (1951) examines the distribution of pay among different types of executives and finds that executive compensation is positively correlated with both profits and growth of the firm. Subsequent studies usually just used data relating to the CEO because of greater ease in obtaining these data. Roberts (1956) and McGuire et al. (1962) find a stronger relationship between sales and compensation than between profits and compensation. In a more recent study, Jensen and Murphy (1990) find the opposite. Ciscel and Carroll (1980) correct econometric problems in these models by using an instrumental variable for profits to reduce multicollinearity between sales and profits. This literature plus more recent studies conclude that both profits and size are positively related to executive compensation. Executives are paid more when the company is more successful and are also paid more when the company is larger. This provides incentives to executives to improve performance, a goal in line with stockholders' interest, but it also provides incentives to increase the size of the company, a goal that might not be in the interest of stockholders.

Other studies have introduced additional explanatory factors. Among these variables are regulatory effects in transportation and utilities (Carroll and Ciscel, 1982), market concentration and barriers to entry (Auerbach and Siegfried, 1974), the gender of executives and capital investment in workers (Bartlett and Miller, 1988), sales growth (Murphy, 1985; Coughlin and Schmidt, 1985), and stock performance instead of accounting performance (Masson, 1971; Murphy, 1985; Deckop, 1988). In this study we follow the lead of previous studies in choosing control variables and use the two types of measures, profitability and size, that have been found to be important determinants of executive compensation.

A second line of research in executive compensation relates corporate performance to ownership dispersion. Demsetz and Lehn (1985) find no relationship between profitability and ownership concentration using a linear model. However, Morck et al. (1988) find a significant non-monotonic relationship between both ownership concentration and profit rates and ownership concentration and Tobin's Q—a measure of market valuation. As ownership concentration increases, Tobin's Q rises, falls, and then rises again.

The last series of studies is most closely related to our study. These studies directly test the agency problem with respect to executive compensation. Stigler and Friedland (1983) examine the relationship between shareholder control and executive compensation for a sample of 92 firms for 1937–1938. They find no significant relationship between the average salary of the top three executives and the percent of stock held by the top 20 shareholders. Santerre and Neun (1989) replicate this study, and after including profits as an additional independent variable, find a negative relationship. Both Santerre and Neun (1986) and Dyl (1988) use more recent data to test the agency problem with respect to executive compensation. Using only data for CEOs, both studies find a negative relationship between ownership concentration and CEO compensation. More recently, Goldberg and Idson (1995) examined the agency question for Fortune 500 companies. This study estimated the relationship between the dispersion of corporate ownership and the compensation of top executives across the executive hierarchy and for different components of the compensation package in contrast to the more limited previous studies. The study found a statistically significant agency effect, though it was small relative to company size. The effects were greatest for salaries, the most liquid form of remuneration, and the executive with the strongest effect was the Chairman of the Board.

Increased attention has been paid to corporate governance issues recently in other countries. However, there are only a limited number of academic empirical investigations of corporate governance in other countries. Germany has probably been the country in which the greatest interest has been shown. Germany has more of a bank dominated financial system in contrast to the market dominated system in the United States. A number of studies, such as Rubach and Sebora (1998), Kim (1995), and Emmons and Schmid (1998), have discussed corporate governance issues in Germany and compared them to the United States. Chirinko and Elston (1996) systematically evaluate German bank influence and find that bank influence does not lower finance costs nor have any discernable effect on profitability. However, they also find that control problems are addressed by concentrated ownership and bank influence. Weigand and Lehmann (1998) examine the impact of ownership structure on the performance of German firms, as measured by return on assets, from 1991 to 1996. They find that corporate structure only affects performance for firms not quoted on the stock exchange. In addition, they show that blockholder ownership results in higher returns and that there are systematic interactive influences of ownership concentration and the identity of owners on performance for the non-quoted companies. Franks and Mayer (1998), however, do not find a significant relationship between board turnover and patterns of ownership.

Schwalbach (1991) was one of the first studies to examine the effects of management interests and profits on compensation in Germany. Using 468 firms in 1988 from the Bonn Data, he shows that size and industry effects are important in determining executive compensation. Conyon and Schwalbach (1999) examine executive pay outcomes in the UK and Germany. Their study finds a positive and significant relationship between pay and company performance in both countries. Finally, using 83 firms from 1968–1990 and 220 firms from 1988–1992, Schwalbach and

Grasshoff (1997) find that firm size and industry are important determinants of compensation for the management board but that performance itself plays only a minor role.

The two previous studies most similar to our current study are FitzRoy and Schwalbach (1990) and Schmid (1997). The first study, using annual data for 95 firms from 1969–1985, finds a negative effect of concentrated ownership on the average annual salary of the management board. Ownership is measured by a Herfindahl index of equity capital distribution in 1982. Since these data are only available for one year, the same ownership distribution variable is employed for every year for each company in the sample. Schmid (1997) provides an alternative approach to the issue by examining the relationship for 1991 between compensation on the two boards of 110 of the largest 120 traded German companies and shareholder structure and firm performance. He tests various hypotheses and finds evidence that the compensation of both boards is affected by performance and by the firms' shareholder structures. His measure of ownership concentration uses a Herfindahl index for 110 firms in 1991 and has some advantages over the measure that we use here. However, his study only covers one year while our study contributes to the literature by conducting a dynamic analysis of corporate governance effects on compensation for a broad panel of German firms over a 17-year time period.

3. GERMAN CORPORATE GOVERNANCE STRUCTURE

There are two main aspects of the German corporate governance structure that are different from the system in the United States. The first is that many large companies in Germany have a 2-tiered board structure comprised of the Aufsichtrat or SB and the Vorstand or managing board (MB). We are primarily interested in the MB rather than the SB. The SB has oversight responsibilities for the corporation similar to the responsibilities of American boards of directors. The SB appoints the MB and also sets the compensation of the members of the MB. The MB is the top management of the corporation and has responsibility for the day-to-day operation of the corporation. Commercial banks have a significant influence on corporate governance in contrast to the United States where the banks are prohibited in general from directly owning equity in corporations.

In Germany only certain legal identities are required to have supervisory and managing boards. These include the common AG (Aktiengesellschaft) or stock held firm, as well as the more rare corporate form, the KgaA (Kommanditgesellschaft auf Aktien).[4] German law dictates that if an AG has fewer than 2000 employees, then the employees elect one third of the members of the SB and two thirds are elected by the shareholders. If the AG has more than 2000 employees, the shareholders appoint half of the SB while the firm employees select the other half. The chairperson of the SB is elected by a two-thirds vote of all board members for a maximum term of five years, with the possibility of reappointment. The law dictates the size of the SB for firms with more than 2000 employees. The SB must have 12 members for firms with 2000–10,000 employees, 16 members for firms with 10,000–20,000 employees, and 20 members for larger firms with over 20,000 employees. The owner appointed members are frequently bank representatives and the employee members are frequently labor representatives. Since SB members are paid an honorarium fee, and all members are paid the same, we are more interested in the relationship of MB compensation and performance. Moreover, the members of the MB are comparable to the top executives including CEOs of American corporations that have been studied previously.

A controversial attribute of the German corporate governance system is the extent to which the German universal banks impact the governance of the firm. While little empirical evidence exists to measure the precise extent of corporate control of

German banks, it is widely believed that these universal bankers have a degree of control that extends beyond the traditional boundaries of the creditor–lender relationship. As specified in Elston (1998), the primary spheres of influence of banks on firms is through (1) bank share ownership and associated voting rights accrued from ownership and proxy votes, (2) through bank representation on the SB (sometimes as chair or deputy chair), and (3) through bank lending and share underwriting. As shareholders, bank representatives regularly participate at annual shareholders meetings, and are frequently represented on the firm's SB with one or more representatives. This multi-faceted role provides a direct line of influence between banks and firms that goes beyond the traditional Anglo-Saxon creditor–firm relationship.

Through the proxy voting system (Depotstimmrecht), banks can also obtain voting rights from shares in trustee accounts of bank customers. These votes count in general board decisions, including appointments to the firm's MB and their salary levels. In fact almost half of the total shares issued are deposited in such bank trustee accounts. Adding the power of the proxy votes to the votes from direct ownership rights, the overall proportion of votes controlled by banks in the largest 100 firms is 36%; and in the top 10 firms this control jumps to over 50%. Thus, though banks may own directly only a small portion of the voting rights of the firm, through the collection of proxy votes, the banks can have a significant influence on the decisions of the firm, including both the composition and compensation of the SB and MBs. From an agency problem perspective, since banks often hold significant shares of the firms over long periods of time, they also have both the incentive and the ability to engage in extensive and ongoing monitoring of the firm. Therefore in analyzing the factors affecting supervisory and managing board salaries in Germany, it is important to consider the unique structure of the German style system of universal banking. Consequently, we include in our analysis a composite variable measuring bank influence.

4. MODEL AND HYPOTHESES

The main objective of this paper is to find the relationship between corporate control factors in Germany and executive compensation. We examine the compensation of members of both the supervisory and the managing boards of German corporations. We are most concerned with the compensation of the MB since its members comprise the top executives of the company. In fact, if there is an agency problem and management is able to extract additional compensation for itself, we would expect this effect to be more pronounced for the MB than for the SB.

The methodology, which is well established in the US compensation literature, requires least-squares analysis of the following regression model:

$$\log(\text{Compensation}) = \beta_0 + \beta_1 \, \text{ROE}_{jt} \\ + \beta_2 \, \text{Conc}_{jt} \\ + \beta_3 \, \log(\text{Size}_{jt}) \\ + \beta_4 \, \text{Bank}_{jt} \\ + \beta_5 D_{jt} + \varepsilon_t \quad (1)$$

where Compensation is the total or per member salaries for the SB or MB, ROE is the return on equity, Conc is the ownership concentration of the firm, Size is the annual firm sales net of value added tax, Bank is the bank influence dummy variable, and D is the vector of industry and time dummy variables.

We employ several variants of this model in order to test a series of related hypotheses and insure robustness of results. Non-reported regression variants, which produced consistent results, included use of return on assets as an alternative measure of returns instead of ROE, number of employees and total assets as alternative firm size measures instead of sales, and lagged independent variables. Correlation matrices were estimated to check for the impact of multicollinearity among independent variables.

Our main analysis contains four different equations, each with a different independent variable. For each of the two boards, SB and MB, we employ two different compensation measures, total compensation of the board and compensation for the average board member. These measures are chosen because the actual compensation is not available for each individual board member. SB members are compensated equally, but MB members are paid differentially. However, these compensation differentials do not approach the differentials among American executives.

We hypothesize a positive relationship between log Compensation and ROE and also a positive relationship between log Compensation and log Sales. This is consistent with the findings of previous studies that have found that executives are paid more when the company is more profitable and when the company is larger.

We cannot employ a Herfindahl index as done by Schmid (1997) and FitzRoy and Schwalbach (1990) because complete data on ownership structure are not available for each firm for the 17-year span of our data panel. This is because those who own less than 25% of a firm are not required to disclose ownership in Germany. We do, however, have complete interval data on ownership percentages greater than 25% for each firm for every year of the study. We therefore construct an alternative concentration measure based on the ranked categorical source data on ownership concentration. The highest numbered concentration category represents the highest degree of owner concentration. Initially we develop a variable that incorporates the rank of the concentration class, and for this variable we would expect a negative coefficient in the regression model because the agency problem is expected to be most important when ownership is more dispersed. That is, in the categories with greater dispersion, management may be able to extract greater compensation. Since this formulation using the ownership categories might assume a particular relationship, we alternatively employ a model with dummy variables for each category, omitting the category with the most dispersed ownership.

The bank influence variable is a dummy variable that takes a value of 1 when a firm is determined to be bank influenced, per our definition in Section 5, and 0 otherwise. The refutable hypothesis is that banks will exert influence and moderate executive compensation. Therefore, a negative coefficient is expected.

We also test the effects on executive compensation of different types of ownership. We employ dummy variables to indicate whether the firm is owned by another firm, owned by foreign interests, owned by a bank, or family owned. Government control, mixed ownership, and management control (no large blocks) comprise the omitted category. Because bank influence has a close relationship with bank ownership, we run regressions including these dummy variables both with and without the bank influence variable. We expect executive compensation to be less when there is strong ownership control in these four categories.

Since agency problems may differ by industry, there may be some heterogeneity in compensation practices across firms. A final analysis examines bank influence by industry group.

5. DATA

One of the greatest impediments to measuring the impact of corporate governance on executive compensation in Germany has been the lack of reliable and comprehensive data. This study uses two non-commercially available sources of unique data. The first is a firm-level database that tracks the financial performance of a comprehensive set of German firms from 1961 to 1986. The second data source is derived from various sources, including Commerzbank's *Wer Gehort zu Wem?*, *Handbuch der Grossunternehemen*, *Leitende Maenner und Frauen der Wirtschaft*, *Aktienfuehrer*, various annual reports of the firm, and Boehm (1992). The combined information in these collected data exceeds the depth and breadth of commercially available data for Germany, enabling us to directly examine the importance of corporate governance on compensation. The bank influence variable for example is a composite measure using information on percent of bank ownership of the firm, percent of bankers on the SB and whether they are chair of the SB, and total number of votes exercised by banks at annual shareholder meetings.[5]

We operationalized this information by defining a dummy bank influence variable. A firm is characterized as bank influenced rather than independent if the bank owns more than 25% of the shares of the firm, if total votes of banks at shareholder meetings (including proxy votes) are greater than 50%, or if total votes are between 25% and 50% and the chair of the SB is a banker.[6] This discrete measure is possibly an imperfect measure of the influence of banks on firms, however it does succeed in incorporating all of the available information on bank–firm relations for each of these firms over each of the 17 years, thereby enabling a dynamic empirical analysis of compensation behavior.[7]

As mentioned above, the data used also include a subset of the Bonn Data that is based on a collection of financial reports of about 700 German industrial corporations quoted on the German stock exchange.[8] Because of mergers, bankruptcies, acquisitions, changes in legal status, and double listing of consolidated and non-consolidated information, about 295 unconsolidated firms remained in 28 industry groups as of 1986.[9] We had information on the ownership identity and concentration for exactly 100 firms over the full time period. This was reduced to 91 firms in the analysis where we had both balance sheet and bank relationship data. Thus we used all firms for which the appropriate data were available rather than using a random sample of firms.[10]

We need to focus on these listed firms in order to study the phenomenon of executive compensation since these are the types of firms for which supervisory and managing boards are mandatory. We used data from 1970 to 1986 because prior to 1970 there were too many missing key variables.[11] Even for this time period, some variables were missing, thus requiring running regressions on smaller subsets of the full sample. Data after 1986 are not used

because of the substantial changes in the German accounting laws, which make it impossible to compare the data without considerable adjustment.[12] The sample time period of 1970–1986 is important not only as point of comparison with current stock of US studies available for this period, but also to understand the pay–performance relationship during this period for Germany.

The number of firms in the sample is also fairly representative because the German exchange is considerably smaller than its American counterpart. For example in 1980 there were only about 459 listed firms incorporated as AG and KgaA.[13]

For these 91 firms we have annual firm-level information detailing the identity of firm owners. These discrete data are reported in mutually exclusive categories defining the identity and concentration of the ownership structure for the firms. Firms categorized as "Firm Controlled" are those in which another domestic firm either owns more than 50% of the outstanding shares or another firm owns at least 25% and no one else owns more than 25%. "Foreign Controlled" firms are those with more than 50% ownership by foreigners. "Bank Controlled" firms are those with more than 50% ownership by financial institutions. "Family Controlled" firms are those with more than 50% ownership by family members, groups, or individuals. "Government Controlled" firms are those with more than 50% ownership by any county or state. "Management Controlled" firms are those which have no block ownership percentage over 25%. Finally "Mixed Control" denotes a situation where different types of the above owners exist, each owning anywhere from 25% to 50% of the shares. We combine the last three groups as the omitted category in the empirical analysis. Most firms in this omitted group have no block ownership over 25%.

The concentration of firm ownership is measured from one to five, where five defines the highest degree of concentration, with a single stockholder holding more than 75% of the firm's shares. If two or three stockholders hold more than 75% of the shares and the firm does not qualify for the higher concentration level, then concentration is set at four. Concentration is set at three if a single stockholder holds more than 50% of the shares, and two, if two or three stockholders own more than 50% of the shares. Concentration is set at one for all cases in which the concentration level is lower than for category two.[14] Note that if the firm satisfies two or more concentration levels, the firm is placed in the higher concentration category.[15] SB and MB pay is defined as total salaries paid to supervisory and managing board members by the firm for which they provided this service.[16] Sales is measured as sales of the firm net of taxes. The data for variables are measured in terms of logs of millions of Deutsche marks. The estimations were run with both time and industry dummy variables in order to control for macroeconomic shocks and industry-specific effects in the model.

6. EMPIRICAL RESULTS

The means and standard deviations of the main variables are presented in Table 17.1.

The number of observations at the bottom of the table indicates the maximum number of observations for each variable; however, the actual regressions generally used fewer observations because of missing data. Note that there appear to be substantial differences across variable means for the levels of ownership concentration. This justifies the separate analysis of each category of ownership concentration. It should be noted that average compensation per board member is lower for the higher concentration ownership categories 3–5. Thus without controlling for other factors, there is some evidence that higher levels of ownership concentration help to control the agency problem.

Table 17.2 contains the results of OLS fixed-effect regressions on the log of compensation measures of the two boards. We are most interested in the results dealing with the MB. Panel A of Table 17.2 reports results for regressions using the log of average salary of a management board member and the log of total salaries of the management board members of each firm as the dependent variables. The results for both measures of compensation are quite

Table 17.1 Decriptive statistics 1970–1986

Variable	All firms	Bank influenced	Independent	Conc = 5 (high)	Conc = 4	Conc = 3	Conc = 2	Conc = 1 (low)
ROA	0.0239	0.0254	0.0337	0.0197	0.0260	0.0224	0.0251	0.0239
	(0.0230)	(0.0166)	(0.0238)	(0.0155)	(0.0184)	(0.0172)	(0.0341)	(0.0639)
ROE	0.0555	0.1013	0.0494	0.1109	0.0396	0.0355	0.0377	0.0363
	(0.2168)	(0.3474)	(0.1921)	(0.4269)	(0.0369)	(0.0315)	(0.0695)	(0.0639)
Net sales	1453.04	808.869	1551.32	965.950	659.265	294.522	1111.32	915.88
	(3869.95)	(1890)	(4080.08)	(2245.39)	(1129.85)	(974.26)	(1968.99)	(1845.21)
Total assets	1149.83	399.2058	1263.91	558.223	732.51	242.6478	672.0945	564.98
	(3136.83)	(862.966)	(3335.37)	(946.81)	(1202.29)	(654.896)	(937.13)	(941.51)
Number of employees	9701.93	6747.21	10148.93	5731.71	3122.28	1891.28	9802.26	7299.25
	(25957)	(15974)	(27126)	(11665)	(4405)	(3914)	(17112)	(12950)
SB salaries	0.2215	0.2306	0.2202	0.1363	0.2014	0.1555	0.3031	0.2492
	(0.2511)	(0.2315)	(0.2539)	(0.1349)	(0.2333)	(0.1628)	(0.2478)	(0.2453)
MB salaries	1.4761	1.1722	1.5208	0.9477	1.2038	0.7049	1.6876	1.3918
	(2.2285)	(1.8093)	(2.2808)	(1.1923)	(1.9360)	(1.0046)	(1.8959)	(1.6029)
Observations	1683	221	1462	517	192	288	257	429

Standard deviation in parenthesis below means. Net sales, total assets, and average board salaries are in logs of millions of DM. Conc stands for ownership concentration: Conc 5 = highest concentration, Conc 1 = lowest concentration. Bank influence is a composite measure of bank influence on the firm, incorporating information on: Ownership structure and concentration, proxy voting by banks, bank representation, and position on SB. Data sample covers 17 years for 100 firms; however, not all firms have data for each year for every variable. Therefore, actual observations used in calculations vary.

Table 17.2 OLS fixed-effects regressions of (Panel A) MB salaries and (Panel B) firm-level SB salaries

Variable	ROE	Sales	Ownership concentration	Bank influence	Adj R^2
Panel A					
Average MB member salary	0.049* (2.326)	0.210* (20.403)	−0.036* (−3.419)	−0.108* (−2.338)	0.4184
Firm total MB salary	−0.027 (−1.100)	0.502* (42.408)	−0.0841* (−7.020)	−0.191* (−3.594)	0.8072
Panel B					
Average SB member salary	0.094* (2.648)	0.1577* (9.096)	−0.114* (−6.471)	−0.002 (−0.019)	0.3425
Firm total SB salary	0.111* (2.937)	0.410* (22.079)	−0.098* (−5.185)	0.1310** (1.570)	0.5304

All equations use time and firm dummies, and White's error correction for obtaining heteroskedastic parameter estimates.
*t-Value indicates variable significant at 5% level and **significant at the 10% level. Observations = 1365.

similar indicating that we are capturing the same compensation process with either definition and can proceed to report results only for the average salary per board member in the following tables. The ownership concentration variable has a negative coefficient and is statistically significant in both equations as predicted by the agency hypothesis. Firms with more concentrated ownership provide less compensation for MB members. ROE has a positive and significant coefficient for the average MB member salary but is insignificant for the firm total MB salary. The Sales variable has a positive and statistically significant coefficient in both equations indicating that larger size leads to greater compensation for the members of the MB.[17] The bank influence dummy variable is negative in both cases at the 5% level. Bank influence appears to reduce management compensation.

Panel B of Table 17.2 presents results for the SB. In both the average salary equation and the total salary equation, the ownership concentration variable again has a negative coefficient that is statistically significant. Greater ownership concentration leads to lower compensation for SB members, confirming the hypothesis that lack of ownership control permits greater personal rewards. Both ROE and Sales are positive and significant in the two regressions,

indicating that better performance and larger size lead to greater compensation for the members of the SB board. However, the bank influence variable is negative and not significant in the average SB member salary equation and positive and significant at the 10% level in the firm total SB salary equation. Since bankers sit on the SB they may have conflicting motives regarding controlling compensation. Clearly bank influence is more important in controlling compensation on the management board. In results not reported here, we have substituted ROA for ROE and Assets or Employees for Sales. The results including these variables were essentially the same as those reported here.

In Tables 17.3 and 17.4 we add additional explanatory variables to the analysis. Instead of using a single summary variable to measure ownership concentration, we employ four dummy variables in order to examine the importance of the different ownership concentration categories and omit the least concentrated category, Conc 1. We also include dummy variables for groups that have ownership control.[18] Table 17.3 analyzes management board salaries and Table 17.4 analyzes SB salaries. In both tables three equations are estimated using OLS fixed-firm effects and generalized method of moments using

Table 17.3 Managing Board (MB) salaries

Dependent variables	OLS MB salaries			GMM MB salaries		
	1	2	3	1	2	3
ROE	0.0091	0.0092	0.0136	0.0885	0.2061	0.0514
	(0.23)	(0.23)	(0.27)	(0.62)	(1.59)	(0.34)
Sales	0.1372*	0.1555*	−0.1495*	−0.0907*	0.2596*	−0.0754*
	(7.01)	(8.16)	(−16.52)	(−7.99)	(10.01)	(−7.87)
Bank	−	−2.6262*	−0.4831*	−	−2.4381*	−0.1113**
influence	−	(−27.77)	(−7.96)	−	(−18.19)	(−1.80)
Concentration (1 = low, 5 = high)						
Conc 5	−0.1045	−	−0.2138*	−0.3204*	−	−0.0552
	(−1.43)	−	(−2.96)	(−3.50)	−	(−0.74)
Conc 4	−0.1182	−	−0.3070*	−0.1392	−	0.0742
	(−1.21)	−	(−2.79)	(−1.25)	−	(0.71)
Conc 3	−0.2085*	−	−0.7625*	−0.5086*	−	−0.6557*
	(−3.81)	−	(−13.73)	(−8.88)	−	(−12.47)
Conc 2	0.1614**	−	−0.09256	0.1858	−	0.0699
	(1.65)	−	(−1.06)	(1.61)	−	(0.62)
Ownership						
Firm	−2.3419*	−2.5311*	−	−0.2597*	−2.5152*	−
	(−18.41)	(−21.98)	−	(−3.25)	(−16.70)	−
Foreign	−2.3792*	−2.6496*	−	−0.5550*	−3.0891*	−
	(−11.32)	(−14.72)	−	(−3.93)	(−12.52)	−
Bank	−2.3848*	−	−	−0.2618*	−	−
	(−20.73)	−	−	(−3.50)	−	−
Family	−2.2640*	−2.4781*	−	−0.2715*	−2.4527*	−
	(−19.18)	(−24.07)	−	(−3.83)	(−17.57)	−
Adj R^2	0.7583	0.7530	0.5935	0.7994	0.8339	0.7705
Sargan	−	−	−	146.693	121.2323	168.1391
(*p*-Value)	−	−	−	(0.2503)	(0.2069)	(0.2869)

All equations use time and firm dummies, and average MB salary.
OLS fixed-effects model reports estimates corrected for heteroskedasticity.
GMM heteroskedastic-consistent estimates use instruments of lagged ROE, ROA, and Sales variables from $t − 2, \ldots, t − 7$.
The Sargan statistic tests for over identifying restrictions in the model.
Regressions 2 and 3 do not have the Bank ownership variable because of the high correlation with the composite bank-influence variable.
*t-Value indicates variable significant at 5% level and **significant at the 10% level. Observations = 1365.

instrumental variables (GMM IV). All reported coefficients are heteroscedastic-consistent parameter estimates. Time dummies were also included in the regressions. The first equation in each set of equations includes the concentration dummies and four ownership dummy variables but excludes the bank influence variable because it is highly correlated with bank ownership. The second equation excludes the concentration dummies and the third excludes the ownership dummies.

The results in Tables 17.3 and 17.4 provide strong support for the agency hypothesis, though the traditional variables, ROE and Sales, do not perform as well as before. For the regressions with the MB average salary, ROE has a positive but non-significant coefficient while Sales is positive and significant in half of the equations but negative and significant in the other half of the equations. The bank influence variable however, has a negative and significant coefficient in all four equations

Table 17.4 Supervisory Board (SB) salary

Dependent variables	OLS SB salaries			GMM SB salaries		
	1	2	3	1	2	3
ROE	0.0889	0.0900	0.1180	0.4408**	0.4130**	0.1113
	(1.36)	(1.36)	(1.34)	(1.88)	(1.74)	(0.37)
Sales	0.0839*	0.1073*	−0.5055*	0.1570*	0.1414*	−0.4828*
	(2.62)	(3.44)	(−35.09)	(2.96)	(3.01)	(−26.25)
Bank influence	−	−4.4983*	−0.3908*	−	−4.3470*	−0.0638
	−	(−29.54)	(−4.14)	−	(−18.24)	(−0.58)
Concentration (1 = low, 5 = high)						
Conc 5	−0.1452	−	−0.9720*	−0.0365	−	−0.8975*
	(−1.31)	−	(−8.32)	(−0.27)	−	(−6.84)
Conc 4	−0.3126*	−	−1.1946*	−0.0597	−	−1.0521*
	(−2.45)	−	(−7.95)	(−0.43)	−	(−6.81)
Conc 3	−0.2517*	−	−1.3873*	0.1708	−	−1.1206*
	(−2.81)	−	(−15.07)	(1.57)	−	(−10.94)
Conc 2	0.5086*	−	−0.0178	0.8345*	−	0.4230**
	(3.40)	−	(−0.13)	(4.43)	−	(1.90)
Ownership						
Firm	−5.0138*	−5.1999*	−	−5.3364*	−5.1337*	−
	(−24.01)	(−27.59)	−	(−15.71)	(−18.80)	−
Foreign	−6.0995*	−6.4531*	−	−6.6204*	−6.5132*	−
	(−17.83)	(−21.87)	−	(−11.63)	(−14.57)	−
Bank	−4.2251*	−	−	−4.5323*	−	−
	(−22.52)	−	−	(−14.18)	−	−
Family	−4.3604*	−4.3692*	−	−4.7789*	−4.6326*	−
	(−22.80)	(−28.37)	−	(−14.88)	(−18.79)	−
Adj R^2	0.7285	0.7200	0.5065	0.7950	0.7865	0.6568
Sargan	−	−	−	403.2899	422.5238	681.5953
(p−Value)	−	−	−	(0.6655)	(0.6972)	(0.1247)

All equations use time and firm dummies, and average SB salary.
OLS fixed-effects model reports estimates corrected for heteroskedasticity.
GMM heteroskedastic-consistent estimates use instruments of lagged ROE, ROA, and sales variables from $t − 2, ..., t − 7$.
The Sargan statistic tests for over identifying restrictions in the model.
Regressions 2 and 3 do not have the Bank ownership variable because of the high correlation with the composite bank-influence variable.
*t-Value indicates variable significant at 5% level and **significant at the 10% level. Observations = 1365.

in which it is included. As expected, the more highly concentrated ownership categories 3–5 have negative coefficients in all but one case and many of the coefficients are significant. All of the ownership dummies are negative as expected and all are statistically significant.

The results are similar for the SB average salary regressions reported in Table 17.4. ROE has a positive coefficient in all cases and is statistically significant in two equations. Sales is positive in four equations and is negative in two, and it is statistically significant in each case. The bank influence variable is negative in all four equations and is statistically significant in three of the equations. The ownership concentration dummies are negative in all but one case for the three most concentrated groups and are significant in many cases. Note that Conc 2 is positive and significant in three of the four cases where it is included. The ownership categories are again negative and significant in all cases.

Table 17.5 Managing Board (MB) salaries by industry

Dependent Variables	Metals and minerals	Chemicals and fiber	Electronic and precision instruments	Motor vehicles	Food and tobacco	Textiles	Other
ROE	−1.765	0.024	0.035	0.253	0.063	0.099	−1.442*
	(−0.56)	(0.56)	(0.06)	(0.32)	(0.35)	(0.30)	(−5.91)
Sales	0.0426	0.148*	0.078*	0.181*	−0.076**	−0.002	0.213*
	(0.29)	(3.32)	(5.41)	(8.64)	(−1.74)	(−0.01)	(9.29)
Bank influence	−0.657**	0.204	−0.948*	−0.948*	−0.780*	−0.204	−2.057*
	(−1.66)	(1.11)	(−5.36)	(−10.00)	(−2.89)	(−0.12)	(−19.62)
Adj R^2	0.5344	0.9472	0.8864	0.8025	0.0966	0.0167	0.5276
Observations	102	221	323	102	235	102	595

All equations use time and firm dummies, and average MB salary.
OLS fixed-effects model reports estimates corrected for heteroskedasticity.
* *t*-Value indicates variable significant at 5% level and **significant at the 10% level. Observations = 1683.

Table 17.5 reports regressions for MB salaries by industry using three independent variables. While ROE is insignificant in all five equations, Sales is positive and statistically significant in three of the five industries. Bank influence is negative and significant in five of the seven industries. Thus, even within most industries banks appear to temper compensation when they have significant influence.

7. CONCLUSION

We have analyzed data on the compensation of members of the supervisory and managing boards of large German corporations in order to satisfy the heightened interest in the compensation of German executives. Most of the empirical work on executive compensation has dealt with the United States. This study extends one important aspect of the research done on American executives to Germany. We find, as do studies on the US, that the greater the ownership concentration the less the ability of executives to extract higher levels of compensation. The agency problem caused by the separation of ownership and control appears to exist in Germany as well as elsewhere. We also find that performance and size are generally positively related to compensation, similar to previous studies in

the United States. There is evidence that banks serve as monitors of executive compensation for the MB and some evidence with respect to the SB. Block ownership by various groups also restrains compensation.

The results of this study are consistent with findings of Schmid (1997) and indicate that in a different institutional setting the same types of economic problems relating to executive compensation hold—that is, there is evidence of agency problems caused by the separation of ownership and control. When ownership is dispersed management can obtain greater monetary compensation. Unfortunately, we do not have information on non-monetary compensation, but we might also expect that lack of control by ownership may enable management to extract greater non-monetary compensation.

This study shows that the agency impact on executive compensation in Germany is similar to that in the United States. In addition we find that bank influence reduces executive compensation and that ownership structure can affect executive compensation practices.

ACKNOWLEDGEMENTS

We would like to thank Joachim Schwalbach, Frank Seger, and three anonymous referees for their insightful suggestions on this research. We would also like to thank conference participants at the May 2000 Financial Management Association meetings in Edinburgh Scotland, the July 2000 Western Economic Association meetings in San Diego, CA, and the November 2000 Southern Finance Association Meetings in Savannah, GA for their useful comments. The first author acknowledges support from the American Institute for Contemporary German Studies for this research.

APPENDIX A. MEANS OF BANK INFLUENCE VARIABLES

Bequity: Bank percentage equity ownership of firm.
Bsuper: Percent of bankers on the firm's SB.
Big Votes: Big 3 banks total percentage of votes at shareholder meetings.
Bchair: Dummy variable = 1 when banker is chair or deputy chair of SB = 0 otherwise.
All Votes: Total percentage votes of all banks at shareholders meetings.

	Bequity	Bsuper	Big Votes	Bchair	All Votes
All Firms	0.0550	0.0889	0.0952	0.2235	0.2072
	(0.1233)	(0.0755)	(0.1743)	(0.4172)	(0.3111)
Bank influence	0.1748	0.1724	0.3206	0.7342	0.6825
	(0.1698)	(0.0770)	(0.2033)	(0.4446)	(0.2224)
Independent	0.0188	0.0630	0.0271	0.0654	0.0627
	(0.0742)	(0.0550)	(0.0842)	(0.7477)	(0.1476)

Own calculations from multiple sources. (See Section 5 for details.)
Standard deviations in parenthesis.
Above data are available for all firms for 1986, except Bequity which is available for all firms over each of the 17 years.
A firm is considered bank influenced if: Bequity >25% or if (All Votes >50%) or (25% < All Votes <50%) and (Chair or Deputy Chair of the SB is a banker).
A firm is Independent if it is not bank influenced.
Big 3 banks include: Commerzbank, Deutsche, and Dresdner.

NOTES

* Corresponding author. Tel.: +1-305-284-1869.
E-mail addresses: julie.elston@osucascades.edu (J.A. Elston), lgoldberg@miami.edu (L.G. Goldberg).
1 Tel.: +1-541-322-3165.
2 Among the most important articles on German compensation are FitzRoy and Schwalbach (1990), Schwalbach (1991), Schwalbach and Grasshoff (1997), and Schmid (1997).
3 Kroll finds no sensitivity of SB compensation to firm performance.
4 The Gesellschaft mit beschraenkter Haftung (GmbH) legal identity is also required to have a supervisory and managing board if the number of employees regularly exceeds 500. However, the rights of the GmbH SB are not as extensive as that of the AG board. For example, the GmbH SB does not appoint the MB. Further, until 1987 only a subset of the GmbHs was even required to adhere to public disclosure law, so that very little information was public before 1987. For these reasons the GmbH firms are not included in this study.
5 Appendix A reports descriptive statistics for bank influence variables. Note that there is a substantial difference between the independent firms and the bank influenced firms. See Seger (1997) for a detailed study of governance effects on the performance of German firms.
6 Voting data are available for 1986 only. Ownership identity and concentration are available for each firm for every year of the study.
7 As a secondary check for accuracy of the bank influence measure, we also checked the results of this characterization on a firm by firm basis over the sample period and found it remarkably consistent with all available information on bank–firm relationships.

8   The main sources for the data was the Bonn Data, constructed at the Business and Economics Institute of the University of Bonn.

9   We use unconsolidated data although there is no theoretical reason to believe that the compensation performance relationship is impacted by the existence of a parent company nor are we aware of any previous research addressing this issue. In fact, Bond et al. (2002) compare investment estimations for both consolidated and unconsolidated firms using these data and fail to find a significant difference in estimation results between groups when examining investment sensitivity to liquidity constraints.

10   Our data represent nearly 20% of what Edwards and Fischer (1994, p. 77), report as the listed stock held by AG firms in Germany in 1980.

11   We use data after 1965 because of the Corporation Act of 1965, under which the accounting rules for the valuation of plant, equipment, and inventories, as well as profits, were tightened. For example, if BASFs 1981 equity was valued under US–SEC rules rather than under German law, the valuation would be 40% higher than reported according to the new German rules.

12   An accounting law provision passed on December 12, 1985 that stated that unconsolidated firms must comply with the new standards by 1/1/1986.

13   See Edwards and Fischer (1994, p. 77) for a detailed discussion on legal incorporations.

14   Note that 25% is a key percentage because it represents a minority blocking vote at shareholders meetings and German law requires disclosure of ownership for any party owning 25% or more of outstanding stock.

15   We do not include data from consolidated annual reports because it represents a different level of firm activity from non-consolidated firms.

16   Note that salary data are reported annually by firms only as a total. Individual salaries were calculated by dividing the corresponding salary by the number of board members. While this was the only option available for these estimations, it makes particular sense in the German context where SB members are paid the same amount (honorarium) and MB have less variation in salaries as compared to US firms.

17   Using sales that were lagged produced essentially equivalent results and these results are available from the authors on request.

18   We examine the correlation between the summary concentration measure and each of the dummy variables for groups that have ownership control. The highest correlation coefficient was 0.3416 between Conc and Firm. The correlation coefficients were respectively 0.2755 for Foreign, 0.1225 for Bank, and 0.0422 for Family. Thus we do not appear to have a multicollinearity problem. A full correlation matrix for all relevant variables is available from the authors.

REFERENCES

Aktienfuehrer, 1970–1986. Hoppenstedt, Darmstadt.

Auerbach, P.R., Siegfried, J.J., 1974. Executive compensation and corporation control. Nebraska Journal of Economics and Business 13, 3–16.

Bartlett, R.L., Miller, T.I., 1988. Executive earnings by gender: A case study. Social Science Quarterly (December), 802–909.

Berle Jr., A.S., Means, G.C., 1932. The Modern Corporation and Private Property. MacMillan, New York.

Boehm, J., 1992. Der Einfluss des Banken auf Grossunternehmen. Duisberger Volkswirtschaftliche Schriften Band 13, S + W Hamburg.

Bond, S., Elston, J.A., Mairesse, J., Mulkay, B., 2002. A comparison of empirical investment equations using company panel data for France, Germany, Belgium, and the UK. Review of Economics and Statistics, forthcoming.

Carroll, T.M., Ciscel, D.C., 1982. The effects of regulation on executive compensation. The Review of Economics and Statistics 64 (August), 505–509.

Chirinko, R., Elston, J.A., 1996. Finance, control, and profitability: An evaluation of German Bank influence. Caltech working paper 96–5.

Ciscel, D.H., Carroll, T.M., 1980. The determinants of executive salaries: An econometric survey. The Review of Economics and Statistics 62 (February), 7–13.

Conyon, M.J., Schwalbach, J., 1999. Executive compensation: Evidence from the United Kingdom and Germany. Manuscript, November 1999.

Coughlin, A.T., Schmidt, R.M., 1985. Executive compensation, management turnover, firm performance: An empirical investigation. Journal of Accounting and Economics 7, 43–66.

Deckop, J.R., 1988. Determinants of chief executive officer compensation. Industrial and Labor Relations Review 41 (January), 215–226.

Demsetz, H., Lehn, K., 1985. The structure of corporate ownership: Causes and consequences. Journal of Political Economy 93, 1155–1177.

Dyl, E.A., 1988. Corporate control and management compensation: Evidence on the agency problem. Managerial and Decision Economics 9, 21–25.

Edwards, J.S., Fischer, K., 1994. The German Financial System. Cambridge University Press, Cambridge.

Elston, J.A., 1998. Investment, liquidity constraints and bank relationships: Evidence from German manufacturing firms. In: Competition and Convergence in Financial Markets: The German and Anglo-Saxon Models. Advances in Finance, Investment, and Banking and Finance Series, vol. 5. Elsevier Science Publishers, Amsterdam.

Emmons, W.R., Schmid, F.A., 1998. Universal banking, control rights, and corporate finance in Germany. In: Federal Reserve Bank of St. Louis Review 80 (4), 19–42.

FitzRoy, F.R., Schwalbach, J., 1990. Managerial compensation and firm performance: Some evidence from West Germany. WZB, Discussion Paper FS IV 90–20.

Focus, 1998. No. 49, pp. 290–297.

Franks, J., Mayer, C., 1998. Ownership, control and the performance of German Corporations. IFA working paper, London.

Goldberg, L.G., Idson, T.L., 1995. Executive compensation and agency effects. The Financial Review 30 (2), 313–335.

Handbuch der Grossunternehmen, 1987. Hoppenstedt, Darmstadt.

Jensen, M.C., Meckling, W.H., 1976. Theory of the firm: Managerial behavior, agency costs, ownership structure. Journal of Financial Economics 3 (October), 305–360.

Jensen, M.C., Murphy, K.J., 1990. Performance pay and top-management incentives. Journal of Political Economy 98 (April), 225–264.

Kim, H.-J., 1995. Markets, institutions, and corporate governance: Perspectives from

Germany. Law and Policy in International Business 26 (2), 371–405.

Kroll, L., 1999. Warning: Capitalism is contagious. Forbes, May 18, 1999.

Leitende Maenner und Frauen der Wirtschaft, 1987. Hoppenstedt, Darmstadt.

Masson, R.T., 1971. Executive motivations, earnings, and consequent equity-performance. Journal of Political Economy (October), 1278–1292.

McGuire, J.W., Chiu, J.S.Y., Elbing, A.O., 1962. Executive incomes, sales and profits. The American Economic Review 52 (September), 753–761.

Morck, R., Shlelfer, A., Vishney, R.W., 1988. Management ownership and market valuation: An empirical analysis. Journal of Financial Economics 20, 293–315.

Murphy, K.J., 1985. Corporate performance and managerial remuneration: An empirical analysis. Journal of Accounting and Economics 7, 11–42.

Patton, A., 1951. Current practices in executive compensation. Harvard Business Review 29 (January), 56–64.

Roberts, D.R., 1956. A general theory of executive compensation based on statistically tested propositions. Quarterly Journal of Economics 70 (May), 270–294.

Rubach, M.J., Sebora, T.C., 1998. Comparative corporate governance: Competitive implications of an emerging convergence. Journal of World Business 33 (2), 167–184.

Santerre, R.E., Neun, S.P., 1989. Managerial control and executive compensation in the 1930s: A reexamination. Quarterly Journal of Business and Economics 28 (Autumn), 100–118.

Santerre, R.E., Neun, S.P., 1986. Stock dispersion and executive compensation. The Review of Economics and Statistics 88 (November), 685–687.

Stigler, G.J., Friedland, C., 1983. The literature of economics: The case of berle and means. Journal of Law and Economics 26 (June), 237–268.

Schmid, F.A., 1997. Vorstandbezuge, Aufsichtsratsvergutung und Aktionarsstruktur. Zeitschrift für Betriebswirtschaft 1, 67–83.

Schwalbach, J., 1991. Principal/agent-problem, Managervergutung und Unternehmenserfolg. WZB, Discussion Paper FS IV 91–5.

Schwalbach, J., Grasshoff, U., 1997. Managervergutung und Unternehmenserfolg. Zeitschrift für Betriebswirtschaft 2, 203–217.

Seger, F., 1997. Einfluss der Banken auf Unternehmenserfolg und Unternehmensfinanzierung. Gabler Publishing, Wiesbaden.

Weigand, J., Lehmann, E., 1998. Does the governed corporation perform better? Governance structures and the market for corporate control in Germany, Unpublished manuscript.

Wer Gehört zu Wem, 1970–1986. Commerzbank, Germany.

## Chapter 18

John E. Core and David F. Larcker[†]

PERFORMANCE CONSEQUENCES OF MANDATORY INCREASES IN EXECUTIVE STOCK OWNERSHIP[*]

Source: *Journal of Financial Economics*, 64(3) (2001): 317–340.

ABSTRACT

We examine a sample of firms that adopt "target ownership plans", under which managers are required to own a minimum amount of stock. We find that prior to plan adoption, such firms exhibit low managerial equity ownership and low stock price performance. Managerial equity ownership increases significantly in the two years following plan adoption. We also observe that excess accounting returns and stock returns are higher after the plan is adopted. Thus, for our sample of firms, the required increases in the level of managerial equity ownership result in improvements in firm performance.

1. INTRODUCTION

DESPITE THE CENTRAL IMPORTANCE OF THE ISSUE to corporate finance researchers, there is no theoretical or empirical consensus on whether managerial equity ownership affects firm performance. Studies of this issue generally take one of two very different directions, as two seminal studies illustrate. On the one hand, Morck et al. (1988) find that managers' equity ownership and firm performance is too low for many firms. On the other hand, Demsetz and Lehn (1985) predict that when firms' ownership levels are optimally determined, there will be no relation between ownership and performance.

These two schools of thought make very different assumptions about the nature of the adjustment costs of correcting suboptimal contracts. For example, Morck et al. implicitly assume that adjustment costs are so great that firms cannot contract optimally. Therefore, some firms deliver poor performance to their shareholders. Conversely, by concentrating on the equilibrium behavior of optimizing firms, Demsetz and Lehn assume that firms can continuously re-contract because there are no adjustment costs. The choice of one of these two extremes drives the design and interpretation of the results of any study that examines the relation between ownership and performance. It is perhaps not surprising that there is no consensus on the performance consequences of managerial equity ownership.

We choose an alternative, middle approach by relaxing some of the strong assumptions of this prior research. Specifically, we assume that firms choose optimal managerial equity incentives when they contract (consistent with the literature that predicts no relation between ownership and performance), but that transaction costs prohibit continuous re-contracting (consistent with the literature that documents a strong relation between ownership and performance). Because ownership is periodically re-optimized, we expect no association between ownership and firm performance in a cross-sectional regression that controls for the endogenous determinants of firms' optimal ownership levels. However, because contracting is not continuous, firms' ownership levels gradually deviate from the optimal level. We predict that firms that are below optimum can improve their performance by increasing ownership levels, and that a subset of these firms can benefit sufficiently from the increased performance that it is worthwhile for them to incur the recontracting costs of mandating the ownership increase. For this sample of firms, required increases in managers' ownership should strengthen firm performance.

We implement our approach by constructing a sample of firms that adopt requirements specifying the minimum amount of stock that must be held by executive officers. These contracts are generally termed "target ownership plans." Before the plan is adopted, these firms deliver low stock returns and have low levels of equity ownership. However, in the two years after the board adopts the plan, managerial stock ownership increases significantly. Finally, excess accounting returns are statistically higher in the two years following plan adoption and excess stock price returns are statistically higher in the first six months of the fiscal year in which the plan is announced. Thus, increases in managerial equity ownership from suboptimal levels appear to result in improvements in firm performance.

One advantage of our approach is that the board of directors is using the target ownership plan to mandate increased equity ownership by executives. Thus, any subsequent changes in firm performance are likely to be related to the shifts in managerial incentives brought about by increases in equity ownership. This approach differs from using a sample in which the top executives voluntarily increase ownership. If we were to use this design, we could not be sure if firm performance improved because of increased ownership or if equity ownership increased in anticipation of performance improvements (e.g., a form of insider trading on private information, as

in Kole (1996)). Accordingly, firms adopting target ownership plans provide a unique and powerful sample for examining the link between managerial ownership and performance.

The remainder of the paper consists of five sections. Section 2 provides institutional background on target ownership plans and develops our three research hypotheses. Section 3 describes the sample selection process and provides descriptive statistics on target ownership plans. Section 4 examines the ability of variables that measure the existence of governance problems to discriminate between adopting and nonadopting firms. Section 5 describes the accounting and stock market performance consequences associated with target ownership plan adoption. A summary of the paper and concluding remarks are provided in Section 6.

2. INSTITUTIONAL BACKGROUND AND RESEARCH HYPOTHESES

The section titled "Corporate Governance" in Campbell Soup Company's 1993 proxy statement illustrates common features of target ownership plans:

> The Company is committed to shareholder-sensitive corporate governance... By the end of 1994, all officers (29 persons), as well as approximately 40 other executives, are required to own outright (i.e., excluding options and restricted stock) Campbell stock valued at one-half to three times base salary, depending on their positions. (Proxy statement dated October 8, 1993, p. 6)

Proxy statement disclosures of target ownership plans vary greatly in the level of detail provided. The most common plan disclosure makes an explicit formal statement of the minimum level of managerial stock ownership, where this ownership requirement must be satisfied by outright ownership of common stock (i.e., stock option holdings do not satisfy the ownership requirements). Seven percent of the plans in our sample express the target as a number of shares. The remaining plans express the target as a percentage of salary, so that the target becomes more difficult to attain if the stock price decreases. Finally, the typical disclosure specifies the maximum time allowed to achieve the ownership goal.

Adopting firms indicate that their motivation for imposing minimum equity ownership levels is to ensure that their managers have the appropriate incentives to increase shareholder value. For example, the 1993 proxy statement of Morrison Restaurants Inc. says:

> Believing that equity ownership plays a key role in aligning the interests of Company personnel with Company stockholders, the Company encourages all employees to make a personal investment in Company stock. The Company's goal is that 10 percent of the Common Stock will be owned by employees by the year 2000 and that 80 percent of employees with more than two years of experience with the Company will own Common Stock. (Proxy statement dated August 26, 1993, p. 12)

Thus, target ownership plans are designed to address the contention of some researchers and governance activists that stock ownership of senior-level executives is "too small" (e.g., Jensen and Murphy, 1990; Jensen, 1993; Norton, 1995).

In addition to the implicit requirement created by the public announcement of the ownership targets, 52 (27%) of our sample firms state an explicit penalty for executives who do not meet the ownership target. The penalty falls into one of three categories, each of which involves changing some aspect of the executive's equity compensation. When executives do not meet their targets, either (1) a fraction of their annual cash pay is paid as restricted stock, (2) their grants of options, restricted stock and cash long-term incentives are reduced or eliminated, or (3) the vesting of their outstanding restricted stock and

options is delayed. Thus, by explicitly linking future equity compensation to a specific minimum ownership goal, these target ownership plans are designed to motivate executives to increase their equity ownership and to maintain this increase.

We hypothesize that target ownership plans are adopted when the board of directors recognizes that the firm has a governance problem. The board adopts the plan in order to move the firm to a more appropriate governance structure. We assume that stock returns that are lower than industry benchmark returns are evidence of potential governance problems. The United Shareholders Association (1992) uses this approach to detect governance problems, and the approach is verified empirically by Core et al. (1999). Another way to detect actual or potential governance problems is to determine whether a firm's managerial stock ownership is low relative to some comparison group. This approach is similar to the method used by governance monitoring groups such as Institutional Shareholder Services (1993). Thus, we predict that if a firm has low managerial stock ownership and poor stock price performance, the board infers that the level of managerial equity is insufficient to motivate good performance. One strategy for mitigating this perceived governance problem is to adopt a target ownership plan that requires managers to own a minimum level of stock. Thus, our first research hypothesis is as follows:

H_1. The likelihood of adopting a target ownership plan is negatively related to prior stock price performance and managerial equity ownership levels.

We hypothesize that the board acts in the interests of shareholders to mitigate a perceived governance problem, and for that reason it adopts a "substantive" target ownership plan that mandates ownership increases by executives.

An alternative to this hypothesis is that management controls the board and convinces the board to adopt a plan that does not actually force the managers to increase their equity ownership. The purpose of this "symbolic" plan is to make it appear that managers have taken steps to improve governance, but without actually having to bear the costs of increased ownership. This hypothesis assumes that managers believe that outside investors are unable to discriminate between symbolic changes and substantive changes (e.g., Pfeffer, 1981).

Another explanation for an association between target ownership plan adoption and equity ownership increases is that management has private information about future firm performance and encourages the board to adopt a target ownership plan. However, if this were true, we would not expect changes in managers' relative ownership positions after plan adoption, because rational managers would take advantage of their superior information and increase their stockholdings prior to the announcement of the plan. Because managers expect to achieve the ownership targets, it will not matter to them whether the plan includes a penalty for noncompliance.

To distinguish between these competing explanations, we examine changes in managerial equity ownership following the adoption of the plan, and our second research hypothesis is as follows:

H_2. Managerial equity ownership increases following the adoption of a target ownership plan.

If target ownership plans improve managerial incentives, adoption should have favorable operating performance consequences for the firm. In saying this, we assume that when a firm with low ownership requires that managers increase their ownership, this increase mitigates agency problems and motivates managers to select actions that are more consistent with shareholder objectives.

The existing literature does not provide consistent evidence on the association between managerial equity ownership and firm performance. The evidence in Morck et al. (1988) and subsequent studies suggests that equity ownership is too low at most firms, and performance will improve if managerial equity ownership increases. For example, McConnell and Servaes (1990) find evidence of a positive relation between increases in ownership and firm performance so long as managerial ownership is less than 50%. Demsetz and Lehn (1985) predict, and Himmelberg et al. (1999) find, that there is no relation between equilibrium levels of ownership and firm performance. In other words, once the researcher recognizes the endogenous nature of equity ownership, there is little evidence to indicate a relation between equilibrium levels of ownership and firm performance (Himmelberg et al.).

In contrast to this prior research, we examine firms that are below equilibrium levels of managerial equity ownership. We predict that as equity ownership rises, there will be an increase in operating performance. In addition, if the stock market does not completely anticipate this contractual change, the firm's stock price will increase when the firm announces to the market that it has adopted a target ownership plan. Thus, our third research hypothesis is as follows:

H_3. Adopting a target ownership plan will have a positive impact on subsequent operating and stock market performance.

3. SAMPLE SELECTION AND DESCRIPTIVE STATISTICS ON TARGET OWNERSHIP PLANS

We identify our initial sample from selected articles that discuss target ownership plans (e.g., Brill, 1993; Reese, 1993; McMillan and Sabow, 1994; Young, 1995) and from a keyword search of all proxy statements on Lexis. We read the proxy statement of each firm in the initial sample to determine whether the firm has actually adopted a target ownership plan, and we check each firm's prior year's proxy statement to ensure that we have the proxy that first announces the plan. The earliest target ownership plan adopters have December 31, 1991 fiscal year-ends. We include plan adopters with fiscal years ending up to and including December 31, 1995. Approximately 1.5% of the sample firms have 1991 fiscal year-ends, 16.9% have 1992 FYEs, 35.5% have 1993 FYEs, 36.9% have 1994 FYEs, and 9.2% have 1995 FYEs. Table 18.1 describes the final sample, which comprises 195 firms across 40 different industrial and service sectors of the economy. There is some concentration

Table 18.1 Industry composition of firms adopting target ownership plans

The sample consists of 195 firms that adopt target ownership plans. This table lists the number of sample firms in each two-digit standard industrial classification (SIC) code, and a description of that industry

SIC code	No. of firms	Industry description
1	2	Agriculture–Crops
10	1	Mining
13	4	Petroleum and natural gas
16	1	Heavy construction
20	8	Foods
22	2	Textile
23	1	Apparel
24	1	Lumber
25	2	Furniture
26	2	Paper
27	5	Publishing and printing
28	20	Chemical
29	4	Petroleum refining
30	3	Tires and rubber
32	2	Stone, metal, and glass
33	3	Steel and nonferrous metals
34	1	Metal fabricating
35	15	Machinery
36	9	Electrical equipment
37	9	Automobile and aerospace equipment
38	8	Instruments and measuring equipment
39	2	Miscellaneous manufacturing
40	3	Railroad
41	1	Bus transit
44	2	Water transportation
48	9	Telephone and broadcast media
49	12	Electric and gas services
50	3	Durable wholesale
51	5	Nondurable wholesale
52	1	Building materials
53	3	Retail merchandise
57	1	Retail home furniture and equipment
58	3	Eating and drinking places
60	16	Commercial banking
61	6	Credit institutions
63	14	Insurance
64	1	Insurance agents
73	8	Business services
75	1	Automobile rental
80	1	Health services

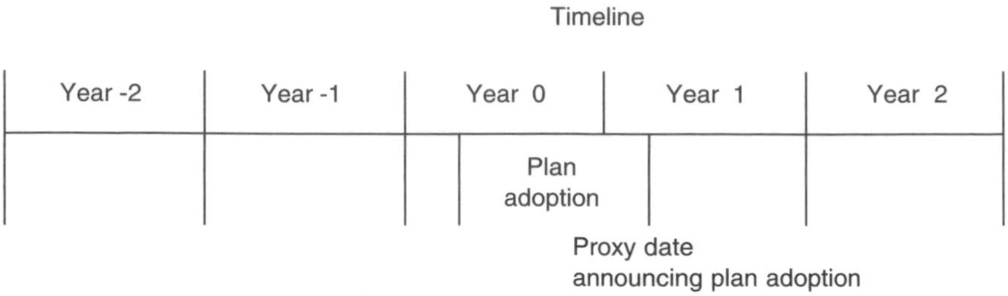

Timeline

Figure 18.1 Timeline.

in the chemical, machinery, utilities, banking, and insurance industries.

We measure variables relative to the fiscal year in which the proxy statement announcing the plan adoption appears. Figure 18.1 provides a timeline and illustration. Proxy statements appear a few months after the fiscal year-end. For example, a firm with a December 1993 fiscal year-end typically issues its proxy in April 1994. We denote the fiscal year in which the proxy statement appears as year 1, and the fiscal year that the proxy describes as year 0. The SEC requires that the year 1 proxy statement describe compensation during year 0, ownership at the end of year 0, and the actions of the compensation committee for the period following the year 0 proxy statement through the year 1 proxy statement. For example, the April 1994 proxy statement would describe compensation payments during the fiscal year ended December 31, 1993 (year 0), executive ownership as of the fiscal year-end (December 31, 1993), and the actions of the compensation committee from May 1993 (year 0) to April 1994 (year 1). It is during this period spanning the latter part of year 0 and the early part of year 1 that the board decides to adopt a plan. Eighty-two firms (42%) do not specify when the board action to adopt the plan took place, 75 (39%) state that the plan was adopted in year 0, and 38 (19%) indicate that the plan was adopted early in year 1.

Table 18.2 provides descriptive statistics for the target ownership plans and actual ownership levels. Recall that the plans require executives to own a target value of

stock, which is expressed as a multiple of base salary. Consistent with the prior survey results in Towers Perrin (1993) and McMillan and Sabow (1994), Panel A shows that for the 138 firms disclosing a target, the minimum level of ownership for the median CEO is four times base salary, and the minimum level of ownership for other top executives is two and a half times base salary. For the nine firms that express the target as a number of shares, we convert the target into a salary multiple using the stock price at the end of year 0. Similar to the survey results in Hewitt Associates (1993) and Towers Perrin, the typical firm allows the executives approximately five years to comply with the minimum level of stock ownership.

Panel B, Table 18.2, presents statistics for the actual ownership multiples of the sample firms. We compute the ownership multiple (value of stock owned/salary) using the salary and shares disclosed in the proxy statement for year 0, and the stock price at the end of year 0.[1] The size of our sample of target ownership firms is slightly less than 195 because we cannot compute the ownership multiple for one CEO (two executive groups) due to insufficient proxy disclosure. To compute the ownership variable for the other (four) top executives, we use the data disclosed in the proxy statement for the (five) most highly compensated executives, and then exclude the CEO. We calculate a weighted average by summing the stock values of each executive and dividing this by their total salaries. The median CEO owns 5.6 times his or her salary in stock. The other executives own a

Table 18.2 Descriptive statistics

The sample consists of 195 firms adopting target ownership plans. Panel A contains descriptive statistics for the ownership multiples (stock value divided by salary) required for the CEOs and the other top executives, and the period allowed for the executives to reach this target. Number is the number of the 195 adopters whose proxy statements provide data. Panel B gives descriptive statistics for the actual multiple for the CEO and the other top executives. For the CEO, the multiple is (value of stock owned/salary). The other executives are the most highly compensated executives as a group, excluding the CEO. The multiple for the other top executives is a weighted average equal to the total value of stock owned by the other executives divided by their total salary. We compute the multiples by using the salary and shares owned as disclosed in the proxy statement for the adoption year 0, and the stock price at the end of year 0. Panel C gives descriptive statistics for the number of firms for which the actual multiple for the CEO and the other top executives is less than the minimum specified by the firm. When no minimum is specified, we impute the minimum using the median values shown in Panel A

Panel A Ownership minimums and compliance periods

	Number	Mean	Median	Min	Max
Ownership minimum multiple of base salary):					
Chief executive officer (CEO)	138	4.0	4.0	0.4	11.0
Other top executives	116	2.5	2.5	0.1	8.6
Compliance period (years)	103	5.0	5.0	0.0	10.0

Panel B Actual ownership multiples

	Number	Mean	Median	Min	Max
Actual ownership (multiple of base salary):					
Chief executive officer (CEO)	194	32.2	5.6	0.0	1,111.7
Other top executives as a group	193	4.7	2.4	0.1	55.0

Panel C Actual ownership multiple is less than minimum multiple

	Number	Number below minimum	Percent below minimum
Chief Executive Officer (CEO)	194	73	38%
Other top executives as a group	193	94	49%
At least one other top executive	193	156	81%
At least one executive (including CEO)	195	163	84%

median of 2.4 times their salary in stock. Because the distributions are skewed by some very large observations, the mean values are much higher than the medians, at 32.2 and 4.7 times salary, respectively.

The median values suggest that it is a minority of CEOs who have not already attained the target, and a minority of other executive teams that have not attained the minimum. To provide more direct evidence, we compare the actual ownership multiple to the actual plan minimum. To do these comparisons, we use the plan targets if disclosed (Panel A, Table 18.2), and if not disclosed we impute a target equal to the medians of 4.0 and 2.5 for the CEO and other executives, respectively. In Panel C, we show that 38% of CEOs are below minimum and that 49% of other executives (on a weighted average basis) are below minimum. Because the weighted average calculation can be distorted by one executive with very large ownership, we also examine whether each other executive meets the minimum. The results of this analysis indicate that for 81% of the firms, at least one other top executive does not meet his or her target. Accordingly, while only 38% of the firms have CEOs that do not exceed their minimums, 84% of the firms have a CEO or at least one other top executive who does not meet his or her minimum.

4. ANALYSIS OF TARGET OWNER-SHIP PLAN ADOPTION

In this section, we describe how we construct a test of Hypothesis 1, which predicts that target ownership adopters have lower pre-plan returns and ownership than a control sample. We define our measures, describe how we construct the control sample, and then describe our test.

4.1. Measures for benchmark-adjusted returns and ownership

We measure firm performance as the stock price return in the two years (years -2 and -1 in Figure 18.1) preceding the adoption year 0, less the median stock price performance during the same time period for the firms on the 1998 Compustat file that have the same two-digit SIC code. We label the resulting variable "prior industry-adjusted returns", and we assume that governance problems are an inverse function of prior industry-adjusted returns.

We compute our ownership benchmark by constructing a regression model comparable to that used by Demsetz and Lehn (1985). Because target ownership plans require executives to own a certain value of common stock directly (exclusive of stock options) that is a multiple of that executive's base salary, we examine the ownership multiple computed at year 0 as described above.[2] To normalize the distribution of this highly skewed variable, we transform it by the natural logarithm and use log(stock value/salary) as the dependent variable in our ownership regression. This transformation

enables us to interpret the residual as the percentage by which actual ownership deviates from expected ownership. We compute this variable for the CEO and for the other top executives.

Following Demsetz and Lehn (1985) and Baker and Hall (1998), we expect that managerial ownership will increase at a decreasing rate as firm size increases. We follow prior researchers in measuring size with the natural logarithm of the market value of equity at the end of year 0, denoted as log(MV equity). Prior researchers such as Murphy (1999) find that executive salaries also increase at a decreasing rate as firm size increases. Because log(stock value/salary) is equal to log(stock value)−log(salary), we do not predict the direction of the association between this variable and log(MV equity).

We expect that equity ownership will increase at a decreasing rate as monitoring costs increase. We also follow Demsetz and Lehn in using stock return volatility as a proxy for noise that increases monitoring costs. We capture the hypothesized concave relation between increases in noise and increases in equity ownership by including the square of stock return volatility. We measure stock volatility by using the standard deviation of daily stock price returns over the six months before the fiscal year-end. Because several of our firms did not trade for all of year 0, we maximize our sample size by measuring daily stock volatility over the six months prior to the fiscal year-end. We predict that stock volatility will be positively associated with log(stock value/salary), and that stock volatility squared will be negatively associated with log(stock value/salary).

Similar to Smith and Watts (1992), we expect that CEO equity ownership will be greater for firms with larger investment opportunity sets. Like Smith and Watts, we use the book value of assets divided by the market value of assets as a proxy for growth opportunities, and expect that firms with greater growth opportunities will have lower book-to-market ratios. We measure the book-to-market ratio at the end of year 0. We expect to find a negative relation between the book-to-market ratio and log(stock value/salary).

To control for industry factors and other unspecified determinants that might affect the level of equity ownership, we also include 23 industry indicator variables. To capture potential temporal differences, we include five indicator variables that correspond to the years of data collected from our sample of plan adopters and ExecuComp. The resulting benchmark model for the level of stock ownership is as follows:

$$
\begin{aligned}
\text{Log(stock value/salary)}_{it} = \beta_0 \\
+ \beta_1 \text{Log(MV equity)}_{it} \\
+ \beta_2 \text{ Stock volatility}_{it} \\
+ \beta_3 \text{ Stock volatility} \\
\text{squared}_{it} \\
+ \beta_4 \text{ Book-to-market}_{it} \\
+ \gamma_{1\ldots5} \text{ year} \\
\text{indicators}_{it} \\
+ \delta_{1\ldots23} \text{ industry} \\
\text{indicators}_{it} + \varepsilon_{it}. \quad (1)
\end{aligned}
$$

We estimate this benchmark model using ordinary least squares. We create an estimation sample by pooling annual ownership data for the target ownership plan adopters for years 0, 1, and 2 with ExecuComp data on managerial ownership for firm-years from 1992 to 1997. Because ExecuComp has no 1991 fiscal year data, we include the 1991 adopters coded with a year indicator of 1992. The ExecuComp database meets our requirement for an accurate, convenient data source for managerial equity ownership. We include data for the years 1996 and 1997 so that we can use these residuals in later tests (described in Section 5.1) of whether the managerial equity ownership of the 1994 and 1995 plan adopters increases in the two years following adoption. To mitigate the influence of outliers, we set the upper- and lower-most percentiles for each variable equal to the values at the first and 99th percentiles in each year, respectively.

Table 18.3 presents the estimation results, which indicate that the models for the CEO and other top executives are statistically significant ($p<0.001$), with adjusted R^2s

of 19.4% and 17.9%, respectively. All of the reported statistical tests are two-tailed. The log of the ownership multiple has a statistically positive relation to firm size. As we expected, we find a negative relation to the book-to-market ratio (or a positive relation to the investment opportunities confronting the firm). We also observe that the log of the ownership multiple has a concave relation to the standard deviation of stock returns. We find less managerial ownership for those firms with very low or very high stock volatility. We label the residual from the benchmark model the "stock value residual", and we assume that governance problems are an inverse function of the stock value residual.

4.2. Results

Because Hypothesis 1 predicts differences between adopting and non-adopting firms, we require a set of control firms that have not adopted a target ownership plan. We create a control sample by deleting from the sample described above all data for 1996 and 1997 and all firms that are included in our sample of target ownership plan adopters. (Because we have the full sample of target ownership adopters prior to 1996, we know that none of our control firms have adopted plans.) A total of 4,498 firm-years on ExecuComp from 1992 to 1995 constitute our control sample. Because some firms are missing data on prior industry-adjusted returns, the target ownership sample reduces to 170 observations and the control sample to 4,022 observations. Again, to mitigate the influence of outliers, we set the upper- and lower-most percentiles for each independent variable equal to the values at the first and 99th percentiles in each year, respectively.

Univariate results are consistent with Hypothesis 1. We find that prior industry-adjusted returns for the target ownership plan sample are significantly lower than those for the control sample by a mean of 4.5 percentage points ($p<0.002$) and median of 0.7 percentage points ($p<0.05$).[3] In addition, the CEO stock value residual for the target ownership plan

Table 18.3 OLS regression models of log(stock value/salary)$_t$

This table summarizes regression results from estimating Eq. (1). The sample consists of 7,373 firm-year observations for years 1992–1997 for the target ownership plan adopters and for firms included on ExecuComp. We base *t*-statistics (in parentheses) on OLS standard errors. Log(CEO stock value/salary) is the natural logarithm of the value of stock owned by the CEO divided by the CEO's salary. Log(other execs' stock value/salary) is the natural logarithm of the total value of stock owned by the other executives divided by the total salary of the other executives. The other executives are the most highly compensated executives, excluding the CEO. We compute these variables by using the salary and shares owned as disclosed in the year *t* proxy statement, and the stock price at the end of year *t*. We compute all the explanatory variables at or for the period ending at year *t*. Log(MV equity) is the natural logarithm of the market value of equity. Stock volatility is the standard deviation of daily stock price returns over six months. Stock volatility squared is the square of stock volatility, and book-to-market is the book value of assets divided by the market value of assets. Coefficients on an intercept, five year indicators, and 23 industry indicators are not shown.

		Dependent variable	
Independent variable	Predicted sign	Log (CEO stock value/salary) (1)	Log (other execs' stock value/salary) (2)
Log(MV equity)$_t$	?	0.16*** (8.17)	0.23*** (13.20)
Stock volatility$_t$	+	5.92*** (9.45)	0.96* (1.80)
Stock volatility squared$_t$	−	−6.06*** (−9.73)	−2.13*** (−4.02)
Book-to-market$_t$	−	−3.17*** (−27.36)	−2.23*** (−22.55)
N		7,373	7,291
Adjusted R^2		19.4%	17.9%

***, **, * significant at a 0.01, 0.05, 0.10 level (two-tailed).

sample is statistically lower than that of the control sample by a mean of 36.0% ($p<0.002$) and median of 32.9% ($p<0.001$).[4] Finally, the other executives' stock value residual for the target ownership plan sample is statistically lower than that of the control sample by a mean of 34.2% ($p<0.002$) and median of 35.0% ($p<0.002$).

Using "Plan" as an indicator variable equal to one if a firm adopts a target ownership plan, and zero otherwise, we can express the adoption decision as follows:

$$PLAN_{it} = \beta_0 + \beta_1 \text{ Prior industry-adjusted returns}_{it} + \beta_2 \text{ Stock value residual}_{it} + \gamma_{1\ldots3} \text{ year indicators}_{it} + u_{it,} \quad (2)$$

where we hypothesize that $\beta_1 <0$ and $\beta_2 <0$.

We estimate this model using logistic regression and present the results in Table 18.4. In Columns 1 and 2, we see that the individual coefficient estimates (and changes in predicted probability) for prior industry-adjusted returns and the stock value residual are statistically negative at conventional levels. The changes in predicted probability for prior industry-adjusted returns indicate that if prior industry-adjusted returns increase from the first quartile to third quartile and the other independent variables remain at their mean values, the predicted probability of the firm having a target ownership plan decreases from 3.8% to 3.0%. Although this decrease seems small, it is arguably more

Table 18.4 Determinants of the decision to adopt a target ownership plan

This table summarizes estimation results of Eq. (2), which is a logistic model in which the dependent variable is equal to one if a firm adopts a target ownership plan and zero otherwise. The sample consists of 4,192 firm-year observations from 1992 to 1996. Δ Pred. Prob. is the change in the predicted probability that occurs when the independent variable increases from its first to third quartile value, and is evaluated at the mean values of the remaining independent variables. We base t-statistics (in parentheses) on maximum likelihood standard errors. The prior industry-adjusted return is the stock price return in the two years preceding the fiscal year in which the plan is adopted, less the median stock price performance during the same time period for all firms contained in the 1998 Compustat file that have the same two-digit SIC code. The stock value residual is the residual obtained from estimating the model described by Eq. (1). We measure the stock value residual at the end of the year in which the plan is adopted. Coefficients on the intercept and three year indicator variables are not shown.

Independent variable	Coefficient estimate [Δ Pred. Prob.] (t-statistic) (1)	Coefficient estimate [Δ Pred. Prob.] (2)	Coefficient estimate [Δ Pred. prob.] (3)
Prior industry-adjusted returns	-1.23^{***} [-0.82%] (-2.92)	-1.26^{***} [-0.84%] (-2.98)	-1.23^{**} [-0.76%] (-2.88)
CEO stock value residual	-0.08^{**} [-0.58%] (-2.06)		-0.05 [-0.34%] (-1.22)
Other execs' stock value residual		-0.12^{**} [-0.69%] (-2.44)	-0.10^{*} [-0.51%] (-1.80)
N	4,192	4,113	4,113
# adopting	170	168	168
# non-adopting	4,022	3,945	3,945
Pseudo R^2	4.1%	4.5%	4.6%
Model p-value	<0.0001	<0.0001	<0.0001

***, **, * significant at a 0.01, 0.05, 0.10 level (two-tailed).

relevant that it represents a relative decline of 21% in the predicted probability (DeAngelo et al., 2000, p. 341). The decreases in predicted probability for CEO stock residual (Column 1) and for other executives' stock residual (Column 2) represent relative declines of 16% and 18%, respectively, in the predicted probability of a target ownership plan.

When we include both the CEO and the other executives' stock value residuals in the same model (Column 3), the coefficient on the other executives' stock residual is significant ($p<0.10$), but the coefficient on the CEO stock residual is insignificant. This evidence suggests that low ownership by executives other than the CEO is a more

important determinant of the decision to adopt than is low ownership by the CEO. We note that there is a 0.39 correlation between the two residuals, and that we also obtain a significant coefficient ($p<0.01$) if we instead include as a single variable a weighted average of the two residuals, in which the CEO (other executives) residual receives a 20% (80%) weight. If we impute a zero value for missing values of prior industry-adjusted returns (and include an indicator variable equal to one when prior industry-adjusted returns are missing), the Table 18.4 results are robust to this change in specification and increase in sample size. The only qualitative change is that the coefficient on the other executives' stock value residual becomes more significant in Column 3 ($p<0.01$).

Although not reported, we also obtain qualitatively similar results if we select the control sample by using a random match that approximates the proportion of target ownership adoptions per year. For example, because 26.3% of the adoptions occur in the Compustat data year 1993, we randomly select 26.3% of all firms on the 1993 ExecuComp file as a control group for the 1993 adoption group, and so forth. Finally, our results are robust to our inclusion of firm size and industry indicators as additional control variables.

Thus, consistent with Hypothesis 1, our results suggest that boards respond to governance problems (as measured by low relative stock price returns and low relative managerial equity ownership) by adopting target ownership plans for senior-level executives.

5. CONSEQUENCES OF TARGET OWNERSHIP PLAN ADOPTION

The majority of this section discusses how we conduct tests of our hypothesis that performance improves for target ownership plan adopters. However, before we examine the performance consequences of plan adoption, we must first determine if target ownership plans actually cause executives to increase their level of stock holdings, as we predict in our second hypotheses. If we do not find that managerial equity ownership increases after the adoption of target ownership plans, we would not expect to find improvements in performance associated with the plans.

5.1. Changes in managerial stock ownership

To test whether equity ownership increases following adoption, we use the stock value residuals described in Section 4.1. We examine the difference between the year 2 residual and the year 0 residual, and test

whether this difference indicates a significant increase. For the sample of firms for which we can obtain proxy statement data on CEO ownership two years after plan adoption ($n = 174$), we observe that the CEO stock value residual increases by a mean (median) of 14.1% (27.5%). The mean is marginally significant ($p = 0.13$), and the median is significant at a 0.001 level. For those firms with data on top executive ownership changes for the two years after the plan adoption ($n = 173$), we find that the other executives' stock value residual increases by a mean (median) of 18.2% (11.7%), which is statistically significant at a 0.07 (0.01) level.

There are three possible limitations to these results. First, the increases that we document above might reflect mean reversion in executive ownership, in which case one would expect to observe increases for a sample of firms known to have a low level of ownership relative to the population. In fact, when we regress the change in ownership for the full sample on the beginning residual, we find a negative and significant coefficient on the beginning residual, which means that firms with lower ownership experience greater subsequent increases. We address this limitation by matching each sample firm to the control firm with the closest ownership residual in the adoption year. We choose from among those control firms for which we can obtain proxy statement data on ownership two years after the plan adoption. We then compute the two-year change in the stock value residual for each sample firm and compare it to the two-year change in the stock value residual for the matched control firm.

Benchmarking sample firm increases against control firm increases also addresses a second limitation, which is that managers' equity ownership is likely to increase with the time they have spent at the firm. This increase over time can occur either because of mechanical reasons related to the accumulation of stock through stock compensation plans (i.e., the exercise of stock options) or because of economic reasons, such as the need to prevent horizon problems with CEOs near retirement. Palia (1998) and Core and Guay (1999) find evidence that CEO ownership increases with the CEO's tenure.

We find that the sample firm increases are significantly greater than those of the control firms. Paired t-tests (z-tests) indicate that the sample firm mean (median) increase of 14.1% (27.5%) in the CEO stock value residual is significantly greater than the control firm mean (median) increase of -9.3% (1.7%) at a 0.04 (0.02) level. The sample firm mean (median) increase of 18.2% (11.7%) in the other executives' stock value residual is also greater than the control firm mean (median) increase of -12.0% (-3.9%) at a 0.02 (0.02) level.

As a second means of controlling for CEO ownership increases over time, we add CEO tenure as an additional control variable in the regression model for log(CEO stock value/salary) described by Eq. (1). We denote the residual from this model as CEO stock value residual$_{tenure}$. Data on tenure for the other executives are not available from most firms' proxy disclosures. Therefore, we cannot control for tenure in the ownership model for the other executives. For the sample firms, we observe that the mean (median) CEO stock value residual$_{tenure}$ increase of 12.4% (5.0%) is significantly greater than zero at a 0.12 (0.09) level, and also significantly greater than the control firm mean (median) change of -15.8% (-12.1%) at a 0.004 (0.001) level.

Another limitation on our results is that the changes in CEO ownership from year 0 to year 2 might be contaminated if a sample firm changes CEO during year 1 or year 2. We delete the 42 firms with CEO turnover, and examine separately the sample of firms with the same CEO from the year of adoption until at least two years after the plan adoption ($n = 132$). For these firms, we observe that the CEO stock value residual increases by a mean (median) of 39.9% (30.3%), which is statistically different from zero at a $p < 0.01$ level. This increase is also greater than the 12.2% (12.0%) increase of the control firms with the same CEO at a $p < 0.01$ level.[5]

Moreover, the ownership residuals for these CEOs are no longer statistically different from zero, indicating that these CEOs' ownership levels have increased to equilibrium levels. We obtain qualitatively the same results if we examine CEO stock value residual$_{tenure}$ instead. The sample firms' mean (median) increase of 15.6% (3.2%) is significantly greater than both zero and the control firms' mean (median) increase of -10.1% (-10.1%), and the year 2 ownership residuals for these CEOs are not statistically different from zero.

This consistent evidence of ownership increases for the CEO and for the other top executives supports Hypothesis 2 that target ownership plans are followed by significant increases in managers' equity ownership.

5.2. Post-adoption operating performance: methodology and results

To examine whether plan adoption improves firm performance, we first look at whether the accounting return on assets (ROA) is statistically positive over the two years (years 1 and 2) following the adoption of the target ownership plan. For accounting returns, we use the industry and performance match suggested by Barber and Lyon (1996) to develop a comparison benchmark. Barber and Lyon find that this approach generates well-specified models that can test future abnormal performance for firms that "...as a group, have historically experienced especially good or poor performance" (p. 378), or whose performance "differs only slightly" from the population (p. 396). Using this benchmark is important, because in the two years prior to adoption, our sample firms underperform the control firms' ROA by a mean of 0.9 percentage points ($p < 0.01$) and median of 0.7 percentage points ($p < 0.01$). Also, by examining the future performance of historical poor performers that are less likely to survive for two future years, this matching procedure mitigates any potential sample selection bias.

To implement this procedure, we select a comparison firm for each adopting firm. We match firms on their two-digit standard industrial classification (SIC) codes, and then select that firm with an ROA closest to the sample firm in the year prior to adoption. We require that the control firm's ROA be within 90% and 110% of the sample firm's ROA. We are unable to match five adopting firms because they have no Compustat data for year 0.

Sometimes, either the sample firm or a control firm is missing data in year 1 or year 2, either because it was acquired or for some other reason. All of the 190 sample firms with year 0 data also have data available for year 1, but nine of the firms have no data available for year 2, so we do not compute the excess ROA for these firms. If a matching firm has no data available for either year 1 or year 2, we use the firm that is in the same SIC code with the ROA next closest to the sample firm in the year of adoption. We still require that the control firm ROA be within 90% and 110% of the sample firm ROA. When we cannot find a matching firm in the same industry, we follow Barber and Lyon (1996) and select the firm with the closest ROA regardless of its SIC code. As discussed below, Vijh (1997) uses a similar splicing method when he computes excess stock returns.

Although Barber and Lyon (1996) base their ROA calculation on operating income before depreciation expense (Compustat data item 13), this data item is not available on Compustat for certain financial institutions. To maximize our sample size, we also compute an ROA using operating income after depreciation expense (Compustat data item 178).

Table 18.5, Panel A, presents the accounting performance comparisons. The

Table 18.5 Two-year post-adoption excess operating and stock performance for target ownership firms

The sample consists of 190 target ownership firms. We calculate excess ROA by using the matched-firm approach of Barber and Lyon (1996), where the matching firm is the firm in the same industry with the closest prior operating performance, and by using both operating income after depreciation and operating income before depreciation. We calculate excess stock returns using the matched-firm approach of Barber and Lyon (1997), where each sample firm is matched to the non-sample firm with the closest book-to-market ratio within that subset of firms whose market value lies between 70% and 130% of the sample firm market value.

	n	Mean	p-value	Median	p-value
Panel A Operating performance					
Excess ROA computed using operating income after depreciation:					
Year 0	190	0.0%	0.552	−0.0%	0.321
Year 1	190	1.2%	0.028	0.5%	0.024
Years 1 and 2	181	1.8%	0.017	0.8%	0.002
Excess ROA computed using operating income before depreciation:					
Year 0	181	0.0%	0.843	−0.0%	0.462
Year 1	181	1.2%	0.049	0.6%	0.017
Years 1 and 2	173	1.4%	0.068	0.7%	0.025
Panel B Stock price performance					
Excess returns:					
First six months of year 1	190	3.8%	0.086	2.9%	0.041
Year 1	190	5.7%	0.161	5.7%	0.160
Years 1 and 2	190	5.3%	0.442	7.9%	0.171

first line of each half of the panel indicates that our matching procedure is successful in creating a control sample whose prior-year performance is insignificantly different from that of our test sample. In the first year after the contractual change and for the cumulated two years after adoption, the target ownership sample has an ROA that is significantly greater than the control firms. The adopting firms statistically outperform the ROA (after depreciation) of the benchmark firms by a mean (median) of 1.2 (0.5) percentage points. In the two years after adoption, the adopting firms statistically outperform the compounded ROA of the benchmark firms by a mean (median) of 1.8 (0.8) percentage points.

The bottom half of Panel A shows that our results are also robust for a reduced sample for which we use ROA before depreciation. Again, the adopting firms statistically outperform the ROA of the benchmark firms by a mean (median) of 1.2 (0.6) percentage points. In the two years after adoption, the adopting firms statistically outperform the compounded ROA of the benchmark firms by a mean (median) of 1.4 (0.7) percentage points. These results are consistent with Hypothesis 3 that target ownership plans are followed by significant increases in operating performance.

5.3. Post-adoption stock performance: methodology and results

We assess stock price performance in the announcement window around the release of the proxy statement and for the six-, 12-, and 24-month periods beginning in year 1, the year after target ownership plan adoption. We first examine stock market returns in the three-day window surrounding the date of the proxy statement in which the target ownership plan is disclosed.[6] Using standard event study methodology (e.g., Brickley, 1986) and the statistical tests described in Patell (1976), we find that over the three-day window, the cumulative average excess return for the adopting firms is 0.15%, which is statistically indistinguishable from

zero ($p > 0.10$). These short-window results do not support Hypothesis 3.

Although target ownership plans lead to improvements in operating performance, we might not see excess stock returns in the short time period around the proxy date. There are two reasons for this. First, although our searches of the Dow Jones and PR newswires reveal no public discussion of the plans prior to the proxy date, managers might have privately communicated the news of the adoption of a target ownership plan to large shareholders. Thus, by the proxy date, the expected benefits of the plan might already be impounded into the stock price.[7]

Second, even if the market knows that the plan exists, target ownership plans represent an innovation, and the positive or negative performance consequences of this innovation become clear only with the passage of time. In this case, when there are improvements in operating performance, the market will be surprised and there will be positive abnormal returns for a period following the plan adoption. For example, the stock market might react to changes in managerial investment and financing decisions, rather than to the contractual change disclosed in the proxy statement. We explore these possibilities by assessing whether stock price returns are statistically positive over the six-, 12-, and 24-month periods starting in the year after target ownership plan adoption (year 1).

Barber and Lyon (1997) and Lyon et al. (1999) show that the use of a control firm matched on size and book-to-market in computing buy-and-hold excess returns (BHERs) for each sample produces test statistics that are well specified in random samples of firms and for almost all non-random samples of firms. We use their methodology to develop our group of control firms. We obtain the matching firms from the list of all Center for Research in Securities Prices firms with price data as of the end of June of year 0 (where year 0 is the year of target ownership plan adoption). We compute market value in June of year 0, and the book-to-market ratio by using the last book value reported prior to

June of year 0. Using the subset of firms whose market value lies between 70% and 130% of the sample firm value, we pair each sample firm with the firm that has the closest book-to-market ratio. (We note that our control group is closely matched to our test sample: on average the percentage difference in firm size is 4.0% and the percentage difference in the book-to-market ratio is -0.0%.) We compute the BHERs starting the first month of year 1, the fiscal year in which the firm releases the proxy statement announcement of the plan. Because the proxy is always released within the first six months of the fiscal year-end, all of our BHER measures can capture any announcement effects related to the plan adoption.

If either a sample or a control firm stops trading because it was acquired (or for some other reason) before the end of our accumulation period, we follow Vijh (1997) by ending the excess return calculation with the delisting month. If a control firm delists, we use the return for a firm that has the book-to-market ratio next closest to the sample firm in the year prior to adoption and a firm size within 70% and 130% of the sample firm size.

Table 18.5, Panel B, presents the stock price performance results. The sample firms statistically outperform the control group for the first six months of the fiscal year of adoption with a mean (median) BHER of 3.8% (2.9%). Although the BHERs for the 12- and 24-month periods are positive, they are insignificant at conventional levels. Combined with our findings of significant and positive operating performance, the BHER results suggest that the market reacts favorably to the adoption of the target ownership plan, and prices its expected benefits in the six-month period around plan adoption. These stock price results support Hypothesis 3.

5.4. Sensitivity analysis

Our sample comprises firms with relatively low levels of management stock ownership prior to the adoption of the new program. However, 70 of the firms have CEOs with positive stock value residuals, 70 of the firms have other top executives with positive stock value residuals, and 38 of the firms have both CEOs and other executives with positive stock value residuals. This observation raises two issues. First, we wish to establish that our results are not driven by observations that already have appropriate equity incentives (for which we expect the incentive effects of establishing minimum ownership levels would be lower). A second issue is that if an executive has a positive stock value residual, the plan could create perverse incentives by forcing him or her to own "too much" stock.

We address the first issue in two ways. First, we delete the 38 firms that have positive stock value residuals for both the CEO and the other executives as a group. We then examine the performance of the remaining 157 firms and find that these firms experience large, significant increases in ownership for both the CEO and the other executives as a group in the two years after plan adoption. For this subsample, all means and medians of the excess performance variables remain positive and significant, with two exceptions. First, while excess ROA using operating income after depreciation remains significant, excess ROA using operating income before depreciation loses significance (this variable is available for fewer observations). Second, the mean excess stock return for the first six months becomes insignificant ($p = 0.152$), although the median remains significant ($p = 0.056$). Thus, our results are robust to deleting the subset of firms with positive stock value residuals.

Second, the plan may not require an increase in ownership even if the ownership residuals are negative (i.e., the plan is not binding). If the plan is not binding on the top executives, one might expect the incentive effects of establishing minimum ownership levels to be lower. To address this issue, we delete from the sample of 157 firms with negative residuals the 15 (42) firms for which the plan does not bind on at least the CEO or *one* of the other top executives (the CEO or the other top executives *as a group*), resulting in a subsample of

142 (115) firms. The inference for the subsample of 142 firms is the same as that reported above for the 157-firm subsample: all of the excess performance variables remain positive and the same variables are significant. For the smaller 115-firm subsample for which the plan is binding on the CEO or the top executives as a group, the inference is qualitatively similar to that reported above for the 157-firm subsample: all of the excess performance variables remain positive, and the same variables are significant except that the mean excess two year ROA using operating income after depreciation becomes insignificant ($p = 0.141$), although the median remains significant ($p = 0.014$). Thus, with the exception that excess ROA using operating income before depreciation loses significance in these subsamples, our results are robust to examining the subsamples of firms obtained by deleting firms with nonpositive stock value residuals and then by deleting firms without binding plans.

The finding that a subset of firms has positive ownership residuals raises another question. If a firm's executives already own a large amount of stock prior to the target ownership plan adoption, the plan could force the executives to own "too much" stock, which could create perverse incentives and lead to lower firm performance. Although this is a possibility, target ownership plans impose a floor on executive ownership levels, and do not require increases in ownership levels for executives whose holdings are already above this floor. Of the 70 sample firms with positive CEO stock value residuals, none of the firms' ownership targets require increases in ownership by the CEO. Similarly, of the 70 sample firms with positive other executive stock value residuals, none of the firms' ownership targets require increases by *all* of the other executives. However, eight of the targets require increases in ownership by *some* of the other executives. Finally, the actual increases in ownership for these firms either are significantly less than zero or are not different from zero, depending on the measure used for the analysis. Thus, it appears that the design of these target

ownership plans does not impose excess ownership on the executives. Moreover, we find no evidence that firms with CEOs or other executives with positive stock value residuals have excess operating or stock price performance that is significantly lower than the remainder of the sample.

Finally, we note the results of two additional sensitivity tests. The two-year CEO turnover rate of 24.1% for the target ownership adopters is greater than the turnover rate of the control sample of 19%, and the difference is marginally significant ($p = 0.12$ from a binomial test of differences). Our accounting and stock price performance results are qualitatively the same as in Table 18.5 if we examine only those firms with the same CEO over the time period used for developing the performance tests. Finally, we note that we have a concentration of financial firms in our sample (as shown in Table 18.1), and these firms have different accounting conventions and operate in a very specific industrial sector. We obtain qualitatively the same performance results if we delete the 36 financial firms and examine separately the non-financial adopting firms; the only difference is that the six-month excess return is only marginally significant ($p < 0.15$).

6. SUMMARY AND CONCLUSION

We construct a powerful test of the hypothesis that re-contracting to require managers to increase equity ownership from suboptimal levels will improve incentives and increase performance. We implement this test by examining a sample of firms that adopt minimum ownership levels for executive officers. Because most managers in our sample have low ownership, these plans generally require increases in managerial ownership. We find that firms that adopt target ownership plans show lower stock price performance than do their industry peers in the time period prior to plan adoption. These firms also have managers who own lower levels of equity relative to our benchmark model, which is similar to that of Demsetz and Lehn (1985). We also find that managers increase their stock ownership following the adoption of a target ownership plan. These results indicate that target ownership plan adoption is an intervention by the board of directors to improve incentives and governance.

More important, we find that excess accounting returns are statistically higher in the two years following plan adoption, and that excess stock price returns are statistically higher in the first six months of the fiscal year in which the plan is announced. These results illustrate that when managers with below-equilibrium equity ownership are required to increase their ownership levels, there are improvements in firm performance.

We contribute to the literature on ownership and performance by suggesting a way to reconcile the starkly contrasting predictions and findings of Morck et al. (1988) and Demsetz and Lehn (1985). Like Demsetz and Lehn, we assume that firms optimize ownership levels when they contract, and that at the optimum there is no association between ownership and firm performance. Like Morck et al. we expect that some firms are below optimum and that their performance can be improved by increasing ownership levels. Consistent with our approach, we find that mandatory increases in suboptimal equity ownership are associated with increases in subsequent firm performance.

NOTES

* A previous version was titled "Performance Consequences of Mandatory Increases in CEO Stock Ownership". We gratefully acknowledge the helpful comments of Stanley Baiman, Wayne Guay, Paul Healy (the referee), Robert Holthausen, Christopher Ittner, and Rebecca Tsui. We thank Howard Yeh and Christine Phillips for research assistance. We gratefully acknowledge the help of John Moyer of Ernst & Young LLP and the financial support of the Wharton School.

† Corresponding author. Tel.: + 1–215–898–4821; fax: + 1–215–573–2054.

E-mail address: jcore@wharton.upenn.edu (J.E. Core).

1 We use the value of stock disclosed in the year 0 proxy (rather than in the year -1 proxy) to maximize the sample size. The disadvantage of the year -1 shareholdings is that they are available for a much smaller group of firms. If we used year -1 numbers, our sample size would be reduced substantially because some sample firms are not public at that time and it is not always possible to determine ownership levels from 1991 proxies for 1992 adopters. Because ExecuComp does not have data prior to 1992 (i.e., prior to the 1992 reforms in proxy disclosure), we also would have no control firms for our 1992 adopters. Although the board does not know the year 0 shareholdings at the time of adoption, the interim ownership numbers that the board considers when it adopts the plan are probably close to the year 0 numbers. If some managers react to the plan adoption in year 0 by increasing their stockholdings, our measure of ownership at the time of adoption will be too large, and this will limit our ability to find significant differences between the adopters and non-adopters and to find significant increases after adoption.

2 While our measure of ownership is consistent with the measure used in the target ownership plans, prior research has concentrated on either the fraction of the firm owned or the value of ownership (not deflated by base salary). In addition, arguably a better proxy for managerial equity incentives would also include the incentives provided by the manager's options (e.g., Core and Guay, 1999). If we use instead the logarithm of the value of managerial stock ownership or the logarithm of the total incentives provided by the manager's stock and option portfolio, our results are qualitatively the same as those discussed below. In particular, the adopting firms' managers have significantly lower equity incentives than the comparison group, and these incentives increase significantly in the two years following adoption.

3 A "percentage point" difference is the difference in two returns, e.g., a 1% return is 1 percentage point lower than a 2% return.

4 As noted above, because our dependent variable is log(stock value/salary), we can interpret the residual as the percentage by which actual ownership deviates from expected ownership. Further, we can interpret the differences in two residuals as percentage differences, e.g., we term the difference in the -0.336 mean residual for the adopters and the 0.026 mean residual for the control samples as a 36.2% difference.

5   The other executives' stock value residual for the 130 of these observations with available data increased by a mean (median) of 16.5% (14.2%), which is significantly greater than both zero and the -19.9% (−5.6%) change for the control sample.

6   There is some debate on the desirability of using proxy statement release dates for detecting the shareholder value consequences associated with changes in compensation contracts; Gaver et al. (1992) discuss this point.

7   As noted above, most of the target ownership plans are adopted in year 0, which raises the possibility that the leakage could have occurred prior to the start of our event window at the beginning of year 1. To address this possibility, we examine excess returns for the six months ending with the start of year 1 for the set of firms (with available return data) that do not state that they adopted early in year 0. We find no significant excess returns for either the sample of 73 firms that specifically disclose that they adopted in year 0, or for the 152-firm subsample that does not state that they adopted in year 1. This finding is consistent with the lack of disclosure of the plans and with the conjecture that the board action to adopt these plans occurs late in year 0.

REFERENCES

Baker, G., Hall, B., 1998. CEO incentives and firm size. NBER Working paper 6868.

Barber, B., Lyon, J., 1996. Detecting abnormal operating performance: the empirical power and specification of test statistics. Journal of Financial Economics 41, 359–399.

Barber, B., Lyon, J., 1997. Detecting long-run stock returns: the empirical power and specification of test statistics. Journal of Financial Economics 43, 341–372.

Brickley, J., 1986. Interpreting common stock returns around proxy statement disclosures and annual shareholder meetings. Journal of Financial and Quantitative Analysis 21, 343–349.

Brill, J., 1993. Stock ownership guidelines for executives. The Corporate Executive (March–April), 381–385.

Core, J., Guay, W., 1999. The use of equity grants to manage optimal equity incentive levels. Journal of Accounting and Economics 28, 151–184.

Core, J., Holthausen, R., Larcker, D., 1999. Corporate governance, CEO compensation, and firm performance. Journal of Financial Economics 51, 371–406.

DeAngelo, H., DeAngelo, L., Skinner, D., 2000. Special dividends and the evolution of dividend signaling. Journal of Financial Economics 57, 309–354.

Demsetz, H., Lehn, K., 1985. The structure of corporate ownership: causes and consequences. Journal of Political Economy 93, 1155–1177.

Gaver, J., Gaver, K., Battistel, G., 1992. The stock market reaction to performance plan adoption. The Accounting Review 67, 172–182.

Hewitt Associates, 1993. Survey Findings: Executive Stock Ownership Guidelines. Hewitt Associates, Lincolnshire, Ill.

Himmelberg, C., Hubbard, G., Palia, D., 1999. Understanding the determinants of managerial ownership and the link between ownership and performance. Journal of Financial Economics 53, 353–384.

Institutional Shareholder Services, 1993. The ISS Proxy Voting Manual. Institutional Shareholder Services, Washington, DC.

Jensen, M., 1993. The modern industrial revolution, exit, and the failure of internal control systems. Journal of Finance 48, 831–880.

Jensen, M., Murphy, K., 1990. Performance pay and top-management incentives. Journal of Political Economy 98, 225–264.

Kole, S., 1996. Managerial incentives and firm performance: incentives or rewards? Advances in Financial Economics 2, 119–149.

Lyon, J., Barber, B., Tsai, C., 1999. Improved methods for tests of long-run abnormal stock returns. Journal of Finance 54, 341–372.

McConnell, J., Servaes, H., 1990. Additional evidence on equity ownership and corporate value. Journal of Financial Economics 27, 595–612.

McMillan, J., Sabow, S., 1994. Encouraging executive stock ownership. The Corporate Board (January/February), 16–20.

Morck, R., Shleifer, A., Vishny, R., 1988. Management ownership and market valuation: an empirical analysis. Journal of Financial Economics 20, 293–315.

Murphy, K., 1999. Executive compensation. In: Ashenfelter, O., Card, D. (Eds.), Handbook of

Labor Economics, Vol. 3. North-Holland, Amsterdam.

Norton, L., 1995. Velvet handcuffs. Barron's (July 24), 21–24.

Palia, D., 1998. The endogeneity of managerial compensation in firm valuation: a solution. Working paper, Columbia University.

Patell, J., 1976. Corporate forecasts of earnings per share and stock price behavior: empirical tests. Journal of Accounting Research 14, 246–276.

Pfeffer, J., 1981. Power in Organizations. Pitman, Boston.

Reese, J., 1993. Buy stock—Or die. Fortune (August 23), 14–15.

Smith, C., Watts, R., 1992. The investment opportunity set and corporate financing, dividends and compensation policies. Journal of Financial Economics 32, 263–292.

Towers, P., 1993. Stocking up in the 90s: how companies are creating managers/owners. CompScan.

United Shareholders Association, 1992. 1992 Shareholder 1,000: rating corporate America's responsiveness to shareholders.

Vijh, A., 1997. Long-term returns for equity carveouts. Journal of Financial Economics 51, 273–308.

Young, L., 1995. The owner mentality. The Wall Street Journal (April 12), R12.

Part 5

Governance, performance and financial strategy

INTRODUCTION

THE PAPERS IN THIS PART DEAL WITH THE IMPACT of governance structure on corporate performance, its investment and financing strategy.

Corporate governance and performance

Erik Lehmann and Jürgen Weigand (Ch.19) focus on the relationship between governance structure in Germany and corporate performance. As noted above, Germany has a unique corporate governance structure and its performance effects are therefore a matter of considerable interest in evaluating the comparative merits of different corporate governance systems. Although there has been an intensive debate on the relative merits of different systems of corporate governance, empirical evidence on the link between corporate governance and firm performance almost exclusively refers to the market-oriented Anglo-American system. This paper, therefore, investigates the more network- or bank-oriented German system. In panel regressions for 361 German corporations over the time period 1991 to 1996, significantly the authors find ownership concentration to negatively affect profitability. However, this effect depends intricately on stock market exposure, the location of control rights, and the time horizon (short-run *vs.* long-run). They conclude that (1) the presence of large shareholders does not necessarily enhance profitability, (2) ownership concentration seems to be sub-optimal for many German corporations, and, finally, (3) having financial institutions as largest shareholders of traded corporations improves corporate performance.

Corporate governance is manifested in a variety of ways and different metrics of corporate governance may offer different, even conflicting, perspectives on the effectiveness of governance. A composite metric that integrates these disparate metrics is therefore a useful step in establishing the relationship between corporate governance and performance. Shareholder rights vis-à-vis the firm are major pillars of corporate governance but vary widely across countries and even within a single country. Paul Gompers, Joy Ishii and Andrew Metrick (Ch.20) measure the level of corporate governance on the basis of shareholder rights that vary across firms in the US. Using the incidence of 24 governance rules, the authors construct a 'Governance Index' to proxy for the level of shareholder rights in about 1,500 large US firms during the 1990s. An investment strategy that bought firms in the lowest decile of the index (strongest rights) and sold firms in the highest decile of the index (weakest rights) would have earned abnormal returns of 8.5 percent per year during the sample period. They found that firms with stronger shareholder rights had higher firm value, higher profits, higher sales growth, lower capital expenditures, and made fewer corporate acquisitions. This study represents a landmark in the way corporate governance is quantified and its methodology can be extended to other countries and to other aspects of corporate governance such as accounting disclosures and creditor rights.

Corporate governance and corporate investment strategy

The governance structure of strategic investments and its impact on both the investment itself and the investing firms is a matter of interest to firms. Often strategic investments may fail due to poor governance structures as evidenced by numerous studies on post-merger integration (Sudarsanam, 2003, ch.22). Such governance problems also plague joint ventures and strategic alliances (Sudarsanam, 2003, ch.10). Gertjan Schut and Ruud van Frederikslust (Ch.21) examine the shareholder wealth effects of 233 joint venture announcements of Dutch public companies in the period 1987 till 1998. They find that on average, establishing joint ventures has a positive effect on the market value of Dutch companies. Using the strategic characteristics of joint ventures it is possible to explain and understand these wealth effects. The authors show that strategic intention, the context in which the strategy is unfolded and the extent to which the company has ownership and managerial control over the implementation of the joint venture, strongly explains the extent to which it can create value.

Financial distress is another context in which the influence of corporate governance on the strategic and other decisions a firm makes can be studied. Firms in performance decline may choose a variety of restructuring strategies for recovery with conflicting welfare implications for different stakeholders such as shareholders, lenders and managers. Choice of recovery strategies is therefore determined by the complex interplay of ownership structure, corporate governance and lender monitoring of such firms. For a sample of 297 UK firms experiencing relative stock return decline during 1987–1993, Jim Lai and Sudi Sudarsanam (Ch.22) examine the impact of these factors as well as other control factors on their turnaround strategies. Strategy choices during the decline year and two post-decline years are modelled with logit regressions. The results show that turnaround strategy choices are significantly influenced by both agency and control variables. While there is agreement among stakeholders on certain strategies there is also evidence of conflict of interests among them. There is further evidence of shifting coalitions of stakeholders for or against certain strategies. This paper points to the rich and complex ways in which different corporate governance mechanisms interact, sometimes conflicting with and, at others, complementing one another.

Corporate governance and corporate financing strategy

Retained profits may create the problem of free cash flow which entrenched managers may invest in value destroying projects such as ambitious acquisitions or reckless R&D. Whether they are allowed to do so or prevented by being forced to return free cash flow to shareholders depends at least partly on the effectiveness of corporate governance. Jorge Farinha (Ch.23) tests the agency explanation for the cross-sectional variation of corporate dividend policy in the UK by looking at the managerial entrenchment hypothesis. Consistent with its predictions, a significant U-shaped relationship between dividend payout ratios and insider ownership is observed for a large sample of over 600 UK companies and two distinct periods. These results strongly suggest the possibility of managerial entrenchment until insider ownership reaches a threshold of around 30 per cent. Beyond this level managers seek to offset the higher agency costs by increasing payout. Evidence is also presented that non-beneficial holdings by insiders can lead to entrenchment in conjunction with shares held beneficially. Farinha also provides evidence, as do Dahya et al. (see Part 3, Ch.13), that compliance with the Cadbury Code after 1992 results in corporate decisions more aligned to shareholder interests, thus testifying to the greater effectiveness of the governance regime introduced by the Code.

Entrenched managers may not only enjoy private benefits of control at the expense of shareholders and capture the pay setting process to award themselves excessive compensation but also prevent shareholders from finding out what they are up to. The earnings they report may have been 'managed' and therefore lack transparency. Whether such creative accounting is feasible depends on the corporate governance structure including shareholder rights (see Gompers et al., (Ch.20) on shareholder rights as a measure of corporate governance). Christian Leuz, Dhananjay Nanda and Peter Wysocki (Ch.24) propose an explanation for the systematic differences they observe in earnings management across 31 countries. Insiders, in an attempt to protect their private control benefits, use earnings management to conceal firm performance from outsiders. Thus, earnings management is expected to decrease in investor protection because strong protection limits insiders' ability to acquire private control benefits, which reduces their incentives to mask firm performance. The findings are consistent with this prediction and suggest an endogenous link between corporate governance and the quality of reported earnings.

REFERENCE

Sudarsanam, P. Sudi (2003), *Creating value from mergers and acquisitions. The challenges, an international and integrated perspective*, New York: FT Prentice Hall.

Chapter 19

Erik Lehmann and Jürgen Weigand

DOES THE GOVERNED CORPORATION PERFORM BETTER? GOVERNANCE STRUCTURES AND CORPORATE PERFORMANCE IN GERMANY

Source: *European Finance Review*, 4(2) (2000): 157–195.

ABSTRACT

Although there has been an intensive debate on the relative merits of different systems of corporate governance, empirical evidence on the link between corporate governance and firm performance almost exclusively refers to the market-oriented Anglo-Saxon system. This paper therefore investigates the more network- or bank-oriented German system. In panel regressions for 361 German corporations over the time period 1991 to 1996, we find ownership concentration to affect profitability significantly negatively. However, this effect depends intricately on stock market exposure, the location of control rights, and the time horizon (short-run vs. long-run). We conclude from our results that (1) the presence of large shareholders does not necessarily enhance profitability, (2) ownership concentration seems to be sub-optimal for many German corporations, and, finally, (3) having financial institutions as largest shareholders of traded corporations improves corporate performance.

> Shareholders are stupid and impertinent – stupid, because they give their funds to somebody else without adequate control, and impertinent, because they clamor for a dividend as a reward for their stupidity.
>
> Carl Fürstenberg (1850–1933), German financier

1. INTRODUCTION

EVER SINCE BERLE AND MEANS (1932) STATED THAT in the modern corporation hired managers have enough discretion for corporate plundering, the issue of separating ownership from control and its resulting impact on corporate performance has been placed high on the agenda of economists. Globalizing product and financial markets have recently triggered renewed interest in the link between corporate governance and performance among academics and business press. As firms face new challenges from increased cross-border competition, pressures to adapt to an internationally integrated environment mount. The question arises naturally whether established systems of corporate finance and corporate governance are still appropriate to cope with the challenges ahead.[1]

Ownership structures are a central distinguishing feature of financial systems (Mayer, 1992; Moerland, 1995). Particular attention has been paid in the corporate governance literature to ownership concentration as a key to more effective corporate governance and shareholder value maximization. The presence of large shareholders may curb managerial discretion, reduce agency costs and enhance performance (Stiglitz, 1985; Shleifer and Vishny, 1986). The existing empirical evidence on the impact of ownership structures on corporate performance refers almost exclusively to Anglo-Saxon firms and is rather mixed.[2] This paper therefore focuses on German corporations. We investigate empirically how ownership concentration, the location of control rights, board representation of owners, and stock market exposure affect firm profitability (return on total assets).

Ownership concentration is low in the Anglo-Saxon countries which rely heavily on stock markets to channel the flow of capital, control its efficient use, and assure outside investors of maximizing the return on their investments.[3] The Anglo-Saxon financial system has been criticized for short-termism, neglect of interests other than shareholders', and inefficiency in delivering effective corporate governance.[4]

By contrast, concentrated ownership is a salient feature of the German system. Non-incorporated small and medium-sized firms tightly held by individuals or families dominate the firm population. German corporations are typically in the hands of large blockholders who often command a super-majority interest. Widely dispersed outside shareholdings as in the USA or UK are rare. Ownership structures hardly change over time, implying that large shareholders stick to their blockholdings even in bad times. An active market for corporate control does not exist yet despite the recent takeover-battle between Mannesmann and Vodafone. Although improving lately, the German stock market is still relatively small regarding listings and market capitalization.[5] Close ties between industrial firms and financial institutions (banks) (e.g., via cross-holdings, long-term lender-borrower relations) apparently foster access to debt capital, thus reducing the need to attract equity capital on the stock market. This network-like structure has effectively thwarted any serious attempts of hostile takeovers in Germany.[6] In view of high unemployment and sluggish growth, critics have pointed to the German network-orientation as a root cause for entrepreneurial inertia, risk aversion, and low investment in emerging new technologies and infant industries.[7]

In the remainder of the paper we discuss in Section 2 the link between corporate governance and firm performance in more detail. Section 3 presents our empirical analysis that employs a panel data set of 361 German corporations over the time period 1991 to 1996. Our main finding is a significantly negative effect of ownership concentration on profitability. However, this effect depends intricately on stock market exposure, the location of control rights, and the time horizon chosen (short-run vs. long-run). Section 4 summarizes and concludes.

2. CORPORATE GOVERNANCE AND FIRM PERFORMANCE

2.1. The governed versus the managed corporation

The separation of ownership and control

A prime element of corporate governance is the alignment of shareholders' interests with the interests of managers hired to run the firm. The major concern is whether managers pursue their own interests (pet projects, empire building, perks etc.) rather than maximize shareholder value. Public corporations with widely dispersed outside shareholdings may be particularly prone to managerial discretion. Such corporations have a clear separation of control and ownership. Shareholders delegate decision-making to managers and control to a supervisory board. Managers are put in place because it is expected that their superior entrepreneurial skills allow them to better achieve success for the firm than the owners. The supervisory board is responsible for selecting, monitoring, and replacing senior managers.

An extensive literature has discussed the pros and cons of separating ownership from control and whether governance of such a "managed" (manager-controlled) corporation is inherently ineffective.[8] Corporate supervisory boards are suspected of being inefficient or 'entrenched' monitors who only take action when true performance disasters have already happened (Warner et al., 1988).[9] In principle, if the corporation does not perform as expected, shareholders can oust the supervisory board in a joint voting effort. However, coordinating a large number of shareholders for joint voting is difficult. The incentive to monitor and take action against the board will be low for shareholders who command only a negligible share in a firm. The costs of such efforts usually outweigh the individual benefits. Moreover, a shareholder gains from any other shareholder's control effort without having to contribute to the incurred costs. This free-rider problem makes it unattractive for a small shareholder to exercise and enforce voting rights. Thus, managerial mistakes can "go uncorrected" in the managed corporation "until they become catastrophes" (Pound, 1995, p. 92). When markets for equity capital are highly liquid, dissatisfied shareholders can easily sell off their holdings. Therefore, shareholders of the managed corporation rather favor a "cheap 'exit'" over an "expensive 'voice'" (Bhide, 1994, p. 132) in times of crisis.

In active markets for corporate control, hostile takeovers may provide an effective mechanism to reign in free-wheeling managers and sanction underperforming firms (Manne, 1965; Jensen and Ruback, 1983). However, as shown by Grossman and Hart (1980), the free-rider problem also besets the takeover mechanism. The threat of shareholders' cheap exit by selling off to a raider may thus be insufficient to discipline management. In addition, incumbent managers can apply anti-takeover strategies to entrench their positions (Stulz, 1988; Shleifer and Vishny, 1988; Jensen, 1988; Fluck, 1999).

The governed corporation

In view of these problems, Pound (1995) has suggested replacing the managed corporation with what he terms the governed corporation. For a corporation to be governed, investors must be different from the investors of the managed corporation. The model of the governed corporation rests on *committed* owners who *actively* participate in governing the firm. Commitment means that investors do not sell out quickly in times of trouble. To guarantee that the company is soundly managed, they participate in selecting the top management and initiate replacements in case of inferior performance.

For having one's interests and concerns respected, the "active" (Jensen 1993, p. 866) or "relationship" (Thompson, 1998, p. 27) investor needs to be a large shareholder, that is, he must have sufficient control over the firm's assets.[10] Only investors who control a substantial part of the voting capital will be able to keep managers from diverting free cash flow into pet projects and force them to distribute profits to shareholders. The incentive to take action should increase with the investor's wealth commitment (Shleifer and Vishny, 1986; Huddart, 1993; Admati et al., 1994). The model of the governed corporation thus suggests concentrating the stakes in a firm in the hands of only a few shareholders. The underlying hypothesis is that by re-integrating ownership and control corporate performance (profitability, productivity, innovative thrust etc.) is going to be enhanced.

Demsetz (1983) has argued that concentrated ownership is no safeguard against corporate plundering: "Where is it written that the owner-manager of a closely held firm prefers to consume only at home?" (ibid., p. 381). Contesting the model of the firm on which both the managerial discretion hypothesis and the agency approach rest, Demsetz states, "It is clearly an error to suppose that a firm managed by its only owner comes closest to the profit-maximizing firm postulated in the model firm of economic theory" (ibid., p. 383).

Theoretically, the impact of ownership concentration on firm value is indeed not definite. Shleifer and Vishny (1986) show that concentrated shareholdings raise firm value. In Huddart (1993) and Admati et al.

(1994) this outcome is reversed because of risk-averse large shareholders. Recent contributions by Pagano and Röell (1998) and Bolton and von Thadden (1998a,b) stress the existence of a trade-off between control and liquidity. As the incentive and the ability to monitor increase with share concentration, control will be more stringent and effective but this comes at the cost of liquidity. Constraining liquidity could affect profitability negatively if the firm cannot fully exploit its investment opportunities. This reasoning may only apply to smaller firms with the intention to go public. In general, mature large corporations hardly face financing constraints and finance investment overwhelmingly from retained earnings.[11] Cash-flush corporations may thus rather overinvest to keep funds in the firm instead of "wasting" them on the shareholders (Jensen, 1986; Hellwig, 2000). Strong owners could prevent managers from stashing money away and thus reduce both free cash flow and inefficient investments. Profitability should then be enhanced, but this is not for sure, since large shareholders may overdo monitoring. As shown by Burkart, Gromb, and Panunzi (1997), too much monitoring can stifle managerial initiative. The governed corporation may then miss out on profitable investment opportunities.

Large shareholders can inflict substantial costs on other shareholders as well as stakeholders (managers, employees, creditors) in the form of an expropriation-like redistribution of wealth if their interests diverge from those of other investors or stakeholders (Shleifer and Vishny, 1997). Further, large share- or stakeholders and managers may collude to keep minority shareholders at bay (Hellwig, 2000). Finally, large shareholders closely associated with the management may refrain from attempts to dismiss underperforming managers if such an intervention puts their own reputation at risk (Mayer, 1996).

The identity of owners

The commitment of owners and their willingness to intervene may crucially depend on who they are. In other words, the location of control rights can be a more important determinant of the degree of control exerted by owners than ownership concentration. Insider (internal) control may represent a higher degree of control at any given level of blockholdings than outsider (external) control (Cubbin and Leech, 1983; Mayer, 1992). Family interests, allied industrial firms, banks, and holdings companies are frequently identified as insiders, while the shareholders of diffusely held firms (e.g., institutional investors such as pensions funds) are viewed as outsiders.

It is not obvious though that insider control enhances performance. For instance, individuals or families are often large blockholders because they are the founders of the company or the heirs. Given an emotional involvement, these owners may be more strongly interested in the success of the firm than investors for which the firm is just one piece in their portfolios. A large shareholder "personally" attached to the firm possibly motivates managers and employees to more commitment and determination so that firm performance improves. The opposite may hold if running the firm is impeded because the owners engage in infighting or take on a know-all attitude and try to "mastermind" decision-making. In this respect, investors without a personal interest may be better for corporate performance. Banks can be such neutral investors. If they are more efficient monitors (Diamond, 1984, 1991) and reduce agency costs, performance should be enhanced. Their actual governance role, either as owners, board representatives or proxy voters, and the impact on corporate performance has been disputed.[12] Not much is known about industrial firms and holdings as blockholders of other industrial firms. Empirical evidence on large diversified US corporations (Lang and Stulz, 1994; Shin and Stulz, 1998) suggests that members of business groups may underperform because internal capital markets do not work efficiently. In short, it is open to empirical testing whether the identity of owners really matters.

Product market competition and endogenous ownership structures

The mode of corporate governance may be less important if there is intensive competition in product markets (e.g., Demsetz, 1983; Hart, 1983; Schmidt, 1997; Allen and Gale, 1998). Competition forces firms to adopt not only cost minimizing methods of production but also efficient governance and organization structures. More efficient firms will steal business from slack firms and drive the least efficient firms out of the market. At least in the longer run when entry is facilitated, this selection effect of competition eliminates inefficient structures and generates effective governance. In the longer run, the mode of corporate governance may be simultaneously determined with firm performance by the forces of competitive markets (Demsetz, 1983; Demsetz and Lehn, 1985).

Conclusion

The debate on the managed versus the governed corporation, or the insider versus the outsider model of the corporate governance, has generated conflicting hypotheses concerning the link between ownership, control, and firm performance. The model of the governed corporation suggests that the tightly-held, insider-controlled firm outperforms the managed, diffusely-held firm. As there are costs of having large shareholders, ownership concentration or increased monitoring through the owners may be beneficial only up to a certain extent. At a given level of wealth commitment, the willingness of owners to control may also be dependent on who they are. It is thus an empirical question which of the advanced hypotheses are valid.

2.2. Empirical evidence

The existing empirical evidence does not allow for clear-cut answers. Short's survey (1994, p. 227) finds no "conclusive evidence either in support of, or in opposition to, the hypothesis that the ownership and control structures of firms materially affect their performance". Mayer (1996, p. 17) interprets the empirical evidence as implying "benefits in the exercise of corporate governance from modest levels of concentrations of ownership", but "exploitation of private benefits" at high levels of ownership concentration.

Considering the high ownership concentration and the presence of presumably strong insiders such as allied industrial firms, banks and families, many German corporations seem to come close to the model of the governed corporation. Only a few empirical studies have focused on German corporations so far to investigate the impact of governance structures on firm performance. The evidence from regression analyses is similarly ambiguous as for Anglo-Saxon firms.[13]

In a pioneering study, Thonet and Poensgen (1979) found significantly lower returns on equity for owner-controlled than for manager-controlled German public companies.[14] Other studies focused on banks as blockholders of industrial firms. Cable (1985), Weigand (1999) and Gorton and Schmid (2000) report a significantly positive impact of bank involvement on firm profitability, whereas profitability differences between bank- and non-bank firms are not significant in Chirinko and Elston (1996).[15] The positive influence of banks is in line with the standard reasoning that banks are better monitors and thus firm performance is enhanced. However, it may very well be that banks were not better in governing but in "picking winners".

Franks and Mayer (1997), analyzing quoted corporations only, and Goergen (1999), focusing on IPOs, could not find a significant impact of ownership indicators on firm performance. Franks and Mayer interpret their results as inconsistent with the view that the German market of corporate control performs a disciplining function. Rather concentration of ownership seems to further rent extraction. Goergen views his results as support for the Demsetz (1983) hypothesis that ownership structures are chosen as to maximize firm value.[16] Gedajlovic and Shapiro (1998) find a significantly negative and non-linear impact of ownership concentration on the return on total assets for a sample of large quoted corporations. Thus profitability first decreases in ownership concentration and then, at higher levels of concentration, rises again.[17] Becht (1999) reports a negative effect of ownership concentration on liquidity (measured by the ratio of turnover to market capitalization) which supports the hypothesis of a control-liquidity trade-off.[18]

In sum, "governed" (more concentrated or owner-controlled) German firms seem to have enjoyed higher returns during the 1970s and early 1980s (Cable, Gorton and Schmid, Weigand). The positive impact vanishes or turns even negative when data from the late 1980s and the 1990s are included (Becht, Chirinko and Elston, Franks and Mayer, Goergen, Gedajlovic and Shapiro). The opening of markets and increased international competition may have altered the profitability-ownership concentration relation since the late 1980s. In the subsequent section we explore this conjecture using a large panel data set of both quoted and non-quoted German corporations for the 1990s.

3. OWNERSHIP CONCENTRATION, INSIDER CONTROL, AND PERFORMANCE OF GERMAN FIRMS

3.1. Data, variables, and sample characteristics

The data set contains 361 firms from the German mining and manufacturing industries. Although 300 of these firms have the legal form of stock corporations (Aktiengesellschaften), only 183 were officially listed and traded on German stock exchanges during the observation period. As we are interested in the importance of stock market exposure, our sample also includes non-traded stock corporations as well as some limited liability corporations (GmbH, 54 firms) and limited commercial partnerships (GmbH & Co. KG, KGaA, 7 firms). The time period covered is 1991 to 1996, which yielded the largest number of

reporting firms with complete and consistent data. According to their main field of economic activity, the sample firms were assigned to 30 different two-digit industries, among them machinery (76 firms), chemicals and pharmaceuticals (60 firms), the electronic products industry (56 firms), and iron and steel (37 firms).

Our preferred measure of corporate performance is the return on total assets (ROA). We also report summary statistics for the return on equity (ROE) but ROE comparisons across firms may be distorted by the leverage effect and differences in the user cost of capital. For both ROA and ROE the numerator is gross profits, calculated as turnover minus expenses for personnel and materials.[19] Equity capital is defined as shareholders' equity plus reserves and pension liabilities.[20]

The firm-specific variables are constructed from balance sheet and profit-and-loss account data as collected from either the Hoppenstedt Bilanzdatenbank (a commercially sold data source), the Bundesanzeiger (a federal gazette, in which corporations are obliged by law to publish their annual financial statements), or annual reports directly obtained from the corporations.[21] We used unconsolidated company data whenever available and excluded pure holding companies.[22]

Secondary sources were consulted for identifying owners, share distributions, and the composition of managing and supervisory boards. The sources are Commerzbank's Wer gehört zu wem? (Who owns whom?, 16th–18th edition), Bayerische Hypotheken- und Wechselbank's Wegweiser durch deutsche Aktiengesellschaften (Guide of German Stock Corporations, "Hypo-Guide", annual issues 1988–1996), and Hoppenstedt's Börsenführer (Stock Market Guide, annual issues, 1988–1998). In combining these data sources it was possible to obtain a fairly precise picture of voting stock ownership.[23] For the purpose of this study, we have defined a 'large' shareholder as one who controls at least 5 per cent of a firm's voting capital. This cut-off point of when a shareholder is large rather than small is less important than in

Anglo-Saxon studies, since almost all sample firms have large shareholders who control at least 25% of the voting capital. As Table 19.1 shows, 65% of the companies in the sample have one large shareholder who, on average, controls 89% of the voting stocks and faces a group of small shareholders with an aggregate share in the voting capital of about 11%.

In the empirical literature ownership concentration is the standard indicator for the extent of "governance" exercised by firm owners. In this study as in previous ones, we measure ownership concentration by the Herfindahl index of outstanding voting stock and, alternatively, by the percentage stake of the largest shareholder. The share of the largest shareholder indicates her fundamental voting power, that is, the ability to outvote other shareholders or initiate major changes by herself (e.g., ousting the supervisors, introduce a new

Table 19.1 Ownership structures: sample of 361 German manufacturing firms, 1991–1996

Number of large shareholders	Group of firms — Full sample Quoted firms Non-quoted firms	Percentage relative to the group of firms	Largest shareholder's stake — Mean (std. dev.) in per cent	Block of widely dispersed shares — Mean (std. dev.) in per cent
0	2	0.55	0.00 (0.00)	100.00 (0.00)
	2	1.09	0.00 (0.00)	100.00 (0.00)
	–	–	–	–
1	235	65.10	89.07 (21.54)	10.93 (21.54)
	100	54.64	76.55 (27.14)	16.50 (27.14)
	135	75.84	98.35 (7.88)	1.65 (7.88)
2	77	21.33	56.55 (18.75)	18.62 (19.45)
	50	27.32	55.08 (20.87)	26.80 (18.53)
	27	15.17	59.26 (13.96)	3.48 (9.60)
3	28	7.76	44.07 (18.41)	24.43 (23.47)
	19	10.38	40.26 (20.01)	36.00 (19.65)
	9	5.06	52.11 (11.65)	0.00 (0.00)
4	15	4.16	52.87 (29.71)	25.67 (25.74)
	11	6.01	43.82 (19.30)	35.00 (23.84)
	4	2.25	77.75 (41.82)	0.00 (0.00)
5	1	0.28	52.00 (NA)	15.00 (NA)
	–	–	–	–
6	1	0.28	55.00 (NA)	0.00 (NA)
	–	–	–	–
	1	0.56	55.00 (NA)	0.00 (NA)
7	2	0.55	53.00 (4.24)	0.00 (0.00)
	–	–	–	–
	2	1.12	53.00 (4.24)	0.00 (0.00)
Total	361	100.00	75.27 (28.72)	14.53 (22.73)
	183	100.00	63.98 (28.56)	27.67 (25.53)
	178	100.00	86.49 (24.39)	1.54 (7.61)

The sample consists of 361 German firms which operated in 30 industries of the mining and manufacturing sector during the period 1991 to 1996. Of the sample firms 300 have the legal form of stock corporations (Aktiengesellschaften) with 183 listed and traded on German stock exchanges. The data set further includes 54 limited liability corporations (GmbH) and 7 limited commercial partnerships (GmbH & Co. KG, KGaA). For identification of owners and share distributions we used Commerzbank, Wer gehört zu wem? (Who owns whom?, editions 16th to 18th, publication years 1988, 1992, 1994), Bayerische Hypotheken- und Wechselbank, Wegweiser durch deutsche Aktiengesellschaften ("Hypo-Guide", Guide of German Stock Corporations, annual issues 1988–1996), and Hoppenstedt's Börsenführer (annual issues, 1988–1998). We define a large shareholder as controlling at least 5 per cent of a corporation's voting capital.

corporate charter). The Herfindahl index, defined as the sum of squared individual stakes, has the advantage of accounting for an asymmetric dispersion of shares among different shareholders.[24]

Ownership concentration may not suffice as an indicator of the degree of "governance". The identity of owners may play a more crucial role. Officially reported shareholdings often do not reflect the true extent of voting control exercised by owners of German corporations (Becht and Boehmer, 1997; Boehmer, 1999). Complex cross-holding arrangements and unreported fiduciary and dormant voting rights complicate the identification of actual controllers. Nevertheless, given the information available, we attempt to assess the relevance of the owner's identity for the link between profitability and ownership concentration.

For the purpose of grouping firms by the location of control rights five broad categories of direct owners can be identified: another industrial firm or holding company (INDFIRM), families or (voting pools of) individuals (FAMILY), financial institutions (banks or bank-owned investment companies, insurance companies, FININST), different large shareholders (MIX, e.g., industrial firms and investment companies), and foreign owners (FOREIGN). A sixth group, CHANGE, is defined to account for 26 firms for which a turnover of blockholdings from one of these owner categories to another was observed during the observation period.

The groups are mutually exclusive. A firm that, for instance, had another industrial firm as largest shareholder in some years and a bank in other years only appears in the CHANGE group but not in the groups INDFIRM or FININST. Due to the lack of detailed ownership information, the foreign-owned firms were also treated as a separate group. A few firms are owned by foundations which have no owner in a strict sense. It is thus unclear who really controls these firms. As the foundations are often close to the founding families of the firms, as in the case of Bosch GmbH (a leading electronic products firm), it seems tenable to assign them to the group of firms controlled by families or (voting pools of) individuals.

For some firms such as Bayer, Mannesmann, Schering, Siemens, or VEBA more than 90% of the voting capital is generally reported as "widely dispersed". The study of Baums and Fraune (1995) shows that in the 1992 annual shareholders' meetings banks controlled an aggregate of more than 90% of those firms' voting capital via associated investment companies and proxy votes. These sample firms were therefore added to the group of firms with financial institutions as largest shareholders.

To relate back to the discussion on the managed vs. the governed firm, or the insider vs. outsider model, corporations having individuals or families (FAMILY), banks (FININST), or different independent large shareholders (MIX) may be interpreted as potentially governed by committed insiders. By contrast, for firms owned by another industrial firm (INDFIRM) it might be managers rather than the ultimate owners who control the managers of the owned company. Firms of this group, mostly subsidiaries of large quoted stock corporations (e.g., BASF, Thyssen), may then be considered as managed. However, we make no attempt here to argue that a certain location of control rights indeed implies "more" or "less" governance. Although we took great efforts to trace ownership back to the ultimate owners for all firms, it is not entirely clear whether these ultimate owners really "govern", or whether hired managers nonetheless exercise control even if ownership concentration is high and firms are owned by families for example.

To investigate whether stock market exposure makes a difference for the potential link between governance indicators and corporate performance we distinguish between corporations traded on the stock exchange (QUOTED) and non-traded or non-stock corporations (NON-QUOTED).

Table 19.2A presents the mean and median values of selected variables for the full sample and the groups of quoted and non-quoted firms. The last column reports

Table 19.2A Summary statistics: sample of 361 German manufacturing firms, 1991–1996. Sample split by stock market exposure

	Group of firms			Test statistics
Variable	All firms (361)	Quoted (183)	Non-quoted (178)	t/Mann-Whitney
Return on total assets (ROA)				
Mean/median	0.2958/0.2875	0.3159/0.3028	0.2755/0.2705	5.39***/5.75***
Return on equity				
Mean/median	0.5515/0.4993	0.5593/0.5475	0.5436/0.5116	0.90/3.09***
Ownership concentration (OC)				
Herfindahl index (bounded)				
Mean/median	7,465/10,000	5,130/4,543	8,628/10,000	27.48***/482.2***
Largest shareholder's stake				
Mean/median	0.8584/1.0000	0.7340/0.7800	0.9787/1.0000	28.91***/29.60***
Board representation (B)				
Mean/median	0.2802/0.0000	0.2811/0.0000	0.2793/0.0000	0.09/0.07
Turnover				
Mean/median	3,283/552	4,327/477	2,221/631	4.95***/0.89
Employment				
Mean/median	11,063/2,094	14,805/2,291	7,259/1,843	5.16***/3.29***
Firm size (S)				
Mean/median	19.897/19.779	19.982/19.621	19.810/19.887	2.25**/0.88
Firm growth (G)				
Mean/median	0.0219/0.0220	0.0359/0.0296	0.0078/0.0159	2.64***/3.06***
Capital intensity (K)				
Mean/median	12.177/12.085	12.088/12.036	12.267/12.144	6.46***/4.82***
Capital structure (C)				
Mean/median	0.5841/0.5974	0.5979/0.6112	0.5699/0.5753	3.49***/2.99***
Market concentration (H)				
Mean/median	579.52/327.70	610.19/316.70	548.33/350.60	1.95*/0.27

Calculations are based on data from annual reports of 361 German corporations (see Table 19.1). The sample split is based on stock market quotation for at least three out of the six sample years. Return on total assets (ROA) is gross profits (calculated from the firms' profit-and-loss statement as turnover minus expenses for personnel and materials) divided by the book value of total assets (as reported in the firms' balance sheet). Return on equity is gross profits divided by equity (calculated as shareholders' equity plus reserves and pension liabilities). Ownership concentration is measured as the sum of squared individual percentage stakes, thus bounded to lie in the interval [0; 10,000], and alternatively, as the percentage stake of the largest shareholder. Board representation is an indicator variable taking on unit value if an identified owner served on the board of executive directors in a certain year, otherwise it has zero value. Turnover is in millions DM. Employment is the reporting year average number of full-time employees as provided in the firms' annual report or in secondary sources. In some cases end-of-the-year figures had to be used because information on average employment was not available. We measure absolute firm size as the natural logarithm (log) of total assets to reduce the skewness of the firm size distribution. Firm growth is the annual logarithmic change in real turnover (turnover deflated by the 1995 GDP deflator, source: German Statistical Office). Capital intensity is defined as log (total assets/employees). Capital structure is equity (as defined above) over total capital (book values). Market concentration is measured by a standard Herfindahl index at the two-digit industry level of the German industry classification for the manufacturing sector ("SYPRO", source: German Statistical Office).

Means and medians of all variables are calculated for the period 1991 to 1996 with the exception of firm growth which, due to its definition, is available for the period 1992 to 1996. We compare the variables' means and medians between the two groups of firms, quoted versus non-quoted firms. The last column of the table provides the t-statistic for the test of equal group means and the Mann–Whitney statistic for the test of equal group medians.

***/**/* Significant at the 0.01/0.05/0.10 error level respectively.

statistics for testing the hypotheses of equal group means (t-statistic) and medians (Mann–Whitney statistic). The table shows that quoted firms have significantly higher average returns on total assets and also higher median returns on equity. The quoted firms are less levered. Further, as measured by turnover, employment, and the natural log of total assets, the quoted firms are substantially larger on average but the median firms do not differ significantly in turnover or total assets. Finally, quoted

firms had significantly higher growth of turnover than non-quoted firms.

Table 19.2B contains summary statistics of selected variables for the groups of firms as classified by the identity of the largest owner. For any pair of owner categories we conducted pairwise t- and median tests for the variables listed in Table 19.2B but do not report these results separately.[25] The tests reveal that the INDFIRM firms have significantly lower rates of return than any other owner group except for the equity

Table 19.2B Summary statistics: sample of 361 German manufacturing firms, 1991–1996. Sample split by the location of control rights

	Location of control rights					
Number of firms	INDFIRM 81	FAMILY 122	FININST 20	MIX 54	FOREIGN 58	CHANGE 26
Return on total assets						
Mean	0.2408	0.3162	0.2725	0.2918	0.3439	0.2913
Median	0.2253	0.3120	0.2536	0.2999	0.3129	0.2844
Return on equity						
Mean	0.4288	0.6359	0.4386	0.5173	0.6084	0.5690
Median	0.3500	0.5626	0.4091	0.5106	0.5487	0.4982
Ownership concentration (bounded Herfindahl index)						
Mean	8,818	7,485	1,897	3,318	9,045	4,078
Median	10,000	9,900	342	3,322	10,000	3,563
Turnover						
Mean	2,880	1,918	16,241	3,427	2,065	3,389
Median	853	333	3,378	889	613	503
Firm growth						
Mean	0.0016	0.0428	0.0363	0.0221	0.0018	0.0204
Median	0.0074	0.0378	0.0256	0.0191	0.0076	0.0082
Capital structure						
Mean	0.5930	0.5541	0.6367	0.5999	0.6115	0.5626
Median	0.6019	0.5666	0.6673	0.6068	0.6264	0.5464

Calculations are based on data from annual reports and secondary sources of 361 German manufacturing firms (see Table 19.1). The sample split is based on the location of control rights (voting stock). We define a large shareholder as controlling at least 5 per cent of a corporation's voting capital and distinguish six identities of large shareholders: 1. INDFIRM is defined as firms having another independent industrial firm or a holding company as largest shareholder (e.g., THYSSEN GUSS AG, subsidiary of THYSSEN concern). 2. FAMILY is defined as firms having (pools of) individuals or families as largest shareholders (e.g., BAUSCH AG, BOSCH GmbH). 3. FININST is defined as firms having banks, insurance companies, or associated investment companies as largest shareholders (e.g., LINDE, larger stakes owned by Deutsche Bank and Commerzbank), or, having widely dispersed shareholdings, but banks control at least 75 per cent of the voting capital through proxy voting rights (e.g., BAYER). 4. MIX is defined as firms having different independent large shareholders (e.g., BOSCH-SIEMENS Hausgeräte GmbH, owned equally by BOSCH GmbH and SIEMENS AG). 5. FOREIGN is defined as firms having foreign companies as largest shareholders (e.g., OPEL AG, owned by GM). 6. CHANGE is defined as firms which experienced a change in the identity of blockholders through turnovers of blocks from one of the owner categories 1–5 to another (e.g., AQUA SIGNAL AG). See Table 19.2A for definitions of the other variables.

return of firms controlled by financial institutions. Ownership concentration is the highest for the managed firms. Family-controlled firms have the highest ROE and the second highest ROA but their share of equity capital is the lowest of all groups. Bank-controlled firms have the highest share of equity capital and thus the lowest degree of leverage. Foreign-owned firms have the highest ROA and the second highest ROE.

3.2. Regression model and hypothesis

Regression model

To investigate the impact of the mode of corporate governance on corporate performance we use the following panel regression

$$\text{ROA}_{it} = b_1 OC_{it} + b_2 B_{it} + b_3 S_{it} + b_4 G_{it} \\ + b_5 K_{it} + b_6 C_{I,t-1} + b_7 H^j_{it} + u_{it}, \quad (1)$$

in which the subscript $i = 1, \ldots 361$ identifies individual firms, $j = 1, \ldots, 30$ indicates the respective two-digit industry a firm operates in, and $t = 1992, \ldots 1996$ denotes time periods.

In model (1) we regress the return on total assets ROA on ownership concentration OC and a set of other variables. For lucidity and space restrictions, we will only present regression results using for OC the unbounded Herfindahl index as in Demsetz and Lehn (1985).[26] B indicates the presence of the largest shareholder on the executive board. The following variables which have frequently been employed in the Industrial Organization (IO) literature to explain profitability differences across firms or industries, serve as right-hand side control variables: absolute firm size S (natural logarithm of total assets), firm growth G (logarithmic annual change in turnover), capital intensity K (log of total assets divided by the number of employees), capital structure C (shareholders' equity plus reserves divided by total capital), and the Herfindahl index of

supplier concentration at the two-digit industry level (source: German Statistical Office). These variables will be discussed in more detail below.[27]

Due to the combination of time series and cross-section data we can decompose the regression disturbance u_{it} into a classical white noise error ε_{it} and effects specific to individual firms, a_{i}, time, λ_{t}, and industries, a_{j}. We use standard panel regression techniques (see Hsiao, 1986; Baltagi, 1995) to estimate (1). As ownership concentration and profitability could be determined simultaneously in competitive and well-functioning markets, we test for simultaneity bias in (1) by applying instrumental variable estimation techniques as well. Details on estimation techniques and specification tests will be provided in the tables.

Hypotheses

1. Ownership concentration, board representation, and stock market exposure

Our main interest lies in estimating the coefficients b_1 and b_2. If ownership concentration indicates tighter and performance-enhancing governance exerted by owners, $b_1 > 0$ is to be expected. If managerial discretion is facilitated in traded corporations because ownership concentration tends to be lower for traded than for non-traded firms, we expect to observe a stronger positive impact of ownership concentration on ROA for the traded firms. However, if there is less asymmetric information in traded corporations because they are more transparent to outside investors than non-traded firms, the differential impact of ownership concentration on ROA between traded and non-traded corporations may go the other way. In the extreme, if the market mechanism indeed provides effective corporate control, as suggested, e.g., by Demsetz and Lehn (1985), $b_1 = 0$ should hold for the traded firms. By contrast, $b_1 < 0$ may indicate inefficiency or rent extraction due to the presence of large shareholders. The same reasoning as for ownership concentration can be applied to the representation of the largest shareholder on the board of executive directors.

2. Firm size and firm growth

Economic theory offers no clear-cut predictions for the impact of firm size and firm growth on profitability. A positive influence of absolute firm size is implied by the economies of scale and scope argument (e.g., Baumol, 1959), while a negative effect may result from organizational inefficiency (X-inefficiency, Leibenstein, 1966). As larger firms tend to be more diversified, lower risk premiums could render b_3 negative. Firm growth may, on the one hand, reflect better investment opportunities and thus higher profitability, $b_4 > 0$. On the other hand, if managers have sufficient discretion to divert free cash flow and overinvest, profitability should be lower for growing firms, $b_4 < 0$.

3. Capital intensity

The coefficient on capital intensity may help to identify overinvestment. If decreasing scale economies prevail, profitability should decrease in capital intensity, $b_5 < 0$. The opposite may hold if high capital intensity is a barrier to entry and exit, which allows incumbents to earn rents, as frequently argued in the IO literature.

4. Capital structure

With imperfect capital markets capital structure matters for investment decisions and firm profitability. Capital structure choices vary across firms and industries depending on informational asymmetries, transaction costs, and growth prospects. If a higher equity share implies lower risk of bankruptcy, an inverse relation between profitability and the share of equity capital, C, can be expected, $b_6 < 0$, since the return on investment required to compensate for risk-taking decreases in risk.[28] To reduce potential simultaneity bias between ROA and capital structure, we use beginning-of-the-period values for C.

5. Market concentration

Supplier concentration is implied by oligopoly theory to be positively correlated with profitability. This prediction is supported by a vast empirical literature. We therefore expect $b_7 > 0$. As it is not the concern of this paper to discuss the appropriate interpretation of the relationship, we take market concentration as a summary measure of industry characteristics, reflecting current production technologies (potential scale economies), demand (price elasticity) as well as the intensity of competition.

6. Industry characteristics

Industry characteristics such as knowledge conditions and technological opportunities may simultaneously determine governance structures, investment, and profitability (Audretsch and Weigand, 1999). In industries such as optical instruments or machinery, production technology or the knowledge on which firm know-how is based does not require large firm size per se. Cost advantages (scale economies) from large-scale operations (production, R&D) are not ubiquitous. Therefore, these industries offer a favorable environment for smaller firms, and indeed that is where we find small family-owned firms to be very common. By contrast, in the chemical and pharmaceutical industry large stock corporations dominate. Clearly, production technologies require larger firm sizes. Different ownership structures are also necessary to satisfy the increased capital needs and to better spread the higher risk involved in large-scale operations. Based on this reasoning we expect industry characteristics, if not fully reflected by market concentration, to affect profitability and ownership structures.

7. Firm-specific effects

The firm-specific effects control for systematic variation in profitability not captured by the explanatory variables (e.g., differences in risk-taking, user cost of capital). If our explanatory variables do miss systematic ROA variation, the firm-specific effects should turn out to be statistically significant.

8. Time-specific effects

The time-specific effects subsume the macroeconomic shocks common to all firms. Their inclusion is suggested by the fact that during the sample period the German economy first experienced the reunification boom of 1990/91 and then slid into the recession of 1992/93, the worst downturn in Germany's post-war history.

3.3. Results

Specifying the relationship between profitability and corporate governance indicators

Table 19.3A summarizes the panel regression estimates for Equation (1), the extended model, which includes the set of variables highlighted in the IO literature, and also for the *parsimonious* variant which excludes the IO variables. Table 19.3B takes ownership concentration as the dependent variable. For now, we selectively focus on the impact of the governance indicators OC and *B*, the importance of individual firm and industry effects as well as the possible simultaneity of OC and ROA.[29]

All regressions in Tables 19.3A and 19.3B imply a negative relation between the return on total assets and ownership concentration. The estimated coefficients on OC in the extended and parsimonious ROA regressions (Table 19.3A) are statistically significant at the 0.05 level in Models C to G which take advantage of the pooled data. With one exception the same holds for ROA in the OC regression (Table 19.3B). Board representation has a positive coefficient in the ROA regression and a negative coefficient in the OC regression in almost all models. However, the statistical significance of the estimated coefficient is clearly affected by the way unobserved systematic influences are modelled. The coefficient of determination (adjusted R squared) reveals how much the respective variables add to the explanatory power of the regression. Beginning with the parsimonious variant in Model C, the governance indicators explain about 1% of the ROA variation, while ROA and board representation are of little help in explaining the variation of ownership concentration across firms and over time. In terms of explanatory power, the combination of random firm-specific and fixed industry-specific effects with other firm variables is not very useful either (Models F and G). By far the highest explanatory power is achieved by including fixed individual firm effects (Model E).

The specification tests show that there is systematic variation in the explained variables picked up by either individual firm or industry effects. Firm-specific effects are fixed rather than random. There is no gain by endogenizing OC. Put differently, OC can be taken as an exogenous variable in the ROA regression. For the OC regression, the specification test indicates simultaneity bias at least in the extended model, that is, ROA should be treated as an endogenous variable.[30] In short, model E is supported. As they lack time series variation, the industry indicator variables cannot be included in Model E because they would be perfectly correlated with the fixed firm effects (see Baltagi, 1995, p. 11). We will return to the problem of estimating the impact of time-constant variables in a fixed effects model below. The time-specific effects are highly significant in the parsimonious variant of Model E but insignificant in the extended variant. Further investigation reveals that including capital intensity in the regression renders the time effects insignificant. We will offer an explanation shortly.

Does stock market exposure affect the profitability-corporate governance relationship?

The negative impact of ownership concentration on ROA supports the view of inefficient ownership concentration and rent extraction. So far it does not refute the Demsetz–Lehn hypothesis which implicitly assumes firms to be exposed to the market for corporate control. This assumption holds only for about half of our sample firms. Therefore, we consider stock market exposure next.

As the Durbin–Watson statistic in Table 19.3A indicates problems of first-order serial correlation in our favored Model E, we used an estimation technique which corrects for both heteroskedasticity and first-order serial correlation. Table 19.4A contains these robust estimates for the extended model. To allow for a comparison with the non-robust coefficient estimates for OC and *B* in Table 19.3A, column 1 of

Table 19.4A ignores stock market exposure. Column 2 then presents the robust estimates for the quoted firms, while column 3 gives the coefficient differences with respect to the (not separately reported) regression coefficients of the non-quoted firms. We also report the group means of the firm-specific effects.

The fixed effects measure the average systematic difference in ROA across groups of firms not accounted for by the model's explanatory variables. There is no statistically significant difference in the means of these firm-specific intercepts between the traded and non-traded firms.[31] Stock market exposure does also not change the profitability-ownership concentration relationship. The negative impact of ownership concentration is a bit weaker for the quoted firms (−0.0027) than for the non-quoted firms (−0.0049) but still significant at the 0.05 error level. The coefficient difference (−0.0022) is not statistically significant. These results contradict both the hypothesis of the beneficial large shareholder as well as the Demsetz–Lehn hypothesis of no ownership effect. However, the estimated coefficient on OC for the full (non-split) sample implies a quantitatively small effect. Evaluated at the sample means, doubling the unbounded Herfindahl index would lower ROA by about 8%.

There is a notable difference between the two groups with respect to board representation. The coefficient on B is insignificantly positive (and remains so when ownership concentration is excluded from the regressions) for the non-split sample and for the quoted firms but significantly positive for the non-traded firms. For the non-traded firms the presence of the largest owner on the board of executive directors thus improves profitability. Assuming that informational problems are more pronounced for non-traded firms this result implies that tighter control through the owner reduces agency costs and improves firm performance. The estimated coefficient on B for the non-quoted firms suggests an increase of average ROA by about 3% if average board representation raises by 1%.

For the IO variables we find that all coefficients except for the one on market concentration are highly significant. Larger firms and firms with a higher share of equity capital (lower leverage) have significantly lower returns, which is consistent with diversification and risk-return considerations. Firm growth affects ROA positively which supports the argument that growing firms have better investment opportunities. The negative coefficient on capital intensity seems to imply decreasing returns to scale. Given the above-mentioned fact that the time effects become insignificant when capital intensity enters the regression, this variable is apparently a proxy for capital utilization and thus picks up business cycle effects. Market concentration has a positive but statistically insignificant effect. Stock market exposure does not change the impact of the IO variables on ROA in any significant way.

Does the identity of owners matter?

As in the case of the industry indicators, we cannot consider the identity of owners in a fixed-effects regression directly, since the indicators for the location of control rights lack time series variation and thus will be perfectly correlated with the firm-specific effects. We therefore follow two approaches. In the first approach, we investigate the indirect impact of the location of control rights on ROA by interacting the identity indicators with all time-varying right-hand side variables of (1).[32] The second approach homes in on the estimated fixed firm effects. The fixed effects can be interpreted as the autonomous component of ROA neither explained by the explanatory variables nor by purely stochastic disturbances. By regressing the fixed effects on the identity indicators we obtain a direct multivariate test on how the location of control rights affects ROA, after having controlled for the time-varying explanatory variables' influence.

The regression results from the indirect approach are contained in Table 19.4B. The group of firms with another firm as largest shareholder, INDFIRM, serves as the base group. Column 1 presents the coefficient estimates for this base group, while the

Table 19.3A Panel regression estimates of the return on total assets equation, 1992–1996. Full sample

Dependent variable: ROA	Regression coefficient (absolute t-statistic) of selected explanatory variables				Regression diagnostics	
	Ownership concentration		Board representation			
Regression model	Extended model	Parsimonious model	Extended model	Parsimonious model	Adj. R sq.	DW
A. Between (cross-section)	−0.0007 (0.87)	−0.0009 (1.04)	0.0309 (1.68)*	0.0375 (2.04)**	0.1016 / 0.0096	– / –
B. Between (cross-section) with fixed industry effects	−0.0007 (0.93)	−0.0009 (1.11)	0.0142 (0.40)	0.0254 (1.49)	0.2939 / 0.2058	– / –
C. Total common intercept and slopes	−0.0008 (2.14)**	−0.0009 (2.27)**	0.0313 (3.59)***	0.0365 (4.19)***	0.1017 / 0.0117	0.3636*** / 0.3646***
D. Total with fixed industry effects	−0.0010 (2.91)***	−0.0009 (2.41)**	0.0187 (2.20)**	0.0247 (2.83)***	0.2829 / 0.2021	0.4509*** / 0.4589***
E. Within (fixed firm effects)	−0.0029 (2.28)**	−0.0030 (1.98)**	0.0098 (0.51)	−0.0009 (0.05)	0.7763 / 0.7302	1.5598*** / 1.6699***
F. RE (random firm effects)	−0.0013 (1.95)*	−0.0014 (2.03)**	0.0137 (0.91)	0.0272 (1.76)*	0.0351 / 0.5005	0.2203*** / 0.2480***
G. RE with fixed industry effects	−0.0014 (2.24)**	−0.0013 (2.05)**	0.0073 (0.52)	0.0198 (1.38)	0.0330 / 0.0071	0.2777*** / 0.3022***
H. Within-2SLS	−0.0079 (0.79)	−0.0078 (0.71)	0.0018 (0.06)	−0.0091 (0.33)	– / –	– / –

(Table 19.3A continued)

Table 19.3A Continued

Specification test	Null hypothesis	Test statistic Extended model Parsimonious model	Accept/Reject null
Model A vs. Model B	No fixed industry effects	$F(29, 325) = 56.24^{***}$	Reject
		$F(29, 330) = 58.79^{***}$	Reject
Model C vs. Model D	No fixed industry effects	$F(29, 1762) = 240.79^{***}$	Reject
		$F(29, 1767) = 228.71^{***}$	Reject
Model C vs. Model E	No fixed firm effects	$F(360, 1431) = 16.01^{***}$	Reject
		$F(360, 1436) = 14.29^{***}$	Reject
Model C vs. Model F	No random firm effects	$Chisq(1) = 66.07^{***}$	Reject
		$Chisq(1) = 49.81^{***}$	Reject
Model D vs. Model G	No random firm effects	$Chisq(1) = 68.91^{***}$	Reject
		$Chisq(1) = 60.58^{***}$	Reject
Model E vs. Model F	Random firm effects	$Chisq(7) = 50.28^{***}$	Reject
		$Chisq(3) = 2.24$	Accept
Model E vs. Model H	No simultaneity bias	$Chisq(6) = 0.4728$	Accept
		$Chisq(4) = 0.8216$	Accept
Model F vs. Model G	No fixed industry effects	$F(29, 1762) = 232.48^{***}$	Reject
		$F(29, 1767) = 193.31^{***}$	Reject
Model D	No time effects	$F(4, 1762) = 3.23^{**}$	Reject
		$F(4, 1767) = 4.72^{***}$	Reject

Model E	No time effects	$F(4, 1762) = 1.69$	Accept
		$F(4, 1792) = 14.66^{***}$	Reject
Model G	No time effects	$F(4, 1762) = 7.13^{***}$	Reject
		$F(4, 1767) = 5.98^{***}$	Reject

The estimating sample contains 361 German firms as described in Table I. The *extended model* is given by

$$ROA_{it} = b_1 OC_{it} + b_2 B_{it} + b_3 S_{it} + b_4 G_{it} + b_5 K_{it} + b_6 C_{I,\,t-1} + b_7 H^i_{it} + u_{it}$$
$$u_{it} = a_i + a_j + \lambda_t + \epsilon_{it} \tag{1}$$

in which ROA, OC, B, S, G, K, C, and H are the return on total assets, ownership concentration (unbounded Herfindahl index), board representation, firm size, firm growth, capital intensity, capital structure, and market concentration of firm i operating in industry j at time t. See Table 19.2A for definitions of variables. In the parsimonious model we only include ownership concentration and board representation as right-hand side variables and ignore all variables implied by the industrial organization literature. The regression disturbance u_{it} can be decomposed into firm-, industry- and time-specific effects, a_i, a_j, λ_t respectively, and a classical white noise regression disturbance ϵ_{it}.

Model A is a standard cross-section regression with the regression variables averaged over the observation period (361 observations). Model B adds 29 industry dummies to Model A. Models C to H use the pooled cross-section time-series data (1805 pooled observations). Model C restricts the firm-specific effects to be constant and identical for all firms. Model D adds 29 industry dummies to Model C. Model E assumes fixed (constant) firm-specific effects (361 firm-specific intercepts). Other time-constant effects (e.g., industries dummies) cannot be included. Model F assumes random firm-specific effects (i.e., a common intercept from which individual firms may deviate randomly). Model G adds 29 industry dummies to Model F. Model H includes fixed firm-specific effects as Model E but treats OC as an endogenous right-hand side variable (i.e., being correlated with ϵ_{it}). Models A, B, C and D are estimated by OLS. Model E is Within-OLS (LSDV, Least Squares Dummy Variables estimator). Models F and G use GLS. Model H is Within-2SLS using the fitted values of OC from the reduced-form (first-stage) regression of OC on all exogenous right-hand side variables in (1), B, S, G, K, C, H plus the number of large shareholders as an additional instrument included to identify the regression equation. The number of large shareholders has been excluded from the second-stage OC regression (to be presented in Table 19.3B). We tested alternative exclusions of variables, since picking a specific variable is – admittedly – arbitrary. The results were not significantly different when any other pair of the IO variables was excluded.

We present specification test statistics for these models. A standard F-test is employed to test a restricted model (e.g., no industry or no time effects) against an unrestricted model (allowing for such effects). To test for random firm-specific effects versus no such effects we use the Lagrange multiplier test suggested by Breusch and Pagan (1980). Hausman's (1978) specification test is used to decide on fixed versus random firm-specific effects. The same test, known in this case under the name "Wu–Hausman" (Wu, 1972) is also applied to compare the Within-OLS estimates (which are inefficient if OC in Equation (1) is endogenous) with the Within-2SLS estimates (which are efficient if OC is indeed endogenous). "Durbin–Watson" tests for first-order serial correlation (AR1) of panel regression residuals (Bhargava et al., 1982). See Hsiao (1986) or Baltagi (1995) for a detailed discussion of panel regression models and specification tests. The estimates' absolute t-statistics as provided in parentheses are based on White's (1980) heteroskedasticity-robust variance-covariance estimator.

***/**/*Significant at the 0.01/0.05/0.10 error level respectively.

following columns contain the estimates of coefficient differences with respect to the other owner categories. The coefficient on ownership concentration is positive but insignificant for this base group of presumably managed rather than governed firms. The negative impact of ownership concentration as reported for the non-split sample (Table 19.4A, column 1) can be traced back to the firms owned, and perhaps governed by FAMILY, MIX, FOREIGN, and CHANGE. The coefficient difference is statistically significant for the FAMILY and MIX firms. Taking the number of shareholders as given, the Herfindahl index is lower when the variance of stakes is lower.[33] Therefore, the higher the stake of the largest shareholder, and the smaller the individual stakes of other shareholders, the larger will be the variance of stakes cet. par. (i.e., the more asymmetric is the stake distribution). In other words, the presence of another large shareholder improves profitability. This result is in line with Boehmer (2000) who finds the presence of a second or third large shareholder to raise firm value.

Interestingly, ownership concentration is beneficial to firms potentially under the control of financial institutions. The coefficient difference is significantly positive. This group of firms has by far the lowest degree of ownership concentration (cf. Table 19.2B) and can, by German standards, be viewed as dispersedly held. The group also includes firms in which banks accumulated proxy votes. The positive impact of ownership concentration suggests that firm performance is enhanced when banks increase their cash flow stakes.

With respect to the IO variables, larger firm size and a higher equity share are significantly more important for FAMILY firms, which are the smallest on average and at the median, than for any other group of firms. The choice of absolute firm size and capital structure can be interpreted as reflecting the risk-return trade-off. As the risk of bankruptcy is lower for larger firms with more equity, the rate of return required to compensate for risk-taking can be lower as well.

Finally, Table 19.4B shows differences in the means of the firm-specific intercepts across the groups. The firms controlled by financial institutions have the highest mean intercept, while the FAMILY and CHANGE firms have the lowest. Compared to the INDFIRM group, FAMILY and CHANGE firms have a signifcantly lower autonomous ROA, while having financial institutions as largest shareholders significantly improves profitability. To investigate these differences further is our second, direct approach to assessing the impact of the identity indicators on ROA.

Ignoring time effects for simplicity, the estimates of the firm-specific fixed effects are given by (see Hsiao, 1986, p. 30)

$$\hat{a}_i = \bar{y}_i - \bar{X}_i' \hat{b}, \qquad (2)$$

where $\wedge$ indicates an estimated parameter, the bar denotes the firm-specific time mean of a variable, y is the dependent variable, X is the matrix of time-varying right-hand side variables, a and b are the vectors of firm-specific effects and slope coefficients. We interpret (2) as depicting the long-term or autonomous component of the ROA model (1). The fixed effects can be regressed on a set of variables, z, which vary across firms but not over time, such as the identity or industry indicators.

$$\hat{a}_i = \mu + z_i' \gamma + \bar{\epsilon}_i. \qquad (3)$$

The coefficient vectors γ and μ in Equation (3) can be consistently estimated by OLS if $\hat{b}$ is a consistent estimate and if the number of cross-section units is large and the time-series component is not tending to infinity (Hsiao 1986, p. 50). The first requirement is satisfied, since we can insert for $\hat{b}$ the estimates described in Table 19.4A. With 361 firms and variables averaged over five years we feel confident that the second condition is not completely violated. Therefore, we present in Table 19.5 the results from estimating regression (3) by OLS.

When we regress the firm-specific effects on the identity indicators only, taking INDFIRM as the base group and

Table 19.3B Panel regression estimates of the ownership concentration equation, 1992–1996. Full sample

Dependent variable: OC

Regression model	Model	Regression coefficient (absolute t-statistic) of selected explanatory variables — Return on total assets	Board representation	Regression diagnostics — Adj. R sq.	DW
A. Between (cross-section)	Extended model	−1.8990 (0.58)	−1.8985 (1.63)	0.1489	—
	Parsimonious model	−3.5145 (1.05)	−0.5887 (0.51)	−0.0014	—
B. Between (cross-section) with fixed industry effects	Extended model	−3.2924 (0.86)	2.0470 (1.69)*	0.1364	—
	Parsimonious model	−4.3864 (1.12)	−0.0471 (0.04)	−0.0088	—
C. Tota (common intercept and slopes)	Extended model	−1.9620 (1.55)	−1.4862 (3.18)***	0.1441	0.0398***
	Parsimonious model	−2.9901 (2.19)**	−0.6368 (1.28)	−0.0003	0.0263***
D. Total with fixed industry effects	Extended model	−2.8930 (2.14)**	1.6834 (3.43)***	0.2082	0.0414***
	Parsimonious model	−3.4874 (2.32)**	−0.1163 (0.22)	0.2021	0.4589***
E. Within (fixed firm effects)	Extended model	−1.4324 (2.32)**	−1.4332 (1.08)	0.9680	0.9930***
	Parsimonious model	−1.1429 (1.90)*	−1.6843 (1.19)	0.9674	0.9793***
F. RE (random firm effects)	Extended model	−1.3055 (2.41)**	−1.2139 (2.40)**	0.323	0.0229***
	Parsimonious model	−1.1929 (2.33)**	−1.4840 (2.89)**	0.4645	0.0219***
G. RE with fixed industry effects	Extended model	−1.3877 (2.52)**	−1.1100 (2.17)**	0.0146	0.0247***
	Parsimonious model	−1.1986 (2.31)**	−1.3782 (2.65)***	−0.0209	0.0234***
H. Within-2SLS	Extended model	−6.9690 (1.58)	−1.3606 (0.97)	—	—
	Parsimonious model	−0.3924 (0.23)	−0.0091 (0.33)	—	—

(Table 19.3B continued)

Table 19.3B Continued

Specification test	Null hypothesis	Test statistic Extended model Parsimonious model	Accept/Reject null
Model A vs. Model B	No fixed industry effects	$F(29, 325) = 11.94^{***}$ $F(29, 330) = 13.19^{***}$	Reject Reject
Model C vs. Model D	No fixed industry effects	$F(29, 1762) = 64.49^{***}$ $F(29, 1767) = 68.51^{***}$	Reject Reject
Model C vs. Model E	No fixed firm effects	$F(360, 1431) = 128.97^{***}$ $F(360, 1436) = 149.05^{***}$	Reject Reject
Model C vs. Model F	No random firm effects	$Chisq(1) = 19.99^{***}$ $Chisq(1) = 7.14^{***}$	Reject Reject
Model D vs. Model G	No random firm effects	$Chisq(1) = 20.27^{***}$ $Chisq(1) = 6.41^{**}$	Reject Reject
Model E vs. Model F	Random firm effects	$Chisq(4) = 3.51$ $Chisq(3) = 0.86$	Accept Accept
Model E vs. Model H	No simultaneity bias	$Chisq(2) = 19.97^{***}$ $Chisq(2) = 0.63$	Reject Accept
Model F vs. Model G	No fixed industry effects	$F(29, 1762) = 66.03^{***}$ $F(29, 1767) = 61.01^{***}$	Reject Reject
Model D	No time effects	$F(4, 1762) = 0.13$ $F(4, 1767) = 0.25$	Reject Reject

Model E	No time effects	$F(4, 1762) = 2.04^*$	Reject
		$F(4, 1792) = 5.63^{***}$	Reject
Model G	No time effects	$F(4, 1762) = 0.73$	Accept
		$F(4, 1767) = 0.51$	Accept

The estimating sample contains 361 German firms as described in Table 1. The extended regression model is given by

$$OC_{it} = e_1 ROA_{it} + e_2 B_{it} + e_3 S_{it} + e_4 G_{it} + e_5 N^{LS}_{it} + e_6 C_{I,t-1} + e_7 H^I_{it} + u_{itv} \qquad (2)$$
$$u_{it} = a_I + a_i + \lambda_t + \epsilon_{it}$$

in which OC, ROA, B, S, G, N^{LS}, C, and H, are ownership concentration (unbounded Herfindahl index), the return on total assets, board representation, firm size, firm growth, the number of large shareholders, capital structure, and market concentration of firm i operating in industry j at time t. As theory is rather silent on potential determinants of ownership concentration, regression (2) is an ad-hoc specification. See Tables 19.1 and 19.2A for definitions of variables. In the *parsimonious* model we only include the return on total assets and board representation as right-hand side variables and ignore all other ad-hoc variables. The regression disturbance u_{it} can be decomposed into firm-, industry- and time-specific effects, $a_I, a_{ji}\ \lambda_t$, respectively, and a classical white noise regression disturbance ϵ_{it}.

Model A is a standard cross-section regression with the regression variables averaged over the observation period (361 observations). Model B adds 29 industry dummies to Model A. Models C to H use the pooled cross-section time-series data (1805 pooled observations). Model C restricts the firm-specific effects to be constant and identical for all firms. Model D adds 29 industry dummies to Model C. Model E assumes fixed (constant) firm-specific effects (361 firm-specific intercepts). Other time-constant effects (e.g., industries dummies) cannot be included. Model F assumes random firm-specific effects (i.e., a common intercept from which individual firms may deviate randomly). Model G adds 29 industry dummies to Model F. Model H includes fixed firm-specific effects as Model F but treats OC as an endogenous right-hand side variable (i.e., being correlated with ϵ_{it}). Models A, B, C and D are estimated by OLS. Model E is Within-OLS (LSDV, Least Squares Dummy Variables estimator). Models F and G use GLS. Model H is Within-2SLS using the fitted values of ROA from the reduced-form (first-stage) regression of ROA on all exogenous right-hand side variables in (2), B, S, G, N^{LS}, C, H plus capital intensity as an additional instrument (included to identify the regression equation). Capital intensity has been excluded from the second-stage ROA regression (Table 19.3A). We tested alternative exclusions of variables. The results were not significantly different when any other pair of variables was excluded.

We present specification test statistics for these models. A standard F-test is employed to test a restricted model (e.g., no industry or no time effects) against an unrestricted model (allowing for such effects). To test for random firm-specific effects versus no such effects we use the Lagrange multiplier test suggested by Breusch and Pagan (1980). Hausman's (1978) specification test is used to decide on fixed versus random firm-specific effects. The same test, known in this case under the name "Wu-hausman" (Wu, 1972) is also applied to compare the Within-OLS estimates (which are inefficient if OC in Equation (1) is endogenous) with the Within-2SLS estimates (which are efficient if OC is indeed endogenous). "Durbin–Watson" tests for first-order serial correlation (AR1) of panel regression residuals (Bhargava et al., 1982). See Hsiao (1986) or Baltagi (1995) for a detailed discussion of panel regression models and specification tests. The estimates' absolute t-statistics as provided in parentheses are based on White's (1980) heteroskedasticity-robust variance-covariance estimator.

***/**/* Significant at the 0.01/0.05/0.10 error level respectively.

Table 19.4A   Robust estimates of the return on total assets equation, 1992–1996. Full sample and sample split by stock market exposure

Dependent variable: ROA Explanatory variable	Regression coefficients (absolute t-statistic)		
	All firms (1)	Quoted firms (2)	Difference to non-quoted firms (3)
Ownership concentration	−0.0031 (2.54)**	−0.0027 (2.00)**	−0.0022 (0.69)
Board representation	0.0113 (0.43)	0.0157 (0.59)	3.0411 (7.35)***
Firm size	−0.0954 (7.69)***	−0.0975 (6.14)***	0.0069 (0.26)
Firm growth	0.1232 (12.49)***	0.1226 (8.33)***	0.0014 (0.07)
Capital intensity	−0.0695 (5.66)***	−0.0793 (4.79)***	0.0196 (0.76)
Capital structure (t −1)	−0.0938 (3.23)***	−0.1375 (3.08)***	0.0830 (1.40)
Market concentration	0.2361 (1.31)	0.3484 (1.45)	−0.2468 (0.68)
Mean firm intercept	3.0996 (183.42)***	3.1038 (188.26)***	−0.0082 (0.36)
Adj. R squared	0.78 (0.78)		
Durbin–Watson	1.56**, 1.86		

The estimating sample contains 361 German firms as described in Table 19.1. The split criterion is stock market quotation which divides the full sample into 183 traded and 178 non-traded firms. The estimating regression is

$$ROA_{it} = b_1 OC_{it} + b_2 B_{it} + b_3 S_{it} + b_4 G_{it} + b_5 K_{it} + b_6 C_{I,t-1} + b_7 H^j_{it}$$
$$+ d_1 D_{it} \times OC_{it} + d_2 D_{it} \times B_{it} + d_3 D_{it} \times S_{it} + d_4 D_{it} \times G_{it}$$
$$+ d_5 D_{it} \times K_{it} + d_6 D_{it} \times C_{i,t-1} + d_7 D_{it} \times H^j_{it} + a_i + \lambda_t + \epsilon_{it}$$

in which ROA, OC, B, S, G, K, C, and H are the return on total assets, ownership concentration (unbounded Herfindahl index), board representation, firm size, firm growth, capital intensity, capital structure, and market concentration of firm i operating in industry j at time t. See Table 19.2A for definitions of variables. a_i is a firm-specific effect, λ_t a time dummy, and ϵ_{it} the stochastic disturbance.

The split sample estimates are based on the full sample regression with the set of explanatory variables (except for the fixed firm-specific effects) interacted with a dummy variable D which takes on unit value for non-quoted firms and zero value for quoted firms. The regression coefficients b estimate the impact of the respective explanatory variables on ROA for the quoted firms, while the coefficients d yield the difference between the coefficients b and the respective coefficients for the non-quoted firms, to be obtained by adding d's to matching b's, or directly, by estimating the regression a second time but with D defined the other way around. The "All firms" estimates (column 1) come from the regression excluding the set of interacted variables. For the governance variables, these latter estimates can be compared to the Within-OLS estimates presented in Table 19.3A (Model E) which are not robust to first-order serial correlation.

The estimates shown above are robust to heteroskedasticity (White, 1980) and first-order serial correlation (AR1) (see Hsiao, 1986, pp. 55). The Within-OLS estimator was employed to generate consistent first-step esti-mates. We used the Within residuals to estimate a firm-specific serial correlation coefficient rho. Alternatively, we restricted the model to have a serial correlation coefficient common to all firms. The rhos were used to trans-form the original data. Regressions based on the transformed data were then estimated by OLS (firm-specific rho) or Maximum Likelihood (common rho). The drawback of the "firm-specific rho" approach is that due to the larger number of firm-specific coefficients to be estimated the coefficient on board representation was not estimable for the group of non-quoted firms. Therefore, we only report the estimates based on the "common rho" approach. However, the coefficients on all other explanatory variables can be estimated in the "firm-specific rho" approach. As these latter coefficient estimates are qualitatively identical and quantitatively only marginally different from those shown below, we do not report them separately. The estimates are available from the authors on request. The first Durbin–Watson statistic refers to the first-step Within-OLS residuals, the second statistic is based on the residuals from the AR1 regression. The adjusted R squared is given for both the original and, in parentheses, the transformed data.
***/**/*Significant at the 0.01/0.05/0.10 error level respectively.

Table 19.4B Robust estimates of the return on total assets equation, 1992–1996. Sample split by location of control rights

Dependent variable: ROA	Regression coefficients (abs. T-statistic)	Coefficient difference (absolute t-statistic)				
Explanatory variable	INDFIRM	FAMILY	FININST	MIX	FOREIGN	CHANGE
Ownership concentration	0.0028 (1.00)	−0.0060 (1.72)*	0.0129 (2.09)**	−0.0146 (2.56)**	−0.0061 (1.14)	−0.0098 (2.73)***
Board representation	0.0852 (1.63)	−0.1024 (1.57)	−0.1242 (1.30)	−0.1176 (1.23)	−	−
Firm size	−0.0529 (1.74)*	−0.0633 (1.74)*	−0.0442 (0.43)	−0.0498 (0.96)	−0.0360 (0.78)	−0.0464 (0.84)
Firm growth	0.1104 (6.50)***	0.0131 (0.48)	0.0822 (1.19)	0.0726 (1.67)*	0.0176 (0.69)	0.0256 (0.68)
Capital intensity	−0.0520 (1.74)*	−0.0023 (0.70)	−0.0634 (1.55)	0.0014 (0.03)	0.0021 (0.54)	−0.1104 (1.69)*
Capital structure (t−1)	0.0180 (0.35)	−0.2539 (3.55)***	−0.1021 (1.15)	−0.0208 (0.16)	−0.0091 (0.75)	0.0655 (0.56)
Market concentration	0.3048 (1.05)	0.2177 (0.39)	−1.3709 (0.78)	−0.7218 (0.77)	−0.2214 (0.54)	0.0010 (0.00)
Mean intercept	3.1126 (136.7)***	−0.0590 (1.94)*	0.1174 (1.97)**	−0.0080 (0.23)	0.0455 (1.15)	−0.0782 (1.64)*
Number of firms (obs.)	81 (405)	122 (610)	20 (100)	54 (270)	58 (290)	26 (130)
adj. R squared	0.78 (0.78)					
Durbin–Watson	1.56**, 1.86					

The estimating sample contains 361 German firms as described in Table I. The split criterion is the location of control rights (identity of voting block owners). The estimating regression is

$$ROA_{it} = b_1OC_{it} + b_2B_{it} + b_3S_{it} + b_4G_{it} + b_5K_{it} + b_6C_{i,t-1} + b_7H^j_{it}$$
$$+ \Sigma^5_{z=1}\Sigma^7_{k=1} + d_{kz}D_{zi} \times x_{kzit} + a_i + \lambda_t + \epsilon_{it}$$

in which ROA, OC, B, S, G, K, C, and H are the return on total assets, ownership concentration (unbounded Herfindahl index), board representation, firm size, firm growth, capital intensity, capital structure, and market concentration of firm i operating in industry j at time t. a_i is a firm-specific effect, λ_t a time dummy, and ϵ_{it} the stochastic disturbance.

The split sample estimates are based on the full sample regression with the set of explanatory variables $x = \{OC, B, S, G, K, C, H\}$ interacted with a set of dummy variables D_z which take on unit value for firms from $z = \{FAMILY, FININST, MIX, FOREIGN, CHANGE\}$ respectively and zero value for other firms. See Tables 19.2A and 19.2B for definitions of variables. The regression coefficients b estimate the impact of the respective explanatory variables on ROA for firms from the INDFIRM group, arbitrarily chosen as the base group, while the coefficients d yield the difference between the coefficients b and the coefficients for other groups of firms as represented by z. Adding the respective "coefficient difference" to the base group's "regression coefficient", yields the regression coefficients for the other groups of firms.

The estimates shown above are robust to heteroskedasticity (White, 1980) and first-order serial correlation (AR1) (see Hsiao, 1986, pp. 55). The Within-OLS estimator was employed to generate consistent first-step estimates. We used the Within residuals to estimate a firm-specific serial correlation coefficient rho. Alternatively, we restricted the model to have a serial correlation coefficient common to all firms. The rhos were used to transform the original data. Regressions based on the transformed data were then estimated by OLS (firm-specific rho) or Maximum Likelihood (common rho). The coefficient on board representation was not estimable for the firms in MIX and CHANGE due to an insufficient number of observations. In line with Table 19.4A, we report the estimates based on the "common rho" approach. Again, the coefficients of all other explanatory variables can be estimated in the "firm-specific rho" approach. These latter coefficient estimates are qualitatively identical and quantitatively only marginally different from those shown below so we do not report them separately. The estimates are available from the authors on request. The first Durbin–Watson statistic refers to the first-step Within-OLS residuals, the second statistic is based on the residuals from the AR1 regression. The adjusted R squared is given for both the original and, in parentheses, the transformed data.
− Not estimable due to an insufficient number of observations in the respective group.
***/**/* Significant at the 0.01/0.05/0.10 error level respectively.

Table 19.5 OLS estimates of the firm-specific fixed effects equation, 1992–1996

Dependent variable: fixed firm-specific effect
           Regression coefficient (absolute t-statistic)

Explanatory variable	(1)	(2)	(3)
INDFIRM (base group)	3.1346 (53.87)***		
FAMILY	−0.0541 (1.70)*		
FININST	0.0996 (1.96)**		
MIX	−0.0279 (0.84)		
FOREIGN	0.0290 (0.74)		
CHANGE	−0.0857 (1.85)*		
QUOTED	0.0140 (0.56)		
QUOTED			
INDFIRM (base group)		3.1406 (37.48)***	0.9066 (4.19)***
FAMILY		−0.0233 (0.48)	0.0368 (1.18)
FININST		0.1432 (2.26)**	0.0593 (1.54)
MIX		0.0373 (0.69)	0.0508 (1.48)
FOREIGN		0.0517 (0.73)	0.1156 (2.24)**
CHANGE		−0.0415 (0.70)	0.0509 (1.44)
Ownership concentration			0.0048 (2.62)***
Board representation			0.0131 (0.55)
NON-QUOTED			
INDFIRM		0.0320 (0.62)	0.1112 (2.61)***
FAMILY		−0.0030 (0.07)	0.0805 (2.00)**
FININST		−0.1009 (1.20)	−0.1021 (1.65)*
MIX		0.0938 (1.98)**	−0.0227 (0.63)
FOREIGN		0.0093 (0.13)	0.0377 (0.64)
CHANGE		−0.0748 (0.59)	−0.0312 (0.78)
Ownership concentration			−0.0066 (2.62)***
Board representation			−0.0079 (0.21)
Firm size			0.0872 (15.42)***
Firm growth			0.1404 (2.01)**
Capital intensity			0.0145 (0.92)
Capital structure			0.2529 (5.83)***
Market concentration			−0.1009 (0.52)
Industry effects		$F(29,326) = 42.91$***	$F(29,312) = 52.49$***
Adj. R^2	0.0377	0.1854	0.6804

The estimating sample contains 361 German firms as described in Table 19.1. The estimating regression is

$$\hat{a}_i = \gamma_1 + \gamma_2 FAMILY_i + \gamma_3 FININST_i + \gamma_4 MIX_i + \gamma_5 FOREIGN_i + \gamma_6 CHANGE_i$$
$$+ d_1 D_i \times INDFIRM_i + d_2 D_i \times FAMILY_i + d_3 D_i \times FININST_i + d_4 D_i \times MIX_i$$
$$+ d_5 D_i \times FOREIGN_i + d_6 D_i \times CHANGE_i + a_j + \epsilon_i$$

with

$$\hat{a}_i = \overline{ROA}_i - \hat{b}_1 \overline{OC}_i - \hat{b}_2 \overline{B}_i - \hat{b}_3 \overline{S}_i - \hat{b}_4 \overline{G}_i - \hat{b}_5 \overline{K}_i - \hat{b}_6 \overline{C}_i - \hat{b}_7 \overline{H}_i^j.$$

The firm-specific effects are denoted by $\overline{ROA}_i$, $\overline{OC}_i$, $\overline{B}_i$, $\overline{S}_i$, $\overline{G}_i$, $\overline{K}_i$, $\overline{C}_i$, $\overline{H}_i^j$ are the time means (1992–1996) of the return on total assets, ownership concentration (unbounded Herfindahl index), board representation, firm size, firm growth, capital intensity, capital structure, and market concentration of firm i operating in industry j. See Table 19.2A for variable definitions. INDFIRM, FAMILY, FININST, MIX, FOREIGN, and CHANGE are the mutually excluding groups referring to the location of control rights as defined in Table 19.2B. a_j is an industry-specific effect and ϵ_i the stochastic disturbance.

The coefficients $\hat{b}_k$ $(k = 1,\ldots, 7)$ are the robust estimates as shown in Table 19.2A, column 1. The coefficients γ_2 to γ_6 estimate the difference between the average fixed firm-specific effect γ_1 of the chosen base group INDFIRM and the average fixed firm-specific effect of the other groups. Adding the respective coefficient difference γ_2 to γ_6 to the base group's regression coefficient γ_1, yields the regression coefficients for the other groups of firms. The dummy variable D takes on unit value for non-quoted firms and zero value for quoted firms. The coefficients d estimate the difference in the coefficients between quoted and non-quoted firms. The OLS cross-section estimates below are robust to heteroskedasticity (White, 1980).
***/**/*Significant at the 0.01/0.05/0.10 error level.

the regression constant μ in (3) as its regression coefficient, we obtain the mean firm-specific effects and the corresponding t-statistics on the differences as reported in Table 19.4B. Column 1 of Table 19.5 adds in stock market exposure and industry indicators as further determinants of autonomous ROA. The coefficient on stock market exposure is positive but not significantly so. This result is consistent with Table 19.4A where we ignored the location of control rights and industry effects when comparing quoted and non-quoted firms. The included industry effects are highly significant.

In column 2 of Table 19.5, we interact the identity and stock market indicators to explore whether there is a combined impact of the location of control rights and stock market exposure on the fixed firm-specific effects. Significant differences emerge for the MIX firms for which the lack of stock market exposure lowers profitability. Further, as previously found, firms with financial institutions as controlling stakeholders perform better than the "managed" base group. However, the regressions of columns 1 and 2 ignore that the firm-specific effects may be correlated with the explanatory variables of the original ROA regression.[34] Therefore, column 3 adds in the regression the time means of these variables, distinguishing also ownership concentration and board representation by stock market exposure.

Ownership concentration significantly improves the autonomous ROA for the quoted firms but lowers it for the non-quoted firms. As the quoted firms are significantly less concentrated (see Table 19.2A), this result supports the view that the presence of large shareholders enhances the long-term performance of traded corporations. For the non-quoted firms higher concentration implies weaker performance both in the short (Table 19.4A) and in the long run (Table 19.5). Board representation, market concentration and capital intensity do not make a difference. Autonomous ROA is significantly larger for larger and growing firms as well as for firms with more equity capital.

Controlling for differences in ownership concentration, firm size and capital structure changes the magnitude, sign and significance of the coefficients on the identity indicators compared with column 2. Our multivariate test now reveals that the non-quoted FININST significantly underperformed with respect to the base group of quoted INDFIRM firms, whereas the quoted FOREIGN firms and the non-quoted INDFIRM and FAMILY firms have significant larger fixed effects than the base group.[35] All other differences are statistically insignificant at conventional error levels.

Summing up, the changes in the estimates on the identity indicators underline that, given firm size, investment opportunities (growth) and capital structure, it is the combination of the size of the equity stake held, the identity of owners and stock market exposure that matters for firm performance in the longer run.

4. SUMMARY AND CONCLUSION

Almost a decade ago Michael C. Jensen (1993, p. 873) laid out the research agenda for the new millenium in the field of corporate governance, corporate finance, and corporate performance:

> For those with a normative bent, making the internal control systems of corporations work is the major challenge facing economists and management scholars in the 1990s. For those who choose to take a purely positive approach, the major challenge is understanding how these systems work, and how they interact with other control forces (in particular the product and factor markets, legal, political, and regulatory systems, and the capital markets) impinging on the corporation.

This paper contributes to the positive approach. We focused on German firms because ownership concentration is an important feature setting the German system of corporate governance apart from the Anglo-Saxon. In the corporate governance literature ownership concentration is often understood as reflecting a stronger governing effort of owners. By reducing informational asymmetries between owners and managers as well as between the firm and external investors ownership concentration is expected to affect firm profitability positively. Contrary to this argument, we find a significantly negative impact of ownership concentration on profitability as measured by the return on total assets. This result holds for both quoted and non-quoted firms and supports the view that large shareholders inflict costs on the firm (e.g., rent extraction, too much monitoring, or infighting).

Ownership concentration can be an insufficient or misleading indicator of the control owners actually exert. We therefore checked the location of control rights and also the time horizon. When focussing on short-run ROA, the negative effect of ownership concentration originates primarily with the firms owned by families (individuals) or different large shareholders as well as firms which experienced a change in owners during the observation period. A positive impact of ownership concentration on profitability is found for firms with financial institutions as largest shareholders. This latter result is consistent with the view that banks are better (more efficient) monitors so that agency costs are lower.

When we look at the long-term performance we find that ownership concentration significantly improves the ROA of firms exposed to the stock market. This result is consistent with the standard view advanced in the literature that in the bank- or network-oriented system of corporate governance, committed owners take a long-term horizon on their investments at the expense of a higher short-term return. However, and the qualification warrants attention, this conclusion does not hold for the non-quoted firms. For the non-quoted firms ownership concentration influences profitability negatively, not only in the short but particularly so in the long run. An interpretation is that the owners favor control over both higher liquidity (by going public) and higher profitability (by exploiting investment opportunities better). The location of control rights seems to be more important for non-quoted firms. While the representation of the largest shareholder on the board of executive directors does not affect the ROA of quoted firms, it makes a significant positive difference for the non-quoted firms in the short run but not in the long run.

Finally, can we answer the question posed in this paper: Do governed corporations perform better? If one is willing to view firms owned by families, financial institutions, or a mix of large shareholders as governed rather than managed, the answer to the question seems to be yes. These groups have significantly higher mean and median profitabilities than the group of firms owned by another industrial firm. After controlling for other potential ROA determinants such as firm size, stock market exposure, industry effects, or the time horizon, these differences between owner categories are less pronounced but still present. Most of the variation in ROA across firms is explained by firm- or industry-specific effects. To get a more comprehensive picture of how governance structures affect firm performance, future research faces the challenge to identify what is behind these effects.

In conclusion, our study finds systematic influences of ownership concentration, stock market exposure, and the location of control rights on the profitability of German corporations. Our results imply that (1) the presence of large shareholders does not necessarily improve performance as measured by ROA, (2) concentrated ownership appears to be a sub-optimal choice for many of the tightly held and non-traded German corporations, and, finally, (3), having financial institutions as largest shareholders of traded corporations enhanced profitability.

ACKNOWLEDGMENTS

The authors are indebted to Bob Chirinko for extensive and insightful comments on the very first draft of the paper and, most of all, for his encouragement. We are also grateful to an anonymous referee for substantial advice which greatly improved the paper. Many helpful suggestions on various drafts were received from Rashjree Agarwal, David Audretsch, Matthew Bennett, Hans Degryse, Paul De Grauwe, Julie Ann Elston, Oliver Fabel, Rainer Feuerstack, Günther Franke, Carolin Frohlin, George Gelauff, Sabine Langner, Manfred Neumann, Marco Pagano, Hans-Jürgen Ramser, and seminar participants at the 1999 Meetings of the European Finance Association (EFA, Helsinki), European Economic Association (EEA, Santiago de Compostela), European Association for Research in Industrial Economics (EARIE, Torino), and Western Economic Association (WEA, San Diego) as well as at the University of Central Florida Orlando, Humboldt University Berlin, University of Konstanz, and Katholieke Universiteit Leuven. The second author would like to thank Ulrich Hege, Piet Moerland, and Luc Renneboog for stimulating discussions on corporate governance. As a matter of fact, any remaining errors are the authors' sole responsibility. Generous financial support was provided by the Bundesland Mecklenburg-Vorpommern (first author) and the German Science Foundation (DFG, second author). Main parts of the paper were written while the second author was visiting Georgia State University (School of Policy Studies, Atlanta) and Indiana University (School of Public and Environmental Affairs, Bloomington). The hospitality and support of these institutions is gratefully acknowledged. This research is not related to any CPB Netherlands Bureau for Economic Policy Analysis projects. The opinions expressed here do not necessarily reflect those of the CPB.

NOTES

1 See for a discussion and references, e.g., Porter (1992), Jensen (1993), Blair (1995), Berglöf (1997), Shleifer and Vishny (1997), Mayer (1998), Hopt et al. (1998), Barca and Becht (1999), OECD (1999), Allen and Gale (2000), and Vives (2000).

2 See Short (1994) and Shleifer and Vishny (1997) for surveys of the field.

3 Allen and Gale (2000, ch. 2 and 3) provide an excellent overview of the financial systems in the USA, UK, Germany, Japan, and France.

4 See, e.g., Porter (1992), Jensen (1993), Roe (1994), Bhide (1994), Pound (1995). As Bhide (1994, p. 129, p. 131) argues, "Unwittingly, the system [of U.S. securities regulations and disclosure rules] nurtures market liquidity at the expense of good governance.... U.S. rules that protect investors don't just sustain market liquidity, they also drive a wedge between shareholders and managers. Instead of yielding long-term shareholders who concentrate their holdings in a few companies, where they provide informed oversight and counsel, the laws promote diffused, arm's length stockholding". The benefits typically attributed to this so-called market-based system are seen in a better provision of finance to innovative start-up firms and higher returns to investors.

5 In December 1998, 323 domestic corporations with an aggregate market capitalization of 1,822,103 million DM (equivalent to 48% of the 1998 German GDP) were quoted and officially traded on the Frankfurt stock exchange. At the same time, 2,399 domestic corporations (3,829,375 million DM, 182% of GDP) were listed on the London stock exchange and 2,722 (17,373,835 million DM, 105% of GDP) on the New York stock exchange. (Source: Deutsche Börse, Factbook, Frankfurt, http://www.exchange.de; own calculations.) Boehmer (1999) provides a thorough analysis of ownership structures and location of control rights for the 430 stock corporations which were officially traded on the Frankfurt stock exchange in 1996. According to this study, banks, industrial firms, holdings, and insurance companies controlled as large blockholders almost 80% of the median firm's voting rights, or roughly 50% of the overall market value of firms officially listed.

6 The high tax on the sale of company cross-holdings (to be abolished soon) and the rigid German takeover code (under revision) which requires shareholders to be bought out with cash have contributed to making takeovers unattractive.

7 See, e.g., Edwards and Fischer (1994), Perlitz and Seeger (1994), Audretsch and Elston (1997), or Wenger and Kaserer (1998). The implementation of the Neuer Markt (new market) on which shares in innovative young firms are traded can be seen as a step in the direction of a more market-based system of corporate finance.

8 See, e.g., Fama and Jensen (1983), Short (1994) and Shleifer and Vishney (1997) for discussion and references to seminal contributions.

9 In Germany, the case of Metallgesellschaft may serve as an example of supervisory board failure. Deutsche Bank, as a major debtholder represented on the supervisory board, was regarded responsible for the disaster and scolded in the business press for insufficient and bad monitoring. See Frankel and Palmer (1996) for further discussion. See also Franks and Mayer (1998) on the dubious role of banks in the few German corporate takeovers.

10 What insufficient control over a firm's assets means, is nicely depicted by the General Motors example cited in Roe (1994, XII). In 1990, two 'large' (relative to all other shareholders) institutional investors, being dissatisfied with the company's bad performance, wanted to negotiate the implementation of a new CEO with GM's leaders. The management could calmly decline the request, since each 'large' shareholder only accounted for less than one per cent of the voting capital. In 1992 GM's top management had to take action after all. As losses piled up to over $6 billion, CEO Robert Stempel was eventually fired.

11 See Hubbard (1998) for a recent survey on investment and capital market imperfections.

12 See, e.g., Edwards and Fischer (1994) or Hellwig (2000) for discussion and references.

13 Boehmer (1999, 2000) provides in-depth descriptive analyses of governance structures and stock market performance of traded German corporations. As his approach is different from the regression studies surveyed here, we will refer to some of his results below.

14 A firm was defined as owner-controlled if individuals or families held at least the blocking minority (25% of voting capital plus one vote). A drawback of the study is that ownership structures were identifiable only for about 90 out of 300 sample firms. Thus in the regression analysis owner-controlled firms had to be compared to a mixture of presumably manager-controlled firms and firms with unknown governance structures, rendering the results questionable.

15 Cable (1985), Chirinko and Elston (1996) and Gorton and Schmid (2000) apply a cross-section regression approach. Cable's analysis for the time period 1968 to 1972 is based on 48 out of Germany's 100 largest corporations in 1970. The Gorton and Schmid study is also based on a very small sample and only two years (82 firms in 1975) and (56 firms in 1986). Chirinko and Elston investigate 300 stock corporations over the observation period 1965 to 1990 but due to incomplete ownership information cannot take advantage of the panel data properties. Weigand uses a panel data set which includes detailed ownership data (identity of owners, outstanding shares) for 240 stock corporations during 1965 to 1986.

16 Franks and Mayer (1997) apply a panel data set of 171 quoted corporations over the period 1989 to 1994 and use a fixed effects panel regression approach. There is only weak evidence of a relationship between either management or supervisory board turnover and performance in firms with concentrated ownership. This result is consistent with Kaplan's (1994) findings. Goergen's (1999) sample consists of 86 IPOs during the period 1981 to 1988. In both static and dynamic panel data regressions, ownership concentration did not have an impact on profitability (measured by cash flow over total assets).

17 Gedajlovic and Shapiro (1998) studied the blockholdings-performance link for the largest firms from five major industrialized countries. Their sample includes 99 publicly traded German stock corporations over the period 1986 to 1991. The U-formed relationship between ownership concentration and ROA was also found for the US firms.

18 Becht (1999) uses the corporations represented in the DAX100 stock market index during 1996 to 1998.

19 This definition is equivalent to earnings before interest, taxes, and depreciation (EBITDA).

20 Pension liabilities have been added for two reasons. First, it is peculiar to the German system of accounting that pension assets and pension liabilities are not netted out in companies' balance sheets. Further, pension liabilities are not paid into a trust (pension fund) but remain within the firm. They are available to the firm as a source of internal long-term finance. Pension liabilities thus can be seen as 'quasi' equity. Second, the shareholders' equity of limited liability companies (GmbH) is, by legal construction, extremely low. Adding reserves and pension liabilities to shareholders' equity helps avoid generating unrealistically high returns on equity for these firms compared to stock corporations.

21 We referred to the Bundesanzeiger or requested annual reports from firms to double-check and correct some entries in the Hoppenstedt Bilanzdatenbank (inconsistencies in reporting, missing values, obviously wrong entries etc.).

22 This exclusion refers to the subsequent empirical analysis of profitability only. Of course, a holding company can be the owner of a sample firm.

23 In many cases the Hypo-Guide also lists blocks smaller than 25% and indicates indirect ownership (voting rights granted to a large shareholder from other shareholders). Sometimes even very small blockholdings (5% and less) are reported.

24 As disclosure of smaller blockholdings was not mandatory during the observation period, the calculated Herfindahl index can only be an approximation to the true degree of ownership concentration. Two alternative Herfindahl indices were constructed for corporations with missing information on this "dispersed" portion of shareholdings. One measure treats the "dispersed" portion as one block. Using the means in Table 19.1 for corporations with only one large shareholder as an example, the Herfindahl index is $(89.07)^2 + (10.93)^2 = 8,053$. The other measure assumes that the dispersed portion is uniformly distributed among an unknown number of shareholders, each holding at most 1% of the shares outstanding, which yields a Herfindahl index of $(89.07)^2 + 10 \times (1.00)^2 + (0.93)^2 = 7,944$. The results to be presented below are not affected by the choice of the calculation method.

25 The results are available from the authors on request.

26 The Herfindahl-Index in its standard definition is restricted to take on values between 0 and 10,000. The logit transformation log $[H/(10,000 - H)]$ yields an "unbounded" variable. In the case of Mannesmann, for which ownership of voting shares is reported to be "100% dispersed", H was set at 1 in the transformation. For firms with only one owner holding 100% of voting stock, H was set at 9,999. In alternative regression runs we used the bounded Herfindahl-Index as well as the share of the largest shareholder plus its squared value as in Gedajlovic and Shapiro (1998). Further, we replaced ROA by ROE. As the estimates with respect to governance indicators do not differ significantly, we do not report the results from these alternative specifications here. They are available from the authors on request.

27 See for a recent discussion, e.g., Church and Ware (2000, ch. 12).

28 See the discussion in Hall and Weiss (1967).

29 We discuss the impact of the IO variables below.

30 With respect to the IO variables in the extended model we find ownership concentration to be significantly lower for firms which are larger, use more capital per employee, have more equity capital, and, hardly surprising, have more large shareholders. By contrast, growing firms and firms operating under more concentrated market structures have more concentrated ownership. In an alternative try, we endogenized board representation and the number of large shareholders. The results were qualitatively identical. The Wu–Hausman test did not indicate the endogeneity of board representation or the number of large shareholders.

31 As some of the variables in the regression are expressed in the natural logarithm, the means of the firm-specific intercepts are of different magnitude than mean ROA in the summary statistics tables.

32 This model specification gives estimates identical to those from separate regressions for each group of owners but considers the across-groups variation of the regression residuals in the variance-covariance matrix.

33 Recall that the Herfindahl index can be decomposed into $n^{-1} + nV$ where, in our case, n and V denote the number of (large) shareholders and the variance of individual stakes respectively.

34 This is suggested by the Hausman specification test in Table 19.3A (model E vs. model F) from which we concluded that the firm-specific effects are fixed rather than random. The test does indeed check whether these effects are correlated with the right-hand variables or not.

35 There are only two non-quoted firms with bank involvement. These two firms operated with mean ROAs of 0.16 and 0.09 respectively in the notoriously declining and restructuring mining industry. The mean ROA for the quoted firms with bank involvement is 0.28.

REFERENCES

Admati, A., Pfleiderer, P., and Zechner, J. (1994), Large shareholder activism, risk sharing, and financial market equilibrium, *Journal of Political Economy* **102**, 1097–1130.

Allen, F. and Gale, F. (1998), *Corporate Governance and Competition*, Working paper, New York University.

Allen, F. and Gale, D. (2000), *Comparing Financial Systems*. MIT Press, Cambridge and London.

Audretsch, D. and Elston, J. (1997), 'Financing the German Mittelstand', *Small Business Economics Journal* **9**, 97–110.

Audretsch, D. and Weigand, J. (1999), *Does Science Make a Difference? Investment, Finance and Corporate Governance in German Industries*, CEPR working paper No. 2056, London.

Baltagi, B. H. (1995), *Econometric Analysis of Panel Data*. Wiley, New York.

Baumol, W. (1959), *Business Behavior, Value, and Growth*. Macmillan, New York.

Baums, T. and Fraune, C. (1995), 'Institutionelle Anleger und Publikumsgesellschaft: Eine empirische Untersuchung', *Die Aktiengesellschaft* **40**, 97–112.

Barca, F. and Becht, M. (eds.) (1999), *Ownership and Control in Europe*. Oxford University Press, Oxford.

Becht, M. (1999), 'European corporate governance: Trading off liquidity against control', *European Economic Review* **43**, 1049–1056.

Becht, M. and Boehmer, E. (1997), *Transparency of Ownership and Control in Germany*, Working paper, Humboldt University, Berlin.

Bergloef, E. (1997), 'Reforming corporate governance: Redirecting the European agenda', *Economic Policy*, 93–123.

Berle, A. and Means, G. (1932), *The Modern Corporation and Private Property*. MacMillan, New York.

Bhargava, A., Franzini, L., and Narendanathan, W. (1982), 'Serial correlation and the fixed effects model', *Review of Economic Studies* **49**, 533–549.

Bhide, A. (1994), 'Efficient Markets, Deficient Governance', *Harvard Business Review*, November–December, 129–139.

Blair, M. (1995), *Ownership and Control: Rethinking Corporate Governance for the Twenty-First Century*, The Brookings Institution, Washington, D.C.

Boehmer, E. (1999), *Who Controls Germany? An Exploratory Analysis*, Working paper, Humboldt University, Berlin.

Boehmer, E. (2000), 'Business groups, bank control, and large shareholders: An analysis of German takeovers', *Journal of Financial Intermediation* **9**, 117–148.

Bolton, P. and von Thadden, E.-L. (1998a), 'Blocks, liquidity, and control', *Journal of Finance* **53**, 1–25.

Bolton, P. and von Thadden, E.-L. (1998b), 'Liquidity and control', *Journal of Institutional and Theoretical Economics* **154**, 177–215.

Breusch, T. and Pagan, A. (1980), 'A simple test for heteroscedasticity and random coefficient variation', *Econometrica* **47**, 1287–1294.

Burkhart, M., Gromb, D., and Panunzi, F. (1997), 'Large shareholders, monitoring, and the value of the firm', *Quarterly Journal of Economics* **112**, 693–728.

Cable, J. (1985), 'Capital market information and industrial performance: The role of West German banks', *Economic Journal* **95**, 118–132.

Chirinko, R. and Elston, J. (1996), *Finance, Control, and Profitability: An Evaluation of German Bank Influence*, American Institute for Contemporary German Studies: The Johns Hopkins University, Working Paper No. 28, Washington, D.C.

Church, J. and Ware, R. (2000), *Industrial Organization: A Strategic Approach*. McGraw-Hill, New York.

Cubbin, J. and Leech, D. (1983), 'The effect of shareholding dispersion on the degree of control in British companies: Theory and evidence', *Economic Journal* **93**, 351–369.

Demsetz, H. (1983), 'The structure of ownership and the theory of the firm', *Journal of Law and Economics* **26**, 375–390.

Demsetz, H. and Lehn, K. (1985), 'The structure of corporate ownership: Causes and consequences', *Journal of Political Economy* **93**, 1155–1177.

Diamond, D. (1984), 'Financial intermediation and delegated monitoring', *Review of Economic Studies* **51**, 393–414.

Diamond, D. (1991), 'Monitoring and reputation: The choice between bank loans and directly placed debt', *Journal of Political Economy* **99**, 689–721.

Edwards, J. and Fischer, K. (1994), *Banks, Finance, and Investment in Germany*. Cambridge University Press, Cambridge.

Fama, E. and Jensen, M. (1983), 'Separation of ownership and control', *Journal of Law and Economics* **26**, 301–325.

Fluck, Z. (1999), 'The dynamics of the management-shareholder conflict', *Review of Financial Studies* **12**, 379–404.

Frankel, A. and Palmer, D. (1998), 'The management of financial risks at

German nonfinancial firms: The case of Metallgesellschaft, in S. Black and M. Moersch, eds., *Competition and Convergence in Financial Markets: The German and Anglo-American Models, Advances in Finance, Investment and Banking*, vol. 5, Elsevier Science, North-Holland, Amsterdam, pp. 41–78.

Franks, J. and Mayer, C. (1997), *Ownership, Control and the Performance of German Corporations, Paper presented at the Center for Financial Studies Conference*, November 19–20, Frankfurt a.M.

Franks, J. and Mayer, C. (1998), 'Bank control, takeovers, and corporate governance in Germany', *Journal of Banking and Finance* **22**, 1385–1403.

Gedajlovic, E. and Shapiro, D. (1998), 'Management and ownership effects: Evidence from five countries', *Strategic Management Journal* **19**, 533–553.

Goergen, M. (1999), *Corporate Governance and Financial Performance*. Edward Elgar, Cheltenham.

Gorton, G. and Schmid, F. (2000), 'Universal banking and the performance of German firms', *Journal of Financial Economics* **58**, forthcoming.

Grossman, S. and Hart, O. (1980), 'Takeover bids, the free-rider problem and the theory of the corporation', *Bell Journal of Economics* **11**, 42–64.

Hausman, J. A. (1978), 'Specification Tests in Econometrics', *Econometrica* **46**, 1251–1272.

Hall, M. and Weiss, L. (1967), 'Firm size and profitability', *Review of Economics and Statistics* **47**, 319–331.

Hart, O. (1983), 'The market mechanism as an incentive scheme', *Bell Journal of Economics* **14**, 366–382.

Hellwig, M. (2000), 'On the economics and politics of corporate finance and corporate control', in Xavier Vives, ed., *Corporate Governance*, Cambridge University Press, Cambridge.

Hopt, K., Kanda, H., Roe, M. J., Wymersch, E., and Prigge, S. (1998), *Comparative Corporate Governance: The State of the Art and Emerging Research*, Clarendon Press, Oxford.

Hsiao, C. (1986), *Analysis of Panel Data*, Cambridge University Press, Cambridge.

Hubbard, R. G. (1990), 'Capital-market imperfections and investment', *Journal of Economic Literature* **36**, 193–225.

Huddart, S. (1993), 'The effects of a large shareholder on corporate value', *Management Science* **39**, 1407–1421.

Jensen, M. C. (1986), 'Agency costs of free cash flow, corporate finance and takeovers', *American Economic Review* **76**, 323–329.

Jensen, M. C. (1988), 'Takeovers: Their causes and consequences', *Journal of Economic Perspectives* **2**, 21–48.

Jensen, M. C. (1993), 'The modern industrial revolution, exit, and the failure of internal control systems', *Journal of Finance* **48**, 831–880.

Jensen, M. C. and Ruback, R. (1983). 'The market for corporate control: The scientific evidence', *Journal of Financial Economics* **11**, 5–50.

Kaplan, S. (1994), 'Top executives, turnover, and firm performance in Germany', *Journal of Law, Economics, and Organization* **10**, 142–159.

Lang, L. and Stulz, R. (1994), 'Tobin's q, corporate diversification, and firm performance', *Journal of Political Economy* **102**, 1248–1280.

Leibenstein, H. (1966), 'Allocative efficiency vs. "X-Efficiency"', *American Economic Review* **56**, 392–415.

Manne, H. G. (1965), 'Mergers and the market for corporate control', *Journal of Political Economy* **73**, 110–120.

Mayer, C. (1992), Corporate finance, in P. Newman, M. Milgate and J. Eatwell, eds., *The New Palgrave Dictionary of Money & Finance*, New York.

Mayer, C. (1996), 'Corporate governance, competition, and performance', *OECD Economic Studies* **27**, 7–34.

Mayer, C. (1998), 'Financial systems and corporate governance: A review of the international evidence', *Journal of Institutional and Theoretical Economics* **154**, 144–165.

Moerland, P. W. (1995), 'Corporate ownership and control structures: An international comparison', *Review of Industrial Organization* **10**, 443–464.

OECD (1999), *Principles of Corporate Governance*, OECD, Paris.

Pagano, M. and Röell, A. (1998), 'The choice of stock ownership structure: Agency costs, monitoring, and the decision to go public', *Quarterly Journal of Economics* **113**, 187–225.

Perlitz, M. and Seger, F. (1994), 'The role of universal banks in German corporate governance', *Business and the Contemporary World 4.*

Porter, M. E. (1992), 'Capital disadvantage: America's failing capital investment system', *Harvard Business Review*, September–October, 65–82.

Pound, J. (1995), 'The promise of the governed corporation', *Harvard Business Review*, March–April, pp. 89–98.

Roe, M. (1994), *Strong Managers, Weak Owners: The Political Roots of American Corporate Finance*, Princeton: Princeton University Press.

Schmidt, K. (1997), 'Managerial incentives and product market competition', *Review of Economic Studies* 64, 191–213.

Shin, H.-H. and Stulz, R. (1998), 'Are internal capital markets efficient?', *Quarterly Journal of Economics* 113, 531–552.

Shleifer, A. and Vishny, R. (1986), 'Large shareholders and corporate control', *Journal of Political Economy* 95, 461–488.

Shleifer, A. and Vishny, R. (1988), 'Management entrenchment: The case of manager-specific investment', *Journal of Financial Economics* 25, 123–139.

Shleifer, A. and Vishny, R. (1997), 'A survey of corporate governance', *Journal of Finance* 52, 737–783.

Short, H. (1994), 'Ownership, control, financial structure, and the performance of firms', *Journal of Economic Surveys* 8, 203–249.

Stiglitz, J. (1985), 'Credit markets and the control of capital', *Journal Money, Credit and Banking* 17, 133–152.

Stulz, R. (1988), 'Managerial control of voting rights: Financing policies and the market for corporate control', *Journal of Financial Economics* 20, 25–54.

Thompson, J. K. (1998), 'Shareholder value and the market for corporate control in OECD countries', *OECD Financial Market Trends* 69, February, 15–37.

Thonet, P. J. and Poengsen, O. (1979), 'Managerial control and economic performance in West Germany', *Journal of Industrial Economics* 28, 23–37.

Vives, X. (ed.) (2000), *Corporate Governance*, Cambridge University Press, Cambridge.

Warner, J., Watts, R., and Wruck, K. (1988), 'Stock prices and top management changes', *Journal of Financial Economics* 20, 461–492.

Weigand, J. (1999): Corporate Governance, Profitability, and Capital Structure, unpublished post-doctoral thesis (Habilitationsschrift), Nuernberg.

Wenger, E. and Kaserer, C. (1998), 'The German system of corporate governance – A model that should not be imitated', in S. Black and M. Moersch, eds., *Competition and Convergence in Financial Markets: The German and Anglo-American Models*, Advances in Finance, Investment and Banking, vol. 5. Elsevier Science, North-Holland, Amsterdam.

White, H. (1980), 'A heteroscedasticity-consistent covariance matrix estimator and a direct test for heteroscedasticity', *Econometrica* 48, 817–838.

Wu, D. (1972), 'Alternative tests of independence between stochastic regressors and disturbances', *Econometrica* 41, 733–750.

## Chapter 20

Paul Gompers, Joy Ishii and Andrew Metrick

CORPORATE GOVERNANCE AND EQUITY PRICES[*]

Source: *The Quarterly Journal of Economics*, 118(1) (2003): 107–155.

ABSTRACT

Shareholder rights vary across firms. Using the incidence of 24 governance rules, we construct a "Governance Index" to proxy for the level of shareholder rights at about 1500 large firms during the 1990s. An investment strategy that bought firms in the lowest decile of the index (strongest rights) and sold firms in the highest decile of the index (weakest rights) would have earned abnormal returns of 8.5 percent per year during the sample period. We find that firms with stronger shareholder rights had higher firm value, higher profits, higher sales growth, lower capital expenditures, and made fewer corporate acquisitions.

I. INTRODUCTION

CORPORATIONS ARE REPUBLICS. THE ULTIMATE authority rests with voters (shareholders). These voters elect representatives (directors) who delegate most decisions to bureaucrats (managers). As in any republic, the actual power-sharing relationship depends upon the specific rules of governance. One extreme, which tilts toward a democracy, reserves little power for management and allows shareholders to quickly and easily replace directors. The other extreme, which tilts toward a dictatorship, reserves extensive power for management and places strong restrictions on shareholders' ability to replace directors. Presumably, shareholders accept restrictions of their rights in hopes of maximizing their wealth, but little is known about the ideal balance of power. From a theoretical perspective, there is no obvious answer. In this paper we ask an empirical question—is there a relationship between shareholder rights and corporate performance?

Twenty years ago, large corporations had little reason to restrict shareholder rights. Proxy fights and hostile takeovers were rare, and investor activism was in its infancy. By rule, most firms were shareholder democracies, but in practice management had much more of a free hand than they do today. The rise of the junk bond market in the 1980s disturbed this equilibrium by enabling hostile-takeover offers for even the largest public firms. In response, many firms added takeover defenses and other restrictions of shareholder rights. Among the most popular were those that stagger the terms of directors, provide severance packages for managers, and limit shareholders' ability to meet or act. During the same time period, many states passed anti-takeover laws giving firms further defenses against hostile bids. By 1990 there was considerable variation across firms in the strength of shareholder rights. The takeover market subsided in the early 1990s, but this variation remained in place throughout the decade.

Most research on the wealth impact of takeover defenses uses event-study methodology, where firms' stock returns are analyzed following the announcement of a new defense.[1] Such studies face the difficulty that new defenses may be driven by contemporaneous conditions at the firm; i.e., adoption of a defense may both change the governance structure and provide a signal of managers' private information about impending takeover bids. Event studies of changes in state takeover laws are mostly immune from this problem, but it is difficult to identify a single date for an event that is preceded by legislative negotiation and followed by judicial uncertainty. For these and other reasons, some authors argue that event-study methodology cannot identify the impact of governance provisions.[2]

We avoid these difficulties by taking a long-horizon approach. We combine a large set of governance provisions into an index which proxies for the strength of shareholder rights, and then study the empirical relationship between this index and corporate performance. Our analysis should be thought of as a "longrun event study": we have democracies and dictatorships, the rules stayed mostly the same for a decade—how did each type do? Our main results are to demonstrate that, in the 1990s, democracies earned significantly higher returns, were valued more highly, and had better operating performance. Our analysis is not a test of market efficiency. Because theory provides no clear prediction, there is no reason that investors in 1990 should have foreseen the outcome of this novel experiment. Also, because this "experiment" did not use random assignment, we cannot make strong claims about causality, but we do explore the implications and assess the supportive evidence for several causal hypotheses.[3]

Our data are derived from publications of the Investor Responsibility Research Center. These publications provide 24 distinct corporate-governance provisions for approximately 1500 firms since 1990.[4] In Section II we describe these provisions and data sources in more detail. We divide the rules into five thematic groups and then construct a "Governance Index" as a proxy for the balance of power between shareholders and managers. Our index construction is straightforward: for every firm we add one point for every provision that reduces shareholder rights. This reduction of rights is obvious in most cases; the few ambiguous cases are discussed. Firms in the highest decile of the index are placed in the "Dictatorship Portfolio" and are referred to as having the "highest management power" or the "weakest shareholder rights"; firms in the lowest decile of the index are placed in the "Democracy Portfolio" and are described as having the "lowest management power" or the "strongest shareholder rights."

In Section III we document the main empirical relationships between governance and corporate performance. Using performance-attribution time-series regressions from September 1990 to December 1999, we find that the Democracy Portfolio outperformed the Dictatorship Portfolio by a statistically significant 8.5 percent per year. These return differences induced large changes in firm value over the sample period. By 1999 a one-point difference in the index was negatively associated with an 11.4 percentage-point difference in Tobin's Q. After partially controlling for differences in market expectations by using the book-to-market ratio, we also find evidence that firms with weak shareholder rights were less profitable and had lower sales growth than other firms in their industry.

The correlation of the Governance Index with returns, firm value, and operating performance could be explained in several ways. Section IV sets out three hypotheses to explain the results. Hypothesis I is that weak shareholder rights caused additional agency costs. If the market underestimated these additional costs, then a firm's stock returns and operating performance would have been worse than expected, and the firm's value at the beginning of the period would have been too high. Hypothesis II is that managers in the 1980s predicted poor performance in the 1990s, but investors did not. In this case, the managers could have put governance provisions in place to protect their jobs. While the provisions might have real protective power, they would not have caused the poor performance. Hypothesis III is that governance provisions did not cause poor performance (and need not have any protective power) but rather were correlated with other characteristics that were associated with abnormal returns in the 1990s. While we cannot identify any instrument or natural experiment to cleanly distinguish among these hypotheses, we do assess some supportive evidence for each one in Section V. For Hypothesis I we find some evidence of higher agency costs in a positive relationship between the index and both capital expenditures and acquisition activity. In support of Hypothesis III we find several observable characteristics that can explain up to one-third of the performance differences. We find no evidence in support of Hypothesis II. Section VI concludes the paper.

II. DATA

II.A. Corporate-governance provisions

Our main data source is the Investor Responsibility Research Center (IRRC), which publishes detailed listings of corporate-governance provisions for individual firms in *Corporate Takeover Defenses* [Rosenbaum 1990, 1993, 1995, 1998]. These data are derived from a variety of public sources including corporate bylaws and charters, proxy statements, annual reports, as well as 10-K and 10-Q documents filed with the SEC. The IRRC's universe is drawn from the Standard & Poor's (S&P) 500 as well as the annual lists of the largest corporations in the publications of *Fortune, Forbes,* and *Businessweek*. The IRRC's sample expanded by several hundred firms in 1998 through additions of some smaller firms and firms with high institutional-ownership levels. Our analysis uses all firms in the IRRC universe except those with dual-class

common stock (less than 10 percent of the total).[5] The IRRC universe covers most of the value-weighted market: even in 1990 the IRRC tracked more than 93 percent of the total capitalization of the combined New York Stock Exchange (NYSE), American Stock Exchange (AMEX), and NASDAQ markets.

The IRRC tracks 22 charter provisions, bylaw provisions, and other firm-level rules plus coverage under six state takeover laws; duplication between firm-level provisions and state laws yields 24 unique provisions. Table 20.1 lists all of these provisions, and Appendix 1 discusses each one in detail. We divide them into five groups: tactics for delaying hostile bidders (*Delay*); voting rights (*Voting*); director/officer protection (*Protection*); other takeover defenses (*Other*); and state laws (*State*).

The *Delay* group includes four provisions designed to slow down a hostile bidder. For takeover battles that require a proxy fight to either replace a board or dismantle a takeover defense, these provisions are the most crucial. Indeed, some legal scholars argue that the dynamics of modern takeover battles have rendered all other defenses superfluous [Daines and Klausner 2001; Coates 2000]. The *Voting* group contains six provisions, all related to shareholders' rights in elections or charter/bylaw amendments. The *Protection* group contains six provisions designed to insure officers and directors against job-related liability or to compensate them following a termination. The *Other* group includes the six remaining firm-level provisions.

These provisions tend to cluster within firms. Out of $(22*21)/2 = 231$ total pairwise correlations for the 22 firm-level provisions, 169 are positive, and 111 of these positive correlations are significant.[6] In contrast, only 9 of the 62 negative correlations are significant. This clustering suggests that firms may differ significantly in the balance of power between investors and management.

The IRRC firm-level data do not include provisions that apply automatically under state law. Thus, we supplement these data with state-level data on takeover laws as

Table 20.1 Governance provisions

	Percentage of firms with governance provisions in			
	1990	*1993*	*1995*	*1998*
Delay				
Blank check	76.4	80.0	85.7	87.9
Classified board	59.0	60.4	61.7	59.4
Special meeting	24.5	29.9	31.9	34.5
Written consent	24.4	29.2	32.0	33.1
Protection				
Compensation plans	44.7	65.8	72.5	62.4
Contracts	16.4	15.2	12.7	11.7
Golden parachutes	53.1	55.5	55.1	56.6
Indemnification	40.9	39.6	38.7	24.4
Liability	72.3	69.1	65.6	46.8
Severance	13.4	5.5	10.3	11.7
Voting				
Bylaws	14.4	16.1	16.0	18.1
Charter	3.2	3.4	3.1	3.0
Cumulative voting	18.5	16.5	14.9	12.2
Secret ballot	2.9	9.5	12.2	9.4
Supermajority	38.8	39.6	38.5	34.1
Unequal voting	2.4	2.0	1.9	1.9
Other				
Antigreenmail	6.1	6.9	6.4	5.6
Directors' duties	6.5	7.4	7.2	6.7
Fair price	33.5	35.2	33.6	27.8
Pension parachutes	3.9	5.2	3.9	2.2
Poison pill	53.9	57.4	56.6	55.3
Silver parachutes	4.1	4.8	3.5	2.3
State				
Antigreenmail law	17.2	17.6	17.0	14.1
Business combination law	84.3	88.5	88.9	89.9
Cash-out law	4.2	3.9	3.9	3.5
Directors' duties law	5.2	5.0	5.0	4.4
Fair price law	35.7	36.9	35.9	31.6
Control share acquisition law	29.6	29.9	29.4	26.4
Number of firms	1357	1343	1373	1708

This table presents the percentage of firms with each provision between 1990 and 1998. The data are drawn from the IRRC Corporate Takeover Defenses publications [Rosenbaum 1990, 1993, 1995, 1998] and are supplemented by data on state takeover legislation coded from Pinnell [2000]. See Appendix 1 for detailed information on each of these provisions. The sample consists of all firms in the IRRC research universe except those with dual class stock.

given by Pinnell [2000], another IRRC publication. From this publication we code the presence of six types of so-called "second-generation" state takeover laws and place them in the *State* group.[7] Few states have more than three of these laws, and only Pennsylvania has all six.[8] Some of these laws are analogues of firm-level provisions given in other groups. We discuss these analogues in subsection II.B.

The IRRC data set is not an exhaustive listing of all provisions. Although firms can review their listing and point out mistakes before publication, the IRRC does not update every company in each new edition of the book, so some changes may be missed. Also the charter and bylaws are not available for all companies and thus the IRRC must infer some provisions from proxy statements and other filings. Overall, the IRRC intends its listings as a starting point for institutional investors to review governance provisions. Thus, these listings are a noisy measure of a firm's governance provisions, but there is no reason to suspect any systematic bias. Also, all of our analysis uses data available at time t to forecast performance at time $t + 1$ and beyond, so there is no possibility of look-ahead bias induced by our statistical procedures.

To build the data set, we coded the data from the individual firm profiles in the IRRC books. For each firm we recorded the identifying information (ticker symbol, state of incorporation) and the presence of each provision. Although many of the provisions can be made stronger or weaker (e.g., supermajority thresholds can vary between 51 and 100 percent), we made no strength distinctions and coded all provisions as simply "present" or "not present." This methodology sacrifices precision for the simplicity necessary to build an index.

For most of the analysis of this paper, we match the IRRC data to the Center for Research in Security Prices (CRSP) and, where necessary, to Standard and Poor's Compustat database. CSRP matching was done by ticker symbol and was supplemented by handchecking names, exchanges, and states of incorporation. These procedures enable us to match 100 percent of the IRRC sample to CRSP, with about 90 percent of these matches having complete annual data in Compustat.

II.B. The Governance index

The index construction is straightforward: for every firm we add one point for every provision that restricts shareholder rights (increases managerial power). This power distinction is straightforward in most cases, as is discussed below. While this simple index does not accurately reflect the relative impacts of different provisions, it has the advantage of being transparent and easily reproducible. The index does not require any judgments about the efficacy or wealth effects of any of these provisions; we only consider the impact on the balance of power.

For example, consider Classified Boards, a provision that staggers the terms and elections of directors and hence can be used to slow down a hostile takeover. If management uses this power judiciously, it could possibly lead to an increase in overall shareholder wealth; if management uses this power to maintain private benefits of control, then this provision would decrease shareholder wealth. In either case, it is clear that Classified Boards increase the power of managers and weaken the control rights of large shareholders, which is all that matters for constructing the index.

Most of the provisions can be viewed in a similar way. Almost every provision gives management a tool to resist different types of shareholder activism, such as calling special meetings, changing the firm's charter or bylaws, suing the directors, or just replacing them all at once. There are two exceptions: Secret Ballots and Cumulative Voting. A Secret Ballot, also called "confidential voting" by some firms, designates a third party to count proxy votes and prevents management from observing how specific shareholders vote. Cumulative Voting allows shareholders to concentrate their directors' votes so that a large minority holder can ensure some board representation. (See Appendix 1 for fuller descriptions.) These two provisions are usually proposed by shareholders and opposed by management.[9] In contrast, none of the other provisions enjoy consistent shareholder support or management opposition; in fact, many of these provisions receive significant numbers of shareholder proposals for their repeal [Ishii 2000]. Also, both Cumulative Voting and Secret Ballots tend to be negatively correlated with the presence of other firm-level provisions (19 negative out of 21 for Cumulative Voting; 11 out of 21 for Secret Ballot). Thus, we consider the presence of Secret Ballots and Cumulative Voting to be *increases* in shareholder rights. For each one we add one point to the Governance

Index when firms do *not* have it. For all other provisions we add one point when firms do have it.[10]

Thus, the Governance Index ("*G*") is just the sum of one point for the existence (or absence) of each provision. We also construct subindices for each of the five categories: *Delay, Protection, Voting, Other,* and *State*. Recall that there are 28 total provisions listed in the five categories, of which 24 are unique. For the state laws with a firm-level analogue, we add one point to the index if the firm is covered under the firm-level provision, the state law, or both.[11] For example, a firm that has an Antigreenmail provision and is also covered by the Antigreenmail state law would get one point added to both its *State*

subindex and its *Other* subindex, but only one point (not two) would be added to its overall *G* index. Thus, *G* has a possible range from 1 to 24 and is not just the sum of the five subindices.

Table 20.2 gives summary statistics for *G* and the subindices in 1990, 1993, 1995, and 1998. Table 20.2 also shows the frequency of *G* by year, broken up into groups beginning with $G \leq 5$, then each value of *G* from $G = 6$ through $G = 13$, and finishing with $G \geq 14$. These ten "deciles" are similar but not identical in size, with relative sizes that are fairly stable from 1990 to 1995. In the remainder of the paper we pay special attention to the two extreme portfolios: the "Dictatorship Portfolio" of the firms with the weakest shareholder rights

Table 20.2 The Governance Index

	1990	1993	1995	1998
Governance index				
Minimum	2	2	2	2
Mean	9.0	9.3	9.4	8.9
Median	9	9	9	9
Mode	10	9	9	10
Maximum	17	17	17	18
Standard deviation	2.9	2.8	2.8	2.8
Number of firms				
$G \leq 5$ (Democracy Portfolio)	158	139	120	215
$G = 6$	119	88	108	169
$G = 7$	158	140	127	186
$G = 8$	165	139	152	201
$G = 9$	160	183	183	197
$G = 10$	175	170	178	221
$G = 11$	149	168	166	194
$G = 12$	104	123	142	136
$G = 13$	84	100	110	106
$G = 14$ (Dictatorship portfolio)	85	93	87	83
Total	1357	1343	1373	1708
Subindex means				
Delay	1.8	2.0	2.1	2.1
Protection	2.4	2.5	2.5	2.1
Voting	2.2	2.1	2.1	2.2
Other	1.1	1.2	1.1	1.0
State	1.8	1.8	1.8	1.7

This table provides summary statistics on the distribution of *G*, the Governance Index, and the subindices (*Delay, Protection, Voting, Other,* and *State*) over time. *G* and the subindices are calculated from the provisions listed in Table 20.1 as described in Section II. Appendix 1 gives detailed information on each provision. We divide the sample into ten portfolios based on the level of *G* and list the number of firms in each portfolio. The Democracy Portfolio is composed of all firms where $G \leq 5$, and the Dictatorship Portfolio contains all firms where $G \geq 14$.

$(G \geq 14)$, and the "Democracy Portfolio" of the firms with the strongest shareholder rights $(G \leq 5)$. These portfolios are updated at the same frequency as G.

Most of the changes in the distribution of G come from changes in the sample due to mergers, bankruptcies, and additions of new firms by the IRRC. In 1998 the sample size increased by about 25 percent, and these new firms tilted toward lower values of G. At the firm level, G is relatively stable. For individual firms the mean (absolute) change in G between publication dates (1990, 1993, 1995, 1998) is 0.60, and the median (absolute) change between publication dates is zero.[12]

Table 20.3 shows the correlations between pairs of subindices. The *Delay, Protection, Voting*, and *Other* subindices all have positive and significant pairwise correlations with each other. *State*, however, has negative correlations with *Delay, Protection*, and *Voting*. It could be that firms view some of the state laws as substitutes for the firm-level provisions, but then it would be surprising that *Other*, which contains three provisions that are direct substitutes for state laws, is the only subindex that is positively correlated with *State*. Overall, it appears that coverage under state laws is not highly correlated with the adoption of firm-level provisions. This fact has implications for the analysis of causality, as is discussed in Section IV.

Table 20.4 lists the ten largest firms (by market capitalization) in the Democracy and Dictatorship Portfolios in 1990 and gives the value of G for these firms in 1990

and 1998. Of the ten largest firms in the Democracy Portfolio in 1990, six of them are still in the Democracy Portfolio in 1998, three have dropped out of the portfolio and have $G = 6$, and one (Berkshire Hathaway) disappeared from the sample.[13] The Dictatorship Portfolio has a bit more activity, with only two of the top ten firms remaining in the portfolio, four firms dropping out with $G = 13$, and three firms leaving the sample though mergers or the addition of another class of stock.[14] Thus, 40 percent (eight out of 20) of the largest firms in the extreme portfolios in 1990 were also in these portfolios in 1998. This is roughly comparable to the full set of firms: among all firms in the Democracy and Dictatorship Portfolios in 1990, 31 percent were still in the same portfolios in 1998.

There is no obvious industry concentration among these top firms; the whole portfolios are similarly dispersed. Classifying firms into 48 industries as in Fama and French [1997], the portfolios appear to be broadly similar to each other in all years, with a mix of old-economy and new-economy industries.[15] Each portfolio has an important technology component. "Computers" is the largest industry by market value in the Democracy Portfolio in 1990, with 22.4 percent of the portfolio, falling to third place with 12.3 percent of the value in 1998. "Communications" does not make the top five in market value for the Dictatorship Portfolio in 1990, but rises to first place with 25.3 percent of the portfolio in 1998.

Table 20.3 Correlations Between the Subindices

	Delay	Protection	Voting	Other
Protection	0.22**			
Voting	0.33**	0.10**		
Other	0.43**	0.27**	0.19**	
State	−0.08**	−0.04	−0.07*	0.05

This table presents pairwise correlations between the subindices, *Delay, Protection, Voting, Other*, and *State* in 1990. The calculation of the subindices is described in Section II. The elements of each subindex are given in Table 20.1 and are described in detail in Appendix 1. Significance at the 5 percent and 1 percent levels is indicated by * and **, respectively.

Table 20.4 The Largest Firms in the Extreme Portfolios

1990 Democracy portfolio

	State of incorporation	1990 Governance index	1998 Governance index
IBM	New York	5	6
Wal-Mart	Delaware	5	5
Du Pont de Nemours	Delaware	5	5
Pepsico	North Carolina	4	3
American International Group	Delaware	5	5
Southern Company	Delaware	5	5
Hewlett Packard	California	5	6
Berkshire Hathaway	Delaware	3	—
Commonwealth Edison	Illinois	4	6
Texas Utilities	Texas	2	4

1990 Dictatorship Portfolio

	State of incorporation	1990 Governance index	1998 Governance index
GTE	New York	14	13
Waste Management	Delaware	15	13
General Re	Delaware	14	16
Limited Inc	Delaware	14	14
NCR	Maryland	14	—
K Mart	Michigan	14	10
United Telecommunications	Kansas	14	—
Time Warner	Delaware	14	13
Rorer	Pennsylvania	16	—
Woolworth	New York	14	13

This table presents the firms with the largest market capitalizations at the end of 1990 of all companies within the Democracy Portfolio ($G \leq 5$) and the Dictatorship Portfolio ($G \geq 14$). The calculation of G is described in Section II. The companies are listed in descending order of market capitalization.

III. GOVERNANCE: EMPIRICAL RELATIONSHIPS

III.A. Summary statistics

Table 20.5 gives summary statistics and correlations for G (and subindices) with a set of firm characteristics as of September 1990: book-to-market ratio, firm size, share price, monthly trading volume, Tobin's Q, dividend yield, S&P 500 inclusion, past five-year stock return, past five-year sales growth, and percentage of institutional ownership. The first four of these characteristics are in logs. The construction of each characteristic is described in Appendix 2. The first column of Table 20.5 gives the correlation of each of these characteristics with G, the next two columns give the mean value in the Democracy and Dictatorship Portfolios, and the final column gives the difference between these means. These results are descriptive and are intended to provide some background for the analyses in the following sections.

The strongest relation is between G and S&P 500 inclusion. The correlation between these variables is positive and significant — about half of the Dictatorship Portfolio is drawn from S&P 500 firms compared with 15 percent of the Democracy Portfolio.

Given this finding, it is not surprising that G is also positively correlated with size, share price, trading volume, and institutional ownership. S&P firms tend to

Table 20.5 Summary Statistics

	Correlation with G	Mean, democracy portfolio	Mean, dictatorship portfolio	Difference
BM	0.02	−0.66	−0.54	−0.12
				(0.10)
SIZE	0.15**	12.86	13.46	−0.60**
				(0.21)
PRICE	0.16**	2.74	3.14	−0.40**
				(0.12)
VOLUME	0.19**	16.34	17.29	−0.95**
				(0.24)
Q	−0.04	1.77	1.47	0.30*
				(0.14)
YLD	0.03	4.20%	7.20%	−3.00%
				(4.34)
SP500	0.23**	0.15	0.49	−0.34**
				(0.06)
5-year return	−0.01	90.53%	85.41%	5.12%
				(20.74)
SGROWTH	−0.08**	62.74%	44.78%	17.96%
				(9.83)
IO	0.14**	25.89%	34.44%	−8.55%*
				(3.36)

This table gives descriptive statistics for the relationship of G with several financial and accounting measures in September 1990. The first column gives the correlations for each of these variables with the Governance Index, G. The second and third columns give means for these same variables within the Democracy Portfolio ($G \leq 5$) and the Dictatorship Portfolio ($G \geq 14$) in 1990. The final column gives the difference of the two means with its standard error in parentheses. The calculation of G is described in Section II, and definitions of each variable are given in Appendix 2. Significance at the 5 percent and 1 percent levels is indicated by * and **, respectively.

have relatively high levels of all of these characteristics. In addition, the correlation of G with five-year sales growth is negative and significant, suggesting that high-G firms had relatively lower sales growth over the second half of the 1980s, the period when many of the provisions were first adopted.

Correlations at other times in the sample period (not shown in the table) are similar. Overall, it appears that firms with weaker shareholder rights tend to be large S&P firms with relatively high share prices, institutional ownership and trading volume, relatively poor sales growth, and poor stock-market performance. The 1990s were a time of rising activism by institutional investors and more attention to governance provisions; thus, we might expect to see some reduction in the institutional ownership of high-G firms. In untabulated tests, we find no evidence of such a reduction, with both pairwise correlations and

multivariate analysis suggesting no robust relationship between G and changes in institutional ownership.

III.B. Governance and returns

If corporate governance matters for firm performance *and* this relationship is fully incorporated by the market, then a stock price should quickly adjust to any relevant change in the firm's governance. This is the logic behind the use of event studies to analyze the impact of takeover defenses. If such a reaction occurs, then expected returns on the stock would be unaffected beyond the event window. However, if governance matters but is not incorporated immediately into stock prices, then realized returns on the stock would differ systematically from equivalent securities.

In this section we examine the relationship between G and subsequent returns. An investment of $1 in the (value-weighted)

Dictatorship Portfolio on September 1, 1990, when our data begin, would have grown to $3.39 by December 31, 1999. In contrast, a $1 investment in the Democracy Portfolio would have grown to $7.07 over the same period. This is equivalent to annualized returns of 14.0 percent for the Dictatorship Portfolio and 23.3 percent for the Democracy Portfolio, a difference of more than 9 percent per year.

What can explain this disparity? One possible explanation is that the performance differences are driven by differences in the riskiness or "style" of the two portfolios. Researchers have identified several equity characteristics that explain differences in realized returns. In addition to differences in exposure to the market factor ("beta"), a firm's market capitalization (or "size"), book-to-market ratio (or other "value" characteristics), and immediate past returns ("momentum") have all been shown to significantly forecast future returns.[16] If the Dictatorship Portfolio differs significantly from the Democracy Portfolio in these characteristics, then style differences may explain at least part of the difference in annualized raw returns.

Several methods have been developed to account for these style differences in a system of performance attribution. We employ one method here and use another in Section V. The four-factor model of Carhart [1997] is estimated by

$$R_t = \alpha + \beta_1 * RMRF_t + \beta_2 * SMB_t + \beta_3 * HML_t + \beta_4 * Momentum_t + \epsilon_t,$$
$$(1)$$

where R_t is the excess return to some asset in month t, $RMRF_t$ is the month t value-weighted market return minus the risk-free rate, and the terms SMB_t (small minus big), HML_t (high minus low), and $Momentum_t$ are the month t returns on zero-investment factor-mimicking portfolios designed to capture size, book-to-market, and momentum effects, respectively.[17] Although there is ongoing debate about whether these factors are proxies for risk, we take no position on this issue and simply view the four-factor model as a method of

performance attribution. Thus, we interpret the estimated intercept coefficient, "alpha," as the abnormal return in excess of what could have been achieved by passive investments in the factors.

The first row of Table 20.6 shows the results of estimating (1) where the dependent variable R_t is the monthly return difference between the Democracy and Dictatorship Portfolios. Thus, the alpha in this estimation is the abnormal return on a zero-investment strategy that buys the Democracy Portfolio and sells short the Dictatorship Portfolio. For this specification the alpha is 71 basis points (bp) per month, or about 8.5 percent per year. This point estimate is statistically significant at the 1 percent level. Thus, very little of the difference in raw returns can be attributed to style differences in the two portfolios.

The remaining rows of Table 20.6 summarize the results of estimating (1) for all ten "deciles" of G, including the extreme deciles comprising the Democracy ($G \leq 5$) and Dictatorship ($G \geq 14$) Portfolios. As the table shows, the significant performance difference between the Democracy and Dictatorship Portfolios is driven both by overperformance (for the Democracy Portfolio) and underperformance (by the Dictatorship Portfolio). The Democracy Portfolio earns a positive and significant alpha of 29 bp per month, while the Dictatorship Portfolio earns a negative and significant alpha of −42 bp per month.

The results also show that alpha decreases as G increases. The Democracy Portfolio earns the highest alpha of all the deciles, and the next two highest alphas, 24 and 22 bp, are earned by the third ($G = 7$) and second ($G = 6$) deciles, respectively. The Dictatorship Portfolio earns the lowest alpha, and the second lowest alpha is earned by the eighth ($G = 12$) decile. Furthermore, the four lowest G deciles earn positive alphas, while the three highest G deciles earn negative alphas. More formally, a Spearman rank-correlation test of the null hypothesis of no correlation between G-decile rankings and alpha rankings yields a test statistic of 0.842, and is rejected at the 1 percent level.

Table 20.6 Performance-Attribution Regressions for Decile Portfolios

	α	RMRF	SMB	HML	Momentum
Democracy- Dictatorship	0.71** (0.26)	−0.04 (0.07)	−0.22* (0.09)	−0.55* (0.10)	−0.01 (0.07)
G ≤ 5 (Democracy)	0.29* (0.13)	0.98** (0.04)	−0.24** (0.05)	−0.21** (0.05)	−0.05 (0.03)
G = 6	0.22 (0.18)	0.99** (0.05)	−0.18** (0.06)	0.05 (0.07)	−0.08 (0.04)
G = 7	0.24 (0.19)	1.05** (0.05)	−0.10 (0.07)	−0.14 (0.08)	0.15** (0.05)
G = 8	0.08 (0.14)	1.02** (0.04)	−0.04 (0.05)	−0.08 (0.06)	0.01 (0.04)
G = 9	−0.02 (0.12)	0.97** (0.03)	−0.20** (0.04)	0.14** (0.05)	−0.01 (0.03)
G = 10	0.03 (0.11)	0.95** (0.03)	−0.17** (0.04)	0.00 (0.04)	−0.08** (0.03)
G = 11	0.18 (0.16)	0.99** (0.05)	−0.14* (0.05)	−0.06 (0.06)	−0.01 (0.04)
G = 12	−0.25 (0.14)	1.00** (0.04)	−0.11* (0.05)	0.16** (0.06)	0.02 (0.04)
G = 13	−0.01 (0.14)	1.03** (0.04)	−0.21** (0.05)	0.14* (0.06)	−0.08* (0.04)
G ≥ 14 (Dictatorship)	−0.42* (0.19)	1.03** (0.05)	−0.02 (0.06)	0.34** (0.07)	−0.05 (0.05)

We estimate four-factor regressions (equation (1) from the text) of value-weighted monthly returns for portfolios of firms sorted by G. The calculation of G is described in Section II. The first row contains the results when we use the portfolio that buys the Democracy Portfolio (G ≤ 5) and sells short the Dictatorship Portfolio (G ≥ 14). The portfolios are reset in September 1990, July 1993, July 1995, and February 1998, which are the months after new data on G became available. The explanatory variables are *RMRF, SMB, HML*, and *Momentum*. These variables are the returns to zero-investment portfolios designed to capture market, size, book-to-market, and momentum effects, respectively. (Consult Fama and French [1993] and Carhart [1997] on the construction of these factors.) The sample period is from September 1990 through December 1999. Standard errors are reported in parentheses and significance at the 5 percent and 1 percent levels is indicated by * and **, respectively.

Table 20.7 reports several variations of the abnormal-return results. In each variation we estimate the performance-attribution regression in equation (1) on the return difference between the Democracy and Dictatorship Portfolios, while changing some aspect of the portfolio construction or return calculation. We perform all of these tests using both value-weighted (VW) and equal-weighted (EW) portfolios. These tests allow us to estimate the fraction of the benchmark abnormal returns that can be attributed to industry composition, choice of cutoffs for the extreme portfolios, new provisions during the decade, legal variation across states, and different time periods.

The first row of Table 20.7 replicates the baseline portfolio construction used above. The remaining rows of the table summarize tests using industry-adjusted returns (row 2), two alternative constructions of the extreme portfolios (rows 3 and 4), fixed portfolios built with 1990 levels of G (row 5), a subsample that includes only Delaware firms (row 6), and subsamples split between the first half and the second half of the sample period (rows 7 and 8). Details of each of these constructions are given in the table note. The main themes of these results are, first, that the VW returns (Democracy minus Dictatorship) are economically large in all cases and, second, the EW abnormal returns are usually about two-thirds of the

Table 20.7 Performance-Attribution Regressions under Alternative Portfolio Constructions

	α, Value-weighted	α, Equal-weighted
(1) Democracy-Dictatorship	0.71**	0.45*
	(0.26)	(0.22)
(2) Industry-adjusted	0.47*	0.30
	(0.22)	(0.19)
(3) Big portfolios	0.47*	0.39*
	(0.21)	(0.19)
(4) Small portfolios	0.78*	0.45
	(0.33)	(0.25)
(5) 1990 portfolio	0.53*	0.33
	(0.24)	(0.22)
(6) Delaware portfolio	0.63	0.42
	(0.34)	(0.26)
(7) Early half	0.45	0.58*
	(0.23)	(0.28)
(8) Late half	0.75	0.04
	(0.40)	(0.27)

This table presents the alphas from four-factor regressions for variations on the Democracy ($G \leq 5$) minus Dictatorship ($G \geq 14$) Portfolio. The calculation of G is described in Section II. The portfolios are reset in September 1990, July 1993, July 1995, and February 1998, which are the months after new data on G became available. The sample period is September 1990 to December 1999. The first row uses the unadjusted difference between the monthly returns to the Democracy and Dictatorship Portfolios. The second row contains the results using industry-adjusted returns, with industry adjustments done relative to the 48 industries of Fama and French [1997]. The third and fourth rows use alternative definitions of the Democracy and Dictatorship Portfolios. In the third row, firms are sorted on G and the two portfolios contain the smallest set of firms with extreme values of G such that each has at least 10 percent of the sample. This implies cutoff values of G for the Democracy Portfolio of 5, 5, 6, and 5 for September 1990, July 1993, July 1995, and February 1998, respectively. The cutoffs for the Dictatorship Portfolio are always 13. In the fourth row, the two portfolios contain the largest set of firms such that each has no more than 10 percent of the sample. The cutoff values of G for the Democracy Portfolio are 4, 4, 5, and 4 for September 1990, July 1993, July 1995, and February 1998, respectively, and they are always 14 for the Dictatorship Portfolio. In the fifth row, portfolio returns are calculated maintaining the 1990 portfolios for the entire sample period. As long as they are listed in CRSP, we neither delete nor add firms to these portfolios regardless of subsequent changes in G or changes in the IRRC sample in later editions. The sixth row shows the results of restricting the sample to firms incorporated in Delaware. In the seventh and eighth rows, the sample period is divided in half at April 30, 1995, and separate regressions are estimated for the first half and second half of the period (56 months each). The explanatory variables are *RMRF*, *SMB*, *HML*, *Momentum*, and a constant. These variables are the returns to zero-investment portfolios designed to capture market, size, book-to-market, and momentum effects, respectively. (Consult Fama and French [1993] and Carhart [1997] on the construction of these factors.) All coefficients except for the alpha are omitted in this table. Standard errors are reported in parentheses, and significance at the 5 percent and 1 percent levels is indicated by * and **, respectively.

VW abnormal returns. Most of the return differential can be attributed to within-state variation already in place in 1990, and this return differential is apparent in both halves of the sample period.

Overall, we find significant evidence that the Democracy Portfolio outperformed the Dictatorship Portfolio in the 1990s. We also find some evidence of a monotonic relationship between G and returns. It would be useful to know which subindices and provisions drive these results. We address this issue in depth within the broader analysis

of causality and omitted-variable bias in Section V, so we defer a detailed analysis until then.

III.C. Governance and the value of the firm

It is well established that state and national laws of corporate governance affect firm value. La Porta et al. [2001] show that firm value is positively associated with the rights of minority shareholders. Daines [2001] finds that firms incorporated in Delaware have higher valuations than other U. S. firms. In this section we study whether variation in firm-specific governance is associated with differences in firm value. More importantly, we analyze whether there was a change in the governance/value relationship during the 1990s. Since there is evidence of differential stock returns as a function of G, we would expect to find relative "mispricing" between 1990 and 1999 as a function of G.

Our valuation measure is Tobin's Q, which has been used for this purpose in corporate-governance studies since the work of Demsetz and Lehn [1985] and Morck, Shleifer, and Vishny [1988]. We follow Kaplan and Zingales' [1997] method for the computation of Q (details are listed in Appendix 2) and also compute the median Q in each year in each of the 48 industries classified by Fama and French [1997]. We then regress

$$Q'_{it} = a_t + b_t X_{it} + c_t W_{it} + e_{it}, \qquad (2)$$

where Q'_{it} is industry-adjusted Q (firm Q minus industry-median Q), X_{it} is a vector of governance variables (G, its components, or inclusion in one of the extreme portfolios) and W_{it} is a vector of firm characteristics. As elements of W, we follow Shin and Stulz [2000] and include the log of the book value of assets and the log of firm age as of December of year t.[18] Daines [2001] found that Q is different for Delaware and non-Delaware firms, so we also include a Delaware dummy in W. Morck and Yang [2001] show that S&P 500 inclusion has a positive impact on Q, and that this impact increased during the 1990s; thus, we also include a dummy variable for S&P 500 inclusion in W.

Using a variant of the methods of Fama and MacBeth [1973], we estimate annual cross sections of (2) with statistical significance assessed within each year (by cross-sectional standard errors) and across all years (with the time-series standard error of the mean coefficient). This method of assessing statistical significance deserves some explanation. In particular, one logical alternative would be a pooled setup with firm fixed effects and time-varying coefficients.

We rejected this alternative mainly because there are few changes over time in the Governance Index, and the inclusion of fixed effects would force identification of the G coefficient from only these changes. In effect, our chosen method imposes a structure on the fixed effects: they must be a linear function of G or its components.

Table 20.8 summarizes the results. The first column gives the results with G as the key regressor. Each row gives the coefficients and standard errors for a different year of the sample; the last row gives the average coefficient and time-series standard error of these coefficients. The coefficients on G are negative in every year and significantly negative in nine of the ten years. The largest absolute value point estimate occurs in 1999, and the second largest is in 1998. The point estimate in 1999 is economically large; a one-point increase in G, equivalent to adding a single governance provision, is associated with an 11.4 percentage point lower value for Q. If we assume that the point estimates in 1990 and 1999 are independent, then the difference between these two estimates ($11.4 - 2.2 = 9.2$) is statistically significant.

In the second column of Table 20.8, we restrict the sample to include only firms in the Democracy and Dictatorship Portfolios. We then estimate (2) using a dummy variable for the Democracy Portfolio. The results are consistent with the previous regressions on G. The point estimate for 1999 is the largest in the decade, implying that firms in the Democracy Portfolio have a Q that is 56 percentage points higher, other things being equal, than do firms in the Dictatorship Portfolio. This compares with an estimated difference of 19 percentage points in 1990. While the difference in coefficients between 1990 and 1999 is not statistically significant, it is similar to the total EW difference in abnormal returns estimated in Table 20.7.[19] There is no real pattern for the rest of the decade, however, and large standard errors toward the end of the sample period prevent any strong inference across years.

The final columns of Table 20.8 give results for a single regression using the five governance subindices: *Delay, Voting,*

Table 20.8 Q Regressions

	(1) G	(2) Democracy Portfolio	(3) Delay	(4) Protection	(5) Voting	(6) Other	(7) State
1990	−0.022**	0.186	−0.015	−0.035	0.015	−0.031	−0.004
	(0.008)	(0.127)	(0.022)	(0.018)	(0.030)	(0.026)	(0.020)
1991	−0.040**	0.302*	−0.033	−0.048	−0.012	−0.059	0.003
	(0.012)	(0.143)	(0.034)	(0.028)	(0.047)	(0.040)	(0.031)
1992	−0.036**	0.340*	−0.041	−0.039	0.021	−0.054	−0.011
	(0.010)	(0.151)	(0.027)	(0.023)	(0.038)	(0.032)	(0.025)
1993	−0.042**	0.485*	−0.023	−0.055*	0.009	−0.060	−0.062*
	(0.011)	(0.204)	(0.029)	(0.026)	(0.038)	(0.035)	(0.027)
1994	−0.031**	0.335*	−0.032	−0.012	−0.032	−0.029	−0.047*
	(0.009)	(0.161)	(0.023)	(0.020)	(0.031)	(0.028)	(0.022)
1995	−0.039**	0.435*	−0.046	−0.062*	−0.086*	0.023	−0.022
	(0.011)	(0.217)	(0.030)	(0.027)	(0.041)	(0.036)	(0.028)
1996	−0.025*	0.299	−0.029	−0.030	−0.078	0.018	−0.024
	(0.011)	(0.195)	(0.031)	(0.028)	(0.041)	(0.037)	(0.028)
1997	−0.016	0.210	−0.017	−0.007	−0.055	−0.001	−0.017
	(0.013)	(0.196)	(0.035)	(0.032)	(0.047)	(0.042)	(0.032)
1998	−0.065**	0.203	−0.023	−0.096*	−0.132	−0.058	0.012
	(0.020)	(0.404)	(0.052)	(0.049)	(0.070)	(0.066)	(0.052)
1999	−0.114**	0.564	−0.067	−0.171*	−0.294**	−0.006	−0.033
	(0.027)	(0.602)	(0.071)	(0.067)	(0.098)	(0.090)	(0.073)
Mean	−0.043**	0.336**	−0.033**	−0.056**	−0.065	−0.025*	−0.020*
	(0.009)	(0.040)	(0.005)	(0.015)	(0.030)	(0.010)	(0.007)

The first column of this table presents the coefficients on G, the Governance Index, from regressions of industry−adjusted Tobin's Q on G and control variables. The second column restricts the sample to firms in the Democracy ($G \leq 5$) and Dictatorship ($G \geq 14$) Portfolios and includes as regressors a dummy variable for the Democracy Portfolio and the controls. The third through seventh columns show the coefficients on each subindex from regressions where the explanatory variables are the subindices *Delay*, *Protection*, *Voting*, *Other*, and *State*, and the controls. We include as controls a dummy variable for incorporation in Delaware, the log of assets in the current fiscal year, the log of firm age measured in months as of December of each year, and a dummy variable for inclusion in the S&P 500 as of the end of the previous year. The coefficients on the controls and the constant are omitted from the table. The calculation of G and the subindices is described in Section II. Q is the ratio of the market value of assets to the book value of assets: the market value is calculated as the sum of the book value of assets and the market value of common stock less the book value of common stock and deferred taxes. The market value of equity is measured at the end of the current calendar year, and the accounting variables are measured in the current fiscal year. Industry adjustments are made by subtracting the industry median, where medians are calculated by matching the four-digit SIC codes from December of each year to the 48 industries designated by Fama and French [1997]. The coefficients and standard errors from each annual cross-sectional regression are reported in each row, and the time-series averages and time-series standard errors are given in the last row. * and ** indicate significance at the 5 percent and 1 percent levels, respectively.

Protection, *Other*, and *State*. The table shows that all subindices except *Voting* have average coefficients that are negative and significant (assuming independence across years). Over the full sample period, *Delay* and *Protection* have the most consistent impact, while the largest absolute coefficients are for *Voting* at the end of the sample period. The subindices are highly collinear, however, and the resulting large standard errors and covariances make it difficult to draw strong conclusions. For example, even in 1999 we cannot reject the null hypothesis that the coefficient on *Voting* is equal to the coefficient on *Delay*.

Overall, the results for returns and prices tell a consistent story. Firms with the weakest shareholder rights (high values of G) significantly underperformed firms with the strongest shareholder rights (low values of G) during the 1990s. Over the course of the

1990s, these differences have been at least partially reflected in prices. While high-G firms already sold at a significant discount in 1990, this discount became much larger by 1999.

III.D. Governance and operating performance

Table 20.9 shows the results of annual regressions for three operational measures on G (or a Democracy dummy). The three operational measures are the net profit margin (income divided by sales), the return on equity (income divided by book equity), and one-year sales growth. All of these measures are industry-adjusted by subtracting the median for this measure in the corresponding Fama-French [1997] industry. This adjustment uses all available Compustat firms. To reduce the influence of large outliers—a common occurrence for all of these measures—we estimate median (least-absolute-deviation) regressions in

Table 20.9 Operating Performance

	(1) Net profit margin	(2)	(3) Return on equity	(4)	(5) Sales growth	(6)
	G	Democracy Portfolio	G	Democracy Portfolio	G	Democracy Portfolio
1991	−0.70	10.61	−1.19*	13.54	−2.30	−3.52
	(0.39)	(7.12)	(0.60)	(11.30)	(1.38)	(17.83)
1992	−0.52	9.45	0.42	2.54	−1.43	0.10
	(0.58)	(10.43)	(0.61)	(9.21)	(1.06)	(11.52)
1993	−0.76	7.77	−0.34	2.51	−3.35**	18.55
	(0.48)	(9.98)	(0.79)	(10.98)	(1.17)	(17.71)
1994	−0.83	10.94	−1.07	2.69	−2.71*	12.58
	(0.48)	(6.59)	(0.61)	(10.36)	(1.10)	(22.81)
1995	−0.72	7.56	−1.39	14.77	−0.89	7.91
	(0.67)	(8.30)	(0.75)	(9.88)	(1.70)	(19.67)
1996	−0.43	−2.17	0.90	2.30	−2.44	14.84
	(0.40)	(7.22)	(0.65)	(12.09)	(1.39)	(19.36)
1997	0.21	−9.61	0.66	−17.54	0.01	−4.28
	(0.55)	(9.99)	(0.81)	(9.83)	(1.64)	(26.61)
1998	−0.73	−3.99	−1.28	13.62	−1.45	−15.65
	(0.63)	(7.15)	(1.01)	(15.10)	(1.50)	(23.36)
1999	−1.27*	4.59	0.93	−15.53	−0.52	15.38
	(0.58)	(11.58)	(0.85)	(10.38)	(1.92)	(26.10)
Mean	−0.64**	3.91	−0.26	1.59	−1.68**	5.10
	(0.13)	(2.46)	(0.33)	(3.98)	(0.37)	(3.84)

The first, third, and fifth columns of this table give the results of annual median (least absolute deviation) regressions for net profit margin, return on equity, and sales growth on the Governance Index, G, measured in the previous year, and the book-to-market ratio, BM. The second, fourth, and sixth columns restrict the sample to firms in the Democracy ($G \leq 5$) and Dictatorship ($G \geq 14$) portfolios and include as regressors a dummy variable for the Democracy Portfolio and BM. The coefficients on BM and the constant are omitted from the table. The calculation of G is described in Section II. Net profit margin is the ratio of income before extraordinary items available for common equity to sales; return on equity is the ratio of income before extraordinary items available for common equity to the sum of the book value of common equity and deferred taxes; BM is the log of the ratio of book value (the sum of book common equity and deferred taxes) in the previous fiscal year to size at the close of the previous calendar year. Each dependent variable is net of the industry median, which is calculated by matching the four-digit SIC codes of all firms in the CRSP-Compustat merged database in December of each year to the 48 industries designated by Fama and French [1997]. The coefficients and standard errors from each annual cross-sectional regression are reported in each row, and the time-series averages and time-series standard errors are given in the last row. Significance at the 5 percent and 1 percent levels is indicated by * and **, respectively. All coefficients and standard errors are multiplied by 1000.

each case. While our sample does not include a natural experiment to identify G as the cause of operational differences, we attempt to control for "expected" cross-sectional differences by using the log book-to-market ratio (BM) as an additional explanatory variable.

The odd-numbered columns give the results when G is the key regressor. We find that the average coefficient on G is negative and significant for both the net-profit-margin and sales-growth regressions, and is negative but not significant for the return-on-equity regressions. The even-numbered columns give the results for the subsample of firms from the extreme deciles, with a dummy variable for the Democracy Portfolio as the key regressor. For all three operating measures, the average coefficient on this dummy variable was positive but insignificant. Thus, these results are consistent with the evidence for the full sample but not significant on their own. In untabulated results, we also regressed these same measures on the five subindices. The results show no clear pattern of differential influence for any particular subindex, with most coefficients having the same sign as G. Overall, we find some significant evidence that more democratic firms have better operating performance and no evidence that they do not.

IV. GOVERNANCE: THREE HYPOTHESES

Section III established an empirical relationship of G with returns, firm value, and operating performance. Since firms did not adopt governance provisions randomly, this evidence does not itself imply a causal role by governance provisions. Indeed, there are several plausible explanations for our results:

HYPOTHESIS I. Governance provisions cause higher agency costs. These higher costs were underestimated by investors in 1990.

HYPOTHESIS II. Governance provisions do not cause higher agency costs, but rather were put in place by 1980s managers who forecasted poor performance for their firms in the 1990s.

HYPOTHESIS III. Governance provisions do not cause higher agency costs, but their presence is correlated with other characteristics that earned abnormal returns in the 1990s.

Most explanations of the Section III results can be fit within these three hypotheses. Under Hypothesis I, a reduction in shareholder rights causes an unexpectedly large increase in agency costs through some combination of inefficient investment, reduced operational efficiency, or self-dealing. If shareholders find it difficult or costly to replace managers, then managers may be more willing and able to extract private benefits. This is the standard justification for takeover threats as the strongest form of managerial discipline [Jensen 1986]. For Hypothesis I to be correct, these additional agency costs must have been underestimated in 1990.

Under Hypothesis II, governance does not affect performance, but there must be a perception that governance provisions are protective for management. In this case, the stock in these companies would have been relatively overvalued in 1990, even though objective measures (e.g., Q regressions) would suggest that it was undervalued relative to observable characteristics. When the poor operating performance occurs, the market is surprised, but the managers are not. The protective provisions then supply a shield, real or imagined, for managerial jobs and compensation.

Under Hypothesis III, all of the results in the previous section would be driven by omitted-variable bias. Since governance provisions were certainly not adopted randomly, it is plausible that differences in industry, S&P 500 inclusion, institutional ownership, or other firm characteristics could be correlated both with G and with abnormal returns. Under this hypothesis, governance provisions could be completely innocuous, with no influence either on managerial power or on agency costs.

Ideally, we would distinguish among these three hypotheses by using random variation in some characteristic that was causal for G. Unfortunately, we have not been able to identify such an instrument. One candidate would be the subset of state laws, with the *State* subindex as a proxy. Though in some states these laws were passed at the urging of large corporations, it seems reasonable to assume that their passage was exogenous to most firms. But the *State* subindex has three flaws as an instrument. First, firms can choose to reincorporate into different states; enough firms have done so that exposure to state laws is not truly exogenous [Subramanian 2001]. Second, many firms have opted out of the protections of some of the most stringent of these laws, so that a firm's state of incorporation is only a noisy measure for its actual legal exposure. Third, as shown in Table 20.3, the *State* subindex is not positively or consistently correlated with the other components of *G*. Other potential instruments have different problems. For example, if takeover protections were adopted during industry-specific takeover waves, then we might be able to use industry as an instrument for *G*. Unfortunately, this would render it impossible to distinguish between *G* or industry as the cause of poor returns in the 1990s.

In Section V our tests consist of a search for evidence supportive of each hypothesis, while acknowledging the impossibility of a perfect test to distinguish among them. First, if Hypothesis I is correct, then we should observe some "unexpected" differences in agency costs across firms. We discuss several previous studies on this topic and look for such differences in our sample by analyzing capital expenditure and acquisition behavior. Second, for Hypothesis II we analyze insider-trading activity as a function of *G*. If governance provisions were put in place by prescient managers, these same managers might be net sellers of the stock in their firms. Finally, for Hypothesis III we test whether a large set of observable firm characteristics can explain the empirical relationship between returns and *G*.

V. GOVERNANCE: TESTS

In this section we examine the evidence for each of the hypotheses described in

Section IV. Subsection V.A covers Hypothesis I, subsection V.B covers Hypothesis II, and subsection V.C covers Hypothesis III. Subsection V.D summarizes and discusses the evidence.

V.A. Evidence on Hypothesis I

Increased agency costs at high-*G* firms can directly affect firm performance in several ways. In the specific case of state takeover laws, where causality is easier to establish, researchers have found evidence of increased agency costs through a variety of mechanisms. Borokhovich, Brunarski, and Parrino [1997] show that compensation rises for CEOs of firms adopting takeover defenses. Bertrand and Mullainathan [1999a, 1999b, 2000] find a similar result for CEOs and other employees in firms newly covered by state takeover laws. They also find that these laws cause a decrease in plant-level efficiency, measured either by total factor productivity or return on capital. Garvey and Hanka [1999] show that state takeover laws led to changes in leverage consistent with increased corporate slack. These studies provide the cleanest evidence in support of Hypothesis I, but, of course, do not make use of the full variation embodied in the *G* index. We supplement these findings by examining the empirical relationship of *G* with two other possible sources of agency costs: capital expenditure and acquisition behavior.

A substantial literature, dating back at least to Baumol [1959], Marris [1964], and Williamson [1964], holds that managers may undertake inefficient projects in order to extract private benefits. This problem is particularly severe when managers are entrenched and can resist hostile takeovers [Jensen and Ruback 1983; Shleifer and Vishny 1989]. Under this view, if capital expenditure increases following the adoption of new takeover defenses, this increase would be a net negative for firm value.[20]

To examine the empirical relationship between capital expenditure and governance, we estimate annual median regressions for capital expenditure (CAPEX), scaled by either sales or assets, and net of the industry median. To control for the different investment opportunities available at value and growth firms, we include the log of the book-to-market ratio (BM) as a control variable in all specifications. Table 20.10 summarizes the results, with BM coefficients omitted. Columns (1) and (3) give results for the full sample, with G as the key regressor; columns (2) and (4) give results for the sample restricted to firms in the Democracy and Dictatorship Portfolios, with a Democracy dummy as the key regressor. The average coefficient on G is positive and

significant in both sets of regressions. Consistent with these results, we find that the average coefficient on the Democracy dummy is negative and significant in both sets of regressions. We conclude that, other things equal, high-G firms have higher CAPEX than do low-G firms.

Another outlet for capital expenditure is for firms to acquire other firms. Some of the strongest evidence for the importance of agency costs comes from the negative returns to acquirer stocks after a bid is

Table 20.10 Capital expenditure

	(1) CAPEX/Assets	(2)	(3) CAPEX/Sales	(4)
	G	Democracy Portfolio	G	Democracy Portfolio
1991	1.32**	−13.02**	0.70*	−9.28
	(0.27)	(4.28)	(0.32)	(4.96)
1992	0.42	−7.03	0.54	−7.23
	(0.35)	(4.86)	(0.35)	(6.01)
1993	0.81*	−6.06	0.09	−1.68
	(0.37)	(4.48)	(0.34)	(4.98)
1994	0.51	−7.84	−0.07	−4.82
	(0.32)	(5.21)	(0.37)	(4.76)
1995	0.35	−3.40	0.32	−9.80
	(0.39)	(6.83)	(0.39)	(5.90)
1996	0.75	−6.90	0.31	−3.26
	(0.39)	(5.55)	(0.33)	(6.36)
1997	0.74*	−4.23	0.70	−8.05
	(0.34)	(3.50)	(0.40)	(5.71)
1998	0.80*	−10.57	0.37	−6.43
	(0.37)	(6.75)	(0.35)	(5.63)
1999	−0.15	3.12	−0.32	3.49
	(0.39)	(4.20)	(0.38)	(5.52)
Mean	0.62**	−6.21**	0.30*	−5.23**
	(0.13)	(1.53)	(0.11)	(1.41)

The first and third columns of this table present the results of annual median (least absolute deviation) regressions of CAPEX/Assets and CAPEX/Sales on the Governance Index, G, measured in the previous year, and BM. The second and fourth columns restrict the sample to firms in the Democracy (G ≤ 5) and Dictatorship (G ≥ 14) portfolios and include as regressors a dummy variable for the Democracy portfolio and BM. The coefficients of BM and the constant are omitted from the table. The calculation of G is described in Section II. CAPEX is capital expenditures, and BM is the log of the ratio of book value (the sum of book common equity and deferred taxes) in the previous fiscal year to size at the close of the previous calendar year. Both dependent variables are net of the industry median, which is calculated by matching the four-digit SIC codes of all firms in the CRSP-Compustat merged database in December of each year to the 48 industries designated by Fama and French [1997]. The coefficients and standard errors from each annual cross-sectional regression are reported in each row, and the time-series averages and time-series standard errors are given in the last row. Significance at the 5 percent and 1 percent levels is indicated by * and **, respectively. All coefficients and standard errors are multiplied by 1000.

announced. Considerable evidence shows that these negative returns are correlated with other agency problems, including low managerial ownership [Lewellen, Loderer, and Rosenfeld 1985], high free-cash flow [Lang, Stulz, and Walkling 1991], and diversifying transactions [Morck, Shleifer, and Vishny 1990]. In addition to negative announcement returns, there is also long-run evidence of negative abnormal performance by acquirer firms [Loughran and Vijh 1997; Rau and Vermaelen 1998].[21] Taken together, these studies suggest acquisitions as another pathway through which governance affects performance.

To analyze the relation between acquisition activity and G, we use the SDC database to identify all transactions in which a sample firm acted as either the acquirer or the seller during the sample period. From January 1991 through December 1999, there are 12,694 acquisitions made by sample firms; SDC gives the acquisition price for just under half of these. For each firm, we count the number of acquisitions ("Acquisition Count"). We also calculate the sum of the price of all acquisitions in each calendar year and divide this sum by the firm's average market capitalization for the first day and last day of the year ("Acquisition Ratio").

Table 20.11 summarizes the results of annual regressions for both Acquisition Count and the Acquisition Ratio in year t on G (or a Democracy dummy), the log of size, the log of the book-to-market ratio, and 48 industry dummies, all measured at year-end $t - 1$. Coefficients on all control variables are omitted from the table. Since many firms make no acquisitions in a year, the dependent variables are effectively left-censored at zero. To account for this censoring, we estimate Poisson regressions for Acquisition Count and Tobit regressions for the Acquisition Ratio. Columns (1) and (3) give results for the full sample, with G as the key regressor; columns (2) and (4) give results for the sample restricted to firms in the Democracy and Dictatorship Portfolios, with a Democracy dummy as the key regressor. For both sets of regressions, the coefficients on G are positive in every

year, and the average coefficient on G is positive and significant. Consistent with this result, the average coefficient on the Democracy dummy is negative for both sets of regressions and is significant for Acquisition Count.

One interpretation of these results is that high-G firms engaged in an unexpectedly large amount of inefficient investment during the 1990s. This interpretation is consistent with contemporaneous unexpected differences in profitability, stock returns, and firm value. This inefficient investment does not necessarily mean that firms are attempting to maximize their size in a form of empire building. Indeed, empire building would be inconsistent with the negative relationship between sales growth and G found in Table 20.9. Instead, managers may be attempting to stave off "empire collapse" with high expenditure and acquisition activity. In that case, the results of this section are consistent with the evidence of Table 20.9.

V.B. Evidence on Hypothesis II

It is well established that insider trading can forecast returns. Firms whose shares have been intensively sold (bought) by insiders tend to underperform (overperform) benchmarks in subsequent periods.[22] If some 1980s insiders forecasted poor performance for their firms, we might expect them to have looked for ways to keep the shareholders from firing them, either through voting or takeovers. In this case, weak shareholder rights would be a symptom of insiders' superior information, but would not necessarily be the cause of the poor performance in the subsequent decade.

To study this possibility, we use data collected by Thomson Financial from the required SEC insider-trading filings. For each firm in our sample, we sum all (split-adjusted) open-market transactions for all insiders in each year, with purchases entering positively and sales entering negatively. We then normalize this sum by shares outstanding at the beginning of the year to

Table 20.11 Acquisitions

	(1) (2) Acquisition count (Poisson regressions)		(3) (4) Acquisition ratio (Tobit regressions)	
	G	Democracy Portfolio	G	Democracy Portfolio
1991	1.58	−50.81	0.51	0.14
	(1.46)	(26.12)	(0.47)	(5.03)
1992	1.64	−31.39	0.10	7.91
	(1.44)	(24.61)	(0.50)	(6.42)
1993	1.75	−47.67	0.70	−6.31
	(1.42)	24.51	(0.56)	(6.85)
1994	4.09**	−13.10	0.75	1.82
	(1.27)	(21.02)	(0.48)	(4.14)
1995	2.57*	−60.92**	0.41	−2.95
	(1.15)	(17.85)	(0.44)	(4.42)
1996	2.69*	−66.06**	1.33*	−24.22**
	(1.14)	(20.48)	(0.60)	(9.41)
1997	2.34*	−63.81**	0.99*	−9.24
	(1.12)	(19.03)	(0.51)	(6.78)
1998	2.42*	−52.03**	1.47	−11.11
	(1.09)	(17.67)	(0.76)	(8.51)
1999	0.52	−47.64**	0.84	−20.87*
	(1.01)	(17.27)	(0.74)	(9.68)
Mean	2.18**	−48.16**	0.79**	−7.21
	(0.33)	(5.60)	(0.14)	(3.49)

The first column of this table presents annual Tobit regressions of the *Acquisition ratio* on the Governance Index, *G*, measured in the previous year, *SIZE*, *BM*, and industry dummy variables. The third column presents annual Poisson regressions of *Acquisition count* on the same explanatory variables. In the second and fourth columns, we restrict the sample to firms in the Democracy ($G \leq 5$) and Dictatorship ($G \geq 14$) Portfolios, and we include as a regressor a dummy variable that equals 1 when the firm is in the Democracy Portfolio and 0 otherwise. The coefficients on *SIZE*, *BM*, and the industry dummy variables are omitted from the table. The calculation of *G* is described in Section II. *Acquisition ratio* is defined as the sum of the value of all corporate acquisitions during a calendar year scaled by the average of market value at the beginning and end of the year. *Acquisition count* is defined as the number of acquisitions during a calendar year. The data on acquisitions are from the SDC database. *SIZE* is the log of market capitalization at the end of the previous calendar year in millions of dollars, and *BM* is the log of the ratio of book value (the sum of book common equity and deferred taxes) in the previous fiscal year to size at the close of the previous calendar year. Industry dummy variables are created by matching the four-digit SIC codes of all firms in the CRSP-Compustat merged database in December of each year to the 48 industries designated by Fama and French [1997]. The coefficients and standard errors from each annual cross-sectional regression are reported in each row, and the time-series averages and time-series standard errors are given in the last row. Significance at the 5 percent and 1 percent levels is indicated by * and **, respectively. All coefficients and standard errors are multiplied by 100.

arrive at a "Net Purchases" measure for each firm in each year. If insiders put new provisions in place when they forecast poor performance, then we would expect Net Purchases to be negatively correlated with *G*.

We employ two regression specifications. First, we estimate OLS regressions of Net Purchases on *G* (or a Democracy dummy), *BM*, and log of size. For some firm-years, the Net Purchase measure is dominated by one large transaction. While large transactions might have information content, they might also reflect liquidity or rebalancing needs. In an OLS regression, firms with large outliers will dominate.

Thus, we also estimate ordered logit regressions on the same OLS regressors, in which the dependent variable is equal to one if Net Purchases is positive, zero if Net Purchases is zero, and negative one if Net Purchases is negative.

Table 20.12 summarizes the results of these regressions. Columns (1) and (3) give results for the full sample, with G as the key regressor; columns (2) and (4) give results for the sample restricted to firms in the Democracy and Dictatorship Portfolios with

a Democracy dummy as the key regressor. Coefficients on all control variables are omitted from the table. We find no significant relationships between governance and insider trading. Two of four sets of regressions have positive average coefficients, two have negative average coefficients, and none of these average coefficients are significant. In untabulated results we also estimated median regressions, replicated all of the above results using all transactions (the main difference is the inclusion of

Table 20.12 Insider Trading

	(1) OLS	(2)	(3) Ordered logit	(4)
	G	Democracy Portfolio	G	Democracy Portfolio
1991	0.07*	−0.14	−8.85	−345.18
	(0.04)	(0.53)	(21.34)	(295.15)
1992	0.10	−1.47	−66.92**	499.93
	(0.07)	(1.50)	(21.70)	(310.53)
1993	0.10	−0.23	−32.40	797.17*
	(0.07)	0.51	(21.41)	(326.87)
1994	0.07	−0.61	−28.09	323.07
	(0.04)	(1.23)	(20.58)	(290.11)
1995	0.04	−0.17	−4.66	−153.33
	(0.02)	(0.20)	(22.00)	(308.90)
1996	0.15	−0.62	12.01	−93.95
	(0.14)	(1.05)	(21.67)	(321.18)
1997	−0.01	0.89	−46.08	781.42*
	(0.10)	(0.66)	(24.33)	(369.78)
1998	−0.12	2.41	−1.88	146.49
	(0.20)	(3.17)	(24.31)	(342.22)
1999	0.36	−1.36	4.41	−117.36
	(0.48)	(2.91)	(21.09)	(323.85)
Mean	0.09	−0.15	−19.16	204.25
	(0.04)	(0.40)	(8.66)	(140.02)

The first and third columns of this table present annual OLS and ordered logit regressions of *Net insider purchases* on G measured in the previous year, *SIZE, BM,* and a constant. In the second and fourth columns, we restrict the sample to firms in the Democracy ($G \leq 5$) and Dictatorship ($G \geq 14$) Portfolios and we include as a regressor a dummy variable that equals 1 when the firm is in the Democracy Portfolio and 0 otherwise. The coefficients on *SIZE, BM,* and the constant are omitted from the table. The calculation of G is described in Section II. *Net insider purchases* is the sum of split-adjusted open market purchases less split-adjusted open market sales during a year scaled by shares outstanding at the end of the previous calendar year. The ordered logit regressions use a dependent variable that equals 1 if *Net insider purchases* is positive, 0 if it is zero, and −1 if it is negative. The data on insider sales are from the Thomson database. *SIZE* is the log of market capitalization in millions of dollars measured at the end of the previous calendar year, and *BM* is the log of the ratio of book value (the sum of book common equity and deferred taxes) in the previous fiscal year to size at the close of the previous calendar year. The coefficients and standard errors from each annual cross sectional regression are reported in each row, and the time-series averages and time-series standard errors are given in the last row. Significance at the 5 percent and 1 percent levels is indicated by * and **, respectively. All coefficients and standard errors are multiplied by 1000.

option-exercise transactions), and estimated long-horizon regressions using all years of data for each firm. In none of these cases did we find a robust relationship between governance and insider trading. Overall, we find no support for Hypothesis II in the insider-trading data.

V.C. Evidence on Hypothesis III

What other factors might be driving the return difference between the Democracy and Dictatorship Portfolios? We saw in Table II that G is correlated with several firm characteristics, including S&P 500 membership, institutional ownership, trading volume, and past sales growth. If returns to stocks with these characteristics differed in the 1990s in a way not captured by the model in equation (1), then a type of omitted variable bias may drive the abnormal-return results. In this section we explore this possibility using a cross-sectional regression approach. In addition to providing evidence on Hypothesis III, this method also supplements the analysis of subsection III.B by allowing a separate regressor for each component of G.

For each month in the sample period, September 1990 to December 1999, we estimate

$$r_{it} = a_t + b_t X_{it} + c_t Z_{it} + e_{it} \qquad (3)$$

where, for firm i in month t, r_{it} are the returns (either raw or industry-adjusted), X_{it} is a vector of governance variables (either G, its components, or inclusion in one of the extreme portfolios), and Z_{it} is a vector of firm characteristics. As elements of Z, we include the full set of regressors used by Brennan, Chordia, and Subrahmanyam [1998], plus five-year sales growth, S&P 500 inclusion, and institutional ownership.[23] Variable definitions are given in Appendix 2.

We estimate (3) separately for each month and then calculate the mean and time-series standard deviation of the 112 monthly estimates of the coefficients. Table 20.13 summarizes the results. The first two columns give the results, raw

and industry-adjusted, for the full sample of firms in each month with G as the key independent variable. In both regressions the average coefficient on G is negative but not significant. The point estimates are not small. For example, the point estimate for the coefficient on G in column (3) implies a lower return of approximately four bp per month (= 48 bp per year) for each additional point of G, but it would require estimates nearly twice as large before statistical significance would be reached.

The next two columns give the results when the sample is restricted to stocks in either the Democracy ($G \leq 5$) or Dictatorship ($G \geq 14$) Portfolios. In the first column the dependent variable is the raw monthly return for each stock. In the second column the dependent variable is the industry-adjusted return for each stock, where industry adjustments are relative to the Fama and French [1997] 48 industries. The key independent variable in these regressions is the Democracy dummy, set equal to one if the stock is in the Democracy Portfolio and zero if the stock is in the Dictatorship Portfolio. For both the raw and industry-adjusted returns, the coefficient on this dummy variable is positive and significant at the 1 percent level. The average point estimate can be interpreted as a monthly abnormal return. These point estimates, 76 bp per month raw and 63 bp per month industry-adjusted, are similar to those found in the factor models, and provide a further robustness check to the benchmark result. Here, industry adjustments explain about one-sixth of the raw result. In the factor-model results of Table 20.7, the industry adjustment explained about one-third of the raw result.

Columns (5) and (6) of Table 20.13 give the results for the full sample of firms when the five subindices are used as the components of X. In principle, these regressions could help us distinguish between Hypotheses I and III. If governance provisions cause poor performance, then we might expect certain provisions to play a stronger role. In the absence of such a finding, we should wonder whether the results are driven by some other characteristic.

Table 20.13 Fama-MacBeth Return Regressions

	(1) Raw	(2) Industry-adjusted	(3) Raw	(4) Industry-adjusted	(5) Raw	(6) Industry-adjusted
G	−0.04 (0.04)	−0.02 (0.03)				
Democracy Portfolio			0.76* (0.32)	0.63* (0.26)		
Delay					−0.03 (0.10)	0.02 (0.07)
Protection					−0.07 (0.08)	−0.01 (0.06)
Voting					−0.08 (0.13)	−0.08 (0.10)
Other					0.01 (0.08)	−0.04 (0.07)
State					0.02 (0.08)	−0.04 (0.06)
NASDUM	−0.83 (6.94)	−0.42 (5.26)	−8.23 (6.45)	−10.36 (5.94)	−2.60 (6.39)	−0.29 (4.98)
SP500	−0.19 (0.49)	−0.20 (0.42)	−0.42 (0.49)	−0.21 (0.41)	−0.19 (0.45)	−0.24 (0.40)
BM	0.04 (0.19)	0.14 (0.12)	0.06 (0.38)	0.11 (0.29)	0.06 (0.20)	0.15 (0.11)
SIZE	0.17 (0.27)	0.22 (0.16)	0.47 (0.38)	0.02 (0.32)	0.19 (0.27)	0.24 (0.17)
PRICE	0.26 (0.26)	0.20 (0.20)	0.28 (0.31)	0.44 (0.31)	0.20 (0.28)	0.16 (0.22)
IO	0.61 (0.47)	0.10 (0.33)	0.78 (0.67)	−0.16 (0.60)	0.59 (0.44)	0.14 (0.33)
NYDVOL	−0.11 (0.29)	−0.21 (0.18)	−0.49 (0.36)	−0.03 (0.31)	−0.13 (0.28)	−0.21 (0.18)
NADVOL	0.01 (0.43)	−0.13 (0.29)	−0.09 (0.41)	0.48 (0.39)	0.06 (0.43)	−0.15 (0.29)
YLD	10.85 (10.54)	10.94 (7.25)	15.74 (14.62)	9.23 (11.56)	6.21 (11.63)	8.76 (7.70)
RET2–3	−0.48 (1.40)	−0.93 (1.04)	−2.04 (2.33)	−1.82 (1.73)	−0.57 (1.43)	−1.03 (1.07)
RET4–6	−0.68 (1.33)	−0.48 (0.92)	−2.21 (1.89)	−1.12 (1.36)	−0.58 (1.33)	−0.55 (0.93)
RET7–12	2.42* (1.00)	0.89 (0.65)	0.12 (1.35)	−1.67 (1.03)	2.69** (0.99)	1.06 (0.65)
SGROWTH	−0.00 (0.26)	0.03 (0.18)	0.75 (0.47)	0.27 (0.40)	−0.01 (0.25)	0.02 (0.18)
Constant	−0.53 (2.55)	−0.18 (1.71)	1.17 (3.43)	−1.86 (2.99)	0.03 (2.39)	−0.16 (1.69)

This table presents the average coefficients and time-series standard errors for 112 cross-sectional regressions for each month from September 1990 to December 1999. The dependent variable is the stock return for month t. The results are presented using both raw and industry-adjusted returns, with industry adjustments done using the 48 industries of Fama and French [1997]. The first and second columns include all firms with data for all right-hand side variables and use G, the Governance index, as an independent variable. In the third and fourth columns, the sample is restricted to firms in either the Democracy ($G \leq 5$) or Dictatorship ($G \geq 14$) Portfolios, and we use the independent variable, *Democracy Portfolio*, a dummy variable that equals 1 when the firm is in the Democracy Portfolio and 0 otherwise. In the fifth and sixth columns, we again include all firms with data for each explanatory variable and use the subindices, *Delay, Protection, Voting, Other*, and *State* as regressors. The calculation of G and the subindices is described in Section II. Definitions for all other explanatory variables are provided in Appendix 2. All regressions are estimated with weighted least squares where all variables are weighted by market value at the end of month $t − 1$. Significance at the 5 percent and 1 percent levels is indicated by* and **, respectively.

For example, some legal scholars argue that the *Delay* provisions are the only defenses with deterrent value [Coates 2000; Daines and Klausner 2001]. If managers also believe this, then the *Delay* subindex should also be the most important driver of the results.

Unfortunately, large standard errors, due in part to the substantial multicollinearity between the regressors, makes it difficult to construct a powerful test. None of the subindex coefficients are statistically significant in either specification, but many of the point estimates are economically large. In the end, we cannot precisely measure the relative importance of *Delay* or any other subindex. This is similar to the problem that occurred in the Q regressions of Table 20.8. For example, in both Tables 20.8 and 20.13 the coefficients on *Voting* suggest potentially enormous economic significance, but large standard errors prevent any meaningful statistical inference.

In untabulated tests, we also included all 28 provisions from Table 20.1 as separate regressors in (3). Regressing raw returns on these 28 provisions plus the same controls as in Table 20.13, we find that 16 of the coefficients are negative, and only one (Unequal Voting) is significant. (With this many regressors, we would expect one to appear "significant" just by chance.) Results for industry-adjusted returns are similar. These results highlight and magnify the lack of power in the subindex regressions. Indeed, many of the point estimates imply return effects above 20 basis points per month (2.4 percent per year), but are still far from being statistically significant. This result also suggests that the Democracy-minus-Dictatorship return differences are not driven by the presence or absence of any one provision.

V.D. Discussion

The evidence in subsections V.A, V.B, and V.C must be interpreted with caution. Since this is an experiment without random assignment, no analysis of causality can be conclusive. The main problem is the possibility that some unobserved characteristic is correlated with G and is also the main cause of abnormal returns. This type of omitted-variable bias could be something prosaic, such as imperfect industry adjustments or model misspecification, or something more difficult to quantify, such as a partially unobservable or immeasurable "corporate culture." Under the latter explanation, management behavior would be constrained by cultural norms within the firm, and democracy and dictatorship would be a persistent feature of a corporate culture; G would be a symptom, but not a cause, of this culture. In this case, all the results of the paper could be explained if investors mispriced culture in 1990, just as they appear to have mispriced its proxy, G. The policy impact of reducing G would be nonexistent unless it affected the culture of managerial power that was the true driver of poor performance.

In addition to the three hypotheses considered above, other explanations fall into the general class of "Type I" error. For example, one could argue that investors in 1990 had rational expectations about the expected costs and benefits of takeover defenses, where the expected costs are more severe agency problems and the expected benefits are higher takeover premiums. Then, when the hostile takeover market largely evaporated in the early 1990s—perhaps because of macroeconomic conditions unrelated to takeover defenses—Dictatorship firms were left with the costs but none of the benefits of their defenses. Over the subsequent decade, the expected takeover premiums eroded as investors gradually learned about the weak takeover market. Simple calculations suggest that this explanation cannot be that important. Suppose that in 1990 the expected takeover probability for Dictatorship firms was 30 percent, and the expected takeover premium conditional on takeover was also 30 percent. Further suppose that both of these numbers were zero for Democracy firms. Then, the unconditional expected takeover premium for Dictatorship firms would have been only 9 percent, which is approximately the relative underperformance of these firms for only a single year.

In sum, we find some evidence in support of Hypothesis I and no evidence in support of Hypothesis II. For Hypothesis III we find that industry classification can explain somewhere between one-sixth and one-third of the benchmark abnormal returns, but we do not find any other observable characteristic that explains the remaining abnormal return. The subindex regressions, which might be helpful in distinguishing between Hypotheses I and III, are not powerful enough for strong inference. We conclude that the remaining performance differences, which are economically large, were either directly caused by governance provisions (Hypothesis I), or were related to unobservable or difficult-to-measure characteristics correlated with governance provisions (Hypothesis III).

What do these hypotheses imply about abnormal returns in the future? None suggests any obvious pattern for the relationship between G and returns. Under Hypothesis I, if we interpret our test as a long-run event study, then there is no reason to expect any relationship once the market has fully priced the underlying "event" of corporate governance. The fact that this price adjustment is taking such a long time does not seem so surprising in light of the lengthy intervals necessary for much more tangible information to be incorporated into prices.[24] Thus, to the extent that end-of-sample price adjustment is incomplete, complete, or has overreacted, the future relationship between G and returns could be negative, zero, or positive. Under Hypothesis II there is a similar dependence on whether past insider information has been fully incorporated into prices. Under Hypothesis III future return differences would be driven by the relevant omitted characteristic; clearly, this hypothesis yields no clear prediction.

VI. CONCLUSION

The power-sharing relationship between investors and managers is defined by the rules of corporate governance. Beginning in the late 1980s, there is significant and stable variation in these rules across different firms. Using 24 distinct corporate-governance provisions for a sample of about 1500 firms per year during the 1990s, we build a Governance Index, denoted as G, as a proxy for the balance of power between managers and shareholders in each firm. We then analyze the empirical relationship of this index with corporate performance.

We find that corporate governance is strongly correlated with stock returns during the 1990s. An investment strategy that purchased shares in the lowest-G firms ("Democracy" firms with strong shareholder rights), and sold shares in the highest-G firms ("Dictatorship" firms with weak shareholder rights), earned abnormal returns of 8.5 percent per year. At the beginning of the sample, there is already a significant relationship between valuation and governance: each one-point increase in G is associated with a decrease in Tobin's Q of 2.2 percentage points. By the end of the decade, this difference has increased significantly, with a one-point increase in G associated with a decrease in Tobin's Q of 11.4 percentage points. The results for both stock returns and firm value are economically large and are robust to many controls and other firm characteristics.

We consider several explanations for the results, but the data do not allow strong conclusions about causality. There is some evidence, both in our sample and from other authors, that weak shareholder rights caused poor performance in the 1990s. It is also possible that the results are driven by some unobservable firm characteristic. These multiple causal explanations have starkly different policy implications and stand as a challenge for future research. The empirical evidence of this paper establishes the high stakes of this challenge. If an 11.4 percentage point difference in firm value were even partially "caused" by each additional governance provision, then the long-run benefits of eliminating multiple provisions would be enormous.

APPENDIX 1: CORPORATE-GOVERNANCE PROVISIONS

This appendix describes the provisions listed in Table 20.1 and used as components of the Governance Index. The shorthand title of each provision, as used in the text of the paper, is given in boldface. These descriptions are given in alphabetical order and are similar to Rosenbaum [1998]. For a few provisions we discuss their impact on shareholder rights or the logic behind their categorization in Table 20.1.

Antigreenmail. Greenmail refers to a transaction between a large shareholder and a company in which the shareholder agrees to sell his stock back to the company, usually at a premium, in exchange for the promise not to seek control of the company for a specified period of time. Antigreenmail provisions prevent such arrangements unless the same repurchase offer is made to all shareholders or approved by a shareholder vote. Such provisions are thought to discourage accumulation of large blocks of stock because one source of exit for the stake is closed, but the net effect on shareholder wealth is unclear [Shleifer and Vishny 1986; Eckbo 1990]. Five states have specific **Antigreenmail laws**, and two other states have "recapture of profits" laws, which enable firms to recapture raiders' profits earned in the secondary market. We consider recapture of profits laws to be a version of Antigreenmail laws (albeit a stronger one). The presence of firm-level Antigreenmail provisions is positively correlated with 18 out of the other 21 firm-level provisions, is significantly positive in 8 of these cases, and is not significantly negative for any of them. Furthermore, states with Antigreenmail laws tend to pass them in conjunction with laws more clearly designed to prevent take-overs [Pinnell 2000]. Since it seems likely that most firms and states perceive Antigreenmail as a takeover "defense," we treat Antigreenmail like the other defenses and code it as a decrease in shareholder rights.

Blank Check preferred stock is stock over which the board of directors has broad authority to determine voting, dividend, conversion, and other rights. While it can be used to enable a company to meet changing financial needs, its most important use is to implement poison pills or to prevent takeover by placing this stock with friendly investors. Because of this role, blank check preferred stock is a crucial part of a "delay" strategy. Companies that have this type of preferred stock but require shareholder approval before it can be used as a takeover defense are *not* coded as having this provision in our data.

Business Combination laws impose a moratorium on certain kinds of transactions (e.g., asset sales, mergers) between a large shareholder and the firm, unless the transaction is approved by the Board of Directors. Depending on the State, this moratorium ranges between two and five years after the shareholder's stake passes a prespecified (minority) threshold. These laws were in place in 25 states in 1990 and two more by 1998. It is the only state takeover law in Delaware, the state of incorporation for about half of our sample.

Bylaw and **Charter** amendment limitations limit shareholders' ability to amend the governing documents of the corporation. This might take the form of a supermajority vote requirement for charter or bylaw amendments, total elimination of the ability of shareholders to amend the bylaws, or the ability of directors (beyond the provisions of state law) to amend the bylaws without shareholder approval.

Control-share **Cash-out laws** enable shareholders to sell their stakes to a "controlling" shareholder at a price based on the highest price of recently acquired shares. This works something like fair-price provisions (see below) extended to non-takeover situations. These laws were in place in three states by 1990 with no additions during the decade.

A **Classified Board** (or "staggered" board) is one in which the directors are placed into different classes and serve overlapping terms. Since only part of the board can be replaced each year, an outsider who gains control of a corporation may have to wait a few years before being able to gain control of the board. This slow replacement makes a classified board a crucial component of the *Delay* group of provisions, and one of the few provisions that clearly retains some deterrent value in modern take-over battles [Daines and Klausner 2001].

Compensation Plans with changes-in-control provisions allow participants in incentive bonus plans to cash out options or accelerate the payout of bonuses if there should be a change in control. The details may be a written part of the compensation agreement, or discretion may be given to the compensation committee.

Director indemnification **Contracts** are contracts between the company and particular officers and directors indemnifying them from certain legal expenses and judgments resulting from lawsuits pertaining to their conduct. Some firms have both "Indemnification" in their bylaws or charter and these additional indemnification "Contracts."

Control-share Acquisition laws (see Supermajority, below).

Cumulative Voting allows a shareholder to allocate his total votes in any manner desired, where the total number of votes is the product of the number of shares owned and the number of directors to be elected. By allowing them to concentrate their votes, this practice helps minority shareholders to elect directors. Cumulative Voting and Secret Ballot (see below) are the only two provisions whose presence is coded as an *increase* in shareholder rights, with an additional point to the Governance Index if the provision is absent.

Directors' Duties provisions allow directors to consider constituencies other than shareholders when considering a merger. These constituencies may include, for example, employees, host communities, or suppliers. This provision provides boards of directors with a legal basis for rejecting a takeover that would have been beneficial to shareholders. Thirty-one states have **Directors' Duties laws** allowing similar expansions of constituencies, but in only two of these states (Indiana and Pennsylvania) are the laws explicit that the claims of shareholders should not be held

above those of other stakeholders [Pinnell 2000]. We treat firms in these two states as though they had an expanded directors' duty provision unless the firm has explicitly opted out of coverage under the law.

Fair-Price provisions limit the range of prices a bidder can pay in two-tier offers. They typically require a bidder to pay to all shareholders the highest price paid to any during a specified period of time before the commencement of a tender offer, and do not apply if the deal is approved by the board of directors or a supermajority of the target's shareholders. The goal of this provision is to prevent pressure on the target's shareholders to tender their shares in the front end of a two-tiered tender offer, and they have the result of making such an acquisition more expensive. Also, 25 states had **Fair-Price laws** in place in 1990, and two more states passed such laws in 1991. The laws work similarly to the firm-level provisions.

Golden Parachutes are severance agreements that provide cash and noncash compensation to senior executives upon an event such as termination, demotion, or resignation following a change in control. They do not require shareholder approval. While such payments would appear to deter takeovers by increasing their costs, one could argue that these parachutes also ease the passage of mergers through contractual compensation to the managers of the target company [Lambert and Larcker 1985]. While the net impact on managerial entrenchment and shareholder wealth is ambiguous, the more important effect is the clear decrease in shareholder rights. In this case, the "right" is the ability of a controlling shareholder to fire management without incurring an additional cost. Golden Parachutes are highly correlated with all the other takeover defenses. Out of 21 pairwise correlations with the other firm-level provisions, 15 are positive, 10 of these positive correlations are significant, and only one of the negative correlations is significant. Thus, we treat Golden Parachutes as a restriction of shareholder rights.

Director **Indemnification** uses the bylaws, charter, or both to indemnify officers and directors from certain legal expenses and judgments resulting from lawsuits pertaining to their conduct. Some firms have both this "Indemnification" in their bylaws or charter and additional indemnification "Contracts." The cost of such protection can be used as a market measure of the quality of corporate governance [Core 1997, 2000].

Limitations on director **Liability** are charter amendments that limit directors' personal liability to the extent allowed by state law. They often eliminate personal liability for breaches of the duty of care, but not for breaches of the duty of loyalty or for acts of intentional misconduct or knowing violation of the law.

Pension Parachutes prevent an acquirer from using surplus cash in the pension fund of the target to finance an acquisition. Surplus funds are required to remain the property of the pension fund and to be used for plan participants' benefits.

Poison Pills provide their holders with special rights in the case of a triggering event such as a hostile takeover bid. If a deal is approved by the board of directors, the poison pill can be revoked, but if the deal is not approved and the bidder proceeds, the pill is triggered. Typical poison pills give the holders of the target's stock other than the bidder the right to purchase stock in the target or the bidder's company at a steep discount, making the target unattractive or diluting the acquirer's voting power. Poison pills are a crucial component of the "delay" strategy at the core of modern defensive tactics. Nevertheless, we do not include poison pills in the *Delay* group of provisions, but include it in the *Other* group because the pill itself can be passed on less than one-day's notice, so it need not be in place for the other *Delay* provisions to be effective. The other provisions in this group require a shareholder vote, so they cannot be passed on short notice. See Coates [2000] and Daines and Klausner [2001] for a discussion of this point.

Under a **Secret Ballot** (also called confidential voting), either an independent third party or employees sworn to secrecy are used to count proxy votes, and the management usually agrees not to look at individual proxy cards. This can help eliminate potential conflicts of interest for fiduciaries voting shares on behalf of others, and can reduce pressure by management on shareholder-employees or shareholder-partners. Cumulative Voting (see above) and Secret Ballots are the only two provisions whose presence is coded as an *increase* in shareholder rights, with an additional point to the Governance Index if the provision is absent.

Executive **Severance** agreements assure high-level executives of their positions or some compensation and are not contingent upon a change in control (unlike Golden or Silver Parachutes).

Silver Parachutes are similar to Golden Parachutes in that they provide severance payments upon a change in corporate control, but differ in that a large number of a firm's employees are eligible for these benefits. Since Silver Parachutes do not protect the key decision makers in a merger, we classified them in the *Other* group rather than in the *Protection* group.

Special Meeting limitations either increase the level of shareholder support required to call a special meeting beyond that specified by state law or eliminate the ability to call one entirely. Such provisions add extra time to proxy fights, since bidders must wait until the regularly scheduled annual meeting to replace board members or dismantle takeover defenses. This delay is especially potent when combined with limitations on actions by written consent (see below).

Supermajority requirements for approval of mergers are charter provisions that establish voting requirements for mergers or other business combinations that are higher than the threshold requirements of state law. They are typically 66.7, 75, or 85 percent, and often exceed attendance at the annual meeting. In practice, these provisions are similar to **Control-Share Acquisition laws**. These laws require a majority of disinterested shareholders to vote on whether a newly qualifying large shareholder has voting rights. They were in place in 25 states by September 1990 and one additional state in 1991.

Unequal Voting rights limit the voting rights of some shareholders and expand those of others. Under time-phased voting, shareholders who have held the stock for a given period of time are given more votes per share than recent purchasers. Another variety is the substantial-shareholder provision, which limits the voting power of shareholders who have exceeded a certain threshold of ownership.

Limitations on action by **Written Consent** can take the form of the establishment of majority thresholds beyond the level of state law, the requirement of unanimous consent, or the elimination of the right to take action by written consent. Such requirements add extra time to many proxy fights, since bidders must wait until the regularly scheduled annual meeting to replace board members or dismantle takeover defenses. This delay is especially potent when combined with limitations for calling special meetings (see above).

APPENDIX 2: DEFINITIONS FOR THE REGRESSION VARIABLES

This list includes all variables used as regressors or for summary statistics in Tables 20.5 and 20.13. All components are drawn from the CRSP monthly files and all variables are in natural logs unless explicitly noted otherwise. Variables are listed in alphabetical order in boldface.

BM — The ratio of book value of common equity (previous fiscal year) to market value of common equity (end of previous calendar year). Book value of common equity is the sum of book common equity (Compustat item 60) and deferred taxes (Compustat item 74). This variable, and all other variables that use Compustat data, are recalculated each July and held constant through the following June.

5-Year Return — The compounded return from month $t - 61$ to month $t - 2$.

IO — Shares held by institutions divided by total shares outstanding (not in logs). Institutional holdings are from SEC Form 13F quarterly filings, as provided by Thomson Financial. We use the most recent quarter as of the end of month $t - 1$, with shares outstanding (from CRSP) measured on the same date.

NADVOL — The dollar volume of trading in month $t - 2$ for stocks that trade on the NASDAQ. Approximated as stock price at the end of month $t - 2$ multiplied by share volume in month $t - 2$. For New York Stock Exchange (NYSE) and American Stock Exchange (AMEX) stocks, NADVOL equals zero.

NASDUM — A dummy variable equal to one if the firm traded on the NASDAQ Stock Market at the beginning of month t and zero otherwise.

NYDVOL — The dollar volume of trading in month $t - 2$ for stocks that trade on the NYSE or AMEX. Approximated as stock price at the end of month $t - 2$ multiplied by share volume in month $t - 2$. For NASDAQ stocks, NYDVOL equals zero.

PRICE — Price at the end of month $t - 2$.

Q — The market value of assets divided by the book value of assets (Compustat item 6), where the market value of assets is computed as book value of assets plus the market value of common stock less the sum of the book value of common stock (Compustat item 60) and balance sheet deferred taxes (Compustat item 74). All book values for fiscal year t (from Compustat) are combined with the market value of common equity at the calendar end of year t.

RET2–3 — Compounded gross returns for months $t - 3$ and $t - 2$.

RET4–6 — Compounded gross returns for months $t - 6$ through $t - 4$.

RET7–12 — Compounded gross returns for months $t - 12$ through $t - 7$.

SGROWTH — The growth in sales (Compustat item 12) over the previous five fiscal years (not in logs).

SIZE — Market capitalization in millions of dollars at the end of month $t - 2$.

SP500 — membership in the S&P 500 as of the end of month $t - 1$. Value is equal to one if the firm is in the index, and zero otherwise. Data are from CRSP S&P 500 constituent file.

VOLUME—The dollar volume of trading in month $t - 2 = $ NADVOL + NYDVOL.

YLD—The ratio of dividends in the previous fiscal year (Compustat item 21) to market capitalization measured at calendar year-end (not in logs).

NOTES

* We thank Franklin Allen, Judith Chevalier, John Core, Robert Daines, Darrell Duffie, Kenneth French, Gary Gorton, Edward Glaeser, Joseph Gyourko, Robert Holthausen, Steven Kaplan, Sendhil Mullainathan, Krishna Ramaswamy, Roberta Romano, Virginia Rosenbaum, Andrei Shleifer, Peter Siegelman, Robert Stambaugh, Jeremy Stein, René Stulz, Joel Waldfogel, Michael Weisbach, Julie Wulf, three anonymous referees, and seminar participants at the University of Chicago, Columbia, Cornell and Duke Universities, the Federal Reserve Board of Governors, Georgetown University, Harvard University, INSEAD, Stanford University, the Wharton School, Yale University, the 2001 NBER Summer Institute, and the New York University Five-Star Conference for helpful comments. Yi Qian and Gabriella Skirnick provided excellent research assistance. Gompers acknowledges the support of the Division of Research at Harvard Business School. Ishii acknowledges support from an NSF Graduate Research Fellowship.

1   Surveys of this literature can be found in Bhagat and Romano [2001], Bittlingmayer [2000], Comment and Schwert [1995], and Karpoff and Malatesta [1989].

2   See Coates [2000] for a detailed review of these arguments.

3   Other papers that analyze relationships between governance and either firm value or performance have generally focused on board composition, executive compensation, or insider ownership [Baysinger and Butler 1985; Bhagat and Black 1998; Core, Holthausen, and Larcker 1999; Hermalin and Weisbach 1991; Morck, Shleifer, and Vishny 1988; Yermack 1996]. See Shleifer and Vishny [1997] for a survey.

4   These 24 provisions include 22 firm-level provisions and six state laws (four of the laws are analogous to four of the firm-level provisions). For the remainder of the paper we refer interchangeably to corporate governance "laws," "rules," and "provisions." We also refer interchangeably to "shareholders" and "investors" and refer to "management" as comprising both managers and directors.

5   We omit firms with dual-class common stock because the wide variety of voting and ownership differences across these firms makes it difficult to compare their governance structures with those of single-class firms.

6   Unless otherwise noted, all statements about statistical significance refer to significance at the 5 percent level.

7   These laws are classified as "second-generation" in the literature to distinguish them from the "first-generation" laws passed by many states in the sixties and seventies and held to be unconstitutional in 1982. See Comment and Schwert [1995] and Bittlingmayer [2000] for a discussion of the evolution and legal status of state takeover laws and firm-specific takeover defenses. The constitutionality of almost all of the second-generation laws and the firm-specific takeover defenses was clearly established by 1990. All of the state takeover laws cover firms incorporated in their home state. A few states have laws that also cover firms incorporated outside of the state that have significant business within the state. The rules for "significant" vary from case to case, but usually cover only a few very large firms. We do not attempt to code for this out-of-state coverage.

8   The statistics of Table 20.1 reflect exactly the frequency of coverage under the default law in each state. A small minority of firms elect to "opt out" of some laws and "opt in" to others. We code these options separately and use them in the creation of our index.

9   In the case of Secret Ballots, shareholder fiduciaries argue that it enables voting without threat of retribution, such as the loss of investment-banking business by brokerage-house fiduciaries. See Gillan and Bethel [2001] and McGurn [1989].

10   Only two other provisions—Antigreenmail and Golden Parachutes—seem at all ambiguous. Since both are positively correlated with the vast majority of other firm-level provisions and can logically be viewed as takeover defenses, we code them like other defenses and add one point to the index for each. See their respective entries in Appendix 1 for a discussion.

11   Firms usually have the option to opt out of state law coverage. Also, a few state laws require firms to opt in to be covered. The firms that exercise these options are listed in the IRRC data. When we constructed the *State* subindex, we ignored these options and used the default state coverage. When we constructed the *G* index, we included the options and used actual coverage.

12   The IRRC gives dates for some of the provision changes—where available, these data

suggest that the majority of the provisions were adopted in the 1980s. Danielson and Karpoff [1998] perform a detailed study on a similar set of provisions and demonstrate a rapid pace of change between 1984 and 1989.

13 Berkshire Hathaway disappeared because it added a second class of stock before 1998. Firms with multiple classes of common stock are not included in our analysis.

14 NCR disappeared after a merger. It reappeared in the sample in 1998 as a spinout, but since it received a new permanent number from CRSP, we treat the new NCR as a different company.

15 The industry names are from Fama and French [1997], but use a slightly updated version of the SIC classification of these industries that is given on Ken French's website (June 2001). In Sections III and V we use both this updated classification and the corresponding industry returns (also from the French website).

16 See Basu [1977] (price-to-earnings ratio), Banz [1981] (size), Fama and French [1993] (size and book-to-market), Lakonishok, Shleifer, and Vishny [1994] (several value measures), and Jegadeesh and Titman [1993] (momentum).

17 This model extends the Fama-French [1993] three-factor model with the addition of a momentum factor. For details on the construction of the factors, see Fama and French [1993] and Carhart [1997]. We are grateful to Ken French for providing the factor returns for *SMB* and *HML*. *Momentum* returns were calculated by the authors using the procedures of Carhart [1997].

18 Unlike Shin and Stulz [2000], we do not trim the sample of observations that have extreme independent variables. Results with a trimmed sample are nearly identical and are available from the authors.

19 Table 20.7, first row, second column, shows an alpha of 45 bp per month for the EW difference between the Democracy and Dictatorship Portfolios. Over 112 months this produces a difference of approximately 50 percent, as compared with the $56 - 19 = 37$ percent difference estimated for the Q regressions. We use the EW alpha as a comparison because the Q regressions are also equal-weighted.

20 For an alternative view, see Stein [1988, 1989]. Empirical evidence on this issue is given by Daines and Klausner [2001], Johnson and Rao [1997], Meulbroek et al. [1990], Pugh, Page, and Jahera [1992], and Titman, Wei, and Xie [2001].

21 Mitchell and Stafford [2000] have challenged the magnitude of this longrun evidence, but still allow for some underperformance for acquisitions financed by stock. A related debate on whether diversifying acquisitions destroy value has grown too large to survey here. The seminal works are Lang and Stulz [1994] and Berger and Ofek [1995]. Recent work is summarized in Holmstrom and Kaplan [2001] and Stein [2001].

22 See Seyhun [1998] for a comprehensive review of this literature and a discussion of SEC rules, filing requirements, and available data.

23 All of these additional variables are correlated with G (see Table 20.3) and, in prior studies, with either firm value or abnormal returns. See Lakonishok, Shleifer, and Vishny [1994] (sales growth), Gompers and Metrick [2001] (institutional ownership), and Morck and Yang [2001] (Q).

24 For example, there is evidence that earnings surprises [Bernard and Thomas 1989], dividend omissions [Michaely, Thaler, and Womack 1995], and stock repurchases [Ikenberry, Lakonishok, and Vermaelen 1995] have long-term drift following the event, and all seem to be relatively simple events compared with changes in governance structure.

REFERENCES

Banz, Rolf, "The Relation between Return and Market Value of Stocks," *Journal of Financial Economics*, XXXVIII (1981), 269–296.

Basu, Sanjoy, "The Investment Performance of Common Stocks in Relation to Their Price-to-Earnings: A Test of the Efficient Markets Hypothesis," *Journal of Finance*, XXXII (1977), 663–682.

Baumol, William, *Business Behavior, Value, and Growth* (New York, NY: Macmillan, 1959).

Baysinger, Barry D., and Henry N. Butler, "Corporate Governance and the Board of Directors: Performance Effects of Changes in Board Composition," *Journal of Law, Economics, and Organization*, I (1985), 101–124.

Berger, Philip G., and Eli Ofek, "Diversification's Effect on Firm Value," *Journal of Financial Economics*, XXXVII (1995), 39–65.

Bernard, Victor, and J. K. Thomas, "Post-Earnings Announcement Drift: Delayed Price Response or Risk Premium?" *Journal of Accounting Research*, Supplement, XXVII (1989), 1–36.

Bertrand, Marianne, and Sendhil Mullainathan, "Is There Discretion in Wage Setting?" *Rand Journal of Economics*, XXX (1999a), 535–554.

Bertrand, Marianne, and Sendhil Mullainathan, "Corporate Governance and Executive Pay: Evidence from Takeover Legislation," Working Paper, MIT Department of Economics, 1999b.

Bertrand, Marianne, and Sendhil Mullainathan, "Enjoying the Quiet Life? Managerial Behavior Following Anti-Takeover Legislation," Working Paper, Department of Economics, Massachusetts Institute of Technology, 2000.

Bhagat, Sanjai, and B. S. Black, "The Relationship between Board Composition and Firm Performance," in *Comparative Corporate Governance: The State of the Art and Emerging Research*, K. Hopt, M. Roe, and E. Wymeersch, eds. (Oxford, UK: Clarendon Press; New York, NY: Oxford University Press, 1998).

Bhagat, Sanjai, and Roberta Romano, "Event Studies and the Law: Part II—Empirical Studies of Corporate Law," Working Paper, Yale University, 2001.

Bittlingmayer, George, "The Market for Corporate Control (Including Take-overs)," in *Encyclopedia of Law and Economics, Vol. III—The Regulation of Contracts*, Boudewijn Bouckaert and Gerrit de Geest, eds. (Cheltenham, UK, and Northampton, MA: Edward Elgar, 2000).

Borokhovich, Kenneth A., Kelly R. Brunarski, and Robert Parrino, "CEO Contracting and Antitakeover Amendments," *Journal of Finance*, LII (1997), 1495–1518.

Brennan, Michael J., Tarun Chordia, and Avanidhar Subrahmanyam, "Alternative Factor Specifications, Security Characteristics, and the Cross Section of Expected Stock Returns," *Journal of Financial Economics*, XLIX (1998), 345–375.

Carhart, Mark, "On Persistence in Mutual Fund Performance," *Journal of Finance*, LII (1997), 57–82.

Coates, John, "Takeover Defenses in the Shadow of the Pill: A Critique of the Scientific Evidence," *Texas Law Review*, LXXIX (2000), 271–382.

Comment, Robert, and G. William Schwert, "Poison or Placebo? Evidence on the Deterrence and Wealth Effects of Modern Antitakeover Measures," *Journal of Financial Economics*, XXXIX (1995), 3–43.

Core, John, "On the Corporate Demand for Directors' and Officers' Insurance," *Journal of Risk and Insurance*, LXIV (1997), 63–87.

——, "The Directors' and Officers' Insurance Premium: An Outside Assessment of the Quality of Corporate Governance," *Journal of Law, Economics, and Organization*, XVI (2000), 449–477.

Core, John E., Robert W. Holthausen, and David F. Larcker, "Corporate Governance, Chief Executive Officer Compensation, and Firm Performance," *Journal of Financial Economics*, LI (1999), 371–406.

Daines, Robert, "Does Delaware Law Improve Firm Value?" *Journal of Financial Economics*, LXII (2001), 525–558.

Daines, Robert, and Michael Klausner, "Do IPO Charters Maximize Firm Value? Antitakeover Protection in IPOs," *Journal of Law, Economics, and Organization*, XVII (2001), 83–120.

Danielson, Morris G., and Jonathan M. Karpoff, "On the Uses of Corporate Governance Provisions," *Journal of Corporate Finance*, IV (1998), 347–371.

Demsetz, Harold, and Kenneth Lehn, "The Structure of Corporate Ownership: Causes and Consequences," *Journal of Political Economy*, XCIII (1985), 1155–1177.

Eckbo, B. Espen, "Valuation Effects of Greenmail Prohibitions," *Journal of Financial and Quantitative Analysis*, XXV (1990), 491–505.

Fama, Eugene F., and Kenneth R. French, "Common Risk Factors in the Returns on Bonds and Stocks," *Journal of Financial Economics*, XXXIII (1993), 3–53.

Fama, Eugene F., and Kenneth R. French, "Industry Costs of Equity," *Journal of Financial Economics*, XLIII (1997), 153–194.

Fama, Eugene F., and James D. MacBeth, "Risk, Return, and Equilibrium: Empirical Tests," *Journal of Political Economy*, LXXXI (1973), 607–636.

Garvey, Gerald T., and Gordon Hanka, "Capital Structure and Corporate Control: The Effect of Antitakeover Statutes on Firm Leverage," *Journal of Finance*, LIV (1999), 519–546.

Gillan, Stuart, and Jennifer Bethel, "Managerial Control of the Proxy Process: The Impact on Shareholder Voting," Working Paper, Babson College, 2001.

Gompers, Paul A., and Andrew Metrick, "Institutional Investors and Equity Prices," *Quarterly Journal of Economics*, CXIV (2001), 229–260.

Hermalin, Benjamin, and Michael Weisbach, "The Effects of Board Composition and Direct Incentives on Firm Performance," *Financial Management*, XX (1991), 101–112.

Holmstrom, Bengt, and Steven N. Kaplan, "Corporate Governance and Merger Activity in the United States: Making Sense of the 1980s and 1990s," *Journal of Economic Perspectives*, XV (2001), 121–144.

Ikenberry, David, Josef Lakonishok, and Theo Vermaelen, "Market Underreaction to Open Market Share Repurchases," *Journal of Financial Economics*, XXXIX (1995), 181–208.

Ishii, Joy L., "Corporate Governance in the 1990s: New Evidence on the Role of Shareholder Proposals," Senior Honors Thesis, Harvard University, 2000.

Jegadeesh, Narasimhan, and Sheridan Titman, "Returns to Buying Winners and Selling Losers: Implications for Stock Market Efficiency," *Journal of Finance*, XLVIII (1993), 65–91.

Jensen, Michael, "Agency Costs of Free Cash Flow, Corporate Finance, and Takeovers," *American Economic Review*, LXXVI (1986), 323–329.

Jensen, Michael, and Richard Ruback, "The Market for Corporate Control: The Scientific Evidence," *Journal of Financial Economics*, XI (1983), 5–50.

Johnson, Mark S., and Ramesh P. Rao, "The Impact of Antitakeover Amendments on Corporate Financial Performance," *Financial Review*, XXXII (1997), 659–690.

Kaplan, Steven N., and Luigi Zingales, "Do Investment-Cash Flow Sensitivities Provide Useful Measures of Financing Constraints?" *Quarterly Journal of Economics*, CXII (1997), 169–216.

Karpoff, Jonathan M., and Paul H. Malatesta, "The Wealth Effects of Second-Generation State Takeover Legislation," *Journal of Financial Economics*, XXV (1989), 291–322.

Lakonishok, Josef, Andrei Shleifer, and Robert Vishny, "Contrarian Investment, Extrapolation, and Risk," *Journal of Finance*, XLIX (1994), 1541–1578.

Lambert, Richard A., and David F. Larcker, "Golden Parachutes, Executive Decision-Making and Shareholder Wealth," *Journal of Accounting and Economics*, VII (1985), 179–203.

Lang, Larry H. P., and René M. Stulz, "Tobin's Q, Corporate Diversification, and Firm Performance," *Journal of Political Economy*, CII (1994), 1248–1280.

Lang, Larry H. P., René M. Stulz, and Ralph A. Walkling, "A Test of the Free Cash Flow Hypothesis: The Case of Bidder Returns," *Journal of Financial Economics*, XXIX (1991), 315–335.

La Porta, Rafael, Florencio Lopez-de-Silanes, Andrei Shleifer, and Robert Vishny, "Investor Protection and Corporate Valuation," Working Paper, Harvard University, 2001.

Lewellen, Wilbur, Claudio Loderer, and Ahron Rosenfeld, "Merger Decisions and Executive Stock Ownership in Acquiring Firms," *Journal of Accounting and Economics*, VII (1985), 209–231.

Loughran, Tim, and Anand M. Vijh, "Do Long-Term Shareholders Benefit from Corporate Acquisitions?" *Journal of Finance*, LII (1997), 1765–1790.

Marris, Robin, *The Economic Theory of Managerial Capitalism* (New York, NY: Free Press of Glencoe, 1964).

McGurn, Patrick S., *Confidential Proxy Voting* (Washington, DC: Investor Responsibility Research Center Inc., 1989).

Meulbroek, Lisa K., Mark L. Mitchell, J. Harold Mulherin, Jeffrey M. Netter, and Annette B. Poulsen, "Shark Repellents and Managerial Myopia: An Empirical Test," *Journal of Political Economy*, XCVIII (1990), 1108–1117.

Michaely, Roni, Richard Thaler, and Kent Womack, "Price Reactions to Dividend Initiations and Omissions," *Journal of Finance*, XXXVIII (1995), 1597–1606.

Mitchell, Mark L., and Erik Stafford, "Managerial Decisions and Long-Term Stock Price Performance," *Journal of Business*, LXXIII (2000), 287–330.

Morck, Randall, Andrei Shleifer, and Robert Vishny, "Management Ownership and Market Valuation: An Empirical Analysis," *Journal of Financial Economics*, XX (1988), 293–315.

Morck, Randall, Andrei Shleifer, and Robert Vishny, "Do Managerial Objectives Drive Bad

Acquisitions?" *Journal of Finance*, XLV (1990), 31–48.

Morck, Randall, and Fan Yang, "The Mysterious Growing Value of the S&P 500 Membership," Working Paper, University of Alberta, 2001.

Pinnell, Maria Carmen S., *State Takeover Laws* (Washington, DC: Investor Responsibility Research Center Inc., 2000).

Pugh, William M., Daniel E. Page, and John S. Jahera Jr., "Antitakeover Charter Amendments: Effects on Corporate Decisions," *Journal of Financial Research*, XV (1992), 57–67.

Rau, P. Raghavendra, and Theo Vermaelen, "Glamour, Value and the Post-Acquisition Performance of Acquiring Firms," *Journal of Financial Economics*, XLIX (1998), 223–253.

Rosenbaum, Virginia, *Corporate Takeover Defenses* (Washington, DC: Investor Responsibility Research Center Inc., 1990, 1993, 1995, 1998).

Seyhun, H. Nejat, *Investment Intelligence from Insider Trading* (Cambridge, MA: MIT Press, 1998).

Shin, Hyun-Han, and René M. Stulz, "Firm Value, Risk, and Growth Opportunities," NBER Working Paper No. 7808, 2000.

Shleifer, Andrei, and Robert Vishny, "Greenmail, White Knights, and Shareholders' Interest," *Rand Journal of Economics*, XVII (1986), 293–309.

Shleifer, Andrei, and Robert Vishny, "Management Entrenchment: The Case of Manager-Specific Investments," *Journal of Financial Economics*, XXV (1989), 123–140.

Shleifer, Andrei, and Robert Vishny, "A Survey of Corporate Governance," *Journal of Finance*, LII (1997), 737–783.

Stein, Jeremy C., "Takeover Threats and Managerial Myopia," *Journal of Political Economy*, XCVI (1988), 61–80.

——, "Efficient Markets, Inefficient Firms: A Model of Myopic Firm Behavior," *Quarterly Journal of Economics*, CIV (1989), 655–669.

——, "Agency, Information, and Corporate Investment," *Handbook of the Economics of Finance*, George Constantinides, Milton Harris, and René Stulz, eds. (Amsterdam: Elsevier Science, 2001).

Subramanian, Guhan, "The Influence of Antitakeover Statutes on Reincorporation Choice: Evidence on the 'Race' Debate and Antitakeover Overreaching," Working Paper, Harvard Business School, 2001.

Titman, Sheridan, K. C. John Wei, and Feixue Xie, "Capital Investments and Stock Returns," Working Paper, University of Texas at Austin, 2001.

Williamson, Oliver, *The Economics of Discretionary Behavior: Managerial Objectives in a Theory of the Firm* (Englewood Cliffs, NJ: Prentice Hall, 1964).

Yermack, David, "Higher Market Valuation for Firms with a Small Board of Directors," *Journal of Financial Economics*, XL (1996), 185–211.

## Chapter 21

Gertjan Schut and Ruud van Frederikslust

SHAREHOLDERS WEALTH EFFECTS OF JOINT VENTURE STRATEGIES[*]

Source: *Multinational Finance Journal*, 8(3–4) (2004): 211–225.

ABSTRACT

We investigate the shareholder wealth effects of 233 joint venture announcements of Dutch public companies in the period 1987 till 1998. The research shows that, on average, establishing joint ventures has a positive effect on the market value of Dutch companies. Using the strategic characteristics of joint ventures it is possible to explain and understand these wealth effects. Our research shows that the factors of strategic intention, the context in which the strategy is unfolded and the extent to which the company has control over the implementation strongly explains the extent to which a joint venture can create value.

I. INTRODUCTION

WE INVESTIGATE SHAREHOLDER WEALTH EFFECTS of 233 joint venture announcements by Dutch public companies in the period 1987 till 1998. The study focuses on joint ventures in which the consequences for the shareholders of the parent companies are central. Setting up a joint venture involves establishing a separate legal entity, with its own identity, liability and share capital. Most companies have experienced stagnation in their market value growth and cash flow margins up to three years before the establishment of a joint venture; e.g., Mohanram and Nanda (1998) and Bergman and Friedman (1977). This article addresses the joint venture strategy factors and how they have an impact on the market value of parent companies. Section II outlines the sample survey and the applied research methodology. Section III presents the findings of the impact of the joint venture strategy on the market value of companies. Section IV presents the summary and conclusions.

II. DATA AND METHODOLOGY

A. Data

This research is based on the event study methodology developed by Fama et al. (1969). The initial announcement of a joint venture is defined as the 'event', while the market value is studied by examining the development of the share price. The announcements were found in the Dutch financial daily *Het Financieele Dagblad*. The study analyzed a sample of 233 non-financial joint ventures whose announcements met the following criteria:

The shares of at least one of the joint venture partners were being traded on

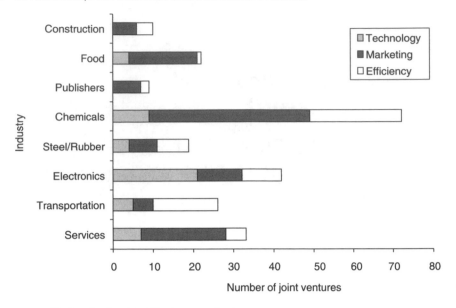

Figure 21.1 Motive for the Joint Ventures by Sector.

Table 21.1 Location of the Joint Venture and Nationality of the Partners

Nationality of Partner	Netherlands	Europe	Nafta	Japan & S. Korea	China	Other	Total
Dutch	25	1	0	0	1	3	30
European	10	27	0	0	2	5	44
Nafta	11	9	11	0	0	2	33
Japanese & S. Korean	3	1	1	13	0	2	20
Chinese	0	0	0	0	21	0	21
Other	0	1	1	0	1	32	35
Total	49	39	13	13	25	44	183

Note: When location could not be clearly identified, the joint venture was not included.

the Amsterdam Stock Exchange at the time of the announcement.

During the (−20, 20) days in which the market reaction was measured, no other relevant announcements regarding the companies participating in the alliance appeared in Het Financieele Dagblad.

The companies involved were not financial institutions[1].Forty-eight Dutch companies, that is, approximately 21% of the public companies in the Netherlands accounted for the 233 joint ventures.

Figure 21.1 shows the motives underlying the joint ventures by sector. Chemical and petrochemical companies are strongly represented in the sample; companies in this sector of industry formed nearly one-third of the total number of joint ventures. The most common motive was market development, followed by technology and efficiency.

Table 21.1 presents the distribution by location of joint ventures and nationality of the partners. Approximately a quarter of the joint ventures are based in the Netherlands. Most of the joint ventures are established in the country of one of the partners. This is due to the fact that the Netherlands is a small country with a long international trading history.

B. Methodology

The analysis of the value effect of joint ventures includes only the abnormal part of the market reaction in respect to the parent company share price.[2] The expected returns on the relevant days were estimated by means of the market model approach. The abnormal return ($AR_{i,t}$) of a share i at time t is calculated as follows:[3]

$$AR_{i,t} = R_{i,t} - (a_i + b_i R_{m,t}), \qquad (1)$$

where $R_{i,t}$ is the effective return of share i at time t, a_i a constant term of share i, b_i is the systematic risk of share i, $R_{m,t}$ is the market return at time t and $a_i + b_{iR}m,t$ is the expected return on share i according to the estimated market model.

To measure the full effect of the announcement, the abnormal return ($AR_{i,t}$) of the announcement day and the following day were computed and averaged for all sample companies to obtain the cumulative abnormal return (CAR). The standard deviation of the abnormal return of each share in the sample was estimated through observations made during the estimation period (from 200 to 51 days before the announcement). A t-test was used to determine whether the market reaction on and around the day of the announcement significantly deviates from zero (Brown and Warner [1985]). In addition to CAR, the standardized cumulative abnormal return, or SCAR, was included in the analysis.[4]

To gain further insight into why some reactions are negative while others are positive, we accomplish a regression analysis of the CARs using several different variables. Joint ventures and similar capital investments come forth out of the strategy process of firms; e.g.; Copeland (1995). To explain wealth effects of joint ventures, the dimensions that characterize the strategy should be able to explain the observed variance in CAR.

In the decision-making process involved in formulating a joint venture, three strategy dimensions are distinguished: Strategy Content, Strategy Context and Strategy Control. The strategy content of a joint venture concerns the characteristics of the actual strategy itself. Two characteristics of the strategy content are taken into account: the functional motive underlying a joint venture and the degree of diversification realized by the joint venture. Research into joint venture motivations distinguishes motives stemming from market and technology developments; e.g., Koh and Venkatraman (1991) and Das, Sen and Sengupta (1998). These studies show that alliances primarily motivated by technological issues have a more positive impact on the market value of companies than marketing-oriented joint ventures. These studies did not examine efficiency improvement as a motive. The influence of the degree of diversification of the joint venture is not clear. Depending on the theoretical concepts used, diversification influences the value effect of the alliance either positively (Balakrishnan and Koza [1993]) or negatively (Koh and Venkatraman [1991]). To explain the value effects, the authors respectively applied the transaction cost approach and the strategic behavior perspective.

The strategy context defines the decision-making parameters of the environment. Important elements are partner selection, the nationalities involved, and the associated cultural differences. Mohanram and Nanda (1998) and Koh and Venkatraman (1991) found that companies gain more excess returns if they enter into an alliance with a larger partner. The relative size of the partner appears to be a relevant factor in establishing the value potential of a joint venture. Closely examined in the relationship between partners is the effect of the relatedness[5] of the partners, i.e., the degree of similarity between their activities.

Research conducted by Koh and Venkatraman (1991) and Balakrishnan and Koza (1993) produced conflicting conclusions and, as a consequence, have been a source of debate. Studies which investigated the nationality of chosen partners and its impact on joint venture wealth effects yielded few results so far. The studies focused on American companies (Lee and Wyatt [1990] and Borde, Whyte, Wiant and Hoffman [1998]) and produced contradictory lists of countries and economic regions where joint ventures were either successful or unsuccessful in generating shareholder value.

Following Datta and Puia (1995) and Kogut and Singh (1988), for the purposes of this study cultural difference, measured by the variable individualism, was selected as the distinguishing indicator of nationality, since it was also used in qualitative studies by Bleeke and Ernst (1993) and others. As a rule, these studies show that cultural differences can lead to management problems. We therefore expected this dimension to have a negative effect.

Finally, Strategic control is the extent to which an enterprise can exert influence on the development of the joint venture. The ownership structure is a clear manifestation of the degree of influence that a company can exert on the joint venture. The distribution of control within joint ventures is discussed in depth in qualitative studies; e.g., Bleeke and Ernst (1993). Koh and Venkatraman (1991) found that one party having more control within an alliance had a positive effect. In contrast, Bleeke and Ernst (1993) argue that an equal balance of control makes it easier to manage a joint venture and consequently increases the probability of success. None of the studies in Table 21.2 developed an integral model to determine the conditions under which a joint venture creates value.

III. RESULTS

A. Results of the event study

Average CAR is positive but there is substantial variance, with 57% of joint ventures associated with positive share price impacts, and 43% negative. Table 21.3 provides the results obtained by testing the CAR and SCAR of the 233 joint venture announcements. Over the two-day testing period positive market reactions were found with a significance level of 0.01 for both performance criteria (CAR and SCAR). The CAR is equal to 0.40%.

Table 21.2 Overview of the Results Found in the Literature

Dimension	Variable	Expectation	Authors
Content	Technology	+	Das, Sen and Sengupta (1998) Chan, Kensinger, Keown and Martin (1997)
	Marketing	−	
	Efficiency	±	
	Diversification	±	Koh and Venkatraman (1991) Mohanram and Nanda (1998)
Context	Partner relatedness	±	Koh and Venkatraman (1991) Balakrishnan and Koza (1993)
	Individualism	−	Datta and Puia (1995) Bleeke and Ernst (1993)
	Relative size	+	Mohanram and Nanda (1998) Koh and Venkatraman (1991) McConnel and Nantell (1985)
Control	Majority	+	Bleeke and Ernst (1993) Copeland et al. (1995)
	Equality	+	
	Minority	−	

Table 21.3 Test Results of CAR and SCAR

Period t(i,j)	CAR (%)	SCAR
(−1,0)	0.40***	3.50***
(−1,1)	0.39***	3.15***
(−2,2)	0.39**	2.15**

Note: The table shows the CAR and SCAR for various event windows for a sample of 233 joint venture announcements by Dutch public companies in the period 1987 to 1998. ***$p \leq 0.01$ and **$0.01 < p \leq 0.05$.

According to CAR, the reactions to joint ventures were both strongly positive (1.77% on average) and negative (−1.34% on average).

To gain further insight into why some reactions are negative while others are positive, we accomplish a regression analysis of the CARs using a strategic explanation model.

B. Impact of the joint venture strategy on CAR

None of the American studies attempted to develop an integrated model that reveals the dynamics among the strategic factors and the value effects of the joint ventures. The distribution of the factors according to strategic dimensions is addressed above in section II. Investor's interpretation of the strategy content, the context in which this strategy must function, and the extent of the company's control over the implementation of the strategic option determine how much shareholder value is generated. The variables investment climate (risk-free rate[6]) and industry were included in the analysis as control variables to ensure that they did not have any impact on the research results.

Joint venture strategy

This section describes the variables used to identify factors that influence the shareholder wealth effects. Each strategic dimension is discussed in terms of what factors were examined and how the variables were examined and calculated. In the regression analysis, the CAR is the dependent variable for the following variables:

$$Car_j = b_0 + b_1 \binom{\text{Technology}}{\text{Dummy}}_j$$

$$+ b_2 \binom{\text{Efficiency}}{\text{Dummy}}_j$$

$$+ b_3 (\text{Diversification})_j$$

$$+ b_4 (\text{Individualism})_j$$

$$+ b_5 (\text{RelSize})_j$$

$$+ b_6 \binom{\text{Majority}}{\text{Dummy}}_j$$

$$+ b_7 \binom{\text{Minority}}{\text{Dummy}}_j$$

$$+ b_8 \binom{\text{Risk-free}}{\text{Rate}}_j$$

$$+ b_9 \binom{\text{Industry}}{\text{Dummy}}_j + e_j \qquad (2)$$

where $e_j \sim N(0,\sigma^2)$. An explanation of the independent variables of the model follows below:

Strategy content

Three dichotomous variables are used to test the impact on the parent company of the underlying motive of the joint venture. The value of the dichotomous variable is 1 if there is a distinguishable motive, otherwise it is 0. The dummy variables are technology, in the case of a technology development joint venture; marketing, for a market development joint venture; and efficiency, for an efficiency-driven joint venture.

The diversification variable represents the relatedness between the activities of the parent company and those of the joint venture. The relatedness is the difference between the primary three-digit US-SIC number for the parent company[7] and the joint venture.[8] The relatedness is divided by 899, the maximum possible distance used by Balakrishnan and Koza (1993) in their research.

Strategy context

The relative size of the partner is calculated by dividing the number of staff the partner employs by the number of staff working for the company whose shares are analyzed.[9]

In discussing the success and failure of cooperative agreements, cultural differences are often used as a reason for failure (Bleeke and Ernst; 1993). Franke, Hofstede and Bond (1991) argue that differences in cultural values, rather than in material and structural conditions, are ultimate determinants of human organization and behavior,

and thus economic growth. In their long term study they find empirical support for their thesis. From the proxies used to characterize cultural distance, it became clear that the cultural dimension Individualism had the most explanatory power in explaining economic growth. The dimension of individualism is a criterion for the way in which an individual views his or her relationship with the rest of the collective[10]. Frank, Hofstede and Bond (1991) constructed scores on this dimension based on most major countries. Datta and Puia (1995), Kogut and Singh (1988), Erramilli (1991) and Shane (1992) used these bipolar scores to investigate cultural distance. This study used these scores in calculating cultural distance measured by the individualism dimension. The variable Individualism is calculated by:

$$Individualism = \frac{(I_j - INL)^2}{V}, \qquad (3)$$

where I_j is an index-score on the individualism index of the country of origin of the partner, INL is the index-score of the

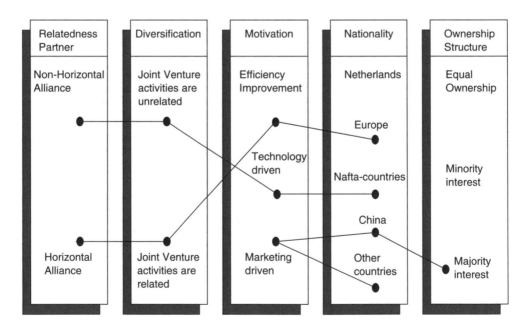

Figure 21.2 Autonomous relationships.

Table 21.4 Estimated Functions and Test Results

			SCAR	CAR
Strategy	Variable	Expected Result	Result	Result
	Constant		1.357***	2.492***
Content	Technology	+	0.832***	1.584***
	Efficiency	±	0.843**	1.570***
	Diversification	±	−2.877***	−5.180***
Context	Inividualism	−	0.287**	0.433**
	Rel. Size	+	0.057***	0.101***
Control	Majority	+	0.975**	2.134***
Control variable	R_f		−0.244**	−0.478**
	Publishers		2.685*	5.245*
R^2			0.492	0.492
Adj.R^2			0.399	0.399
F-value			5.530***	5.303***
N			110	110

Note: This table shows the results of the estimated functions of the cumulative abnormal returns of a sample of 110 joint venture announcements of Dutch public companies in the period 1987 till 1998. ***$p \leq 0.01$, **$0.01 < p \leq 0.05$ and *$0.05 < p \leq 0.10$.

individualism index of the Netherlands and V is the variance of individualism scores of all countries.

Strategy control

The ownership structure within the joint venture is represented by three dummy variables. Three structures are possible: the company can have a majority, a minority or an equal distribution of shares in the joint venture. It is assumed that the ownership structure correlates with the degree of control in the joint venture. The dummy variables take the value of one if the firm has that particular ownership structure and the value of zero, otherwise.

Control variables

In order to prevent investment climate and industry specific factors to influence the overall results of this study we control for them by using control variables in the regression. To measure the effect of investment climate the variable risk-free rate (R_f) is added to the model. This

return is equal to the yield of ten-year government bonds.

The study also takes industry effects into account. Based on SIC number,[11] the companies in the sample are classified into the following sectors of industry: construction, food, publishing, (petro) chemical, steel and rubber, electronics, logistics, and services. Industry effects are measured using dummy variables which take the value of one if the firm is in that particular industry otherwise zero.

Autonomous relationships

Figure 21.2 shows the autonomous relationships uncovered by the study. Technology joint ventures are mostly initiated between non-horizontal partners in NAFTA territory. Efficiency driven joint ventures are often between horizontal partners within the E.U. region. Marketing driven joint ventures are frequently setup in emerging markets where for China the Dutch firms mostly have a majority stake. In China it is still obligatory to form joint ventures; the Chinese government prevents foreign firms to have full control of Chinese subsidiaries.

Estimated functions and testing results

A regression analysis was conducted to measure the explanatory power of the synthesis model (2). There appeared to be little difference between the results of the various performance criteria. The results presented here are based on the CAR and SCAR performance criteria. Only the significant effects are shown in table 4. The results reveal that all the given strategic factors help to explain the performance of joint ventures. The model that incorporates the strategic dimensions provides a stronger, more substantial explanation for the variation in the cumulative abnormal returns than the control variables alone.

The contribution of the control variables on R^2 of the estimated functions is 5% on average. The variables from the synthesis model appear to be relevant to the explanation of the shareholder wealth effects of joint ventures. The estimated regressions are checked for multicollinearity using VIF-statistics. The few correlations between the explanatory variables are not significant, as the value of VIF-statistics of approximately 1 is low.

IV. SUMMARY AND CONCLUSIONS

On average the joint ventures that Dutch companies entered in the period 1987–98 generated value. Notably, companies tended to enter joint ventures when their performance was less than adequate. The statistics show that on average the company performance was below the average stock market performance in the years before the joint venture announcement. This means that we now have an explanation for the negative relationship between return and joint venture activities observed by Berg and Friedman (1977). Our results demonstrate that companies were already performing poorly prior to deciding to enter a joint venture and that joint venture decisions were a reaction to the poor results rather than their cause. In bad times, when shareholder value is deteriorating, joint ventures can provide rays of hope. In this study, the intensity of these rays is expressed through characteristics of the strategy dimensions: Strategy Content, Strategy Context and Strategy Control.

A. Strategy content

The substantive function that a joint venture fulfils for a company is an important component in the evaluation of a joint venture. As shown by the results of Koh and Venkatraman (1991) for joint ventures and Das, Sen and Sengupta (1998) for alliances without share participation, technology development joint ventures have a higher impact on a company's market value than market development joint ventures. The average value created by efficiency-driven joint ventures lies somewhere in between.

The less the activities of the joint venture are related with those of the parent company, the less enthusiastic the investor reacts. In order to create shareholder value it is essential for a company to utilize its core competencies. With an increasing distance between the new activities comes increasing difficulty in effectively deploying the company's competencies. Moreover, there is less potential for the joint venture to affect the core activities and, since most of the corporate value stems from the core activities, a distant joint venture is less likely to be able to generate significant impact. It seems that there is an optimal degree of diversification for joint venture contracts. Investors are usually not in favor of companies using joint ventures for reasons of strong diversification.

B. Strategy context

The American studies show the various impacts of partner nationality. In our study we found that joint venture partners that scored high on individualism have a positive impact on value creation. As no other economic variables appear to make any contribution, it is plausible that investor reactions are partly based on the perception of the economic power of the partner's country of origin and business location.

Research shows that the relatedness of the partner's activities is of less importance in determining the value generated by a joint venture. Investors focus on the activities of the joint venture. However, the analysis reveals that horizontal partners are usually selected for horizontal joint ventures and vice versa. Neither conventional testing of differences in means nor regression analysis uncovered any impact on value creation by joint ventures. The overlap in the partners' activities is the result, rather than the cause, of the joint venture and its objective. The debate conducted in the literature on the impact of overlapping strategic activities appears to be irrelevant in our research.

Partner size has a strong effect on the performance of a joint venture. The variable is highly significant and positive for all performance criteria. In their qualitative study, Bleeke and Ernst (1993) concluded that a stronger partner is a prerequisite for a successful joint venture. The regression results and the univariate tests support this theory. The results of this study show that venturing with relative large partners result in higher wealth effects. For smaller firms the joint venture can underline the value of its business proposition through the acceptance of larger partners. The initial impact of venturing with smaller partners doesn't seem to be very high. When there is much excitement surrounding a joint venture with a smaller partner, this can be attributed to the promise of technology/innovation.

C. Strategy control

Joint venture announcements with an unequal partner shares gain higher wealth effects then with an equal (50/50) partner share. From the data observed, it seems that joint ventures with an equal share distribution receive a negative premium. Minority partner shares receive on average positive wealth effects, but report less strong significance in the multivariate regression tests. The valuation of a joint venture is especially positive for companies that have a majority interest. A majority interest gives a company a dominant position in the collaboration, ensuring that the company has more control over the achievement of the objectives of the joint venture. The results contradict the prevailing paradigms that assert the importance of equality in cooperative alliances. Bleeke and Ernst (1993), Harrigan (1988) and Copeland et al. (1995) underlined the importance of equality in the ownership structure. If shareholder value is the target, then equality within an alliance is not essential. It is more important that the ratios should be fair and bear a connection to the value of the resources (knowledge, capital and other assets) in which each party invests in the joint venture. It appears that the equal distribution of share capital at any cost is not appreciated by investors and has a negative impact on market value. Furthermore, investors have more confidence in joint ventures with one captain than those with two.

The synthesis of the aggregate strategic dimensions explains a great deal of the share price reaction. Clearly, investors respond consistently enough to joint venture announcements to justify the development of an analytical model based on these factors.

NOTES

* We acknowledge comments on prior drafts by the anonymous referee and the editor Peter Theodossiou.

1 Financial institutions were not included in the sample because they are not comparable to other sectors in that they are regulated by the Dutch Central Bank. Moreover their annual accounts differ strongly from those of other companies.

2 In order to verify the stability of the estimated market model, Cannella and Hambrick (1993), three alternative performance criteria have been calculated. They are based on the following: (i) Returns corrected for the market. This method comprises the effective return minus the market return, i.e. without estimating the parameters alpha and beta as in performance criteria (1). (ii) Returns corrected for the

average. The return is calculated by subtracting the average return of the share in the estimation period from the effective return. (iii) Effective return. The uncorrected return during the announcement. In addition a verification analysis was also performed based on the 'buy and hold' investment strategy. The extraordinary buy and hold return is also based on the market model; however a composite return is the starting point. The results of the alternative methodologies are similar to those reported in the paper.

3   The parameters a and b were estimated using the least square method, based on observations made during the estimation period. The estimation period runs from 200 to 51 days before the announcement day.

4   Unlike CAR, SCAR is normally distributed for each hypothesis (Strong [1992]).

5   To avoid confusion the term relatedness is used to characterize similarities between parents and the term diversification is reserved to characterize similarities between the activities of the joint venture and the parent that is under investigation.

6   In accordance to economic theory, when the risk free rate lowers, so does the cost of capital. With the cost of capital lower it is more attractive for companies to invest. So the risk free rate is a proxy of the investment climate. This control variable helps in identifying over-or undervaluation of the venture due to the economic situation at that particular time.

7   Source: Worldscope.

8   Source: KPMG Dealwatch.

9   Das el al. (1998) also used this proxy for the partners in the joint venture.

10   Also used in Hofstede (1980).

11   Standard industry classifications.

REFERENCES

Balakrishnan, S. and Koza, M.P. 1993. Information asymmetry, adverse selection and joint-ventures. *Journal of Economic Behavior and Organization* 20: 99–117.

Berg, S. and Friedman P. 1977. Joint ventures, competition and technological complementaries. *Southern Economic Journal* 43: 1330–1337.

Bleeke, J. and Ernst D. 1993. *Collaborating to Compete.* John Wiley & Sons, Inc: New York.

Borde, S.F.; Whyte, A.M.; Wiant, K.J; and Hoffman L.L. 1998. New evidence on factors that influence the wealth of international joint ventures. *Journal of Multinational Financial Management* 8: 63–77.

Brown, S.J. and Warner, J.B. 1985. Using daily stock returns: The case of event studies. *Journal of Financial Economics* 14: 3–31.

Cannella Jr, A.A. and Hambrick, D.C. 1993. Effects of executive departures on the performance of acquired firms. *Strategic Management Journal* 14: 137–152.

Chan, S.H.; Kensinger, J.W.; Keown, A.J; and Martin J.D. 1997. Do strategic alliances create value? *Journal of Financial Economics* 46: 199–221.

Copeland, T.; Koller, T.; and Murrin J. 1995. *Valuation: Measuring and managing the value of companies.* John Wiley & Sons, Inc: New York.

Das, S.; Sen, P. K.; and Sengupta, S. 1998. Impact of strategic alliances on firm valuation. *Academy of Management Journal* 41: 27–41.

Datta, D.K. and Puia G. 1995. Cross-border acquisitions: an examination of the influence of relatedness and cultural fit on shareholder value creation in U.S. acquiring firms. *Management International Review* 35: 337–359.

Erramilli, M.K. 1991. The experience factor in foreign market entry behavior of service firms. *Journal of International Business Studies* 22: 479–501.

Fama, E.F; Fisher, L.; Jensen, M.C.; and Roll, R. 1969. The adjustment of stock prices to new information. *International Economic Review* 10: 1–21.

Franke, R.H; Hofstede, G.; and Bond, H. 1991. Cultural roots of economic performance: A research note. *Strategic Management Journal* 12: 165–173.

Harrigan, K.R. 1988. Joint ventures and competitive strategy. *Strategic Management Journal* 9: 141–158.

Kogut, B. and Singh, H. 1988. The effect of national culture on the choice of entry mode. *Journal of International Business Studies* 19: 411–432.

Koh, J. and Venkatraman, N. 1991. Joint venture formations and stock market reactions: An assessment in the information technology sector. *Academy of Management Journal* 34: 869–892.

Lee, I. and Wyatt S.B. 1990. The effects of international joint ventures on shareholder wealth. *The Financial Review* 25: 641–649.

McConnell, J.J and Nantell, T.J. 1985. Corporate combinations and common stock returns: The case of joint ventures. *The Journal of Finance* 40: 519–536.

Mohanram, P. and Nanda, A. 1998. When do joint ventures create value? Working paper. Harvard Business Studies.

Shane, S.A. 1992. The effects of cultural differences in perceptions of transaction costs on national differences in the presence for licencing. *Management International Review* 32: 295–311.

Strong, N. 1992. Modeling abnormal returns: A review article. *Journal of Business Finance and Accounting* 19: 533–553.

## Chapter 22

Jim Lai and Sudi Sudarsanam

CORPORATE RESTRUCTURING IN RESPONSE TO PERFORMANCE DECLINE: IMPACT OF OWNERSHIP, GOVERNANCE AND LENDERS[*]

Source: *European Finance Review*, 1(2) (1997): 197–233.

ABSTRACT

Firms in performance decline may choose a variety of restructuring strategies for recovery with conflicting welfare implications for different stakeholders such as shareholders, lenders and managers. Choice of recovery strategies is therefore determined by the complex interplay of ownership structure, corporate governance and lender monitoring of such firms. For a sample of 297 U.K. firms experiencing relative stock return decline during 1987–93, we examine the impact of these factors as well as other control factors on their turnaround strategies. Strategy choices during the decline year and two post-decline years are modelled with logit regressions. Our results show that turnaround strategy choices are significantly influenced by both agency and control variables. While there is agreement among stakeholders on certain strategies there is also evidence of conflict of interests among them. There is further evidence of shifting coalitions of stakeholders for or against certain strategies.

1. INTRODUCTION

FIRMS WHICH HAVE EXPERIENCED SUBSTANTIAL decline in their financial performance adopt a variety of strategies to reverse that decline. These strategies range from operational actions to rationalise production and reduce costs, changes to financial and management structure to asset sales. Some of these strategies are of a fire fighting nature with a short term cash flow increasing focus whereas others are of a longer term strategic nature with no immediate cash flow implications.

A firm faced with performance decline may choose operational restructuring to improve its efficiency and profitability, asset sales to raise cash to meet its financial commitments to, say, lenders, renegotiate its debt to relieve the immediate burden of financial commitments, issue new equity to finance its operations or reconfigure its business strategy by making strategic disposals of businesses or investing in new businesses. A precondition to firm revival may often be the removal of existing management. These strategies may be grouped broadly into an operational, asset, financial and managerial restructuring.

Operational, asset, financial and managerial restructuring may be motivated by the need to get the firm back on its feet.

However, any restructuring strategy has different implications for different stakeholders – shareholders, lenders, managers and employees often leading to conflict of interests among them. While one stakeholder group may find its control diluted or investment eroded, another group may have its stake strengthened.

An understanding of the nature of the restructuring process – the range of restructuring choices available, the determinants of these choices and the relative effectiveness of different types of restructuring – enables firms suffering performance decline to design feasible and effective restructuring programmes to achieve turnaround. The extant literature in finance and strategy provides a fragmented perspective on the issues raised by firm performance decline and turnaround. In this study we attempt a more comprehensive and integrated analysis of corporate restructuring in response to performance decline.

We examine the restructuring strategy choices made by firms which have experienced relative performance decline in terms of stock market returns to equity holders. These choices are made by managers who are subject to a variety of pressures from different stakeholders and also to conflicts of interest. The choices made by declining firms are analysed within the agency model of the relationship among shareholders, lenders and managers. The central thesis of this paper is that these different stakeholders have preferences for different restructuring strategies. We hypothesise that choice of recovery strategies is determined by the complex interplay of the ownership structure, corporate governance and lender monitoring of the firms in decline.

For a sample of 297 U.K. firms whose stock returns declined from being in the top 50% of all U.K. listed firms to the bottom 20% we assemble empirical evidence on the extent and variety of restructuring undertaken by declining firms. The impact of ownership, governance and lender monitoring on the restructuring strategic choices is examined for a variety of strategies.

Our results show that turnaround strategy choices are significantly influenced by both agency variables and control variables. While there is agreement among stakeholders on certain strategies there is also evidence of conflict of interests between lenders and managers and between managers and some block shareholders. Lenders' preference for cash generative action is in direct conflict with shareholders' incentive to avoid such action. Entrenched managers are less likely to restructure the firm and replace themselves. Non-institutional rather than institutional shareholders appear to be active monitors. Independent non-executive directors, however, seem to be effective in their oversight of managers as they instigate more turnaround strategies.

The paper is organised as follows. Section 2 discusses the theoretical framework for the choice of turnaround strategies by declining firms. The methodology and data for our empirical analysis are described in Section 3. The results are presented and interpreted in Section 4. Section 5 provides a summary and the conclusions.

2. THEORETICAL FRAMEWORK

The choice of turnaround strategies is contingent upon a number of factors. Since different strategies may have different, and often conflicting, welfare implications for managers, shareholders and lenders, the choice of any strategy can only be made as a trade off among these contending stakeholders. The restraints on any single stakeholder group such as managers maximising their own self-interest to the detriment of other stakeholders is a function of the governance structure and the mechanics of agency monitoring in a firm (Gilson, 1990). Thus, an understanding of the nature and sources of these restraints is necessary to make the appropriate turnaround strategy choices.

2.1. Impact of agency conflicts on turnaround strategy choice

The restraints on managerial choice of turnaround strategies may be examined within the context of the agency conflicts among shareholders, managers and lenders. The motivations of these players also provide the impetus to the pursuit of turnaround strategies so that firm value is enhanced and its ability to meet its financial commitments is restored.

While both lenders and shareholders have a common interest in restoring firm viability and its ability to generate adequate returns to their investment in the firm, in the turnaround process either group may gain at the expense of the other. Shareholders may benefit from a transfer of wealth from creditors when managers undertake risky investments (Myers, 1977). Likewise, lenders may benefit from a wealth transfer from shareholders when sale of assets to pay off debts eliminates the option value of those assets (Lang et al., 1995). Similarly, managers may pursue turnaround strategies which least harm them while the burden of turnaround is borne by shareholders or lenders or both. Managers' pursuit of self-serving objectives may manifest itself in their choice of strategies. However, managerial discretion in choice of strategy may be tempered by the agency control mechanism in place in the firm.

Broadly, the turnaround options available to declining firms include: operational, business strategic, managerial and financial restructuring. Not all of these actions will appeal equally to shareholders, managers and lenders since they demand different degrees of sacrifice from these stakeholders during the turnaround process.

Managerial restructuring, e.g. replacement of the top managers, is obviously unlikely to be favoured by managers and where the governance structure is weak and the management is entrenched such replacement may not happen. Similarly, where financial restructuring involves additional borrowing or dilution of the covenants protecting existing lenders they are likely to resist such debt restructuring. On the other hand, turnaround based on fresh infusion of equity is likely to be preferred by lenders but frowned upon by shareholders. Dividend cuts may be loathed by shareholders but supported by lenders.

Strategic or asset restructuring in the form of divestments may be favoured by shareholders provided the divestment proceeds are not used to pay down debt. Lenders may support divestment provided their debt is paid off. New investments of a high risk nature may be preferred by shareholders but not necessarily by lenders (Myers, 1977).

2.2. Impact of lender monitoring on managerial choice

In the agency model of the firm posited by Jensen (1989a) a highly leveraged firm will react faster to poor performance than less leveraged ones due to a desire to avoid breaching debt covenants. This early response preserves the going-concern value of highly leveraged firms as compared to less-leveraged firms.

Ofek (1993) examines the role of lender monitoring within the agency paradigm in influencing the choice of restructuring strategies of poorly performing companies in the U.S.A. He finds that high gearing significantly increases the probability of financial and operational restructuring. Gilson, John and Lang (1990) find no relation between gearing and financial restructuring.[1]

High leverage is also found by Storey et al. (1987) to be more positively associated with equity rights issues (i.e. financial restructuring) in failing firms than in non-failing firms. They attribute this to the monitoring pressure from bank creditors who are only willing to continue financial support conditional upon shareholders sharing a part of the burden of turnaround.

Impact of debt on managerial choice of turnaround strategies may depend on the characteristics of debt such as ownership, maturity structure and security available. Debt ownership by informed bank creditors promotes more effective monitoring than by other types of debt holders. This increased effectiveness arises from the banks' close relations with firms and their access to private information, a right established by loan covenants or through ongoing bank relationship.

Banks' reputational capital provides them with the economic incentives to monitor firm actions. Hirschey et al. (1990) find that the higher the proportion of bank debt in total debt the higher is the positive return on announcement of a sell-off to the divestor shareholders. This superior valuation is attributed to the more effective and credible monitoring by banks with a large stake.

James (1987) argues that banks provide some special service not available from other lenders. He finds evidence of a larger positive stock price reaction to new bank credit agreements than to announcement of private placements or public straight debt offerings. In Gilson's (1989) study bank lenders frequently initiate senior management changes in financially distressed firms.

Maturity structure of debt is likely to influence the borrower firm's restructuring decisions since the greater the proportion of short term debt the greater should be the level of monitoring. The credit renewal process associated with short-term debt subjects firm managers to more frequent monitoring than long-term debt and increases the bargaining power of banks over managerial decisions such as liquidation (Diamond, 1993; Rajan, 1992; Gertner and Scharftein, 1991) and the use of proceeds from asset sales (Brown et al., 1994). Empirically, Ofek (1993) finds that short-term leverage increases the probability of all the restructuring strategies examined by him except financial restructuring.

In addition to debt ownership and maturity structure, the security for the debt may also impact on the restructuring decision. A high proportion of unsecured debt is likely to be associated with more effective monitoring because of the unprotected nature of this debt. Lack of security may induce more intense monitoring by unsecured lenders.

The efficiency of lender monitoring is almost beyond question. Leverage may have a positive and significant relation with the incidence of all four generic turnaround strategies. The primary motivation is debt repayment. Lenders are expected to favour asset sales proceeds to be applied to debt repayment rather than retained by the firm (Slatter, 1984; Lang et al., 1995). They are likely to favour cut or omission of dividends to conserve cash or equity issues to increase liquidity (Storey et al., 1987). Lenders may expect extensive asset sales, operational cost cutting and management changes as a prerequisite for debt restructuring. Debt restructuring may be the last resort after exhausting other forms of restructuring.

2.3. Impact of ownership structure on managerial choice

The share ownership in the declining firm may provide an agency mechanism for controlling managerial discretion in the choice of turnaround strategy. Block shareholders may provide effective oversight leading to value maximising behaviour on the part of managers (Shleifer and Vishny, 1986). Where managers hold significant shares, their interests may be aligned to those of shareholders in general.

The role of block shareholders as agency monitors has been studied by many researchers. Large shareholders provide an efficient mechanism for resolving the agency conflict which arises in a firm owned by atomistic shareholders (Jensen and Meckling, 1976). Demsetz and Lehn (1985) argue that as the size of large shareholding increases, monitoring effectiveness also increases. Block shareholders may be institutional or non-institutional, and associated to incumbent management or independent of it. Agency monitoring effectiveness varies across these different blockholder categories.

For the U.S., Hill and Snell (1989) find a positive relation between large shareholding and firm productivity. McConnell and Servaes (1990) find a significant relation between Tobin's q and the level of institutional block shareholding. Agrawal and Mandelker (1990) provide evidence of a positive relation between institutional ownership and stockholder wealth effects of various types of anti-takeover amendments in target companies. Jarrel and Poulsen (1987) show that firms that adopt the most value-reducing forms of anti-takeover charter amendments also have lower institutional shareholding than do other firms. Brickley et al. (1988) find evidence that institutional investors who do not have business dealings with corporate management are more likely to vote against anti-takeover amendments. All these U.S.-based results are consistent with the reduction of agency costs due to large shareholders monitoring.[2]

The positive valuation impact of large share acquisitions has been evidenced in a number of studies. Barclay and Holderness (1991), Mikkelson and Ruback (1985), Holderness and Sheehan (1985) and Choi (1991) report, for the U.S., that block acquisitions in excess of 5% generate significant wealth gains for target shareholders. For the U.K., Sudarsanam (1996) reports similar results.

Shivdasani (1993) emphasises the need to differentiate associated from non-associated non-institutional block holders. Shareholders associated with incumbent management, e.g. family trusts or company pension funds are less likely to provide effective monitoring of managers. Shivdasani (1993) finds evidence that unassociated shareholders increase the probability of hostile takeovers, invoking their disciplinary motives.

Bethel and Liebeskind (1993) report that block share ownership is associated with corporate restructuring. Sudarsanam (1995) finds substantial asset, financial and managerial restructuring following large block acquisitions and value increases attendant upon such acquisitions are maintained or enhanced over the following three years.

In contrast, shareholders are also known to frown upon certain strategies which are painful to themselves such as dividend cut/omission (Asquith and Mullins, 1986; DeAngelo and DeAngelo, 1990), rights issue (e.g. Schipper and Smith, 1986) and asset sales where proceeds are utilised to pay down debts (Lang et al., 1995).

2.4. Impact of corporate governance structure

Corporate governance structure as a monitoring mechanism to reduce the agency problem between shareholders and managers has recently received much attention (Cadbury Report, 1992). Composition of the board of directors is an important part of this structure, influencing its policing effectiveness. Board composition is therefore likely to impact significantly on the choice of turnaround strategies.

Boards of directors differ in a number of ways: the relative importance of executive versus non-executive directors; the leadership of the board by an executive or non-executive chairman and the separation of the roles of the chairman of the board and the CEO. In the context of declining firms, their performance decline may have been caused by managerial entrenchment and weak governance structure may have contributed to this entrenchment. Turnaround may, therefore, demand managerial restructuring with the top management being replaced. Whether managerial restructuring can be carried out depends upon the independence and strength of the board as well as the power of block shareholders and lenders.

According to Fama and Jensen (1983), the separation of decision management and decision control in the decision-making process can alleviate the agency problem. Whilst inside directors are responsible for decision management, decision control should be left with outside directors. Outside directors has an incentive to monitor management actions since they have staked their reputation as professional corporate referees. Consequently, the higher the proportion of non-executive to executive directors, the more effective would be the board monitoring of management.

Empirically, Weisbach (1988) finds that CEO turnover is highly correlated with proportion of outside directors to inside directors. The monitoring function of outside directors is also supported by Rosenstein and Wyatt (1990), who find positive share price reactions to the appointment of outside directors. Further, Boeker and Goodstein (1993) report that strong insider presence significantly influences CEO replacement decisions. However, Mallette and Fowler (1992) observe empirically that the proportion of outside directors has no bearing on the adoption of poison pills. Hermalin and Weisbach (1992) and Shivdasani (1993) are unable to document any systematic relation between outside directors, firm performance and the probability of hostile takeovers.[3]

Where one person combines the roles of board chairman and CEO his or her powers are considerable. This duality of roles can promote focused objectives and a clear line of command. On the other hand, duality may entrench the top manager to the detriment of shareholders and possibly lenders, reduce the oversight function of the board and weaken the governance structure.

The role of board Chairman is to oversee the performance of board members from an informed perspective. Therefore, if the board is chaired by a non-executive Chairman, the external and part-time nature of his position coupled with information asymmetry problems can present him with difficulty in effectively controlling the board. Consequently, a non-executive Chairman strengthens CEO control and contributes to potential managerial entrenchment. An executive Chairman, on the other hand, is likely to strengthen the board's monitoring role.

Mallette and Fowler (1992) find support for the entrenchment hypothesis in their empirical study with duality increasing the probability that poison pills are adopted whereas separation diminishes the probability. However, Rechner and Dalton (1989) find no significant difference in firm performance between dual and non-dual firms.

The primary focus of this study is the impact of three broad categories of agency monitoring mechanisms – ownership, leverage and board composition – on the turnaround strategies of poorly performing firms. We examine the individual as well as the combined effects of the three mechanisms.

2.5. Impact of multiple agency control mechanisms

In the choice of restructuring strategies, the influences representing ownership, board composition and lenders may often be reinforcing but at other times working at cross purposes. In other words, the monitoring role of owners, governance and lenders may be complementary, substitutory or contradictory. Lenders and outside directors may complement each other, say in forcing management changes in declining firms. However, high leverage and high lender influence on management change may also substitute for the lack of pressure from outside directors for the same action, where the proportion of outside directors in the board is low. An example of contradictory influence arises when lenders press for asset sales and rights issue to generate cash for the purpose of paying down debt. Lenders' preference, in the latter case, clearly contradicts owners' desire to avoid injecting fresh equity funds and their preference for lenders to increase or at least maintain financial support.

2.6. Impact of dominant stakeholders

Our discussion so far has ignored the relative bargaining powers of the different stakeholder groups in declining firms when strategy choices are made. The choice of a strategy is likely to be decided by the relative strength and dominance of these stakeholders. We develop the concept of stakeholder dominance to take into account the complex interactions between the various stakeholders or agency monitors indicated above. Five types of stakeholder dominance are examined – lender, manager-owner, blockholder, CEO and collective board dominance.

2.6.1. Lender dominance

Where a firm is highly leveraged and has suffered a severe decline, lenders[4] are deemed dominant in influencing the firm's decision-making machinery. Recent work by Jensen (1989a,b) suggests that leverage is an important determinant of how decision rights are allocated among claimholders. Therefore, when a firm is severely distressed, with equity shareholders occupying a very low position in the repayment queue, lenders have the ultimate say and influence on the firm's restructuring choice.

Lenders would generally prefer cash generative strategies to facilitate debt repayment. They may frequently insist on removal of top managers and freeze in investments as a condition for continuing financial support. Removal of top managers poses a serious conflict with managers' interest, but if the firm's finance is dire, managers have little power to avoid displacement even when they hold a high equity share holding. Asset sales may pose a weak conflict of interest with block shareholders as they deem the sale of assets extinguishes the option value attached to assets sold. In the final analysis, lender dominance prevails over other stakeholders' preferences as lenders' continued support is key to the survival of the firm. Management may therefore be forced to implement cash generative actions and refrain from cash consuming asset investment and operational strategies.

2.6.2. Manager-owner dominance

If the firm's decision-making process is not dominated by lenders, and managerial and associated shareholdings are high, manager-owners are deemed to be entrenched and possess dominant influence. In the circumstance, entrenched managers are expected, in the least, to refrain from adopting managerial restructuring strategies. The literature (e.g. Maris, 1964) suggests that entrenched managers favour large size as power and compensation are related to size. Consequently, dominant managers may refrain from downsizing their operations

through operational restructuring or asset divestment and prefer size increasing acquisitions or capital expenditure.

Likewise, dominant managers are likely to disfavour the 'final resort' strategy – debt restructuring – which is adopted only when all efforts to pay off (or buy out) creditors fail. In a debt restructuring exercise, lenders frequently insist on dealing with a credible management team leading to installation of a new management team. Gilson (1989, 1990), and Murphy and Zimmerman (1993) find lenders to instigate significant top management changes in distressed firms.

2.6.3. Blockholder dominance

Where neither lenders nor manager-owners are dominant, and unassociated block-holding is high, blockholders may dominate. Operational restructuring, which is the least controversial of all strategies, is expected to be favoured by dominant block-holders. Extant literature (e.g. Schipper and Smith, 1986; Asquith and Mullins, 1986) indicating shareholders' dislike for equity-based strategies such as dividends cut and omission and equity issue, would mean that they are shunned by dominant blockholders. As discussed above, shareholders also shun asset sales as they extinguish the option value attached to the assets sold. Following from dominant shareholders' dislike for cash generative actions (equity issues and asset sales), we can expect them to disfavour investments which necessitate such cash generative actions.

Dominant blockholders are expected to favour debt restructuring as lenders frequently provide additional working capital, forgive loans or interests or make other form of concessions, though reluctantly, in the hope of realising higher debt repayments when the distressed firm is eventually turned around. Similarly, dominant block-holders who possess significant influence over management are expected to initiate top management replacement.

In summary, blockholder dominance is expected to be positively associated with operational, managerial and debt restructuring but negatively associated with all other strategies.

2.6.4. CEO and collective board dominance

When the firm is not lender, manager-owner or blockholder dominated, corporate control is expected to lie with the board of directors. However, where the board is chaired by a dual CEO, the dual CEO is expected to dominate the board and hence the firm's decision-making process. CEO board dominance is expected to favour strategies akin to manager-owner dominance firms, i.e. shun managerial restructuring, prefer investments, avoid operational restructuring and cash generative actions.

When the firm is not lender, manager-owner, blockholder or CEO dominated, corporate control is expected to lie 'collectively' with the board of directors. Since the collective interests of all stakeholders are in the avoidance of a crisis and recovery, collective board dominance is expected to be positively associated with all restructuring strategies.

No study to date has examined the relationships between agency monitors' motivations and restructuring strategy choice in a comprehensive manner. Although Ofek (1993) finds that different agency variables are associated with different restructuring strategies, his approach lacks a robust theoretical underpinning. More importantly, Ofek does not examine the relative dominance of stakeholders in shaping restructuring strategy choices. This research attempts to fill the empirical gap by exploring the impact of agency monitoring on specific strategy choice and the role of dominant stakeholders.

3. METHODOLOGY AND DATA

The first step in our empirical analysis is to devise an operational definition of performance decline. In the turnaround literature in corporate strategy and finance a range of definitions has been used, some based on

change in either simple or industry adjusted accounting ratios such as return on assets and some others based on stock returns. Given the central importance of value maximisation as an objective function within the agency model, we prefer to define performance decline in terms of stock market value changes i.e. stock returns.

Ofek (1993) defines performance decline in terms of the change in the annual stock return ranking of a firm among all the firms in the market from being in the top 67% in one year (the base year) to the bottom 10% in the following year (the distress year). This decline may range from a maximum of 100% to a minimum of 23%. This steep fall in value is regarded as sufficient to trigger various restructuring actions by the distressed firms.

We employ a definition broadly similar to Ofek's but arguably more stringent. A firm is defined as having experienced performance decline when it falls in stock return ranking of all firms on the London Stock Exchange to the bottom 20% in a year (the decline year) after having been in the top 50% in each of the two preceding years. In the decline year the maximum decline is 100% and the minimum is 30%. With this definition, in contrast to Ofek's, the fall in rank has to be much steeper for inclusion in our sample. Further, the fall is from a stable high performance. This condition avoids sampling companies whose performance decline is due to short term volatility of their share prices.[5]

Firms satisfying the above criterion of performance decline are sampled and the restructuring actions they take subsequent to decline are tracked. The agency monitoring determinants of choice of these actions by the sample firms are identified using the logit regression methodology.

3.1. Definitions of dependent variables

The various restructuring actions declining firms choose are the dependent variables for the logit regressions. These actions fall into the four generic strategies – operational, asset, managerial and financial. Ofek (1993) distinguishes between actions resulting in short term cash inflow and those with no such cash inflow since cash generation to meet the firm's financial commitments may be necessary to alleviate financial distress and avoid default on them. Accordingly, we define combinations of restructuring strategies which generate cash and those which do not.

Operational restructuring covers cost reduction, improved financial control, and closures and integration of production and other facilities. Asset restructuring includes both asset reduction and new investment. Asset reductions comprise divestment, management buy-out, spin off, sale and leaseback, and other asset sales. Investment includes acquisitions and internal capital expenditures. Internal capital expenditure is measured by significant expenditure in plant and machinery, exceeding routine asset replacements. Significant expenditure is taken as that in excess of 10% of the pre-decline year total assets.[6]

Managerial restructuring covers replacement of Chairman or CEO or managing director. Financial restructuring refers to both equity- and debt-based strategies. Equity issues (excluding those issued in an acquisition-related share exchange) and dividend cuts and omission are part of an equity-based restructuring. Debt restructuring includes debt refinancing and renegotiation of the terms of existing debt. Cash generating strategies include asset sales and equity issues. Managerial and operational changes are deemed non-cash generative in the short term. The above restructuring actions are summarised in Table 22.1. In the logit regressions each restructuring action is coded as a dummy variable.

3.2. Explanatory variables

The main explanatory variables are the agency monitoring variables representing different aspects of share ownership, leverage and board composition. Leverage is book value of total debt over book values of debt and equity. The total debt is also decomposed into bank debt, short-term debt and unsecured debt (as a proportion of debt and equity). Debt comprises all interest-bearing liabilities. Equity refers to shareholders funds i.e. equity and reserves. Short-term debt is any debt that matures in less than 12 months.

Share ownership categories are proxied by directors' shareholding and block holding in excess of 5% prior to 1990 and 3% after 1990. Block holding is divided into shareholding by financial institutions and non-institutional holding. The latter is further split into associated and unassociated blocks. Associated blocks are held by families or trusts associated with the directors and company pension schemes.

Board composition is proxied by three variables: proportion of outside or non-executive directors on the board, whether the board is chaired by a non-executive director, CEO cum Chairman (CEO duality) where the two posts are held by the same person.

The empirical literature suggests that turnaround strategy choices are also dictated by non-agency monitoring factors. These additional variables are included in our regressions as control variables. Severity of decline dictates both the pace of restructuring and choice of particular actions. For example, asset investment or acquisitions may be less likely in more seriously distressed firms as they consume scarce cash resources.

Economic and industry condition also may influence choice of strategy. For example, where the industry as a whole is depressed, asset sales and divestments may not raise as much cash as otherwise (Shleifer and Vishny, 1992). Economic downturns may emphasise the need for operational cost cutting actions and preclude equity issues with depressed stock markets. Economic condition is measured by the Gross Domestic Product (GDP) growth rate whilst industry condition is represented by the firm's Financial Times-Actuaries (FTA) industry return. Size of the firm is a proxy for both the flexibility and internal slack available to the declining

Table 22.1 Definition of restructuring strategies

Restructuring strategies selected by firms experiencing stock return performance decline are identified and defined. Information on strategies is from press releases to the London Stock Exchange which are documented by Extel Financial News Summary from 1987, with the exception of capital expenditure. Capital expenditure is based on annual reports and accounts. Supplementary information is also collected from Andersen Corporate Register and Hambro Company Guide, Datastream International, and Company Reports and Accounts. These alternative sources are also used for cross-checking information reported in the Extel Financial News Summary.

Strategy	Definition
Operational restructuring	
Operational restructuring	Cost rationalisation, layoffs, closures and integration of business units.
Asset restructuring	
Asset sales	Divestment of subsidiaries, management buy-outs, spin-offs, sale-and-leaseback, and other asset sales.
Acquisitions	Full and partial acquisitions of businesses.
Capital expenditure	Internal capital expenditure on fixed assets such as plant and machinery.
Managerial restructuring	
Managerial restructuring	Removal of Chairman or Chief Executive Officer Officer/Managing Director (retirement under the age of 65 is included).
Financial restructuring	
Dividend cut or omission	Omission or reduction of dividends from previous year.
Equity issue	Issue of equity for cash.
Debt restructuring	Debt refinancing involving extending, converting or forgiving of debt and interest.
Combination strategies	
Cash generative actions	Asset sales and cash equity issue.

firm and the opportunities for certain strategies such as divestment. A large firm may be able to negotiate debt restructuring and may be able to avoid dividend cuts.

Where the firm's performance decline has been caused by internal, firm-specific factors such as mistaken business strategy, bad implementation of strategy or lack of financial control, any restructuring has to reverse the firm specific causes. Again, the choice of restructuring will be dictated by the existence of significant internal causes of decline.

The above explanatory variables are summarised in Table 22.2. Chairman cum CEO, non-executive Chairman and internal cause of decline are each represented by a dummy variable.

3.3. DATA

As stated earlier, sample firms are those which experience a sharp decline in their relative stock return performance. On a ranking of annual stock returns of all London Stock Exchange listed firms, firms which fall into the bottom 20% in the decline year after having been in the top 50% in the previous two years (base years) are sampled. This sampling criterion is called the 50 : 50 : 20 rule. The sample covers the period 1985–1993, with 1985–1991 as the base years and 1987–1993 as the decline years.

Datastream International is the data source for annual stock returns. An initial sample of 415 declining firms satisfying

Table 22.2 Definition of explanatory variables

The table defines three groups of variables representing firms' agency monitoring mechanism which are expected to influence the choice of restructuring strategies by poor performing firms. Debt structure is based on accounting information provided by Datastream International and Extel Company Research. Ownership and governance data are extracted from Andersen Corporate Register, Hambro Company Guide and Annual Reports and Accounts. Block shareholding is holding of 5% or more (3% or more since 31st May 1990) as disclosed in the company annual reports. Industry is the Financial Times-Actuaries Index industry group to which the sample firm belongs.

Variable	Definition
Debt structure	
Leverage	Total book debt over total book debt and equity
Short term leverage	Short term debt over total book debt and equity
Bank leverage	Bank debt over total book debt and equity
Unsecured leverage	Unsecured debt over total book debt and equity
Ownership structure	
Managerial shareholding	Shareholding by members of the board of directors
Associated block shareholding	Shareholding by family members or trusts of members of the board and company pension plans
Institutional block shareholding	Shareholding by institutional investors
Non-institutional unassociated block shareholding	Shareholding by non-institutional blockholders unassociated with management
Governance structure	
Chairman cum CEO	Combined role of Chief Executive and Chairman (CEO duality)
Non-executive Chairman	Chairman in a non-executive capacity
Proportion of outside directors	Non-executive directors as a percentage of total number of directors
Control variables	
Economic condition	GDP growth in the restructuring year
Industry condition	FTA industry return in the restructuring year
Internal cause of decline	Reported internal problems such as project failures, bad acquisitions or poor financial control
Severity of decline	Stock returns ranking in the year of decline
Size	Log of market value of equity at the end of pre-decline year

our 50 : 50 : 20 rule is assembled from a total of 3706 firms covered by Datastream over the period 1985–1993. Sampling excludes financials, utilities and firms with a market capitalisation of less than £10m. Small firms are excluded for want of sufficient data on their restructuring.

Data on the sample firms' restructuring activities and on the explanatory variables are collected from Datastream International, company annual reports and Extel Annual News Summaries. Such data were not available for all companies defined as declining. The final sample consists of 297 poor performing firms.

3.4. Sample characteristics

3.4.1. Performance decline

Table 22.3 provides the descriptive statistics for the sample. From Panel A, the mean (median) annual log returns for the sample in the base and distress years are: 42% (36%) (base year −2), 33% (28%) (base year −1) and −51% (−38%) (decline year). The returns to the Financial Times All Share (FTALL) Index in the same years are: 16%, 15% and 16% respectively. The sample firms clearly outperform the market in the base years and under perform it in the decline year.

Moreover, the decline in performance for the sample is also very steep. This pattern of steep decline is repeated for each of the sample decline years 1987 to 1993. The sample median returns in the base years for the sample range from −6% in 1990, a recession period, to 53% in 1986. In the decline years the median return ranges from −12% in 1993 to −112% in 1990.

Panel B of Table 22.3 gives the performance statistics based on accounting variables. Both profitability and cash flows deteriorate significantly in the decline year. The median fall in the profitability measures − operating margin, earnings per share, return on equity and return on asset − ranges from 18% to 22%, all significant at 1%. Median fall in operating cash flows − profit before interest, tax and depreciation deflated by total assets − is 15%, significant at 1%. The accounting-based performance measures thus reflect the stock return decline. Our sample thus captures both operating performance and stock return performance decline.[7] Excess volatility of stock returns does not appear to cause the performance decline in our sample firms. Indeed, the sample betas are not unusual (mean and median values are both less than 1) and likely to cause the stock return decline.

3.4.2. Agency monitoring mechanisms

Table 22.4 provides descriptive statistics on the leverage, share ownership and governance structure in base year −1. The median leverage, total book debt to book debt and equity, is 27% and median short-term debt, bank debt and unsecured debt as proportions of book debt and equity are in the range 12% to 16%. The leverage variables are not entirely mutually exclusive. For example, there may be an overlap between short term and bank leverage. This implies that when all the leverage variables are included in a regression, the empirical result has to be interpreted cautiously.

Median directors' shareholding is 9.5% and associated block holding is negligible. Institutional ownership amounts to a median value of 6.9%. Non-institutional but unassociated block holding has a median of 0% (but a mean of 7%).

Comparison with the only other study by Ofek (1993) that examines the determinants of restructuring strategy choice during performance decline reveals interesting differences in agency mechanism between U.S. and U.K. firms. Ofek reports median leverage, managerial shareholding and outside (non-managerial) shareholding of 31%, 22% and 6% respectively. This compares with our sample's 27%, 9.5% and 15.7% (not shown in Table 22.4). U.S. firms have apparently higher levels of managerial shareholding but lower levels of outside or non-managerial shareholdings. The difference may lie in difference between sampling criteria as firms studied by Ofek are in the bottom 10% in the decline year. When we test for this difference by selecting only firms that fall to the bottom 10% ie. 50 : 50 : 10 firms the statistics are respectively 27%, 11% and 16%. Therefore, the differences between the two studies are more likely to stem from market differences than sampling criterion differences.

As regards board composition, in 44% of sample firms one person plays the dual roles of Chairman and CEO. Non-executive Chairmen preside over the board in 24% of the companies. The median proportion of outside directors in the sample boards is 22%.

3.4.3. Frequency of turnaround strategies

Panel A of Table 22.5 reports the frequencies of sample firms undertaking different turnaround strategies in the decline year and in the two post-decline years. We find that the most frequent form of restructuring is operational with 59% of the sample firms undertaking it in the decline year and 47% and 52% of the firms in the two following years. This is comparable to Ofek's 53% for the decline year.

Asset sales are carried out by between 27% and 38% of the firms in those years. This is much higher than the 15% rate reported by Ofek (1993) for the decline year.

Table 22.3 Descriptive statistics for stock returns and accounting performance

Panel A shows the sample firms' stock log returns in the two years prior to and including the year of decline. Return on the Financial Times All Share Index (FT-AII), a value-weighted index based on around 800 firms covering in excess of 90% of stock market capitalisation in the London Stock Exchange, is provided for comparison. Panel B shows changes in accounting based performance in the year of decline. PBIT = profit before interest and tax. EPS = profit after tax, minority interests and preference dividends but before extraordinary items/the average number of shares in issue in the year. Return on equity = profit attributable to shareholders/share capital and reserves less intangibles. Return on assets = profit before interest and tax/total assets less current liabilities. PBITD = profit before interest and tax plus depreciation (proxy for cash flows). Total debt is the total of all interest-bearing debt, i.e. short, long and subordinated debt. Capital employed is the sum of book debt plus book equity. Beta is based on figures computed by the Risk Measurement Service of London Business School, at the beginning of the year prior to decline. Size is market capitalisation at the beginning of the year of decline. in Panel B the mean and median are tested using the t-test and the Mann-Whitney Wilcoxon test.

Panel A: Annual stock returns in the year of, one year prior to, and two years prior to, decline

	No.	Returns in decline year-2		Returns in decline year-1		Returns in decline year	
		Mean	*Med.*	*Mean*	*Med.*	*Mean*	*Med.*
Total sample	297	42.20	35.56	32.63	28.07	-51.12	-37.87
FT-All Share		16.15		14.59		16.29	
Decline year, 1987	41	40.30	33.65	50.20	41.20	-30.10	-23.97
FT-All Share		18.3		24.3		7.7	
Decline year, 1988	55	61.10	52.86	49.20	40.49	-39.70	-33.41
FT-All Share		24.3		7.7		11.0	
Decline year, 1989	54	44.10	39.46	28.70	23.61	-50.20	-41.72
FT-All Share		7.7		11		30.8	
Decline year, 1990	32	38.40	35.14	32.70	25.98	-131.00	-112.31
FT-All Share		11		30.8		-10.3	
Decline year, 1991	28	23.90	20.58	-7.00	-6.19	-59.20	-54.03
FT-All Share		30.8		-10.3		18.9	
Decline year, 1992	19	1.60	2.79	36.00	24.88	-95.70	-80.53
FT-All Share		-10.3		18.9		18.7	
Decline year, 1993	68	47.20	40.51	27.10	23.06	-20.40	-11.58
FT-All Share		18.90		18.70		25.10	

Panel B: Changes in profitability and cash flows in the year of decline

	Mean (t statistics)	Median* (Z statistics)
PBIT/Sales	−19.1 (9.42)[a]	−17.6 (−10.34)[a]
Earnings per share	−25.6 (4.49)[a]	−19.6 (−7.17)[a]
Return on equity	−23.5 (7.21)[a]	−21.6 (−7.93)[a]
Return on assets	−22.4 (8.80)[a]	−20.9 (−8.85)[a]
PBITD/Capital employed	−15.3 (7.30)[a]	−14.7 (7.52)[a]
PBITD/Total debt	−27.6 (8.23)[a]	−26.8 (−8.30)[a]
Risk (beta)	0.95 Min (0.05)	0.96 Max (1.49)

a Indicates significance at 1%.

Table 22.4 Descriptive statistics for agency and control variables

The table shows the descriptive statistics for the explanatory variables in the pre-decline year. For definitions of the variables see Tables 22.1 and 22.2. Chairman cum CEO, Non-executive Chairman and internal cause of decline are dummy variables coded as 1 when these are present and 0 if otherwise. Source: Hambro Company Guide and Corporate Register, Datastream International and Company Reports and Accounts

Agency variables	*Pre-decline year*	
	Mean	Median
Capital structure	0.29	0.27
Leverage	0.15	0.12
Short leverage	0.19	0.16
Bank leverage	0.17	0.12
Unsecured leverage		
Ownership structure (%)		
Managerial shareholding	19.90	9.5
Associated block shareholding	0.71	0.0
Institutional block shareholding	12.2	6.9
Non-institutional unassociated	7.1	0.0
block shareholding		
Governance structure		
Chairman cum CEO	44.1%	–
Non-executive Chairman	24.2%	–
Proportion of outside directors	0.20	0.22
Control variables		
Internal cause of decline	0.30	–
Severity of decline	10.8	10.9
Size (£M)	344.2	54.8

	Decline year		*Decline year + 1*		*Decline year + 2*	
	Mean	*Median*	*Mean*	*Median*	*Mean*	*Median*
Economic condition	2.27	2.34	2.08	2.34	0.68	0.70
Industry condition	7.80	11.29	3.60	7.80	−32.75	−16.88

Surprisingly, acquisitions do not cease when firms hit trouble and they are carried out by nearly 50% of the sample firms in the decline year and by 36% and 27% of the firms in the post-decline years. Internal capital expenditure, again surprisingly, does not cease but is incurred by 62% of firms in the decline year and by 50% and 48% in the following years.

Removal of top management is observed in 20% (in decline year) to 26% (in decline year + 1) of the sample firms. Again, Ofek (1993) reports a similar 21% of top management replacement in the year of decline. Debt restructuring is quite infrequent with only 2% of sample firms in the decline year and 3% and 7% in the following years respectively taking recourse to it. In contrast, Ofek (1993) finds 11% of his sample firms restructure their debt in the year of decline. Debt restructuring appears to be more common among U.S. than U.K. firms (only 4% of firms declining to the bottom 10%, i.e. 50 : 50 : 10 firms, adopt it). Equity issues are made by 20% of sample firms in the decline year but by only about 10% in the following years. The most frequently employed financial restructuring device is dividend cut or omission. The proportions of firms adopting this strategy in the three years are: 24%, 27% and 34%.

Table 22.5 Descriptive statistics for restructuring strategies and frequency of restructuring strategies pursued by U.K. listed firms during 1989–1994

This table shows the distribution of corporate restructuring actions in the year of decline, one year, and two years post-decline. Frequency is the proportion of sample firms adopting the strategy. Sample size declines in post-decline years due to failure of firm, takeover or where no data is available, i.e. firms declining in 1993 (68 firms) are excluded from decline year + 2 analysis. Source: Company press releases and Company Reports and Accounts.

Panel A: Descriptive statistics for restructuring strategies in the year of, one and two years after decline

Restructuring strategy	Decline year, frequency(%)	Decline year + 1, frequency (%)	Decline year + 2, frequency (%)
Operational restructuring			
Cost rationalisation, closures and integration of business units	58.6	46.7	51.6
Asset restructuring			
Asset reduction	26.6	37.8	35.6
Acquisition	50.2	35.9	27.1
Capital expenditure	61.6	50.4	47.9
Managerial restructuring			
Remove top management	19.5	25.9	21.8
Financial restructuring			
Dividend cut or omission	23.6	27.0	34.0
Equity issue	20.2	10.4	13.3
Debt restructuring	2.4	3.3	7.4
Cash generative actions	40.1	44.1	43.6
Sample size	297	270	188

Panel B: Frequency of restructuring strategies pursued by U.K. listed firms during 1989–1994

Asset sales cover divestments, management buy-outs and other asset sales. Acquisitions represent full and partial acquisitions. Dividend cut/omission refers to cut/omission in dividends per share over the previous year. Rights issues encompass rights issue, rights offer, offer for sale, open offer and placing of firm shares with institutions and financial intermediaries. Source: Financial Times Extel Company Research and Company Analysis.

Average no. of firms	Asset sales %	Acquisitions %	Dividend cut/ omission %	Rights issue %	Cash generative actions %
1521	19.6	34.5	20.8	15.2	31.6

An interesting question to ask is how does the frequency of strategies followed by performance decline firms compare with that in the population of firms listed in the U.K. Do these frequencies differ from the population benchmarks and why? Panel B of Table 22.5 provides answers to these questions where population data are available. From an extensive and rigorous search of financial news reported by firms and reported by FT Extel in their Company Research CD-ROM, we compile the average number of firms in the population adopting asset sales, acquisition, dividend cut/omission, rights issue and cash generative actions, during the period 1989–1994. The period broadly coincides with the period under study, and the year 1989 is the first year covered by the Company Research CD-ROM.

Unsurprisingly, a higher proportion of our sample firms (34%) sell their assets than in the population (20%),[8] from the year of decline to two years thereafter. In the case of acquisitions, sample firms clearly overtake the population with 50% versus 35% of firms in the population making acquisitions in the year of decline. However, with the onset of decline, sample firms reduce their rate of acquisitions to the population rate one year after decline. Two years post-decline, far fewer sample firms seek acquisitions compared to the population. A similar pattern is observed with regard to equity issue. More sample firms tap the market than the population at large, 20% in the decline year, versus 15%. However, sample firms are less likely to be successful in raising finance from equity investors subsequent to performance decline than the firm in the population. Finally, more sample firms resort to cash generative actions than the population with an annual average of 43% of sample firms taking it compared to only 32% of firms in the population. Overall, our sample of declining firms carries out various restructuring activities more intensively than the firm population at large.

4. RESULTS

4.1. Impact of stakeholder dominance on turnaround strategy choice

We divide our sample into two groups – one stakeholder dominated and the other non-dominated by that stakeholder. For each stakeholder group – lenders, manager-owners, block shareholders, CEO and collective board of directors – we examine the likelihood of a given strategy being chosen. The difference in the proportions of sample firms in the dominated and non-dominated groups choosing a strategy is tested for statistical significance. Any significant difference reflects the influence of the dominant stakeholder.

Table 22.6 shows the proportions of sample firms pursuing a given strategy in the decline and two post-decline years when the differences in these proportions

between dominant and non-dominant groups are significant. Sample firms are lenders dominated when their leverage is in the top quartile of all the sample firms and they are in severe decline (bottom 50% in sample stock ranking in the year of decline). Lenders under such circumstances are likely to have high stakes in recovery and to exercise their priority rights. Sample firms are manager-owner dominated when they are not lender dominated according to the above definition and the managerial and associated shareholdings are in the top quartile of all sample firms.

Where neither lenders nor manager-owners are dominant according to the above definitions and the unassociated block shareholding is in the top quartile of all sample firms, the firms are deemed block shareholders dominated. Finally, the sample firms not dominated by lenders, manager-owners and block shareholders, they are deemed to be under the control of the board of directors. In turn, the board may be dominated by a dual CEO or collectively by the board members.

Panel A of Table 22.6 shows the effect of lender dominance on strategy choice. To summarise, lender-dominated firms are more likely to opt for operational restructuring, cash generative actions, dividend cut/omission and debt restructuring. They are less likely to approve of cash-consuming strategy such as capital expenditure. They have little influence on management changes.

In Panel B, the effects of manager-owner dominance are shown. Manager-owner dominated firms are more likely to undertake capital expenditure and less inclined to pursue operational restructuring and acquisitions. They are also less likely to sack their top management!

When firms are dominated by blockholders, their influence is less pronounced and limited to two strategies as shown in Panel C. These shareholders make operational restructuring and capital expenditure less likely. CEO dominant board influence is also limited but stronger than with blockholder dominance. Declining firms dominated by their CEOs prefer capital expenditure but disfavour dividend cut/ omission. They understandably reduce the chances of managerial restructuring. Collective board dominance again influences only three strategies. With little conflict of interests in the board, operational restructuring, cash generative actions and acquisitions are favoured by the board collectively.

Having explored the impact of stakeholder dominance on restructuring strategy choice, we now examine the individual and joint impact of agency monitoring mechanisms on strategy choice.

4.2. Impact of individual agency monitoring mechanisms on turnaround strategy choice

Tables 22.7–22.9 report the model coefficients for the logistic regressions of corporate restructuring strategy choices on the agency and control variables. A separate regression is run for each strategy and for each of the following years: year of performance decline (the decline year), the year after the decline year (decline year + 1) and the second year after the decline year (decline year + 2).

We model the strategy choices in each year, rather than over a single period covering the three years, to examine whether there is a time lag in the impact of the agency and control variables. It is plausible that certain drastic strategies like top managerial change or asset reduction may be undertaken after strategies such as operational restructuring.

In the decline year, in Table 22.7, the logistic models are significant (based on the Chi-square statistic) in all except where managerial restructuring and debt restructuring are the dependent variables. Significance of the individual variables is tested for using the Wald statistic.[9] The explanatory power of the models, measured by McFadden's R^3, ranges from 4% to 24%.

It appears that in the decline year itself significant restructuring begins to take place and the impact of several agency and control variables is felt. Lenders increase the probability of cash generative and debt

restructuring strategies. They, however, disfavour capital expenditure.

Associated shareholding significantly influences the choice of several strategies. It reduces the probability of the declining firm pursuing operational restructuring, cash generative actions and acquisitions. Unassociated shareholders, however, have no influence whatsoever in the year of decline.

As regards the governance structure, declining firms with CEO duality are more likely to increase capital expenditure and less likely to take cash generative actions. Non-executive Chairmen and the proportion of outside directors on the board have little Influence in the choice of turnaround strategy, at least in the decline year.

The control variables have varying impact on strategy choice. Where firm decline coincides with an economic downturn, firms react with several strategies. They resort to more operational restructuring, managerial restructuring and dividend cut/omission. However, cash generative actions and investments are less likely during an economic downturn. On the other hand, if the whole of their industry suffers decline, the sample firms are more likely to increase their capital expenditure perhaps to gain a competitive advantage, cut/omit their dividends, and restructure their debts. Where decline has resulted from firm specific internal problems, operational restructuring is more likely.

The more severely declining firms (represented by low ranking on stock returns in the decline year) are more likely to go for operational restructuring, top management replacement, dividend cut/omission and debt restructuring. Finally, large companies are more likely to avoid the need to cut/omit dividends.

The strategy choices made in the second year of decline are shown in Table 22.8. All logit models are significant at the 5% level or better. McFadden's R^2 ranges from 7% to 27% and for most of the models the explanatory power is much higher than of their counterparts in the decline year in Table 22.7. It appears that agency and control variables exercise their influence more strongly in the second year of decline

Table 22.6 Stakeholder dominance and choice of restructuring strategy

The choice of restructuring strategies is determined by the relative bargaining powers of various stakeholders in the firm. The table compares the choice of strategy between stakeholder dominated and non-dominated groups of declining firms. Four stakeholder groups are identified: lenders, managers, block-holders and board of directors. Where a firm is highly leveraged (i.e. top quartile of sample firms ranked on leverage) and has suffered a severe decline (bottom 50% of sample stock ranking in year of decline), leaders are deemed dominant in influencing the type of actions the firm takes. If the firm's decision-making process is not dominated by lenders, and managerial and associated shareholding are high (i.e. top quartile of sample firms ranked on such shareholding), manager-owners are deemed to be entrenched and possess dominant influence. Where neither lenders nor manager-owners are dominant, and unassociated blockholding are high (i.e. top quartile of sample firms) relative to the total of all significant shareholders, blockholders are deemed dominant. The remaining firms, which are not lenders, manager-owners or blockholders dominated, are deemed to be controlled by the board. The board is deemed to be CEO dominated if Chairman is also the CEO and collectively dominated, otherwise. The table shows the proportion of sample firms in each group choosing the strategy. Only variables for which there is a significant difference between dominant and non-dominant groups are shown. Z is the absolute value of test statistic for the Mann–Whitney Wilcoxon test.

Strategies	Year of decline			Year of decline+1			Year of decline+2		
	Yes Mean	No Mean	Z	Yes Mean	No Mean	Z	Yes Mean	No Mean	Z
Panel A: Lender dominance									
Operational restructuring	0.73	0.56	1.94**	0.69	0.43	2.78***	0.47	0.53	0.59
Cash generative actions	0.49	0.39	1.27	0.69	0.40	3.13***	0.53	0.42	1.17
Capital expenditure	0.53	0.63	1.18	0.31	0.53	2.39**	0.33	0.51	1.73*
Dividend cut/omission	0.44	0.20	3.44***	0.51	0.23	3.48***	0.37	0.34	0.33
Debt restructuring	0.09	0.01	3.24***	0.17	0.01	4.87***	0.10	0.07	0.58
Sample size	43	254		35	235		30	158	
Panel B: Manager-owner dominance									
Operational restructuring	0.41	0.63	3.13***	0.36	0.49	1.80*	0.50	0.52	0.24
Capital expenditure	0.20	0.45	3.64***	0.22	0.50	3.74***	0.25	0.49	2.84***
Acquisitions	0.36	0.54	2.47**	0.22	0.39	2.42**	0.23	0.28	0.75
Managerial restructuring	0.15	0.21	1.05	0.16	0.29	2.04**	0.23	0.22	0.17
Sample size	61	236		58	212		44	144	

Panel C: Blockholder dominance

Operational restructuring	0.55	0.51	0.59	0.33	0.50	2.34**	0.43	0.50	1.00
Capital expenditure	0.51	0.65	2.03**	0.40	0.53	1.81*	0.53	0.48	0.24
Sample size	65	232		60	210		28	160	

Panel D: CEO board dominance

Capital expenciture	0.81	0.57	3.29***	0.67	0.46	2.58***	0.56	0.46	1.19
Managerial restructuring	0.18	0.20	0.42	0.16	0.28	1.85*	0.26	0.21	0.65
Dividend cut/omission	0.11	0.27	2.58**	0.19	0.29	1.32	0.38	0.33	0.65
Sample size	57	240		51	219		39	149	

Panel D: Non-CEO board dominance

Operational restructuring	0.73	0.54	2.89***	0.50	0.46	0.62	0.64	0.48	1.93*
Cash generative actions	0.52	0.36	2.37**	0.53	0.42	1.68*	0.51	0.41	1.18
Acquisitions	0.61	0.47	2.00**	0.47	0.32	2.15**	0.26	0.28	0.28
Sample size	71	226		66	204		47	141	

***, **, * indicate significance at 1%, 5% and 10% respectively.

Table 22.7 Logistic regression of restructuring strategies on agency and control variables (year of decline)

Coefficients of the logistic regressions of restructuring strategies on agency and control variables are presented. The dependent variable equals one if a strategy is taken, and zero if otherwise. The sample consists of 297 declining firms over the period 1987 to 1993. The decline year refers to the year in which a firm declines to the bottom 20% ranking in stock returns, in the market, after having been in the top 50% for two previous consecutive years. Coefficients are tested for significance using the Wald test statistic.
Model: Restructuring strategy = f (Debt, ownership, governance and control variables)

Explanatory variables	Operational restructuring	Cash generation	Acquisition	Capital expenditure	Managerial restructuring	Dividend cut/omission	Debt restructuring
Leverage	0.63	2.58**	0.08	-1.76**	-0.86	0.45	4.63*
Associated shareholding	-0.02**	-0.02***	-0.02**	0.00	0.00	0.01	-0.01
Unassociated shareholding	-0.01	-0.01	-0.01	-0.01	0.01	0.01	0.01
Chairman cum CEO	-0.36	-0.58*	-0.21	-0.71**	-0.09	-0.61	0.97
Non-executive Chairman	-0.05	-0.28	-0.19	0.24	-0.19	-0.69	0.11
Proportion of outside directors	1.45	-0.21	0.21	1.78	-0.54	-0.36	0.63
Economic condition	-0.15**	0.13*	0.13**	0.22***	-0.13*	-0.50***	-0.18
Industry condition	-0.01	-0.01	0.00	-0.01**	0.00	-0.02**	-0.04*
Internal problem	1.12***	0.24	-0.01	0.38	0.02	0.44	-1.05
Severity of decline	-0.05**	0.02	0.01	0.02	-0.07**	-0.12***	-0.13*
Size	-0.10	-0.05	0.07	-0.04	0.14	-0.30**	-0.06
Constant	1.69**	-0.37	-0.09	-0.13	-0.86	2.20**	-3.92
McFadden's R-square	12.1%	13.0%	5.9%	12.0%	4.4%	23.9%	4.7%
Chi-square	38.2	41.2	18.0	38.1	13.3	81.2	14.2
Regression p-value	0.00	0.00	0.08	0.00	0.27	0.00	0.22

*** , ** , * indicate significance at 1%, 5% and 10% respectively.

Table 22.8 Logistic regression of restructuring strategies on agency and control variables (year 1 after decline)

Coefficients of the logistic regressions of restructuring strategies on agency and control variables are presented. The dependent variable equals one if a strategy is taken, and zero if otherwise. The sample consists of 270 declining firms which are neither insolvent (bankrupt) nor acquired, one year post decline, in the period 1987 to 1993. Coefficients are tested for significance using the Wald test statistic.
Model: Restructuring strategy = f (Debt, ownership, governance and control variables)

Explanatory variables	Operational restructuring	Cash generation	Acquisition	Capital expenditure	Managerial restructuring	Dividend cut/omission	Debt restructuring
Leverage	0.85	2.27***	0.81	-0.83	-0.50	1.41	10.83**
Associated shareholding	-0.02***	-0.02**	-0.01	0.01	-0.01	-0.00	-0.10**
Unassociated shareholding	-0.03***	-0.01	0.00	0.00	0.00	0.00	0.05
Chairman cum CEO	0.07	-0.49	-0.04	0.60*	-0.87**	-0.36	-1.09
Non-executive Chairman	0.24	-0.91**	0.73*	0.61	-0.48	0.47	-7.36**
Proportion of outside directors	-0.14	3.35***	0.81	0.57	2.47*	0.27	2.43
Economic condition	-0.52**	0.00	0.29***	0.31***	-0.07	-0.43***	-0.55**
Industry condition	0.02**	0.01	0.01	0.00	0.00	-0.01**	0.10**
Internal problem	0.38	0.47	-0.47	-0.21	0.02	0.05	-10.47
Severity of decline	-0.06**	0.03	0.05*	0.02	-C.03	-0.12***	-0.50**
Size	-0.11	0.03	0.22**	0.30***	-C.10	-0.08	0.84
Constant	2.60***	-0.46	-3.20***	-2.46***	-0.04	0.84	-7.86*
McFadden's R-square	26.5%	16.5%	14.0%	14.0%	6.8%	19.4%	17.7%.
Chi-square	83.0	48.8	40.8	40.7	19.1	58.3	52.5.
Regression p-value	0.00	0.00	0.00	0.00	0.05	0.00	0.00.

*** ** * indicate significance at 1%, 5% and 10% respectively.

Table 22.9 Logistic regression of restructuring strategies on agency and control variables (year 2 after decline)

Coefficients of the logistic regressions of restructuring strategies on agency and control variables are presented. The dependent variable equals one if a strategy is taken, and zero if otherwise. The sample consists of 188 declining firms which are neither insolvent (bankrupt) nor acquired, two years post-decline. The sample covers only firms in decline in the period 1987 to 1992, as firms declining in 1993 have only one year post-decline strategies to the end of the analysis period i.e. December 1994. Sample size is therefore reduced. Coefficients are tested for significance using the Wald test statistic.
Model: Restructuring strategy = f (Debt, ownership, governance and control variables)

Explanatory variables	Operational restructuring	Cash generation	Acquisition	Capital expenditure	Managerial restructuring	Dividend cut/omission	Debt restructuring
Leverage	-0.20	1.32	0.71	-1.96**	-0.24	1.19	3.36*
Associated shareholding	-0.01	-0.02*	0.00	0.00	0.00	0.00	-0.01
Unassociated shareholding	-0.01	-0.02*	0.00	0.00	-0.01	0.02	0.00
Chairman cum CEO	-0.54	-0.25	0.37	0.68*	0.05	-0.07	0.56
Nonexecutive Chairman	0.07	0.19	0.46	0.55	0.06	0.15	-0.18
Proportion of outside directors	0.55	2.61*	3.13**	2.55*	-0.24	0.57	-0.43
Economic condition	-0.51***	-0.02	0.22***	0.34***	-0.08	-0.31***	0.07
Industry condition	0.01*	0.00	0.00	0.00	-0.01***	-0.01***	-0.01*
Internal problem	0.81**	0.41	-0.44	-0.16	0.07	-0.66	0.06
Severity of decline	-0.04	0.03	0.02	0.04	-0.02	-0.06*	0.00
Size	0.17	0.13	0.11	0.23	0.15	-0.15	0.22
Constant	0.27	-1.48	-3.03***	-2.71	-1.86	-0.44	-4.96***
McFadden's R-square	22.2%	12.9%	9.7%	19.3%	7.0%	27.2%	5.4%
Chi-square	47.1	25.9	19.2	40.2	13.6	59.8	10.6
Regression p-value	0.00	0.00	0.05	0.00	0.25	0.00	0.47

***, **, * indicate significance at 1%, 5% and 10% respectively.

suggesting delayed reaction to the onset of decline.

Unsurprisingly, lenders continue to press for cash generative actions. They are also more likely to resort to debt restructuring. Ownership continues to influence strategy choices in the second year. Associated shareholding decreases the probability of operational restructuring and cash generative actions. Thus, management-associated shareholders' resistance to these strategies in the decline year is reinforced in the second year. Interestingly, associated shareholders resist debt restructuring. Unassociated shareholding begins to influence adoption of strategies in the second year. They are negatively related to the choice of operational restructuring. CEO- duality continues to increase the chances of capital expenditure but, unsurprisingly, reduces the probability of managerial restructuring. Non-executive Chairmen make cash generative actions and debt restructuring less likely but capital expenditure more likely. More outside directors now means greater chances of cash generative actions and managerial restructuring. Outside directors' activism in the second year is in stark contrast to their passivity in the decline year.

The effects of economic downturn are equally significant in the second year. It continues to increase the probability of operational restructuring, dividend cut/omission and debt restructuring, but reduces the probability of investments both acquisitions and capital expenditure.

Industry downturn makes operational and debt restructuring less likely and dividend cut/omission more likely. Severity of decline impacts further in the second year. It continues to make operational restructuring, dividend cut/omission and debt restructuring more likely. In addition, the more severely declining firms are also less likely to undertake acquisitions. Internal cause of decline has little influence on strategy choice in the second year of decline. Finally, large firms increase the probability of investments in the form acquisitions and capital expenditure.

The logit models of strategic choices made in the third year of decline (decline year + 2) are shown in Table 22.9. In contrast to the model for the previous year in table 8, only five of the third year models are significant at least at the 10% level. McFadden's R^2 ranges from 5% to 27%. The third year models thus generally have less explanatory power than the models for the first two decline years. It appears that the influence of the agency and control variables on strategy choices is waning. Nevertheless, some of these variables continue to exert significant impact.

Lenders continue to restrict capital expenditure. Debt restructuring is again made more likely by lenders. Associated shareholders stubbornly resist cash generative strategies. Interestingly, unassociated shareholders join associated shareholders in resisting cash generative strategies.

As regards governance structure, dual CEOs are still more likely to go for capital expenditure. Non-executive Chairmen, however, are quite inactive. With more outside directors a poorly performing firm is now more likely to undertake not only more cash generative actions but acquisitions and capital expenditure too, perhaps to expand the firm after two years of restructuring.

The impact of external environment is still important in the third year. Economic downturn still increases the probability of operational restructuring and dividend cut/omission, and reduces the probability of acquisitions and capital expenditure. If the industry is depressed in the third year, sample firms would be inclined to remove top management, cut/omit dividends and restructure their debts. Operational restructuring, however, is less likely to be needed. Sample firms are still constrained in their strategy by the existence of an internal cause of decline and severity of the initial decline. Firms with an internal cause of decline are still more likely to restructure their operations. Severe decline firms are still more likely to cut/omit their dividends. Firm size, however, ceases to have any impact in the third year.

4.3. Summary of the impact of agency and control variables

In Table 22.10 the results of the logit models of turnaround strategy choice reported in Tables 22.7–22.9 are summarised to highlight the impact of each agency or control variable on the probability of choosing or avoiding different strategies. A striking feature of the results is that certain stakeholder groups seem to act in

similar ways to reduce or increase the probability of certain restructuring actions. Associate and unassociated shareholders make operational restructuring and cash generative actions less likely. This coalition in resisting cash-generative actions stems from owners' desire to avoid option value-destroying asset sales and stump up new cash in the form of equity injections.

Similarly, Chairmen cum CEOs and non-executive Chairmen seem to prefer

Table 22.10 Summary of the effect of each explanatory variable on the choice of restructuring strategies

This table summarises the results in Tables 22.7–22.9 The multiple influences of each explanatory variable on the probability of various restructuring actions occurring are highlighted. Variables that are significantly positively/negatively related to particular strategies (i.e. increasing/decreasing the probability of those actions occurring) in the logistic regression models in Tables 22.7–22.9, are separately listed.

	Probability of restructuring action	
Explanatory variable	*Increased*	*Decreased*
Leverage	Debt restructuring Cash generation	Capital expenditure
Associated shareholding		Acquisitions Operational restructuring Debt restructuring Cash generative actions
Unassociated shareholding		Operational restructuring Cash generative action
Chairman cum CEO	Capital expenditure	Managerial restructuring Cash generative actions
Non-executive Chairman	Acquisitions	Debt restructuring Cash generative actions
Proportion of outside directors	Cash generative actions Acquisitions Capital expenditure Managerial restructuring	
Economic downturn	Operational restructuring Dividend cut/omission Debt restructuring	Cash generative actions Acquisitions Capital expenditure
Industry downturn	Capital expenditure Dividend cut/omission Managerial restructuring Debt restructuring	Operational restructuring Debt restructuring
Internal problem	Operational restructuring	
Severe decline	Operational restructuring Managerial restructuring Dividend cut/omission Debt restructuring	Acquisitions
Size	Acquisitions Capital expenditure	Dividend cut/omission

investments but dislike cash-generative actions. Outside directors appear to side with lenders in pressing for cash-generative actions. However, only outside directors do not disfavour any particular strategies, and favour both cash-generating and cash-consuming actions, and more importantly, instigate managerial restructuring. This lends support to the effectiveness of a governance structure characterised by a substantial independent director presence. In contrast, lenders appear to be primarily concerned with conserving or augmenting the cash position of declining firms and are neutral towards management change.

Declining firms react differently to deterioration of the business environment. Faced with an economic downturn, they resort to operational restructuring, dividend cut/omission and debt restructuring. Cash generative actions, however, are also more difficult in depressed economic climates. Investments are also less likely in harsh economic conditions. In contrast, when their industry as a whole experiences a downturn, these firms pursue capital expenditure, dividend cut/omission, managerial and debt restructuring. Operational restructuring, however, is less needed during an industry downturn. Firms with an internal cause of decline are more likely to restructure their operations. The response to severe decline takes the form of operational restructuring, dividend cut/omission, debt restructuring and a reduction in acquisitions. More interestingly, management replacement is also more likely in such firms. This suggests that top managers are able to fend off attempts to replace them until the firm situation deteriorates perilously. Large firms, being more resourceful, are also less likely to resort to dividend cut/omission and are more able to afford investments.

Table 22.11 summarises the joint impact of one or more agency or control variables on the probability of choosing or avoiding a particular strategy. It answers the questions 'which factors make a given restructuring strategy more likely and which factors make it less likely?' and 'what is the coalition of stakeholders bearing on the adoption of a given strategy?'

None of the strategies is favoured by all stakeholders. Strategies such as cash-generative actions are favoured or opposed by different coalitions of interests. While bank creditors' push for cash-generative actions, they are supported by outside directors but the coalition of associated and unassociated shareholders, Chairman cum CEO and non-executive Chairmen makes it less probable. Associated and unassociated shareholding jointly resist operational restructuring.

While capital expenditure is favoured by Chairmen cum CEO and outside directors, lenders seem opposed to the strategy. Similarly, Chairman cum CEO and outside directors' preference for acquisitions is matched by associated shareholders resistance to the same strategy. Managerial replacement is made more likely by outside directors, but it is, predictably, opposed by Chairmen cum CEOs. Our results thus reveal shifting coalitions of stakeholders vis-à-vis different turnaround strategies.

The results based on logit regression models are consistent with those discussed earlier under stakeholder dominance and thus add to the robustness of our conclusions about the impact of stakeholder dominance on restructuring strategy choice.

4.4. Impact of lender and ownership types on restructuring strategy choice

We know that when lenders dominate firms' decision-making process, they demand operational restructuring, cash-generative actions, dividend cuts/omissions and cut in cash-consuming capital expenditure. We also know that when manager-owners dominate firms' decision-making process, they refrain from adopting operational restructuring, acquisitions and managerial restructuring strategies, and opt instead for capital expenditure. Similarly, when blockholders dominate the firm's decision-making process, they disfavour operational restructuring and capital expenditure. The logit regression results on the effects of lender and shareholders monitoring on strategy choice

Table 22.11 Joint impact of explanatory variables on individual restructuring strategy choice

As explanatory variables collectively influence the choice of restructuring strategies, the combined impact of explanatory variables on the choice of a specific restructuring strategy is summarised from the results reported in Tables 22.7–22.9. Explanatory variables that are significantly positively/negatively related to a specific strategy, in the logistic regression models in Tables 22.7–22.9, increase/decrease the probability of that action occurring.

	Explanatory variables	
Restructuring strategy	*Probability increasing*	*Probability decreasing*
Operational restructuring	Industry condition Internal problem	Associated shareholding Unassociated shareholding Economic condition Severity of decline
Acquisitions	Non-executive Chairman Proportion of outside directors Severity of decline Economic condition Size	Associated shareholding
Capital expenditure	Chairman cum CEO Proportion of outside directors Economic condition Size	Leverage Industry condition
Managerial restructuring	Proportion of outside directors	Chairman cum CEO Economic condition Industry condition Severity of decline
Dividend cut/omission		Economic condition Industry condition Severity of decline Size
Debt restructuring	Leverage Industry condition	Associated shareholding Non-executive Chairman Economic condition Industry condition Severity of decline
Cash generation	Leverage Proportion of outside directors Economic condition	Associated shareholding Unassociated shareholding Chairman cum CEO Non-executive Chairman

broadly confirm these tendencies. The question then is which type of lenders and owners favour which type of strategy. To test for these individual impacts we rerun all the regressions in Tables 22.7–22.9 with three types of lenders instead of one, short term lenders, bank lenders and unsecured lenders, and four types of shareholders instead of two, manager shareholders, associated block shareholders, institutional block shareholders and non-institutional unassociated block shareholders.

The results show that short term and unsecured lenders are the parties behind lenders' demand for operational restructuring.[10] Bank and short term lenders jointly press for cash generative actions. However, only bank lenders have the clout to restrict firms' capital expenditure.

Manager shareholders alone resist operational restructuring, cash generative and acquisition strategies. Conversely, associated block shareholders prefer acquisitions and surprisingly, in a show of independence, managerial restructuring.

Institutional block shareholders and non-institutional unassociated block shareholders jointly resist operational restructuring and cash-generative actions. However, non-institutional block shareholders also make managerial restructuring more likely. They are also supportive of declining firms, in terms of dividend cut/omission.

5. SUMMARY AND CONCLUSIONS

Firms which experience performance decline may choose a variety of alternative methods of restructuring themselves to restore their financial health. These restructuring strategies for poorly performing companies include operational, asset, financial and managerial restructuring. However, any restructuring strategy has different, and often conflicting, welfare implications for the different stakeholders in firms – shareholders, lenders and managers. Within the agency model of the firm the strategy choices made by managers may benefit one group of stakeholders at the expense of the other groups. However, managerial choices are also constrained by the agency monitoring embodied in the firms. Agency monitoring may be embodied in the rights of lenders, the power and influence of large block shareholders or in the oversight function and independence of the board of directors. The choice of recovery strategies is, therefore, determined by the complex interplay of the ownership structure, corporate governance and lender monitoring of the firms in decline.

For a sample 297 U.K. firms which experienced stock return performance decline during the period 1987–1993, we examine the impact of agency monitoring on the turnaround strategies selected by them. Performance decline is defined as the fall into the bottom 20% of the ranking of all U.K. listed firms on annual stock market returns from being in the top 50% in the preceding two years. A number of variables proxying for different lender types, for different types of block shareholders and for the strength and independence of the

board as well as control variables to allow for the external economic and industry environment, severity of decline and firm size are included as explanatory variables. The impact of these variables on turnaround strategy choices in the decline year and in the two post-decline years is modelled with logit regressions.

Our results show that turnaround strategy choices are significantly influenced by both agency variables and control variables. While there is agreement among stakeholders on certain strategies there is also evidence of conflict of interests between lenders and managers and between managers and some block shareholders. Lenders' preference for cash-generative actions are in direct conflict with shareholders' preference. Weak governance structure helps entrench managers and perpetuate their self-serving behaviour resulting in less restructuring and top management replacement. Non-institutional rather than institutional shareholders appear to be active monitors and influential in instituting top management changes. However, all types of shareholders disfavour any type of costly strategy such as operational restructuring or option value-destroying strategies such as asset sales. Boards of directors, however, seem to be effective in their oversight of managers, as they intensify adoption of generic turnaround strategies. There is evidence of shifting coalitions among lenders, managers and directors in the choice of recovery strategies. Institutional shareholders generally seem to go along with management shareholders. Response of non-executive Chairmen and CEO cum Chairman to turnaround is broadly similar.

The results also show the effects of dominance by certain stakeholder groups. Lenders' tight financial reigns through wholesale bans on investments can cause an under investment problem. Lenders may not only be depriving firms of vital resources necessary to compete and reverse decline but also side lining their longterm health by favouring short-term cash generative measures to facilitate debt repayment. It raises the question if banks are too keen to pull the plug on ailing firms which lack short-term cash generation ability in spite of their healthy long-term potential. Entrenched managers' inaction to performance decline may lead a downward spiral to failure. Blockholders have a weak influence on a limited range of turnaround strategies. Consequently, corporate failures can potentially be explained by poor management of stakeholders' interests during decline, resulting in poor selection of turnaround strategies.

NOTES

* This paper has benefited from the comments of Richard Brealey, Julian Franks, Michel Habib, Mezzaine Lasfer, Paul Marsh, Colin Mayer, John McGinnes, Ayo Salami, Henri Servaes, Richard Taffler, Dylan Thomas, seminar participants at City University Business School and London Business School, and conference participants at the 1996 European Finance Association Meeting and the 1996 Midwest Finance Association Meeting. We are grateful to the Chartered Association of Certified Accountants, U.K. for partially funding this research.

1   A potential explanation for this inconsistency lies in the difference in length of distress examined in the two studies. Ofek (1993) studies the short-term restructuring actions in the year of performance decline whereas Gilson et al. (1990) examine firm actions following three years of low performance.

2   Pound (1988) provides counter-arguments for a less effective monitoring role for institutional and large shareholders due to their being passive investors or having other business dealings with the company which lead to a conflict of interest detracting from effective monitoring. Mallette and Fowler (1992) also report that high levels of institutional shareholdings are more positively associated with the adoption of anti-takeover poison pills than lower levels of institutional shareholding.

3   There are impediments to effective monitoring by non-executive directors. Baysinger and Hoskisson (1990) cite information asymmetry whereby outside directors do not possess all the information that executive directors have. Moreover, the insiders may have packed the board with outside directors who are beholden to them in some way and therefore subservient.

4   In the U.K., secured creditors are frequently blamed for pulling the plug on firms too soon.

The appointment of a receiver by secured lenders, or an administrative receiver when a floating charge is held, effectively bankrupts the distressed firm.

5   The literature on stock price overreaction (De Bondt and Thaler, 1985) raises the concern that a stock return based measure of performance decline may merely represent a correction for the earlier overreaction. The condition of two consecutive years' good performance preceding the decline which we have applied in our sampling mitigates this problem. Further, anecdotal evidence suggests that stock market performance decline is not greeted with inertia and indifference by managers who smugly attribute such decline to the stock market whims such as overreaction. It appears that such performance decline causes managerial concern and triggers remedial action including corporate restructuring.

6   Routine replacements proxied by sample firm annual depreciation charge average 6.5%.

7   The similarity of performance decline in both stock return and accounting terms suggests that the stock return decline is no freak caused by correction of stock market overreaction in the base years unrelated to underlying operating performance.

8   The population frequency is the average for the period 1989–1994. The same benchmark population is used in the rest of this section. It should be noted that the population includes the sample firms. Hence, comparison is not between two independent groups. Managerial and operational restructuring are not examined due to lack of details in the Extel CD-ROMs.

9   To simplify the tables, the Wald statistic is not reported and only its level of significance indicated when it is significant at least at the 10% level.

10   Due to space constraints the tables are not presented in the paper. The results are available from the authors.

REFERENCES

Agrawal, A. and Mandelker, G. (1990) Large shareholders and the monitoring of managers: The case of anti-takeover charter amendments, *J. Financ. Quantitat. Analysis* 25(2), June.

Asquith, P. and Mullins, D. W., Jr. (1986) Signalling with dividends, stock repurchases and equity issues, *Financ. Managt* Autumn, 27–44.

Barclay, M. and Holderness, C. (1991) Negotiated block trades and corporate control, *J. Finance* **46**, 861–878.

Baysinger, B. D. and Hoskisson, R. E. (1990) The composition of boards of directors and strategic control: Effects on corporate strategy, *Academy of Managt Rev.* **15**, 72–87.

Bethel, J. E. and Liebeskind, J. (1993) The effects of ownership structure on corporate restructuring, *Strategic Managt J.* **14**, 15–31.

Boeker, W. and Goodstein, J. (1993) Performance and successor choice: The moderating effects of governance and ownership, *Academy of Managt J.* **36**, 172–186.

Brickley, J. A., Lease, R. C., and Smith, C. W. (1988) Ownership structure and voting on anti-takeover amendments, *J. Financ. Econom.* **20**, 267–292.

Brown, D. T., James, C. M., and Mooradian, R. M. (1994) Asset sales by financially distressed firms, *J. Corporate Finance* **1**, 233–257.

The Cadbury report on the Financial Aspects of Corporate Governance, Institute of Chartered Accountants, England and Wales, 1992.

Choi, D. Toehold acquisitions, shareholder wealth and the market for corporate control, *J. Financ. Quantitative Anal.* **26**(3), Sep.

De Angelo, H. and De Angelo, L. (1990) Dividend policy and financial distress: An empirical investigation of troubled NYSE firms, *Journal of Finance* **45**, 1425–1431.

De Bondt, W. F. M. and Thaler, R. H. (1985) Does the stock market overreact?, *Journal of Finance* **40**, 793–805.

Demsetz, H. and Lehn, K. (1985) The structure of corporate ownership: Causes and consequences, *J. Polit. Econ.* **93**, 1155–1177.

Diamond, D. (1983) Seniority and maturity of debt contracts, *J. Financ. Econom.* **33**, 341–368.

Fama, E. F. and Jensen, M. C. (1993) Separation of ownership and control, *J. Law Econom.* **26**, 301–325.

Gertner, R. and Scharfstein, D. (1991) A theory of workouts and the effects of reorganization law, *J. Finance* **XLVI**(4), September, 1189–1222.

Gilson, S. C. (1989) Management turnover and financial distress, *J. Financ. Econom.* **25**, 241–262.

Gilson, S. C. (1990) Bankruptcy, boards, banks, and bondholders – Evidence on changes in corporate ownership and control when firms default, *J. Financ. Econom.* **27**, 355–387.

Gilson, S. C., John, K., and Lang, L. H. P. (1990) Troubled debt restructuring: An empirical study of private reorganization of firms in default, *J. Financ. Econom.* **27**, 315–353.

Hermalin, B. and Weisbach, M. (1992) The effects of board composition and direct incentives on firm performance, *Financ. Managt* **20**, 101–112.

Hill, C. W. L. and Snell, S. A. (1989) Effects of ownership structure on corporate productivity, *Academy Managt J.* **32**, 25–46.

Hirschey, M., Slovin, M. B., and Zaima, J. K. (1990) Bank debt, insider trading and the return to corporate sell-offs, *J. Banking and Finance* **14**, 85–98.

Holderness, C. G. and Sheehan, D. P. (1985) Raiders or saviours?: The Evidence on six controversial investors, *J. Financ. Econom.* **14**, 555–579.

James, C. (1987) Some evidence of the uniqueness of bank loans, *J. Financ. Econom.* **19**, 217–235.

Jarrell, G. A. and Poulsen, A. B. (1987) Shark repellents and stock prices: The effects of anti-takeover amendments since 1980, *J. Financ. Econom.* **18**, 127–168.

Jensen, M. C. and Meckling, W. H. (1976) Theory of the firm: Managerial behaviour, agency costs and ownership structure, *J. Financ. Econom.* October, 305–360.

Jensen, M. (1989a) Active investors, LBO's and privatisation of bankruptcy, *J. Appl. Corporate Finance* **2**, 35–44.

Jensen, M. (1989b) Eclipse of the public corporation, *Harvard Bus. Rev.* 61–74, Sep./Oct.

Lang, L., Poulsen, A., and Stulz, R. (1995) Asset sales, firm performance, and the agency costs of managerial discretion, *J. Financ. Econom.* **37**, 3–37.

Mallette, P. and Fowler, K. L. (1992) Effects of board composition and stock ownership on the adoption of poison pills, *Academy Managt J.* **35**(5), 1010–1035.

Marris, R. (1964) *The Economic Theory of Managerial Capitalism*, Free Press, New York.

McConnell, J. J. and Servaes, H. (1990) Additional evidence on equity ownership and corporate value, *J. Financ. Econom.* **27**, 595–612.

Mikkleson, W. H. Ruback, R. S. (1985) An empirical analysis of the interfirm equity investment process, *J. Financ. Econom.* **14**, 523–553.

Murphy, K. J. and Zimmerman, J. L. (1993) 'Financial performance surrounding CEO turnover', *Journal of Accounting and Economics* **16**, 273–315.

Myers, S. C. (1977) Determinants of corporate borrowing, *J. Financ. Econom.* November, 147–176.

Ofek, E. (1993) Capital structure and firm response to poor performance: An empirical analysis, *J. Financ. Econom.* **34**, 3–30.

Pound, J. (1988) Proxy contests and the efficiency of shareholder oversight, *J. Financ. Econom.* **20**, 237–265.

Rajan, R. (1992) Insiders and outsiders: The choice between informed and arm's-length debt, *J. Finance* **47**, 1367–1400.

Rechner, P. L. and Dalton, D. R. (1989) The impact of CEO as board chairperson on corporate performance: Evidence vs. rhetoric, *Academy Managt Exec.* **3**, 141–143.

Rosenstein, S. and Wyatt, J. H. (1990) Outside directors, board independence, and shareholder wealth, *J. Financ. Econom.* **26**, 175–191.

Schleifer, A. and Vishny, R. W. (1986) Large shareholders and corporate control, *J. Polit. Economy* **94**, 461–488.

Schipper, K. and Smith, A. (1986) A comparison of equity carve-outs and seasoned equity offerings: Share price effects and corporate restructuring, *J. Financ. Econom.* **15**, 153–186.

Shivdasani, A. (1993) Board composition, ownership structure, and hostile takeovers, *J. Account. Econom.* **16**, 167–198.

Slatter, S. (1984) *Corporate Recovery: Successful turnaround strategies and their implementation*, Penguin.

Storey, in Keasey and Watson (1987) *J. Banking and Finance* **14**(3), Autumn, 335–350.

Sudarsanam, S. (1995) Large shareholders, corporate restructuring and target valuation, Paper presented to Financial Management Association Annual Meeting, New York.

Sudarsanam, S. (1996) Large shareholders, takeovers and target valuation, *J. Busin. Finance Account.* **23**(2), March.

Weisbach, M. (1989) Outside directors and CEO turnover, *J. Financ. Econom.* **20**, 431–460.

## Chapter 23

Jorge Farinha[*]

DIVIDEND POLICY, CORPORATE GOVERNANCE AND THE MANAGERIAL ENTRENCHMENT HYPOTHESIS: AN EMPIRICAL ANALYSIS

Source: *Journal of Business Finance & Accounting*, 30(9–10) (2003): 1173–1210.

1. INTRODUCTION

THIS PAPER PROVIDES AN EMPIRICAL ANALYSIS of the agency theory explanation for the cross-sectional distribution of dividend payouts in the United Kingdom (UK). This perspective asserts that cash payments to shareholders may help to reduce agency problems either by increasing the frequency of external capital raising and associated monitoring by investment bankers and investors (Easterbrook, 1984), or by eliminating free cash-flow (Jensen, 1986).

Although other theories have been proposed to explain cross-sectional dividend policy (notably those based on signalling and tax clienteles), the existing empirical literature typically finds that the observed dividend behaviour is consistent with more than a single theory, and therefore usually fails to dismiss alternative explanations. However, the managerial entrenchment hypothesis taken from the agency literature offers a distinctive set of predictions that cannot be found in other competing stories for the explanation of cross-sectional dividend policy behaviour. Consistent with such hypothesis, this paper finds evidence of a strong U-shaped relationship between dividend payouts and insider ownership in the UK. Specifically, these findings show

that after a critical entrenchment level estimated in the region of 30%, the coefficient of insider ownership changes from negative to positive. In addition, the analysis suggests that directors' control over non-beneficial shares managed on behalf of other shareholders (typically the company's pension fund, charity trusts or employee stock ownership plans) can also lead to managerial entrenchment.

The remainder of this paper is organised as follows. Section 2 presents a summary of previous literature and outlines the research motivation. Section 3 describes the research design, sampling procedures and data characteristics. Main empirical results and several robustness checks are reported in Sections 4 and 5, respectively. The final section summarises the paper and its main conclusions.

2. PREVIOUS LITERATURE AND RESEARCH MOTIVATION

(i) Agency theory view of dividend policy

Easterbrook (1984) argues that dividends play a role in controlling equity agency problems by facilitating primary capital market monitoring of the firm's activities and performance. The reason is that higher dividend payouts increase the likelihood that the firm will have to sell common stock in primary capital markets. This in turn leads to an investigation of management by investment banks, securities exchanges and capital suppliers. Studies by Baghat (1986), Smith (1986), Hansen and Torregrosa (1992) and Jain and Kini (1999) have recognised the importance of monitoring by investment bankers in new equity issues. Recent theoretical work by Fluck (1998), and Myers (2000) also presents agency-theoretic models of dividend behaviour where managers pay dividends in order to avoid disciplining action by shareholders.

Additionally, Jensen (1986) sees expected, continuing dividend payments as helping to dissipate cash which might otherwise have been wasted in non-value maximising projects, therefore reducing the extent of overinvestment by managers.

In Rozeff's (1982) model, an optimal dividend policy is the outcome of a trade-off between equity agency costs and transaction costs. Consistent with such trade-off model, Rozeff reports evidence of a strong relationship between dividend payouts and a set of variables proxying for agency and transaction costs in a large sample composed of one thousand US firms for the period 1974 to 1980.

A cross-sectional analysis of dividend policy by Crutchley and Hansen (1989) also shows results consistent with dividend policy acting as a corporate monitoring vehicle and with substitution effects between dividend payments and two other control mechanisms, managerial ownership and leverage.

(ii) The managerial entrenchment hypothesis

Following Jensen and Meckling (1976), when managers hold little equity and shareholders are too dispersed to take action against non-value maximisation behaviour, insiders may deploy corporate assets to obtain personal benefits, such as shirking and perquisite consumption. As insider ownership increases, agency costs may be reduced since managers bear a larger share of these costs. However, as Demsetz (1983) and Fama and Jensen (1983) point out, managers holding a substantial portion of a firm's equity may have enough voting power to ensure that their position inside the company is secure. As a result, they may become to a great extent insulated from external disciplining forces such as the takeover threat or the managerial labour market. Stulz (1988) presents a model where high ownership by managers can effectively preclude the possibility of a takeover, in accordance with an entrenchment hypothesis. Consistent with this, Weston (1979) reports that firms where insiders held more than 30% have never been acquired in hostile takeovers. Morck et al (1988) and McConnel and Servaes (1990) find an inverted U-shaped relationship between insider ownership and firm performance in accordance with the existence of managerial entrenchment above a critical level of ownership.

This entrenchment hypothesis taken from the agency literature is particularly interesting since it has consequences for dividend policy which are distinct from other competing theories of dividend behaviour. Specifically, the prediction is that below an entrenchment level insider ownership and dividend policies can be seen as substitute corporate governance devices, therefore leading to a negative relationship between these two variables. After such critical entrenchment level, however, when insider ownership increases are associated with additional, entrenchment-related, agency costs, dividend policy may become a compensating monitoring force and, accordingly, a positive relationship with insider ownership would be observed. This prediction is a distinctive one given that signalling, tax clienteles or other competing theories for dividend behaviour do not predict such U-shaped relationship between insider ownership and dividend policy.

Schooley and Barney (1994), using US data, document a U-shaped relationship between dividend yield and CEO ownership. That study suffers from several limitations. CEO ownership is not always the best measure of insider ownership as in frequent cases board members other than the CEO hold significant amounts of a firm's equity. Apart from using a relatively small sample size (235 firms against our sample in excess of 600 firms) Schooley and Barney's data is confined to large firms with a small number of cases where the CEO holds substantial holdings (the average CEO ownership in their sample is 2.5% against our mean insider ownership of 16% (in 1991) and 13% (in 1996). Finally, they do not control for alternative monitoring mechanisms on managers which have been recognised in the literature.

Also, no studies have analysed, in the context of dividend policy, the possibility that beneficial and non-beneficial insider holdings may be conducive to entrenchment. Such possibility has, however, been suggested by previous research from Gordon and Pound (1990), Chang and Mayers (1992) and Cole and Mehran (1998), who find evidence that manager's voting control over Employees Stock Ownership Plans (ESOPs) can contribute to managerial entrenchment.

3. RESEARCH DESIGN

(i) General model specification

The general model specified for this analysis is represented by a single-equation cross-sectional regression between dividend payouts and a set of variables related to Rozeff's (1982) trade-off argument. This trade-off is between the marginal benefits of dividend payouts (a reduction in agency costs) and respective marginal costs (an increase in the so-called 'transaction costs'). 'Transaction costs' here relate to the direct or indirect costs of external equity financing and potential tax costs associated with dividend payouts. Implicit

is the notion that dividend policy is set up optimally so as to minimise total agency and transaction costs.[1]

Additionally, given that the presence of other managerial monitoring devices is likely to affect the usage of any particular mechanism for reducing agency costs (Hart, 1995), allowance is made for the presence of such variables when modelling dividend policy. In line with previous research, it is possible that not just inverse relationships, or substitution effects, exist between different governance mechanisms. In fact, Rediker and Seth (1995) argue that different control mechanisms may be complementary, and not just alternative, instruments for corporate governance. The other monitoring mechanisms considered in the analysis are debt, analysts following, institutional ownership, the presence of outsiders in the board and compliance with Cadbury (1992) Code of Best Practice.

The formal basic model used, along with the variables employed, is described in sub-section 3 (iii).

(ii) Testable hypotheses

A particular concern of this paper is an attempt to distinguish the agency perspective of dividend policy from other competing explanations by focusing on the relationship between insider ownership and dividend payouts. Following the discussion above, it is likely that managers controlling large holdings in the firm can to a significant extent insulate themselves from other disciplining mechanisms. If dividend policy and insider ownership both perform a monitoring role, one might expect that before a critical level of entrenchment, dividend policy and insider ownership could be substitute monitoring mechanisms. As such, increasing insider ownership would be accompanied by decreasing dividend payouts. After a critical level of ownership, however, larger dividend payouts may be needed to compensate for entrenchment-related agency costs arising from larger (above critical level) insider holdings.

This leads to the following testable hypothesis:

H_1:   The cross-sectional distribution of dividend payouts, all else constant, is negatively related to beneficial insider ownership below an entrenchment level of ownership, and positively related above that level.

Hypothesis H_1 can be modelled by using a second-degree polynomial specification for the insider ownership variable and testing the expectation of a negative sign for the first term and a positive one for the second. However, the positive sign predicted after the critical level of insider ownership could alternatively be explained by a managerial desire to diversify their wealth by increasing liquidity (Beck and Zorn, 1982) when their shareholdings in the firm are large, rather than by an entrenchment explanation. To control for this possibility, it is hypothesised that in a setting where insiders control shares on non-beneficial terms at the same time that their beneficial stakes are too small to enable entrenchment, a similar U-shaped relationship will still be observed between dividend payouts and total (beneficial or not) holdings with the turning point above the level of beneficial holdings. This is because both categories of holdings can bring control and, therefore, potential entrenchment. In other words, this hypothesis looks at the possibility that managers may use not just beneficial but also non-beneficial holdings to entrench themselves. This leads to the following testable hypothesis:

H_2:   For low (below critical entrenchment point) levels of beneficial insider ownership, dividend payouts have a U-shaped relationship with total (beneficial and non-beneficial) insider ownership, all else constant, as predicted in Hypothesis H_1 for beneficial ownership, with a turning point above the level of beneficial holdings.

Hypothesis H_2 can thus also be seen not just as a test for an alternative explanation

for the U-shaped relationship, but also as a test for the proposition that non-beneficial holdings can be conducive to entrenchment by insiders.

A final test is to analyse whether compliance with Cadbury (1992) Code of Best Practice affects dividend policy. Since the Code was published in 1992, this is done in the 1996 regression only. That document reviewed the role of corporate boards in corporate governance and provided a set of recommendations of best practice to enhance the accountability and monitoring function of the directors of UK firms. After publication of the report, the London Stock Exchange required listed firms to state their compliance, and reasons for not complying, with the Code's prescriptions. The analysis of the relationship between dividend policy and Cadbury (1992) compliance is a novel way of testing the agency explanation for dividend policy given the Cadbury (1992) recognised role in corporate governance in the UK.[2] If dividend policy is a substitute (complementary) disciplining mechanism to compliance with the Cadbury (1992) Code, then a negative (positive) association between dividend payouts and Cadbury (1992) compliance should be apparent. Since none of these two alternative possibilities can be ruled out, the null hypothesis is that there is no association between Cadbury (1992) compliance and dividend payouts. The corresponding testable hypothesis is thus:

H_3:   Compliance with the Cadbury (1992) Code of Best Practice has a zero impact on dividend payouts, all else constant.

The cross-sectional analyses in this paper are reported for 1991 and 1996. Using two periods provides a robustness check on the results obtained for a single year. It also enables a control for possible structural changes, particularly those potentially arising from the intense academic and public debate on corporate governance in the UK since the early nineties. A five-year interval between the two cross-sections was considered because the construction of some variables, notably the dividend payout measure, required computations over five years.

(iii) Formal model and variables employed

The empirical mode model used in the analysis can be described as follows:

$$
\begin{aligned}
MNPAY_i = {} & \beta_0 + \beta_1 INSBEN_i \\
& + \beta_2 INSBEN^2_i \\
& + \beta_3 GROW1_i \\
& + \beta_4 GROW2_i + \beta_5 DEBT_i \\
& + \beta_6 VARIAB_i + \beta_7 CASH_i \\
& + \beta_8 DISPERS_i \\
& + \beta_9 INSTIT_i \\
& + \beta_{10} NONEXPCT_i \\
& + \beta_{11} IACT_i + \beta_{12} SIZE_i \\
& + \beta_{13} LANALYST_i \\
& + \beta_{14} ROA_i \\
& + \beta_{15} ROAxDUMNEG_i \\
& + \beta_{16} CADBURY_i \\
& + \sum_{j=1}^{n} \beta_j INDUMMY_{j,i} + \epsilon_1
\end{aligned}
$$

where: β = regression coefficients,

i = index of the ith firm,

j = sector index,

n = number of sector dummies (2-digit AIC codes),

ϵ_1 = error term.

The dependent variable, MNPAY is the dividend payout ratio, constructed as a five-year mean ratio of total ordinary annual dividends declared (interim plus final) to after-tax earnings (before extraordinary items).[3] Similar to Rozeff (1982), a mean payout ratio is preferred to annual payout figures, to reduce the effects of transitory and noisy components in short-term earnings. Thus, the focus is on a measure of long-term dividend payout, given the evidence, from a series of studies dating back to Lintner (1956), that firms typically stabilise dividends around a long-term payout objective.[4] Observations with mean dividend payout ratios in excess of one or negative are excluded due to the lack of economic significance of these values. The

choice of a five-year period balanced the trade-off between the advantage of using a longer period to provide a more accurate measure of the long term dividend payout ratio, and the costs associated to the survivorship bias problems arising from the requirement of longer series of data for each firm in the sample.

Beneficial insider ownership, INSBEN, is defined as the percentage of the company's shares directly or indirectly controlled by the firm's managers, their families or family trusts (as disclosed in firm's annual reports). Jensen and Meckling (1976) posit a negative relationship between insider equity ownership and agency costs while Morck et al. (1988) and McConnel and Servaes (1990) present evidence consistent with that assertion. Within certain ownership ranges, higher insider ownership can reduce expected agency costs and hence dividend policy may becomes less important as a monitoring vehicle. Therefore, the expected sign for the coefficient of INSBEN in the regression is negative. A square term for insider ownership is included, as discussed above, to account for the possibility of managerial entrenchment, which translates into the expectation of a positive sign. This follows, in particular, arguments and evidence by Morck et al (1988) and McConnel and Servaes (1990) that the effect of insider ownership in the reduction of agency costs may change its sign after a certain critical level of ownership.

The remaining variables are control factors that either (i) have been observed in the literature to influence dividend payments, (ii) can be seen as alternative or complementary managerial monitoring vehicles or (iii) can proxy for the presence of potential agency problems.

Past growth (GROW1), defined as the geometric mean rate of growth of the firm's total assets for the last five years, is included on the grounds that higher historic growth may render dividend policy less relevant for inducing primary market monitoring vehicle given the likelihood that growth may already be inducing external fund raising (and associated monitoring).

Hence, a negative sign is expected.[5] A similar argument applies to GROW2, a variable proxying for future growth opportunities, measured as the ratio of market to book value of equity). Consistent with these assertions, Rozeff (1982) reports a negative association between dividend payouts and variables proxying for past or future growth opportunities.

The inclusion of DEBT, the book value of total debt deflated by the market value of equity is mainly motivated by its potential monitoring role on managers. In particular, financial leverage has been argued by Jensen and Meckling (1976), Jensen (1986) and Stulz (1988), among others, to play a role in reducing agency costs arising from the shareholder-manager conflict. Debt may also have an impact on dividends because of debt covenants and related restrictions imposed by debtholders.[6] Thus a negative sign is expected.

The total variance of a firm's stock returns, VARIAB, is also included in the analysis. High fixed operating costs or business risk may affect the firm's dividend payout, all else constant, to the extent that these will increase the frequency of costly additional external financing. This is due to the greater variability in earnings and funding needs that high operating leverage or business risk may induce in a firm. The same reasoning applies to interest charges, which are characterised by Rozeff (1982) as 'quasi-fixed costs'. Both these operating and financial risks should translate into a high total risk (or variance) of the firm's stock returns. In addition, as observed by Holder et al. (1998), transaction costs of new issues in the form of underwriting fees are usually larger for riskier firms. The expected sign of the coefficient of VARIAB in the regression is thus negative.

To the extent that high figures of CASH, defined as a five-year average of cash and cash equivalents as a percentage of a firm's assets represent, or are correlated with, a firm's free cash-flow in the Jensen (1986) sense and associated agency costs, expected dividend payouts will be higher. Thus, greater payouts might be associated with higher figures of CASH and so the expected sign for its regression coefficient is positive.

Shareholder dispersion (DISPERS), represents a measure of stock ownership diffusion. This variable is defined as 100% minus the accumulated sum of the ownership by individual entities with more than 3% of the firm's stock in 1991 or 1996. The existence of a large number of (small) shareholders (or a low level of ownership concentration) increases the potential agency costs given the free-rider problem associated with higher ownership diffusion. The predicted sign for the coefficient of DISPERS is thus positive.

INSTIT measures total institutional blockholder ownership of the firm's shares. Institutional blockholders may act as a monitoring device on the firm's managers, as argued by Demsetz and Lehn (1985) and Schleifer and Vishny (1986), thus dampening in principle the need for high dividend payouts. However, it is possible that institutions may influence higher dividend payouts by a company to enhance managerial monitoring by external capital markets, namely if they believe their own direct monitoring efforts to be insufficient or too costly. In this case a complementarity between these alternative governance mechanisms could be apparent. Thus, the expected sign for this coefficient may be positive or negative.

Following Winter (1977), Fama (1980) and Weisbach (1988), the percentage of non-executives on the firm's board, NON-EXPCT, is also included to account for the possibility that such outside directors may act as management monitors. Thus, the expected sign for this coefficient is negative, unless the same observations referred about INSTIT apply, in which case a positive relationship might emerge.

IACT is a control variable defined as the cumulative 5-year sum (1987–91 or 1992–96) of the amounts shown in a firm's accounts as irrecoverable Advance Corporate Taxation (ACT), deflated by total assets. The usage of a cumulative sum instead of single-year figures is mainly to account for the often observed situation of a firm declaring in one year surplus ACT which eventually is written off in following years. If a company has had significant irrecoverable ACT in the past then it is likely that this should translate into a higher perceived cost of paying dividends[7] (or dividend 'transaction costs'). A negative sign is thus expected for this variable's coefficient.

The control variable firm size (SIZE) is defined as the log of market capitalisation. Size may be an important factor not just as a proxy for agency costs (which can be expected to be higher in larger firms) but also because transaction costs associated with the issue of securities are also (negatively) related to firm size as documented, among others, by Smith (1977). However, as Smith and Watts (1992) point out, the theoretical basis for an impact of size on dividend policy is not strong, and indeed some negative relationships have been observed (Allen and Michaely, 1995; and Keim, 1985). Therefore, the inclusion of size may be best regarded as a simple control variable, with no particular sign expectation.

LANALYST is the log of the number of analysts (ANALYSTS) following a particular firm (as taken from *I/B/E/S*). Former research suggests that financial analysts may constitute a source of managerial monitoring. Specifically, Moyer, Chatfield and Sisneros (1989) and Chung and Jo (1996) present evidence consistent with the number of financial analysts following a firm having a negative impact on agency costs. The expected sign for the impact of analysts following can either be positive or negative, in accordance with the Rediker and Seth (1995) argument. A logarithmic transformation is used because it is likely that the impact of an additional analyst may become smaller as the number of analysts following a firm increases.

Return on assets, ROA, is defined as the mean ratio between after-tax earnings before extraordinary items and total assets calculated over a 5-year period (1987–91 or 1992–96). In general accordance with a signalling perspective (Miller and Rock, 1985), dividend payouts may be positively related with measures of profitability.

Jensen et al. (1992) find evidence of a positive association between return on assets and dividend payouts. To the extent, however, that there are links between past profitability and current or expected growth, such measures of profitability may have a different impact on payouts. For instance, past profitability may capture information on growth prospects missed by other variables (namely GROW2), possibly because more profitable firms may be more (or less) likely to grow in the future. In addition, higher profitability may be evidence that agency problems are not very relevant so that monitoring mechanisms such as dividend policy are less needed. Therefore, the sign for this control variable can either be negative or positive. A problem arises, however, because firms may face constraints to pay dividends when their earnings are negative. DeAngelo and DeAngelo (1990) and DeAngelo et al. (1992) document that a significant proportion of firms having losses over a 5 year period tend to omit their dividends entirely. Similarly, Baker (1989) finds that an important reason cited by firms for not paying dividends is 'poor earnings'. Therefore, small or zero dividend payouts could reflect not high levels of alternative monitoring mechanisms included in equation (1) but simply be the result of negative earnings. Given such possible non-linearities, ROA is included in the analysis along with a dummy (DUMNEG) accounting for the existence of any negative earnings during the period used for the calculation of ROA, as well as an interactive term between such dummy and the ROA measure.

The final independent variable is CADBURY, which consists of a dummy term taking the value of 1 if the firm states its full compliance, in the 1996 regression, with the Cadbury (1992) Code of Best Practice. Since the purpose for the introduction of this Code was the improvement of firm's corporate governance practices, an impact may be expected on firm's dividend payouts. The sign of this impact is, however, unclear, as discussed in the statement of Hypothesis H_3.

INDUMMY represents industry dummies using two-digit AIC–Actuaries Industry Classification codes published by the London Stock Exchange and obtained from LSPD. Michel (1979), among others, shows evidence that industry classification may have an impact on dividend policy, an effect which is usually attributed to industry-related growth opportunities but that also can be related to industry-specific level of competition or takeover threat.

4. SAMPLE SELECTION AND DATA SOURCES

The sample of firms used for the subsequent analysis was taken from Standard and Poor's (S&P) *Global Vantage* Database. Financial data was obtained from *Global Vantage, Datastream* and from companies' annual reports. Market statistics were drawn from *LBS Risk Measurement Service*. Ownership data was compiled from companies' annual reports. Board data was obtained from *Datastream* and companies' reports. Information on the number of analysts following a particular firm was taken from the *I/B/E/S* database.

The selection procedure can briefly be described as follows. In a first stage, all firms incorporated in the United Kingdom and listed on the London Stock Exchange with complete data were taken from the Industrial Active and Industrial Research (Dead) *Global Vantage* files. Firms with Sector Index Codes (SIC) between 6000 and 6999 (financials) and between 4800 and 4941 (regulated utilities) were excluded. Also excluded were firms that were involved in major mergers or demergers in the period 1987–91 or 1992–96. The final number of firms in the sample are 693 in 1991 and 609 in 1996. Table 23.1 depicts the sector distribution of the final samples.

5. EMPIRICAL RESULTS

(i) Descriptive statistics

The sector distribution of the sample is shown in Table 23.1. Comparison with the sector distribution of LSPD's non-financial constituents (not shown) reveals no obvious differences between this and our sample's. Descriptive statistics are presented in Table 23.2, while Table 23.3 provides a detailed breakdown of insider ownership variables. The dependent variable shows considerable cross-sectional variation, as does the insider ownership variables. In particular, it should be noticed the large number of firms with relatively high levels of ownership by insiders. For example, in more than 20% (or 152 firms) of the sample in 1991 beneficial insider ownership exceeds 25%, while in 1996 such figure is around 15% (or 92 firms).

(ii) Ordinary least-squares (OLS) results

Table 23.4 reports the results of cross-sectional OLS regressions of dividend payouts (MNPAY) on the set of variables defined in sub-section 3(*iii*). Different specifications are considered (models 1, 2, 3, 4 and 5). It can be seen in models 2 to 5, that the insider ownership variable (INSBEN) and its square are signed as expected (in models 4 and 5 the *p*-values are in the region of 1% in 1996, and even lower in 1991). Overall, the regressions yield remarkably high adjusted *R*-squares (around 33% in 1991 and 44% in 1996). Such results are in accordance with the notion that an alignment of interests caused by increased levels of insider ownership makes dividends less needed for monitoring purposes, but only up to a certain point. Indeed, after a critical level of holdings by managers, companies feel the need to compensate potential managerial entrenchment with increased dividend payouts to shareholders. In other words, the results are consistent with the expected U-shaped relationship between dividend payouts and the level of ownership by managers as predicted in our Hypothesis H_1.

Given the link between dispersion and associated potential agency costs, an important result to the agency perspective of dividends is also the positive and significant (*p*-value close to 1%) impact of shareholder dispersion variable on dividend

Table 23.1 Sector Distribution of Sample According to AIC-Actuaries Industry Classification Codes

		1991		1996	
AIC	Sector Name	Frequency	%	Frequency	%
12	Extractive Industries	6	0.9	4	0.7
15	Oil, integrated	4	0.6	3	0.5
16	Oil exploration and production	14	2.0	9	1.5
21	Building and construction	37	5.3	39	6.4
22	Building materials and merchants	38	5.5	33	5.4
23	Chemicals	23	3.3	21	3.4
24	Diversified industrials	25	3.6	10	1.6
25	Electronic and electrical equipment	58	8.4	39	6.4
26	Engineering	89	12.8	79	13.0
27	Engineering, vehicles	10	1.4	10	1.6
28	Paper, packaging and printing	31	4.5	26	4.3
29	Textiles and apparel	47	6.8	0	0.0
32	Alcoholic beverages	8	1.2	4	0.7
33	Food producers	37	5.3	29	4.8
34	Household goods	21	3.0	58	9.5
36	Health care	15	2.2	15	2.5
37	Pharmaceuticals	6	0.9	8	1.3
41	Distributors	39	5.6	40	6.6
42	Leisure and hotels	25	3.6	16	2.6
43	Media	28	4.0	34	5.6
44	Retailers, food	19	2.7	14	2.3
45	Retailers, general	37	5.3	38	6.2
47	Breweries, pubs and restaurants	14	2.0	15	2.5
48	Support services	45	6.5	50	8.2
49	Transport	17	2.5	15	2.5
	Total	693	100.0	609	100.0

payouts, either for 1991 or 1996. In economic terms, an increase in dispersion of 10 p.p. increases on average the dividend payout ratio in about 1 p.p.

Other variables included in the regressions are, in general terms, either signed as expected or insignificant. An exception to this is the Irrecoverable Advance Corporate Taxes variable, where its transaction cost role for dividends generated the expectation of a positive sign but the results yield a positive coefficient (in the 1991 regression only). Such result is, however, consistent with Adedeji (1998), who finds a similar association between irrecoverable ACT and dividend payouts and interprets that evidence as related to firms seeing irrecoverable ACT as a tax allowance that can enhance distributable earnings. It also

should be mentioned that modelling the impact of profitability with a ROA variable, a dummy for negative earnings and an interactive term provides a significantly better fit, either for 1991 or 1996, but particularly so in 1991 (where adjusted R-square increases from 20.64% in model 3 to 32.93% in model 4).

Consistent with Allen and Michaely (1995) and Keim (1985), a significant negative relationship between firm size and dividend payouts is observed for 1991 and 1996. An interesting result also is that full compliance with the Cadbury (1992) Report has a positive impact on dividend payouts (with a p-value close to 1%) as well as economic significance (compliance with Cadbury increases payouts in around 4% of earnings).[8] This result is consistent

Table 23.2 Summary Descriptive Statistics

Variable	Mean	Std. Dev.	Max.	Q3	Med.	Q1	Min.	Skew.	Kurt.
Panel A: 1996									
Sample (N = 609)									
MNPAY	0.373	0.228	0.999	0.517	0.379	0.205	0.000	0.295	-0.305
INSBEN	10.804	15.747	75.243	14.000	3.585	0.347	0.001	1.848	2.692
INSNONB	2.333	7.163	67.489	0.813	0.000	0.000	0.000	5.050	30.115
INSIDER	13.137	17.861	82.861	18.916	4.410	0.417	0.001	1.574	1.565
GROW1	0.108	0.188	1.921	0.147	0.078	0.018	-0.374	3.575	25.633
GROW2	1.820	1.217	12.664	2.050	1.515	1.123	0.555	3.742	21.642
DEBT	0.819	11.233	276.412	0.354	0.161	0.057	0.000	24.376	598.737
VARIAB	37.036	16.394	110.000	46.000	32.000	25.000	16.000	1.264	1.577
CASH	11.102	10.981	70.209	15.294	8.025	3.155	0.000	1.886	4.557
DISPERS	55.273	21.348	99.985	71.247	54.175	38.840	5.838	0.062	-0.765
INSTIT	23.665	16.767	78.770	35.890	21.300	9.990	0.000	0.483	-0.567
DIR	7.433	2.531	25.000	9.000	7.000	6.000	2.000	1.447	4.585
NONEX	3.174	1.550	10.000	4.000	3.000	2.000	0.000	0.972	1.510
NONEXPCT	0.424	0.144	0.857	0.500	0.429	0.333	0.000	-0.048	0.260
IACT	0.120	1.119	22.722	0.000	0.000	0.000	-3.661	14.081	276.736
MKCAP	720.350	3,055.271	39,544.000	336.000	87.000	24.000	0.310	9.679	105.307
SEQ	228.586	953.304	14,887.000	125.400	33.852	11.411	-1,034.400	10.744	143.768
AT	559.758	1,961.070	32,572.000	298.800	81.517	31.730	0.562	9.635	129.445
ANALYSTS	5.814	5.945	27.000	9.000	3.000	1.000	0.000	1.086	0.167
LANALYST	1.509	0.948	3.332	2.303	1.386	0.693	0.000	-0.059	-1.085
SIZE1	4.560	1.933	10.585	5.817	4.466	3.178	-1.171	0.268	-0.072
SIZE2	4.646	1.707	10.391	5.700	4.401	3.457	-0.576	0.411	0.246
ROA	3.844	12.960	31.414	8.424	5.643	2.199	-217.692	-9.650	146.947
DUMNEG	0.388	0.488	1.000	1.000	0.000	0.000	0.000	0.463	-1.792
CLOSE	0.084	0.277	1.000	0.000	0.000	0.000	0.000	3.013	7.101
CADBURY	0.486	0.500	1.000	1.000	0.000	0.000	0.000	0.056	-2.003
Panel B: 1991									
Sample (N = 693)									
MNPAY	0.375	0.194	0.997	0.481	0.355	0.247	0.000	0.537	0.440
INSBEN	14.412	19.487	79.570	21.370	5.290	0.410	0.000	1.511	1.179

INSNONB	2.166	5.848	1.150	50.910	0.000	0.000	0.000	4.464	24.944
INSIDER	16.578	20.656	26.640	79.570	6.760	0.530	0.000	1.287	0.504
GROW1	0.201	0.218	0.251	2.202	0.152	0.083	−0.260	3.220	18.224
GROW2	1.421	0.790	1.622	9.123	1.252	0.957	0.420	3.792	24.175
DEBT	0.987	8.247	0.542	209.378	0.248	0.091	0.000	23.611	592.204
VARIAB	40.329	12.973	46.000	92.000	38.000	31.000	13.000	1.111	1.457
CASH	10.022	10.373	13.282	70.994	6.973	2.825	0.470	2.073	5.704
DISPERS	50.361	22.333	65.810	99.900	49.160	33.000	0.470	0.163	−0.772
INSTIT	22.667	16.415	32.900	90.430	20.360	9.600	0.000	0.746	0.350
DIR	7.339	2.613	9.000	21.000	7.000	6.000	3.000	1.188	2.594
NONEX	2.657	1.716	4.000	9.000	2.000	1.000	0.000	0.803	0.710
NONEXPCT	0.349	0.170	0.462	0.800	0.375	0.250	0.000	−0.176	−0.275
IACT	0.093	0.826	0.000	6.926	0.000	0.000	−5.135	1.519	23.079
MKCAP	399.560	1,626.134	176.000	25,638.000	46.000	15.000	0.540	9.487	114.211
SEQ	199.929	757.814	96.790	11,561.000	30.442	10.886	−455.883	9.968	128.868
AT	470.385	1,740.742	218.600	31,792.000	68.556	25.141	1.356	11.042	167.806
ANALYSTS	5.023	5.501	8.000	21.000	3.000	1.000	0.000	1.019	−0.192
LANALYST	1.336	0.999	2.197	3.091	1.386	0.693	0.000	0.055	−1.327
SIZE1	3.988	1.882	5.170	10.152	3.829	2.708	−0.616	0.374	0.007
SIZE2	4.423	1.714	5.387	10.367	4.228	3.225	0.305	0.510	0.112
ROA	6.472	6.949	9.520	24.885	6.749	4.362	−49.127	−3.282	21.119
DUMNEG	0.227	0.419	0.000	1.000	0.000	0.000	0.000	1.309	−0.286
CLOSE	0.121	0.327	0.000	1.000	0.000	0.000	0.000	2.326	3.421

Notes: MNPAY = 5-year mean of the ratio of interim plus final ordinary dividends divided by after-tax earnings before extraordinary items; INSBEN = Percentage of the firm's shares controlled beneficially by board directors; INSNONB = Percentage of the firm's shares controlled on non-beneficial terms by board directors; INSIDER = Sum of INSBEN and INSNONB; GROW1 = 5-year geometric mean rate of growth in total assets; GROW2 = market to book value, defined as market capitalisation of equity plus book value of assets minus book value of equity, divided by book value of total assets; DEBT = Total debt deflated by market capitalisation; VARIAB = 5-year volatility of stock returns; CASH: 5-year mean of the ratio of cash plus cash equivalents deflated by total assets; DISPERS = Percentage of the firm's shares owned collectively by entities (non-insiders) with less than 3% individual stakes; INSTIT = Percentage of firm's shares owned collectively by institutions with 3% or more of the firm's stock; DIR = Number of directors in the board; NONEX = Number of external directors in the Board; NONEXPCT = Percentage of external directors on the board; IACT = Sum of consecutive five years of irrecoverable advance tax deflated by total assets; MKCAP = Market capitalisation of a firms's equity as of 31 December; SEQ = Book value of equity; AT = Book value of total assets; ANALYSTS; Number of one year ahead earnings forecasts by analysts; LANALYST = Natural log of ANALYSTS; SIZE1 = Natural log of the firms's market capitalisation; SIZE2: Natural log of the book value of total assets; ROA: 5-year mean return on assets; DUMNEG: Dummy of 1 if at least some of the earnings are negative in the 5-year period and 0 otherwise; CLOSE: Dummy taking the value of 1 if the company has a close company status, and zero otherwise; CADBURY: Dummy taking the value of 1 of the company complies in full with the Cadbury (1992) Code of Best Practice, and zero otherwise.

Table 23.3 Beneficial and Non-beneficial Insider Ownership Statistics

Ownership Range	1991 Beneficial No.Firms	%	1996 Beneficial No.Firms	%	1991 Non-Beneficial No.Firms	%	1996 Non-Beneficial No.Firms	%
0%	3	0.4	0	0.0	392	56.6	331	54.4
>0%–5%	335	48.3	337	55.3	216	31.2	206	33.8
>5%–10%	91	13.1	79	13.0	36	5.2	33	5.4
>10%–15%	57	8.2	48	7.9	19	2.7	13	2.1
>15%–20%	29	4.2	27	4.4	13	1.9	7	1.1
>20%–25%	26	3.8	26	4.3	7	1.0	7	1.1
>25%–30%	25	3.6	18	3.0	4	0.6	2	0.3
>30%–35%	21	3.0	11	1.8	2	0.3	1	0.2
>35%–40%	13	1.9	9	1.5	1	0.1	1	0.2
>40%–45%	12	1.7	11	1.8	0	0.0	3	0.5
>45%–50%	8	1.2	14	2.3	2	0.3	2	0.3
>50%–55%	18	2.6	12	2.0	1	0.1	2	0.3
>55%–60%	21	3.0	7	1.1	0	0.0	0	0.0
>60%–65%	12	1.7	6	1.0	0	0.0	0	0.0
>65%–70%	14	2.0	2	0.3	0	0.0	1	0.2
>70%–75%	6	0.9	1	0.2	0	0.0	0	0.0
>75%	2	0.3	1	0.2	0	0.0	0	0.0
Total	693	100.0	609	100.0	693	100.0	609	100.0

with the idea that firms with better internal corporate governance rules are also those that use dividend payouts more intensely, suggesting that these two monitoring forces act as complements rather than substitutes. This is similar in spirit to findings by Laporta et al. (2000), who observe that in countries where investor protection is greater, dividend payouts tend to be higher as well, suggesting that the legal environment and dividend policy may complement each other in terms of their disciplining effects on managers. Thus, Hypothesis H_3 of no impact of compliance with Cadbury on dividend policy can be rejected.

(iii) Critical entrenchment levels

From the results in Table 23.4, critical entrenchment levels can be derived as the turning points in the U-shaped relationship between dividend payouts and beneficial insider ownership. The estimated critical entrenchment levels for beneficial insider ownership are approximately 32% in 1991 (model 4) and 25% in 1996 (model 5). These numbers are intuitively plausible and in line with Weston's (1979) observation of no hostile takeovers occurring in firms where insiders hold 30% or more of the equity.

An important question that could be asked is whether the number of firms above the estimated critical entrenchment level is sufficiently significant to make the results reliable. In 1991, 120 firms have beneficial insider ownership in excess of the estimated critical level of 32%, which corresponds to about 17% of the firms in the sample. In 1996, 92 firms (15% of the sample) have ownership above the 25% threshold. Overall, this suggests that the estimated turning points are driven by a non-negligible number of observations.

The hypothesis that size may affect the critical level of entrenchment was investigated as one might expect that in larger firms less ownership would be needed to achieve entrenchment. This could happen, for instance, because larger firms may be more difficult to acquire by means of hostile takeovers, so that insulation from such

disciplinary force could eventually be possible with a smaller share ownership by insiders. Accordingly, and using a procedure employed by Peasnell et al. (1998), a dummy variable was created taking the value of 1 if a company's measure of size is above the sample median and zero otherwise. This binary variable was then made to interact with the insider ownership variables as for 1991 and 1996. Results are reported in Table 23.5 (Panel A). Contrary to the hypothesis that critical entrenchment levels vary according to firm size, small and large firms have virtually identical estimated critical entrenchment levels in 1991 (around 32%). In 1996, however, it can be observed that the U-shaped relationship between dividend payouts and insider ownership is confined to larger firms (above the size median), where it is significant at the 1% level, with an estimated entrenchment level almost identical to that of 1991. The number of firms in 1996 where insider ownership levels are higher than 32% is 66 (about 11% of the sample). Thus, results suggest that an entrenchment level slightly above 30% is a consistent feature for all firms in 1991 and large firms in 1996. From the findings above it can be inferred that either some structural change affected the U-shaped relationship between insider ownership and dividend policy for small firms or that some empirical problems might be affecting the significance of the estimated coefficients for small firms in 1996.

To analyse this issue in a somewhat different way, the sample was split in two according to size. Regressions were then re-run separately for firms below and above the size median in 1991 and 1996. Results are reported in Panel B of Table 23.5 and it can be seen they are very close to those presented in Panel A.

(iv) Entrenchment versus liquidity hypothesis

A possible alternative explanation to the entrenchment hypothesis for the U-shaped relationship between dividend payouts is the possibility of liquidity motivations.

Table 23.4 OLS Regression Results: All Firms Dependent Variable: Dividend Payout Ratio (MNPAY)

Variable	Expected Sign	1991 (1) Coefficient / p-value	1991 (2) Coefficient / p-value	1991 (3) Coefficient / p-value	1991 (4) Coefficient / p-value	1996 (1) Coefficient / p-value	1996 (2) Coefficient / p-value	1996 (3) Coefficient / p-value	1996 (4) Coefficient / p-value	1996 (5) Coefficient / p-value
INTERCEPT		***0.5485 / 0.0001	***0.5893 / 0.0001	***0.5362 / 0.0001	***0.6052 / 0.0001	***0.6433 / 0.0001	***0.6942 / 0.0001	***0.6747 / 0.0001	***0.7033 / 0.0001	***0.7129 / 0.0001
INSBEN	(−)	−0.0003 / 0.5726	***−0.0041 / 0.0019	***−0.0044 / 0.0009	***−0.0049 / 0.0001	0.0004 / 0.5445	*−0.0031 / 0.0926	*−0.0031 / 0.0930	**−0.0042 / 0.0107	**−0.0039 / 0.0157
INSBEN^2	(+)	***0.0001 / 0.0018	***0.0001 / 0.0018	***0.0001 / 0.0012	***0.0001 / 0.0001	**0.0001 / 0.0368	**0.0001 / 0.0368	**0.0001 / 0.0404	***0.0001 / 0.0028	***0.0001 / 0.0045
GROW1	(−)	***−0.1318 / 0.0001	***−0.1182 / 0.0005	***−0.1271 / 0.0002	***−0.1443 / 0.0001	−0.0316 / 0.4792	−0.0190 / 0.6729	−0.0229 / 0.6092	**−0.0859 / 0.0354	**−0.0780 / 0.0560
GROW2	(−)/(+)	**−0.0252 / 0.0169	**−0.0237 / 0.0240	***−0.0273 / 0.0093	0.0046 / 0.6801	0.0027 / 0.7366	0.0036 / 0.6545	0.0024 / 0.7638	0.0097 / 0.2237	0.0104 / 0.1923
DEBT	(−)	−0.0010 / 0.2571	−0.0011 / 0.1878	−0.0010 / 0.2347	−0.0006 / 0.4532	0.0001 / 0.8703	0.0000 / 0.9629	0.0001 / 0.9069	−0.0003 / 0.6390	−0.0002 / 0.7156
VARIAB	(−)	***−0.0038 / 0.0001	***−0.0039 / 0.0001	***−0.0028 / 0.0001	*−0.0012 / 0.0730	***−0.0076 / 0.0001	***−0.0077 / 0.0001	***−0.0072 / 0.0001	***−0.0037 / 0.0001	***−0.0036 / 0.0001
CASH	(+)	−0.0006 / 0.4217	−0.0006 / 0.3574	−0.0011 / 0.1178	−0.0005 / 0.4111	0.0001 / 0.9143	0.0001 / 0.9042	0.0001 / 0.9454	0.0007 / 0.3659	0.0007 / 0.3295
IACT	(−)	**0.0186 / 0.0280	**0.0173 / 0.0394	*0.0163 / 0.0514	**0.0197 / 0.0105	0.0000 / 0.9980	−0.0009 / 0.8971	−0.0008 / 0.9114	0.0071 / 0.2784	0.0080 / 0.2176
DISPERS	(+)	0.0008 / 0.1021	*0.0008 / 0.0936	*0.0009 / 0.0682	**0.0009 / 0.0192	**0.0014 / 0.0200	**0.0014 / 0.0216	**0.0015 / 0.0166	**0.0014 / 0.0109	***0.0013 / 0.0146
INSTIT	(−)/(+)	0.0005 / 0.3758	0.0004 / 0.4852	0.0003 / 0.5605	0.0005 / 0.2619	0.0009 / 0.1589	0.0007 / 0.2300	0.0008 / 0.2143	**0.0014 / 0.0116	**0.0014 / 0.0097
NONEXPCT	(−)/(+)	0.0566 / 0.1856	0.0451 / 0.2907	0.0513 / 0.2265	0.0470 / 0.2278	−0.0174 / 0.7707	−0.0360 / 0.5492	−0.0327 / 0.5852	−0.0087 / 0.8717	−0.0431 / 0.4362
LANALYST	(−)/(+)	0.0208 / 0.1237	0.0211 / 0.1174	0.0163 / 0.2239	0.0076 / 0.5419	**0.0335 / 0.0478	**0.0340 / 0.0445	*0.0326 / 0.0534	**0.0376 / 0.0129	**0.0340 / 0.0246

	Pred. sign	(1)	(2)	(3)	(4)	(5)	(6)	(7)	(8)	(9)
SIZE	(−)/(+)	−0.0103 (0.2181)	−0.0146* (0.0833)	−0.0142* (0.0899)	−0.0190** (0.0142)	−0.0290*** (0.0022)	−0.0329*** (0.0007)	−0.0331*** (0.0006)	−0.0357*** (0.0001)	−0.0381*** (0.0001)
ROA	(−)/(+)		3.0039*** (0.0013)	−0.0116*** (0.0001)			0.0015** (0.0420)		−0.0112*** (0.0001)	−0.0111*** (0.0001)
DUMNEG	(−)/(+)				−0.2762*** (0.0001)				−0.3094*** (0.0001)	−0.3086*** (0.0001)
ROA x DUMNEG	(−)/(+)				0.0158*** (0.0001)			0.0120*** (0.0120)	0.0120*** (0.0120)	0.0120*** (0.0001)
CADBURY	(−)/(+)									0.0423** (0.0163)
R^2		22.54%	23.68%	24.88%	36.71%	32.89%	33.40%	33.88%	47.21%	47.74%
Adjusted R^2		18.41%	19.49%	20.64%	32.93%	28.79%	29.21%	29.60%	43.59%	44.06%
N		693	693	693	693	609	609	609	609	609
F		5.462	5.654	5.864	9.711	8.024	7.966	7.909	13.047	12.973
F test for signif. of ind.dummies		2.7495	2.7519	2.2381	2.2657	1.6349	1.7009	1.5779	2.5958	2.6132
(p-value)		0.0001	0.0001	0.0010	0.0009	0.0344	0.0244	0.0460	0.0001	0.0001
Estimated critical entrenchment level (No. Firms above critical level)		–	33.14% (111)	34.26% (107)	31.99% (120)	–	23.93% (98)	24.34% (98)	25.37% (90)	25.25% (92)

Notes: MNPAY = 5-year mean of the ratio of interim plus final ordinary dividends divided by after-tax earnings before extraordinary items; INTERCEP: Intercept term; INSBEN = Percentage of the firm's shares controlled on beneficial terms by board directors; GROW1 = 5-year geometric mean rate of growth in total assets; GROW2 = market to book value, defined as market capitalisation of equity plus book value of assets minus book value of equity, divided by book value of total assets; DEBT = Total debt deflated by market capitalisation; VARIAB = 5-year volatility of stock returns; CASH: 5-year mean of the ratio of cash plus cash equivalents deflated by total assets; DISPERS = Percentage of the firm's shares owned collectively by entities (non-insiders) with less than 3% individual stakes; INSTIT = Percentage of firm's shares owned collectively by institutions with 3% or more of the firm's stock; NONEXPCT = Percentage of external directors on the board; IACT = Sum of consecutive 5-years of irrecoverable advance tax deflated by total assets; LANALYST = Natural log of ANALYSTS; SIZE = Natural log of the firm's market capitalisation; ROA: 5-year mean return on assets; DUMNEG: Dummy of 1 if at least some of the earnings are negative in the 5-year period and 0 otherwise; CADBURY: Dummy taking the value of 1 of the company complies in full with the Cadbury (1992) Code of Best Practice, and zero otherwise. The critical entrenchment level (last line) is computed as the turning pont where the relationship between the dividend payout ratio (MNPAY) and beneficial insider ownership changes from negative to positive, as implied by the estimated coefficients for INSBEN and $INSBEN^2$. *, ** and *** indicate two-tailed significance at the 10%, 5% and 1% levels, respectively.

Table 23.5 Critical Entrenchment Levels: Small (below median size) versus Large (above median size) Firms

Panel A: estimates from the inclusion of an interactive term between a size dummy and beneficial insider ownership (INSBEN) variables
Panel B: estimates from restricting the regression to either large or small firms

	1991 Estimated Critical Level	p-value of INSBEN	p-value INSBEN²	1996 Estimated Critical Level	p-value of INSBEN	p-value of INSBEN²
Panel A						
All firms	31.99%	0.0001	0.0001	25.25%	0.0157	0.0045
Small	32.03%	0.0017	0.0011	16.48%	0.4688	0.1989
Large	31.45%	0.0014	0.0044	32.08%	0.0003	0.0181
Panel B						
Small	30.92%	0.0142	0.0062	20.44%	0.1707	0.0406
Large	31.07%	0.0030	0.0037	33.40%	0.0072	0.0251

Notes: The model used in Panel A is:
$$\text{MNPAY} = \alpha_1 \text{INSBEN} + \alpha_2 \text{INSBEN}^2 + \alpha_3 \text{INSBEN} \times \text{DUMMYLARGE} + \alpha_4 \text{INSBEN}^2 \times \text{DUMMYLARGE} + \text{control variables, where}$$
DUMMYLARGE = 1 if SIZE > median SIZE. else DUMMYLARGE = 0.
Expected coefficient on INSBEN:
- for small firms: α_1
- for large firms: $\alpha_1 + \alpha_3$
Expected coefficient on INSBEN:[2]
- for small firms: α_2
- for large firms: $\alpha_2 + \alpha_4$

P-values are obtained from computing the following *t*-statistics:
$$\frac{\alpha_1 + \alpha_3}{\text{STD}(\alpha_1 + \alpha_3)} \text{ and } \frac{\alpha_2 + \alpha_4}{\text{STD}(\alpha_2 + \alpha_4)}$$

where STD = standard deviation, and $\text{STD}(\alpha_i + \alpha_j) = \sqrt{\text{VAR}(\alpha_i) + \text{VAR}(\alpha_j) + 2 \times \text{COV}(\alpha_i \alpha_j)}$
VAR = variance
COV = covariance

In firms where insider holdings are relatively high, managers could be tempted to increase dividend payouts to obtain liquidity in order to diversify their personal wealth by investing elsewhere the cash received without reducing their share of the firm. However, this liquidity argument would lose most of its power if one could demonstrate a similar upward swing driven by shareholdings that were controlled (in terms of voting power), but not beneficially owned, by insiders. This is the basis for the statement of Hypothesis H_2.

To test for this hypothesis, models 4 in 1991 and 5 in 1996 were re-run with the restriction that beneficial insider ownership is below the estimated entrenchment level and by substituting beneficial insider ownership with total (beneficial and non-beneficial) holdings by directors. If again a U-shaped relationship is observed with the turning point above the maximum level allowed for beneficial holdings, one would conclude that the upward swing in the dividend/insider ownership curve can only be driven with the contribution of non-beneficial holdings. This would then contradict the liquidity hypothesis.

Table 23.6 reports the results. Regressions from Table 23.4 are re-run with the substitution of beneficial insider ownership for total (beneficial and non-beneficial) holdings by insiders. The results in model 1 (1991) and 2 (1996) show that the U-shaped relationship between dividend payouts and insider ownership is still strong for the new definition of insider ownership. The new critical entrenchment points are now 36.43% and 30.47% for 1991 and 1996, respectively. Next, in regressions 3 and 4, the calculations are repeated with the exclusion of firms for which beneficial ownership by insiders (INSBEN) is below estimated entrenchment levels (given that these levels are estimated with a degree of error, the restriction on INSBEN was arbitrarily set at 1.5 p.p. below the estimated entrenchment levels).[9] One can see that the U-shaped relation is still apparent, with the crucial difference that the upward movement in the dividend-insider ownership curve cannot now be driven

without the contribution of non-beneficial holdings. The number of firms for which, in regressions 3 and 4, total insider ownership exceeds the critical turning is around 3% of the sample in either 1991 (16 firms) or 1996 (18 firms). Although the number of observations above the turning points is not large, the consistent results across the two cross-sections and the significance of the coefficients lend some support to Hypothesis H_2, i.e., the proposition that liquidity is not behind the upward movement in dividend policy after the turning points.

The results above also offer an interesting insight on the role of non-beneficial insider ownership that has been little addressed in the literature. Specifically, they show that non-beneficial holdings where insiders can control voting rights (but not cash-flow rights) can be used as an entrenchment tool, along with their beneficial holdings. Such findings are consistent with Gordon and Pound's (1990) and Cole and Mehran's (1998) results that managers can use their voting control over ESOPs (Employee Stock Ownership Plans) as a management entrenchment device against takeovers. They are also in accordance with Chang and Mayers' (1992) finding that the usage of ESOPs is especially prone to provoke entrenchment when insiders already have substantial voting rights. However, our results are more general than these given that our data on non-beneficial holdings includes holdings owned not just by ESOPs but also by a number of other entities (like charity trusts, founder trusts and company pension funds).

Since our results on the liquidity hypothesis, although consistent along the two cross-sections, rely on a relatively small number of observations above the turning points, an additional test was made to test the robustness of the findings. Specifically, if diversification driven-liquidity needs are deemed to increase dividend payouts when holdings by insiders are large, then one should expect that the larger the market value of insider holdings, the larger dividend payouts should be, all else constant. Therefore, a positive relationship between

Table 23.6 OLS Regression Results with Insider Ownership Defined as Total (beneficial and non-beneficial) (models 1 and 2) and with the Restriction that INSBEN < Turning Points (models 3 and 4) Dependent Variable: MNPAY

Variable	Expected Sign	1991 (1) Estim. Coefficient	p-value	1996 (2) Estim. Coefficient	p-value	1991 (3) Estim. Coefficient	p-value	1996 (4) Estim. Coefficient	p-value
Restriction on INSBEN		None		None		<35%		<29%	
INTERCEP		***0.6509	0.0001	***0.7282	0.0001	***0.6993	0.0001	***0.7419	0.0001
INSIDER	(−)	***−0.0053	0.0001	**−0.0036	0.0140	***−0.0068	0.0005	**−0.0043	0.0169
INSIDER^2	(−)	***0.0001	0.0001	***0.0001	0.0097	*0.0001	0.0569	*0.0001	0.0751
GROW1	(−)	***−0.1439	0.0001	**−0.0804	0.0482	***−0.1376	0.0001	−0.0615	0.1562
GROW2	(−)/(+)	0.0038	0.7328	0.0107	0.1795	−0.0034	0.7899	*0.0159	0.0687
DEBT	(−)	−0.0006	0.3970	−0.0003	0.7047	−0.0006	0.4165	−0.0002	0.7472
VARIAB	(−)	**−0.0014	0.0417	***−0.0036	0.0001	**−0.0019	0.0159	***−0.0041	0.0001
CASH	(+)	−0.0005	0.4541	0.0007	0.3601	−0.0008	0.2748	−0.0001	0.8826
IACT	(−)	**0.0197	0.0101	0.0080	0.2189	**0.0205	0.0169	0.0085	0.1939
DISPERS	(+)	0.0008	0.1010	**0.0012	0.0486	*0.0008	0.0931	*0.0011	0.0683
INSTIT	(−)/(+)	0.0002	0.6743	**0.0012	0.0391	0.0001	0.8255	*0.0011	0.0774
NONEXPCT	(−)/(+)	0.0421	0.2776	−0.0373	0.5005	0.0363	0.3982	−0.0274	0.6513
LANALYST	(−)/(+)	0.0069	0.5741	**0.0351	0.0202	0.0045	0.7416	***0.0431	0.0083

		(1)	(2)	(3)	(4)
SIZE1	(−)/(+)	** −0.0198	*** −0.0383	** −0.0218	*** −0.0416
		0.0103	0.0001	0.0118	0.0001
ROA	(−)/(+)	*** −0.0114	*** −0.0110	*** −0.0113	*** −0.0098
		0.0001	0.0001	0.0001	0.0014
DUMNEG	(−)/(+)	*** −0.2752	*** −0.3080	*** −0.2787	*** −0.2851
		0.0001	0.0001	0.0001	0.0001
ROAxDUMNEG	(−)/(+)	*** 0.0154	*** 0.0120	*** 0.0147	*** 0.0105
		0.0001	0.0001	0.0001	0.0009
CADBURY	(−)/(+)		** 0.0399		** 0.0424
			0.0243		0.0253
R^2		37.14%	47.60%	39.00%	48.44%
Adjusted R^2		33.39%	43.91%	34.65%	44.25%
N		693	609	587	533
F		9.895	12.899	8.967	11.555
Estimated critical entrenchment level		36.43%	30.47%	37.90%	33.76%
(No. Firms above critical level)		(124)	(99)	(16)	(18)

Notes: MNPAY = 5-year mean of the ratio of interim plus final ordinary dividends divided by after-tax earnings before extraordinary items; INTERCEP: Intercept term; INSIDER = Percentage of the firms's shares controlled on beneficial and non-beneficial terms by board directors; $GROW_1$ = 5-year geometric mean rate of growth in total assets; GROW2 = market to book value, defined as market capitalisation of equity plus book value of assets minus book value of equity, divided by book value of total assets; DEBT = Total debt deflated by market capitalisation; VARIAB = 5-year volatility of stock returns; CASH: 5-year mean of the ratio of cash plus cash equivalents deflated by total assets; DISPERS = Percentage of the firm's shares owned collectively by entities (non-insiders) with less than 3% individual stakes; INSTIT = Percentage of firm's shares owned collectively by institutions with 3% or more of the firm's stock; NONEXPCT = Percentage of external directors on the board; IACT = Sum of consecutive five years of irrecoverable advance tax deflated by total assets; LANALYST = Natural log of ANALYSTS; SIZE = Natural log of the firms's market capitalisation; ROA: 5-year mean return on assets; DUMNEG: Dummy of 1 if at least some of the earnings are negative in the 5-year period and 0 otherwise; CADBURY: Dummy taking the value of 1 if the company complies in full with the Cadbury (1992) Code of Best Practice, and zero otherwise. The critical entrenchment level (last line) is computed as the turning point where the relationship between the dividend payout ratio (MNPAY) and insider ownership changes from negative to positive, as implied by the estimated coefficients for INSIDER and $INSIDER^2$.
*, **, and *** indicate two-tailed significance at the 10%, 5% and 1% levels, respectively.

dividend payouts and the market value of insider holdings should emerge.

Accordingly, regressions were re-run with the inclusion of MKVINS, a variable constructed as the product between SIZE (the market value of the company) and INSBEN, while keeping in the regression the ownership variables INSBEN and $INSBEN^2$. The null hypothesis to test is whether MKVINS enters the regression with a significant positive slope. Also, if the documented positive coefficient of $INSBEN^2$ is due to liquidity rather than entrenchment, one would expect that the inclusion of MKVINS would alter the significance of $INSBEN^2$. Unreported results show that MKVINS has either an insignificantly different from zero coefficient (in 1991) or a significantly negative one (in 1996), and in this last case the slope of INSBEN is no longer significant (most likely as a result of the correlation between MKVINS and INSBEN). As for $INSBEN^2$, its slope remains positive and significant throughout. Also, an attempt was made to see if results would change with the omission of $INSBEN^2$, so as to analyse if potential correlation problems between $INSBEN^2$ and MKVINS are affecting the significance of MKVINS. Results show, however, that MKVINS remains insignificantly different from zero in 1991 and significantly negative in 1996. The slope on INSBEN in 1996 becomes significantly positive but this is most likely biased due to the misspecification arising from the omission of $INSBEN^2$. One can thus conclude that, once again, the liquidity hypothesis stated above is contradicted by the data.

To summarise, our tests offer some support for the notion that liquidity is not behind the U-shaped relationship documented between dividend payouts and insider ownership. Results show in fact that the same relationship can be observed for a restricted sample where non-beneficial holdings are essential to achieve total insider holdings above the critical turning points. Secondly, the quadratic term for $INSBEN^2$ remains significantly positive when a variable controlling for the market value of insider holdings (MKVINS) is

entered in the regressions and this variable, when significant, is negatively, not positively, signed.

(v) Alternative specifications

The general reasoning behind the way the variables were defined above was to consider contemporaneous variables (at 1991 or 1996) in both sides of equation (1). However, in the definition of the dividend payout and cash variables, the annual figures were observed to be remarkably unstable so in those cases a mean was judged, as referred above, to be the best estimate for the value of each of those variables in 1991 or 1996. Given that the dividend payout variable was thus defined as a mean over a five-year period (1987–91 or 1992–96), while some of the variables (e.g., debt, the number of analysts or ownership variables) relate to either 1991 or 1996, a degree of look-ahead bias could occur, although the direction of such potential bias is undetermined. However, when alternative definitions of dividend payout were attempted (defining it, in the 1991 cross-section, as either the mean over the 1989–93 or the 1991–95 period), the results were similar so any possible look-ahead bias was dismissed as not serious.

Several other robustness checks were made to see if the conclusions above were sensitive to the usage of other specifications or when considering other potentially relevant factors. Regressions were thus repeated by excluding firms having close company tax status[10] which could affect the relative transaction costs of dividends. Results were, however, unchanged.

A piecewise linear regression was also performed allowing for one turning point in the vicinity of the estimated critical entrenchment levels in Table 23.4. The hypothesis of changing slopes under this new specification was confirmed with significance levels and R-squares very close to those under the quadratic specification. The usage of switching regimes to analyse alternative critical entrenchment points under the piecewise linear regression did not produce results that could contradict the existence of a negative slope followed by a positive one after a critical level. Such alternative specifications did not yield, however, higher *R*-squares than the quadratic specification used before. Since it is reasonable to think that in general terms a piecewise linear regression imposes a much stricter structure than the quadratic specification used above, our preference goes to this one.

Collinearity diagnostics prescribed by Belsley et al. (1980) and VIF (variance inflation factors) analysis were used to observe if multicollinearity problems could be obscuring some of the results. The conclusion was that the statistically insignificant variables in Table 23.4 were not significantly affected by collinearity problems.

In addition, log transformations was used in all variables for which skewness was seen as relatively high but again no relevant departures from former results were observed. Also, since some evidence of non-normality in the residuals was observed that could be a symptom of misspecification, a robust estimation analysis was performed. Specifically, a rank regression procedure by which all variables (except dummies) were converted into their respective ranks (and INSBEN^2 was redefined as the square of the rank of INSBEN). The results of using this procedure revealed that the insider ownership variables were still highly significant at the 1% level or very close to it.

Finally, no evidence of significant heteroskedasticity was found when using a White (1980) test, which is also a test for misspecification. In spite of this, White (1980) adjusted *t*-statistics were used but, as expected, did not reveal any significant departures from the significance levels observed before.

7. SUMMARY AND DISCUSSION OF FINDINGS

This paper provides an empirical examination of the agency theory explanation for the cross-sectional distribution of dividend policies in the UK. Using data for two five year periods (1987–91 and 1992–96) and a considerably large sample (in excess of 600 firms), it tests the hypothesis that insider ownership affects dividend policies in a manner consistent with a managerial entrenchment perspective, drawn from the agency literature.

In line with predictions, and controlling for other factors, strong evidence is found that after a critical entrenchment level of insider ownership estimated in the region of 30%, the coefficient on insider ownership changes from negative to positive.

The hypothesis that liquidity needs on the part of insiders are responsible for the positive association between dividend payouts and insider ownership after the critical turning point was also investigated. The conclusion was the rejection of the liquidity explanation given that a similar relationship is also observed when insiders hold non-beneficial holdings in addition to beneficial holdings that alone are below the critical turning point. This point was also reinforced when no positive association was observed between dividend payouts and the market value of beneficial insider holdings. The analysis suggested that holdings over which insiders have control, but not cash-flow rights, can be conducive to entrenchment.

Consistent with the existence of links between corporate governance and dividend policy, compliance with the Cadbury (1992) Code of Best Practice was observed to have a statistically and economically significant impact on dividend payouts. Also in accordance with an agency perspective, strong evidence was produced that shareholder dispersion has a significant positive impact on dividend policy.

The main results presented in this paper vindicate the agency explanation for cross-sectional dividend policy. Some limitations of the analysis should, however, be kept in mind. First, the non-insider ownership data does not include ownership levels below 3%. In principle, it is possible that allowing for a finer partition could alter the significance of some of the ownership variables. In addition, the results may not be easily extrapolated to the smallest firms. Indeed, the analysis of interactions between insider ownership and size for the 1996 sample suggested that in smaller firms a U-shaped relationship between dividend policy and insider holdings might not hold.[11] Finally, the results on the usage by managers of non-beneficial holdings as an entrenchment vehicle rely on a relatively small number of observations above the critical levels of insider ownership, suggesting therefore a degree of caution in the interpretation of these particular findings.

A final issue regards the existing literature on the simultaneous determination, or endogeneity, of several alternative or complementary corporate governance mechanisms (see for instance Agrawal and Knoeber, 1996). Specifically, and in the spirit of Jensen et al. (1992), a simultaneous specification for the joint determination of dividend policy and other monitoring devices with allowance for the entrenchment effects suggested in this paper, might yield some incremental explanatory power.

NOTES

*   The author is from CETE-Centro de Estudos de Economia Industrial, do Trabalho e da Empresa, Faculdade de Economia, Universidade do Porto, Portugal. This paper is based on part of his PhD dissertation at Lancaster University, UK. He is particularly grateful to his supervisors, Ken Peasnell and Peter Pope, and also to Sudi Sudarsanam, Steve Young, Sanjay Unni, Massoud Mussavian, Robin Limmack, Abe de Jong, participants at the 1998 EFA-European Finance Association Meeting, the 1998 BAAICAEW Doctoral Colloquium, the Accounting and Finance Seminar Series at Lancaster University, the 2002 PFN-Portuguese Finance Network Meeting, the 2002 EFMA-European Financial Management Association Conference, and the 2002 1st International Conference on Corporate Governance at the University of Birmingham, for all the helpful comments received. He is thankful to I/B/E/S International Inc. for allowing the usage of the I/B/E/S database and also gratefully acknowledges the generous financial support received from Fundação para a Ciência e Tecnologia/ Praxis XXI Programme and from Faculdade de Economia, Universidade do Porto.

1   In the UK, dividends are proposed by directors and no dividends can be approved by shareholders if they exceed the amount proposed (see Companies Act 1985, Table A, article 102).

2   For an analysis of the Cadbury (1992) report in the context of UK corporate governance see Sheikh and Rees (1995).

3   DeAngelo et al. (1992) point out that, consistent with arguments by Modigliani and Miller (1959), discarding unusual income items provides a better explanation for firm's dividend decisions.

4   An attempt was also made to use annual cross-sections as an alternative to the specification above. As predicted, the noisiness of dividend payout ratios in the short term reduced dramatically the overall significance of the equation. Results became, however, closer to those presented in the text (albeit with much lower significance levels), when annual regressions were restricted so as to exclude firms whose short-term earnings were more volatile.

5   In a questionnaire survey of companies' reasons for not paying dividends, Baker (1989) observes that growth and expansion through investment is a reason listed by 76% of the respondents.

6   Baker (1989) documents that 22% of companies inquired on the reasons for paying no dividends cite debt covenants and restrictions.

7   Surplus ACT can arise when dividends are paid in excess of the maximum amount of taxable profits that the UK tax system allowed ACT to be set against. This surplus can be the result of a variety of situations, namely when the company pays dividends out of reserves, when the tax system allows capital to be written off at a different rate than that used in the accounts, or when dividends are paid out of foreign income. Although this surplus can, with some limitations, be relieved by carrying it back or forward, permanent differences between dividends paid and taxable profits can occur that lead to structural irrecoverable ACT surplus. See Freeman and Griffith (1993) for a description of the mechanics of ACT.

8   It should be noted, however, that one cannot reject the possibility of inverse causality.

9   Using or benchmarks set at 0.5, 1, or 2 p.p. below estimated entrenchment levels yielded similar results.

10   For a description of this tax condition see, for instance, Whitehouse et al. (1993, pp. 514–18).

11   Also, in a (unreported) more detailed analysis of the sample, comparison between firms in the LSPD-London Share Price

Database (excluding utilities and financials) suggests that the proportion of small firms in the sample is lower than in the LSPD, although firms from basically all size categories are present.

REFERENCES

Adedeji, A. (1998), 'Does the Pecking Order Hypothesis Explain the Dividend Payout Ratios of Firms in the UK?', *Journal of Business Finance & Accounting*, Vol. 25, pp. 1127–55.

Agrawal, A. and C.R. Knoeber (1996), 'Firm Performance and Mechanisms to Control Agency Problems Between Managers and Shareholders', *Journal of Financial and Quantitative Analysis*, Vol. 31, pp. 377–97.

Allen, F. and R. Michaely (1995), 'Dividend Policy', in R. Jarrow et al. (eds.), *Finance, Vol. 9 of Handbooks in Operations Research and Management Science*, (North Holland), pp. 793–837.

Baker, H. (1989), 'Why Companies Pay No Dividends', *Akron Business and Economic Review*, Vol. 20, pp. 48–61.

Beck, P. and T. Zorn (1982), 'Managerial Incentives in a Stock Market Economy', *Journal of Finance*, Vol. 37, pp. 1151–67.

Belsley, D., E. Kuh and R. Welsh (1980), *Regression Diagnostics* (New York, Wiley).

Cadbury Committee (1992), 'The Financial Aspects of Corporate Governance'.

Chang, S. and D. Mayers (1992), 'Managerial Vote Ownership and Shareholder Wealth: Evidence from Employee Stock Ownership Plans', *Journal of Financial Economics*, Vol. 32, pp. 103–31.

Chung, K. and H. Jo (1996), 'The Impact of Security Analyst's Monitoring and Marketing Functions on the Market Value of Firms', *Journal of Financial and Quantitative Analysis*, Vol. 31, pp. 493–512.

Cole, R. and H. Mehran (1998), 'The Effect of Changes in Ownership Structure on Performance: Evidence from the Thrift Industry', *Journal of Financial Economics*, Vol. 50, pp. 291–317.

Crutchley, C. and R. Hansen (1989), 'A Test of the Agency Theory of Managerial Ownership, Corporate Leverage and

Corporate Dividends', *Financial Management*, Vol. 18, pp. 36–76.

DeAngelo, H. and L. DeAngelo (1990), 'Dividend Policy and Financial Distress: An Empirical Investigation of Troubled NYSE Firms', *Journal of Finance*, Vol. 45, pp. 1415–31.

Demsetz, H. (1983), 'The Structure of Ownership and the Theory of the Firm', *Journal of Law and Economics*, Vol. 26, pp. 301–25.

—— and K. Lehn (1985), 'The Structure of Corporate Ownership: Causes and Consequences', *Journal of Political Economy*, Vol. 93, pp. 1155–77.

Easterbrook, F.H. (1984), 'Two Agency-Cost Explanations of Dividends', *American Economic Review*, Vol. 74, pp. 650–59.

Fama, E. and M. Jensen (1983), 'Separation of Ownership and Control', *Journal of Law and Economics*, Vol. 26, pp. 327–49.

Fluck, Z. (1998), 'Optimal Financial Contracting: Debt Versus Outside Equity', *Review of Financial Studies*, Vol. 11, pp. 383–418.

Freeman, H. and R. Griffith (1993), 'Surplus ACT – A Solution in Sight?', *Fiscal Studies*, Vol. 14, pp. 58–73.

Gordon, L. and J. Pound (1990), 'ESOPs and Corporate Control', *Journal of Financial Economics*, Vol. 27, pp. 525–55.

Hansen, R.S. and P. Torregrosa (1992), 'Underwriter Compensation and Corporate Monitoring', *Journal of Finance*, Vol. 47, pp. 1537–56.

Hart, O. (1983), 'The Market Mechanism as an Incentive Scheme', *Bell Journal of Economics*, Vol. 74, pp. 42–64.

—— (1995), 'Corporate Governance, Some Theory and Applications', *The Economic Journal*, Vol. 105, pp. 687–89.

Holder, M., F. Langrehr and J. Hexter (1998), 'Dividend Policy Determinants: An Investigation of the Influences of Stakeholder Theory', *Financial Management*, Vol. 3, pp. 73–82.

Jain, B. and O. Kini (1999), 'On Investment Banker Monitoring In the New Issues Market', *Journal of Banking and Finance*, Vol. 23, pp. 49–84.

Jensen, G., D. Solberg and T. Zorn (1992), 'Simultaneous Determination of Insider

Ownership, Debt and Dividend Policies', *Journal of Financial and Quantitative Analysis*, Vol. 27, pp. 247–63.

Jensen, M. (1986), 'Agency Costs of Free Cash-flow, Corporate Finance and Takeovers', *American Economic Review*, Vol. 76, pp. 323–29.

—— (1993), 'The Modern Industrial Revolution, Exit and the Failure of Internal Control Systems', *Journal of Finance*, Vol. 48, pp. 831–80.

—— and W. Meckling (1976), 'Theory of the Firm: Managerial Behavior, Agency Costs and Ownership Structure', *Journal of Financial Economics*, Vol. 3, pp. 305–60.

Keim, D.B. (1985), 'Dividend Yields and Stock Returns: Implications of Abnormal January Returns', *Journal of Financial Economics*, Vol. 14, pp. 473–89.

Laporta, R., F. Lopez-de-Silanes, A. Shleifer and R. W. Vishny (2000), 'Agency Problems and Dividend Policies Around the World', *Journal of Finance*, Vol. 55, pp. 1–33.

Lintner, J. (1956), 'Distribution of Incomes of Corporations Among Dividends, Retained Earnings and Taxes', *American Economic Review*, Vol. 46, pp. 97–113.

McConnel, J.J. and H. Servaes (1990), 'Additional Evidence on Equity Ownership and Corporate Value', *Journal of Financial Economics*, Vol. 27, pp. 595–612.

Michel, A. (1979), 'Industry Influence on Dividend Policy', *Financial Management*, Vol. 8, pp. 22–26.

Miller, M. and K. Rock (1985), 'Dividend Policy Under Asymmetric Information', *Journal of Finance*, Vol. 40, pp. 1031–51.

Morck, R., A. Schleifer and R. Vishny (1988), 'Managerial Ownership and Market Valuation', *Journal of Financial Economics*, Vol. 20, pp. 293–315.

Moyer, R., R. Chatfield and P. Sisneros (1989), 'Security Analyst Monitoring Activity: Agency Costs and Information Demands', *Journal of Financial and Quantitative Analysis*, Vol. 24, pp. 503–12.

Myers, S. (2000), 'Outside Equity', *Journal of Finance*, Vol. 55, pp. 1005–37.

Peasnell, K., P. Pope and S. Young (1998), 'Managerial Ownership and the Demand for Outside Directors', Working Paper (Lancaster University).

Rediker, K.J. and A. Seth (1995), 'Board of Directors and Substitution Effects of Alternative Governance Mechanisms', *Strategic Management Journal*, Vol. 16, pp. 85–99.

Rozeff, M. (1982), 'Growth, Beta and Agency Costs as Determinants of Dividend Payout Ratios', *Journal of Financial Research*, Vol. 5, pp. 249–59.

Schooley, D.K. and L.D. Barney, Jr. (1994), 'Using Dividend Policy and Managerial Ownership to Reduce Agency Costs', *Journal of Financial Research*, Vol. 17, pp. 363–73.

Sheikh, S. and W. Rees (eds.) (1995), *Corporate Governance and Corporate Control* (London, Cavendish Publishing).

Shleifer, A. and R. Vishny (1986), 'Large Shareholders and Corporate Control', *Journal of Political Economy*, Vol. 94, pp. 461–88.

Smith, C.W., Jr. (1977), 'Alternative Methods for Raising Capital: Rights Versus Underwritten Offerings', *Journal of Financial Economics*, Vol. 5, pp. 273–307.

—— and R. Watts (1992), 'The Investment Opportunity Set and Corporate Financing, Dividend and Compensation Policies', *Journal of Financial Economics*, Vol. 32, pp. 263–92.

Stulz, R.M. (1988), 'Managerial Control of Voting Rights: Financing Policies and the Market for Corporate Control', *Journal of Financial Economics*, Vol. 20, pp. 25–54.

Weisbach, M. S. (1988), 'Outside Directors and CEO Turnover', *Journal of Accounting and Economics*, Vol. 20, pp. 431–60.

Weston, J. (1979), 'The Tender Takeover', *Mergers and Acquisitions*, pp. 74–82.

White, H. (1980), 'A Heteroskedasticity-Consistent Covariance Matrix Estimator and a Direct Test for Heteroskedasticity', *Econometrica*, Vol. 48, pp. 817–38.

Whitehouse, C., L. Watson and N. Lee (1993), *Revenue Law: Principles and Practices* (11th ed., Butterworths).

Winter, R. (1977), 'State Law, Shareholder Protection and the Theory of the Corporation', *Journal of Legal Studies*, Vol. 6, pp. 251–92.

## Chapter 24

Christian Leuz[†], Dhananjay Nanda and Peter D. Wysocki

EARNINGS MANAGEMENT AND INVESTOR PROTECTION: AN INTERNATIONAL COMPARISON*

Source: *Journal of Financial Economics,* 69(3) (2003): 505–527.

ABSTRACT

This paper examines systematic differences in earnings management across 31 countries. We propose an explanation for these differences based on the notion that insiders, in an attempt to protect their private control benefits, use earnings management to conceal firm performance from outsiders. Thus, earnings management is expected to decrease in investor protection because strong protection limits insiders' ability to acquire private control benefits, which reduces their incentives to mask firm performance. Our findings are consistent with this prediction and suggest an endogenous link between corporate governance and the quality of reported earnings.

1. INTRODUCTION

THIS PAPER PROVIDES COMPARATIVE EVIDENCE on corporate earnings management across 31 countries. At a descriptive level, we find large international differences across several earnings management measures, including loss avoidance and earnings smoothing. Our descriptive evidence suggests that firms in countries with developed equity markets, dispersed ownership structures, strong investor rights, and legal enforcement engage in less earnings management. We then delve deeper and present an incentives-based explanation for these patterns.

Based on prior research that identifies investor protection as a key institutional factor affecting corporate policy choices (see Shleifer and Vishny, 1997; La Porta et al., 2000), we focus on investor protection as a significant determinant of earnings management activity around the world.[1]

We argue that strong and well-enforced outsider rights limit insiders' acquisition of private control benefits, and consequently, mitigate insiders' incentives to manage accounting earnings because they have little to conceal from outsiders. This insight suggests that the pervasiveness of earnings management is increasing in private control benefits and decreasing in outside investor protection. Our empirical results are consistent with this prediction and suggest that investor protection plays an important role in influencing international differences in corporate earnings management.

Following Healy and Wahlen (1999), we define earnings management as the alteration of firms' reported economic performance by insiders to either mislead some stakeholders or to influence contractual outcomes. We argue that incentives to misrepresent firm performance through earnings management arise, in part, from a conflict of interest between firms' insiders and outsiders. Insiders, such as controlling owners or managers, can use their control over the firm to benefit themselves at the expense of other stakeholders. Examples of such private control benefits range from perquisite consumption to the transfer of firm assets to other firms owned by insiders or their families. The common theme, however, is that some value is enjoyed exclusively by insiders and thus not shared with non-controlling outsiders.

Insiders have incentives to conceal their private control benefits from outsiders because, if these benefits are detected, outsiders will likely take disciplinary action against them (see, e.g., Zingales, 1994; Shleifer and Vishny, 1997). Accordingly, we argue that managers and controlling owners have incentives to manage reported earnings in order to mask true firm performance and to conceal their private control benefits from outsiders. For example, insiders can use their financial reporting discretion to overstate earnings and conceal unfavorable earnings realizations (i.e., losses) that would prompt outsider interference. Insiders can also use their accounting discretion to create reserves for future periods by understating earnings in years of good performance, effectively making reported earnings less variable than the firm's true economic performance. In essence, insiders mask their private control benefits and hence reduce the likelihood of outside intervention by managing the level and variability of reported earnings.

Legal systems protect investors by conferring on them rights to discipline insiders (e.g., to replace managers), as well as by enforcing contracts designed to limit insiders' private control benefits (e.g., La Porta et al., 1998; Nenova, 2000; Claessens et al., 2002; Dyck and Zingales, 2002).[2] As a result, legal systems that effectively protect outside investors reduce insiders' need to conceal their activities. We therefore propose that earnings management is more pervasive in countries where the legal protection of outside investors is weak, because in these countries insiders

enjoy greater private control benefits and hence have stronger incentives to obfuscate firm performance.

Our analysis is based on financial accounting data from 1990 to 1999 for over 8,000 firms from 31 countries. To measure the pervasiveness of earnings management in a country, we create four proxies that capture the extent to which corporate insiders use their accounting discretion to mask their firm's economic performance. As it is difficult to specify ex ante which techniques firms use to obfuscate firm performance, our earnings management proxies are designed to capture a variety of earnings management practices such as earnings smoothing and accrual manipulations.

We begin with a descriptive country cluster analysis, which groups countries with similar legal and institutional characteristics. Three distinct country clusters are identified: (1) outsider economies with large stock markets, dispersed ownership, strong investor rights, and strong legal enforcement (e.g., United Kingdom and United States); (2) insider economies with less-developed stock markets, concentrated ownership, weak investor rights, but strong legal enforcement (e.g. Germany and Sweden); and, (3) insider economies with weak legal enforcement (e.g., Italy and India). These clusters closely parallel simple code-law and common-law as well as regional characterizations used in prior work (e.g., La Porta et al., 1997; Ball et al., 2000). We find significant differences in earnings management across these three institutional clusters. Outsider economies with strong enforcement display the lowest level of earnings management and insider economies with weak enforcement the highest level of earnings management. That is, earnings management appears to be lower in economies with large stock markets, dispersed ownership, strong investor rights, and strong legal enforcement.

To examine more explicitly whether differences in earnings management are related to private control benefits and investor protection, we undertake a multiple regression analysis. We measure outside investor protection by both the extent of minority shareholder rights as well as the quality of legal enforcement. Our results show that earnings management is negatively related to outsider rights and legal enforcement. These results remain significant after we control for the endogeneity of investor protection as well as for differences in economic development, macroeconomic stability, industry composition, and firm characteristics. We also provide direct evidence that earnings management is positively associated with the level of private control benefits enjoyed by insiders. While these results highlight insiders' incentives to manage earnings as a way to conceal their private control benefits, we acknowledge that accounting rules may limit insiders' ability to manage earnings. We therefore attempt to control for cross-country differences in accounting rules that potentially affect insiders' ability to manage earnings and find that our results are robust to the inclusion of this control. Finally, we demonstrate that our results are not sensitive to the inclusion or exclusion of any particular country (in particular, the U.S.) in our sample.

This study builds on recent advances in the corporate governance literature on the role of legal protection for financial market development, ownership structure, and private control benefits (e.g., Shleifer and Vishny, 1997; La Porta et al., 2000). We extend this literature by presenting evidence that the level of outside investor protection endogenously determines the quality of financial information reported to outsiders. These results add to our understanding of how legal protection influences the agency conflict between outside investors and controlling insiders. Weak legal protection appears to result in poor-quality financial reporting, which likely undermines the development of arm's length financial markets.

Our work also contributes to a growing literature on international differences in firms' financial reporting. Prior research has analyzed the relation between earnings and stock prices around the world, only implicitly accounting for international differences in institutional factors (e.g., Alford et al., 1993; Joos and Lang, 1994; Land and Lang, 2002). Our results suggest that a country's legal and institutional environment influences the properties of reported earnings. In this regard, our study complements recent work by Ali and Hwang (2000), Ball et al. (2000), Fan and Wong (2001), and Hung (2001), which documents that various institutional factors explain differences in the price-earnings association across countries.[3] However, the price-earnings relation of a country reflects both its prevailing pricing mechanism and earnings quality. Consequently, it is important to understand the effect of institutional factors on *reported* earnings when examining the relation between stock prices and *managed* earnings.

Our empirical findings are subject to several caveats. First, earnings management is difficult to measure, especially as it manifests itself in different forms. We attempt to address this issue by computing several proxies for earnings management and we obtain consistent results across all measures. However, our findings are contingent on the ability of these measures to appropriately and consistently capture earnings management activities around the world. Second, we acknowledge that other institutional factors correlated with investor protection may also affect insiders' earnings management incentives. Since institutional factors are often complementary, it is difficult to fully control for the potential impact of other factors and to disentangle them from the direct effect of investor protection. Moreover, the existence of complementarities raises concerns about endogeneity bias. We attempt to address these concerns with two-stage least squares (2SLS) estimation. However, as the relations among the institutional factors are difficult to model, we acknowledge that other endogenous interactions may still exist. Finally, we note that, holding private control benefits constant, strong investor protection potentially encourages earnings management because insiders have greater incentives to hide their control benefits when faced with higher penalties. While we acknowledge the potential existence of such a penalty effect, the empirical evidence suggests that it is dominated by international differences in private control benefits, and thus the negative relation between investor protection and earnings management prevails.

The remainder of the paper is organized as follows. Section 2 describes the construction of our earnings management measures. In Section 3, we describe the sample and provide descriptive statistics. Empirical tests and results are presented in Section 4. Section 5 concludes.

2. EARNINGS MANAGEMENT MEASURES

This section describes the earnings management measures used in our empirical analysis. Drawing on the existing earnings management literature (see Healy and Wahlen, 1999; Dechow and Skinner, 2000), we develop four different country-level measures of earnings management that capture various dimensions along which insiders can exercise their discretion to manage reported earnings. The four measures capture outcomes of insiders' earnings management activities and avoid the problem that stated accounting rules can be (and often are) circumvented by insiders and hence do not reflect firms' actual reporting practices (see also Ball et al., 2003).

2.1. Smoothing reported operating earnings using accruals

Insiders can conceal changes in their firm's economic performance using both real operating decisions and financial reporting choices. Focusing on insiders' reporting choices, our first earnings management measure captures the degree to which insiders "smooth", i.e., reduce the variability of reported earnings by altering the accounting component of earnings, namely accruals. The measure is a country's

median ratio of the firm-level standard deviation of operating earnings divided by the firm-level standard deviation of cash flow from operations. Scaling by the cash flow from operations controls for differences in the variability of economic performance across firms. Low values of this measure indicate that, ceteris paribus, insiders exercise accounting discretion to smooth reported earnings.

Cash flow from operations is computed indirectly by subtracting the accrual component from earnings because direct information on firms' cash flows is not widely available in many countries. Following Dechow et al. (1995), we compute the accrual component of earnings as

$$Accruals_{it} = (\Delta CA_{it} - \Delta Cash_{it})$$
$$- (\Delta CL_{it} - \Delta STD_{it}$$
$$- \Delta TP_{it}) - Dep_{it}, \quad (1)$$

where ΔCA_{it} = change in total current assets, $\Delta Cash_{it}$ = change in cash/cash equivalents, ΔCL_{it} = change in total current liabilities, ΔSTD_{it} = change in short-term debt included in current liabilities, ΔTP_{it} = change in income taxes payable, and Dep_{it} = depreciation and amortization expense for firm i in year t. Changes in short-term debt are excluded from accruals because they relate to financing transactions as opposed to operating activities. If a firm does not report information on taxes payable or short-term debt, then the change in both variables is assumed to be zero.

2.2. Smoothing and the correlation between changes in accounting accruals and operating cash flows

Insiders can also use their accounting discretion to conceal economic shocks to the firm's operating cash flow. For example, they may accelerate the reporting of future revenues or delay the reporting of current costs to hide poor current performance. Conversely, insiders underreport strong current performance to create reserves for the future. In either case, accounting accruals buffer cash flow shocks and result in a negative correlation between changes in accruals and operating cash flows. A negative correlation is a natural result of accrual accounting (see, e.g., Dechow, 1994). However, larger magnitudes of this correlation indicate, ceteris paribus, smoothing of reported earnings that does not reflect a firm's underlying economic performance (see Skinner and Myers, 1999).[4] Consequently, the contemporaneous correlation between changes in accounting accruals and changes in operating cash flows is our second measure of earnings smoothing. The accrual and operating cash flow components of earnings are computed as in equation (1) and the correlation is computed over the pooled set of firms in each country.

2.3. Discretion in reported earnings: The magnitude of accruals

Apart from dampening fluctuations in firm performance, insiders can use their reporting discretion to misstate their firm's economic performance. For instance, insiders can overstate reported earnings to achieve certain earnings targets or report extraordinary performance in specific instances, such as an equity issuance (see, e.g., Dechow and Skinner, 2000). Accordingly, our third earnings management measure uses the magnitude of accruals as a proxy for the extent to which insiders exercise discretion in reporting earnings. It is computed as a country's median of the absolute value of firms' accruals scaled by the absolute value of firms' cash flow from operations. The scaling controls for differences in firm size and performance. It should be noted that managers can sometimes use discretionary accruals to increase the informativeness of financial reports. In fact, the evidence for the U.S. suggests that, on average, managers use their discretion in a way that increases the informativeness of earnings (e.g., Watts and Zimmerman, 1986). These findings, however, may be the result of effective outside investor protection and therefore may not extend to countries with weak investor protection.

2.4. Discretion in reported earnings: small loss avoidance

Degeorge et al. (1999) and Burgstahler and Dichev (1997) present evidence that U.S. managers use accounting discretion to avoid reporting small losses. While one may argue that managers have incentives to avoid losses of any magnitude, they only have limited reporting discretion and are consequently unable to report profits in the presence of large losses. Small losses, however, are more likely to lie within the bounds of insiders' reporting discretion. Thus, in each country, the ratio of small reported profits to small reported losses reflects the extent to which insiders manage earnings to avoid reporting losses.

Following Burgstahler and Dichev (1997), the ratio of "small profits" to "small losses" is computed, for each country, using after-tax earnings scaled by total assets. Small losses are defined to be in the range [− 0.01, 0.00) and small profits are defined to be in the range [0.00, 0.01]. In order to reliably compute this ratio, we require at least five observations of small losses for a country to be included in the sample.

2.5. Aggregate measure of earnings management

Finally, to mitigate potential measurement error, we construct an overall summary measure of earnings management for each country. For each of the four earnings management measures, countries are ranked such that a higher score suggests a higher level of earnings management. The aggregate earnings management score is computed by averaging the country rankings for the four individual earnings management measures.

3. SAMPLE SELECTION AND DESCRIPTIVE STATISTICS

Our data are obtained from the Worldscope Database, which contains up to ten years of historical financial data from annual reports of publicly traded companies around the world. Banks and financial institutions are excluded from the empirical analysis. To be included in the sample, a country must have at least 300 firm-year observations for a number of accounting variables, including total assets, sales, net income, and operating income. Each firm must have income statement and balance sheet information for at least three consecutive years. Finally, Argentina, Brazil, and Mexico experienced hyperinflation over the sample period and are excluded from the main sample because high inflation may unduly affect our earnings management measures. However, the results are qualitatively unchanged if these countries remain in the sample. The final sample consists of 70,955 firm-year observations, across 31 countries and 8,616 non-financial firms for the fiscal years 1990 to 1999.

Table 24.1 presents the number of firm-year observations per country as well as descriptive statistics for the sample firms and countries. There is significant variation in the number of firm-year observations across countries due to differences in capital market development, country size, and the availability of complete financial accounting data. Note that the U.S. version of the Worldscope Database includes only U.S. firms belonging to the S&P 500 index. However, our results are not sensitive to the inclusion of the U.S. (or any particular country). To allow for direct firm size comparisons across countries, the median firm's sales in US$ is reported for each country. Based on the large differences in the median firm size across countries, we scale all financial variables by the lagged value of total assets. Scaling by other variables such as lagged sales or market value of equity does not affect the results. Table 24.1 also shows a substantial cross-country variation in capital intensity, the fraction of manufacturing firms, per capita GDP, inflation and volatility of growth. We address the potentially confounding effects of cross-country differences in these variables in subsequent multiple regressions.

Panel A of Table 24.2 provides descriptive statistics for the four individual earnings management measures as well as the aggregate earnings management score. The countries are sorted in descending order based on their aggregate score. The four individual earnings management measures exhibit striking differences across countries, but similar patterns in terms of their relative magnitudes. The statistics of the first measure (EM1) show that earnings are smoother in Continental Europe and Asia than in Anglo-American countries, after controlling for the volatility of cash flows. Similarly, large negative correlations between changes in firms' accruals and cash flows (EM2) indicate that earnings smoothing is more pervasive in, for instance, Greece and Japan than in Canada and the U.S. With regard to accounting discretion, the third measure (EM3) shows that the magnitude of firms' accruals, relative to the magnitude of their operating cash flows, is small in the U.K. and the U.S. compared to Austria, Germany, and South Korea. Similarly, the fourth measure (EM4) reveals that European and Asian firms exhibit a greater degree of loss avoidance than Anglo-American firms.[5]

The earnings management measures are highly correlated and the rankings corresponding to the four individual measures and the aggregate earnings management score are similar. Factor analysis suggests that a single factor represents the four individual measures. Thus, it seems appropriate to combine the four measures into a single summary measure of earnings management. Our results hold for the smoothing and discretion measures separately, as well as for the single factor identified by factor analysis. The last column of Table 24.2 Panel A presents a country ranking based on this aggregate earnings management score, showing high ranks for countries such as Austria, Italy, and South Korea, and low ranks for countries such as Australia, the U.K. and the U.S.

Panel B of Table 24.2 provides descriptive statistics on the institutional characteristics of each country in the sample and is sorted based on countries' aggregate

Table 24.1 Descriptive statistics of sample firms and countries

The full sample consists of 70,955 firm-year observations for the fiscal years 1990 to 1999 across 31 countries and 8,616 non-financial firms. Financial accounting information is obtained from the November 2000 version of the Worldscope Database. To be included in our sample, countries must have at least 300 firm-year observations for a number of accounting variables, including total assets, sales, net income, and operating income. For each firm, we require income statement and balance sheet information for at least three consecutive years. We discard three countries (Chile, New Zealand, Turkey) because of an insufficient number of observations to compute the loss avoidance measure, and three countries (Argentina, Brazil, Mexico) due to hyperinflation. Firm size is measured as total US$ sales (in thousands). Capital intensity is measured as the ratio of long-term assets over total assets. The fraction of manufacturing firms is the percentage of firm-year observations with SIC 2000 to 3999. Average per capita GDP in constant 1995 US$ is computed from 1990 to 1999. Inflation is measured as the average percentage change in consumer prices from 1990 to 1998. Volatility of GDP growth is measured as the standard deviation of the growth rate in real per capita GDP from 1990 to 1998.

Country	# Firm-years	Median firm size in US$	Median capital intensity	Fraction of mfg. firms	Per-capita GDP in US$	Inflation (%)	Volatility of GDP growth (%)
AUSTRALIA	1,483	233,344	0.425	0.319	20,642	2.62	2.01
AUSTRIA	564	213,101	0.313	0.710	29,287	2.62	1.22
BELGIUM	727	277,510	0.280	0.563	27,357	2.26	1.45
CANADA	3,322	271,287	0.465	0.381	19,687	2.25	1.92
DENMARK	1,235	119,113	0.344	0.573	34,163	2.07	1.23
FINLAND	854	308,974	0.345	0.618	26,296	2.25	4.69
FRANCE	4,404	178,163	0.187	0.548	26,960	2.04	1.42
GERMANY	4,440	336,894	0.282	0.637	30,166	2.51	1.46
GREECE	858	38,305	0.295	0.568	11,393	12.06	1.48
HONG KONG	1,483	167,754	0.376	0.513	21,610	4.10	3.89
INDIA	2,064	63,027	0.409	0.859	374	10.09	2.32
INDONESIA	787	75,502	0.361	0.694	961	13.86	7.26
IRELAND	436	124,021	0.386	0.438	18,707	2.38	3.03
ITALY	1,213	350,380	0.280	0.721	19,025	4.40	1.25
JAPAN	16,475	463,191	0.289	0.583	41,200	1.38	2.29
KOREA (SOUTH)	1,692	452,349	0.382	0.724	10,250	6.28	4.64
MALAYSIA	2,036	81,407	0.403	0.557	4,043	3.97	4.35
NETHERLANDS	1,561	349,909	0.333	0.503	27,037	2.48	1.07
NORWAY	988	104,483	0.356	0.410	33,189	2.46	1.28
PAKISTAN	508	24,907	0.432	0.913	488	10.34	2.25
PHILIPPINES	429	60,814	0.460	0.500	1,093	9.80	2.42
PORTUGAL	460	97,229	0.412	0.545	10,942	6.40	1.68
SINGAPORE	1,100	104,187	0.377	0.472	22,721	2.15	2.66
SOUTH AFRICA	1,043	380,644	0.327	0.445	3,914	10.41	1.92
SPAIN	1,082	333,207	0.424	0.492	15,092	4.43	1.64
SWEDEN	1,384	261,343	0.295	0.505	27,350	3.59	2.29
SWITZERLAND	1,320	377,488	0.394	0.626	44,485	2.51	1.65
TAIWAN	1,001	208,798	0.357	0.809	11,893	3.37	0.80
THAILAND	1,529	55,344	0.433	0.578	2,570	5.50	3.28
UNITED KINGDOM	10,685	109,337	0.335	0.430	19,126	3.95	2.03
UNITED STATES	3,792	3,597,429	0.333	0.556	27,836	3.09	1.64
Mean	2,289	316,756	0.358	0.574	19,028	4.76	2.34
Median	1,235	208,798	0.357	0.557	19,687	3.37	1.92
Min	429	24,907	0.187	0.319	374	1.38	0.80
Max	16,475	3,597,429	0.465	0.913	44,485	13.86	7.26

Table 24.2 The variables are computed from 70,955 firm-year observations for fiscal years 1990 to 1999 across 31 countries and 8,616 non-financial firms. Data are obtained from the Worldscope Database (November 2000). EM1 is the country's median ratio of the firm-level standard deviations of operating income and operating cash flow (both scaled by *lagged* total assets). The *cash* flow from operations is equal to operating income minus accruals, where accruals are calculated as: (Δtotal current assets − Δcash) − (Δtotal current liabilities − Δshort-term debt − Δtaxes payable) − depreciation expense. EM2 is the country's Spearman correlation between the change in accruals and the change in cash flow from operations (both scaled by lagged total assets). EM3 is the country's median ratio of the absolute value of accruals and the absolute value of the cash flow from operations. EM4 is the number of "small profits" divided by the number of "small losses" for each country. A firm-year observation is classified as a small profit if net earnings (scaled by lagged total assets) are in the range [0,0.01]. A firm-year observation is classified as a small loss if net earnings (scaled by lagged total assets) are in the range [−0.01,0]. Net earnings are bottom-line reported income after interest, taxes, special items, extraordinary items, reserves, and any other item. The aggregate earnings management score is the average rank across all four measures, EM1-EM4. The sign in the column heading indicates whether *higher* scores for the respective EM measure imply *more* earnings management (+) or *less* earnings management (−).

Panel A: Country scores for earnings management measures (Sorted by aggregate earnings management)

	Earnings smoothing measures		Earnings discretion measures		
	EM1 σ(OpIncl)/ σ(CFO) (−)	EM2 ρ(ΔAcc, ΔCFO) (−)	EM3 |Acc|/ |CFO| (+)	EM4 # of SmProfit/ # of SmLoss (+)	Aggregate earnings management score
AUSTRIA	0.345	−0.921	0.783	3.563	28.3
GREECE	0.415	−0.928	0.721	4.077	28.3
KOREA (SOUTH)	0.399	−0.922	0.685	3.295	26.8
PORTUGAL	0.402	−0.911	0.745	3.000	25.1
ITALY	0.488	−0.912	0.630	4.154	24.8
TAIWAN	0.431	−0.898	0.646	2.765	22.5
SWITZERLAND	0.473	−0.873	0.547	5.591	22.0
SINGAPORE	0.455	−0.882	0.627	3.000	21.6
GERMANY	0.510	−0.867	0.848	3.006	21.5
JAPAN	0.560	−0.905	0.567	3.996	20.5

BELGIUM	0.526	−0.831	0.677	3.571	19.5
HONG KONG	0.451	−0.850	0.552	3.545	19.5
INDIA	0.523	−0.867	0.509	6.000	19.1
SPAIN	0.539	−0.865	0.514	6.000	18.6
INDONESIA	0.481	−0.825	0.506	7.200	18.3
THAILAND	0.602	−0.868	0.671	3.136	18.3
PAKISTAN	0.508	−0.913	0.513	2.643	17.8
NETHERLANDS	0.491	−0.861	0.480	3.313	16.5
DENMARK	0.559	−0.875	0.526	2.708	16.0
MALAYSIA	0.569	−0.857	0.578	2.658	14.8
FRANCE	0.561	−0.845	0.579	2.370	13.5
FINLAND	0.555	−0.818	0.517	2.633	12.0
PHILIPPINES	0.722	−0.804	0.555	2.455	8.8
UNITED KINGDOM	0.574	−0.807	0.397	.802	7.0
SWEDEN	0.621	−0.764	0.466	2.568	6.8
NORWAY	0.643	−0.722	0.556	1.235	5.8
SOUTH AFRICA	0.649	−0.840	0.297	1.667	5.6
CANADA	0.607	−0.759	0.478	2.338	5.3
IRELAND	0.625	−0.788	0.371	1.667	5.1
AUSTRALIA	0.765	−0.790	0.450	1.486	4.8
UNITED STATES	0.541	−0.740	0.311	1.631	2.0
Mean	0.541	−0.849	0.558	3.196	
Median	0.539	−0.861	0.552	3.000	
Standard Deviation	0.100	0.056	0.128	1.413	
Min	0.345	−0.928	0.297	1.235	
Max	0.765	−0.722	0.848	7.200	

(Table 24.2 continued)

Table 24.2 Continued

Panel B: Institutional characteristics of the sample countries (Sorted by aggregate earnings management)

Countries are sorted based on the aggregate earnings management score tabulated in Panel A of Table 24.2 The classification of the Legal Origin and the Legal Tradition are based on La Porta et al., (1998). CD (CM) indicates a code-law (common-law) country. The Outside Investor Rights variable is the anti-director rights index created by La Porta et al. (1998); it is an aggregate measure of minority shareholder rights and ranges from zero to five. Legal Enforcement is measured as the mean score across three legal variables used in La Porta et al. (1998): (1) the efficiency of the judicial system, (2) an assessment of rule of law, and (3) the corruption index. All three variables range from zero to ten. The Importance of Equity Market is measured by the mean rank across three variables used in La Porta et al. (1997): (1) the ratio of the aggregate stock market capitalization held by minorities to gross national product, (2) the number of listed domestic firms relative to the population, and (3) the number of IPOs relative to the population. Each variable is ranked such that higher scores indicate a greater importance of the stock market. Ownership Concentration is measured as the median percentage of common shares owned by the largest three shareholders in the ten largest privately owned non-financial firms (La Porta et al., 1998). The Disclosure Index measures the inclusion or omission of 90 items in the 1990 annual reports (La Porta et al., 1998); it is not available (NA) for three countries in our sample.

Country	Legal Origin	Legal Tradition	Outside Investor Rights	Legal Enforcement	Important of Equity Market	Ownership Concentration	Disclosure Index
AUSTRIA	German	CD	2	9.4	7.0	0.51	54
GREECE	French	CD	2	6.8	11.5	0.68	55
KOREA (SOUTH)	German	CD	2	5.6	11.7	0.20	62
PORTUGAL	French	CD	3	7.2	11.8	0.59	36
ITALY	French	CD	1	7.1	6.5	0.60	62
TAIWAN	German	CD	3	7.4	13.3	0.14	65
SWITZERLAND	German	CD	2	10.0	24.8	0.48	68
SINGAPORE	English	CM	4	8.9	28.8	0.53	78
GERMANY	German	CD	1	9.1	5.0	0.50	62
JAPAN	German	CD	4	9.2	16.8	0.13	65
BELGIUM	French	CD	0	9.4	11.3	0.62	61
HONG KONG	English	CM	5	8.9	28.8	0.54	69
INDIA	English	CM	5	5.6	14.0	0.43	57
SPAIN	French	CD	4	7.1	7.2	0.50	64
INDONESIA	French	CD	2	2.9	4.7	0.62	NA
THAILAND	English	CM	2	4.9	14.3	0.48	64
PAKISTAN	English	CM	5	3.7	7.5	0.41	NA
NETHERLANDS	French	CD	2	10.0	19.3	0.31	64
DENMARK	Scandinavian	CD	2	10.0	20.0	0.40	62
MALAYSIA	English	CM	4	7.7	25.3	0.52	76
FRANCE	French	CD	3	8.7	9.3	0.24	69

FINLAND	Scandinavian	CD	3	10.0	13.7	0.34	77
PHILIPPINES	French	CD	3	3.5	5.7	0.51	65
UNITED KINGDOM	English	CM	5	9.2	25.0	0.15	78
SWEDEN	Scandinavian	CD	3	10.0	16.7	0.28	83
NORWAY	Scandinavian	CD	4	10.0	20.3	0.31	74
SOUTH AFRICA	English	CM	5	6.4	16.3	0.52	70
CANADA	English	CM	5	9.8	23.3	0.24	74
IRELAND	English	CM	4	8.4	17.3	0.36	NA
AUSTRALIA	English	CM	4	9.5	24.0	0.28	75
UNITED STATES	English	CM	5	9.5	23.3	0.12	71

Panel C: Correlation between earnings management and institutional characteristics

The table presents Spearman correlations and significance levels (in parentheses) between the following measures. The aggregate earnings management score is the average rank of all four earnings management measures, EM1–EM4. Outside Investor Rights is the anti-director rights index from La Porta et al. (1998). It is an aggregate measure of (minority) shareholder rights and ranges from zero to six. Legal Enforcement is measured as the mean score across three legal variables used in La Porta et al. (1998): (1) the efficiency of the judicial system, (2) an assessment of rule of law, and (3) the corruption index. All three variables range from zero to ten. The Importance of the Equity Market is measured by the mean rank across three variables used in La Porta et al. (1997): (1) the ratio of the aggregate stock market capitalization held by minorities to gross national product, (2) the number of listed domestic firms relative to the population, and (3) the number of IPOs relative to the population. Each variable is ranked such that higher scores indicate a greater importance of the stock market. Ownership Concentration is measured as the median percentage of common shares owned by the largest three shareholders in the ten largest privately owned non-financial firms (La Porta et al., 1998). The Disclosure Index measures the inclusion or omission of 90 items in the 1990 annual reports (La Porta et al., 1998).

	Outside Investor Rights	Legal Enforcement	Importance of Equity Market	Ownership Concentration	Disclosure Index
Aggregate Earnings Management	−0.538 (0.002)	−0.291 (0.112)	−0.418 (0.019)	0.434 (0.015)	−0.686 (0.000)
Outside Investor Rights		−0.026 (0.888)	0.515 (0.003)	−0.344 (0.058)	0.568 (0.002)
Legal Enforcement			0.522 (0.003)	−0.396 (0.028)	0.393 (0.038)
Importance of Stock Market				−0.315 (0.084)	0.647 (0.000)
Ownership Concentration					−0.398 (0.036)

earnings management scores presented in
Panel A. The institutional variables are
drawn from La Porta et al. (1997, 1998).
The Legal Origin and Legal Tradition
assignments are presented in columns 2
and 3 of Panel B. The proxy for Outside
Investor Rights is an anti-director rights
index that captures the voting rights of
minority shareholders. The Legal
Enforcement measure for each country is
the average score across three variables:
(1) an index of the legal system's efficiency; (2) an index of the rule of law; and,
(3) the level of corruption. The Importance
of Equity Markets is measured by a country's average rank based on: (1) the ratio
of the aggregate stock market held by
minorities to gross national product;
(2) the number of listed domestic stocks
relative to the population; and, (3) the
number of IPOs relative to the population.
Ownership Concentration is measured as
the median percentage of common shares
owned by the largest three shareholders, in
the ten largest privately owned non-financial
firms. Finally, the Disclosure Index measures
the inclusion or omission of 90 accounting
items in firms' 1990 annual reports, and
hence captures firms' disclosure policies at
the country level.

Simple correlations among institutional
variables and the aggregate earnings
management score for each country are
presented in Panel C of Table 24.2
Consistent with our hypothesis, there is a
strong negative correlation between the
aggregate earnings management measure
and both the outside investor rights and
enforcement proxies. However, there are
also significant correlations between the
earnings management measure and other
institutional factors, suggesting that
earnings management is more pervasive in
countries characterized by less developed
stock markets, more concentrated ownership and lower disclosure levels. The latter
correlation suggests that firms engaging in
earnings management also provide fewer
disclosures. This finding questions the use
of disclosure indices as exogenous variables
in prior research.

4. EMPIRICAL RESULTS

4.1. Descriptive cluster analysis

To provide descriptive evidence on the
systematic patterns in earnings management
across groups of countries with similar institutional characteristics, we begin with a
cluster analysis. Our aim is to first identify
country clusters with similar institutional
features such as the level of investor protection, stock market development, and ownership concentration, and then to examine
whether earnings management varies across
these clusters. This approach, while descriptive in nature, captures interactions among
institutional factors and documents systematic patterns in earnings management
without relying on specific hypotheses.

The cluster analysis is based on nine
institutional variables from La Porta et al.
(1997, 1998). We use those variables prior
to the aggregation presented in Table 24.2
because it is preferable for cluster analysis
to have a large set of variables. However,
the results are similar if only the five
variables from Table 24.2 are used. The
variables are standardized to z-scores,
and a k-means cluster analysis with three
distinct country clusters is conducted.
Panel A of Table 24.3 reports the means
of each institutional variable for each of
the three clusters. The first cluster is
characterized by large stock markets, low
ownership concentration, extensive outsider
rights, high disclosure, and strong legal
enforcement. The second and third clusters
show markedly smaller stock markets,
higher ownership concentration, weaker
investor protection, lower disclosure levels,
and weaker enforcement. Based on institutional characteristics, we refer to countries
in the first cluster as "outsider economies."
The countries in the second and third
clusters are referred to as "insider
economies," with the distinction that
countries in the second cluster have significantly better legal enforcement than
countries in the third cluster. While cluster 2
seems "in-between" cluster 1 and 3,
a comparison of the Euclidean distances

Table 24.3 Earnings management and institutional clusters

The table presents results from a k-means cluster analysis using three distinct clusters and nine institutional variables from La Porta et al., (1997, 1998). See Panel B of Table 24.2 for details. The variables are standardized to *z*-scores. Panel A reports the means of the institutional variables by cluster. Panel B reports the cluster membership for the 31 sample countries based on the cluster analysis performed on the variables in panel A. Countries in each cluster are sorted by the aggregate earnings management score from Panel A in Table 24.2. CD (CM) indicates a code-law (common-law) tradition. This variable is *not* used in the cluster analysis. Panel C reports the mean aggregate earnings management score for each cluster. The last row reports one-sided p-values for differences in the means of the aggregate earnings management across clusters using a *t*-test.

Panel A: Mean values of institutional characteristics by cluster

Institutional Variables	Cluster 1	Cluster 2	Cluster 3
Stock Market Capitalization	0.82	0.46	0.21
Listed Firms	49.56	18.58	9.50
IPOs	4.04	0.55	0.37
Ownership Concentration	0.34	0.37	0.50
Anti-Director Rights	4.50	2.62	2.90
Disclosure Index	74.38	66.67	58.13
Efficiency of Judicial System	9.78	9.04	5.50
Rule of law	9.02	9.07	5.65
Corruption Index	8.80	9.09	5.13
	Outsider features	↔	Insider Features

Panel B: Cluster membership of countries

Institutional variables	Cluster 1	Cluster 2	Cluster 3
Countries Sorted by Aggregate Earnings Management Score	Singapore (CM)	Austria (CD)	Greece (CD)
	Hong Kong (CM)	Taiwan (CD)	Korea (CD)
	Malaysia (CM)	Switzerland (CD)	Portugal (CD)
	UK (CM)	Germany (CD)	Italy (CD)
	Norway (CD)	Japan (CD)	India (CM)
	Canada (CM)	Belgium (CD)	Spain (CD)
	Australia (CM)	Netherlands (CD)	Indonesia (CD)
	USA (CM)	Denmark (CD)	Thailand (CM)
		France (CD)	Pakistan (CM)
		Finland (CD)	Philippines (CD)
		Sweden (CD)	
		South Africa (CM)	
		Ireland (CM)	

Panel C: Pervasiveness of earnings management by cluster

	Cluster 1	Cluster 2	Cluster 3
Mean Aggregate Earnings Management Score	10.1	16.1	20.6
Tests of EM differences between clusters	C1 vs. C2	C2 vs. C3	C1 vs. C3
(*p*-values)	(0.044)	(0.059)	(0.003)

between the cluster centers supports our interpretation that clusters 2 and 3 are closer to each other than clusters 1 and 2. Overall, the results in Table 24.3, Panel A are consistent with the existence of institutional complementarities.

Table 24.3, Panel B shows the cluster membership of the sample countries. Groupings are consistent with the common- and code-law as well as regional distinctions used in prior research to classify countries (see, e.g., Ball et al., 2000; Ball et al., 2003). As indicated in Panel B, all countries in the first cluster with the exception of Norway have a common-law tradition. The three Southeast Asian countries (Hong Kong, Malaysia, and Singapore) in this cluster were formerly under British rule and have inherited parts of the Anglo-Saxon institutional framework. The fact that the three East Asian countries have by far the worst earnings management ratings in this group is consistent with Ball et al. (2003) who argue that, despite the common-law influence, reported earnings do not exhibit common-law properties (i.e., asymmetric timeliness). Fan and Wong (2001) present similar findings. In the second cluster, all countries except Ireland and South Africa have a code-law tradition. This cluster contains most of the Northern European and Scandinavian countries. The third cluster consists of several Asian and Southern European countries with both common- and code-law traditions. Thus, the cluster approach suggests that the common- and code-law distinction matters only when legal enforcement is relatively high, as in the first and second clusters. In the third cluster, for which the quality of legal enforcement is low, legal tradition seems unrelated to cluster membership.

Panel C of Table 24.3 shows that differences between the clusters' average earnings management scores are statistically significant. Outsider economies (cluster 1) exhibit lower levels of earnings management than insider economies (clusters 2 and 3). Thus, even after controlling for interactions among various institutional factors, earnings management appears to be lower in economies with strong investor protection, large stock markets and dispersed ownership. The third cluster exhibits significantly higher earnings management than the second cluster, highlighting the salient importance of legal enforcement.

4.2. The role of investor protection: multiple regression analysis

The previous analyses suggest that the pervasiveness of earnings management is systematically related to a country's institutional characteristics. A key question, however, is: Which institutional factors are primary determinants of earnings management and which are correlated outcomes? We posit that better investor protection results in less earnings management because insiders enjoy fewer private control benefits and hence have lower incentives to conceal firm performance from outside investors. This hypothesis ties in closely with findings in Nenova (2000) and Dyck and Zingales (2002), suggesting that private control benefits decrease in the level of investor protection. The notion of investor protection as a key primitive is also reinforced by recent work relating to capital market development (e.g., Beck et al., 2003), corporate policy choices around the world (e.g., La Porta et al., 2000), and cross-listing in the U.S. (e.g., Doidge et al., 2003; Lang et al., 2003). Consistent with this literature, we view low earnings management, large equity markets, and dispersed ownership patterns as complements and joint outcomes of strong investor protection. This view is in contrast to La Porta et al. (1997, 1999) who treat the level of disclosure as an exogenous factor in explaining financing and ownership patterns. Our results suggest, however, that the quality of reported earnings and financial disclosure is endogenous and hence a joint outcome.

Our multiple regressions examine the relation between earnings management and investor protection. Column 1 of Table 24.4 reports a rank regression using the aggregate earnings management measure as the dependent variable. Results show that outside investor protection explains a substantial portion (39%) of the variation in earnings management. Outsider rights and legal enforcement both exhibit a significant negative association with earnings management. Ordinary least squares (OLS) regressions of the aggregate earnings management score on the unranked variables yield similar results in this and in subsequent regressions.

The multiple regressions assume, however, that outside investor rights and legal enforcement are exogenous variables. If, on the other hand, outsider protection and earnings management are simultaneously determined, our results suffer from an endogeneity bias. We address this concern by using countries' legal origins and wealth as instruments for the investor protection variables as suggested by Levine (1999). While related to the level of investor protection (see La Porta et al., 1998), a country's legal origin can be considered as predetermined and exogenous to our analysis because the origins of most legal systems are several centuries old and many countries obtained their legal system through occupation and colonization. We use three dummy variables, indicating English, French, German, and Scandinavian legal origins, as instrumental variables. In addition, we use a country's average per capita GDP — measured prior to our sample period, 1980 to 1989 — as an instrument because an effective legal infrastructure is costly to create and maintain, and hence a country's wealth potentially influences the level of legal enforcement.

Column 2 of Table 24.4 reports results of a 2SLS regression using ranked variables. The regression results support our hypothesis that the pervasiveness of earnings management decreases in the level of investor protection, and suggest that this relation is not driven by the potential endogeneity of investor protection.

Finally, we attempt to provide more direct evidence on the hypothesis that insiders' private control benefits are positively related to earnings management. In the previous regressions, we employ an indirect approach by using the investor protection variables. An alternative approach is to directly estimate the relation between earnings management and private control benefits, explicitly accounting for the effect of investor protection on the level of private control benefits. We use a country's average block premium estimated by Dyck and Zingales (2002) as a proxy for the level of private control benefits. We estimate a 2SLS regression of the aggregate earnings management score on the control benefits proxy using the level of outsider rights and legal enforcement as instruments. The results presented in column 3 of Table 24.4 show that earnings management and private control benefits exhibit a significantly positive association as predicted by our hypothesis. Similar results are obtained if the legal origins and per capita GDP are used as instruments (as in column 2).

4.3. Robustness checks

Prior work shows that per capita GDP explains differences in financing, ownership, and payout policies across countries. Consequently, we re-estimate our primary regressions using *contemporaneous* per capita GDP as an additional explanatory variable (not reported). While GDP is marginally significant in this regression ($p = 0.140$), the negative relation between investor protection and earnings management is robust to the inclusion of this proxy.

Another potential concern is that our results are driven by economic heterogeneity across countries. Although we control for economic differences across firms by scaling our earnings management measures by firms' operating cash flows, variation in industry composition and firm size across countries can potentially affect our results. Since Table 24.1 shows that the fraction of manufacturing firms and median firm size vary considerably across countries, the regressions are re-estimated using two subsamples comprised exclusively of manufacturing firms (SIC 2000–3999) and medium-size firms from each country, respectively. The medium-size firm subsample also eliminates many multinationals operating in several institutional settings. The regression results for these subsamples

Table 24.4 Earnings management, outside investor protection and private control benefits

The table presents coefficients and two-sided *p*-values (in parentheses) from rank regressions with the Aggregate Earnings Management Measure as the dependent variable, which is created by averaging the ranks of all four earnings management measures, EM1–EM4 (see Table 24.2). Outside Investor Rights are measured by the anti-director rights index from La Porta et al., (1998), which ranges from zero to five. Legal Enforcement is measured as the average score across three legal variables used in La Porta et al., (1998): (1) the efficiency of the judicial system, (2) an assessment of rule of law, and (3) the corruption index. All three variables range from zero to ten. Private Control Benefits are measured at the country level as the average block premium estimated by Dyck and Zingales (2002) based on transfers of controlling blocks of shares. The first column presents a simple rank regression. The second regression is estimated using two-stage least squares. Instrumental variables are the rank of the country's real per capita GDP averaged from 1980 to 1989, and three binary variables indicating an English, German, French, or Scandinavian legal origin based on the classification in La Porta et al., (1998). The third regression is also estimated using two-stage least squares. The instrumental variables are the Outsider Rights Index and the Legal Enforcement.

	Aggregate Earnings Management Measure	Aggregate Earnings Management Measure -2SLS-	Aggregate Earnings Management Measure -2SLS-
Constant	28.605	31.421	3.128
	(<0.001)	(<0.001)	(0.463)
Outside Investor Rights	−0.499	−0.641	—
	(<0.001)	(0.001)	
Legal Enforcement	−0.289	−0.322	—
	(0.025)	(0.025)	
Private Control Benefits	—	—	0.931
			(0.004)
Adjusted R^2	0.389	0.359	0.272
Number of Observations	31	31	26

(not reported) are essentially the same as those presented in Table 24.4, alleviating concerns that international differences in firm size and industry composition drive our findings.

Finally, we are concerned that differences in firm characteristics and macroeconomic stability affect our inferences. For instance, larger firms have smoother earnings, and operating leverage is positively related to earnings volatility. Similarly, inflation rates and growth rate volatility influence the variability of accounting earnings. Consequently, we re-estimate the regressions using median firm size, median capital intensity, a country's average yearly inflation rate, and the standard deviation of the real GDP growth rate as additional controls. The results (not reported) are consistent with our original findings in Table 24.4. In particular, outside

investor rights and legal enforcement continue to have a significantly negative relation with earnings management.

4.4. The role of other institutional factors

While the robustness checks in the previous section suggest that our findings are not driven by economic heterogeneity across countries, we must still address the concern that other institutional variables, which are correlated with investor protection, are responsible for our main findings. In particular, we are concerned about the influence of accounting rules and firms' ownership structures on earnings management.

First, accounting rules can both limit a manager's ability to distort reported earnings, and affect the properties of reported earnings. But the extent to which accounting rules influence reported earnings and curb earnings management depends on how well these rules are enforced. Moreover, accounting rules likely reflect the influence of a country's legal and institutional framework and are therefore endogenous in our analysis. Countries with strong outsider protection are expected to enact and enforce accounting and securities laws that limit the manipulation of accounting information reported to outsiders. Consistent with this view, Enriques (2000) argues that U.K. and the U.S. laws on director self-dealing are stricter and are more reliant on disclosure than those in Germany or Italy. Similarly, d'Arcy (2000) shows that Anglo-American countries have stricter accounting rules with respect to explicit accounting choices than Continental European countries with less effective investor protection.

Ultimately, however, it is an empirical matter whether our results are robust to the inclusion of controls for countries' stated accounting rules. To address this issue, we re-estimate the main regression and include an accrual rules index constructed by Hung (2001) as a control variable. This index captures the use of accrual rules to accelerate the recognition of economic transactions (e.g., R&D activities or pension plans) in accounting, and it proxies for the extent

Table 24.5 Earnings management and outside investor protection: Controlling for differences in the accounting rules and ownership concentration

The table presents coefficients and two-sided p-values (in parentheses) from rank regressions of the Aggregate Earnings Management Measure on Outside Investor Rights and Legal Enforcement controlling for other institutional factors. Outside Investor Rights is the anti-director rights index from La Porta et al., (1998), which ranges from zero to five. Legal Enforcement is measured as the average score across three legal variables used in La Porta et al. (1998): (1) the efficiency of the judicial system, (2) an assessment of rule of law, and (3) the corruption index. All three variables range from zero to ten. The Accrual Rules variable captures the extent to which accrual rules accelerate the recognition of economic transactions (e.g., R&D activities or pension obligations) in accounting. It is constructed by Hung (2001). Ownership concentration is measured as the median percentage of common shares owned by the largest three shareholders in the ten largest privately owned non-financial firms (La Porta et al., 1998). The regressions in columns 2 and 4 are estimated using two-stage least squares. Instrumental variables are the rank of the country's real per capita GDP averaged from 1980 to 1989, and three binary variables indicating an English, German, French, or Scandinavian legal origin based on the classification in La Porta et al. (1998).

	Aggregate Earnings Management Controlling for Accounting Rules	Aggregate Earnings Management Controlling for Accounting Rules -2SLS-	Aggregate Earnings Management Controlling for Ownership	Aggregate Earnings Management Controlling for Ownership -2SLS-
Constant	30.974	34.591	24.333	47.261
	(<0.001)	(<0.001)	(<0.001)	(0.002)
Outside Investor Rights	−0.285	−0.501	−0.444	−0.774
	(0.079)	(0.044)	(0.003)	(0.007)
Legal Enforcement	−0.297	−0.420	−0.228	−0.571
	(0.080)	(0.048)	(0.101)	(0.048)
Accrual Rules	−0.689	0.125	—	—
	(0.016)	(0.313)		
Ownership Concentration	—	—	0.151	−0.609
			(0.302)	(0.225)
Adjusted R^2	0.584	0.468	0.392	0.214
Number of Observations	20	20	31	31

to which a country's stated accounting rules are intended to produce timely and informative reported earnings.

The results presented in Table 24.5, column 1, show that the coefficients on the accounting rules variable and the outsider rights and legal enforcement variables are significant. However, as shown in column 2, the coefficient on the accounting rules variable is insignificant in the 2SLS regression specification, whereas the investor protection variables remain significant. These results support our view that accounting rules are endogenous and suggest that investor protection is a more fundamental determinant of earnings management across countries. A related concern is that the use of earnings for tax and financial accounting purposes may introduce earnings management and in particular smoothing incentives unrelated to investor protection. We therefore re-run the main regression including a proxy for the degree of a country's tax-book conformity (e.g., Alford et al., 1993; Hung, 2001). In this regression (not reported), the tax variable is not significant while the results for the investor protection variables are similar to those reported in Table 24.4.

Finally, we examine the incremental impact of ownership concentration on insiders' earnings management incentives since prior research highlights the relation between firms' ownership structures and the properties of reported earnings (e.g., Fan and Wong, 2001; Ball et al., 2003). We re-estimate our main regressions using a proxy for ownership concentration constructed by La Porta et al. (1998) as an additional control variable. Neither the rank regression nor the 2SLS regression presented in columns 3 and 4 of Table 24.5 indicate any incremental explanatory power of the ownership variable. Thus, while differences in ownership concentration may be related to cross-sectional variation in earnings management *within* a country, our country-level tests suggest that average ownership patterns are not a primary determinant of systematic earnings management *across* countries.

In summary, the regression results are consistent with the hypothesis that weak outsider protection and private control benefits create incentives to manage earnings. We acknowledge, however, that institutional factors are complementary and hence difficult to isolate.

5. CONCLUSION

This paper documents systematic differences in the level of earnings management across 31 countries. We perform a descriptive cluster analysis to identify groupings of countries with similar institutional characteristics and then show that earnings management varies systematically across these institutional clusters. The analysis suggests that outsider economies with relatively dispersed ownership, strong investor protection, and large stock markets exhibit lower levels of earnings management than insider countries with relatively concentrated ownership, weak investor protection, and less developed stock markets.

As prior work shows that investor protection is a key primitive driving corporate choices such as firms' financing and dividend policies as well as ownership structures, we explore the relation of legal investor protection and firms' earnings management practices. The analysis is based on the notion that insiders, i.e., managers and controlling shareholders, have incentives to acquire private control benefits. However, the ability of insiders to divert resources for their own benefit is limited by legal systems that protect the rights of outside investors. As outsiders can only take disciplinary actions against insiders if outsiders detect the private benefits, insiders have an incentive to manipulate accounting reports in order to conceal their diversion activities. Thus, we expect that earnings management decreases in legal protection because, when investor protection is strong, insiders enjoy fewer private control benefits and consequently incentives to mask firm performance are moderated.

Consistent with this hypothesis, the regression results show that earnings management is negatively associated with the quality of minority shareholder rights and legal enforcement. The findings highlight an important link between investor protection and the quality of accounting earnings reported to market participants, and complement both finance research that treats the quality of corporate reporting as exogenous and accounting research that documents systematic patterns in the relation between stock returns and accounting numbers.

Our findings are robust to the inclusion of controls for country wealth, economic heterogeneity across countries, and international differences in accounting rules and ownership concentration. They should nevertheless be interpreted cautiously as earnings management is difficult to measure and the theoretical relations among institutional factors are not yet well understood and hence difficult to disentangle.

NOTES

* This paper was previously circulated and presented under the title "Earnings Management Around the World" at the 2000 European Accounting Association meetings in Munich. It has also benefited from presentations at the Duke/UNC Fall Camp, the EAA meetings in Athens, the European Finance Association meeting in Berlin, the Financial Economics and Accounting conference at the University of Michigan, Goethe University Frankfurt, MIT, London Business School, New York University, University of Vasa, University of Virginia, the Wharton School, and the College of William and Mary. We are grateful to Stan Baiman, Sudipta Basu, Phil Berger, Larry Brown, Willem Buijink, Elroy Dimson, Simeon Djankov, Richard Frankel, Wayne Guay, Juha Kinnunen, David Larcker, Christian Laux, Martien Lubberink, Peter Pope, Bill Schwert, Weiling Song, Ross Watts, and especially Bob Holthausen and an anonymous referee for helpful comments.
1 Corresponding author. Tel.: +1-215-898-2610; fax: +1-215-573-2054. E-mail address: leuz@wharton.upenn.edu (C. Leuz).

1 While the investor protection literature acknowledges the importance of accounting information, it typically treats the quality of this information as exogenous and does not distinguish between stated accounting rules and firms' actual reporting practices (e.g., La Porta et al., 1998).

2 Outsiders are also expected to price protect themselves, leading to more internal financing, smaller arm's length financial markets and higher cost of outside capital (see, for example, La Porta et al., 1997). Bhattacharya et al. (2002) replicate our earnings management measures and provide evidence that firms' earnings management activities appear to be priced in capital markets.

3 See also Basu et al. (1998) and Hope (2003) relating the properties of analyst forecasts to institutional factors.

4 As accounting systems likely underreact to economic shocks, insiders using accruals to signal firm performance induce on average a less negative (and in specific cases even positive) correlation with cash flows.

5 Our loss avoidance results may appear to contradict the finding of Brown and Higgins (2001) that earnings *surprise* management is more pronounced in the US than in other countries. However, the two findings are compatible. Brown and Higgins (2002) show that US firms engage in more *expectations* management, i.e., downward guidance of analysts, to meet or beat analysts' earnings forecasts, rather than earnings management.

REFERENCES

Alford, A., Jones, J., Leftwich, R., Zmijewski, M., 1993. The relative informativeness of accounting disclosures in different countries. Journal of Accounting Research 31 (Suppl.), 183–221.

Ali, A., Hwang, L., 2000. Country-specific factors related to financial reporting and the value relevance of accounting data. Journal of Accounting Research 38, 1–23.

Ball, R., Kothari, S., Robin, A., 2000. The effect of international institutional factors on properties of accounting earnings. Journal of Accounting and Economics 29, 1–52.

Ball, R., Robin, A., Wu, J., 2003. Incentives versus standards: properties of accounting income in four East Asian countries. Journal of Accounting and Economics, forthcoming.

Basu, S., Hwang, L., Jan, C., 1998. International variation in accounting measurement rules and analysts' earnings forecast errors. Journal of Business, Finance and Accounting 25, 1207–1247.

Beck, T., Demirgüe-Kunt, A., Levine, R., 2003. Law, politics, and finance. Journal of Financial Economics, forthcoming.

Bhattacharya, U., Daouk, H., Welker, M., 2002. The world price of earnings opacity. Unpublished working paper, Indiana University.

Brown, L., Higgins, H., 2001. Managing earnings surprises in the U.S. versus 12 other countries. Journal of Accounting and Public Policy 20, 373–398.

Brown, L., Higgins, H., 2002. Managers' guidance of analysts: international evidence. Unpublished working paper, Georgia State University and Worcester Polytechnic Institute.

Burgstahler, D., Dichev, I., 1997. Earnings management to avoid earnings decreases and losses. Journal of Accounting and Economics 24, 99–129.

Claessens, S., Djankov, S., Fan, J., Lang, L., 2002. Disentangling the incentive and entrenchment effects of large shareholdings. Journal of Finance 57, 2741–2772.

d'Arcy, A., 2000. The degree of determination of national accounting systems — an empirical investigation. Schmalenbach Business Review 52, 45–67.

Dechow, P., 1994. Accounting earnings and cashflows as measures of firm performance: the role of accounting accruals. Journal of Accounting and Economics 18, 3–42.

Dechow, P., Skinner, D., 2000. Earnings management: reconciling the views of accounting academics, practitioners, and regulators. Accounting Horizons 14, 235–250.

Dechow, P., Sloan, R., Sweeney, A., 1995. Detecting earnings management. The Accounting Review 70, 193–225.

Degeorge, F., Patel, J., Zeckhauser, R., 1999. Earnings manipulation to exceed thresholds. Journal of Business 72, 1–33.

Doidge, C., Karolyi, A., Stulz, R., 2003. Why are firms listed in the U.S. worth more? Journal of Financial Economics, forthcoming.

Dyck, A., Zingales, L., 2002. Private benefits of control: an international comparison. Unpublished NBER working paper (8711).

Enriques, L., 2000. The law on company directors' self-dealing: a comparative analysis. International and Comparative Corporate Law Journal 2, 297–314.

Fan, J., Wong, T., 2001. Corporate ownership structure and the informativeness of accounting earnings in east asia. Journal of Accounting and Economics 33, 401–426.

Healy, P., Wahlen, J., 1999. A review of the earnings management literature and its implications for standard setting. Accounting Horizons 13, 365–383.

Hope, O., 2003. Disclosure practices, enforcement of accounting standards, and analysts' forecasts: an international study. Journal of Accounting Research 41, 235–272.

Hung, M., 2001. Accounting standards and value relevance of financial statements: an international analysis. Journal of Accounting and Economics 30, 401–420.

Joos, P., Lang, M., 1994. The effects of accounting diversity: evidence from the European Union. Journal of Accounting Research 34(Suppl.), 141–168.

La Porta, R., Lopez-de-Silanes, F., Shleifer, A., Vishny, R., 1997. Legal determinants of external finance. Journal of Finance 52, 1131–1150.

La Porta, R., Lopez-de-Silanes, F., Shleifer, A., Vishny, R., 1998. Law and finance. Journal of Political Economy 106, 1113–1155.

La Porta, R., Lopez-de-Silanes, F., Shleifer, A., Vishny, R., 1999. Corporate ownership around the world. Journal of Finance 54, 471–517.

La Porta, R., Lopez-de-Silanes, F., Shleifer, A., Vishny, R., 2000. Investor protection and corporate governance. Journal of Financial Economics 58, 3–27.

Land, J., Lang, M., 2002. Empirical evidence on the evolution of global accounting. Accounting Review 77(Suppl.), 115–133.

Lang, M., Raedy, J., Yetman, M., 2003. How representative are cross-listed firms? An analysis of firm performance and accounting quality. Journal of Accounting Research 41, 363–386.

Levine, R., 1999. Law, finance and economic growth. Journal of Financial Intermediation 8, 8–35.

Nenova, T., 2000. The value of corporate votes and control benefits: a cross-country analysis. Unpublished working paper, Harvard University.

Shleifer, A., Vishny, R., 1997. A survey of corporate governance. Journal of Finance 52, 737–783.

Skinner, D., Myers, L., 1999. Earnings momentum and earnings management. Unpublished working paper, University of Michigan and University of Illinois.

Watts, R., Zimmerman, J., 1986. Positive Accounting Theory. Prentice-Hall, Englewood Cliffs, NJ.

Zingales, L., 1994. The value of the voting right: a study of the Milan stock exchange experience. Review of Financial Studies 7, 125–148.

Part 6

On takeover as disciplinary mechanism

INTRODUCTION

IN PART 3 WE COLLECTED PAPERS THAT EXAMINE the relationship between different corporate control devices and top management turnover as a manifestation of their disciplinary effect. The control devices are generally internal to the control or ownership structure of the underperforming firms. In this part, we present papers that deal with an external control device. This is the market for control in which management teams compete for control of corporate assets. Manne (1965) was the first to conceptualise the market for corporate control as a managerial disciplinary device with underperforming firms becoming targets of bidders with presumably greater ability to correct under-performance and create greater value for target shareholders.

Hostile takeover is the means by which corporate control is wrested from the underperforming target managers. In theory such an external disciplinary device may be considered redundant if the internal control mechanisms are effective. The incidence of a hostile takeover may thus be an indictment of the failure of the internal controls. This argument pre-supposes that internal controls and hostile takeover are substitutes. A contrary perspective is that efficient internal controls facilitate hostile takeovers by preventing the entrenched incumbent management at the target firm from raising the barricades against managerial change. In this view hostile takeover and robust internal controls are complementary tools serving the same purpose. The papers in this part deal with the role of hostile takeovers as a disciplinary device and how governance regimes in certain countries substitute for them or facilitate them.

Rezaul Kabir, Dolph Cantrijn and Andreas Jeunink (Ch.25) empirically examine the relationships between a firm's takeover defences, its ownership structure and stock returns in Holland. Analysing data of Dutch listed companies, they find that these firms increasingly adopt multiple anti-takeover defences when such firms are characterised by relatively lower ownership concentration. The evidence supports the hypothesis that more concentrated ownership of shares provides more effective monitoring of managers. Issue of preferred shares has recently been the most widely adopted anti-takeover defence mechanism in the Netherlands and its impact on shareholders' wealth is also analysed. The adoption of stringent anti-takeover measures (e.g. the issue of preference shares to friendly investors) leads to a mixed reaction from the stock market. While in the period immediately prior to the issue the reaction is favourable, in the post-issue period it is negative. It appears that the move to adopt the defensive measure signals an impending takeover bid thereby raising the value of the issuing firm, but the actual adoption reduces the chances of such a bid thereby leading to value decline.

Another European country with a similar governance and ownership structure and where hostile takeovers are rare is Germany. However, Tim Jenkinson and Alexander

Ljungqvist (Ch.26) provide clinical evidence to show that the German market for corporate control and the governance system are characterised by both more active and more hostile deals than previously believed. Their study provides a complete breakdown of ownership and takeover defence patterns in German listed companies and finds highly fragmented (but not dispersed) ownership in non-majority controlled firms. The paper documents how the accumulation of hostile stakes can be used to gain control of target companies given these ownership patterns. The article also suggests an important role for banks in helping predators accumulate, and avoid the disclosure of, large stakes.

Jens Köke (Ch.27) also focuses on Germany and examines whether changes in ultimate firm ownership (control) play a disciplinary role in a bank-based economy. Germany is the prototype of a bank-based system and the study finds that poor performance makes a change in control more likely. This suggests a disciplinary role for managerial control. Tight shareholder control acts as a substitute for control changes beside strong creditor control as a complement for shareholder control. Following a change in control, management turnover increases, but not as a consequence of poor performance, and performance does not improve significantly. These findings are inconsistent with a disciplinary role of the market for corporate control in bank-based Germany.

Julian Franks and Colin Mayer (Ch.28) test an important assumption about the motivation for hostile takeovers (i.e. a superior management team seeks to take control of poorly performing target firms and replace the inefficient incumbent management). Their paper examines the disciplining function of hostile takeovers in the UK in 1985 and 1986. It reports evidence of high board turnover and significant levels of post-takeover restructuring. Large gains are anticipated in hostile bids as reflected in high bid premiums. However, there is little evidence of poor performance prior to bids, suggesting that the high board turnover does not derive from past managerial failure. Hostile takeovers do not therefore perform a disciplining function. Instead, rejection of bids appears to derive from opposition to post-takeover redeployment of assets and renegotiation over the terms of bids.

Overall there is some evidence that market for corporate control is active in both Germany and the UK but in Germany it is minority stakes that are traded, whereas in the UK trading it is majority control of target firms. There is mixed evidence regarding the disciplinary motivation for hostile bids. There is also mixed evidence concerning the substitutability or complementarity of internal and external control devices.

REFERENCE

Manne, Henry G. (1965), 'Mergers and the market for corporate control' *Journal of Political Economy*, 73: 110–120.

Chapter 25

Rezaul Kabir, Dolph Cantrijn and Andreas Jeunink

TAKEOVER DEFENSES, OWNERSHIP STRUCTURE AND STOCK RETURNS IN THE NETHERLANDS: AN EMPIRICAL ANALYSIS

Source: *Strategic Management Journal,* 18(2) (1997): 97–109.

ABSTRACT

This study empirically examines the relationships between a firm's takeover defenses and its ownership structure and stock returns. Analyzing data of Dutch listed companies, we find that multiple antitakeover defenses are increasingly adopted when firms are characterized by relatively lower ownership concentration. The evidence supports the hypothesis that more concentrated ownership of shares provides more effective monitoring of managers. As defense by issuing preferred share has recently been the most widely adopted mechanism in the Netherlands, its impact on shareholders' wealth is also analyzed. We observe the presence of two opposing effects of this antitakeover measure.

INTRODUCTION

HOSTILE TAKEOVER BIDS ARE RARE IN THE Netherlands, and were successful, at most, on a few occasions. The reason is that stock exchange listed companies are protected by multiple takeover defenses. Around the turn of the twentieth century, defense mechanisms started to be used to protect Dutch corporations from foreign influences. Later on, they were applied to restrict the power of common shareholders. The use of defense measures to repel corporate raids and unfriendly takeovers has become more important since the 1960s, and has received both criticism and support from various interest groups. Public corporations have been devoting time and resources toward developing diverse tactics to defend against unfriendly takeovers. As a result, the external market for corporate control plays a diminished disciplinary role in the Netherlands. An issue deserving investigation is under what circumstances this disciplinary mechanism becomes ineffective. To address this issue, we investigate virtually the whole population of Dutch listed industrial companies which have adopted multiple defense mechanisms.

The issue of corporate governance is also interesting in an international setting because it differs from country to country. For example, there is an active takeover market in the U.S.A. and the U.K., but this is not so in many other countries. There, as for example, shareholders are considered to be one group of stakeholders in a firm next to employees, suppliers and customers. The equity ownership is also concentrated in the hands of a few investors. Although the pattern of cross-shareholdings in German and Japanese companies may look similar, the governance structures are quite dissimilar. German firms have close relationships with banks which supply both equity capital and debt. In contrast, Japanese firms are characterized by large industrial groups with interlocking directorships. Hostile takeovers are virtually nonexistent in Germany and the Netherlands, but due to two different reasons. Extensive cross-shareholdings provide German companies with a strong defense, while Dutch companies are protected by multiple antitakeover devices. These and other differences imply that the influence of various disciplinary mechanisms will vary from country to country. The takeover market is a relatively more important disciplinary mechanism in the U.S.A. and the U.K. But, for Germany and the Netherlands, concentrated ownership and supervisory boards exert a relatively more important role. Various antitakeover measures are adopted in the U.S.A. to protect the interests of shareholders during takeover bids. But, in the Netherlands these measures are primarily directed to limit the power of common shareholders.

A vast literature addresses the interrelationship between ownership structure and different corporate governance devices. Walsh and Seward (1990) examine different internal and external mechanisms of corporate control used in aligning the diverse interests of managers and shareholders. Important internal control mechanisms include the control function of the board of directors, competition within the managerial team, and the monitoring role of large shareholders. The external control mechanisms, on the other hand, are the market for corporate control and the competition in the product market. Walsh and Seward (1990) argue that the failure of one control mechanism triggers the presence of another mechanism. Studies by Jarrell and Poulsen (1987), Ambrose and Megginson (1992), and Gordon and Pound (1993)

also suggest that differences in firms' ownership structure (internal control aspect) can explain observed variations in antitakeover defenses (external control aspect). The notion can be illustrated in the following way.

Shareholders with large stakes are expected to participate actively in managerial decision making (Demsetz, 1983; Shleifer and Vishny, 1986). They will not in their own interest allow managers to adopt defensive measures, as disciplining will be more difficult. The same is true for large but passive shareholders who will also try to resist any attempt by managers to adopt defenses. This is because any future possibility of gain through facilitating a third-party takeover will then be reduced. Shareholders with small holdings, on the other hand, may not take an active interest in monitoring management, perhaps because of the 'free-rider' problem. Defense measures are then relatively easily adopted by managers because there are no large shareholders to counteract management's attempt. The purpose of the study is, therefore, to test empirically this theoretically predicted relationship between firms' ownership concentration and takeover defense measures.[1]

Incentives as well as the degree of monitoring can vary depending on the stakes and the types of shareholders. One may be interested to know how institutional shareholders, as a separate group, affect corporate decision making. These investors— usually banks, insurance companies, pension funds and mutual funds—are expected to play a more active role in the affairs of a company. They are in a better position to invest resources for increased monitoring so that management's inclination to adopt defense mechanisms decreases. On the other hand, some institutional investors may align with management because of commercial ties and profitable business opportunities. The role actually played by institutional shareholders, therefore, becomes an empirical issue.[2]

Although it has been argued that large shareholders who are effective monitors will prevent managers from adopting defensive measures, one can not be sure if shareholders in general are harmed by such adoptions. In fact, adoption of takeover defenses is usually explained under two competing hypotheses (DeAngelo and Rice, 1983; Mahoney and Mahoney, 1993). According to the managerial entrenchment hypothesis, defense measures primarily protect poorly functioning management by reducing the probability of potential takeover. These measures help incumbent management to abuse their power by acting in their own interest at the expense of shareholders. On the other hand, the shareholder interest hypothesis postulates that adoption of defense measures allows current management to focus on long-term strategies of the firm while remaining protected from the worry of hostile takeovers. Through a strong negotiating position, managers can also help shareholders to obtain a fairer/higher premium if a takeover does take place.

Empirical studies from the U.S.A. document that while some defense mechanisms are harmful for shareholders, others are not.[3] This study, therefore, reexamines the valuation impact of defense measures, using the Dutch data. If shareholders of Dutch companies interpret the adoption of defense measures as managerial entrenchment, stock prices should decline. Alternatively, if these measures allow management to bargain for a higher takeover premium, share prices should increase.

The wealth effect of defense measures needs to be examined in conjunction with the ownership structure of firms. Jarrell and Poulsen (1987) document that value-reducing takeover defenses are adopted by firms with larger insider holdings and smaller institutional holdings. McWilliams (1990) finds that defense measures induce positive effects on shareholder wealth for firms with low insider share ownership. Agrawal and Mandelker (1990) report that the effect is more favorable the larger the level of institutional ownership. Song and Walkling (1993) find that managerial ownership is related both to the probability of being a takeover target and to increments

in target shareholder returns. Given these findings, we examine if the shareholders wealth effect of takeover defenses is related to ownership structure.

The remainder of the paper is organized as follows. Important takeover defense measures are first discussed with particular emphasis on those prevailing in the Netherlands. The following two sections describe the sample and the methodology. The results are presented in the next section. A brief summary of the study and the research implications are presented in the final section.

TAKEOVER DEFENSE MEASURES

Takeover defense measures help to make acquisition of a company more difficult, if not impossible, and thereby serve to insulate managers from the free market for corporate control. These measures vary from country to country depending on institutional features and corporate governance systems (Franks and Mayer, 1990). Moerland (1995) distinguishes two basic types of corporate systems: the market-oriented system (prevailing in the U.S.A. and the U.K.) and the network-oriented system (prevailing in, for example, the Netherlands, Germany, France and Japan). The former is characterized by relatively developed financial markets, large-scale presence of corporations with widely dispersed ownership, and active markets for corporate control. The latter system, on the other hand, features closely held corporations, group membership of corporations, and substantial involvement of banks in corporate financing and corporate control. These differences in governance systems are also reflected in differences in adoption of specific defense devices.

There exist a variety of ways to classify takeover defenses. These can be either structural or technical. The first type arises from prevailing structures of stock market and equity ownership (e.g., relative importance of debt financing, crossholdings). The second type of defenses are specifically directed to impede hostile takeover attempts (e.g., issuing preferred defense shares, limiting voting power). According to one study,[4] structural barriers to takeovers are relatively strong in Italy, France, Germany and Switzerland, and of medium strength in Spain and Sweden, but weak in the Netherlands and the U.K. Technical measures, on the other hand, are relatively strong in the Netherlands, Germany and Switzerland, of medium strength in Italy, France, Spain and Sweden, and weak in the U.K.

Defense mechanisms are also classified according to shareholders' approval (Ruback, 1988). Some defenses require shareholders' approval before adoption. These include super-majority provisions, fair-price amendments and classified boards. Other measures may be adopted by management without requiring shareholders' approval. Examples include poison pills and targeted share repurchases.

The Dutch situation offers companies numerous possibilities of defense mechanisms, many of which do not exist in the U.S.A. These include (a) legal measures such as the creation of structure companies ('structuur vennootschappen'); (b) statutory measures such as issuing preferred defense shares, issuing priority shares, making binding appointments of directors and limiting voting power per shareholder; and (c) nonstatutory measures such as the issue of depository receipts of shares ('certificaten van aandelen'). Some important features of these antitakeover devices are explained below.

The law on 'structure companies' compels a large firm to establish a 'supervisory board' (consisting of outsiders and different interest group representatives). This board (thus, not the shareholders of the company) in turn appoints a 'management board' to run day-to-day affairs of the firm. Many decisions of the 'management board', such as adoption of annual accounts, investment plans and company restructuring, require approval of the 'supervisory board', which meets on a few occasions per year. Priority shares are issued to a friendly foundation which reserves the right to approve any amendment

of a company's charter. Therefore, the power of the general meeting of common shareholders is restricted. The approval of priority shareholders is also needed for decisions such as hiring or firing of company directors and issuing new common shares. Depository receipts are issued by an administrative office to investors after detaching the voting rights from ordinary shares. The holder of depository receipts has all economic rights attached to common shares, except for the voting right (which rests with the administrative office). Binding appointments of new directors are made by the management board, thereby strengthening their own control. Ordinary shareholders are, thus, deprived of the possibility to appoint their own directors. Only a two-third majority at the shareholders meeting can overrule the binding appointment. Limited voting power mechanism restricts the maximum number of votes that can be cast by one shareholder, regardless of the number of shares actually held.

Besides the above-mentioned takeover defenses, the issue of preferred defense shares is the most widely adopted defense mechanism in the Netherlands. These shares are issued in the name of the holder (usually friendly parties) because of their *control* function, with only the statutory minimum of 25 percent of par value to be paid up. Even though they are not fully paid up, preferred shares have the same voting rights as common shares. In order to resist any unfriendly takeover attempt, common stockholders authorize company management to issue preferred shares whenever necessary and thus, grant substantial voting power to another entity.

The procedure of defense with preferred shares takes place in three consecutive steps. First, common shareholders approve the necessary charter amendment to *create* the possibility of issuing preferred shares. Second, company management *grants* the option to a friendly party—usually a specially created foundation and/or an institutional investor. Third, management decides to *issue* preferred share. This usually happens when there is a fear of unfriendly takeover attempt. These three steps follow one after another, but do not necessarily take place simultaneously. A company may create the possibility to issue preferred defense shares at a certain point of time, while the shares are actually issued several years later (depending on any threat of hostile takeover).

DATA

Inspired by the European Community initiative, shareholders with holdings of 5 percent or more in Dutch listed companies have been required to disclose their holdings publicly since February 1992. Before that, there was no mandatory disclosure of share ownership, and no way existed even to identify shareholders.[5] The data on block-holdings are collected from the Dutch financial daily *Het Financieele Dagblad*. In total, we obtained a sample of 177 companies listed on the Amsterdam Stock Exchange. These companies represent more than 90 percent of the Dutch stock market capitalization. Data on takeover defense measures associated with these companies are collected from Voogd (1989) and other publications. Our findings are presented in Tables 25.1 and 25.2.

Table 25.1 shows that more than 90 percent of Dutch companies are protected by at least one defense measure. We find that while only 16 (9%) companies are without any of these defenses, 52 (29%) companies have one defense mechanism, 62 (35%) firms have two defense mechanisms, and as many as 47 (27%)

Table 25.1 Number of takeover defenses adopted by Dutch companies

No. of measures	No. of firms	%
0	16	9.1
1	52	29.4
2	62	35.0
3	39	22.0
4	8	4.5
Total	177	100

Table 25.2 Distribution of different takeover defenses

	Official market[a]	Parallel market[a]	Total
Total number of firms	141	36	177
Priority shares	63	16	79
Preferred shares	89	16	105
Binding appointment	49	15	64
Limited voting power	7	0	7
Depository receipts	41	19	70

a The official market is the first-tier market for larger companies, while the parallel market is for smaller companies.

firms are protected by three or more defense devices. Table 25.2 presents a list of widely used antitakeover measures in the Netherlands. We find that 105 (32%) firms have adopted defense mechanism with preferred shares, 79 (24%) firms have issued priority shares, 70 (22%) companies have issued depository receipts, 64 (20%) firms have made binding appointments of directors, and seven (2%) companies have imposed restrictions on voting rights.

After searching sources like the stock exchange publication *Beursplein 5* and the financial daily *Het Financieele Dagblad*, we find that 79 *new* defense mechanisms were announced by Dutch companies during 1984–90. Defense with preferred share was the most frequently announced mechanism—on 52 occasions, which represents 66% of the total. The next most important antitakeover devices were the issues of priority shares and depository receipts. Both were adopted on seven occasions each. No new defense measure was announced during 1991–92 because of restrictions imposed by the Amsterdam Stock Exchange. Many companies accelerated the adoption of new antitakover devices before the restriction took effect.

Out of the 52 announcements of defense with preferred shares during 1984–90, we select a sample of 47 to analyze shareholder wealth effect.[6] The sample is further divided into three groups based on the announcement of three steps followed during the issuing process. The statutory possibility to defend with preferred shares was created for the first time during 1984–90 by 17 companies. During the same period, the announcement of granting an option allowing friendly parties to own preferred shares was made by 12 companies (these 12 companies have taken the first step either during 1984–90 or earlier). Finally, during the period of our investigation, there were 18 companies which actually announced the issue of preferred shares.

We collect daily share price data from Datastream. These are adjusted for stock splits and other capital changes. We also adjust for cash dividends and then compute continuously compounded stock returns for the analysis.

METHODOLOGY

We first divide the aggregate sample into groups with cumulative takeover defense measures, and then determine the average ownership concentration for each group. We calculate ownership concentration of a firm in several ways: the percentage of shares held by the largest block-holder[7] (C_1), the share of the three largest blockholders (C_3), and the share of all blockholders (C_{block}). We also separately calculate a concentration measure ($C_{inst.}$) to represent institutional ownership (estimated by blockholdings held by major Dutch banks and insurance companies). On the basis of a t-test we then find out whether average ownership concentration significantly varies among groups of companies with different takeover defenses.

The above analysis is performed by comparing two sample averages at a time. In order to examine the effect of firms' ownership structure on the likelihood of adopting *individual* takeover defense, we estimate the following logistic regression:[8]

$$p \text{ (defense measure)} = f \text{ (ownership concentration)}$$

Here the dependent variable is equal to 1 if a firm has a particular defense measure and 0 otherwise. Several new proxies are

used to calculate ownership concentration. In addition to the four concentration measures defined earlier, we use the logarithmic transformation of these variables as well as the Herfindahl measure of concentration in the regression analysis.[9]

To examine whether shareholders experience any change in their wealth when new takeover defense measures are announced, we follow the conventional event study methodology. This methodology has been widely used in the financial economics literature (e.g., DeAngelo and Rice, 1983; Linn and McConnell, 1983). Recently, it has also become popular in the strategic management literature (e.g., Mahoney and Mahoney, 1993). The purpose of this method is to estimate the deviation of actual stock returns (consequent upon the announcement of a specified event) from expected stock returns. We employ the Market Model and the Market Adjusted Returns Model to estimate these deviations for each stock.

The Market Model supposes that the return on an individual stock is linearly related to the market return. The relationship is written as follows:

$$R_{jt} = \alpha_j + \beta_j R_{mt} + e_{jt}$$

where

R_{jt} = the continuously compounded return of stock j in period t;

R_{mt} = the continuously compounded market return in period t;

$\alpha_j \beta_j$ = security specific and time independent parameters;

e_{jt} = the error term of stock j in period t.

The period to estimate the Market Model parameters is selected as the period of 100 days before the start of the event (or announcement) period. We also estimate the parameters using 100 days of data from the postevent period. A period of 20 days before the announcement until 20 days after the announcement is selected as the event period. The impact of takeover defense announcements on stock returns is measured over this period. The parameters are estimated by using the ordinary least squares method. We use the 'CBS-Total Return Index' to calculate the market returns used in the model.[10] The abnormal return (also called excess return or prediction error) is the difference between the actual return during the event period (-20, $+20$) and the return predicted from the estimation period:

$$AR_{jt} = R_{jt} - \hat{\alpha}_j - \hat{\beta}_j R_{mt}$$

The abnormal returns for individual stocks are then averaged across all stocks to obtain average abnormal returns for each day. The excess returns for each stock are also compounded over different time intervals around announcement date to calculate cumulative abnormal returns. A t-test is performed to test whether the average abnormal returns are significantly different from zero. The t-value is obtained by dividing average daily abnormal returns by its standard deviation calculated from the estimation period.

In order to check the robustness of our results, we also perform the stock return analysis using the Market Adjusted Returns Model. The model predicts individual stock return to be equal to the corresponding market return, or in other words,

$$R_{jt} = R_{mt}$$

This model is distinct from the Market Model in the sense that here all stocks are assumed to be of average risk. The abnormal returns are calculated as the difference between the actual stock return and the corresponding market return:

$$AR_{jt} = R_{jt} - R_{mt}$$

The average abnormal returns and cumulative average abnormal returns are then computed as described previously.

EMPIRICAL RESULTS

Ownership structure

A descriptive analysis on Dutch ownership structure is presented in Table 25.3. We find that blockholders hold more than half of all shares in Dutch companies. The average share of the largest blockholder is 31 percent, that of the three largest blockholders is 45 percent, and the average share of all blockholders together is 51 percent. It appears that the group with the three largest shareholders dominates ownership concentration of Dutch firms. The correlations between these variables are, as expected, very high. Our results show that ownership concentration in the Netherlands is higher than in the U.S.A., the U.K. and Japan, but lower than in Sweden.[11] The variation within each measure of ownership concentration is also higher in the Netherlands. The standard deviation of percentage of shares held by the top five blockholders in our sample is 26 percent compared with Prowse's (1995) findings of 16 percent in the U.S.A. and the U.K. and 14 percent in Japan.

Analyzing the distribution of shareholdings, we find that the largest shareholder has more than 25 percent of shares in 52 percent of the firms in the sample, and more than 50 percent of shares in 22 percent of the firms. A majority of the companies

Table 25.3 Means, medians, standard deviations, and correlations

Variables	Mean	Median	S.D.	C_1	C_3	C_5	C_{block}	$C_{inst.}$
C_1	30.8	25.5	1.68	1				
C_3	45.1	42.5	24.9	0.89	1			
C_5	49.2	49.8	25.8	0.81	0.97	1		
C_{block}	50.9	55.1	26.5	0.75	0.93	0.90	1	
C_{inst}:	9.9	6.0	12.5	-0.16	-0.02	0.06	0.08	1

The table reports the results of different ownership concentration variables: C_1, C_3, C_5, C_{block} and $C_{inst.}$ represent the percentage of shares held by the largest blockholder, the three largest blockholders, the five largest blockholders, all blockholders, and institutional blockholders, respectively. The sample consists of 177 industrial companies listed on the Amsterdam Stock Exchange in 1992.

has a blockholding in excess of 50 percent. After searching the identity of these blockholders, we find that the average shares of management and family members, companies, and individual blockholders are 8 percent, 20 percent and 5 percent, respectively. The average share of financial institutions (banks and insurance companies) in our sample is almost 10 percent. The combined share of these investors is less than 25 percent for 90 percent of the companies. The sample contains 18 companies in which banks and insurance companies are the only blockholders. The average share of other institutional blockholders is 6 percent.

In Table 25.4 we present the average ownership concentrations of companies with cumulative defense mechanisms. We also report in the lower panel corresponding t-values testing the difference in average ownership concentrations. Our results show that the concentration of the largest shareholder for firms without any defense measure is almost 13 percentage points higher than that for firms with only one measure. Similarly, for companies with one takeover defense device, the concentration of the largest shareholder is 11 percent age points higher than that for firms with two devices. Both differences in concentration are statistically significant. In general, we find that the lower the ownership concentrations are, the more takeover defenses companies adopt. This phenomenon is valid for all three measures of ownership concentration. Our evidence is consistent with Bergström and Rydqvist (1990), who observe that Swedish firms with high concentration of equity ownership rarely adopt antitakeover devices. These findings suggest that firms adopt multiple takeover defenses when shareholdings are diffuse.

Table 25.4 also reports the results for institutional blockholders (banks and insurance companies). The concentration of these institutional shareholders does not show any particular relationship with multiple takeover defenses. The share of these investors in firms with one defense mechanism is five percentage points higher than in firms without any defense. Afterwards, as institutional ownership concentration declines, firms adopt a higher number of defenses. These differences are not statistically significant.

Next, we examine if the general finding on the negative relationship between

Table 25.4 The difference in ownership concentration of firms with cumulative takeover defenses

| No. of defenses | No. of firms | Measures of concentration | | | |
		C_1	C_3	C_{block}	$C_{inst.}$
0	16	48.51	65.21	73.08	7.83
1	52	35.88	53.01	59.78	12.16
2	62	24.99	37.59	41.48	9.36
3	39	28.99	42.24	49.93	9.01
4	8	20.33	27.04	29.99	7.45
t (0, 1)		2.00**	1.91*	2.17**	−1.27
t (1, 2)		2.78**	3.46**	3.92**	1.11
t (2, 3)		−0.78	−0.96	−1.59	0.13
t (3, 4)		0.95	1.72*	2.02**	0.35

** Statistically significant at the 5% level.
* Statistically significant at the 10% level.
The table reports results of four concentration variables—C_1, C_3, C_{block} and $C_{inst.}$—representing the percentage of shares held by the largest blockholder, the three largest blockholders, all blockholders, and institutional blockholders, respectively. The t-statistic reported in the lower panel tests for the difference of means between two measures of ownership concentrations.

ownership concentration and defense mechanisms also holds for *individual* takeover defenses. The analysis is carried out by performing a logit regression. The estimated regression coefficient expresses the relationship between the likelihood of choosing one particular defense mechanism and a measure of firms' ownership concentration. The results are presented in Table 25.5.[12] The reported coefficient estimates are obtained from running regressions with one explanatory variable at a time. We find that the results are generally consistent with earlier findings. The probability of a firm adopting any one takeover defense mechanism is negatively related to ownership concentration. The finding is robust to all variables used in computing ownership concentration, including the logarithmic transformations

of the Herfindahl measures. The results with institutional concentration variables alone are, however, once again mixed.

Wealth effects

The sample here consists of 44 new preferred defenses announced during 1984–90.[13] Table 6 presents the cumulated average abnormal returns based on the Market Model for several intervals in the event period. The results from the aggregate sample indicate that the announcement of the preferred share defense mechanism is, on average, associated with a decline in common share price. During the 2-day announcement period [0, 1], shareholders suffer a statistically significant return decline of 1.18 percent. The result is not driven by a few outliers as the number of

Table 25.5 Estimates of logistic regressions relating the likelihood of adopting a specific takeover defense mechanism to ownership concentration

Measures of concentration	Priority share		Preferred share		Depository receipts	
	Intercept	Coefficient	Intercept	Coefficient	Intercept	Coefficient
C_1	0.06	−0.01	0.94**	−0.02**	0.40	−0.03**
	(0.24)	(1.32)	(3.45)	(2.54)	(1.47)	(3.46)
C_3	0.30	−0.01*	1.40**	−0.02**	0.50	0.02**
	(0.97)	(1.87)	(3.99)	(3.33)	(1.55)	(3.16)
C_{block}	0.31	−0.01*	1.65**	−0.02**	0.37	−0.02**
	(0.93)	(1.78)	(4.26)	(3.72)	(1.12)	(2.67)
$C_{inst.}$	0.08	−0.03**	0.23	0.01	−0.67**	0.02*
	(0.41)	(2.24)	(1.18)	(1.16)	(3.34)	(1.95)
$LN(C_1)$	0.63	−0.27	1.89**	−0.48**	1.26**	−0.55**
	(1.17)	(1.63)	(3.06)	(2.58)	(2.19)	(3.04)
$LN(C_3)$	0.97	−0.33*	2.48**	−0.58**	0.94	−0.39**
	(1.53)	(1.93)	(3.06)	(2.69)	(1.48)	(2.21)
$LN(C_{block})$	0.93	−0.31*	2.66**	−0.61**	0.73	−0.32*
	(1.48)	(1.88)	(3.16)	(2.82)	(1.18)	(1.93)
$LN(C_{inst.})$	0.19	−0.27**	0.15	0.15	−0.85**	0.26**
	(0.85)	(2.36)	(0.66)	(1.31)	(3.43)	(2.28)
H_{block}	−0.06	−0.90	0.76**	−2.22**	0.11	−3.51**
	(0.31)	(1.09)	(3.54)	(2.58)	(0.50)	(3.15)
$H_{inst.}$	−0.14	−5.41	0.29*	6.34	−0.45**	1.55
	(0.87)	(1.04)	(1.77)	(1.13)	(2.68)	(0.35)

** Statistically significant at the 5% level.
* Statistically significant at the 10% level.
The concentration variables are defined as follows. The variables C_1, C_3, C_{block}, and C_{inst}. represent the percentage of shares held by the largest blockholder, three largest blockholders, all blockholders, and institutional blockholders, respectively. The LN and H variables are logarithmic transformed and Herfindahl concentration measures, respectively. Absolute t-values are shown in parentheses beneath each coefficient.

negative abnormal returns dominates the sample. This is also found to be statistically significant at the 5 percent level after conducting a sign test (Z-statistic = 2.34). Over the 6-day postannouncement period, the cumulative abnormal return is −2.27 percent (with a t-value of −2.97).[14]

Although the above result tends to support the managerial entrenchment hypothesis, further analysis of the sample reveals some interesting findings. We split the aggregate sample into three subsamples based on the three steps followed in the issuing process. With the announcement of the first step towards defense (creating the possibility of preferred share issue), a positive and statistically significant stock price effect is observed. This evidence does not support the managerial entrenchment hypothesis. Shareholders do not experience any wealth decline from the charter amendment leading to takeover defense. On the contrary, they appear to benefit as there is a signficant increase in stock returns (1.23% in 2 days).[15] All other postannouncement intervals also reveal positive (but not significant) price increases. This result indicates that defense measures are indeed adopted allowing shareholders to benefit from increased takeover premiums.

The almost negligible stock price impact with respect to the second step announcement is not surprising, since granting a purchase option to a friendly party is an obvious outcome of the charter amendment.

Another interesting finding is obtained when we look at the third step of the defense process. The negative announcement effect of the aggregate sample is in fact determined by the issue of the preferred share itself. We find that the announcement of a preferred share issue is associated with a strong excess decline in stock returns (−4.09%), which is statistically significant (with a t-value of −4.94). For the 6-day period [0, 5], the excess decline in shareholders' wealth amounts to 6.40 percent.[16] However, we find a significant price increase before the announcement of the preferred share issue. This increase in share price could be an indication of a takeover attempt that eventually led managers to issue the preferred shares.[17] Interestingly, the post-announcement periods indicate a significant decline in shareholders' wealth. This decline might provide an estimate of the lost premium incurred by common shareholders—since the chance of eventual takeover was eliminated by actually issuing preferred shares.[18] Our finding is consistent

Table 25.6 Cumulative abnormal returns around the announcement of defense with preferred share issue

	(−20, −1)	(0, 1)	Return intervals (−1, 1)	(0, 5)	(−20, 5)	(0, 20)
Full sample	1.06	−1.18**	−1.17**	−2.27**	−1.52	−3.56**
(n = 44)	(0.76)	(2.67)	(2.18)	(2.97)	(0.96)	(2.49)
Create possibility	−3.11	1.23*	0.71	0.60	−2.51	1.43
(n = 17)	(1.41)	(1.77)	(0.83)	(0.01)	(1.00)	(0.64)
Grant option	0.50	−0.41	−0.10	−0.42	0.08	−2.81
(n = 10)	(0.22)	(0.57)	(0.12)	(0.33)	(0.03)	(1.20)
Actual issue	4.93*	−4.09**	−1.70*	−6.40**	1.21	−9.64**
(n = 17)	(1.88)	(4.94)	(1.68)	(4.46)	(0.41)	(3.59)
First issue	4.36	−4.18**	−2.20*	−7.03**	1.42	−11.73**
(n = 13)	(1.32)	(4.00)	(1.72)	(3.88)	(0.38)	(3.46)
Second issue	6.78**	−3.79**	−0.09	−4.37**	0.52	−2.85
(n = 4)	(2.30)	(4.06)	(0.08)	(2.71)	(0.16)	(0.94)

** Statistically significant at the 5% level.
* Statistically significant at the 10% level.
Abnormal returns are computed employing the Market Model, and are shown as a percentage. Results are presented for six different intervals. The numbers in parentheses below the coefficients are absolute t-values.

with prior studies showing that stock prices increase with takeover bids but then decline if they do not materialize. In sum, the evidence provided here suggests that, although defense measures are beneficial to a certain extent, the benefits do not remain when they are used to fend off takeover attempts.

We also examine whether there is a difference in the results between the first preferred share issue and a subsequent issue. The issue sample is further divided into a subsample of 13 companies that issued preferred shares for the first time and a subsample of four companies with a subsequent issue. We find that the first issue is more damaging for shareholders. The abnormal return in the 5-day post-announcement period is -7.03 percent (t-value $= -3.88$) in case of the first-time issue, compared to -4.37 percent (t-value $= -2.71$) in case of a subsequent issue. This difference is statistically very significant (with a t-value of -6.24).[19] Other post-announcement return intervals show similar results.

CONCLUSIONS AND IMPLICATIONS

This paper empirically analyzes the relationship of takeover defenses with firms' ownership structure and shareholders' wealth. A sample of Dutch industrial companies is selected for the study. The Dutch scenario is particularly interesting because almost all listed companies have adopted multiple takeover defenses.

We find that firms with a relatively lower ownership concentration are the ones with a larger number of defense measures. Our analysis suggests that firms with disperse ownership adopt more defense tactics. The analysis also shows that the likelihood for a firm to adopt takeover defenses is inversely and significantly related to ownership concentration. The result is robust to different ways of measuring ownership concentration. Overall, our evidence is consistent with the hypothesis that company management is more likely to adopt defensive measures when a firm is characterized by diffuse shareholdings. We do not find any significant relationship associated with institutional stock ownership. The evidence provided here, therefore, does not strongly support the hypothesis that institutional shareholders provide better monitoring than other blockholders.

We also conduct a stock return analysis in the case of defense with preferred share—the most widely used takeover defense device in recent years in the Netherlands. Our results indicate two opposing effects of defense on shareholders' wealth: in one situation, the stock market reacts positively, seemingly to allow managers to bargain for a higher premium in takeover bids. In another situation, the stock market reacts negatively as potential takeover attempt appears to be eliminated.

Alternative disciplinary mechanisms have been an area of extensive scrutiny. In this paper, we document that low (high) ownership concentration is associated with greater (smaller) use of antitakeover devices which affect the functioning of the market for corporate control. We also provide evidence on the existence of positive and negative share price effects of takeover defense measures. Some implications of our findings are discussed below.

The empirical results obtained in this study reconfirm the need of analyzing firms' ownership structure as a mechanism to control the agency conflict between shareholders and managers. Other such mechanisms include the capital market, the market for corporate control, the managerial labor market and the product market. Similar to Walsh and Seward (1990), we believe that much can be learned about one control mechanism when it is analyzed in and around another mechanism. Managers in the Netherlands seem to be immune from the disciplinary threat of the market for corporate control. Since the takeover market is just one disciplinary mechanism, we would expect other control mechanisms to be at work too. Our results in this paper demonstrate this—for example, monitoring by concentrated ownership. As Prowse (1995) points out, concentrated shareholdings are important because they provide investors with both the incentive and the ability to monitor and influence the management. Without such concentration, again other mechanisms of corporate control must be relied upon.

It is usually believed that institutional investors find it in their best interest to more effectively monitor company managers. In the U.S.A., institutional shareholdings have increased over the last years, and a few institutional shareholders have emerged as very active monitors. The findings of Duggal and Millar (1994) suggest that researchers should better split aggregate institutional ownership into different categories to obtain correct results. The results of this study show that in the Netherlands institutional shareholders like banks and insurance companies do not have large holdings, and these have no relationship with the adoption of antitakeover devices. An implication of this finding is that active monitoring by institutional shareholders may not take place in many countries. It is highly unlikely that Dutch institutional shareholders lack the expertise and the ability to serve as effective monitors. Rather, the presence of small stakes may explain why passivity remains the norm. It is also possible that active institutional monitoring may not be a representation of the general pattern in the U.S.A.

There are many types of defense measures, and their effects also depend on situation like the manner in which a particular device is introduced. Our analysis shows that it is difficult to say *a priori* whether defense measures are good or bad for shareholders. Even takeover defenses that are approved by shareholders have the potential to reduce shareholder wealth. This lack of conclusive evidence regarding the stock price reaction could also be attributed to the limitations of event-study methodology and the additional need of analysis using other characteristics of firms that propose takeover defense measures.

Although the results presented here show that one monitoring mechanism has been substituted by another, these do not imply one mechanism being better than another. Analyzing the cost—benefit aspects of each monitoring mechanism is an issue which was beyond the scope of the paper. According to Moerland (1995), there exists a trade-off in the sense that the advantages of one mechanism will generally be the disadvantages of the other. Questions also remain relating the effectiveness of monitoring with corporate performance. Are firms with concentrated ownership more profitable than firms in which ownership is not concentrated? If incumbent managers use defense tactics to deter takeovers, are they completely insulated from the consequences of poor firm performance? The usual finding has been that takeover threat improves performance of a firm. But, as has been mentioned by Walsh and Seward (1990), if managers in a poorly performing firm anticipate a takeover contest, they may adopt antitakeover devices to protect them. On the other hand, managers could be more frequently dismissed when they perform poorly because another disciplinary mechanism—the managerial labor market—then starts functioning. A further analysis of the role of different corporate governance mechanisms represents an interesting area of future research.

ACKNOWLEDGEMENTS

We would like to thank Tom Berglund, Associate Editor Richard Bettis, Marc Zenner and two anonymous referees for useful comments and suggestions. We have also benefited from the comments of seminar participants at Tilburg University, the Workshop on Corporate Finance at the European Institute for Advanced Studies in Management (Brussels), the International Meeting of the French Finance Association (La Baule), the Symposium on Money, Finance, Banking and Insurance (Karlsruhe) and the Eastern Finance Association Meeting (Boston) where previous versions of this paper were presented.

NOTES

1   Although several studies have examined empirically the relationship between equity ownership and firm value (e.g., McConnell and Servaes, 1990; Slovin and Sushka, 1993), limited attention has been given to explore ownership concentration vis-à-vis multiple defense measures.

2   Empirical evidence on the mixed role of institutional shareholders can be observed from different studies, such as Agrawal and Mandelker (1990), Bhagat and Jefferis (1991), Brickley, Lease, and Smith (1988), Duggal and Millar (1994), Pound (1988), Shivdasani (1993) and Van Nuys (1993).

3   DeAngelo and Rice (1983) and Jarrell and Poulsen (1987) find an insignificant price effect; Linn and McConnell (1983) find a weak positive effect; and Jarrell and Poulsen (1988), Mahoney and Mahoney (1993), Malatesta and Walkling (1988) and Ryngaert (1988) find a significant negative share price effect.

4   Effect of 'Bangeman Proposal' on Barriers to Takeovers in the European Community, Coopers & Lybrand Management Consultants, Amsterdam, 1990.

5   Public corporations in the Netherlands issue predominantly bearer shares.

6   We could not find a definitive announcement date for two companies; three companies were closely involved in a merger or takeover.

7   Blockholders are owners of 5 percent or more of the outstanding equity.

8   The logistic analysis is chosen here because the dependent variable is a binary, qualitative variable.

9   As the variable C_{block} combines both institutional and blockholders' shares, we have constructed another variable which estimates the share of all blockholders other than those held by institutional blockholders. The Herfindahl measure was calculated by summing squared percentage of shares owned by each blockholder.

10   The CBS-Total Return Index is a value-weighted index representing all listed stocks. It is the only market index available in the Netherlands which covers all listed companies. In addition, the index is adjusted for cash dividends.

11   Prowse (1995) reports average ownership concentration of the five largest shareholders to be 25 percent in the U.S.A., 21 percent in the U.K. and 33 percent in Japan. According to Bergström and Rydqvist (1990), the average ownership concentration of the largest shareholder in Sweden is 43 percent.

12   Because of space limitation and qualitatively similar findings, the regression results of only a limited number of variables are presented.

13   Three measures could not be included in the sample because the market model parameters' estimation period coincided with the event period of a previous measure.

14   The finding is robust as the two other methodologies (the Market Adjusted Returns Model and the Market Model using postevent period data) show that stock prices decline by 1.50 percent and 1.85 percent, respectively.

15   The Market Adjusted Returns Model and the Market Model using postevent period data show that stock prices increase by 1.33 percent and 1.27 percent, respectively.

16   Once again, the results are materially indifferent to one particular methodology used in calculating abnormal returns. The Market Adjusted Returns Model and the Market Model using postevent period data also show a decline in stock returns (−5.06% and −5.62%, respectively).

17   The increase in stock price followed by a decline on the announcement of share issue could also be seen as an indication of the breakdown of takeover negotiations. To verify this, we searched the financial press throughout the event period, and found no report on any negotiation. This, of course, does not rule out the possibility of undisclosed information.

18   We also searched the financial press to check if any specific event followed the announcement, but were unable to find any.

19   We also investigate whether the market reaction varies with firms' ownership concentration. The sample is divided into three portfolios: portfolio 1 contains firms with the lowest concentration, portfolio 3 contains those with the highest concentration, and portfolio 2 is between them. We do not find statistically significant differences in cumulative abnormal returns among these portfolios. Therefore, the results are not reported here. A cross-sectional regression between ownership structure and announcement period abnormal return also yields insignificant results. Our analysis, however, should be interpreted with caution because the sample size is small and only one defense mechanism is examined.

REFERENCES

Agrawal, A. and G. N. Mandelker (1990). 'Large shareholders and the monitoring of managers: The case of antitakeover charter amendments', *Journal of Financial and Quantitative Analysis*, **25**, pp. 143–161.

Ambrose, B. W. and W. L. Megginson (1992). 'The role of asset structure, ownership structure, and takeover defenses in determining acquisition likelihood', *Journal of Financial and Quantitative Analysis*, **27**, pp. 575–589.

Bergström, C. and K. Rydgvist (1990). 'Ownership of equity in dual-class firms', *Journal of Banking and Finance*, **14**, pp. 255–269.

Bhagat, S. and R. H. Jefferis (1991). 'Voting power in the proxy process', *Journal of Financial Economics*, **30**, pp. 193–225.

Brickley, J. A., R. C. Lease and C. W. Smith (1988). 'Ownership structure and the voting on antitakeover amendments', *Journal of Financial Economics*, **20**, pp. 276–291.

DeAngelo, H. and E. M. Rice (1983). 'Antitakeover charter amendments and stockholder wealth', *Journal of Financial Economics*, **11**, pp. 329–359.

Demsetz, H. (1983). 'The structure of ownership and the theory of the firm'. *Journal of Law and Economics*, **26**, pp. 375–390.

Duggal, R. and J. A. Millar (1994). 'Institutional investors, antitakeover defenses and success of hostile takeover bids', *Quarterly Review of Economics and Finance*, **34**, pp. 387–402.

Franks, J. and C. Mayer (1990). 'Capital markets and corporate control: A study of France, Germany and the UK', *Economic Policy*, **5**, pp. 191–231.

Gordon, L. A. and J. Pound (1993). 'Information, ownership structure, and shareholder voting: Evidence from shareholder-sponsored corporate governance proposals', *Journal of Finance*, **48**, pp. 697–718.

Jarrell, G. A. and A. B. Poulson (1987). 'Shark repellents and stock prices: The effects of antitakeover amendments since 1980', *Journal of Financial Economics*, **19**, pp. 127–168.

Jarrell, G. A. and A. B. Poulsen (1988). 'Dual-class recapitalizations as antitakeover mechanisms, the recent evidence', *Journal of Financial Economics*, **20**, pp. 129–152.

Linn, S. C. and L J. McConnell (1983). 'An empirical investigation of the impact of "antitakeover" amendments on common stock prices', *Journal of Financial Economics*, **11**, pp. 361–399.

Mahoney, J. M. and J. T. Mahoney (1993). 'An empirical investigation of the effect of corporate charter antitakeover amendments on stockholder wealth', *Strategic Management Journal*, **14**(1), pp. 17–31.

Malatesta, P. H. and R. A. Walkling (1988). 'Poison pill securities: Stockholder wealth, profitability and ownership structure', *Journal of Financial Economics*, **20**, pp. 347–376.

McConnell, J. and H. Servaes (1990). 'Additional evidente on equity ownership and corporate value', *Journal of Financial Economics*, **27**, pp. 595–612.

McWilliams, V. B. (1990). 'Managerial share ownership and the stock price effects of antitakeover amendment proposals', *Journal of Finance*, **45**, pp. 1627–1640.

Moerland, P. W. (1995). 'Alternative disciplinary mechanisms in different corporate systems', *Journal of Economic Behaviour and Organization*, **17**, pp. 17–34.

Pound, J. (1988). 'Proxy contests and the efficiency of shareholder oversight', *Journal of Financial Economics*, **20**, pp. 237–265.

Prowse, S. (1995). 'Corporate governance in an international perspective', *Financial Markets, Institutions and Instruments*, **4**, pp. 1–63.

Ruback, R. S. (1988). 'An overview of takeover defenses'. In A. J. Auerbach (ed.), *Mergers and Acquisitions*. University of Chicago Press, Chicago, IL, pp. 49–67.

Ryngaert, M. (1988). 'The effect of poison pill securities on shareholder wealth', *Journal of Financial Economics*, **20**, pp. 377–417.

Shivdasani, A. (1993). 'Board composition, ownership structure, and hostile takeovers', *Journal of Accounting and Economics*, **16**, pp. 167–198.

Shieifer, A. and R. W. Vishny (1986). 'Large share holders and corporate control', *Journal of Political Economy*, **94**, pp. 461–488.

Slovin, M. B. and M. E. Sushka (1993). 'Ownership concentration, corporate control activity, and firm value: Evidence from the death of inside blockholders', *Journal of Finance*, **48**, pp. 1293–1321.

Song, M. H. and R. A. Walkling (1993). 'The impact of managerial ownership on acquisition attempts and target shareholder wealth', *Journal of Financial and Quantitative Analysis*, **28**, pp. 439–457.

Van Nuys, K. (1993). 'Corporate governance through the proxy process: Evidence from the 1989 Honey well proxy solicitation', *Journal of Financial Economics*, **34**, pp. 101–132.

Voogd, R. P. (1989). 'Statutaire beschern-ingsmiddelen bij beursvennootschappen', doctoral dissertation, University of Nijmegen, Kluwer.

Walsh, J. P. and J. K. Seward (1990). 'On the efficiency of internal and external corporate control mechanisms', *Academy of Management Review*, **15**, pp. 421–458.

Chapter 26

Tim Jenkinson and Alexander Ljungqvist[*]

THE ROLE OF HOSTILE STAKES IN GERMAN CORPORATE GOVERNANCE

Source: *Journal of Corporate Finance*, 7(4) (2001): 397–446.

ABSTRACT

This article uses clinical evidence to show how the German system of corporate control and governance is both more active and more hostile than has previously been suggested. It provides a complete breakdown of ownership and takeover defence patterns in German listed companies and finds highly fragmented (but not dispersed) ownership in non-majority controlled firms. We document how the accumulation of *hostile stakes* can be used to gain control of target companies given these ownership patterns. The article also suggests an important role for banks in helping predators accumulate, and avoid the disclosure of, large stakes.

1. INTRODUCTION

THERE IS A WIDESPREAD BELIEF THAT THE German system of corporate governance exhibits a very low level of hostility. In the stereotypical view of German finance, hostile tender offers are virtually unheard of, with banks (rather than markets) assumed to play an important role in both the financing and control of German corporations.[1] This article challenges some important elements of this view. It is certainly true, notwithstanding the recent successful tender offer for Mannesmann by Vodafone–Airtouch, that hostile tender offers have played almost no role in disciplining incumbent management.[2] However, we suggest that there is a much greater incidence of outsiders accumulating *hostile stakes* or blocks in an attempt to gain control. Hostile stakes are often built by coalitions of large investors who share dissatisfaction with the incumbent management, or have other motives for seeking control. One such

particularly important motive may be the expropriation of minority shareholders. The dynamics of hostile stakebuilding are complex and difficult to observe—in many cases it is not possible simply to look at a share register and infer who is exerting control over the company. This opaqueness derives from the low level of transparency of share stakes and weak regulation of parties acting in concert. Our article seeks to overcome this opacity by taking a "clinical", or case study approach, looking in detail at the dynamics of stake accumulation, and the control battles that ensued.

This approach is both a strength and weakness of the paper. We identify 17 cases of hostile stakebuilding over an 8-year period. This is clearly not a large number in absolute terms, or relative to the total number of listed companies in Germany (fewer than 600 at the time). However, one should not jump to conclusions too quickly. In common with a number of other countries in Europe (excluding the UK) ownership concentration is very high in Germany.[3] In Section 2 we look in detail at the ownership structure, and takeover defences, of all German listed companies and find that as few as 64 German companies may be vulnerable to hostile attack. The resulting 3–4% per annum incidence of hostile stakebuilding is surprisingly similar to the incidence of hostile tender offers in, for example, the UK.[4]

However, while we argue that this incidence is economically significant, and has not previously been identified, the low absolute number of cases precludes econometric testing of formal hypotheses. On the other hand, we are able, through the clinical approach, to analyse in considerable detail the behaviour of the various parties involved in the control contest. For example, we analyse the behaviour of banks in such battles and find their role to be much more complex than has previously been documented. Far from protecting incumbent management, on a number of occasions, German banks have been actively involved in bringing about hostile changes of control by facilitating stakebuilding. We show how banks can assist predator companies in the accumulation of hostile stakes, and how beneficial ownership can be obscured. We also consider how the regulatory environment allows such stake accumulation to occur and whether recent important changes—such as the introduction of Germany's first Takeover Code—will influence the way that corporate control is exercised in the future.

The contributions of this article are, therefore, empirical. The findings are relevant to a number of different areas of research. First, there is a rich literature, mainly focused on US companies and markets, which investigates the links between ownership structure and corporate performance. Most of this literature takes as its starting point, the Berle and Means (1932) thesis that dispersed ownership leads to an agency conflict between (weak) owners and (strong) managers. Blocks in this context are typically thought to perform one of two roles: a toehold prior to a hostile takeover (Shleifer and Vishny, 1986;

Bulow et al., 1999) or a way to mitigate the free-rider problem in monitoring management (Butz, 1994; Mørck et al., 1989). The second of these roles has recently attracted a lot of attention. One strand of the literature looks at acquisitions of 5% or more in the US, that is, the emergence of new blocks. These 'partial acquisitions' are typically greeted with positive share price responses both for the target and the buyer (see Mikkelson and Ruback, 1985, for public 13-D acquisitions, Wruck, 1989, for private placements), indicating that increases in ownership concentration are value-increasing. Moreover, consistent with the Berle–Means thesis, targets tend to have performed poorly prior to the partial acquisition (Choi, 1991; Bethel et al., 1998) and be more diversified (Bethel et al., 1998), while subsequent target firm operating and financial behaviour is positively affected (Spencer et al., 1998) and CEO turnover increases substantially (Bethel et al., 1998).

A second, and related, literature focuses on existing blocks. Perhaps surprisingly, significant share blocks are common even in the US, where corporate ownership is typically more dispersed than in Germany and other continental European countries (Barclay and Holderness, 1989).[5] Trading in such blocks is about twice as frequent as hostile tender offers (Barclay and Holderness, 1991), and typically takes place at a premium to the post-trade market price (Barclay and Holderness, 1989). Since trading of existing blocks leaves ownership concentration unchanged, Barclay and Holderness (1989) suggest the block premium is consistent with private benefits of control rather than value-increasing monitoring, though the two are not mutually exclusive: block trades are followed by an increase in CEO turnover, of a magnitude usually only seen in hostile tender offers (Barclay and Holderness, 1991), and are associated with subsequent business restructuring (Denis and Serrano, 1996). A look at the treatment of minority shareholders when block trades are followed by tender offers suggests that the block premium is not entirely due to private benefits: minorities are typically bought out at a premium to the block price, despite the absence of any legal compulsion (Barclay and Holderness, 1991, 1992). In contrast, in Germany, minorities are vulnerable to expropriation by majority owners: there is no legal requirement to buy-out minority stakes, and when offers to minority shareholders are made, they are typically at a large discount to the price paid by the controlling shareholder.

There are some important differences between the block trades discussed in the US literature and our cases. First, US Securities and Exchange Commission (SEC) regulations have tended to result in block trades being negotiated and publicised rather than covert. Second, partial acquisitions or trades of existing blocks take place against the background of an ownership structure that is significantly more dispersed in the US than in Germany, particularly for large firms.[6] Therefore, the economically significant block size is likely to be different in the US and Germany, and should depend on the concentration and composition of the remaining ownership structure. Third, three-quarters of the US cases involve a simple sale of one existing block (Barclay and Holderness, 1991), while our article documents a much richer dynamic of blocks being built from open-market purchases acquired from existing blockholders and combined with other blocks. In that sense, we look at block-building, rather than block transfers. There has, to date, been little analysis of block accumulation tactics, in the US or elsewhere.[7]

Finally, our article is also related to the literature on optimal takeover regulation, since we focus particularly on the ability to build hostile stakes without the knowledge of other market participants—something that the existing block literature assumes away. For example, as Burkart (1996) notes, it is critical whether stakebuilding, and hostile intentions, can be obscured because as soon as such a strategy becomes transparent, free-riding (along the lines suggested by Grossman and Hart, 1980) is likely to result. Loose disclosure and regulation of acting in concert will provide the

opportunity for hostile control changes to be effected via stakebuilding and for such behaviour to be profitable. Such loose regulation exists in a number of continental European countries including Germany. Hence, the behaviour that we focus on in this article is, in a sense, quite predictable, although no previous paper has, to our knowledge, provided systematic evidence on the importance of hostile acquisitions in Germany via stakebuilding. Our article complements that of Franks and Mayer (2001), who consider the importance of share stakes in Germany. They document a large incidence of stake changes and suggest that such changes are the most significant influence on the turnover of supervisory board members. However, Franks and Mayer consider the incidence and observed response to sales of share stakes in general, without distinguishing between the nature of these sales. In contrast, we focus exclusively on hostile stakebuilding, where the objective is to influence control.

The remainder of the article is organised as follows. In Section 2, we start by discussing the rules governing corporate control in Germany, in particular, the control rights associated with share blocks of various sizes. We also provide a snapshot of the actual ownership patterns in Germany, which demonstrates the importance of large share blocks. In Section 3, we outline our research methodology and data sources. Section 4 presents evidence on hostile stake accumulation for a number of recent cases, detailed chronologies of which are provided in Appendix A (in alphabetical order by target company, for ease of reference). Section 5 concludes.

2. OWNERSHIP AND CONTROL OF GERMAN COMPANIES

Ownership of German companies is highly concentrated, certainly in comparison with US or UK companies. We document later on in this section just how concentrated ownership structures are, but we begin by explaining the control rights associated with different-sized share blocks in Germany.

In many cases, the hostile stakebuilding that we document later in the article does not involve building a majority stake, but rather takes the form of building a stake with sufficient control rights to exert a major influence on the incumbent managers and other shareholders. The rules regarding these control rights therefore play a critical role in hostile stakebuilding strategies.

2.1. Control rights

There are five economically significant block sizes as defined by the rights of minorities and the discretionary powers of the dominant blockholders. These are summarised in Table 26.1. One important feature of corporate control in Germany is the existence of *pooling contracts.* Pooling contracts are agreements between shareholders that oblige them to pool their votes. Hence, share blocks can be built directly via purchase and/or indirectly via a pooling contract. Either way, the control rights summarised in Table 26.1 would apply to the single or pooled block. The pooling

contracts have no special legal standing, and are typically renewable every 4–5 years.

We start by considering the rights associated with dispersed shareholdings. In Germany, no special rights are attached to share blocks of below 25%. Indeed, in common with many other EU countries, small minority shareholders are afforded little in the way of protection, either from expropriation by controlling shareholders, or equal treatment. For example, there is no legal requirement to buy-out minority stakes when a party acquires a stake in excess of 50%. While the recently introduced, and voluntary, Takeover Code does introduce such a requirement, it is noticeable that the offer to minority shareholders can be at a discount (of up to 25%) to the price paid in acquiring the controlling stake (see footnote 27 for more details).

The first important threshold in terms of control rights applies to blocks of 25% or more. Such a shareholding is referred to as a blocking minority and gives veto powers on corporate charter amendments, supervisory board changes, and profit transfer and

Table 26.1 Control rights in Germany

The control rights associated with certain block sizes are related to the minimum required percentage of the votes cast at an annual or extraordinary general meeting. Corporate charters may in certain cases specify higher thresholds, for instance regarding changing the composition of the supervisory board.

Block size	Control rights
< 25%	No major formal rights other than voting pro rata. Shareholders who control at least 5% of the equity capital can demand that an annual general meeting be called.
25%	Blocking minority control. Power of veto over corporate charter amendments, supervisory board changes, and profit transfer and control agreements. Stakes above 24.9% must be reported to the Cartel Office and to the target company, which in turn has a duty to publish a notification in certain newspapers.
50%	Management control, although the existence of another block of 25% would limit discretion.
75%	Super-majority control. Enables the blockholder to amend the corporate charter, change the composition of the supervisory board, and enter into profit transfer and control agreements. The lack of any blocking minority (25%) stake thus significantly increases effective control.
95%	The blockholder can force a merger and minority shareholdings can be compulsorily purchased. The law requires that minority shareholders be paid 'adequate' compensation in the form of cash or shares in the parent company. The level of compensation is largely left unregulated.

control agreements. The latter agreements are an important way by which the claims of minority shareholders can be diluted. Subject to ensuring the economic survival of the dominated company, a controlling shareholder can dilute minorities in a variety of ways. First, group losses can be foisted disproportionately onto minorities, while profits can be transferred out of the dominated company. Second, hidden reserves (typically land and share stakes whose book value is below market value) can be sold and the proceeds transferred to the majority owner. Third, group assets can be bought and sold at prices that are advantageous to the dominant shareholder.[8] Fourth, while minority shareholders must be offered the alternative of a guaranteed fixed dividend should they wish not to sell out to the controlling shareholder, neither the bid price nor the guaranteed dividend need in any way be related to the share price, or the price the bidder paid to acquire control.[9] Both options are, in most cases, relatively unattractive: Wenger and Hecker (1995) show that for 45 buy-out bids made to minority shareholders between 1983 and mid-1992, the price offered was 27.1% *below* the market price 2 days before the announcement.

Minority shareholders have no right of legal appeal against any such transfer of assets or profits per se, but can litigate against the level of compensation (dividend or buy-out bid) offered within 2 months of the date of the offer. Many such offers (such as the Boge case we examine below) do indeed result in lengthy litigation during which minority shareholders attempt to increase the attractiveness of the terms they are offered. The average court case takes 5.3 years to conclude (Wenger and Hecker, 1995). There is, in general, no right of final appeal to the Supreme Court, which has led to different second-level courts of appeal passing contradictory verdicts, all of which have binding character. Neither the law nor the courts have established any consistent framework for valuing a company or assessing its risk.[10] As to offers being made below trading prices, the courts have adopted the line that market prices have nothing to do with fundamental value—which can 'only' be found by accountants acting as expert witnesses. Even when the courts do find in the plaintiffs' favour, the average imposed increase in bid prices or guaranteed dividends of 25% (Wenger and Hecker, 1995) is not sufficient to close the discount to the market price before the buy-out announcement. Finally, the law explicitly gives the majority owner the right to cancel the control and/or profit transfer agreement if the court's decision is unfavourable.[11]

Hence, the ability to veto a profit transfer and control agreement represents an important control threshold. It is also worth noting that, in the absence of other large shareholders, a 25% stake can in practice provide more than mere veto influence, given an average presence of no more than 57% of votes at AGMs (Baums and Fraune, 1994).

The next threshold in terms of control rights occurs with blocks of 50% or more. Such a block gives management control of the company, but is subject to limits on the controlling party's discretion due to the existence of a blocking 25% minority. In practice, 50% may not be enough to dismiss incumbent management quickly if the supervisory board is not on the controlling party's side: it is the supervisory board which appoints and dismisses the management, and the supervisory board in turn can only be dismissed with a 75% super-majority.

Given the various control rights that accrue to blocking minority stakes of 25% or more, the next important control threshold occurs with blocks of more than 75%. Such super-majority blocks give the controlling party complete discretion in matters of supervisory board elections and profit transfer and/or control agreements. However, the incremental control rights associated with blocks of 75% accrue entirely from the impossibility of a rival blocking minority stake, rather than additional legal rights. The final control threshold occurs with 95% ownership, when the remaining minority shareholders can be compulsorily bought out on disadvantageous terms.

2.2. Ownership structure and takeover defences

Given the various control thresholds identified, how frequently are blocks of each size observed? Table 26.2 gives a complete breakdown of the ownership structure of all listed German firms in September 1991 by the size of the largest disclosed block, or pooled block where a pooling contract exists. As can be seen from Panel A of Table 26.2, 72% of all listed companies have a majority owner: 17% have blocks in excess of 95% of capital (or votes, if different), 24.6% are super-majority controlled, and 30.5% have a simple majority owner. Therefore, only 28% of companies — 141 firms — are not at least majority controlled by one blockholder. Panels B and C take a closer look at these 141 firms. 86 of these have one or more blocking minority stakes (Panel B), where, of course, two or three such stakes would have amounted to combined majority or super-majority control had the various blockholders pooled their votes (which to our knowledge they had not).[12] The remaining 55 firms, in Panel C, have no stakes in excess of 25%. Thirty-seven of these have one or more disclosed non-blocking stakes, while 18 firms are classified as widely held because no stakes were disclosed at all (though Baums and Fraune, 1994, claim that banks, despite only owning an average of 13% of widely held firms' equity, control more than 80% of votes via proxies). Mannesmann, the target of Vodafone–Airtouch's recent successful hostile tender offer, was one of those rare widely held companies.

From the point of view of corporate governance, the firms in Panels B and C are very interesting. In the absence of a majority owner, there are three alternatives for how these companies are controlled. They may either be (i) run by a coalition of non-pooling blockholders, (ii) controlled by the dominant blockholder with the connivance of the remaining blockholders, or (iii) run by management without much shareholder influence at all, in a way reminiscent of widely held firms in the US or the UK. Given the presence of sizeable and often multiple blocks, ownership in these firms is not usually dispersed, but rather fragmented. This, we would argue, increases the scope for hostile stakebuilding, especially where blockholders are in disagreement over corporate policy or where blocks come up for sale.

Table 26.3 lists the frequency of four types of takeover defences amongst the population of all German listed companies in September 1991: instances where only non-voting preference shares are publicly traded; voting right restrictions which cap the number of votes any individual shareholder can cast; limitations on the transferability of shares (which give the target's board the option not to register the shares in the new shareholder's name, thus effectively disenfranchising the stake); and departures from the principle of one-share-one-vote, as when certain classes of shares (usually held by friendly parties and not traded) have greater voting power at all times or under certain circumstances (for instance, for the purpose of supervisory board elections). Not surprisingly, few of the 402 majority controlled firms have takeover defences: 8.2% list only non-voting shares, 3.5% restrict the transferability of stock, and 4.7% have stock with differential voting rights (Panel A). Limits on transferability and differential voting rights are the main takeover defences amongst the 86 firms without majority owners but with one or more blocking-minorities (Panel B). However, 79% of these 86 firms have no formal takeover defences. It is amongst the firms without blocking-minority stakes that takeover defences are most common. 42% of these 55 firms have defensive share structures, with voting right restrictions being the most popular (Panel C).

How many of the 141 non-majority controlled firms in Panels B and C could potentially become targets of hostile stakebuilding? Clearly not all of them: firms with three blocking-minority shareholders would be relatively hard to buy into, if only because each blockholder, being pivotal, would demand a control premium. To answer the question, we propose four possible stakebuilding strategies (see Table 26.4).

Table 26.2 Ownership of German stock exchange listed companies (1991)

Panel A: Majority control		Number of firms	(%) of sample
Single or formally pooled 95% + block		95	17.0%
Single or formally pooled super-majority (75% +) owner of which have...		137	24.6%
One additional disclosed blockholder	11		
Two or more additional blockholders	2		
Single or formally pooled majority (50% +) owner of which have...		170	30.5%
One additional disclosed blockholder	59		
Two or more additional blockholders	22		
Total with majority control		402	72.0%

Panel B: Blocking-minority control		Number of firms	(%) of sample
One blocking minority (25% +) block of which have...		47	8.4%
One additional disclosed blockholder	8		
Two or more additional blockholders	12		
Two blocking minority (25% +) blocks of which have...		28	5.0%
One additional disclosed blockholder	8		
Two or more additional blockholders	3		
Three blocking minority (25% +) blocks of which have...		11	2.0%
One additional disclosed blockholder	3		
Total with blocking-minority control		86	15.4%

Panel C: No blocking-minority control		Number of firms	(%) of sample
One or more non-blocking blocks (< 25%) of which have...		37	6.6%
One block	12		
Two blocks	9		
Three blocks	5		
Four or more blocks	11		
Widely held (no blocks disclosed at all)		18	3.2%
Total with no blocking minority control		55	9.8%
Ownership information not available		15	2.7%
Grand total		558	100.0%

Source: Own calculations based on "Saling, 1992," Hoppenstedt's stock market yearbook.

Notes: The law requires disclosure of blocks of more than 25% and more than 50%. Frequently, smaller blocks are also disclosed (as in Panel C). Non-disclosure need not imply non-existence.

Table 26.3 Defensive share structures of German stock exchange listed companies (1991)

Number of firms with...	Only non-voting shares listed	Cap on voting rights	Limited share transferability	Departures from one-share-one-vote
Panel A: Majority control (402 firms)				
Single or formally pooled 95% + block	21		3	2
Single or formally pooled super-majority (75% +) owner	7		6	6
Single or formally pooled majority (50% +) owner	5		5	11
Total	33		14	19
(% of all firms with majority owner)	8.2%		3.5%	4.7%
Panel B: Blocking-minority control (86 firms)				
One blocking minority (25% +) block	1	2	3	3
Two blocking minority (25% +) blocks	1	1	3	4
Three blocking minority (25% +) blocks				
Total	2	3	6	7
(% of all firms with a blocking-minority)	2.3%	3.5%	7.0%	8.1%
Panel C: No Blocking-minority control (55 firms)				
One or more non-blocking blocks (< 25%)		10	3	1
Widely held (no blocks disclosed at all)		7		2
Total	0	17	3	3
(% of all firms with no blocking minority)	0%	30.9%	5.5%	5.5%
Ownership information not available (15 firms)	2	1	2	3
Grand total	37	21	25	32
(% of all German listed companies)	6.6%	3.8%	4.5%	5.7%

Source: Own calculations based on "Saling, 1992," Hoppenstedt's stock market yearbook.

Table 26.4 Potential targets for hostile stakebuilders

Firms which could become the target of hostile stakebuilding (in order of increasing difficulty)	Total number of firms	Impediments to hostile stakebuilding				Number of firms without takeover defences
		Only non-voting shares listed	Cap on voting rights	Limited share transferability	Departures from one-share-one-vote	
Strategy 1: could (potentially) take over in the open-market (free float > 50%) • Widely held firms • Firms with one blocking-minority stake and a free float of 50%+ • Firms with one or more non-blocking stakes and free float of 50%+	79	0	17	2	1	59
Strategy 2: in addition, could (potentially) take over if bought out one or more or all existing non-blocking stakes • The remaining firms with one or more non-blocking stakes	7	0	1	1	0	5
Strategy 3: in addition, could (potentially) take over if bought out one existing blocking-minority stake plus open-market purchases • Firms with one blocking-minority stakes and a free float of 25%+ • Firms with two blocking-minority stakes and free float of 25%+	30	1	1	3	0	25
Strategy 4: in addition, could (potentially) take over if bought out two existing blocking-minority stakes • Firms with two blocking-minority stakes and a free float of less than 25%+ • Firms with three blocking-minority stakes and a free float of less than 25%+	25	1	1	2	0	21
Grand total (% of all German listed companies)	141 25.3%					110 19.7%

Notes: This table is based on an analysis of the companies which appear in Panels B and C in Table 26.1. In the final column, the number of potential takeover targets was reduced if and only if the existing limits to share transferability or multiple voting rights applied to a sufficiently large number of votes to effectively rule out hostile stakebuilding.

First, a hostile bidder could attempt to build stakes in firms that have a free float of 50% or more, without buying any existing blocks. The companies that potentially fall into this category are widely held firms; companies with one blocking-minority stake; and firms with one or more non-blocking-minority stakes. Both Mannesmann and Thyssen belong in this category. Checking for the presence of additional disclosed stakes and computing free float, we find 79 companies with a free float of 50% or more.[13] Second, a bidder could take over a company by buying one or more or all existing non-blocking stakes; there were seven firms potentially at risk from this strategy. A third takeover strategy is to buy-out one existing blocking-minority stake and to make up the difference to 50% via open-market purchases. Thirty firms had one or two blocking minority stakes and enough free float for this strategy potentially to allow a majority takeover. The final strategy involves a bidder buying out two existing blocking minority stakes, for instance, in companies which have two or three such stakes and too little free float to make any of the other strategies viable. Therefore, of the 141 non-majority controlled, some are much more vulnerable to hostile stakebuilding than others. In practice, the first two strategies look much more feasible than the last two, suggesting the potential takeover targets might number around 86, which represents just 15.4% of the total number of listed German firms.

If the defensive features summarised in Table 26.3 are effective, some of these 86 firms are unlikely to be taken over. Table 26.4 takes this into account by looking in detail at the nature of any takeover defences. Two companies, for instance, listed only non-voting preference shares, making them virtually immune to hostile stakebuilding.[14] A further 20 had voting right restrictions, though we will argue later that the empirical effectiveness crucially depends on the level of the cap. Of the 11 companies with limited share transferability, eight restricted transferability sufficiently to make a bidder's life difficult. Finally, of the 21 companies that had multiple classes of

stock, one had sufficiently privileged stock to block hostile approaches. Depending on the effectiveness of each of these takeover barriers, the number of firms at risk from hostile stakebuilding could fall to 110 (if all takeover strategies are considered) or as low as 64—just 11% of all German listed firms—if only the first two strategies are considered realistic.

3. DATA AND METHODOLOGY

The cases for our clinical analysis were identified using the Financial Times Mergers and Acquisitions (FTMA) database. FTMA contains structured templated information on changes in the ownership structure of European firms, covering (i) listed and unlisted firms; (ii) takeover bids and stake purchases; and (iii) transactions which are completed as well as those merely rumoured or still under negotiation. All 'forms' compiled by FTMA between January 1988 and December 1996 were obtained for transactions involving German companies as targets. This yielded 2511 forms, some of which pertain to the same firm at different points in time, or to different bidders for the same firm at the same point in time. Two types of filters were used to manage this very large amount of raw data. 'Negative' filters were used to eliminate, without further investigation, FTMA-reported transactions with a low likelihood of being motivated by 'hostility'. These negative filters were:

1. cases of apparent initiation of cross-shareholdings (which require both parties' agreement)
2. "participation in capital increases via subscription" (which presumably are agreed between buyer and target, and thus not hostile)
3. unlisted companies other than those captured using a positive filter (see below)
4. complete or partial disposals of divisions or other operating units
5. privatisations by the Treuhandanstalt

Second, we used positive filters designed to identify cases with a high probability of being motivated by hostility, and devoted more time to these cases:

1. firms known to be potential takeover targets using our knowledge of their ownership structure discussed above (no majority owner, no pooled majority etc.)
2. multiple filings over time for the same firm
3. cases where FTMA reported transactions by 'undisclosed bidders'

For firms not eliminated by the negative filters, all electronically available news story headlines were read, and where appropriate, the story itself,[15] around the year indicated in FTMA to establish the nature of transaction: friendly, negotiated, don't know, openly hostile, etc. At this stage, a 6th negative filter was used to exclude companies in financial distress as the change in ownership structure presumably reflects rescue operations. Most effort was spent reading about transactions that passed the positive filters.

In common with existing research in the area of hostile takeovers, we do not have a precise definition of hostility. Instead, we look for such 'telltale signs' as *public* resistance by target management to block-building, for instance taking the form of verbal exchanges or actions designed to ward off further block-building (e.g. discouraging further stake sales) or reduce the new blockholder's influence (e.g. imposition of voting restrictions). Clearly, this unavoidably biases our sample identification since we must rely on reportable and reported reactions by target management. Where disputes take place, and stay, behind closed doors, we are unable to establish the blockbuilder's intent and the target's reaction. While this is unavoidable, a potentially more serious concern is Comment and Schwert's (1997) argument that using press coverage to distinguish between hostile and friendly tender offers may be misleading. Comment and Schwert find little economic difference between

deals conventionally classified as friendly and hostile, and suggest that both management resistance and publication thereof are strategic bargaining ploys to improve the bid terms for target shareholders. While this point is pertinent to situations where stakebuilding is followed by tender offers (which affect target shareholders), very few of our cases involve subsequent tender offers (and those that do offer minority shareholders very poor terms).

On the basis of the news stories, 17 prima facie hostile cases were identified. We make no claims as to the comprehensiveness of our search strategy: our filters may well have filtered out hostile cases, particularly amongst unlisted firms. The filters were necessary, however, given the otherwise unmanageably large number of FTMA filings, each of which would have required a news search to establish the background.

All news stories before and after the FTMA date were then read *line by line* for the 17 cases. In some instances, this involved reading more than 1000 articles (e.g. 1283 articles on the Continental case). From these readings, we established the players, the sequence of events, information on ownership changes and prices paid (where available), the bidder's (apparent) motivation, the target's response, the outcome, etc. We augmented the news information with security price data (from Datastream) where we had information on dates (e.g. date of block purchase) and with ownership data from the standard German sources: Hoppenstedt's *Saling* stock market yearbook; Com-merzbank's *Wer gehört zu wem?* Tri-annual register of corporate ownership; and the electronic *Amadeus* database, which uses ownership files compiled by Creditreform, a credit reference agency.

We refrain from performing an event study on our cases for three main reasons. First, in contrast to the US or the UK, where event dates are easy to identify from SEC or stock exchange filings, it is extremely difficult to identify the dates of German block trades: the notification requirement is to the target company in the first instance. Second, the way blocks are acquired is often, and deliberately, covert, even where formal notification would in principle be required. Finally, block trades often receive press coverage only once further buying activity or target responses add up to a pattern, resulting in substantial reporting delays.

4. THE CASE STUDIES

The 17 cases of hostile stakebuilding provide an insight into the way corporate governance is exercised in Germany. Brief summaries of each individual case are provided in Appendix A. In this section, we first describe the sample companies in terms of firm characteristics, shareholder structure, and defences in place. We then turn to the various strategies employed by hostile stakebuilders, including the formation of coalitions, the role of banks and ways to avoid disclosure. We next consider the defensive actions taken by targets, including voting restrictions, denial of board representation and the use of defensive coalitions and white knights. Finally, we discuss the outcomes of the different types of control battle that are observed.

4.1. Company characteristics

Table 26.5 lists the 17 targets and their respective suitors. The control contests were initiated between 1987 (Axel Springer Verlag) and 1994 (Kolbenschmidt) though, due to the often covert nature of stakebuilding, precise dating is difficult. The targets are invariably from 'traditional' industries, ranging from construction (Philipp Holzmann and Dywidag) to insurance (AMB and DBV). One of the most noticeable characteristics of the case studies is that the stakebuilders mostly operate in the same industry as their targets. Indeed, many cases are reminiscent of Jensen's (1993) over-capacity argument, for instance, the two construction cases, the Krupp–Hoesch steel case, or any of the car

industry cases. In only two instances are the control contests of a conglomerate nature. This suggests that the bidders' motivation may often be industrial or strategic rather than disciplinary: stakebuilders may seek to reduce overcapacity in their industry or increase market power rather than 'punish' wayward managers. Since target managers would expect to lose their jobs whatever the stakebuilders' motivation, their resistance to the control changes is not surprising. The strong horizontal (and vertical) bias results in the Cartel Office being involved in a relatively high proportion of the cases. Indeed, the Cartel Office's frequent involvement supports the view that market concentration or consolidation motives play an important role in our cases.

The final column of Table 26.5 attempts to categorise the stakebuilders' apparent motivations. In their study of the US block market, Bethel et al. (1998) distinguish between 'activist' block-buyers (usually individuals whose announced intention is to influence firm policy) and 'strategic' block-buyers (other companies whose purchases are unopposed by target management). Our stakebuilders do not easily fit this distinction: most of the stakebuilders are companies— not individuals as documented in the US by Holderness and Sheehan (1985) and Bethel et al. (1998)—but we cannot call them 'strategic' since they *were* opposed by target management and announced 'activist' style intentions. The classifications we offer are instead based on the *extent* to which the stakebuilders sought to become involved—ranging from gaining *influence* over corporate decision-making via blocking minority stakes (as in the AMB, Buderus, Th. Goldschmidt and Holzmann cases) to gaining majority *control* (as in the Axel Springer Verlag case) or effecting a *takeover* (as in the Asko, BIFAB, Boge, Bopp and Reuther, Conti, DBV, Dywidag, Hoesch, and Kolbenschmidt cases). We label six of the nine intended takeovers as 'consolidating takeovers' because the stakebuilders—all of whom operated in the same industry—made public statements concerning the need to remove overcapacity (steel being an obvious example). The large

Table 26.5 Stakebuilders and targets

Base year[a]	Target company	Industry	Stakebuilder	Country of origin	Industry	Industrial relationship with target	Stakebuilder's apparent motive
1991	AMB Aachener und Münchener Beteiligungen	insurance	AGF	France	insurance	horizontal	gaining influence over corporate decision-making
1992	Asko	retailing	Metro	Switzerland	retailing	horizontal	consolidating takeover
1987	Axel Springer Verlag	media/publishing	Kirch group vs. Burda brothers vs. Springer heirs	all from Germany	media/publishing	horizontal	gaining control over corporate decision making
1988	Bibliographisches Institut and F.A. Brockhaus (BIFAB)	publishing	Maxwell Communication	UK	media/publishing	horizontal	takeover
1988	Boge	car parts	Sogefi	Italy	car parts	horizontal	consolidating takeover
1989	Bopp and Reuther	process engineering	IWKA	Germany	process engineering	horizontal	consolidating takeover
1994	Buderus	heating systems/metal products	Bilfinger and Berger	Germany	construction	vertical	"long-term strategic investment" via 25% block
1989	Continental	tires	Pirelli	Italy	tires	horizontal	consolidating takeover
1993	Deutsche Beamten–Versicherung (DBV)	insurance	Commerzbank/Winterthur	Germany/Switzerland	bank/insurance	horizontal	takeover
1988	Dyckerhoff und Widmann (Dywidag)	construction	Walter Group	Germany	construction	horizontal	consolidating takeover
1988	Feldmühle Nobel	conglomerate	Veba vs. Stora vs. SCA	Germany/Sweden/Sweden	conglomerate/pulp and paper/pulp and paper	–	disciplining target management
1991	Th. Goldschmidt	metallurgy/industrial chemicals	VIAG vs. Veba/Rütgers	Germany/Germany	conglomerate/conglomerate	–	gaining influence, possibly takeover
1991	Hoesch	steel	Krupp	Germany	steel	horizontal	consolidating takeover
1989	Philipp Holzmann	construction	Hochtief	Germany	construction	horizontal	gaining influence
1994	Kolbenschmidt	car parts	T&N	UK	car parts	horizontal	takeover
1988	Seitz–Enzinger–Noll (SEN)	process engineering	Klöckner Werke vs. APV	Germany/UK	machine tools	vertical	possibly greenmail
1992	Wünsche	conglomerate	WCM and Diekell	Germany/Germany	conglomerate/individual	–	disciplining target management

a Base year is defined as the year in which the control contest began.

number of such 'consolidating takeover' bids lends further support to the importance of 'industrial' rather than disciplinary motivations as the primary driver of hostile stake-building. Only the two cases involving targets that were conglomerates appear to have been motivated by a desire to remove 'underperforming' management. Finally, APV's stakebuilding in the SEN case is perhaps best understood as an instance of intended greenmail, as we will show later on.

A final striking feature of the stake-builders is their nationality: nine cases involved non-German stakebuilders, including most of the earliest cases. This is consistent with 'outsiders' undermining the prevailing 'governance consensus'.

In line with our discussion in Section 2.1, in Table 26.6, we classify the target companies according to their shareholding structure in the run-up to their control contests. Three of the companies were majority controlled prior to the control contest. SEN had a 50.01% owner but still became the target of a control contest. Wünsche was majority controlled by two brothers who later fell out. Bopp and Reuther, the only non-listed target in our sample, was controlled by a large number of family shareholders and one outside 25% + blockholder, who originally pooled their votes. Of the remaining 14 companies, there was a blocking minority shareholder in six cases, and in the remaining eight companies, ownership was initially dispersed.

The middle block of Table 26.6 documents the takeover defences in place in the run-up to the control contests. Eight of the 17 targets had some form of takeover defence. Not surprisingly, the three majority controlled firms in Panel A had no formal takeover defences. Amongst the six companies in Panel B, which initially had blocking minority shareholders, two (Axel Springer Verlag and DBV) limited the transferability of shares, and one (Th. Goldschmidt) had differential voting rights. The most popular defence for companies with fragmented ownership structures appears to be caps on voting rights, which were in place in four of the eight companies in Panel C (Asko, Continental,

Feldmühle Nobel and Hoesch). This is not surprising as such caps clearly make it more difficult (although as we shall see later, not impossible) for a stakebuilder to establish a controlling interest.

The final block of Table 26.6 provides some performance indicators prior to the control contests. The targets are mostly large companies, with nominal annual sales averaging DM 3.6 billion in the 3 years prior to the control contests. The smallest target (BIFAB) had annual sales of DM 44 million, and the largest target (Asko) had DM 13.2 billion. All but four of the targets had experienced positive sales growth in the 3 years leading up to the control contests, with double-digit growth rates in five cases. The earnings dynamic is more mixed, with three firms moving into losses over the 3 years pre-contest, three firms experiencing negative earnings growth, and the remaining 11 seeing sometimes quite substantial increases in earnings. In the year their control contests began, four firms were loss-making and six firms earned less than an 8% return on equity. The remaining seven, however, would appear to be performing healthily, with return on equity ranging from 10% to 22%.

4.2. Stake accumulation tactics

Hostile stakes can be formed either via open-market purchases or by purchasing blocks from existing shareholders. As Table 26.7 shows, stakes are often built partially through open-market purchases, but limited secondary market liquidity typically precludes a controlling stake being accumulated without also buying (or forming coalitions with) existing blocks. In contrast to the predictions of the theoretical literature (such as Zwiebel, 1995) there are usually *multiple* large blockholders in our cases. This greatly increases the complexity of the game for each individual blockholder. In particular, each blockholder will fear *not* being part of a controlling coalition when a hostile stakebuilder emerges, given the high risk of being diluted in Germany. It is not altogether surprising, therefore, that in a large number of cases

Table 26.6 Pre-contest target company ownership structure, takeover defenses, and performance

Target company	Shareholder structure prior to stakebuilding	Defenses[a]			Performance prior to stakebuilding				
		Cap on voting rights	Limited share transferability	Departure from one-share-one-vote	Sales[b] DM million	Sales growth[c] (%)	Earnings growth[c] (%)	Return on equity[b] (%)	Return on sales[b] (%)
Panel A. Majority controlled, prior to stakebuilding									
Bopp and Reuther	several family shareholders, bound by a pooling contract, had majority control, one outside blocking minority				185	−10.8	move into losses	n.a.	−5.1
SEN	one 50.01% stake, one blocking-minority stake				378	−7.3	move into losses	n.a.	−0.3
Wünsche	two blocking-minority stakes with pooling contract				1833	6.6	29.5	21.2	1.5
Panel B. Blocking minority stake(s), prior to stakebuilding									
Axel Springer Verlag	one blocking-minority stake, several smaller stakes		yes		2220	28.4	218.8	19.1	2.6
BIFAB	two blocking-minority stakes, one smaller stake				44	8.1	51.8	n.a.	−0.7
Buderus	one blocking-minority stake, several smaller stakes				2696	3.9	11.4	16.2	2.5

DBV	two blocking-minority stakes	yes		2199	12.6	35.8	4.7	1.7
Th. Geldschmidt	one blocking-minority stake, several smaller stakes		yesᵈ	1197	7.2	16.0	22.0	4.1
Kolbenschmidt	one blocking-minority stake, several smaller stakes			1449	−3.9	move into losses	n.a.	−3.8

Panel C. Fragmented ownership, prior to stakebuilding

AMB	several small stakes	yes		n.a	n.a.	4.8	5.4	n.a.
Asko	several small stakes	5%		13,188	20.1	−29.6	3.3	0.1
Boge	two non-blocking stakes			537	8.8	25.4	7.3	1.0
Continental	at least two non-blocking stakes	5%		6588	21.2	26.2	16.0	2.6
Dywidag	several small stakes			1459	9.2	−25.9	2.7	0.4
Feldmühle Nobel	several small stakes	5%ᵉ		8846	−3.0	−4.7	10.2	2.3
Hoesch	at least one non-blocking stake	15%		10,426	8.7	29.7	5.3	0.9
Philipp Holzmann	at least one non-blocking stake			3937	32.3	142.7	12.9	1.2

Source: accounting data comes from Hoppenstedt Bilanzdatenbank and various issues of the Saling stock market yearbook.

a None of the target firms we analyse have only non-voting shares listed.
b Measured as the average in the base year and the previous 3 years.
c Measured as the average growth rate in the base year and the previous 2 years.
d 1.3% of shares have 11.6% of votes.
e Adopted in response to stakebuilding rumours.

Table 26.7 Stakebuilding strategy

Target	Source of stake	Acting in concert	Bank stake	Bank assists stake-builder	Disclosure problems
Panel A: Majority controlled, prior to stakebuilding					
Bopp and Reuther	IWKA bought stake from a group of family shareholders, despite pooling agreement	✓			
SEN	APV offered options on 40% holding by SEN minority shareholders (stake held by Badische Kommunale Landesbank) to foil forced merger of SEN with KW's subsidiary (KW had bid for the 40% block); APV tender for remainder at DM175	✓	✓	✓	
Wünsche	possibly to end a long-standing feud with his brother, W-J. Wünsche sold 25%+1 share stake (of which 6% were parked with a bank) to WCM and Dieckell, who pooled; this sale was welcomed by brother Kai Wünsche, the CEO of Wünsche. The stake was allegedly sold at a 25% discount to market price	✓	✓	✓	
Panel B: Blocking minority stake(s), prior to stakebuilding					
Axel Springer Verlag	Kirch bought 10% at the IPO; claimed also to have option on 16%, source unclear; Burda brothers bought 24.9% stake from Axel Springer (the deceased founder)	✓			✓
BIFAB	Langenscheidt bought initial stake from Meyer family in response to Maxwell's targeted bid	✓			
Buderus	unknown, but possibly at time of IPO		✓	✓	
DBV	Commerzbank took a stake at the IPO, ostensibly to protect DBV from takeover threats; bought a further stake later to gain majority control		✓	✓	
Th. Goldschmidt	Veba: 20% from Metallgesellschaft, increased to 25%+ from family shareholders; origin of VIAG's	✓			

Kolbenschmidt	rival 20% unknown; the two new blockholders emerged when there were rifts in the family shareholder coalition and rumours of a rift between management and family shareholders T&N bought stakes from Metallgesellschaft (47%) who were in liquidity crisis; Magna International Canada (2.5%); and other institutional investors (3%)	✓

Panel C: Fragmented ownership, prior to stakebuilding

AMB	AGF bought 1.8% block from Skandia AB (with whom they acted in concert) and boosted this via open-market purchases	✓ ✓
Asko	Metro and its house bank, WestLB, bought 10% each from Asko (which Asko owned via a subsidiary) to cement a joint venture; however, Metro then bought further shares in the open-market	✓ ✓
Boge	open-market	✓ ✓
Continental	open-market	✓ ✓
Dywidag	hostile stakebuilder, Walter, acquired a total of 38% from the founding family, Siemens and its house bank; "white knight" Advanta bought Holzmann's pivotal 24.9% stake; Holzmann's intentions were to prevent Walter from gaining control by selling stake to white knight—who sold stake on to Walter	✓ ✓
Felmühle Nobel	Stora bought out the two nephews of former owner and their coalition of five others (40%, originally secretly assembled) once the coalition failed to win the proxy contest due to house bank supporting incumbent management	✓ ✓
Hoesch	open-market purchases	✓ ✓ ✓
Holzmann	Hochtief bought (options on) stakes from Advanta (10%) and Commerzbank (4.9%), its house bank	✓ ✓ ✓

existing pooling agreements break down in the face of a hostile stakebuilder. For example, in the Th. Goldschmidt case, the family shareholders had a pooling agreement with Allianz that gave the coalition majority control. When VIAG emerged as a stakebuilder, Allianz let its pooling contract expire and sold out to VIAG, who thereby gained control. In the Bopp and Reuther case, the pooling agreement that established majority control was actually violated by certain shareholders, which precipitated the control battle in the first place.

It is also interesting to observe the role of banks during the control contests. As Table 26.7 shows, banks held significant stakes in 12 of the 17 cases, and often sided with the predator (either through sale or pooling). In some cases, the bank stakes appear to have been held for a long time, although there are also examples where investment banks essentially built stakes in partnership with a predator, and appear to play a pivotal role in brokering a controlling coalition. Perhaps the most interesting example is the Hoesch case, where three banks held significant stakes: Deutsche Bank (Hoesch's house bank); WestLB (Krupp's—the stakebuilder's—house bank) and Credit Suisse (who was acting for Krupp). Credit Suisse, on behalf of Krupp, secretly accumulated an initial 24.9% stake. Later in the battle, Credit Suisse accumulated a further 20% stake, pledging it in support of Krupp. While WestLB did not declare its 12% stake in support of Krupp during the battle (to avoid voting restrictions), it later worked with Krupp to have voting restrictions removed and seal the takeover. Interestingly, Krupp also enjoyed the support of Deutsche Bank—Hoesch's house bank—which was estimated to control around 12% of the votes (partly via proxies).[16]

The secretive nature of stakebuilding in the Krupp case is a common feature of our case studies. There is clearly much to be gained from not alerting other shareholders that a significant stake, or coalition of stakes, is being assembled. Two particularly relevant considerations in this respect are, first, the rules governing disclosure of stakes and acting in concert, and second,

given the horizontal nature of many of these takeovers, the threshold beyond which Cartel Office approval is required.

Disclosure problems are of particular concern since most German companies—unlike British or American ones—issue bearer shares, making it hard to identify one's shareholders. During the period of our investigation, company law required only holdings in excess of 25% and 50% to be revealed. This contrasts with the 5% threshold in the US (Regulation 13-D) and the 3% threshold in the UK. The ability of a predator to build a stake without other market participants realising is important as it reduces the likelihood of other shareholders eliminating potential takeover gains by free-riding,[17] and it prevents the potential target from initiating some form of anti-takeover protection such as limiting the votes that can be cast by any individual shareholder. Germany's disclosure rules have been progressively tightened in recent years,[18] but it is unclear whether this in itself limits the ability to build a secret stake: as our cases demonstrate, banks or other friendly parties can act in concert to help companies build large stakes by combining a number of smaller stakes that individually do not have to be disclosed. Note also that the law requires no notification for block increases between 25% and 49.9%, so a stakebuilder could secretly build a near-controlling block.

Our case studies show how weak, in practice, disclosure rules are in Germany. For example, by splitting up his 38% stake between himself and some of his companies and two children, Walter avoided revealing his ownership interest in Dywidag. In the Feldmühle Nobel case, the Flick brothers were able to assemble a secret 40% stake via open-market purchases and undisclosed agreements with institutional blockholders. Indeed, having sold this stake to Veba, the Flick brothers secretively assembled a *second* stake, which they used to extract further surplus from Veba. Effective stakes can also be hidden by the use of option contracts, such as in the Axel Springer Verlag case, where the predator had a disclosed stake of 10% but an undisclosed option on a further 16%.

Stakes in excess of 24.9% must be reported to the Cartel Office, whose permission is required before they are increased. However, even the Cartel Office rules can be stretched. For example, in the Hochtief case, Commerzbank enabled its client to acquire an effective stake in excess of the 24.9% threshold by purchasing an additional block and granting a call option on it to Hochtief. Commerzbank was paid an undisclosed fee to finance the cost of carry; hence, all the economic risks were borne by Hochtief who, in all but title, thus 'owned' the stake.[19] Monopolies Commission reports have highlighted a number of other such cases. A particularly interesting—albeit extreme-case is the 1985 takeover of Deutsche SB-Kauf by Asko, a rival retailer. Acting in concert with three banks, Asko avoided a Cartel Office investigation by arranging for all parties to hold no more than 24.9% each, thus accumulating a stake of 99.6%!

The critical issue is clearly the regulation of parties acting in concert, which historically has been very weak in Germany. Such matters are beginning to come under review by the German courts in the wake of the case brought by the Cartel Office in the Hochtief–Holzmann bid. However, while there may be some tightening of the rule regarding breaching the Cartel Office's 24.9% threshold, it seems less likely that regulations regarding the disclosure of beneficial ownership or, more crucially, effective control, will be changed sufficiently to remove the ability to build secret stakes in excess of the formal disclosure limits.

4.3. Defensive actions

During our sample period, German firms were prevented by law from using such popular US defence tactics as share buy-backs, issuing shares with multiple voting rights, poison pills or recapitalisations targeted at white knights. However, they did have a number of other defences against hostile stakebuilders. We distinguish between pre-existing takeover defences, such as the voting restrictions that we documented in Table 26.6, and defensive actions taken in response to the emergence of an unwanted stakebuilder. The main defensive actions are to forge an alliance with friendly blockholders, seek the assistance of the house bank, line up a white knight, and reduce the stakebuilder's influence by denying him a supervisory board seat. As Table 26.8 shows, almost all the target companies in our sample attempted to forge (or maintain) a defensive alliance of friendly blockholders. In many cases, white knights were sought by the incumbent management, in some cases apparently motivated, at least in part, by a desire to thwart a foreign suitor. This was certainly the case in the battle for BIFAB, where the board "resisted a takeover by a foreign firm" and found a white knight in Langenscheidt, who ultimately took the firm private. Similarly, the attempted takeover of Boge by Italian rival Sogefi was resisted in favour of a German white knight (Mannesmann). However, white knight defences do not always work as expected. For example, Advanta adopted the role of white knight in defence of Dywidag against the unwelcome attention of Walter, but then sold the critical controlling stake to Walter!

The other main defence that we observe is denial of representation on the supervisory board. As noted in Section 2, the supervisory board appoints, or removes, the management board, and a blocking minority can prevent changes in the supervisory board. Hence, we tend to see such defences employed where initial ownership includes a blocking majority. The Dywidag case illustrates how powerful a blocking minority can be in this respect: even a stake as large as 40% need not guarantee even a single seat on the supervisory board in the face of target opposition. Denial of supervisory board representation can certainly thwart a blockholder's attempts to change management or corporate strategy. However, in some cases where the initial goal of the stakebuilder was "co-operation and influence" such denial by the target can provoke a full takeover. For example, the board of Th. Goldschmidt denied major blockholders Veba and VIAG (who between them, held nearly 46% of the shares) representation

Table 26.8 Defensive actions

Target	Defensive actions			Voting restrictions		
	Defensive alliances	Bank assists target	White Knight	Deny supervisory board seat	Caps on total votes per block	Limited transferability of stock
Panel A: Majority controlled, prior to stakebuilding						
Bopp and Reuther	✓		✓			
SEN	✓		✓	✓		✓
Wünsche						
Panel B: Blocking minority stake(s), prior to stakebuilding						
Axel Springer Verlag	✓			✓		
BIFAB	✓		✓			✓
Buderus						
DBV				✓		
Th. Goldschmidt	✓					
Kolbenschmidt	✓		✓			
Panel C: Fragmented ownership, prior to stakebuilding						
AMB	✓					
Asko	✓				✓	✓
Boge	✓		✓			
Continental	✓	✓	✓		✓	
Dywidag	✓	✓	✓	✓		✓
Feldmühle Nobel	✓	✓			✓	
Hoesch					✓	
Holzmann						

on the supervisory board. Initially Veba and VIAG were demanding a "change of direction" but their frustration ultimately resulted in VIAG assembling a controlling stake, without offering to buy-out the family blockholders who had denied it a seat on the supervisory board.

A more potent form of defence, frequently employed by companies with fragmented ownership, can be the use of voting restrictions. While it is not unheard of that a company institutes voting restrictions *after* a hostile stakebuilder has emerged, as in the Feldmühle Nobel case, more usually restrictions are already in place.[20] Such restrictions typically limit the proportion of votes that can be cast by any individual shareholder or in some cases, groups of shareholders operating under a pooling agreement. However, voting restrictions can also take the form of limited transferability of voting rights. For example, Continental had a restriction that no shareholder could exercise more than 5% of the votes. Not surprisingly, this resulted in numerous blockholders holding precisely 5% blocks. When the Pirelli bid emerged, a group of minority shareholders demanded an extraordinary general meeting to remove the voting right restriction. This required a simple majority and was duly carried. However, this decision was later overturned in the courts when Continental alleged that Pirelli had acted in concert with its allies.[21] The predator group should, therefore, have been subject *collectively* to a 5% voting limit. Continental continued to deny Pirelli and its allies votes in excess of 5%, and this restriction was clearly critical in thwarting the attempted takeover.

Voting restrictions appear, however, to be much less potent as a defence when they are set at slightly higher levels. For example, the 15% voting right restriction in Hoesch's corporate charter was not an effective defence against Krupp. The 15% restriction meant that it was only necessary for Krupp (with its 24.9% stake) to convince two other significant blockholders to vote in favour of removal of the voting restriction. One of these was WestLB, its house bank, who had a 12% stake but, significantly, at no stage declared its support for Krupp—thus avoiding accusations of acting in concert. Surprisingly, Deutsche Bank, who controlled about 12%, also sided with Krupp despite being Hoesch's house bank. Hence, this case illustrates the significant difference between voting restrictions of 5%, which can be a major impediment to hostile stakebuilders, and restrictions of 15%, which are typically much less effective in defending a target company.[22] It also illustrates that a target cannot, as a matter of course, rely on its house bank for its defence. In general, proxy votes give banks both substantial influence (because voting restrictions do not apply to proxy votes which are ultimately not owned by the banks themselves) and valuable information about changes in ownership, which could be used to obstruct, or accelerate, a bid's progress. However, proxies are not always effective. While Deutsche Bank successfully used its proxy votes to defend Continental against Pirelli, its proxies proved ineffective in defending Feldmühle Nobel once shareholders themselves had decided to accept Stora's bid.

4.4. Outcomes

Classifying the outcomes of the control contests requires some care, as the 'success' of a stakebuilder's control challenge must be measured against his initial intentions. For instance, where stakebuilders intended to gain 'influence' (or, perhaps, co-operation) rather than majority control, a measure of their success is whether they gain seats on the supervisory board, or whether they can effect changes in management or corporate strategy. In this spirit, Table 26.9 summarises the outcomes of the 17 control contests. Judged relative to the initial intentions, the original hostile stakebuilder was successful in 10 of the 17 cases. It is noticeable that there is no apparent relationship between initial ownership structure and the success of the stakebuilding: the two main reasons for failure in our cases are either the intervention of the Cartel Office or the appearance of a second 'white knight' stakebuilder.

Table 26.9 Outcomes

Target	Summary	Original apparent motive	Outcome relative to original apparent motive	Control outcome	Management board changes	Supervisory board changes	Tender to minorities	Return on equity		Return on sales	
								Average of 3 years pre-contest (%)	Average of 3 years post-contest (%)	Average of 3 years pre-contest (%)	Average of 3 years post-contest (%)
Panel A: Majority controlled, prior to stakebuilding											
Bopp and Reuther	IWKA bought 43% stake. Defensive pooling agreement broke down when Hannover Finanz sided with IWKA who then bought remaining stakes	consolidating takeover	stake-builder succeeded	control change	management dismissed		×	n.a.	n.a.	−5.1	−4.1
SEN	rival stakebuilder opposed controlling shareholder Klöckner Werke, but ultimately sold its stake to the latter	possibly greenmail	stake-builder succeeded	control change	management board opposed forced merger	rival bidder vetoed seats for controlling shareholder	yes, at 18% discount	n.a.	1.6	−0.3	0.0
Wünsche	a family feud resulted in one brother being removed from the management board. He then sold his 26% stake to two	disciplining target management	stake-builders succeeded	control change	CEO resigned		×	21.2	24.0	1.5	2.1

outsiders, who pressured the CEO to resign. Rumours about the CEO change led to 28% share price rise. The stakebuilders sold out once the CEO was removed

Panel B: Blocking minority stake(s), prior to stakebuilding

Axel Springer Verlag	Kirch and Burda family initially pooled stakes against the Springer family. This broke down when part of the Burda stake was sold to the Springer family, who ultimately co-operated with Kirch	gaining control over corporate decision-making	stake-builders succeeded: co-operation	co-operation	multiple CEO resignations	bidder initially denied then given seat		19.1	25.0	2.6	2.9
BIFAB	the stakebuilding prompted the breakdown of a pooling agreement, with Langenscheidt gaining control and later taking BIFAB private	takeover	stake-builder un-successful: sold to white knight	control change			Yes, at 10% premium	n.a.	17.8	−0.7	4.4

(Table 26.9 continued)

Table 26.9 Continued

Target	Summary	Original apparent motive	Outcome relative to original apparent motive	Control outcome	Management board changes	Supervisory board changes	Tender to minorities	Return on equity Average of 3 years pre-contest (%)	Average of 3 years post-contest (%)	Return on sales Average of 3 years pre-contest (%)	Average of 3 years post-contest (%)
Buderus	stakebuilder bought a 15% stake, tried to increase it to 25% but was blocked	"long-term strategic involvement" via 25% block	stake-builder un-successful: blocked by Cartel Office stake-builder succeeded	no change		bidder given seat		16.2	21.4	2.5	3.4
DBV	Commerzbank held a 25% stake, which it undertook not to increase. The stake was gradually increased to 50% and then sold on to a Swiss insurer	takeover	stake-builder succeeded	control change			X	4.7	8.0	1.7	2.5
Th. Gold-schmidt	VIAG and Veba both bought stakes, which they pooled and sought board representation. This was denied. VIAG then	gaining influence, possibly takeover	stake-builder succeeded	control change		bidders initially denied seat (despite 45.8% stake)	X	22.0	15.2	4.1	3.2

		takeover	gaining influence	stake-builder	control change			
Kolben-schmidt	bought Veba's stake and a stake owned by Allianz to gain majority control T&N built a controlling block, but were prevented from taking control by the Cartel Office. Pending an appeal, Commerzbank acquired the block and granted options to T&N. Ultimately, Commerzbank placed 25% with Rheinmetall, later also acquired the remaining 25%	X		stake-builder un-successful: blocked by Cartel Office. Controlling block sold to 2nd bidder	control change	n.a.	11.9	−3.8	2.1

Panel C: Fragmented ownership, prior to stakebuilding

			gaining influence	stake-builder				
AMB	AGF won voting rights on blocking stake after AMB's supervisory board turned against CEO		X	stake-builder succeeded: co-operation	co-operation CEO resigned	5.4	6.2	n.a.	n.a.

(Table 26.9 continued)

Table 26.9 Continued

Target	Summary	Original apparent motive	Outcome relative to original apparent motive	Control outcome	Management board changes	Supervisory board changes	Tender to minorities	Return on equity		Return on sales	
								Average of 3 years pre-contest (%)	Average of 3 years post-contest (%)	Average of 3 years pre-contest (%)	Average of 3 years post-contest (%)
Asko	supervisory board chair ousted. Voting restrictions then removed and takeover welcomed	consolidating takeover	stake-builder succeeded	control change		chairman removed	X	3.3	5.5	0.1	0.5
Panel C: Fragmented ownership, prior to stakebuilding											
Boge	a defensive coalition successfully formed. The controlling group sold out to Mannesmann. initial stake-builder Sogefi also sold out to Mannesmann a few months later	consolodating takeover	stake-builder un-successful: defensive coalition sold to "grey knight"	control change			yes, initial offer at 64% discount	7.3	5.7	1.0	0.5
Con-tinental	Pirelli and allies each bought 5% stakes, but were ultimately defeated by the	consolodating takeover	stake-builder un-successful: court upholds	no change	CEO removed; management board split			16.0	10.9	2.6	1.0

Company	Description									
	fall in Continental's share price and the failure to remove voting restrictions			voting right cap						
Dywidag	Walter constructed a 40% stake in Dywidag with a view to takeover. Dywidag responded by welcoming "white knight" Advanta, who then sold on a critical 25% stake to Walter	consolidating takeover	stake-builder succeeded	control change	bidder denied seat (despite 40% stake)	X	2.7	5.0	0.4	0.4
Feldmühle Nobel	Initial stake-building by Veba blocked by voting restrictions. Flick brothers then built a stake in opposition to Veba. Stora took control by buying both stakes	disciplining target management	stake-builder un-successful: 2nd stake-builder gains control	control change		yes, at 15% discount	10.2	13.4	2.3	2.1
Hoesch	Krupp built a 24.9% stake and its advisor,	consolidating takeover	stake-builder succeeded	control change	yes, share offer	management board members	5.3	n.a.	0.9	−0.6

(Table 26.9 continued)

Table 26.9 Continued

Target	Summary	Original apparent motive	Outcome relative to original apparent motive	Control outcome	Management board changes	Supervisory board changes	Tender to minorities	Return on equity		Return on sales	
								Average of 3 years pre-contest (%)	Average of 3 years post-contest (%)	Average of 3 years pre-contest (%)	Average of 3 years post-contest (%)
	Credit Suisse, also took a 20% stake. With help from other blockholders, a voting rights restriction was removed. Among Krupp's allies were its house bank and the target's house bank				suspended						
Holzmann	Hochtief prevented from increasing its long-held 20% stake via exercising options on stakes held by banks	gaining influence	stake-builder un-successful: blocked by Cartel Office	no change				12.9	15.1	1.2	1.0

Source: for accounting data: Hoppenstedt Bilanzdatenbank and various issues of the Saling stock market yearbook.

An alternative way to assess the outcome of the control contests is to look at actual changes in control. Consider first the three companies that were initially majority controlled (see Panel A). It is noticeable that control changed hands in each case, which demonstrates that pooling agreements can break down when rival stakebuilders appear, and that blocking minority stakes can have considerable influence even when there is a controlling stake or coalition. The stakebuilders' apparent motivations in this group were very heterogeneous, ranging from IWKA's consolidating takeover bid to APV's greenmail and the disciplinary actions taken in the Wünsche case. Four of the six targets in Panel B, which initially had one or more blocking minority stakes (but no controlling stake), saw control change, though in two cases it was parties other than the original stakebuilders who gained control. In one case (Axel Springer Verlag) the target finally agreed to 'co-operate' with the stakebuilder. In the final case (Buderus) the Cartel Office effectively blocked a change in control (the Cartel Office also blocked T & N's stakebuilding in Kolbenschmidt, although this simply led to control passing to a third party).

Of the eight cases in Panel C, where the initial ownership structure was fragmented, the initial stakebuilder took control in three cases, a rival stakebuilder took control in two cases, and in one case (AMB) the target company agreed to cooperate with the stakebuilder. In the remaining two cases (Holzmann and Continental), control did not change hands. In the Holzmann case, the attempt by Hochtief to gain control was effectively blocked by the Cartel Office. In the remaining case, involving Continental, court decisions on voting restrictions were the decisive factor in thwarting the predator—though Continental's supervisory board nevertheless dismissed the CEO for his alleged intransigence in dealing with Pirelli's bid.

Overall, therefore, we observe control changes in 12 cases, co-operation with the stakebuilder in two cases, and no change in control in the remaining three cases. Table 26.9 also documents management

changes resulting directly from the control contest. We find senior management changes in seven[23] of the 17 cases. This rate of post-contest management turnover is roughly comparable to the finding of Bethel et al. (1998) that about 22% of US CEOs are replaced following 'activist' or 'strategic' block purchases. German CEOs appear to be at risk even when the stakebuilders ultimately do not gain control, as in the Continental case.

How were minority shareholders treated in those cases where majority control was gained? As noted in Section 2, German corporate law neither requires that minority shareholders be made a buy-out offer nor that they receive 'equal treatment' in the terms offered. As can be seen from Table 26.9, in the few cases where tender offers were made to minority shareholders, such offers have typically been at a significant discount to the price offered to block sellers in the course of gaining control. Specifically, in three of the five cases where offers were made to minorities, the discounts ranged from 15% to 64%. Only in one case (BIFAB) were minorities offered a *premium* to the market price, of 10%. The implications of the rules regarding minorities can be seen in the takeover of SEN by KW. Rival stakeholder APV had no realistic chance of taking majority control of SEN since KW owned 50.01%. However, its 40% stake had considerable value as it could be used to block KW's merger with SEN. Blocking minority stakes can, therefore, potentially be used for greenmail: in the event, KW bought APV's stake at a premium to its purchase price and then proceeded to offer a coercive dilution deal to the remaining (non-blocking) minorities. The Feldmühle Nobel case similarly involved a substantially lower bid to minorities once Stora had gained control.

This evidence contrasts with the US, where most of the blockholders investigated by Barclay and Holderness (1992) voluntarily buy out the minorities at a premium to the block price. The ability to dilute the value of minority shareholdings in Germany does, of course, provide a powerful incentive for takeover and is likely to reduce Grossman and Hart (1980) free-rider problems. However, the sense of inequity resulting from such dilution frequently results in protracted lawsuits, and is likely to have been a reason why the Ministry of Finance recently introduced its voluntary Takeover Code, which limits (but specifically does not remove) the ability to dilute minority shareholdings.[24]

Finally, we consider how the control contests affected the performance of the target companies. Given our small sample size and the uncertainty about precise event dates, we cannot offer formal statistical tests. Instead, the final columns of Table 26.9 offer an impressionistic glance at performance changes by comparing return on sales (RoS) and return on equity (RoE) in the 3 years before and the 3 years after the control contests began. On average across the sample, RoE hardly changed (11.3% before, 12.5% after)—mirroring Bethel et al.'s US findings that 'activist' and 'strategic' block purchases lead at best to modest performance gains—but RoS nearly doubled (from 0.7% to 1.3%). At the individual company level, nine firms increased their RoE and eight firms increased their RoS. Although this suggests that stakebuilding had some positive effect on target financial performance, the predominantly horizontal nature of the control contests cautions against attributing this necessarily to enhanced efficiency. Also, the signs of the performance changes do not appear to correlate with the control contest outcomes: half of the cases in which control changed hands experienced a decline in RoS, while the other half saw an increase. So, to the extent that hostile stakebuilding has an effect on financial performance, it appears unrelated to the final outcome and it is uncertain whether it derives from increases in market power or in efficiency.

5. CONCLUSIONS

In some countries, notably the US and UK, ownership of companies is dispersed and control is exercised, at least in part, through tender offers to shareholders. However, such

a pattern of ownership is the exception rather than the rule. In many other countries, ownership is concentrated in large blockholders who, either individually or in coalition, exercise control. If the US/UK corporate governance problem is one of "strong managers, weak owners", as suggested by Roe (1994), in continental Europe, and many other countries, the corporate governance problem is rather one of "strong block owners, weak minorities." While a theoretical literature on blocks has recently developed, there is little systematic empirical evidence on their importance or their impact on corporate control. This article provides such evidence for Germany.

The article challenges a number of conventional views of the way corporate control is exercised in Germany. First, there is a widespread belief that there is a very low incidence of hostile acquisition. While there have, to date, been only two cases of hostile *tender offers* for German companies, we have documented a more important and common means of gaining control: through the building of hostile stakes. Given the pattern of ownership of German listed companies (summarised in Section 2), with around 87% of firms having at least one blockholder owning 25% or more, it is not surprising that a relatively active market exists in stakes, both for liquidity reasons and for friendly as well as hostile changes in control. We identify 17 cases over an 8-year period that can be classified as hostile stakebuilding. At first sight, this may look like an insignificant threat. However, our analysis of the ownership structure of German companies suggests that the number of firms facing a realistic risk of hostile acquisition may be as low as 64. This suggests a much higher incidence (at around 3–4% per year) of hostility in Germany than has previously been suggested, and is of a similar magnitude to the incidence of hostile takeovers in the UK.

Second, these cases reveal the considerable power that can be associated with blocking minority stakes, even in cases where a controlling shareholder, or coalition of shareholders, exists. The incremental control rights associated with 25% + stakes derive, in the main, from the ability to block transactions such as profit transfer and control agreements that can be used to reduce the value of minority shareholdings. Establishing a blocking minority stake is, therefore, frequently the initial stage in a control contest, and is often followed by an attempt to build a coalition with other large stakeholders with a view to gaining control. As we see from the cases, the emergence of a rival coalition can even cause existing pooling agreements between stakeholders to collapse.

Third, we have illustrated the complex role that banks can play in corporate governance. The dominant role accorded to German banks in much of the academic literature is as major providers of finance and also—via their representation on supervisory boards, their direct equity ownership and their control of proxy votes—as important monitors of corporate performance. We believe that this stereotype is, at best, only partially accurate. There is growing evidence that banks do *not* provide a higher proportion of finance for investment in Germany than elsewhere, and that the effectiveness of the monitoring role has often been overstated.[25] In this paper, we identify another important role for banks, namely their role in assisting companies pursuing a strategy of hostile stakebuilding. We document many cases where banks play a pivotal role in building, brokering and concealing stakes. In contrast, it is striking how few examples we find of banks actively *defending* target companies from a hostile stakebuilder. Such behaviour may, of course, be compatible with the view that banks actively monitor German companies and help to effect changes in corporate governance in the case of failing firms. However, it is important to recognise that this role is performed not by the companies' *house banks* (who are often believed to be acting as monitoring intermediaries drawing on their privileged information), but by the banks assisting the predator. This role has not previously been recognised.

An important question remains: given the ownership structure that exists in Germany, how efficient is the system of corporate control we observe? A full answer is beyond the scope of the present article, but there are certainly a number of areas of concern. First, the ability of a controlling blockholder to expropriate minorities could significantly raise the cost of capital. It is interesting to observe that the recently introduced Takeover Code in Germany—the adoption of which is voluntary[26] for firms—makes some attempt to protect minorities. Companies acquiring stakes in excess of 50% are now *required* (provided they have adopted the Code) to make an offer for the outstanding shares, but the regulations regarding the terms of such offers provide very little, if any, additional protection for minorities and are far weaker than those operating in other countries.[27]

Second, corporate governance in Germany is both unpredictable and lacking in transparency. Battles often involve a protracted, and clandestine, shuffling of stakes between rival coalitions and the revising of pooling agreements. Even large blockholders can find themselves, apparently without warning, as members of the suppressed minorities. Furthermore, once a hostile stakebuilder appears there is frequent recourse to the courts, whose decisions are, on occasion, unpredictable and lack consistency. As a result, some of the bids considered in this paper took over 5 years to reach their conclusion. If a guiding principle for the design of corporate governance systems is reasonable speed and certainty, the German system frequently fails to achieve either.

Germany's market for stakes is becoming more liquid. Banks are, in general, reducing their stakes in companies, in response to tax changes and a general shift in opinion regarding their role in corporate governance. The latter has many roots: the recent string of embarrassing failures of control and monitoring at Schneider, Balsam, Metallgesellschaft and Klöckner–Humboldt–Deutz; the increasingly global financial outlook of many large German companies; and the new focus on shareholder value permeating many German companies and banks. As banks reduce their stakes, and their influence over corporate governance, cases of hostile stakebuilding will surely increase. An important gap in the existing theoretical literature is the analysis of control battles where *multiple* large blocks exist, and this remains an area for future research.

ACKNOWLEDGEMENTS

The paper has benefited from helpful discussions at Birkbeck College, Humboldt University Berlin, London Business School, Lund University, Oxford's Saïd Business School, Stockholm School of Economics, the 1997 European Corporate Governance Network conference (Milan), the 1997 European Finance Association meetings (Vienna), and the 1997 TMR Network Conference (Florence). We are grateful to Patrick Bolton, Ernst-Ludwig von Thadden, Ekkehart Boehmer, Colin Mayer, Mike Burkart, Luc Reeneboog, and Dr. Ruppelt (head of the policy unit of Germany's Federal Cartel Office) for useful comments and to Dirk Schiereck for generously making the accounting data available. Any views expressed herein are ours alone, as are any remaining errors. Finally we thank the Editor and an anonymous referee for particularly useful comments and suggestions.

APPENDIX A

A.1. Aachener und Münchener Beteiligungen (AMB)

The control contest began when French insurer AGF built a 25% + 1 share stake in a bid to become "actively involved in insurer AMB's management", but was rebuffed by AMB's board who refused to register AGF's votes (though the board could not prevent AGF from voting Skandia's 1.8% stake with whom AGF was acting in concert). AGF's legal challenge against AMB's refusal to register failed in a lower court on the grounds that a "board has a legitimate duty to defend itself against a hostile takeover." Part of AMB's cross-shareholdings unravelled when Royal Insurance decided to sell its 18.8% stake. Fondiaria, the third party

to the original cross-shareholding structure, exercising its right of refusal, bought part of this stake (at a 5.5% premium over the market price), increasing its 6% holding to 21%. Meanwhile, another 10% block came on the market which AMB was eager for another German insurer, Volksfürsorge, to buy (AMB had recently acquired a majority interest in Volksfürsorge thanks to Fondiaria). Hostilities ended when the chairman of AMB's supervisory board brokered a deal with AGF, against the opposition of his own CEO, who subsequently resigned. The peace agreement entailed a partial registration of AGF's votes, operational co-operation, and a commitment by AMB to take a 5% noyeau dur stake in AGF in preparation for AGF's planned privatisation. Fondiaria, opposed to AGF's accommodation, sold its 21% holding to a consortium of German banks and insurers (in preference to AGF's counter-offer). These German institutions then controlled 38%, in response to which AGF increased its stake to 33.55% via purchases from UK institutional investors (at the time, a draft EC Directive suggested harmonising the blocking minority threshold to 33 1/3%). Following subsequent skirmishes between AGF and the German institutions over the chairmanship of the supervisory board, AGF finally entered into a standstill agreement not to increase (or decrease) its block (with a registered 27.49% of the votes) until December 1999, forestalling — at least for some time — a majority takeover of AMB.

A.2. Asko

The control contest began when rival retailer Metro increased its declared (and indeed so far friendly) 10% stake in open-market purchases, while two close allies of Metro (including its house bank) also held 10% each. Asko's supervisory board chair (who was CEO for 18 years and founded the firm) opposed Metro's bid for control, despite Asko's financial difficulties. In an attempt to fight off the predator, Asko revealed that 50% of the votes in its main trading subsidiaries were held by a foundation close to members of its supervisory board, implying that a new owner could not control Asko's operations (this was part of a defence structure erected in response to two hostile takeover attempts by rival retailer co-op AG in 1978 and 1981). Asko itself had a 5% voting restriction. The battle ended once the supervisory board removed its chairman in a vote of confidence, unravelled the special rights of the foundation, and removed the voting right restriction. Metro then increased its stake to 55%, in the open-market and from other blockholders (believed to be its associates, though the sellers' identity was never confirmed).

A.3. Axel Springer Verlag

The control contest began when, following the flotation of the company and the death of its founder, three rival blockholders emerged at this publishing house: the family (which, though in a minority, controlled the boards), the Burda brothers Franz, Frieder and Hubert (to whom the late founder had tried to give majority control, which was blocked by the Cartel Office), and an outsider, Leo Kirch. Initially, Franz and Frieder Burda co-operated with the family to contain Kirch's influence, denying him a seat on the supervisory board and not removing the CEO, as he demanded. Then they surprisingly agreed to pool their 25.9% stake with Kirch's declared 10% and his undeclared option on a further 16%, giving the new coalition majority control. Only a month later, however, Franz and Frieder Burda sold their block to the family. The family was not yet safe, though: claiming he had first refusal on his brothers' stake, Hubert Burda challenged the sale in court. As defensive measures, the Springer family refused to register Kirch's additional 16% of votes, signalled they would not register Hubert's block should he win in court (which he finally did not), and entered into a cross-shareholding agreement with Monti of Italy (in a further twist, the family and Monti later fell out, with Monti threatening to sell its 10% to Kirch). Eventually, Kirch

and the family came to an arrangement, electing first one of his associates and later Kirch himself onto the supervisory board. Throughout the 10 years of control battles, there was extremely high turnover amongst top executives, including four fired CEOs in one 12-month period.

A.4. Bibliographisches Institut and F.A. Brockhaus (BIFAB)

The control contest began when Maxwell Communications privately approached BIFAB's board with a takeover offer at a 53% premium to the share price. At the time, there were three blockholder groups: the Brockhaus family with around 15%, its pooling partner the Meyer family with around 38%, and Rheinpfalz Verlag with 27.34%. While it is not known what prompted Maxwell's bid, the fact that the Meyer family did eventually sell out hints at either of: (i) its desire to divest its stake for some unknown reason, which put BIFAB in play and prompted Maxwell's bid; (ii) the imminent breakdown of the controlling coalition of the two families; or (iii) the possibility that the large premium Maxwell was willing to offer tempted the Meyer family into considering a sell out. BIFAB's board responded to Maxwell's approach by saying it "resisted a takeover by a foreign firm" and was reported to be looking for a (German) white knight to stave off Maxwell's "hostile takeover bid." The Brockhaus family added to this opposition claiming it would not sell under any circumstances, nor would it tolerate a sale to Maxwell by the Meyer family. A white knight was quickly found in rival publishing house Langenscheidt, which bought the Meyer family's 38%, giving it majority control in coalition with the Brockhaus family (whose patriarch joined Langenscheidt's board). Langenscheidt shortly afterwards increased its stake to 65.34% by buying out Rheinpfalz. One year later, Langenscheidt and Brockhaus jointly took BIFAB private; the buy-out offered minority shareholders a 10% premium to the trading price.

A.5. Boge

The control contest began when rival car parts company Sogefi, controlled by Carlo de Benedetti, emerged as the holder of a 24.9% block in Boge, assembled in the open-market. In response to Sogefi's acquisitions and newspaper speculation that de Benedetti sought a majority stake, Commerzbank and Boge's industrial partner VDO Adolf Schindling, who at Boge's flotation 18 months earlier, had each taken a 10% stake, increased their stakes to 15% and 17.5%, respectively, and claimed that they, together with an unnamed third blockholder, controlled a majority of Boge's votes. Both Boge and VDO rejected Sogefi's proposal for a three-way merger, stating they wished to remain independent. At Boge's subsequent AGM, Sogefi disclosed an increased stake of 28.3%, which they increased to over 45% over the following year. Meanwhile, doubts had emerged over the actual existence of that third blockholder and thus over Boge's ability to muster a friendly majority coalition against Sogefi. Boge's management eventually placed a 6% stake with its US joint venture partner, TRW, openly expressing its preference for closer co-operation with TRW over Sogefi. When Sogefi further boosted its stake, to 47.88%, Commerzbank revealed that a friendly pool now controlled a slim majority: Commerzbank (24%), VDO (17.6% plus 2.5% held by its Swiss subsidiary) and TRW (6%). Free float at this point was a mere 2%, down from 80% when the company went public 3 years earlier. When over the following year, the co-operation with TRW went sour and TRW put its stake up for sale, Commerzbank sought a friendly buyer of the 50.1% pooled block (TRW's 6% was clearly pivotal. However, it is likely that TRW was prevented by the pooling contract from selling it to the highest bidder if that bidder was unacceptable to its pooling partners). One bidder, US car parts group Arvin Industries, was publicly rebuffed, prompting Arvin to consider a public counter-offer or to buy Sogefi's near-majority block. Interestingly, while Boge's management favoured Arvin as its new majority owner, its current majority owners, led by Commerzbank, instead sold their stakes to Mannesmann (to whom Commerzbank shortly afterwards also brokered the sale of VDO) at an undisclosed price in a deal described as "a defensive measure to prevent de Benedetti from taking over." A few months later, Sogefi also sold its stake to Mannesmann. Mannesmann proceeded to offer to buy-out the remaining 2% minority shareholders, at a 64% discount to the price it paid Sogefi, offering one Mannesmann share for every two Boge shares (1:2). Though a shareholder lawsuit aimed at annulling the forced integration of Boge was unsuccessful, Mannesmann nevertheless increased its offer to 1:1 plus a cash payment of DM 80/Boge share. The control contest lasted 2.5 years in total.

A.6. Bopp and Reuther (B & R)

The control contest began when IWKA acquired a 42.9% block from a group of family shareholders following years of poor performance. Two years earlier, the family owners of B & R had sold a 25.1% stake to financial investor Hannover Finanz (HF) in preparation for a possible subsequent stock market listing. The twenty-odd family shareholders and HF had signed a pooling agreement which secured pre-emptive rights over share stakes and "a say in any important decisions affecting the company's future." This pooling agreement was violated when some family members sold their 42.9% block without notifying either the company's board or their pooling partners. Hinting at resistance against IWKA's intrusion from the remaining 32% family blockholders (led by B & R managing director Carl-Friedrich Reuther), IWKA affirmed its wish to majority-control B & R and to "exercise its influence on the management or supervisory board with a view to improving the company's poor operating performance," and consequently offered to buy-out the remaining shareholders. B & R's board countered by pointing out that a 54% majority was still bound via a pooling contract between some of the remaining family shareholders and HF (though that contract was due to expire within 11 months and even the board had to admit that the pool did not agree on the desirability of IWKA's new stake; the 54% figure also suggests that 3.1% of the family holdings did not rally around Reuther's defence). Reuther himself was engaged in negotiating the sale of the combined 54% block held by the remaining family shareholders and HF to Britain's Siebe (it later emerged that the family had offered to buy-out HF at 170% of book value, and that Siebe's 195% bid for the 54% majority stake valued the company more highly than IWKA's 180%). However, within 2 weeks, IWKA had secured HF's support (in spite of the latter's pooling commitment) and intended to dismiss B & R's board at the forthcoming extraordinary annual meeting. The deal with Siebe fell through once HF switched its support to IWKA, and HF was later sued by family members for violation of the pooling contract (the outcome of this suit is unknown). Following the EGM, the remaining family shareholders gave up and sold their 32% stake to IWKA at the lower price of 180% of book value. IWKA exchanged the management, began to restructure the company, and a few years later also bought out HF.

A.7. Buderus

The control contest began shortly after Metallgesellschaft floated its 79.9% stake in Buderus in a public offering lead-managed by Deutsche Bank and co-managed by Dresdner Bank and Commerzbank with a mandate to spread the shares widely. At the time of the book-building, Buderus announced that a number of institutional investors had taken stakes of between 1% and 3% and jointly (though not in coalition) controlled a majority of votes. Buderus' management welcomed the fact that the company no longer had a majority owner; it is known that Buderus' management and Metallgesellschaft had considered selling to a single investor instead of placing the shares in the market, but that

this option had been rejected to ensure Buderus' independence. However, shortly afterwards, Commerzbank and Dresdner revealed they had each taken a 10% stake "as a long-term financial investment and not for resale to potential takeover bidders." A month later, Bilfinger and Berger (B & B) revealed at Buderus' AGM that it had assembled a 15% block and planned to discuss its long-term strategic vertical involvement with Buderus' management. While Buderus did not openly condemn the emergence of this block, its management did declare their intention to keep the company independent of outside influence (curiously motivated as being in the interest of Buderus' core customers!). Significantly, Dresdner Bank acted as B & B's house bank, was its only declared blockholder (25.1%), and chaired its supervisory board. This constellation led to speculation that Dresdner Bank had facilitated the assembly of B & B's 15% stake (possibly in connection with the IPO) and might have taken its own 10% stake for the benefit— if not on behalf of—B & B. Not surprisingly, therefore, B & B applied to the Federal Cartel Office to increase its Buderus stake to 25%, prompting Buderus to declare that it could not see any synergy gains and did not need B & B as a strategic partner. Only once the Cartel Office ruled against the stake increase did Buderus soften its tone and entered into a dialogue with its 15% shareholder and supervisory board member B & B. To date, B & B has not divested its Buderus stake.

A.8. Continental (Conti)

The control contest followed a year of heavy trading (7.6 times total Conti share capital) and persistent stock market rumours—repeatedly denied by Conti and the subsequent bidder, Pirelli—that a takeover bid was imminent. In the run-up to Pirelli's intentions being confirmed, the Italian tyre manufacturer—faced with worldwide over-capacity in the tyre industry—privately approached Conti with a merger proposal, and reportedly received encouragement from two members of the supervisory board: Ulrich Weiss, of Deutsche Bank (Deutsche Bank was Conti's house bank, chaired the supervisory board, and held 5% of its shares) and Friedrich Schiefer, a management board member of 5% shareholder Allianz, the insurance company. Having assembled a 5% stake in open-market purchases, Pirelli eventually announced its bid for control in the form of a reverse takeover by Conti of Pirelli's tyre division, adding that it had already secured the support of an unnamed majority of Conti's shareholders; Conti's share price fell by 7%. Pirelli was at pains to stress that its proposal was friendly. Behind the scenes, Conti CEO Horst Urban enlisted Morgan Grenfell (Deutsche's investment banking division) to advise on the takeover defence and lobbied his board to reject the proposed merger. Urban also promised his unions that there would be no redundancies if Conti stayed independent—which is a significant form of defence as employee representatives controlled half the supervisory board. Though allegedly originally in favour of Pirelli's approach, supervisory board chairman Weiss helped defeat (with the votes of the employee representatives) the other board members' suggestion that management be instructed to negotiate with Pirelli. Urban then publicly declared the proposal "a hostile takeover attempt, despite all assurances to the contrary." The share price continued to fall. Over the following few months, stakes of up to 5% each were disclosed by some of Pirelli's backers, including two of Pirelli's own shareholders (Italian merchant bank Mediobanca and Sopaf), Fiat, Allianz' Italian subsidiary and Merrill Lynch, Pirelli's advisors. After an unusually public war of words, Conti demanded a standstill agreement as a pre-condition for talks, including a commitment that Pirelli abstain from attempting to remove Conti's 5% voting right restriction. Pirelli rejected this demand. Morgan Grenfell was actively engaged in finding a white knight or at least a 25% blocking coalition, a solution publicly favoured by Urban. Pirelli had still neither named its alleged majority supporters nor

launched a public tender offer. Events took an unexpected turn when a group of minority shareholders demanded an extraordinary general meeting to repeal the voting right restriction (which required a simple majority) and force a decision on the merger proposal (which required the approval of 75% of votes at the EGM). Deutsche Bank and Morgan Grenfell put together a defensive coalition of banks, proxy votes and car manufacturers large enough to block the merger proposal: Daimler Benz (in which Deutsche Bank held a 28.3% stake and whose supervisory board it chaired), Volkswagen (whose CEO was Urban's predecessor at Conti), and BMW; Conti's share price fell by 5.5%. Nevertheless, at the EGM, the voting restriction was overturned with a 65.97% majority (though this was later to be opposed in the courts by a minority shareholder as well as Conti itself); Conti's share price rose 5.2%. Conti still vowed to defend its independence. Interestingly, the arithmetic of the EGM indicates that Pirelli did not in fact control a majority of votes. Shortly afterwards, Conti's supervisory board relieved CEO Urban of his duties, reportedly for his continued opposition to talks. Unconditional talks were resumed and continued over the next 8 months, though the management board was still publicly divided on the merits of a merger. Conti began to restructure by closing overseas factories and selling off non-core divisions. Just before a cross-shareholding deal between Conti and Pirelli was to be announced, it emerged that Pirelli had given its backers indemnity guarantees to reimburse any losses on Conti shares. As Conti shares had lost roughly 45% of their value since Pirelli and its partners bought their stakes, Pirelli came under pressure from its banks to find funds to cover its position and was eventually forced to call off the deal and restructure and refinance its balance sheet. However, Pirelli also bought options on its allies' combined 32.4% in Conti. At that point, Conti appealed to the courts alleging Pirelli had broken securities laws by acting in concert and not disclosing the contracts with its allies. This challenge, later accepted by the court, invalidated the EGM's decision to remove the voting right restriction. Over the next 4 months, new Pirelli allies bought stakes in Conti and Pirelli tried again: at the next AGM, it moved to have the restriction lifted, a proposal deemed "hostile" by Conti's new CEO who called Pirelli's intentions "sinister." Conti refused to let Pirelli and its allies vote all their shares at the AGM, on the grounds that they constituted a concert party and as such were limited to 5%; Pirelli's motion was defeated, though Pirelli managed to obstruct Conti's proposed capital increase. When finally a superior court resurrected a decision of a pre-bid AGM to raise the majority required to remove the voting right restriction from 50% to 75%, Pirelli gave up and let its 5% stake and the options it held be placed by Deutsche Bank with German companies friendly to Conti. These placements were supported by a financial guarantee from the state of Lower Saxony where Conti is headquartered. The control contest lasted 2.5 years in total.

A.9. Deutsche Beamten–Versicherung (DBV)

The control contest began soon after public sector insurer DBV was privatised via a public offering of 50% minus 2 shares. The IPO was lead managed by Commerzbank, which not only took a 25% + 1 share stake (another 25% + 1 share block still being in the public sector) but also bound itself not to increase the size of its block and agreed that DBV was to remain independent. One way to ensure independence was the choice of restricted transferability of shares, which requires the board's registration before votes can be exercised. However, when DBV's share price soon began to fall below the offer price, Commerzbank, perhaps in an effort to support the share price, acquired a further 23.3% over the following few months from an unnamed investor. This stake increase ostensibly had the approval of DBV's board, and anyway was accompanied by Commerzbank's pledge not to have the votes of the additional shares registered, its assurance that

the overall stake would be reduced back to 25.1% in due course, and, it appeared later, its agreement that DBV could veto Commerzbank's choice of buyer. When Zurich Insurance emerged as a possible buyer, DBV's management expressly declared they would block any attempt at a hostile takeover and that they would not allow any shareholder to build up a majority or dominant stake —which would seem a credible threat given (i) the restrictions on votes, (ii) the free float of below 50%, and (iii) Commerzbank's earlier commitment to ensure DBV's independence. The talks with Zurich Insurance collapsed, partly because DBV opposed Zurich Insurance's insistence on majority control. Four months later, in spite of its long-standing commitment not to hold more than a blocking minority stake, Commerzbank increased its stake to 50% + 1 share via open-market purchases. Once it controlled DBV, the bank swiftly proceeded to sell majority control to Winterthur, a Swiss insurer. As DBV's CEO was chosen to head all of Winterthur's German subsidiaries, it seems unlikely that DBV objected to the sale; however, since Commerzbank had acquired majority control opposition on DBV's part was, one presumes, no longer an attractive proposition.

A.10. Dyckerhoff und Widmann (Dywidag)

The control contest began at a time when Dywidag's ownership structure was highly fragmented, with a maximum free float of only 21% and the two largest blocks owned by Holzmann, a rival construction company whose shareholding was viewed as friendly, and industrialist Max Aicher. During the late 1980s, Ignaz Walter, acquisitive owner of several regional construction companies, embarked on what he later called a 'strategy of slow takeover' of Dywidag by clandestinely buying up minority blocks from various sources, including a stake held by his house bank, Bayern LB, and 2% bought on the open-market. While there was speculation that Walter was behind the stake purchases, he repeatedly denied being a blockholder in Dywidag. By the end of 1991, Walter controlled 40% of Dywidag's votes, which he had previously failed to declare, and explicitly denied having; it appears that technically, he never crossed the 24.9% disclosure rule simply by spreading the 40% stake over various associated parties, including his children. Once Walter declared his stake as well as his intention to take over the company, Dywidag's management strongly and publicly resisted his hostile endeavours. Despite being the largest shareholder, Walter was denied a seat on the supervisory board. In December 1991, a financier called Dieter Bock proposed a "friendly" takeover of Dywidag, a move that was welcomed by the board. Rather than inviting all Dywidag's shareholders to tender their shares, Bock proposed to consummate the takeover via the negotiated friendly acquisition of two key shareholders' large stakes: the 24.9% stake held by Holzmann, and the Aicher block, which by now had been increased to 24.7%, along with the small stake owned by Dumez of France via a cross-shareholding arrangement. This 51% stake would block the 40% stake owned by Walter. However, events did not turn out as expected. Bock duly acquired the Holzmann stake, but then announced, in May 1992, that Advanta had failed to complete the assembly of a controlling stake in Dywidag, blaming Max Aicher for reneging on the sale contract (a view disputed by Aicher). Bock also disclosed that Advanta had sold the 24.9% stake in Dywidag it had acquired from Holzmann to Walter, finally giving Dywidag's hostile suitor majority control! Dywidag's CEO resigned. No buy-out offer was made to minority shareholders. The Cartel Office subsequently fined Walter DM 500,000 for failure to register changes in its ownership interest in Dywidag.

A.11. Feldmühle Nobel (FeNo)

The control contest began when the Flick brothers, Friedrich Christian and Gert-Rudolf (the former owner's grand-nephews) accused the management of not maximising the sale price of various assets. When a hostile tender offer was rumoured, FeNo's management restricted voting rights to a maximum of 5% per shareholder, aided by Deutsche Bank which controlled about 55%, mostly via proxies but also via its 8% stake in FeNo. A year later, the Flicks and five associated parties sold a previously undisclosed 40% block (assembled with the help of Merrill Lynch via open-market purchases and secret direct agreements with institutional blockholders) to Veba, which Veba then boosted to 51%. However, when Veba failed to remove the 5% restriction and take control of FeNo, the Flicks assembled another stake of between 10% and 20% and began to oppose Veba for not launching a full bid. The Flicks' actions are consistent with a strategy of trying to maximise the bid value in the ensuing auction, which they were well-placed to do given that their 10–20% stake, spread over several parties, gave them more clout than Veba derived from its 51% stake. Two further suitors emerged in the form of Sweden's Stora Kopparberg and SCA, both of which bid for the company. Veba eventually sold its block to Stora, who also bought out the block jointly held by the Flicks and Merrill Lynch, as well as SCA's 5% toehold stake. Once Stora owned 85%, minority shareholders were offered a buy-out price 15% below the bid price paid to Veba. The firm was split up and restructured, in spite of the management's opposition. The control contest lasted 15 months.

A.12. Th. Goldschmidt

The control contest began when two conglomerates, VIAG and Veba, independently and potentially in rivalry, bought stakes from an existing corporate shareholder and part of the family. When management and the remaining family shareholders affirmed their desire to remain independent, the new blockholders pooled their 45.8% stakes and demanded "a change of direction," but were kept at bay by the insiders who refused to grant representation on the supervisory board. The contest was resumed when (i) Veba came under pressure from its shareholders to sell its 27.95% stake (25.02% of votes) and (ii) the family's coalition with insurer Allianz broke down, when Allianz chose to let its pooling contract (via which the family controlled the firm) expire in 1996 and put its 10.38% stake (9.29% of votes) on the market. VIAG beat the family to both stakes, and in April 1997, controlled 50.34% of the votes to the family's 39.94%. No offer to the minority shareholders was made. The control battle lasted 5 years in total.

A.13. Hoesch

The control contest began when high trading volumes in Hoesch shares throughout 1991 prompted speculation of a possible (foreign) takeover bid. In October 1991, Krupp, a rival steel maker, revealed it had bought a 24.9% stake secretly accumulated on its behalf by Credit Suisse. Hoesch's share price fell by 9.7% in response, while Krupp's rose by 8.6%. Krupp made clear its intention to acquire a majority block, a plan for which it claimed to have received the prior support of various banks and financial institutions with holdings in Hoesch. One of these was WestLB, Krupp's house bank and chair of its supervisory board, which declared it had a 12% Hoesch stake on its trading books, though it denied to have pledged the shares or the votes to Krupp. This is not altogether surprising, since a formal agreement would have reduced Krupp's influence given Hoesch's corporate charter, which capped the votes of any stake or formal pooling of votes at 15%. Deutsche Bank was Hoesch's house bank and chaired its supervisory board. Nevertheless, there were persistent rumours that Deutsche Bank controlled a block of perhaps 10% which was friendly to Krupp! Krupp's CEO, Gerhard Cromme, was at pains to stress this was no hostile bid, but a defensive move as Krupp would have suffered had Hoesch been taken over by a (foreign) rival. The initial reaction from Hoesch's management was muted with no particular indication of opposition, except perhaps grumblings about not having been informed until a few days before Krupp made its public announcement. Initially, it was only Hoesch's unions which called Krupp's bid a hostile takeover. Hoesch's CEO, Kajo Neukirchen, subsequently developed a more confrontational tone in public, and eventually Hoesch's supervisory board declared its opposition to the clandestine nature of Krupp's stake-building, though it was in principle willing to consider merger plans on the basis of a voluntary discussion amongst equals. At the same time, it took the unusual step of suspending two members of the management board who were believed to favour Krupp's bid, widely seen as a hardening of positions. For a brief moment, it looked as if British Steel might step in as a white knight to rescue Hoesch. Krupp's Cromme reacted by noting that he would take over Hoesch whether or not Hoesch co-operated. Significantly, he also claimed Deutsche Bank had been notified of the impending bid some 2 weeks in advance, and had welcomed it, which contradicted Deutsche Bank's public insistence on its uninformed and neutral role. When Hoesch demanded evidence of Krupp's alleged majority coalition, Cromme provided notary evidence of the support of a further 30.4% of the votes, including a 20% block held at Credit Suisse, but excluding WestLB's 12%. Shortly afterwards, Krupp announced it had bought a further 26% (likely to have included at least part of Credit Suisse's 20% stake) at an undisclosed price, thus increasing its 24.9% stake to a majority block; Hoesch's share price fell by 4%. Krupp had still not made a formal tender offer. Over the next few months, Krup and its allies removed the voting right restriction, sealed a merger agreement and saw off legal challenges from three minority shareholders. Amongst its allies were not only WestLB, its own house bank, but also Deutsche Bank, Hoesch's house bank, which controlled an estimated 12% of Hoesch via proxies. Hoesch's CEO Neukirchen resigned. Krupp's CEO Cromme was elected "Manager of the Year" by TopBusiness and Manager Magazin. The contest only lasted a few months.

A.14. Philipp Holzmann

The control contest began when Advanta, a company controlled by financier Dieter Bock (see above: Dywidag), announced it had acquired, from an unnamed source, a 10.25% stake in Holzmann, Germany's largest construction company by turnover. At the time, a key 20% Holzmann shareholder was Hochtief, Germany's second-largest construction company. Bock's ultimate intentions were unclear until Advanta sold its stake to BfG, one of its house banks. That BfG simultaneously granted Hochtief a call option on the stake only became apparent when Hochtief notified the Federal Cartel Office of its intention to raise its 20% stake via exercising the BfG option, thus triggering a mandatory anti-trust review. Furthermore, Hochtief declined to rule out increasing its stake further, raising the prospeck of a takeover. While analysts welcomed the potential bid, Holzmann's board issued a statement reaffirming its commitment to remaining independent. At the same time, there was speculation—first denied and later confirmed—that Deutsche Bank, Holzmann's house bank, dominant shareholder and chair of supervisory board, was willing to contemplate reducing its 25.9% to 10%, thus deserting its client (Deutsche Bank was doing brisk trade with Hochtief's majority owner, RWE). Holzmann's main line of defence, therefore, was the anti-trust card which duly paid off: the Cartel Office ruled against Hochtief on competition grounds, blocking any future increase in Hochtief's Holzmann stake from the pre-bid level of 20%. Hochtief arranged for Commerzbank, its house bank and minority shareholder, to purchase the 10.25% block from BfG, paid Commerzbank an undisclosed fee to finance the cost of carry, and eventually signed a purchase agreement for the stake with Commerzbank contingent on Hochtief winning its appeal against the Cartel Office's ruling before the superior court in Berlin. When these transactions came to light, the Cartel Office started an investigation into the legality of Hochtief's dealings with Commerzbank and BfG, threatening the three companies' managers with fines of up to DM 1 million each. Simultaneously, Hochtief also purchased the 4.9% stake in Holzmann, which Commerzbank had acquired 13 years earlier. In a filing with the Cartel Office, Hochtief later disclosed it had held a call option on the 4.9% stake all along, though neither Hochtief nor Commerzbank had previously disclosed this. Indeed, Commerzbank had declared the disputed stake as its own until the very onset of hostilities, thus helping Hochtief obscure its true ownership interest in Holzmann. These revelations followed assurances by Commerzbank and Hochtief that there were no undisclosed stakes or contracts pertaining to such stakes; Commerzbank and Hochtief only eventually disclosed their contractual arrangements due to requirements under the new securities trading law.

A.15. Kolbenschmidt

The control contest began when T & N acquired options on a combined 52.5% block after financially troubled Metallgesellschaft put its 47% block on the market (the remainder were options on 2.5% from Magna International of Canada, and 3% from institutions which held a combined stake of 10%). As a horizontal merger, the deal was subject to Cartel Office approval. Within 3 months, target management asserted their desire to remain independent of any majority shareholder, sought a different, friendly but minority buyer (Dana) for a 25% block, and organised a workforce petition in protest against T & N's planned takeover. Due to Cartel Office opposition and problems over its UK asbestos liabilities, T & N failed to exercise its options by their expiry, prompting its bank, Commerzbank, to acquire a total of 49.99% on T & N's behalf and grant T & N a new option (Magna's 2.5% option was extended). Shortly afterwards, the Cartel Office blocked the deal and T & N appealed. After a further options extension, T & N appealed—unsuccessfully—to the EU competition authorities to overrule the

German decision. Finally, Commerzbank placed half of its stake with Rheinmetall, another car parts maker, which subsequently received Cartel Office clearance to take management control of Kolbenschmidt. Within a few months, Rheinmetall took management control by purchasing T & N's option on the remaining 24.99% stake still held by Commerzbank and buying a further 3% in the open-market.

A.16. Seitz–Enzinger–Noll (SEN)

The control contest began when SEN's minority shareholders, and then its own board, objected to the forced merger with a division of its 50.01% parent, Klöckner-Werke (KW). In that climate, APV managed to acquire a 40% block from a local savings bank (BaKoLa) and the Seitz family, and offered to buy-out both KW's controlling block and outside shareholders (prompting KW to offer to match APV's bid. APV won support for this deal from the SEN board and the trade unions, arguing that unlike KW, APV would not rationalise the firm. In coalition with the remaining minority shareholders, APV then obstructed KW's attempts at controlling SEN, for instance by voting against supervisory board appointees; while KW sought an EGM to sack the 10 out of 12 supervisory board members hostile to it. In the end, APV abandoned its control bid and sold out to KW, making a 14.6% return over 1 year on the stake sale. Controlling 90% of votes, KW then forced a profit transfer and control agreement on SEN, and offered to buy-out minorities at a 12.9% discount to the price it paid APV, and an 18% discount to the market price.

A.17. Wünsche

The control contest began when the family coalition, which in total controlled over two-thirds of votes, broke down. After being dismissed from the management board by his brother Kai Wünsche (the CEO and 44% blockholder) for alleged insider dealing, W-J. Wünsche became a vociferous critic of the management and supervisory boards, lobbying to oust the supervisory board for failing to carry out its control duties. Wünsche eventually sold his 26% blocking minority stake to two outsiders at a 24% discount to the market price. The new blockholders, one of whom wanted the company broken up, pooled their votes and—even though they were still bound by Wünsche's original pooling agreement with his brother—put pressure on the CEO to eventually step down. Once Kai Wunsche had agreed to resign as CEO to move onto the supervisory board, the two outside blockholders sold their stakes to a new financial investor group, who also acquired a 4.9% stake from WestLB to form a blocking minority stake of 25.1%. The new CEO acquired a 10% stake on assuming office, while Kai Wünsche reduced his then 42% stake to 30%. When the CEO change was first rumoured, the share price rose 28% in 1 day. The new CEO proceeded to sell off a string of peripheral businesses with a view to refocusing the company.

NOTES

* Corresponding author. Finance Department, Stern School of Business, New York University, 44 West Fourth Street, Suite 9–190, New York, NY 10012-1126, USA. Tel.: +1-212-998-0304; fax: +1-212-995-4233.
E-mail address: aljungqv@stern.nyu.edu (A. Ljungqvist).

1 The following illustrate this conventional wisdom: Carney (1997, p. 78), "...no market for corporate control exists in Germany to cure even the most extreme monitoring problems." Grundfest (1990, p. 105), "...in both Germany and Japan, corporate investors and intermediaries are able to reach deep into the inner workings of portfolio companies to effect fundamental management change. They do so without the need for a hostile takeover or proxy contest." Allen and Gale (1994, p. 9): "Banks are heavily involved in the control of industry and form long-term relationships with firms. There is little publicly available information about firms and there is no active market for corporate control." Franks and Mayer (1990, p. 208) "...banks protect firms from interference from

external parties, in particular from hostile takeovers."

2   Krupp's recent (ultimately unsuccessful) bid for rival steel producer Thyssen was possibly Germany's first-ever truly Anglo–U.S. tender offer: being open to all shareholders and offering a 25.5% premium. Vodafone's tender offer for Mannesmann was, in our view, the first *successful* hostile tender offer for a German company.

3   See Becht and Roell (1999).

4   The incidence of hostile takeovers is quite variable over time, but Jenkinson and Mayer (1994) report an average of 40 hostile bids per annum in the U.K. over the period 1984–1989. Taking the number of potential targets as around 1500 (excluding investment trusts), this would result in an incidence of under 3% per annum in the U.K.

5   They quote figures from a 1984 survey by the SEC that around 20% of NYSE and AMEX companies have at least one outside shareholder owning more than 10% of the common stock.

6   It should be noted that many small to medium sized firms in the U.S. have concentrated shareholding structures.

7   There has, however, been some interesting analysis of optimal ownership structure in the presence of blockholders (e.g. Bolton and von Thadden, 1998; Zwiebel, 1995). Zwiebel assumes that there are private benefits of control that can be divided and shared amongst blockholders who form controlling coalitions. Zwiebel suggests that the existence of a large blockholder will tend to discourage small blockholders, who would then find it more difficult to form controlling coalitions. Hence, large blockholders tend to 'create their own space'. In contrast, our article documents the existence of multiple competing large blockholders who are engaged in trades (often of a clandestine nature). The apparent motivation for block building is not Zwiebel's pursuit of a share in the (divisible) private benefits of control, but to effect a control change via the accumulation of a majority or controlling stake.

8   For instance, minority shareholders in Volksfürsorge, an insurance company, recently suffered dilution twice within a short space of time. Volksfürsorge was first made to buy a stake in its parent's health insurance subsidiary, which KPMG had valued using a particularly low discount rate of 2.9%. Subsequently, Volksfürsorge was ordered to sell its legal insurance subsidiary to its parent who had commissioned a valuation on the basis of a much higher discount rate of 12%!

9   There is a third option: minorities can be offered a certain fraction of the controlling parent's dividend, which, since the law does not specify what dividend policy the parent has to follow, allows for minorities to be diluted without any compensation whatsoever.

10   One appeals court decided in 1990 that the compensation should be based solely on the basis of future cash flows, without regard to hidden reserves or other peripheral assets, both of which could be realised solely for the benefit of the majority shareholder. Recently, another appeals court chose a discount factor significantly above the risk-free rate to calculate the required minority compensation, after having used a discount factor *below* the risk-free rate in a previous decision.

11   This option will be optimally exercised once the dependent company has insufficient capacity to generate enough cash to pay the guaranteed dividend post-dilution.

12   Thyssen, the target of Krupp's unsuccessful 1997 hostile bid, would feature in our Panel B, given its two non-majority blockholders: an investment company (controlled by Allianz, Germany's largest insurer, and Commerzbank) with a 25% + stake and the Thyssen family trust holding under 9%.

13   This is the maximum number of firms with free float of 50% +. Where there are undisclosed stakes, true free float may be less than the level we calculated.

14   Non-voting shares need not always be an effective takeover barrier, as the experience of computer manufacturer Nixdorf illustrates. Nixdorf became the target of takeover rumours when one family (voting) shareholder was alleged to be looking to sell out. The reason why Nixdorf's CEO, Klaus Luft, took these rumours seriously enough to declare his opposition is a German corporate law stipulation that preference shares become enfranchised if a company passes the preferred dividend in two consecutive years—a condition which in the Nixdorf case was met. As soon as Luft resigned from the board (without giving any reasons), Siemens took over control by buying 51% of the voting shares from Deutsche Bank, the family and a charitable trust in a move apparently masterminded by Deutsche Bank. (As we cannot attribute hostile intentions to Siemens, we do not include this case in our clinical analysis below.)

15   Electronically available news sources are: Reuters Textline, German and international newspapers, and newswires such as Press Association.

16   This case demonstrates that the conventional view that a German house bank will

defend its client from takeover is not generally accurate. In an interview with the Frankfurter Allgemeine Zeitung, Hilmar Kopper, then chief executive of Deutsche Bank, said he had known of Krupp's planned takeover of rival steel group Hoesch beforehand. "It has my full support because it makes good industrial sense," Kopper said. In his view, Deutsche Bank (whose management board member, Herbert Zapp, headed Hoesch's supervisory board) had no obligation to defend Hoesch against the bid: "How [should Deutsche Bank have defended Hoesch]? Everyone knew someone was buying shares, but no one knew who. Secondly, why should Deutsche Bank defend Hoesch? Does Hoesch have a right to a defence? Or is Deutsche Bank obliged to maintain [industrial] structures?"

17   As suggested, for example, by Shleifer and Vishny (1986). However, incentives for minorities to free-ride in Germany are likely to be small relative to the fears of expropriation.

18   The new securities trading law has introduced two lower reporting thresholds of 5% and 10%. In addition, the Berlin Supreme Court ruled in 1991 that if asked at their AGMs, companies have a duty to disclose shareholdings of (i) 10% or more or (ii) a minimum market value of DM 100 million. The market value threshold means that share stakes of less than 1% in DAX-30 companies are declarable.

19   Hochtief later went a step further and signed a purchase agreement for the stake with Commerzbank, effectively raising its holding in Holzmann to 35.15%. The agreement and exchange of title and consideration were contingent on Hochtief winning its appeal against the Cartel Office's ruling that it should not be allowed to increase its stake above 20%. This ruling prevented Hochtief voting the additional stake pending regulatory approval, but the purchase agreement bound Commerzbank 'not to act against Hochtief's interests', a clause which would almost certainly tie Commerzbank's hands at Holzmann's AGM. When these transactions came to light, the Cartel Office started an investigation into the legality of Hochtief's dealings with Commerzbank and another bank (BfG), threatening the three companies' managers with fines of up to DM 1 million each.

20   A Frankfurt court recently ruled a charter amendment inadmissible, that would have allowed the Dresdner Bank management board to institute a *contingent* 10% voting right restriction in the event of a hostile bidder emerging, subject only to the supervisory board's approval.

21   This information came to light when it emerged that Pirelli had entered into contracts with some of its allies guaranteeing to compensate them for any fall in Continental's share price. Fall it duly did (by around 45%) and Pirelli's exposure became known when its banks exerted pressure to cover its position.

22   Limiting the transferability of shares can also be a major impediment to a predator, as in the case of AGF's stake in AMB. In this case, the court upheld the refusal of AMB's board to register the shares on the grounds that a board has a right to defend itself against a hostile stakebuilder.

23   Counting Asko's supervisory board chairman as 'management', which he de facto appeared to be.

24   The Takeover Code was introduced in October 1995, and includes a requirement that minorities should receive an offer when majority control changes hands. However, its adoption is voluntary, and the rules provide little protection for minorities. See footnote 27 for more details.

25   See, for example, Rajan and Zingales (1995), Corbett and Jenkinson (1996) and Edwards and Fischer (1994).

26   By September 1996, 1 year after it came into force, only around one-third of listed companies in Germany had actually adopted the Code. The Takeover Commission reviewed 12 cases in its first year, only one of which led to a public censoring.

27   A party that acquires a stake in excess of 50% (via open-market purchases or a private deal) must offer to buy out minority shareholders *unless* the acquiring company has merged with the target company or entered into a profit transfer and/or management control agreement within the first 18 months after gaining control. In the absence of a merger or control agreement, the controlling company is required to make a public offer for the remaining shares within the next 3 months. If, during the initial 18 month period after having gained control, the acquiring company has not bought additional shares, the price offered to minorities must not be less than the price paid on purchases during the 6 months before gaining control *minus 25%* (denote this price P_1). If the acquiring company has made additional purchases since gaining control, the price offered to minorities must be the maximum of P_1 and the weighted average of the prices paid on such additional purchases. To those who have grown accustomed to observing bid *premia* being offered to shareholders in the event of a takeover, such arrangements will

hardly appear too onerous for the bidder! This contrasts, for example, with the U.K. City Code on Takeovers, which demands a full bid once a shareholder obtains a stake in excess of 30%, at a price no worse than the highest price that the bidder paid during the previous 12 months.

REFERENCES

Allen, F., Gale, D., 1994. A welfare comparison of the German and US financial systems, LSE Financial Markets Group Discussion Paper no. 191.

Barclay, M.J., Holderness, C.G., 1989. Private benefits from control of public corporations. Journal of Financial Economics 25 (2), 371–395.

Barclay, M., Holderness, C.G., 1991. Negotiated block trades and corporate control. Journal of Finance 46 (3), 861–878.

Barclay, M., Holderness, C.G., 1992. The law and large-block trades. Journal of Law and Economics 35, 265–294.

Baums, T., Fraune, C., 1994. Institutionelle Anleger and Publikumsgesellschaft. Die Aktiengesellschaft 3, 106–124.

Becht, M., Roell, A., 1999. Blockholdings in Europe: an international comparison. European Economic Review 43, 1049–1056.

Berle, A., Means, G., 1932. The Modern Corporation and Private Property. Macmillan, New York.

Bethel, J.E., Liebeskind, J.P., Opler, T., 1998. Block share purchases and corporate performance. Journal of Finance 53 (2), 605–634.

Bolton, P., von Thadden, E.-L., 1998. Blocks, liquidity and corporate control. Journal of Finance 53 (1), 1–26.

Bulow, J., Huang, M., Klemperer, P., 1999. Toeholds and takeovers. Journal of Political Economy 107 (3), 427–454.

Burkart, M., 1996. Economics of takeover regulation, mimeo. Stockholm School of Economics.

Butz, D.A., 1994. How do large minority shareholders wield control? Managerial and Decision Economics 15 (4), 291–298.

Carney, W.J., 1997. Large bank stockholders in Germany: saviours or substitutes? Journal of Applied Corporate Finance 9 (4), 74–81.

Choi, D., 1991. Toehold acquisitions, shareholder wealth and the market for corporate control. Journal of Financial and Quantitative Analysis 26, 391–407.

Comment, R., Schwert, G.W., 1997. Hostility in takeovers: In the eyes of the beholder? mimeo, University of Rochester.

Corbett, J., Jenkinson, T.J., 1996. The financing of industry, 1970–1989: an international comparison. Journal of the Japanese and International Economies 10 (1), 71–96.

Denis, D.J., Serrano, J.M., 1996. Active investors and management turnover following unsuccessful control contests. Journal of Financial Economics 40 (2), 239–266.

Edwards, J.S.S., Fischer, K., 1994. Banks, Finance and Investment in West Germany Since 1970. Cambridge Univ. Press, Cambridge.

Franks, J., Mayer, C.P., 1990. Capital markets and corporate control: a study of France, Germany and the U.K. Economic Policy 10, 191–231.

Franks, J., Mayer, C.P., 2001. Ownership and control of German corporations. Review of Financial Studies, forthcoming.

Grossman, S., Hart, O., 1980. Take-over bids, the free-rider problem and the theory of the corporation. Bell Journal of Economics 11, 42–64.

Grundfest, J.A., 1990. Subordination of American capital. Journal of Financial Economics 27 (1), 89–114.

Holderness, C.G., Sheehan, D.P., 1985. Raiders or saviors? The evidence on six controversial investors. Journal of Financial Economics 14 (4), 555–579.

Jenkinson, T.J., Mayer, C.P., 1994. Hostile Takeovers — Defence, Attack and Corporate Governance. McGraw-Hill, London.

Jensen, M., 1993. The modern industrial revolution, exit, and the failure of internal control systems. Journal of Finance 48 (3), 831–880.

Mikkelson, W., Ruback, R., 1985. An empirical analysis of the interfirm equity investment process. Journal of Financial Economics 14, 523–553.

Mørck, R., Shleifer, A., Vishny, R.W., 1989. Alternative mechanisms for corporate control. American Economic Review 79 (4), 842–852.

Rajan, R.G., Zingales, L., 1995. What do we know about capital structure? Some evidence from international data. Journal of Finance 50 (5), 1421–1460.

Roe, M.J., 1994. Strong Managers, Weak Owners: The Political Roots of American Corporate Finance. Princeton Univ. Press, Princeton.

Shleifer, A., Vishny, R., 1986. Large shareholders and corporate control. Journal of Political Economy 94 (3), 461–488.

Spencer, C., Akhigbe, A., Madura, J., 1998. Impact of partial control on policies enacted by partial targets. Journal of Banking and Finance 22, 425–445.

Wenger, E., Hecker, R., 1995. Übernahme-und Abfindungsregeln am deutschen Aktienmarkt— Eine kritische Bestandsaufnahme im internationalen Vergleich. Ifo Studien 41, 51–87.

Wruck, K.H., 1989. Equity ownership concentration and firm value: evidence from private equity financings. Journal of Financial Economics 23, 3–28.

Zwiebel, J., 1995. Block investment and partial benefits of corporate control. Review of Economic Studies 62 (2), 161–185.

## Chapter 27

Jens Köke

THE MARKET FOR CORPORATE CONTROL IN A BANK-BASED ECONOMY: A GOVERNANCE DEVICE?

Source: *Journal of Corporate Finance,* 10(1) (2004): 53–80.

ABSTRACT

This study examines whether changes in ultimate firm ownership (control) play a disciplinary role in a bank-based economy. We focus on Germany as the prototype of a bank-based system. We find that poor performance makes a change in control more likely; this suggests a disciplinary role. Tight shareholder control acts as a substitute for control changes, strong creditor control as a complement. Following a change in control, management turnover increases, but not as a consequence of poor performance, and performance does not improve significantly. These findings are inconsistent with a disciplinary role of the market for corporate control in bank-based Germany.

1. INTRODUCTION

THE MARKET FOR CORPORATE CONTROL represents an important governance device. For market-based economies, the disciplinary role of control changes is well documented (see Jensen and Ruback, 1983; Jarrell et al., 1988 for the US, and Franks and Mayer, 1995 for the UK). To a large extent, this market is based on hostile takeovers in both countries. For bank-based economies, the typically low frequency of hostile takeovers suggests that there is no market for corporate control (OECD, 1998). But other forms of control changes may also play a disciplinary role (see Schwert, 2000 who shows that hostile and friendly takeovers in the US are not distinguishable in economic terms). Overall, systematic evidence on the nature of control changes in bank-based countries is sparse.

This study aims to fill this gap. The question it tries to answer is: 'Does the market for corporate control fulfill a disciplinary function in a bank-based economy?' To address this question, we examine the frequency, causes, and consequences of changes in ultimate firm ownership for Germany. We choose Germany because it is often regarded as the prototype of a bank-based country (OECD, 1995). We investigate changes in ownership because this should capture all forms of control changes. And we define a change in control as a change in *ultimate* ownership because ownership patterns in bank-based countries are often complex (La Porta et al., 1999), making changes in *direct* ownership less meaningful.

An important characteristic of bank-based economies is that there is a number of alternative governance mechanisms to changes in control. For Germany, the most relevant are tight shareholder control, continuous creditor control, and control by the supervisory board. These nonmarket mechanisms might act as a substitute for disciplinary control changes. Therefore, we examine whether their presence makes control changes less likely to occur. Another characteristic of bank-based countries is the large number of nonlisted corporations. We take advantage of this characteristic. If a stock market listing provides for an extra monitoring tool (e.g. via regular analysts' reports), we should expect nonmarket governance devices to be stronger for nonlisted firms. Therefore, we investigate whether the causes and consequences of control changes differ between listed and nonlisted firms.

The empirical analysis is based on a sample of almost 1000 listed and non-listed German corporations for the years 1987–1994. Our main findings are: (1) poor performance makes a change in control more likely, being a necessary condition for control changes to be disciplinary; (2) tight shareholder control (creditor control) has a negative (positive) impact on the probability of control change, indicating that shareholder control (creditor control) acts as a substitute (complement) for control changes; (3) following a change in control management turnover increases, but irrespective whether performance was good or poor before the transaction; and (4) performance does not improve signifi-cantly after a change in control. We con-clude from these results that the market for corporate control in Germany does not work as a governance device.

This study contributes to the literature in several ways. First, previous evidence on ownership changes almost exclusively refers to market-based economies; closely related studies are Bethel et al. (1998) and Denis and Sarin (1999). This study examines a typical bank-based economy. Second, previous studies on Germany provide valuable insights into the nature of ownership changes; Jenkinson and Ljungqvist (2001) assemble case study evidence on hostile stake-building, and Franks and Mayer (2001) examine

changes in block ownership and their relation to management turnover for a small sample of listed firms. This study is the first to provide systematic evidence on the causes and consequences of control changes, based on a large sample of listed and nonlisted firms. Third, this study identi-fies changes in ultimate firm ownership based on individual shareholder data. Therefore, it allows for changes *within* shareholder categories and in this sense extends the work of Denis and Sarin (1999) who examine changes *between* shareholder categories. It improves on Franks and Mayer (2001) whose work is based on changes in *direct* ownership.

The study proceeds as follows: Section 2 reviews the literature on control changes and other governance devices to formulate testable hypotheses. Section 3 describes the data used for this study and defines the concept of control that is applied to iden-tify the ultimate owner. Section 4 describes the frequency of control changes in Germany as well as the type of buyers and sellers of control blocks. Section 5 analyzes the causes and consequences of control changes and compares the results with evidence from market-based countries. Section 6 concludes.

2. HYPOTHESES

As a starting point of our analysis, we hypothesize that changes in control have a disciplining function in bank-based as well as market-based economies. To make this working hypothesis testable, we now develop more specific hypotheses. Basically they say when firms are likely to experience a change in control and what the conse-quences of a control change are likely to be. We pay particular attention to key characteristics of the German system of corporate governance.

Hypothesis 1. Poorly performing firms are more likely to experience a change in control. It is widely recognized that firm perform-ance may suffer if management does not act in the interest of shareholders. The market for corporate control moderates this divergence of interest because managers who fail to create shareholder value can be disciplined by shareholders acquiring control. This discipline can take the form of a takeover, closer shareholder monitoring, or dismissing management (Shleifer and Vishny, 1986; Jensen, 1988; Scharfstein, 1988). Hence, we expect control changes to affect particularly poorly performing firms.

Hypothesis 2. The availability of nonmarket governance devices makes firms less likely to experience a change in control.

For market-based economies, the market for corporate control is often described as a critical governance mechanism (Jensen, 1988; Shleifer and Vishny, 1997). For a bank-based economy such as Germany, non-market monitoring devices can be expected to play a larger role because hostile control transactions are rare (Franks and Mayer, 1998) and because other constituencies such as large shareholders or large creditors typically have considerable power (Mayer, 1988; OECD, 1995). Key characteristics of the German system of corporate governance are: (a) highly concentrated share ownership, allowing for tight shareholder control, (b) close relationships to banks, allowing for tight creditor control and long-term lending, and (c) a two-tier board structure with representatives of banks and shareholders on the supervisory board, supporting tight control by creditors and shareholders. We expect that a firm will be less likely to experience a change in control if these alternative governance mechanisms are present.

Concentrated share ownership is an important vehicle to overcome the traditional free-rider problem (Shleifer and Vishny, 1986). A large shareholder has the incentive to collect information and to monitor management because the expected private benefits from monitoring exceed the expected costs. Hence, agency problems should be smaller for firms with concentrated ownership, making a disciplinary change in control less profitable. But

concentrated ownership also has costs: First, shareholders owning large blocks are poorly diversified. This may render their monitoring too risk-averse (Fama and Jensen, 1983). Second, the interests of the concentrated shareholder do not need to coincide with those of other investors. This may allow the concentrated owner to redistribute wealth from others (Shleifer and Vishny, 1997). Third, disciplinary action via takeovers becomes more difficult because incumbent large shareholders must be willing to sell their blocks. Regardless of whether concentrated ownership is good or bad, we expect changes in control to be less likely if ownership is concentrated. For Germany, this negative relation between shareholder concentration and the probability of a change in control should be particularly pronounced because share concentration is comparatively high (see, for example, Becht and Böhmer, in press).

The second characteristic concerns lending relationships. Shleifer and Vishny (1997) argue that large creditors are similar to large shareholders because they have large investments in the firm and therefore a strong incentive to monitor. Additionally, large creditors typically have a variety of control rights and therefore sufficient power to monitor. Hence, agency problems should be smaller for firms under strong bank influence, making a disciplinary change in control less profitable. For Germany, we might expect that bank influence is particularly strong. One reason is that historically German banks have acted as so-called house banks, providing long-term loans to long-term clients (Baums, 1994). Another reason is that German banks traditionally have owned large equity positions in other German corporations and therefore have been represented on many supervisory boards. Mayer (1988) characterizes these lending relationships as an integral part of the German system of corporate finance.

The third characteristic concerns the two-tier board structure of German corporations (see Hopt, 1997 for a detailed description). The management board

(*Vorstand*) manages the firm according to its own business judgement, and the supervisory board (*Aufsichtsrat*) oversees management. The supervisory board has the legal duty to supervise management, and its directors are not allowed to simultaneously serve on the management board. This strict separation of management and control makes the supervisory board a potentially strong monitoring institution, and its presence should reduce the scope for performance improvements following a change in control. However, German supervisory boards are subject to codetermination. This might weaken the board's monitoring function because it tends to slow decision-making processes and endangers confidentiality. Therefore, we expect the supervisory board's impact on the probability of a control change to be weak.

Hypothesis 3. The availability of nonmarket governance devices has a stronger negative impact on the probability of a control change for nonlisted firms than for listed firms.

A fourth characteristic of bank-based governance systems is that their stock markets are smaller and less liquid than the stock markets in market-based economies (OECD, 1995). In turn, the number of nonlisted corporations is typically large. Whereas listed and nonlisted corporations are similar regarding regulatory characteristics (see below), we expect their governance structures to differ for two reasons. First, nonlisted firms lack the monitoring function of the stock market, for example in form of regular analysts' reports. This makes it more difficult for investors to recognize the necessity of a change in control (Holmström and Tirole, 1993). Second, nonlisted firms are likely to have higher shareholder concentration and higher leverage because they did not sell their shares to the public and thus need to rely on debt. This implies that both shareholder control and creditor control are likely to be stronger, and that the scope for profitable control changes is accordingly smaller. In summary, we expect that the negative impact of nonmarket governance devices

on the probability of a control change is more pronounced for nonlisted firms.

Hypothesis 4. Changes in control are followed by corporate restructuring and improvements in performance.

If changes in control have a monitoring function, we will expect operational changes to take place after a control change. Jensen and Ruback (1983) argue that the market for corporate control is part of the managerial labor market, in which alternative management teams compete for the right to manage corporate resources. Hence, we expect increasing turnover rates for the management board. Turnover rates for the supervisory board should also increase because it comprises shareholders' representatives. But bringing an organization back on track requires further organizational changes. Jensen (1986) argues that management is likely to invest free cash flow in inefficient projects if monitoring is not strict enough. Reverting these investments should be accompanied by asset sales or layoffs. Ultimately, we expect performance to improve after a change in control.

Irrespective whether control changes are disciplinary or not, there are reasons to expect other firm characteristics to be related to the probability of a change in control. Among these characteristics are insider ownership, ownership complexity, and firm size. Insider ownership can weaken the ability of investors to take over the firm, for example because the insiders belong to the founder's family and want to keep the business 'within the family'. Based on disciplinary arguments, the role of insider ownership is not clear. Insider ownership aligns managers' and shareholders' interests (Jensen and Meckling, 1976), but it also restricts optimal governance due to risk-averse monitoring (Fama and Jensen, 1983); the first scenario decreases the need for disciplinary action, the second scenario increases it. Regarding ownership complexity, Bebchuk et al. (2000) predict that cross ownership and pyramid structures may deter control changes; both types of complexity are well documented for Germany (La Porta et al., 1999). Finally, large firms may be less likely to experience a change in control due to wealth constraints or diversification strategies of investors. Shleifer and Vishny (1992) show that the market for corporate control is less liquid as firm size increases.

3. DATA AND MEASUREMENT ISSUES

We examine the frequency, causes, and consequences of control changes using a sample of listed and nonlisted German firms for the years 1987–1994. Firms from former Eastern Germany are included after 1990. We use only incorporated firms because disclosure requirements are the strictest for them. The inclusion of nonlisted firms is essential because the determinants of control changes might differ between listed and nonlisted firms, particularly for a bank-based economy such as Germany. To identify changes in control, we apply a concept of control that is based on *ultimate* share ownership (see Section 3.3). This is significant because German corporations are often owned through pyramids or cross-ownership structures (La Porta et al., 1999), making changes in *direct* share ownership less meaningful.

3.1.   Sample

In total, the analysis of the frequency of control changes (Section 4) is based on data from 946 firms (4882 firm years). This sample (in the following, Sample I) includes firms with at least two continuous years of data because changes in ownership must be calculated. The analysis of causes and consequences of control changes (Section 5) is based on a subsample and encompasses data from 664 firms (4433 firm years). This sample (in the following, Sample II) includes firms with at least four continuous years of data because analyzing the consequences of control changes requires data on the year prior and the

2 years after change in ownership. In Section 3.2, we investigate whether dropping firms with fewer continuous years of data introduces a selection bias, particularly which variables are most likely to be affected.

The sample is fairly representative for the universe of large German corporations. Taking the number of all incorporated German firms in the year 1992 as a benchmark, coverage is high for listed firms (66.6%), all of which are public corporations.[1] For nonlisted firms, coverage is small for public corporations (13.9%) and weak for private corporations (0.03%). Controlling for firm size, the sample includes 48% of all public corporations with total sales exceeding 100 million DM, and more than 3% of large private corporations. Industry coverage is sufficiently representative for manufacturing industries. There is also a significant number of firms from other industries such as wholesale trade and construction. Details on sample selection and data sources are provided in Appendix A.

This study does not distinguish between private and public corporations because they are similar in many regulatory characteristics (e.g., liability status, disclosure requirements, and taxation).[2] But it does distinguish between listed and nonlisted corporations because their governance structures are likely to differ.[3] As argued above, we expect tighter shareholder control and creditor control for nonlisted firms, reflected in differences of ownership and capital structure. For the present data set, we find that shareholder concentration is significantly higher for nonlisted firms (Table 27.1). But we do not find that creditor control is tighter, at least when measured by leverage or the ratio of bank debt to total debt. However, we find major differences between listed and nonlisted firms regarding ownership complexity and types of owners. At this point, we take these observed differences as indicative for differences in governance structures. The observed differences are generally robust to excluding nonlisted subsidiaries, which were increasingly sampled (by the data provider) during the early 1990s. Whether

Table 27.1 Characteristics of listed and nonlisted firms

	Listed firms	Nonlisted firms	
	All	All	Without subsidiaries
Ownership structure			
Largest block	60.6%	85.9%***	70.0%***
Ownership concentration	47.3%	80.3%***	58.1%***
Cross ownership	6.6%	9.5%***	6.8%
Pyramid	35.6%	57.0%***	50.9%***
Type of owner			
Individual	33.5%	28.1%***	31.5%
thereof: insider	22.5%	12.0%***	12.9%***
Financial firm	9.2%	9.2%	7.1%***
Nonfinancial firm	24.0%	48.6%***	38.2%***
Government	1.9%	4.7%***	3.4%***
Dispersed shares	31.5%	9.3%***	19.8%***
Capital structure			
Leverage	41.3%	39.0%***	39.0%***
Bank debt	35.8%	20.7%***	27.4%***
Number of observations	2460	2422	1141

Comparison of listed and nonlisted firms, based on the mean of various firm-specific characteristics. All characteristics are defined in Appendix A. The types of owners are: individual (family, partnership, or foundation), financial firm (bank, insurance company, or investment fund), nonfinancial firm, government authorities, and dispersed shares (shares not held in a block). Insiders are executive and nonexecutive directors (or members of their families). The test statistics are heteroscedastic *t*-tests of equal means; the tests compare listed firms (column 2) with nonlisted firms (columns 3 and 4, respectively).
The sample comprises 946 firms (Sample I).
*** Significant at the 0.01 level.

this sampling procedure induces some type of sampling bias is examined next.

3.2. CHARACTERISTICS OF ENTERING AND EXITING FIRMS

Next we check for a sampling bias. For example, if poor performance increased the likelihood of firm failure or takeover, the sample could contain systematically fewer poorly performing firms. This would bias any observed correlation between performance and the likelihood of a control change towards zero.

First, we examine whether Sample II, which is used for the analysis of causes and consequences of control changes (Section 5), systematically excludes some type of firms. Comparing firms with at least four continuous years of data (Sample II) with firms that have fewer than four observations

we find some differences that are statistically as well as economically significant: For nonlisted firms, firms in Sample II have lower leverage (measured by debt to assets), better performance (measured by industry-adjusted return on assets, return on equity, or earnings loss), and larger firm size (measured by total assets). For listed firms, we find no systematic difference between the two samples except for firm size, which is larger in Sample II.[4]

Second, we examine what type of firms enter and exit the full sample (Sample I) during the years 1987–1994 (Table 27.2). For firms entering in year *t*, the comparison group is firms in year *t* that are in the sample at least since year $t - 1$. For firms exiting at the end of year *t*, the comparison group is firms in year *t* that are still in the sample in year $t + 1$. We find that entering firms tend to be smaller and have higher ownership concentration. Listed firms

Table 27.2 Characteristics of entering and exiting firms

	Entry analysis		Exit analysis	
	Firms entering in year t	Firms in sample at least since year t − 1	Firms exiting at end of year t	Firms still in sample in year t + 1
Listed firms				
Largest block	67.3%	60.8%***	84.0%	60.3%*
Ownership concentration	54.5%	47.5%***	73.8%	47.2%
Debt-to-assets ratio	41.0%	41.6%	41.1%	41.2%
Return on assets (ROA)	4.6%	1.2%***	0.1%	1.5%
Return on equity (ROE)	6.9%	1.3%***	0.2%	1.8%
Change in ROA	0.4%	−0.3%	4.6%	−0.6%
Change in ROE	0.4%	−0.9%	3.3%	−1.6%
Earnings loss	3.5%	10.1%***	20.0%	8.9%
Total assets (mn DM)	527.5	2714.2***	27.0	2518.4***
Number of observations	171	2094	5	2094
Nonlisted firms				
Largest block	89.1%	85.7%***	82.1%	84.8%
Ownership concentration	85.1%	79.8%***	75.5%	78.6%
Debt-to-assets ratio	43.8%	37.9%***	47.2%	37.8%**
Return on assets (ROA)	0.1%	0.8%	−0.4%	1.0%
Return on equity (ROE)	1.7%	1.3%	−3.9%	1.6%
Change in ROA	0.9%	−0.2%*	2.3%	−0.4%
Change in ROE	1.7%	−0.2%	−1.3%	−0.6%
Earnings loss	20.0%	13.0%***	19.3%	12.3%
Total assets (mn DM)	692.4	1453.6***	461.8	1379.3***
Number of observations	448	1842	60	1842

Characteristics of firms entering the sample after 1987, the first year of the sample, or exiting the sample before 1994, the last year of the sample, compared with characteristics of firms that do not enter or exit the sample, separately for listed and nonlisted firms. For firms entering in year t, the comparison group is firms in year t that are in the sample at least since year t − 1. For firms exiting the sample at the end of year t, the comparison group is firms in year t that are still in the sample in year t + 1. Firms are compared at the mean of each firm characteristic. All characteristics are defined in Appendix A. All performance measures except the loss indicator are calculated as the difference to median industry performance (two-digit industry level). The test statistics are heteroscedastic t-tests of equal means.
The sample comprises 946 firms (Sample I).
* Significant at the 0.10 level.
** Significant at the 0.05 level.
*** Significant at the 0.01 level.

typically show better performance when entering, whereas nonlisted firms show poorer performance. Regarding exiting firms, the main difference to firms remaining in the sample is firm size, which tends to be smaller for listed and nonlisted firms leaving the sample.

There are two lessons from this sample composition analysis. First, it is possible that Sample II is somewhat biased towards well-performing firms, but only for nonlisted firms. As discussed above, this can reduce the explanatory power of poor performance in a regression explaining the probability of control change. Second, a systematic bias due to sample attrition is unlikely because, with the exception of firm size, exiting firms are not significantly different from other sample firms. This result could be expected because 60% of sample exits are cases of nonreporting due to name changes, and not due to bankruptcy or ownership change (see Appendix A).

3.3. CONCEPT OF CONTROL

The identification of the ultimate owner for each firm is based upon German corporate law and involves two steps. First, we identify the ultimate owner for every direct shareholder of a firm using the following three rules:

- Rule 1 (strong ownership rule): A chain of control is pursued to the next level if the shareholder being analyzed is owned to 50% or more by a shareholder on the next level, while all other shareholders on the next level own less than 50%.
- Rule 2 (weak ownership rule): If rule 1 does not apply, a chain of control is pursued to the next level if the shareholder being analyzed is owned to 25% or more by a shareholder on the next level, while all other shareholders on the next level own less than 25%.
- Rule 3 (stop rule): If neither rule 1 nor rule 2 applies, a chain of control is not pursued further.

These rules guarantee that no more than one ultimate owner is identified for every direct shareholder. Note that if a shareholder has split his ownership stake in a particular company into several smaller stakes, for example into two blocks of 50% held by two subsidiary firms, we combine these smaller stakes into one single block. We set the first cutoff point at 50% because German law allows an investor owning 50% of all shares to appoint management.[5] The second cutoff point is set at 25% because an investor owning 25% of the shares has the right to veto decisions. After having identified the ultimate owner of every direct shareholder, the second step is to apply the three rules to all direct shareholders.[6] This allows to identify one single shareholder that is in ultimate control. When no single shareholder fulfills the criteria, the respective firm is seen to have no ultimate owner.

For illustration, consider the example of Dornier Aeronautics, a nonlisted mediumsized firm in the aeronautics industry (Figure 27.1). It is 100% owned by Dornier, the *direct* shareholder (level 1). In turn, Dornier is owned by the Dornier family (42.4%) and by Deutsche Aerospace (57.6%) (level 2). This latter firm is part of the Daimler-Benz conglomerate, being owned with 83.0% by the automobile giant (level 3). Daimler-Benz itself is in the hands of Deutsche Bank (28.2%), Mercedes Automobil-Holding (25.2%), and the Emirate of Kuwait (14%). The rest of the shares is dispersed. Applying our concept of control, we find a continuous chain of majority stakes between Dornier Aeronautics and Daimler-Benz, but several shareholders owning minority stakes larger than 25% in Daimler-Benz. Hence, we identify Daimler-Benz as the *ultimate* owner of Dornier Aeronautics.

The strength of our concept of control is that it clearly identifies one single ultimate owner and at the same time accounts for complex ownership structures. Identifying one controlling shareholder is important for this study because it allows to examine changes in control. If instead multiple controlling shareholders were defined, for example by pursuing *each* ownership chain to its end, it would remain unclear which of the so-defined controlling shareholders actually controls the respective firm. Taking into account complex ownership structures is important because pyramid structures are widespread in bank-based economies. If instead control were strictly defined at the direct level of ownership, this would assume that shareholders on higher levels cannot influence decisions at the base level. Whereas control might be partially diluted in pyramids, for example due to information asymmetries or transaction costs, full dilution is unlikely since pyramids are attractive forms of organization.

One weakness of our concept of control could be that it uses fixed thresholds. We recognize that the selection of these thresholds to some extent is arbitrary (see also Short, 1994). But as argued above, these thresholds are based on German corporate law and therefore associated with explicit control rights. In addition, the size

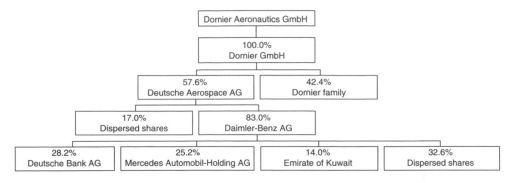

Figure 27.1 Ownership structure of Dornier in 1992.

distribution of share blocks for German corporations shows large peaks at exactly these thresholds, indicating that shareholders hold these blocks in awareness of the associated control rights (Köke, 2001; Becht and Böhmer, in press). Therefore, varying these thresholds should not significantly change the main findings of this study.

Another weakness could be that the concept of control is based on officially reported ownership rights instead of voting rights.[7] Ownership rights do not need to coincide perfectly with voting rights for two reasons: First, shares might have voting caps or carry multiple voting rights. Second, shares that are officially reported as dispersed might be under de facto control of banks because the German system of proxy voting gives banks the right to execute voting rights of deposited shares. Unless shareholders have given instructions, banks can multiply their influence this way. We believe that these weaknesses do not induce a systematic bias. Although legal during 1987–1994, limitations on voting rights do not seem to be widespread. Gorton and Schmid (2000) report that only 14 of the largest German firms had voting rights restrictions. Hence, for the vast majority of sample firms, voting rights do coincide with ownership rights. As for proxy voting, recent evidence suggests that proxy voting is extremely unlikely to enhance German banks' voting power considerably (Edwards and Nibler, 2000). In addition, only few of our sample firms have a dispersed shareholder base, which is

the precondition for bank voting power based on proxy rights. Hence, if there is a discrepancy between German banks' ownership rights and voting rights, it is probably small. In summary, the concept of control has potential weaknesses. But these weaknesses do not appear to induce a systematic bias in the identification of the ultimate owner for each sample firm.

4. FREQUENCY OF CONTROL CHANGES

In this section, we determine the frequency of changes in ownership, the size of traded blocks, and the types of buyers and sellers of control blocks. We distinguish between changes in the ultimate owner of each direct share block (*block trades*) and changes in the ultimate owner of each sample firm (*control changes*). For illustration, consider the following example (Figure 27.2). In the year 1990, Boge, a large nonlisted firm in the rubber industry, is owned by four large shareholders. Applying the concept of control, we identify Carlo de Benedetti as the ultimate owner of Boge. In the year 1991, Mannesmann becomes the new ultimate owner of VDO Adolf Schindling, a direct shareholder of Boge. This is a block trade from the Schindling-Rheinberger family to Mannesmann. Note that de Benedetti remains the ultimate owner of Boge. In the year 1992, Mannesmann acquires almost all shares of Boge, becoming

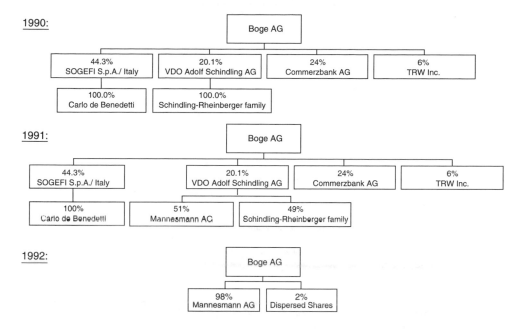

Figure 27.2 Ownership structure of Boge AG in 1990, 1991, and 1992.

its new ultimate owner. These block trades lead to a change in control.

In total, the sample encompasses 2460 firm years for listed firms and 2422 firm years for nonlisted firms. This is the total number of cases in which block trading could occur. For listed firms, in 258 cases (10.5% on average in any given year), we observe that a block is purchased by a new shareholder, who did not own a block before the purchase. For nonlisted firms, the respective rate of block purchases is 7.3%. Table 27.3 shows the size distribution of blocks purchased by new shareholders. For listed firms, the purchased block is a majority block in 107 cases (41.5%), and a minority block in 62 cases (24.0%). This strongly suggests that new shareholders come in *because* they want to take over control of the respective firm.

To put these results into perspective, we compare them with evidence from other countries. For Germany, we find that a new shareholder purchases a block larger than 10% in 9.9% of listed firms, on average in any given year. This rate of block purchases compares to 12.4% for Belgium

(Renneboog, 2000) and 9.0% for the UK (Franks et al., 2001). For the US, Bethel et al. (1998) report a rate of 6.6% for blocks larger than 5%. Hence, the frequency of block trades in Germany is similar to other countries. For nonlisted firms, the respective annual rate is 7.0%; no comparable figures from other countries are available.

As exemplified by the case of Boge (Figure 27.2), the trade of a large block does not need to be associated with a change in control over the entire firm. An example of this is a new shareholder purchasing a large block, while the majority of shares remains in the hands of the ultimate owner. To identify changes in control, we check for name changes of the ultimate owner. We find that a change in control takes place in 205 cases in listed firms (8.3% on average in any given year), and in 146 cases in nonlisted firms (6.0%).[8] Hence, the frequency of control changes is somewhat lower than suggested by the number of blocks traded. We conclude that not all block trades lead to change in control but that a large part does.

To see whether a particular shareholder type dominates control changes, we explore

Table 27.3 Size distribution of blocks purchased by new shareholders

| | | Size of purchased block | | | | | | | |
| | | [5%; 10%] | | [10%; 25%] | | [25%; 50%] | | [50%; 100%] | |
	Total number of purchases	Total	Percentage (%)	Total	Percentage (%)	Total	Percentage (%)	Total	Percentage (%)
Listed firms	258	11	4.3	74	28.7	62	24.0	107	41.5
Nonlisted firms	178	6	3.4	24	13.5	21	11.8	125	70.2

Size distribution of blocks that are purchased by a new shareholder (i.e. a shareholder that did not own a block before the transaction) for the period 1987–1994, separately for listed and nonlisted firms. Block size is observed at the direct level of ownership, block ownership is determined at the ultimate level, applying the concept of control. Therefore, purchases by new shareholders refer to changes in ultimate ownership of direct share blocks. Column 2 shows the total number of block purchases by new shareholders. Columns 3, 5, 7, and 9 disaggregate these purchases into four size classes. Columns 4, 6, 8, and 10 relate the disaggregate number of blocks to the number of all block purchases by new shareholders (column 2). The sample comprises 946 firms (Sample 1).

the transaction partners more closely. For listed firms, most control blocks are sold by nonfinancial firms (33.2%) and individuals (29.3%). In turn, the largest number of control blocks is purchased by nonfinancial firms (41.5%) and individuals (25.9%). Compared to the fraction of listed firms under ultimate ownership of nonfinancial firms (28.6%) and individuals (42.4%), it becomes clear that nonfinancial firms trade control blocks more often than would be expected by their frequency as ultimate owners. In comparison with all other shareholder types, nonfinancial firms are the most active traders of control blocks. For nonlisted firms, nonfinancial firms buy an even larger fraction of control blocks (56.8%), more than three times the fraction individuals purchase. These findings stand in sharp contrast to evidence from market-based governance systems. For the US, Bethel et al. (1998) report that 13.1% of share blocks are purchased by strategic investors such as Gulf and Western or IBM. For the UK, Franks et al. (2001) report a comparable ratio of 14.5%. In summary, although the frequency of control changes is similar for bank-based and market-based economies, the players differ fundamentally. Whether this affects the mechanics of control changes is examined next.

5. CAUSES AND CONSEQUENCES OF CONTROL CHANGES

In the following, we analyze the causes and consequences of control changes (Sections 5.1 and 5.2, respectively). The aim is to test the hypotheses lined out in Section 2. The analysis is based on Sample II, which contains firms with at least four continuous years of data. Throughout, we distinguish between listed and nonlisted firms. In Section 5.3, we compare our findings from the bank-based German economy to previous findings from market-based economies.

5.1. Causes of control changes

To examine the antecedents of control changes, we apply a univariate and a multivariate analysis. The univariate analysis provides first evidence on the relation between control changes and key firm characteristics such as performance and governance structure. The multivariate analysis investigates the causes of control changes in a more systematic fashion using a logistic regression model.

5.1.1. Univariate analysis

Table 27.4 compares firms that experience a change in ultimate ownership in year 0

Table 27.4 Causes of control changes: univariate results

		Listed firms		Nonlisted firms	
		No change in control	Change in control	No change in control	Change in control
Return on assets (ROA)	year − 2		1.3%		1.3%
	year − 1		0.8%		0.3%
	year 0	1.8%	0.9%	0.9%	−1.0%
Earnings loss	year − 2		9.9%		6.2%**
	year − 1		13.7%**		12.4%
	year 0	8.0%	11.8%*	13.8%	15.5%
Ownership concentration	year − 2		36.1%***		60.2%***
	year − 1		36.3%***		61.4%***
	year 0	49.8%	40.2%***	82.1%	68.3%***
Bank debt	year − 2		39.3%***		29.8%***
	year − 1		40.6%***		31.2%***
	year 0	33.7%	40.3%***	18.8%	30.8%***
Supervisory board	year − 2		100.0%		67.0%*
	year − 1		100.0%		67.0%*
	year 0	100.0%	100.0%	56.8%	67.0%*
Insider ownership	year − 2		14.6%***		12.6%
	year − 1		12.2%***		10.3%
	year 0	27.3%	9.7%***	13.5%	5.4%***
Cross ownership	year − 2		6.8%		7.2%
	year − 1		6.2%		7.2%
	year 0	5.8%	8.1%	10.2%	7.2%
Total assets (mn DM)	year − 2		1327.7***		960.2***
	year − 1		1426.8***		1030.0***
	year 0	3089.1	1630.9***	1598.0	1012.8***
Number of observations		1443	978	1391	621

Characteristics of firms that experience a change in ultimate ownership (control) in year 0 (columns 4 and 6), compared with characteristics of firms that do not experience such a change in any year (columns 3 and 5), separately for listed and nonlisted firms. Firms are compared at the mean of each firm characteristic. For firms with a change in control, statistics are calculated for the 2 years preceding the change (year − 1 and year − 2) and the year of change (year 0). For other firms, statistics refer to the whole period of observation. All characteristics are defined in Appendix A. The test statistics are heteroscedastic *t*-tests of equal means. The sample comprises 664 firms (Sample II).
* Significant at the 0.10 level.
** Significant at the 0.05 level.
*** Significant at the 0.01 level.

(*change in control*) with firms that do not experience such a change in any of the sample years (*no change*). We find that profitability (measured by industry-adjusted return on assets) is weaker during the 2 years preceding a change in control (year −1, year −2). But the difference to firms not experiencing a change in control is statistically insignificant. The proportion of loss-making listed firms is significantly higher among firms in which a control change is going to occur within 1 year (13.7%) than in firms without a control change (8.0%). These purely descriptive results suggest that poor profitability generally does not induce a change in ultimate ownership. Only in case of an earnings loss a change in control becomes more likely. We take these results as indicative that the German market for corporate control (measured by changes in ultimate ownership) addresses governance problems (reflected in poor performance) and thus potentially works as a disciplining device.

Next, we consider three alternative governance devices: (1) shareholder control,

(2) creditor control, and (3) supervisory board control. Concerning shareholder control, we find that ownership is significantly less concentrated in firms experiencing a change in control. This finding is consistent with the view that concentrated ownership ensures good governance, making a disciplinary change in control less profitable and therefore less likely. It is also consistent with the view that concentrated ownership makes it more difficult for outside investors to assemble a controlling block.

Concerning creditor control, we find that the ratio of bank debt to total debt is significantly higher among firms experiencing a change in control. Taking bank debt as a proxy for bank influence, this implies that control changes are more likely for firms under bank influence. This result is inconsistent with the view that strong creditors continuously monitor borrowers and thereby reduce the need for disciplinary control changes. Rather, banks appear to assist control changes.

The supervisory board is mandatory for listed firms. Thus, we cannot determine whether its presence is related to the probability of a control change for listed firms. For nonlisted firms, there is weak evidence that a larger proportion of firms experiencing a change in control has a supervisory board than firms not experiencing a change in control. Hence, the presence of a supervisory board does not appear to make control changes less likely. This finding is inconsistent with the view that monitoring by a board modifies the need for disciplinary action. As argued in Section 2, some firm characteristics can be expected to reduce the probability of a change in control, irrespective whether these changes are disciplinary or not: insider ownership, ownership complexity, and firm size. Measuring firm size by total assets, we find that firm size tends to be larger for firms that do not experience a change in control. This supports the view that firm size deters control purchases, for example due to wealth constraints of investors. Furthermore, measuring insider ownership by the fraction of shares owned by members of the management or supervisory board (or their families), we find that firms not experiencing a change in control tend to show higher insider ownership; but this holds only for listed firms. This result suggests that insiders try to hinder changes in control. Finally, measuring ownership complexity by a dummy that indicates whether the ultimate owner belongs to the well-known web of German financial and nonfinancial firms (Wenger and Kaserer, 1998)[9], we find no evidence that complex ownership structures deter control purchases.

5.1.2. Multivariate analysis

The above univariate analysis provides a first indication of the determinants of control changes. To take into account that different variables can simultaneously affect the probability of a control change, we examine the determinants of control changes using a logistic regression model (Table 27.5). This model predicts control changes using 1-year-lagged measures of performance, alternative governance devices, and other deterrents of control changes. To investigate the difference between listed and nonlisted firms, we run the regression on the pooled sample and include interaction terms for nonlisted firms, i.e. a dummy that indicates a nonlisted firm multiplied by the respective firm characteristic. Hence, the columns for nonlisted firms in Table 27.5 show to which extent their slope parameters *differ* from those for listed firms.

Model (1) confirms that firms making earnings losses are more likely to experience a change in control. Tight shareholder control, measured by ownership concentration, serves as an alternative governance device, reducing the probability of a control change. Tight creditor control does not reduce the probability of a control change. To the contrary, firms with strong creditors are more likely to experience a change in control. We find no evidence that the supervisory board acts as a substitutive governance device to changes in control. As argued in Section 2, this lack of monitoring power may be due to co-determination of supervisory boards. Among the other deterrents of control changes, only insider ownership is significantly negatively related to the probability of a control change. The determinants of control changes do not differ between listed and nonlisted firms as the column for nonlisted firms shows. The only exception is the dummy indicating earnings losses, which is significantly smaller for nonlisted firms. In fact, taking the sum of both earnings loss coefficients, we obtain the respective slope parameter for nonlisted firms; this parameter is not statistically different from zero at the 0.10 level. Hence, for nonlisted firms, poor performance does not affect the probability of a change in control. As argued in Section 3.2, this result might be due to a selection problem because our sample contains systematically fewer poorly performing nonlisted firms.

Model (2) investigates the positive impact of bank debt on the probability of a control change more closely. The aim is to see whether this effect is due to the creditor position of German banks or to their shareholder position. As argued in Section 2, German banks are often large creditors as well as large shareholders. To examine this issue, we interact bank debt with the total burden of debt (leverage) and with the fraction of shares ultimately owned by banks (bank ownership). Table 27.5 shows that bank debt looses its explanatory power. Instead, the interaction of leverage and bank debt is significantly positive. This indicates that the banks' role in promoting control changes comes from their strong creditor position. In comparison, banks do not appear to enhance their monitoring role based on their shareholder position. In summary, we find support for H1 that poor performance makes firms more likely to experience a change in control, but only if the firms' financial difficulties are severe. We find partial support for H2 because tight shareholder control functions as a substitutive governance device to control changes. But we find no support for the view that creditors or the supervisory board act as alternative governance devices. These findings are consistent with Edwards and Nibler (2000) who show that shareholder control is more important than

creditor control for addressing governance problems in large German firms. Our finding that strong creditor control enhances the probability of a control change is consistent with recent case-study evidence: Jenkinson and Ljungqvist (2001) document many cases where German banks play an assisting role in building hostile stakes. Finally, we do not find evidence that the determinants of control changes differ between listed and nonlisted firms. Thus, we do not find support for H3.

5.1.3. Sensitivity of results

To test the sensitivity of our results, we conduct a number of robustness checks (Table 27.6). Our benchmark is Model (2) from Table 27.5. First, we examine whether our results depend on the choice of the performance measure. Choosing a dummy that indicates low interest coverage instead of an earnings loss leaves all results qualitatively unaffected (Model 2a). When using industry-adjusted return on assets, we find that the performance variable looses its significance, but the other results remain qualitatively unaffected (Model 2b).[10] These findings confirm that poor performance makes a control change more likely, but only if performance is very poor. Model (2c) examines whether our results depend on the choice of the measure for shareholder control. We find that measuring shareholder concentration by the size of the largest share block instead of the Herfindahl concentration index does not affect our findings qualitatively. This result could be expected because shareholder concentration in Germany is typically very high (see also Table 27.1).

Next, we examine the impact of ownership complexity more closely. Replacing the dummy that indicates cross ownership with a dummy that indicates pyramid structures, we find essentially the same results (not tabled). In particular, the impact of ownership complexity remains insignificant. These findings stand in contrast to the popular view that complex German ownership structures hinder control changes.

Table 27.5 Causes of control changes: multivariate results

	Model (1)		Model (2)	
	Listed firms	Nonlisted firms	Listed firms	Nonlisted firms
Earnings loss	0.863** (0.034)	−1.300* (0.052)	0.791** (0.050)	−1.261* (0.062)
Ownership concentration	−0.992*** (0.000)	−0.353 (0.384)	−0.981*** (0.000)	−0.352 (0.388)
Bank debt	1.072*** (0.001)	0.191 (0.701)	−0.160 (0.815)	1.040 (0.346)
Bank debt × leverage			2.114** (0.031)	−1.310 (0.460)
Bank debt × bank ownership			−0.378 (0.695)	−0.176 (0.932)
Supervisory board		−0.013 (0.952)		−0.018 (0.934)
Insider ownership	−0.797*** (0.006)	−0.845 (0.165)	−0.821*** (0.005)	−0.836 (0.172)
Cross ownership	−0.053 (0.874)	0.342 (0.459)	−0.014 (0.968)	0.327 (0.486)
Log (total assets)	−0.050 (0.130)	0.017 (0.293)	−0.040 (0.234)	0.013 (0.435)
Number of observations	4181		4181	
Log likelihood	−1030.9		−1028.4	

Results of logistic regression models predicting changes in control by various firm characteristics. The models estimate the slope parameters for listed firms (column *listed firms*) and the *difference* in slope parameters compared to nonlisted firms (column *nonlisted firms*). All characteristics are defined in Appendix A. Both models include an intercept and time dummies (not reported). The *p*-values (reported in parentheses) are based on robust standard errors, which are calculated using the White/Huber sandwich estimator for the variance–covariance matrix.

* Significant at the 0.10 level.
** Significant at the 0.05 level.
*** Significant at the 0.01 level.

Finally, we run Model (2) on two subsamples. First, we exclude all nonlisted subsidiary companies because their disclosed annual reports could to some extent be influenced by biased transfer prices within conglomerates. Then, these reports would not reflect the subsidiaries' true financial status. Second, we exclude all firms from Eastern Germany for which data are included since 1990. The reason is that their governance structures might be fundamentally different from those in Western Germany. Both corrections do not change the results of Model (2) estimated on the full sample (not tabled). In summary, we are confident that our main findings from Section 5.1.2 are robust to alternative definitions of explanatory variables as well as the inclusion of potentially questionable types of firms.

5.2. Consequences of control changes

To analyze the consequences of control changes, we compare firms that experience a change in ultimate ownership with firms that do not experience such a change in any of the sample years. Table 27.7 examines the effects of control changes on corporate restructuring; Table 27.8 the effects on performance. All figures are calculated for the year of ultimate ownership change (year 0), the two following years (year 1, year 2), and the year prior to the change (year − 1).

Regarding corporate restructuring, we use the following measures: management turnover, asset divestitures, employment growth, and cutting of labor costs. Concerning management turnover, we

Table 27.6 Causes of control changes: robustness tests

	Model (2)		Model (2a)		Model (2b)		Model (2c)	
	Listed	Nonlisted	Listed	Nonlisted	Listed	Nonlisted	Listed	Nonlisted
Earnings loss	0.791** (0.050)	−1.261* (0.062)					0.717* (0.079)	−1.199* (0.076)
Low interest coverage			0.952*** (0.006)	−1.383** (0.021)				
Industry adjusted ROA					−0.405 (0.443)	0.873 (0.212)		
Ownership concentration	−0.981*** (0.000)	−0.352 (0.388)	−0.979*** (0.000)	−0.408 (0.321)	−0.927*** (0.001)	−0.443 (0.276)		
Largest block							−0.923*** (0.001)	−0.760* (0.091)
Bank debt	−0.160 (0.815)	1.040 (0.346)	−0.190 (0.779)	1.084 (0.326)	−0.246 (0.717)	1.193 (0.273)	−0.125 (0.854)	1.019 (0.356)
Bank debt × leverage	2.114** (0.031)	−1.310 (0.460)	2.139** (0.029)	−1.318 (0.458)	2.113** (0.032)	−1.404 (0.425)	2.117** (0.030)	−1.268 (0.475)
Bank debt × bank ownership	−0.378 (0.695)	−0.176 (0.932)	−0.367 (0.703)	−0.033 (0.987)	−0.279 (0.771)	−0.283 (0.891)	−0.393 (0.683)	−0.267 (0.897)
Supervisory board		−0.018 (0.934)		0.012 (0.957)		−0.005 (0.980)		−0.006 (0.977)
Insider ownership	−0.821*** (0.005)	−0.836 (0.172)	−0.829*** (0.005)	−0.843 (0.171)	−0.826*** (0.005)	−0.823 (0.179)	−0.838*** (0.004)	−0.770 (0.205)
Cross ownership	−0.014 (0.968)	0.327 (0.486)	−0.031 (0.927)	0.370 (0.432)	0.013 (0.969)	0.296 (0.527)	0.031 (0.928)	0.280 (0.551)
Log (total assets)	−0.040 (0.234)	0.013 (0.435)	−0.033 (0.329)	0.015 (0.364)	−0.044 (0.185)	0.011 (0.523)	−0.050 (0.135)	0.027 (0.158)
Number of observations	4181		4145		4181		4181	
Log likelihood	−1028.4		−1015.3		−1029.6		−1029.1	

Results of logistic regression models predicting changes in control by various firm characteristics. The models estimate the slope parameters for listed firms (column *listed firms*) and the *difference* in slope parameters compared to nonlisted firms (column *nonlisted firms*). All characteristics are defined in Appendix A. The benchmark model for the robustness checks is Model (2), which is taken from Table 27.5. All models include an intercept and time dummies (not reported). The *p*-values (reported in parentheses) are based on robust standard errors, which are calculated using the White/Huber sandwich estimator for the variance–covariance matrix.

* Significant at the 0.10 level.
** Significant at the 0.05 level.
*** Significant at the 0.01 level.

Table 27.7 Corporate restructuring following control changes

		Listed firms		Nonlisted firms	
		No change in control	Change in control	No change in control	Change in control
Turnover of CEO	year −1		10.2%		12.8%
	year 0	14.0%	21.1%**	14.2%	17.9%
	year 1		19.5%*		25.6%**
	year 2		21.1%**		20.5%
Turnover of executive directors	year −1		10.9%		11.2%
	year 0	11.9%	19.6%***	11.5%	20.6%***
	year 1		15.8%*		23.4%***
	year 2		16.5%**		16.2%
	year −1		6.9%		6.0%
Sales of fixed assets	year 0	6.2%	8.8%**	6.6%	5.2%*
	year 1		7.4%		8.5%
	year 2		7.3%		5.8%
	year −1		16.5%		12.1%
Sales of financial assets	year 0	16.2%	20.0%	14.8%	16.7%
	year 1		18.6%		13.8%
	year 2		17.4%		17.7%
	year −1		4.6%		−0.1%
Growth rate of employment	year 0	4.6%	5.5%	−1.3%	−3.2%
	year 1		1.1%		1.1%
	year 2		−2.0%***		−3.2%
	year −1		4.6%		3.3%**
Growth rate of labor costs	year 0	4.6%	4.3%	6.4%	4.9%
	year 1		10.9%**		13.6%**
	year 2		4.3%		6.8%
Number of observations		1443	978	1391	621

Characteristics of firms that experience a change in ultimate ownership (control) in year 0 (columns 4 and 6), compared with characteristics of firms that do not experience such a change in any year (columns 3 and 5), separately for listed and nonlisted firms. Firms are compared at the mean of each firm characteristic. For firms with a change in control, statistics are calculated for the year preceding the change (year −1), the year of change (year 0), and the 2 years following the change (year 1 and year 2). For other firms, statistics refer to the whole period of observation. All characteristics are defined in Appendix A. The test statistics are heteroscedastic *t*-tests of equal means.
The sample comprises 664 firms (Sample II).
* Significant at the 0.10 level.
** Significant at the 0.05 level.
*** Significant at the 0.01 level.

observe that the replacement rates of the CEO and other executive directors strongly increase following control changes. For example, for listed firms that experience a change in control CEO turnover rates more than double from 10.2% in the year preceding the change to 21.1% in the year of change. This turnover rate is significantly above average CEO turnover in listed firms that do not experience a change in control.

For the supervisory board, we also find strongly increasing turnover rates, both for the chairman and the other board members (not tabled).

Concerning asset divestitures, we find that control changes are accompanied by increasing sales of fixed assets, but only for listed firms. Specifically, sales rates of fixed assets increase from 6.9% in year − 1 to 8.8% in year 0. The difference in the rate of asset sales to firms without a change in control is significant at the 0.05 level. Regarding employment, we find that in the second year after the control change, the average growth rate of employment is negative for listed and nonlisted firms, but the difference in growth rates between firms with and without a change in control is significant only for listed firms. Hence, employee layoffs increase, but not before 2 years after the change in control. This time lag suggests that adjustment costs play a role in reorganizing a firm. Concerning cost cutting, we find no evidence of decreasing labor costs. On the contrary, labor costs per employee significantly increase after a change in ultimate ownership. This might reflect that the new owner is working to improve incentives for employees.

Finally, the evidence does not support the view that control changes improve performance (Table 27.8). Neither for listed firms nor for nonlisted firms we observe significant improvements in operating performance following control changes. Only the fraction of loss-making listed firms declines to a level that is comparable to the industry benchmark. In summary, we find no support for H4.

Table 27.8 Performance following control changes

		Listed firms		Nonlisted firms	
		No change in control	Change in control	No change in control	Change in control
Return on assets (ROA)	year −1		0.8%		0.3%
	year 0	1.8%	0.9%	0.9%	−1.0%
	year 1		1.0%		1.9%
	year 2		1.1%		0.4%
Return on equity (ROE)	year −1		2.7%		−0.3%
	year 0	2.1%	0.1%	1.4%	−4.6%**
	year 1		2.4%		2.1%
	year 2		2.4%		−2.6%
Change in ROA	year −1		−0.6%		−1.1%
	year 0	−0.4%	0.3%	−0.1%	−1.6%
	year 1		0.4%		2.3%**
	year 2		0.2%		−1.5%
Change in ROE	year −1		1.0%		2.0%
	year 0	−0.4%	−5.0%	0.2%	−8.6%*
	year 1		0.2%		6.0%
	year 2		−0.7%		−7.2%
Earnings loss	year −1		13.7%**		12.4%
	year 0	8.0%	11.8%*	13.8%	15.5%
	year 1		11.2%		11.0%
	year 2		11.8%		11.9%
Number of observations		1443	978	1391	621

Performance of firms that experience a change in ultimate ownership (control) in year 0 (columns 4 and 6), compared with performance of firms that do not experience such a change in any year (columns 3 and 5), separately for listed and nonlisted firms. Firms are compared at the mean of each performance measure. For firms with a change in control, statistics are calculated for the year preceding the change (year − 1), the year of change (year 0), and the 2 years following the change (year 1 and year 2). For other firms, statistics refer to the whole period of observation. All performance measures are defined in Appendix A; all except for the loss indicator are calculated as the difference to median industry performance (two-digit industry level). The test statistics are heteroscedastic *t*-tests of equal means.
The sample comprises 664 firms (Sample II).
 * Significant at the 0.10 level.
 ** Significant at the 0.05 level.

5.3. Comparison with market-based economies

To put our findings into perspective, we compare them to evidence from market-based economies. Regarding the causes of control changes, Bethel et al. (1998) show for the US that poor performance makes block purchases more likely (see also Denis and Sarin, 1999; Maksimovic and Phillips, 2001). Unlike in the US, ownership changes in Germany become more likely only if performance is extremely poor. This suggests that control changes in a bank-based economy are not well suited to address regular performance declines. But they might come into play when all other governance mechanisms clearly have failed.

An alternative monitoring device to control changes is tight shareholder control. We are not aware of any study that tests for a substitutive relationship between these two governance mechanisms for a market-based economy. For Germany, we find that tight shareholder control makes control changes less likely, and we take this as evidence for this substitutive relationship. To explicitly test for the disciplinary role of both shareholder control and control changes, we examine their joint impact on management turnover in a multivariate framework. We look at management turnover because it is often regarded as a key indicator of disciplinary action (Bethel et al., 1998; Denis and Sarin, 1999). Table 27.9 confirms that changes in control are associated with higher rates of CEO turnover. The impact of ownership concentration is also positive but insignificant. When we interact both governance devices with a dummy that indicates an earnings loss in the previous year, we find that the interaction term is insignificant for control changes but significant for ownership concentration. These findings suggest that control changes as well as tight shareholder control make CEO turnover more likely, but only tight shareholder control disciplines poor performance. The beneficial role of tight shareholder control stands in contrast to Kaplan (1995) and Franks and Mayer (2001) who find no relation between ownership and disciplinary action against management for Germany. In turn, our finding that changes in ownership are not related to the dismissal of poorly performing management is consistent with Franks and Mayer (2001). This questions the disciplinary nature of control changes in a bank-based economy.

What is similar to market-based economies is the role of insider ownership. For the US, Barber et al. (1995) and Bethel et al. (1998) show that insiders can deter changes in control when owning large blocks. This is consistent with our evidence from Germany. Likewise, consistent with Bethel et al. (1998) and Mulherin and Boone (2000), we document that larger firms are less likely to experience a change in control, although the impact of firm size disappears in the multivariate analysis.

Regarding the consequences of control changes, recent studies on market-based economies document various types of restructuring. CEO turnover strongly increases following block purchases of activist investors (Bethel et al., 1998) and following large increases or decreases in insider ownership (Denis and Sarin, 1999). Similarly, asset divestitures and employee layoffs increase, and the frequency of mergers and acquisitions decreases after changes in ownership (Bethel et al., 1998, for the US; Franks and Mayer, 1995, for the UK). For Germany, we also observe higher rates of management turnover. Sales of fixed assets increase as well, but only weakly, and employee layoffs increase, but not before 2 years after the control change. In contrast to the US (Bethel et al., 1998), the impact on performance is weak. Only the fraction of loss-making firms declines after control changes.

In summary, some of the causes and consequences of control changes are similar for bank-based and market-based economies. But since we cannot find evidence that control changes help discipline poorly performing management, we cannot support the working hypothesis of this study. Control changes in bank-based Germany do not play the disciplinary role that they play in market-based economies.

Table 27.9 Logistic regressions predicting CEO turnover

	Listed firms	Nonlisted firms
Change in control	0.612*** (0.001)	0.049 (0.888)
Change in control × earnings loss in $t - 1$	−0.563 (0.536)	1.558 (0.370)
Ownership concentration	0.247 (0.153)	−0.044 (0.792)
Ownership concentration × earnings loss in $t - 1$	0.958** (0.026)	−0.058 (0.937)
Number of observations		3187
Log likelihood		− 1335.9

Results of logistic regression model predicting CEO turnover by two governance devices (change in control, tight shareholder control) and their interaction with poor performance (earnings loss in previous period). The model estimates the slope parameters for listed firms (column *listed firms*) and the *difference* in slope parameters compared to nonlisted firms (column *nonlisted firms*). All characteristics are defined in Appendix A. The model includes an intercept and time dummies (not reported). The *p*-values (reported in parentheses) are based on robust standard errors, which are calculated using the White/Huber sandwich estimator for the variance–covariance matrix.

** Significant at the 0.05 level.
*** Significant at the 0.01 level.

6. SUMMARY AND CONCLUSIONS

This paper sheds light on the market for corporate control in a bank-based country. We focus on Germany because high ownership concentration and tight bank relationships make it the prototype of a bank-based system. We examine the frequency, causes, and consequences of changes in corporate control and compare our findings to those from market-based countries.

In contrast to the common perception, Germany has an active market for large share blocks. We find that the frequency of block trades is similar to the US and the UK. Since the traded blocks are typically very large, block trades usually lead to a change in control. The most active traders of control blocks are nonfinancial firms. This stands in contrast to market-based economies where nonfinancial firms play only a minor role in control transactions.

Regarding the causes of control changes, we find that poor performance makes a change in control more likely. This indicates that control changes in Germany may play a disciplinary role as in market-based economies. We also find that high ownership concentration makes control changes less likely. This is consistent with the view that tight shareholder control acts as a substitute for disciplinary control changes. The presence of a supervisory board does not make control changes less likely. This suggests that the board cannot substitute for control changes; this stands in contrast to evidence from the US (Kini et al., 1995). Codetermination may explain the weak monitoring power of German supervisory boards. Contrary to our expectation, we find that control changes are more likely for firms under strong creditor influence. This suggests that creditor control and control changes are complementary; this assertion is supported by recent case-study evidence on hostile stake-building in Germany (Jenkinson and Ljungqvist, 2001).

Whereas the observed causes of control changes are consistent with a disciplinary role of control changes, the observed consequences are not. We find that following a change in control management, turnover increases, but irrespective whether performance was good or poor before the control transaction. For listed firms, also sales of fixed assets and layoffs increase. In contrast to evidence from the US (Bethel et al., 1998; Denis and Sarin, 1999), we cannot confirm that sales of financial assets increase or labor costs decrease. Similarly, we cannot confirm that performance significantly improves after a change in control. In summary, although there is an active market for corporate control in Germany and although there are some indications that control changes address poor performance, the evidence on the consequences is inconsistent with a disciplinary role of control changes.

Finally, we find that the causes and consequences of control changes do not differ between listed and nonlisted firms. Even more, the impact of nonmarket governance devices (such as shareholder control) on the probability of control change or managerial turnover is quantitatively similar for listed and nonlisted firms. These results suggest that a stock market listing does not provide for an extra monitoring tool, and nonmarket governance devices need to be similarly strong for listed and nonlisted firms to have a disciplinary impact. We take this as additional evidence for the weakness of market-based governance devices in Germany.

Thus, can we answer the question posed in this paper: Does the market for corporate control fulfill a disciplinary function in a bank-based economy? The answer seems to be no. Nonetheless, our results should be interpreted with some caution. First, it is possible that the results of a disciplinary change in control are not observable within our 2-year time horizon; major performance improvements may need several years to materialize. In Germany, it is difficult to conduct extensive restructuring rapidly, for example due to legal protection against dismissal. Hence, turning around an ailing firm may indeed take longer than in market-based economies (see Denis and Kruse, 2000 for evidence from the US). Second, we do not know whether our results are unique to the period of 1987–1994 examined in this study. It may be that recent changes in capital market regulation and the emergence of the European Monetary Union have changed the nature of the German market for corporate control. For example, increasing competition may have strengthened managers' focus on shareholder value and therefore the disciplinary characteristic of control changes. Therefore, it would be interesting to investigate the causes and consequences of control changes during other time periods and for other countries.

ACKNOWLEDGEMENTS

Financial support from the German Science Foundation (DFG) is gratefully acknowledged (grant no. BO 934, 7-2). Comments from Axel Börsch-Supan, Dirk Guennemann, Silke Januszewski, Melanie Lührmann, Mattias Nilsson, Joachim Winter, an anonymous referee, seminar participants at the University of Mannheim and the Centre for European Economic Research in Mannheim, and participants of the Financial Management Association meeting in Paris and the European Finance Association meeting in Barcelona are highly appreciated. Matthias Braun, Gregor Führich, and Heiko Truppel provided excellent research assistance.

APPENDIX A

The first main pillar of data comes from Hoppenstedt's Balance Sheet Database (BSD). An important feature of this data source is that it contains information on listed and nonlisted corporations, both public (AG) and private (GmbH). We take 1986 as the starting year because a change in disclosure rules hinders comparability of the annual reports before and after the year 1986.[11] The last year of the sample is 1994 because publication of our main source of ownership data has been discontinued in this year. For the period 1986–1994, BSD contains 5222 firms (22, 732 firm years) for which consolidated balance sheet data are available (Table 27.10). We eliminate firms from the utility, traffic, and telecommunications industries because they were still predominantly government-owned during the period of observation. As a matter of comparability, we also eliminate firms that primarily operate in the banking and insurance business, while operating little in nonfinancial activities. Selection by industry causes 1752 firm deletions.

The second main pillar—data on ownership structures—is obtained from annual reports published by Bayerische Hypotheken-und Wechsel-Bank (in short,

Table 27.10 Data selection procedure

Selection criterion	Firms	Firm years
Consolidated balance sheet data for the years 1986–1994	5222	22,732
Mining, manufacturing, construction, and trade	3470	15,148
Ownership data	1485	6367
No missing values	1455	6205
Sample I (at least two continuous years of data)	946	4882
Sample II (at least four continuous years of data)	664	4433

Hypobank). These reports contain information on direct ownership of common stock (*Stammaktien*) for all listed German corporations. In addition, Hypobank provides information on direct ownership of common stock for large nonlisted corporations (*Stammaktien* for the nonlisted AG and *Gesellschafteranteile* for the GmbH which cannot be listed). Hypobank reports the size and the name of a direct owner when the size of the ownership block exceeds 5%. In general, ownership rights as reported by Hypobank correspond to voting rights (see Section 3.3).

Ownership information from Hypobank cannot readily be used in our analysis for three reasons. First, ownership information from Hypobank only refers to the *direct* level of owners. But this analysis requires to identify the *ultimate* owner of each sample firm. In contrast to Becht and Böhmer (in press), who rely on voting rights information provided by the German Securities Exchange Commission (*Bundesaufsichtsamt für den Wertpapierhandel*), this study reconstructs voting rights information in a bottom-up approach from information on direct ownership rights. Our concept of control, as outlined in Section 3.3, represents the methodological tool to achieve this aim. A second drawback is that Hypobank does not directly reveal ownership information on medium-sized nonlisted firms. Therefore, we construct the relevant ownership structures by searching the information on investments in subsidiaries and affiliated companies, which is given in the appendix to each company in Hypobank. To further enlarge our sample, we search the Mannheim Company Database (MUP) located at the ZEW in Mannheim. We thereby obtain ownership structures on many medium-sized

nonlisted firms, mainly for private corporations (GmbH). Third, some firms changed their names during the period of observation, for example following takeovers or restructuring of conglomerates. Since changes in ownership are crucial to the data collection procedure, we adjust for name changes and obtain a panel on ownership structures through the years 1986–1994.

In consequence, we are left with ownership data for 1485 firms (6367 firm years). Because of missing values for important balance sheet items, another 30 firms must be eliminated. This selection procedure generates a sample of 1455 firms (6205 firm years) with at least 1 year of balance sheet and ownership data during the years 1986–1994. As this study examines changes in ownership, we further eliminate 509 firms for which we have only 1 year of data. For almost all of these 509 firms, the year 1994 is the single year. This is due to the fact that Hoppenstedt substantially increased firm coverage in 1994. The resulting sample that contains 946 firms (4882 firm years) is labeled 'Sample I' in this study. For the analysis of causes and consequences of control changes (Section 5), we require firms to display at least four continuous years of data. This generates 'Sample II' which contains 664 firms (4443 firm years). Table 27.10 summarizes the sample selection procedure.

To test for a potential sample selection bias, we collect data on the firms' survival status. For firms leaving the sample before 1994, information is obtained from the BSD and MUP databases and from telephone interviews. We find that 39 out of 65 firms that exit the sample before 1994 still existed in 1994 without a change in ultimate

Table 27.11   Definition of variables

Performance

Return on assets (ROA)	Earnings before interest, taxes, depreciation and amortization (EBITDA) divided by total assets
Return on equity (ROE)	EBITDA/total equity
Change in ROA	$\Delta ROA_t = ROA_t - ROA_{t-1}$
Change in ROE	$\Delta ROE_t = ROE_t - ROE_{t-1}$
Earnings loss	EBITDA < 0

Ownership structure

Largest block	Size of largest share block
Ownership concentration	Herfindahl index $H = \sum_{j=1}^{n} P_j^2$, with P_j proportion of a firms' shares owned by shareholder j
Insider ownership	Fraction of shares owned by executive and nonexecutive directors or their families
Cross ownership	Cross $= 1$ if ultimate owner is part of the web of firms identified by Wenger and Kaserer (1998) and if ultimate owner indirectly owns a share block in itself, 0 otherwise
Pyramid	Pyramid $= 1$ if ultimate owner is located on the second or higher level in the ownership structure

Capital structure

Bank debt	Bank debt to total debt
Leverage	Total debt to total assets
Interest coverage	EBITDA/interest payments; interest coverage is low if EBITDA/interest payments < 1

Board structure

Turnover of CEO	$CEO_t = 1$ if chairman of management board (*Vorstand*) changes from year $t-1$ to t, 0 otherwise.
Turnover of executive directors	$(J_t + L_t)/(E_t + E_{t-1})$ with J_t (L_t) $=$ number of joining (leaving) directors executive directors and $E_t =$ number of executive directors
Supervisory board	Board $= 1$ if firm has a supervisory board, 0 otherwise

Restructuring

Sales of assets	$s_{jt} = S_{jt}/T_{jt}$ with $S_{jt} =$ sales of asset class j in year t and $T_{jt} =$ stock of asset class j at the beginning of year t
Growth rate of employment	$n_t = (N_t - N_{t-1})/(N_{t-1})$ with $N_t =$ total number of employees in year t
Growth rate of labor costs	$c_t = (C_t - C_{t-1})/(C_{t-1})$ with C_t total labor expenditures in year t

---

ownership, but simply changed their name or quit reporting due to reasons determined within the firm. In 11 cases, operation was shut down due to liquidation or bankruptcy. In 14 cases, the respective firm had been taken over by another entity. And in one case, operation was shut down voluntarily. Hence, 60% of firm exits during the sample period are not related to bankruptcy or ownership change.

We recognize that the selection procedure of nonlisted medium-sized firms does not generate a random sample of nonlisted medium-sized firms. Given that we include only medium-sized firms that are subsidiaries of conglomerates, our sample might be biased. For example, we lack medium-sized firms that are directly owned by families. But given the advantage of a smaller average firm size in the total sample, we regard this as a necessary cost to be incurred.

All variables used in this study are defined in Table 27.11.

NOTES

1 The database includes all firms listed on any German stock exchange that do not belong to the financial industry and industries under strict regulation such as utility, traffic, and telecommunications (see Appendix A).

2 One major difference between private (GmbH) and public corporations (AG) is that in private corporations, the general meeting of shareholders can give instructions to management, but not in public corporations. Therefore, management could in principle be under tighter control in GmbH firms. This difference is unlikely to be of major relevance in our sample because ownership concentration is high for both types of firms.

3 Regulatory characteristics of listed and nonlisted corporations are also very similar. One difference is that disclosure rules are more strictly enforced for listed corporations. However, after inspecting the annual reports, we cannot find evidence that the nonlisted sample firms do not meet the exchanges' listing requirements.

4 Detailed results are available upon request.

5 A 50% majority is sufficient to dismiss management after its regular period of office, and a majority of 75% to dismiss management during its period of office (§103 (1) AktG).

6 Of course, this step is required only if there is more than one direct shareholder.

7 Information on voting rights is provided by the German Securities Exchange Commission (BAWe) and is used by Becht and Böhmer (in press). Unfortunately, this information is available only from 1996 onwards, and the methodology applied by the BAWe to attribute voting rights in complex ownership structures has serious drawbacks, as shown by Becht and Böhmer.

8 Overall, 73.2% of sample firms do not experience any change in control. For about 20% of firms, the ultimate owner changes once, for about 6% twice. Hence, several consecutive changes in control are not very likely.

9 Originally, the web described by Wenger and Kaserer (1998) consists of 39 firms. From these firms, we select those that own shares in each other because only those are truly 'cross-held'. We identify the following web members: (a) financial corporations: Allianz, Commerzbank, Deutsche Bank, Dresdner Bank, Münchner Rück, and the predecessors of Hypovereinsbank; (b) nonfinancial corporations: Linde, Siemens, and VIAG.

10 When we do not correct for industry performance, we also obtain an insignificant coefficient for performance. The same holds when we use other measures of performance such as return on equity, return on sales, or 1-year changes in each of these measures of performance.

11 In 1985, several changes were introduced in German corporate law (§289 HGB), most of them triggered by the European Community's Fourth Company Law Directive on the harmonization of national requirements pertaining to financial statements.

REFERENCES

Barber, B.M., Palmer, D., Wallace, J., 1995. Determinants of conglomerate and predatory acquisitions: evidence from the 1960s. Journal of Corporate Finance 1, 283–318.

Baums, T., 1994. The German banking system and its impact on corporate finance and governance. In: Aoki, M., Patrick, H. (Eds.), The Japanese Main Bank. Oxford Univ. Press, Oxford, pp. 409–449.

Bebchuk, L.A., Kraakman, R., Triantis, G., 2000. Stock pyramids, cross ownership, and dual class equity. In: Morck, R.K. (Ed.), Concentrated Corporate Ownership. University of Chicago Press, Chicago, pp. 295–315.

Becht, M., Böhmer, E., 2002. Voting control in German corporations. International Review of Law and Economics (in press).

Bethel, J.E., Liebeskind, J.P., Opler, T., 1998. Block share purchases and corporate performance. Journal of Finance 53 (2), 605–634.

Denis, D.J., Kruse, T.A., 2000. Managerial discipline and corporate restructuring following performance declines. Journal of Financial Economics 55, 391–424.

Denis, D.J., Sarin, A., 1999. Ownership and board structures in publicly traded corporations. Journal of Financial Economics 52, 187–223.

Edwards, J., Nibler, M., 2000. Corporate governance: banks versus ownership concentration in Germany. Economic Policy 15 (2), 237–267.

Fama, E.F., Jensen, M.C., 1983. Separation of ownership and control. Journal of Law and Economics 26, 301–325.

Franks, J., Mayer, C., 1995. Ownership and control. In: Siebert, H. (Ed.), Trends in Business Organization. Mohr, Tübingen, pp. 171–200.

Franks, J., Mayer, C., 1998. Bank control, takeovers, and corporate governance in Germany. Journal of Banking and Finance 22, 1385–1403.

Franks, J., Mayer, C., 2001. Ownership and control of German corporations. Review of Financial Studies 14, 943–977.

Franks, J., Mayer, C., Renneboog, L., 2001. Who disciplines the management of poorly performing companies? Journal of Financial Intermediation 10, 209–248.

Gorton, G., Schmid, F.A., 2000. Universal banking and the performance of German firms. Journal of Financial Economics 58, 29–80.

Holmström, B., Tirole, J., 1993. Market liquidity and performance monitoring. Journal of Political Economy 101 (4), 679–709.

Hopt, K.J., 1997. The German two-tier board: a German view on corporate governance. In: Hopt, K.J., Wymeersch, E. (Eds.), Comparative Corporate Governance: Essays and Materials. Walter de Gruyter, Berlin, pp. 3–20.

Jarrell, G.A., Brickley, J., Netter, J., 1988. The market for corporate control: the empirical evidence since 1980. Journal of Economic Perspectives 2, 49–68.

Jenkinson, T., Ljungqvist, A., 2001. Hostile stakes and the role of banks in German corporate governance. Journal of Corporate Finance 7 (4), 397–446.

Jensen, M.C., 1986. Agency costs of free cash flow, corporate finance, and takeovers. American Economic Review 76, 323–329.

Jensen, M.C., 1988. Takeovers: their causes and consequences. Journal of Economic Perspectives 2, 21–48.

Jensen, M.C., Meckling, W.H., 1976. Theory of the firm: managerial behavior, agency costs, and ownership structure. Journal of Financial Economics 3, 305–360.

Jensen, M.C., Ruback, R., 1983. The market for corporate control. Journal of Financial Economics 11, 5–50.

Kaplan, S.N., 1995. Corporate governance and incentives in German companies: evidence from top executive turnover and firm performance. European Financial Management 1, 23–36.

Kini, O., Kracaw, W., Mian, S., 1995. Corporate takeovers, firm performance, and board composition. Journal of Corporate Finance 1, 383–412.

Köke, J., 2001. New evidence on ownership structures in Germany. Kredit und Kapital 34 (2), 257–292.

La Porta, R., Lopez-de-Silanes, F., Shleifer, A., 1999. Corporate ownership around the world. Journal of Finance 54 (2), 471–517.

Maksimovic, V., Phillips, G., 2001. The market for corporate assets: who engages in mergers and asset sales and are there efficiency gains? Journal of Finance 56 (6), 2019–2065.

Mayer, C., 1988. New issues in corporate finance. European Economic Review 32, 1167–1189.

Mulherin, J.H., Boone, A.L., 2000. Comparing acquisitions and divestitures. Journal of Corporate Finance 6, 117–139.

OECD, 1995. Financial markets and corporate governance. Financial Market Trends 62, 13–35.

OECD, 1998. Shareholder value and the market in corporate control in OECD countries. Financial Market Trends 69, 15–37.

Renneboog, L., 2000. Ownership, managerial control, and the governance of companies listed on the Brussels stock exchange. Journal of Banking and Finance 24 (12), 1959–1995.

Scharfstein, D., 1988. The disciplinary role of takeovers. Review of Economic Studies 55, 185–199.

Schwert, W.G., 2000. Hostility in takeovers: in the eyes of the beholder? Journal of Finance 55 (6), 2599–2640.

Shleifer, A., Vishny, R.W., 1986. Large shareholders and corporate control. Journal of Political Economy 94 (3), 461–488.

Shleifer, A., Vishny, R.W., 1992. Liquidation values and debt capacity: a market equilibrium approach. Journal of Finance 47 (4), 1343–1366.

Shleifer, A., Vishny, R.W., 1997. A survey of corporate governance. Journal of Finance 52 (2), 737–783.

Short, H., 1994. Ownership, control, financial structure, and the performance of firms. Journal of Economic Surveys 8 (3), 203–247.

Wenger, E., Kaserer, C., 1998. The German system of corporate governance: a model which should not be imitated. In: Black, S.W., Moersch, M. (Eds.), Competition and Convergence in Financial Markets. Elsevier, Amsterdam, pp. 41–78.

## Chapter 28

Julian Franks[*] and Colin Mayer

HOSTILE TAKEOVERS AND THE CORRECTION OF MANAGERIAL FAILURE

Source: *Journal of Financial Economics*, 40(1) (1996): 163–181.

ABSTRACT

This paper examines the disciplining function of hostile takeovers in the U.K. in 1985 and 1986. We report evidence of high board turnover and significant levels of post-takeover restructuring. Large gains are anticipated in hostile bids as reflected in high bid premiums. However, there is little evidence of poor performance prior to bids, suggesting that the high board turnover does not derive from past managerial failure. Hostile takeovers do not therefore perform a disciplining function. Instead, rejection of bids appears to derive from opposition to post-takeover redeployment of assets and renegotiation over the terms of bids.

1. INTRODUCTION

HOSTILE TAKEOVERS ARE CONTROVERSIAL. To some, takeovers are an important method of correcting managerial failure. Rappaport (1590), for example, believes that the recent wave of takeover activity 'has changed the attitudes and practices of U.S. managers'. He argues (p. 100) that 'it represents the most effective check on management autonomy ever devised. And it is breathing new life into the public corporation'. Grossman and Hart (1980, p. 329) associate this discipline with hostile takeovers: '...since the threat of raids encourages good management and raids only occur in events where the company is worth more to the raider than it is currently worth, there is no reason on efficiency grounds for society to restrict raids'.

To others, takeovers are a poor form of corporate governance. Peter Drucker has declared that 'there can be absolutely no doubt that hostile takeovers are exceedingly bad for the economy.' Herzel and Shepro (1990, p. 3) believe that they are 'a tremendously expensive and imprecise solution.' Shleifer and Summers (1988, p. 37) take a wider social perspective and 'see hostile takeovers as destructions of valuable corporate cultures...which have extremely serious allocative consequences'.

This paper addresses the disciplining function of takeovers, specifically examining whether hostile takeovers are associated with the dismissal of the management and prior poor performance. Evidence on poor performance of target firms comes from pre-bid measures of financial performance as well as bid premiums and post-takeover restructurings. We find clear evidence of high board turnover and significant levels of restructuring in hostile takeovers. Large gains are anticipated, as reflected in high bid premiums paid to target shareholders. However, using a number of different benchmarks, we find little evidence that hostile takeovers are motivated by poor performance prior to bids. We therefore reject the view that hostile takeovers perform a disciplinary role. Instead, we argue that opposition to bids by incumbent management reflects disagreement over the price the bidder is willing to pay and its intentions to restructure the company.

Section 2 describes the sample and the methodology. Section 3 reports results on hostile takeovers and managerial control changes. Section 4 provides evidence on the bidding process in hostile bids. Section 5 concludes the paper.

2. DATA, HYPOTHESES, AND METHODOLOGY

The U.K. and U.S., unlike many other countries, have active markets for corporate control. In 1985 and 1986 there were 80 hostile bids in the U.K. Jensen (1988) reports that there were 40 hostile tender offers in the U.S. in 1986. In contrast, Germany has had just three cases of hostile acquisitions of nonfinancial corporations in the whole of the post-Second World War period. The absence of a market for corporate control in most of continental Europe is attributable to the structure of capital markets, with small numbers of quoted companies and ownership of quoted companies concentrated in the hands of a small number of investors (see Franks and Mayer, 1994).

The U.K. is thus one of the few countries other than the U.S. whose market for corporate control can be studied. In fact, the U.K. has certain advantages over the U.S. in that there are fewer antitakeover provisions enshrined in either corporate charters or state legislation. For example, the Takeover Code in the U.K. explicitly prevents the application of poison pills once a takeover bid has been launched.

This paper examines hostile takeovers in the U.K. in 1985 and 1986. A hostile takeover is defined as one in which the first offer is opposed by the incumbent management. A bid is successful if the bidder acquires the target on the basis of its first or a revised offer. A bid is unsuccessful if the target firm remains independent or is subsequently acquired by another bidder in a later bid battle. There were a total of 325 bids for listed companies, including unsuccessful bids. Of the 80 hostile bids, 35 were successful, 23 remained independent (to July 1990), and 22 were subsequently acquired. In five cases there were multiple bids involving more thann one bidder. If two companies bid for one target and the target management rejected one bid but accepted the other, then the former bid was classified as 'rejected' and the latter as 'accepted'. This occurred only once in our sample. The level of hostile takeover activity is similar to prior years: according to the annual report of the U.K. Takeover Panel, 23% of bids for publicly listed targets in 1969–1971 were classified as hostile. The level of hostile takeover activity is also not dissimilar to that recorded in the U.S. by Bhagat, Shleifer, and Vishny (1990), who find 63 successful hostile takeover bids and 22 unsuccessful contests during the three years 1984–1986.[1]

The sample data is drawn from AMDATA, a database of takeover bids, buyouts, and divestments. The sample includes all 35 successful hostile take overs, all 23 unsuccessful hostile takeovers, a set of 35 randomly selected accepted bids from AMDATA, and a group of nonmerging firms over the performance period 1980 to 1986. The nonmerging sample was matched by industry (London Stock Exchange Industry Classification) and size (equity market capitalization in 1990) with the targets of hostile bids (and of uncontested bids) using the London Share Price Data Base (LSPD).

The unsuccessful hostile takeovers, the randomly selected accepted bids, and the nonmerging firms provide benchmarks of comparative performance for the sample of successful hostile takeovers. We compare the performance of firms involved in successful hostile bids with the performance of firms involved in other takeovers (accepted bids). We also compare targets of hostile takeovers and nonmerging firms to see how firms that become hostile takeover targets perform relative to other firms of similar size in the same industry. Finally, we compare successful hostile takeovers and failed hostile takeovers. Failed takeovers provide evidence of target management's response to the threat of a hostile bid and can be compared with the bidder's response in a successful takeover.

2.1. Board turnover and post-takeover restructuring

If hostile takeovers perform a disciplinary role, we should see a high level of managerial turnover followed by large-scale restructuring. These actions are necessary but not sufficient conditions for takeovers to be disciplinary because they could reflect disagreement over a strategic redeployment of assets. To evaluate management turnover, we collect data on all members of the board of directors of the target firm, including the name of the director, the date of resignation or retirement, and the eventual position of the director in the merged company.

Our information comes from company accounts of the target and bidder firms and from company announcements issued by the Stock Exchange. The number of target company board members promoted to the acquiring company's board comes from accounts of the target company and the acquiring firm. Telephone interviews with company representatives corroborated and supplemented the data. The directors' histories were followed for two years after the takeover.

We use two measures of post-takeover restructuring. The first measure is significant sales of assets during the two years after takeover. Asset sales for successful hostile and friendly bids are classified as significant if more than 10% of the total fixed assets of the merged firm are sold in the corresponding year. Data on asset sales are based on annual accounts and telephone interviews with company secretaries to the board of directors or equivalent persons.

Post-bid studies of successful takeovers suffer from the difficulty of separately identifying asset sales in the target firms from those of the bidder, since the financial accounts are reported on a consolidated basis. In contrast, the post-bid asset sales of targets of unsuccessful bids are readily observable. Consequently, we also analyze the asset sales of targets of unsuccessful bids over a period of five years around the bid.

2.2. Anticipated bid benefits and prebid performance measures

If hostile bids serve a disciplinary function there must also be evidence of anticipated gains associated with the restructurings and poor performance prior to the takeover Anticipated merger benefits are measured using bid premiums based on abnormal share price returns in the month of the first bid. If bids are revised. we examine the month of the first bid to the month of the last bid.

We use four measures of pre-bid financial performance. The first is share price returns over five years prior to the month of the announcement of the initial bid. The bid announcement date is from Financial Times Mergers & Acquisitions (FTM&A). If bids are revised, the date of the first bid is obtained from FTM&A, London Stock Exchange Microfiches, and Textline. Textline provides extracts from newspapers such as the *Financial Times*. Returns are based upon share price and dividend data collected from LSPD and Datastream. Abnormal returns are calculated using a market model ($\alpha = 0, \beta = 1$). The second measure of financial performance is based on changes in dividends per share and dividend omissions in each of the two years prior to the financial year in which the takeover occurred. The third measure of pre-bid financial performance is the cash flow rate of return on assets employed in 1980 and in the last accounting year before the bid, calculated from the cash flow gross of interest and depreciation divided by the sum of the market value of equity and the book value of debt. The last measure is based on Tobin's Q ratio, the ratio of the market value to replacement cost of a firm's assets. The ratio is calculated for 1980 (or the first year of the listing) and the last accounting year before the bid. The market value of equity and book value of debt proxy for the numerator. The replacement cost of each company's assets was taken from its annual accounts. Until 1985, companies in the U.K. were required to report the current cost of their assets. Current cost is the replacement cost based on an up-to-date cost of the assets, after providing for depreciation to reflect the age and usage of the assets. Replacement costs are based on an index of prices of new assets.

3. TEST RESULTS

Sections 3.1 and 3.2 examine the extent to which hostile takeovers give rise to management board turnover and post-takeover restructuring. Sections 3.3 and 3.4 evaluate the extent to which hostility and managerial control changes are associated with higher bid premiums and poor pre-bid performance.

3.1. Board turnover

Table 28.1 reports that 50% of the directors resign after accepted bids, compared with 90% after successful hostile bids. If outside directors are excluded, the difference barely changes. According to panel 2, the differences in proportions between successful hostile and accepted bids are significant at the 1% level for both total and inside board resignations.

The levels of inside director resignations in both successful and unsuccessful hostile bids are higher than in nonmerging firms. For example, in a sample of ten nonmerging firms drawn from the lowest decile of share price performance in 1985, only 19% of the board resigned during the year of bad performance and the subsequent year, compared with 90% in successful hostile bids and 39% in unsuccessful bids. Clearly, hostile takeovers are associated with a high level of board turnover. These results are consistent with Klein and Rosenfeld (1988) who find that firms successfully defending themselves through greenmail experience above-average management turnover. The high turnover of the executive members of the boards in unsuccessful hostile bids is also consistent with Hirshleifer and Thakor's (1994) prediction that hostile bids reveal information about the quality of management to the monitors of the firm.

3.2. Post-takeover asset sales

Hostile takeovers are also associated with restructurings. Based on accounts of merged companies and telephone interviews, asset sales exceed 10% of the value of total fixed assets of the merged firms in 53% of

Table 28.1 Proportion of directors who resigned in the targets of accepted and successful and unsuccessful hostile bids (size of sample, *n.* in parentheses)

Panel 1. Resignations	Accepted	Successful hostile	Unsuccessful hostile
All directors	50% (34)	90% (31)	39% (23)
Inside directors	50% (26)	88% (26)	36% (22)

Panel 2: t-statistic: difference in proportions	All directors	Inside directors
Successful hostile vs. accepted	3.52[a]	3.00[a]
Unsuccessful hostile vs. successful hostile	−4.01[a]	−3.76[a]

Source: Annual reports. Stock Exchange microfiches. Part of the source data for 1986 is contained in appendices A and B of Franks and Mayer (1990). It includes resignations in the two years subsequent to takeover.

a Significant at the 1% level.

successful hostile bids. In contrast, only 26% of accepted bids had significant asset sales, a difference that is statistically significant at greater than the 5% level. The high level of asset disposals is consistent with the results of Dann and DeAngelo (1988, p. 88), who find that 'the median restructuring involves assets constituting 23% of the target's pre-offer equity value'. It is also consistent with Bhide (1989) who finds more evidence of sales of assets arising from past acquisitions of targets in hostile than in friendly bids.

Table 28.2 provides a detailed examination of the proportion of asset disposals for unsuccessful hostile bids. The table suggests that prior to the bid and in the year of the bid, annual sales of assets total 8–9% of total fixed assets. Post-bid asset sales are larger, with the proportion increasing from 13% in the year after the acquisition to 19% three years after takeover. In the third year after the acquisition, asset sales are significantly greater than 10% (at the 5% significance level), with 60% of companies having sold more than 10% of their assets. This finding is consistent with the observation of Dann and DeAngelo (1988, p. 88) that 'hostile bids rarely prevail in cases in which the planned restructurings were implemented by target managers'.

3.3. Anticipated benefits and bid premiums

It might be expected that the higher levels of restructurings in hostile takeovers would create greater shareholder, value than in other takeovers. Furthermore, if takeovers are disciplinary, then takeovers which give rise to managerial control changes should have higher bid premiums than those which do not. Table 28.3 finds that anticipated benefits are higher in successful hostile bids than in other bids: bid premiums average 30% in the month of a bid compared with only 18% for accepted bids. [By way of comparison, Franks and Harris (1989) report premiums of 42% for hostile bids and 28% for uncontested and unrevised bids in the U.S.] The difference of 12 percentage points is statistically significant at the 5% level. When bid premiums are computed for a period which includes any bid revisions, the difference is 15 percentage points and is significant at the 1% level. There is therefore some support for the proposition that bid premiums are higher in hostile bids. Bradley, Desai, and Kim (1988) suggest that competition in the bidding market may produce benefits to the target shareholders at the expense of the shareholders of the bidder.

Unsuccessful hostile bids have bid premiums that are considerably lower than those in successful hostile bids. In fact, they are much closer to the bid premiums in accepted bids, suggesting that the market is anticipating some restructuring after unsuccessful bids but not at as high a level as in successful hostile bids.

We also examine whether the high level of board turnover in hostile bids (reported earlier) is associated with high bid premiums.

Table 28.2 Asset disposals for a five-year period around the bid for unsuccessful bids occurring in 1985 and 1986 (size of sample. *t*-statistic, and proportion >10% in parentheses)

	$B - 1$[a]	B	$B + 1$	$B + 2$	$B + 3$	*Average*[b]
Asset disposals as a % of tangible fixed assets	8.5% (32, − 1.0,0)	9.2% (24, − 0.4,25)	13.3% (19,1.0,42)	17.2% (17,1.6,53)	19.4% (15,2.2.60)	11.0% (33,0.7.42)

Source: Annual reports. *t*-statistic indicates whether the figure is different from 10%.

a *B* is the year of the bid.

b Firms for which data do not exist for some of the five years have been included for the calculation of the average.

Table 28.3 Bid premiums for three samples: targets of accepted bids, successful hostile bids, and unsuccessful hostile bids (sample size, t-statistic, and proportion positive in parentheses)

Panel 1. Eid premiums

	Accepted	Successful hostile	Unsuccessful hostile
Bid month	18.44%	29.76%	21.50%
	(34,6.09,88)	(32, 8.30, 100)	(43, 6.27, 87)
Initial bid to final bid month	18.44%	33.88%	22.40%
	(34, 6.09, 88)	(33, 7.39,97)	(46, 5.98, 89)

Panel 2: t-statistic: difference in bid premiums

	Bid month	Initial bid to final bid month
Successful hostile vs. accepted	2.29[a]	2.80[b]
Unsuccessful hostile vs. successful hostile	−1.41	−1.94[c]

Source: LSPD. Bid premiums in panel 1 are calculated using a market model with parameter values of $\beta = 1$ and $\alpha = 0$.

a Significant at the 5% level.
b Significant at the 1% level.
c Significant at the 10% level.

We define a change in managerial control as occuring when either the chief executive or the chairman of the target firm resigns *or* when there are no promotions from the target to the main board of the acquiring firm. This happens in 88% of successful hostile bids and 60% of accepted bids. The difference is statistically significant at the 2% level. We also repeat the analysis using an alternative definition: a control change occurs when either the chief executive or the chairman resigns *and* there are no promotions to the main board of the acquiring firm. According to this definition, there are control changes in 24% of accepted bids and 66% of successful hostile bids. Since the subsequent results are similar we report the evidence from the first test only.

Bid premiums for targets with control changes are almost identical to those without control changes: 25.23% versus 25.25%. This result is similar to Martin and McConnell (1991) who report abnormal returns of 31.33% for the sample in which there is turnover of the top manager and 33.77% when there is no change; they find that the difference is not statistically significant. Thus, while hostile takeovers give rise to higher bid premiums, the higher premiums are not attributable to the high

level of managerial control changes. This evidence is not consistent with a disciplinary role for hostile takeovers. Section 4 provides an alternative explanation for the high bid premiums in hostile takeovers based on bargaining over the terms of the offer.

3.4. Pre-bid performance

Finally, if hostile bids are disciplinary, we would expect high board turnover to be associated with poor performance of the target prior to the bid. We use four measures of performance: share prices, dividend changes, cash flow rates of return, and Tobin's Q.

3.4.1. Pre-bid share price performance

The first panel of Table 28.4 reports abnormal share price performance for successful hostile bids, unsuccessful hostile bids, and accepted bids, as well as for two samples of nonmerging firms paired by industry and size with the samples of accepted bids and successful hostile bids. Abnormal returns are shown for five years, two years, and one year prior to the date when the market first began to anticipate the bid which is

Table 28.4   Abnormal share price returns for the period up to five years before the bid for various samples of merging and nonmerging firms (size of sample, *t*-statistic, and proportion positive in parentheses)

Panel 1. Abnormal returns

	Accepted bids	Matched nonmerging sample[a]	Successful hostile bids	Matched nonmerging sample[a]	Unsuccessful hostile bids
Average over 5 years[b]	4.53% (28, 0.99, 64)	0.83%[b] (19, 0.23, 53)	−0.14% (32, −0.04, 50)	0.14% (26, 0.03, 38)	2.71% (34, 0.72, 50)
2 years prior	7.75% (32, 1.10, 53)	−7.84% (18, −0.67, 50)	−6.09% (34, −0.84, 38)	2.26% (25, −0.84, 38)	5.07% (44, 0.78, 41)
1 year prior	7.77% (35, 1.11, 51)	1.99% (19, 0.22, 58)	−7.68% (34, −1.17, 41)	7.90% (26, 1.14, 54)	−2.84% (44, −0.57, 48)

Panel 2. t-statistic: difference in abnormal returns

	Average over 5 years	2 years prior	1 year prior
Successful hostile less accepted	−0.79	−1.37	−1.61
Accepted less nonmerging	0.46	1.14	0.51
Successful hostile less nonmerging	−0.05	−0.83	−1.63
Successful hostile less unsuccessful hostile	−0.53	1.15	0.60

Source: LSPD and own calculations. Abnormal returns in panel 1 are calculated using a market model with parameter values of $\alpha = 0$ and $\beta = 1$.

a Based upon the same industry using the Stock Exchange Industrial Classification and the company with the closest market equity capitalisation.

b Some companies had incomplete data for the five years because they were not listed at the beginning of the period.

c One company has been excluded because it was an outlier showing an abnormal return of 161% over five years.

assumed to be three months prior to the announcement date as reported by the London Stock Exchange. Results are reported on an equally weighted basis. The *t*-statistics in the second panel test the hypothesis that the average abnormal returns in the two relevant samples are equal. The *t*-statistics are calculated as $t = (M_1 - M_2)/SD$, where M stands for the cell mean $SD = \sqrt{(S_1^2/N_1 + S_2^2/N_2}$, with N the number of observations averaged in a cell mean and S the cross-sectional deviation about the cell mean.

A comparison of accepted bids with successful hostile bids in panel 1 suggests that the pre-bid performance of targets of successful hostile bids is worse than that of accepted bids: in each of the periods described as one and two years prior to the bid, the difference is around 14 percentage points. Although economically meaningful, panel 2 records that this difference is not significant at the 5% level. The difference in returns is reduced to less than 5 percentage points when abnormal returns are estimated over the five years prior to the bid.

When matching the accepted and hostile bids with nonmerging firms of equivalent size and industry, nonmerging firms record almost identical performance to successful hostile bids over the five years prior to a bid and somewhat worse (but not statistically significantly so) performance than accepted bids. Abnormal returns are higher for unsuccessful bids than for successful bids, although the difference over five years is small and none of the differences are statistically significant. An analysis of medians discloses similar differences between accepted and successful hostile bids on an equally weighted basis two years prior to a bid and a smaller difference one year before a bid. Using the Wilcoxon test, the differences in median are significant at the 13% level two years before a bid and at the 14% level one year before a bid.

3.4.2. Dividend changes

The second measure of financial performance reports firms' dividend decisions in each of the two years prior to a bid using four classifications: omission, increase, decrease, or no change. Poor performance should be associated with reductions and omissions in dividends. Panel 1 of Table 28.5 shows that in the two years prior to a bid a majority of companies in all three samples of bids (successful hostile, unsuccessful hostile, and accepted bids) increased their dividends; very few reduced them. The dividend was omitted entirely in only six cases. A similar pattern emerges in the second panel for dividends declared over the one

prior to a bid. The dividend behavior of targets of unsuccessful hostile bids is very similar to targets of successful bids.

Differences in dividend policy may reflect changes in payout policy rather than differences in underlying performance. However, the payout ratios of the three samples calculated for the six-year period 1980–85 (or 1981–86 for 1986 bids) are similar: 38.3% for accepted bids, 40.4% for successful hostile bids, and 43.3% for unsuccessful hostile bids. The differences in the payout ratios between the three samples are not statistically significant and the t-statistics are all less than one. The results suggest that there is little difference in performance between the samples.

This result stands in marked contrast to the dividend behavior of a sample of 80 firms in the lowest quintile of shareprice performance reported by LSPD in 1985. The sample had an average abnormal return of −63%. Dividends were omitted or reduced in 41% of cases compared with 12% for successful hostile bids. In the remaining cases, dividends were held constant (29%) or increased (30%) For 80 firms with zero abnormal returns, dividends

Table 28.5 Proportion of companies omitting or changing dividends in accepted and hostile bids (size of sample, *n*, in parentheses)

Panel 1. 2 years prior

	Accepted	Successful hostile	Unsuccessful hostile
Omitted	5.6% (3)	5.9% (2)	2.8% (1)
Decrease	14.3% (5)	2.9% (1)	5.7% (2)
No change	22.9% (8)	14.7% (5)	17.1% (6)
Increase	51.4% (18)	73.5% (25)	71.4% (25)
N/A	2.9% (1)	2.9% (1)	2.8% (1)

Panel 2. 1 year prior

	Accepted	Successful hostile	Unsuccessful hostile
Omitted	2.9% (1)	5.9% (2)	2.9% (1)
Decrease	8.6% (3)	5.9% (2)	5.7% (2)
No change	11.4% (4)	11.8% (4)	11.4% (4)
Increase	77.1% (27)	76.5% (26)	74.3% (26)
N/A	0.0% (0)	0.0% (0)	5.7% (2)

Source: Annual reports.

were omitted and reduced in 9% of cases and increased in 77% of the cases. These results are remarkably similar to the dividend performance of the sample of hostile takeover targets reported in Table 28.5. This evidence suggests that when there is poor performance as measured by share prices, dividends are more likely to be omitted or reduced. The results strongly suggest that the sample of targets of hostile bids with its very low level of dividend reductions or omissions is not representative of firms with poor share price performance.

3.4.3. Pre-bid cash flow rates of return

Table 28.6 reports cash flow rates of return on capital for 1980 and 1985/86. Rates of return for targets for successful hostile bids (17.82%) are similar to those of accepted bids (20.25%) as well as to their matched sample of nonmerging companies (17.15%). None of the differences is statistically significant. Rates of return for targets for

successful hostile bids are not statistically different from those of unsuccessful bids.

3.4.4. Tobin's Q

The failure to uncover differences in pre-bid rates of return between targets of hostile bids and other firms may be due to the stock market capitalizing poor performance at the start of the period. If this is the case, then there will be differences in the Tobin's Q ratios, the ratio of market to replacement cost valuations of firms. Table 28.7 shows that the Q ratios of targets of successful and unsuccessful hostile bids in 1980 are similar to those of accepted bids. Thus the difference in abnormal returns between hostile and accepted bids revealed in Table 28.4 is not a consequence of differences in initial market values. However, the nonmerging sample has a significantly higher Tobin's Q than the successful hostile bids. There is, therefore, some evidence that poor performance is

Table 28.6 Cash flow to asset ratios in 1980 and 1985/1986 for various samples of merging and nonmerging firms (size of sample, *t*-statistic, and proportion positive in parentheses)

Panel 1. Cash flow/(market value of equity + book value of debt)

	Accepted bids	Matched nonmerging sample[a]	Successful hostile bids	Matched nonmerging sample[a]	Unsuccessful hostile bids
1980	28.20%	21.74%	22.28%	18.24%	24.49%[b]
	(23, 6.04, 96)	(18, 8.81, 100)	(27, 6.69, 100)	(23, 6.42, 100)	(26, 8.66, 100)
1985, 1986	20.25%	21.61%	17.82%	17.15%	17.50%
	(30, 5.73, 97)	(18, 5.27, 94)	(29, 8.72, 100)	(24, 10.3, 100)	(30, 13.67, 100)

Panel 2. t-statistic: difference in cash flow ratio of two samples

	1980	1985, 1986
Successful hostile less accepted	−1.03	0.60
Accepted less nonmerging	1.28	−0.22
Successful hostile less nonmerging	0.92	0.25
Successful hostile less unsuccessful hostile	−0.51	0.13

Source: Datastream. LSPD, own calculations.

Definitions: Cash flow = Profit after tax + Depreciation + Interest payments, Book value of debt = ST loans + LT loans − Cash balances + Deferred tax.

a Based upon the same industry, using the Stock Exchange Industrial Classification and the company with the closest market equity capitalization.
b One company has been excluded from the sample because it showed a cash flow ratio of 306.64%.

Table 28.7   Tobin's Q for 1980 (or first year of listing) and 1985/1986 (or last year of listing/annual report) for various samples of merging and nonmerging firms (size of sample, t-statistic, and proportion with Tobin's $Q > 1$ in parentheses)

Panel 1 Tobin's Q

	Accepted bids	Matched nonmerging sample[a]	Successful hostile bids	Matched nonmerging sample[a]	Unsuccessful hostile bids
1980	0.72%	0.92%	0.82%	1.12%	0.80
	(23, −3.8, 26)	(17, −1.0, 47)	(27, −2.7, 19)	(24, 1.0, 38)	(24, −3.1, 25)
1985, 1986	1.35	1.25	1.04	1.11	1.22
	(29, 3.7, 76)	(18, 2.1, 73)	(29, 1.0, 55)	(25, 2.0, 60)	(27, 3.0, 74)

Panel 2. t-statistic: difference in Tobin's Q of two samples

	1980	1985, 1986
Successful hostile less accepted	0.92	−2.95[c]
Accepted less nonmerging	−1.73[b]	0.67
Successful hostile less nonmerging	−2.12[d]	−1.06
Successful hostile less unsuccessful hostile	−0.21	−2.20[d]

Source: Datastream, LSPD, own calculations. t-statistic indicates whether Tobin's Q is different from one.

Definition: Tobin's Q = (Market value of equity + Book value of debt)/Replacement cost of assets.
a Based upon the same industry using the Stock Exchange Industrial Classification and the company with the closest market equity capitalization.
b Significant at the 10% level.
c Significant at the 1% level.
d Significant at the 5% level.

being capitalized in the targets of hostile bids when the comparison is made with firms in the same industry.

For 1985 and 1986 the Tobin's Q ratios of targets of hostile bids are lower than those of accepted bids in the year of the merger (1.04 versus 1.35); the t-statistic for the difference is −2.95. In addition, the Q ratio of successful hostile bids is lower than that for the targets of unsuccessful hostile bids (1.04 versus 1.22, t-statistic = −2.2). Thus, the performance of targets of hostile takeover bids is significantly worse than that for the other two samples. However, the average Q ratios of the targets of accepted and hostile bids are both greater than one, providing evidence of poor relative, rather than poor absolute, performance.

3.5. Summary of findings

To summarize, three different measures indicate that the pre-bid financial performance

of targets of hostile bids is not easily distinguished from that of targets of accepted bids. The performance of targets of hostile bids is not inferior to that of a nonmerging sample of firms matched on the basis of size and industry; the only exception is for Q ratios. This evidence is consistent with Martin and McConnell (1991) who find no difference in pre-bid performance of targets of accepted and rejected bids.

These findings raise the question of whether poor pre-bid performance is more closely associated with managerial control changes than with the hostility of bids. We examine this proposition by repeating the above pre-performance tests on the sample of all takeovers partitioned by control changes. A very similar picture to that described for the hostile and accepted partition emerges. (Tables relating to this section are available from the authors on request.)

Over five and two years prior to the bid, takeovers with control changes display superior abnormal share price performance to those without control changes, the opposite of the result predicted by evidence of managerial failure. Only in the year prior to the bid is there worse performance although the difference is not statistically significant. [Kini, Kracaw, and Mian (1993) record an inverse relation between performance and CEO turnover for insider-dominated boards and no relation for outsider-dominated boards.] The proportion of firms cutting or omitting dividends is very small in relation to the proportion raising dividends for both samples. There is slightly more evidence that firms omit dividends prior to control change bids but no evidence that they cut them. Cash flow rates of return are lower in the control change sample both five years before the bid and in the year of the bid. However, the differences are not statistically significant. Finally, five years prior to the bid the Tobin's Q ratio of control change targets is slightly higher (0.79) than that of noncontrol change targets (0.70), although in the year of the bid it is lower (1.17 versus 1.32); the differences are not statistically significant. In both cases, the Q ratios are greater than one and therefore suggest profitable investment opportunities rather than poor performance.

In summary, there is little evidence that takeovers with control changes are the result of poor past performance. Several studies examine the relation between board turnover and performance. Weisbach (1988) finds a strong association between prior performance and the probability of director resignations for companies with outsider-dominated boards. Warmer, Watts, and Wruck (1988) only find an inverse relation between the probability of a management change and a firm's share price performance when the latter is extremely good or bad. Gilson (1989) finds a significantly higher level of executive turnover in financially distressed than nondistressed firms.

Whereas the last two studies find a relation between very poorly performing companies and high board turnover. we show that the targets of hostile take-overs are performing neither poorly nor worse than the targets of accepted bids. However,

Martin and McConnell's (1991) finding of worse pre-bid performance in takeovers where there are high executive changes stands in contrast to our results for the U.K.

4. REVISED BIDS

The previous section reports a high level of board turnover in hostile take-overs, associated with high levels of sales of assets and high bid premiums. However, there is no evidence of high bid premiums when takeovers are partitioned on the basis of control changes. In addition, neither hostile take-overs nor control changes are associated with poor pre-bid performance. The evidence therefore strongly suggests that hostile takeovers are not associated with a disciplinary role in this sample of U.K. takeovers.

The evidence of a high level of post-takeover restructuring in conjunction with high board turnover is more consistent with board dismissal being a result of disagreement with the bidder over the future restructuring of the company. Another explanation, consistent with the high bid premiums in hostile bids, is that rejection of bids is part of the process of negotiating the terms of bids. To evaluate this possibility, we collected data on bid revisions for our sample of successful and unsuccessful bids. In Table 28.8, we show that hostile bids were revised in 25 out of the 35 successful hostile bids. When the hostile bidder did not revise the terms after rejection by the target, there was a high rate of bid failure (20 out of 30 cases).

If rejection of bids were a matter of negotiation over price. we would expect to observe bids being rejected, revised, and then accepted (if the bid succeeded); alternatively, the bid would fail because other bidders would emerge in the same or in a subsequent bid. The 13 successful hostile bids that were finally accepted (and therefore recommended) by target management can be interpreted in this way. However, we also observe 12 successful hostile bids being rejected to the end, even after the

Table 28.8 Number of bids subject to revision partitioned by hostility of bid

	Revised	Unrevised
Accepted	0	35
Successful hostile: finally accepted	13[b]	0
Successful hostile: contested to the end	12[c]	10
Unsuccessful hostile bids[a]	15[d]	20

Source: Financial Times Mergers & Acquisitions, Extel and Textline.

a Some data on revisions of unsuccessful bids missing.

b Average length of the window: approximately 45 days.

c Average length of the window: approximately 75 days. In three cases, the length was greater than 100 days. One of them was referred to the Monopolies and Mergers Commission, another was referred to the Takeover Panel because of alleged irregularities with the offer, and the other was subject to multiple bidders.

d Average length of the window: approximately 78 days. In two of them the length was greater than 100 days. One of them was referred to the Monopolies and Mergers Commission and the other was subject to multiple bidders.

bids were revised. For this sample, rejection may reflect the breakdown of the bargaining process or outright hostility towards the particular bidder. The latter is consistent with a disciplinary role for takeovers or disagreement over the redeployment of assets after the takeovers.

A further test of the disciplining function involves examining whether a sample of hostile bids that were ultimately rejected had worse performance than a sample of revised bids that were ultimately accepted. Table 28.9 reports three measures of performance Tobin's Q, abnormal share price returns, and cash flow rates of return. If initial rejection but ultimate acceptance of bids has to do with bargaining over price, then we would predict (i) higher Q ratios for bids that are ultimately accepted (S.2 in table 28.9), (ii) larger abnormal returns and (iii) higher cash flow rates of return.

The sample sizes are small, between 10 and 15 for each partition of hostile bids. Table 28.9 reports that the pattern of results is not consistent for any of the three measures, except that the Q ratios for contested bids that are ultimately accepted are greater (0.87) than for the sample of bids that are ultimately rejected (0.73) in 1980. In 1985/86, the Q ratios are almost identical. Abnormal returns are smaller for ultimately accepted bids over five years, though the difference in averages is not statistically significant. Cash flow rates of

return are higher in ultimately accepted than in rejected bids in 1980 but lower in 1985/86.

In sum, there is no evidence of poor pre-bid performance in ultimately rejected bids. Continuing opposition to the bid appears to reflect a breakdown over negotiations or disagreement over the redeployment of assets after the takeover. The fact that post-takeover restructuring is significantly higher in hostile than accepted takeovers points to the latter as being an important consideration.

5. CONCLUSION

This paper examines whether hostile takeovers act as a discipline on management. Evidence comes from the performance of targets of hostile takeovers before, during, and after acquisition. We report that hostile takeovers are associated with high levels of boardroom changes, higher in hostile than accepted bids and higher in targets of successful than unsuccessful hostile bids. There are also larger asset disposals and bid premiums in hostile takeovers. However, targets of hostile takeovers do not perform worse prior to bids than either targets of other acquisitions or nonmerging firms. By only one measure (Tobin's Q) is there any evidence of statistically significant worse performance

Table 28.9 Tobin's *Q*, abnormal returns, and cash flow rates of return for (i) revised successful hostile bids which are ultimately rejected by the incumbent management (S.1), and (ii) revised successful hostile bids which are ultimately accepted by the incumbent management (S.2) (size of sample, *t*-statistic, and proportion with Tobin's *Q* > 1 or abnormal returns and cash flow rates of return > 0 in parentheses)

Panel 1. Tobin's Q, abnormal returns, and cash flow rates of return

	Tobin's Q		Abnormal returns			Cash flow rates of return	
	1980	1985/86	− 5 years	− 2 years	− 1 year	1980	1985/86
S.1: Ultimately rejected bids	0.73% (10, −3.1, 10)	1.02% (11,0.2,45)	0.50% (12, −0.28,47)	−5.31% (12, −0.58, 46)	0.85% (12, 0.09, 31)	18.72% (10, 7.07, 100)	21.60% (11, 4.79, 100)
S.2: Ultimately accepted bids	0.87% (10, −1.0, 30)	1.08% (11, 1.2, 64)	−4.20% (13, −1.40, 47)	−3.00% (13, −0.28, 47)	−8.33% (13, −0.87, 40)	27.12% (10, 3.06, 100)	13.92% (11, 7.82. 100)

Panel 2 t-statistic

	Tobin's Q		Abnormal returns			Cash flow rates of return	
	1980	1985/86	− 5 years	− 2 years	−1 year	1980	1985/86
S.1 less S.2	−0.87	−0.64	0.98	−0.14	0.69	−0.91	1.59

Source: Datastream, LSPD, own calculations. Abnormal returns are based on a market model with parameter values α = 0 and β=1.

Definitions: Tobin's *Q* = (Market value of equiry + Book value of debt). Replacement cost of assets. Cash flow = Profit after tax + Depreciation + Interest payments. Book value of debt = ST loans + LT loans − Cash balances + Deferred tax. Cash flow rates of return = Cash flow (Market value of equity + Book value of debt).

of targets of hostile bids. There is no evidence of either high bid premiums or poor pre-bid performance when takeovers involve managerial control changes. The market for corporate control does not therefore function as a disciplinary device for poorly performing companies.

Rejection of bids is more consistent with opposition to the anticipated redeployment of assets by the bidder and negotiation over the terms of bids. We find that there is a high level of bid revisions and large bid premiums in hostile takeovers out no evidence of poor performance where negotiations over the terms of the bid break down. Thus, our results provide a picture of a market for corporate control In the U.K. that is more consistent with dissatisfaction over the bid terms and the redeployment of assets after the takeover than with a disciplinary role.

NOTES

* Corresponding author.
This paper is part of an ESRC funded project, number W102251003, on 'Capital Markets, Corporate Governance, and the Market for Corporate Control'. We are grateful to Nick Carrick, Luis Corrcia da Silva, and Marc Goergen for valuable research assistance. We wish to thank John Chown for financial assistance on this project and for helpful discussions.
The paper has been presented at the 1993 Annual Meeting of the American Finance Association in Anaheim, at the Annual Meeting of the French Finance Association in Paris, at the Annual Meeting of the European Finance Association in Athens, at a conference on European Restructuring at INSEAD and at seminars in Essex, Keele, Oxford, Paris, and Warwick. We are particularly grateful to discussants Patrick Bolton, Stuart Gilson, Kristian Rydgvist, and Paul Seabright for valuable suggestions. We are also grateful for comments from Swami Bhaskaran, Michael Brennen, Michel Habib, David Hirsbleifer, Ernst Maug, Narayan Naik, Kjell Nyborg, and Walter Torous. We also wish to thank Richard Ruback (the editor) and John Pound (the referee) for many helpful comments in the revision of the manuscript.
1   Their sample includes hostile takeovers for targets with a value greater than $50 million.

The definition of hostility is similar to that in this paper, where the target management initially expressed opposition to the bid.

REFERENCES

Bhagat, Sanjay, Andrei Shleifer, and Robert W. Vishny, 1990. Hostile takeovers in the 80s: The return to corporate specialization, Brookings Papers on Economic Activity, 1–72.

Bhide, Amar, 1989, The causes and consequences of hostile takeovers, Journal of Applied Corporate Finance 2, 36–59.

Bradley, Michael, Anand Desai, and E. Han Kim, 1988, Synergistic gains from corporate acquisitions and their division between the stockholders of target and acquiring firms, Journal of Financial Economics 21, 183–206.

Dann, Larry and Harry DeAngelo, 1988, Corporate financial policy and corporate control: A study of defensive adjustments in asset and ownership structure, Journal of Financial Economics 20, 87–127.

Franks, Julian R. and Robert Harris, 1989. Shareholder wealth effects of corporate takeovers: The UK experience 1955–1985, Journal of Financial Economics 23, 225–249.

Franks, Julian R. and Colin P. Mayer, 1990, Capital markets and corporate control: A study of France, Germany and the UK, Economic Policy 10, 191–230.

Franks, Julian P. and Colin P. Mayer, 1994, Ownership and control in Germany, Working paper (London Business School, London).

Gilson, Stuart C., 1989, Management turnover and financial distress. Journal of Financial Economics 25, 241–267.

Grossman, Sanford J. and Oliver D. Hart, 1980, Takeover bids, the free rider problem, and the theory of the corporation, Bell Journal of Economics 11, 42–64.

Herzel, Leo and Richard W. Shepro. 1990. Bidders and targets: Mergers and acquisitions in the U.S. (Blackwell, Oxford).

Hirshleifer, David and Anjan Thakor, 1994, Managerial performance, boards of directors and takeover bidding, Journal of Corporate Finance 1, 63–90.

Jensen, Michael, 1988, Takeovers: Their causes and consequences, Journal of Economic Perspectives 2, 21–48.

Klein, April and James Rosenfeld, 1988, Targeted share repurchases and top management changes. Journal of Financial Economics 20. 493–506.

Kini, Omesh, William Kracaw, and Shehzad Mian, 1993. Corporate takeovers, firm performance and board composition. Working paper (Pennsylvania State University. University Park, PA).

Martin. Kenneth J. and John J. McConnell, 1991, Corporate performance, corporate takeovers and management turnover. Journal of Finance 46. 671–687.

Rappaport, Alfred, 1990, The staying power of the public corporation. Harvard Business Review 1. 96–104.

Shleifer, Andrei and Larry H. Summers, 1988, Breach of trust in hostile takeovers, in: A.J. Auerbach ed., Corporate takeovers: Causes and consequences (National Bureau of Economic Research, Chicago, IL).

Warner, Jerold B., Ross L. Watts, and Karen H. Wruck. 1988, Stock prices and top management changes, Journal of Financial Economics 20, 461–492.

Weisbach, Michael S. 1988, Outside directors and CEO turnover, Journal of Financial Economies 20, 431–460.

Name index

Wizman, T. 43n, 70
Woltenzon, D. 99, 182, 257, 275
Wolff, E. 43n
Wolfram, C. 77, 396n
Wolken, J. 114–115
Womack, K. 553n
Wong, T. 62, 625, 636, 640
Woodburn, L. 115
Wruck, K. 16, 26, 38, 43n, 44n, 45n, 63, 69, 364, 663, 744
Wu, D. 507, 519n
Wuh Lin, J. 111–130
Wulf, H. de 305
Wurgler, J. 101
Wyatt, J. 364, 573
Wyatt, S. 560
Wymeersch, E. 289, 310n
Wysocki, P. 489, 623–641

Xie, F. 553n

Yafeh, Y. 66, 69, 102
Yang, F. 535, 553n
Yermack, D. 58, 229–230, 243, 261, 395n, 410, 411, 413, 416n, 417n, 431, 436–437, 441, 552n
Yeung, B. 199
Young, L. 470

Zechner, J. 138, 147, 149, 154n, 307n
Zeckhauser, R. 126
Zellner, W. 43n
Zenner, M. 364, 396n
Zervos, S. 101
Zhou, X. 394
Zimmerman, J. 287, 290, 305, 364, 574, 627
Zingales, L. 52, 56, 60, 62, 69, 74, 78, 99, 101, 107n, 175, 182, 192, 199, 210, 217n, 258, 260, 535, 624, 636–638, 705n
Zorn, T. 602
Zwiebel, J. 675, 704n